IACOCCA

IACOCCA

David Abodaher

A STAR BOOK

published by

the Paperback Division of
W.H. ALLEN & Co. PLC

A Star Book
Published in 1986
by the Paperback Division of
W.H. Allen & Co. PLC
44 Hill Street, London W1X 8LB

Copyright © David Abodaher, 1982

Typeset by Phoenix Photosetting, Chatham
Printed in Great Britain by
Cox & Wyman Ltd, Reading

ISBN 0 352 31835 X

For David and Jane Gillespie,
my world's most beautiful people

ACKNOWLEDGMENTS

First I must thank John J. Morrissey, chairman of the board of Kenyon & Eckhardt Advertising. As a member of his staff, it was incumbent on me to clear through the agency any outside work related to an agency account. Mr Morrissey's enthusiasm during the writing calls for this special expression of thanks. Without him the book never would have been written.

I also feel indebted to Lee Iacocca, who while not directly supplying any material used in the writing, did allow me to interview members of his family, including his wife, mother, and sister.

I am grateful to Bill Winn and Frank Zimmerman for much of the material delineating Iacocca's early times at Ford. Others involved with Lee Iacocca at Ford or Chrysler to whom I am obliged include Harold Sperlick, Gar Laux, Walter Murphy, L. H. McCormick-Goodheart, and Wes Small. I owe particular thanks to Jay Dugan and gratitude to Bill Fugazy.

I am obliged to my colleagues at Kenyon & Eckhardt. Leo-Arthur Kelmenson of the New York office, president of K & E, provided me with important background on Lee Iacocca and on his arrival at Chrysler. Don Grant of the New York office was also quite helpful.

Among my colleagues in the Detroit K & E office I thank Paul Stevens, Linda Kuzawinski, Wayne Saylor, and Michelle Nosco for their encouragement and Bill O'Neill (now heading the Minneapolis office) for providing valuable information.

For help in proofreading, thanks are owed to Carol Yavruian. For typing and retyping through six tedious months my love and appreciation go to my daughter, Lynda. I am grateful to her husband, Bob Henderson, for sparking me into action when spirits sagged.

Lastly I wish to express my gratitude to a number of men at Ford Motor Company who wish to remain anonymous.

PROLOGUE

The tinted windows of Ford Motor Company's world headquarters reflected the glare from a blazing, early-morning midsummer sun as Lido Anthony Iacocca wheeled his Continental Mark down the southbound Southfield Freeway. Mildly aware of the cars whizzing past at more than the fifty-five-mile-an-hour speed limit, he turned into the Ford Road exit in Dearborn. That morning, Thursday, July 13, 1978, Lee, who preferred the Americanisation of his given name, expected to arrive at his office in the northeast corner of the building's twelfth floor at his usual time. Someone privy to the circumstances, but unfamiliar with Lee Iacocca, might have been amazed that the president of the Ford Motor Company was following his normal routine on this day of all days.

A lesser man might not have bothered to show up at all, much less endure what had to be an anxious, even bewildering, twenty-five-mile drive from his home in Bloomfield Hills, a posh suburb north of Detroit. Most would have found it far less agonising to chuck it, to walk away from the emotional roller coaster that the day promised. But to Lee Iacocca it was, at the least, an uncomfortable situation, at the most a crisis to meet head-on.

His bland, almost tranquil expression belied the inner fire that might be expected from his Italian heritage, nor did it betray the resentful bitterness fuelled by the painful prospect that awaited him. But from his youth Lee Iacocca had never dodged a bad situation. This unhappy Thursday would be no different.

Despite the inescapable hornet's nest towards which he was heading, here he was – as he had been daily through twenty-two years – in the very heart of 'Ford Country.' And no one could mistake the fact that in this sector of Dearborn, Michigan, everything in sight – north, south, east, and west – bore the Ford brand.

On the right, south of the Ford Road exit, even such non-Ford enterprises as the Hyatt Regency Hotel and the sprawling Fairline Shopping Center stood on Ford land, as did the low-rise building to the left of the freeway, which housed the J. Walter Thompson Company, the advertising agency for the corporation's Ford Division. Beyond the Thompson facility, also on the left, were the Ford-built, Ford-owned, and Ford-leased Parklane Towers, twin high-rises that were dubbed the Washer and Dryer by some, the Salt-and-Pepper Shakers by others, because of their architectural conformation.

In one of the twin towers were the offices of Kenyon & Eckhardt, the ad agency that served various other Ford Motor Company activities, including the Parts and Service, Glass, and Lincoln-Mercury divisions. Locating offices in the heart of Fordland was, of course, a convenience and time-saver for the executives and account representatives of the agencies who shuttled back and forth daily, visiting clients for programme approvals.

While their physical closeness is a practical and generally accepted business set-up in doing business with a giant, even in spheres other than advertising, it is more than just political expediency. The rental and lease revenues that accrue to Ford Land Development, in this instance from J. Walter Thompson and Kenyon & Eckhardt, substantially influence the bottom line in corporate profits.

Directly south of the Parklane Towers, also on the east side of the freeway, stood the building to which Lee Iacocca was headed, the centrepiece of Ford Country, a long, rectangular structure with exterior walls that appeared to be unbroken expanses of reflective glass. It is appropriately known as the Glass House.

The top floor of the Glass House is the twelfth, although there is a penthouse-type structure above that houses executive dining rooms and sleeping quarters for busy executives or visiting dignitaries. Ford employees called the suite in the southeast corner of the twelfth floor, the one next to Iacocca's own, the place 'where God lives.' From this suite Henry Ford II ruled the Ford empire like an autocrat, more in the mould of his legendary grandfather than his father.

No other automobile executive ruled his fiefdom with the absolute power of Chairman of the Board Henry Ford II. Not Thomas Murphy, chairman of General Motors, not John Riccardo of Chrysler Corporation, not Gerald Meyers of American Motors. These men held their posts by the grace of directors' votes and shareholder acquiescence.

Of course, Ford Motor Company also had its stockholders and board of directors. Thanks, however, to the establishment of the Ford Foundation in January, 1956, the Ford family had firm control of voting shares in the company. Henry II, as a result, wielded unchallenged authority by virtue of the prepotent Ford name, one that checkmated directors and stockholders alike. If any dared question Henry's right to make a final decision, his irrefutable answer was quick in coming.

'Look whose name is on the building!'

Henry meant this often-made pronouncement literally. At the top right of the wide exterior of the Glass House is the familiar Ford trademark, a royal-blue oval bearing the Ford name in white script, a symbol instantly recognisable anywhere in the free world.

This Thursday morning the traditional emblem looked down on Lee Iacocca as he guided his car around the building and down into the executive parking area. With an unchanging expression he parked and walked briskly to the executive elevator. He was ready for whatever Henry Ford II had wrought the night before.

As was his custom when business didn't have him in some far off hamlet talking to dealers or overseas checking on operations at one of Ford's worldwide facilities, Lee had spent the previous evening quietly at home with his wife and younger daughter, Lia. Kathy, the fourth member of the family, was away at school.

Late that evening, when the telephone rang, Mary Iacocca answered and heard a voice she recognised as that of Keith Crain, publisher of the Detroit-based *Automotive News*, the automobile industry's leading weekly. The caller asked to speak to Mr Iacocca.

Lee took the receiver and, after a few pleasantries, heard Crain say he had just received a puzzling phone call from Henry Ford II.

'What the hell's going on?' was the gist of the publisher's message. 'Henry told me he's going to fire you tomorrow.'

Lee was visibly shocked as he recradled the phone, but not totally surprised. He was shocked to hear such news from a third party, and a company outsider to boot. But not really surprised because he had been aware for some time that Henry, for no legitimate reason he could fathom, had been manoeuvring to force him out of the company presidency.

Lee had first sensed the manoeuvres to oust him when he had heard repetitions of what he had originally passed off as idle rumours. All started from sources he was unable to identify. Most were inconsequential, possibly intended to encourage him to resign or take early retirement.

Too busy to consider them any more than irritations, Lee ignored them and went about his work. Ultimately he had to acknowledge, to himself at least, that something odious was indeed in the wind.

Lee could discount the stories no longer when he discovered that Henry Ford actually had begun his oust-Iacocca campaign as early as three years after he had named Iacocca president. He had ordered an audit of Iacocca's expenses and dealings with certain suppliers, hoping to find evidence of kickbacks.

In any large organisation such actions could not be kept secret for long. When Lee first learned of Henry's demeaning tactics, he was embittered and furious enough to consider resigning, but only momentarily. A resignation might be construed as an admission of guilt, and he knew he had done nothing to degrade himself. He also knew that he had made far-ranging contributions to the company, that he had fought and worked too hard to make his boyhood dream a reality to just give up and walk away. As far back as his sophomore year in college he had said he would get a vice-presidency at Ford before he was thirty-five. He would not taint his achievement with a resignation.

No naïve neophyte in corporate life, he was now past the age of fifty. More than thirty of those years had been spent in the service of the Ford Motor Company. The automobile industry was little different from other big businesses – the climb to the top had been hazardous, an everyday battle for survival. Each successive rung up the ladder added pressure from below as well as from above.

One's immediate superior controlled a man's future, demanding action and accomplishment. And those below on the stairway to the executive suite waited for the slip that might enable them to leapfrog ahead.

Lee Iacocca had made it as far as he could go in the Ford Motor Company. He knew it, and was fully content. He was president and had no illusions about the next highest position, that of chairman of the board. That post, by virtue of the Ford stockholdings, would remain in the Ford family. He had known that when he came in. He was even more aware of it now.

As Lee had turned from the phone that Wednesday evening, the questions he couldn't answer – all things considered – were 'Why this?' and 'Why now?'

Despite knowing of Henry's tactics over the past few years, the message from Keith Crain still had come as a thunderbolt. It made no sense. Less than a month earlier Iacocca had taken part in planning for ceremonies celebrating the Ford Motor Company's diamond jubilee. He had felt a surge of pride in the contributions he had made during thirty-two of the company's seventy-five years of building automobiles for the world.

The gratification he had felt made this news from an outsider harder to take. It was possible, of course, that Henry's harassment had gone underground only because of the extensive preparations for the big anniversary ceremonial. Then, too, it was possible – even probable – that Crain was merely fishing, as newspeople so often do to get a scoop.

Crain simply could have mistaken something Henry had told him, or, having heard revivals of the earlier rumours, he might have been trying to weasel a confirmation out of Iacocca himself. Knowing Keith Crain, however, that was hardly likely. The man had a reputation for being a straight shooter.

Whatever the answer, Henry's lengthy campaign had never made much sense. Even those at Ford who were aware of Henry's not-too-subtle plotting were hard put to understand why he wanted to dump his second in command. Next to Ford himself, Lee Iacocca was the best-known individual in the entire industry. And he alone brought the company more favourable publicity than the heads of all the other auto manufacturers combined.

Auto-industry executives respected Iacocca for his abilities, his driving force, and his accomplishments. If a reporter had approached any of them on this July night in 1978 and said that Lee Iacocca was to be fired, he would have found his sanity questioned.

The very thought of firing Mr Mustang was laughable. How could Henry Ford II afford to give up the man who had stood automobiledom on its ears in 1964 with his marketing of the pony car? Such a dismissal would send shock waves through the business and financial worlds.

Then, too, with his stock options and contract that reputedly would not expire for another four years or so, Lee Iacocca seemed as rock-steady at Ford as Henry himself.

Even before he took over the presidency, Iacocca had put his brand on Ford profitability. As vice-president and general manager at Ford Division he had given General Motors and its Chevrolet Division plenty to worry about. His Mustang had clobbered its come-after Chevy counterpart, the Camaro. His Maverick had multiplied Chevrolet concerns as well as helped stem the early-1960s trend towards the small imports from Germany and Japan. Later, after his promotion to president of Ford, Iacocca had breathed new life into its Lincoln-Mercury Division.

Lee Iacocca had given the Ford Motor Company what it needed most at a time when it was most needed, a healthy bottom line in profits. While 1974 and 1975 were not good years, a period of slight recession, under Iacocca the company had achieved a record $938 million profit in 1976. That mark was shattered the following year as Ford racked up sales totalling $37.8 billion and profits of $1.7 billion. And the projected figures for 1978, as of July 1, clearly indicated that profits for 1978 might set a new record were it not for the lengthy and costly strike at Ford's English subsidiary. Such numbers made Henry's itch for Iacocca's scalp incomprehensible.

The burning question was 'Why?' One possible answer lay in the natures of the two men. While they are similar in many ways, in essence they are as different as chalk from cheese. Both are strong, hard-nosed and blunt-speaking, but poles apart in background and character.

Henry Ford II is the gregarious, curt, often caustic aristocrat, a charmer and a community-minded citizen who put his talents and money to work to help revitalise Detroit, even though his home, offices, and factories were located outside the city. Although silver-spooned from birth, he has never projected the picture of a pampered son of opulence.

Conversely, Lee Iacocca was not born to inherited wealth. But he did not come from what is generally termed a 'poor' family from the other side of the tracks. At the time of his birth in 1924 his father, Nicola, was considered well to do.

Incongruities in the temperaments of Henry Ford II and Lee Iacocca are made more evident by their intra-family relationships. Henry loved his father, Edsel, but it was his uneducated, acerbic, and provocative grandfather, the very antithesis of Edsel, on whom Henry doted and who more surely shaped his mind and personality. The entire Ford family, except for the till-death-do-us-part devotion of the first Henry and Edsel for their wives, has been loosely knit. Months may pass with no contact between the Ford brothers and sisters other than in business.

On the other hand, the Iacoccas' background is that of their motherland, where family is paramount, whatever the circumstance. Lee more than loved his father; he revered him. Some claim he was dominated by Nicola. If so, the dominance was born of Lee's respect and reverence. From his earliest teens Lee strove hard to be like his father, a hard-charging doer.

Phlegmatic though he seems at times, Henry Ford II is not callous and insensitive, but often a kind and thoughtful man who takes the time to stop and chat with the grubbiest worker on an assembly line. He is the unabashed extrovert, a man who projects an image of the glad-handing travelling salesman.

Iacocca is no less kind, but he is not so outgoing. He is a warm, impassioned, and zealous individual who is extremely protective of his privacy and that of his family and who is fiercely loyal to his friends. Always maintaining a sense of quiet dignity in public, he is nonetheless a witty and charming man.

Gar Laux, who came to Ford about the same time as Iacocca and climbed the corporate ladder a step behind him, says that, contrary to press caricatures of him as a tough, salty-tongued enigma, Lee is easy to understand and like. He is, says Laux, what he has to be, a demanding man at the office and a loving husband and father at home.

In every aspect the Lee Iacocca lifestyle is far more conservative than that of Henry Ford II. Henry has always been the sociable, fun-loving cosmopolite, a man who loves a practical joke and could not care less about dignity. Once, in his early adult years, Henry stood outside a fine restaurant in Grosse Pointe, the elegant Detroit suburb in which he lived, and blew a loud, shrill blast on a police whistle to shake up the diners inside. On another occasion, at a party overseas, he duelled with an Italian count, riposting the nobleman's tosses of ice cream with a soda siphon.

While Lee Iacocca was happily married to his first sweetheart, Henry is twice divorced and three times married. He is a dedicated girl-watcher who has not lost his zest for a pretty face and trim figure. Unruffled, however embarrassing the situation, he lives and plays by his own rules, offering no excuses.

In February, 1975, while his second wife, Cristina, was in Katmandu attending the coronation of the king of Nepal, Henry was arrested in Goleta, California, and charged with drunk driving. His companion in the car was Kathy DuRoss, a redhaired model who had worked for the Ford Motor Company and later would become his third wife.

Henry was given a blood test and offered release on a $375 cash bond. After stubbornly refusing to post bail, he was jailed for four hours. Finally he paid. As he left the jail, he found reporters waiting for a juicy tidbit or, at least, a roasting of the police. Henry gave them neither. He merely waved and went his way.

The next day Henry was scheduled to address the Society of Automotive Engineers at Detroit's Cobo Hall Convention Center, and he flew back to meet his speech commitment. During his talk someone in the hall shouted out a question referring to the previous night's happening in California.

'Never complain, never explain,' Henry answered with a laugh. He received a standing ovation from the hundreds of engineers gathered at dinner.

Henry Ford II is a newsmaker whatever he does, but a man little concerned whether the attendant publicity is embarrassing or complimentary. Invariably he is insulated from any lasting harm by his name, position and nonchalance.

Lee Iacocca entered his twelfth-floor office that Thursday morning still mystified and bewildered by the turn of events. Had Henry, the night before, really initiated another bit of headline news, one that would startle and galvanise the entire business world? Keith Crain had told him that a board of directors meeting had been called hastily by Henry and that Lee was finished as president of the Ford Motor Company.

Whether any or all of Crain's report was valid hardly mattered now. Lee would soon know. And he was ready for the phone call that would come if Crain was right, ready also for the walk to the suite next door.

He sat at his desk waiting, realising he could do nothing, that he had no way to exorcise the spectre that hovered over his shoulder. Only Henry could do that.

He took care of routine business. The phone rang often, but every call was from an associate with a report or a question. Obviously, the word had not been spread around the Glass House. The hours passed, and though he wondered, Lee was not overly surprised at the delay in hearing from the chairman. Henry was not one to worry about hours.

'I don't like to get up early if I don't have to,' Henry once said. 'It gets you into crazy habits. If I've got a meeting at nine, I'll get there at nine o'clock. But if I don't, what's the use of sitting behind my desk waiting for somebody to ask a question he ought to answer himself?'

Obviously Henry had set no definite time for giving Lee Iacocca the news. It was possible, too, that contrary to Henry's avowed statement that he would never pass the buck and would do what had to be done himself, he hoped that Iacocca, alerted by Keith Crain, might not show up. But certainly, after so many years Henry should have known Lee Iacocca well enough to know that that was highly unlikely.

At noon Iacocca was still waiting. He had lunch in the penthouse dining room. Henry was not to be seen. Lee finished his light meal and returned to his office.

Lee's secretary had placed an afternoon newspaper on his desk. Its headline story seemed a most fitting one. Andrew Young was being edged out as the US ambassador to the United Nations.

Iacocca sat back in his chair to wait. Many things crossed his mind as the minutes ticked by. In any such situation there are always bits and pieces that might suggest a reprieve.

The phone call of the night before might not have been what it was purported to be. It might not have been hard fact. Also, considering Henry's past vacillations, he might have had a change of heart. The three years or so that Henry had done much to encourage Iacocca's resignation lent credence to a possible change of mind.

In midafternoon the phone rang.

'Mr Ford wants to see you in his office,' his secretary reported.

CHAPTER 1

Lido Anthony Iacocca was born in Allentown, Pennsylvania, on October 12, 1924. An astrological enthusiast might see astral influences at work, for 1924 was a year of coincidental significance to the adult life of the newborn infant.

That year the Ford Motor Company set a record in building its ten millionth car, and while the first Henry Ford's beloved 'tin lizzie' would live for another three years, the death knell had already sounded for the legendary Model T. And not long after baby Lido was first placed in his crib, another automobile company was being established.

Walter P. Chrysler had taken over the dying Maxwell – the very Maxwell later made famous by Jack Benny's humour and the driving of Benny's chauffeur, Rochester – and brought it to profitability. Chrysler, one of the foremost engineers in automobile history, bought out the Maxwell company and made it the foundation of his own Chrysler Corporation.

Lido was the second child born to Nicola and Antoinette Iacocca. Nicola Iacocca – the correct Italian pronunciation of the last name is Ee-a-ko-ka- – most influenced his son's life, encouraging the determination, persistence, and ambition that would make the name Lee Iacocca a household word.

Nicola first came to the United States from San Marco, a village in Italy's Campania province, as a restless, energetic youth of thirteen. The town, in the foothills of the Apennine Mountains about 100 kilometres northeast of Naples, had

1

nothing to offer a boy of ambition.

Life in Campania at the turn of the century was more barbarous than civilized. Naples was a hellhole of tuberculosis, where too many lived a hopeless existence underground in caves. In Benevento, a few kilometres from San Marco and the nearest town of any size, a young person might find himself auctioned off as a farm labourer. And wild, overcrowded Rome, far too dangerous for a lone thirteen-year-old, was a world away.

There was one answer to Nicola's itch for adventure agreeable to his mother. A prosperous half-brother of Nicola lived in the United States. So Nicola Iacocca, a credulous adolescent, came to Garrett, a Pennsylvania mining town southeast of Pittsburgh and a short distance from the Maryland border.

Nicola found Garrett a dirty town on the way to oblivion. No more populous than San Marco, it was also in a mountainous area, enough to make him feel at home, but Nicola soon hated the coal-dust-polluted atmosphere of the northern Appalachians. And he had problems.

Nicola's half-brother owned the mining camp's supply store. About twice Nicola's age and married, he was impatient with the hyperactive, impetuous youngster, Nicola's sister-in-law, irritated by his ebullience and ever-present ear-to-ear grin, made him feel uncomfortable and unwelcome.

It was too much for the happy-go-lucky young Italian immigrant. He ran away, not caring where, and was caught. He disappeared again and again, but was always found and brought back. Warnings had no effect.

'If you keep on doing this,' the half-brother threatened, 'I don't want the responsibility. You'll have to go back home to your mother.'

Nicola returned to Italy. Within two years he was back in America, this time accompanied by his two older brothers and sponsored by an uncle in Allentown. This, Nicola found, was a city of love. Here, he could learn, work, enjoy life, be somebody.

Allentown, a historic city on the Lehigh River in eastern

Pennsylvania, then had a population of about 70,000. Its hilly terrain and fresh air reminded him of the Apennine foothills where he once roamed. He loved crossing the bridge over the Lehigh and walking into the country where an occasional deer might be seen. He enjoyed Allentown's clean, neat streets that took him up hillsides covered with brick and frame row houses, so different from the little houses in San Marco.

Nicola listened in awe to stories of the American Revolution, of how the famous Liberty Bell was smuggled into Allentown from Philadelphia in 1777, when the British threatened the headquarters of the Continental Congress. He visited the church in which the Liberty Bell had been hidden and the Liberty Bell Shrine, where he saw a replica of the symbol of America's fight for freedom.

To the uneducated but ambitious Nicola, Allentown was just this side of heaven, a place where he quickly made himself self-supporting. Working in his uncle's hot dog restaurant he began to save money. His charisma, infectious grin, and jolly nature – destined to be the hall marks of his future success – made him a customer favourite.

The Nicola who had been a problem in Garrett two years earlier had matured into a serious young man of sixteen. Allentown, with its beautiful hills, its metal and textile industries, and its many people, unlike Garrett or San Marco, was exciting, a place where money could be made. Like so many immigrants to America in the early years of the twentieth century, young Nicola was determined to be somebody the American way.

Like so many of those immigrants, he soon realised that the way to achievement in America was to work hard, save money, and make that money make more money. He was also determined to be American, act American. It would be all right for his brothers and uncle and the other Italians to call him Nicola, but around Allentown calling himself Nick would better show his mushrooming love for his new country.

When Nick had saved enough money working for his uncle, he opened a hot dog restaurant of his own, the first of many steps he would take towards becoming Allentown's premier entrepreneur, a thinking, speculative, and innovative businessman with a Midas touch. An early decision, a portent of the future, was his purchase of an automobile, a Ford Model T.

One of the few in Allentown to own a car, Nick Iacocca was making himself visible, while rushing along the road to success. His restaurant was doing so well that profits built quickly. He began looking for new ventures for investment.

New ventures, however, had to wait. Calamitous events had taken place overseas. On June 28, 1914, Archduke Francis Ferdinand, heir apparent to the Austrian throne, was assassinated, and World War I erupted. America became directly involved on March 18, 1917, when three United States merchant ships were sunk by German submarines. President Woodrow Wilson immediately called for a declaration of war against Germany.

Nick was not yet an American citizen. But seeing the Uncle Sam 'I Want You!' posters, he quickly made up his mind. He would not wait for the draft process. He volunteered.

Because he was one of the few able to drive an automobile, his army service was spent at Camp Crane in Allentown, a training centre for the United States Ambulance Corps. Located on the fairgrounds, the camp had been named for Dr Charles Henry Crane, US Army Surgeon General in 1882.

Nick did double duty at Camp Crane. He helped train ambulance drivers and used his Model T to drive doctors and surgeons to duty during training manoeuvres. As a resident of Allentown he could have slept at home, but he refused. He insisted on sharing quarters with other soldiers, tents hastily constructed in front of the fairgrounds' bleachers.

Another occupant of the huge bleacher tent was Adolphe Menjou, the motion picture character actor who later starred in such films as *The Front Page* with Pat O'Brien, *Little Miss Marker* with Shirley Temple, and, among many others, *A Star Is Born* with Fredric March and Janet Gaynor. Evenings, the tent was a hotbed of hilarity when the jolly, uninhibited Italian immigrant and the suave, debonair French-American exchanged quips.

After the war Nick returned to his hot dog restaurant. His older brother had maintained the business and its level of profit so well that Nick opened a second restaurant.

Having done so well, Nick decided that his mother, alone in San Marco, should come to the United States. As an American citizen now he could have arranged for her entry. In his early thirties at the time, a touch of nostalgia and a desire to surprise his mother convinced him he should bring her back himself. He left his brothers to manage his enterprises and sailed for Italy.

When Nick arrived in San Marco, his intention was to spend no more than two weeks visiting relatives and friends. He was impatient to get back to business. His first visit to the family of a shoemaker he had known as a boy erased all thoughts of a quick return. The moment he saw sixteen-year-old Antoinette Perotto, the shoemaker's eldest daughter, he became determined not to return to America without her.

Courtship in the Italy of the day was no simple boy-meets-girl-boy-gets-girl procedure. It was a lengthy, involved process where one did not go to call on the girl of one's dreams, but rather made courtesy calls ostensibly to honour the parents. One visit led to another, with Nick in a trance as Antoinette entered and reentered the room setting the table and serving the meal, seldom glancing in his direction.

As the reason for his many visits became obvious, young Antoinette would suddenly disappear, running across the street to the village church. She felt she was too young to marry. She feared leaving her home and going to a strange country. Always when she returned home, Nick was still there, enchanted by the grace with which this tiny girl with the angelic face moved about and by the sparkle in her dark eyes the few times they met his squarely.

At the proper time he talked to Antoinette's father, who told Nick that if Antoinette agreed, he had his permission. Antoinette could not deny her own feelings. There was something about this happy man with the laughing eyes she could not resist.

Nick had arrived at San Marco in April. In July he and Antoinette were married in the San Marco church across the street from the Perotto home.

Preparing to leave for the United States, Nick Iacocca took his new bride on a honeymoon to Rome and Capri. Nick's mother joined them in Naples for the trip across the Atlantic.

Just as Nick, Antoinette, and Mamma were ready to board the ship, Antoinette became ill. It may have been the blistering heat of a southern Italian July or the trepidation of leaving home for a strange land, or a combination of both, but she came down with typhoid fever, which was not diagnosed until the ship had left the harbour.

The frail newlywed, just turned seventeen, was placed in quarantine on the ship for twenty-two days, transforming the jolly, lively Nick into a frantic bridegroom. Not until two weeks passed could he see his bride, and then only through a tiny window.

Nick's brothers came to New York to bring the three travellers back to Allentown. Antoinette recovered fully after a three-month convalescence. Nick remained at her bedside every possible moment until she was well.

Nick then found a new home for them, a brick row house on a quiet Allentown street. It was in this house that their first child, a daughter they named Delma, was born. She was followed less than two years later by the boy they christened Lido Anthony Iacocca.

Newspaper reporters and magazine writers have romanticised Nick's and Antoinette's naming of their son Lido, writing that he was so named because of his father's memories of a glamorous honeymoon spent on the Lido at Venice. Actually Nick and Antoinette's brother had taken a trip to Venice and the Lido before the wedding, and Nick had not forgotten the beauty of the spot.

Nick's business ventures mushroomed. He opened a new hot dog restaurant in Allentown after his return. Located on Sixth Street, a few blocks from his new home, he called it the Orpheum House. When Antoinette was well enough, she came to help, even though she was still learning English.

Lido was a handsome two-year-old when his father, whose brain was always awhirl with new business ideas, came upon a moneymaking idea that would later blossom into one of the world's great enterprises. He was driving his Model T through Allentown one day when the thought struck him that many people could use temporary transportation.

Never one to let a potentially profitable idea lie dormant, Nick established a business he called U-Drive-It, very likely the first rent-a-car business in America, perhaps the world. This new enterprise may have provided the spark that influenced his son's future. From the time Lido was four years old he was taken often to his father's U-Drive-It. Certainly, as youngsters beg to do, young Iacocca often sat behind the wheel of Model T's and later Model A's, for Nick's rental cars were almost exclusively Ford. Lee Iacocca figuratively teethed on Fords.

The U-Drive-It business was no less a success than his Orpheum Wiener House, so the enterprising Nick was able to move into real estate development, a dream he had been nuturing for some time. By the late 1920s Nick Iacocca had grown wealthy.

Nick Iacoca was not so much all business that he neglected his family to build a fortune. On the contrary, he loved his family, and togetherness was the rule when the business day ended. On Sundays at the Iacoccas it was open house, with friends and relatives overflowing the small rooms from mid-morning until late in the evening. Everybody was welcome for Sunday dinner, with the pasta ready at all hours for Antoinette's own spicy tomato sauce.

The environment was ideal for a growing Lido, shy and reserved. On the one hand was the spirited character of his father, garrulous, warm, and hospitable. On the other was a family intimacy and love that would last his lifetime, an atmosphere underscored by Nick's personal philosophy that when it's time to work, give the job your all, and when it's time to play, relish it.

Nick Iacocca felt strongly that no place was better for his maturing son than Allentown. An Italian, born to the thrills of soccer, he found that Italian and other immigrants who had come to work in Allentown's mills had brought Europe's favourite sport with them. So Lido could play soccer. And softball. Even though Nick was vague about any form of baseball, softball was an American game and something his all-American boy should enjoy.

Then, too, not far from Allentown were hiking trails, camping sites, and boating and fishing to be enjoyed at Leaser Lake. And, less than an hour and a half drive in his Model T, were the beautiful Poconos, mountains that rivalled the Apennines back home.

Few father-son relationships are more steadfast than that between Nick and Lido, a closeness Nick initiated from Lido's early years. Lee rarely went anywhere without his father, for whom he had an abiding respect and love. Through his school years and later in the business world, whenever Lee received an award or promotion, he made sure his dad could be there to share in the joy of his achievement.

Nick – tough, hard-nosed and proud – even ruthless – in business was a caring, loving father who impressed his son at every turn with the importance of standing by your guns when you know you are right. It was the sure path to accomplishment, Nick emphasised. This resoluteness in Nick's character saved the Iacocca family from disaster in 1929.

The Great Depression brought the American economy crashing, and Nick Iacocca's hard-won fortune was washed away with those of thousands of other Americans. Nick, never one to curse bad luck, didn't despair, nor did he permit his family to lose hope, even though his situation became more desperate each day.

A building he had constructed on Sixth Street and three apartment houses were lost. Tenants who had operated restaurants in two buildings Nick owned lost their business and moved out. Nick took over the restaurants in the hope of recouping some of his losses, but it was not to be. Losing money day by day, he ultimately lost ownership of the buildings.

Lido, only five years of age at the time of the Crash, was hardly aware of the family misfortune. Nick, meanwhile, took a long look at what seemed a hopeless situation. There had to be some way to start back up. Real estate was out of the question. He had no money to invest. There was another possibility.

'People have got to eat,' he told Antoinette, and finding a promising location, he opened the State Restaurant. He was right back where he had started.

Nick Iacocca had been a food expert, and the people of Allentown remembered. With Antoinette at his side, he worked hard. He saved every cent possible without depriving his family of their needs. Nick still had his touch. The restaurant did so well that he was able to buy two motion picture theatres, one of which – the Franklin – still stands in Allentown.

Profits from the restaurant and the theatres sent Nick Iacocca back to his great love, real estate. He purchased 200 acres of land in East Allentown and developed a fine residential area he called Midway Manor. He began by building one home at a time, then two. As profits permitted, he increased construction. (Midway Manor is today one of the finest residential districts in the Allentown area. Nick had kept one prime corner lot on which he built, in 1950, a castlelike architectural gem of brick for himself and Antoinette, a beautiful home in which Nick's cordial, genteel, and active widow still lives.)

Lido was in the third grade at Allentown's Stephens School when his father began his climb back to prosperity. Throughout his school years he made fine grades, which pleased his father. Having accomplished what he had without a formal education, Nicola believed there was no limit to what his son could become with good schooling.

Lido was a bookworm, but not in the accepted sense. He had his moments for play and recreation. He liked sports. He was no hell-raiser, but he did get into the minor scrapes typical of a growing youngster, though Nick's shadow over his shoulder was a deterrent. Anything his father said was law.

Nick had told Lido that whenever he was in any trouble, got involved in any fight, or fell or got hurt, he should come to him immediately. One day when Lido was about eight years old he was jostling with a friend when the other boy accidentally pushed him through a basement window. The window broke, and Lido cut his hand.

Lido did not go home. He ran to his father's restaurant, his hand bleeding. When his father asked him why he had come there instead of home, Lido answered: 'You always told me when I get hurt I should come to you.' What Nick said Lido invariably took as gospel.

So when Nick Iacocca said Lido must study, Lido studied and let nothing interfere. Often his friends would stand outside his window and call, 'Lido! Lido! Come on out!' Lido ignored the voices, and when they would continue calling, he finally would get up and shout from the window: 'Go away! I've got to study.'

For Lido there was always a time for play and a time for work. It was his father's dictum, and that was enough.

Lido sailed through grade school, a model student. And in junior high, where he earned an overall average of 95, his two lowest grades were 88, one in music, the other in physical education.

'Lido was a rare student,' says Carroll Parks, his eighth-grade English and Latin teacher. 'Not a hell-raiser. Not colourful. He was all business, with a lot of initiative, a boy who knew what he had to do, and did it. Maybe a little shy, too much reserved for his young age.'

Lido took after his hard-driving father, and this probably contributed to his diffidence, since he respected his dad too much to get into the usual rough-and-tumble antics typical of a youngster in his early teens. He may well have been in awe of Nick, an industrious human dynamo who elbowed his way past obstacles.

Gar Laux, who worked with and for Lee many years, knew Nick intimately and had great affection for him. He tells of an incident that graphically portrays Nick's intensity, his ethic for making it in a tough world.

Laux and Iacocca were attending a meeting of Ford dealers in Palm Springs, California, one summer, and Nick Iacocca was invited by his son to join him there for a vacation. Neither Laux nor Iacocca were avid golfers, but during a business break they went out for the exercise, taking Nick with them.

'I'll never forget,' Laux says, 'that after we got Nick to hit the ball, he took off in a speedy run. And we yelled at him,

"No! No! You don't run after the ball, you walk! Walk!" But that's the kind of man Nick was. He just had to go, go one hundred percent.'

This spirit Nick Iacocca hoped to instil in his son. Lido had to learn that the soul of success was vigorous action. It was the way in which his son could become the renowned and powerful man he wanted him to be.

When Lido entered Allentown High School he began to lose his shyness. He began to take part in sports, enjoyed baseball and football, but found swimming and ice-skating gave him the greatest pleasure. In both he was far better than average.

Unfortunately, when he was a sophomore the thrills of swimming, skating – any kind of sports activity – were taken away. He came down with a severe case of rheumatic fever and was bedridden for three months. Unable to move his legs and in pain most of the time, he was as worried about losing time in school as his parents and sister were concerned about his recovery.

Pain wasn't going to stop Lido. If he couldn't get to school, he devised a plan to have school – so to speak – come to him. He had his sister, Delma, then a senior at Allentown High, bring him his assignments day after day. Despite the discomfort he did the required work, and each morning Delma delivered it to Lido's teacher.

Three months in bed did not lower his scholastic average. He was placed on the honour roll that sophomore year.

But he was finished as far as participation in sports was concerned. He had recovered, but he had lost so much weight he resembled a toothpick. Even more distressing, his passions for swimming and skating were now restricted to those of a spectator. It was not enough. He channelled his love for sports into managing the school team.

Lido graduated from Allentown High School in June, 1942, second highest on the class honour roll. *Comus*, the Yearbook, lists Lido Iacocca as a member of the National Honor Society, president of the senior class, member of the Oratan Debating Society and of the Latin Club, and manager of the swimming team.

His picture in *Comus* shows a good-looking, thin young man with dark hair and penetrating dark eyes. Under the name Lido Anthony Iacocca a caption indicates his interests in life to be engineering and science, beneath which is Lido's quote: 'When you aim at anything you are sure to hit it,' a fitting preamble to his future. The brief analysis of Lido's character that follows is also, oddly enough considering his age at the time, a prognostic of the Iacocca to be.

'Lee is a raconteur extraordinary,' it reads, 'and not only can he quip with the best, but he can pun with the worst. If knowledge really is power, he is omnipotent. This, together with the ability he has developed in managing and directing school affairs, will prove a great asset in his career of engineering.'

It was the first time that Lido Anthony Iacocca had been openly referred to in print as 'Lee,' for like his father before him, though he was proud of and would never deny his Italian background, he preferred the more American version of his name. Whether Lee to his friends or Lido to his parents, graduation day was Nick's to relish, though his heart was bursting and his eyes were tear-filled. The boy he had nurtured was now a young man much in his own image.

And it was a somewhat more capricious young man who emerged as Lee Iacocca, high school graduate. He became more outgoing, like his father, enjoying parties and dances. One evening, when Nick and Antoinette went visiting, Lee invited some friends to the house. There was music, dancing, a little beer, but overall it was just a good time.

'They made such a mess,' Antoinette Iacocca says, 'I'll never forget it. When we got home, and it was pretty late, the house was upside-down. Nick really said plenty to Lee.'

Nick, she points out, never laid a hand on either of his children, but there was punishment. When they were young, it was usually the 'go to your room' or 'no outside play today' type. On this occasion Nick had his say and sent Lee to his room, depriving him of the family car for a few days.

Nick being Nick, it was taken for granted that when Lee graduated from high school the next step would be college. The matter of where he should go was one Nick believed

12

deserved serious thought.

It had to be the finest engineering college in the country, Nick insisted, and Lee should pick the one he liked best. Lee was partial to the Massachusetts Institute of Technology but really preferred Lehigh, which was practically next door in Bethlehem, Pennsylvania.

Lee, though he wanted it, resisted a decision for Lehigh because it was known as a rich man's engineering university and thus would be too expensive. That was no argument as far as Nick was concerned. In his eyes the best was none too good for his son. Besides, Lehigh's location meant he could see his son more often.

Once Lehigh was decided on, another determination had to be made. Lee, conscious of the great expense his father would undertake in sending him to such a college, felt that with Lehigh so near, he should live at home.

Nick would have none of it. The added expense of living in a dormitory on campus was little compared to Lee's need to get out into the world. Much as he would have liked to have his son home every night, he insisted that Lee live on campus. Lee finally deferred to his father's wish with the proviso that he would come home on weekends and holidays.

During his first year at Lehigh the budding engineer, who was banned from taking part in any sport by his bout with rheumatic fever, buried himself in his studies. Monday through Thursday the hours away from classrooms were spent in his dormitory room with his books. When classes were finished on Friday, Nick would be waiting in his Ford to take him the ten miles back to Allentown. Early Monday morning the trip was reversed.

Lee's dedication to his books earned him relentless teasing from his dormitory mates, but he shrugged it off. He knew what he was aiming for. Ever since his high school days he had been in love with Fords. Now, at Lehigh, he became all but obsessed with becoming an engineer at the Ford Motor Company, and – as the quote in high school yearbook said – he was going to hit his target.

When the dormitory joshing continued, Lee stopped the jokers with the remark that became his challenge. 'You wait,' he declared. 'I'm going to be a vice-president at Ford before I'm thirty-five!' The statement was made with such seriousness it stopped his friends in their tracks.

Having lost much of his early reticence, Lee was now a more outgoing person, although his classmates at Lehigh still thought him restrained and reserved.

But Lee had a reason for his standoffishness. He was determined to finish his course in industrial engineering in three years, not the usual four. That meant piling up credits, which in turn called for extra hours of hard work. In his sophomore year, by then almost assured of receiving his degree after his third year, he grew more involved in university affairs and became an active member of the Lehigh student government.

One morning in the late spring of 1945, Lee's graduation year from Lehigh, a long, shiny black 1942 Lincoln Continental came to a stop in front of the university's administration building. Out from behind the steering wheel stepped a short, smartly dressed, dignified gentleman with the unlikely name of Leander Hamilton McCormick-Goodheart. His objective was the office of the Dean of Engineering. 'If possible I would like to talk to engineering graduates you consider have the most potential,' McCormick-Goodheart said after introducing himself as supervisor of the Ford Motor Company's personnel planning department. 'Perhaps those at the top in their respective engineering courses.'

Lee Anthony Iacocca was the first Lehigh student to be interviewed by McCormick-Goodheart. Since his early teens Lee, who had idolised Henry Ford as the maker of the Model T that Nick featured at the U-Drive-It, could hardly contain himself. He knew little or nothing of Henry Ford II, who had just been made executive vice-president of Ford, but it had been his dream to work for the Ford Motor Company. And this man with the longest name he had ever heard was offering him the possibility of a job as a Ford trainee.

McCormick-Goodheart explained the great opportunity at Ford for bright young engineers, and though he might have saved his breath, he enthusiastically sold the virtues of the Ford Motor Company. Lee listened intently. However much

14

he had hoped to have Ford in his future, the picture painted by this nattily dressed man with the singular, almost musical name reinforced his determination to go Ford.

McCormick-Goodheart offered Lee a position as an engineering trainee at the hardly munificent salary of $185 a month. The small salary didn't matter, but Lee had a problem. He had already been granted a fellowship at Princeton to get his master's degree, an honour he wanted to accept. Yet his desire to join Ford was equally, if not more, resolute.

He quickly made up his mind. If he had to, it would be Ford, not Princeton. He explained his dilemma and his decision to McCormick-Goodheart.

'One of the remarkable things about Lee Iacocca,' McCormick-Goodheart reported to Henry Ford II, 'is his tremendous, driving sincerity. He didn't "yes" me along or anything. He said "I want very much to work for Ford, but if it doesn't affect me adversely, I want to go on to Princeton for my master's in mechanical engineering."'

'Go to Princeton and get your master's,' Lee was notified. 'A year from now your job will be waiting for you.'

Lee could not have been happier at this turn of events, as was his father. For one thing Nick was glad to have his son home for the summer. It provided an opportunity to further strengthen the unbreakable bond that already existed between them.

The first order of business after Lee's arrival in Allentown after receiving his degree from Lehigh was a graduation party. Nick went all out. The Iacocca home was jammed through the evening. Nick had invited everyone who knew him or Lee, young or old.

Near the end of the evening Nick presented his son with his graduation present, a prewar used Ford. The gift was as much a benefit for Nick as for Lee. Princeton was more than fifty miles away, and if Lee had no car to drive home on weekends, there would have been lengthy separations that both were happy to avoid.

Lee's year at Princeton passed quickly. Typically, he kept his head buried in studies. Months went by without a word from McCormick-Goodheart or anyone at Ford, giving Lee cause for some worry. But early in the spring of 1946 a man named Olen Peters came to see Lee at Princeton. Peters, assistant to McCormick-Goodheart, had been sent to confirm Lee's job as well as check on his progress in mechanical engineering.

Peters had taken the entire file on Lee Iacocca, including a photograph, with him to Princeton. Though shocked by the long, lean, almost anaemic-looking young man, he was impressed especially when he heard Lee reaffirm his great desire to work for Ford. Peters suggested that Lee come to Dearborn as soon after graduation as possible.

When Peters reported back to Ford's personnel planning office in Dearborn, McCormick-Goodheart asked him, 'What did you think of this Lee Iacocca?'

'He's super,' Peters replied. 'We should get him going right away.'

McCormick-Goodheart agreed. 'When I first saw him, I noticed a tremendous directivity in the young man, a tremendous awareness of where he was going. He had a goal, and it stuck out, as much as saying "I know what I'm going to do with myself." At his age I found that unusual.'

'He made no bones about the fact that he really wants to become a part of Ford,' Peters remarked. 'I learned that he'd told classmates that he was going to be a vice-president here by the time he was thirty-five. And he meant it according to some of his classmates!'

'He seemed to me the type of guy who'd say a thing like that,' McCormick-Goodheart said. 'But you know, I think he's also the kind of guy to go ahead and do it. He's got a very strong, serious personality, unusually serious for a kid of twenty-one.'

McCormick-Goodheart had been riffling through the Iacocca file and stopped for a moment to look at Lee's picture. He looked up at Peters.

'You know, Olen,' he said, 'there's only one thing that bothers me about him, especially about his entering the executive world. Look at this picture of him with its head-on look and piercing eyes. Doesn't the expression on his face tell you something? And consider how skinny he is!'

'What do you mean?' asked the puzzled Peters.

McCormick-Goodheart laughed. 'Why, he looks like the American bald eagle that found some other bird's egg in his nest.' After a moment he added: 'Ach, it's stupid of me to say that. He's a goodlooking kid with ability, and it's the ability that counts. And he'll put some weight on his bones, I'm sure.'

'But not before he takes more off in the open hearth,' Peters added. 'And that'll make him all bones before he's hardly started. Can he hold up, I wonder?'

Lee Iacocca was awarded his master's degree in mechanical engineering at Princeton in the early summer of 1946. He was not yet twenty-two. Typically, he had chosen as the subject of his graduation thesis the function and use of torque converters.

After a few weeks at home in Allentown Lee reported to the Ford River Rouge plant in August to begin his role as an engineering trainee. He was the last to report of the fifty-man group recruited by McCormick-Goodheart.

The routine for an engineering trainee began with a ten-day indoctrination designed to make the potential executives familiar with the basic phases of car manufacture. Each ten-day phase was under the tutelage of a different safety engineer, each with responsibility for one area in the sprawling Rouge plant.

In order for the trainees to get to know and understand the work done in each area, as well as to acquaint them with the layout of the far-reaching Rouge, they spent a full day with each of the ten safety engineers. This not only oriented them to the plant but also gave them a physical taste of the various jobs being done.

On his first day Lee Iacocca was taken through the Rouge plant by a safety engineer named Malakas, who explained the different phases of the programme as they walked along. As they went through the open hearth of the steel mill, they passed huge blast furnaces, which were kept scorching hot, their heat bouncing back in searing blasts at anyone within five feet.

Iacocca's escort stopped him. Pointing at one of the furnaces he said: 'You'll be starting here in the morning.'

They then proceeded up to a balcony overhang that provided a good view of the open hearth and also shielded them, to some degree, from the incredible heat.

'Do you know any of the guys in the programme?' Malakas asked. When the new trainee shook his head, the engineer indicated the young man below, no older than Iacocca himself, and added: 'That's Frank Zimmerman.'

Zimmerman, a graduate of the University of Connecticut, was the first man signed for Ford by McCormick-Goodheart. He had already spent ten months in the programme.

Iacocca looked down at the young man, hardly believing his eyes. This smallish youth, who looked like he weighed no more than 105 pounds, was stripped to the waist.

'What's he doing?' Iacocca asked the engineer.

'He's a number-three melter's helper,' Malakas answered, 'and he feeds coke breeze into the furnace.'

Malakas explained that coke breeze was coke ground to a granular consistency, and that the furnace at which Zimmerman was working had been 'tapped-out' – drained of the melted steel. Shovelling coke breeze onto the still-red-hot inner surface of the furnace prevented leakage when smelting was resumed.

Iacocca was awestruck. The furnace door was about four feet off the floor, and Zimmerman, short in stature and so lean one could see the outline of his ribs, could hardly get the shovel up to the furnace opening.

'My God!' exclaimed Iacocca, who hardly weighed more then Zimmerman, 'what did he look like when he first got here?' He then turned to Malakas. 'Tell me, how long does it take to get from number-three to number-two helper?'

Zimmerman, hearing from below, looked up and laughed. The only difference between him and this long, lean Italian Ichabod Crane, as he described Iacocca, was height. It was the beginning of an unending friendship born of mutual respect.

The two had contrasting natures: Lee was quiet, burning with ambition, impatient to get his career moving forward and to a great degree an introvert with a wry sense of humour;

18

Zimmerman was loquacious, a dedicated, innovative practical joker with a sense of the dramatic.

When Lee first arrived in Dearborn, he had taken a room at ten dollars a night in East Dearborn's Fordson Hotel. When Zimmerman had first arrived, unable to find a room, he reputedly slept on the city hall steps. Both later moved to Ann Arbor, some thirty miles west of the Ford headquarters, Lee sharing an apartment with three other trainees, Zimmerman taking a furnished room.

Zimmerman visited the Iacocca apartment almost every evening, playing cards with the three trainees. Lee, who had not learned to relax at a game of cards, made coffee for the group.

Lee had Iacocca cousins studying at Notre Dame, but it was Zimmie – as Lee began to call Frank – who suggested drives to South Bend to see Lee's cousins and not incidentally watch the fighting Irish play football. Zimmie, aware of Lee's passion for sports he could not play, knew such suggestions were certain to get him out of his shell.

Zimmie also twisted Lee's arm into double-dating. Lee was the one with a car, a not-so-new Ford convertible. The pair began taking out two girls from the YWCA. Lee's date, according to Zimmie, was a knockout. Zimmie's girl, however, was described by Lee as a girl already down for the count of ten.

So it went for the remaining year of Zimmerman's training period. Fun-provoking Zimmie slowly transformed the serious-minded Lee into a relaxed young man who appreciated a zany outing now and then. He also interlaced pleasure periods with the engineering talk Lee enjoyed.

Zimmerman had already joined the Society of Automotive Engineers and had SAE friends in Ann Arbor, professors and instructors at the University of Michigan. With these friends he and Lee would spend many hours in shoptalk. Of course Zimmie often spiced up the discussions by suggesting a night on the town.

'As a matter of fact,' Zimmerman recalls, 'we spent Lee's twenty-second birthday at the Pretzel Bell in Ann Arbor throwing hard-boiled eggs at the ceiling.'

The trainee period at Ford was eighteen months, during which each recruit worked in every conceivable area of the Rouge plant. They stoked the coke ovens in the steel mill, forged metal in the blacksmith shop, tightened screws on the assembly line, even worked on the Ford-owned lake boats that brought iron ore from Michigan's Upper Peninsula. They also did duty on the test track and in the Rouge hospital.

It was the most phenomenal education in automobile know-how imaginable, one especially advantageous to both Iacocca and Zimmerman, by a few years the youngest among the fifty then going through the system. Both had been unusually young as college graduates, Lee with a master's degree at twenty-one, and Zimmerman with his bachelor's at twenty.

'We had it made,' Zimmerman says. 'For young kids who had a lot of book learning but didn't know beans about automobiles, it was a tremendous opportunity. A superb education in the practical side of building automobiles, why cars are what they are, and what they should be. And Lee was running away from the rest of us.'

With Zimmie planning to leave when his training time was exhausted, Lee met a man destined to be another close friend, one who would take over where Zimmerman left off in keeping Lee alive and vibrant in what is normally a dull, unexciting routine.

Al Henderson, a Ford man who knew Lee, was making a trip to Chicago for the 1947 All Star baseball game with Bill Winn, a young promotion man who did not work for Ford. Knowing Lee's love of sports, Henderson decided to stop in Ann Arbor and invite him to join them. Lee needed no second invitation.

The threesome drove to the Windy City and saw the American League trounce the National, 2–1. After the game Henderson had some personal business to take care of. Lee and Bill Winn took off together to look over America's second-largest city.

They did the Chicago scene, laughing, joking, getting acquainted. They passed Soldier Field, visited the Field Museum of Natural History and the Shedd Aquarium. The more they walked and talked, the more impressed Lee became with Bill Winn, who was in sales promotion. Winn was a gentle individual, soft-spoken, and with a puckish charm. He was nowhere near as tall, a young man of quiet reserve like Lee, but with a roguish wit.

On Michigan Avenue they suddenly decided to go shopping, to find hats as gifts for their girlfriends. They went from store to store, looking, comparing, kidding. Finally each made a purchase.

'We made quite a picture,' Bill Winn says, 'with people staring at us, two guys walking by carrying two pink hatboxes.'

The weekend in Chicago was the beginning of a lasting friendship. With two of his apartment mates moving on at Ford, Lee was looking for a new apartment, as was Bill, so they joined forces. Remaining together through the balance of Lee's training period helped complete what Zimmerman had begun, the emergence of Lee Iacocca as a resolute, self-reliant young man.

Frank Zimmerman, who had started his trainee period ten months before Lee's arrival, completed his eighteen-month course in November, 1946. He wanted to be nearer his Connecticut home and headed east, applying for a job in Ford's New York district. Short and trim, even younger looking than his twenty-one years, he had to talk the district manager into assigning him to truck sales.

Lee, whose training period would not end before January, 1948, itched to get his career in high gear. He had seen the group called the "Quiz Kids" come into the training centre, punch the same time clock he had punched – while making much more money than his $185 a month – and move out of training in a matter of weeks. They were out of the army and few, if any, had a better education than he.

He had an advantage over them in the time he already had spent learning the reality of making automobiles, something the Quiz Kids really could not have absorbed in their short training periods. To remain until August and cover every single facet of the manufacturing business seemed a waste of time.

Lee talked the matter over with his superiors and was able to convince them that with a master's degree he hardly needed the full eighteen-month indoctrination. They agreed and cut his training period to one year. In August, 1947, his trainee days were over.

He was now face to face with his future in the Ford Motor Company. But what turn should it take? In what area could he make the most meaningful contributions to the company and, at the same time, help himself achieve his goal at Ford?

One possibility was engineering, which had been his major, but as far as he could see, few engineers made it to the top of the industry. Styling was another course, but it had its limitations, too. There also were finance, product development and planning, sales and marketing, and a half-dozen or so other areas for which he felt himself suited.

The question was: 'Where do I go from here?'

CHAPTER 2

Iacocca decided that his best prospects for progress at the Ford Motor Company lay in sales and marketing. The number of motor vehicles registered in the United States was nearing the 47-million mark in 1947, a leap of 15 million since 1940. More than 10 million of this increase was in passenger cars.

Phenomenal changes were also taking place in American highways. Fast, smooth freeways and toll roads had begun to crisscross the continent. It was being said that one could drive from New York to Los Angeles someday soon in three days or less. A 'See America First' spirit, already taking hold, indicated that automobile sales would skyrocket year by year.

In addition the potential for corporate profits in the automobile industry had been increased substantially when a Republican-dominated Congress passed, over President Truman's veto, the Taft-Hartley bill, which abolished some of the restrictions on management imposed by the Democratic administration of Franklin Roosevelt and added several restraints on labour unions. Business in general, and the automobile industry in particular, should enjoy a productive shot in the arm.

Frank Zimmerman was already settled in the truck sales department in Ford's New York district office at Edgewater, New Jersey, on the Hudson River just north of Manhattan. Zimmerman suggested that Lee follow the same course.

Anxious to get back east and closer to home, Iacocca headed for Edgewater to see the district manager.

When he arrived, he found the manager away, and was interviewed by two assistants. One assistant manager, as Lee tells it, 'never put down the *Wall Street Journal*, he never saw me,' and the other said 'If you're a college graduate, number one, and from the home office, number two, get the hell out and go back to Detroit.'

Lee was taken aback somewhat by such cavalier treatment, but waited and finally was interviewed by the district manager. Lee was with him for some while, answered the questions asked, and waited for the verdict.

'Well, Iacocca,' the manager said, 'I'm impressed with what I hear, but my advice to you is that you'll never make it in sales. I think you ought to try to get into engineering.'

The irony of the situation is that the manager told Iacocca, who would be one of the greatest marketing geniuses since Phineas T. Barnum, that he couldn't cut the mustard.

Whether or not the assistants were merely playing a joke on a rookie or the manager did not know what he was talking about, Lee was crushed momentarily. The reaction was anything but what he expected, but it was enough to make him consider – if only for a moment – resigning from the Ford Motor Company. Imbued from his earliest days by his father's often-repeated 'You never give up. You *never* quit!' Lee decided to try again.

This time he approached Charles Beacham, sales manager of the Ford Eastern regional office at Chester, Pennsylvania, a small city near Philadelphia. Beacham, who was very likely the most astute sales manager in the Ford empire, and who was to achieve a vice-presidency in the near future, saw in young Iacocca a latent driving force and a determination to make it whatever the cost in physical energy – qualities he demanded in the men who worked for him.

Lee was able to go home to Allentown for a two-week visit with his family before he started at Chester. Nick Iacocca was overjoyed at having his son to himself for fourteen days, proudly showing him off to friends, relatives, and any strangers they happened to meet.

24

When Lee reported at Chester, his assignment was that of field manager, a job considered by those who held it 'the lowest form of life in sales,' despite the title. It involved visiting different dealers in a particular zone – for Lee it was southeastern Pennsylvania – and doing everything possible to stimulate sales by influencing dealers to promote and advertise.

'Low-life' assignment or not, Chester was the ideal starting point for Lee Iacocca's first job. It not only was near enough to Allentown to permit spending every weekend at home, it also put him in the hands of a mentor who was tailor-made to develop his innate talents.

The rebuff and discourtesy he had suffered at the New York office were the best bad luck of his life. Beacham, a hard-driving, ply-the-hammer man in the mould of Nick Iacocca, was just what Lee needed. Beacham was tough and demanding as well as understanding and fair.

Gar Laux, who also worked for him, paints a clear picture of the man in action. 'One day Mr Beacham called me into his office and took me apart,' he recalled. 'It got to the point where I said "Mr Beacham, I don't have to take this from you or anybody else." I turned and walked to the door, and just as I got to the door, Beacham said, "Come back here. Damn it, if I didn't think you had anything worthwhile, I wouldn't waste my damn time with you. Now get the hell out of here and do your job." Beacham was the kind of man who was always on your tail to make you do better, *if* you can do better. If you can't, you don't belong.'

Exposed as he was day-in and day-out to a Charley Beacham, and determined to do the best he could as soon as he could, Lee not only came out of his shell but also absorbed what Ford people have called 'Beachamism' – an intuitive knowledge that 'you've got to move fast to catch the weasel asleep.'

Gar Laux carries Charley's influence on Iacocca a step further. 'Between them Lee's dad and Mr Beacham did a helluva job with Lee. But I'll tell you, they had a helluva lot of guy to do something with.'

Lee's exposure to the many dealers, sales managers, and

other dealership personnel in his assigned territory, with their divergent personalities and educational levels, sparked his inherent talent for communication. That valuable experience, coupled with the tough but reasonable prodding of Charley Beacham, early on proved Iacocca to be a comer who bore watching – a 'remarkable young man,' in Beacham's words.

One of Lee's co-workers at Chester was a former newspaper editor named Jay Dugan. Dugan, who left Ford soon after Iacocca's arrival to open his own ad agency in the Philadelphia area, helped implement many of Iacocca's future promotions. He, too, was thoroughly impressed with the newcomer to Chester.

'In the few months I was at Chester after Lee's appointment,' Dugan says, 'I found him to be very forthright, candid, and straight-on in his approach to dealers. He was disarming in his candour when talking to his dealers, or anybody. He could tell you something you might not want to hear, but he could tell it in such a way that you accepted it as something constructive, which it was, he was that sharp.'

In two months Beacham promoted Iacocca into the truck sales department, with a territory spreading into southern New Jersey and Delaware. After a few meetings with truck salesmen Lee saw a need for putting into print the important do's and don't's for successful truck merchandising and selling. He took it upon himself, with some editing help from Jay Dugan, to write *Hiring and Training Truck Salesmen*, a handbook for use by dealers and their sales managers.

Each discussion he had with dealership executives, each meeting he conducted for truck salesmen and sales managers, further sharpened his speaking skills. At training meetings he was a spellbinder, with a sharp, sometimes caustic wit. His sphere of action broadened to include the South Atlantic states.

Typical of his ability to take advantage of any situation was his opening gambit at a truck sales meeting he conducted in Atlanta, Georgia. He called the meeting to order and wrote his name LEE IACOCCA in large letters on a blackboard. As if a light had been turned on in his brain, he turned suddenly and erased his last name.

'Now that's better,' he said, pointing at the blackboard where only the word LEE remained. 'That's a name that really means something down in this country.'

It was Iacocca at his best. Throughout that meeting, and in all meetings he conducted in the South, this little touch held attention and produced results.

Whether in the Chester office or on the road, Iacocca took few breaks. He worked long hours, studied the automobile business, particularly sales and marketing techniques, non-stop. Now and again he and his friend Jay Dugan, whose ad agency was now established in nearby Jenkintown, would sit late into the night devising gimmicks that would increase automobile sales.

One afternoon in late spring of 1948, about three months after he started working for Charley Beacham, Lee Iacocca was in a hallway at the Chester office talking to a co-worker in truck leasing, when an extraordinarily pretty redhead was passing through a corridor straight ahead.

'Now there's somebody you should check on,' Iacocca's companion said.

The young lady was Mary McCleary, a receptionist at the Ford assembly plant in Chester. She was heading for the medical dispensary located in the same building as Lee's office, a victim of too much exposure to a sun lamp. She did not see Lee, but he was immediately impressed.

About a month later, on June 9, the Ford Motor Company introduced its new 1949 models to the Philadelphia district in a gala reception at the elegant Bellevue Stratford Hotel. All Ford employees in the area were invited to attend the company party marking the new car introduction.

After a motion picture preview of the new cars, everyone converged on the Bellevue Stratford cocktail lounge. On entering, Mary McCleary was intercepted by a married man with a reputation bordering on the lecherous. One of the Chester secretaries, who was seated at a table that included Lee Iacocca, saw the man take Mary's arm. She quickly had her rescued, brought to the table, and introduced to Lee.

As he stood to acknowledge the introduction, one he had hoped for since she was pointed out in the Chester office hallway, Mary's first impression was 'Oh, my! He's as skinny as a beanpole!' Iacocca was so tall and so thin, weighing, she says, 'maybe a hundred and eighteen pounds soaking wet. And very shy.'

But Lee was not too shy to show his interest by asking to take Mary McCleary home that evening. They began to date, but irregularly. Lee was tied up with his work most of the week, and on weekends he drove back to Allentown to see his father, mother, and sister. The weekend trips began with his first week at Chester, months before he met Mary, and it was a routine he did not break.

'Must you go to Allentown?' became a regular Friday-afternoon plea.

Mary wanted to visit friends with Lee, have dinner occasionally, go to the theatre or even sports events in Philadelphia, since Lee was such an avid sports fan. Finally, eager to spend time with the man she had come to love, she agreed to accompany him on a few trips home.

Mary got on well with the Iacocca family. She quickly grew to love Nick, Antoinette, and Delma, and they her, but even so the weekends at Allentown were often depressing. It seemed that the only time she had alone with Lee was on the drive there and back. So when the question of marriage came up, as it often did, Mary was uneasy. She would not say yes even though she wanted to. Lee, completely taken by Mary's good sense and waiflike charm, continued to ask.

He also continued to work hard, making himself more valuable by the day to Charley Beacham and to the Ford Motor Company. Suddenly, in the early 1950s a slowdown in sales hit the Ford Division. In 1950 total Ford new-car registrations in the United States numbered 1.5 million, but they dropped to under 1.25 in 1951 and plummeted below the million mark in 1952.

The trauma in these numbers, so far as Ford headquarters in Dearborn was concerned, was not so much in the loss of sales. The economy had been sluggish, and Chevrolet, the Ford Division's most formidable competition, had suffered proportionately. The real agony lay in the fact that when sales for both leaped back over the million mark in 1953, the Ford

Division, which had gained on Chevy to the tune of 134,000 between 1950 and 1952, fell back some 106,000 in registered sales.

For the executives at Ford Division headquarters in Dearborn losing ground after coming within a hair of topping Chevy was the real cause for alarm. They ordered an austerity programme across the board. The Chester office was forced to cut back on personnel. Lee did not lose his job, but he was dropped a notch in grade.

Taking that one step back on the promotion ladder just as he began moving ahead fast was a crushing blow. For a short time he began to have doubts about his future at Ford, but the realist in Iacocca prevailed.

After all he was still with the company he had longed to work for since his teens, and a setback wasn't the end, but something that could be turned into a plus if he applied himself. This was Nick Iacocca's philosophy filtering through Lee's brain. As his father did after the Crash of '29, Lee went after his job with intensified effort.

The success of his talks to dealer groups had instilled an intrepid and spirited self-confidence and had given him the on-the-stump charisma of a spellbinding preacher. What he said made sense and stimulated sales managers and salesmen to increase closings on car deals. His hard work paid off. Within six months he was restored to the grade he held before the rollback. Beacham's faith in the marketing neophyte he had hired had been more than justified. In another six months Lee Iacocca was named assistant sales manager of the Philadelphia district.

Meanwhile the romance between Lee and Mary McCleary had run hot and cold into its seventh year. Things had not changed for Mary as Lee continued his weekend drives to Allentown, failing to do so only once in about six months.

When the winter winds ease up and the grass begins to green, the automobile industry traditionally begins planting the seeds of promotion for the oncoming model year. On the national level corporate sales and marketing executives work in concert with their major advertising agencies. Their aim is a broad-scale concept to position the virtues of their four-wheel offerings more dramatically than the competition.

On more local levels, particularly district offices, the emphasis is on support for the national effort, based on observations that stress sales in tune with the buyers of the immediate area. At the Chester office Lee Iacocca buried himself in finding the sales stimulus that would best serve the Philadelphia district in moving the upcoming 1956 models. Mary saw even less of Lee than usual as he thought of and discarded idea after idea.

He spent days patiently searching for the surest way to thaw public resistance to the purchase of new cars. He was born in the area, knew its people – the German, Italian, and Irish immigrants and their first-generation offspring. He talked the matter over with his friend, Jay Dugan.

What, he wondered, could influence car buyers whose paycheques had to cover rent, food, and clothing, in addition to car payments? Lee took pencil in hand and began doodling figures. He analysed the buyers in his area and their reticence in saddling themselves with car payments.

The base for the ideal sales stimulus was right there. The car payment. People who needed or wanted a new car were less likely to worry about the sticker price – the total they had to pay – as long as they knew they could afford the monthly instalments.

'That is the genius of Iacocca,' Jay Dugan insists. 'The capacity to visualise a need, to prepare a plan and implement that plan to meet the need long before anybody else sees there is a need for it.'

The idea proposed by Iacocca, commonplace today, had marketing men throughout the industry shaking their heads. It was so simple, so obvious – why hadn't they thought of it?

The heart and guts of the Iacocca promotion was its theme: '56 for 56.' People could buy a brand-new 1956 Ford for $56 a month after a moderate down payment. Only $56 a month? It was peanuts for the average working man.

The idea, revolutionary in its day, took hold in the Philadelphia district like a brushfire. Dealers loved it. The '56 for 56' really sold cars. But Lee was not content to rest with the concept alone. To milk every possible sale it had to be merchandised and given maximum impact and visibility. Just as visibility makes a man better known by selling him to his superiors, putting a good idea squarely in the public's eye would generate interest and, in turn, generate sales.

He talked over merchandising ideas with Jay Dugan, and they came up with a gimmick they called 'wujatak' – a play on the phrase 'would-you-take.' On streets and on parking lots throughout the district cards attractively designed by the Jay Dugan Agency were placed on automobiles by Ford salesmen. The card asked the car owner 'wujatak' a specified number of dollars, based on the value of the particular automobile, 'for your car on a new 1956 Ford.'

Attached to the wujatak was a small bag of potato chips bearing the words 'The chips are down. We're selling cars for $56 a month' and the name and address of the Ford dealer in the specific sector.

Potato chips were hard to come by in the Philadelphia area for some time. Jay Dugan had cornered the market as he bought trailerload after trailerload to give Lee's promotion a rousing and stimulating send off.

'You should have seen us,' Dugan laughs, 'me, my wife and sons, sitting in our kitchen night after night stapling wujataks to potato chip bags.'

The slogan '56 for 56' proved to be a blockbuster, one of the most innovative and successful promotions in the history of automobile sales. The 139 dealers in the Ford Philadelphia district could not keep up with demand. Chester led the nation in Ford sales. Lee Iacocca's name was heralded at Ford's Dearborn headquarters as well as at Chester.

Robert S. McNamara, then vice-president in charge of the Ford Division, took Lee's programme and made it a nationwide campaign for 1956 Ford cars. It produced extra sales approaching 75,000.

The gratification and pleasure Lee enjoyed as his '56 for 56' swept the country was not without pain, partly caused by his inability to get Mary McCleary's consent to marry him. His courtship took a turn for the worse in the spring of 1956.

On one of the rare weekends he did not drive back to Allentown, he and Mary joined a group of married couples on a trip to the Poconos. Mary, perhaps envious of the way the marrieds enjoyed the outing, was distressed by the thought that such wished-for happiness was denied her. Lee, whom she could not stop loving, was wedded to his parents and his job. When Lee dropped her at her home after the mini-vacation, they decided they would not see each other again.

The morning after their return Mary came down with a high fever. She called her office to report being sick. Throughout the day she had an insatiable thirst. She drank water, Pepsi, Seven-Up, any liquid available. Nothing helped. She became weaker as the day went on. When her brother came home, Mary's mother insisted he take the girl to the hospital immediately.

Lee himself had spent an apprehensive day in his Chester office, boggled in mind, saddened by the decision made the night before. He did not want to lose the one girl in his world. At five o'clock he phoned Mary's home and learned from her father that she was in the hospital. Lee wasted no time in getting there.

Mary's illness had been diagnosed as a severe case of pneumonia. Throughout her stay in the hospital Lee was there every possible moment. The hours he spent at her bedside made him more determined. For him there was no one but Mary McCleary. And Mary, seeing his concern, loved him more dearly. Yet . . .

After Mary came home from the hospital, her mother sat and talked to her at length. The mental anguish her daughter was suffering had to end. While she had vowed earlier not to interfere, she believed now was the time to say what she felt.

She told Mary how much she loved and respected Lee Iacocca, that the love Lee had for his father was a good thing, not parental dominance, because Lee had proved himself a strong man in his own right. Besides, she pointed out, a man who had such high regard for his parents made the best kind of husband.

Lee and Mary were engaged on Mother's Day and began their plans for a September wedding.

Lee arrived at his office the next day, buoyed up and exultant. After calling Nick to give him the news, he went at his job with a vengeance. The demotion that had dashed his hopes a couple of years back had taught him that one should have no illusions about instant progress, that perseverance could turn a seeming failure into a conquest. Getting Mary back was proof enough.

In July came a sweet yet saddening surprise. Charley Beacham, who was now at Ford Division headquarters, notified Lee to pack his bags and move from the banks of the Delaware River to the shores of the Potomac. He had been promoted to manage the Washington district office.

It was the development he needed to get back on track toward his goal, a giant step towards that vice-presidency he aimed for. Yet, with the wedding almost two and a half months in the offing, it also meant seeing less of Mary. Their only chance to be together would be on weekends or at such times as Mary could come to Washington or his work take him back to Chester.

Hard work provided the healing balm for Lee's temporary separations from Mary. There were problems in Washington, and thinking about possible solutions kept his mind occupied. It was his first full-charge management position, and Lee made the most of it, putting the Washington office on a crash status for improved productivity. His growing reputation as a marketing expert was not overlooked.

On the Wednesday before his wedding day he began a short leave of absence, arriving in Chester that evening. Thursday morning he and Mary went to the courthouse for their marriage licence, after which Lee took Mary home and then paid a visit to the Chester office. He was surprised to find Charley Beacham waiting for him.

'Pick up your paycheque and forget about Washington,' Beacham told Lee. 'When you come back after your wedding, you'll be coming to Dearborn. You're my new truck marketing manager.'

Lee was speechless. Too much was happening too fast. Or was it? In less than four weeks he would be thirty-two, which left him a bare three years to hit the target he had predicted while at Lehigh.

'But don't tell Mary until after the wedding,' Beacham

added. 'She's got enough on her mind right now.'

Lee kept the good news secret from Mary, but, as he had with every promotion and award he had ever received, he could not wait to tell his father. It was a lengthy phone call of repeated congratulations. Nick, naturally, was overjoyed. His unequivocal pride in his son's future, boasted of for years as a sure thing, was now substantiated. Certainly almost everyone in Allentown became aware of Lee's good fortune before Mary.

September 29, 1956, Mary K. McCleary and Lido Anthony Iacocca were married by Father Michael McNicholas in Chester's St. Robert Catholic Church. At the reception no man, other than Lee himself, was happier or danced more than Nick Iacocca.

Because of Lee's promotion the honeymoon was necessarily brief. The couple came back to Chester, where Mary remained with her mother. Lee went on to Dearborn, eager to start his new assignment and to search for a house.

Charles Beacham had been significantly responsible for the transformation, so he was not surprised at the difference between the Lee Iacocca who had returned to his Chester office nine years earlier and the well-tailored, confident Iacocca who reported to his office at Ford Division in October, 1956. Beacham was sure that this young man who had proved himself a wunderkind in the marketing of automobiles, an art vital to Ford at that time, was just the one to bring Ford sales back to respectability.

The Ford Motor Company had closed out 1956 with a market share 22.3 percent below that of General Motors and not quite 13 percent above Chrysler's share of the American market. The company badly needed a stimulating shot in its selling arm.

It was the kind of challenge Iacocca had hoped for. Only by doing the thorough job he had been doing – thus making himself visible – could he possibly come close to his pledge of a vice-presidency by his thirty-fifth birthday.

Those who knew of his aspiration called it an illusion, a grasping at shadows. An objective look at the situation made it an improbable, even impossible dream.

'A lot of us snickered behind his back,' said one of his contemporaries. 'He was such a gung-ho guy on the job, and he let you know it with his sharp duds and big cigar. What's his hurry, we said. As the new kid on the block, he had a lot of bodies to leapfrog. And no way could he shortstop any of the Whiz Kids.'

'Whiz Kids' was a more dignified name for the group originally called the Quiz Kids, the same intellectuals who were privileged with brief indoctrination while Lee spent a full year as trainee. Lee was familiar with the achievements of a few, particularly Robert McNamara, now his top boss as vice-president of Ford and general manager of Ford Division. McNamara, along with Arjay Miller, Ed Lundy, Ben Mills, Francis Reith, and James Wright were indeed a formidable group.

Nothing could be gained by worrying about anyone else. The realities be damned – what he had to do was charge ahead. His nature thrived on seemingly irrational challenges. His dream might be called a fantasy, but even fantasies had a way of becoming fact. It counted for something that he had devotedly loved the Ford Motor Company as far back as when he sat in Model T's in his father's U-Drive-it. He had idolised the first Henry Ford for accomplishing what he had without an education and for having the courage to go ahead and do what he wanted. That devil-take-the-hindmost spirit of old Henry appealed to Iacocca.

He knew it would not be easy to reach his goal, which made it all the more exciting – as did the existing situation at Ford, with its up-one-year-and-down-the-next history.

During the first two decades of the twentieth century the Ford name had been synonymous with automobile. Ford was the royal family of the industry. In many ways the chronology of the company's activities over a half-century was a blend of genius and idiocy.

CHAPTER 3

People on seven continents know that the Ford Motor Company was given birth by Henry Ford. Strong parallels exist in the characters of Henry, a product of the nineteenth century, and the twentieth-century Iacocca, but they also had dissimilarities, such as those that existed between Iacocca and Henry Ford II

Henry the first, no blueblood, although he came to see himself as the equivalent, began with only an idea and no money. From a humble start he built one of the world's best known organisations. Yet he all but destroyed the company through bad judgment and his increasingly obstreperous nature.

Henry Ford was born July 30, 1863, the eldest son of William Ford, who farmed a few acres just west of the city of Detroit. Because young Henry detested farming and was interested only in things mechanical, his father and two brothers, John and William, shared a dislike for Henry that verged on hatred as the years passed. Henry had as little regard for his father and brothers.

'John and William are all right,' Henry's father once declared. 'But I'm worried about Henry. I don't know what will become of him.'

What became of Henry is history. He made himself the wealthy eccentric who changed the world's way of life by putting it on wheels. A man with the courage of his convictions and rare foresight, he was nonetheless the same Henry who also blundered and made almost as many turns down the wrong road as up the right.

He frequently refused sound advice. Too often he put his trust where it was not warranted, which proved to be his Achilles heel.

Henry's lone stabilising influence, the one person whose judgment could override his own, was common-sensed Clara Bryant, the tiny, chestnut-haired girl he met at a square dance and married when he was twenty-eight. From the start of their courtship Clara, whom he always called 'Mother,' was his heart, mind, and often his voice. Characteristically, he did not marry Clara until she assured him that she, unlike his father and brothers, understood and appreciated his obsession with mechanics.

Henry Ford made the automobile an affordable means of transportation rather than a plaything of the wealthy, but he was not its inventor. Nor was he the originator or first builder of the internal combustion engine or the first to drive a 'horseless carriage.'

In April, 1866, two Germans, Nikolas Otto and Eugen Langen, were granted a patent for a gasoline-powered engine. Gottlieb Daimler and Karl Benz, also Germans, produced efficient engines as early as 1885. And in the United States, Charles Duryea chugged through the streets of Springfield, Massachusetts, in his self-built gas-buggy on September 22, 1893.

Henry Ford was working for the Edison Illuminating Company in Detroit in 1893 when he was inspired by an article in the *American Machinist*, which described how to construct a gasoline engine. Henry built his machine in the basement of his home from an old piece of gas pipe and bits of scrap iron.

On Christmas Eve, 1893, about two months after his son Edsel was born, Henry carried his device upstairs to the kitchen. He connected a wire from the contrivance to an electric light to create an ignition. He started the engine with Clara carefully squeezing drops of gasoline into the pipe.

Henry worked in a small shed behind his home for another two and one-half years, refining his engine and building a four-wheeled cycle-type body. Early on the morning of June 4, 1896, he installed the engine in the makeshift body.

A happy Henry started the engine and prepared to mount the box that served as the quadracycle's only seat. Though it was after three in the morning, Clara could not keep him from taking the loud, clattering vehicle for a test drive. Henry started up to the seat and suddenly realised that his creation was far too big to pass through the shed's single door. Yet, galvanised by his inner excitement, Henry was not to be deprived of his ride. He grabbed an axe and demolished the front wall of the outbuilding.

Henry's quadracycle was a primitive contraption, boxy in appearance and without brakes. It had no reverse gear. Its deficiencies mattered little to Henry as he bounced through the rough Detroit streets, imagining himself building hundreds of cars at prices so low any working man could afford one.

But Henry had quit his job at Edison to work full-time on his quadracycle, and building cars would take money. He needed cash support, investors who had faith in him and in his dream.

His first patron was William Murphy, a Detroit lumber baron. Murphy believed in profits. Henry enjoyed tinkering with his 'toy' rather than going into immediate production. The Detroit Automobile Company established by Murphy lost $100,000 in its first year, and Murphy went one way, Henry another.

Other investors came and went. Finally Murphy, who had not lost faith in Henry Ford's contraption, put together another group of investors, with Henry as chief engineer holding 1,000 shares of stock in the company. To keep Ford in line Murphy and his group hired Henry Leland, a highly respected engineer, to keep Henry enthusiastic about building cars.

Henry resented the intrusion. He ignored Leland and went along dreaming and not producing. He was, and would remain through his lifetime, a recalcitrant, iron-willed autocrat. 'I'll do it my way or not at all.'

It was too much for the Murphy investors, who bought

Henry's shares for $9.00 each and then dissolved the Detroit Automobile Company. With Henry Leland as the new head, an organisation was established as the Cadillac Motor Company. Henry's refusal to accept Leland was to cost the future Ford Motor Company. He not only lost the help of one of the most brilliant automobile minds the industry would know but would, in a few years, spend $8 million in Ford money to take over the Lincoln Motor Company eventually established by Leland.

The world mistakenly sees Henry Ford as an engineer with incomparable foresight, an organisational genius who built a worldwide industrial giant. Henry undeniably knew engines, and he did have the foresight to recognise a need for inexpensive automobiles. It was this latter fact which brought him his fame as well as his fortune. Despite his engineering knowhow he was perhaps the most disorganised carmaker in automobile history.

Henry Ford could build engines, but his talents ended there. Someone else was needed to build the body and machine parts to precise specifications. This need brought about another of the freakish situations in which the Ford Motor Company would become involved.

John and Horace Dodge, hell-raising, heavy-drinking brothers who had come from Canada to open a machine shop in Detroit, were producing parts for Oldsmobile. They were approached by Alexander Malcomson, a coal merchant who delivered fuel for the Ford fireplace, and became Henry's new financial backer. Malcomson asked the Dodge Brothers to provide Ford Motor with 650 full chassis a year at $250 each. They hesitated but finally agreed to leave Oldsmobile when Malcomson sweetened the pot with fifty shares of Ford stock for each brother.

With the Dodge brothers in the fold, the Ford Motor Company became a going concern. Within thirty-seven days the first Ford car, a two-cylinder dubbed the Model A, was sold for $850. By October 1 the fledgling company had delivered 195 Model A cars to show a profit of approximately $37,000 and orders began to pour in.

In the spring of 1903, Malcomson, excited by the

potential, established a partnership that gave Henry his head and promised no interference. James Couzens, Malcomson's hot-tempered bookkeeper, would manage the Malcomson interests in a new company named after Henry.

The Ford Motor Company was established on June 16, 1903, capitalised at $150,000, with Henry Ford as vice-president and chief engineer. More than one-third of the original stock sold was held by John Gray, a Detroit banker, who was named president. With the filing of the corporate papers the Ford legend was born. The Ford name was on the way to international fame.

Henry, however, soon found Malcomson and other board members of the company bearing his name as difficult to please as William Murphy. Other automobile makers were building big cars, and the Ford directors soon understood that the bigger the car produced, the higher the selling price and the larger the profit margin. This did not fit Henry's concept. He wanted to build low-cost small cars that the average man could buy. He argued that building more and selling for less would balance out profits in the long run. The board would not agree.

Henry, realizing that he was at the mercy of the board, quietly began buying up stock. By October, 1906, he owned 58½ percent of all Ford stock and took over as president. He could now do what *he* wanted without question. The only man among the Malcomson group he retained was James Couzens, who later made millions thanks to Ford, yet subsequently, as a member of the United States Senate, fought Henry Ford at every turn.

Within one year, remembering the hard farm work he had hated, Ford introduced a mechanised tractor to ease the farmer's workload. Before the turn of another calendar year, Detroit set eyes on his most memorable contribution to the world, a car people began writing about, singing about, and joking about.

It was Henry Ford's Model T, his fabulous 'tin lizzie,' the first production-built automobile model with the steering wheel on the left. Its cost was $850. Lizzie made her bow on October 1, 1908, Henry telling buyers, with a twinkle in his eyes, that they could have her 'in any colour they wanted as long as it was black.'

The Model T sold well from the start, even though the rest of the infant auto industry laughed at it and downgraded Lizzie behind Henry's back. They called it no more than a pile of sheet metal strung together with baling wire. But Henry had the last laugh.

He entered his Model T in a New York-to-Seattle endurance race open to all car-makers, giving its critics a field day. No way, they said, could this plain, ugly-structured horseless carriage make it from New York to New Jersey, much less across the continent.

Lizzie proved equal to the task. Twenty-two days after the competition got under way on June 1, 1909, she had conquered rutted dirt and mud-filled roads from the Atlantic to the Pacific, arriving in Seattle far in front of the few others able to withstand the rigours of the still primitive American roads. She had proved herself a durable, versatile automobile that people could depend on.

The success story of the tin lizzie is the success story of Henry Ford, a story too well known to bear repetition. In Henry's Highland Park Plant in 1910, 21,000 Model T's rolled off the newly designed production assembly line, where cars could be put together in minutes instead of days. Called the greatest of all engineering achievements, Henry's new line, which could assemble a complete car in ninety-three minutes, had cost more that $7 million. By 1912 the line was creating some 200,000 cars a year, and romanticists began calling it the eighth wonder of the world.

Henry Ford tossed another bombshell into the automobile industry on January 5, 1914, by announcing a $5 daily wage for eight hours' work, earnings that more than doubled the industry scale of $2.34 for a nine-hour day. On January 6 10,000 labourers, including hundreds from General Motors, stormed the Ford plants for jobs.

Henry's only son, Edsel, married Eleanor Lowthian Clay on November 1, 1916. As a wedding gift Edsel was brought into the Ford Motor Company as secretary. Bright, intelligent, and already a carwise young man at twenty-two, Edsel

41

was happy for the opportunity. His pleasure was short-lived, however. He had a title but no authority. What say-so Henry did not keep for himself he gave to Danish-born Charley Sorenson, his right-hand man. It was the start of a lifelong heartbreak for young Edsel, whose automotive expertise would never be acknowledged by his father.

It was also the forerunner of a series of other blunders by Henry Ford, almost all in the nature of disastrous ego trips.

One was his leasing a ship named *Oscar II* and sailing with a group of pacifists across the Atlantic to convince the Kaiser to stop World War I. The well-intentioned peace effort failed, and Henry never fully recovered from the fiasco.

On September 4, 1917, Edsel's first son, named Henry II for his grandfather, was born. Not long after that the Ford family was subjected to a trauma that plagues the wealthy. A man named Jacob Yellin threatened to kidnap Edsel in an extortion attempt. Though the man was quickly arrested and sent to prison, Henry, with the added worry of a new grandson, decided special security was needed, a bodyguard.

His choice was another horrendous mistake, one destined to bring the wrath of the workingman down on his family and the company. He hired Harry Herbert Bennett, ex-boxer, ex-navy man, a bully, and a trigger-tempered opportunist who quickly made himself indispensable to the 'boss.'

Bennett became untouchable at Ford, exempt from any responsibility and accountable only to the elder Henry, hired to serve as Henry's eyes and ears as to what went on within the company as well as to provide protection for the family.

Edsel, whose eagerness to work with his father in the company pre-empted his desire for a college education, continued to be ignored by his father, but persistence eventually brought him some responsibility. Henry finally permitted Edsel to hire Ernest Kanzler, his brother-in-law and friend, as treasurer. Edsel, feeling the company needed experienced men, also suggested hiring a tried and capable automobile man, William S. Knudsen, a thoroughly professional automobile executive with a genius for organisation, a quality lacking in the Ford structure. Knudsen was hired.

Henry was pleased at what he perceived as his son's interest in the welfare of the company, but he was not convinced that Edsel had what it took to run the company once he was gone. He called in Charley Sorenson, telling him to 'make a man out of Edsel.' Henry believed that Sorenson was ideal to put 'guts and grit' into mild-mannered Edsel.

'Edsel's too soft,' was Henry's appraisal of his only son and heir.

Henry Ford – interestingly – displayed the same toughness towards his son Edsel that Nicola Iacocca showed his Lido, but the important healing salve was lacking. The open, honest, and vital love and pride that Nicola always had for Lee was denied Edsel.

The Model T meanwhile had sent Henry's ego sky-high, transforming the introverted farmboy into a man in the world's spotlight. The name Ford, thanks to the Lizzie, had become a synonym for automobile. The Model T was busy doing what it was born to do, on the streets of Killarney, Glasgow, and Prague as well as on Broadway, State Street, or the backroads of Iowa and Kansas.

Henry Ford's spirit thrived on the international reputation brought him by the Model T. He came to believe that he could do anything, even run the United States government if need be, a fantasy given impetus by President Woodrow Wilson.

When World War I ended in 1918, Wilson was desperately trying to get congressional approval for American participation in the League of Nations. He invited Ford to the White House. Needing every possible Democratic vote to offset the isolationist bloc in the Republican Party, he told Henry, nominally a Republican, 'You are the only man in Michigan who can be elected.' Wilson knew how to appeal to Henry, who still felt the sting of ridicule from the Peace Ship failure. He added: 'You can help bring about the peace you so much desire.'

Henry went home to think it over. He had obviously made up his mind to accept when on January 1, 1919, he resigned as president of the Ford Motor Company and named Edsel to succeed him. It was a serious mistake, not because Edsel could not handle the responsibility, but because Ford assigned Henry Bennett to manage things. Edsel never had the authority that should have gone with the office.

Throughout the industry the paraphrased cliché became 'Edsel proposes, but Bennett disposes.' Everyone seemed to know. It was not Edsel, but Harry Bennett who actually piloted the ship.

During Edsel's first year as president Charley Sorenson proved to be as great a worry to him as Bennett. Charley was disappointed at losing the presidency and tried to undercut Bill Knudsen, who, with Edsel and Kanzler, was building a smoothly operating organisation. Edsel and Kanzler soon realised what was going on and developed a plan to save the capable Knudsen for the Ford Motor Company.

To get Knudsen away from Sorenson's snooping and back-biting, Edsel planned to name Knudsen as manager of Ford's growing English subsidiary. Edsel intended to approach his father without Sorenson's or Bennett's knowledge.

The wily Sorenson had an ace in the hole: Henry's private secretary, Ernest Liebold, a Sorenson-Bennett stooge. When Liebold heard why Edsel wanted to see Henry, he put him off for a day to let Sorenson in on the planned reassignment.

Sorenson scurried to Henry's Fair Lane home. He, not Knudsen, Sorenson told Henry, deserved to head the British operation, if only on the basis of seniority. Henry, who always admired Sorenson's toughness and audacity, seldom denied him anything. He not only overruled Edsel's decision but also made another of his many tactical errors that kept Ford Motor Company foundering. He ordered Sorenson to fire Bill Knudsen.

To Henry's chagrin Knudsen went on to become one of the giants of the industry at General Motors, especially in his role as vice-president in charge of its Chevrolet Division. Before Knudsen took over Chevrolet, it had been so thoroughly smothered by Ford in the marketplace that GM seriously considered eliminating Chevy from the GM line.

In less than three years Knudsen had Chevrolet on the move. Within seven years he brought so much strength back into the division that Chevy sailed past Ford to become the best-selling car in the United States. Having listened to the toadying Sorenson rather than his own son, Henry gave his competition an edge it would never relinquish. Henry was ruining his business.

He seemed not to care. President Wilson's words had had a telling effect on his already inflated ego, and he was set to run for the US Senate. He accepted the Democratic nomination to battle Truman H. Newberry, who had served as secretary of war in Theodore Roosevelt's cabinet.

It was a challenge without confrontation. Henry considered himself too important to stump and refused to campaign. His name, he said, was enough to engulf Newberry. Actually, inarticulate Henry dreaded making public appearances. He declared openly that 'he would never make a public speech to get elected.'

Even without campaigning Henry lost by less than 6,000 votes. His pride was strong as ever. Hadn't he proved the power of this name by coming so close without lifting a finger?

He did not leave well enough alone. He blamed the loss not on his failure to campaign but on the concerted efforts of 'Jewish capitalists who made billions during the war.' He also declared that he would show those 'avaricious bankers and all America' the truth not found in the 'capitalistic press owned or controlled by Jews.'

Edsel was aghast at his father's escalating boorishness, but he could do nothing. There was no stopping Henry's purchase of a small weekly newspaper published near the Ford home at Fair Lane, a journal called the *Dearborn Independent*, which Henry boasted would quickly rival the *New York World* in circulation.

The May 18, 1920, edition of Henry's *Independent* carried a front-page editorial headed: 'The International Jew: The World's Problem.' It was the first of many anti-Semitic blasts to come.

The vicious editorials had their effect on Model T sales. Jews and Jewish organisations stopped buying Fords. Thousands of non-Jews, including Christian businessmen who did not wish to alienate Jewish customers, boycotted the Ford Motor Company.

To improve sales Edsel suggested improved steering and braking and replacement of the four-cylinder engine with a six. But a six-cylinder engine was a horror to the farm-raised Henry.

'I've got no use,' he snorted, 'for an engine that's got more spark plugs than a cow has teats.'

Henry forgot his disapproval of more spark plugs when an opportunity arose to turn the tables on an old adversary, Henry Leland, who had replaced Ford in the Detroit Automobile Company. Leland had built a luxurious car with a V-8 engine and incorporated his Lincoln Motor Company in early 1920. Now, his board of directors, led by one of Henry's former investors, was squeezing Leland out.

Desperate, Leland came to Ford for help. At the receivership sale Henry bought the Lincoln company for $8 million. In what seemed a magnanimous gesture at the time he named Henry Leland president, Leland's son Wilfred first vice-president, with Edsel to serve as second vice-president.

It was a short-lived, unhappy marriage. Soon Henry tried to force the Lelands out. Henry Leland, unable to face the loss of the company he started, sent his son to Ford with an offer to buy back Lincoln for the $8 million Henry had paid plus a fair interest.

'Mr Leland,' Henry said. 'I wouldn't sell the Lincoln plant for five hundred million dollars.'

With Edsel busy at the Lincoln plant Henry Ford was relieved, at least for a time, of listening to his son's practical suggestions which he almost always turned down. But one day he recalled his son's solid arguments in favour of advertising as a means of getting more people to know and buy the Model T. Henry had always been a confirmed and blatant publicity seeker if it cost nothing, and advertising cost money. Now he had what he thought was a better idea.

Henry had taken a number of camping trips with such good friends as Thomas Edison and Harvey Firestone, provider of tyres for his Lizzie. Why not, he thought, invite the President of the United States, Warren Harding, to join them in a week of outdoor relaxation. A swarm of newspapermen would follow them.

Harding accepted the invitation, the campers made for the wilderness in a cavalcade of Model T Fords. As Henry expected, the ruggedness and durability of Lizzie received as much attention as did the country's chief executive.

The trip brought Henry Ford the sales he expected from the free publicity. It also infected him with the germ of a new ambition. If a farmboy like Warren Harding – none too bright, as Henry saw him – could sit in the White House, there was no reason why he, one of the best-known men in the world, could not become President of the United States himself.

Harding was expected to run for a second term, but his chances for re-election began to dim soon after his return to Washington, as the country heard rumblings of 'Teapot Dome,' a scandal within the Harding cabinet. Almost simultaneously a 'Henry Ford for President' boom got under way, sparked by Henry's secretary, Ernest Liebold, and by Charley Sorenson. Henry told Charley he would name him his secretary of war.

Ernest Liebold, doing double duty in public relations, got the word out. 'Henry Ford for President' became a growing battle cry in rural America and spread into the cities. There were more poor in the cities than rich, and Henry had relentlessly cut costs so that a Model T was within reach of almost anyone. They would back him solidly.

But fate stepped in. What might well have been the tragedy of a Ford presidency was averted when Warren Harding, stung by the growing Teapot Dome scandal, died on August 2, 1923, and Calvin Coolidge was sworn in as President.

Coolidge had an appeal that transcended that of Henry Ford. He had a solid background in politics. His combination of homey simplicity, honesty, sincerity, and quiet humour made him an ideal candidate for the Republicans. The Ford balloon deflated quickly.

Edsel was still president of the Ford Motor Company and responsible, at least on paper, for all the company's activities. However, he had found himself happiest at the Lincoln plant. Only there did he have the semblance of a free hand.

But whatever he planned, whatever he accomplished, Harry Bennett still haunted him. And now there was another concern: Ford's competition was picking up steam.

Chevrolet, under Bill Knudsen, was making worrisome inroads on Ford sales, turning out slightly under half a million units in 1923 and moving ahead rapidly. In June of 1924, when the 10 millionth Ford rolled off the assembly line – and even though the Model T still outsold Chevrolet by a million and a half cars and more – Henry finally listened to Edsel. He admitted that the Lizzie's days were numbered and gave his son the go-ahead to design a new car.

The last of more than 15 million Model T Fords came off the assembly line in May, 1927. On December 2 of that year its successor made its bow. The Model A – the second Ford to carry that designation – was a robust, stylish car for its day, with a redesigned four-cylinder engine that gave it more speed than Chevrolet. In included revolutionary new features such as the first laminated safety glass windshield ever offered as standard equipment.

The Model A was an immediate success. As many as 400,000 people placed orders, including cash deposits, within two weeks of its announcement. Before 1930 bowed out, four million had been produced, with model choices increased to nine. Edsel's green light for the Model A was taken so literally that a town-car version was produced, a car with chauffeur's seat and roof, isolating the passenger compartment, priced at $1,200. At the lower end of the price scale was the Model A Tudor at $500, available in grey and green as well as Henry's traditional black.

Even though the 5 millionth Model A was produced in 1931, a plunge in sales brought on by the nationwide depression led to the development of a new car. Henry Ford was ready for change with a revolutionary idea that proved a sensation. He introduced a V-8 engined Ford at a price only slightly higher than that of the four-cylinder Model A. This automobile carried Ford Motor Company into the next decade.

Despite the Depression the sales side of the Ford Motor Company ledger had held up. Even so, a storm was brewing within its offices. The ageing Henry was slipping badly in judgment and losing his grip. Harry Bennett, the ex-boxer and bully whose rowdy nature contrasted severely with that of the sensitive and cultured Edsel Ford, took charge.

Thanks to Bennett, 1937 became a year not to remember, for it was one stigmatised by his abuse of power, the year of the infamous 'Battle of the Rouge Overpass.'

The United Auto Workers' Ford local, headed by Walter Reuther, had been granted permission by the City of Dearborn for a peaceful demonstration at the Ford Rouge gates the afternoon of May 26. Reuther, aware of Bennett's cadre of guards identified as 'bruisers, ex-baseball and -football players and jailbirds,' and of Bennett's impulsive, intemperate, violent reactions, had carefully planned the move on the Rouge.

Reuther and his volunteers, who included a number of women, arrived at the Rouge plant area about three o'clock to pass out their printed pieces during Ford's 4:00 p.m. shift change. They headed for an overpass leading to a streetcar stop used by incoming and outgoing workers. At the other end a gate led into the Ford grounds, but the union organisers were to go no further than the middle of the overpass.

Reuther led his group up the bridgelike structure. Near the centre they were met by a band of goons and musclemen led by Angelo Caruso, a known hoodlum hired by Harry Bennett.

'Get the hell out of here!' Caruso screamed. 'This is Ford property.'

Reuther wanted no confrontation. He ordered his people to back down towards the streetcar stop. They were faced suddenly with a second group of Ford bruisers, who began beating the retreating unionists with clubs and fists.

One grabbed Reuther from behind, knocked him to the ground, and, after kicking his head and body, flung him down the steel steps. Another unionist had his jacket pulled over his head to immobilise his arms and was then beaten. A woman was kicked in the stomach. Another union man had his back broken.

Newspaper photographers, who had gathered to catch the confrontation on film, were the next targets. They were beaten, and their cameras confiscated. But enough escaped to provide front-page coverage of the vicious assault for the next day's newspapers and for national magazines. Their pictures were so graphic that the National Labor Relations board found the Ford Motor Company guilty of using terror tactics to prevent union organisation.

Henry accepted the government's decision with ill grace, blaming it all on the 'capitalist' press as usual. But he refused to knuckle under. He bestowed greater powers than ever on Harry Bennett, ordering him to stamp out the least trace of union activity. Bennett obeyed with sadistic pleasure despite public disgust at the unneeded brutality. He was little concerned over the boycott of Ford products that sky-rocketed General Motors past Ford and dropped Henry's company into third place behind Chrysler.

Edsel was horror-stricken by his father's cavalier reaction to the brutality as well as by his refusal to honour the terms of the new labour law. It took four years of insistent pleading, and his mother's help, before Henry capitulated.

Clara was worried over Edsel's health and concerned over the corrosive and detrimental effect of the violence on the company. She declared to her husband that if he didn't do something about Harry Bennett's violence and sign the union agreement, she would leave him. That threat finally brought peace to the Ford Motor Company.

Henry's obstinacy, which Bennett encouraged during the lengthy strife, ate at Edsel's heart like the yet-undiagnosed cancer that was shortening his life. He worried about the workers in the plant, about the company's image, and about its plummeting profits. A compassionate man, he detested the useless violence triggered by Bennett's goons, which he was unable to halt.

There had never been much warm communication between Edsel and his father. And when Henry suffered his first of two strokes, the rift widened. The old man refused to admit even to himself that he was incapable of running the company, and he continued making important decisions and interfering with the execution of almost every suggestion Edsel offered. Bennett was always at hand, ready and willing to relay Henry's orders. Too often they were not Henry's, but Bennett's, made in the old man's name.

Harry Bennett could do no wrong in Henry's eyes, but the wrongs Bennett committed had put the company well on the way to bankruptcy. The security men he controlled hauled tons of company property through the gates without a check. An inventory of parts and accessories taken later revealed shortages of over a million dollars.

One bright spot for Edsel in the last half of the thirties was the 1936–1939 four-year period in which Lincoln topped Cadillac in sales. Another was the completion of a personal car, built specifically for him, a Lincoln with the 'long, low, continental' look Edsel so much admired.

Weakened by his worries over the slippage in Ford sales, the repercussions from the shameful incident at the Rouge overpass, and his unending and fruitless struggle with his father, Edsel visited Florida for a rest when the car was completed. Prenamed Lincoln Continental by him, the car was brought there in March, 1939.

From the moment it arrived, the stunning grey coupé caught the fancy of everyone who saw its fine craftsmanship. Edsel sensed the widespread interest and ordered it produced in a limited edition. It was introduced to the public in October, each car virtually hand built. America's reigning architect, Frank Lloyd Wright, described it as the most beautiful car ever made.

The hallmark of Edsel's Lincoln Continental Mark was the spare tyre mounting at the rear of the car. Not a truly new concept, it had been commonplace in the 1920s but had gone out of favour in the early 1930s. Since the introduction of Edsel's car, any automobile with the tyre so placed has been called continental. Years later Lee Iacocca would give the tyre-placement image and the Continental name a new and meaningful success on American roads.

This Lincoln Continental may well be termed Edsel Ford's swan song. His illness, finally diagnosed as inoperable cancer, continued for another four years, though the bulldog in his father refused to face up to the seriousness of his son's condition.

It was only the 'softness' in Edsel, Henry kept saying. If the boy would only toughen up like a man, he would be hale and hearty. Milk delivered directly from Henry's dairy farm to his son's home would make Edsel healthy and strong again.

Unfortunately Henry had a nature fetish that would not countenance pasteurisation. When Edsel developed increased fever and pain and uncontrolled perspiration, doctors discovered that contamination in the unhomogenised milk was responsible for the undulant fever. Early on the morning of May 26, 1943, Edsel died at age forty-nine.

Edsel's wife, Eleanor, was never sure whether illness caused her husband's death or whether heartbreak had brought on the illness. But she was grateful that he had lived long enough to see his oldest son, Henry II, marry beautiful and gentle Anne McDonnell, father a daughter, and be named a director of the Ford Motor Company. Henry II, who had been drafted into the navy with the outbreak of the Second World War, returned from the Great Lakes Naval Training Station for his father's funeral.

Once Edsel was buried, his family realised how serious a problem now confronted them. A meeting of the Ford board of directors was scheduled for June 1, at which Edsel's successor as president would be chosen. They were worried, and with good reason, that the ageing and incapacitated Henry might order the appointment of Henry Bennett. In some way the Edsel Ford family was determined to maintain control of the board.

The block of stock bequeathed to Eleanor by Edsel enabled her to win a seat on the board before the members broke for lunch. Then, with Sorenson's help, she was able to manoeuvre the appointments of Henry II and her second-oldest son, Benson, to the board. But her victory was not total. Bennett and two of his cronies were also named directors.

Overall, the best the Edsel clan could do during the election of company officers was to have the older Henry restored to his earlier position as president, with Charley Sorenson as vice-president. B. J. Craig, a Bennett man, was elected second vice-president and treasurer.

Henry II had to return to his duties in the navy after the funeral, but he had seen and heard enough to disturb him. He asked Russell Gnau, Sorenson's secretary, to keep him advised of everything happening at the plant, unaware that he would learn only what Bennett wanted him to know. Gnau was another of Harry's many agents.

Bennett, realising that the family plan was to move Henry II into his grandfather's position when the older Henry died, looked for ways to sidetrack the young heir. Bennett wanted to run the Ford Motor Company himself.

He asked the advice of I. A. Capizzi, a Ford attorney who had always been friendly to him, implying that Eleanor's brother, Ernest Kanzler, wanted control of the company. With so much voting stock in his sister's hands, Kanzler might easily succeed, Bennett pointed out.

Capazzi suggested a codicil to Henry's will that could clear Bennett's way by wiping out the Ford Foundation and its block of non-voting stock. Then a trusteeship could be established to run the corporation for a period after Henry's death.

Bennett, pleased at the prospect, began composing a list of trustees. He would be secretary of that board. Others would include Capizzi, Ernest Liebold, and Frank Campsall, old Henry's current private secretary. Sorenson, however, could not be excluded, even though he also had his eye on the company presidency.

A drama of intrigue was in the making, and Harry Bennett was writing the script.

Ernest Kanzler, who had been ousted from his Ford position through Bennett's efforts, read Bennett's mind. He quickly sensed that a plan with ominous overtones for the Edsel Ford family was in the wind.

Kanzler was well aware that the company was in dire straits, its future resting in the hands of two men. One, Henry Ford, had been pronounced by his own physician, Dr Roy McClure, to be too ill to leave his home or to be consulted on decisions. The other, devious Harry Bennett, wielded the actual power.

There was only one way, Kanzler decided, to deal Bennett a knockout blow. First he would need the combined support of Clara, old Henry's wife, and Eleanor, Edsel's widow. But just as critical to a successful sabotage of whatever Bennett had in mind was the presence on the scene of Henry II, whose release from the navy was years away.

Kanzler pleaded with Frank Knox, Franklin Delano Roosevelt's secretary of the navy. The deterioration in Henry Ford's physical and mental capacities, and his dependence on the ambitious and unscrupulous Harry Bennett, was reason enough to arrange a discharge from the navy for young Henry Ford. The company needed the strength of an untarnished, visible, and sane Ford to manage its government contracts and commercial future.

Knox agreed, and Henry Ford II won a naval discharge and came to the Ford Rouge plant in August, 1943. At twenty-six he was thrust into a position he was hardly qualified to fill, and his playboy reputation provided little assurance that a young Henry Ford could do better than the senile old one.

Did he have the strength and talent to make order out of the chaos within the Ford Motor Company? Could he stand up to the wily Harry Bennett? It seemed too much to ask of someone whose life had been one of ease since birth, with never a worry or confrontation.

CHAPTER 4

What had perhaps been Henry Ford II's most significant exposure to the dominion he one day would rule had come at the age of two years and eight months, on the morning of May 17, 1920. Smartly attired, his chubby face topped by a hat made of beaver fur, he was brought to the newly built Rouge plant to christen its first blast furnace. Carried by his grandfather for the ceremony, little Henry couldn't handle the match to set the furnace ablaze. So it was the grandfather, not the heir, who struck the match.

Precociousness best describes Henry's growing years. He was never awed by rank, royalty, or fame. When Henry was six years old. Edward, Prince of Wales, heir to the British throne, was expected as a dinner guest at Edsel's home. Henry and his brother, Benson, four at the time, were promised a look at the future king of England.

Since their royal guest was late in arriving, Edsel's wife asked her mother to take the boys to their bedroom, assuring them that the prince would come in to bid them goodnight. Sometime later Edsel escorted the English heir up the stairs to the accompaniment of snickers, chuckles, and booming laughter echoing loudly from the boys' room.

Edsel opened the door and looked around. His mother-in-law was nowhere to be seen. Flustered by the arrival of royalty she had taken cover behind a screen.

'What's going on?' Edsel demanded as Prince Edward preceded him into the bedroom.

Young Henry, unabashed by the royal presence, blurted out: 'Benson was so excited he threw up.' He then let out another guffaw and added: 'You'll find grandmother hiding over there.'

There is no denying the brilliance of today's Henry Ford II, but his prep-school years at Hotchkiss, the prestigious Connecticut academy for the sons of wealth, were unimpressive. Hitting the books was never the favourite pastime of this pudgy adolescent with a puckish sense of humour.

'He was not noted for his intellectual brilliance,' is the evaluation of his headmaster of Hotchkiss.

However mediocre his Hotchkiss years may have been, Grandfather Henry and Grandmother Clara gave him a memorable graduation present, a trip to Europe. It was during this summer vacation, when he was nineteen, that he first met Anne McDonnell, the lovely and elegant blonde socialite who would become his first wife.

Henry's four years at Yale were even less noteworthy than his terms at Hotchkiss, except for his second meeting with Anne and his resolve to marry her. Otherwise his eight semesters at one of America's finest institutions of learning were a washout.

'I didn't learn anything, except maybe from my courses in sociology,' Henry has admitted. 'They were a bit of fun, and I took them because the guys told that sociology was a breeze, and I'd already flunked engineering. Hell, I also flunked sociology.'

Henry failed his sociology course because his eagle-eyed professor decided the thesis he submitted was too well done to be Henry's own work. Confronted by the instructor, uninhibited, straightforward Henry made no excuse.

'I got some help,' he confessed readily. 'And when the prof said I couldn't get my degree unless I wrote a new thesis on a different subject, I said to hell with it. Besides, I didn't want to lose any time getting married.'

There was a distressing hitch in Henry's prospect of marrying Anne. Grandfather Henry would have called it an insurmountable obstacle, if he had only known in time. Anne was the daughter of William McDonnell, a Wall Street heavyweight. She was also a Roman Catholic.

A Wall Street connection was enough in itself to send the older Henry into a rage. But he also categorised Catholics with the hated Jews, Communists, and union leaders.

Edsel had no objections, but McDonnell family details had to be kept from his father until it was too late. So careful were Eleanor and Edsel around old Henry that the remaining obstacle to the wedding was overcome without his knowledge: This was young Henry's conversion to Catholicism under the tutelage of world-respected Monsignor Fulton J. Sheen.

Henry Ford II and Anne McDonnell were married June 13, 1940, in what was reported as 'the wedding of the year.' Gifts from friends and relatives were worth over a million dollars. From Henry's parents the bridal couple received a palatial Grosse Pointe residence. Edsel, in addition, transferred to Henry 25,000 shares of Ford stock valued at more than $3.2 million. With the stock came a note announcing that after his marriage Henry 'will join the Ford Motor Company as your future business,' and also noting the fact that Henry had been a director of the company for over two years.

Henry II arrived at the Rouge after discharge from the navy in the summer of '43 as guardian of his family's company. It was a weighty burden to place on the shoulders of a young man who had little or no experience in so competitive a business. He underestimated neither the importance of the job ahead nor the tangled skein that had to be unravelled. He had seen enough while on furlough for his father's funeral to realise that things were not right.

When Henry reported in for his first day, he had no definite assignment, not even a desk, much less an office. Grateful that Harry Bennett had made himself scarce, he roamed the plant asking questions of assembly-line workers and keeping his eyes open.

Finally Laurence Sheldrick, who had not been aware of Henry's arrival, took him in hand. Sheldrick, no Bennett hanger-on, had been Edsel's chief designer. He not only filled Henry in on what was going on, he also suggested a look at the Army Proving Grounds in Aberdeen, Maryland.

The trip didn't take place. Before they could start out, Sheldrick was summoned at Harry Bennett's orders to Sorenson's office.

'What the hell do you think you're doing?' Sorenson stormed. 'Leave the kid alone, and don't go stuffing him with your crazy ideas about building modern cars after the war's over.'

'All I've done,' Sheldrick said, holding his temper, 'is tell him about ideas Edsel was working on that he already knew about.'

Sorenson's face turned red. 'Then why did you go against Mr Ford's wishes and take him to Aberdeen to make a warmonger out of him?'

Sheldrick's answer did him in. 'All I was doing was showing young Henry that Ford's as much interested in helping the government as General Motors.'

Sorenson exploded. 'If GM's that goddamn good, why don't you go work for them!'

'All right,' Sheldrick replied, 'if that's the way it is, I'm through.'

Sorenson had achieved what Bennett hoped, disposal of another of Edsel's few remaining loyalists. Furious as he was when he heard of it, Henry II held himself in check, biding his time.

Four months later, at a meeting of the board of directors, his family's votes brought him a vice-presidency, and Henry II moved into his father's old office. He kept Edsel's remaining staff and added a few of his own choices. Though he had to work closely with Charley Sorenson, he had little use for the man after the Sheldrick incident. As for Harry Bennett, Henry loathed his name and discounted Harry's egocentric claim to at-will entrée to his ailing grandfather.

Henry II was not convinced that Bennett had his grandfather's ear and carte blanche to relay orders in the old man's name. He often had heard his father, Edsel, speak of Bennett's devious nature and was prepared to evaluate Bennett's manipulation of the truth.

'When an important policy matter came up,' young Henry

once reported, 'Bennett would get into his car and disappear for a few hours. Then he would come back and say "I've been to see Mr Ford and he wants us to do it this way."'

Henry did his best to maintain pleasant relations with his grandfather and visited him often. Old Henry would hear no bad word against Bennett. 'He's a good man,' he told his grandson. But young Henry did ask questions at appropriate moments and did get Bennett-damning answers.

'I checked with my grandfather,' he said, 'and found out that Bennett had not been to see him on the occasions he claimed.'

Henry II knew only too well that something had to be done about the older Henry, growing more senile and making decisions through Harry Bennett. He was ruling the company with passion rather than reason. More than a little frustrated, Henry II moved carefully, albeit his thinking was clear and incisive. In many ways he had the compassion and charm of his father. In others he exhibited the bulldog resolution of his grandfather.

Sorenson and Bennett cared little that Henry was a vice-president. They saw him as powerless, even during board meetings. As for young Henry, it grieved him to see his grandfather hobble in to the meetings against the will of his doctor, always accompanied by the inevitable Bennett. He was sure it was Bennett who insisted on the old man's attendance.

The board meetings were travesties. His grandfather would merely walk around the table, shake hands with each director, and then turn to Bennett.

'Come on, Harry,' he would say. 'Let's get the hell out of here. We'll probably change everything they do, anyway.'

Henry II watched with growing contempt for both Sorenson and Bennett. Charley had engaged himself in an unequal power play, trying to outdo the well-entrenched Bennett in pleasing Henry's ailing grandfather. Both had eyes on the presidency that could never be theirs. The end result was a rash of firings, each guillotining qualified men he believed might be loyal to the other.

Bennett disposed of A. M. Wibel, a responsible and

dedicated purchasing, production, and financial wizard, as well as Eugene Gregorie, one of the most capable designers in the industry. Sorenson already had drawn first blood by getting rid of Laurence Sheldrick.

Sorenson, who had been a loyal Ford man since 1905, was himself on the way out without realising it. He had done an admirable job co-ordinating defence work, and now the Allies were gaining ground in Europe. Roosevelt, Churchill, and Chiang Kai-shek had met in Cairo for a strategy conference, and Roosevelt and Churchill had gone on to Tehran for a meeting with Joseph Stalin.

Sorenson was tired and badly in need of a rest, and there was little for him to do as 1943 wound down. He went to see old Henry.

'Everything's caught up,' he told his longtime boss, 'so I think I'll take a trip to Miami.'

Henry's quick acquiescence should have been a warning, but tired as he was, Charley didn't read anything into the old man's hasty goodbye. He drove a company car south and had barely arrived when he heard that his office was being occupied by Ray Rausch, a Bennett crony.

Shocked and tormented by such treatment, a despicable trick in character with Harry Bennett, he burned up the telephone wires in vain. Henry refused to speak to him or return his calls.

Flustered and frustrated, Sorenson hastily drove back north. When he reached the gates of the Rouge, a Bennett security guard refused him entrance and took the car.

On January 23, 1944, Henry Ford II was elected executive vice-president of the Ford Motor Company. Despite the new title, which placed him second only to his grandfather, he was helpless in trying to alleviate the chaotic situation.

His grandfather remained in command, but his mind was fast deteriorating. He was too feeble to come to the office often. When he did, he could not remember the names of his most familiar executives and had to be reminded of their identity. All except the hovering Harry Bennett.

However hard he tried, Henry II could not pass the Bennett barrier. The confusion and mismanagement at every

60

level made no sense. Bennett laughed off Henry II's concern by pointing out that it was 'always done that way.'

Young Henry was also sickened by the brutality of the foreman in the plant. Bennett's reaction to his complaint was that it was necessary to keep lazy workers on the job.

His hands tied, Henry could do little more than shake his head, wondering how anything got accomplished. Good workers either rebelled at the harsh treatment and were fired, or they quit in disgust. They were losing too many good men, and not merely in the plant. Bennett's high-handed measures also disenchanted upper-echelon executives, who went off the payroll.

Not long after Henry II was elected vice-president, he made it clear that he did not have all the answers, that with his inexperience he needed all the help he could get. 'One man can't do it alone,' he said again and again. But, whether or not it was part of a Bennett-planned campaign, he was losing too many of the men who had tried to give him a hand.

He became particularly upset when Harry Doss, Ford's capable sales manager, told Henry he could no longer tolerate Bennett interference. Bennett and his cohorts, Doss said, were putting the best dealerships in the hands of friends.

'I don't want to quit, but I've got to,' Doss told Henry. 'And I wouldn't if something could be done about Bennett's interference.'

Henry tried to change Doss's mind, but without success. 'I can't blame you one damn bit,' Henry finally said. 'There's not a damn thing I can do about it right now, but I guarantee you someday I will.'

Henry discussed the problem with his uncle, Ernest Kanzler. He had to have a dependable, loyal, and able sales manager. Kanzler reminded Henry that the Doss resignation was hardly the first, and as a matter of fact, John Davis, whom Doss replaced, had taken a demotion to get away from Bennett. Davis, with Edsel's help, had remained with the company and was managing a branch office in California.

'He's the best man for the job in the country, if you can get him,' Kanzler told Henry.

Henry phoned Davis, but Davis refused to come back to

Dearborn. 'I'll never do it if I have to deal with Harry Bennett again,' he said.

Henry flew out to Long Beach, California, to talk to Davis. Strong-willed Jack Davis would not be budged, but Henry did not let him go. 'I'll tell you what,' he said. 'Come on back. Hell, if Bennett makes trouble, you quit, and I'll quit too.' Davis returned to Dearborn.

A month or so later Henry was approached by Leander Hamilton McCormick-Goodheart, then managing a small department called Personnel Planning. In 1939 McCormick-Goodheart had been about to begin his last year at England's Cambridge University when Germany invaded Poland, triggering World War II. A native American whose mother was English, McCormick-Goodheart had been refused a visa by the State Department to return to Cambridge because of the outbreak of hostilities.

McCormick-Goodheart's father had been a frequent golfing partner of Edsel Ford during Edsel's vacation periods at Bar Harbor, Maine. After graduation from the New York Institute of Photography, he was able, through Edsel, to join the Ford factory training programme in September, 1940. He had worked himself up to his present position in the five intervening years.

'Mr Ford,' McCormick-Goodheart told Henry, 'if I may suggest it, I believe it would be to the company's advantage to rejuvenate the student orientation programme. The way it has evolved it has too many deficiencies, too many tool and die people and mechanics playing engineer. They're not professionals, which is really what the company needs.'

Henry listened, liking what he heard. 'Well, what are your ideas?' he asked. 'What can you do about it?'

'I'd like to build the programme back up,' McCormick-Goodheart said. 'I think it was an excellent programme when it began, but it's become a dumping ground for Harry Bennett's pets, men who just spend time to pick up a paycheque. To me, that's most unproductive for the company. I'd like to revamp the whole programme, streamline it, put some order and sense into it.'

'How would you go about it?' Henry asked.

'I'd like to go to the major universities,' McCormick-Goodheart replied, 'and bring in some young professional engineers, hand-pick young men who are mechanical engineers because they want to be.'

Henry was impressed by the loyalty and concern for the company evidenced by the young man about his own age. It was a practical, sound idea.

'Go do it,' he told McCormick-Goodheart, little realising the far-reaching, down-the-road impact it would have on the Ford Motor Company. Lee Iacocca was the brightest of the many gems McCormick-Goodheart discovered during that summer of 1945.

Harry Bennett, meanwhile, had done a little hiring on his own, adding an ingredient to his cadre that he believed was a necessary protective measure. He took on tough, vigorous John S. Bugas, a Wyoming lawyer who had been the head of the Detroit FBI office for about five years.

For the last of those years his office, because of the war contracts awarded the Ford Motor Company, had kept a watchful eye on the company and had uncovered thefts of war matériel as well as the bootlegging and black market sale of parts. Bugas could not turn down the salary offered by Bennett to supervise labour relations for Ford.

Bugas had come in as a Bennett man, but to Harry's surprise Bugas was more his own man, honest and dedicated to his job. When he revealed his straight stripes by firing one of Bennett's cronies, Harry put him in a deep freeze. 'Bennett had me as isolated as a tuberculosis bug,' Bugas said.

Disgusted with Bennett's pattern of shortsighted, self-centred policies, Bugas became one of young Henry's best allies. Hiring John Bugas was to become Harry Bennett's passport to exile.

On June 28, 1945, the Ford Motor Company completed its war contracts when the last Liberator bomber was assembled at its Willow Run facility, ending a government assignment that had produced 8,600 bombers, 57,000 aircraft engines, and 278,000 jeeps and seeps (amphibious jeeps). Five days later Henry II ordered the resumption of passenger-car production, but he needed someone trustworthy to replace Ray

Rausch, a Bennett confidant, as head of manufacturing.

The best man for the job, whom he could trust and who was not a Bennett stooge, was Mead Bricker, formerly Sorenson's assistant, now in charge at the Willow Run bomber plant.

First Henry wanted to sound out the only ones in whom he had faith, John Bugas and John Davis, his sales manager. He decided to invite all three men to dinner at the Dearborn Inn, the posh hotel his grandfather had built for the convenience of visitors to Dearborn.

'My God, no!' Bugas exploded when Henry suggested the inn. 'Every corner in that dining room is bugged.'

They finally decided on a corner table in the dining room of the Detroit Club in downtown Detroit. As they sat down, Henry wasted no time in getting to the nub of the matter.

'I've asked you to come here because I have confidence in you,' he said. 'I want you to help me rebuild the Ford Motor Company.'

Bricker, who knew the high regard in which Henry held John Bugas, realised he would not have been there without Bugas's approval. He let out a roar and turned to the former FBI man.

'You son of a bitch,' he said to Bugas, smiling broadly, 'I thought you distrusted me!'

'What the hell can we do?' Henry asked the other three men at the table.

His grandfather might have run the company single-handed, but young Henry knew he didn't have the experience to do it. Besides, times had changed. The day was long gone when a business like Ford Motor Company could be run single-handed.

Bugas had an answer. 'First,' he said, 'get your grandfather to sign an order stating that nobody can get fired anymore without your permission.' Bugas firmly believed it was the only way to water down Bennett's influence.

'All right,' Henry agreed. 'But then what?'

'Clean house,' Bugas replied. 'Better still, tell me to do it.'

Henry shook his head. 'If I did that,' he said, I'd be known around the company as a guy who passed the buck.'

Here Henry II exhibited a characteristic at odds with his grandfather's way of getting rid of the unwanted by not facing them directly.

At that time the Red Army had already taken Warsaw from the Germans and the Americans had crossed the Rhine at Remagen. By VE Day Henry was back at the Rouge with the order suggested by Bugas, signed by his grandfather.

The first firing salvo at Ford came when Mead Bricker entered Rausch's office to find that Bennett crony chatting with some of his lieutenants. In minutes after Bricker closed the door Rausch and his crew shot out into the corridor. Bricker remained inside, in charge.

The revitalisation of Ford was progressing smoothly, perhaps too smoothly, since Henry was unaware of Harry's trump card, a codicil to his grandfather's will. It had been prepared by old Henry's lawyer, I. A. Capizzi, at Bennett's insistence. Suddenly rumours about this secret document, one that would put Ford Motor Company in control of a board of trustees after the aged Henry's death, began to float through the industry.

No one in the Edsel Ford family was aware of such a document, but young Henry quickly realised that if indeed such a codicil existed, it would probably make Harry Bennett head man. The thought sickened and angered him.

Henry II sought out John Bugas. If the rumours were true, he told Bugas, he was going to resign and sell his stock. He would also recommend that Ford dealers dump their franchises. Better that there be no Ford Motor Company than one with Harry Bennett running it.

'Wait,' Bugas suggested. 'Let me find out from Harry if it's true.'

Bugas charged into Bennett's office and confronted him. Redfaced, caught short by Bugas' obvious knowledge of the codicil, Bennett told Bugas to come back the next day and he would have the matter straightened out.

The next morning, when Bugas entered Bennett's office, Bennett was holding two legal-looking papers, one the alleged codicil to Henry's will, the other a carbon copy. He let Bugas see the original, then set a match to it. When it had been reduced to ashes, Bennett swept the ashes into an envelope.

'Here,' he said, handing Bugas the envelope. 'Take these back to Henry.'

Bugas waited, his lips tight. Bennett finally handed over the carbon. There was no way of knowing whether the codicil had actually been signed by Henry Ford or if it was a clever forgery. But that mattered little now since the original had been destroyed.

Bennett continued to be Henry's prime hindrance in operating the company, and removing him while his grandfather was alive called for finesse. Yet the only way in which young Henry could exercise control was to send Bennett packing.

It was Henry II's mother, Eleanor, who tipped the scales. She made certain that old Henry was in full control of his senses before she made her move and visited the Ford patriarch.

She minced no words. In firm tones she told the bedridden old man that he must step down and that her son, Henry II, must become president of the company.

'If this is not done,' she warned, emphasising each word. 'I shall sell my stock.'

Old Henry had no choice. If Eleanor sold her stock, the Ford Motor Company would certainly pass from family control. On September 20, 1945, a tired, stringbean-thin Henry Ford sent for his grandson. In faltering words he told young Henry that he would be elected president the following day. The younger Henry made it clear to the older: He would take the job only if he had complete freedom to do what he felt necessary. The old man made no objection.

At the hastily called board meeting the next day old Henry and Bennett were both in attendance. The moment the secretary of the board began reading the aged Ford's letter of resignation, Bennett, his face flaming red, jumped to his feet.

'Congratulations!' he snapped angrily in young Henry's direction.

He started to leave the room but was held back by other directors in order to make the vote unanimous. The moment it was over, he bolted toward his own office. Henry Ford II was now president of the Ford Motor Company, and Bennett realised his hours were numbered.

The elder Henry Ford was helped from the meeting room. As the door closed behind him, the last page in a historical saga had seemingly been turned. Although Henry Ford lived on for another seventeen months, an unparalleled career in the automobile industry had come to an end. His grandson was now the man of the hour and the man with the power. As soon as the boardroom was clear, Henry II made his way to Harry Bennett's office. He found Harry in a state of shock.

'We've got to part company,' Henry told Bennett. 'I'll keep you on salary for a year and a half until your retirement pay begins, but stay off of Ford property.'

Bennett, not surprised, took the news in his usually graceless manner. 'You're taking over a billion-dollar organisation you haven't contributed a thing to,' he shrieked at Henry.

As he promised, Henry had not passed the buck, but he did leave it to John Bugas to see that Bennett left the premises by day's end. Aware than Bennett always had a .45 handy, Bugas holstered a .38 automatic inside his coat. He would be ready if Bennett tried anything.

Bugas opened the door to Bennett's office, entered, and stood there for a moment as he closed it. Bennett sat at his desk, his eyes flaming. Bugas walked toward the desk, and as he reached it, Bennett leapt to his feet, pulling his blunt-nosed .45 from his desk drawer.

'You're behind all of this, you son of a bitch!' he screamed at Bugas.

Bugas waited, alert and ready, but Bennett's explosion seemed to have taken the steam from his anger. He unceremoniously dropped the gun on his desk and walked out. That same night he caught a train for California, never again to be seen at the Ford Motor Company. Soon after, as quickly as Henry could replace them, the rest of the Bennett squad disappeared from Ford.

Assuming the power of company president, Henry II had his hands full. He had inherited a crippled Ford Motor Company. He had an outmoded plant that would cost millions to modernise and millions more to retool for new cars. Losses were averaging about $10 million a month.

He had taken on a giant assignment, one he was unsure he could handle. The important thing was that he cared, cared for the company and for the thousands of people the company supported. His comparatively short time around the Rouge had made him aware of his priorities.

Fortunately cash was on hand for operating expenses, over $68 million. His first priority was men, good, qualified men in tune with the times.

In November Henry received an enigmatic telegram. Its presumptuous, arrogant wording read, in part: 'We have a matter of management importance to discuss with you.' It was signed simply Charles Bates Thornton, Colonel US Army Air Force, a name unknown to Henry or any of his men. But the telegram included as a reference the name of Robert Lovett, the secretary of defense.

Charles Thornton, who liked to be called 'Tex,' was reputed to be the only Air Force officer ever to reach the rank of full colonel by the age of twenty-five. He headed the Air Force Office of Statistical Control in Washington. To improve efficiency in that office he selected promising young officers and sent them to the Harvard Business School for quick courses in economics and business management. The brightest and most accomplished he brought back to Washington to serve on his staff.

As World War II wound down, Thornton selected his nine most brilliant aides. He told them that their exceptional and varied abilities could bring challenging and rewarding jobs in private industry. He also pointed out that since they all had worked together and knew each other's abilities so well, they could make a great splash in positions within the same company if they worked as a team of ten.

When Henry Ford II first received the telegram, his inclination was to throw it away. With the war over, even full colonels were a dime a dozen, and this Charles Thornton was an unknown. But he did know Robert Lovett well enough to give the telegram a second thought. He had one of his subordinates contact Thornton and invite him to Dearborn.

Thornton arrived with seven of his ten men in tow. Henry was flabbergasted, not only by the number of men, but also by the demand that all ten would have to be hired en masse. He was willing, however, to listen.

He had inherited a company badly in need of bright new men, and while he was being offered a most unconventional deal, it was worth exploring. The 'rah-rah, let's-get-the-job-done' attitude of Thornton and his men was contagious. Despite his own problems at Yale Henry had been impressed by the dedication of the 'genius types' in his classes. He decided Ford could use some of the do-or-die spirit that this infusion of new blood might bring the company. If only one of them made a contribution to help restore Ford leadership in the industry, it would be a profitable investment.

'Thornton came up with ideas that made a lot of sense to me,' Henry said. 'He convinced me that he and his men could make military management systems work in private industry, and improve cost-efficiency. That kind of talk appealed to me. So I hired 'em all.'

The Thornton crew reported for assignment in Dearborn on February 1, 1946. In addition to Tex Thornton they included George Moore, J. E. Lundy, Wilbur Andreson, Charles E. Bosworth, Ben Davis Mills, Francis C. Reith, James O. Wright, Arjay Miller, and Robert S. McNamara. Their wide-ranging knowledge covered business, law, economics, and finance. Not one had an automobile background.

At the start they were given an abbreviated version of the in-plant training received by Frank Zimmerman, Lee Iacocca, and other McCormick-Goodheart discoveries. An orientation period followed to learn the business side of automobile production as well as the structure of the Ford Motor Company. They were given carte blanche to roam the vast Ford complex, to move from one department to the other, asking pertinent questions as they went.

For a time they were a thorn in the sides of department heads and their personnel. Some considered them company spies or, at best, young, wet-behind-the-ears, inquisitive meddlers. They soon earned the nickname 'Quiz Kids,' a term they resented.

'I hate it,' one of them complained. 'We aren't kids and we're not quizzing anybody. We're just asking questions because that's the only way we can get the information to do a good job.'

As they became better known and respected for their abilities, the hated appellation was varied to 'Whiz Kids,' a name that suited them better. Henry Ford was pleased with their dedication, for within four months they proved themselves to be indeed 'whizzes' who knew considerably more about Ford Motor Company operations than employees of twenty years' service. He had little doubt that more than one of the ten would play major roles in the future of Ford.

Henry also realised that their inexperience in the automobile industry meant it would be years before they could make major contributions. His immediate need was a solid automotive-oriented man who could work closely with him.

He found the ideal candidate with the help of his uncle, Ernest Kanzler, then a director of the Bendix Aviation Corporation. The man was an ex-General Motors executive, Ernest R. Breech, president of Bendix. Breech, reluctant to leave Bendix where he was happy as top man, at first refused Ford's offer, then accepted it as a challenge despite the pitiful conditions he knew existed at Ford.

Five months after the Whiz Kids bowed in, Breech joined Ford as Henry's executive vice-president. It was July 1, 1946, a date most automotive experts call the day of first salvation for the Ford Motor Company.

In September, 1945, when Henry Ford II took over the company presidency, he had said that his one aim was to make Ford number one among American automobile manufacturers. Now, in July, 1946, Ernest Breech let it be known that he had taken what appeared a thankless job with one thought in mind, that of helping Ford become 'the leading automobile manufacturer in the United States.' It was an off-the-cuff excuse for his leaving Bendix, so far as reporters were concerned. Who in his right senses would leave a secure position for such a doubtful future?

The press was wrong. Breech knew what he was doing. He had analysed the situation at Ford, knew what he had to do, knew how to get it done. Ford was trying to bridge the gap between wartime and peacetime production, and this was the kind of challenge Breech enjoyed. In the interim between accepting Ford's offer and actually joining the company he made important decisions as to the people he needed.

One must be a forward-looking, innovative, yet down-to-earth chief of engineering. He had in mind Harold T. Youngren, a top-notch chief engineer with Borg-Warner, who had earlier been at the Oldsmobile Division of General Motors. Youngren, unhappy that he was doing more desk work that engineering, readily gave both Breech and Henry II an unqualified yes.

Finance, in as much a muddle as engineering, also needed a man of high calibre. Breech wanted Lewis Crusoe, who had been controller of GM's Fisher Body Division and assistant treasurer for General Motors itself. Crusoe had retired and only recently had come to Bendix as Breech's assistant.

Mead Bricker and Logan Miller had been doing an acceptable job in manufacturing, but Breech saw that a more hard-driving chief with up-to-date knowhow could move Ford forward faster. He made his feelings known to Henry and told him that Delmar S. Harder, who had spent some years supervising production for GM, would supply the experience needed. After some reluctance, and with the offer of a five-year contract, Harder joined the Breech team.

Even before he began his reconstruction at Ford, Breech knew it would take more than changes in high-level management. One vital problem was worker morale, which he'd seen at first hand on a chance visit to the Rouge plant. He and Mead Bricker were taken on a tour by a production supervisor. At one point, as they passed between the machines silent during the lunch break, they noticed a young man reading a newspaper. Unceremoniously the supervisor kicked the newspaper from the worker's hands and screamed at the surprised employee: 'Get out! Don't you ever let me see you in here again!'

Later in the tour another worker who had not seen them

coming accidentally blocked their path. Without a word the supervisor picked up the young man and flung him out of the way. Seething, Bricker fired the supervisor on the spot.

As they left the building, Breech told Bricker that he thought Henry II had outlawed the plant brutality for which the company had become infamous. Bricker agreed that Henry had.

'But you can't change some of these men,' Bricker said. 'The fact is that five years ago supervisors would have been fired if they *didn't* act that way.'

On November 15, 1946, not long after Lee Iacocca began his training period in the Rouge plant, Breech brought all supervisors and department heads together. He had in his hands an Elmo Roper report on employee impressions of working conditions at Ford. Almost 85 percent of the near 25,000 who responded criticised the treatment by their foremen and supervisors. In addition over 81 percent expressed dislike of what they considered management's attitude toward them.

Breech made it clear that the supervisors in front of him had to stop their abuse of men on the line, whose work was as important, maybe even more so, than that of the supers who abused them. The Ford Motor Company was not an army encampment, he told them.

'We won't have an "officer caste" here,' he emphasised. 'We won't have any brass-hat-ism.'

Backing Breech to the hilt, Henry II made it equally clear that while the Ford Motor Company had operated on, and exploited, the fear of its workers during the past twenty years, those days were gone.

'No company,' he said, 'can operate when relationships inside the company are predicated on fear.' He also pointed out the waste that came from working under such conditions, that cars could not be built as cheaply as when good human relations existed inside the company.

However imperious and obdurate Henry II may have been in later years, he was no autocrat as he went about restoring the company left ravaged by his grandfather. He knew his limitations, admitted them, and sought the help of men

72

knowledgeable enough to keep him on the right track. He read business publications, books, and magazines, searching for the surest and quickest course to make Ford competitive in an industry made more complex by government rulings.

A czar or a young Caesar would have feared a strong, dominant, and dedicated Ernest Breech, but Henry trusted Ernie and leaned heavily on his experience. He immediately agreed that the company's most conspicuous need was a decentralisation of authority; that no one man could oversee the hydra-headed monster into which the Ford Motor Company had evolved.

No longer was there only a Model T production to manage. Now there were Fords, Mercurys, Lincolns. There were steel mills, rubber plantations, soybean farms, and dozens of sidelines begun as his grandfather's avocations. Some were millstones that should be discarded. The others needed single-authority management to ensure efficient control of production and cost-efficiency.

Under Henry I the only consideration had been overall profit. Little attention was given to losses sustained by one or another of the widespread enterprises. Good sense dictated keeping and making the winners more productive while disposing of the non-essentials and the losers. Company losses were holding at about $10 million a month. Selling the off-shoots not germane to building cars would help cut losses, perhaps even provide operating cash.

Henry III went down the line with an axe. Ford-owned shops that turned out nuts, bolts, gauges, wheels, and other components were sold. The Brazilian government bought the Ford rubber plantations, which had amassed losses of $20 million and more. Soybean farms and processing plants went on the block.

With Breech at his side Henry charged ahead with a vengeance, but he had so much to do and so little time in which to get it done. High in priority was the production of the company's all-new 1949 model. The postwar cars already built were little more than the prewar 1942s offered the public. Something striking and totally different would be their salvation, a product the public would flock to as they had to the Tin Lizzie, one that would be a blockbuster in the marketplace.

It had to be a car without the 'tin' connotation of old Lizzie, one strongly built, whose doors would close with the solid but soft thud that indicated quality construction. Henry was obsessed with the belief that only such a car could bring substantial profits.

In 1946 Ford sustained a $50 million loss. A price increase of $62.50 per car approved by the OPA brought a $5 million profit in September, enabling the company to post a modest $2,000 profit before year's end.

Henry also realised that it would take more than good-quality construction to sell cars. He remembered his father's firm declaration, never agreed to by his grandfather, that a car also had to be pleasing to the eye. The new 1949 had to offer both.

Automobiles were no longer being made directly from design prints as in the days of the first Henry Ford. Now the company followed a multistep procedure before a car was actually produced. Small-scale models were made to vividly show the styling concept. When they were approved, full-size models were constructed from wet clay, enabling the stylist to make minor changes in the car's exterior lines through the use of a spatula.

Old Henry would have been shocked, but he was too ill and too unconcerned as his mind continued to deteriorate. Clara had taken her husband to Georgia for two months in the warm sun and brought him back to Fair Lane in April. He died in his bed of a cerebral haemorrhage the night of April 7, 1947. He was eighty-three.

Young Henry and Ernie Breech – while also finalizing plans for the new 1949 Ford – had restructured the company. Each major facet of the company's operations would be called a division, with a single executive responsible for each; every division head was answerable to the policy committee, which in turn reported to Ford and Breech.

The various divisions, each to be managed by a vice-president, were automotive engineering, industrial relations, manufacturing, purchasing, finance, and sales. A Lincoln-

Mercury Division, headed by Benson Ford after his father's death, had been set up in late 1925. Ford Division had not yet been formed but was being considered.

As the finishing touches were being applied to the 1949 Ford, styled by Henry's new designer George Walker, Benson Ford, vice-president in charge of the Lincoln-Mercury Division, had his new offerings ready. On April 11, 1948, the 1949 Lincoln and Lincoln Cosmopolitan were introduced to the public. Eighteen days later, on the 29th, Benson revealed his personal pride, the stylish and comfortable 1949 Mercury.

None of the Lincoln-Mercury cars received the introduction fanfare accorded the new Ford when it was unveiled on June 10. For this gala event only the gold-and-white grand ballroom of New York's Waldorf-Astoria would do.

The New York showing was lavish. Before the grand opening for the public, radio, television, and newspaper reporters enjoyed a preview complete with music, champagne, and a miniature replica of the 1949 Ford presented to each member of the media in attendance.

They saw the first of the totally new postwar automobiles, for Ford had the jump on the competition, and the car was hardly recognisable as a Ford product. It was lower to the ground, neatly designed with minimum chrome trim, offered greater seating capacity than previous Fords, and had a larger windshield with more side glass for increased visibility. The running boards had vanished.

Throughout the six-day show the Waldorf-Astoria ballroom was jammed with the curious, thousands ready to buy. Before the books were closed on the '49, more than 800,000 were sold. Total Ford Motor Company passenger car sales, which included Lincoln and Mercury units, broke the million barrier. Henry Ford II had the company back on its feet.

The 1949 Ford proved, however, not to have the high-quality construction Henry had envisioned. The body did not fit solidly to the chassis, and dealers began to relay buyer complaints of dirt and water seeping into the interior. After talking it over with Ernie Breech, Henry decided that the time had come to form a separate division to oversee Ford vehicle production. On February 11, 1949, Ford Division was organised to handle all aspects of production, assembly, and marketing of all passenger cars and trucks bearing the Ford nameplate. Lewis D. Crusoe, who had headed planning for the contemplated organisation for two years, was named vice-president in charge. He was to supervise the division as a totally separate function, a company within the company.

Crusoe and his assistant general manager at the new Ford Division, staid and scholarly Robert S. McNamara, were both cost-conscious executives. Tex Thornton had resigned, and McNamara was top man among the Whiz Kids. McNamara, with his roundish face, rimless glasses, and straight hair flat against his scalp, hardly fitted so playful a term as 'whiz kid,' but he had an incisive, finance-oriented mind.

Both men, Crusoe in particular, felt the 1949 Ford was too expensive to compete with Chevrolet. John Davis, the sales manager, was not so sure.

'Remember,' he pointed out, 'that when we were first in sales Chevrolet took our leadership away from us even when their car cost a hundred dollars more than ours. They made real profits because they had a good gross margin.'

Crusoe and McNamara believed that higher grosses came by reducing production costs. They had their engineers dismantle Fords and Chevrolets, then compared the parts from both cars as to size and number and actual cost, getting the figures down to within one cent.

'You know,' Crusoe said, 'this is a nickel-and-dime business. If we save a dime on each of a million units, we've saved $100,000 in production costs. I'll tell you, we'll practically cut your throat around here for a quarter.'

His final comparative figures had shown him that a Chevrolet was less costly to produce than a Ford, about $84 cheaper. He and McNamara set about to lower that differential, but it would take time.

The outbreak of the Korean War in June of 1950 upset their timetable. While automobile production was not halted, a crimp was put into making cars by government restrictions on aluminium and steel. Not until after the end of the conflict, three years later, could they get back into high gear.

Planning for war's end, Ford Division was ready in 1953 to surprise the market with a new series of two better styled cars that offered roomier interiors and better handling and roadability. One, the lower of the two in price, was the Ford Mainline. The second, which would take its place among the company's more successful products, was the Ford Fairlane. Sales of the 1954s hit 267,799, only 25,280 less than Chevrolet. They had made the kind of inroads Ford had hoped for.

In the meantime Ford was making great strides with its overseas operations. What had started as far back as 1904 with the granting of a franchise to sell Fords throughout Europe to a man named Percival Perry, had later been broadened into Ford of Britain acting as a holding company for facilities developed in Germany, Denmark, Spain, Holland, and France. In the early fifties Ford bought out minority interests in their foreign subsidiaries to form Ford of Europe, with headquarters in London. The company was now literally worldwide.

General Motors and Chrysler also had highly successful European operations. Inevitably the European manufacturers began testing the waters of the American market. The little MG Midget began it in 1946, with Jaguar following soon after, its XK120 at around $4,000 hitting it big from the start. Americans were not only talking about, but also buying, cars that were winners at LeMans and in European Grand Prix races.

The minor flood of sporty imports opened the eyes of the American automakers. Their designers began emulating the imports, scrapping the big, high-off-the-ground styling, lowering the overall height and rounding out sharp body corners to minimise wind drag.

Chevrolet beat Ford to the draw, unveiling its dream car, the Corvette, at the 1953 Motorama. Its most unusual features were body construction of reinforced fibreglass on a conventional frame, with seating for only two. It was acclaimed as the most striking American sports car since the classic Stutz Bearcat, which had died in the Depression.

Lewis Crusoe was not to be outdone. On October 22, 1954, less than two years after the Corvette debut, Ford answered the Chevrolet challenge with its Thunderbird two-seater. It offered a full range of transmissions – automatic, manual synchromesh, and overdrive – and the availability of options such as power brakes, power steering, and power seats.

Corvette, in the $5,000 bracket, had first-year problems in performance and manoeuvrability that were quickly corrected. However, its first-year production totalled only 300, while Thunderbird hit the road with 11,000 during its initial year at a basic price under $2,700.

On February 1, 1955, changes were made in the corporate structure of the Ford Motor Company. One of the executive promotions more than likely triggered a reversal in the temperament of Henry Ford II, while another proved significant to the future of Lee Iacocca. Ernest R. Breech moved up from executive vice-president to the newly established post of chairman of the board. While Breech and Ford continued handling major management decisions together, the titles in effect made Ernie Breech Henry's superior.

The position of executive vice-president was filled by Lewis Crusoe, who was replaced as the head of Ford Division by Robert S. McNamara.

Ford Division designers had no totally new car on the drawing boards for the 1956 model year when Bob McNamara took over. However, new models for 1956 were introduced in late 1955 for the Mercury and the Lincoln/Continental divisions. Mercury brought out two, the more luxurious of which was the Monterey, planned to compete with Buick and Oldsmobile. William Clay Ford, Henry's brother and head of Lincoln/Continental, offered the Continental Mark II.

McNamara's most serious concern at Ford Division in his first year as its head was to try to close the widening gap between Ford and Chevrolet. In 1954 Ford had closed in on Chevy, coming within 17,013 units after a disastrous 1953, when Chevy had beaten Ford by 226,213 sales. In 1955 the hopes of the previous year were dashed as Chevrolet retightened its lead to the tune of almost 67,000.

Lee Iacocca's fabulous promotion for the Philadelphia district, '56 for 56,' had set new records for the area. McNamara was impressed by the sales in Philadelphia and picked up the '56 for 56' idea for national use. Although sales increased by some 72,000 sales that might not otherwise have been made, Ford's 1956 model year was disheartening. Chevrolet's edge had stretched to 190,056 over Ford.

It became obvious to Bob McNamara that his Ford Division needed a heavy charge. He was hopeful that the young marketing genius in the Chester office, who had just been promoted to head the Washington district, was the man to turn things around. He sent Charley Beacham to Chester during the week of Lee Iacocca's wedding to bring the young man, nurtured by Beacham, back to Ford Division headquarters in Dearborn as Ford's new marketing manager for trucks.

CHAPTER 5

Jubilant as a newlywed, and hopeful that his career was on the rise, Lee Iacocca arrived in Dearborn on November 1, 1956, to take up his new duties. He was confident that here, in the thick of things at Ford, he could make his mark in the big leagues of the automobile business. He checked in with Charley Beacham at Ford Division, the low-rise structure less than a mile south of Ford's new twelve-storey world headquarters. The imposing Glass House had been dedicated just three days before his marriage to Mary McCleary.

The ebullient spirit of his strikingly beautiful and under-standing wife had increased his own zest for life and his love of the challenge ahead. He missed her tremendously, and his first priority had to be finding a home so that she could join him.

With Beacham's help good luck came his way within a week. Another Ford executive was being transferred, and his house was available. Lee, certain that Mary would like the rambling ranch house on Orchard Lake, about twenty miles north of his Dearborn office, rented it. Mary arrived by the middle of the month.

When he first stepped into the Ford Division offices, Lee found the Ford complex in an upbeat state. The previous year had set a record in car and truck production. More than 2.5 million vehicles had rolled off the assembly lines despite the company's slippage in its battle with General Motors and Ford Division's inability to close in on Chevrolet. Amazingly, Ford had paid out over $1 billion in wages to 180,000 employees in the one year.

On March 7 the Ford Motor Company had become a public corporation when the Ford Foundation released 10 million shares for sale. No longer was it a wholly family-owned company, even though the Fords still controlled a majority of the voting stock. The day Ford shares went on sale, the floor of the New York Stock Exchange was a madhouse. Ford's first annual report, reflecting a $437 million profit, made investors eager to buy pieces of the pie. Over 235,000 individuals bought one or more shares of stock within a week.

The year 1956 had begun and progressed right into fall as a year of milestones. On June 19 a Ford had set the 500-mile stock car record at the Indianapolis Speedway. The world took note, and Ford stock went up. Then, on September 28, the day after Lee heard of his promotion, Ford had received even more worldwide publicity as it made its first public showing of cars in Moscow. Henry Ford II had been there, a capitalist or not, to be regaled by the Soviet communist leaders.

On November 16 Henry presided over another big Ford event, one that – unsuspected at the time – would become one of the company's biggest flops. It was the introduction of the Edsel.

The Edsel was named for the first Ford who believed in the value of automobile styling. Edsel's father had not agreed, but now Henry II was bringing out an automobile that he confidently expected would become the styling sensation of the decade.

It was not. The Edsel had been designed in group sessions, with too many fingers leaving their mark on its identity. It came to life, as one wag put it, like a camel, which is really a horse created by committee.

The Edsel did have a different, innovative style, much too different for the times, and it came on the market with three strikes against it. The car had been rushed through and had far more defects than the normal few usually expected in new automobiles. Its front end was strange looking with a 'horsecollar' grille that turned off many buyers. And the Edsel was offered in so many models at such varying prices that prospective purchasers were confused.

The Edsel was also unlucky. It made its bow just before a recession hit the nation, so that even later refinements in its styling and correction of its defects could not save it. An expensive fiasco – its tooling and production costs were estimated at $350 million – it died an ignominious death soon after its second birthday.

The optimism Lee sensed when he first arrived had turned to ashes, but with his new responsibilities he could not let the pall that hung over the company affect his work. He attacked his job head-on, not conservatively and feeling his way as most newcomers to responsibility are wont to do. For him today was already yesterday if he were to reverse Ford's bad second in truck sales to Chevrolet. A look at the charts revealed that Chevrolet had averaged 50,000 more sales a year for each of the last five. Ford had come closest in 1954, when it had been only 25,280 behind.

Iacocca quickly discovered that the source of the problem nationwide was little different from what he had found in the Philadelphia district. Dealer apathy had relegated truck merchandising to the status of stepchild in relation to cars. Most dealerships who sold both cars and trucks found selling five or more automobiles easier than making a single truck sale, and few urged their salesmen to give equal emphasis to trucks.

The solution, then, lay in dealership-level training. Both dealers and salesmen had to be sensitised to the importance of truck volume to their own profitability. Iacocca would have to re-emphasise the specific knowledge needed to sell cargo carriers in contrast to those necessary for passenger car sales.

Lee went into the field himself. He paid hard-sell visits to dealers. He held forceful seminars for salesmen, speaking his mind toughly and tersely, sure that only a get-with-it honest approach could succeed. He organised a task force to follow up his personal visits and check on progress.

His programme worked. In his first year as truck marketing manager he chopped Ford's truck sales deficit to within 14,000 of Chevrolet, an astounding success when balanced against the miseries of the five previous years.

This startling turnaround was not lost on Robert McNamara, and before the year's end he promoted Lee Iacocca to marketing manager for cars.

Lee could hardly contain himself. It was a giant step toward his goal, and he could not wait to phone his father. Nick's Italian blood raced with pride. He had always said there was no stopping his son, and he urged Lee to go for the top.

Lee swung into his new assignment with his usual total commitment, giving more evidence of his ability to cope with the demands of the increasingly complex automobile business. In 1957, for the first time in twenty-two years, Ford new-car registrations topped those of Chevrolet. In one year Ford Division shot 50,000 units ahead of the enemy. It was a master achievement, a historic landmark for the Ford Motor Company, and one that helped ease the agony over the Edsel.

The normally imperturbable McNamara was enthusiastic in his praise. His protégé had achieved a long-sought goal. Ernest Breech came by personally with a salute. Even Henry Ford II phoned to congratulate Lee. If cloud nine exists, Lee Iacocca was riding it.

A few days later Lee had a more personal cause for celebration. Mary had returned home from a visit to her doctor to say she was pregnant. Lee's spirits sky-rocketed, looking ahead to the one blessing that outweighed his progress at Ford.

It was not something for him to delight in alone. Nick and Antoinette would have to come. So, too, would Mary's mother. And, he told Mary, it was time that they bought their own house, since his promotion made it financially feasible. A finer, larger home was found in Birmingham, the suburb north of Detroit that housed many of the industry's executives.

Back at his desk in Ford Division, Lee busily prepared for the introduction of McNamara's brainchild, the Ford Falcon. The more McNamara saw of Iacocca, the more he liked the straightforward, dogged honesty of the young man from Allentown. He was particularly impressed by the fact that Iacocca was no sycophant. If he disagreed with something, he spoke up, even when his position was counter to that of his boss.

McNamara had planned the Falcon, the first American compact, as a car that would enable Ford to beat all other major carmakers in offering a smaller-sized automobile, and he wanted a solid marketing strategy for its introduction. McNamara told his planning committee that he thought 'safety' was the basis on which the new car should be sold. He was concerned over the public's perception of the automobile as a killer since congressional hearings on the subject began in 1956. In his view the public would react favourably to positioning the safety features of the Falcon as the base of its promotion and advertising.

'Safety won't sell cars,' was Iacocca's unhesitant reaction.

Safety, he was convinced, would only rub salt in an already festering wound and make the buyer more wary. Besides, legal problems might accrue from advertising safety. An accident victim might prove a case against the company, claiming that 'advertised safety' was tantamount to a guarantee against injury. McNamara saw the point and dropped the idea.

Lee and his staff plunged full speed ahead in search of a promotion so electrifying it would receive broadscale coverage in newspapers as well as on radio and television. It was a trying time for Lee, spearheading the structure of the promotion while spending as much time as possible with Mary, now in her ninth month of pregnancy.

Lee's father and mother arrived from Allentown, and Mary's mother from Chester, to help. On June 29, 1959, less than five weeks before the unveiling of the Falcon, Kathy Iacocca introduced herself to the world at Detroit's Henry Ford Hospital. The tiny girl had upstaged the spectacular Lee was planning for Ford's newest car.

When Mary came home with the Iacocca firstborn, holding the beautiful, dark-haired baby girl became a source of competition between Lee and the grandparents. Never was a child more loved and coddled, and no home echoed more with happiness and joy.

The exultation at the Iacocca home in Birmingham was in sharp contrast to the fretful spirit that marked the Henry Ford II mansion in Grosse Pointe. Anne, the dazzling socialite Henry had given up his college degree to marry, had wearied of him. She had given Henry two daughters – Charlotte, born in 1941, and Anne, in 1943, as well as a son, Edsel II, in 1945 – but had enough of Henry's peccable ways.

The beginning of the end had come when Henry met Cristina Vettore Austin, an Italian divorcee, at a Parisian party given by Ernest Kanzler's fourth wife. With the once rhapsodic union of Anne McDonnell and Henry Ford II turning sour, Henry was hardly aware of the plans for the presentation of his newest automobile.

Bob McNamara enthusiastically approved the Falcon introduction promo, conceived by Iacocca, and gave Lee a hearty go-ahead. The setting was to be a small town in the centre of the United States, Flora, a city of 5,000 population in the heart of the dairy and farming area of southern Illinois.

On a bright, hot day in August a procession of new Falcons paraded into the usually quiet town, now festooned with flags and bunting heralding the honour bestowed on it by the Ford Motor Company. On their arrival the Falcons were distributed among the townspeople, one for each family in Flora and the adjacent area, and one for each single adult.

Throughout the morning and afternoon Lee Iacocca moved among the citizens and business establishments of Flora, asking their personal opinions of the cars they drove. What did they like about them? What didn't they like? Would they suggest any changes? It was an attention-getter never before experienced in the automobile industry, and it was enjoyed vicariously by all America via television.

Flora's gala day sparked a Falcon sales record unequalled in the industry, with first-year registrations of 417,174. A testimonial to the skill with which Lee Iacocca executed the campaign, it was also a triumph for Robert McNamara, who described Lee Iacocca as a man worth his weight in gold. It had not been easy to sell Henry Ford II on the value of offering the American public a smartly styled, low-priced, six-cylinder car as a choice against the gas-guzzlers of the day.

Less than three months after his phenomenal success at Flora, Lee Iacocca celebrated his thirty-fifth birthday. He experienced a tinge of disappointment at not having earned a vice-presidency by then, but his regret was alleviated by the happy birthday greetings at home and by tiny Kathy, not yet four months old. He also took solace in the fact that he had come a long way in a short time.

Unaware that Henry Ford II was sharpening his guillotine for a series of decapitations, Iacocca continued to work hard. Henry had felt for some time that he had had enough of Ernest Breech, that the time was ripe to bid him goodbye.

Breech had been more instrumental than Henry himself in saving the Ford Motor Company after the death of the first Henry Ford. Henry II had leaned on his knowledge and expertise and had given Breech the post of chairman, a step higher than his own as president. For Henry this was no longer a healthy situation.

Henry had been usurping many of Breech's prerogatives as chairman. With private innuendos he began downgrading the man who had done so much for the company, while in public utterances he continued to praise Breech. Increasingly Henry exhibited traits that reminded his associates of his grandfather.

In the summer of 1960 he finally let Ernie Breech know that he was no longer wanted. The professional and tactful Breech quietly submitted his resignation to Henry in mid-July. In the subsequent corporate realignment Henry II served for a time both as president and chairman.

Soon, however, the burden proved too great for a man with an impending divorce who was drinking more heavily. Robert McNamara was named president, which created an opening in the post of vice-president and general manager of Ford Division.

On the morning of November 11, 1960, Lee Iacocca was summoned to Henry's office in the Glass House. The job was his. He had achieved the vice-presidency, not by his thirty-fifth birthday as he had predicted so long ago, but less than two weeks after his thirty-sixth.

Lee returned to Ford Division as its boss. Driving the short distance back from the Glass House, he realised that his takeover of Bob McNamara's office was bound to breed bitterness and animosity. He had leapt past older men with longer tenure. Keeping them in line would take strong, unsubtle measures.

'Get with it,' he told the men now under his command. 'You're being observed closely. Guys who don't get with it don't play on the team after a while.' It worked because, as Iacocca says, 'all of a sudden a guy is face to face with the reality of his mortgage payments.'

From the moment he returned to Ford Division as its head, Lee Iacocca set about to get a firm grip on everything affecting his responsibilities. He made certain that he knew all that happened in the ranks, and he let his men know he knew. He developed an evaluation process for his department heads, preparing what came to be known as Iacocca's 'black book' – a journal that held each department chief's objectives for the quarter ahead. At the end of each three-month period he graded each man on the extent to which those objectives had been met.

He stretched his people to their limits and threw himself into the battle with equal intensity, spurred on by an ego that matched his position. He had a large group of varied and conflicting personalities to manage and control. Those who knew and respected his integrity were inspired by his dedication. Any who harboured resentment at his meteoric climb were pulled quickly in line by the force of his magnetism or were soon gone.

Lee Iacocca's toughness and resoluteness of purpose brought distinction and panache to Ford Division. 'So much panache,' said Hal Sperlick, a product planner and engineer at Ford since 1957, 'that along with John Kennedy, who hit the world about the same time, he was like a breath of fresh air. They were both young for the responsibilities they were to have. They brought a little bit of Camelot, Kennedy to Washington and Iacocca to Ford Division. With Lee's young, new kind of management, things were pretty exciting.'

Excitement was the norm throughout the Ford Motor Company during the final months of 1960. President-elect John F. Kennedy wanted the man who was president of Ford in his cabinet.

Despite having been given the choice of heading the Treasury or Defense departments, Robert McNamara was reluctant to leave Ford so soon after attaining its presidency. Sargent Shriver, sent by Kennedy to make the offer, persisted, but McNamara refused the Treasury appointment, claiming no expertise in fiscal affairs or banking. Nor did he want Defense. He did, however, promise to meet with John Kennedy the following day.

It took a second meeting with the President-elect before McNamara accepted the post of secretary of defense. He submitted his resignation to Henry Ford II, and John Dykstra, not Lee Iacocca, was named to succeed him at Ford.

Early in 1961 Lee Iacocca stirred up excitement at Ford with a dynamic promotion that overshadowed the pageantry of the pilgrimage to Flora, Illinois. He had added a convertible to the Falcon, giving the line a sporty flair that included bucket seats. The Falcon's inaugural at Flora had been all-American. This new Falcon with touches of European styling deserved a continental presentation.

On New Year's Eve two airliners with more than 200 men and women aboard, including Lee Iacocca, Gar Laux, Walter Murphy, Wes Small, and Tom Kierney of Ford Division, as well as Bill Winn and Bob Castle representing Ford promotion agencies, took off for Europe. Also aboard were a variety of Ford automobiles, not the least of which were several new Falcon convertibles, and 120 press people, which included representatives of prestigious magazines such as *Newsweek* and *Time*.

The entourage arrived at Monaco, the tiny principality overlooking the Mediterranean, at six in the morning New Year's Day. The all-night ride, spiced by many beverages, was a loud, happy, and wakeful one. The hour of arrival, however, allowed little time for freshening up, much less a catnap. A reception was scheduled for ten o'clock at the royal palace of Prince Rainier and Princess Grace.

In the great hall of the palace, awaiting the appearance of the royal family, the Ford people and the news people were served champagne in huge beer mugs. 'The last thing we needed after that plane ride,' Walter Murphy said. At ten o'clock sharp huge golden doors opened, framing Princess Grace, former American movie star.

Princess Grace, followed by Prince Rainier and three-year-old Prince Albert, greeted Lee Iacocca and the entire American group. There was an instantaneous rapport between Iacocca and the ruler of the world's smallest principality. They talked at length about automobiles. Rainer, Lee discovered, had a well-rounded knowledge of engineering.

Iacocca presented His Serene Highness with a new Ford Thunderbird and Princess Grace with a Ford station wagon for her Red Cross charity. To their heir, Prince Albert, he gave a specially handcrafted, miniature Thunderbird.

The unveiling of the new Falcon convertible and other Ford products to the press was scheduled for that afternoon in the grounds of the Place du Casino de Monte Carlo, high above the Mediterranean, and although Monaco has no more that sixty days of rain in a year, that day it poured. A large tent was erected on the Casino grounds for the product presentation presided over by Gar Laux.

At the conclusion of the formalities members of the press took part in a ride-and-drive exercise to give each an opportunity to evaluate the car. Starting at the casino, a seventy-five-mile route road-rally course had been laid out that took the riders through the town and out into the Maritime Alps.

Lee Iacocca rode in a Falcon piloted by Timo Makinen, a Finnish race driver. At one point as they made a turn in the mountains, the driver lost control momentarily. For seconds the car seemed headed off the crest of a mountain into a gully hundreds of feet down.

The car was righted just in time and brought to the finish line undamaged. 'Well, I at least found out what the car can do,' was all a still-shaking Iacocca could say as he stepped out of the Falcon.

In the evening most of the Ford and press people congregated in the world's most famous casino. As he stood watching the milling crowd, Walter Murphy, Iacocca's public relations chief, was approached by a dark-haired, dark-skinned man.

'My boss would like to talk to your boss,' the man told Murphy in broken English.

'Who's your boss?' Murphy asked. The request seemed strange, coming at such an inappropriate time.

The man pointed toward the entrance where Murphy could see a dignified, grey-haired, smartly attired, obviously well-to-do individual. 'It is Mr Aristotle Onassis,' the man explained.

Knowing that Iacocca did not stand on protocol, Murphy indicated the table at which Lee stood. 'There's my boss,' he told the man. 'Take him over and introduce him.'

It was definitely not the way of Ari Onassis. 'No! No!' the dark-skinned man said almost fearfully. 'It is not right. You must introduce him.'

Murphy shrugged his shoulders. The man must be one of the Onassis servants or bodyguards, he decided. He agreed to introduce the famous Greek shipping tycoon to Lee Iacocca, vice-president of the Ford Motor Company.

Once he had done the honours, Murphy walked out onto the balcony overlooking the basinlike harbour of Monte Carlo. Moored there, far below, was the Onassis yacht – as big as the *Queen Mary*, Murphy thought – festooned with strings of sparkling lights from prow to stern, which illuminated a huge banner bearing a welcome to Ford and Lee Iacocca.

Lee found Ari Onassis a charming and enchanting conversationalist. He was fascinated by this Greek who had spent little time in the United States, yet knew more about American history than he did. Onassis began with the causes of the American Revolution and ticked off, in year-by-year chronology, historic events through the election of John Fitzgerald Kennedy.

The stay in Monaco lasted two weeks. During that period Ford cars were entered in the annual Monaco Grand Prix, the twisting, treacherous, around-the-houses race now a fixture on the Grand Prix circuit. The Ford cars were not expected to win – they were entered only as a test of the cars' durability for the benefit of the press. The race was won by England's great driver, Stirling Moss, in a Lotus-Climax.

Ford automobiles also took part in the Paris-to-Monaco leg of the Monte Carlo Rally, one of the oldest and best known of all rallies. The principal purpose was to get film footage of Ford cars in action, with Bill Winn supervising the crew that photographed the full run. This time a Falcon won in its class.

The Ford session in Monaco and its entries in the Grand Prix and Monte Carlo Rally received worldwide attention and so was judged an overwhelming promotional success. Once back in America, Lee Iacocca had other attention-getters ready for the same model year. One, designed to add zest to the Falcon's introduction to Ford dealers, made a new Falcon convertible available to airline stewardesses who had a day off between flights in cities where Ford dealer meetings were being held. The stewardesses had the car for their personal use and visited the ceremonies presenting the Falcon to the Ford dealers.

It was also in 1961 that Lee Iacocca produced another promotion that would continue bringing prospects into Ford dealerships. This was the highly motivating Punt, Pass, and Kick programme, providing youngsters nine through thirteen the opportunity to show their abilities in three facets of football. Produced in co-operation with the National Football League, the Punt, Pass, and Kick competition began in local Ford dealerships.

Winners at the local level went on to compete in district challenges. District victors met other district winners for zone competitions. The latter were held during half times of scheduled NFL games, with the champions in each age group going on to vie for national honours during half time of the Super Bowl.

Youngsters qualified for PP&K participation by visiting their local Ford dealership in the company of fathers or related adults, a factor that in itself packed a powerful promotional punch. Over the fifteen-year span of the programme more than 20 million car buyers visited Ford

91

dealerships with PP&K hopefuls, a good percentage of whom might not otherwise have been exposed to a Ford product. No valid estimate can be made of the probably many thousands of sales that were generated.

Punt, Pass and Kick exemplifies Lee Iacocca's perception of what stimulates public interest and produces sales. It also reflects his awareness of what it takes to stir public interest and excitement. In this instance the passion of young America for sports competition could become an asset for Ford because Iacocca understood the public as well as his relationship to those who implemented the programmes.

No one else in the industry came close to achieving the success of the promotional themes conceived by Lee Iacocca. His campaigns combined good, practical, utilitarian sense with drama.

In methodical, systematised fashion Lee Iacocca went about planning for automobiles that would carry his personal totem. When he took over Ford Division, he had to work with automobiles conceived by others. He gave McNamara's Falcon a few new touches, added the successful convertible to the line, but a car that was distinctly an Iacocca creation would take time. In the automobile industry an incubation of three years was necessary to take a car from design to final production.

Moving from the first scratches on the drawing board to a finished automobile is a long, laborious, and tedious process that in more recent years has been speeded up by computer and other technological advances. First is the planning. What kind of car will have public appeal? What dimensions? What power? What basic features are needed to make it an attractive buy at a marketable price?

Only after most of these fundamentals have been resolved, production costs estimated, is the next step – designing – taken. This in itself is no simple, one-time go-through. Refinements and adjustments in styling lines, often in the preset dimensions and other elements, are made, altered, and re-altered until the powers are satisfied. Then prototypes are constructed of wood and clay. And again changes may be needed. At the same time dies to make the body components are created. All this is necessary before a driveable prototype can be built, because the final product represents an investment of millions of dollars.

Lee realised that Ford could not afford another bomb like the Edsel. Planning for his own car of the future had to begin with positive indications of its viability in the market. Meanwhile, business had to proceed as usual.

He supervised the final touches on the new Ford Fairlane series, which entered the market with some success on November 16, 1961, as one of the Ford entries for the 1962 model year. For 1963 he restyled the Falcon and the standard Ford model rooflines to provide a more contemporary look, and he added a V-8 to give Falcon better performance. To give the 'new-look' Falcon exposure Iacocca had it driven to college campuses throughout the country accompanied by a 'Hootenanny Folk Sing.'

Iacocca was also determined to dispel the public's image of Ford cars as stodgy, unimaginative vehicles and to give the cars' fresh, modern styling and improved performance more visibility. Where better, he thought, than on the racetrack?

European Fords had done their part over the years. In 1936, 1938, and 1953 English Fords won the Monte Carlo Rally and other races on the continent. In 1955 another English Ford won the rough, tough, East African Safari through Kenya and Uganda.

Before 1960, the year in which the American automobile industry agreed not to sponsor racing events, American Fords had done extremely well. The 1,913-mile Pan-Americana race through Central America was won by Lincolns in 1952–53–54, and from 1956 through 1959 Ford racked up hundreds of wins in NASCAR (National Association for Stock Car Auto Racing) competition. And in 1962 an unsponsored Ford-powered car won the three-hour continental race at Daytona.

Iacocca looked on the three-year-old agreement as an exercise in hypocrisy. Many manufacturers still clandestinely underwrote race expenses. He believed Ford should come out in the open with company sponsorship and approached Henry Ford II with his idea. Automotive racing attracted more people than baseball and football combined, making it ideal for the exposure of Ford cars.

Henry was enthusiastic. He had already been excited by the nearly endless Grand Prix and LeMans wins by Ferrari, so much so that he had tried to buy Enzo Ferrari's company and make Ferrari director of operations for automobiles that would be called Ford-Ferraris.

Ferrari had turned him down, irritating Henry. A few weeks later Ferrari changed his mind, but Henry took no chances on a second rebuff. He refused to buy. He gave Lee Iacocca carte blanche to get into racing, especially to build Ford cars that would whip Ferrari's best.

Henry's quick agreement may have been triggered by other matters that occupied his mind. For one thing he made it clear on May 1, 1963, that uneasy would lie the head of anyone he made president of the Ford Motor Company. He announced that John Dykstra had been replaced by Arjay Miller, one of the original Whiz Kids. Miller took office as the seventh president in the history of the company, the fifth to hold that office in the seventeen years since Henry II took over.

The following months were especially troublesome for Henry. His marriage to Anne had finally collapsed. His affair with the Italian divorcee had become too much of an embarrassment to Anne McDonnell Ford. On August 3, 1963, she and Henry had legally separated, she to go her way, he to pursue the indomitable Cristina.

Lee went back to work not only to prepare the Ford Motor Company for racing wars, but to make final decisions on his personal contribution to the Ford line, a car to be called – after many other names were discarded for one reason or another – the Ford Mustang.

CHAPTER 6

Unaware that he was creating a legend, Lee Iacocca initiated plans for the first automobile he could call his own. His primary objective was to give American car buyers the kind of automobile they wanted. Iacocca was determined that his new car would be something special. It had to be, for he sensed that the American public had become more demanding and more quality conscious, that a change in public tastes was in the air.

A significant factor in Iacocca's thinking were the imports, which were eating up an increasingly large share of the American market. The import invasion had begun after World War II when England's manufacturers returned to car production before their counterparts in the United States were given the go-ahead by Washington.

The perky and sporty MG led the way, sending one-third of its 1946 production, 500 cars, across the Atlantic. Jaguar quickly followed. American GIs in Europe had been exposed to the sportier styling of British and European cars, many of which, like the MG, were smaller that US models, and they had learned to like them. Given a choice between a used American car and a new European model, many opted for the latter. In no time MG's most profitable market was the United States. Jaguar also found a bonanza on the western shores of the Atlantic. When its XK120, a stock car that sold for about $4,000, was delivered in the United States, it became an overnight sensation among fine-car buffs.

By 1948 the imports had achieved the modest American market penetration of 0.46 percent. It was so small, compared to GM's more than 40 percent, Chrysler's over 21 percent, and even Ford's near 19 percent, that American carmakers had not been concerned. Nor were they worried in 1956, when the import share climbed to 1.65 percent of American sales, even though it was more than double that of the previous year.

Volkswagen's Beetle and its smart Kharmann-Ghia coupé had hit American buyers in 1955, accounting for the sharp rise in import sales. Toyota and Datsun, from Japan, followed in 1957 and 1958, respectively. By the end of 1959 imports had achieved a startling 10.17 percent of American car sales, taking just over 4.25 percent from General Motors and over 2.5 percent from Chrysler. Thanks to Falcon, Ford earned a 1.68 percent increase.

A sharp diagnostician, Iacocca found further reinforcement for his concept of a new car in the sales figures for 1960, a year in which both GM and Chrysler introduced new compact cars to increase their shares of the American market at the expense of the imports and Ford.

Just a few months before Lee Iacocca's promotion to general manager of Ford Division – a pressure-laden responsibility since Ford Division produced 80 percent of the company's car – Chrysler had brought out its compact Plymouth Valiant, with a 101-horse-power, six-cylinder engine and a revolutionary electrical alternator. The new Valiant helped boost Plymouth sales by 55,486 in 1960.

At about the same time GM's Chevrolet Division offered its air-cooled, independently sprung, rear-engined Corvair. Corvair sold surprisingly well – it would be some time before Ralph Nader's book *Unsafe at Any Speed* would deal it a death blow – boosting Chevy's 1960 sales 277,794 over the previous year.

One factor in Corvair's sales charts particularly intrigued Iacocca. The highest number of Corvair sales went to its sporty version called Monza, a car that to a great degree reflected the styling of the European imports. But Lee was not totally convinced that the Corvair Monza provided a barometer for what Americans hungered for in an automobile. Certainly, Monza's success indicated that Ford Motor Company's lack of sportily styled automobiles had caused its decrease in 1960 of more than 50,000 sales while Chevy registrations shot up over a quarter-million. Yet Iacocca felt that sportiness alone was not the complete answer.

A somewhat clearer picture emerged from a survey taken of the extra equipment ordered for Ford Falcons. A great percentage of buyers had paid extra for more powerful engines, automatic transmissions, power features, and decorative items such as paint stripes and white sidewall tyres. Americans, it seemed, did not want plain, unexciting cars.

Nonetheless, the picture of trends in American buyer wants in automobiles was still cloudy. Iacocca needed a sharper focus to avoid an Edsel fiasco. The Edsel's styling had not been thoroughly researched.

To get a handle on public preference Lee gathered a staff of twenty young researchers and put them on a crash schedule. He told them to find out what kind of car Americans wanted. How big or small? How much power? What kind of styling? What special equipment?

His researchers polled students, young marrieds, the middle-aged, Korean veterans, even Monza buyers. Surprisingly few interviewees cared for anything then on the market. Some pointed to the small, jazzy Europeans as 'maybe' their kind of car. Most said only that they would like 'something different.'

Early on in his new position Lee Iacocca had put together a staff of capable aides, specialists in engineering, product planning, styling, and merchandising. Hal Sperlick was one. Gar Laux, Don Frey, and Joe Oros were others. Together with Lee they analysed the research results in depth.

They soon noted that a new market segment, with its own buying patterns, had been growing gradually among young buyers, the eighteen- and nineteen-year-olds ready for their first car, as well as the young marrieds who were then taking on family responsibilities at an earlier age. They wanted a car with flair in its styling.

As the Iacocca team dug further, it discovered that this

same sportiness was desired by a sizeable percentage of the middle-aged and older, the 'young at heart' who wanted to express their youthful spirit in a car with gusto. Television had proved to be the foundation of youth that washed away the stodgy and dull in their lives and instilled a passion for excitement and adventure.

The research revealed another important factor. A growing economy was producing a more affluent middle class. The number of two-car families was growing, and they preferred a smaller, personalised automobile for their second car.

These multiple findings established a profile of the automobile Lee's intuition told him would please American buyers. This would be his first contribution to the Ford product line. Plan a car that is easy to handle, he ordered his team, a car styled with zip and class, lower and longer in front than other American makes, and shorter in the rear deck. Make it an automobile that performs with dash, that can go from zero to sixty in seven or eight seconds. And, very important, he emphasised, produce a car affordable for young America.

'Lee was very much personally involved in every phase of the car right from scratch,' Hal Sperlick said. 'He wanted to pave some fresh ground as the new vice-president of Ford Division. He wanted this car to hit a ready market and make the statement that Ford really was back in the mainstream of the automobile business.'

Iacocca was not looking for a small car *per se*, Sperlick made clear. 'There were some small cars out, like the Falcon and Monza,' he said. 'But Lee was looking for a distinctive kind of car. From cars already on the market you could buy only either a big car or a smaller, plain kind, and there wasn't a really nice smaller car available. If you wanted a nice car, you had to buy a Lincoln or Cadillac, but that was it.'

In late October of 1961 Iacocca approved the specifications for the car as recommended by Sperlick and his product-planning team. It should weigh no more than 2,500 pounds and be no more than fifteen feet (180 inches) in overall length. And its retail price should be $2,500 or less.

The next step was to create a clay model based on the specifications. Lee discussed the matter with Eugene Bordinat, Ford Motor Company's chief designer. Bordinat arranged a competition between the company's three design studios, the Ford Division, Lincoln-Mercury, and Corporate studios. Each would take the specifications and come up with one or more clay models reflecting their individual conceptions of how the car should look.

Within two weeks the studios had seven clay models ready for inspection by Iacocca and his team. The one designed by Joe Oros, Ford Division's head stylist, had the lines and smart styling Lee wanted. It was a different, unique breed of automobile that measured less than twenty-nine inches from the ground to the top of the hood and only 154 inches in overall length, twenty-six inches shorter than the original specifications called for.

Lee was pleased with Oros's design at first sight. His initial plan had been a two-seater, much like the original Thunderbird, but he had changed his mind, asking that a small back seat be added. His gut reaction as he examined the clay model of a convertible was that they were on the right track.

But what about Henry Ford II? How would he look on this project, which had been put together secretly? It would take many millions of dollars to tool up for and put into production such a car, and Henry's yes or no meant its life or death.

Protocol demanded that Iacocca approach Arjay Miller, the company president, before going to Ford, the board chairman. But Lee, impatient at any small delay, went directly to Henry's suite in the Glass House. Henry all but literally threw him out of the office. He had absolutely no interest.

Lee returned to Ford Division undismayed. He knew he was right, and however long it took, he would prove it. In a week he was back at the Glass House, trying to persuade Henry that the market was ready for this type of smaller car. An angry Henry again showed Lee the door, making it clear he was not interested in a small car.

A third and fourth trip found Henry gradually weakening, showing a bit of interest, but still opposed. But Lee, realising that he was developing a sort of inevitability for the success of his project, persisted. The fifth time at Henry's office he was able to outline details of the research he had conducted. Henry finall agreed to at least come and take a look.

At the Styling Center, surrounded by Iacocca, Sperlick, and other Ford Division men, Henry still shook his head. Neither Lee Iacocca nor Hal Sperlick could convince Henry, however aggressively they sold the concept of the new automobile or the need for it in the marketplace. Henry was nervous over the failure of the Edsel and the resulting cash drain on the company, yet he finally agreed to think it over.

Iacocca already had set himself a timetable that would be shattered if he had to wait for Henry's final decision. He took a chance and gave his team a go-ahead to proceed to the next phase, building an actual-size model from laminated hardwoods.

He had good reasons for his seeming impatience. As vital as secrecy is in the highly competitive automobile business, where every security precaution possible is taken, word of activity on anything new does leak out. Lee already knew that Chevrolet was considering a scaled-down version of the successful Corvette, and he was determined to beat them into the market.

Lee also realised that rumours were buzzing around Detroit about an unusual new two-seater sports-type car on the Ford drawing boards. He hoped that these fast-spreading but unconfirmed reports would not send Chevrolet into a crash programme that would upset his own schedule. He had to have a prototype ready the moment Henry approved funding for production – if, indeed, he gave the go-ahead.

Speculation about the new one from Ford escalated throughout the industry, and Lee had a plan to feed those rumours. Dependent on Henry II's decision, he intended to unveil a prototype of some kind during the annual running of the 1962 American Grand Prix at Watkins Glen, New York, on October 7.

Meanwhile Iacocca and his team busied themselves with deciding on a name for his creation. The name of a new car is vitally important to its marketability and sales success. In order to stir buyer enthusiasm it had to be catchy, memorable, and meaningful in terms of the car's image, a name that could be translated into advertising impact.

Merely for identification Iacocca's team referred to the new automobile as the Special Falcon. But nothing like the name Falcon was to be considered. Falcon was a Bob McNamara offering, and the all-new concept had to be perceived as an Iacocca production. Lee ordered the Ford Division advertising agency, J. Walter Thompson, to suggest names. The agency reported back with a list numbering more than 5,000. On the list were Colt, Bronco, Cheetah, Torino, Cougar, and Mustang.

Joe Oros had referred to his clay model as Cougar, and for a time that name was considered. Then a decision was made to call the car Torino, since it had a Ferrari flavour and Ferrari was built in Turin, a city the Italians call Torino. Torino was considered so seriously that J. Walker Thompson prepared potential advertisements using that name.

Despite all the pre-preparation the name Torino was suddenly dropped. One Ford executive said that the name had become an embarrassment since Henry Ford II was at the time pursuing Cristina all over Europe while his divorce was still pending. Iacocca, it was said, feared that the press would play the Italian connection to the hilt, making a mockery of the car's introduction.

Gar Laux, who was close to Lee throughout the car's development, is inclined to discount that story. 'Look at the car,' he said. 'Look at the first prototype, then the second, and finally the car that was introduced. It looked, that first little one at Watkins Glen, like an Italian import. But when the car went on the market, it was all-American. Its looks had changed, so the name had to change. It became the Yankeedoodle car, and a name like Torino didn't fit. Mustang did. Made you think of wild charging horses and the wide-open west. The name and the car, they were both as American as all hell!'

Getting the approval of Henry Ford II to build Mustang took time and some doing on Lee Iacocca's part. As structured under Henry Ford II the Ford Motor Company was heavily finance-oriented, in sharp contrast to the fiscal looseness of the company under his grandfather. As a result every major investment was a difficult sell. Henry was not about to commit millions of dollars to produce anything but a sure hit. Undismayed, Iacocca collared Henry at every opportunity, either alone or with Hal Sperlick's backing. Sperlick was as confident in, and as excited about, their planned car as was Lee. But Henry continued to hold out, demanding solid facts and figures to justify spending millions.

Yet, when Lee and Sperlick provided the facts and figures and peppered Henry with the results of their surveys, Henry remained opposed. Sure of his ground, Lee did not give up.

On September 10, 1962, Lee made another trip to the Glass House office of Henry Ford II. He again presented his case for a car that his gut feeling told him would bowl over the industry.

This time Henry, obviously weakening, agreed to take another look. He went with Lee to the Styling Center and examined the prototype from bumper to bumper. Finally he opened the passenger-side door and sat in the rear seat.

Henry, as the story goes, frowned for a moment. The back seat did not have enough room, he said. The car should provide an additional inch of space in the rear.

Iacocca, Sperlick, and the design team surrounding the car disagreed. Adding even that inch of space would destroy the styling, they all agreed. Henry would not listen. It had to be his way or there would be no new car.

Losing a small battle was better than total defeat. The designers and stylists added the extra space. Iacocca's persuasiveness had paid off at small cost. Henry approved an appropriation of $51 million for production of the new Mustang.

Iacocca and Sperlick were jubilant as they rushed back to Ford Division, but they had little time to savour their victory because a lot of work remained before the blue prototype could be shipped under wraps to Watkins Glen. After nearly a month's work around-the-clock, everything was ready.

The afternoon of October 7, 1962, 35,000 race buffs filled

the Watkins Glen grandstand as a hard rain swept across the oval. They were there primarily to see some of the world's greatest race drives compete in the American Grand Prix, but for hours curious eyes were focused on a platform in the infield where something was shrouded in canvas.

After Scotland's champion driver Jim Clark swept across the finish line as winner in his Lotus-Climax, the tarpaulin was removed. There it stood, now identified as Experimental Mustang I. In minutes thousands of spectators sloshed through mud and wet grass to get a close-up view of the little blue car with a Ferrari flair.

Standing no higher than a baby's crib, it had a long, sloping front end that ended hardly a foot from the platform floor. It had no headlights. It was equipped with a V-4 engine installed, not under the hood like most American cars, not at the rear like a Volkswagen Beetle or Corvair, but in the middle like many classic European cars.

It had been planned as a smoke screen, a showcase car displayed to throw all competition off base, one with just enough of the future Mustang to whet the appetite – if indeed American car buyers reacted with pleasure. It was there to give Iacocca the assurance that he was on the right track.

At the unveiling Lee knew he was. The enthusiasm of the thousands crowding around the platform oblivious of the torrential rain gave him his answer. The hundreds in the crowd trying to place orders immediately buttressed his confidence.

Of course it was impossible to take orders, however loudly the crowd clamoured. The real Mustang would not be ready for sale for almost two years.

After his return to Dearborn Iacocca realised that a way would have to be found to maintain and nourish the astounding interest generated at Watkins Glen in a car not yet ready for final production. A means had to be found for placating the media, which was bombarding him, Walter Murphy, and his Ford public relations staff with questions.

Iacocca could not afford to dampen this mounting Mustang momentum. Since he was not ready to release details about his final product, he decided on preparing another red herring to keep curiosity boiling. He ordered the building of a second Mustang prototype.

The front and back ends of Experimental Mustang I were chopped and pointed fenders added to give the new showpiece a different look. Since Mustang I, with its aerodynamic front end, had no headlights, recessed headlamps with glass covers were installed. Experimental Mustang II was also given an open-mouthed grille in which was centred the soon-to-become-ubiquitous galloping pony emblem.

Iacocca was playing a cloak-and-dagger game to give himself time to produce the real Mustang while throwing competition off. So he created Experimental Mustang II as another hybrid, part real Mustang and part fantasy, though less a phantom of the mind than the first.

No secret was made of the plan to reveal the new prototype. It was sent off with panoply and fanfare to the 1963 Watkins Glen American Grand Prix. Unlike 1962, this showing was not intended as a sneak preview. Newspapers, television, and radio reported the upcoming event. Journalists speculated as much about the car as about the race itself. Not surprisingly, attendance at Watkins Glen was far greater than in 1962.

Iacocca had hoped for a large crowd, for the reaction of the thousands at Watkins Glen would reassure him that his new car had what would be needed to crowd Ford showrooms once the real Mustang was introduced.

Iacocca need not have worried. A hungry, eager crowd swarmed excitedly about the platform displaying his four-wheeled offspring. Not only young people, but men and women of middle age and older, shouted at anyone who appeared to be a Ford representative demanding, as hundreds had done the year before, to place orders.

The usually impassive Iacocca could not suppress a smile. If only Henry Ford II, who had fought production of Mustang for so long, were there to see.

Back at the Ford Division offices Iacocca, Sperlick, Laux, and others on his Mustang team sat around a conference table relishing their victory. They had many things to discuss, including the refinements that would transform Experimental Mustang II into the real thing. Just as important was the matter of Mustang's introduction.

New car models were at the time normally introduced in the fall, which would mean a year's wait. Iacocca was not about to have Mustang's debut diluted by other car intros. He put production on an all-out basis. 'Make Mustang happen,' he told his staff. 'And make it quick.'

Lee Iacocca had involved himself in all levels leading to the creation of the Mustang, a rarity in the industry. Now his primary efforts could be directed toward promotion and marketing, at which he was a master. The two exposures at Watkins Glen were just the forerunners of a promotion blitz unequalled in any area of the business world.

Lee did not permit any letdown after the smash success at Watkins Glen. Within weeks he had his staff invite fifty young, middle-income couples to the Ford Styling Center as a means of confirming consumer reactions to Mustang. They came in small groups, they looked and admired. Almost to a couple their only negative reaction was to what they believed such a fine car would cost. Their estimates ranged from $4,000-$7,000, hardly practical for middle-incomes of the time.

When they heard that the base price was somewhat under $2,500, they expressed amazement and disbelief. At such a price, all agreed, Mustang was a car that they would like to own. This simple master stroke sent 100 voices out of the Ford Styling Center to spread the word of Mustang through fifty American cities.

To further bridge the gap before Mustang's official introduction, Iacocca brought 200 of the nation's most listened-to radio disc jockeys to the Ford test track opposite Ford Division. Each test-drove a Mustang, and each was promised the use of a Mustang for a week after his return home. All any d.j. needed to do was contact the local Ford dealer and pick up the car.

At the turn of the year, Iacocca brought in Frank Zimmerman, who had joined Ford as a trainee just before Lee himself, to work with him as general marketing manager. As Mustang Day neared, promotions were stepped up.

Mustangs were displayed at 200 Holiday Inns and in major airport terminals, shopping centres, and business lobbies.

On Monday April 13, 1964, Mustang Introduction Day, a press preview preceded the public showing in the Ford Pavilion at the New York World's Fair. Newspaper, radio, and television representatives from the United States and Canada heard briefings on Mustang and then participated in a road rally that took them from the pavilion to Ford headquarters in Dearborn, Michigan.

A reporter at the Ford Pavilion asked Lee Iacocca how many Mustangs he expected to sell in its first year.

'How many Falcons were sold?' Lee asked.

The automotive journalist rattled off the Falcon sales record, as yet unequalled in the industry. He told Lee, '417,174.'

'Mustang will go 417,175,' Lee said. (Actual sales figures for Mustang's first year were 417,800!)

Mustang mania took hold of America when the car was officially introduced to the public on April 17 at the New York World's Fair. Visitors packed into the Ford Pavilion in near hysteria. That same evening a Mustang served as pace car for a race in Huntsville, Alabama. More than 7,500 enthusiasts leapt over the retaining wall to form a phalanx around the Mustang, holding it in place and delaying the race for over an hour.

Car buffs swarmed into Ford dealerships from coast to coast in such numbers that business was halted. A Ford dealer in Pittsburgh was unable to get a Mustang off a wash rack because of people crowding around the car. In Chicago a dealer was forced to lock his doors, the crush of Mustang lookers was so great.

Henry Ford II was on hand at the Ford Pavilion, but Lee Iacocca was the man in demand. His picture made the cover of the April 17 issue of *Time*, and the cover feature of *Newsweek* was the Iacocca story. He had produced a spectacular car with a name that would soon be familiar in Rio, Rome, and Rangoon as well as Racine.

Mustang was quickly perceived as the all-American, all-purpose automobile. It could be seen at country clubs, outside famous restaurants and churches, as well as at drag strips and on boulevards. It was the right car at the right time, a sizzler with four-on-the-floor that appealed to a full spectrum of drivers from eighteen to eighty.

Such terms as 'Mustang mystique,' 'Mustang mania,' and 'Mustang generation' became everyday expressions, the latter first used by a California real estate developer named Howard Ruby. In brochures advertising apartments for young singles he offered 'A country club atmosphere catering to the champagne tastes of the Mustang generation.'

Mustanging became a way of life in America and throughout the world, and erased the dull and the humdrum replacing them with glamour and excitement. It was a Cinderella slipper on wheels, magically converting reserved Walter Mitty types into debonair men-about-town, as pictured in one of the early television commercials approved by Iacocca.

In the one-minute commercial Henry Foster, staid and prim in rimless pince-nez spectacles, derby hat, and dark suit, was seen leaving his shop. He was carrying something in a brown paper bag. He turned the sign that read 'open' to 'out to lunch' and securely locked the door. In the background was a wispy old lady who operated a nearby shop. 'Have you heard about Henry Foster?' she asked.

Henry then walked stiffly until he turned the corner. There, in sight of his new red Mustang he became a different man. Off went his pince-nez glasses, his derby hat, his dark suitcoat. On went a bright plaid hat, red vest, and dark goggles, all taken from the brown paper bag. As he got behind the wheel of the Mustang, the old lady's voice was heard saying: 'Something's happened to Henry.'

The screen then showed Henry braking his Mustang in a park area as a soft, seductive voice said, 'A Mustang's happened to Henry.' On a grassy plot in the park a sexy young woman waited with a picnic basket and bottle of wine. Henry leapt from his Mustang to join the young lady, now totally uninhibited, happy and laughing.

'Mustang made it happen' became the battle cry of the 'in' people of the mid-sixties, whatever their age. Lee Iacocca's desk at Ford Division was flooded with letters from young and old telling how much Mustang was loved. One forty-four-year-old bachelor from Texas wrote that he had a 'pony V-8 in Rangoon Red with accent paint stripes, moulding, and air conditioning, and man, this is the greatest. A widow with seven thousand acres came sixty miles so I could take her riding in it.'

It was a Mustang world from its first day in the showroom, and Lee Iacocca took every advantage to keep the magic full force. The day Mustang was born he agreed to co-operate with the newly formed National Council of Mustang Clubs headquartered in the shadows of Ford Division. It was an extension of the firmly rooted car club traditions in Europe.

The National Council of Mustang Clubs brought the hundreds of such clubs throughout the United States under one umbrella, sponsoring activities that ran the gamut of motorsport action. Its big day through the following years was April 17, a nation-wide celebration of Mustang's birthday.

On that day rallies were held by the hundreds of clubs associated with the National Council. From the final results of each year's rallies a national winner was determined and presented with a new Mustang. All the proceeds generated by rallies supervised by the National Council on that day were donated by the individual clubs to local charities.

Club activities took place year-round. On any weekend one might find a beach gathering in Florida or California. There would be local slaloms, gymkhanas, and hill climbs almost anywhere. The National Council even developed a 'Braille rally' for youngsters at schools for the blind. Club members would bring their Mustangs and each select a blind boy or girl to serve as navigator using instructions prepared in braille.

Iacocca also created the Society of Mustangers, a no-constitution and no-by-laws groups of Mustang owners brought together about the time the millionth Mustang came off the assembly line. It was established only after Mustang owners in Chicago, Philadelphia, and Los Angeles were mailed a brochure explaining the plan and asking their reaction.

The only obligation, as stated in the brochure, was a two

108

dollar annual fee, for which members would receive quarterly issues of *The Mustanger*, a magazine that would serve as the official voice of the society, as well as a membership card and a decal for their car. Other incentives were discounted tour and travel rates; hotel, motel, restaurant, and nightclub discounts; specially arranged Mustanger pleasure trips; and quality merchandise items at about half the normal retail cost, all explained and displayed in *The Mustanger*.

The recipients of the brochures were asked only to mail in a 'no' or 'yes' indication of their interest in this type of organisation. So strong was the magnetism of Mustang that not only were 'yes' votes unexpectedly large, 16 percent of those answering also included two dollars, even though the society had not yet been established. One month later an actual solicitation mailing was made, and over 35,000 Mustang owners became members of the Society of Mustangers.

One of the surprising facts discovered in the creation of the society was that as many as 8 percent of members were between fifty-five and sixty-five years of age, and 2 percent were over sixty-five. As was expected, 67 percent were under forty-five. Not expected were such revealing figures as those that showed 51 percent had annual incomes of $10,000 or over, and 36 percent were professional or managerial types. The college educated accounted for 58 percent.

Lee Iacocca had stunned the automobile industry with his Mustang, the car that made its debut at a time when America was ready for an automobile with a change of pace in styling and performance. General Motors, Chrysler, and American Motors were not about to stand by stoically watching Mustang sales spiral steadily upward without doing something.

Chevrolet had a similar car on its drawing boards when Mustang exploded on the market, but it did not make its bow for two years. Mustang sales had soared past a half-million before Chevy brought out its Camaro, another jazzy, sleek machine that symbolised youthfulness.

To a degree the 1967 Camaro was a Mustang copy. It fitted the long-hood, short-deck design and came on the scene gunning for Mustang's record. While 100,000 Camaros did hit the road within seven months, Chevy's entry was unable to outsell Mustang in any one sales period for almost three years.

General Motors tossed another competitor into the ring with its Pontiac Firebird. Chrysler entered the sports car field about the same time with refined versions of the Plymouth Barracuda and Dodge Charger, neither of which was a completely new car. A year after Camaro American Motors produced two 'muscle' cars, as Mustang types were being called, the Javelin and the AMX. None came near matching Camaro, and Camaro was hard put to come close to Mustang in popularity.

The phenomenon that was Mustang, especially with spirited, powerful engines offered as options, could not be restricted to the street scene. Inevitably it progressed from street to drag strip and from drag strip to racing oval.

'Race 'em on Sunday, and sell 'em on Monday,' was Lee Iacocca's philosophy. Mustangs raced and sold.

On drag strips, where it takes brute horsepower to eat up 1,320 feet of hot asphalt in the shortest time, Mustangs were fierce competitors, thanks to Iacocca's support and a supercharged 427-cubic-inch single overhead cam engine. Mustangs won class championships in the spring nationals of the National Hot Rod Association. In the American Hot Rod Association winter championship races a Mustang equipped with a 429-cubic-inch Cobra jet engine achieved an estimated 114 miles per hour, turning in an elapsed time of 12.5 seconds for the 1,320-foot dash.

From drag strip to road racing is a natural progression, and there, too, Mustang could not be denied. The Sports Car Club of America opened the door when it established the Trans-American sedan series. In a '24-hours at Daytona' race Mustang blew its Trans-Am competitors, including Camaro, figuratively into the Atlantic as it finished first in class, and fourth overall, behind three Porsche 907 coupes.

Ford Motor Company's re-entry into the racing scene actually had taken place early in the summer of '64, two months after Mustang's introduction. Henry Ford II, anxious to upstage Enzo Ferrari after the Italian carmaker's

Walter P. Chrysler, founder of Chrysler Corporation (*National Automotive History Collection Photo, Detroit Public Library*)

Lee Iacocca, the new president of the Ford Motor Company in 1970 (*National Automotive History Collection Photo, Detroit Public Library*)

Lee Iacocca on his arrival at Ford headquarters in 1956 (*National Automotive History Collection Photo, Detroit Public Library*)

Lee Iacocca (*right*) with Bill Winn during the Cougar introduction in the Caribbean (*Photo courtesy of Bill Winn*)

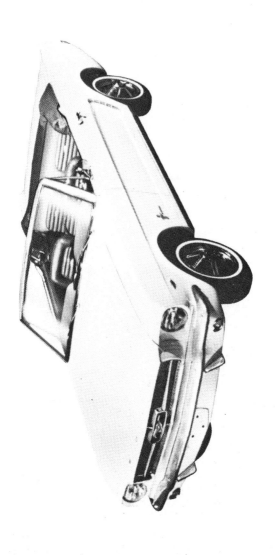

The real first Mustang as introduced at the New York World's Fair in April, 1964 (*National Automotive History Collection Photo, Detroit Public Library*)

Lee Iacocca with wife Mary and daughter Lia in the living room of their Bloomfield Hills home (*Photo by John Collier*, Detroit Free Press)

Lee at home in Lido's Lounge, as wife Mary and daughter Lia watch a news report showing a televised Iacocca appearance before a congressional committee (*Photo by John Collier*, Detroit Free Press)

Henry Ford II as he took over the Ford Motor Company after discharge from the Navy in 1946 (*National Automotive History Collection Photo, Detroit Public Library*)

The first Henry Ford in his original Model A (*National Automotive History Collection Photo, Detroit Public Library*)

Lee Iacocca, Frank Sinatra, and Leo-Arthur Kelmenson during discussion of Sinatra's TV appearances for Chrysler Imperial (*Photo courtesy of Kenyon & Eckhardt Public Relations*)

Iacocca and the first K-car off the assembly line (*Photo by John Collier*, Detroit Free Press)

Iacocca answering questions at a news conference (*Photo by John Collier*, Detroit Free Press)

A moment at home with younger daughter, Lia (*Photo by John Collier*, Detroit Free Press)

Left to right: Bill Winn, Lee Iacocca, Frank Zimmerman, and Larry Domegal (Ford's fleet and lease manager) at a cocktail reception following a Mustang introduction *(Photo courtesy of Bill Winn)*

initial refusal to sell the Ferrari plant to Ford, had pressured Iacocca's Ford Division team to produce a car for the 1964 LeMans twenty-four hour race.

Iacocca's engineers produced three cars dubbed the Ford GT40 for the confrontation with Ferrari. The first Ford-built, Ford-sponsored cars ever to race on an international circuit, they were equipped with 4.2-litre (256-cubic-inch) V-8 engines. Their GT40 designation deceived few at the famous French race. Most saw them as experimental Mustangs with special bodies.

Also included among the fifty-five starters in the competition were two cars with 427-cubic-inch Ford Cobra Jet engines. Neither was an official Ford Motor Company entry. Enzo Ferrari's entries included two new V-12 Ferraris with 3.3- and 4-litre displacement. Triumphs, Porsches, Alfa Romeos, and Jaguars were among the other racers ready for the twenty-four-hour run.

As far as the press and the public were concerned, the focus of the race was on the Ferrari-Ford confrontation. Henry Ford II, in typical fashion, pulled no punches. He was out to humiliate Ferrari, and he was confident it could be done. In substance the race had developed into a struggle between American cars and the European.

For the first hour after the fall of the starter's flag – and despite two of the Ford GT40s being boxed in by other cars – the third GT40, driven by Richie Ginther and Gaston Gregory (both Americans), held the lead over a Ferrari 330P, handled by Lorenzo Bandini of Italy and England's John Surtees. Before it was over, however, all three GT40s had broken down, and Ferrari ran away with the honours.

It was a bitter defeat for Henry Ford II, tempered little by the fact that one of the unsponsored Cobra Jets had won first place in the GT category. Henry vowed to be back next year.

The defeat at LeMans in no way tarnished 1964 as Lee Iacocca's year of glory. Before year's end the Mustang was acclaimed an international success, visible almost everywhere in the free world. And everywhere the Ford Motor Company was perceived in connection with Lee Iacocca as much as Henry Ford. Iacocca was lauded as Mr Mustang.

Everyone close to Lee Iacocca knows, however, that the birth of the Mustang was not his most treasured memory of 1964. On July 16 Mary Iacocca had presented him with his second daughter. She was named Lia, after her now famous father.

CHAPTER 7

For Lee Iacocca the birth of his second daughter had a bittersweet tinge. Tiny Lia, with reddish hair and pretty features much like her mother's, seemed likely to be their last child, an unhappy prospect for a man so family-oriented. But Lee was worried about his wife. Mary Iacocca had been a diabetic for some time, and recently her condition had worsened.

Lee's devotion to his wife of more than two and one-half decades was in the classic, biblical mode, a total commitment that places her welfare above his own. For him she was a friend, companion, and confidante. And he was her balm during hours of pain, anxious when he must leave town without her, and making contingent plans before he did leave. Friends like Bill Winn and Gar Laux were always ready if an emergency arose. Both tell of rushing her to a hospital in a diabetic coma when Lee had been away.

Time and again Lee had left important meetings abruptly after getting word that Mary had been stricken. At a most critical moment during the Chrysler Corporation loan-guarantee hearings in January, 1979, he left Washington the moment his secretary notified him that Mary had suffered a heart attack, rushing to the hospital in Boca Raton, Florida, the site of their winter home, where Mary sought relief from the bitter Michigan cold.

Lee also accompanied his wife on all her visits for tests or treatment at Boston's Joslin Clinic for Diabetes Research.

He was dedicated no only to helping her get well, but also to helping solve the problem of diabetes. For some time he contributed a significant part of his salary to the Joslin Clinic. He also served on the board of directors of the President's Advisory Council of the American Diabetes Association.

'Some of the men he works with call him the Iron Chancellor or the Ayatollah at the office,' Mary said with a laugh, 'but around the house he's a lamb. He calls Kathy "Olive Oyl" and Lia "Sweet Pea." They call him "Wimpy."'

Iacocca is proud of his role as a dedicated father. Though his two daughters, Kathy and Lia, seem to have the world on a string, both know the value of money and like to do things on their own. The spirit of independence and the emotional drive to be a doer, inherited by Lee from his father, is also apparent in the two girls.

When twenty-one-year-old Kathy went to work at Chrysler as part of a college course, she insisted it be without pay. She was not only concerned over her father's being accused of nepotism but felt it wrong when Chrysler workers made sacrifices to keep the company going. Yet, when her six-week course took her into sales and she joined the sales staff of a Chrysler dealership away from the Detroit area, she accepted commissions for cars she sold.

'She moved four cars in one week's time,' the dealer reported. 'More than my best salesman, so she earned it.'

Just before turning seventeen Lee's younger daughter, Lia, also wanted to earn her own money during summer vacation. To go to work at Chrysler in a depressed economy and with people out of work was unthinkable. She did ask her father to help her get work at Kenyon & Eckhardt, Chrysler's ad agency. Lee said no, that would not be proper, at the same time wondering if she understood his refusal to help.

Lia did understand. On her own she found and took a summer job with an art studio as an apprentice and messenger.

Understandably, since Lee is so much a reflection of his father, his family is close-knit. On Sundays when Mary's health permitted, all four may have been seen together at St. Hugo of the Hills Catholic Church for mass. Holidays, birthdays, anniversaries, any special occasion within the family, were spent together as a foursome.

Lee allowed no circumstance, however urgent, to interfere with a promise to Mary or the children. On one occasion while he was president of Ford a mixup in the scheduled date of a high-level meeting with Henry Ford conflicted with an afternoon off on which he had promised to take the children on an outing.

As he prepared to leave his office for the day, his secretary told Lee that he was expected at the meeting.

'I'm not going to the meeting,' he told her.

The secretary reminded him of its importance. 'Mr Ford said . . .' she insisted.

Lee cut her off. 'I don't really give a damn,' he said. 'I promised my daughters I was taking them out, and I'm going to take them. This damn place could burn down before I'd break my promise.'

With Lee Iacocca his family comes before everything else. 'He is very protective of us,' Mary Iacocca said. 'Maybe too much so. He telephoned every day, maybe three or four times. And it doesn't matter where he is, at a dealer meeting in California or over in Europe. He was also that way with Kathy when she was at college in California. And his mother, too. At least once a week he phoned Antoinette to see how she was.'

Iacocca has always had an abiding preference for his home fireside. On normal days he makes every effort to leave his office as soon after six as possible. And, unlike many of his contemporaries, he never stops at some watering place on the way home. Eager to get there, he immediately headed his car north on the Southfield Freeway, heading for the comfortable, quietly elegant nineteen-room home in Bloomfield Hills.

There was peace and serenity in the very location of the house, sitting back from the road and framed by tall and stately trees. Its large sunken living room with huge picture windows overlooking the green of a Michigan spring or summer, the multicoloured leaves of fall, or the white snows of winter, was not furnished for show but for easy conversation among friends and family.

Iacocca's home life was easy, happy, and uncomplicated,

except for his continuing concern over Mary's health. There was no formality even when Mary and he entertained, no fancy feasts. Most dinners, even when such close friends as the Bill Winns and there, have a family flavour reminiscent of those in the Allentown row house when Lee was a young man.

When Lee arrived home, he was most likely pulling off his tie as he walked in the door. Relaxing before dinner he may have had a bit of cheese, a glass of wine, and perhaps a few moments alone. More often than not he would sip as he helped in the kitchen, for at the Iacoccas' getting dinner was a family affair.

Naturally, pasta was a frequent fare. Lee and Mary would jointly get it ready, as Lia – when Kathy was away at school – made the salad and set the table. Noodles for the spaghetti were Mary's own home-made. The sauce varied from time to time, but Lee's preference was one without tomatoes, with the noodles simmered in broth and topped with a creamy sauce over which grated cheese and crumbled bacon was generously sprinkled.

After dinner it may have been just casual conversation in the living room, a game of gin with Mary, or – as Lee so much enjoys – an hour or two alone in his den, which was located on a lower level. Iacocca called this fully equipped haven Lido's Lounge. It was filled with mementoes of his life, pictures of his family and friends, a game table, and a soundproof booth holding a sixteen-millimetre projector for Saturday-night showing of carefully chosen motion pictures. There, too, was Lee's special pride, an excellent stereo system.

Lido's Lounge was Iacocca's 'think tank' hideaway. One of his greatest pleasures was to lie back in a comfortable chair and listen to tapes of the music he loves best, the big-band sound of the forties era, Tommy Dorsey, Les Brown, Paul Whiteman.

'Lee has always been a jazz buff,' says Bill Winn, who shared an apartment with Lee in his earliest Ford days. After Lee completed his training period and began work at Ford's Philadelphia District office, Winn visited Iacocca. 'We went to New York for a weekend,' he says. 'Lee really wanted to see the *Andrea Doria*, which was then making its maiden voyage. After all, it's an Italian ship and was docking at New York and allowing visitors aboard.'

Winn and Iacocca did board the *Andrea Doria* and were impressed, but the most memorable event of the weekend was their stop at a small club where the great Dizzy Gillespie was featured. 'Once Lee knew Gillespie was there, we had to go,' Winn says.

They arrived at the club so early that no one was there but Gillespie himself, sitting on the bandstand with his horn. The sweet Gillespie tones mesmerised Iacocca, according to Winn, but only until Dizzy began eating a sandwich while he played.

'We sat there, I don't know how long, just waiting for part of the sandwich to come blowing out of that horn,' Winn laughs. 'It's something Lee has never forgotten. And Dizzy Gillespie has been a favourite ever since.'

Their beautiful home notwithstanding, the Iacoccas did little socialising. A dinner out now and then when Mary felt well enough, and a gathering of their closest friends once in a while. When not in Washington fighting government regulation, or away on other business inside or outside the country, Lee's evenings were spent quietly at home.

Except Friday. That was Lee's night, reserved for a friendly game of poker either in Lido's Lounge or at the home of one of the other men with whom he played. Even during the most amicable game Lee's shrewdness was evident.

'You can never get by with a bluff with him,' says Gar Laux. 'That computer mind of his has your hand pegged from your first raise. But he's really a softie, a good human being under that hard-nosed exterior. It's not in his nature to hurt a person's feelings.'

Laux himself was a volunteer aide in helping solve a problem caused by Lee's inability to harm someone who had served him well. For some weeks Laux had seen that Lee's secretary, an older woman who had been at the job for years, had become too slow to keep up with Iacocca's fast-charging dictation. He finally suggested that it wasn't fair to keep the woman in a job for which she was no longer suited, that it would be best to let the secretary go.

'I just can't do it,' Lee told Laux. 'I haven't got the heart to hurt her.'

'You know, you're not being mean to the woman,' Laux pointed out. 'She's a nice lady, but she's having a hard time. If you can't do it, would you like me to handle it?'

Lee nodded. 'But be sure she's transferred to a job that pays at least the same,' he said. 'Something she can hold until her retirement.'

Men like Gar Laux, Bill Winn, Hal Sperlick, and Leo-Arthur Kelmenson, who have known Iacocca and worked closely with him for thirty-five years or more, describe him as the most loyal and protective of his friends of anyone they have ever known. Each always is careful to point out that he shouldn't be looked on as a saint, a man without blemish who never makes a wrong judgment.

'Sure he does things wrong,' Gar Laux is quick to say. 'We all do. The only guy who didn't died on a cross, and the world has seen only one of those. But hell, he's right so damn much more than he's wrong.' Rough and gruff himself, Laux holds nothing back. 'He's the roughest s.o.b. I've ever worked for,' he adds. 'In a second he can make you feel like shinola if you've goofed somewhere. A minute later he's asking you how's the wife! Or reminding you about Friday night's poker game.'

On the job Lee Iacocca is tough and uncompromising. He expects much and demands much of the men who work with and for him. What his people learn from him is to keep reaching, never to stop reaching. He is never satisfied with a man just doing his job, even if he does it well. A man must reach beyond the limits of his immediate work.

He preaches two philosophies. One is that he doesn't pay any man on his team merely for what he does. More important is what the man gets others to accomplish. Anyone working for Lee at a supervisory level has to give management of subordinates his highest priority. In a business as complex as the automobile industry no department can be a one-man operation and run smoothly. And that leads to Iacocca's second doctrine, the need for management development.

118

Lee is adamant that his department heads not only manage their people but they also develop personnel who can climb up the corporate ladder, individuals who at the very least can replace their immediate supervisors.

Each of his department heads is required to turn in quarterly evaluation forms of the people they manage. If he receives a form indicating that a worker in the department has remained too long in one capacity, Lee's reaction is that the department head has not done his job in bringing the subordinate along.

'That's one of the keys to Iacocca's success,' Gar Laux says. 'Even if a man is an expert in one phase of the business, he wants him to progress to another and become equally expert. Everybody working for him has to move forward, expect to be the head honcho someday.'

Iacocca also instituted a requirement that department heads submit quarterly plans indicating what they intend to accomplish in the following three-month period. At the end of each quarter he expects an evaluation by each individual of his own work. He is more likely to accept total failure if the man evaluates his accomplishment as zero and can explain the reasons, than if one says 50 percent and has managed only 40 to 45 percent. He is that tough a taskmaster. He wants honesty at all times and from everybody, whether employees or suppliers.

Leo-Arthur Kelmenson discovered this Iacocca characteristic the first time they met. Kelmenson had just joined Kenyon & Eckhardt and arrived at Lee's office to introduce himself and assure Iacocca that he would carry on the advertising agency's work on behalf of Ford with the same high level of quality as his predecessor. After an hour of give and take Kelmenson said goodbye and started for the door.

'Kelmenson!' Iacocca called as Kelmenson reached the door. Kelmenson turned and waited. 'One thing,' Iacocca added. 'Don't ever bullshit me.'

Kelmenson, a positive-thinker and doer in his own right, answered: 'Okay, that's a deal. But you don't bullshit me either.'

Based on a more-than-twenty-year working association

through good times and bad, one that brought about a close-knit family-to-family relationship, Kelmenson draws a graphic picture of Lee Iacocca. He sees him as a farsighted, hardheaded, often abrasive executive, and a bit of an egomaniac.

Iacocca's biggest problem, in Kelmenson's view, is people who don't really do their work as they should and do only what they think he wants. He is a man who abhors sycophants, who wants his people to fight with him and take a position, to be strong and smart and prove they are right in their stand.

'He's enigmatic, he's wild, he's a hip-shooter, a dreamer,' Kelmenson says, 'but in spite of all those things he's pragmatic as hell. If he has fifty, a hundred, or a thousand ideas, he knows they're not all good. He knows some are disastrous. But he expects people around him to tell him. But there are far more brilliant strokes of genius that come out of those ideas than from any other man I have ever met.'

Iacocca has indeed proved his brilliance again and again. The broadness of his capacity to store information is awesome, as is his ability to use it in daily conversations, speeches, and meetings. He has made himself one of the easiest to listen to, most persuasive public speakers in the industry.

Almost to a man those who have worked with him at Ford, and who now make up his team at Chrysler, say he is an easy leader to follow, an inspiration to do their jobs. He never asks a man to do anything he can't or won't do himself. They also emphasise his phenomenal memory. Make a slip, and at one time or another he'll drag it out of his brain and slap you with it. But they insist, he does it always in a man-to-man confrontation. He never embarrasses a person in public.

Hal Sperlick, who has worked directly with Iacocca longer than any other single individual – he was at Iacocca's side as product planner throughout the development of Mustang – makes an interesting observation about Lee. 'There is a piece of him that is General Patton when he's at work,' Sperlick says. 'Cocky and a great leader, he's the kind of man men follow through hell and high water.'

Sperlick also describes Iacocca as a blend of many other personalities, an unusual character aside from his enormous business strength. There's a piece of him that's kind and very, very gentle, a gentleness not only with his family, where he is extraordinary, but with the men he works with.

You see both sides of his character in business, Sperlick elaborates, the very concerned, gentle man and the tough, hard-riding general. And it's a truly interesting kind of man who can be both at the same time. Cars are Iacocca's life. He's a car man through and through. 'He awakens in the morning with the car business, and he falls asleep at night in the car business.' Sperlick further thinks that what creates a man of such diverse natures would take a mind-boggling depth of psychology to fathom.

Jay Dugan has a somewhat different assessment of the Iacocca character. Other than Bill Winn, Dugan has known Lee Iacocca longer (and knew him earlier in his career) than any of Lee's other contemporaries. Dugan calls Iacocca's 'genius a simple genius,' the ability to design cars and marketing campaigns that are ahead of his time.

'He is always thinking way ahead of anybody,' Dugan says. 'It's not as if he gets messages carried by angels. His ideas are simple damn things, but they're so simple they're good, and you wonder why you didn't think of them yourself.'

On the more personal side Dugan says that he has never met anyone who has had personal contact with Iacocca, worked for him or with him or was a social friend, who had anything but admiration for the man. 'That's rather unique in today's business,' Dugan says, 'because you've got to be pretty iron-butt, bash in a lot of heads and kick a lot of asses. With it all Lee still has the capacity to engender respect and admiration.'

There are those, however, who do not share the near hero worship Jay Dugan, Hal Sperlick, and Gar Laux feel for Iacocca. A good number – and former colleagues at Ford, most of whom came along for the Chrysler ride – disagreed in their evaluations of Iacocca as a man and as a boss, although all attested to his phenomenal ability.

One former vice-president of Ford said, 'Unless you were one of Iacocca's inner circle, you always got the short end of the stick. As an executive I expected being called down for serious mistakes, but for even the smallest, often insignificant error, there was a viciousness in his eating out that was humiliating and abusive. You had to take it without a word of rebuttal or you'd find yourself knocked down a few notches.'

'Lee was never what you'd call a jolly, warm kind of guy,' another said. 'But he was on the friendly side when he first came to Ford Division. The minute he was named vice-president of the company in charge of the division, an icky kind of ego seemed to mushroom overnight. He'd walk by you with that big cigar as if you didn't exist. One thing I'll say for Henry. He always had a nod or a smile.'

Two other interviewees said they felt demeaned when Iacocca kept them cooling their heels in an outer office after calling them in. 'Maybe he was busy,' said one of the two, 'but it happened too often. After all I had work to do, too.'

One former high-level Ford executive who was put through this 'wait' routine turned the tables on Iacocca in early 1982. Ben Bidwell, who had headed both Ford car divisions at one time or another and rose to vice-president in charge of Ford's North American car and truck operations, gave Iacocca a dose of his own medicine.

Bidwell left the Ford Motor Company in 1981 and took over the presidency of the Hertz Corporation. In January, 1982, Iacocca paid a visit to Bidwell's Madison Avenue office in New York. He was there to convince his old employee to add more Ford-built cars to the Hertz inventory. Iacocca was kept waiting for some twenty minutes in an anteroom of the Hertz headquarters before Bidwell signalled his secretary to usher in his former boss.

Bidwell, a pleasant, pixieish man with a well-known sense of humour, looked up with a smile, as the story goes, and said: 'Sorry, Lee. It was the devil made me do it!'

Two others were sharply critical of Iacocca's role in the Pinto rear-end collision crisis. 'It was hell around the Glass House in early 1978 when the Pinto problem hit high C,' said one. 'Pinto sales pooped out like a deflated balloon, and

Pinto was really Lee's baby. He got all the kudos when Pinto hit the market, but he never acknowledged any blame for the big trouble we had.'

'The Pinto problem would not have happened,' the second of the two pointed out, 'if the company hadn't tried to save seven or eight dollars a car. Iacocca was the boss, so it was his responsibility. The money it cost Ford could have paid the bill to make two million Pinto gas tanks safe in a rear-end collision. We saved the money and lost the war.'

However one views Lee Iacocca, the fact remains that because of Mustang he burst on the world scene as an automotive sage, a rare species in the manner of a Karl Benz or Enzo Ferrari, a farsighted innovator ahead of his times. The often incompatible images of Iacocca drawn by his contemporaries paint him as a hard-driving, often cruel, sometimes sadistic entrepreneur or as a demanding taskmaster fair in his treatment of subordinates, a loyal friend, a warm and loving husband and father.

Too tough though he may be, and sometimes impatient and uncomfortable with those he deems unimportant, the fact remains that, on the job at least, he is in a class by himself. He handles his team like a sharp quarterback, running his offence with imagination and courage.

Unlike his counterparts at other automobile companies Iacocca is publicly perceived as a lively, spirited man and a battler. He maintains a visibility the others lack and has made himself a national – even international – personality. When it is to his advantage, and when the spirit moves him, he can be a humorous, warm, and winning individual, 'a guy who can charm the hide off a bull elephant,' as one Ford vice-president expressed it, a man at ease with the likes of high-powered types like Gay Talese, Frank Sinatra, and George Steinbrenner.

Incompatible as the varied images of him drawn by his contemporaries may be, he is a loyal friend, an affectionate and dedicated husband and father. For him, his family remains his first priority.

To understand Iacocca the man one must begin with the shy youth, the teenager in a sickbed doing his homework so

123

as not to lose time from his classes. One must then place him in proper perspective as the son of a strong, imperious, often arrogant, loving, overprotective father, as a son who idolised that father and absorbed much of his drive, ambition, and determination.

CHAPTER 8

The year 1965 began on a high note for both the Ford Motor Company and Lee Iacocca. Figures released on January 2 revealed that the company had set a record in worldwide sales – 3,952,727 automobiles, trucks, and tractors. Of the more than 2.5 million units sold within the United States, Lee Iacocca's Ford Division had accounted for about three-fourths, an undeniable affirmation of the Iacocca marketing magic.

This achievement deserved recognition and promotion, and Iacocca received both. On January 15, Henry Ford II appointed Lee vice-president of the corporate car and truck group. This step up the corporate ladder also meant a move to world headquarters, an office in the Glass House.

In this new position Iacocca's responsibilities were broadened extensively. He now had overall supervision of planning, production, and marketing of all vehicles offered by the Lincoln-Mercury and Ford divisions. He also would control the advertising and promotion activities of Kenyon & Eckhardt, the advertising agency for Lincoln-Mercury, as well as those of J. Walter Thompson, the agency for Ford Division products.

The promotion brought Lee Iacocca within a step or two of the company presidency. This high on the ladder of succession he certainly would be more vulnerable than ever to demoralising snipings of fearful or jealous executives. He was aware that in just such a way the dismissal of a good and capable man had been engineered during his second year at Ford Division.

James J. Nance, who had been president of the Packard Motor Car Company, had been persuaded by Ernest Breech to leave the post and come to Ford as vice-president of marketing. Breech, thinking of Ford's future, wanted an experienced man available to replace him.

At that time, Robert S. McNamara, one of the original Whiz Kids, held the position to which Lee Iacocca had just been promoted. Some of McNamara's associates considered Jim Nance a roadblock to their own progress and searched for means to remove him. With the probably unwitting help of Charles F. Moore, Jr., vice-president for public relations, they manoeuvred Nance into a newspaper press conference and then accused him of violating Ford policy by not getting prior approval. Henry Ford II, who was soon to dispose of Breech, probably welcomed the opportunity to fire Nance, which he did.

To protect himself Iacocca surrounded himself with men he could trust, including Hal Sperlick, Gar Laux, Frank Zimmerman, and Walter Murphy. He installed John B. Naughton as general manager of Ford Division, Matthew S. McLaughlin to head Lincoln-Mercury, and Theodore Mecke, Jr., as vice-president for public relations. All three were graduates of the Philadelphia district office at Chester, where Lee had got his start.

Iacocca had been long aware that too many car buyers harboured an unfavourable perception of Ford Motor Company engineering. In his newly expanded role he now could do something about correcting that impression.

From its earliest years Ford had been the most innovative of carmakers in America. An extensive list of firsts to enhance driving performance, convenience, and safety began developing as early as 1904. The innumerable innovations, which were later utilised by other manufacturers, included Ford's production of the two-door body type, application of a baked-enamel finish for bodies, safety-glass windshields as standard equipment, and the one-piece windshield.

Ford had also been first with the fingertip, push-button

starter; first to position passengers between axles rather than over them, for better riding comfort; first with a three-speed torque-converter automatic transmission and with an all-synchro three-speed manual transmission. In more recent years the company had introduced power front-disc brakes, self-adjusting brakes, rack-and-pinion steering for American cars, and many other innovations that the public took for granted, without knowing they originated with Ford.

Iacocca was determined that the public know. He called on Kenyon & Eckhardt for a campaign that would focus on Ford as the industry's foremost innovator. In the process of planning this advertising campaign one of the most memorable slogans in automobile history was created.

A group in the New York office of K & E headed by Ronald DeLuca developed an appropriate concept and produced a number of ads stressing Ford as the company that had conceived and implemented many of the most important refinements in automotive engineering. While working on one of the many ads produced for the campaign, a copywriter in DeLuca's group came up with a phrase that ranks with the previously most memorable of all time: 'Ask the man who owns one,' which had been conceived for the long-gone Packard. The new slogan, 'Ford Has a Better Idea,' still serves the company well after more than sixteen years.

Iacocca's appointment of Matt McLaughlin to head Lincoln-Mercury Division fitted in with another of his priorities, to give Lincoln-Mercury greater significance as a division within the company, and to restore it to the status planned for it by Henry's two brothers, Benson and William Clay. For too many years the division had been little more than a company stepchild. To a great degree it had been a dumping ground for Ford Division executives who were deemed incapable of future progress, or a farm club for men believed to be promising material for Ford Division.

Lincoln sales were usually about one-fifth of those of Cadillac, Lincoln's prime competitor. And Mercury was always beaten substantially by Buick and Oldsmobile and by more than two to one by Pontiac. Iacocca could not stomach that situation. He knew that the fault lay in product quality.

127

Mercury had neither good looks nor a comfortable ride.

The reasons for the division's position were obvious. Sufficient money was never allocated to improve product quality, and Lincoln-Mercury advertising budgets were kept too low for effective merchandising. Further erosion had resulted from complacency among Lincoln-Mercury dealers.

'Iacocca took the necessary steps to make Lincoln-Mercury a significant division,' according to Leo-Arthur Kelmenson, president of Kenyon & Eckhardt. 'He committed the resources to improve product quality. To whatever degree he could, he was the one who supported a clear separation of the two divisions by making the cosmetic and engineering changes needed to give Lincoln and Mercury cars their own image and justify making Lincoln-Mercury a totally separate division within the company.'

Iacocca encountered little resistance from Henry Ford II in his efforts to revitalise Lincoln-Mercury and in the appointment of his experienced loyalists to important positions. For one thing, in early 1965 Henry was busy trying to placate his mother, who made no secret about her displeasure over Henry's insistence on marrying Cristina Vettore Austin. Henry became even more preoccupied when he was actually married to Cristina by a District of Columbia justice the night of February 19. The couple went off on an extended honeymoon to England, France, and Switzerland.

Henry was unable to remain long around the Glass House even after his return to Dearborn. During the honeymoon he had set the stage for another family problem by inviting his two daughters, Charlotte and Anne, to come to Europe and get to know the new Mrs Henry Ford II. While there Charlotte met Stavros Niarchos, the Greek multimillionaire.

The romance that blossomed was not much to Henry's liking. Niarchos was not only eight years older than Henry himself, but he was already married. Henry spent much time flying to New York and to Europe to dissuade his daughter, but to no avail.

Meanwhile Lee Iacocca pursued his ambition to improve Lincoln-Mercury's share of the car market quite unhindered. He directed his product-planning group headed by

Hal Sperlick to work toward two new cars far different from the dull, unimaginatively styled, and hard-riding products then being offered by the division.

At the same time he had his racing team at Ford Division make refinements on the Ford GT40 that might bring Henry his desperately wanted victory over Enzo Ferrari at the 1965 LeMans, to be run June 19 and 20. The fleet of GT40s headed for LeMans were to carry the further designation of Mk.2.

Seven GT40 Mk.2 prototypes were sent to LeMans for the round-the-clock race. Hopes were highest for one powered by a seven-litre V-8 and driven by Philip Hill, the first American ever to win a Grand Prix Championship.

During practice sessions Hill's Ford lapped 5.1 seconds faster than the quickest Ferrari, and also set a lap record during the actual race. Through the first half of the twenty-four-hour competition a happy Henry Ford II anxiously awaited the chequered flag. Unfortunately the Ford V-8 engined poured out too much power for the car's transmission and clutch, which broke down.

Enzo Ferrari had turned back Ford for the second successive time and, to embarrass Henry further, had not only done it with a smaller (3.3 litre) engine, but had had his Ferraris finish one-two-three. Irritated, but still stubborn, Henry promised to be back with a winner.

It was an angry Henry Ford II who returned to the Glass House demanding that the Ford racing cars be ready for the 1966 running of the LeMans twenty-four-hour race and placing the burden of getting the job done on Iacocca. Even though Lee was deeply involved in the planning of cars for both Ford and Lincoln-Mercury three years into the future, as well as in completing production of the two Mercurys for introduction in 1966, he could not let Henry down.

He worked with the Ford racing team to produce a fleet of GT40 Ford cars capable of giving Ferrari a run for his money. Exhaustive tests were given each racer to make sure that transmission and clutch performance were compatible with the power of the 427-cubic-inch V-8 engines installed in the cars. Heads would roll if Henry had to eat crow for a third time.

Iacocca further strengthened the 1966 assault on the

twenty-four hours of LeMans by approving the signing of three of the finest race-driver teams available. Ken Miles, who had won with a GT40 at Daytona, was paired with Denis Hulme, a Grand Prix champion from New Zealand. Two other New Zealanders who were also Grand Prix winners, Chris Amon and Bruce McLaren, would drive another Ford entry. A third would be handled by Dan Gurney, one of America's greatest drivers, and Jerry Grant, another American.

It was a confident Ford team that arrived in LeMans. In practice sessions before the race Dan Gurney's GT40 Mk.2 turned in the fastest officially timed lap, 142.5 miles per hour, but since Phil Hill had about the same record the year before, Henry Ford II – who was in attendance – reserved judgment. After all there were fifty-five starters in the race, seven of which were Ferraris, three of them new P3 models with four-litre V-12 engines equipped with fuel injection.

Henry should not have worried. While one Ferrari held the lead briefly during the night, the Fords swept the boards, finishing first, second, and third. Porsches took the next four positions. Only one of the seven Ferraris was able to finish.

Having earned some measure of revenge for the Ferrari snub of three years past and for the drubbings in the two previous years' races, Henry was happy but cautious. Remembering that Ferrari had beaten him two in a row, he was determined to even the score. He told Iacocca to have Ford entries ready for the 1967 LeMans.

But in his World Headquarters office Lee finished preparations for the introduction of his new Mercury cars. One was the Mercury Marquis, a luxurious car designed as a fullsized, middle-priced competitor to Buick, Olds, and Pontiac, and Mercury Cougar, America's first luxury sports car.

Earlier in the year, in order to build dealer enthusiasm for the new Mercurys, Iacocca had called on Bill Winn and Bill Fugazy and asked them to produce the most unusual and dramatic dealers-only introduction in automobile history. Both men were trusted friends and capable entrepreneurs. Winn was a creator of spectaculars, Fugazy a developer of exciting travel-incentive programmes.

130

Lee had added some personal touches to the introduction plans and approved them before leaving for LeMans. On his return he found that Fugazy had implemented a competition among dealers to select the group which would be present for the two-car introduction. And Bill Winn had hired Bob Castle and a crew from Wilding Division of Bell & Howell to handle the introduction staging.

Iacocca had planned to reveal the new Lincoln-Mercury products to the public on September 30, 1966. The dealers who had met their assigned sales quotas, and thus were to participate in the preview spectacular, would see their new '67 products two weeks earlier.

In mid-September Iacocca, his Lincoln-Mercury team, the selected dealers, and the staging crew boarded the luxury liner, *S.S. Independence* at New York. Their destination was the Caribbean. However, as the ship entered tropical waters, a little more than halfway from New York, she was turned so the stern faced the sunset. Her engines were then silenced.

As the sun slid low on the horizon, the dealers assembled at the stern of the ship. There they saw a mound of helium-filled balloons that was some ten feet long, five feet wide, and five feet high. Suddenly, to a fanfare of music, the balloons were released to reveal the 1967 Mercury Marquis, one of the two cars that were to bring Lincoln-Mercury Division back to a semblance of respectability.

Matt McLaughlin and Lee Iacocca described the car and its features. The dealers cheered. This car, they agreed, was what they needed. Once the ceremonies were concluded, the *S.S. Independence* reset a course for St Thomas, one of the American Virgin Islands. Two days later it docked at Charlotte Amalie on the island's southern shore.

The first full day at Charlotte Amalie was spent in playing golf and tennis, swimming, and sightseeing. The second day everyone was bussed to the island's north side, bordering the Atlantic Ocean. There, along the rounded end of horseshoe-shaped Magens Bay, discovered by Christopher Columbus in 1493, a luau and beach party was laid out.

Throughout the afternoon members of the entourage swam and, between dips in the bay or the ocean, discussed with Iacocca and other Lincoln-Mercury officials their high expectations for the Marquis and the division. Each conversation usually included an assurance that there was more to come.

As evening approached, the group enjoyed an out-door cookout of barbecued ribs and chicken. Local people made tours through the area leading mules, each of which carried two bottles of brandy around its neck. As it turned dark, five hundred torches were lit.

Suddenly the sounds of an engine came from the middle of the bay, and what looked to be a banana boat soon appeared. Actually it was a World War II LST covered with leaves and banana stalks and outfitted with lights. The landing craft came right to the beach and lowered its front end.

A bright new automobile rolled out of the LST, over the beach, and up a six-foot-high ramp onto a thatched, hutlike structure that had been erected at the centre of the bay's curve. As the car came to a stop on stage, the interior of the thatched hut came ablaze with lights.

Out of the car stepped Vic Damone, who introduced the new Mercury Cougar to the attending dealers in song. Damone had become a friend of Iacocca's in 1964 while starring in an NBC network programme called *The Lively Ones*, which was sponsored by Ford Division for Iacocca's record-breaking Mustang.

Returning to the United States by plane, the Lincoln-Mercury dealers were unstinting in their praise for Lee Iacocca. They were impressed by the theatrics that introduced Marquis and Cougar, but even more so with the cars themselves. Iacocca made it clear, however, that a division that had lain dormant for so long would not spring back to life overnight.

It would, and did, take a few years of intensive planning and hard work before the Lincoln-Mercury Division reached an appreciably profitable stage. The buying public had to be convinced that the quality, so long missing, was back. It took the concerted efforts of Lee Iacocca, Matt McLaughlin's Lincoln-Mercury staff, and Kenyon & Eckhardt.

Marquis, as a full-size family car appealing primarily to

older buyers, had to be positioned as a dependable, smooth-riding automobile, something previous Mercurys had not been. After much trial and error Iacocca approved a memorable campaign that in time accomplished what he wanted.

Kenyon & Eckhardt chose television as the medium for this new approach because of its high visual impact, and the agency produced a commercial promoting the comfort and smoothness of the Mercury Marquis ride. It portrayed a Dutch diamond cutter riding in the back seat of a Marquis. He was about to split a large, precious gem while the car travelled rough roads. The diamond, after moments of suspense, was precisely cut without difficulty.

Shown across the nation for a year and more, it was one of the most effective, most talked-about commercials ever produced, one so well known that it earned a spoof on *Saturday Night Live*. In the tricked-up version an imaginary car called the 'Royal DeLuxe' was seen on the same type of rough roads. However, the diamond cutter was supplanted by a man posing as a rabbi performing a successful circumcision on an infant.

Promoting Mercury Cougar was another matter. Cougar was a different automobile, a sporty type aimed at the youthful and youthful-feeling who wanted luxury in their automobiles. Its buyers were similar to Mustangs, but more affluent.

The assignment was so challenging to both Kenyon & Eckhardt and the Lincoln-Mercury promotion staff that to ease the tension, Frank Zimmerman at Lincoln-Mercury suggested to Lee Iacocca that he hire a trained orangutang to drive a Cougar from New York to San Francisco. The animal, said Zimmerman, tongue in cheek, would be trained to sit behind the wheel and simulate driving. A man hunched under the dash would use specially installed equipment to do the actual driving.

Think of the drama in such a situation, Zimmerman said, the perception it would give people of how simple and safe it is to drive a Ford-built car. As he made a hasty retreat out of the office, he reminded Lee of the hundreds of newspaper reporters and camera crews followed the car from coast-to-coast.

The idea, ludicrous as it was, triggered a stroke of marketing genius. Why not a real cougar to suggest the image of the new car?

The idea that the cougar is the most graceful of all large cats in the New World could be used in advertising to reflect the smoothness of the car's ride and its ability to conquer American roads with a touch of elegance. The silken sleek look and fluid motion of the cat could be suggestive of the Cougar's ride. And the growl might well symbolise the power of the car.

The go-ahead from Iacocca placed the responsibility for implementing the concept on the shoulders of Bill Suchman, creative director of Kenyon & Eckhardt's New York office. Suchman recommended that the cat be used not only in print and broadcast advertising to identify the new Cougar, but also to symbolise the Mercury line of the Lincoln-Mercury Division. The latter could be accomplished by placing the animal atop the sign identifying dealerships.

Finding the suitable trained animal was one thing, but getting it up on the sign to photograph was something else. It took weeks of work and more than a few dangerous scrapes, but the animal's trainer finally managed to get the animal up and to emit the desired growl. It was another Iacocca-inspired triumph. 'The Sign of the Cat' became a nationwide trademark, and despite the change in advertising agencies from Kenyon & Eckhardt to Young and Rubicam in 1979, the cat continues to give an identity to Mercury automobiles.

The two new Mercurys, Marquis and Cougar, helped Iacocca bring profitability to the Lincoln-Mercury Division as well as recognition within the Ford Motor Company. Nevertheless it did not, and probably never could, match Ford Division in sales. But where Lincoln-Mercury sales had seldom topped 300,000 annually, they began to nudge the half-million mark, cutting into the market shares of Buick, Oldsmobile, and Pontiac.

It was a fine start toward a meaningful increase in market penetration, the symbol of success in the auto industry. Chrysler was so far behind it could be discounted, but Iacocca knew that to battle General Motors for further increases both the Ford and Lincoln-Mercury divisions needed new and saleable competitors for Chevrolet in particular, and all GM divisions in general. The gulf between Ford and General Motors was too wide to expect miracles. But Iacocca had narrowed the gap between Ford Division and Chevrolet. Even though Chevy was still ahead by 167,291 registrations in 1966, Ford Division had gained over a quarter-million in that one year.

That made Chevrolet Iacocca's prime target for the upcoming 1968 model year. He gave both Ford and Lincoln-Mercury divisions products aimed to fight Chevy head-to-head. They were Ford Torino and Mercury Montego, each already in production. But in those early months of 1967, Iacocca had another important responsibility.

The twenty-four-hours at LeMans was scheduled for June 10 and 11, and Henry Ford II was determined to defeat Enzo Ferrari for the second year in a row. Lee had to keep an eye on the refinements being made for the new GT40s, which would be designated M4. He had ordered the horsepower increased and the GT40 Mk.4s made heavier than the Mk.2s of 1966. He also had the new versions equipped with cast-iron cylinder heads instead of the aluminium used the previous year. The cars were also given larger brakes to compensate for their increased speeds.

A win at LeMans would not only make Henry happy, it also could lead to greater sales in the 1968 model year. It had always been Iacocca's contention that more people watch automobile racing than baseball, football, and basketball combined, and those millions would have their attention focused on LeMans in June.

He was determined to leave as little as possible to chance and he authorised the managers of the racing group to hire the finest teams of drivers. Signed for LeMans were Dan Gurney and A. J. Foyt as one, Mark Donahue and Bruce McLaren for the second, Mario Andretti and Lucien Bianchi as a third, and Roger McCluskey and Jo Schlesser as a fourth team. All but Bianchi, McLaren, and Schlesser were Americans.

Both Henry Ford and Lee Iacocca were on hand for the

start of the race on June 10. The four GT40 Mk4 racers for Ford were backed up by three Mk2s that had been modified. Seven Ferraris were among the fifty-four starters, which also included Chaparral, Matra, Peugeot, and Renault.

All the Fords and Ferraris got away well when the starter's flag was dropped, with the Chaparral, driven by America's Grand Prix Champion Phil Hill, in close pursuit. Two Ferraris soon moved in ahead of the Chaparral. The hours passed with Fords and Ferraris alternating in the lead. After midnight three of the GT40s were in front, a Ferrari was fourth, the Chaparral fifth. The closest other Ferrari was running seventh.

Suddenly serious trouble hit the Ford teams. The McLaren-Donahue car developed clutch trouble and was forced into the pits. Lucien Bianchi, in another Ford, came in and turned the driving over to Mario Andretti. Andretti snapped on his helmet, goggles, and harness and sped out onto the road. He took his GT40 up a rise and started down the hill at about 160 miles an hour.

As he approached a series of S-turns, he jammed on the brakes too quickly. The left-front brake locked, and the GT40 skidded around. It hit the bank on one side of the road, then skidded across to bounce off the opposite bank into the middle of the road, where it stalled. Alarmed that other cars would soon be bearing down on the GT40, Andretti leapt from the car and ran clear off the road.

Within a half-minute Roger McCluskey's GT40 came barrelling over the top of the hill. Fearful that the driver might still be in the cockpit of the stalled car visible in his headlights, McCluskey rammed the GT40 into the road bank.

A few seconds later Jo Schlesser's GT40 caught the two disabled vehicles in its headlights as it came over the hill. Schlesser made a valiant effort to drive between the two disabled Fords and missed, crashing into McCluskey's. Three out of the four most powerful GT40s were out of the race.

The one remaining Ford GT40 Mk4, driven by the Dan Gurney-A. J. Foyt team, managed to slide by the damaged threesome. It was the only hope for a Ford victory. Gurney and Foyt were in the lead, but two more power-laden Ferrari P4s were after them. As the Ferraris passed their pits, they were signalled by Enzo Ferrari to speed up. His strategy was to get close to the lone Ford, driven by Gurney, and tease him into an all-out race that might punish the Ford engine enough to disable it. One of the Ferraris pulled up beside Gurney's Ford. Gurney, aware of a ploy he had often used himself, merely smiled and waved the Ferrari on. But the second the Ferrari passed his GT40, Gurney jammed the accelerator to the floorboard and roared past the Ferrari driver. Gurney did not let up and opened an increasing lead each second. He completed the 3,200-mile course and crossed the finish line more than thirty miles ahead of the nearest Ferrari.

Iacocca stood by silently as Henry accepted the honours. If it was revenge over Enzo Ferrari that Henry wanted so badly, it was his. He had defeated the Italian master two in a row, which really amounted to a standoff, since Ferrari had also defeated Ford twice.

LeMans 1967 was Ford's last company-sponsored European race, though the American racing schedule was carried on for the balance of the year. Thereafter the money spent on racing was to be diverted to achieving the emissions and safety standards required by the government. Iacocca returned to his Glass House office and a heavy workload, soon to be made heavier as the Detroit area, and the auto industry, experienced an unexpected blow.

The disastrous summer of 1967 race riots, which almost wrecked Detroit, also took their toll on automobile production. New-car registrations for each of the Big Three dropped substantially from 1966 with almost every car line suffering equally, except for one surprising difference. GM's Cadillac and Chrysler's Imperial divisions revealed appreciable increases. The one luxury car line showing a loss was Ford's Lincoln, dropping almost 15,000 sales from 1966.

Ford Motor Company suffered another blow during 1967, one not shared by the other automobile manufacturers. The Arab-Israeli war brought about a boycott of Ford products in all Arab countries because Ford Motor Company operated an assembly plant in Israel. This exclusion of Ford products was destined to last at least into the eighties and barred all Ford cars from Lebanon, Syria, Saudi Arabia, the Arab Emirates, Yemen, Iraq, and Egypt. It meant a tremendous loss in revenue, since Ford products, especially Mustang, had been favourites in the Middle East.

For Iacocca 1967 was a debilitating year even though he had introduced two new cars to the public. Ford sold about 500,000 fewer units in 1966, and its profits dropped proportionately. In midsummer the United Auto Workers called a strike that closed all Ford plants for fifty-three days, an action that intensified the problems caused by the race riots.

As if that was not enough, shoddy workmanship by Ford plant workers produced another business setback. About one-third of all the cars built, including every one of 447,000 Mustangs, had to be recalled to correct various defects. Over and above the cost of repairs Ford Motor Company paid out a quarter-million dollars in postage fees to notify owners to return their cars.

Iacocca had yet another problem as the year ended. Henry had insisted that the Mustang planned for the following year be longer and heavier, and Lee now deeply regretted that he had let himself be persuaded. The car that had knocked the industry on its ears in 1965 was no longer the smart little muscle car that reflected the spirit of American youth.

It was almost a tradition in the industry to enlarge successful automobiles, lengthening them, increasing their overall size and weight, and adding to their cost to increase profit. With Mustang, this idea backfired. Sales dropped. Individuals trading in their original Mustangs complained about the new models.

Iacocca felt something had to be done. He could not bear to see his classic little pony fade from the scene through impractical design. He had to find a way to convince Henry that the old premise – bigger is better – no longer held true, at least to the medium- and lower-priced cars.

In analysing the market over the previous few years, Iacocca had noted a resurgence in the luxury-car segment. Ever on the alert to taking advantage of market changes, he was ready. The new car he had waiting in the wings not only should please Henry, it should also soften his resistance to downsizing the Mustang.

Planned for a 1968 introduction, the new Mark III was an up-to-date version of Edsel Ford's Continental Mark discontinued some years earlier. Iacocca had predicted a return to prominence of luxurious automobiles as early as 1965 and had his product planners design a car that would compete with Cadillac's Eldorado.

The Mark II Continental had been discontinued in 1957 even though many acknowledged it the most beautiful, as well as the most expensive and heaviest, car on the road. Other luxury cars were overstyled and ostentatious, but the Mark had a classic simplicity, with good taste in its design, an understated dignity and elegance. However, the mid-fifties had proved to be bad years for a car that sold for $10,000.

Iacocca saw the market in the late sixties as being just right, and how better to make an impact in the luxury-car field than with the revival of an acknowledged classic? Cadillac's Eldorado needed an American competitor, and Iacocca wanted to improve the Lincoln's market share, which had rarely been better than 4 percent.

Henry Ford II found no fault with Iacocca's plan to revive the Continental Mark. He endorsed it heartily as a worthy successor to his father's Mark I and the Mark II in which his brother William Clay was so thoroughly involved.

Iacocca's star glittered brightly along the corridors of the Glass House as 1967 came to a close. Executives at all levels below Lee's executive vice-presidency were giving odds that the next president of the Ford Motor Company would be none other than the man from Allentown. With Henry's unpredictability a change might come at any moment.

Lee himself felt certain that he would not be overlooked when the time came for a change. He had proved himself the most capable man in the history of the company. Businessmen throughout the nation considered him the most important man in the entire automobile industry. There was no doubt in his or anyone else's mind (except perhaps Henry II) that the Ford presidency would go to him soon.

Mercurial Henry Ford II did have a different, if not a better, idea. It was one made possible by the sudden resignation of Semon E. (Bunkie) Knudsen as executive vice-president of General Motors. Bunkie, whose father had been fired by Henry Ford I and then gone on to become president of General Motors, expected to follow in his father's footsteps.

In the normal course of events the new president of GM would have been Bunkie Knudsen. But for some reason Edward Cole was named. To bypass a man in direct line for promotion is tantamount in the automobile industry to telling the skipped-over executive that he has reached his peak. Knudsen, realising this, resigned.

Henry Ford II had just returned from a vacation with Cristina in the British West Indies when he heard of Bunkie's resignation. Knudsen, of course, was no stranger to him. During Bunkie's thirty years at General Motors their paths had crossed many times, and Henry felt that Ford could use a man with Knudsen's experience. Besides, Henry had his hands full with some outside interests.

Earlier in the year President Lyndon Johnson had asked Henry to chair his newly created National Alliance of Businessmen, the stated function of which was to hire and train about a half-million ghetto youths. It was a three-year assignment and would demand much of Henry's time, visiting businessmen throughout the country and getting their pledges to make good use of the millions of dollars appropriated by Congress. Yes, Henry decided, he needed Bunkie Knudsen.

He phoned Bunkie and asked to meet with him. Knudsen quickly agreed to come to Henry's home in Grosse Pointe, but Henry wanted to keep the meeting secret, and Grosse Pointers have a way of learning too much too soon. It was decided that Henry would visit Bunkie at his home in Bloomfield Hills. He arrived there in a rented GM car to throw off any nosy neighbours.

Bunkie Knudsen was willing to come to Ford, but he knew Henry too well. He accepted a salary and bonus comparable to Henry's, but he was not about to make himself a well-paid sacrificial lamb. He said yes only after Henry agreed to give him a protective contract. Besides, Knudsen couldn't help but wonder why Ford needed him with Iacocca in the wings. Was it because Henry felt Bunkie could really help the company? Or was it a kind of atonement for the treatment given his father by Henry's grandfather about four decades earlier?

The morning of February 6, 1968, Henry Ford II held a press conference to announce the elevation of Arjay Miller (a token promotion to ease the way for his resignation) to vice chairman of the board, and the appointment of Semon E. Knudsen as president of Ford Motor Company. During the press conference Henry praised his new second in command.

'Today the flow of history has been reversed,' Henry told the assembled reporters. 'Another Knudsen, having left General Motors, has been elected president of the company his father helped build. I am delighted to have him because he is a strong and resourceful executive, brought up in a great automotive tradition. He will be a fine asset to management at Ford.'

The unexpected announcement was a blow to Lee Iacocca's ego. Bringing in an outsider to fill a position he felt eminently qualified for – and entitled to – was infuriating. Reporters, wondering whether Iacocca might resign, didn't leave Henry off the hook.

'Why?' they asked the Ford chairman. Henry weaselled. His unconvincing answer was that Iacocca was still needed where he was. Besides, he added, another year or so of experience would make him even more valuable when his time came.

Henry's reasoning seemed downright ludicrous. If Lee Iacocca had not yet proven himself capable of running the Ford Motor Company, he never would. Had Bunkie Knudsen done as much for General Motors as Lee had for Ford? Nobody with knowledge of the inner workings of the industry bought Henry's lame excuse.

Possibly Henry had begun to fear Iacocca's strength within the company. Or maybe Henry had decided on this way to let Iacocca know that he was not indispensable, to pierce what many at Ford were calling an inflated ego.

'Lee had become as imperialistic as Henry himself,' said one man who was close to Lee at Ford. 'He had become, well you might say a little big for his breeches. He was a good and brilliant man, no doubt about that, but what bothered a lot of people was that he let you know it.'

Another Ford executive, now retired, said, 'Lee had changed quite a bit from the time he hit it big with Mustang. At one time he had a smile and a good word for lower-echelon people, but all of a sudden he would walk by them, ignore them, his head held high like a royal personage expecting a curtsy. He gave you the feeling that you didn't exist, that the only ones who mattered were the men on his team. None of the rest of us were surprised when Henry detoured around him to name a new president.'

Iacocca's reactions to Henry's appointment of Knudsen have been kept within him. Perhaps Henry's statements to the press, holding out hope for another day, may have mollified Lee. Whatever his feelings, he decided to bide his time and returned to work no doubt determined to make Henry regret the Knudsen appointment.

Two months after Knudsen took office Iacocca presented America's luxury-car buyers with the Continental Mark III. Lee had supervised its design and production, taking it through all channels – market research, design reviews, marketing and advertising strategy – and with appropriate panoply and fanfare introduced it as an automobile of distinctive personality on April 5, 1968. The car had an attractively sculpted low profile, a hood longer than any other American car, and a short rear deck distinguished by a continental spare tyre reminiscent of the early Marks.

Powered by a 460-cubic-inch overhead-valve, V-8 engine, the 1969 Continental Mark III was a rarity among heavy luxury cars, able to get from zero to sixty miles an hour in nine and one-half seconds, from zero to ninety in under twenty-one. Iacocca positioned it as a personal luxury car available in one body style, a two-door coupe.

The Continental Mark III did what Iacocca hoped it would, increasing Lincoln's prestige in the luxury-car market by outselling the Cadillac Eldorado by 30 percent in its first year. It also helped achieve the highest single-year sales for Lincoln in 1969, and despite a depressed economy in 1970 and 1971, the car also enjoyed increased sales in those years.

Iacocca had another car ready for the 1969 model year. September 27, 1968, he brought out the Marauder to give the Mercury line a shot in the arm. Marauder offered some of the luxury of Marquis and a bit of the sportiness of Cougar to attract the older buyers who wanted a performance image in their car.

Overall, 1968 was such a good year that Iacocca was able to forget the humiliation of being passed over for Bunkie Knudsen. Henry was away so often that Lee had few problems from that quarter. The chairman was enjoying his fling in the political arena despite his unhappiness over Lyndon Johnson's having announced in March that he would not seek re-election. With a strong distaste for Richard Nixon Henry immediately supported Hubert Humphrey for the nation's highest office.

The year was also a comeback year for the Ford Motor Company and the city of Detroit. By June indications were strong that Ford would top the 2.25 million mark in new-car registrations in the United States. And Detroit was rebounding from the calamitous effects of the previous year's race riots.

In fact a spirit of oneness developed between whites and blacks as Detroit's professional baseball team, the Tigers, charged toward the American League championship. Al Kaline, Mickey Lolich, Willie Horton, and Gates Brown helped propel a team to a world's championship in defeating the National League's St Louis Cardinals, which pointed up Iacocca's farsightedness. He had established a sports panel for Lincoln-Mercury that included Al Kaline, a contender for the Baseball Hall of Fame.

Looking ahead, Lee was concerned over government standards for the automobile industry as well as the mush-rooming sales of imports. To help satisfy one and offset the effects of the other he began plans for small cars with improved mileage. One, for Ford Division, would be all-new, with a name that would have a marketing rub-off from Mustang, the Pinto. The second, for the Mercury line, was a newly designed car along the lines of Pinto, and on a Pinto chassis, that would retain the somewhat successful name Comet. Later it would become Mercury Bobcat.

Pursuing these ideas, Iacocca again locked horns with Henry Ford II, who had little interest in small cars. Lee argued that Ford had to bring out fuel-efficient cars to combat imports. In the previous six years, he told Henry, imports had doubled their share of the American market, from under five percent in 1962 to a near 10.5 percent in 1968.

Henry, as he usually did when Iacocca initially suggested a policy change, disagreed. He reminded Lee of the Mustang as well as another car smaller than other Ford models ready for the following year, Lee's own 1970 Maverick. Maverick, Lee countered, would be a fine car and a good seller, but it was not the kind of car to match Volkswagen or compete with Toyota. Henry remained unconvinced.

As he had done with Mustang, Iacocca kept at Henry, often backed up in his arguments by Hal Sperlick. 'Our insistence that small cars were the wave of the future led to Iacocca and Sperlick not being much admired by Mr Ford,' Hal Sperlick says. Admired or not, Henry finally gave in to the two men and agreed to fund production of Pinto and the restyled Comet, both of which were introduced as 1971 models on September 11, 1970.

Bunkie Knudsen, meanwhile, had stormed into his presidency at Ford like a lion on the loose. Henry Ford II had described him to the press as 'strong and resourceful,' and he was all of that. He looked into everything – planning, styling, engineering, production – and made changes, often without consulting Henry, much less Iacocca.

At General Motors Knudsen had shown himself competent in managing GM's international operations, which were smaller than Ford's. So he made himself visible throughout the thirty-odd countries where Ford owned business. He was an obsessive achiever, perhaps too much like

Iacocca himself. Morning, noon, and night he could be found in the foundry, at the Styling Center, anywhere in the Ford empire, suggesting a change here, a change there. He made at least one design variation that had the Styling Center up in arms, placing a GM-type grille on the Ford Thunderbird.

No one could deny that Bunkie Knudsen was a sincere, hard-working Ford man, but perhaps he worked too hard, so hard that Henry, remembering the dedication of the Ernest Breech he had ousted, began to fear him. Rumours began floating about the Glass House that Henry indeed was concerned and that his fears were being fed by some members of Lee Iacocca's team.

Knudsen, unintentionally, made one serious mistake. As April 17, 1969, introduction day for the new Maverick approached, Bunkie began singing the praises of the fine new Ford entry, which might possibly give Mustang a run for its money in sales. Then, on introduction day, Bunkie was there in the forefront answering reporters' questions and being very presidential, as though he were offering the new Maverick as his creation, not Iacocca's.

In early summer Glass House corridors echoed with whispers that about a dozen Ford men – Iacocca stalwarts? – had prepared a list of Knudsen misdemeanours for presentation to Mr Ford. True or not, early on the morning of September 1, Ted Mecke, an Iacocca man who had been promoted two weeks earlier to vice-president of public affairs, visited Bunkie Knudsen at his home.

The word is that Mecke went to alert Knudsen that Henry Ford II was going to fire him that day. And Knudsen says that the following day Ford came into his office and told him that 'things had not worked out' as Henry had hoped and that he would be fired.

Knudsen was speechless for a moment. Perhaps his mind focused on the day when he was about ten or eleven and his father was just as summarily fired by the grandfather of the man who was now giving him his walking papers. He asked Henry II to give him a reason. Henry did not. Maybe, as in previous such circumstances, he couldn't.

Within two weeks Henry Ford II called a press conference

and announced that his board of directors had voted to terminate the nineteen-month presidency of Semon E. Knudsen. Even though Knudsen was absent, reporters made it rough for Henry, asking for reasons. Bunkie Knudsen was no ordinary executive to be brushed off so easily.

Henry had trouble answering. It was not a resignation – he had made that clear. In fact, as Knudsen said later, Ford had not even given him a chance to resign, although if he had, Knudsen would have refused it. As reporters kept hammering for a reason, Henry finally said only that 'sometimes these things don't work out.'

Bunkie Knudsen, however, had an answer to explain Henry's arbitrary manoeuvre. 'Henry was afraid of losing his Tinkertoy,' he told friends the night of the firing.

Whatever the reason for Knudsen's dismissal, it cost the Ford Motor Company a bundle of money. According to the settlement Knudsen would continue to receive his $600,000 salary until the end of 1972. In addition he would also receive his 1969 share of the annual bonus given Ford executives, a figure that could approach $500,000. Knudsen also retained the 15,000 shares of Ford stock he received on joining Ford and kept options to purchase, if he wished, another 75,000 shares at slightly less than $50 each.

For Henry Ford II and his company the severance proved expensive, but, as might be expected, it brought jubilation to the Iacocca camp. They had no doubt that now their champion would get his just reward. As for Lee himself he remained primly guarded as to his inner feelings. When reporters asked how he felt about the Knudsen firing, his answer was 'I've never said "no comment" to you before, but I'll say "no comment" this time.'

Iacocca wanted to be certain that his time had come, even though it was definitely his turn to serve as second in command to Henry Ford II. But Henry had another surprise up his sleeve.

He did not name a new president for the Ford Motor Company, he named three men to handle the duties of the office. Iacocca was one, with the title of executive vice-president of the Ford Motor Company and president of Ford's North American automotive operations. The other two were Robert Stevenson, president of Ford's international automotive operations, and Robert Hampson, president of non-automotive operations. The three were to operate as equals in authority, all answerable to Henry Ford II.

This unusual and strange turn of events was a bitter pill for Iacocca. Not only did this three-way split deprive him of the office he believed he deserved, it also represented a watering down of his authority. It mattered little that as president of Ford's North American operations he headed the most important phase of the company's activities. He actually had occupied that seat for the past two years, so Henry's action was hardly in the nature of a favour.

Agonising questions flooded his mind. Was Henry trying to tell him something? That he should resign? That he had come as far as he ever would at Ford? Then maybe he was just plain lucky. The president's chair at Ford, to judge by the short tenures of the men who had occupied it, was a hot one. Henry was living proof that the closer one got to the king's throne the more vulnerable one became to his fancies and foibles.

Iacocca would not remember 1969 as a particularly happy year, even though his Maverick had already run up six-month sales that rivalled those of the record-holding Mustang. One of his most valuable lieutenants, Gar Laux, had been relieved of his duties as vice-president for sales, and he would be sorely missed.

Henry kept himself too busy during the last months of 1969 and the early months of 1970 to see much of Iacocca. In April of 1970 he took Cristina with him to the Soviet Union for a nine-day business trip. Vodka mixed well with Henry's gregarious personality, and he returned home with Soviet approval to build a huge truck-manufacturing plant.

Henry's ebullience at this master stroke of business was short-lived – President Richard Nixon killed it. He sent his secretary of defense, Melvin Laird, to Detroit to chastise Henry. At a press conference he embarrassed the chairman of the board of the Ford Motor Company for having the audacity even to consider such a deal without clearing it with the government, while 'the Soviet Union is sending trucks by the shipload to North Vietnam.'

Somehow, during the trip to Russia, Henry had also had a change of mind. And, no doubt forgetting that Iacocca had been preaching the same sermon for some time, Henry began sounding off about the harm to the American economy from the onslaught of imports, especially those from Japan.

He now bemoaned the fact that Japanese imports were coming into the United States too freely, while American cars sent to Japan were subjected to so many restrictions and taxed so heavily that the Japanese could not afford them. 'We are certainly being discriminated against by the Japanese,' he told reporters.

Another problem, government intervention in the automobile business – politely categorised as 'regulation' – was escalating. Nixon had appointed scrappy, abrasive John Volpe as secretary of transportation, and he was setting deadlines for meeting emission standards that were unrealistic if production costs were to be held in check. And Volpe's insistence that all cars had to be equipped with air bags before 1972 would shoot car prices up even further.

Those rising costs would play havoc with Iacocca's plans for the years ahead. For one thing his hopes for Pinto as a car affordable by people with modest incomes – he had expected to give it a sticker price of about $2,000 – would be dashed, and September 11, 1970, announcement day for Pinto and Comet, was closing in.

The fun in the fight for success was being diminished by outside forces, and Lee began to wonder if the prize was worth the battle. He was still bitter over Henry's reluctance to give him the presidency, and he did not like the hassle of making long-range plans with two other individuals. Management by trio was inefficient, ineffective, and confusing. Both Stevenson and Hampson followed Henry, not Iacocca, in their thinking, and little progress was being made in meeting the public's growing demand for smaller, higher-gas-mileage cars.

Lee was tiring of Henry's repeated refusal to consider approval of research towards the more fuel-efficient front-wheel-drive concept. Henry had spoken out against the unfair advantage given Japanese imports through government-mandated inequities, but when Lee and Hal Sperlick argued for a change in policy, his response was negative.

Import sales had skyrocketed during the previous five years. From 1965 through 1967 their sales increases had averaged 100,000 and more over each previous year, and in 1968 the increase was 200,000 above that of 1967. In 1969, for the first time, foreign car sales had topped the million mark.

Henry's answer was an even larger Mustang for introduction in the fall of 1970. The new pony car was to be almost eight inches longer, six inches wider, and about 600 pounds heavier than Lee's original Mustang. Burning inside at this desecration, Lee wondered whether the time had come to leave Ford.

Public utterances by Henry Ford gave the fire building inside Iacocca no chance to burn out. Henry, it seemed, used every opportunity to fuel further doubts about Lee's tenure with the company. The chairman's interviews with the press could be perceived as messages to Iacocca, reminders not to hold his breath waiting for better things.

Out of the blue Henry had begun giving attention to the prospects of his son, Edsel II, as the Ford heir apparent. 'I think he would like to come into the company someday,' Henry was quoted by one reporter.

For those who knew young Edsel as a mild-mannered, sincere youth, that 'someday' seemed far in the future. No more brilliant a student than his father, Edsel was just finishing prep school prior to enrolment at the none-too-demanding Babson Institute. A certain charisma and the Ford name had been his primary assets in education, according to his counsellors. After Babson it was expected that young Edsel might sign on as a sales trainee at Ford. Insiders at the Glass House considered Henry's references to his son's future as little more than a subtle harassment of Lee Iacocca.

In such an atmosphere it would be natural for Iacocca to consider a change. And, if he did decide to leave Ford, plenty of positions were certainly available for a man of his reputation and stature, and not only in the industry he so passionately loved.

As the 1970 clock ticked toward September, Iacocca was busy preparing for the introduction of his Pinto. Conceived as the first truly small car by an American manufacturer, it was so new in concept it would take exceptional stimulation to earn enthusiasm from the Ford dealer body.

Bill Winn, at Iacocca's direction, was once again to develop the most spectacular show ever put together for the automobile industry's introduction of a car to its dealers. The locale selected for the dealer meeting was the Las Vegas Convention Center, where Winn's group built a theatre to accommodate nearly 2,000 Ford dealers and their wives.

The entire floor of the convention centre's auditorium was restructured to provide seating in tiers beginning at the balcony and sloping down to the main arena floor. A giant theatre was created, including an elliptical stage with a motion picture screen 128 feet wide that enabled simultaneous use of three projectors to produce a panoramic effect.

The first American subcompact, Pinto, was scheduled to be the climax of the show. First, however, would be the showing of the new four-door Maverick that Iacocca had added to the original line, brought out only as a two-door compact less than a year earlier.

A two-door Maverick was driven on stage and 'magically' converted into a four-door before the dealers' eyes. Winn had the Dearborn Steel Tubing Company create a Maverick prototype with two doors on the passenger side and one door on the driver's side. This one-door driver's side would face the audience at the start of the presentation.

To the accompaniment of specially orchestrated live music the driver's side of the Maverick was dismantled by actors posing as technicians. When the door and side panels were removed, a billowing puff of smoke concealed the car. Under the cloak of smoke the car was revolved to appear, once the billows cleared away, as a four-door automobile transformed on the spot.

The piece de resistance from outer space was the introduction of the all-new and perky little Pinto. With the arena in darkness dealers suddenly saw whirling lights similar to those on police cars lighting up the ceiling of the convention centre dome. The lights were attached to a simulated flying saucer, a canopied half-spaceship with its rounded, finished side facing the arena floor.

Building this 'spaceship' and raising it to the top of the dome had been a chore for Bill Winn and his people. It was about twenty-four feet in length and had considerable depth. It was huge and heavy, with canisters of carbon dioxide as well as the whirling lights fixed at the bottom. Winn's men had actually restructured the dome to accommodate the weight.

A large cast danced on stage to music from the orchestra as the spiralling lights illuminated the 'flying saucer' for the first time. Then spotlights from the saucer were directed toward centre stage. Suddenly carbon dioxide exploded from the tanks under the spaceship to create a fog bank for the launch. The spaceship, engulfed in carbon dioxide, landed on the stage, then immediately lifted off again to the roar of another blast of carbon dioxide.

The music, with outer-space tonality, built to a crescendo as the saucer soared back toward the ceiling and the carbon dioxide fog dissipated to reveal a bright-yellow Pinto. The difficult manoeuvring had been so well executed it produced the desired illusion of a Pinto brought down on a spaceship. It actually had been driven on stage while the carbon dioxide fog was at its heaviest.

The Ford dealers had come to Las Vegas more in anticipation of a good time than in expectation of a new car with obvious potential for good sales and profits. As the curtain came down on the show finale, they went wild, giving Iacocca a rousing tribute for providing them with what they felt would be their best seller since the Mustang.

In fact the Pinto proved to be exactly that. Even though only one quarter of the year remained after the public introduction on September 11, the year 1970 proved to be Ford Division's best in sales since Mustang's second year.

Iacocca noted the heavy traffic into dealerships throughout the country for weeks after the introduction and the burgeoning sales of Pinto with a feeling of self-satisfaction. With deep regret he had become serious about leaving the Ford Motor Company. During the months leading to Pinto's introduction prospects for an improved working atmosphere had become bleaker, and the tug of war between Iacocca and the other members of the troika-presidency, Stevenson and Hampson, was wearing him down. Pinto was making it possible for him to say his goodbyes on a high note.

'Lee definitely intended to leave Ford and work for another company,' said Bill Fugazy, Iacocca's close friend. 'He had some fine offers – one that was particularly good and interested him.'

Fugazy did not identify either the company or its location. 'I went around with him looking for houses for him to relocate,' he added, 'but I suggested that he first show the offer to Henry Ford.'

Iacocca did reveal his prospective job to Henry Ford II, and a series of discussions ensued. Surprisingly, Henry acted as if determined to keep him at Ford. Lee, no doubt remembering the Knudsen situation, insisted on a contract with long-range terms. Henry resisted but finally gave in.

Lee's first moves after agreeing to the terms set for his presidency of the Ford Motor Company were to tell his wife and to call his father in Allentown. Nick and Antoinette Iacocca caught the first plane out to help their son celebrate.

Henry Ford II called a press conference for the morning of December 10, 1970. With Lee Iacocca at his right, and with Nick Iacocca seated in the back of the room and smiling broadly, he introduced the new president of the Ford Motor Company. He told the media representatives present that he needed a strong president because 'Ford operations in Europe are expanding, and I've got to devote more of my time to that.'

Turning to Iacocca he expanded further. 'I've reached the point where I need some help,' he said, 'but now Lee's here, and I won't have to worry about it.'

It was done. At the age of forty-six Lido Anthony Iacocca, who had predicted he would be vice-president of Ford before he was thirty-five and missed by less than a year, had finally made it to the presidency of the company he had loved since his boyhood.

Now his office would be located right next to Henry's, in the northeast corner of the Glass House. Now, with salary and bonuses, he would be earning some $600,000 a year or more for some time to come.

'That was one helluva Christmas present,' Iacocca told reporters.

CHAPTER 9

Lee Iacocca had climbed as far up the Ford mountain as he had a right to expect. The name in the blue oval atop the Glass House all but precluded the final step up the ladder to chairman of the board whatever his personal expectations might have been. It seemed improbable, however, that the man Gar Laux describes as 'forever running' could stand still.

As Lee Iacocca took his new office, he realised that the coming decade of the seventies would be a difficult one. Profits would not be easy to come by as the federal government increased pressures for costly safety and pollution standards. Keeping pace with the regulations and the increasing production and labour costs were bound to erode the company's earnings. Now the burden was his, a weight certain to be increased thanks to Henry's vacillating judgments.

His first important job for 1971 may have seemed contradictory to his rarely heeded plea for small, easy-on-the-gas automobiles, but Iacocca had never discounted the public's desire for full-size luxury cars. A full half-century had passed since the first Lincoln was produced by Henry's father, Edsel. Over and above pleasing Henry, Lee enjoyed his part in bringing out the golden-anniversary Lincoln Continental.

The Continental Mark III, which had made its debut two years earlier, had given Lincoln a viable competitor for Cadillac Eldorado. Lee was now determined that the Lincoln

Continental would make the same inroads on Cadillac's most luxurious limousine, the DeVille.

Under Iacocca's watchful eye the new Lincoln emerged, to be positioned in advertising as a refined luxury car of tasteful simplicity with a rich interior, driver and passenger comfort conveniences that made riding in it as restful as sitting in one's living room. Its engine was the most powerful available to the public, a 460-cubic-inch V-8 that developed 365 horsepower at 4,600 revolutions per minute. With an overall length of 225 inches and a total kerb weight for the four-door of 5,072 pounds, ads proclaimed, it offered a smooth, quiet ride unparalleled in the American industry.

The moneyed aficionados who demanded the new and prestigious in their motor cars reacted as Iacocca had expected. The golden-anniversary Lincoln Continentals, four-door limousine and two-door town car, made inroads on Cadillac's DeVille in about the same proportions as Continental Mark III had on Cadillac Eldorado. Together the Continental and Mark tripled Lincoln sales by the end of 1973.

Ford and Mercury car sales also swung upwards due to a highly charged national economy. With profits reaching record figures, Henry kept himself busy building a reputation as a civic-minded citizen dedicated to restoring Detroit's inner city.

Detroit needed a renaissance, he told the city's business community, and he was going to spearhead a downtown development called the Renaissance Center. Along the Detroit River waterfront a cluster of high-rise buildings, a seventy-storey hotel flanked by four office towers, was to be built. The Ford commitment for the start of the project was $6 million.

Ford had no plants or properties to speak of within Detroit's city limits, but the city was the headquarters of its rival automotive giant. General Motors, therefore, could not be left out and matched Henry's investment. In one month Henry had more than two-thirds of the money needed to get the project under way. Not a resident of the city – he lived in Grosse Pointe – Henry Ford II was nonetheless the Lion of the Motor City and was hailed as its potential saviour.

With Henry so preoccupied, Lee Iacocca had nearly a free hand in moving the Ford Motor Company ahead. Late in 1970 Matt McLaughlin, head of Lincoln-Mercury Division, had returned from a trip to Ford's subsidiary in Cologne, Germany, and reported that there was an automobile built by Ford of Germany that Lee should look at.

At his first opportunity Iacocca flew to Cologne. The car, the Capri, was a natural to combat Japanese and European imports on their own turf.

Lee made the necessary arrangements to import the Capri and assigned the merchandising of the car to Lincoln-Mercury Division. The jazzy little import, promoted in advertising as 'the sexy European car', added to Iacocca's laurels, helping to lift Mercury car sales by some 75,000 in 1971 and enabling Mercury to rack up its three best consecutive years.

Ford Motor Company's annual report to stockholders for 1970, a handsome brochure with a bright-yellow Pinto on the cover, carried the signatures of both Henry Ford II and Lee A. Iacocca. Its figures were a glowing testimonial to Iacocca's management. The company's combined sales for the year were a record $15 billion.

The next year's report, which included glamorous shots of Capri as well as Pinto on the cover, provided even better news for stockholders: '1971 was a year of record sales and near-record earnings . . .' it read, again over the dual signatures. Net income was reported as 27 percent more than that of the previous year.

In 1972, even though Ford's new-car registrations in the US went up an additional 186,000 and stockholders were told it was 'the most successful year in your company's history', all was not wine and roses. That same year the Ford Motor Company was subjected to the most humiliating embarrassment in its sixty-nine-year existence.

Congress had instituted Environmental Protection Agency requirements for tests to ensure that 1973-model engines met air-pollution standards before they were approved for installation. Evidently some Ford technicians had found engines failing the tests, so they refined the prototype engines to meet the standards before filing their reports.

When this was discovered and splashed in newspaper headlines across the nation. Henry and Iacocca were livid. Both claimed not to have known about the infractions. Henry himself took the blame, thinking that perhaps the many speeches he had made criticising the government's 'stupid' standards led his workers to take the chance.

'I still don't like the law,' Henry told a press conference, 'and I think it ought to be changed. But you have to play by the rules. You don't cheat.'

The government assessed a $7-million fine against the Ford Motor Company and permitted correction of the faulty reports rather than totally withhold approval, an act that would have barred Ford cars from the market. Though the fine ate into company profits, 1972 was still a very good year for Ford.

Throughout most of the tumult over the emissions fiasco Lee Iacocca kept himself busy with a labour of love. Since 1967 the company had received hundreds of letters bemoaning the change in Mustang. Those letters finally brought about a change of mind by Henry, and now Mustang was already in the process of being rebuilt on a shorter wheelbase, planned for introduction in September of 1973 as a 1974 model. It was to be called Mustang II.

Iacocca had worked closely with Ben Bidwell, who had succeeded John Naughton as head of Ford Division, in determining what kind of small car the new Mustang should be. Their early inclinations were to produce it as a compact, the size of Maverick, five inches shorter than the original Mustang.

When the Capri, a subcompact, was introduced so successfully, Iacocca changed his mind. Germany could supply only a limited number of Capris per year, and if the young who flocked to buy it were so intrigued by its size, perhaps Mustang II should be sized as a subcompact as well. Surveys also bore out Iacocca's decision. Subcompact sales in 1970 far exceeded compact purchases.

Iacocca then made another decision. Circumstances in the

seventies were much different from those of the mid-sixties, when the first Mustang had made its bow. The car buyers of the seventies had become more sophisticated. Looks alone no longer would sell them. A letter received from a customer in Greenville, South Carolina, triggered Iacocca's thinking.

'I would like to suggest several things that I feel would increase the overall appeal of the new Mustang,' said the letter. 'The car should offer enough luxury such as AM/FM stereo, custom interior with cut-pile carpeting, complete instrumentation.'

Definitely, Iacocca decided, the car had to have shock value in its appointments. As with the first Mustang, it had to look more expensive than its sticker price. A check on the small cars that were selling the best strengthened his belief. Expensive Capris were selling as fast as dealers could get them. The more expensive models of Japanese imports such as the Datsun 240-Z and Toyota Celica were also outselling their cheaper counterparts.

Iacocca placed responsibility for making Mustang II a sporty subcompact in the image of the best-sellers on the shoulders of Hal Sperlick, his vice-president for product planning, who had played a major role in the development of the original Mustang.

Sperlick turned to one of the most famous automobile design studios in the world, the fifty-year-old Ghia studios at Turin, Italy, which had created bodies for Alfa Romeo, Porsche, Maserati, and Rolls Royce. It had also produced the most expensive Volkswagen, the Kharmann-Ghia.

Some weeks before Iacocca was promoted to president of Ford, he and Sperlick had flown to Italy to discuss their plans for Mustang II with Alejandro deTomaso, head of Ghia. They commissioned deTomaso to build a Ghia-styled, operable Mustang II with a European fastback look. Less than two months later, with Iacocca now president, the prototype arrived in Dearborn.

Ford's executives, used to the two- or three-year lapse between design and complete prototype, were amazed at the speedy production of the handsomely styled Mustang II, painted in a striking red and black, with a sloping rear that swept gracefully down from roof-line to bumper. Iacocca and others, including Sperlick, drove the Ghia model.

In late March deTomaso sent another model to Ford's Dearborn headquarters, this one in the traditional notchback styling that featured a squared rear window vertical to the rear deck. This second model brought on heavy debate among the designers, stylists, and planners. Should the new Mustang II be a fastback or a notchback? Both were attractive. The question was which would appeal more to the American public.

Following the procedure used in building the first Mustang, Iacocca put the various design studios to work making clay models of the 1974 Mustang as they perceived it based on the deTomaso cars. Within three months the four design groups had four clay models ready. Oddly, only one of the four had chosen to build a notchback, a model that offered much of the flair that distinguished the first Mustang. Of the three fastbacks submitted one stood out for its sportiness and overall features.

Iacocca would not make a final choice without getting some measure of public reaction. He had the fastback and notchback sent to San Diego for some buyer impressions of the two. There the preference was overwhelming in favour of the fastback.

Still not fully satisfied, Iacocca had another survey conducted at Anaheim, California. The car buyers there also made the fastback their odds-on choice. The fastback went into production with some minor styling changes.

The front end was modified to give it a wider grille, the top of which was even with the top of the headlamps. Iacocca also decided that side scoops, a distinctive feature of the first Mustang, should also be included in the new version.

Another decision was made to redesign the Mustang emblem, the galloping pony that graced the centre of the grille. Many Mustang buyers had complained that the original emblem did not have the excitement generated by the Mustangs of the old West and that the Mustang's legs were sculpted with an awkward gallop. A new, more faithful reproduction of a galloping Mustang was made for the new Mustang II.

Iacocca is like a proud father when it comes to one of his automobiles, fretting over it until its birth is finally achieved. So it was no surprise when he suddenly decided that one more survey of customer preference for fastback or notchback would be worthwhile. For a third study of buyer reaction to the cars he shipped two Mustangs, one fastback and one notchback, to San Francisco.

From the start he had had been intrigued with the notchback designed by deTomaso and could not get it out of his mind. He could put his worry to rest if San Franciscans, a different breed of buyers, agreed with those of San Diego and Anaheim.

They were different without question. The San Francisco judgment was a near 100 percent in favour of the spectacular notchback with lines so smoothly blended that it created the illusion of motion while standing.

The survey results did not bring about a total shift to the notchback. Iacocca felt certain that markets existed for both. Mustang II would be produced with a 50-percent mix of each. Once this decision was made, production for the first year was increased from 250,000 units to 300,000, with each body style available in two models.

The fastback, with its third door at the rear, would be offered as a four-passenger car with folding rear seats to provide storage space and as a performance-type sports car. The notchback would have two four-passenger models, one of which would offer special luxury features and be known as the Mustang Ghia, perhaps the most elegant subcompact available anywhere.

Iacocca's greatest concern as Mustang II took shape was its riding characteristics. He was determined that his new pony car be everything the public expected, and a smooth ride was essential. Small American cars, especially those powered by four-cylinder engines, had front-end suspensions incapable of absorbing the ups and downs of front wheels as they met bumps and dips in the road. He put his engineers to work on the problems.

In the midst of his worries over the riding comfort for the Mustang Lee sustained the most crushing blow of his life.

The father whom he loved and revered, and who had suffered for some years with leukaemia, suddenly died. Lee returned to Allentown immediately to console his mother and help arrange for Nick's funeral.

Following Nick's interment the spacious home he had built for Antoinette in Midway Manor was filled with friends and relatives of the Iacocca family as well as many of Lee's own friends and co-workers. Henry Ford himself had come from Grosse Pointe to pay his respects.

It was a strange Henry who was there, according to Antoinette Iacocca. He stood quietly during the after-burial gathering, the only man among the many mourners without a drink. Lee, according to his mother, came up to Henry.

'Henry,' Lee said – and it may have been the only time Iacocca ever addressed his chairman as other than Mr Ford – 'if my father could see you standing here without a drink in your hand, he would turn over in his grave.'

Lee felt the death of his father deeply and remained reserved and largely unapproachable for months after he returned to Dearborn. It was to be expected. Nick's part in Lee's life was more that of a beloved brother and friend than father.

Lee immersed himself in work. His engineers had solved his worries over the riding qualities of Mustang II by adopting a concept used for some expensive European cars. Called a 'subframe', it added the equivalent of a second miniframe, isolated from the body of the car. The front-suspension system worked off this subframe, not off the body itself, and took up the shocks occasioned by bumps and ruts, thus minimising their impact on driver and passenger.

On December 8, 1972, Iacocca test drove the Mustang II. He was satisfied. The car had a solid feel as well as a smoothness and quietness as it travelled over rough areas, an uncommon quality in a subcompact.

Mustang II was introduced to the public on September 21, 1973. For three weeks its sales spiralled upward. Then on Friday, October 19, the roof started to fall in on the American economy when Libya shut off all oil shipments to the United States because of American support for Israel in the Yom Kippur war.

The Libyan action began a domino effect as Saudi Arabia followed suit the next day, and on Sunday Kuwait and the emirates of Abu Dhabi and Qatar made the oil embargo complete. Gasoline pumps dried up. Long lines formed as service stations doled out what was becoming a precious fuel.

Although the automobile industry was hard hit, it had enjoyed nine months of escalating sales. Ford Motor Company had its best year ever, topping even 1972 by over 100,000 units sold. It was Lee Iacocca's third straight year of record-setting sales as president of the company.

The oil embargo made Lee Iacocca a prophet to be reckoned with. He, along with Hal Sperlick, had been preaching the need for small, more fuel-efficient cars for some years. Now big Detroit cars were being dubbed gas-guzzlers, and the average American shied away.

The cars selling best were Volkswagens, Toyotas, Hondas, and Datsuns. Overall it was, if only for a time, an all-out import market. Foreign-made cars, which already had dented American sales more heavily year by year, beat the great sales year of 1972 by about 200,000.

The only American dealership selling in at least fair numbers were those with foreign-made models. Among these were Lincoln-Mercury dealers with the European Capri, Buick with the German Opel, and Dodge with the Japanese Colt. Like the other foreign-made cars they offered twenty or more miles to a gallon.

It was not a happy new year for American car manufacturers as 1973 slipped into 1974; a year of disaster for the automobile market. General Motors dropped almost 1.5 million registrations. Ford fell back 500,000, Chrysler more than 300,000.

In self-defence the carmakers of America began to adopt the small-is-best philosophy. In this Iacocca already had built an edge for Ford. He had two beautifully styled, easy-on-the-gas cars ready in 1974, one for Ford Division and one for Lincoln-Mercury. Both were brought out on September 27, 1974, as 1975 models.

For Ford Division he had the Granada, a luxury-oriented small car with a Rolls Royce look in the front end. In fact it was merchandised as being as quiet as a Rolls, and television commercials showed decibel meters measuring the noise level in each. Built on the same chassis, but with a more expensive range of interior appointments, was the Mercury Monarch, with its 'Mercedes' appeal.

Even in the depressed market of 1974 Ford Granada racked up more than 150,000 sales in its first six months. The more expensive Mercury Monarch totalled 50,000 for the same period. Small was where the action was, and other makers began to fall in line with down-sized models. Even Cadillac got into the act with a car they named Seville, but at $14,000.

Along with Granada and Monarch a third new car was presented to the public on September 27, 1974. Not small in the manner of Monarch, but not large, the Ford Elite was on the 'smaller' side, with fair gas mileage. Iacocca had done his homework well in a year when America faced up to the fact that bigger was not the better way to car sales.

While Iacocca was showing his mettle on the automobile front, his boss was obviously having some trouble in the marital area. Henry being Henry, his difficulties with Cristina came with him to the Glass House. As 1975 got well under way the chairman of the Ford Motor Company reverted to his inexplicable harassment of his president.

CHAPTER 10

One morning early in 1975 the telephone rang in the office of Leo-Kelmenson, president of Kenyon & Eckhardt. He had no chance to complete his hello before the gravelly voice of Henry Ford II cut him off.

'Kelmenson, keep that son-of-a-bitch Winn the f— out of my company!'

The K & E president was shocked. Only a day or so earlier Kenyon & Eckhardt had added the Bill Winn promotion house as a subsidiary, and Winn had just completed staffing his organisation.

Henry did not give a reason, and before Kelmenson could react, Henry had slammed his phone back into its cradle. Startled and appalled by the brief explosion, Kelmenson replaced his own phone, bewildered.

He wondered if Henry was drunk. The one-sided conversation had been too brief to get a line on Henry's condition, but something certainly had happened to the Ford chairman. One thing was certain! Whatever caused Henry's action was hardly due to displeasure with Bill Winn or his work.

Winn, a quiet-demeanoured, kindly man, scrupulously honest, went about his work efficiently without making waves. He had proved himself an asset to the Ford Motor Company in producing shows that stimulated Ford and Lincoln-Mercury dealers to sales never before achieved. Whatever had evoked Henry's anger, his phone call was a cruel and harsh attack on a good man.

Most perplexing was the fact that Henry Ford had taken this indirect means of getting rid of Winn. One would expect the macho, second-best-to-nobody Henry to take his beef directly to Iacocca or to Winn himself. Passing the buck in this way, Henry reemphasised weakness in his character. His intention could have been nothing more than a secondhand demeaning of Iacocca.

Kelmenson could do nothing but call Iacocca and tell him they would have to get along without Winn in the future, even though the cost to Winn would be considerable. To defy Henry would mean the loss of Kenyon & Eckhardt's most valuable account.

Henry never did mention his axing of Bill Winn as a Ford Motor Company supplier to Iacocca, yet he must have realised the shabbiness of his action. However, three years passed before he recanted his dismissal of Winn, and even then it was not done directly.

Doug McClure had taken over the marketing position at Ford. Aware of Winn's contributions to the company, he asked Henry's brother, William Clay Ford, to intercede on Winn's behalf. Bill Ford succeeded in softening Henry, but again it was not Henry who delivered the news. McClure himself talked to Kelmenson and Iacocca. Bill Winn was restored to a persona grata status at Ford.

Lee, naturally, was grieved at the injustice done his friend, but, like Kelmenson, he could do nothing about it at the time. With so much work ahead he buried his anger in efforts to minimise the company's losses in the depressed economy of the mid-seventies.

As the oil embargo passed into history, it left after effects that, combined with the stringent government standards for control of emissions, had a crippling effect on the industry. Gasoline prices maintained an upward spiral that helped bring about double-digit inflation. Rising car prices added to the problem.

Gerald Ford of Michigan had taken over the country's highest office after Richard Nixon's resignation over the Watergate scandal. Ford, determined to lower gasoline consumption and help halt the rising inflation, succeeded in setting a nationwide speed limit on automobiles to conserve gasoline use. People began to drive less and to buy fewer cars. Then, as unsold cars piled up, the automakers laid off workers by the thousands, further damaging an already sick economy.

By the first of March, 1975, nearly 135,000 General Motors workers and over 120,000 at Ford and Chrysler were on the streets without jobs. This was just the tip of the iceberg; throughout the country other industries dependent on the automobile business also cut their work forces.

However unfavourable the market was, scrapping existing plans would mean added losses. On March 21 Lee Iacocca brought out his newest small car, a Lincoln-Mercury Division counterpart of the Ford Pinto, the Mercury Bobcat. As might be expected, its sales were not spectacular, but they did help Mercury show an increase over the previous year, while Ford Division fell back a quarter-million units. Bobcat provided one more small, fuel-conserving automobile for Lee Iacocca's stable.

Other than in meetings or an occasional pass-by in the corridors, there had been little personal contact between Iacocca and Henry Ford since Henry's rash and unreasonable expulsion of Bill Winn. Iacocca, for one, preferred it that way. Now, however, the need to protect one of his most capable and loyal protégés made it necessary to see the chairman of the board.

Iacocca had sensed for some time that Henry was disenchanted with Hal Sperlick, who had backed Lee in his battles to downsize Ford cars. Having Sperlick away from Henry's daily view would be safer, and besides, in Lee's opinion his good right hand deserved a promotion.

Iacocca resolved to put Sperlick in charge of Ford's extensive overseas operations with headquarters in London, the one area of Ford operations that had shown a substantial profit in 1974 and was well on its way to help save 1975. Lee would need Henry Ford's approval for the appointment.

Lee sought out his boss and made a good case for Sperlick, but Henry would have none of it. Then, without Iacocca's knowledge, Ford named Philip Caldwell, a quiet uncontroversial man loyal to Henry to fill the post. Iacocca bit his lip.

Customarily the chairman, president, and other high officers of Ford joined a new overseas head in London on the occasion of his taking over his new duties. Since the wives and families of those concerned were usually invited, Lee arrived in London with Mary, Kathy, and Lia.

One evening four couples, including the Iacoccas, were at dinner at the Caldwells' London home. While the elders dined together Iacocca's two daughters ate in the library. After dinner the ladies left the men to their cigars and brandy. Mary Iacocca went into the library to see how the children were.

Sometime later, as Mary stood in the library, Henry entered and from behind put his arms around her and nuzzled her neck.

'Mary, have I ever told you,' Henry whispered in her ear, 'what your husband has done for us? He has done more to help the Ford Motor Company than anybody ever.'

Mary Iacocca was dumbfounded. Here was the chairman of the Ford Motor Company, a man who was often denigrating her husband, telling her what a great man Lee was. Henry had had more than a little to drink, as she could tell from his breath.

In recounting the incident years later Mary Iacocca said: 'My mother told me when I was quite young that the truth always comes out when a man has had too much to drink.' But she could not understand why, if Henry were indeed telling the truth while drunk, he had been treating Lee as he had.

Lee had walked into the library while Henry still had his arms around Mary and suggested that it was time to go.

'I'm talking to Mary,' Henry said to Lee over his shoulder, 'and when I'm finished, you can go.'

When the Iacoccas were settled in their limousine, eleven-year-old Lia blurted out: 'Daddy! Did you see Mommy with Mr Ford? If you saw him keep kissing her on the neck, you'd divorce Mommy!'

The two faces of Henry Ford were always difficult to fathom, according to Mary Iacocca. Sober or not, when he

167

was with other Ford people his innuendos often cut Lee down, as they would hear later from friends. But with the Iacoccas at any social or business gathering, after a few drinks he would describe Lee as the saviour of the Ford Motor Company.

'One time Henry was in Texas,' Mary recounted, 'and our phone rang at three o'clock in the morning. The phone was beside my bed so I grabbed it. "Is Lee there?" Henry asked. I said, "Who is this?" He said, "Henry." I knew very well who Henry was, but I said, "Henry who?" Then he continued talking to me, telling me he was going to write me a letter to let me know what Lee had done for the company and what a great man he was. I never did get the letter.'

As 1975 moved towards its close, it became obvious that Henry Ford's inner agitation over his home life was taking its toll. He was as irascible in his Glass House suite as in his Grosse Pointe mansion. His marriage to Cristina had been damaged by the Kathy DuRoss affair to such an extent that a formal announcement of separation became inevitable.

It was first made public by a columnist in the *New York Daily News* and confirmed the same afternoon by Henry's lawyer. Ford himself was away on an overseas trip with Kathy DuRoss at the time, and the Glass House buzzed with anticipation of what might happen once Henry returned.

Henry did not keep people guessing for long after his return to Dearborn. He barged into Iacocca's office one morning. 'Get rid of Sperlick!' he told Lee. 'I don't want him around here.'

It is reported that without another word he charged out the door, leaving Iacocca stupefied, not only by the demand that Lee fire one of his most capable aides, but also by the inexplicable speed with which he came in and went out.

For Iacocca it was both a shock and a bitter pill, and he lacked the heart to relay such devastating news to someone with so much talent, ability, and professionalism, and whom he had admired so much. He called in Bill Bourke, one of Henry's partisans, and had him tell Sperlick. The outspoken Sperlick took his expertise in the development of small cars and joined the Chrysler Corporation.

If it had not occurred to him earlier, Iacocca now had little doubt that Henry Ford was out to get him and was using every trick possible to pressure him into resigning. If so, Henry underestimated Iacocca's strongmindedness. He had lived by his father's dictum never to quit, and to do so under such circumstances would play into Henry's hands.

Grim-faced and resolute, Iacocca went about his responsibilities and had a down-sized and comparatively inexpensive luxury-type car ready for release in the fall of 1976, the 1977 Ford LTD II. And three others were on the drawing boards for 1977 introduction, one – the Lincoln Versailles as competition for Cadillac Seville – to be shown to the public in April.

An upward turn in the economy was reversing the sales slump of the previous year. Especially heartening to Iacocca was the Mercury and Lincoln sales figures, which matched their best years ever. But the potential increase in Ford profits seemed to have no effect on Henry's determination to get Iacocca to leave.

Henry initiated an investigation into Iacocca's personal and business life and had the respected law firm that handled Ford Motor Company matters conduct the probe.

Iacocca was furious when he became aware of Henry's order, but kept quiet, confident it would prove to be a wild goosechase.

Henry had his investigators request a review of the J. Walter Thompson advertising agency books. According to a former executive of the agency, JWT refused permission, and as a result Henry took away their budget for small-car promotion and gave it to Grey Advertising, only to give it back to JWT a year or so later, after the books were checked and revealed nothing helpful.

Bill Fugazy's office in New York was bugged and broken into. Henry was convinced that because Fugazy got so much business from Iacocca and other Ford executives he was funnelling part of his profits back to men he dealt with.

The investigators dug up nothing, a boner on Henry's part that cost Ford Motor Company more than $1.5 million. That nonbusiness expenditure soon would come back to haunt

Henry in a lawsuit brought against him by his nephew, Benson Ford II.

The American automobile industry was buzzing over Henry Ford's incomprehensible doings. As chairman of the board of Ford Motor Company and a man in control of enough stock to wield dictatorial powers, it was inconceivable that he would resort to such tactics. A strong man, as he was reputed to be, would have just fired Lee Iacocca without need for a reason. He certainly had done it to others often enough in the past.

Iacocca became so angered at Henry's tactics that he discussed his problems on several occasions with individual members of the board of directors. Most of them were strongly in Lee's corner. The most supportive was Henry's own brother, William Clay Ford.

The directors with whom Lee talked suggested patience. They knew Henry's vacillating and vindictive nature and listened politely to his unsubstantiated charges. As one director said: 'Henry would come on with a blazing cannon, but he'd leave with a peashooter.'

Henry obviously was willing to try anything that might outrage Iacocca enough to make him quit when he came up with another blow below the belt. Having failed to discover any skulduggery in Lee's business dealings with Bill Fugazy, Henry did what many around the Glass House had predicted he would do. He demanded that Iacocca dissolve Fugazy's agreement with the Ford Motor Company.

Bill Fugazy, who operated a limousine service in the New York City area, had proved himself as friendly and loyal to Ford as to Iacocca. Thirteen years earlier Fugazy had made Lincoln Continentals the backbone of his own fleet.

'I had expected it for some time,' Fugazy said. 'Henry always used the back door when he came down on somebody stronger than he was.'

The situation became so ludicrous, according to one minor executive still at Ford, that a few men were making book on who would crack first, Henry or Lee. The payoff was made when Henry was struck down with angina and hospitalised for almost two weeks.

Henry's sudden attack of angina pectoris did not result from the tension between him and Iacocca, though that may have contributed. Henry for years had suffered from a heart condition. His high living and heavy drinking didn't help – nor did the scandal leading to his separation from Cristina, the stormy months preceding the breakup of their marriage, the problems that had surfaced in his running the vast Ford complex, as well as the hitches in his pet community-service project.

One such problem inside the company concerned the number of Pintos and Bobcats whose gasoline tanks had burst into flames after rear-end collisions. While the problem was kept secret within the Glass House for some time, deaths resulting from a number of the collisions brought it into the open.

Henry's extracurricular activities also played a part in his problems. He enjoyed the front-page newspaper stories and television interviews that heralded him as the saviour of Detroit, but he had been called to task for diverting company funds into the project, which, on paper at least, was his personal baby.

Henry had also used the vast buying power of the Ford Motor Company to influence suppliers to help bail out the Renaissance project when more financing was needed to complete its construction. Many of the companies who did business with Ford complained to the press – with names withheld, of course. Henry's image was thus further tarnished.

Whichever of his worries, singly or in combination, caused the heart attack, it must have made Henry think more seriously about the future of his company. If something happened to him, it might well mean the end of family control.

His brother Benson also had a heart problem and was seldom seen around the Glass House. His other brother, William Clay, was more interested in his Detroit Lions professional football team than in automobiles, and while Bill still attended board meetings and maintained a cursory interest in company affairs, he had made it clear in an interview with the automotive writer for the *Detroit News* that he would not want to actually run the Ford Motor Company. He would accept the chairmanship, he told the reporter, if it meant 'simply serving as chairman, chairing the company and shareholders' meetings.'

Henry also had to face the possibility that the post would not be offered to his brother. William was such a staunch supporter of Iacocca's that, having made it clear he would not run the company, operations would definitely be in Iacocca's hands. That was something Henry could not abide, especially since he realised also that his son Edsel was too young and inexperienced to have much of chance with the board.

In mid-May of 1977 Henry watered down Iacocca's authority by naming Philip Caldwell vice-chairman of the board, thus placing his own man, and one who had been reporting to Lee, between himself and his president. Henry then restored the troika, creating a triumvirate to operate the company under the broad title of 'Office of the Chief Executive.' It would consist of himself, Caldwell, and Iacocca.

If Henry expected this new slap to drive Iacocca into a resignation, he was again mistaken. Lee was still determined to stay on, at least for another two years, when he would be fifty-five and qualify for his pension.

The manoeuvre that dropped him a rung down the ladder was a cheap shot in Iacocca's eyes as well as in those of other executives within Ford. Nor did the media treat Henry kindly for this move.

The next day Iacocca brought out the new Lincoln Versailles. To the automotive writers he presented his usual genial public self, telling them that his new small luxury car would give Cadillac's Seville a run for its money. He uttered no word of recrimination, only enthusiasm for a new product.

Iacocca, however, pulled no punches with Henry. He let him know that the troika had not worked before and would not work now. He called it a three-headed monster that would not be able to make the decisions necessary to keep Ford afloat in the government-controlled atmosphere of the times. Henry shrugged him off. He was the boss, and the decision had been made.

Iacocca had expected nothing else, and as always he went back to his work. Already in production and scheduled to be released in the fall were two cars of special significance for him. Though they would be presented under his aegis as president of Ford, they were two of the last three for which his staunch supporter, Hal Sperlick, was responsible.

One was the Ford Fairmont, the other the Mercury Zephyr. Introduced on October 7, 1977, they were small yet roomy enough to be ideal family cars. The kind of automobiles Iacocca and Sperlick had been fighting for, their styling was fresh, and they offered good mileage. Sperlick's third offering would be the Ford Fiesta, the first front-wheel-drive offered by Ford in America.

Fairmont and Zephyr were as warmly accepted as Iacocca hoped, helping Ford Division to enjoy its best sales year since Mustang II's bow in 1973. But even more heartening were the 1977 record-setting numbers for Lincoln-Mercury Division. And sales for both Lincoln and Mercury attained an even higher return in the early months of 1978.

Ford Division, however, was not quite so fortunate. Sales decreased slightly from the previous year, beginning a worrisome downward slide that would last into the eighties. The culprit was Pinto, whose sales plummeted because of its gas-tank fires and the resultant bad publicity.

Henry could have used the Pinto problem as an excuse to get rid of Iacocca, but no dout he realised he also had to shoulder some of the responsibility. He held the purse strings, and a few dollars more per car would have provided a different and safer gas tank. Instead of getting rid of Iacocca altogether early in June, 1978, Henry dropped him another notch down the ladder.

Henry named William Clay Ford as chairman of the executive committee while still maintaining the troika setup. In effect this dropped Iacocca another step in the pecking order, making him fourth to Henry, William Clay, and Philip Caldwell.

As if to make Lee Iacocca more aware of the hopelessness of his future at Ford, Henry also announced to the press that he would give up his post as chief executive officer of the company at the 1980 annual stockholders' meeting and retire as chairman of the board no later than 1982. Under this new line of authority William Clay Ford would succeed him as chairman of the board in 1982, and Philip Caldwell would take over as chief executive officer.

This further undercutting of Iacocca's position did not alter Lee's determination to stick it out. Working under Caldwell would not be his cup of tea, but he felt that things would change for the better once Bill Ford became top man. Nor did Lee permit this latest setback to lessen his pleasure in anticipating the graduation of his eighteen-year-old daughter, Kathy, from the highly regarded Kingswood School.

It is a Kingswood tradition during graduation week festivities that the parents of one of the graduates host an after-midnight party called 'Afterglow' following the senior prom. The hosts in 1978 were the Robert McGregors, whose daughter Molly was a classmate of Kathy Iacocca's. (Ironically, Bob McGregor was then head of the Detroit office of a San Francisco-based advertising agency that worked for Chrysler Corporation.)

The McGregor home grounds were not spacious enough to accommodate the huge tent usually erected to house the Kingswood seniors and their dates and parents. Even though Mary Iacocca was ill at the time, she and Lee volunteered the broad expanse outside their home on Edgemere Court.

Lee Iacocca was the proud father rather than the beleaguered president of the Ford Motor Company throughout the early-morning hours of the Afterglow party. He entertained the fathers inside and helped serve the young guests mountains of food outside. At 5:30 that morning he was laughing and joking at the kitchen sink as he washed dishes with the help of Bob McGregor.

Lee spent the few weeks following quietly and uneventfully at his Glass House desk. Henry was away most of the time, and Lee was occupied with plans for the fall television spectacular commemorating the seventy-fifth anniversary of the founding of the Ford Motor Company. There were many conferences with Leo-Arthur Kelmenson and other Kenyon

& Eckhardt people charged with supervising production of the star-studded two-hour programme to be titled 'A Salute to American Imagination.'

Wednesday, July 12, Lee was aware of the presence of Henry Ford in the suite next to his, but they had no contact throughout the day. Lee left for home about six-thirty, unaware that Henry had called an emergency meeting of the board of directors for that evening. Usually Lee took part in such meetings, but this session with the board was to be highly unusual.

That evening loud, angry voices echoed from the boardroom in the penthouse above the twelfth floor of the Glass House. Henry, as chairman, demanded that the board approve his firing of Lee Anthony Iacocca. Most of the board members argued against such a move. Henry's brother, William Clay, and George Bennett – representing a Boston investment house that held a great many Ford loans – were most vehement in their arguments against Henry's proposal.

The debate continued for over an hour with neither the board nor Henry giving ground. Finally Henry gave the directors an ultimatum.

'It's either him or me!' he shouted.

The board gave in.

Later that evening Lee Iacocca recradled the phone after his conversation with Keith Crain and turned to his wife. 'It may be all over tomorrow,' he said.

The following afternoon he again hung up a telephone, this time in his Glass House suite after hearing his secretary's words: 'Mr Ford wants to see you in his office.'

His face grim, Iacocca walked the few feet down the corridor to the suite in the southeast corner and entered. Ford's secretary glanced at him for a moment, then looked away as she told him to go right in.

(The following scene in Mr Ford's office is a recreation based on knowledge privy to various individuals close to both Ford and Iacocca. To some degree it is a fictionalised overview of the meeting.)

Lee turned the knob and walked into the plush surroundings of Henry's inner sanctum. Henry was seated behind his desk. In the background, making no effort to hide his feelings, stood teary-eyed William Clay Ford. Obviously Henry's younger brother had been making a last-ditch effort on Iacocca's behalf.

As Lee closed the door, Bill Ford's choked voice entreated in low tones, 'Don't do it, Henry.'

Iacocca had barely taken a step inside the office when Henry, ignoring his brother, barked: 'You're fired.'

Iacocca froze momentarily but recovered quickly and continued toward Henry's desk. He took a chair, determined not to leave without making Henry squirm a little. Lee, with deliberation, took a cigar from his pocket and lit it.

'Why are you doing this, Mr Ford?' he asked finally.

When Henry merely glared, Iacocca took a puff on his cigar.

William Ford's voice came from the back of the room. 'Henry, you've got to give him an answer.'

Henry, looking at Iacocca, said: 'I just don't like you!'

Henry Ford II denied this account months later in an interview with Barbara Walters on ABC television.

'Did you fire him just because you didn't like him?' Walters asked Henry on camera.

'Well, that's been said,' Henry answered, 'but that isn't true. He said to me, as I recall, "why are you doing this? Don't you like me?" and as far as I can remember, I didn't answer the question.'

The morning after the confrontation in Henry's office, the usual bland excuses for a sudden, and requested, resignation were fed to the press at a news conference. Reporters, wise in the ways of business, did not believe that a friendly parting of the ways had come about.

One newspaper columnist, Nicholas Von Hoffman wrote: '. . . the firing of Iacocca has the look of an act of spite, by a petulantly selfish rich kid.' Newspapers across the country covered the event under big headlines. Radio and television reports made it their lead story. Walter Cronkite, the dean of television newsmen, relating the axing of Lee Iacocca to such sensational books about the automobile business as *Wheels* and *The Betsy*, told the public on his CBS news broadcast, 'It sounds like something from one of those enormous novels about the automobile industry.'

The automobile industry itself was stunned, even though Henry had shown himself to be a fractious individual who had not hesitated in the past to dump Ford presidents on what were perceived to be impulses. But Lee Iacocca had outserved them all. In his thirty-fourth year with the company, almost eight as president, and with his tremendous record of achievement, if any man should have felt secure, it was Lee Iacocca.

As for Lee himself, one of his closest friends says that on his way home from the Glass House that Thursday afternoon his reaction had been one of relief. 'Thank God that bullshit is over,' he had said to himself.

For Henry Ford II it must have been a different matter. He had some concerns about his action, and perhaps a touch of conscience. Whatever his thoughts, it seems he may have drunk a little more than usual that night.

Sometime around three o'clock the next morning he called the residence of Walter Murphy, the Ford vice-president for public relations and an Iacocca ally. Murphy, who had spent almost as many years with the Ford Motor Company as Iacocca, was awakened from a deep sleep. He picked up the receiver and was given hardly a chance to speak.

'Walter,' said the blurred but unmistakable voice of the Ford chairman, 'do you like Iacocca?'

Murphy, though still not fully awake, answered without hesitation. 'Why, yes, Mr Ford,' he said. 'I do like and respect Mr Iacocca.' 'Then you're fired!' was the responding blast, followed by the slam of the phone.

If Henry had followed through immediately on Murphy's dismissal, Walter would have been deprived of the pension for which he would be eligible in April, 1979. Ford, however, showed some compassion in this instance, allowing Murphy to remain at work until the first of December, after which he would be put on leave until his pension became active.

Iacocca did not receive such consideration. His separation from the Ford Motor Company was set for mid-October, three months after the fateful confrontation. Then, as if to remind the former president of Ford that he was persona non grata around the Glass House, he was assigned a desk in a cubicle at the Ford parts facility on Detroit's Telegraph Road.

It was a needless further abasement of a man who had loved the Ford Motor Company and had worked hard to make it a success. The new office not only embittered Iacocca all the more, but also had other Ford executives muttering imprecations about their chairman. As one Ford vice-president put it: 'If this kind of thing could happen to as big a man as Iacocca, what security did any of us have?'

One somewhat embarrassing aspect to Henry's ridding himself of Iacocca resulted from its timing. Lee had been preparing for the introduction of his newest Mustang, the 1979 downsized pony car. Press kits promoting the Mustang subcompact had already been sent to automotive writers. Featured in them was a picture of Iacocca beside his newest car and smiling proudly. Henry sent Bill Bourke scurrying to retrieve the brochures featuring Iacocca.

Closing the books on Lee Iacocca was not as simple for Henry as in the case of Walter Murphy. Iacocca's contract and his stock options gave him great leverage towards a substantial settlement with the company. To handle the details Lee engaged the services of one of the country's great attorneys, Edward Bennett Williams of Washington, D.C.

Williams did a masterful job for Iacocca. When the haggling ended, he had a separation agreement that called for Ford to pay Lee Iacocca one million dollars per year until the end of 1980. The sole proviso was that Lee not work for any automobile company in competition with the Ford Motor Company.

This restriction meant little to Iacocca in the early weeks after the firing ordeal. He was tired of the rat race, and a long rest was beautiful to contemplate. He could spend more time with his wife, whose condition, while fairly stable, had not improved appreciably. He could give more attention to his daughters. And he had no worries about money. Even without the severance settlement, Iacocca was already well off.

Once the axe had fallen, Lee's most distressful moments

were those spent trying to understand the fickleness of one-time friends. Men he had worked with closely, vice-presidents and others he had appointed to responsible positions, many J. Walter Thompson advertising executives he had worked with – fearful of recrimination from Henry Ford – abandoned him, afraid to be seen with him publicly for fear of losing their jobs.

At dinner one night with Leo-Arthur Kelmenson, Lee saw Max Fisher, a wealthy Detroit real estate developer, local entrepreneur, and bosom friend of Henry Ford in the same restaurant.

Kelmenson, still involved with the Ford Motor Company as president of its Lincoln-Mercury agency, joked about Fisher's presence with Iacocca. 'Now,' he said, 'we can expect Max to run to Henry and tell him Leo was having dinner with Lee.'

'Don't you care?' Lee asked.

'I don't give a damn,' Kelmenson answered.

Expanding on the incident, Kelmenson later said, 'Many of us valued our friendship with Iacocca more than we valued any reprisals by Henry Ford.'

Henry Ford II had always been irritated by Iacocca's socialising with people he did business with, some of whom were among Lee's closest friends. 'Mr Ford used to criticise Lee for having too many friends in the business,' says Kelmenson. 'Lee's response to Ford was, "When you work twenty hours a day, when do you have time to develop friends who are not in the business?"'

Kelmenson was one of the first friends with whom Iacocca talked at length after the firing. The following weekend the Iacocca family were guests at the Kelmenson home on Long Island. After dinner on Saturday Iacocca and Kelmenson sat on the deck facing the sea talking about Lee's future plans.

Iacocca told Kelmenson that he was going to do nothing for a while. He was going to take time to think. After so long on an emotional roller coaster, he needed to clear his mind. Yet, as the conversation progressed – mostly reflections on what had happened and how – one thing became clear to Kelmenson. The life of the idle rich was not for Lee Iacocca.

One way or another he had to keep moving.

'I was, of course, a very prejudiced listener,' Kelmenson said. 'Because I felt that of all the things that Henry Ford had ever done, firing Lee was no doubt the most ill advised.'

They sat looking out at the Atlantic for hours, with 'Lee fantasising about the future of the automobile industry,' Kelmenson added. 'Lee felt that there had to be a whole new concept in the manufacturing, sales, and distribution of automobiles. He was gone from Ford, but he was still living and breathing the business.'

Back home in Bloomfield Hills Iacocca could not help but begin to sense a void. He missed the early-morning drives to Dearborn and the challenges that faced him each day. He had never cared much for golf, so his days would not be filled in the way of so many of his retired contemporaries. And the daytime hours were the ones most difficult to fill. Evenings friends could visit or be visited. He spent many hours reminiscing and pondering the future with Bill Winn.

One evening in early October Iacocca received a phone call from J. Richardson Dilworth, a director of Chrysler Corporation and investment counsellor to the Rockefellers of New York. Chrysler, Dilworth told Lee, was on the verge of bankruptcy. Would he consider bringing it back to life?

Lee was well aware of Chrysler's mounting difficulties, as was everyone involved with the automobile industry. It was a stew pot of seething toil and trouble to which an ordinary man would not give a second thought. Iacocca, no doubt itching to get back in harness, told Dilworth that he would like to think about it.

Over the next week or two he discussed the situation with his closest friends, Winn and Kelmenson. The more they talked, the more surely Chrysler seemed an impossible situation. Did he dare jeopardise his hard-earned reputation as an automobile marketing genius by taking on an almost certain failure?

There was, he told his wife one evening, an overriding factor that could not be ignored. To let Chrysler go down the drain without doing everything possible to save it would add hundreds of thousands of workers to the unemployment rolls. It would also have a devastating effect on the city of Detroit, already in dire straits, as well as the state of Michigan and the nation as a whole.

When John Riccardo, Chrysler's chairman of the board, called Iacocca at Dilworth's suggestion, Lee agreed to discuss the matter. He talked to Riccardo, to other members of the Chrysler board, to Winn and to Kelmenson, even though Kelmenson was still involved with the Ford Motor Company as president of its Lincoln-Mercury and corporate advertising agency. Their personal friendship obviated any accusation of unethical conduct.

Should he or shouldn't he? The decision pulled Iacocca emotionally this way and that. For one thing, not enough time had passed since his release from Henry Ford's whirlpool of controversy for him to savour and enjoy a little peace of mind.

Then, too, there was his pride. Should he take a chance on an impossible job when other fine offers outside the automobile industry were being handed to him? His ego also had its say. He was confident that if anybody could do it, he could, and what great satisfaction there would be in putting a few more grey hairs into the head of Henry Ford II. It was already an open secret that the Ford Motor Company itself was in trouble.

And there was his settlement with Ford. If he took on the presidency at Chrysler, he was not only inheriting a can of worms deemed unsalvageable by many of the best economic brains in the country, he would also be forfeiting more than $2 million guaranteed by Ford.

In the end all the negatives were overridden by two factors. One, he was an automobile man pure and simple. He could be happy in no other business. Even more important was the catastrophic effect on the American economy if hundreds of thousands of workers who depended on Chrysler lost their jobs in one fell swoop.

On November 2, 1978, John Riccardo introduced Lee Iacocca as the new president and chief operating office of the deficit-ridden Chrysler Corporation.

CHAPTER 11

Chrysler Corporation had not always been the frail and feeble third among the big three of the automobile industry. In 1936 Chrysler had catapulted past Ford into second place and held on through 1949, thanks to the engineering genius of its founder, Walter Chrysler, the first Henry Ford's floundering management, and the tottering empire Ford left his grandson.

Unlike William Durant and the first Henry Ford, who established the other two automotive giants, Walter P. Chrysler was not only a farsighted engineering wizard, but also a tough, no-nonsense, innovative marketer of automobiles. In this he was much like Lee Iacocca.

Walter Percy Chrysler was born April 2, 1875, in Wamego, a small town in east-central Kansas. He was the son of an engineer for a Union Pacific passenger train, who moved his family 500 miles west to Ellis, Kansas, when Walter was about five years old. Young Walter's greatest pleasure was riding in the steam engine's cab with his father, an enjoyment that planted the seed for his love of engineering.

While still in high school he worked in the Union Pacific railroad shops, beginning as an engine cleaner. He didn't hesitate when he was offered a job as a machinist apprentice. He advanced to machinist when an opportunity arose in Wellington, a somewhat larger town in southern Kansas.

At the age of twenty-six he returned to Ellis to marry Della

Forker, his high school sweetheart. It was now 1901, and with all the interest in internal combustion engines throughout the country Walter Chrysler went with the tide. On a visit to the Chicago Auto Show he fell in love with a $5,000 Locomobile.

Though he had only $700, the enterprising Chrysler bought the car, borrowing the needed $4,300 from a banking friend. He disassembled the car's engine, examined its components and their function carefully, then put it back together again. He became an automobile enthusiast on the spot, deciding that if automobile engines were designed and built with the same precision as a steam locomotive engine, the four-wheel vehicle indeed would supplant the horse and buggy.

As a stepping-stone to entering the still fledgling automobile industry, Chrysler took a job as plant manager for the Providence, Rhode Island, subsidiary of the American Locomotive Works. The plant was building replicas of the French Berliet, chain-driven, four-cylinder machines with twenty-four and forty horsepower that were sold under the name Alco. With Chrysler in charge of the plant, the Alco was given a shaft drive in 1907. In 1909 the most famous Alco was produced, a sixty-horsepower six that won the Vanderbilt Cup race in both 1909 and 1910. The Alco passed from the scene in 1913, but by then Walter Chrysler had gone on to better things.

While at the Alco plant Chrysler had met James J. Storrow, a director of the American Locomotive Works who was also the chairman of the General Motors Finance Committee and president of a Boston banking house. Storrow had been brought in to General Motors to help salvage the company, which had been brought to the brink of bankruptcy by William Durant.

Chrysler accepted Storrow's offer of a job as assistant to Charles Nash, who headed the Buick facility of GM in Flint, Michigan. Chrysler started at Buick in 1912, when fewer than fifty Buicks per day were being built, a pitiful figure compared to the thousand and more produced daily by Ford. He brought to Buick a dedication for engineering precision and the moving assembly line initiated by Ford.

Within four years Walter Chrysler made Buick the most profitable division in General Motors and became its president and general manager. In 1916 Bill Durant regained control of General Motors and again started the giant on a downward slide by getting into unprofitable ventures such as the making of farm machinery and tractors. Chrysler fought Durant on these acquisitions in vain. Down the GM drain went $30 million. Chrysler, with a flamboyant personality, pride, a hot temper, and an equally hot vocabulary, gave Durant a blistering lecture and resigned.

Immediately Walter Chrysler was offered $1 million to save Willys-Overland, a car-manufacturing company that had suffered during the economic slow-down after World War I. Chrysler could not turn it down when he found that the Chicago banker who had lent him the money to buy his Locomobile was one of the men asking for help. Though it seemed an impossible task going in, Walter Chrysler restored Willys-Overland to profitability.

Even before he had finished his work at Willys-Overland, the same banking group asked Chrysler to take on the Maxwell, a popular car that was not selling as well as it once had because its axles often broke. Something needed to be done with the huge inventory of unsold Maxwells. Chrysler simply redesigned the axles, and Maxwell's reputation was saved, and the stockpiled cars were sold. After less than two years under Chrysler, Maxwell showed a profit of more than $2.5 million. The following year its profit level was $4 million.

Almost from the day Walter Chrysler purchased his Locomobile in Chicago, his dream had been to one day have an automobile-manufacturing company bearing his own name. He wanted to design automobiles that would, first and foremost, be examples of engineering excellence. The time was now ripe.

Chrysler had brought with him to Maxwell three brilliant young engineers who had helped him at Willys-Overland. They were Fred M. Zeder, Owen R. Skelton, and Carl Breer. Together the four of them began work on a new six-cylinder automobile featuring the high-compression type of engine

184

developed during the war. Zeder produced a six-cylinder with a high-compression cylinder head that offered seventy-miles-per-hour performance.

The 'Chrysler Six', as it was to be called, was also fitted with four-wheel hydraulic brakes, something unique and new to the American market, as well as aluminium pistons, shock absorbers, and oil filters that could be replaced. Chrysler had a prototype of his car ready for exhibit at the New York Auto Show in January, 1924, but auto-show officials denied Chrysler exhibit space because his car was not yet in production. Undaunted, he leased the lobby of the Commodore Hotel, where many newsmen were staying. The Chrysler Six, priced at $1,565, was so well received that a banking syndicate offered Walter a $5-million loan to start production. With so much power and styling at so low a price, Chrysler's car gave buyers the feeling of driving a far more expensive car. In twelve months 32,000 were sold, setting an industry record of $50 million in sales within one year.

In 1925 Walter P. Chrysler bought out Maxwell and discontinued its name, forming the Chrysler Corporation with its headquarters in Highland Park, Michigan, a suburb of Detroit. When profits neared $50 million in 1927, Chrysler expanded and modernised his factory facilities.

By 1928 the complete Chrysler line consisted of the seventy-horsepower Chrysler Six, the four-cylinder Chrysler 58, and a luxury model, the Imperial Six, priced at about $3,100. Walter was also planning to introduce a new, lower-priced model, the DeSoto.

In establishing his Chrysler Corporation Walter Chrysler surrounded himself with capable men. One was B. E. Hutchinson, who had been his treasurer at Maxwell. Hutchinson's first name was Bernice, which he detested, and so he insisted on being referred to by his initials. Another of Chrysler's team, one who had been with him at General Motors, was Kaufman T. Keller, who also disowned his first name and became known solely as K. T. Keller. Keller was placed in charge of manufacturing by Chrysler.

Hutchinson, tight-fisted when it came to expenditures,

pointed out that DeSoto could not be produced with cost-efficiency because the company, lacking facilities for forging iron and steel and making castings, had to buy many components. Until Chrysler Corporation could increase factory capacity, it would never be able to adequately compete with Ford, much less General Motors.

It would cost $75 million to bring facilities to efficient size, Hutchinson told Chrysler, and that would mean such a drain on cash reserves that DeSoto could not be produced at the low price hoped for. Chrysler feared that a delay in expansion would destroy any chance to move ahead in the industry. He decided that the only answer was a merger with another automobile maker.

A company-saving opportunity surfaced in 1928. The Dodge Brothers Company was for sale. After John and Horace had died in 1920 the company had been operated by their widows. Their management didn't work out and Dodge was then taken over by the prestigious New York investment firm of Dillon, Read. In May 1928, Clarence Dillon offered the Dodge name and facilities to Walter Chrysler.

The merging of Dodge into Chrysler Corporation was Walter Chrysler's greatest single achievement, even though the Dodge line still consisted of only its original four-cylinder model available as either a sedan or truck. The greatest asset in the Dodge acquisition was the company's huge facility in Hamtramck, another Detroit suburb not far from the Chrysler headquarters. It was one of the world's largest and most efficiently organised automobile factories, covering fifty-eight acres and employing a work force of 2,000. The moment the deal was consummated Chrysler appointed K. T. Keller as the Dodge production chief. Keller wasted no time. As he took control of Dodge on July 30, 1928, he had huge signs reading 'Chrysler Corporation – Dodge Division' strung across all entrance gates.

Walter Chrysler, earlier in the month of July, went into head-to-head competition with Henry Ford's Model A, the car brought out just eight months earlier as the successor to the Model T. Chrysler's new car, named Plymouth, was a six-cylinder, as against the Model A's four. It was rakishly styled in comparison with the Ford and was priced at $670.

'Chrysler has gone into the low-priced field with throttle wide open,' was *Time*'s reaction to Plymouth. Nonetheless it took about a year for the car to catch on, and then only after Chrysler demonstrated the reliability and performance of his six-cylinder engines to the world by entering two Plymouths in a race at LeMans. Neither won – an English Bentley finished first and an American Stutz second – but the two Plymouths did make remarkable showings, coming in third and fourth.

The acquisition of Dodge for about $70 million in Chrysler stock and the assumption of a Dodge debt that ran about $56 million made Chrysler Corporation the third largest automaker, behind General Motors and Ford. The added facilities also made it possible for Chrysler to break into a new segment of the market with the DeSoto, an automobile that represented the very latest in engineering.

Styled to resemble the Chrysler, its 21.6-horsepower engine was a side-valve six mounted on rubber insulators to reduce vibration. It was also equipped with full force-feed lubrication, four-wheel hydraulic brakes, a ribbon-styled chrome radiator, and rear-mounted spare tyre. DeSoto's 90,000 first year sales made 1929 a banner year for Walter Chrysler.

Chrysler and Dodge cars were as great successes in England as in the United States, with European car makers quickly copying the narrow-shell 'ribbon' type radiators that distinguished Chrysler cars. For 1931 Chrysler brought out two new straight eights and a new styling look reminiscent of the long, low Cord. One of the new eights was the 125-horsepower Imperial with a four-speed, silent third-gear transmission.

Experimentation and research were important to Walter Chrysler, but when the economy became seriously depressed after the Crash of '29, he considered closing the research department. He changed his mind when Harold Hicks, a research engineer who had come to Chrysler from Ford, described some recent experiments.

Hicks had become intrigued with automobile body

streamlining. He had discovered that when the body of a car was altered to provide a smoother airflow, the fuel consumption dropped and maximum engine speed increased.

'If that's what research can do,' Chrysler told Hicks, 'we will always have research.' For the rest of Walter Chrysler's life he believed strongly in the value of research. And it led to many innovations that helped Chrysler supplant Ford as America's number-two automaker.

Among these innovations were 'Floating Power', (which was achieved through the use of cushioned engine mounting), automatic clutches, synchromesh transmissions, and automatic overdrive.

Research was also responsible for one of Chrysler's greatest and most farsighted technical successes – which also proved its worst commercial failure – the controversial 'Airflow' design concept discovered in wind-tunnel tests. Chrysler researchers experimented with various makes and found that the cars were aerodynamically more efficient going backwards.

This discovery led to the Chrysler Airflow model, designed with a fully streamlined body and sloping front and rear ends, a styling that proved too extreme for the car buyers of the day. Even though the Chrysler Airflow joined Ford's Edsel as one of the great sales flops in automobile history, it did not halt Chrysler research. In 1937 an independent front suspension was developed, followed two years later by steering-column gear shift and fluid drive.

While Edsel put a crimp in Ford's challenge to General Motors, the Airflow's effect on Chrysler was negligible. It maintained its second-place share of the American market until 1950, when Ford again shot past Chrysler. By that time Walter Chrysler had passed from the scene, having died on August 18, 1940, of a cerebral hemorrhage.

The prolonged illness that led to Chrysler's death had impelled him to turn the company presidency over to K. T. Keller in July of 1935, while Chrysler held onto the post of board chairman. Keller had done such a magnificent job in coordinating Chrysler and Dodge production that the business world had expected the company to maintain the hard-won progress begun by Walter Chrysler.

Unfortunately Keller lacked the vision, patience, creativity, and tenacity of Chrysler. The corporation's downward slide, which culminated in the disastrous nosedive Lee Iacocca would be called upon to end a near half-century later, began during Keller's twenty-one-year control of the company.

World War II helped camouflage many of the Keller inefficiencies. In early 1942, Chrysler, in common with all American automakers, shut down civilian car production in favour of war matériel. K. T. Keller proved himself an organisation genius in supervising Chrysler's part in the war effort.

Chrysler Corporation had been designing, engineering, and producing military vehicles since 1934, building armoured cars capable of mobility and manoeuvrability under the most demanding conditions and over the most rugged terrain. In 1941 it was awarded a multitude of military contracts, including production of tanks in its newly built Detroit Tank Arsenal.

By 1942 Chrysler produced 2,486 twenty-nine-ton General Grant M-3 tanks and 2,388 of the famous thirty-two-ton Sherman tanks. Before the end of 1945 Chrysler's production of tanks in various designs and for a variety of uses reached 25,000. In addition Dodge Division's newly built plant near Chicago turned out an amazing 18,413 Wright Cyclone 2,200-horsepower engines designed for the B-29 Super-fortress.

Chrysler's war involvement under K. T. Keller was mind-boggling. It included production of 18,000 engines for the B-29s, 438,000 army trucks in various sizes, 60,000 Bofors anti-aircraft guns, more than 3 billion rounds of small-arms ammunition, almost 2 million 20-mm shells, 101,000 incendiary bombs, and 1,500 searchlight reflectors, which were ultimately replaced by 2,000 radar antennae units and mounts. Also included in this partial list were 100 miles of submarine nets, 20,000 land mine detectors, and 1,000 rail carloads of precision machinery for the gaseous-diffusion plant at the government's atomic bomb project at Oak Ridge, Tennessee.

President Harry S. Truman awarded Keller the Medal of Merit for his war work, then appointed him head of the United States guided-missile programme, an area in which Chrysler Corporation also played a prominent role.

The return to car production at Chrysler, as at all manufacturing companies, was a slow process. No new cars were on drawing boards, and time permitted only minor changes in the cars offered the public.

Ford and General Motors went to work planning new cars. Chrysler, under Keller, remained content to continue slightly changed models long after its competition brought out new models. After the production drought during the war Americans were eager to trade in their old models. With cars selling as fast as they reached dealer showrooms, Keller was in no hurry to make changes. Three sales-record-breaking years provided K.T.'s justification. In 1947 Chrysler profits were about $63 million, 1948 topped $89 million, and 1949 brought the company over $132 million.

K. T. Keller, the industry said, had a hat fetish. He was so seldom seen without a fedora covering his squarish-shaped head that the joke around Detroit was that he slept with his hat on. This hat obsession carried over into his car-design philosophy. Every car Chrysler built, he vowed, would have a roof high enough to permit a man with a hat to sit up straight in his seat.

'We build cars to sit in, not piss over,' was his rejoinder when asked why Chrysler's share of the American car market, which reached a high of 25.7 percent, gradually slipped to under 18 percent in 1950. During the same period Ford, with new V-8s sporting longer and lower silhouettes, shot up from from its low of 18 percent to 24 percent in 1950.

Keller's most serious blunder was his challenge to the United Auto Workers in 1949 and his refusal to accept the terms related to pension funding already agreed to by Ford and General Motors. The result was a 100-day strike beginning in January, 1950, that cost Chrysler Corporation over $1 billion in lost production. And in the end he was forced to accept a pension plan approximately the same as the one he had rejected.

Keller retired as president of Chrysler that same year, with Lester L. 'Tex' Colbert taking over. K.T., however, remained as chairman of the board and retained as firm a control over the company as he had as president.

Colbert had moved up to the corporate presidency after serving as president of Dodge Division for four years, after which he was elected a vice-president and director of Chrysler Corporation. While at Dodge he had been concerned by the lack of styling that resulted from Fred Zeder's obstinacy and B. E. Hutchinson's tight grip on finances. As he took over the corporation presidency on November 3, 1950, he quickly discovered that making any policy decision called for a battle with Keller and Hutchinson.

Colbert fought for $900 million to modernise Chrysler's antiquated plants. Determined to show Keller the far-ranging weaknesses in the corporation, he hired McKinsey and Company, one of the nation's most respected consulting firms, to do an in-depth study of Chrysler operations. When the study was completed, he had all the ammunition he needed.

The McKinsey report criticised the design and engineering policies of Keller and Zeder and emphasised the need for cars that were competitive in performance and appearance. It also underlined the vital need of Chrysler Corporation for international expansion.

Colbert's plans were given a boost in 1953 when B. E. Hutchinson retired. Then, by hiring away from Studebaker a forward-thinking designer named Virgil Exner, he negated the Zeder influence on styling.

Keller retired in 1956, and Colbert assumed the role of chairman as well as president. In midyear Exner revealed a new 'Fleet Sweep' styling that incorporated rear-end fins. The 1957 models were attractive enough to boost sales.

The US government had maintained the Keller-started military involvement with Chrysler Corporation by bringing the company into America's missile and space activity. Begun in 1952 with only twenty-six engineers, it was by 1956 the most profitable segment of the corporation. It produced the Redstone and Jupiter missile systems that would later act as vehicles in the many 'firsts' achieved by the American space programme. Chrysler Space Division later engineered and built the Saturn, one of which sent up the first Apollo manned flight.

Chrysler's space and defence contracts helped keep the company afloat with Tex Colbert at the helm, although a succession of tragedies in 1956 hurt the corporation considerably. Three of the company's most important officers died within six months: Carl Snyder, vice-president for manufacturing, in a plane crash; George Troost, vice-president for finance, after brain surgery; and Cecil Thomas, vice-president for international affairs, to gangrene. Colbert had a difficult time filling their posts, but one replacement, Lynn Townsend, who took over finance, would play a major role in Chrysler's future troubles.

However he tried, Colbert was unable to halt the Chrysler slide. He enjoyed a short period of success in 1957, when his fin-designed cars produced a profit of more than $125 million, but the euphoria was short-lived. The cars had been produced without sufficient testing in order to make their introduction date, and the result was a torrent of complaints.

The cherished reputation of a company dependable for engineering excellence was blemished. Chrysler sales dropped so low in 1958 that the year showed a loss of about $130 million. In market share the company dropped to 14 percent, while Ford pulled away to over 26 percent.

On April 28, 1960, Colbert, now desperate, named William C. Newberg as president. But Newberg had stock in companies that supplied Chrysler, and he became a target at the 1960 stockholders' meeting. Charged with conflict of interest, he was deposed within two months of his appointment.

Colbert, thoroughly disoriented by the turn of events, voluntarily gave up both the chairmanship and the presidency he had reassumed after Newberg's firing. To fill his time until he reached retirement age he took the post of chairman of Chrysler of Canada. Lynn Townsend was named executive vice-president to run Chrysler, pending the appointment of a new president.

Townsend, at heart a finance man with a sharp knife to cut costs, wanted the presidency, but his vain, contemptuous nature and acid tongue made him unacceptable to the Chrysler board. The job was offered to executives at Ford and at General Motors, including Semon 'Bunky' Knudsen. None took it.

In the end Lynn Alfred Townsend was elected president, an action that was to haunt Chrysler Corporation through fifteen increasingly distressful years. One of Townsend's first orders was the firing of about 7,000 office workers to effect a $50-million-per-year cut in budget.

Townsend's greatest mistake, not evident at the time, was his scattered efforts to increase the Chrysler international division begun by Tex Colbert. In 1964 he expanded English facilities with a takeover of the Rootes Group of Great Britain, makers of the Sunbeam, Hillman, Humber, and Singer cars. After a total investment of $47 million, Chrysler United Kingdon Limited evolved as a wholly owned subsidiary of the Chrysler Corporation.

Townsend also acquired the French Simca facilities, which had a previous association with Ford and Fiat of Italy. Before he was finished Chrysler Corporation had dealings in six continents. By 1965 foreign countries accounted for more than one-third of all Chrysler sales and one-fifth of all Chrysler vehicles built, but each of Townsend's acquisitions abroad further weakened Chrysler's financial picture at home, a deterioration not immediately felt. Chrysler's continuing and exceedingly profitable ties with the United States government as the prime defence contractor for combat tanks and space projects helped conceal Chrysler's crumbling position in the industry.

In 1967 Townsend moved up to chairman of the board, and Virgil Boyd, who had come from American Motors to shore up Chrysler's dealer body, was named president.

Townsend brought Chrysler into the muscle car market in 1968 with the Plymouth Road Runner, described by a national car-buff magazine as 'the ultimate put-on' when it was first announced. It was, nonetheless, a no-nonsense, high-performance car aimed at the sporty-minded eighteen-to-twenty-two-year-old male, designed to please him with solid performance and good looks. Road Runner's first year sales of 45,000 units produced record-making profits of over $300 million.

These 1968 profits, however, proved to be one-time only. Chrysler slid back into its losing ways as Townsend brought out new full-size cars including Imperial, Plymouth Fury, and Dodge Polara, none of which satisfied the public's preference for smaller cars.

Townsend's principal reaction as sales again plummeted was to cut the Chrysler workforce, adding more than 11,000 to the unemployment rolls in a year of slumping economy. He also replaced Virgil Boyd with John J. Riccardo, like himself a former finance-oriented accountant. Townsend believed that with a cost-slasher at his side he could bring Chrysler quickly back to profitability. It was a vain hope.

Riccardo recognised the trend to smaller cars, but the corporation was too deeply in debt and unable to secure the funds necessary to tool up for so radical a change. He did the next best thing, consummating an arrangement with Mitsubishi, a Japanese automaker, to sell its small imports through the Chrysler dealer network. Meanwhile Chrysler would slowly bring out intermediate-sized cars of its own.

By the time this line of cars was ready, the market did an about-face, and larger cars were again in demand. It seemed like a pendulum with Chrysler the loser at each swing. In the summer of 1973 Chrysler was ready to bring out new full-sized cars, but the Arab petroleum exporting countries announced an oil embargo, which sent American car buyers scurrying for small cars. Chrysler lost $52 million in 1974 and had its greatest loss ever in 1975, over $259 million.

The company's future was made even more insecure by the governmental regulations setting mileage and pollution standards for the industry. Chrysler simply did not have the money to comply. At this point Lynn Townsend left the sinking ship totally in John Riccardo's control by retiring.

Operating cash was Chrysler's most vital need, and Riccardo sold off everything Chrysler owned not directly connected to production of cars for the United States and Canada and fulfilment of its defence obligations. Actually the company's Defense Division was the only profit-producer.

The end of the oil embargo brought Chrysler a new but brief lease on life. The car buyers of America swung back to larger cars, and Riccardo could show a near $423-million profit for 1976. While 1977 also showed in the black, the figure dropped to just over $163 million. But 1978, with the company already committed to spending huge sums for plant modernisation and for production costs for a new line of cars, had to be projected as a year heavily in the red.

Hal Sperlick, whom Henry Ford kicked out of the Ford Motor Company for arguing the cause of small, fuel-efficient, front-wheel-drive cars, had won his battle at Chrysler. Given a free hand he was primarily responsible for the introduction of Plymouth Horizon and Dodge Omni the year before. They proved to be the kind of car he had insisted would give imports a battle. But they were not enough.

Dissension at the highest level of Chrysler Corporation did its part in diminishing any possible upturn in company hopes. The naming of John Riccardo as Chrysler chairman and chief executive officer had not been a unanimous action of the board. Many had preferred Eugene Cafiero, an executive vice-president who had been moved up to the presidency when Riccardo succeeded Lynn Townsend as chairman.

Cafiero was continually at odds with Riccardo's hit-and-miss plans for the company's recovery and his doomsday attitude towards possible success. Riccardo had come to Chrysler from an accounting firm and thus was a penny-pincher – a 'bean-counter,' as a finance-orientated individual is referred to in business. Cafiero had been an automobile man from the start, a Chrysler mover and shaker since 1953, a product-based engineer.

Riccardo kept busy trying to drum up money to bail out Chrysler. In doing so he failed to maintain control of production and product quality. The more he looked for financial help, the more financial help became needed to offset delays in manufacture of products and getting them to market. Riccardo tried one banking and investment firm after another in search of $7.5 billion to put Chrysler on its feet.

He was turned down by all.

In desperation he turned to the federal government. As a prelude to his assault on Washington, he collared senators from states in which Chrysler plants were located, twisting their arms for backing on the premise that a Chrysler failure meant economic problems for their constituencies.

Then, too, Riccardo believed he had an ace in the hole in W. Michael Blumenthal, former head of Detroit's Bendix Corporation, who had been appointed secretary of the treasury by President Carter. Blumenthal, having problems of his own within the Carter cabinet, agreed to help, figuring that it would give him added stature in Carter's eyes. Carter was going to need all the votes possible to win re-nomination, much less re-election, and a good deed for America's labourers would not hurt.

Another stalwart in Riccardo's camp was Douglas Fraser, head of the powerful United Auto Workers. Fraser's prime interest was keeping his union members at work in a revitalised Chrysler Corporation.

Any hope that Blumenthal might be of help faded when President Carter replaced him with G. William Miller, chairman of the Federal Reserve Board. While still with the Federal Reserve Board Miller had expressed himself as against government help to bail Chrysler out of its difficulties, and had actually mentioned bankruptcy as a way out. To place what seemed the final nail in the coffin Miller, soon after he took office as secretary of the treasury, made it clear he was unalterably opposed to help for Chrysler Corporation.

Even when it should not have been, John Riccardo's luck was all bad. In early February of 1978 the new XM-1 combat tank produced by Chrysler was ready for release to the United States government. Heralded as the world's greatest combat weapon, the XM-1 was reputed to be bigger, more formidable, and better than anything the Soviets had or could come up with in the foreseeable future.

Extensive and colourful ceremonies were planned for the transfer of the tank of the government-owned, Chrysler-operated plant in Lima, Ohia. An assistant secretary of the Army was on hand, along with a number of generals, the widow of General Creighton Abrams (after whom the tank would be named), and representatives of the press, radio, and television.

When the presentation ceremonies were concluded, the public, press, and dignitaries present were treated to a demonstration of the fifty-nine-ton behemoth. It got under way without trouble as hundreds watched in awe. But suddenly it stopped and could not be moved. Its gears had been locked in reverse. Red-faced Chrysler officials ordered it returned to the plant for further work.

As if that embarrassment was not enough, the fates delivered another cruel blow to Chrysler prestige a few months later. The corporation was bringing out its two new cars for 1979, the Chrysler New Yorker and the Dodge St Regis. William Milliken, Michigan's governor, and Coleman Young, Detroit's mayor, were to drive the first of each off the assembly line.

Governor Milliken was first with the New Yorker. He settled himself in the plush velour seat behind the steering wheel and, with a smile towards the cameras as hundreds applauded and bulbs flashed, he turned the ignition switch. Nothing happened. Sheepishly, he tried again. The engine still did not roar to life. The car had been equipped with a dead battery.

John Riccardo must certainly have felt himself accursed. It was the last straw. As he turned away to head back to his office in Highland Park, he may have been sending up prayers of thanks that Lee Iacocca had been fired by Henry Ford II a month or so earlier.

CHAPTER 12

Traders at the New York Stock Exchange paid Lee Iacocca a high compliment when he accepted the Chrysler challenge. Showing confidence in his ability to bring the ailing corporation back to life, they sent Chrysler stock up one point per share.

Reactions were more reserved in America's business community in general and the automobile industry in particular. Many hard-nosed businessmen found it inconceivable that any man would give up $1 million a year to take on the thankless job of reviving a company already in its death throes. And within the automobile industry responses ran from sheer amazement at General Motors to trepidation at Ford and American Motors.

GM was far too big to fear substantial inroads, however successful Iacocca might be at Chrysler. At Ford, already in a downward slide, overt bluster was tinged with covert concern based on firsthand knowledge of Iacocca's ability.

'Don't use my name, but we weren't really worried,' one Ford executive reminisced in early 1981. 'Only God can make a tree, and Lee Iacocca isn't God.'

Another man with even more reason to desire anonymity had a more realistic view. 'We're still in trouble, and if it wasn't for our international operation, we might be worse off than Chrysler,' he said. 'We're so vulnerable that if Iacocca performs the miracle he's capable of – well, number three is just a step down from number two.'

How much of a miracle it would take not even Iacocca fully realised until he met for the first time with the full complement of Chrysler Corporation officers about a week after his acceptance. The meeting began on a peculiar note.

Without realising it, Iacocca initiated the first of many changes he would make at Chrysler the moment he sat at the conference table with Riccardo and all other high-level officers. He lit one of his big cigars, unaware of the startled sensibilities all around.

Smoking during company meetings had been a strictly enforced John Riccardo no-no for a long time. And trigger-tempered Riccardo had more than once exploded at an officer who lit up a smoke in a moment of forgetfulness. This time Riccardo bit his lip.

'Well, I guess rules have to change sometime,' he sheepishly commented as he brought the meeting to order.

As Riccardo proceeded to outline all the problems that led to the company's untenable situation, Iacocca sat puffing on his cigar, dumbfounded. He had studied the company's background and had been briefed by Riccardo, but what he was hearing was a startling litany of blunders and mis-management.

Chrysler had a huge backlog of unsold cars that should never have been built, automobiles produced only to make the books look good, to justify the bonuses paid to executives. These cars represented far more than production hours and dollars, they also accounted for millions of dollars for storage space.

Parked on open lots throughout the Detroit area, spilling across the river into Canada, standing there through rain, snow, blistering heat, and bitter cold, they were indicative of further waste running into the hundreds of thousands of dollars for damaged paint surfaces, broken windshields and windows, and slashed tyres.

The ridiculous inventory build-up concept dated back to Lynn Townsend's days. Chrysler's cash drain was further increased by recalls of its 1978 models, all because of hurry-up production that resulted in poor quality.

As he went on, Riccardo noted that the quarter just ended

showed a loss approaching $160 million. Iacocca was astonished. The same quarter just two years before had brought Chrysler a $155-million profit. So great a reverse in a two-year period was incredible. The answer lay in gross inefficiency. If ever a company cried for sweeping changes, it was Chrysler Corporation.

It was unbelievable that the third-largest automobile manufacturer in America, a company as old as Iacocca himself, fifty-six, and doing business on six continents, could be in such bottomless trouble. A thorough housecleaning at top levels was called for.

Fortunately, there was one executive around whom Iacocca could build, Hal Sperlick, his coworker on Mustang, who had joined Chrysler in 1977 after Henry Ford II demanded that he be fired. Sperlick, like Iacocca, was sensitive to the automobile market. He had seen the growing need for smaller cars and for the efficiency that front-wheel drive brought to driving. He had fought for progress at Ford, but despite the backing of Iacocca, had lost.

He was Iacocca's kind of executive, one Lee described as 'having a fire in his belly,' a tense, impatient man who drove himself and others equally hard. With Sperlick as his chief of product planning and development, Iacocca could proceed to fill out his executive staff with men equally dedicated and equally competent.

Because Sperlick had been able to further his conviction that small, front-wheel-drive cars were the wave of the future, Chrysler was two years ahead of General Motors and three years ahead of Ford in bringing this more space- and fuel-efficient kind of automobile to the American market. It gave Lee Iacocca his one plus for the future.

To improve quality of car construction as quickly as possible Iacocca persuaded Hans Matthias, who had spent twenty-six years at Ford as chief engineer and head of car manufacture, to come to Chrysler. He was to work with Richard Vining on production and quality control. Matthias was an expert in fit and finish of body components, an area that had cost Chrysler dearly in warranty claims.

To handle purchasing and cost control Iacocca brought

Paul Bergmoser out of retirement. Bergmoser had thirty years of experience at Ford. Gerald Greenwald was induced to resign his post as president of Ford's subsidiary in Venezuela and come aboard as controller. Gar Laux, another one-time Ford vice-president, was brought out of retirement to take on the Chrysler vice-presidency for sales.

'My friends in Houston couldn't understand why I'd give up the easy life and come to Chrysler,' Laux said. 'But I figure that if Lee could do what he was doing to save 150,000 people their jobs, who was I to say no? Lee's a rare man, and it's a privilege to work for him anytime.'

Laux, a huge, friendly bear of a man, was also a specialist in dealer relations, and one of Chrysler Corporation's most vital needs was a boost in dealer morale. Inventories at most dealerships were at record highs. Dealer orders to the factory had been badly handled. Many were delivered late, some without equipment a customer had ordered, others with equipment not asked for, thus changing the original price quoted to the buyer.

Something needed doing, and Iacocca did it. He called a meeting of the Chrysler Dealer Council, a committee of dealers who spoke for the entire dealer body. He asked them for a list of their complaints, any possible area where the corporation's activities had brought them hardship.

Two weeks after his get-together with this council Iacocca invited every Chrysler-Plymouth and Dodge dealer in the country to meet with him in a week-long grievance session in Las Vegas. He addressed the group in the opening session, holding nothing back. In his usual crisp and dramatic fashion he laid out the grim picture of the corporation's condition, its failures, and its faults in placing the dealers in an untenable position, and he made it clear that it would not be an overnight return to solvency.

'Let me start off with that old Chinese proverb,' he said to the assembled dealers, 'that says even a thousand-mile journey begins with a single step. I honestly believe that this meeting with you is that first step and the most important one . . .'

One by one he went through the lengthy list of complaints

201

provided him by the Dealer Council and pointed out what he would do to rectify each situation. He showed slides of the 1980 car lineup to be introduced that fall and explained in detail the features of each that would make them marketable and start Chrysler on the road back. He outlined an incentive plan to help the dealers dispose of their heavy inventories.

It was an inspirational let's-go-get-'em speech that Lee Iacocca delivered with wit and persuasiveness in an attempt to rouse a cynical group. He stood at the podium like a football coach in the locker room exhorting his players at half time to overcome a 40-0 deficit. Sports enthusiast that he is, he injected a football parallel into his talk.

'One night at dinner,' he said, 'I asked Vince Lombardi, the great coach of the Green Bay Packers, who was a friend of mine, why he always seemed able to produce a winner.'

Iacocca then went on to expand on Lombardi's three-point formula for winning in sports, business, or life. First, the need for talent. Second, discipline. And 'the third priceless ingredient to win,' Iacocca pointed out, quoting Lombardi, 'is you have to care for each other. For the entire team to win, every time a man makes a move, he has to consider the effect on the rest of the guys on the field.'

He compared Chrysler's position to being in the fourth quarter of a do-or-die Super Bowl: 'In the fourth quarter, when you are bone-tired, the only thing that keeps you going is your feeling for the other guy. Miss your block, and your buddy gets decked.'

Chrysler has talent, Iacocca emphasised, and it was getting the needed discipline slowly but surely. 'But now,' he said, 'we need to care about each other and help each other.'

Automotive dealers are normally blasé and sceptical, unmoved by rhetoric and paying allegiance only to the profits, but as one Midwestern Dodge dealer said, 'He had us mesmerised. We were hypnotised, and when he got to the last part of his talk, we were all ready to go out and slay the dragon.'

'Everybody's looking at us,' Iacocca told the dealers as he neared the conclusion of his speech, 'and they are betting on us. Betting that we are going to win, and that we're going to bring Chrysler Corporation back to where it belongs in this business.

'We have a fountain of goodwill going for us. Coleman Young, the mayor of Detroit, called me. He wants us to win for the future of Detroit.

'Doug Fraser, the head of the UAW called me. He wants us to win because 150,000 jobs are at stake.

'Hell, even Tom Murphy and Pete Estes called me. They want us to win because they think it will be good for General Motors and the whole industry.'

Lee Iacocca is a master of dealer relations, an expertise honed in his early days with Ford in the Philadelphia District. He knew, however, that he alone could not maintain the vital person-to-person relationships that would keep enthusiasm at a high level in each of the thousands of Chrysler-Plymouth and Dodge showrooms throughout the country. He needed an organisation like the one at Lincoln-Mercury. There, under the overall supervision of David Gillespie, chairman of the board of Kenyon & Eckhardt, and the day-to-day management of John Hickey, he had the finest, most aggressive dealership activity in the industry.

Even before he accepted the Chrysler presidency, Iacocca felt certain that he would need help from people he had worked with before. And on March 1, 1980, Chrysler Corporation called a news conference at New York's Waldorf-Astoria Hotel. The site, the timing, and the purpose were a puzzle to the ever-speculating press.

Was Chrysler Corporation announcing bankruptcy, as so many American economists were predicting it would ultimately do? Had it finally achieved an agreement with another automobile company to merge? Perhaps Lee Iacocca had changed his mind and wanted out of an untenable situation – and who would blame him if he did?

The questions and the wonderment had a startling effect on the business community. The New York Stock Exchange, in a rare move, delayed trading in Chrysler stock until after the purpose of the news conference was made clear.

It was not John Riccardo, Chrysler chairman, who opened the meeting, but Lee Iacocca, its president. In itself this raised eyebrows. Iacocca did not keep his audience in the dark. He came straight to the point.

'I am pleased to announce,' he told the crowded room, 'that we are appointing Kenyon & Eckhardt as Chrysler's single advertising agency, effective just as soon as is practicable.'

The journalists were surprised. Kenyon & Eckhardt had served as the prime Ford agency for thirty-four years. It had been a long, friendly, and safe relationship, despite the foibles of Henry Ford II. Why would they give up so large and profitable an account, one they had little fear of losing, to take on a question mark, the struggling, near-death Chrysler Corporation? It defied understanding until later facts emerged.

Kenyon & Eckhardt was granted a five-year contract with Chrysler Corporation, a first for the advertising industry. Agency firings and resignations are customarily on a ninety-day basis. An even more unusual aspect of the relationship would be K & E's direct involvement with Chrysler's future product planning and marketing. The agency was to serve as a permanent member of corporate committees responsible for those vital functions. In effect an unusual partnership had been created between Chrysler and its advertising agency.

Meanwhile, John Riccardo, still Chrysler chairman but not directly involved in the agency switchover, was busy in Washington, still trying to get government help. Riccardo's chances for success had dwindled appreciably when G. William Miller took over as secretary of the treasury in Jimmy Carter's cabinet. Miller quickly made his opposition to the loan plan clear. He had also recommended to Carter that any loan amount should be scaled down from a billion or more to only $750 million.

Riccardo faced another stumbling block when Senator Proxmire of Wisconsin succeeded Long of Louisiana as chairman of the Senate Banking Committee. Long had supported Chrysler aid. Proxmire was dogmatically opposed, although he had earlier helped American Motors, which employed more people in his state than any other private corporation.

Before Labor Day, 1979, Riccardo and Chrysler were in

an even more tenuous position. With Congress in its summer recess weeks would pass before anything was resolved. Banks clamped down on new loans to Chrysler, and to save cash reserves Chrysler began a series of layoffs. Further diminishing the hopes for Chrysler's future, Mitsubishi of Japan, builders of some of Chrysler's bestselling cars, threatened to stop shipments if cash was not forthcoming. A rumour that Mitsubishi would welcome a termination of its agreement to supply Chrysler with fuel-efficient small cars added to the pall hanging over Iacocca.

To boost sagging morale, as well as to conserve cash for operating expenses, Iacocca announced that he would reduce his salary to $1 a year and that pay cuts averaging 5 percent would apply to management personnel. Riccardo also became a $1-per-year man. If and when the company rebounded, the salaries would be reevaluated in proportion to the increased value of Chrysler stock.

One bright spot in the dreary picture was the continued support of a man who had no ties to the automobile business. It was Edward J. Piszek, a Polish-American patriot who was president of the Philadelphia-based Mrs Paul's Kitchens. Piszek, who had built a fortune from a $250 start as a creator and seller of fish cakes, started investing in Chrysler stock about the time Iacocca joined the company. He kept buying through the worst of times, his faith in Chrysler's survival unshaken, and now he was the major Chrysler stockholder with one million shares.

Did Piszek buy his stock in Chrysler because he knew Lee Iacocca personally? 'No, I did not know him,' Piszek said. 'I just felt from my observations, and what I had read, that Mr Iacocca was an unusually gifted natural leader and an accomplished business person. By his very nature I felt he could handle anything he put his mind to.'

Piszek did meet Lee Iacocca later during filming of a series of motion pictures he sponsored, produced by James Michener, author of *Hawaii* and a bookshelf of other bestsellers. Michener's series, based on American life and living, featured Iacocca in one of five devoted to American transportation.

205

'Mr Iacocca was what I expected, a dynamic man,' Piszek recalls. 'And I've met him many times since, several times in Washington and several times in Detroit, and he has impressed me more each time. He's a thinker and a doer, but he needs some luck. If the economy settles down and interest rates level off, he won't be able to build enough cars to meet the demand.'

In late summer of 1979 Iacocca needed a carload of good luck. Enough cars sat on lots and in dealer showrooms to satisfy the greatest demand, but operating capital to run the company and move those cars was in short supply. John Riccardo's efforts in Washington seemed stalemated, and the worries and pressures took their toll on him. Earlier in the year Riccardo had to cancel a trip to the White House because of hospitalisation due to a heart problem.

By September 18, 1979, Riccardo could take no more. He retired, leaving the financial problems and the chairmanship of the company to Iacocca. The added role was a lot for one man to carry, but Iacocca welcomed it. He was now in full charge of Chrysler, finally able to run the corporation without hindrance.

His first move was to name Paul Bergmoser president. With the experienced Bergmoser at the helm, Lee could turn to the fight in Washington for the loan guarantees that would bring Chrysler back to life.

On his trips to the nation's capital John Riccardo had hammered hard that the government regulations, including unrealistic emissions and mileage standards, were responsible for Chrysler's dilemma, and since the government was the cause, it should help in the cure. The concept enraged many legislators, who hardened their stand against helping.

Iacocca's diplomacy in Washington softened the stand of some senators and congressmen, although hardliners such as Proxmire in the Senate and Kelly in the House became even more adamant. Florida's Kelly was later convicted of bribery as a result of the Abscam scandal. Even a congressman from Michigan, David Stockman, openly decried any help for Chrysler. The lead article in a Sunday edition of the *Washington Post*, written by Stockman, was headed: 'Let Chrysler Go Bankrupt.'

Legislators from states in which Chrysler plants were located, spearheaded by Congressman Blanchard and Senators Reigle and Levin of Michigan, lined up against the Proxmires, Kellys, and Stockmans. Iacocca also had another battler in his corner. It was Douglas Fraser, head of the powerful United Auto Workers, with a stake equal to Chrysler's in the outcome. For Fraser the jobs of nearly 150,000 union members were on the line.

There was, however, a negative side to Fraser's support. He and his union were at odds with the Carter administration, which held life-and-death power over any final loan guarantee approval. Fraser was known to support Senator Edward Kennedy of Massachusetts against Jimmy Carter's 1980 bid for reelection.

As an offset Fraser and Vice-President Walter Mondale were close friends. Mondale, held in high esteem by President Carter, might appeal to Carter's humanitarian instincts on the basis of the plight of laid-off workers and the effect on the nation's economy should Chrysler fail.

Time was critical. Carter was leaning towards help for Chrysler, but he was moving inch by inch, far too slowly to make possible the granting of funds in time to save the company.

His advisers, the domestic experts in charge of finding alternative means to a loan guarantee, if there was one, were taking their time. Somehow the Carter administration had to openly endorse help for Chrysler.

To push matters along Mondale scheduled a breakfast meeting at his home in Washington, inviting both Fraser and Secretary of the Treasury Miller. Miller, who remained dubious about the loan guarantees and continued to hem and haw as time passed, could accelerate action if he could be convinced of the urgency.

Miller circled the issues between sips of coffee. The genial yet tough-talking Fraser impatiently portrayed the dire consequences to the American economy of a Chrysler failure, and the need for quick action.

Miller warned Fraser against haste, emphasising the need for proper timing in getting Congress to accept any recommendation made by the president.

'The pear must be ripe,' he said at one point. 'If you bite too early, you will become ill.'

It was a bit much for the realistic, down-to-earth head of the United Auto Workers. He answered Miller with an icy edge: 'The pear, Mr Miller,' he said, 'is already rotten. The fruit flies are all over it. Now, when in the hell are you going to bite?'

At a subsequent meeting of Carter's staff the chief adviser on domestic policy, Stuart E. Eisenstat, called the bickering to a halt.

'The nation's tenth largest industrial corporation is not going to go bankrupt during the Carter administration,' he announced, ending the discussion with a fist slammed hard against the meeting table.

Within days President Carter sent a message asking Congress to pass a loan-guarantee bill that would provide $1.5 billion in relief for the Chrysler Corporation. It was considerably more than the company had asked for but also included a number of stringent requirements. Chrysler's future now rested with the Senate and the House of Representatives.

To bring about the President's approval Douglas Fraser meanwhile had yielded vital concessions from his United Auto Workers. He had had to make wage concessions from his union that would represent operating savings for Chrysler. Without them Congress was hardly likely to approve Carter's request.

The existing Chrysler contract with the union had expired in September, 1979, but Chrysler workers had not walked out. Fighting with his membership for cuts in the pay scale would be agonising for Fraser. But he was a realist, a new breed of union leader, and knew that it was give a lot or have thousands of his men jobless.

On October 25 he brought new hope to Chrysler with a contract that offered concessions totalling about $400 million, part of which represented deferred payments to the Chrysler workers' pension fund. As part of the agreement it was understood that Fraser would become a member of the

Chrysler board of directors, an unprecedented event in the history of American business.

The 256-member Chrysler Council of the United Auto Workers approved Fraser's recommendation on October 31 with little argument. Chrysler workers, with faith in their leaders, decided that saving their jobs was worth the cut in wages and benefits and later voted for the Fraser concession package.

This expression of confidence on the part of Chrysler employees led the House of Representatives to pass the loan-guarantee bill. The House measure provided Chrysler with $1.5 billion in loan assistance if the corporation could raise an equal amount from other sources, such as suppliers and state and local governments where Chrysler did business. The amount saved through the concessions by the union would be part of the company's $1.5 billion.

The Senate proved a tougher nut to crack. Many senators insisted that the Chrysler work force should sacrifice at least $1 billion rather than the $400 million set down in the House bill. After much argument the Senate accepted the $400-million union contribution, and a bill that satisfied both House and Senate was passed on December 21. It was signed into law by President Carter on January 7, 1980.

While Congress was debating the Chrysler rescue, an emotionally drained Lee Iacocca analysed Chrysler's position. He saw an immediate need for an intense campaign that would bolster worker morale as well as public confidence in Chrysler. A loan guarantee even in the billions would be money down the drain if Chrysler did not build good cars and sell them.

The quality of the cars was important to Iacocca. He was greatly concerned that Chrysler workers might have become careless or uncaring. That at least some employees took pride in their work despite the precarious position of the company was made clear to Iacocca by what Chrysler executives call the 'Case of the Iacocca Cake.'

Lillian Zirwas, a maintenance clerk at Chrysler's Lynch Road plant in Detroit, had written an article that was published in the *Axle News*, the plant newspaper. In it Mrs

Zirwas bemoaned the shoddy work being done by some of her fellow employees and boldly told them to shape up or the company would certainly fail.

As might be expected, Mrs Zirwas was given a rough time for a while by some of her coworkers. The criticism didn't faze her since as many applauded her action. Then one day Mrs Zirwas was told that she should report the next morning at Lee Iacocca's office. The chairman wanted to thank her personally.

Lillian Zirwas felt she could not go to so important a meeting emptyhanded, so she baked a cake, a special cake based on a personal recipe that included a can of beer and chocolate icing.

Iacocca accepted the cake graciously and thanked her for her devotion to Chrysler Corporation. Mrs Zirwas told him that she would name the cake after him if he saved Chrysler.

Iacocca took the cake home. The next morning he described it around his office as 'the best goddamn cake I ever ate.' Soon after Mary Iacocca wrote Mrs Zirwas, asking for the recipe.

Not long after her meeting with Iacocca Mrs Zirwas baked the same cake for the wedding of a friend's daughter. A guest at the wedding was so excited about the cake's unusual flavour that he told his sister he wanted the same cake served at his own wedding.

The sister approached Mrs Zirwas, promising to buy a Chrysler car if Mrs Zirwas would provide the cake for her brother's wedding reception. Lillian Zirwas baked a three-tier version of the Iacocca cake, and the sister purchased a new Plymouth.

Employee morale was only one of Lee Iacocca's many worries. He was equally concerned with the public's possible reticence in purchasing Chrysler cars, its fear of being left out in the cold for service and parts if the company failed. It was a justifiable fear, one that was becoming more difficult to counteract because of the news stories that continually emphasised Chrysler's difficulties.

A 'Chrysler should be let to die' campaign by the prestigious *Wall Street Journal* was echoed throughout the country.

Even in Detroit the media highlighted Chrysler's problems rather than items that gave hope for its survival.

In mid-December, 1979, Iacocca called on Kenyon & Eckhardt to devise a morale-boosting programme that would raise the spirits of Chrysler employees as well as public confidence in the corporation's future. The Bill Winn Group spent the entire weekend devising and rejecting concepts that might instil belief in Chrysler's ability to weather the storm.

'We went round and round with some pretty high-falutin ideas,' Bill Winn recalled, 'but in the end it was a simple and, luckily, effective declaration that came out of the hopper.'

'We Can Do It!' was the battle cry decided upon as the basic theme for an all-out campaign. 'Consider It Done!' was the backup phrase to give the programme a positive emphasis.

Banners bearing each statement were displayed throughout Chrysler Corporation plants and dealerships in North America. Showrooms, parts and service departments, and used-car lots reflected Chrysler's belief in itself for employees and customers to see.

The dedication of Lillian Zirwas spread throughout Chrysler factories. No worker dared to be careless or go goldbrick on the job without earning the wrath of fellow employees. An upgrading of Chrysler quality became noticeable in almost every facet of production. This was especially heartening to Iacocca, since the K-cars, which he hoped would cause Chrysler sales to soar, were being readied for 1980 introduction.

'We Can Do It' was only part of Iacocca's initial confidence building campaign. He also searched for other means.

From the beginning it had been agreed that the basic name of the company could not be changed. The name Chrysler, remindful of the automotive genius of Walter P. Chrysler, the company's founder, was worth millions.

In the end, as with the 'We Can Do It' slogan, simplicity won out. Chrysler Corporation the company would remain, but it would be the *New* Chrysler Corporation, a name that would not only remind the American public that new management was at the helm, but also that this new guardianship was dedicated to restoring the company to its glory days under its founder.

Iacocca, Kelmenson, and John Morrissey, K & E chairman, then considered means of getting the new identity across to the general public and decided on full-page newspaper and magazine advertisements.

Unlike typical ads selling a product, these would be in the form of letters to the public from Lee Iacocca, as chairman of the New Chrysler Corporation. Carefully prepared by K & E and meticulously screened by Iacocca himself, the ads were designed also to serve as a subtle lobbying aimed at Congress and the Carter administration. Since the loan guarantees were still being held up, the ads might well put gentle pressure on the legislators and the President.

Reaction to these Iacocca letter-ads was so favourable that Kenyon & Eckhardt executives decided that the same personal approach should be used in the electronic media. They were convinced that to get maximum mileage from the campaign the chairman had to be seen and heard on television and radio.

Iacocca balked at this approach. High-echelon executives of major corporations seldom acted as barkers, selling their own products. Lee also feared that such ads might add to public perception of Chrysler desperation and imminent failure. Besides, he told Kelmenson and Morrissey, he didn't have the time. He was too busy getting the company in shape and fighting for the loan guarantees in trip after trip to Washington.

It was not an easy sell, but K & E had taken a survey that included showing pictures of Iacocca. A remarkably high 40 percent of the people identified Iacocca. Over three-fourths called him by name. Others said he was 'boss man at Chrysler' or used similar terms. Some said he was the man who was trying to save Chrysler. Others called him the man who built Mustang and was fired by Henry Ford.

The K & E executives told Iacocca that this was proof that he had become a national figure. His appearance and voice could help immeasurably in convincing American car buyers that he was dedicated to winning Chrysler's struggle for survival. People like former baseball player Joe Garagiola and actor Riccardo Montalban might sell cars well, but Lee

Iacocca himself could best sell the future of the New Chrysler Corporation. No one else would have his credibility or would better present the company's plans and potential.

Iacocca finally agreed, and the broadcast announcements were prepared with Lee himself carefully weighing every word. Some television commercials began with him in a chair behind his desk. In others he was seen sitting on the edge of the desk or walking through one of the Chrysler plants.

In every one, as well as in radio spots, he came across as a confident man, comfortable in his role, talking forcefully and straight from the shoulder.

'When we first conceived the idea of using Mr Iacocca,' Ron DeLuca said, 'the fundamental consideration was that the public needed to know that Chrysler had a leader, had somebody who could speak in a different way on behalf of Chrysler its products. There isn't a better spokesman. We couldn't have gone out and hired anybody to do as Lee did in isolating Chrysler's problems and what it's doing to face up to those problems. We just put him in front of the cameras and let him talk.'

The dynamic qualities that inspired hard-nosed dealers were not lost on the man in the street. He empathised when he heard Iacocca say: 'If you buy any car without considering Chrysler, that'll be too bad – for both of us,' and when Iacocca said: 'I'm not asking you to buy one of our cars. I'm asking you to compare,' many did just that.

As the year 1979 wound down, Lee Iacocca's face was more familiar than that of any businessman to the television viewers of America. His appearances before Congress began it. The commercials did the rest.

The campaign apparently also had an effect within Chrysler plants. A cheerful eagerness supplanted spiritless indifference. Absenteeism, which had been running exceedingly high, was more than halved. Nonetheless, each of Iacocca's days had its frustrations. The New Chrysler Corporation was no better off than the old when it came to money for operating expenses. A cash flow from the loan guarantees could not begin too soon.

Equally frustrating – perhaps even more so – were the

thousands of new 1979 cars sitting in open lots, some 80,000 unordered automobiles. Remnants of the old system of building automobiles before receiving orders from dealers, they drained about $2 million each week in costs for interest and maintenance.

With the 1980 models already introduced, moving these quickly was essential. To do so called for a dramatic, hard-sell campaign that combined immediacy, low prices, and an exciting environment, one that would stimulate dealers to all-out participation.

Iacocca approved a K & E concept that called for tent sales conducted in a carnival atmosphere. But rather than commit to a nationwide clearance all at once it was decided to test the idea in a single market. If the plan bombed, losses would be minimal.

The Minneapolis-St. Paul metropolitan area was chosen for the test sale. A huge tent was set up on the extensive parking lot of Metropolitan Stadium, the playing field of the Minnesota Twins and the Vikings.

All Chrysler-Plymouth and Dodge dealers in the area were invited to participate. Most took advantage of the opportunity and sent salesmen to close car and truck purchases for their own dealerships. A special trailer was set up on the grounds to provide on-the-spot financing.

For three days prior to the opening of the twenty-four hour 'Let's Make a Deal' event, the air-waves of the Minneapolis-St. Paul area were saturated with teaser commercial announcements.

This test sale proved a huge success, with thousands swarming over the stadium parking lot and examining automobiles in a carnival atmosphere complete with rousing music and circus-type barkers. Hundreds of cars were disposed of in that single day. It told Iacocca enough to approve extending the concept nationwide.

Tents were set up in appropriate areas in almost every major American city. Special announcements for television and radio were recorded by Joe Garagiola inviting listeners from coast-to-coast to 'Let's Make a Deal.'

In the end 55,000 of the 1979 models were sold along with

hundreds more from dealer stock. This blitz type of marketing proved such a smash hit that soon both General Motors and Ford produced their own versions of the tent sale.

As Iacocca was telling America in his personal commercials, Chrysler was certainly 'doing business like Detroit's never done it before.' Indeed it was.

CHAPTER 13

At times Lee Iacocca looked back with some fondness on the comparatively serene days at Ford. Now he seemed to be on an unending treadmill.

A typical week had him in Washington on Monday, perhaps into Tuesday, pushing for action on the loan guarantees. Then it would be back to his desk in Highland Park, seeing to company business. Another day would be spent in New York for lengthy strategy conferences with Kenyon & Eckhardt executives and taping his commercials. Late in the week he might be back in Washington.

He had few breaks in his merry-go-round routine. One was a sudden, agonizing trip to Boca Raton, Florida, where his wife had gone for relief from Michigan's cold. When Iacocca received word that Mary had suffered a heart seizure and had been rushed to the hospital, he dropped everything, remaining with her until she was out of danger.

Another interruption in his weekly round, one of the few for sheer relaxation, resulted in a near-crippling accident. During one of his sessions in New York he took off with his friend Bill Fugazy to visit Lake Placid during the 1980 Olympics.

For more than a year he had had few opportunities to enjoy watching sports events. After one of the early wins by the United States Olympic hockey team, he stepped on the ice as he and Fugazy were getting ready to leave the arena. Iacocca's feet went out from under him on the slippery surface, and he bruised a hip.

216

He laughed it off as retribution for having taken time off. And when the Americans dramatically upset the Soviet team, he considered the hurt worthwhile.

Still walking with a limp, Iacocca returned to his desk. The 'Let's Make a Deal' promotion had sold an appreciable number of the 1979 overstock. The confidence- and morale-boosting campaigns had done reasonably well, but there was still much to be done to encourage the belief that Chrysler products were of good quality.

Soon after Lee had joined Chrysler, he had initiated a quality-control programme by hiring Hans Matthias to oversee manufacturing procedures for the 1980 products, the new models of the Chrysler New Yorker and Dodge St Regis as well as the all-new Chrysler Cordoba and Dodge Mirada. Double and triple quality checks had been set up for major systems such as engine, electrical, emissions, and air conditioning, as well as for protection against wind noise and water leaks, and for the fit and finish of doors and bodies. Matthias established permanent task forces to study defects in sheet metal and paint jobs, to eliminate squeaks and rattles, and to devise corrections for other problems that denote a poorly built automobile.

To top off his quality crusade Iacocca also had not only installed the industry's most advanced computer testing system, but had stolen a march on General Motors and Ford, by being the first to install an automatic welding system. Called the Robotgate by Chrysler engineers, this new means of assembling body components helped ensure construction of solid, rattle-and-leak-proof bodies.

With all the innovative equipment and control checks in place, Iacocca now could take a chance and introduce the buyer-guarantee he and K & E had been working on since autumn.

On January 24, 1980, an advertising push announced the 'Chrysler Guarantees' programme, which included rare buyer protections that Chrysler's competition considered potentially ruinous.

One phase of these guarantees offered a thirty-day or 1,000-mile money-back guarantee if the buyer did not like the car. Another offered $50 to anyone who took a test drive in a Chrysler Corporation vehicle – car or truck – and then purchased either the Chrysler or a competitor's make.

'We're not foolish. We're just confident,' Iacocca told the American public in his televised messages.

Ford and GM didn't think Iacocca was foolish. They thought he was crazy. The $50 giveaway was bad enough, but money back in thirty days? The returns were certain to kill Chrysler Corporation.

Iacocca, however, had the last laugh. He had projected a possible return of 1 percent of the cars sold. Less than .2 percent were actually returned.

'Really, some of that .2 percent didn't literally return their cars for a refund,' John Morrissey reported. 'There was one buyer, for example, who brought back his Omni because it was too small for his family. He merely traded for a larger car.'

Thanks to the unheard-of 'guarantees' Chrysler was selling cars, but lack of cash still continued to be Iacocca's great concern. Though $1.5 billion waited, not one cent could be touched until that figure was matched by Chrysler, and little more than the $400 million represented by union concessions was already on the table.

Of the $250 million expected to be committed by the states in which Chrysler did business, only $150 million had been tentatively approved. This was the amount offered by Chrysler's home state, Michigan, where Governor Milliken was in favour of the plan. The seven other states involved were moving slowly due to logistic and legal problems. Legislative approval was necessary, and their legislatures were in recess.

The week ending February 1 brought some cause for celebration. Chrysler stock, which had become the biggest loser in corporate history, had taken a healthy rise during that week's trading on Wall Street.

Chrysler's common shares, which had reached a low of $5.50 in late November, had jumped 25 percent during the week to close at $10.75 per share. Preferred stock, which no longer paid dividends, closed $12.87, up $2.50.

The following week a beaming Lee Iacocca addressed the annual convention of the National Automobile Dealers Association in New Orleans. He was now confident that Chrysler would raise the money needed to qualify for the federally guaranteed loans, and he was brimming with ideas to revive the depressed automobile market.

In his succinct, pointed style he told the thousands of dealers representative of all car lines that the government should enact a ten-cent-per-gallon tax on gasoline as a stimulant for the economy. This, he said, would add up to $10 billion, which could be funnelled back to the public with a $1,500 credit for purchase of an American-made car.

'This would stimulate the market for new domestic cars, probably to the tune of a million units,' he claimed. 'It would create jobs. It would conserve fuel by making people more prudent in buying gas.' And, suggesting that the Congress might have to pass laws controlling foreign import sales, he added that a programme such as his 'would be a clear signal to foreign manufacturers that we can make things tougher for them' if some balance wasn't made in the Japanese tax structure that makes American cars too expensive for Japanese buyers, yet gives Japanese cars a competitive edge in America.

As for Chrysler Corporation's future prospects, Iacocca reported that on Monday following the meeting in New Orleans he would be in Washington to meet with the Loan Guarantee Board. He would be notifying the board that $125 million in concessions had been made through a wage freeze on Chrysler white-collar workers and that another $100 million was available through a loan from Europe's largest auto manufacturer, Peugeot-Citroën, pending approval by Chrysler's banks and the government.

Later the same week Iacocca received even more hopeful news when sales figures for the first ten days of February were released. It was the kind of win-while-still-losing good news that only an automobile man could appreciate. In comparison with the same ten-day period in 1979 Chrysler Corporation had lost 11 percent. But GM's drop was 14.9 percent, Volkswagen of America dropped 23.7 percent and

Ford Motor Company a whopping 42.8 percent.

There was still a long way to go, of course, and money remained in short supply, but Lee Iacocca could be forgiven for gloating over those figures and wondering what Henry Ford was thinking. The report was even more gratifying because they did not include any sales from a new incentive announcement before their release.

To help dispose of the more than 100,000 Chrysler 1979 models still in dealer stocks, Iacocca initiated a rebate programme. Buyers were offered from $200 to $700 back, depending on the vehicle, on the purchase of any car or truck, domestic or import, included in the programme. The rebate could be used by the buyer as cash or applied to the down payment or purchase price.

This new rebate programme to clear 1979 stocks was to continue at least through March 20. Co-ordinated with the revolutionary Chrysler guarantees on 1980 models, it offered great expectations for a surge in overall sales, a two-way effort that Iacocca hoped would not only reduce inventories but also increase Chrysler's share of the market.

If Lee Iacocca had been inclined to give it consideration, the time was ideal for a concerted charge against Ford sales. Henry was now in trouble on two fronts. For more than a month the Ford Motor Company had been involved in a damage suit related to the Pinto's susceptibility to fire in a rear-end collision. And media reports were giving lead attention to the sensational aspects of the divorce trial between Henry and Cristina due to begin on February 19.

Rumours were afloat that Henry's sale of a huge block of Ford stock was to provide her with an out-of-court settlement of about $5 million. Cristina, however, was believed to be asking for twice that amount.

Iacocca, however, had worries of his own and was too busy to give much thought to the woes of his former boss. There was an immediate need for cash, and the remaining commitments necessary to meet the requirements of the loan-guarantee bill were not yet in place. The only hope for quick money was action by the Michigan legislature to approve the $150 million recommended by Governor William Milliken.

If that did not come soon, the company would have to close down, if only temporarily.

Still another urgent concern faced Iacocca. The XM-1 combat tank, which had embarrassed Ricardo the previous year, was now ready for acceptance by the US Army. The defence arm of Chrysler had, they hoped, corrected the defects that aborted the 1979 presentation.

February 28 was the date set for the XM-1 unveiling. A tour of the Lima facility preceded a press conference at which more that 150 journalists and all three major television networks were present. With Lee Iacocca delayed at Highland Park on company business, the news conference was chaired by J. Paul Bergmoser, Chrysler president.

Ready to answer questions of the press, in addition to Bergmoser, were O. G. White, director of Chrysler's Defense Manufacturing Division; P. W. Lett, director of the company's Defense Engineering Division; Dr Percy Pierre, Assistant Secretary of the Army for Research and Development; and General E. C. Meyer, US Army chief of staff.

Most of the questions were directed to General Meyer, since the press had concern about the reliability of the tank's engine under combat conditions. One question was whether the tank was indeed ready for production.

'The soldiers who have used it are satisfied, and then I'm satisfied,' Meyer replied.

When asked whether the XM-1 was better than anything the Soviets now had or was in the works, Meyer told the newsmen: 'The new tank will be better than anything the Russians have or anything we know they have on the drawing board.' He also admitted that it was possible the Soviets had a more sophisticated tank, but American Intelligence was not aware of it.

General Meyer also reported that the army had asked that 7,058 XM-1 tanks be built within the next ten years. He refused to give a price estimate for each tank, although it was generally believed to be $1.5 million for each. One enterprising newsman asked whether Chrysler's assets in the tank plant (the plant is actually owned by the government but operated by Chrysler) could be mortgaged to provide some of the cash Chrysler needed. General Meyer's answer was that it was probably illegal to try and mortgage assets that were partially or jointly owned by the army.

The rollout ceremony following the press conference was held inside the huge tank plant, where a large area near the back had been cleared and where Bill Winn's men had erected a reviewing stand and bleachers. The platform had been set directly between two doors through which two of the massive tanks would be driven on cue.

Lee Iacocca, suffering from a cold, arrived in time for the ceremony. With him on the platform, in addition to the general and assistant secretary, were the former astronaut, John Glenn, now senator from Ohio, and the mayor of Lima, Harry Moyer. The mayor welcomed the dignitaries and, in his brief talk, reminded Lee Iacocca that Lima was probably the only city in the United States where Chrysler was showing a profit. Iacocca bristled slightly at the ill-timed remark.

Senator Glenn's remarks were more circumspect, congratulating Chrysler and the Army for tanks that were 'peacemakers and peacekeepers, which by their very existence would no doubt prevent the need for their ever being used in combat.'

As the army band struck a stirring Sousa march, the doors flanking the dais rolled up to reveal an XM-1 combat tank in each doorway. The tanks roared in beside the platform and came to a stop, their 105mm cannons and machine guns pointed at the audience.

Iacocca stepped to centre stage to heavy applause. In his opening remarks he apologized for his cold and joked about his slipping on the ice at Lake Placid during the Olympics.

'I want to present the US Army the first two XM-1 production tanks,' he concluded. 'The quality of their manufacture is outstanding. I am sure that their performance in the field will measure up to the same high standards.'

General Meyer accepted the tanks on behalf of the United States Army and then told the assemblage that the XM-1 would then and there be renamed the 'Abrams Tank' in honour of General Creighton W. Abrams. A veteran of three wars with army service of forty-two years, Abrams had been commander of the forces in Vietnam from 1967 to 1972 and was named Army Chief of Staff in 1972, two years before his death.

General Abrams, Meyer recounted, was widely known as one of the army's most aggressive and successful armoured vehicle commanders, of whom General George S. Patton, Jr., once said: 'I'm supposed to be the best tank commander in the army, but I have one peer – Abe Abrams. He's the world champion.'

Meyer then escorted General Abrams' widow, Julia Harvey Abrams, to the tank at the left of the platform. Handed a bottle of champagne swathed in red, white, and blue, Mrs Abrams smashed the bottle over the tank's cannon. She brought a laugh from the crowd as she licked a finger dripping with champagne.

As Mrs Abrams walked back to her seat, a tank corps enlisted man came forward and attached to the tank a decal imprinted with a bolt of lightning piercing a white cloud to nickname the tank 'Thunderbolt,' which had been the name of the tank Abrams commanded during the Battle of Bastogne in 1944. And to ensure that Chrysler was not forgotten, a K & E staffer took the liberty of applying a decal reading 'Ram Tough,' the ad slogan for Dodge trucks.

The ceremonies concluded with a demonstration of some of the tanks' capabilities on a small test track next to the plant. An enlisted man, Sp/4 William Watson, put the 59.9-ton, 387-inch-long (with cannon forward) tank through its paces, speeding around the track at 45 miles an hour, running through a series of waist-high obstacles, and climbing a steep grade.

'It goes like hell,' twenty-four-old Watson said after the demonstration. 'I love this tank. I drove an M60 at only ten miles an hour over rough terrain, and I was all black and blue from bouncing around. You hardly feel it in the XM-1, it just seems to float.'

Iacocca returned to his home base with a sigh of relief. A failure by the tank could have crippled his hopes for the money needed to keep Chrysler going.

But there was no peace of mind back in his Highland Park

office. The money expected from the state of Michigan had yet to be approved by the legislature as the month of March got underway. Things were at a do-or-die stage. The federal guarantees would slip down the drain without the Michigan loan, which was also needed for even more immediate needs.

On March 6 the Michigan legislature approved the loan for $150 million. The signature of Governor William Milliken was still needed, and the governor was away from the state capital and would not be back before Monday, March 10.

Michigan's governor enjoys the panoply of office and prefers signing important bills with press cameras flashing and TV cameras rolling. But March 10 would be too late to do Chrysler the good it needed. It was imperative that the bill be signed before the banks opened on that Monday.

Milliken was finally located at his home in Traverse City. He agreed to forgo any ceremony and had the Chrysler-aid bill brought to him from Lansing. He signed the bill without fanfare on Saturday, March 8.

The pressure eased, but only a little and only temporarily. To intensify Iacocca's problems in getting the concessions needed to complete the terms of the federal loan guarantees, the First Security Bank of Utah, one of Chrysler's smaller creditors, began suit in federal court seeking repayment of $1 million owed the bank.

March was not going out like a lamb. During the last week of the month a Belgian bank, Banque Bruxelles Lambert S.A., filed a similar action in New York to force payment of $10 million plus interest that had been due the end of January.

Chrysler had been able to convince most of the 150 world-wide banks to whom it owed over $1 billion to forgo any action until it met the loan-guarantee requirements. If the action by these two small institutions had a domino effect, disaster would ensue.

Iacocca's never-give-up temperament kept him going. There were some bright breaks in the clouds. Household Finance Corporation, America's largest maker of loans to the general public, was seriously considering the purchase of Chrysler Financial Corporation, the company's financial arm, which lends money to dealers and individuals to purchase cars.

Then, too, Iacocca's meeting in Ottawa with Herb Gray, Canada's industry minister, on March 24 had offered hope for a multimillion-dollar loan that would keep Chrysler's engine plant in Windsor, Ontario, in operation. A two-hour meeting with Gray had ended with favourable overtones.

The rosy bloom, slight as it was, faded in April as Chrysler sustained a double-barrelled blow. On April 11 Household Finance released a statement to the press that it had notified Chrysler 'of its determination that an investment in Chrysler Financial Corporation is not appropriate at this time.'

Public knowledge of Household Finance's decision came two days after Chrysler reported that its 1980 losses likely would reach $750 million, $100 million more than had been estimated less than three months earlier. At about the same time the company was ordered by the Federal Trade Commission to replace rusted fenders on 200,000 1976 and 1977 Volares and Aspens. The cost to the company would be about $45 million, already figured as part of its estimated year's loss of $750 million.

The Household Finance turndown was the more serious of the two for Iacocca. The funds from the sale were a significant part of the amount needed to qualify for the loan guarantees, and the Loan Guarantee Board had already reported to Congress that Chrysler had commitments for less than one-third of the money needed. Sale of just 51 percent of the financial subsidiary would have offset the $300 million demanded by the board from sale of Chrysler assets.

Expectedly, Iacocca was a bit testy when he addressed the Automotive Service Industry Association convention in Chicago later in the month, telling the ASIA members that no industry in America had been battered by the government as had the automobile industry, and that Chrysler had sustained the worst beating of all because of its limited capital.

'Our government has added $600 to the price of every car built in this country this year because of regulations that include emissions, safety, and gas mileage,' he said, later adding: 'It is only a matter of time before American companies will find themselves in the same position as Chrysler, and when it happens, those companies will learn, just as Chrysler did, that the root of the problem is government regulations.'

Iacocca further pointed out that Chrysler has had to pay out $160 million every month to comply with federal regulations that had raised the price of American automobiles from $1 to $3 a pound. Because of this, he said, America was losing great shares of its market to imports.

'I worry about this,' he added, 'because we aren't in a position to compete with them on an equal basis. Government officials say that we, the American automobile industry, are out of touch with the automobile market. We're not out of touch. We're out of money.'

As April yielded to May, there was no underestimating the near death of Chrysler Corporation. The company would not survive the month without the loan guarantees.

It was the Canadian government that came to the rescue. An emergency Saturday meeting was called in Toronto on May 10, at which Canada approved $200 million in loan guarantees. This, combined with a separate $10-million guarantee by the province of Ontario, pushed Chrysler over the top as to 'outside' help requirements.

That same day the Loan Guarantee Board approved granting the $1.5 billion authorised by Congress, also voting to appropriate an immediate $500 million. Immediate, in this instance, meant a delay of the weekend and more, thanks to Secretary Miller.

'That entire weekend,' one official close to the action said, 'the Treasury Department insisted that every piddling paper and detail be specific and in order, so that the interests of the taxpayers were fully protected.'

A situation that led to another agonising delay occurred on Monday night, May 12 in New York. Hurrying to get hundreds of documents signed for the next day's meeting in Washington, Chrysler officials and lawyers were startled when a cleaning woman came in screaming that the skyscraper in which they were working was on fire.

The man signing the papers, Steve Miller, Chrysler's assistant treasurer, and thirty lawyers bolted for the stairs, leaving the documents behind. After scrambling down thirty-three flights, they dashed out into New York's Park Avenue to a hail of falling glass.

An hour later they were able to retrieve the precious documents that held the fate of Chrysler Corporation, but they had to convince the Manhattan firefighters of the urgency before they were allowed back in the building.

Once an elevator was activated for their use, the men were back on the thirty-third floor, stuffing papers into boxes and mail carts, not knowing whether they had everything or not.

Serious at the time, the picture of straitlaced lawyers pushing mail carts down Park Avenue to the offices of another law firm amused many in legal circles.

During the finalisation of the loan guarantees the next morning, May 13, 1980, Senator Donald Riegle of Michigan took advantage of the near-tragic consequences the fire could have occasioned.

'The fire shows,' he said, 'that not even an act of God can stop the Chrysler recovery.'

CHAPTER 14

Iacocca could now breathe more freely. It had been a traumatic eight months of waiting, wondering, and fighting, eight months that took their toll. At one point it seemed as though he might have a nervous breakdown.

'I was scared,' he has said. 'Afraid inside that the whole thing would come down before we had a chance. That the whole thing would collapse, and I would cut out physically.'

He had been in Washington on one trip after spending many weeks of reviewing his answers to questions he would be asked at the congressional hearings. Almost immediately on his arrival he was taken into the Surgeon General's office.

'I was sort of seeing double,' Iacocca explained. 'All the stuff suddenly hit me, and I got fuzzy-brained.'

That was over now. The chips were down, and Chrysler's fate was to a great degree dependent on Iacocca. If the company could overcome the depressed climate in the automobile business and the assault of the import cars, which was increasing monthly, and if the new Chrysler cars would do the job, the agony would have been worthwhile. The near-dead Chrysler Corporation would be resuscitated as a healthy New Chrysler Corporation.

However, if Iacocca's aim was off target, even $1.5 billion in loan guarantees wouldn't put the company back together again. For the immediate present the company badly needed a drop in interest rates to make purchase of a new automobile practical for the average wage-earner.

The company needed sales to provide a cash flow. A huge payroll had to be met each week. Operating expenses and the continuous planning for new products that ate up more millions each month added to the problems.

Iacocca made it clear to the press that if the loan guarantees had not been approved, Chrysler's cash on hand would have been exhausted before the end of May and the company would have indeed ceased operations. Hundreds of thousands of people would have been out of work, and the American economy would have been in straits more desperate than any since the 1930s. That had been made clear by the secretary of the treasury as soon as the long battle had been resolved.

'If we had let Chrysler go bankrupt,' G. William Miller had emphasised, 'it would have cost the taxpayers three billion dollars over two years in welfare, lost revenue and unemployment.' Simple arithmetic said that that was twice the cost of the loan guarantees if they were never repaid by Chrysler.

Thus the government's help made it possible for Iacocca to offer real hope to Chrysler stockholders at the annual meeting on May 30, 1980, despite the previous year's loss of more than $1 billion.

As Douglas Fraser, head of the United Auto Workers, put it: 'If you look at Chrysler today and Chrysler of a year ago, you're looking at vastly different companies.'

The most startling change, as the meeting in Rockford, Illinois came to a close, was in the makeup of Chrysler's newly elected board of directors. Never before had the board of a corporation been weighted so heavily with former executives of a competing organisation.

In addition to Lee Iacocca as chairman, the new directors included the president, Paul Bergmoser, and Gerald Greenwald, Gar Laux, and Hal Sperlick, elected that same day as executive vice-president of finance, sales and marketing, and engineering, respectively. All were one-time Ford Motor Company executives.

This new Chrysler board also reflected a historic first. Nominated to the board by Lee Iacocca, and elected, was Douglas Fraser. Never before in the annals of American business had any union leader penetrated the upper echelons of management in any major corporation.

The Chrysler comeback, Iacocca assured the stockholders, was on its way. A penetrating look at the company's immediate past showed it to be not so much a helpless concern, but one that – through mistakes and misman-agement – had been rendered financially anaemic. The loan guarantees would provide a strength-restoring transfusion.

The year 1979, Iacocca made clear, was a year to forget. Chrysler's mind-boggling difficulties that year had come about as a result of a combination of situations beyond anyone's control. Escalating gasoline prices and gasoline shortages, rising inflation, record-high interest rates, and a fear of recession had slowed car sales to a trickle.

Operating expenses, of course, continued despite the dras-tic drop in car sales. The company was forced to spend some $160 million a month, even though operations had been restructured to cut costs.

Chrysler's multiplying problems had dropped it in 1979 from tenth to seventeenth among America's largest manufac-turers. Yet, through its worst times it had managed to meet its high monthly cash payouts. Even though 1979 losses were a staggering $1 billion, the company had good reason to hope for better times. Its worldwide sales in an agonising year had totalled $12 billion.

Iacocca assured the stockholders that plans were in the works to further reduce costs and increase operating efficien-cies. Three plants had already been closed down, and the closing of a fourth, the Detroit facility where Chrysler's full-size cars were assembled, was but a week away. Three others were scheduled for shutdown in the fall. The stock-holders were assured that these closings would not cripple the company's manufacturing capabilities. Seventeen factories would still be operating in Michigan, eleven in the metropolitan Detroit area.

Chrysler also had twenty-three plants located in twelve other states. And it still held substantial interests in foreign firms, holding – for one thing – an equity position of about 14 percent in France's Peugeot-Citroën, the largest European automobile company. Of immediate and continuing value and importance to Chrysler was its 15 percent interest in Japan's Mitsubishi Motors. Chrysler, of course, marketed Mitsubishi-manufactured cars in the US and Canada. These included the Dodge and Plymouth pickup trucks, Plymouth Champ, Arrow, and Sapporo passenger cars, and the Dodge Colt and Challenger. Chrysler worldwide sales in 1979 included over 270,000 of these.

Iacocca returned from the stockholders' meeting to put the finishing touches on the new cars he believed would bring Chrysler back to profitability. These were the K-cars, roomy front-wheel-drive automobiles whose engineering was in the hands of Hal Sperlick. Plans called for three body styles, two- and four-door sedans and a station wagon, for both Plymouth and Dodge nameplates.

The 'K' designation was originally a code, not expected to be part of the cars' identity. But it had been presented so forcefully to the loan-guarantee committee as Chrysler's salvation, and the media had speculated so widely about them, that American became K-car conscious.

Iacocca, considering the coverage already given the unborn car, decided sometime before it was ready for the market that it would be a mistake not to take advantage of the built-in familiarity. He decided that the letter 'K' had to be part of the names given the new cars. In the final determination the Plymouth version came to be called Reliant K and the Dodge Aries K.

Iacocca was not too worried about the K-cars' acceptance, but he was concerned about the state of the economy. If it was no shakier than it had been in the spring, sales of about 500,000 for both Plymouth and Dodge versions seemed right. Marketing expert that he was, Iacocca was sure that the American public was ready for front-wheel-drive compacts like the K's.

If his estimate proved right, and if the economy held up, there was hope. K-car acceptance added to the projected sales of the hot Omni and Horizon subcompacts, other Chrysler-built cars and trucks, and the Mitsubishi imports would get Chrysler moving.

Iacocca also had another automobile in the works for introduction during 1980. A couple of conservatives on his staff believed this car a mistake, for it was a reach-for-the-moon kind of luxury automobile to compete with Cadillac Eldorado and the Continental Mark. It was important to Iacocca that the public see the New Chrysler Corporation as a full-line producer of cars.

Iacocca originally called this new personal luxury car La-Scala. The silvery model shown during a private preview for ad agency personnel had a Rolls-Royce aura in its styling. It seemed to have what was needed to compete with Cadillac and Lincoln.

When the car was ready for production, the LaScala name was discarded. In the old Chrysler Corporation's heyday one of the world's finest luxury cars was named Imperial, so the new luxury car was given the advantage of a known and respected name.

Iacocca's Imperial was to be built unlike any other American luxury car. And it was to be marketed unlike any other. It would be a complete car, an automobile that left the showroom equipped with every accessory normally desired by buyers and paid for as extra options. Its equipment was to include the fuel-efficient 318-cubic-inch V-8 engine and the most sophisticated, technologically advanced instrumentation in the industry. And its price, about $20,000, would be competitive with Cadillac Eldorado and Continental Mark.

Luxury cars, with their higher use of fuel as well as high prices, were frowned on by the government. Let the Europeans build Mercedes, Rolls Royce, and BMW, but American carmakers, especially a Chrysler in such financial trouble, should forgo them. Nevertheless, a sizeable percentage of Americans want the prestige of luxury cars, so a market does and will exist, and the more luxurious and expensive automobiles make a higher ratio of profit than the smaller, more mundane models. For Chrysler each Imperial sold – and Iacocca limited production to 25,000 units – would provide profit equivalent to as many as five or more Omnis, Horizons, or K-cars.

All of this planning and execution of plans by Iacocca and his staff was still very much on a speculative basis. Chrysler was still waiting for $500 million of the cash due under the loan-guarantee bill. It would not be forthcoming until about 400 banks involved in the company's refinancing signed off on the concessions included in the loan guarantee. Too many were still reluctant, and just as many were taking their time.

Though it was a suspenseful, nerve-racking, nail-biting wait, there was nothing to do but continue as though the loan guarantee money would be forthcoming soon. Business had to go on as usual. Cars had to be sold.

Gasoline prices had continued to rise, having climbed considerably over the dollar-per-gallon mark. Miles-per-gallon had become the number-one criterion for car purchases by lower- and middle-income Americans. And Chrysler had high-mileage cars.

Plymouth Horizon and Dodge Omni offered thirty-plus miles per gallon, more than any other American-built automobiles. As for imports, the Mitsubishi cars such as Dodge Colt and Plymouth Arrow gave other imports a good run for their money when it came to mpg.

Here, then, was an obvious and built-in plus to be emphasised in an advertising blitz. Kenyon & Eckhardt developed a campaign that both waved the flag and pinpointed the mileage advantages in buying Chrysler products. A red-white-and-blue motif was used in advertisements in newspapers and on television. The high-mileage Dodge and Plymouth car names were projected as 'The American Way to Beat the Pump.' Graphics for the ads and commercials featured situations in which men and women smashed service station gas pumps with clenched fists.

Then, just as the month of May neared its end, Iacocca was faced with a more personal concern. On Memorial Day his wife entered Massachusetts General Hospital in Boston for a new and still somewhat experimental treatment for arteriosclerosis, or hardening of the arteries. Lee remained with Mary at the hospital. She had suffered from this ailment, in addition to her other afflictions, for over three years. The aorta, the main artery that carried blood from her heart, was blocked, severely reducing the blood flow to the legs and producing constant pain.

Until recently the only recourse had been bypass surgery, a dangerous and difficult procedure. It had not been recommended for Mrs Iacocca. Because of her diabetic condition and heart attacks, the risk was too great. So she and Lee came to Boston for a nonsurgical technique called angioplasty.

The treatment, which involved pushing a catheter through the artery to relieve the blockage, was a success. One week after Mary's admission to the hospital, she was able to return home with a much relieved Lee.

Iacocca's most pressing business preoccupation on his return was the quality of his K-cars, the keystone of Chrysler's renaissance. Their new 2.2-litre, four-cylinder engine had to be the best it could be, providing better mileage than might be offered by the four-cylinder engine in GM's X-cars. Iacocca and Chrysler had little to fear from Ford, which was way behind in plans for front-wheel drives.

To ensure top-quality construction for this new engine, Iacocca had ordered modernisation of the Trenton, Michigan, engine plant. Its new assembly line now included thirty-four automatic inspection stations as well as a computer-controlled 'hot' test that automatically examined more than thirty engine functions.

Iacocca was leaving nothing to chance. Since the days of Walter P. Chrysler, engineering had been perceived by the public as the one certain Chrysler plus over its competition. He was determined to build on that decades-long perception with quality cars that were precisely assembled and now, strikingly styled. Styling, for years, had been a Chrysler short-coming.

A soon-to-be initiated change in the company's labour relations, one exclusive to Chrysler and part of its concessions to the United Auto Workers, was expected to go a long way in improving production quality. In mid-summer almost every Chrysler employee in the United States would become a part owner of the company as over $1.5 million in common stock would be distributed among workers over a four-year period.

Employees who had accepted salary and benefit cuts – virtually everyone in the company – were eligible for these stock shares. Already evident in the plants was an increased dedication among workers, a self-interest in doing a better job to produce better automobiles.

Whatever incentives had produced this turnaround, Chrysler people were already doing their best to refute the belief that if an automobile was built by American labour, it was one of inferior quality. They were exhibiting a sense of pride and self-confidence in the cars they turned out.

These workers were showing a high degree of personal involvement in their work, and a team concept had been instituted to increase motivation and dedication. Groups of a dozen or more called 'quality circles' debated ways to do specific jobs more efficiently.

With this attention to detail Chrysler-built cars were coming off the assembly road-ready. Yet, particularly in the case of newly designed automobiles, such as the Imperial and the K-cars, automobiles that had not had the benefit of thousands of miles of actual use, more checks were necessary. These, called 'car evaluation and reliability tests,' were the final quality checks before a car line was released for sale.

For the new Imperial, a special quality-assurance centre had been built adjacent to the plant in Windsor, Ontario, where the car was assembled. Here, after assembly, each individual Imperial – which had already been subjected to countless inspections – was given additional examinations with a warm engine. After an underbody fluid-leak inspection utilising a high-pressure water spray, the car was checked for front-end alignment and given a tough 5.5-mile road test over a special track that included almost every possible type of terrain. At each inspection step the Imperial received a sign-off if everything was in order. Otherwise it was not approved for shipment.

The evaluation and reliability tests for mass-production models like the K-cars were necessarily different. Single body styles for each car line, Plymouth and Dodge, were given round-the-clock 5,000-mile driving tests at the Chrysler Proving Grounds near Chelsea, Michigan, just west of Detroit.

The 5,000-mile test was planned to be equal to 12,000 miles of actual driving. The extensive proving grounds are laid out with two-lane blacktop roads, with roads that have circular pieces of asphalt set irregularly so that jouncing, jarring rides are simulated, with gravel roads complete with chuckholes and loose stones, with hills of varied grades, with roads that curve, and with a six-lane, high-speed concrete, track about five miles long.

At the conclusion of the test, cars were examined meticulously. Rattles, loose fittings, brakes, transmission, and body condition were points of concern after the gruelling run.

Writers for car-buff magazines such as *Motor Trend*, *Road & Track*, and *Car and Driver* were the first outsiders to see the already widely heralded K-cars. Iacocca invited about a hundred of the journalists to a ride-and-drive get-together at the proving grounds.

At a luncheon for the assembled writers Iacocca expressed high expectations for public acceptance of the cars. 'I predict that a guy investing in a K-car will probably drive it a year and sell it for more than he paid for it.'

He also reported that he believed Chrysler could sell at least a million cars in 1981, with perhaps 600,000 being front-wheel drives from the K-car, Omni, and Horizon lines. It could be done, he assured the crowd, if only the nation's economy would show an upturn.

'If that doesn't happen,' he added, 'we're bankrupt. We're wiped out. And Ford will probably be wiped out and be in the same position we are in today, struggling, loaning, borrowing, selling off assets. And GM will be badly wounded. No question about it.'

There was much more that Iacocca could have said, but he put it off for another time. He had seen the trend fifteen years earlier while at Ford and had tried, with Hal Sperlick's backup, to do something about it. He had found himself hamstrung at the time.

In order to improve Chrysler's cash position, and to concentrate on the automobile business, in June Iacocca decided to separate Chrysler's Defense Division from the parent corporation. Defense was the most profitable division in the company. Setting it up as a separate corporation would save it in the event that the corporation itself was forced into bankruptcy. Not that Iacocca thought failure was imminent, but he thought it better to be cautious.

In a speech at San Diego, Iacocca acknowledged being 'in the import capital of the world.' In the state of California imports were taking almost 50 percent for the car market, as against twenty-seven percent nationwide. Another point he made was that American carmakers had abdicated the American market to the imports.

Iacocca went on to say that the priority of the moment was to 'anticipate and meet the needs of the today's fast-changing automobile market.' Consumer attitudes had shifted. Where the buyer's previous experience with a car make was first consideration in deciding on a new-car purchase, it had slipped to sixteenth in importance. Exterior styling had dropped from second to ninth. Value for the money, which had been eighth in importance, was now number one, and quality of workmanship had leaped from sixteenth to second as one of the primary new-market values. The K-cars, which would be introduced in the fall, would put Chrysler 'in an absolutely ideal position.'

That introduction represents, he went on, 'our first major step in meeting the Japanese challenge. When added to the models we already produce, Reliant and Aries will give Chrysler the capacity to produce nearly one million front-wheel-drive small cars a year, starting this fall. That puts us in a position to take on the imports, head to head.'

Iacocca called solving the explosion of the Japanese imports as the first of two major problems to be faced in the following two years. The second was that the total number of new-car sales in the US was declining. One solution for this problem was an innovative suggestion he had made to the government and that he emphasised at every opportunity.

The problem, he said 'can be resolved through a $1,500 personal-investment tax credit for the purchase of fuel-efficient equipment, new automobiles, when pre-1976 cars are traded in. There are 42 million pre-1976 cars still on the road averaging 12.9 miles per gallon.'

New automobiles like the K-cars with average mileage in the twenties could 'save up to 450 million gallons of gasoline a year' if they replaced the pre-1976 gas-eaters on the road. The tax credit would make it worthwhile for Americans to trade in their older cars, thus increasing sales of new American-built cars by up to 1.5 million and enabling the automobile industry to call back to work nearly 200,000 laid-off workers.

As the weeks in June ticked off, the agony of waiting for the loan money increased for Iacocca. Many of the 400 banks continued to drag their feet. To add to his worries, in mid-month the Michigan National Corporation, a bank holding company, confiscated $900,000 of Chrysler funds on deposit in its banks as partial payment for outstanding loans. The next day the bank reversed its position and freed the funds. It was none too soon. The $900,000 was for operating expenses, including suppliers' bills, debts that had been deferred the previous week, when for the first time Chrysler failed to pay its suppliers on the date due.

One worry over Michigan National's action was its effect on other banks still uncommitted to the loan guarantees. Reportedly the banks had secretly agreed among themselves that if one bank held out, all would do so. Michigan National's manoeuvre could have dealt Chrysler a deathblow.

For Iacocca June seemed to be busting out all over with reversals. Another was a missing $8 million Volkswagen had paid for Chrysler's share in its Brazilian subsidiary. VW had made an unfortunate choice in its bank to handle the transfer of funds, the Deutsche Genossenschaftsbank, which held past due notes against Chrysler in approximately that same $8-million amount. The German bank simply seized the money rather than complete the transfer to Chrysler in New York.

More than half of the month had passed, and still some banks continued to hold out against acceptance of concessions that would minimise the amount owed them by Chrysler. The unyielding were only a few among the 400 needed for agreement – two large European banks and a handful of small institutions in the United States – but they were more than enough to force a Chrysler bankruptcy. To forestall disaster the loan guarantee board postponed a meeting scheduled for June 18 to approve $500 million as a first instalment to Chrysler.

Whatever his inner feelings, Lee Iacocca remained outwardly optimistic and unflappable. With the bravado of a man sure he would win, he ordered production of his K-cars to begin two weeks ahead of schedule. This new timetable would permit building 180,000 K-cars by the end of 1980, 30,000 more than originally planned. It also meant that the first K would roll off the assembly line in Detroit on July 29 rather than on August 12.

As if there were no problems and Chrysler was indeed a going concern, he invited 280 of America's largest fleet buyers to a preview of prototypes of his Plymouth and Dodge K-cars. In typical Iacocca oratory he had the car buyers reacting more like people trying to sell him rather than as typically reluctant customers.

'You wouldn't believe the reaction unless you saw it,' Fran Hazelroth, Chrysler's director of fleet sales, reported. 'He had them – people we wanted to sell to – eating out of his hand. When he finished his talk, they gave him a standing ovation like you never saw.'

The fleet buyers did more than that. They bought K-cars on the spot, ordering almost 50,000, with one firm signing up for 5,000 K-wagons without asking the price. 'Imagine, all this while the company was still struggling for help,' Hazelroth added.

Iacocca's seeming confidence proved justified. On June 20 the last two holdout banks agreed to the terms of the loan-guarantee bill. The final approval was that from the Deutsche bank in Germany that had held onto the $8 million.

The loan guarantee board held its approval meeting a little after eleven on the morning of June 24 and quickly voted the immediate issuance of the first $500 million of Chrysler. Lee Iacocca, in Mexico completing plans for an engine plant to be built in that country, and Gerald Greenwald, executive vice-president for finance, were the first Chrysler recipients of the news.

The following day a jubilant Iacocca was on hand in New York to receive a check for the $500 million as well as to chair a news conference in the Waldorf-Astoria Hotel. He projected a picture of the never-say-die optimist as he answered reporters' questions, sidestepping everything negative.

'I am no longer talking about how things are going with the banks,' he said. 'The financial episode is over.'

He tabbed as heroes the hundreds of individuals inside and outside Chrysler who had worked so hard to make the day possible, calling them the saviours of hundreds of thousands of jobs in American industry. He told reporters that it was time that industry in the United States worked closely with labour and the government to solve its problems.

'We already have a tripartite group running Chrysler,' he pointed out, 'one in place to further the reindustrialisation of America.'

With that reference to Douglas Fraser's position as a member of Chrysler's board of directors and the government's part in helping Chrysler, he brought the news conference to a close and left to film a television commercial with Frank Sinatra.

A month or so earlier Sinatra had had dinner with Bill Fine, a friend of his, when Iacocca appeared on a television interview. After watching the TV screen for a moment, Sinatra, who did not know Iacocca at the time, turned to Fine. 'You know,' Sinatra told his friend, 'I really want to help that guy.'

Fine set things in motion. He phoned Leo-Arthur Kelmenson at Kenyon & Eckhardt. Kelmenson phoned Iacocca. Iacocca called Kelmenson back and told him: 'Get this in the works.'

Iacocca met with Frank Sinatra, and the two sons of Italian immigrants hit it off from the start. Iacocca could not commit Chrysler to Sinatra's normal fee, but America's best-known singer did not care. He agreed to promote the New Chrysler Corporation for $1 a year, the same salary being accepted by Iacocca himself. The Chrysler chairman added a new Imperial to the dollar.

The TV commercial filmed that June 25 at the Waldorf, later expanded to newspaper and magazine double-page spreads, showing one 'chairman of the board' (Sinatra's nickname) discussing Chrysler's future with another chairman of the board, Iacocca.

Later Sinatra would film and record a full series promoting the new Chrysler Imperial in song with the theme: 'It's time for Imperial.' With Sinatra's help other stars came aboard, including Gregory Peck, all of whom recognised Chrysler's shaky financial position and made the commercials for the basic union scale.

For Lee Iacocca rays of light were finally penetrating the gloom of his first year and a half at Chrysler. His company had been given a life-restoring transfusion, and he was getting added help from unexpected quarters. Production of his K-cars was in high gear. Yet, as the summer of 1980 moved into its hottest months, he was becoming increasingly irritable at the constant sniping of the media.

Commentators and reporters continued to accentuate the negative of Chrysler's situation in an economic climate that forecast losses of $1 billion or more during the year for both General Motors and Ford. Under such circumstances they thought Chrysler's survival impossible.

In addition Iacocca's launching of the K-cars at a time of recession was severely criticised. The production costs were projected to be a noose for quick strangulation. And Chrysler facilities were described as antiquated relics of a bygone age, despite the millions spent for their modernisation.

The *Wall Street Journal*, bible of the business world and read by many of Chrysler's dealers, suppliers, and customers, had been especially negative in editorials and reports. In July Iacocca sent a long letter to the editor 'to set straight the very serious false impression about Chrysler.'

After its explanatory introduction the letter read: 'But the *Wall Street Journal* won't leave it alone. We continue to have served up to us a daily barrage of negative tidbits from the inch-thick report to Congress, pointing out that even though we have the money we need, even though we have a restructured company, even though we have new management, the right product and great quality, lightning *could* strike! The economy *could* get worse! Car sales *could* be even lousier! It's time to lay out some facts.'

Iacocca's letter, published in the *Journal's* July 31 edition, closed with:

'In spite of recession, in spite of the brickbats, in spite of inflation, we are on our way back. The only thing that could possibly stop us is a constant recitation of the possible pitfalls that lie ahead. Well, life is full of pitfalls. The *Journal* can concentrate on nothing else if it wants to. But life is also full of opportunities – and we're making the most of ours.

'Let me make one final suggestion. Get your reporters started working on a story for next summer – the turnaround story on Chrysler Corporation. We'll be there, getting ready to introduce a 1982 line of products that will knock your eyes out.'

CHAPTER 15

Sports enthusiast that he is, Lee Iacocca was well aware that
'K' is the symbol for strikeout in baseball. But not believing
in superstition, he went ahead and used the letter 'K' to
denote the cars meant to save Chrysler. General Motors had
introduced its X-cars, leading off with the Chevrolet
Citation, one year earlier, marketing its first front-wheel
drives. Nevertheless, thanks to Hal Sperlick's Omni and
Horizon, the giant was a tardy second in entering the domestic front-wheel derby.

Omni and Horizon were compacts, and GM had no front-
wheel products in that class. The K-cars would put Chrysler
toe-to-toe against the GM X-cars in the mid-size front-wheel-
drive category. Here the K's had an edge, not only over the
X's, but over almost all imported front-wheel drives, whatever their class.

Plymouth Reliant K and Dodge Aries K were more spacious than the GM X-cars, holding six passengers rather than
five. The K-car two- and four-door sedans offered trunk
space. The hatchback-type X did not. And the K-cars,
unlike the X's of GM, offered a station wagon model, which
had appreciably more cargo space than any X would provide.

Since 'value' was now the public's top criterion for a
new-car purchase, Iacocca was sure he had little to fear from
X-car competition if the public would only heed his request
that they 'compare.'

While some months would pass before the K-cars would

enter the market. Iacocca felt that whetting the public's appetite might hold back a few potential X-car sales. Accordingly, he announced a public showing of the first K-cars off the assembly line. Wednesday, August 6, 1980, was billed as K-day.

Chrysler's Jefferson Avenue plant in Detroit was gaily festooned for the occasion. Red, white, and blue bunting was everywhere. Over one entrance was a huge 'We Can do It!' banner. Another banner read 'Consider It Done!' The entrances and the streets were jammed with onlookers, the general public as well as Chrysler workers. Flanking the end of the assembly line inside were Lee Iacocca, other Chrysler executives, and politicians.

Michigan's Governor Milliken and Detroit's Mayor Young were on hand, as they had been two years earlier at John Riccardo's ill-fated introduction of new Chrysler models. Donald Riegle and Carl Levin, the senior and junior senators from Michigan, had come from Washington for the ceremonies. Douglas Fraser was there, too, representing the men and women who were building the K-cars.

Iacocca had reserved for himself the distinction of driving the first car off the line. Far better that he be embarrassed if there were a battery failure or other malfunction. As the car, a cream-coloured Plymouth Reliant K two-door came to the end of the assembly line, Iacocca stepped toward it with a broad smile and opened the driver-side door.

'Here we are,' he said, 'two years and a couple of billion dollars later, and ahead of schedule.' With that he entered the driver's seat and turned the ignition switch. As the Reliant's engine came alive with a muffled roar, the crowd, led by the governor and mayor, cheered.

Iacocca put the car in gear and slowly pulled away flashing a V for victory as television cameras recorded the moment. His Plymouth Reliant K was the first in a series of K-cars to drive down Detroit's Jefferson Avenue. Governor Milliken, Mayor Young, Senators Riegle and Levin, and Douglas Fraser followed in Dodge Aries K's and other Reliants.

When they returned to the plant and got out of the cars, there was much joshing all around. Senator Riegle told

Iacocca that he was going to drive a K-car to Washington and give a ride to Sentor Proxmire of Wisconsin, the major stumbling block in the fight for the loan guarantees. Not to be outdone, Senator Carl Levin claimed he would change the spelling of his first name to have it start with a K rather than a C.

Iacocca had set October, the traditional time for presention a new car to the public, for the national introduction of his 1981 model cars, but the K-cars were already known from coast to coast. Not only had the designation been heard repeatedly on network news programmes during the congressional hearings on the loan guarantees, but a teaser campaign had swept the country as early as July.

It began during the Republican National Convention held in Detroit. Banners reading 'K-cars are coming!' were towed by airplanes throughout the Detroit downtown area for the benefit of the hundreds of delegates in general and Ronald Reagan in particular.

'K-cars are coming' teasers then blitzed the national scene in newspapers and on radio and television, while a pertinent campaign was being prepared for the fall introduction. This, Iacocca told his agency, should be one that would do double duty: awaken American car buyers to the benefits of front-wheel drive and, at the same time, launch an assault on imports.

The new slogan, 'America is not going to be pushed around any more,' told the country two things. One, the K-car with front-wheel drive pulled, not pushed as did rear-drive cars. Two, Chrysler was one American automaker that had no intention of abandoning the small-car field to imports.

Beginning on September 7 the 'K-cars are coming' ad campaign was made more specific. Now newspaper ads and radio and television commercials were naming names. 'Aries is coming!' and 'Reliant is coming!' Where colour was possible, the ads and TV commercials were asplash with red, white, and blue. Messages had patriotic connotations supporting 'the American way to beat the pump' and 'America is not going to be pushed around any more.'

Iacocca's own personal television commercials had the

same format. In mid-September, during Chrysler's sponsorship of the movie *Shogun* he appeared on screen to the tune of 'Yankee Doodle' and told his huge audience that in early October Chrysler would be offering the American car buyer 'the red, white, and blue Yankee Doodle direct-power drive system,' a reference to Chrysler's American-designed front-wheel-drive technology.

Surveys had shown that 30 percent of Americans already were aware the K meant a new car from Chrysler. With the preintroduction ads blanketing the print and broadcast worlds, that figure was expected to grow appreciably and send hundreds of thousands of potential buyers into Chrysler-Plymouth and Dodge showrooms.

To give this growing awareness a boost before the first public showing of the K-cars, Iacocca had a special press preview in the nation's capital in mid-September. More than fifty of the country's leading automotive writers showed up at Washington's Shoreham Hotel to inspect and drive Iacocca's great hope.

While *Motor Trend* magazine would later name the Chrysler K as the 1981 'Car of the Year,' few of the writers made any definitive assessments of the car concept as such. Typical was an article by Charles Williams in the *Washington Post*, 'Iacocca's Cure for What Ails Us.'

Williams drove a Dodge Aries K Special Edition and began his story with some high-powered prose. 'It resembles,' he wrote, 'somewhat an un-Sanforized Cadillac Seville but it corners flat, this boxy, sexy Glencoe Green Metallic 1981 Chrysler K-car, squealing towards the light at the end of the Shoreham parking garage tunnel like a snakebit mongoose circling back to even the score.'

The closest he came to an evaluation of the car or its prospects came in two paragraphs near the end of his lengthy article. 'If the K-car succeeds,' he wrote, 'it will be because Chrysler has accurately read the New American car buyer. He is fed up and he is not going to take it any more, and the price he is willing to pay is a car with a trunk as big as the Ritz and a hood as long as a Steinway grand.

'What he gets in return is 25 miles per gallon city and 41

miles per gallon highway, depending on how you drive, and a car that has everything he is used to except size. It has plush sets and imitation walnut panelling and a pretty peppy response when you mash the accelerator, and it looks not like a Mercedes Benz, as Ford's Granada was alleged to when it came out, but like a real American car.'

And, of course, an American automobile is what Iacocca wanted it considered, a Yankee Doodle car. If only it could do for Chrysler what Mustang did for Ford, and do it as quickly, his worries would be over.

As introduction day for the K-cars neared, Iacocca found good reason for bolstered hope. An upturn in the economy seemed imminent, and there were positive indicators for a resurgence in the automobile industry. The inflation rate had declined. Interest rates, which had reached a horrendous 19.8 percent in April, were levelling off at 12 to 13 percent. And fuel costs seemed to have stabilized. In some states gasoline prices had dropped as much as four or five cents per gallon.

Also heartening – and especially gratifying to Iacocca, who had given priority to improving product quality – were the recently released results of a buyer survey conducted by an independent research firm. The survey showed Chrysler to be the 1980 leader in eight out of eleven categories related to quality production.

New-car buyers who were surveyed called Chrysler cars better than those produced by General Motors or Ford in such important areas as quality of workmanship, condition on delivery, paint, fit of body panels, chrome, mouldings, and value. In a similar 1979 survey Chrysler had been shut out by GM in all eleven categories.

Iacocca was confident that his 1981 K-cars – and all other Chrysler-Plymouth and Dodge cars and trucks – would also show up the competition. After all, he had invested over $1 billion in 1980 to upgrade plants by installing the most sophisticated electronic equipment available. This, plus the dedication of his workers, would assure even more improved product quality than in 1980.

Iacocca's exhaustive and expensive efforts to upgrade product quality for 1981 were no longer an in-company secret. Newspapers and magazines were giving it wide exposure.

In hailing the impending introduction of Chrysler's K-cars *Motor Trend* reported in September, 1980: 'Surely these must be indicators of quality, signs of times that have come. But more than this, they reveal that maybe for the first time an American automaker has calculated the demeanour of the general car-buying public. With the Aries and Reliant, New Chrysler will be able to serve us a substantially better car that will last longer in the face of heavy rock salt *and* traditional buyer neglect.'

The *Motor Trend* piece hailed the K's: 'These are the cars we need.' And, in closing his statements prior to an in-depth evaluation of the Plymouth Reliant he test drove, Ro McGonegal, the writer, noted:

'The only thing that will prevent these cars from becoming saviours is a chronic worsening of the economic situation. New Chrysler is still under the avalanche, and they, like the other American carbuilders, will need the next four years just to dig their way to the surface. Cars that are built and presented like the Aries/Reliant will assure them a broad power base from which to start climbing.'

This was a heady, confidence-building reporting – just what Iacocca needed as the New Chrysler Corporation's 1981 product line, including the K-cars, was introduced on October 2. On the same day advertising picked up steam as a number of celebrities joined Frank Sinatra in publicising new Chrysler-built automobiles.

Gregory Peck, Steve McQueen, Angie Dickinson, Sammy Davis Jr., Muhammad Ali, and others gave the K-cars a send-off by telling TV viewers that 'America's not going to be pushed around anymore.'

Throughout the first two weeks of October Chrysler-Plymouth and Dodge showrooms throughout the United States and Canada were jammed. Sales of K-cars broke Chrysler's records during their first ten days of public sale, then tapered off alarmingly. Iacocca's merchandising instincts told him that he had made one of the few marketing mistakes in his long career. He had permitted the K-cars to be delivered to dealers with too much added-cost equipment, thus putting their prices out of reach of many buyers.

Base prices for the K-cars with standard equipment were in the $5,000 range, which not only broadened their market but also allowed buyers to add special equipment they could afford. Too many of the Reliant K and Aries K models in dealer showrooms were tagged at $8,000 or more.

Purchase of the cars at such prices was made more difficult for the average buyer by a new reversal in the economy. In late fall of 1980 the inflation spiral resumed, and interest rates increased. The fickle economy was again a roadblock to Chrysler's resurgence.

Iacocca could do little about the high-priced K-cars already in showrooms. He did, however, call in groups of dealers for a series of personal meetings to impress on them the need for making price concessions. Better, he reminded them, to sell a car at a lesser profit than not to sell at all. Iacocca had already ordered that a high percentage of future cars be shipped as the lower-priced base models.

The dealers reacted to Iacocca with confidence. More than a few of them had had previous exposure to Iacocca, having come over to Chrysler after operating Ford and Lincoln-Mercury dealerships during his tenure at Ford. In Iacocca's first year at the Chrysler helm more than 100 Ford and General Motors dealers had taken on Chrysler-Plymouth or Dodge dealerships. And their respect seemed justified when Chrysler revealed one of the biggest and most spectacular tie-in campaigns in advertising history. This was the 'K-car Comes to K-Mart' promotion, devised in co-operation with North America's largest over-the-counter retailer, with 1,700 stores in the United States and Canada. The millions who visited K-Mart stores were exposed to Plymouth Reliant K and Dodge Aries K and given incentives to visit local showrooms.

Even with these successes Chrysler remained in serious trouble. It was little consolation that GM was no better off and Ford was in even worse straits. The record ten-day sales at introduction time of 10,000 K-cars had not held up, slipping badly in mid-October. Sales recovered slightly in mid-November, then dipped again.

Sales of other products were even more disheartening. Omni and Horizon, the next-best sellers, rose and fell in almost the same proportion as the K-cars. Other Chrysler-built cars suffered more drastically.

In 1980's closing months trepidation grew on Chrysler's executive row. The steadily souring economy seemed about to kill the new-car market and force Chrysler into the bankruptcy that had been evaded a year earlier.

In the third quarter, the three-month period immediately preceding the new-car introductions, Chrysler Corporation had registered a $490-million loss. Ford went $595 million into the red, and GM ran a $567-million deficit, the largest quarterly loss in its history.

'Now those kind of losses can't be the result of just bad planning or bad management or just plain stupidity,' Iacocca told a newspaper Advertising Bureau luncheon on November 13. 'Maybe, just maybe we knew what we were talking about last year [when Iacocca had also addressed the group]. Something is wrong. Something was wrong a year ago, it's still wrong today. . . .'

One major culprit was still the uncertain, still exorbitant interest rates, at that time near 17 percent and heading towards 20 percent. 'The car and house buyers don't want twenty-percent mortgages or twenty-percent car interest rates. So they're all walking away from the market. . . . A lot of people will wind up with car payments that are bigger than their house payments.'

Fate, partially in the form of unconscionably high interest rates, was working against Iacocca's dream of a Chrysler rescue, but, always searching for solutions, he came up with a way to beat the interest blockade. He called a press conference for December 4, 1980, to announce his untried idea.

'When we announced our third-quarter results just one month ago,' he told the assembled reporters, 'we said that if there was some moderation in interest rates in the weeks ahead, Chrysler Corporation would report a profit for the fourth quarter of 1980.'

He went on to point out that at the time the prime rate was

at 13 percent and his hopes had been for a drop to at least 12 percent. 'Instead,' he said, 'it went to eighteen-and-a-half percent – seven moves up in four weeks! It is now very clear, to me at least, that if the prime rate had in fact stayed at thirteen percent, Chrysler would have been substantially in the black in the fourth quarter.'

Bemoaning 'an ill-conceived federal effort to control inflation through monetary policy alone,' he reminded the media that the last time the prime rate exceeded 12 percent was in 1865 – 'one hundred fifteen years ago.'

'We can't change the prime rate,' he added, 'but starting today – and continuing until January 20, when the new administration takes over – Chrysler Corporation will help make up the difference between what the cost of credit for a new car should be and what it actually is.'

Ita was an innovative yet simple plan. Anyone buying a domestic Chrysler car (other than Imperial) with a commercial loan would receive a cash allowance based on the difference between the current interest rate and what was considered a normal 12 percent. For example, a car purchased with the interest rate at 18 percent would earn the buyer a 6 percent allowance, or $420 on a $7,000 car. The rebate would fluctuate with the movement of the prime rate.

'That puts us in the business of helping to stabilise a roller coaster money market that's gone out of control,' Iacocca summed up. 'But the Lord helps those that help themselves. It is up to us to do what the federal government can't do for itself. . . .'

Iacocca's revolutionary form of rebate helped provide a bright spot in an otherwise dismal business period. Chrysler was the only American carmaker to show a sales increase in December, 1980, over December, 1979. Even though the increase was a meagre 2.6 percent it brought smiles: GM had *dropped* 6.2 percent and Ford's loss was a scary 12.6 percent.

The year did not close without another attempt by the *Wall Street Journal* to urge a premature burial for Chrysler. An editorial on December 11 asked that the outgoing Secretary of the Treasury G. William Miller 'put Chrysler Corporation out of its misery' by denying extra funds available under the provisions of the loan-guarantee bill.

'What the country needs now,' the editorial read, 'is someone with the courage to stand up and do what needs to be done with Chrysler. This means saying no more federal loan guarantees.'

Fuming, Iacocca again replied to the *Journal* in a letter the newspaper published on December 26. He told the *Journal* editors they should have titled their editorial 'They Shoot Horses, Don't They?' 'You have announced,' Iacocca wrote, 'that because the patient has not yet been restored to full health by the ingestion of half the prescribed medicine, he should be put to death. I am grateful you are not my personal physician.' He further said that the editorial was 'A mean-spirited broadside against an organisation of human beings who are fighting to preserve American jobs.'

As if to shove the *Wall Street Journal*'s words down its editorial throat, he subsequently did not wait for the usual time to report Chrysler's December good news. During one ten-day period that month sales had totalled 21,296, including 7,096 K-cars, the best ten-day increase since Iacocca's heralded K-Day introduction. Just as important as the K-car sales was the fact that Dodge Omni and Plymouth Horizon buyers numbered 42 percent more than those in the same period of the previous year.

Obviously consumers believed that Chrysler would stay in business. With sales holding up so well in a depressed economy, Iacocca felt a boost in spirits. There was a good chance that the final quarter of 1980 would show a profit. And with his 1981 product line there was an even better chance for a good first quarter.

In addition to the K-cars and the luxury Imperial, new vehicles for 1981 included a new line of light-duty Dodge trucks, built to be better buys than comparable Fords or Chevys. There were also two new sport-utility vehicles, one for each division, a Dodge Ramcharger and a Plymouth Trail Duster, as well as a Dodge Mini-Ram wagon to compete directly against VW's Vanwagon.

What Iacocca had to do was build onto December's sales. He told the press that '1981 belongs to Chrysler, because no

American car company is better equipped to meet the new market requirements of the eighties than the New Chrysler Corporation.' This confidence helped make Christmas merrier for Chrysler employees.

For Lee Iacocca, however, Christmas was not a joyous holiday. His wife Mary was forced to spend Christmas Day in a suburban Detroit hospital. Earlier in December, on the 14th, she had been admitted to the hospital's cardiac unit. By the 18th she had improved enough to go home, but on the 20th she had suffered a relapse.

Christmas cheer for the Iacocca family was set aside until the day after Christmas, when Mary Iacocca was judged well enough to return home.

CHAPTER 16

Lee Iacocca was now into his third year as head of Chrysler. He could only hope that 1981 would bring the turnaround that had so far eluded him. Holding the company together as well as he had under the worst of circumstances was a minor miracle in itself.

Despite the tenuous position in which Chrysler still found itself, Iacocca had accomplished a great deal. He had brought out cars suited to the altered American lifestyle. He had instituted cost-saving measures while building employee confidence. He was selling more cars than the year before, while both General Motors and Ford were selling fewer.

Yet Iacocca felt as though he was walking into quicksand. On January 20 a new administration was taking over in Washington, and each passing day meant a day less for the Loan Guarantee Board to issue additional funds before Ronald Reagan took office.

At the moment there was no telling what Reagan or his secretary of the treasury designate, Donald Regan, might do. The new President had been heard to say that he saw nothing wrong in a bankruptcy for Chrysler. And his choice for secretary of the treasury was an out-and-out foe of the loan-guarantee philosophy.

'Those who live by the sword,' Donald Regan had pontificated, 'and you can finish that statement for yourself.' The implication was clear.

The month of January was slipping away far too fast to suit

Lee Iacocca. Even should the Loan Guarantee Board approve the issuance before the 20th, there was a mandated fifteen-day wait before the actual cash would be available, and there was always the chance that the new secretary of the treasury would undo the work of G. William Miller. Should that happen, the New Chrysler Corporation would be in serious trouble. It would run out of operating funds before the end of January.

Iacocca had talked with Ronald Reagan during the Republican national convention in Detroit in July. At that time Reagan had assured Iacocca of his support, but there was no ironclad guarantee that the new President would not change his mind or that his secretary of the treasury would not take it on himself to reverse the approval of the Carter administration.

That Chrysler sales were on an upswing might not be enough for Donald Regan, particularly if he took overall industry figures for 1980 into consideration – they were the worst in twenty years. Iacocca could only wait and hope.

Merely holding base without reminding the Carter government, and the Reagan group waiting in the wings, of the need for action was not Iacocca's way. One year earlier he had acquainted the Carter administration with his suggested programme for easing the problems facing the automobile industry. The time had come, he decided, to make a further move, one that would bring his proposal directly to Congress and to the incoming President and his staff.

Iacocca prepared and mailed under the date of January 12, 1981, a letter to senators and United States representatives. With that letter he included a seven-page 'white paper' outlining his three-point programme in detail. 'It was a good programme when it was first proposed,' his letter told the members of Congress. 'As events have developed, it is even more critical now.'

In what he suggested as a 'National Automotive Recovery Act' he reiterated the three needs he had preached for three years and which had been given the Carter administration the year before: (1) a two-year agreement with Japan to stop shipping vehicles built on overtime; (2) providing the

$1,500 tax credit for anyone buying a new American car when a pre-1976 model was traded in; and (3) a freeze on all environmental and safety regulations for two years.

'Some people,' he told congressmen in closing his letter, 'are afraid this programme unfairly favours the automobile industry, even though it clearly benefits the national economy. To those people, I would suggest that any industry which can promise the restoration of 250,000 jobs and the saving of 300 million gallons of fuel be given the same kind of assistance.'

The nature of Congress being what it is, Iacocca had little hope that anything would be done. At least he had made his views known to people who could, if they would, do something about the problems.

The first half of January was a roller coaster of good and bad signals as to the loan guarantee. G. William Miller repeatedly postponed approval, asking for revised plans from Chrysler, the UAW, and Chrysler suppliers. On January 13 the union made further concessions. On the 14th Chrysler gave its lending banks a revised schedule for the repayment of loans.

That same day industry sales for the first two weeks of January showed that Chrysler continued on the upgrade with a 4.7-percent increase over the 1980 period, while Ford, GM, AMC, and even VW sustained substantial losses. Of special interest to Iacocca was the fact that over half of the more than 16,000 Chrysler units sold were K-cars, and 4,000 were Omnis and Horizons. Obviously his faith in front-wheel drive was not misplaced, and Chrysler had an excellent chance to survive.

January 14 was also the day G. William Miller called a meeting of the Loan Guarantee Board to discuss granting the additional $400 million. If the board approved the grant, and if the incoming Reagan administration did not block the issuance of funds, Chrysler would have the money before month's end and continue to operate.

Iacocca was waiting with Douglas Fraser outside the boardroom at four in the afternoon. For three long hours they waited. Not until seven o'clock that evening were they called into the boardroom and told that formal approval, which was dependent upon acceptance of the plan by the union, banks, and suppliers, would be announced the next day. Due to the mandatory fifteen-day delay before issuance of the funds, everything now lay in the hands of the new President and his secretary of the treasury designate, if Iacocca could negotiate the additional concessions from the union and banks.

Iacocca did not have to wait long for an indication of Ronald Reagan's position. In an interview published in *U.S. News & World Report* that same week, Reagan, in referring to Chrysler Corporation, was quoted as saying:

'There is a reason to believe that government mandates have had something to do with troubles in the auto industry. If so, government has two responsibilities. The first is to bail out or help bail out a company that's suffered because of that. The second is to do away with the mandates and the regulations that cause the trouble in the first place.'

They were beautiful words to Iacocca. If Reagan could do something about the regulations that had escalated the production costs of an automobile, it would go a long way in bringing not only Chrysler but the entire industry back to profitability.

On January 16, G. William Miller called the Loan Guarantee Board to order, ready to formalize approval of the $400 million to Chrysler. Suddenly he was forced to close the meeting and postpone action until Monday the 19th. A break had developed in the long Iranian hostage crisis, and Miller was needed to help release some of the Iranian assets held by American banks since the seizure of the hostages in November, 1979. Return of the assets was a condition for the freedom of the illegally detained hostages.

Over the weekend Douglas Fraser worked tirelessly to get new concessions to Chrysler from his membership. Chrysler workers had been asked to take wage and benefit cuts that added up to $9,600 per year for each Chrysler worker as an alternative to no work should Chrysler fail.

It was to be a month-long wait before final action. The Reagan administration had taken over, and not until February 27 did Donald Regan, the new secretary of the treasury, call a meeting of the Loan Guarantee Board. Even then he did not approve the issuance of the additional loan guarantees without taking a swipe at Iacocca and Chrysler, charging that the Carter administration had let things slip through and warning that under his chairmanship of the board Chrysler would have a much tougher time getting added money.

The new loan guarantees gave the New Chrysler Corporation another lease on life. Now $300 million more was still available, but in an interview published in a March issue of *Fortune* Iacocca disavowed any possibility of asking for that money. 'I would sell my kids before I went back to Washington for that next $300 million,' he told the interviewer.

The February issue of *Fortune* he had included 'Chrysler on the Brink,' an article that echoed the *Wall Street Journal*'s disbelief in Chrysler's survival even with the loan guarantees. It was not something that a Lee Iacocca would accept without rebuttal. The published interview resulted.

All of the questions asked by the interviewer, Pamela Sherrid, were provocative. At one point she asked: 'Chrysler has shown all its product for this model year. What will happen in the spring, when GM introduces its subcompact J-car and Ford its sporty version of the Escort/Lynx?'

Iacocca's answer was a product blueprint through Chrysler's 1984 model year. 'Chrysler can produce 1.2 million front-wheel-drive cars a year, averaging 30 miles a gallon,' he said. 'Nobody else in Detroit can make that statement, even after the J-cars come in. Ford has no response to our K-car compact until late '83. You may say "You're in for a tough fight. It's dog eat dog." Well, the business has always been that way.'

He then proceeded to lay out Chrysler's product plans. A front-wheel-drive LeBaron and Dodge 400 to be introduced as 1982 models in the fall of 1981, with a LeBaron convertible 'that will knock your eyes out' in the spring of '82. Also in spring 'a sporty pickup on the Omni-Horizon base that will be the first little truck to get 50 miles per gallon on the highway.'

For the 1983 model year Iacocca promised a 'stretched K'

– two-door, four-door, and wagon models with wheelbases three inches longer than the current K-cars. As a 1983½ model (the designation usually used for models introduced in the spring) he predicted 'a super Mercedes-type coupe' and a sports car, a two-door, front-wheel-drive fastback that would finally bring all Chrysler-Plymouth and Dodge vehicles into the FWD category. Another, for 1984, was what Iacocca described as a 'unique new vehicle that is half-van and half-bus.'

'We didn't take the millions from the government and buy new drapes for the offices,' he reminded the *Fortune* interviewer, 'we are spending $160 million a month on future product.'

Iacocca's confidence in his company's survival was backed up by Chrysler sales during the first ten days in March. They were up 51.2 percent over the same period the year before, while GM posted only a modest 7 percent gain and Ford sustained a loss of 3.6 percent.

With a look to the future Iacocca now did some executive restructuring. Gar Laux, his vice-chairman, and Paul Bergmoser, president, had both come out of retirement to help him in his early months as Chrysler's head man. They had served him well and deserved a rest. Besides, it was time to infuse the top levels of his New Chrysler Corporation with young blood that would keep the company on course for years.

Iacocca named Gerald Greenwald, forty-five years old and a financial expert, as his new vice-chairman, and Hal Sperlick, fifty-one, as president. Both had been his long-time trusted lieutenants. Both held philosophies of business identical to his and had comparable confidence that Chrysler would become highly profitable in two to three years.

Speculation was rife among members of the press and other automobile executives as to Iacocca's purpose in making the change at that particular time. Was he contemplating retirement in a year or two and preparing his heirs for their future assignments? One thing seemed certain: Whatever Iacocca's personal plans might be, Greenwald and Sperlick would be the two men to carry on at Chrysler once

Iacocca decided he had had enough.

At any rate, with two trusted men in position to oversee the corporation's day-to-day operations, Iacocca could now free himself to keep an eye on the broad picture . . . and, perhaps, find it possible to spend more time with his family.

There were many elements of consideration for Iacocca in his look at the future. One was completion of his $75-million conversion of the St Louis assembly plant to the production of front-wheel-drive cars for 1982 model, the 'Super K' or 'stretched K' cars for Chrysler LeBaron and Dodge cars three inches longer in wheelbase than the original K's.

Another important matter was increasing the Chrysler-Plymouth and Dodge dealer bodies. While over 100 new dealers had turned to Chrysler within Iacocca's first year, there had since been some attrition. He decided that a dealer-recruitment campaign with large ads in *Automotive News*, the weekly read by almost everyone in the automobile business, was necessary.

Because of the depressed economy and insufficient sales to cover operating costs, many dealerships in America had closed their doors. Not one of the domestic carmakers had been spared, but Chrysler had suffered the least. Iacocca hoped to attract an influx of new dealers with financial backing that would keep them afloat.

Iacocca's next move was aimed at a resumption of marketing Chrysler products in Europe. Chrysler had been out of that market since John Riccardo's sale of European operations to Peugeot-Citroën in 1978. To launch the K-car sales in Western Europe Kenyon & Eckhardt opened an office in Brussels on April 16. An all-out campaign in Holland, northern France, and Belgium would begin in May. Then, as Chrysler established distributor and dealer facilities, the effort would be expanded to include other Western European countries.

Iacocca set in motion the same sales strategy used successfully by the Japanese in the competitive Continental market. They had moved into one country at a time, progressing to another only after success in the first.

Once acceptance of Chrysler products was evident in the

first target nations, Iacocca planned to move into Norway, Sweden, and Switzerland, and then, by 1982, into Austria, Germany, Italy, and Spain. Great Britain would have to wait because no right-hand-drive models were yet set for production.

On the home front full-page newspaper advertising was aiming at the Japanese imports. One ad, signed by Iacocca, featured him smiling confidently. The headline, positioned as a message from Iacocca himself, read: 'To anyone in America who thinks Japanese cars are better than ours I'll give you fifty dollars to compare ours against theirs or any competitive car. And I'll give it to you no matter whose car you buy. We're not foolish. We're confident.'

Meanwhile, sales were picking up, a 24-percent increase over the previous year in the first ten days of April. To get national attention for Chrysler's up-swing as well as exposure for its new 1982 products he invited newspaper, magazine, and broadcast reporters to the Styling Dome in Highland Park. They came from across the country, and most wrote glowing reports about Chrysler's rise from the ashes.

Indicative of the majority reaction was the report of John R. White, published in the *Boston Globe*. He wrote, in part: 'If you think Chrysler is ready to roll over and play dead, guess again . . . Chrysler is up and about, planning for the get well party. . . . The company is building some pretty attractive stuff with some very attractive mileage numbers. And more is yet to come. . . .'

It was this kind of publicity, 180 degrees opposite to the *Fortune* story of a few months earlier and the *Wall Street Journal*'s two-year pro-bankruptcy campaign, that Iacocca hoped for and Chrysler needed. A month after the *Boston Globe* story *Business Week* pinpointed the value to Chrysler of this about-face in the media.

'Industry analysts say,' *Business Week* reported in its issue of June 1, 1981, 'much of the spurt in sales is simply the result of Chrysler's financial travails moving off the front page and out of the 6 o'clock news. Without such bad publicity, the company found it easier to market the inherent appeal of its new front-wheel-drive K-cars.'

261

Chrysler sales, in relation to the previous year, continued to improve, but not enough to ensure profitability with the corporation's huge debt. Interest rates, which had resumed their climb, had risen to 19 percent on May 4. At that figure a $6,000 automobile would cost the buyer an additional $1,140 in one year's interest. Such a high level of interest scared off buyers.

Also of no help to Chrysler was the introduction of General Motors' new series of front-wheel drives, their J-cars, on May 21. With the automotive giant's million-dollar advertising blitz there was no telling how many front-wheel-drive Chevrolets, Pontiacs, and Cadillacs would fill American garages instead of Chrysler's Omnis, Horizons, and K-cars. A weakened Chrysler Corportion could not match General Motors in advertising dollars, even though it did enjoy advantages over General Motors and Ford as well. Even before Iacocca took over, Chrysler had established a lead in front-wheel-drive experience thanks to Hal Sperlick's Dodge Omni and Plymouth Horizon. Iacocca's introduction of the K-cars increased public perception of Chrysler's leadership in front-wheel-drive knowhow. Johnny-come-latelys such as the GM J-cars and Ford's Escort and Lynx would be suspect for months.

Another Chrysler advantage lay in the price. Iacocca had promised in April that Chrysler would not raise prices, as GM and Ford had done. GM's increase was 9.4 percent, Ford's 6.5 percent. As a result Chrysler K-cars – with six-passenger roominess as against five for the J's and four-passenger for some Ford front-wheel-drive vehicles – enjoyed a $1,000 price advantage.

Despite the early introduction of the GM J-cars as 1982 models – Chrysler 1982 cars would come in the fall – Chrysler sales for May of 1981 showed a higher increase over May of 1980 than the increases posted by General Motors or Ford. This made Iacocca's forecast of a profitable second quarter, made at the 1981 annual meeting, believable.

The annual shareholders' meeting was held the same day that the May figures were released, June 4. Some 800 stockholders, gathered at Wilmington, Delaware, applauded as Iacocca reported that 'we've overhauled the entire operation, improved all of our operations, and lowered our break-even point to nearly half of what it was just one year ago.'

It was a pleasant and jovial meeting overall, with Chrysler's continuing problems placed on a back burner. The attending stockholders praised Iacocca, even though their prospects for dividends seemed negligible for years to come. Their smiles and good-natured banter contrasted sharply with the scowls, angry shouts, and bitter denunciations of previous meetings that had brought John Riccardo to the brink of nervous breakdowns.

The shareholders lauded Iacocca's TV commercials. They laughed at his one-liners. Many sought him out once the meeting was adjourned to say they considered his K-cars to be the finest Chryslers ever built.

In late July Iacocca confirmed a second-quarter profit of $11.6 million. This was no great shakes as automotive profits go, but it was enough for a smiling Iacocca to boast of the achievement before a meeting of reporters at the National Press Club in Washington. After nine successive quarters deep in red ink one in the black was something to crow about.

'To do it against all the odds, in spite of double-digit inflation and a twenty-percent prime rate, and in the most depressed market in fifty years, is a little miracle,' he said.

It was a moment to bask in the sun, and Iacocca took advantage of the opportunity. With plants shut-down in the current quarter for model changeovers a loss was expected. The fourth quarter, too, would be a question mark.

'If interest rates fall to fifteen percent or less, we'll have a brilliant fourth quarter,' he told the reporters. 'At twenty percent, it'll be a disaster.'

Iacocca was not far wrong. The sales figures for the third quarter, ending September 30, revealed a near-disastrous loss of about $200 million. The prime interest rate had not hit twenty percent but had come perilously close.

The one bright spot in the gloom was Chrysler's performance through the summer and into early fall. Each month showed an increase over the equivalent month of the previous year, while neither GM or Ford could match the struggling

Chrysler. September, 1981, sales were 2.33 percent over September, 1980. General Motors' were down 2 percent, and Ford had an infinitesimal increase of .3 percent.

Meanwhile Iacocca had continued the personal public relations campaign that he had begun with his appearance at the National Press Club. He scheduled meetings with dealers, Chrysler suppliers, and bankers. He followed his National Press Club appearance with talks to the Empire Club in Toronto, the National Advertisers in San Francisco, and the Newspaper Publishers in Detroit. He made countless trips to the nation's capital.

In Washington he talked with Ed Meese, President Reagan's right-hand man, with Treasury Secretary Donald Regan, Transportation Secretary Drew Lewis, and the head of the Federal Reserve Board, Paul Volcker, the man most responsible for control of the prime interest rate. He discussed strategies with Senators Riegle and Levin and Congressman Blanchard, all from Michigan, and sought out senators and congressmen from other states in which Chrysler employed thousands of workers.

At every meeting and in every talk he sold the strength of the struggling New Chrysler Corporation and the improved quality of its products as evidence in independent surveys. He pointed out that these surveys showed that car buyers rated Chrysler ahead of both General Motors and Ford in product quality.

Chrysler, he told all he met with, was also ahead of GM and Ford in fuel economy, and left both far behind in front-wheel-drives, with 90 percent of its production for 1982 based on this technology. All these Chrysler pluses were advanced to prove Chrysler's ability to weather the storm if only it would get some help from Washington, help that would also give a shot in the arm to the entire industry and the American economy.

It was not money that Chrysler needed, Iacocca emphasized. Even though more millions were still available in loan guarantees, Chrysler did not plan to tap that source again. What Chrysler and the entire industry needed was realisation in Washington that 'they better not wait for the effects of supply-side economics to trickle down to the little guy who wants to buy a car or a house.'

Expanding on that premise in a report to his executive management committee, Iacocca said: 'The administration and Congress have caught hell from the public for interest rates that are the highest since the Civil War. And they're beginning to question monetary policies that divert money away from housing and autos where the jobs are, and into nonproductive areas like corporate acquisitions, short-term money markets, and interest on the national debt.'

Again and again in his talks Iacocca reminded his listeners of the substantial advantage enjoyed by the Japanese in marketing their cars in the United States, an advantage initially created by America in helping Japan recover from the war. In America's determination to establish and hold ties to Japan and maintain it as a Far East buffer against Communism, the United States set trade agreements without thought to reciprocity.

Encouraging Japan's industrial growth, America not only helped them build their automobile plants, it also permitted them to ship their Toyotas, Datsuns, and Subarus with export advantages not enjoyed by American carmakers shipping to Japan. Combined with the lower wage scale in Japan, which permitted the production of a Japanese car at $1,000 or more less than an equivalent American car, these factors impaired the American car industry.

Some measure of relief, Iacocca preached, was essential to help the domestic automakers compete on an even basis with the imports. About two million Japanese cars were sold in the United States in 1981, a year in which American carmakers lost about $2 billion in the first nine months.

Iacocca took time off from his ceaseless travels to introduce Chrysler's 1982 product line on October 1. He brought out the 1982 Plymouth Reliant K and Dodge Aries K, as well as Plymouth Horizon and Dodge Omni, all little changed from their 1981 counterparts. Four weeks later he presented Chrysler Corporation's all-new models for 1982, a redesigned LeBaron Series and a Dodge 400, both of which represented Iacocca's commitment to 90 percent front-wheel-drives for 1982.

The 1982 front-wheel-drive LeBarons were offered in two- and four-door models and a special-edition convertible, the latter a daring move on Iacocca's part. American convertibles had been all but extinct for years. Testing the waters, Iacocca found that young (and youthful-thinking) drivers yearned for a return to open-air motoring. Though he realised it was a limited market, Iacocca built a car that, as he put it, would bring 'fun back to driving.'

The rakish two-seater LeBaron convertible was on the expensive side, sticker-priced in the neighbourhood of $14,000, a cost according to detractors that would make it the equivalent of a Chrysler Edsel. The expense of producing such a luxury might be enough, they said, to drag Chrysler into failure.

Iacocca, however, had not miscalculated the hunger for an upscale open-air car. Not long after its introduction it claimed more than 200 orders, with $200,000 in deposits in the bank. One of the orders carried the name of Brooke Shields, the teenage motion-picture star.

As if to forecast a future phasing out of the Chrysler Cordoba, Iacocca named Ricardo Montalban as broadcast spokesman for the LeBaron Series. 'My new car,' Montalban told TV viewers, was the realisation of 'Lee Iacocca's dream to combine luxury with mileage.'

The Dodge 400 was Dodge Division's answer to Chrysler LeBaron, a sporty four-wheel-drive two-door aimed at the younger, less affluent buyer group. Shown on television, it was featured with Kelly Harmon behind the wheel. The beautiful blonde identified the Dodge 400 as 'America's personal driving machine.'

Advertising strategy for the all-new cars was the subject of a long conference between Iacocca and his marketing staff and his agency. John Morrissey, chairman of Kenyon & Eckhardt Advertising, suggested that the most powerful approach would be Iacocca's own presence in newspaper ads and television commercials. Having done well with earlier efforts, Iacocca was easily persuaded.

Kenyon & Eckhardt proceeded to develop hard-sell, full-page newspaper ads utilising a quote from Iacocca made to reporters on September 28, 1981, as a lead-in statement beside Iacocca's picture.

The newspaper ad layouts featured glamour shots of the specific cars being advertised along with their suggested retail prices and a bold headline that said: ''82 cars at '81 prices!' – a competitive edge for Chrysler, since General Motors and Ford had announced price increases not long before. The advertisements also proudly proclaimed that buyers would receive 'Chrysler Savings Certificates worth $300 to $1,000 on all these cars and trucks,' a rebate offering that enabled Iacocca to steal another march on GM and Ford.

Both competitors had been receiving flak from the Federal Trade Commission over their own rebate plans. Their varied money-back offers often required a dealer contribution, which was not allowed by the FTC unless the fact was clearly spelled out. The FTC had discovered that some GM and Ford dealers victimised the customers by raising their sticker prices to compensate for their contributions.

Iacocca's 'money-back from Chrysler' plan made it clear that every cent of cash rebated came totally from the New Chrysler Corporation, and that sticker prices would be no higher – and might even be lower, at the dealer's discretion – than listed in the ad.

The same theme was utilised for television and radio promotion of Chrysler's 1982 products. Again, Lee Iacocca was the spokesman. TV saturation reached its peak during the final weeks of 1981 and the first of 1982. Iacocca was seen and heard time and again on college bowl games and in National Football League playoff games.

Sales figures show that the ad campaign's success was limited by the depressed state of the economy. November, 1981, sales for all manufacturers were down from the previous years, with Chrysler showing the lowest loss among the Big Three. For the eleven months to November 30 Chrysler was the only one to show an increase, a modest .8 percent, as GM sustained a 1.6-percent drop and Ford a .5-percent loss.

When the full results for 1981 were announced on January 5, 1982, Chrysler was the only American car manufacturer to show an increase in sales over the previous year, 10.9 percent, while GM reported a 7.5-percent loss and Ford a 6.1-percent decline.

Under the existing economic conditions it was an achievement for Iacocca, a tribute to his business acumen and initiative in a crisis-ridden industry that had suffered its worst sales record in twenty years. The American carmakers indeed had fallen on hard times, dropping from an all-time high in 1973 of more than 11 million sales to little more than 6.2 million in 1981.

Iacocca's tightfisted policies had not only enabled his corporation to pay its bills, but had also produced enough revenue to repay the loans still owed to American banks. In late January Chrysler announced that the final $47 million still owed on the $1.3 billion deferred during the loan-guarantee fight would be paid six weeks before its due date. This early retirement of the debt owed to 150 banks resulted in a saving of over $2 million in interest costs.

Nonetheless the New Chrysler Corporation was hardly out of hot water. The Federal Reserve Board's tight-money policy kept interest rates on the rise, and the 1983 budget submitted to Congress by President Reagan did not promise any help.

As January faded into February, there seemed little hope that the car market would take an upturn. People just couldn't afford to buy even the lowest-priced cars when interest rates could add $2,000 and more to the already inflated initial cost.

The first ten days of February were disastrous for the entire automobile industry, with sales sinking to the lowest levels for that period in twenty years. Chrysler was down 4.5 percent, Ford 14.8 percent, and Volkswagen of America a horrendous 56.5 percent. Gereral Motors, however, had only a minor loss of 0.4 percent.

In February's second ten-day sales period Chrysler suffered the most among the big three, falling 14.2 percent behind the same period the previous year, as both General Motors and Ford posted gains, the former 3.9 percent, the latter 4.6 percent.

Iacocca, while concerned about the economy and interest rates, remained optimistic, promising a turnaround in 1982 with a return to the profit column. His only 'if' was that there be no further deterioration in the economy.

In a letter to Chrysler shareholders Iacocca wrote: 'Given even a modest upturn in the economy in 1982, we look forward to a year of full recovery.'

Cash flow was the primary concern. He still had $300 million available from the original $1.5 billion assured by the Loan Guarantee Board. But Iacocca had been saying for a year and more that he would never go back to Washington for money – the trauma of his first go-around was still fresh in his mind.

To provide sufficient cash to keep operating until the economy made its expected swing upward, the New Chrysler Corporation got out of the defence business, its most profitable asset. On February 20 Iacocca announced that Chrysler's lucrative tank-building subsidiary was being sold to the General Dynamics Corporation for $348.5 million. That should keep Chrysler afloat long enough to weather the current storm. It had to be done, Iacocca told a group of newspeople, as a protective move to provide Chrysler with cash.

'What if,' he told the press, 'interest rates go back to twenty percent? What if the ten-percent tax cut in July doesn't kick in – that was the subject of our White House luncheon with the President. . . .'

It was Iacocca at his best, winning points with the reporters with hard-hitting rhetoric. 'I'm a businessman,' he went on. 'I've got to have a sheet to windward. What if the industry drops below five million in March and April? Possible? You're damn right if it's twenty-percent interest. So we don't live in any fool's paradise. We have to look ahead at the next three months, and this is the best insurance policy we have. So we need that kind of cash infusion.'

Iacocca displayed confidence throughout the news conference. Referring to the Defense Division sale he said: 'I really think this was necessary for us, at the threshold of having good products, of having enough cash to do things from a profit-and-loss standpoint, rather than how much cash we need next Friday to survive. So I want to end on the note that we feel healthy, we feel good about it. . . .'

Iacocca had valid reasons to 'feel good about it,' especially if the 'it' was his accomplishment to date, even though Chrysler was by no means totally healthy as yet. Whatever else may lie ahead, he had done a remarkable job.

He had brought a company with terminal illness a long way despite the deepest automotive recession in a half-century. He had restructured Chrysler Corporation through one of the most comprehensive programmes in the history of world business.

He had inherited a cancer-ridden company and restored it to a semblance of health. Based on his record in 1981 – twelve months of increased sales over the previous year while seemingly healthy GM and Ford lost ground month after month – Iacocca had accomplished the near-impossible.

The government had helped with its $1.2 billion in loan guarantees, but he had put that money to good use. He shut down old, outmoded, costly plants and modernised others with new technologies that rivalled the best in the world.

He led the way among American carmakers in converting to front-wheel drive, and he developed new high-quality products, among them the acclaimed K-cars, and improved the quality of the others.

Lee Iacocca had done what he set out to do in late 1978 when he agreed to try saving Chrysler. Only one factor had prevented a full cure – excessive interest rates.

On March 1, 1982, prospects for Chrysler solvency were given a substantial boost by Michael Driggs, executive director of the Chrysler Loan Guarantee Board in Washington. In a January report to a subcommittee of the House of Representatives Appropriations Committee the Loan Guarantee Board was guarded in commenting on Chrysler's survival. Driggs's report on March 1 cited Chrysler as being 'in a better position than it has been since before the beginning of the loan guarantee program.'

Chrysler's top management, the Loan Guarantee Board found, had cut costs across the board so thoroughly that its break-even point was reduced drastically. This low break-even figure indicated to the board that Chrysler Corporation might well record a profit for 1982, despite the condition of the economy and the certainty that the first and second quarters would reflect substantial losses.

Operating cash, once counted on a day-to-day basis, had now reached $750 million, including the near $350 million from General Dynamics for the purchase of the Chrysler defence subsidiary. Thanks to that infusion of cash Iacocca was able to report a profit, not the expected loss, for the first quarter of 1982.

The report, made as April came to a close, revealed that Chrysler had enjoyed a quarterly profit for the first time since the January-March quarter of 1977. The profit figure was $149.9 million, almost double the 1977 pre-Iacocca first quarter profit of $75.4 million.

On the face of it, Chrysler also had again bested its Big Two competitors during the quarter, as it had done every quarter in 1981. General Motors had posted $128 million in profit for the quarter. Ford had sustained a $355 million loss.

Chrysler's survival now seemed assured according to business analysts. They were finally echoing what Lee Iacocca had been preaching all along. He had been telling anyone who would listen that his company's cash position was good, that Chrysler was now dealing from strength and would certainly post a profit in calendar year 1982.

Since all this has come to pass, Lee Anthony Iacocca has performed the most amazing feat in American business history.

EPILOGUE

Inevitably there will come a day when Chrysler Corporation will have to do without Lee Iacocca. As a matter of fact early in 1981 one of the men close to him said that Lee Iacocca would probably resign in 1983. The same individual pointed to Iacocca's appointment of Gerald Greenwald and Harold Sperlick to the number-two and number-three posts in the company as evidence of his intention to retire.

Iacocca himself somewhat confirmed it in an interview published in the August 3, 1981, issue of *Newsweek*, and again in late September with Michael Robinson, a reporter for the *Detroit News*. The *Newsweek* story reported that 'Iacocca plans to stay until 1983 and then ask the Chrysler directors to turn the company over to Greenwald and Sperlick.'

That he would step down at Chrysler in 1983 seemed likely, barring any unforeseen circumstance. But retire? Hardly. A dynamo keeps going until its power is spent. At fifty-nine, his age in 1983, a man with the drive of a Lee Iacocca was hardly ready to sit in a rocking chair, to tend roses, or to chase a golf ball.

Leo-Arthur Kelmenson, president of Kenyon & Eckhardt and one of Iacocca's closest friends, says Lee pondered his future to some degree the evening they sat on the deck of Kelmenson's Long Island home a week after Iacocca was fired by Henry Ford. Kelmenson says that as they looked out over the waters, Lee mentioned a grandiose dream, establishing a world-encompassing automobile company.

'He called it Global Motors,' Kelmenson said. 'Then he laughed as he realised the initials were GM, the same as General Motors.'

'Global Motors' – if that was Iacocca's way to go after retirement from Chrysler – could be a totally new organisation, or it might be formed of a merger of selected present-day carmakers, American and foreign. He shelved the idea when he accepted the Chrysler challenge in 1978, but rumours of such a possibility surfaced in 1979.

In June *Automotive News* featured an article that said Volkswagen was buying Chrysler Corporation. It implied that since Volkswagen's chairman, Toni Schmuecker, was a close friend of Lee Iacocca's, such a purchase would be more in the nature of a merger of Volkswagen and Chrysler. When no such thing happened, the rumour died.

In any event, once Iacocca leaves Chrysler, he might resurrect the idea of a Global Motors. While that is no more than speculation, people who know Iacocca best will lay odds that he will not remain idle for long.

At one time in the summer of 1981 a Detroit columnist suggested that Lee Iacocca was seriously considering politics, with the governorship of Michigan in his sights. Iacocca laughed it off, and one of his close friends reported that in no way would Lee Iacocca consider running for governor in Michigan. After Chrysler such a move would be the equivalent of leaping from one erupting volcano into another. The state was in as much financial trouble as Chrysler Corporation when Iacocca took it over.

The United States Senate is not beyond possibility. Neither is the White House. And certainly, in these days of budget crunches, international problems, and humanitarianism, a Lee Iacocca might well fit the bill. As a businessman who cuts costs with efficiency and resolved to keep a dying Chrysler Corporation afloat, as a dynamic, self-made man, he might very well have appeal for the electorate. His lack of political background should not be a drawback. As recently as the Eisenhower presidency a nonpolitical figure was elected. Nonpolitical though he may be on the surface,

Iacocca has not hesitated to speak out on political matters, particularly as they affect the economy and the automobile industry.

In 1980 he proposed legislation that would help offset the high interest rates that prevented lower-income buyers from the purchase of a car. He called on the President and Congress to provide a $1,500 tax deduction for Americans who bought a new American-built automobile.

More recently Iacocca has suggested a twenty-five-cent-a-gallon tax on gasoline as a means of raising revenue to help balance the budget. He has offered, as an alternative, a year-long excise tax on such products as oil, liquor, gasoline, cosmetics, and tobacco, while warning against any extension of the excise tax to include living essentials such as housing, medicine, and food.

'I'm all for controlling inflation through a programme of fiscal and monetary control,' he said during a lengthy New York interview in January 1982. 'But it can't be done that fast. It took forty years to create the havoc we have today. It cannot be undone overnight, yet that is precisely what we're trying to do. We're embarked on a policy of instant solutions to long-range problems, and it won't work.'

Through necessity Iacocca has made himself the consummate politician, and talks like one. He is the unyielding salesman, decisive and forceful. A Franklin Roosevelt with a brash street-wise and street-talking style that mesmerises audiences. What he believes, he says directly, yet he employs the philosophic trappings of a man stumping for office.

'What the Japanese do have that is better [than we have],' he says, 'is a combined labour and business policy that sets long range goals and provides the means to achieve them. We don't have in this country a national policy that helps solve any basic problems. And if we ever hope to give American ingenuity the chance it needs to restore the strength of this country's basic industries we had better develop such a national policy – and fast!'

In an equally incisive and provocative vein he has pointed out: 'We need a management attitude in this country, starting with guys like me, and the wisdom to avoid preaching doctrinaire free enterprise. . . . Adam Smith went out of style decades ago. This is not a *laissez faire* society of 1890. Don't kid yourself. Our world-wide competition learned that lesson a long time ago. They know how to work together to meet a national goal – and it's time we learned how to do that here!'

These are the kinds of statements one would expect from Ted Kennedy, Walter Mondale, or Bob Dole, not from an automobile executive.

Iacocca does not mince words. 'The Federal Reserve Board should establish a policy of credit conservation,' he says. 'They should nudge the banking community into supplying credit at favourable rates to job-creating industries. Tilt money away from investments that don't create jobs or increase production.'

It is the sort of talk one might hear from a candidate for public office. 'I asked Paul Volcker,' Iacocca adds, 'how much of the available money supply this week went into creating one job through investment in productivity? I asked that a year ago and still haven't got an answer.'

Though Volcker paid no heed to Iacocca, the Reagan administration obviously recognised his multi-faceted abilities. In May 1982 he was named to head a cabinet-level commission charged with the refurbishing of Ellis Island.

It seems that James Watt, former secretary of the interior, who was assigned by President Reagan to search for a man capable of dedicating himself to such a task, decided on Iacocca after seeing him in one of his television commercials.

When advised that the purpose of the new commission was to restore the deteriorating gateway for so many thousands of immigrants into America, Iacocca eagerly accepted. After all, his father had come through Ellis Island twice and his mother once.

Thus, Lee Iacocca is being indoctrinated into the Washington scene in a role other than that of a man fighting for the survival of his company. This new challenge might prove to be just what is needed to whet his appetite.

If an office such as the presidency of the United States is indeed in Lee Iacocca's future plans, a realistic timetable would set it for 1988, or perhaps as late as 1992. Even then he would be five years younger than Ronald Reagan when he became President.

Democrat? Republican? People who know Iacocca intimately say he is ideologically neither or either, with reservations. Liberal-conservative or conservative-liberal, either would suit him well. Thus, he could be wooed by both parties.

In 1980 a motion-picture actor born in Illinois, near the banks of the Mississippi, made it to the White House. What then, would stop a nationally known, highly regarded, successful businessman from near Pennsylvania's Lehigh River from doing the same?

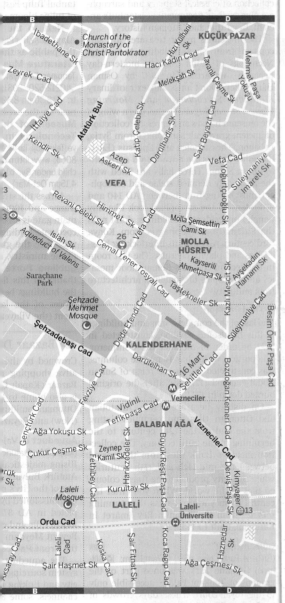

Süleyman the Magnificent. It now houses a splendid collection of artefacts, including exquisite calligraphy and one of the world's most impressive antique carpet collections. The collection is a knockout with its palace carpets, prayer rugs and glittering artefacts, such as a 17th-century Ottoman incense burner.

Born in Greece, İbrahim Paşa was captured in that country as a child and sold as a slave into the imperial household in İstanbul. He worked as a page in Topkapı Palace, where he became friendly with Süleyman, who was the same age. When his friend became sultan, İbrahim was made in turn chief falconer, chief of the royal bedchamber and grand vizier. This palace was bestowed on him by Süleyman the year before he was given the hand of Süleyman's sister, Hadice, in marriage. Alas, the fairy tale was not to last for poor İbrahim. His wealth, power and influence on the monarch became so great that others wishing to influence the sultan became envious, chief among them Süleyman's powerful wife, Haseki Hürrem Sultan (Roxelana). After a rival accused İbrahim of disloyalty, Roxelana convinced her husband that İbrahim was a threat and Süleyman had him strangled in 1536.

Artefacts in the museum's collection date from the 8th to the 19th century and come from across the Middle East. They include *müknames* (scrolls outlining an imperial decree) featuring the sultan's *tuğra* (calligraphic signature); Iranian book binding from the Safavid period (1501–1722); 12th- and 13th-century wooden columns and doors from Damascus and Cizre; Holbein, Lotto, Konya, Uşhak, Iran and Caucasia carpets; and even a cutting of the Prophet's beard. Sections of the Hippodrome walls can be seen near the entrance.

Arasta Bazaar
MARKET

(Map p88; off Torun Sokak; 🚇 Sultanahmet) This historic arcade of shops was once part of the *külliye* (mosque complex) of the Blue Mosque (Sultanahmet Camii). Mosques built by the great and powerful usually included numerous public-service institutions, including an *arasta* (row of shops) such as this, as well as hospitals, soup kitchens and schools. The *arasta* is now home to some of Sultanahmet's most alluring boutiques.

Little Aya Sofya
MOSQUE

(Küçük Aya Sofya Camii, SS Sergius & Bacchus Church; Map p88; Küçük Ayasofya Caddesi, Küçük Ayasofy; ⏰ sunrise-sunset; 🚇 Sultanahmet, Çemberlitaş) **FREE** Justinian and his wife Theodora built this little church sometime between 527 and 536, just before Justinian built Aya Sofya. You can still see their monogram worked into some of the frilly white capitals. The building is one of the most beautiful Byzantine structures in the city despite being converted into a mosque in the early 16th century and having many of its original features obscured during an extensive restoration in 2007.

★ Topkapı Palace
PALACE

See p72.

★ İstanbul Archaeology Museums
MUSEUM

(İstanbul Arkeoloji Müzeleri; Map p88; 📞 0212-520 7740; www.muze.gov.tr; Osman Hamdi Bey Yokuşu Sokak, Gülhane; adult/child under 8yr ₺36/free; ⏰ 9am-7pm Tue-Sun Apr-Sep, to 4.30pm Tue-Sun Oct-Mar; 🚇 Gülhane) The city's foremost archaeological museum is housed in three buildings close to Topkapı Palace. There are many highlights, but the sarcophagi from the Royal Necropolis of Sidon are particularly striking. Currently undergoing a massive renovation, much of the main building is closed and only the Tiled Pavilion, Museum of the Ancient Orient and Ancient Age Sculpture section (where the sarcophagi are displayed) can be visited.

The complex has three main parts: the Museum of the Ancient Orient (Eski Şark Eserler Müzesi), the Archaeology Museum (Arkeoloji Müzesi) and the Tiled Pavilion (Çinili Köşk). These museums house the palace collections formed during the late 19th century by museum director, artist and archaeologist Osman Hamdi Bey. The complex can be easily reached by walking down the slope from Topkapı's First Court, or by walking up the hill from the main gate of Gülhane Park.

➡ **Museum of the Ancient Orient**

Located immediately on the left after you enter the complex, this 1883 building has a collection of pre-Islamic items gathered from the expanse of the Ottoman Empire. Highlights include an 8th-century BC Hittite moulding of a rock relief depicting the storm god Tarhunza and a series of large

MARKET

...iye Caddesi, Zeyrek; ...a wonderful spot ...vibrant Women's ...-hearted. Freshly ...ses swing in the ...ed sheep heads,

pungent *tulum* cheese and other unusual produce. Most shopkeepers are from the southeastern corner of Turkey – specifically Siirt – and the tasty food served at the bazaar's eateries reflects this. It's open daily though hours vary between the various shops.

İSTANBUL'S CONTEMPORARY ART SCENE

İstanbul Modern (İstanbul Modern Sanat Müzesi; Map p100; ☑ 0212-334 7300; www.istanbul modern.org; Meşrutiyet Caddesi 99, Asmalımescit; adult/student/child under 12yr ₺72/54/free; ◷10am-6pm Tue, Wed, Fri & Sat, to 8pm Thu, 11am-8pm Sun; Ⓜ Şişhane, Ⓣ Tünel) This lavishly funded and innovative museum has an extensive collection of Turkish art and also stages a constantly changing and uniformly excellent program of mixed-media exhibitions by high-profile local and international artists. Its permanent home is next to the Bosphorus in Tophane, but the massive Galataport redevelopment project currently under way has led to it temporarily relocating to this site in Beyoğlu.

ARTER (Map p84; ☑ 0212-708 5800; www.arter.org.tr; Irmak Caddesi 13, Dolapdere; adult/child & student ₺25/15, free on Thu; ◷ 11am-7pm Tue-Sun, to 8pm Thu, extended hours 1st Sat of month; 🚌 54KT from Taksim) Opened to great fanfare in September 2019, the new home of the Koç Foundation's collection of contemporary art – one of the most impressive in Turkey – was designed by London-based Grimshaw Architects and is located 1km north-west of Taksim Sq, in the Dolapdere district. It incorporates exhibition spaces, a sculpture terrace, performance halls, a library, an arts bookstore and a cafe, and its exhibition program is sure to be as impressive as its six-floor building, which has a shimmering facade of glass-fibre mosaics. Free shuttle buses run from the Taksim metro station and Pera Museum in Tepebaşı; check the website for details.

SALT Beyoğlu (Map p100; ☑ 0212-377 4200; www.saltonline.org; İstiklal Caddesi 136; ◷noon-8pm Tue-Sat, to 6pm Sun; Ⓜ Şişhane, Ⓣ Tünel) With a brief to explore critical and timely issues in visual and material culture, the İstiklal branch of the SALT cultural centre is one of the city's most interesting arts-focused institutions. Occupying a former apartment building dating from the 1850s, it houses exhibition spaces, a cinema, a bookshop and a reading room popular with students. Exhibitions tend to be dominated by photographic and multimedia works.

Galata Rum Okulu (Galata Greek School; Map p100; www.galatarumokulu.blogspot.com.tr; Kemeraltı Caddesi 25, Tophane; ◷noon-6pm Tue-Sat; 🚉Tophane) With works displayed under glass on top of worn wooden desks or lecterns, and exhibition titles written on blackboards, the historical atmosphere of the former Greek Primary School – now a venue for shows by local contemporary artists – often becomes part of the visual experience. The space also hosts big art events, occasional conferences and lectures.

Anna Laudel Contemporary (Map p100; ☑ 0212-243 3257; www.annalaudel.gallery; Bankalar Caddesi 10, Karaköy; ◷noon-7pm Tue-Sat, to 6pm Sun; 🚉Karaköy) Contemporary Turkish and international artists are featured in the shows at this gallery space, opened in late 2016 in one of the historic buildings in İstanbul's old finance district. Though the gallery covers five floors, each is small, making for an intimate viewing experience. A shop sells jewellery, prints and other small artworks.

Depo (Map p100; ☑0212-292 3956; www.depoistanbul.net; Lüleci Hendek Caddesi 12, Tophane; ◷11am-7pm Tue-Sun; 🚉Tophane) Occupying a former tobacco warehouse, this alternative space is operated by Anadolu Kültür (www.anadolukultur.org), a not-for-profit organisation that facilitates artistic collaboration, promotes cultural exchange and stimulates debates on social and political issues relevant to Turkey, the South Caucasus, the Middle East and the Balkans. It hosts a wide range of talks, art exhibitions and film screenings.

---

blue-and-yellow glazed-brick panels that once lined the processional street and the Ishtar gate of ancient Babylon. The latter depict real and mythical animals such as lions, dragons and bulls.

➤ Archaeology Museum

On the opposite side of the column-filled courtyard to the Museum of the Ancient Orient is this imposing neoclassical building, parts of which were undergoing renovation when we visited. It houses an extensive

collection of classical statuary a agi plus exhibits documenting İ cient, Byzantine and Ottoman h

The museum's major treasu cophagi from sites including Necropolis of Sidon (Side in Lebanon), unearthed in 1887 Hamdi Bey. Don't miss the e *Alexander Sarcophagus* and *Women Sarcophagus*. The north the museum houses an impressi of ancient grave-cult sarcophagi Lebanon, Thessalonica and Eph including impressive **anthropoi agi** from Sidon. Three halls are the amazingly detailed stelae a agi, most dating from between 270. Many of the sarcophagi lo temples or residential buildings. the **Sidamara Sarcophagus** f (3rd century AD) with its interlo es' legs and playful cherubs. Th in this section contains Roman ics and examples of Anatolian a from antiquity.

➤ Tiled Pavilion

The last of the complex's museu is this handsome pavilion, con 1472 by order of Mehmet the The portico, which has 14 marbl was constructed during the reig Abdül Hamit I (1774–89) after t burned down in 1737.

On display here are Seljuk, and Ottoman tiles and ceram from the end of the 12th centu beginning of the 20th century. T tion includes İznik tiles from t between the mid-14th and 17th when that city produced the fine ed tiles in the world. When you central room you can't miss the *mihrab* from the İbrahim Bey Karaman, built in 1432.

Gülhane Park

(Gülhane Parkı; Map p88; ◷7am-10p hane) Gülhane Park was once pa grounds of Topkapı Palace, acces to the royal court. These days locals come here to picnic under trees, promenade past the formall flowerbeds, and enjoy wonderful the Bosphorus, Sea of Marmara an Islands from the park's northeast The park is especially lovely duri

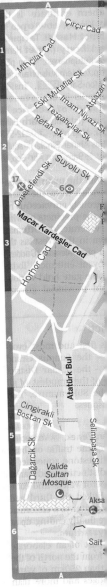

Bazaar District

Çırçır Cad
Mıhçılar Cad
Eski Mutafları Sk
İmam Niyazi Sk
Tezgahçılar Sk
Refah Sk
Ömerefendi Sk
Suyolu Sk
Macar Kardeşler Cad
Horhor Cad
Atatürk Bul
Cıngıraklı Bostan Sk
Dağarcık Sk
Selimpaşa Sk
Valide Sultan Mosque
Aksa
Sait

Women's Bazaar
(Kadınlar Pazarı; Map p9 Ⓜ Vezneciler) Though to observe local life, Bazaar isn't for the slaughtered sheep c wind and shops se

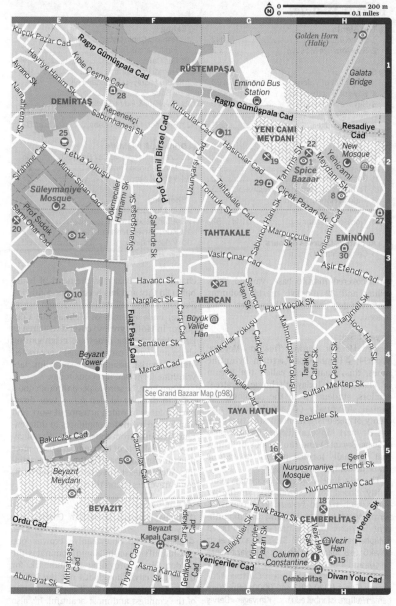

See Grand Bazaar Map (p98)

Şerefiye Cistern HISTORIC BUILDING
(Map p88; ☏ 0212-568 6080; www.serefiyesarnici.istanbul; Pierre Loti Caddesi 2/1, Binbirdirek; ⊗9am-7pm Sun-Fri, to 3pm Sat; ☐Çemberlitaş) **FREE** When an unremarkable 1950s municipal building on this site was demolished in 2010, the construction crew made an excit-

ing subterranean discovery: a Byzantine cistern dating from the reign of Emperor Theodosius. Research has found that the structure was built between 428 and 443 and was known as the Constantinus or Theodosius Cistern. Now restored, a wooden walkway allows visitors to easily admire the

Bazaar District

water-covered marble base, vaulted brick ceiling and 32 massive marble columns (unfortunately marred with modern metal braces).

Beyazıt Square   SQUARE
(Beyazıt Meydanı, Hürriyet (Freedom) Meydanı; Map p94; Beyazıt-Kapalı Çarşı) In Byzantine times, this square was called the Forum of Theodosius. Today it's home to street vendors, students from the adjoining İstanbul University (Laleli-Üniversite) and plenty of pigeons. The main structures are the Beyazıt Mosque (Beyazıt Camii, Mosque of Sultan Beyazıt II) and the various buildings that originally formed part of its *külliye* (mosque complex).

These include a *medrese* (seminary; currently closed for restoration); an *imaret* (soup kitchen) and *kervansaray* (caravanserai) complex now housing the magnificent Beyazıt State Library (Beyazıt Devlet Kütüphanesi; 0212-522 3167; Turan Emeksiz Sokak 6; 8.30am-5pm Mon-Fri; Beyazıt-Kapalı Çarşı); and a handsome double hamam now housing the Turkish Hamam Culture Museum (ext 16120 0212-440 0000; http://turk hamamkulturu.istanbul.edu.tr; Kimyager Derviş Paşa Sokak; 9.30am-4pm Tue-Sun; Laleli-Üniversite) FREE.

★**Grand Bazaar**   MARKET
(Kapalı Çarşı, Covered Market; Map p98; www.ka palicarsi.org.tr; 8.30am-7pm Mon-Sat, last entry 6pm; Beyazıt Kapalıçarşı) The colourful and chaotic Grand Bazaar is the heart of İstanbul's Old City and has been so for centuries. Starting as a small vaulted *bedesten* (warehouse) built by order of Mehmet the Conqueror in 1461, it grew to cover a vast area as lanes between the *bedesten,* neighbouring shops and *hans* (caravanserais) were roofed and the market assumed the sprawling, labyrinthine form that it retains today.

When here, be sure to peep through doorways to discover hidden *hans,* veer down narrow lanes to watch artisans at work and wander the main thoroughfares to differentiate treasures from tourist tack. It's obligatory to drink lots of tea, compare price after price and try your hand at the art of bargaining. Allow at least three hours for your visit; some travellers spend three days!

★**Süleymaniye Mosque**   MOSQUE
(Map p94; Professor Sıddık Sami Onar Caddesi, Süleymaniye; sunrise-sunset; Vezneciler, Eminönü) The Süleymaniye crowns one of İstanbul's seven hills and dominates the Golden Horn, providing a landmark for the entire city. Though it's not the largest of the Ottoman mosques, it is certainly one of the grandest and most beautiful. It's also unusual in that many of its original *külliye* (mosque complex) buildings have been retained and sympathetically adapted for reuse.

Commissioned by Süleyman I, known as 'the Magnificent', the Süleymaniye was the fourth imperial mosque built in İstanbul;

the mosque's four minarets with their 10 beautiful *şerefes* (balconies) are said to represent the fact that Süleyman was the fourth of the Osmanlı sultans to rule the city and the 10th sultan after the establishment of the empire. The mosque and its surrounding buildings were designed by Mimar Sinan, the most famous and talented of all imperial architects. Construction occurred between 1550 and 1557.

Inside, the building is breathtaking in its size and pleasing in its simplicity. Sinan incorporated the four buttresses into the walls of the building – the result is wonderfully 'transparent' (ie open and airy) and highly reminiscent of Aya Sofya, especially as the dome is nearly as large as the one that crowns the Byzantine basilica.

The *mihrab* (niche indicating the direction of Mecca) is covered in fine İznik tiles, and other interior decoration includes window shutters inlaid with mother-of-pearl, gorgeous stained-glass windows, painted *muqarnas* (corbels with honeycomb detail), a spectacular persimmon-coloured floor carpet, painted pendentives and medallions featuring fine calligraphy.

Süleyman specified that his mosque complex should have a *külliye* with *imaret* (soup kitchen), *medrese* (seminary), hamam, *darüşşifa* (hospital), *tabhane* (inn for travelling dervishes) etc. The *imaret* and *tabhane* are on the northwestern edge of the mosque and the main entrance to the mosque is accessed from Professor Sıddık Sami Onar Caddesi, formerly known as Tiryaki Çarşışı (Market of the Addicts). The buildings here once housed three *medreses* and a primary school; they're now home to the Süleymaniye Library and a raft of popular streetside *fasulye* (bean) restaurants that used to be teahouses selling opium (hence the street's former name). The *darüşşifa* is on the corner of Professor Sıddık Sami Onar Caddesi and Şifahane Sokak.

Sinan's *türbe* (tomb) is just outside the mosque's walled garden, next to a disused *medrese* building.

The still-functioning **Süleymaniye Hamamı** is on the eastern side of the mosque. To the right (southeast) of the mosque's main entrance is the cemetery, home to the octagonal **tombs** of Süleyman and his wife Haseki Hürrem Sultan (Roxelana). The tile work surrounding the entrances to both is superb and the ivory-inlaid panels in Süleyman's tomb are lovely.

The streets surrounding the mosque are home to what may well be the most extensive concentration of Ottoman timber houses on the historical peninsula, many of which are currently being restored as part of an urban regeneration project.

Rüstem Paşa Mosque MOSQUE

(Rüstem Paşa Camii; Map p94; Hasırcılar Caddesi, Rüstem Paşa; ⊠Eminönü) Nestled in the middle of the busy Tahtakale shopping district, this diminutive mosque is a gem. Dating from 1560, it was designed by Sinan for Rüstem Paşa, son-in-law and grand vizier of Süleyman the Magnificent. A showpiece of the best Ottoman architecture and tile work, it is thought to have been the prototype for Sinan's greatest work, the Selimiye Camii (p150) in Edirne. At the time of research restoration works were underway and the mosque was closed to the public.

The mosque is easy to miss because it's not at street level. There's a set of access stairs on Hasırcılar Caddesi and another on the small street that runs right (north) off Hasırcılar Caddesi towards the Golden Horn. At the top of the stairs, there's a terrace and the mosque's colonnaded porch. Exquisite panels of İznik tiles are set into the mosque's facade. The interior is covered in more tiles and features a lovely dome, supported by four tiled pillars.

The preponderance of tiles was Rüstem Paşa's way of signalling his wealth and influence, with İznik tiles being particularly expensive and desirable. It may not have assisted his passage into the higher realm though, because by all accounts he was a loathsome character. His contemporaries dubbed him Kehle-i-Ikbal (the Louse of Fortune) because he was found to be infected with lice on the eve of his marriage to Mihrimah, Süleyman's favourite daughter. He is best remembered for plotting with Roxelana to turn Süleyman against his favourite son, Mustafa. They were successful and Mustafa was strangled in 1553 on his father's orders.

★ Spice Bazaar MARKET

(Mısır Çarşısı, Egyptian Market; Map p94; ☎0212-513 6597; www.misircarsisi.org; ⊙8am-7.30pm; ⊠Eminönü) Vividly coloured spices are displayed alongside jewel-like *lokum* (Turkish delight) at this Ottoman-era marketplace, providing eye candy for the thousands of tourists and locals who make their way here every day. Stalls also sell

Grand Bazaar

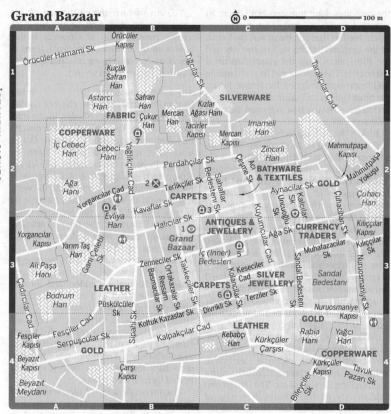

caviar, dried herbs, honey, nuts and dried fruits. The number of stalls selling tourist trinkets increases annually, yet this remains a great place to stock up on edible souvenirs, share a few jokes with vendors and marvel at the well-preserved building.

The market was constructed in the 1660s as part of the New Mosque, with rent from the shops supporting the upkeep of the mosque as well as its charitable activities, which included a school, hamam and hospital. The market's Turkish name, the Mısır Çarşısı (Egyptian Market), references the fact that the building was initially endowed with taxes levied on goods imported from Egypt. In its heyday, the bazaar was the last stop for the camel caravans that travelled the Silk Road from China, India and Persia.

Above the main entrance and accessed via a steep flight of stairs, is **Pandeli** (📞 0212-527 3909; www.pandeli.com.tr; mezes ₺15-38, mains ₺28-68; ⊙ 11am-6.30pm), a historic restaurant with three stunning dining salons encrusted with turquoise-coloured İznik tiles. Sadly, the quality of food served here is average at best, so we don't recommend dining here.

On the west side of the market there are outdoor produce stalls selling fresh foodstuff from all over Anatolia, including a wonderful selection of cheeses. Also here is the most famous coffee supplier in İstanbul, **Kurukahveci Mehmet Efendi** (☏ 0212-511 4262; www.mehmetefendi.com; Tahmis Sokak 66; ⊙ 8am-8pm Mon-Sat), established over 100 years ago. This is located on the corner of Hasırcılar Caddesi, which is full of shops selling food and kitchenware.

Hünkâr Kasrı
MUSEUM

(Hünkâr Mahfili; Map p94; www.facebook.com/hunkarkasr; Arpacılar Caddesi 29, Eminönü; ⊙ 10am-5pm Mon-Sat during exhibitions; ᪧ Eminönü) **FREE** Built over a grand archway attached to the New Mosque, this small *kasrı* (pavilion) or *mahfili* (loge) dates from the same period and functioned as a waiting area and retreat for the sultans. It comprises a salon, bedchamber and toilet and is decorated with exquisite İznik tiles throughout. Entry is via an extremely long and wide staircase that is now ulitised by the İstanbul Ticaret Odası (Chamber of Commerce) as a temporary exhibition space.

The *kasrı* opens when exhibitions are being staged. These tend to open on the second Thursday of each month and have a life of two weeks. Check the Facebook page for details.

Hatice Turhan Valide Sultan Tomb
TOMB

(Map p94; www.istanbulturbelermuzesi.gov.tr; cnr Yenicami Meydanı/Bankacılar Sokak & Yeni Cami Caddesi, Eminönü; ⊙ 9am-5pm Tue-Sun; ᪧ Eminönü) **FREE** Reopened in 2019 after a decade-long restoration, this 17th-century imperial *türbe* (tomb) with its gorgeous İznik tiles and mother-of-pearl inlaid woodwork was commissioned by Turhan Hatice Sultan, mother of Sultan Mehmet IV, and is part of the New Mosque complex. It is the final resting place of Turhan Hatice Sultan, Mehmet IV, Mustafa II, Ahmet III, Mahmut I and Osman III, as well as many princes, princesses and *valide sultans* (mothers of reigning sultans).

Galata Bridge
BRIDGE

(Galata Köprüsü; Map p94; ᪧ Eminönü, Karaköy) To experience İstanbul at its most magical, walk across the Galata Bridge at sunset. At this time, the historic Galata Tower is surrounded by shrieking seagulls, the mosques atop the seven hills of the city are silhouetted against a soft red-pink sky and the evocative scent of apple tobacco wafts out of the nargile cafes under the bridge.

◉ Beyoğlu & Around

Though short on historic monuments, Beyoğlu has an embarrassment of riches when it comes to art galleries and cultural centres. The most prominent of these are the Pera Museum (p103) and İstanbul Modern (p92), but there are others scattered across every district, mostly established and endowed by major Turkish banks and corporations.

Galata Tower
TOWER

(Galata Kulesi; Map p100; www.galatakulesi.org; Galata Meydanı, Galata; adult/child under 12yr ₺35/15; ⊙ 9am-8.30pm; ᪧ Karaköy, ᪧ Tünel) The cylindrical Galata Tower stands sentry over the approach to 'new' İstanbul. Constructed in 1348, it was the tallest structure in the city for centuries and it still dominates the skyline north of the Golden Horn. Its vertiginous upper balcony offers 360-degree views of the city, but we're not convinced that the view (though spectacular) justifies the steep admission cost, especially as the underwhelming on-site helicopter tour simulator costs an extra ₺15/12/10 per adult/student/child.

Be warned that queues can be long and the viewing balcony can get horribly overcrowded; there was a death when someone fell from here in 2019. An elevator goes most of the way to the top, but there is one flight of stairs to climb.

Museum of Turkish Jews
MUSEUM

(500 Yil Vakfi Türk Musevileri, The Quincentennial Foundation Museum of Turkish Jews; Map p100; ☏ 0212-292 6333; www.muze500.com; Büyük Hendek Caddesi 39, Şişhane; adult/child under 12yr ₺30/free; ⊙ 10am-4.15pm Mon-Thu, to 12.30pm Fri, to 4.15pm Sun; Ⓜ Şişhane, ᪧ Tünel) Housed in a building attached to the Neve Shalom synagogue near the Galata Tower, this museum was established in 2001 to commemorate the 500th anniversary of the arrival of the Sephardic Jews in the Ottoman Empire. The imaginatively curated and chronologically arranged interactive collection comprises photographs, video, sound recordings and objects that document the history, language and culture of the Jewish people in Turkey. Visitors must have a passport to enter.

Galata Mevlevi House Museum
MUSEUM

(Galata Mevlevihanesi Müzesi; Map p100; ☏ 0212-245 4141; www.muze.gov.tr; Galipdede Caddesi

Beyoğlu

İSTANBUL

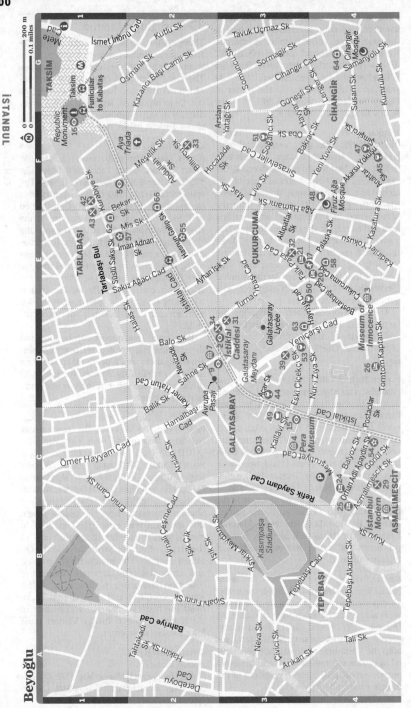

200 m
0.1 miles

TAKSİM

Mete Cad
İsmet İnönü Cad
Kutlu Sk
Osmanlı Sk
Tavuk Uçmaz Sk
Sormagir Sk
Kazancı Başı Camii Sk
Cihangir Cad
CİHANGİR
Cihangir Mosque 64
Samanyolu Sk
Güneşli Sk
Oba Sk
Susam Sk
Soğancı Sk
Yen Yuva Sk
51
Zümrüt Sk
Akarsı Yokuşu
Arslan Yatağı Sk
Sıraselviler Cad
Firuz Ağa Mosque 48
Knahtar
47
45
Maç Sk
Liva Sk
Ağa Hamamı Sk
Kasatura Sk
Hocazade Sk
Meselik Sk
Abdullah Sk
33
Aya Triada
Bilirci Sk
Republic Monument
16
Funicular to Kabataş
Taksim
ÇUKURCUMA
Altıpatlar Sk
Palaska Sk
32
21
17
Faik Paşa Cad
58
Çukurcuma Cad
Bostanbaşı Cad
Museum of Innocence 3
50
Hayriye
63
Yeniçarşı Cad
Nuri Ziya Sk
26
Tomtom Kaptan Sk
42
43
62
5
66
55
Kurabiye Sk
Bekar Sk
Mis Sk
Süslü Saksı Sk
İman Adnan Sk
Saksı Sk
TARLABAŞI
Tarlabaşı Bul
Sakız Ağacı Cad
İstiklal Cad
Hasnun Galip Sk
Ayhan Işık Sk
Haraccı Sk
Balo Sk
Balık Sk
Kamer Hatun Cad
Sahne Sk
Avrupa Pasajı
9
7
34
İstiklal Caddesi 31
Galatasaray Meydanı
Galatasaray Lycée
39
Galatasaray
44
Açar Sk
53
Eski Çiçekçi Sk
GALATASARAY
13
49
15
4
Pera Museum
Kallavi Sk
Meşrutiyet Cad
24
25
Orhan Adli Apaydın Sk
Balyoz Sk
Göndil Sk
54
29
Asmalımescit Sk
Kuyu Sk
İstanbul Modern
ASMALIMESCİT
Refik Saydam Cad
İstiklal Cad
Postacılar Sk
Ömer Hayyam Cad
Emin Camii Sk
Arslan Sk
Hamalbaşı Cad
Aynalı Çeşme Cad
Işık Çık
Işık Sk
Kasımpaşa Meydanı
Aşıklar Meydanı
Kasımpaşa Stadium
Sıpahi Fırını Sk
Tepebaşı Cad
Neva Sk
TEPEBAŞI
Tepebaşı Akarca Sk
Tahtakadı Cad
Hakim Sk
Bahriye Cad
Dereboyu Cad
Çivici Sk
Arikan Sk
Tali Sk

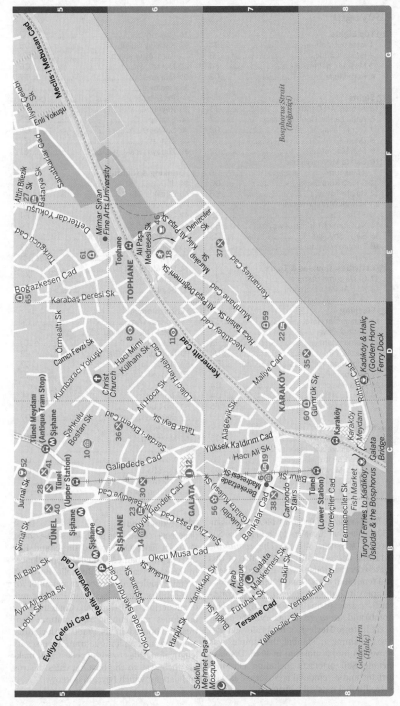

Beyoğlu

15, Tünel; adult/child under 8yr ₺14/free; ⊙9am-4.30pm Tue-Sun Oct-Mar, to 6.30pm Tue-Sun Apr-Sep; ⓜŞişhane, ⓕTünel) The *semahane* (whirling-dervish hall) at the centre of this *tekke* (dervish lodge) was erected in 1491 and renovated in 1608 and 2009. It's part of a complex including a *meydan-ı şerif* (courtyard), *çeşme* (drinking fountain), *türbesi* (tomb) and *hamuşan* (cemetery). The oldest of six historic Mevlevihaneleri (Mevlevi *tekkes*) remaining in İstanbul, the complex was converted into a museum in 1946. Displays include Sufi artefacts including clothing, turbans and ceremonial accessories, as well as traditional musical instruments.

★**İstiklal Caddesi** STREET
(Independence Ave; Map p100; ⓜTaksim, Şişhane, ⓕTaksim, Tünel) Once called the Grand Rue de Pera but renamed İstiklal (Independence) in the early years of the Republic, Beyoğlu's premier boulevard is a perfect metaphor for 21st-century Turkey, being an exciting mix of modernity and tradition. Contemporary boutiques and cutting-edge cultural centres are housed in its grand 19th-century buildings, and an antique tram traverses its length alongside crowds of pedestrians making their way to the bustling cafes, bistros and bars for which Beyoğlu is known.

At the boulevard's northern end is frantically busy **Taksim Meydanı** (Map p100; Ⓜ Taksim), the symbolic heart of the modern city and the scene of often-violent protests in recent years. Another square, Galatasaray Meydanı, is at the boulevard's midpoint, close to Beyoğlu's much-loved **Fish Market** (Balık Pazarı; Map p100; Şahne Sokak; Ⓜ Taksim, 🚋 Taksim) and **Çiçek Pasajı** (Flower Passage; Map p100; Ⓜ Taksim, 🚋 Taksim). At its southern end is Tünel Meydanı and the relatively tranquil district of Galata, home to atmospheric lanes and traces of a fortified settlement built by Genoese merchants in the 13th century.

★**Pera Museum** MUSEUM
(Pera Müzesi; Map p100; 🖉 0212-334 9900; www.peramuseum.org; Meşrutiyet Caddesi 65, Tepebaşı; adult/student/child under 12yr ₺25/10/free; ⊙10am-7pm Tue-Thu & Sat, to 10pm Fri, noon-6pm Sun; Ⓜ Şişhane, 🚋 Tünel) There's plenty to see at this impressive museum, but its major draw is undoubtedly the 2nd-floor exhibition of paintings featuring Turkish Orientalist themes. Drawn from Suna and İnan Kıraç's world-class private collection, the works provide fascinating glimpses into the Ottoman world from the 17th to 20th centuries and include the most beloved painting in the Turkish canon – Osman Hamdi Bey's *The Tortoise Trainer* (1906). Other floors host high-profile temporary exhibitions (past exhibitions have showcased Warhol, de Chirico, Picasso and Botero).

Permanent exhibits on the 1st floor concentrate on Kütahya tiles and ceramics, as well as Anatolian weights and measures. The ground floor is home to the popular **Pera Café** (sandwiches ₺22-25, pastas ₺25-30, cakes ₺12-20), a comfortable space decorated in art deco style to reflect the fact that the building originally housed the swish Bristol Hotel.

Students are given free entry to the museum every Wednesday, and all visitors have free entry from 6pm to 10pm on Friday. The museum is associated with the nearby **İstanbul Araştırmaları Enstitüsü** (İstanbul Research Institute; Map p100; 🖉 0212-334 0900; www.iae.org.tr; Meşrutiyet Caddesi 47, Tepebaşı; ⊙10am-7pm Mon-Sat) FREE, which includes a research library and temporary exhibition space. Visitors with a Museum Pass İstanbul are given a 20% discount on their entry ticket.

★**Museum of Innocence** MUSEUM
(Masumiyet Müzesi; Map p100; 🖉 0212-252 9738; www.masumiyetmuzesi.org; Dalgıç Çıkmazı 2, cnr Çukurcuma Caddesi; adult/student ₺40/30; ⊙10am-6pm Tue-Sun, to 9pm Thu; 🚋 Tophane) The painstaking attention to detail in this fascinating museum/piece of conceptual art will certainly provide every amateur psychologist with a theory or two about its creator, Nobel Prize–winning novelist Orhan Pamuk. Vitrines display a quirky collection of objects that evoke the minutiae of İstanbul life in the mid- to late 20th century, when Pamuk's novel *The Museum of Innocence* is set.

Occupying a modest 19th-century timber house, the museum relies on its vitrines, which are reminiscent of the work of American artist Joseph Cornell, to retell the story of the love affair of Kemal and Füsun, the novel's protagonists. These displays are both beautiful and moving. Some, such as the installation using 4213 cigarette butts, are as strange as they are powerful.

Pamuk's 'Modest Manifesto for Museums' is reproduced on a panel on the ground floor. In it he asserts: 'The resources that are channelled into monumental, symbolic museums should be diverted to smaller museums that tell the stories of individuals'. The individuals in this case are fictional, of course, and their story is evoked in a highly nostalgic fashion, but in creating this museum Pamuk has put his money where his mouth is and come out triumphant. Hiring an audio guide (₺5) provides an invaluable commentary and is highly recommended.

⊙ The Golden Horn

In addition to the appeal of experiencing life off the tourist trail in everyday İstanbul, the Golden Horn area offers a number of significant and fascinating sights, including churches, mosques and hoards of glittering Byzantine mosaics and frescoes.

Fatih Mosque MOSQUE
(Fatih Camii, Mosque of the Conqueror; Map p84; Fevzi Paşa Caddesi, Fatih; ⊙sunrise-sunset; 🚌 31E, 32, 90 from Eminönü, 87 from Taksim) The Fatih was the first great imperial mosque built in İstanbul following the Conquest. Mehmet the Conqueror chose to locate it on the hilltop site of the ruined Church of the Apostles, burial place of Constantine and other Byzantine emperors. Mehmet decided to be buried here as well; his tomb is behind the mosque and is inevitably filled with worshippers.

Wednesday Market

MARKET

(Fatih Pazarı; Map p84; Fatih; ⊘8am-3pm Wed; 🚊31E, 32, 90 from Eminönü, 87 from Taksim) This busy weekly market sells food, clothing and household goods. It's held in the streets behind and to the north of Fatih Mosque.

Yavuz Sultan Selim Mosque

MOSQUE

(Sultan Selim Camii, Mosque of Yavuz Selim; Map p84; Yavuz Selim Caddesi, Çarşamba; ⊘tomb 9am-5pm; 🚊90, 90B from Eminönü) The sultan to whom this mosque was dedicated (Süleyman the Magnificent's father, Selim I, known as 'the Grim') is famous for having killed two of his brothers, six of his nephews and three of his own sons in order to assure his succession and that of Süleyman. He did, however, lay the groundwork for his son's imperial success and, to this day, İstanbullus love his mosque.

Patriarchal Church of St George

CHURCH

(St George in the Phanar; Map p84; 📞0212-531 9670; www.ec-patr.org; Sadrazam Ali Paşa Caddesi, Fener; ⊘8.30am-4.30pm; 🚊44B, 48E, 99, 99Y & 399B/C from Eminönü, 🚢Fener) Dating from 1836, this church is part of the Greek Patriarchate (Rum Ortodoks Patrikhanesi) compound. Inside the church are artefacts including Byzantine mosaics, religious relics and a wood-and-inlay patriarchal throne. The most eye-catching feature is an ornately carved wooden iconostasis (screen of icons) that was restored and lavishly gilded in 1994.

Phanar Greek Orthodox College

HISTORIC BUILDING

(Megali School, Great School, Kırmızı Mektep; Map p84; Sancaktar Caddesi, Fener; 🚢Fener) Rising Hogwarts-like from the urban jumble, this Fener landmark, known locally as *kırmızı kale* (the red castle) for its castellated redbrick facade, still functions as a Greek school. A small student body of some 50 pupils studies here. Built in the early 1880s, it was designed by Ottoman Greek architect Konstantinos Dimadis, who is known for his European chateaux. The institution within predates the Ottoman arrival in Constantinople, making it Turkey's oldest educational body.

Fethiye Museum

MUSEUM

(Fethiye Müzesi, Church of Pammakaristos; Map p84; 📞0212-635 1273; www.muze.gov.tr; Fethiye Caddesi, Çarşamba; ₺6; 🚊99, 99A, 99Y from Eminönü, 55T from Taksim) Not long after the Conquest, Mehmet the Conqueror visited this 13th-century church to discuss theological questions with the Patriarch of the Orthodox Church. They talked in the southern side chapel known as the **pareclesion**, which is decorated with gold mosaics. This part of the building, which functions as a museum and is overseen by Aya Sofya, was closed for restoration at the time of research for an indefinite period.

Church of St Stephen of the Bulgars

CHURCH

(Sveti Stefan Church; Map p84; Mürselpaşa Caddesi 10, Balat; ⊘10am-5pm; 🚊44B, 48E, 99, 99Y & 399B/C from Eminönü, 🚢Balat, Fener) Known as the 'Iron Church', this Gothic Revivalstyle building on the Golden Horn has an extremely beautiful interior, with its gilded iron screens, balcony and columns glinting in the hazy light that filters in through stained-glass windows. It looks set to stay that way for years to come after an extensive restoration completed in early 2018.

★ Kariye Mosque (Chora Church)

MUSEUM

(Kariye Camii; Map p84; 📞0212-631 9241; Kariye Camii Sokak 18, Edirnekapı; ⊘Closed during daily prayer times; 🚊28, 31, 37, 336 from Eminönü, 87 from Taksim, 🚢Ayvansaray) İstanbul has more than its fair share of Byzantine monuments, but few are as drop-dead gorgeous as this mosaic- and fresco-laden mosque. Nestled in the shadow of Theodosius II's monumental land walls, the Chora Church was converted into a mosque during the Ottoman era, designated a museum in 1945 and turned back into a working mosque in 2020. It's currently closed for restoration work to conserve its foundations from water damage. The expected reopening is pegged for 2022.

The best way to get to this part of town is to catch the T5 tram from Cibali to Ayvansaray and walk up the hill along Dervişzade Sokak, turn right into Eğrikapı Mumhane Caddesi and then almost immediately left into Şişhane Caddesi. From here you can follow the remnants of Theodosius II's land walls, passing the Palace of Constantine Porphyrogenitus on your way. From Hoca Çakır Caddesi, veer left into Vaiz Sokak just before you reach the steep stairs leading up to the ramparts of the wall, then turn sharp left into Kariye Sokak and you'll come to the mosque.

The building was originally known as the Church of the Holy Saviour Outside

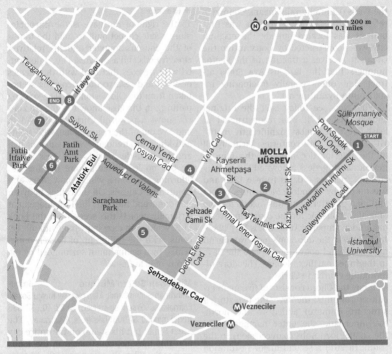

City Walk
Ottoman Heartland

START SÜLEYMANIYE MOSQUE
END WOMEN'S BAZAAR
LENGTH 2KM; TWO HOURS

Start at the magnificent **1 Süleymaniye Mosque** (p96). From Professor Sıddık Sami Onar Caddesi, enter narrow Ayşekadın Hamamı Sokak (it's opposite the main gate to the mosque) and follow it and Kayserili Ahmetpaşa Sokak down through the Molla Hüsrev district, which is slowly being restored. Kayserili Ahmetpaşa Sokak is home to a number of pretty timber houses built in the late 19th and early 20th centuries. These include the **2 Kayserili Ahmet Paşa Konağı**, a three-storey mansion that is now the headquarters of the city's Directorate of Inspection of Conservation Implementation.

Follow the street and veer right, passing the soccer pitch, until you come to the **3 Ekmekçizade Ahmetpaşa Medresesi**, built between 1603 and 1617 by the son of a baker from Edirne who rose up the ranks of Ottoman society to become a *defterder* (first lord of the treasury). From here, turn right and follow

Cemal Yener Tosyalı Caddesi until you come to a junction with Vefa Caddesi. The famous **4 Vefa Bozacısı** (p131) is close by – consider stopping to sample a glass of its *boza* (drink made from water, sugar and fermented grain). Back on Cemal Yener Tosyalı Caddesi, turn left into Şehzade Camii Sokak and go under the stone arch to reach the rear gate of the pretty **5 Şehzade Mehmet Mosque**. If the gate is closed, you will need to backtrack along Cemal Yener Tosyalı Caddesi and turn right into Dede Efedi Caddesi to access the main entrance on Şehzadebaşı Caddesi.

After visiting the mosque, head west and you'll see remnants of the Byzantine Aqueduct of Valens to your right. Cross Atatürk Bulvarı and then head towards the aqueduct through **6 Fatih Anıt (Monument) Park**. The huge monument in the middle of the park shows Mehmet the Conqueror (Fatih) astride his horse. Passing an Ottoman Revivalist building housing the **7 Fatih İtfaiye (Fire Station)** on your left, head under the aqueduct and into the **8 Women's Bazaar** (p94) on İtfaiye Caddesi, a vibrant local shopping precinct where there are a number of excellent eateries.

the Walls (Chora literally means 'country'), reflecting the fact that when it was first built it was located outside the original city walls constructed by Constantine the Great. It receives a fraction of the visitor numbers that the famous Aya Sofya attracts but offers equally fascinating insights into Byzantine art.

What you see today isn't the original church. Instead, it was reconstructed at least five times, most significantly in the 11th, 12th and 14th centuries. Virtually all of the interior decoration – the famous mosaics and the less renowned but equally striking frescoes – dates from c 1320 and was funded by Theodore Metochites, a poet and man of letters who was *logothetes,* the official responsible for the Byzantine treasury, under Emperor Andronikos II (r 1282–1328). One of the museum's most wonderful mosaics, found above the door to the nave in the inner narthex, depicts Theodore offering the church to Christ.

Today the Chora consists of five main architectural units: the nave, the two-storied structure (annexe) added to the north, the inner and the outer narthexes and the chapel for tombs (parecclesion) to the south. In 2013 a second major restoration commenced. This ongoing process is happening in stages, and involves closure of parts of the building; the nave, two-storey annexes on the northern side of the building and most of the inner narthex have been completed.

➡ Mosaics

Most of the interior is covered with mosaics depicting the lives of Christ and the Virgin Mary. Look out for the *Khalke Jesus,* which shows Christ and Mary with two donors: Prince Isaac Comnenos and Melane, daughter of Byzantine emperor Michael VIII Palaiologos. This is under the right dome in the inner narthex. On the dome itself is a stunning depiction of Jesus and his ancestors *(The Genealogy of Christ).* On the narthex's left dome is a serenely beautiful mosaic of *Mary and the Baby Jesus Surrounded by her Ancestors.*

In the nave are three mosaics: *Christ; Mary and the Baby Jesus;* and the *Dormition of the Blessed Virgin (Assumption)* – turn around to see the latter, as it's over the main door you just entered. The 'infant' being held by Jesus is actually Mary's soul.

➡ Frescoes

To the right of the nave is the **pareccle-sion,** a side chapel built to hold the tombs of the church's founder and his relatives, close friends and associates. This is decorated with frescoes that deal with the themes of death and resurrection, depicting scenes taken from the Old Testament. The striking painting in the apse known as the *Anastasis* shows a powerful Christ raising Adam and Eve out of their sarcophagi, with saints and kings in attendance. The gates of hell are shown under Christ's feet. Less majestic but no less beautiful are the frescoes adorning the dome, which show Mary and 12 attendant angels. On the ceiling between this dome and the apse, the Last Judgement strikingly depicts this scene from the Book of Revelation in dazzling white with gilt accents, with the rolling up of heaven represented by a coiling motif surrounded by the choirs of heaven.

Mihrimah Sultan Mosque   MOSQUE
(Mihrimah Sultan Camii; Map p84; Ali Kuşçu Sokak, Edirnekapı; ☉ sunrise-sunset; ◻ 28, 31, 37, 336 from Eminönü, 87 from Taksim, ⛴ Ayvansaray) The great Sinan put his stamp on the entire city and this mosque, constructed in the 1560s next to the Edirnekapı section of the historic land walls, is one of his best works. Commissioned by Süleyman the Magnificent's favourite daughter, Mihrimah, it features a wonderfully light and airy interior with delicate stained-glass windows and an unusual 'birdcage' chandelier.

Eyüp Sultan Mosque   MOSQUE
(Eyüp Sultan Camii, Mosque of the Great Eyüp; Map p84; Camii Kebir Sokak, Eyüp; ☉ tomb 9.30am-4.30pm; ◻ 44B, 48E, 99, 99Y & 399B/C from Eminönü, ⛴ Eyüp) This important complex marks the supposed burial place of Ebu Eyüp el-Ensari, a friend of the Prophet who fell in battle outside the walls of Constantinople while carrying the banner of Islam during the Arab assault and siege of the city (AD 674 to 678). His tomb is İstanbul's most important Islamic shrine.

Eyüp's grave was identified in a location outside the city walls immediately after the Conquest, and Sultan Mehmet II decided to build a grand tomb to mark its location. The mosque complex that he commissioned became the place where the Ottoman princes came for the Turkish equivalent of a coronation ceremony: girding the Sword of Osman to signify their power and their title as *padişah* (king of kings) or sultan. In 1766 Mehmet's building was levelled by an earthquake; a new mosque was built on the site by Sultan Selim III in 1800.

Be careful to observe Islamic proprieties when visiting, as this is an extremely sacred place for Muslims, ranking fourth after the big three: Mecca, Medina and Jerusalem. It's always busy on weekends and religious holidays.

Mihrişah Valide Sultan Complex
HISTORIC BUILDING

(Map p84; Sultan Reşat Caddesi, Eyüp; 🚌 44B, 48E, 99, 99Y & 399B/C from Eminönü, 🚊 Eyüp) Commissioned by Mihrişah Valide Sultan, mother of Sultan Selim III, this late-18th-century complex includes a baroque-style *türbe* (tomb), *medrese* (seminary) and *sebil* (fountain). Its centrepiece is a magnificent *imaret* (soup kitchen) built around a courtyard, which was under restoration at the time of research.

★ Rahmi M Koç Museum
MUSEUM

(Rahmi M Koç Müzesi; Map p84; ☎ 0212-369 6600; www.rmk-museum.org.tr; Hasköy Caddesi 5, Hasköy; museum adult/student/child under 7yr ₺21/9/free, steam-tug cruise ₺10/7/free; ⊙ 9.30am-4.30pm Tue-Fri, to 5.30pm Sat & Sun Oct-Mar, to 6.30pm Sat & Sun Apr-Sep; 🚌 38T, 54HT from Taksim, 47E from Eminönü, 🚊 Hasköy) This splendid museum is dedicated to the history of transport, industry and communications in Turkey. Founded by the head of the Koç industrial group, one of Turkey's most prominent conglomerates, it exhibits artefacts from İstanbul's industrial past and is highly interactive, making it a particularly enjoyable destination for those travelling with children.

⊙ The Bosphorus Suburbs

★ Dolmabahçe Palace
PALACE

(Dolmabahçe Sarayı; Map p84; ☎ 0212-327 2626; www.millisaraylar.gov.tr; Dolmabahçe Caddesi, Beşiktaş; adult/student/child Selamlık ₺60/20/free, Harem ₺40/20/free, joint ticket ₺90/20/free; ⊙ 9am-4pm Tue-Sun; 🚊 Kabataş) These days it's fashionable for architects and critics influenced by the less-is-more aesthetic of Bauhaus masters to sneer at buildings such as Dolmabahçe. However, the crowds that throng to this imperial palace with its neoclassical exterior and over-the-top interior clearly don't share that disdain, flocking here to tour its **Selamlık** (Ceremonial Quarters)

and **Harem**. Both are visited on a self-guided audio tour (included in ticket cost). Of the two, the Selamlık is the more interesting.

More rather than less was certainly the philosophy of Sultan Abdül Mecit I (r 1839–61), who decided to move his imperial court from Topkapı to a lavish new palace on the shores of the Bosphorus. For a site he chose the *dolma bahçe* (filled-in garden) where his predecessors, Sultans Ahmet I and Osman II, had filled in a little cove in order to create a royal park complete with wooden pleasure kiosks and pavilions.

Abdül Mecit commissioned imperial architects Nikoğos and Garabed Balyan to construct an Ottoman-European palace that would impress everyone who set eyes on it. Traditional Ottoman palace architecture was eschewed – there are no pavilions here, and the palace turns its back on the splendid view rather than celebrating it. The designer of the Paris Opera was brought in to do the interiors, which perhaps explains their exaggerated theatricality – the huge Hereke carpets, crystal staircase and chandeliers in the Selamlık are particularly resplendent. Construction was completed in 1854, and the sultan and his family moved in two years later. Though it had the wow factor in spades, Abdül Mecit's extravagant project precipitated the empire's bankruptcy and signalled the beginning of the end for the Osmanlı dynasty. During the early years of the republic, Atatürk used the palace as his İstanbul base. He died here on 10 November 1938.

The tourist entrance to the palace grounds is the ornate imperial gate, with an equally ornate clock tower just inside. Sarkis Balyan designed the tower between 1890 and 1895 for Sultan Abdül Hamit II (r 1876–1909). There is an outdoor cafe near here with premium Bosphorus views.

Set in well-tended gardens, the palace is divided into three sections: the Selamlık, Harem and **Veliaht Dairesi** (Apartments of the Crown Prince). In the Selamlık, a self-guided audio tour takes visitors through huge, ornately furnished reception halls and past a series of more-intimate salons. There are also two exhibition halls here where precious objects from the palace collections are displayed. The Harem is arranged as it was when the sultans and their families lived here, and also has a room dedicated to Atatürk. The Veliaht Dairesi is now home to the **National Palaces Painting Museum** (Milli Saraylar Resim Müzesi; ☎ 0212-236 9000;

Bosphorus

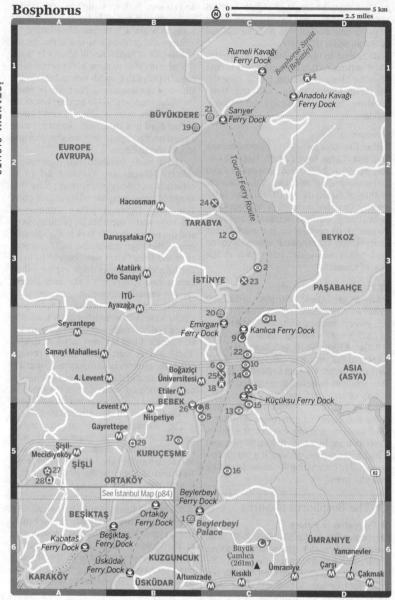

adult/student/child ₺25/10/free; ⊙9am-4pm Tue-Sun; ☐43 from Taksim to Akaretler; ☐Beşiktaş), which is visited on a separate ticket. Buildings in the palace grounds include a **Clock Museum** filled with 19th-century clocks; entry here is included in the palace tickets.

Note that visitor numbers in the palace are limited to 3000 per day and this ceiling is often reached on weekends and holidays – come midweek if possible, and even then be prepared to queue (often for long periods and in full sun). Also note that admission here is not covered by the Museum Pass İstanbul.

Bosphorus

Just outside the gate, the Dolmabahçe Mosque (Dolmabahçe Camii) on Muallim Naci Caddesi was designed by Nikoğos Balyan and completed in 1853.

Palace Collections Museum   MUSEUM
(Saray Koleksiyonları Müzesi; Map p84; ☑ 0212-236 9000; www.millisaraylar.gov.tr; Beşiktaş Caddesi, Beşiktaş; adult/student/child ₺20/5/free; ☉ 9am-5pm Tue-Sun; ☐ 43 from Taksim, ⬛ Beşiktaş) Occupying the warehouse-like Dolmabahçe Palace kitchens, this museum exhibits items used in the royal palaces and pavilions during the late Ottoman Empire and early Turkish Republic. It is a fascinating hotchpotch of some 5000 objects, including palace portraits and photos, tea sets, tiled Islamic wall inscriptions, prayer rugs and embroidery. Hereke carpets and Yıldız Porselen Fabrikası porcelain are also here.

İstanbul Naval Museum   MUSEUM
(İstanbul Deniz Müzesi; Map p84; ☑ 0212-327 4345; https://denizmuzesi.dzkk.tsk.tr/en; Beşiktaş Caddesi 6, Beşiktaş; adult/student & child under 12yr ₺10/free; ☉ 9am-5pm Tue-Fri, 10am-6pm Sat & Sun; ☐ 22, 22B, 25E from Kabataş to Bahçeşehir Üniversity, ⬛ Beşiktaş) Established over a century ago to celebrate and commemorate Turkish naval history, this museum's architecturally noteworthy copper-clad exhibition hall opened in 2013 and showcases a spectacular collection of 19th-century imperial caiques, ornately decorated wooden rowboats used by the royal household. Temporary exhibitions take place in the downstairs gallery.

★ **Beylerbeyi Palace**   PALACE
(Beylerbeyi Sarayı; ☑ 0212-327 2626; www.milli saraylar.gov.tr/saraylar/beylerbeyi-sarayi; Abdullah Ağa Caddesi, Beylerbeyi; adult/student/child under 7yr ₺40/20/free; ☉ 9am-4.30pm Tue-Sun; ☐ 15 from Üsküdar, ⬛ Beylerbeyi) This opulently furnished 1865 building was designed by Sarkis Balyan, brother of Nikoğos (architect of Dolmabahçe Palace). It delighted both Sultan Abdül Aziz (r 1861–76), who commissioned it, and the many foreign dignitaries who visited. Its last imperial 'guest' was former Sultan Abdül Hamit II, who spent the last five years of his life under house arrest here. Look for the whimsical marble bathing pavilions by the water's edge; one was for men, the other for women of the harem.

Assisted by an informative audio tour (included in ticket price) you'll pass through rooms decorated with frescoes of naval scenes, Bohemian crystal chandeliers, Ming vases and sumptuous Hereke carpets, exploring both the grand *selamlık* (ceremonial quarters) and the small but opulent harem. Highlights include the downstairs hall with the huge marble pool used for cooling during summer, the elaborately painted and gilded sultan's apartment, and the wood-panelled sultan's audience room with its Baccarat chandelier, Hereke carpet and magnificent

Bosphorus view. After the tour, you can enjoy a glass of tea in the garden cafe.

The easiest way to visit Beylerbeyi is to take the Dentur Avrasya hop-on/hop-off tour from Kabataş. If coming from Üsküdar by bus, alight at the Beylerbeyi Sarayı stop.

⊙ Kadıköy

Kadıköy's produce market is the neighbourhood's top sight, with its impressive array of street-art an edgy runner-up. Most of the latter is found in the Yeldeğirmeni district directly in front of the ferry docks.

★ **Kadıköy Produce Market**   MARKET
(Kadıköy Pazarı; Map p84; streets around Güneşlibahçe Sokak; ⊙8am-7pm Mon-Sat; ⊠Kadıköy, Ⓜ Kadıköy) An aromatic, colourful and alluring showcase of the best fresh produce in the city, the Kadıköy Pazarı is foodie central for locals and is becoming an increasingly popular destination for tourists. Equally rewarding to explore independently or on a guided culinary walk, it's small enough to retain a local feel yet large enough to support a variety of specialist traders.

Getting here involves crossing from Europe to Asia and is best achieved on a ferry – from the deck you'll be able to admire the domes and minarets studding the skylines of both shores and watch seagulls swooping overhead. Once you've arrived, cross Rihtim Caddesi in front of the main *iskele* (ferry dock) and walk up Muvakkithane Caddesi or Yasa Caddesi to reach the centre of the action. The best produce shops are in Güneşlibahçe Sokak – you'll see fish glistening on beds of crushed ice, displays of seasonal fruits and vegetables, combs of amber-hued honey, tubs of tangy pickles, bins of freshly roasted nuts and much, much more.

Eating and drinking opportunities in and around the bazaar are plentiful: creamy yoghurt and honey at **Etabal** (☑0533 515 8888; www.honeyci.com.tr; Güneşlibahçe Sokak 28; yogurt & honey tub ₺10; ⊙9am-10pm; ☑), regional Anatolian specialities at Çiya Sofrası (p130), crispy *lahmacun* (Arabic-style pizza) at **Borsam Taş Fırın** (☑0216-337 0504; www.borsamtasfirin.com; Güneşlibahçe Sokak 22; lahmacun ₺7-10; ⊙10am-10pm), the catch of the day at **Kadı Nımet Balıkçılık** (☑0216-348 7389; www.kadinimet.com; Serasker Caddesi 10a; fish dishes ₺32-59; ⊙noon-midnight; ⊛☎), ice-cream sundaes at **Baylan Pastanesi** (☑0216-346 6350; www.baylanpastanesi.com.tr; Muvakkithane Caddesi 9a; parfaits ₺30-32, cakes ₺18-32; ⊙7am-10pm) and the city's best Turkish coffee at Fazıl Bey (p133). For gifts to take home, consider *lokum* (Turkish delight) from **Ali Muhıddın Hacı Bekir** (☑0216-336 1519; Muvakkithane Caddesi 6; ⊙8am-8pm), coffee from Fazıl Bey or olive-oil soap from one of the herbalists in Güneşlibahçe Sokak.

For a serious immersion into the local food culture, sign up for a walk with Culinary Backstreets (p118), Turkish Flavours (p119) or İstanbul on Food (p119) – all three companies pride themselves on knowing the best local places to eat and shop.

🏃 Activities

🏃 Bosphorus Ferry Tours

Divan Yolu and İstiklal Caddesi are always awash with people, but neither is the city's major thoroughfare. That honour goes to the mighty Bosphorus Strait, which joins the Sea of Marmara (Marmara Denizi) with the Black Sea (Karadeniz), 32km north of the Galata Bridge. Over the centuries the Bosphorus has been crossed by conquering

---

DON'T MISS

KADIKÖY STREET ART

Kadıköy is the centre of the city's street-art scene, and the streets of the Yeldeğirmeni district near the *iskele* (ferry dock) are where many huge and impressive works by local and international artists are located, many created for the Mural İstanbul Festival (www. muralistanbul.org) supported by the local municipality; head to Karakolhane Sokak near the railway tracks, Misak-ı Milli Sokak, İzzettin Sokak and Macit Erbudak Sokak to see spectacular works by artists including **Chazme & Sepe** (Map p84; Misak-ı Milli Caddesi), **Dome** (Map p84; Misak-ı Milli Caddesi), **Fintan Magee** (Map p84; Nakil Sokak), **PixelPancho** (Map p84; İzzettin Sokak) and **INTI** (Map p84; Macit Erbudak Sokak). Other examples are on or near Moda Caddesi; Rustam Qbic's **'Miracle' mural** (Map p84; Mektebi Sokağı, Moda) is particularly impressive.

WORTH A TRIP

ÜSKÜDAR

Located on the Anatolian (Asian) side of the city, Üsküdar is a short but atmospheric ferry ride from Eminönü or a swift metro ride from Sirkeci. Exploring its rich array of Ottoman mosques – most commissioned by pious *valide sultans* (mothers of reigning sultans) – is a rewarding way to spend half a day.

Şakirin Mosque (Map p84; cnr Nuhkuyusu Caddesi & Dr Burhanettin Üstünel Sokak, Barbaros; ⬜9A, 11P, 12A, 12C) One of the few architecturally notable modern mosques in İstanbul, this 2009 building was designed by Hüsrev Tayla and its interior is the work of Zeynep Fadıllıoğlu, best known for her glamorous restaurant and nightclub fit-outs. The building itself has a wonderful transparency, but the highlight is the interior, which features a gorgeous turquoise-and-gold *mihrab* (niche indicating the direction of Mecca) and a magnificent 'dripping glass' chandelier.

Şemsi Ahmed Paşa Mosque (Şemsi Paşa Camii, Kuskonmaz Camii; Map p84; Paşa Limanı Caddesi; ☉sunrise-sunset; 🚢Üsküdar, Ⓜ Üsküdar) This charming mosque complex on the waterfront was designed by Mimar Sinan and built in 1580 for one of Süleyman the Magnificent's grand viziers, Şemsi Ahmed Paşa. It is modest in size and decoration, reflecting the fact that its benefactor (whose tomb has an opening into the mosque) only occupied the position of grand vizier for a couple of months.

Çinili Mosque (Çinili Camii, Tiled Mosque; Map p84; Çinili Hamam Sokak; ☉sunrise-sunset; 🚢Üsküdar, Ⓜ Üsküdar) This little mosque is fairly unprepossessing from the outside, but the interior is a totally different story. The walls are decorated with gorgeous İznik tiles, the bequest of Mahpeyker Kösem (1640), wife of Sultan Ahmet I and mother of sultans Murat IV and İbrahim I ('İbrahim the Crazy'). It's a 10-minute walk to get here from the Atik Valide Mosque.

Atik Valide Mosque (Atik Valide Camii; Map p84; Valide İmaret Sokak, Valide-i Atik; ☉sunrise-sunset; 🚢Üsküdar, Ⓜ Üsküdar) This is one of the two great İstanbul mosque complexes designed by Mimar Sinan. Though not as spectacular as the Süleymaniye (p96), it was designed to a similar plan and built in a similarly commanding location. Its extensive *külliye* (mosque complex) includes a now decommissioned hamam on Dr Fahri Atabey Caddesi and, closer to the mosque, an *imaret* (soup kitchen), *medrese* (Islamic school of higher studies), *darüşşifa* (hospital) and *han* (caravanserai). All were being restored at the time of research.

Getting There & Away

Ferry Frequent İstanbul Şehir Hatları passenger ferries travel between Üsküdar and Eminönü. Services commence at 7.30am; the final return service is at 10pm. There is also an hourly service to the Haliç (Golden Horn) suburbs via Karaköy. Turyol ferries sail to/from Eminönü and Karaköy, and Dentur ferries sail to/from Beşiktaş, the Adalar and the Bosphorus.

Metro The Marmaray metro travels between Kazlıçeşme in the Old City and Ayrılık Çeşmesi, stopping at Üsküdar, Sirkeci and Yenikapı en route.

Bus Lines 12 and 12A link Üsküdar and Kadıköy. Catch them from the bus stands on Paşa Limanı Caddesi in front of the *iskele* (ferry dock).

armies, intrepid merchants and many an adventurous spirit. These days, thousands of İstanbullus commute along it; fishing vessels try their luck in its waters; huge tankers and container ships make a stately progress down its central channel; and tourists ride the excursion ferries that ply its length. On one side is Europe, on the other Asia – both shores are lined with historic *yalıs* (seafront mansions) and have loads of attractions. As a result, a day spent exploring by ferry and/or bus is enormously rewarding.

This tour follows the route of the Long Bosphorus Tour (p116).

Eminönü to Beşiktaş

Hop onto the boat at the Boğaz İskelesi (Bosphorus Ferry Dock) on the Eminönü

ⓘ BOSPHORUS TOUR ITINERARY TIPS

If you buy a return ticket on İstanbul Şehir Hatları's Long Bosphorus Tour (adult/child under 12 years ₺25/12.50), you'll be forced to spend three hours in the tourist-trap village of Anadolu Kavağı. It's much better to buy a one-way ticket (₺15/7.50) and alight there, or at Rumeli Kavağı, Sarıyer or Kanlıca, and make your way back to İstanbul by bus, stopping at the Sadberk Hanım Museum, the Sakıp Sabancı Museum, Borusan Contemporary, the fortress at Rumeli Hisarı and the waterside suburbs of Bebek, Arnavutköy and/or Ortaköy on the way. To spend a day exploring the Asian shore, purchase a one-way ticket for the Long Bosphorus Tour ferry trip leaving from Eminönü, alight at Anadolu Kavağı and work your way back along that shore by bus, stopping to visit Hıdiv Kasrı, Küçüksu Kasrı and Beylerbeyi Palace before getting off the bus at Üsküdar and catching a ferry or the metro back to town.

Alternatively, you can take the İstanbul Şehir Hatları commuter ferry service from Eminönü (₺5) that stops at Beşiktaş, Arnavutköy, Emirgan, İstinye, Sarıyer and Rumeli Kavağı.

quay near the Galata Bridge. It's always a good idea to arrive 30 minutes or so before the scheduled departure time and manoeuvre your way to the front of the queue that builds near the doors leading to the dock. When these open and the boat can be boarded, you'll need to move fast to score a good seat. The best spots are on the sides of the upper deck at the bow or stern, but note that this deck has no roof or awning so you'll need sunscreen, a sunhat and sunglasses.

The Asian shore is to the right side of the ferry as it cruises up the strait; Europe is to the left. When you start your trip, watch out for the small island of **Kız Kulesi**, just off the Asian shore near Üsküdar. One of the city's most distinctive landmarks, this 18th-century structure has functioned as a lighthouse, quarantine station and restaurant. It also featured in the 1999 James Bond film *The World Is Not Enough*.

Just before the first stop at Beşiktaş, you'll pass the grandiose Dolmabahçe Palace (p107), built on the European shore of the Bosphorus by Sultan Abdül Mecit between 1843 and 1854.

Beşiktaş to Kanlıca

Nineteenth-century French writer Pierre Loti described the stretch of the Bosphorus shore between Beşiktaş and Ortaköy as featuring 'a line of palaces white as snow, placed at the edge of the sea on marble docks'. After brief stops at Beşiktaş and Üsküdar, the ferry heads towards the Bosphorus Strait and one of these palaces, **Çırağan** (Çırağan Sarayı; Map p84; Çırağan Caddesi 84, Ortaköy; 🚌 22, 22B, 25E from Kabataş, 🚢 Beşiktaş), looms on the left. Next to it on the left is the Four Seasons Hotel; on the right is the **Feriye Palace**

(Feriye Sarayı; Map p84; Çırağan Caddesi, Ortaköy), a complex of three buildings commissioned by Sultan Abdül Aziz in 1871 to house members of the royal family who could not be accommodated in Dolmabahçe or Çırağan (the word *feriye* meant 'auxiliary' in the Ottoman language). The palace has been occupied by Galatasaray University since 1992; sadly, its main building was extensively damaged by fire in 2013 and is still awaiting restoration. Across the strait on the Asian shore is the **Fethi Ahmed Paşa Yalı** (Map p84; Paşa Limanı Caddesi, Kuzguncuk; 🚌 15 from Üsküdar), a wide white building with a red-tiled roof that was built in the pretty suburb of Kuzguncuk in the late 18th century. The word *yalı* comes from the Greek word for 'coast', and describes the summer residences along the Bosphorus built by Ottoman aristocracy and foreign ambassadors in the 17th, 18th and 19th centuries. There are now 667 *yalıs* on the Bosphorus, around 200 of which are in foreign ownership. All are protected by the country's heritage laws.

A little further along on your left is the pretty baroque-styled **Ortaköy Mosque** (Ortaköy Camii, Büyük Mecidiye Camii; Map p84; İskele Meydanı, Ortaköy; 🚌 22, 22B, 25E from Kabataş to Ortaköy, 🚢 Ortaköy). The mosque's dome and two minarets are dwarfed by the adjacent **Martyrs of July 15 (Bosphorus) Bridge**, opened in 1973 on the 50th anniversary of the founding of the Turkish Republic.

Under the bridge on the European shore are two huge *yalıs:* the red-roofed **Hatice Sultan Yalı** (Map p84; Ortaköy; 🚌 22 & 25E from Kabataş, 22RE & 40 from Beşiktaş, 40, 40T & 42T from Taksim), once the home of Sultan Murat V's daughter, Hatice; and the **Fehime Sultan Yalı** (Map p84; Muallim Naci Caddesi, Ortaköy;

22 & 25E from Kabataş, 22RE & 40 from Beşiktaş, 40, 40T & 42T from Taksim), home to Hatice's sister Fehime. Both are undergoing massive restorations. On the Asian side is the ornate Beylerbeyi Palace (p109) – look for its whimsical marble bathing pavilions on the shore; one was for men, the other for the women of the harem. On the hill way above Beylerbeyi is Çamlıca Tepesi (Çamlıca Hill), one of the highest points in the city and since 2019 home to the **Çamlıca Mosque** (Çamlıca Camii; Map p108; Ferah Yolu Sokak, Büyük Çamlıca; ☉ sunrise-sunset; 14F from Kadıköy, 14FD from Üsküdar), the largest mosque in the country. A project commissioned by the ruling AKP government, its massive platform base is topped by a cascade of domes and six white minarets.

Past the small village of Çengelköy on the Asian side is the imposing **Kuleli Military School** (Kuleli Askeri Lisesi; Map p108; Kuleli Caddesi 56, Çengelköy; 15, 15E, 15H, 15KÇ, 15M, 15N, 15P, 15ŞN, 15T, 15U from Üsküdar, 15F from Kadıköy), built in 1860 and immortalised in İrfan Orga's wonderful memoir *Portrait of a Turkish Family*. Look out for its two 'witch hat' towers.

Almost opposite Kuleli on the European shore is **Arnavutköy** (Albanian Village), which boasts a number of gabled Ottoman-era wooden houses and Greek Orthodox churches. On the hill above it are buildings formerly occupied by the American College for Girls. Its most famous alumni was Halide Edib Adıvar, who wrote about the years she spent here in her 1926 work *The Memoir of Halide Edib*. The building is now part of the prestigious **Robert College** (Map p108; Kuruçeşme Caddesi 87, Arnavutköy; 22, 22B & 25E from Kabataş, 22RE from Beşiktaş, 40, 40T & 42T from Taksim; Arnavutköy).

Arnavutköy runs straight into the glamorous suburb of **Bebek**, known for its upmarket shopping and chic cafe-bars such as Lucca (p132). Bebek's shops surround a small park housing the Ottoman Revivalist–style **Bebek Mosque** (Map p108; Bebek Parkı, Cevdet Paşa Caddesi; 22, 22B & 25E from Kabataş, 40, 40T & 42T from Taksim) and a lovely waterside *çay bahçesi* (tea garden) – look for its yellow umbrellas in front of the mosque; to the east of these is the ferry dock, to the south is the **Egyptian consulate building** (Map p108; Cevdet Paşa Caddesi 12, Bebek; 22 & 25E from Kabataş, 22RE & 40 from Beşiktaş, 40, 40T & 42T from Taksim), thought by some critics to be the work of Italian architect Raimondo

D'Aronco. This gorgeous art nouveau mini-palace was built for Emine Hanım, mother of the last khedive (viceroy) of Egypt, Abbas Hilmi II. It's the white building with two mansard towers and an ornate wrought-iron fence.

Opposite Bebek on the Asian shore is **Kandilli**, the 'Place of Lamps', named after the lamps that were lit here to warn ships of the particularly treacherous currents at the headland. Among the many *yalıs* here is the huge red **Kont Ostrorog Yalı** (Map p108; Kandilli-Göksu Caddesi 19, Kandilli; 15, 15F & 15T from Üsküdar), built in the 19th century by Count Leon Ostorog, a Polish adviser to the Ottoman court; Pierre Loti visited here when he visited İstanbul in the 1890s. A bit further on, past Kandilli, is the long white **Kıbrıslı** ('Cypriot') **Yalı** (Map p108; Kandilli-Göksu Caddesi 23, Kandilli; 15, 15E, 15H, 15KÇ, 15M, 15N, 15P, 15ŞN, 15T, 15U from Üsküdar, 14R & 15YK from Kadıköy), which dates from 1760.

Next to the Kıbrıslı are the **Büyük Göksu Deresi** (Great Heavenly Stream) and **Küçük Göksu Deresi** (Small Heavenly Stream), two brooks that descend from the Asian hills into the Bosphorus. Between them is a fertile delta, grassy and shady, which the Ottoman elite thought perfect for picnics. Foreign residents referred to it as 'The Sweet Waters of Asia'. If the weather was good, the sultan joined the picnic, and did so in style. Sultan Abdül Mecit's answer to a simple picnic blanket was **Küçüksu Kasrı** (Map p108; ☎ 0212-327 2626; www.millisaraylar.gov.tr/saraylar/kucuksu-kasri; Küçüksu Caddesi, Küçüksu; adult/student/child under 7yr ₺20/5/free; ☉ 9am-4.30pm Tue-Sun; 15, 15E, 15H, 15KÇ, 15M, 15N, 15P, 15ŞN, 15T, 15U from Üsküdar, 14R & 15YK from Kadıköy, Küçüksu), an ornate hunting lodge built in 1856–57. Earlier sultans had wooden kiosks here, but architect Nikoğos Balyan designed a rococo gem in marble for his monarch. You'll see its ornate cast-iron fence, boat dock and wedding-cake exterior from the ferry.

Close to the Fatih Sultan Mehmet Bridge are the majestic fortress structures of **Rumeli Hisarı** (Fortress of Europe; Map p108; ☎ 0212-263 5305; Yahya Kemal Caddesi 42; adult/child under 8 yr ₺18/free; ☉ 9am-4.30pm Thu-Tue Oct-Mar, to 6.30pm Apr-Sep; 22 & 25E from Kabataş, 22RE & 40 from Beşiktaş, 40, 40T & 42T from Taksim) and **Anadolu Hisarı** (Fortress of Anatolia; Map p108; 15, 15KÇ & 15ŞN from Üsküdar, 15F from Kadıköy). Mehmet the Conqueror had Rumeli Hisarı built in a mere four

DON'T MISS

CROSS-CONTINENT FERRY RIDE

Every day **ferries** (Map p84; one way ₺5, using İstanbulkart ₺2.60) operated by İstanbul Şehir Hatları and Turyol ply a short stretch of the Sea of Marmara between İstanbul's European and Asian shores. The 25-minute ride to Kadıköy from Eminönü or Karaköy offers wonderful views, a ubiquitous escort of seagulls and an occasional dolphin sighting. You can even enjoy a cheap glass of tea on board some boats.

months in 1452, in preparation for his siege of Byzantine Constantinople. For its location, he chose the narrowest point of the Bosphorus, opposite Anadolu Hisarı, which Sultan Beyazıt I had built in 1394. By doing so, Mehmet was able to control all traffic on the strait, cutting the city off from resupply by sea.

To speed Rumeli Hisarı's completion, Mehmet ordered each of his three viziers to take responsibility for one of the three main towers. If his tower's construction was not completed on schedule, the vizier would pay with his life. Not surprisingly, the work was completed on time. The useful military life of the mighty fortress lasted less than one year. After the conquest of Constantinople, it was used as a glorified Bosphorus toll booth for a while, then as a barracks, a prison and finally as an open-air theatre.

Within Rumeli Hisarı's walls are park-like grounds, an open-air theatre and the minaret of a ruined mosque. Steep stairs (with no barriers, so beware!) lead up to the ramparts and towers; the views of the Bosphorus are magnificent. Just next to the fortress is a clutch of cafes and restaurants, the most popular of which is **Sade Kahve** (Map p108; ✆0212-263 8800; www.sadekahve.com.tr; Yahya Kemal Caddesi 20a, Rumeli Hisarı; set breakfast ₺57, gözleme ₺18-22; ⊙7am-12.30am; ☒22 & 25E from Kabataş, 22RE & 40 from Beşiktaş, 40, 40T & 42T from Taksim).

Between Rumeli Hisarı and the **Fatih Sultan Mehmet Bridge** is an eccentric-looking turreted building known locally as the Perili Köşk (Haunted Mansion), but properly referred to as the Yusuf Ziya Pasha mansion. The building's construction kicked off around 1910 but was halted in 1914 when the Ottoman Empire was drawn into WWI and

all of its construction workers were forced to quit their jobs and enlist in the army. Work on the 10-storey building came to a standstill and it remained empty, leading to its 'Haunted Mansion' tag. Eighty years later, work finally resumed and the finished building became the home of **Borusan Contemporary** (Map p108; ✆0212-393 5200; www.borusancontemporary.com; Perili Köşk, Baltalimanı Hisar Caddesi 5, Rumeli Hisarı; adult/student/child under 12yr ₺20/10/free; ⊙10am-6pm Sat & Sun; ☒22 & 25E from Kabataş, 22RE & 40 from Beşiktaş, 40, 40T & 42T from Taksim), a cultural centre.

The ferry doesn't stop at Rumeli Hisarı; you can either leave the ferry at Kanlıca and catch a taxi across the Fatih Bridge (this will cost around ₺30 including the bridge toll) or you can visit on your way back to town by bus from Sarıyer. Though Anadolu Hisarı is not open as a museum, visitors are free to wander about its ruined walls.

There are many architecturally and historically important *yalıs* in and around Anadolu Hisarı. These include the **Köprülü Amcazade Hüseyin Paşa Yalı** (Map p108; Körfez Caddesi, Anadolu Hisarı; ☒15, 15KÇ & 15ŞN from Üsküdar, 15F from Kadıköy), a cantilevered box-like structure built for one of Mustafa II's grand viziers in 1698. The oldest *yalı* on the Bosphorus, at the time of research it was undergoing a major renovation. Next door, the **Zarif Mustafa Paşa Yalı** (Map p108; Körfez Caddesi, Anadolu Hisarı; ☒15, 15KÇ & 15ŞN from Üsküdar, 15F from Kadıköy) was built in the early 19th century by the official coffee-maker to Sultan Mahmut II. Look for its upstairs salon, which juts out over the water and is supported by unusual curved timber struts. Closer to the bridge, the large 18th-century **Hekimbasi Salih Efendi Yalı** (Map p108; Körfez Caddesi 53, Anadolu Hisarı) was extensively damaged in 2018 when an out-of-control Maltese-flagged tanker crashed into the shore. The incident has renewed calls for big ships and boats – particularly those carrying oil or chemical cargoes – to be banned from sailing the strait.

Almost directly under the Fatih Bridge on the European shore is the huge stone four-storey **Tophane Müşiri Zeki Paşa Yalı** (Map p108; Balta Limanı Hisar Caddesi 16, Rumeli Hisarı; ☒22 & 25E from Kabataş, 22RE & 40 from Beşiktaş, 40, 40T & 42T from Taksim), a mansion built in the early 20th century for a field marshal in the Ottoman army. Later, it was sold to Sabiha Sultan, daughter of Mehmet VI, the last of the Ottoman sultans, and her husband İmer Faruk Efendi, grandson of Sultan Abdül Aziz. When the sultanate was abolished in 1922, Mehmet walked from this palace onto a British warship, never to return to Turkey.

Past the bridge on the Asian side is **Kanlıca**, the ferry's next stop. This charming village is famous for the rich and delicious yoghurt produced here, which is sold on the ferry and in two cafes on the shady waterfront square. The small **Gâzi İskender Paşa Mosque** (Map p108; Barış Manço Caddesi 4, Kanlıca; ⊟15, 15KÇ & 15ŞN from Üsküdar, 15F from Kadıköy, ⊠Kanlıca) in the square dates from 1560 and was designed by Mimar Sinan. There are excellent views of a number of yalıs as the ferry arrives and departs here.

High on a promontory above Kanlıca is **Hıdiv Kasrı** (Khedive's Villa; Map p108; ☑0216-413 9664; www.beltur.com.tr; Çubuklu Yolu 32, Çubuklu; ⊘9am-10.30pm; ⊟15E from Üsküdar, ⊠Kanlıca), a gorgeous art nouveau villa built by the last khedive of Egypt as a summer residence for use during his family's annual visits to İstanbul. You can see its square white tower (often flying a Turkish flag) from the ferry.

Kanlıca to Sarıyer

On the opposite shore to Kanlıca is the wealthy suburb of Emirgan, home to the impressive **Sakıp Sabancı Museum** (Map p108; ☑0212-277 2200; www.sakipsabancimuzesi.org; Sakıp Sabancı Caddesi 42, Emirgan; adult/student/child under 14yr ₺30/20/free, Wed free; ⊘10am-5.30pm Tue, Thu & Fri-Sun, to 7.30pm Wed; ⊟22 & 25E from Kabataş, 22RE & 40 from Beşiktaş, 40, 40T & 42T from Taksim, ⊠Emirgan). This museum has a permanent collection showcasing Ottoman manuscripts and calligraphy, but is best known for its blockbuster temporary exhibitions. The permanent collection occupies a 1925 mansion designed by Italian architect Edouard De Nari for the Egyptian Prince Mehmed Ali Hasan, and the temporary exhibitions are staged in an impressive modern extension designed by local firm Savaş, Erkel and Çırakoğlu.

On the hill above Emirgan is **Emirgan Korusu (Woods)**, a huge public reserve that is particularly beautiful in April, when it is carpeted with thousands of tulips.

North of Emirgan, there's a ferry dock near the small yacht-lined cove of **İstinye**. Nearby, on a point jutting out from the European shore, is the suburb of **Yeniköy**. This was a favourite summer resort for the Ottomans, as indicated by the cluster of lavish 18th- and 19th-century yalıs around the ferry dock. The most notable of these is the frilly white **Ahmed Afif Paşa Yalı** (Map p108; Köybası Caddesi, Yeniköy; ⊟25E from Kabataş, 40B from Beşiktaş, 40T & 42T from Taksim), designed by Alexandre Vallaury, architect of the Pera Palas Hotel in Beyoğlu, and built in the late 19th century. Look for its two onion-domed towers.

On the opposite shore is the village of **Paşabahçe**, famous for its glassware factory. A bit further on is the fishing village of **Beykoz**, which has a graceful ablutions fountain, the İshak Ağa Çeşmesi, dating from 1746, near the village square. Much of the land along the Bosphorus shore north of Beykoz is a military zone.

Originally called Therapia for its healthy climate, the little cove of **Tarabya** on the European shore has been a favourite summer watering place for İstanbul's well-to-do for centuries, though modern developments such as the multistorey Grand Hotel Tarabya right on the promontory have lessened much of its charm. Look for the cream-coloured, red-roofed **Huber Yalı** (TC Cumhurbaşkanlığı Huber Köşkü; Map p108; www.tccb.gov.tr/en/presidency/campuses/tarabya; Köybaşı Caddesi, Tarabya; ⊟22 & 25E from Kabataş, 22RE & 40 from Beşiktaş, 40, 40T & 42T from Taksim) south of the village, which has a distinctive gold-topped onion dome. The Turkish flags flying in front signal the building's status as the presidential residence in İstanbul. Close by is a white yalı that houses the German consulate and once functioned as the summer residence of the German embassy.

For an account of Therapia in its heyday, read Harold Nicolson's 1921 novel *Sweet Waters*. Nicolson, who is best known as Vita Sackville-West's husband, served as the third Secretary in the British embassy in Constantinople between 1912 and 1914, the years of the Balkan Wars, and clearly knew Therapia well. In the novel, the main character, Eirene, who was based on Vita, spent her summers here.

North of Tarabya are more of the old summer embassies of foreign powers. When the heat and fear of disease increased in the warm months, foreign ambassadors would retire to palatial residences, complete with lush gardens, on this shore. The region for such embassy residences extended north to the village of **Büyükdere**, notable for its churches, summer embassies and the **Sadberk Hanım Museum** (Map p108;

☑ 0212-242 3813; www.sadberkhanimmuzesi.org.
tr; Piyasa Caddesi 25-29, Büyükdere; adult/child
₺10/3; ☉ 10am-4.30pm Thu-Tue; ☐ 22, 22B & 25E
from Kabataş, 22RE from Beşiktaş, 40, 40T & 42T
from Taksim, ⛴ Sarıyer). Named after the wife
of the late Vehbi Koç, founder of Turkey's
foremost commercial empire, this museum
is housed in two late-19th-century *yalıs* and
is a showcase of both Turkish-Islamic artefacts collected by Mrs Koç and antiquities
from the noted Hüseyin Kocabaş collection.
Objects include İznik and Kütahya ceramics;
Ottoman silk textiles and costumes; glass
from the early Greek, Hellenistic and Roman periods; and an exquisite collection of
jewellery and diadems from the Mycenaean,
Archaic and Classical periods. To get here,
alight from the ferry at Sarıyer and walk left
(south) from the ferry dock for approximately 10 minutes; if your ferry stops at Büyükdere, which occasionally happens, alight
there instead.

Further on, towards Sarıyer, is another
Koç museum, the **Vehbi Koç Büyükdere
Evi** (Map p108; ☑ 0212-242 3815; www.vkv.org.
tr; Piyasa Caddesi 109, Büyükdere; ☉ 10am-5pm
Thu-Tue; ☐ 22, 22B & 25E from Kabataş, 22RE from
Beşiktaş, 40, 40T & 42T from Taksim, ⛴ Sarıyer)
FREE. Housed in the Koç family's former
summer house, it has a notable collection
of 36 Anatolian kilims (pileless woven rugs)
that was compiled by American photographer and ethnographer Josephine Powell
(1919–2007), the first foreigner allowed to
travel across Turkey and explore the country after the founding of the Republic. Most
of the rugs date from the 19th century and
are displayed alongside informative panels
in both English and Turkish that explain the
motifs used in their designs.

The residents of **Sarıyer**, the next village
up from Büyükdere on the European shore,
have traditionally made a living by fishing
and it is still possible to see fisherfolk mend-
ing their nets and selling their catch north
of the dock.

Sarıyer to Anadolu Kavağı

From Sarıyer, it's a short trip to **Rumeli
Kavağı**, a sleepy place where the only excitement comes courtesy of the arrival and
departure of the ferry. Just before arriving
in this village the new Yavuz Sultan Selim
(Third) Bridge, which opened in 2016,
comes into view. Located near the mouth of
the Black Sea, it's an attractive suspension
bridge but views of it and the strait have
been dreadfully marred by the power lines

and towers that the authorities have built in
its immediate vicinity.

Anadolu Kavağı, on the opposite shore,
is where the Long Bosphorus Tour finishes
its journey. Once a fishing village, its local
economy now relies on the tourism trade
and its main square is full of mediocre fish
restaurants and their touts.

Perched above the village are the ruins
of **Anadolu Kavağı Kalesi** (Yoros Kalesi; Map
p108; Anadolu Kavağı; ⛴ Anadolu Kavağı), a medieval castle overlooking both the Black Sea
and the Bosphorus. The castle originally had
eight massive towers in its walls, but little
of the original structure has survived. First
built by the Byzantines, it was restored and
reinforced by the Genoese in the 1300s, and
later by the Ottomans. An archaeological
excavation is currently underway and as a
result access is limited. There are, however,
great views of the Third Bridge. It takes 30
to 50 minutes to walk up to the fortress from
the town. Alternatively, taxis wait near the
fountain in the town square just east of the
ferry dock; they charge around ₺25 for the
return trip with 30 minutes' waiting time.
Restaurants and *çay bahçesi* (tea gardens)
along the walking route serve overpriced
food and drink.

GETTING THERE & AWAY

Be sure to check the websites of all companies
as schedules and routes change regularly.

Long Bosphorus Tour

Many day trippers take this ferry trip operated
by **İstanbul Şehir Hatları** (İstanbul City Routes;
☑ 153; www.sehirhatlari.com.tr). Known as both
the Uzun Boğaz Turu (Long Bosphorus Tour) and
the Nostaljik Tur (Nostalgic Tour), it travels the
entire length of the strait in a 95-minute one-way
trip, departing from the *iskele* (ferry dock) at
Eminönü daily at 10.35am and returning from Anadolu Kavağı (Map p108) at 3pm. A return *(çift)*
ticket costs adult/under six years/child six to 11
years ₺25/free/12.50; a one-way *(tek yön)* ticket
costs ₺15/free/7.50. The ferry stops at Beşiktaş
(Map p84), Üsküdar (p111), Kanlıca (Map p108),
Sarıyer (Map p108), Rumeli Kavağı (Map p108)
and Anadolu Kavağı (Map p108). It's not possible
to get on and off the ferry at stops along the way
using the same ticket.

Short Bosphorus Tour

From early March to May and from mid-September
to October, İstanbul Şehir Hatları offers a two-hour
tour (called the Kısa Boğaz Turu) leaving Eminönü
daily at 2.35pm, picking up passengers in Ortaköy
(Map p84) 20 minutes later. It travels as far as the
Fatih Sultan Mehmet Bridge before returning to

Eminönü. Tickets cost adult/child under six years/ child six to 11 years ₺12/free/6. From November to early March the service is limited to Saturdays, Sundays and holidays.

Private company **Dentur Avrasya** (☏ 0216-444 6336; www.denturavrasya.com) operates a tour (₺20) departing at 11.15am daily from its *iskele* (ferry dock) at Kabataş and stopping to pick up passengers in Beşiktaş (Map p84).

Hop-on Hop-off Palace Tour

Departing from the *iskele* behind the petrol station at Kabataş, this tour operated by Dentur Avrasya costs ₺25 (free for children under six years), leaves seven times daily at 11.45am, 12.45pm, 1.45pm, 2.45pm, 3.45pm, 4.45pm and 5.45pm. It picks more passengers up at Beşiktaş and then allows passengers to alight at Emirgan (Map p108), Küçüksu Kasrı (Map p108) and Beylerbeyi Palace (Map p108) and reboard on the same ticket. It would be very rushed to make three stops in one afternoon but two stops is achievable. Be aware that Küçüksu Kasrı and Beylerbeyi Palace close at 4.30pm.

Excursion Tours

A number of companies offer short tours from Eminönü, Karaköy and Üsküdar travelling to Anadolu Hisarı and back without stopping; of these **Turyol** (☏ 0212-251 4421; www.turyol. com) is probably the most reputable. The entire trip from Eminönü takes about 90 minutes (less from Karaköy and Üsküdar) and tickets usually cost adult/child ₺25/12.50.

Commuter Ferries

İstanbul Şehir Hatları operates commuter ferries from Eminönü (₺5) stopping at Beşiktaş, Arnavutköy, Emirgan, İstinye, Sarıyer and Rumeli Kavağı. These depart every hour or so between 11am and 8pm, with the last service returning from Rumeli Kavağı at 4.05pm or from Sarıyer at 6.30pm.

Bus

All commuter ferry trips cost ₺5 (₺2.60 with an İstanbulkart). You'll need an İstanbulkart to take a bus; each trip costs ₺2.60.

From Rumeli Kavağı The bus stop is in the square just in from the *iskele* (ferry dock), in front of the Rumeli Kavağı Ulu Cami.

From Sarıyer Buses 25E and 40 head south to Emirgan.

From Emirgan Buses 22, 22RE and 25E head to Kabataş, and 40, 40T and 42T go to Taksim. All travel via Rumeli Hisarı, Bebek, Ortaköy, Yıldız and Beşiktaş.

From Anadolu Kavağı Bus 15A leaves from the square straight ahead from the ferry terminal en route to Kavacık. Get off at Kanlıca to visit Hıdıv Kasrı or transfer to bus 15 at Beykoz, which will take you south to Üsküdar

via Çengelköy, the Küçüksu stop (for Küçüksu Kasrı) and the Beylerbeyi Sarayı stop (for Beylerbeyi). Bus 15F and 15BK take the same route but continue to Kadıköy.

🛁 Hamams

Succumbing to a soapy scrub in a steamy hamam is one of İstanbul's quintessential experiences.

★ **Kılıç Ali Paşa Hamamı** HAMAM
(Map p100; ☏ 0212-393 8010; www.kilicalipasa hamami.com; Hamam Sokak 1, off Kemeraltı Caddesi, Tophane; traditional hamam ritual ₺310, massages ₺220-520; ⏱ women 8.15am-4pm, men 4.45-11.30pm; 🚇 Tophane) It took seven years to develop a conservation plan for this 1580 Mimar Sinan–designed building and complete the meticulous restoration. Fortunately, the result was well worth waiting for. The hamam's interior is simply stunning and the place is run with total professionalism, ensuring a clean and enjoyable Turkish bath experience.

Ayasofya Hürrem Sultan Hamamı HAMAM
(Map p88; ☏ 0212-517 3535; www.ayasofya hamami.com; Aya Sofya Meydanı 2; bath treatments €55-160, massages €40-75; ⏱ 8am-10pm; 🚇 Sultanahmet) This meticulously restored twin hamam dating to 1556 offers the most luxurious traditional bath experience in the Old City. Designed by Mimar Sinan, it was built just across the road from Aya Sofya by order of Süleyman the Magnificent and named in honour of his wife Haseki Hürrem Sultan, commonly known as Roxelana.

Cağaloğlu Hamamı HAMAM
(Map p88; ☏ 0212-522 2424; www.cagaloglu hamami.com.tr; Professor Kazım İsmail Gürkan Caddesi 24, Cağaloğlu; bath packages €50-180, self-service €30; ⏱ 9am-10pm Mon-Fri, to 11pm Sat & Sun; 🚇 Sultanahmet) Built in 1741 by order of Sultan Mahmut I, this gorgeous hamam offers separate baths for men and women and a range of bath packages incorporating services including foam massage and scrub, foot massage, collagen face mask and aromatherapy massage.

Çemberlitaş Hamamı HAMAM
(Map p94; ☏ 0212-522 7974; www.cemberlitas hamami.com; Vezir Han Caddesi 8, Çemberlitaş; self-service ₺160, bath, scrub & soap massage ₺255; ⏱ men 6am-midnight men, women from 7.30am; 🚇 Çemberlitaş) There won't be too many times in your life when you'll get the opportunity

to have a Turkish bath in a building dating back to 1584, so now might well be the time to do it – particularly as this twin hamam was designed by the great architect Sinan and is among the most beautiful in the city.

Çukurcuma Hamamı
HAMAM

(Map p100; ☑0212-243 6480; www.cukurcuma hamami.com; Çukurcuma Caddesi 43, Çukurcuma; bath treatments ₺310-660, massages ₺250-320; ⊙8.30am-10pm; 🚇Tophane) Opened in 2018 after a long and careful restoration, this 1831 hamam in the residential district of Çukurcuma has one mixed bath, a small *camekan* (entrance hall) and upstairs massage rooms. A traditional 30-minute bath treatment costs ₺310 and the deluxe 'Süreyya Dream' package (₺660, 80 minutes) includes a traditional bath treatment, hand and feet peeling, and oil body-massage. Bookings recommended.

Mihrimah Sultan Hamamı
HAMAM

(Map p84; ☑0212-523 0487; www.mih rimahsultanhamami.com; Fevzi Paşa Caddesi 333, Edirnekapı; bath ₺40, incl scrub & massage ₺70; ⊙men 7am-11pm, women 9am-8pm; 🚌28, 31, 37, 336 from Eminönü, 87 from Taksim, 🚇Ayvansaray) Visit this restored hamam for an affordable and authentic experience. It lacks the architectural beauty of its counterparts in Sultanahmet, but is satisfyingly clean and has a friendly neighbourhood atmosphere. There are separate sections for men and women – men enter from the street entrance and women from the door around the corner.

🍃 Courses

Cooking Alaturka
COOKING

(Map p88; ☑0539 982 3360, 0212-458 5919; www. cookingalaturka.com; Akbıyık Caddesi 72a, Cankurtaran; classes per adult/child under 12yr incl meal €65/46; ⊙10.30am & 4.30pm by reservation Mon-Sat; 🚇Sultanahmet) The first English-language cookery school to open in İstanbul changed hands recently but is still cooking up a storm under its new Turkish-Italian ownership. The convivial classes, which run for two to three hours and are suitable for novices, offer a great introduction to home-style Turkish cuisine. The results are then enjoyed over a meal with wine. Cash payment only.

The school also offers food tours (₺75 to ₺100, Monday to Saturday) visiting produce and spice markets, sampling street food and even visiting a historic brewery. There's a popular package that includes a tour to the

Spice Market followed by a cooking class (₺100). Children aged under 12 receive a 30% discount on tour prices.

1200 Derece
ARTS & CRAFTS

(Map p84; ☑0537 501 7708, 0549 300 1200; www.1200derece.com; Vodina Caddesi 60a, Balat; courses ₺135-540; ⊙10am-9pm; 🚇Balat) The name of this hybrid cafe and glassblowing studio means '1200 Degrees', the degree to which raw materials must be heated before being blown into glass. Aspiring glass artists can come in for a coffee and a short guided try-out in blowing and creating glass beads (₺25), or sign up for a one-hour (₺135) or full-day (₺540) guided workshop.

It's also possible to pop in to enjoy a coffee and cake while watching workshops that are underway and browsing the glass creations on sale.

Tours

See p110 for information on Bosphorus ferry tours.

★ İstanbul Walks
WALKING

(Map p88; ☑0212-516 6300, 0554 335 6622; www. istanbulwalks.com; 1st fl, Şifa Hamamı Sokak 1, Küçük Ayasofya; tours €35-140; 🚇Sultanahmet) Specialising in cultural tourism, this company is run by history buffs and offers a large range of half- and full-day walking tours conducted by knowledgeable English-speaking guides. Tours concentrate on İstanbul's various neighbourhoods, but there are also food tours, Bosphorus and Golden Horn cruises, and a tour to the Princes' Islands (p145).

All tour participants are picked up at their hotels; free transfers back to the hotel are provided if you choose a full-day tour.

The company also operates day tours to Bursa (₺100) and Gallipoli (₺100).

★ Culinary Backstreets
FOOD & DRINK

(www.culinarybackstreets.com/culinary-walks/ istanbul; tours per person US$110-125) These enjoyable culinary walks around the Old City, Bazaar District, Beyoğlu, Kadıköy and the Bosphorus suburbs are conducted by the dedicated foodies who produce the excellent multi-country blog of the same name, and involve lots of eating. Also on offer is a market visit and cooking class held in the vibrant residential suburb of Kurtuluş.

★ Alternative City Tours
TOURS

(☑0535 675 6491; www.alternativecitytours.com; tours per group of 2/4 people €125/150) Having lived in İstanbul for two decades, New York–

born photographer Monica Fritz now shares many of the secrets she has learned about the city with fellow shutterbugs. Her informed and enjoyable tour portfolio covers the European and Asian shores and beyond, and she provides plenty of cultural and historical context.

Popular tours include one that introduces participants to the hidden *hans* (caravanserais) and passageways of the Grand Bazaar, as well as taking to the roof à la James Bond in *Skyfall*. Other destinations include the streets surrounding the Süleymaniye Mosque in the Old City, and the suburbs of Kadıköy, Kuzguncuk and Moda on the Asian side.

İstanbul on Food FOOD & DRINK
(www.istanbulonfood.com; tours adult US$69-100, child 6-12yr US$39-60) This outfit offers four culinary tour options, including a three-hour 'Twilight at Taksim' walk, six-hour 'Flavours of the Old City' and 'Taste of Two Continents' tours (the latter visits Eminönü and Kadıköy), and a three-hour 'Kadıköy Street Food' experience. Tours have a maximum of eight participants and are slightly cheaper than those offered by the company's major competitor, Culinary Backstreets.

Urban Adventures CULTURAL
(☑0532 641 2822; www.urbanadventures.com/destination/istanbul-tours; tours adult/child from US$36/24) This highly professional outfit runs a number of cultural and foodie tours including an 'Istanbul Uncovered' tour visiting Old City highlights and a 3½-hour night tasting walk in Beyoğlu that includes a stop in a traditional *meyhane* (tavern).

Turkish Flavours FOOD & DRINK
(☑0532 218 0653; www.turkishflavours.com; tours per person US$80-125, tour & cooking class US$100) A well-regarded outfit offering foodie walks and cooking classes, Turkish Flavours has offerings including a five-hour 'Market Tour' that starts at Eminönü's Spice Bazaar and then takes a ferry to Kadıköy, where it tours the produce market and finishes with lunch at Çiya Sofrası (p130). Other tours include a vegetarian gourmet walk through Karaköy and Kadıköy, and a traditional sweets tour.

Vegetarians, vegans and those who are gluten-free can be accommodated in cooking classes, as can children (child five to 12 years US$50).

Festivals & Events

İstanbul Tulip Festival CULTURAL
(☺Apr) FREE The tulip (*lâle* in Turkish) is one of İstanbul's traditional symbols, and the local government celebrates this fact by planting over 10 million of them annually. These bloom in April, endowing almost every street and park with vivid spring colours and wonderful photo opportunities. The main display is in Emirgan Park on the Bosphorus.

İstanbul Film Festival FILM
(http://film.iksv.org; ☺Apr) If you're keen to view the best in Turkish film and bump into a few local film stars while doing so, this is the event to attend. Held in the first half of April in cinemas around town, it's hugely popular. The program includes retrospectives and recent releases from Turkey and abroad.

İstanbul Music Festival MUSIC
(http://muzik.iksv.org/en; ☺Jun) The city's premier arts festival includes performances of opera, orchestral concerts and chamber recitals. Acts are often internationally renowned and the action takes place at atmosphere-laden venues such as Aya İrini (p72) in Sultanahmet and the **Süreyya Opera House** (Map p84; ☑0216-346 1531; www.sureyyaoperasi.org; Gen Asim Gündüz/Bahariye Caddesi 29; ☺ticket office 10am-6pm; ☷Kadıköy, ⓂKadıköy) in Kadıköy.

Chill-Out Festival MUSIC
(www.chilloutfest.com; ☺Jun) A two-day event featuring a concept stage, cultural and artistic activities, yoga programs and plenty of music (everything from soul to funk to world beats). It's held at Garden Fiesta in Sarıyer on the Bosphorus and moves to Bodrum in July.

İstanbul Jazz Festival MUSIC
(http://caz.iksv.org/en; ☺late-Jun–mid-Jul) This festival showcases an exhilarating hybrid of conventional jazz, electronica, drum and bass, world music and rock. Venues include Nardis Jazz Club (p134) in Galata, Salon (p134) in Şişhane, and parks around the city.

İstanbul Biennial ART
(http://bienal.iksv.org/en; ☺mid-Sep–mid-Nov odd-numbered years) Now entrenched in the international arts calendar, the city's visual arts biennale sees an international curator or panel of curators nominating a theme

and putting together a cutting-edge program that is then exhibited in a variety of venues around town and on the Princes' Islands.

İstanbul Design Biennial   DESIGN
(http://bienal.iksv.org/en; ⊙ Sep-Nov even-numbered years) This themed event sees the city's design community celebrating its profession and critically discussing its future.

Akbank Jazz Festival   MUSIC
(Akbank Caz Festivali; www.akbanksanat.com; ⊙ Oct or Nov) Now heading towards its third decade, this popular festival features local and international acts performing traditional and avant-garde jazz, as well as Middle Eastern fusions. Venues include **Akbank Art** (Akbank Sanat; Map p100; ☑ 0212-252 3500; www.akbanksanat.com; İstiklal Caddesi 8, Taksim; ⊙ 10.30am-7.30pm Tue-Sat; Ⓜ Taksim) **FREE**, **Zorlu Center** (Map p108; ☑ 0212-924 0100; www.zorlucenter.com; Koru Sokak 2, Beşiktaş; Ⓜ Gayrettepe) and Babylon Bomonti (p134).

FotoIstanbul   ART
(www.fotoistanbul.org; Palanga Caddesi 37, Ortaköy; ⊙ Oct) **FREE** This excellent (and free) annual photography festival displays diverse work by Turkish and international artists at gallery venues in the Beyoğlu, Beşiktaş and Ortaköy neighbourhoods, as well as in outdoor installations. The don't-miss venue is always the Ortaköy Yetimhanesi, a century-old former orphanage where photos are innovatively displayed over three storeys of the atmospherically crumbling building.

🛏 Sleeping

Every accommodation style is available in İstanbul. You can live like a sultan in a world-class luxury hotel, bunk down in a dorm bed or settle into a stylish boutique establishment. The secret is to choose the neighbourhood that best suits your interests and then look for accommodation that will suit your style and budget. During peak tourism periods, such as spring, autumn and Christmas, it's important to book ahead.

🛏 Sultanahmet

Sultanahmet is the heart of Old İstanbul and the city's premier sightseeing area, so hotels here and in the adjoining neighbourhoods to the east (Cankurtaran), south (Küçük

Ayasofya), north (Sirkeci) and northwest (Binbirdirek, Çemberlitaş, Alemdar and Cağaloğlu) are supremely convenient. The area's main drawbacks are carpet touts and the dearth of decent bars and restaurants. Some Cankurtaran hotels can also be noisy, with loud music coming from the bars and hostels on Akbıyık Caddesi. Early in the morning you may be woken by the call to prayer issuing from mosques such as İshak Paşa Mosque (at the northeastern end of Akbıyık Caddesi).

⭐ **Marmara Guesthouse**   PENSION $
(Map p88; ☑ 0212-638 3638; www.marmaraguesthouse.com; Terbıyık Sokak 15, Cankurtaran; s/d/tr/f €55/65/75/85; ❀ ❇ 🛜; 🚊 Sultanahmet) Few of Sultanahmet's family-run pensions can compete with the Marmara's cleanliness, comfort and thoughtful details. Owner Elif and team go out of their way to welcome guests, offering advice aplenty and serving a delicious breakfast on the sea-facing roof terrace. The 15 rooms have comfortable beds, good bathrooms (small in some cases), satellite TVs and double-glazed windows. Expect lots of stairs.

Members of the same family operate the similarly impressive Saruhan Hotel (p122) in the predominantly residential pocket of Kadırga.

⭐ **Hotel Alilass**   DESIGN HOTEL $
(Map p88; ☑ 0212-516 8860; www.hotelalilass.com; Bayram Fırını Sokak 9, Cankurtaran; s/d standard €75/79, deluxe €90/98; ❀ ❇ 🛜; 🚊 Sultanahmet) One of Sultanahmet's few budget boutique hotels, the Alilass offers rooms decorated with evocative Ara Güler prints of Old İstanbul. Standard rooms are small but have kettles and satellite TVs; bathrooms are modern and very clean. For a bit more space, upgrade to the deluxe category. Facilities include a stylish lobby cafe and a breakfast gazebo in the rear garden.

⭐ **Hotel Şebnem**   HOTEL $
(Map p88; ☑ 0212-517 6623; www.sebnemhotel.net; Adliye Sokak 1, Cankurtaran; s/d/tr/f €55/65/75/90; ❀ ❇ 🛜; 🚊 Sultanahmet) A simple but elegant decor gives the Şebnem an edge over nearby budget hotels. Rooms have wooden floors, modern bathrooms and comfortable beds with good-quality bed linen; two have a private courtyard garden. The large upstairs terrace has a breakfast room

and outdoor area with views over the Sea of Marmara. Excellent value.

Cheers Hostel HOSTEL $

(Map p88; ☎0212-526 0200; www.cheershostel.com; Zeynep Sultan Camii Sokak 21, Alamdar; dm €15-20, s €42, d/tw €49-58, tr €90-105; P ⊖ ❄ @ ≋; ⓖGülhane) The four- to 10-bed dorms at Sultanahmet's best hostel are worlds away from the barrack-like quarters at many of its competitors. Bright and airy, they feature air-conditioning, lockers and comfortable beds. Bathrooms (one shower per eight beds) are clean. The excellent central location is a major draw, as is the cosy rooftop bar with its open fire and great view.

Big Apple Hostel HOSTEL $

(Map p88; ☎0212-517 7931; www.hostelbigapple.com; Bayram Fırını Sokak 12, Cankurtaran; dm €10-15, s/d/tw €45/55/65; ⊖ ❄ @ ≋; ⓖSultanahmet) It may lack a backpacker vibe, but the compensations at this comfortable hostel include four-, six- and 14-bed dorms with curtained bunk beds, lockers, individual power points and en-suite bathrooms so clean they gleam. There are also hotel-style private en-suite rooms with satellite TV. Added to this is a rooftop bar-breakfast room with sea views.

Ahmet Efendi Evi PENSION $

(Map p88; ☎0212-518 8465; www.ahmetefendievi.com; Keresteci Hakkı Sokak 31, Cankurtaran; s €40, d €55-60; ⊖ ❄ ≋; ⓖSultanahmet) Mr Ahmet's House has an appealing home-away-from-home feel and is a great choice for those travelling with children, with a warm welcome from hostess Gönül and family. In a predominantly residential area (a rarity in Sultanahmet), its nine rooms of various sizes have modern decor; one has a terrace with views of the Blue Mosque and Sea of Marmara.

Hotel Peninsula HOTEL $

(Map p88; ☎0212-458 6850; www.hotelpeninsula.com; Adliye Sokak 6, Cankurtaran; s/d & tw/tr/f €40/50/60/90; ⊖ ❄ ≋; ⓖSultanahmet) Hallmarks here are friendly staff, comfortable rooms and bargain prices. Start your day on the sea-facing roof terrace with its sociable breakfast room and outdoor tables. Basement rooms are dark, but have reduced prices (single €35, twin €40, family €75).

> **RATES & RESERVATIONS**
>
> Hotels here are usually busy, so you should book your room as far in advance as possible, particularly if you are visiting during the high season (Easter to May, September to October and Christmas/New Year). Recent years have seen significant fluctuations in tourist numbers in İstanbul, so most hotels now use yield management systems when setting their rates. This means that in quiet times prices can drop dramatically (sometimes by as much as 50%) and in busy times they can skyrocket. As a result, you should treat our prices as a guide only – it is possible that the price you are quoted will be quite different. Note that most hotels in İstanbul set their prices in euros, and we have listed them as such here.

The same crowd operates the **Hanedan** (Map p88; ☎0212-516 4869; www.hanedanhotel.com; Adliye Sokak 3; s €40, d €50-55, tr/f €70/85; ⊖ ❄ ≋) opposite and the **Grand Peninsula** (Map p88; ☎0212-458 7710; www.grandpeninsulahotel.com; Cetinkaya Sokak 3; s €45, d €45-65, tr/f €75/80; ⊖ ❄ ≋) nearby, both also recommended.

Bahaus Hostel HOSTEL $

(Map p88; ☎0212-638 6534; www.bahausistanbul.com; Bayram Fırını Sokak 7, Cankurtaran; dm €11-16, r with shared bathroom €38; ⊖ ❄ @ ≋; ⓖSultanahmet) Small, clean and secure, Bahaus stands in stark and welcome contrast to the huge institutional-style hostels on nearby Akbıyık Caddesi. The four- to 14-bed dorms (including two female-only options) have curtained bunks with good mattresses, reading lights and lockers; they can be hot in summer. Top marks go to the plentiful bathrooms, entertainment program and rooftop terrace bar.

★Sirkeci Mansion HOTEL $$

(Map p88; ☎0212-528 4344; www.sirkecimansion.com; Taya Hatun Sokak 5, Sirkeci; s/d & tw/f from €120/140/190; ⊖ ❄ @ ≋ ≈; ⓖGülhane) Travellers love this terrific-value hotel overlooking Gülhane Park, with its impeccably clean, well-sized and amenity-laden rooms, some with park-facing balconies. It has a restaurant where a lavish breakfast is served, an indoor pool and a hamam. Top marks go to the attention to detail, the helpful staff and the complimentary entertainment program, which includes walking tours and afternoon teas.

★ Hotel Empress Zoe   BOUTIQUE HOTEL $$

(Map p88; ☑ 0212-518 2504; www.emzoe.com; Akbıyık Caddesi 10, Cankurtaran; s €95, d €130-170, ste €230-280; ⊛ ❋ @ ☎; ⌂ Sultanahmet) Named after the feisty Byzantine empress, this is one of İstanbul's most impressive boutique hotels. The four buildings house 26 diverse rooms joined by lots of stairs. The enticing garden suites overlook a gorgeous flower-filled courtyard where breakfast is served in warm weather. You can enjoy an early evening drink there, or while admiring the sea view from the terrace.

★ Hotel Ibrahim Pasha   BOUTIQUE HOTEL $$

(Map p88; ☑ 0212-518 0394; www.ibrahimpasha. com; Terzihane Sokak 7, Binbirdirek; r standard/deluxe €170/245; ⊛ ❋ ☎; ⌂ Sultanahmet) Cultural tomes are piled in reception and throughout the 24 rooms of this exemplary design hotel, which also has a comfortable lounge with open fire, and a terrace bar with knockout views of the nearby Blue Mosque and Hippodrome. Rooms are gorgeous but some are small, with more space in the deluxe options and those in the new section.

Hotel Amira   HOTEL $$

(Map p88; ☑ 0212-516 1640; www.hotelamira.com; Mustafa Paşa Sokak 43, Küçük Ayasofya; s €100, d €110-160; ⊛ ❋ @ ☎; ⌂ Sultanahmet) A consistent performer, Amira has 34 comfortable, well-equipped rooms. The standard rooms are cramped, so it's worth paying extra for a deluxe version. Service levels are impressive, as is the breakfast spread, which includes freshly made *gözleme* (stuffed flatbreads). The rooftop terrace bar overlooks the Little Aya Sofya and the Sea of Marmara.

Arcadia Hotel Blue   HOTEL $$

(Map p88; ☑ 0212-516 9696; www.hotelarcadiablue.com; İmran Öktem Caddesi 1, Binbirdirek; r economy/standard/sea view/deluxe from €95/118/153/160; ℗ ⊛ ❋ ☎; ⌂ Sultanahmet) This modern hotel has memorable views of Aya Sofya, the Blue Mosque, the Bosphorus and the Sea of Marmara from its rooftop bar-restaurant, and other facilities include a hamam, spa and cafe where a complimenta-

ry glass of wine and snack buffet are served each afternoon. All rooms are extremely comfortable, but it's worth paying extra for a sea view.

Saruhan Hotel   HOTEL $$

(Map p84; ☑ 0212-458 7608; www.saruhanhotel. com; Cinci Meydanı Sokak 34, Kadırga; s €110, d €120-140; ⊛ ❋ @ ☎; ⌂ Çemberlitaş) Hitherto bereft of hotels, the quiet residential pocket of Kadırga is inching its way into the limelight, courtesy of impressive family-run operations like this one. The Saruhan offers 17 comfortable and well-equipped rooms and a lovely terrace with a sea view. It's a 20-minute walk to the sights in Sultanahmet and a shorter (but steep) walk to the Grand Bazaar.

Sarı Konak Hotel   BOUTIQUE HOTEL $$

(Map p88; ☑ 0212-638 6258; www.istanbulhotelsarikonak.com; Mimar Mehmet Ağa Caddesi 26, Cankurtaran; economy r €70, r €75-95, f €140; ⊛ ❋ ☎; ⌂ Sultanahmet) Guests here enjoy relaxing on the roof terrace with its Sea of Marmara glimpses, but also take advantage of the comfortable lounge and courtyard downstairs. With Ottoman touches and prints of Old İstanbul, bedrooms are attractive but looking a bit worn; the economy rooms have particularly small bathrooms.

Four Seasons İstanbul at Sultanahmet   HOTEL $$$

(Map p88; ☑ 0212-402 3000; www.fourseasons. com/istanbul; Tevkifhane Sokak 1, Cankurtaran; r from €440; ℗ ⊛ ❋ @ ☎; ⌂ Sultanahmet) This luxurious hotel has an excellent position near Aya Sofya and the Blue Mosque, with views of both and of the Bosphorus from its **rooftop bar** (⊙ 5-11pm). Facilities include a spa and a restaurant in the leafy inner courtyard. Even the entry-level superior rooms are serene havens, with original Turkish artworks and handwoven kilims.

Ottoman Hotel Imperial   HOTEL $$$

(Map p88; ☑ 0212-513 6151; www.ottomanhotelimperial.com; Caferiye Sokak 6; r from €190; ⊛ ❋ @ ☎; ⌂ Sultanahmet) This four-star hotel is in a wonderfully quiet location just outside the Topkapı Palace walls. Its large and comfortable rooms have plenty of amenities, including minibars and coffee machines, and are decorated with Ottoman-style objets d'art; opt for one facing the neighbouring Aya Sofya or in the rear annexe. No roof terrace, but on-site **Matbah** (☑ 0212-514

6151; www.matbahrestaurant.com; mezes ₺20-35, mains ₺65-98; ☺noon-10.30pm; 🖥) restaurant compensates.

🛏 Beyoğlu

The first European hotel in Beyoğlu, Hôtel d'Angleterre, opened in 1841 and accommodation options in every budget category have been flourishing ever since. There's a preponderance of boutique options, especially in the fashionable districts of Cihangir, Çukurcuma and Karaköy, and a wide array of apartment rentals.

★ Louis Appartements HOTEL $$

(Map p100; 🖊0212-293 4052; www.louis.com.tr/galata; İlk Belediye Caddesi 10, Şişhane; d from €80; ☺✳🖥; Ⓜ Şişhane, 🚡 Tünel) The tower suite at this meticulously maintained and keenly priced hotel near the Galata Tower is the knockout option among the 12 suites and rooms on offer. All have a large bed, TV/DVD player, ironing set-up and kitchenette equipped with appliances, including an espresso machine. Decor is understated but pleasing; staff are helpful. An optional breakfast costs €6 per person.

★ Witt Istanbul Hotel BOUTIQUE HOTEL $$

(Map p100; 🖊0212-293 1500; www.wittistanbul.com; Defterdar Yokuşu 26, Cihangir; d ste/terrace ste from €155/385; ✳@🖥; Ⓜ Taksim, 🚡 Tophane) Showcasing nearly as many designer features as an issue of *Architectural Digest,* this stylish apartment hotel in Cihangir offers spacious suites with seating area, CD/DVD player, espresso machine, king-size bed and swish bathroom. Most have kitchenettes and a few have panoramic terraces (there's also a communal rooftop terrace). It's a short but steep climb from the Tophane tram stop.

★ Casa di Bava BOUTIQUE HOTEL $$

(Map p100; 🖊0538 377 3877; www.casadibavaistanbul.com; Bostanbaşı Caddesi 28, Çukurcuma; 1-bedroom apt/2-bedroom penthouse from €75/130; ☺✳🖥🖥; Ⓜ Taksim) The two-bedroom penthouse apartment at this wonderfully located suite hotel is an absolute knockout, and the 11 one-bedroom apartments in the 1880s building are impressive, too. All are stylishly decorated and well appointed, with original artworks, fully equipped kitchenettes and washing machines. The basement suites are smaller and

less expensive; all have daily maid service. No breakfast.

Karaköy Rooms BOUTIQUE HOTEL $$

(Map p100; 🖊0212-252 5422; www.karakoyrooms.com; Galata Şarap İskelesi Sokak 10, Karaköy; r €135-150; ☺✳🖥; 🚡 Karaköy) Occupying five floors above one of the city's best-loved restaurants, Karaköy Lokantası (p129), this splendid hotel has only 12 rooms – book well in advance. The double and deluxe rooms are spacious and comfortable, with lots of amenities. The pricier studios are enormous, with well-equipped kitchenettes. Decor is super-stylish throughout. No breakfast.

Hamamhane BOUTIQUE HOTEL $$

(Map p100; 🖊0212-293 4963; www.hammamhane.com; Çukurcuma Caddesi 45, Çukurcuma; studio/ste €110/130; ☺✳@🖥; 🚡 Tophane) Çukurcuma is one of the few enclaves in Beyoğlu to retain an authentic neighbourhood feel, so it's a great spot for a city sojourn. Each of the spacious studios and suites at this keenly priced hotel come with a fully equipped kitchenette and clothes washer/dryer. Decor is Ikea-stylish and there's an extremely pleasant ground-floor dining room and terrace.

Bankerhan Hotel BOUTIQUE HOTEL $$

(Map p100; 🖊0212-243 5617; www.bankerhan.com; Banker Sokağı 2, Galata; r standard/deluxe from €85/105; ☺✳@🖥; 🚡 Karaköy) Budget and boutique aren't concepts that sit comfortably together, but this hotel on the edge of Galata and Karaköy can legitimately claim to be both. The owners have a notable contemporary-art collection that is scattered throughout the building, and the 36 rooms are both stylish and comfortable. The cheapest options are cramped – upgrade if possible.

Istanbul Place Apartments APARTMENT $$

(🖊0506 449 3393; www.istanbulplace.com; apt 1-bed €60-140, 2-bed €80-160, 3-bed €100-290; ✳🖥) Operated by a British-Turkish couple, this apartment-rental company has 12 well-appointed and beautifully presented properties in historic buildings across Galata and Taksim.

TomTom Suites BOUTIQUE HOTEL $$

(Map p100; 🖊0212-292 4949; www.tomtomsuites.com; Tomtom Kaptan Sokak 18, Tophane; ste from €160; ☺✳🖥; 🚡 Tophane) We're more than happy to beat the drum about this hotel, occupying a former Franciscan nunnery off

İstiklal Caddesi. Its contemporary decor is understated but elegant, levels of service are high and the suites are spacious and beautifully appointed. A delicious and generous breakfast is served in the rooftop restaurant with its panoramic view. Sadly, dinner is considerably less impressive.

Marmara Pera HOTEL **$$**
(Map p100; ☑0212-251 4646; www.themarmara hotels.com; Meşrutiyet Caddesi 1, Tepebaşı; r/f/ste from €130/285/380; P🐕😊❄@🛜🏊🎀; Ⓜ Şişhane, 🚇Tünel) A great location in the midst of Beyoğlu's major entertainment enclave makes this high-rise modern hotel an excellent choice. Added extras include a health club, a tiny outdoor pool, a truly fabulous buffet breakfast spread (€15 per person) and the fashionable Mikla (p132) rooftop bar and restaurant. Rooms with a sea view are approximately 30% more expensive.

Manzara Istanbul APARTMENT **$$**
(☑0212-252 4660; www.manzara-istanbul.com; apt from €80; 🛜) Turkish-German architect and artist Erdoğan Altindiş has renovated eight residential apartments in Beyoğlu and rents them out to holidaymakers. Sleeping between one and six people, they offer well-priced alternatives to hotels in the area. A number of the apartments have extraordinary views, some have wi-fi and a few have air-con and private terraces.

★**Pera Palace Hotel** HISTORIC HOTEL **$$$**
(Map p100; ☑0212-377 4000; www.perapal ace.com; Meşrutiyet Caddesi 52, Tepebaşı; r/ste from €170/280; P🐕😊❄@🛜🏊🎀; Ⓜ Şişhane, 🚇Tünel) This famous hotel underwent a €23-million restoration in 2010 and the result is simply splendiferous. Rooms are luxurious and extremely comfortable, and facilities include an atmospheric bar and lounge (the latter often closed for private functions), spa, gym and restaurant. The most impressive feature of all is the service, which is both friendly and efficient. Breakfast costs €22.

🛏 The Golden Horn

This neighbourhood is home to a greater number of self-catering accommodation options than hotels or hostels. It has less tourist facilities and atmosphere after dark than if you stay in, say, Beyoğlu or Sultanahmet, but if you are keen to bed down in this area, home-sharing services such as Airbnb feature properties in Fener and Balat.

Akın House APARTMENT **$**
(☑0530 877 1855; www.akin-house.hotel-istanbul. net/en; Balat; s €25, d €25-35, tr €40; P😊🛜; 🚢Balat) To experience local life in the Golden Horn's most atmospheric neighbourhood, book a room in one of these traditional wooden houses near the Fener ferry stop. All have a fridge and kettle; some have a kitchenette. Exposed brick, wooden floors, rugs and brass beds give plenty of character. The Turkish-Australian managers go out of their way to assist guests. Sensational value.

🛏 Kadıköy

Hush Hostel Moda HOSTEL **$**
(Map p84; ☑0216-330 1122; www.hushhostels. com; Güneşlibahçe Sokak 50b; dm from €13, s without bathroom €22, d €36-44; 😊❄@🛜; 🚢Kadıköy, Ⓜ Kadıköy) Located in the thick of Kadıköy's entertainment district, this is a party hostel – expect plenty of noise. Private rooms with bathroom have air-con (dorms and rooms without bathroom don't) and there's a convivial terrace bar. The produce market is conveniently close, so the communal kitchen sees lots of cooking action. Guests can sign up for bike tours to Kuzguncuk (₺40).

🍴 Eating

🍴 Sultanahmet

Sultanahmet's lovely settings and great views are too often accompanied by disappointing meals. That said, we've eaten our way through the neighbourhood and, fortunately, there are a few decent eateries to be found.

If you're in the Sirkeci neighbourhood at lunchtime, join the locals in Hocapaşa Sokak, a pedestrianised street lined with cheap eateries. Here, *lokantas* (eateries serving ready-made food) offer *hazır yemek* (ready-made dishes), *köftecis* dish out flavoursome meatballs, *kebapçıs* grill meat to order and *pidecis* serve piping-hot pides (Turkish-style pizza).

The Küçük Ayasofya neighbourhood is another good option for more authentic and affordable eateries.

★**Bitlisli** ANATOLIAN **$**
(Map p88; ☑0212-513 77 63; www.bitlisli.net; Hocapaşa Camii Sokak 2b, Sirkeci; pides ₺22-28, kebaps ₺28-55; ⊙10.30am-10.30pm; 🚇Sirkeci) Those keen on robust flavours and the

liberal application of chilli in their food will be instantly enamoured of the dishes served at this bustling eatery in Hocapaşa. Choose from an array of liver options, meat kebaps, pides and *lahmacun* (Arabic-style pizza), and be sure to start with a delicious *sarımsaklı Antep lahmacin* (thin, crispy Antep-style pizza; ₺9). No alcohol.

Erol Lokantası
TURKISH $
(Map p88; ☑ 0212-511 0322; Çatal Çeşme Sokak 3, Alamdar; soup ₺6.50, portions ₺12-26; ☺ 11am-6pm Mon-Sat; ✻ ☑; ☐ Sultanahmet) One of Sultanahmet's last remaining *lokantas*, Erol is recommended for both its food and its warm welcome. The meat and vegetable stews in the bain-marie are made fresh daily using seasonal ingredients by the Erol family members, who have collectively put in several decades in the kitchen. Enjoy them with a side order of pilaf or bulgur.

Şehzade Cağ Kebabı
KEBAP $
(Map p88; ☑ 0212-520 3361; Hocapaşa Sokak 6/4, Sirkeci; kebap portion ₺24; ☺ 11am-9.30pm Mon-Sat; ☐ Sirkeci) Cooked on a horizontal spit, the Erzurum-style lamb kebap that this joint is known for is tender, very slightly charred and very tasty. Served on *lavaş* bread with a side-serve of tangy lemon, it has many local fans. Get here early at lunchtime to score one of the streetside tables, or order a *dürüm* (wrap) to go. No alcohol.

Tarihi Sultanahmet Köftecisi Selim Usta
KÖFTE $
(Map p88; ☑ 0212-520 0566; www.sultanahmet koftesi.com; Divan Yolu Caddesi 12, Alemdar; köfte ₺24, beans ₺8, çorba ₺7; ☺ 10.30am-11pm; ✻; ☐ Sultanahmet) Not to be confused with the nearby Meşhur Sultanahmet Köftecisi, this no-frills place near the Sultanahmet tram stop is the most famous eatery in the Old City. It has been serving its slightly rubbery *ızgara köfte* (grilled meatballs) and bean salad to ultra-loyal locals since 1920, and shows no sign of losing its custom – there's often a queue outside.

Başka Şubemiz Yoktur Karadeniz Aile Pide ve Kebap Salonu
PIDE $
(Map p88; ☑ 0212-522 9191; www.karadenizpide. net; Hacı Tahsinbey Sokak 7, off Divan Yolu Caddesi, Alemdar; pides ₺16-27, kebaps ₺20-59; ☺ 6am-11pm; ☐ Sultanahmet) Serving tasty pides and kebaps since 1985, the original Karadeniz (Black Sea)–style pide joint in this enclave is a hit with local shopkeepers. You can claim a table in the utilitarian interior (women usually sit upstairs) or on the lane. No alcohol.

Sefa Restaurant
TURKISH $
(Map p88; ☑ 0212-520 0670; www.sefarestaurant. com.tr; Nuruosmaniye Caddesi 11, Cağaloğlu; soups ₺7-15, portions ₺13-38; ☺ 7am-4.30pm Mon-Sat; ☎ ☑; ☐ Sultanahmet) Located between Sultanahmet and the Grand Bazaar, this clean and popular place offers *hazır yemek* (ready-made dishes) at reasonable prices. You can order from an English menu, but at busy times you may find it easier to just pick daily specials from the bain-marie. Try to arrive early-ish for lunch because many dishes run out by 1.30pm. No alcohol.

Güvenç Konyalı
TURKISH $$
(Map p88; ☑ 0212-527 5220; www.guvenckonyali. com.tr; Hocapaşa Hamam Sokak 4, Sirkeci; soup ₺15, pides ₺24-60, kebaps ₺22-50; ☺ noon-9pm Mon-Sat; ☐ Sirkeci) Specialities from Konya in Central Anatolia are the draw at this bustling place just off the much-loved Hocapaşa Sokak food strip. Regulars come for the spicy *bamya çorbası* (sour soup with lamb and chickpeas), *etli ekmek* (flatbread with meat) and meltingly soft slow-cooked meats from the oven. No alcohol.

★ Balıkçı Sabahattin
SEAFOOD $$$
(Map p88; ☑ 0212-458 1824; www.balikcisabahat tin.com; Şeyit Hasan Koyu Sokak 1, Cankurtaran; mezes ₺15-50, fish mains ₺60-90; ☺ 1pm-1am; ☎; ☐ Sultanahmet) Balıkçı Sabahattin is an enduring favourite with discerning Turks from near and far, who enjoy the limited but delicious menu of mezes and seafood. This is Sultanahmet's most prestigious restaurant and its best food, although the service can be harried. You'll dine under a leafy canopy in the garden (one section smoking, the other nonsmoking) or in the historic *konak* (house).

Deraliye
TURKISH $$$
(Map p88; ☑ 0212-520 7778; www.deraliyeres taurant.com; Ticarethane Sokak 10, Alemdar; mezes ₺21-56, mains ₺48-135; ☺ noon-11pm; ✻ ☎; ☐ Sultanahmet) Offering a taste of the sumptuous dishes once served in the great Ottoman palaces, Deraliye offers diners the chance to order delights such as the goose kebap served to Süleyman the Magnificent or Mehmet II's favourite lamb stew. Those with less adventurous palates can opt for modern standards such as kebaps. There's live music on Friday and Saturday evenings.

✖ Bazaar District & Around

★ Fatih Damak Pide
PIDE $

(Map p94; ✆ 0212-521 5057; www.facebook.com/fatihdamakpide; Büyük Karaman Caddesi 48, Fatih; pides ₺18-28; ⏱ 7am-11pm; Ⓜ Vezneciler) It's worth making the trek to this *pideci* overlooking the Fatih İtfaiye Park near the Aqueduct of Valens. Its reputation for making the best Karadeniz (Black Sea)–style pide on the historic peninsula is well deserved and the pots of tea served with meals are a nice touch (the first pot is free, subsequent pots are charged). Toppings are mostly standard – the *sucuklu-peynirli* (sausage and cheese) option is particularly tasty – but there's also an unusual *bafra pidesi* (rolled-up pide). On weekends, it offers a Black Sea–style breakfast buffet (₺40) between 7am and 1.30pm. No alcohol.

★ Salloura Oğlu
SWEETS $

(Map p84; ✆ 0553 680 0800; www.facebook.com/sallouraoglu1870; Turgut Özal Millet Caddesi 60, Fındıkzade; kadayıf & künefe ₺25, baklava ₺20; ⏱ 8am-1am; ⓕ Haseki) Transplanted from Aleppo to İstanbul in 2014, this 150-year-old institution is known for speciality sweet cheese desserts such as *kadayıf* and *peynirli künefe* and also makes delectable baklava. It's hugely popular with the many Syrian refugees in the city, but has also built a loyal following among locals. Two branches have opened in this neighbourhood; both are well worth the tram trip.

Dönerci Şahin Usta
KEBAP $

(Map p94; ✆ 0212-526 5297; www.donercisahinusta.com; Kılıççılar Sokak 9, Nuruosmaniye; döner kebap from ₺15; ⏱ 11am-3pm Mon-Sat; ⓕ Çemberlitaş) Turks take family, football and food seriously. And when it comes to food, few dishes are sampled and assessed as widely as the humble döner kebap. Ask any shopkeeper in the Grand Bazaar about who makes the best döner in the immediate area, and you are likely to get the same answer: 'Şahin Usta, of course!' Takeaway only.

Pak Pide & Pizza Salonu
PIDE $

(Map p94; ✆ 0212-513 7664; Paşa Camii Sokak 16, Mercan; pides ₺13-18; ⏱ 11am-3pm Mon-Sat; ⓕ Eminönü) Finding this worker's *pideci* is an adventure in itself, as it's hidden in the steep narrow lanes behind the Büyük Valide Han. Fortunately, your quest will pay off when you try the fabulous pides, which are served straight from the oven.

Burç Ocakbaşı
KEBAP $

(Map p98; Parçacılar Sokak 12, Grand Bazaar, off Yağlıkçılar Caddesi; kebaps ₺20-30, dolması ₺25; ⏱ noon-4pm Mon-Sat; ⓕ Beyazıt-Kapalı Çarşı) The *usta* (grill master) at this simple place presides over a charcoal grill where choice cuts of meats are cooked to perfection. You can claim a stool, or ask for a *dürüm* (meat wrapped in bread) kebap to go. We particularly recommend the spicy Adana kebap and the delectable *dolması* (eggplant and red peppers stuffed with rice and herbs).

Kuru Fasülyeci Erzincanlı Ali Baba
TURKISH $

(Map p94; ✆ 0212-514 5878; www.kurufasulyeci.com; Professor Sıddık Sami Onar Caddesi 11, Süleymaniye; beans with pilaf & pickles ₺30; ⏱ 8am-9pm; ✍; Ⓜ Vezneciler, ⓕ Eminönü) Join the crowds of hungry locals at this long-time *fasülyeci* (restaurant specialising in beans) opposite the Süleymaniye Mosque. It's been dishing up its signature *kuru fasülye* (white beans cooked in a spicy tomato sauce) accompanied by pilaf (rice) and *turşu* (pickles) since 1924. The next-door *fasülyeci* is nearly as old and serves up more of the same. No alcohol.

★ Hatay Haskral Sofrası
SYRIAN $$

(Map p84; ✆ 0210-534 9707; www.hatayhaskralsofrasi.com; Ragıb Bey Sokak 25, Aksaray; mezes ₺18-22, mains ₺38-99; ⏱ 10am-midnight; ⊕ ⓕ; ⓕ Aksaray) In 'Little Syria', this barn-like eatery offers a marvellously varied range of mezes, salads and kebaps. Specialities include *tuzda kuzu kol* and *tuzda tavuk* (whole chicken or lamb shoulder baked in a salt crust; ₺145 to ₺210). Finish with a crispy *künefe* (*kadayıf* layered with sweet cheese, doused in syrup and served hot with a sprinkling of pistachio; ₺16). No alcohol.

Note that you'll need to call 2½ hours in advance to order the *tuzda kuzu kol* and *tuzda tavuk*.

★ Siirt Şeref Büryan Kebap
ANATOLIAN $$

(Map p94; ✆ 0212-635 8085; www.serefburyan.org; İtfaiye Caddesi 4, Kadınlar Pazarı, Fatih; büryan ₺25, perde pilavi ₺22, kebaps ₺22-30; ⏱ 9.30am-10pm Sep-May, to midnight Jun-Aug; Ⓟ ⊕; Ⓜ Vezneciler) Those who enjoy investigating regional cuisines should head to this four-storey eatery in the Women's Bazaar (p94) near the Aqueduct of Valens. It specialises in two dishes that are a speciality of the southeastern city of Siirt: *büryan* (lamb slow-cooked in a pit oven) and *perde pılavı* (chicken and rice cooked in pastry). Both are totally delicious.

Fes Cafe
CAFE $$

(Map p94; ☑0212-526 3070; www.facebook.com/cafefes; Alibaba Türbe Sokak 25-27, Nuruosmaniye; sandwiches & wraps ₺15-30, salads ₺32-36; ⊙9am-6pm Mon-Sat; ☑; ☒Çemberlitaş) After a morning spent trading repartee with the touts in the Grand Bazaar, you'll be in need of a respite. And where better than this Western-style cafe off nearby Nuruosmaniye Caddesi, which offers a menu of sandwiches, wraps, salads and soups. The tiny attached Abdulla boutique stocks top-quality towels, *peştemals* (cotton bath wraps) and olive-oil soap.

Hamdi Restaurant
KEBAP $$

(Map p94; ☑0212-512 1144; www.hamdirestorant. com.tr; Kalçın Sokak 11, Eminönü; mezes ₺19-50, kebaps ₺52-62; ⊙noon-11.30pm; ☑☀☜; ☒Eminönü) One of the city's best-loved restaurants, this place near the Spice Bazaar is owned by Hamdi Arpacı, who started out as a street-food vendor in the 1960s. His tasty Urfa-style kebaps were so popular that he soon graduated to this multistorey restaurant, which has views of the Old City, the Golden Horn and Galata from its top-floor terrace. The food here is excellent.

✖ Beyoğlu

★Hayvore
TURKISH $

(Map p100; ☑0212-245 7501; www.hayvore.com. tr; Turnacıbaşı Sokak 4, Galatasaray; soups ₺10-15, pides ₺24-35, portions ₺14-30; ⊙8am-11pm; ☀☜☐; ☒Taksim, ☒Taksim) Notable *lokantas* are rare in modern-day Beyoğlu, so the existence of this bustling place next to the Galatasaray Lycée is to be wholeheartedly celebrated. Specialising in Black Sea cuisine, its delicious pilafs, pides, *hamsi* (fresh anchovy) dishes, and vegetable and fish soups are best enjoyed at lunch – go early to score a table.

★Karaköy Güllüoğlu
SWEETS $

(Map p100; ☑0212-293 0910; www.karakoygulluoglu.com; Katlı Otopark, Kemankeş Caddesi, Karaköy; portion baklava ₺13-23, portion börek ₺11-12; ⊙7am-midnight Mon-Sat, from 8am Sun; ☒Karaköy) This much-loved *baklavacı* (baklava shop) opened in 1949 and was the first İstanbul branch of a business established in Gaziantep in the 1820s. There are other Güllüoğlu offshoots around town, but this remains the best. Pay for a *porsiyon* (portion) of whatever takes your fancy at the register, then order at the counters.

Galaktion
GEORGIAN $

(Map p100; ☑0537 573 7600; www.facebook.com/cafegalaktion; Billurcu Sokak 18a, Cihangir; soups ₺10-13, mains ₺15-30; ⊙noon-midnight, reduced hours summer; ☒Taksim, ☒Taksim) This cosy Caucasus kitchen serves up delicious, hearty Georgian favourites: fist-sized *khinkali* dumplings, divinely gooey *khachapuri* (cheese-filled bread), *lobio* (herby, garlicky red-bean stew) and tender eggplant rolls filled with walnuts and cheese. No alcohol is served but you can try a minerally Georgian lemonade or Batumi-style coffee.

Zencefil
VEGETARIAN $

(Map p100; ☑0212-243 8234; www.facebook.com/zencozencefil; Kurabiye Sokak 8, Taksim; soups ₺13-19, mains ₺19-28; ⊙9.30am-11.30pm Mon-Sat, from 4pm Sun; ☜☑; ☒Taksim, ☒Taksim) We're not surprised this vegetarian cafe has a loyal following. Its interior is comfortable and stylish, with a glassed courtyard and bright colour scheme, and its food is 100% homemade, fresh and varied. Dishes are either vegetarian or vegan. 'Zencefil' means 'ginger' in Turkish, and the cafe makes its own ginger ale, as well as detox drinks.

Asmalı Canım Ciğerim
ANATOLIAN $

(Map p100; Minare Sokak 1, Asmalımescit; half/full portion ₺25/35, dürüm ₺16; ⊙noon-11pm; ☒Şişhane, ☒Tünel) The name means 'my soul, my liver', and this small place behind the Ali Hoca Türbesi specialises in grilled liver served with herbs, *ezme* (spicy tomato sauce) and grilled vegetables. If you can't bring yourself to eat offal, fear not – you can substitute the liver with lamb. No alcohol, but *ayran* (yoghurt drink) is the perfect accompaniment.

★Cafe Privato
CAFE $$

(Map p100; ☑0212-293 2055; www.privatocafe. com; Tımarcı Sokak 3b, Galata; breakfast ₺70; ⊙9am-10pm; ☜☑; ☒Şişhane, ☒Tünel) Located in an enclave off Galipdede Caddesi in Galata, this friendly, slightly ramshackle cafe is much loved for its exceptionally delicious and huge *köy kahvaltısı* (village breakfast), which includes spinach and cheese *gözleme*, eggs, house-baked bread, jams, fried haloumi cheese, pancakes, olives and more. Regulars tend to order one breakfast to share between two persons, or two between three.

★Zübeyir Ocakbaşı
KEBAP $$

(Map p100; ☑0212-293 3951; www.zubeyirocakbasi.com.tr; Bekar Sokak 28; mezes ₺14-15, kebaps ₺37-80; ⊙12.30pm-11.30pm; ☀☜; ☒Taksim,

Taksim) Every morning the chefs at this popular *ocakbaşı* (grill house) prepare fresh, top-quality meat – spicy chicken wings and Adana kebaps, flavoursome ribs, pungent liver kebaps and well-marinated lamb *şış* kebaps (roast skewered meat) – to be grilled over handsome copper-hooded barbecues that night. The offerings are famous throughout the city, so booking a table is essential.

Reyhun
IRANIAN $$

(Map p100; 0212-245 1500; www.iranyemekleri.com; 1st fl, Yeni Çarşı Caddesi 26, Galatasaray; stews ₺25-35, kebaps ₺27-97; noon-11.30pm; M Şişhane, Tünel) Head up the red-carpeted stairs of this restaurant next to the Galatasaray Garaj to find İstanbul's best Iranian eatery, which boasts a noisy dining salon and large greenery-filled terrace. Authentic stews include a deliciously sour *ghorme sabzi* (fresh herbs, kidney beans and lamb) and there's a huge choice of kebaps. Finish with *shole zard* (rice, saffron and nut dessert). No alcohol.

Sahrap
MODERN TURKISH $$

(Map p100; 0212-243 1616; www.sahraprestaurant.com; General Yazgan Sokak 13a, Asmalımescit; mezes ₺17-25, mains ₺29-65; noon-11pm Mon-Sat, 6-11pm Sun; M Şişhane, Tünel) Popular cookbook writer and TV chef Sahrap Soysal oversees the menu here, and the result is a tasty and well-priced introduction to modern Turkish cuisine. The two-level dining space is attractively decorated and Sahrap's food is fresh and full of flavour, with an emphasis on legumes, seasonal vegetables and seafood.

Çukur Meyhane
TURKISH $$

(Map p100; 0212-244 5575; www.cukurmeyhane.com; basement, Kartal Sokak 1a, Galatasaray; mezes ₺10-35, mains ₺20-50; 6pm-1am Mon-Sat; M Taksim, Taksim) Despite their long and much-vaunted tradition in the city, it is becoming increasingly difficult to find *meyhanes* (taverns) serving good food. Standards have dropped in many of our old favourites (sob!), and we're constantly on the search for replacements. Fortunately, Çukur fits the bill. On offer are a convivial cafeteria-style atmosphere, great food and relatively cheap prices. No English spoken.

Mavra
CAFE $$

(Map p100; 0212-252 7488; Serdar-ı Ekrem Caddesi 31, Galata; breakfast ₺20-55, sandwiches ₺20-34, pastas ₺24-28; 9.30am-10.30pm Fri-Wed, to

8.30pm Thu; M Şişhane, Tünel) Serdar-ı Ekrem Caddesi is one of the most attractive streets in Galata, full of ornate 19th-century apartment blocks and avant-garde boutiques. Mavra was the first of the cafes to open on the strip, and remains one of the best, offering simple food and drinks amid decor that is thrift-shop chic. Vegetarians and vegans are particularly well catered for.

Sofyalı 9
TURKISH $$

(Map p100; 0212-252 3810; www.sofyali.com.tr; Sofyalı Sokak 9, Tünel; mezes ₺9-36, mains ₺32-60; 12.30pm-11.30pm Tue-Thu & Sun, to 1am Fri & Sat; M Taksim, Tünel) Tables at this *meyhane* are hot property on a Friday or Saturday night, when locals flock here to enjoy the tasty food and convivial atmosphere. Regulars tend to stick to mezes, choosing cold dishes from the waiter's tray and ordering *kalamar tava* (fried calamari), *folyoda ahtapot* (grilled octopus in foil) and *Anavut ciğeri* (Albanian fried liver) from the menu.

★ Mürver
TURKISH $$$

(Map p100; 0212-372 0750; www.murverrestaurant.com; Kemankeş Caddesi 57-59, Novotel İstanbul Bosphorus Hotel, Karaköy; mezes ₺33-105, mains ₺85-230; noon-3pm & 6-11pm; Tophane) A notable recent addition to the local restaurant scene, this rooftop restaurant at the Novotel is sustaining its initial hype. The menu is dominated by meat dishes such as lamb cooked in a *tandir* (clay oven) or steak and chicken grilled over coals, but there are also delicious seafood and vegetable options – don't miss the octopus cooked in ash. Book ahead.

★ Neolokal
MODERN TURKISH $$$

(Map p100; 0212-244 0016; www.neolokal.com; 1st fl, SALT Galata, Bankalar Caddesi 11, Karaköy; mezes ₺46-57, mains ₺94-98; 6-11pm Tue-Sun; Karaköy) Chef Maksut Aşkar has been wowing diners with his exciting rifts on traditional Turkish food since 2014, gaining an entry on the San Pellegrino World's Best Restaurant list in the process. Utilising ingredients listed on the Slow Food Foundation's Ark of Taste, his refined creations are enjoyed alongside the spectacular Old City views offered from the dining room and terrace.

★ Antiochia
ANATOLIAN $$$

(Map p100; 0212-244 0820; www.antiochiaconcept.com; General Yazgan Sokak 3, Tünel; mezes & salads ₺26-35, pides ₺30, kebaps ₺40-80;

noon-midnight Mon-Fri, from 3pm Sat; ✸☀; Ⓜ Şişhane, 🚡 Tünel) Dishes from the southeastern city of Antakya (Hatay) are the speciality here. Cold and hot mezes are equally delicious (try the grilled cheese), pides and *lahmacun* are flavoursome and the kebaps are exceptional – try the succulent *şiş et* (grilled lamb). The set menus of mezes and a choice of main dish (₺65 to ₺105) offer excellent value.

Cuma MODERN TURKISH $$$
(Map p100; 📋 0212-293 2062; www.cuma.cc; Çukurcuma Caddesi 53a, Çukurcuma; breakfast plate ₺55, starters ₺38-49, mains ₺45-77; ☉ 9am-midnight Mon-Sat, to 8pm Sun; ✸☀📋; Ⓜ Taksim, 🚡 Taksim) Banu Tiryakioğlu's laid-back foodie oasis in the heart of Çukurcuma has one of the most devoted customer bases in the city. Tables are on the leafy terrace or in the atmospheric upstairs dining space, and the healthy, seasonally driven menu is heavy on flavour and light on fuss – breakfast is particularly delicious (regulars tend to share the *kahvaltı* – breakfast – plate).

Karaköy Lokantası TURKISH $$$
(Map p100; 📋 0212-292 4455; www.karakoy lokantasi.com; Kemankeş Caddesi 37a, Karaköy; mezes ₺8-40, lunch portion ₺17-36, mains ₺38-59; ☉ noon-4pm & 6pm-midnight Mon-Sat, 4pm-midnight Sun; ✸☀; 🚡 Karaköy) Known for its gorgeous tiled interior, genial owner and bustling vibe, Karaköy Lokantası serves tasty and well-priced food to its loyal local clientele. It functions as a *lokanta* during the day, but at night it morphs into a *meyhane*, with slightly higher prices. Bookings are essential for dinner.

🍴 The Golden Horn

★ Primi ITALIAN $$
(Map p84; 📋 0549 805 4545; www.primibalat.com; Yıldırım Caddesi 23, Balat; breakfast ₺42, salads ₺14-29, pastas ₺23-37; ☉ 8.30am-10pm Thu-Tue; ☀; 🚌 44B, 48E, 99, 99Y & 399B/C from Eminönü, 🚢 Fener) Primi has a casual cafe ambience but a serious focus on food. Breakfast is Turkish (and very good), but other meals are emphatically Italian, featuring house-made pasta, eggplant parmigiana and salads (try the delectable caprese with tomato and burrata). Pasta choices include classics such as carbonara and pesto as well as filled varieties such as raviolini with artichoke. No alcohol.

★ CookLife CAFE $$
(Map p84; 📋 0212-982 1578; www.cooklife.com; Akçin Sokak 3, cnr Vodina Caddesi, Balat; breakfast dishes ₺14-35, pastas ₺26-34, burgers ₺35-45; ☉ 9am-7pm Tue-Sun; ✸☀; 🚌 44B, 48E, 99, 99Y & 399B/C from Eminönü, 🚢 Fener) Some of the best coffee on the Golden Horn can be enjoyed at this photogenic place in the thick of Balat's fashionable cafe scene, as can well-executed cafe-style food (smashed avocado, burgers, pastas, acai and matcha bowls). Beans are sourced from third-wave coffee specialists Kimma Coffee Roasters and are used in espresso, Chemex and Aeropress brews.

Asitane TURKISH $$$
(Map p84; 📋 0212-635 7997; www.asitaneres taurant.com; Kariye Oteli, Kariye Camii Sokak 6, Edirnekapı; mezes ₺30-48, mains ₺54-69; ☉ noon-10.30pm; 📋; 🚌 28, 31, 37, 336 from Eminönü, 87 from Taksim, 🚢 Ayvansaray) This elegant restaurant next to the Kariye Mosque (Chora Church) serves Ottoman dishes devised for the palace kitchens at Topkapı, Edirne and Dolmabahçe. Its chefs have been tracking down historic recipes for years, and the menu is full of versions that will tempt most modern palates, including vegetarian.

🍴 The Bosphorus Suburbs

★ Apartıman INTERNATIONAL $$$
(Map p108; 📋 0212-223 4477; www.facebook.com/apartimanyenikoy; Köybaşı Caddesi 153, Yeniköy; starters ₺17-49, mains ₺48-82; ☉ 10am-midnight Tue-Thu, to 1am Fri & Sat, to 11pm Sun; ✸☀; 🚌 25E from Kabataş, 42T from Taksim) Reinventing herself as a chef, former industrial designer Burçak Kazdal brings a pronounced designer approach to the decor and menu of her upmarket brasserie-cafe-bar on Yeniköy's fashionable main strip, offering customers chic contemporary surrounds and a carefully curated and stylishly presented array of French-accented dishes. Seating is arranged over three levels, with both indoor and outdoor options.

★ Kıyı SEAFOOD $$$
(Map p108; 📋 0212-262 0002; www.kiyi.com.tr; Haydar Aliyev Caddesi 186, Tarabya; mezes ₺15-70, seafood mains by weight; ☉ noon-11pm; ✸; 🚌 22, 25E & 29C from Kabataş, 22RE & 40 from Beşiktaş, 40, 40T & 42T from Taksim) Named after a species of freshwater whitefish, this large and often boisterous restaurant has been serving excellent seafood to locals since the 1960s

and remains popular with many of the city's movers and shakers. In summer, the upstairs terrace is the place to be; during winter the action moves into the art-adorned dining room. Menu items are standard but delicious.

✖ Kadıköy

There's only one place to eat when in Kadıköy, and that's in the streets in or around the market. These are full of quality fast-food stands, fish restaurants and *lokantas* (eateries serving ready-made food).

★ Küff
CAFE $

(Map p84; ☑ 0542 778 1800; www.facebook. com/kuffcafe; Karakolhane Caddesi 54a & 49b, Yeldeğirmeni; sandwiches ₺15-20, burgers ₺17-32, pizzas ₺18-27; ⊙ 8am-1.30am; 🕾 🖉; 🖺 Kadıköy, Ⓜ Kadıköy) Ticking all of the hipster boxes (third-wave coffee, vegan food, tattooed baristas, indoor plants), this hugely popular cafe spreads over spaces on both sides of Karakolhane Caddesi in up-and-coming Yeldeğirmeni, one of the city's most bohemian enclaves. You'll have to queue on weekends, when young locals flock here to enjoy cheap and tasty Turkish breakfasts (₺38/60 for one/two persons).

Basta! Street Food Bar
TURKISH $

(Map p84; ☑ 0216-414 0865; www.bastafood. com; Sakız Sokak 1; wraps ₺26-30, hummus ₺15; ⊙ noon-10pm Mon-Sat, to 9pm Sun; 🖺 Kadıköy, Ⓜ Kadıköy) Grabbing a *dürüm* (grilled meat in a flatbread wrap) on the go in İstanbul is a quick way to refuel, but Basta offers a very different eating experience. Young chefs Kaan Sakarya and Derin Arıbaş bring their fine-dining training to this humble street food, offering red meat, chicken and vegetarian versions, as well as *kuzu* (lamb) burgers and delicious hummus.

★ Çiya Sofrası
ANATOLIAN $$

(Map p84; ☑ 0216-330 3190; www.ciya.com. tr; Güneşlibahçe Sokak 43; small meze plate ₺12-15, portions ₺18-55; ⊙ 11am-9pm; 🌂 🖉 🖐; 🖺 Kadıköy, Ⓜ Kadıköy) Known throughout the culinary world, Musa Dağdeviren's *lokanta* showcases dishes from regional Turkey and is an essential stop for foodies, particularly those of the vegetarian variety. Start at the DIY meze bar, and then ask the chefs to explain the daily specials in the bain-marie. Excellent *lahmacun*, kebaps and desserts can be ordered at your table.

Drinking & Nightlife

▼ Sultanahmet

Most Sultanahmet restaurants are licensed, but there are few dedicated bars. Those that do exist are in no way on a par with those in Beyoğlu so it's worth considering substituting caffeine for alcohol and instead relaxing in one of the atmospheric *çay bahçesis* (tea gardens) dotted around the neighbourhood.

Derviş Cafe & Restaurant
TEA GARDEN

(Map p88; cnr Dalbastı Sokak & Kabasakal Caddesi; ⊙ 24hr, closed in winter; 🖺 Sultanahmet) Superbly located directly opposite the Blue Mosque, the Derviş beckons patrons with its comfortable cane chairs and shady trees. Efficient service, reasonable prices and peerless people-watching opportunities make it a great place for a leisurely çay, coffee or fresh juice.

Kybele Cafe
BAR

(Map p88; ☑ 0212-511 7766; Yerebatan Caddesi 23, Alemdar; ⊙ 9am-11.30pm; 🕾; 🖺 Sultanahmet) This hotel lounge bar–cafe close to the Basilica Cistern is chock-full of antique furniture, richly coloured rugs and old etchings and prints, but its signature style comes courtesy of the hundreds of colourful glass lights hanging from the ceiling.

Caferağa Medresesi Çay Bahçesi
TEA GARDEN

(Map p88; ☑ 0212-513 3601; www.tkhv.org; Soğukkuyu Çıkmazı 5, off Caferiye Sokak; ⊙ 9am-6pm Tue-Sun; 🖺 Sultanahmet) On a fine day, sipping a çay or freshly squeezed orange juice in the gorgeous courtyard of this Sinan-designed *medrese* is extremely pleasant. Located close to both Aya Sofya and Topkapı Palace, it houses a craft centre and serves simple food (*tost* ₺9 to ₺10, soup ₺9) for breakfast and lunch.

▼ Bazaar District

Like most parts of the Old City, the area around the Grand Bazaar is conservative and there are few places serving alcohol. There are loads of *çay bahçesis* (tea gardens), nargile cafes and *kahvehanesis* (coffeehouses) to visit, though.

★ Mimar Sinan Teras Cafe
CAFE

(Map p94; ☑ 0212-514 4414; Mimar Sinan Han, Fetva Yokuşu 34-35, Süleymaniye; ⊙ 10am-midnight; 🕾; Ⓜ Vezneciler, 🚢 Eminönü) A magnificent panorama of the city can be enjoyed from the spacious outdoor terrace of this popular student cafe in a ramshackle building located in the shadow of Süleymaniye Mosque. Head here during the day or in the evening to admire the view over a coffee, unwind with a nargile (₺45) or enjoy a glass of çay and game of backgammon.

★**Erenler Nargile ve Çay Bahçesi** TEA GARDEN
(Çorlulu Ali Paşa Medresesi Nargile ve Çay Bahçesi; Map p94; Yeniçeriler Caddesi 35, Beyazıt; ☺8.30am-midnight; 🚇Beyazıt-Kapalı Çarşı) Set in the vine-covered courtyard of the historic Çorlulu Ali Paşa Medresesi, this nargile cafe near the Grand Bazaar is the most atmospheric in the Old City. Nargiles cost ₺35 and are best enjoyed with a glass of çay (₺2.50) or *Türk kahve* (Turkish coffee; ₺7).

Vefa Bozacısı BAR
(Map p94; ☑0212-519 4922; www.vefa.com.tr; 66 Vefa Caddesi, Molla Hüsrev; boza ₺5; ☺8am-midnight; 🚇Vezneciler) This famous *boza* bar was established in 1876 and locals still flock here to drink its viscous non-alcoholic tonic, which is made from water, sugar and fermented barley and has a slight lemony tang. Topped with dried chickpeas and a sprinkle of cinnamon, it has a reputation for building up strength and virility, and tends to be an acquired taste.

🍷 Beyoğlu

There are hundreds of bars in Beyoğlu, with the major bar strips being Balo, Nevizade, Gönül and Sofyalı Sokaks. As a rule, drinks are much cheaper at street-level venues than at rooftop bars. Note that many of the Beyoğlu clubs close over the warmer months (June to September), when the party crowd moves down to Turkey's southern coasts.

★**Coffee Sapiens** CAFE
(Map p100; ☑0212-244 1296; www.coffeesapiens.com; Kılıç Ali Paşa Mescidi 10, Karaköy; ☺8.30am-9.30pm Sun-Thu, to 10.30pm Fri & Sat; 🚇Tophane) Serving coffee home-roasted at their facility in Hasköy, these sapiens have well and truly wised up to the science behind the brew. Choose from Aeropress, Chemex, cold brew, French press, espresso or siphon, and drink it takeaway, standing at the bar or at an outdoor table overlooking goings-on in Karaköy's hippest lane.

★**Solera** WINE BAR
(Map p100; ☑0212-252 2719; www.facebook.com/solerawinery; Yeniçarşı Caddesi 44, Galatasaray; ☺noon-2am; 🚇Şişhane, 🚇Tünel) Stocking more than 300 Turkish wines and pouring an extraordinary 47 by the glass, this atmospherically lit cavern is the city's best wine bar. Regulars tend to head here after work for a glass accompanied by a cheese plate (₺35); many stay on for a bowl of homemade pasta (₺29 to ₺32) or perfectly cooked steak (₺49). Bookings advisable.

★**Geyik** BAR
(Map p100; ☑0532 773 0013; Akarsu Yokuşu 22, Cihangir; ☺4pm-1.30am; 🚇Taksim, 🚇Taksim) Getting our endorsement as the home of İstanbul's best cocktails, this place is so crowded on Friday and Saturday evenings that the action spills out of the cosy wood-panelled interior onto the street. The bartenders really know their mixology – drinks are expertly shaken, stirred and poured. Beers come from the city's own Bomonti Brewery.

★**Parantez** BAR
(Map p100; ☑0212-245 7513; crn Sofyalı & Jurnal Sokaks, Asmalımescit; ☺4pm-4am; 🚇Şişhane, 🚇Tünel) Asmalımescit's most popular bar is tiny, so on weekend evenings the action spills out into Jurnal Sokak and a party atmosphere ensues. Fight your way to the bar to order a cocktail or bottled beer – if it's too crowded there are plenty of other bars in the immediate vicinity.

Kronotrop CAFE
(Map p100; ☑0212-249 9271; www.kronotrop.com.tr/en; Firuzağa Cami Sokak 2b, Cihangir; ☺7.30am-9pm Mon-Fri, 10am-10pm Sat, to 9pm Sun; 🚇; 🚇Taksim, 🚇Taksim) Specialty coffee bars have proliferated in İstanbul in recent years, spearheaded by businesses such as this hip place opposite the Firuz Ağa Mosque in Cihangir. Owned by noted restaurateur Mehmet Gürs, it sources beans from across the globe and roasts them in a purpose-built facility in nearby Maslak. Choose from espresso, cold-drip, filtered, Aeropress, Chemex and traditional Turkish varieties.

Manda Batmaz COFFEE
(Map p100; ☑0212-243 7737; www.mandabatmaz.com.tr; Olivia Geçidi 1a, off İstiklal Caddesi; ☺9am-midnight Mon-Thu, to 1am Fri & Sat, 10am-midnight Sun; 🚇Şişhane, 🚇Tünel) Bored with contemporary coffee culture? Don't care where your beans have been roasted, or whether the milk has been heated to the

prerequisite 54°C? If so, this local institution is for you. Serving Beyoğlu's best Turkish coffee since 1967, it recently expanded into a modern next-door extension, but its cups of ultra-thick and aromatic coffee are as good as ever.

Mikla
BAR

(Map p100; ☎0212-293 5656; www.miklarestau rant.com; Marmara Pera Hotel, Meşrutiyet Caddesi 15, Tepebaşı; ⊗6pm-2am Mon-Sat summer only; ⊛; Ⓜ Şişhane, 🚠 Tünel) Excellent cocktails and what could well be the best view in İstanbul await you on the top floor of the Marmara Pera Hotel. In winter the drinking action moves to the bar in the upmarket restaurant one floor down.

Markus Tavern
PUB

(Map p100; ☎0544 252 0062; www.markusribs. com/tavern; Hayriye Caddesi 16, Galatasaray; ⊗6pm-2am Thu-Sat; ⊛; Ⓜ Taksim, 🚠 Taksim) Tucked in an avant-garde enclave behind the Galatasaray Lycée, this hipster watering hole is known for its beef burgers (₺19) and tacos (₺25 to ₺28), the latter of which are filled with pulled ribs or braised lamb and hummus. The beer on tap is local favourite Bomonti, and there's also a range of local and imported beers available by the bottle.

Cihangir 21
BAR

(Map p100; ☎0212-251 1626; Coşkun Sokak 2/1, Cihangir; ⊗8am-4am; ⊛; Ⓜ Taksim) The great thing about this neighbourhood place is its inclusiveness – the regulars include black-clad boho types, besuited professionals, ex-pat loafers and quite a few characters who defy categorisation. There's beer on tap (Efes and Miller), a smokers' section and a bustling feel after work hours; it's quite laid-back during the day.

MiniMüzikHol
CLUB

(MMH; Map p100; ☎0212-245 1996; www.mini muzikhol.com; Soğancı Sokak 7, Cihangir; no cover; ⊗midnight-5.30am Fri & Sat; Ⓜ Taksim, 🚠 Taksim) Once the mother ship for inner-city hipsters, this small temple to house and techno near Taksim isn't the hot spot it once was, but retains a crew of devoted regulars. It's home to İstanbul DJs Barış K, Mini Başhekim, DJ Tutan, Subsky and Undomondo.

360
BAR

(Map p100; ☎0533 691 0360; www.360istan bul.com; 8th fl, İstiklal Caddesi 163, Galatasaray; ⊗noon-2am Sun-Thu, to 4am Fri & Sat; ⊛; Ⓜ Şişhane, 🚠 Tünel) İstanbul's most famous

bar, and deservedly so. If you can score one of the bar stools on the terrace you'll be happy indeed – the view is truly extraordinary. It morphs into a club after midnight on Friday and Saturday, when a cover charge of ₺60 applies (this includes one drink). The food is overpriced and underwhelming – don't bother with dinner.

Note that from noon to 6pm you can take the elevator to the 8th floor but from 6pm you'll need to go to the 6th floor and walk up the stairs.

⬤ The Golden Horn

Pierre Loti Café
CAFE

(Map p84; Gümüşsuyu Balmumcu Sokak 1, Eyüp; ⊗8am-midnight; 🚌44B, 48E, 99, 99Y & 399B/C from Eminönü, ⛴Eyüp) Many visitors head to this hilltop cafe after visiting the Eyüp Sultan Mosque (p106). Named for the famous French novelist who is said to have come here for inspiration, it offers views across the Golden Horn and is a popular weekend destination for locals, who relax here over cheap tea, coffee and ice cream. A cable car (p144) to the cafe leaves from near the mosque.

⬤ The Bosphorus Suburbs

Craft Beer Lab
CRAFT BEER

(Map p84; ☎0212-236 9192; www.facebook. com/craftbeerlab; Şair Nedim Caddesi 4, Akaretler, Beşiktaş; ⊗11.30am-2.30am Sun-Thu, to 3.30am Fri & Sat; 🚌43 from Taksim, ⛴Beşiktaş) There's a long list of bottled international beers and a good selection of international and local brews on tap at this lively Beşiktaş pub and brewery, which has an industrial-chic interior and a big backyard equipped with umbrellas and heat lamps for outdoor drinking in any weather. The extensive food menu (mains ₺28 to ₺65) features international selections including pastas and burgers.

Lucca
BISTRO

(Map p108; ☎0212-257 1255; www.luccastyle.com; Cevdetpaşa Caddesi 51, Bebek; ⊗noon-2am Mon, from 10am Tue-Sun; ⊛⛱; 🚌22, 22B & 25E from Kabataş, 22RE & 40 from Beşiktaş, 40, 40T & 42T from Taksim) Ecstatically embraced by the in crowd since 2005, Lucca's star shows no sign of waning. Glam young things flock here on Friday and Saturday nights to see and be seen on the famous street terrace, but the mood is more relaxed during the week. Food choices are global (burgers, tacos, poke, sushi) and both coffee and cocktails are well made.

🍽 Kadıköy

The two major bar strips are Kadife Sokak (aka Barlar or Bar Sokak) and the southern end of Güneşlibahçe Sokak, although the streets off Moda Caddesi are starting to give them a run for their money.

★ Fazıl Bey
COFFEE

(Map p84; 🗗 0216-450 2870; www.fazilbey.com; Serasker Caddesi 1; ⏰ 8am-11pm; 🚊 Kadıköy, Ⓜ Kadıköy) Making the call as to who makes the best Turkish coffee in İstanbul is no easy task, but our vote goes to Fazıl Bey, the best-loved *khavehan* (coffeeshop) on Serasker Caddesi. Enjoying a cup while watching the passing parade of shoppers has kept locals entertained for decades. There are other, less atmospheric, branches in Tavus Sokak and Bağdat Caddesi.

Viktor Levi Şarap Evi
WINE BAR

(Map p84; 🗗 0216-449 9329; www.viktorlevimoda.com; Damacı Sokak 4, Moda; ⏰ 11.30am-2am; 🚊 Kadıköy, Ⓜ Kadıköy) Established by Jewish wine merchant Viktor Levi in 1914, this wine bar has a shady, flower-filled rear garden that is a popular drinking spot in the warmer months. In winter, regulars congregate in the attractive upstairs salon instead. There's a large selection of wine by the glass and bottle, and a food menu offering both snacks and full meals.

Bina
BAR

(Map p84; 🗗 0216-330 8466; Kadife Sokak 26; ⏰ 10am-midnight Mon-Thu, to 4am Fri & Sat, 11am-4am Sun; 🎵; 🚊 Kadıköy, Ⓜ Kadıköy) One of the most popular bars on the Kadife Sokak drinking strip, Bina attracts regulars from across the city, who love its rear garden, upstairs arts and performance space, regular DJ sets, well-made cocktails and menu of burgers, pastas and other alcohol-friendly eats (₺30 to ₺40).

Moda Çay Bahçesi
TEAHOUSE

(Map p84; 🗗 0216-337 9986; Ferit Tek Sokak 7, Moda; ⏰ 7am-11.30pm; 🚊 Kadıköy, Ⓜ Kadıköy) The plastic chairs and tables here are decidedly no-frills, but the shady mastic trees and million-dollar views over the Sea of Marmara towards the minarets of İstanbul's Old City make it one of the city's best-loved *çay bahçesi*. It's perfectly acceptable to bring your own picnic food and restrict your order to a tea or Turkish coffee.

Arkaoda
BAR

(Map p84; 🗗 0216-418 0277; www.arkaoda.com; Kadife Sokak 18; ⏰ 4.30pm-2am Sun-Thu, to 3am Fri & Sat; 🎵; 🚊 Kadıköy, Ⓜ Kadıköy) A hub of indie music and art, this relaxed place hosts concerts, DJ sets, festivals, parties, themed markets and film screenings. Sit on the comfortable couches in the upstairs lounge or in the rear courtyard, which is covered in winter.

Karga Bar
BAR

(Map p84; 🗗 0216-449 1725; www.karga.com.tr; Kadife Sokak 16; ⏰ noon-2am Sun-Thu, to 4am Fri & Sat; 🎵; 🚊 Kadıköy, Ⓜ Kadıköy) Multistorey Karga is one of the most famous bars in the city, offering cheap drinks, alternative music (DJs downstairs, live acts upstairs) and avant-garde art on its walls. It's not signed well – look for the small metal sign of a crow.

🍽 Nişantaşı, Bomonti & Harbiye

Most of the action is in the Teşvikiye enclave, with plenty of fashionable young things gravitating to Fırın Sokak and its immediate area. The scene is more staid (and expensive) on Abdi İpekçi Caddesi in Nişantaşı proper.

Populist
BREWERY

(Map p108; 🗗 0212-296 2034; www.thepopulist.com.tr; Tarihi Bomonti Bira Fabrikası, Birahane Sokak 1-D, Bomonti; ⏰ noon-midnight Sun-Thu, to 2am Fri & Sat; Ⓜ Osmanbey) One of the few brewpubs in İstanbul, the Populist became a hot spot as soon as it opened in 2016. A seasonally changing craft-beer list that includes selections such as Scotch ale and stout offers a welcome alternative to the ever-present Efes. A brisket sandwich, artichoke dip, or other choices on the heavily American-style menu pair well with the brews.

Klein
CLUB

(Map p84; 🗗 0212-291 8440; www.facebook.com/istanbulklein; Cebel Topu Sokak 4, Harbiye; cover ₺60; ⏰ 11pm-4am Fri & Sat; Ⓜ Taksim) A subterranean space with a huge dance floor and top-notch sound system, Klein has DJs who spin techno and electronica, two bars and a dance-focused crowd. Check the Facebook feed for events.

Love Dance Point
GAY

(Map p84; 🗗 0212-232 5683; www.lovedp.net; Cumhuriyet Caddesi 349, Harbiye; ⏰ 11.30pm-5am Fri & Sat; Ⓜ Taksim, Osmanbey) Well into its second decade, LDP is the most Europhile of the local gay venues, hosting gay musical icons and international circuit parties. Hard-cutting techno is thrown in with gay anthems and Turkish pop.

☆ Entertainment

It's rare to have a week go by without a range of special events, festivals and performances being staged in İstanbul. Locals adore listening to live music (jazz is a particular favourite), attend multiplex cinemas on a regular basis and support a small but thriving number of local theatre, opera and dance companies.

Biletix BOOKING SERVICE
(🖉 0216-556 9800; www.biletix.com) The number-one web-based resource when sourcing tickets for concerts and events across the city.

★ Babylon Bomonti LIVE MUSIC
(Map p108; 🖉 0212-334 0190; www.babylon.com.tr; Tarihi Bomonti Bira Fabrikası, Birahane Sokak 1, Bomonti; varies; ⏱ Tue-Sat; Ⓜ Osmanbey) İstanbul's pre-eminent live-music venue has been packing the crowds in since 1999 and shows no sign of losing its mojo, especially now that it has moved to a larger space in an atmospheric old beer factory in the upmarket arts enclave of Bomonti, reasonably close to the Osmanbey metro stop.

Borusan Art PERFORMING ARTS
(Borusan Sanat; Map p100; 🖉 0212-705 8700; www.borusansanat.com/en; İstiklal Caddesi 160a; Ⓜ Şişhane, 🚠 Tünel) An exciting privately funded cultural centre on İstiklal, Borusan is housed in a handsome building and hosts classical, jazz, world and new music concerts in its music hall. The occasional dance performance is included in its schedule.

Nardis Jazz Club JAZZ
(Map p100; www.nardisjazz.com; Kuledibi Sokak 8, Galata; cover varies; ⏱ 8.30pm-12.30am Mon-Thu, 9.30pm-1.30am Fri & Sat, closed Aug; Ⓜ Şişhane, 🚠 Tünel) Named after a Miles Davis track, this intimate venue near the Galata Tower is run by jazz guitarist Önder Focan and his wife Zuhal. Performers include gifted amateurs, local jazz luminaries and visiting international artists. It's small, so you'll need to arrive early if you want a decent table (no bookings). There's a limited dinner/snack menu.

Spoken Word Istanbul LIVE PERFORMANCE
(Map p100; www.facebook.com/spokenwordistanbul; Arsen Lüpen, Mis Sokak 15, Taksim; ⏱ 8.30-10.30pm Tue; Ⓜ Taksim, 🚠 Taksim) FREE Poets, improv actors, musicians and storytellers all feature at this multilingual open-mike night that draws a lively young crowd of expats and Turks each week to watch, listen and mingle. Show up early if you want to try and

---

DON'T MISS

SEEING THE DERVISHES WHIRL

If you thought the Hare Krishnas or the Harlem congregations were the only religious groups to celebrate their faith through music and movement, think again. Those sultans of spiritual spin known as the 'whirling dervishes' have been twirling their way to a higher plane ever since the 13th century and show no sign of slowing down.

There are a number of opportunities to see dervishes whirling in İstanbul. The best known of these is the weekly ceremony in the *semahane* (whirling-dervish hall) at the **Galata Mevlevi House Museum** (Galata Mevlevihanesi Müzesi; Map p100; Galipdede Caddesi 15, Tünel; adult/child under 7 ₺100/free; ⏱ performances 5pm Sun; Ⓜ Şişhane, 🚠 Tünel) in Tünel. This one-hour ceremony is held on Sunday at 5pm and costs ₺100 per person. Come early to buy your ticket.

For a more touristy experience, the **Hodjapasha Culture Centre** (Map p88; 🖉 0212-511 4626; www.hodjapasha.com; Hocapaşa Hamamı Sokak 3b, Sirkeci; performances adult ₺125-160, child 7-12yr ₺90-110; ⏱ 7pm whirling dervishes, 8.30pm folk dance; 🚠 Sirkeci), housed in a beautifully converted 15th-century hamam near Eminönü, presents whirling-dervish performances at least three evenings per week throughout the year. There are also weekly performances held on Thursdays at 8pm in one of the halls at the historic Sirkeci train station.

Remember that the ceremony is a religious one – by whirling, the adherents believe they are attaining a higher union with God. So don't talk, leave your seat or take flash photographs while the dervishes are spinning or chanting.

get a performance slot, or just sit back and enjoy a window into one of İstanbul's alternative scenes.

Munzur Cafe & Bar
LIVE MUSIC

(Map p100; ☑0212-245 4669; www.munzurcafe bar.com; Hasnun Galip Sokak 17, Galatasaray; ⊙1pm-4am, music from 9pm; ⓂTaksim, ⓑTaksim) Hasnun Galip Sokak in Galatasaray is home to a number of *türkü evleri*, Kurdish-owned bars where musicians perform live, emotion-charged *halk meziği* (folk music). This simple place, which is two decades old, has a regular line-up of singers and expert *bağlama* (lute) players.

Vodafone Arena
STADIUM

(İnönü Stadyumu; Map p84; www.vodafonearena. com.tr; Kadırgalar Caddesi 1, Beşiktaş; ⓑBeşiktaş) This is the home of one of the top football clubs in Turkey's Super League (Süper Lig), Beşiktaş (the Black Eagles). Matches usually take place at the weekend, often on a Saturday night, between August and May. Tickets are sold at the stadium on the day of the match, but most fans buy them in advance through Biletix.

🛍 Shopping

İstanbullus have perfected the practice of shopping over centuries, and most visitors to the city are quick to follow their lead. Historic bazaars, colourful street markets and an ever-expanding portfolio of modern shopping malls cater to every desire and make sourcing a souvenir or two both easy and satisfying.

🛍 Sultanahmet

The best shopping in Sultanahmet is found in and around the Arasta Bazaar, a historic arcade of shops that was once part of the *külliye* (mosque complex) of the Blue Mosque (Sultanahmet Camii).

★ Jennifer's Hamam
HOMEWARES

(Map p88; ☑0212-516 3022; www.jennifers hamam.com; Öğül Sokak 20, Küçük Ayasofya; ⊙8.30am-8.30pm Apr-Oct, to 7pm Nov-Mar; ⓑSultanahmet) Owned by Canadian Jennifer Gaudet, this shop stocks top-quality towels, *peştemals* (traditional bath wraps) and robes for both adults and children. All are produced using certified organic cotton and silk on old-style shuttled looms, and come in a huge range of colours and styles. This is the main showroom; there is anoth-

er branch in the **Arasta Bazaar** (Map p88; Arasta Bazaar 135; ⊙8.30am-8.30pm Apr-Oct, to 7pm Nov-Mar; ⓑSultanahmet). Note that prices are set; no bargaining.

★Mehmet Çetinkaya Gallery
CARPETS, JEWELLERY

(Map p88; ☑0212-517 6808, 0212-517 1603; www.cetinkayagallery.com; Tavukhane Sokak 5-7; ⊙9.30am-7.30pm; ⓑSultanahmet) Mehmet Çetinkaya is one of the country's foremost experts on antique oriental carpets and kilims. One of his two Tavukhane Sokak galleries is built over the ruins of an ancient temple complete with columns; these can be viewed under a glass floor. Both galleries are filled with alluring items of artistic and ethnographic significance, including antique and modern rugs.

As well as the rugs and a wide range of textiles, the gallery sells jewellery designed by daughter Zehra and clothing designed by son Said. The clothing, which utilises richly coloured and embroidered fabrics sourced from countries as diverse as Uzbekistan and Japan, is extremely beautiful. A small branch in the **Arasta Bazaar** (Map p88; ☑0212-458 6186; Arasta Bazaar 58; ⊙9am-8pm; ⓑSultanahmet) sells textiles and jewellery.

İznik Classics
CERAMICS

(Map p88; ☑0212-516 8874; www.iznikclassics. com; Utangaç Sokak 17, Cankurtaran; ⊙9am-8pm, closes 6.30pm winter; ⓑSultanahmet) İznik Classics is one of the best places in town to source hand-painted collector-item ceramics made with real quartz and using metal oxides for pigments. Admire the range here or at the branch in the **Grand Bazaar** (Map p98; ☑0212-520 2568; Şerifağa Sokak 188, İç Bedesten; ⊙8.30am-6.30pm Mon-Sat; ⓑBeyazıt-Kapalı Çarşı). The shop next door at number 13 sells Kütahya ceramics, including tiles, plates and bowls.

ATA Textiles
TEXTILES

(Map p88; ☑0535 924 7309; www.atatextiles.com; Arasta Bazaar 7, Cankurtaran; ⊙8.30am-9pm; ⓑSultanahmet) Those heading to the Turkish coast after their İstanbul visit may want to purchase one of the colourful woven-cotton beach robes sold at this boutique in the Arasta Bazaar. Available in adult and child sizes, they are displayed alongside similarly colourful and attractive towels and *peştemals*.

Nakkaş
CARPETS

(Map p88; ☑0212-516 5222; www.nakkasrug.com; Nakilbent Sokak 13; ⊙9am-7pm; ⓑSultanahmet)

Nakkaş sells carpets, textiles, ceramics and jewellery. Its varied collection of more than 20,000 carpets and kilims includes antique rugs, hand-woven pieces and traditional Anatolian carpets. A few have even won design awards. Underneath the store is a restored Byzantine cistern, which staff will sometimes show to customers.

Khaftan ARTS & CRAFTS
(Map p88; ☑0212-458 5425; Nakilbent Sokak 16; ⊙9am-6.30pm; ⓖSultanahmet) Gleaming Russian icons, delicate calligraphy (old and new), ceramics, *karagöz* (shadow-puppet theatre) puppets, Ottoman prints and contemporary paintings are all on show in this attractive shop.

🔒 Bazaar District

The city's two most famous shopping destinations – the Grand and Spice Bazaars – are in this district. In between the two is the vibrant local shopping neighbourhood of Tahtakale.

Haşimi Mücevherat ARTS & CRAFTS
(Map p98; Yorgancılar Caddesi, Grand Bazaar; ⊙9.30am-6pm Mon-Sat; ⓖBeyazıt-Kapalı Çarşı) Beautifully decorated antique wooden boxes and carved fabric stamps from Afghanistan are the major drawcard here, but there's also some nice silver and amber jewellery on offer.

Altan Şekerleme FOOD & DRINKS
(Map p94; ☑0212-522 5909; Kıble Çeşme Caddesi 68, Eminönü; ⊙8am-8pm Mon-Sat, 9am-7pm Sun; Ⓜ Haliç, ⓖEminönü) Kids aren't the only ones who like candy stores. İstanbullus of every age have been coming to this shop in the Küçük Pazar (Little Bazaar) precinct below the Süleymaniye Mosque since 1865, lured by its cheap and delectable *lokum* (Turkish delight), *helva* (sweet made from sesame seeds) and *akide* (hard candy).

Mekhann TEXTILES
(Map p98; ☑0212-249 7849; www.facebook.com/mekhann; Divrikli Sokak 49, Grand Bazaar; ⊙8.30am-6.30pm Mon-Sat; ⓖBeyazıt-Kapalı Çarşı) Bolts of richly coloured, hand-woven silk from Uzbekistan and a range of finely woven shawls join finely embroidered bedspreads and pillow slips on the crowded shelves of this Grand Bazaar store, which sets the bar high when it comes to quali-

ty and price. There's another **branch** (Map p100; www.mekhann.com; Boğazkesen Caddesi 32a; ⊙10.30am-6.30pm; ⓖTophane) near the tram stop in Tophane.

Derviş HOMEWARES
(Map p98; ☑0212-528 7883; www.dervis.com; Halıcılar Sokak 51, Grand Bazaar; ⊙9am-7.30pm Mon-Sat; ⓖBeyazıt-Kapalı Çarşı) Raw cotton and silk *peştemals* share shelf space here with traditional Turkish dowry vests and engagement dresses. If these don't take your fancy, the pure olive-oil soaps and old hamam bowls are sure to step into the breach.

Yazmacı Necdet Danış TEXTILES
(Map p98; Yağlıkçılar Caddesi 57, Grand Bazaar; ⊙8.30am-7pm Mon-Sat; ⓖBeyazıt-Kapalı Çarşı) Fashion designers and buyers from every corner of the globe know that, when in İstanbul, this is where to come to source top-quality textiles. It's crammed with bolts of fabric of every description – shiny, simple, sheer and sophisticated – as well as *peştemals,* scarves and clothes. Murat Danış next door is part of the same operation.

Ali Muhiddin Hacı Bekir FOOD
(Map p94; ☑0212-522 8543; www.hacibekir.com.tr; Hamidiye Caddesi 33, Eminönü; ⊙8am-8pm Mon-Sat, from 9am Sun; ⓖEminönü) Many people think that this historic shop, which has been operated by members of the same family for over 200 years, is the top place in the city to buy *lokum* (Turkish delight). Our samplings indicate it's certainly up there with the best. Decide for yourself, choosing from *sade* (plain), *cevizli* (walnut), *fıstıklı* (pistachio), *badem* (almond) or *roze* (rose water).

Vakko İndirim FASHION & ACCESSORIES
(Vakko Outlet; Map p94; ☑0212-522 8941; www.vakko.com; Sultan Hamamı Caddesi 24, Eminönü; ⊙10am-6.30pm Mon-Sat; ⓖEminönü) This remainder outlet of İstanbul's famous fashion store should be on the itinerary of all bargain hunters. Top-quality men's and women's clothing – often stuff that's been designed and made in Italy – is sold here for a fraction of its original price. There are bargains to be had for those willing to spend the time exploring.

Beyoğlu

★ Özlem Tuna
HOMEWARES
(Map p100; ☑ 212-527 9285; www.ozlemtuna.com; Boğazkesen Caddesi 63a, Tophane; ⊙ 9.30am-7pm Mon-Fri, from 10am Sat; ⬚ Tophane) A leader in Turkey's contemporary-design movement, Özlem Tuna produces super-stylish homewares and jewellery and sells them from her retail space near the Tophane tram stop. Her pieces use forms and colours that reference İstanbul's history and culture (tulips, seagulls, Byzantine mosaics, *nazar boncuk* 'evil eye' charms) and include hamam bowls, coffee and tea sets, coasters, rings, earrings, cufflinks and necklaces.

3rd Culture
HOMEWARES
(Map p100; ☑ 0543 732 3633; www.3rdculture project.com; Çukurcuma Caddesi 38b, Çukurcuma; ⊙ 10am-7pm Mon-Sat, from 11am Sun) Having returned to İstanbul after many years living and working around the globe, siblings Emre and Zeynep Lale Rende decided to open a concept store specialising in homewares and furniture made in İstanbul but inspired by their global travels. There's lots to tempt shoppers here, including stunning limited-edition photographs by Emre, who is a photojournalist by profession.

Eyüp Sabri Tuncer
COSMETICS
(Map p100; ☑ 0212-244 0098; www.eyup sabrituncer.com; Mumhane Caddesi 10, Karaköy; ⊙ 10am-7pm; ⬚ Karaköy) Turks of every age adore the colognes and beauty products produced by this local company, which was established in 1923. Its *doğal zeytınyağlı* (natural olive oil) body balms and soaps are wonderfully inexpensive considering their quality.

Pandora Kitabevi
BOOKS
(Map p100; ☑ 0212-243 3503; www.pandora.com. tr; Büyük Parmakkapı Sokak 3, Taksim; ⊙ 10am-8pm Mon-Wed, to 9pm Thu-Sat, 1-8pm Sun; Ⓜ Taksim, ⬚ Taksim) A long-standing business with three floors of books – head to the 3rd floor for English-language titles.

Nilüfer Karaca
CLOTHING
(Map p100; ☑ 0212-251 8614; www.nilufer karaca.com.tr; Yenicarşı Caddesi 9, Galatasaray; ⊙ 10.30am-8pm Mon-Sat, noon-7pm Sun; Ⓜ Taksim, ⬚ Taksim) Local designer Nilüfer Karaca creates sculptural pieces in muted tones that customers can purchase off the rack or have made to measure in two or three days. Her form-hugging summer frocks and statement winter coats are particularly desirable. Also on offer here are stylish shoes, bags and hats.

Opus3a
MUSIC
(Map p100; ☑ 0212-251 8405; www.opus3a.com; Cihangir Caddesi 3a, Cihangir; ⊙ 11am-8pm Mon-Sat, noon-7pm Sun; Ⓜ Taksim, ⬚ Taksim) Those keen to supplement their CD or vinyl collections with some Turkish music should head to this large shop in Cihangir, where knowledgable English-speaking staff can steer you towards the best local classical, jazz, alternative and pop recordings.

Mabel Çikolata
FOOD
(Map p100; ☑ 0212-244 3462; www.mabel.com.tr; Gümrük Sokak 11, Karaköy; ⊙ 9am-7pm Mon-Sat; ⬚ Karaköy) The city's most beloved chocolate company started trading in 1947 and neither its logo nor this flagship store have changed much since that time. The milk, dark and flavoured varieties are equally delicious, and retro treats such as the chocolate umbrellas are perennially popular. There's another branch in Nişantaşı.

Nahıl
HANDICRAFTS
(Map p100; ☑ 0212-251 9085; www.nahil.com.tr; Bekar Sokak 17, Taksim; ⊙ 10am-7pm Mon-Sat; Ⓜ Taksim, ⬚ Taksim) ✐ The felting, lacework, embroidery, all-natural soaps and soft toys in this lovely shop are made by economically disadvantaged women in Turkey's rural areas. All profits are returned to them, ensuring that they and their families have better lives.

Kadıköy

Brezilya Kurukahve ve Kuruyemiş
FOOD
(Map p84; ☑ 0216-337 6317; Güneşlibahçe Sokak 21-23; ⊙ 8.30am-8.30pm; ⬚ Kadıköy, Ⓜ Kadıköy) Located on the produce market's main strip, this shop has been selling coffee beans, nuts, dried fruit (including particularly delicious plums from Nevşehir in Cappadocia) and a range of teas since 1920. Its original owner was the first business person in the city to begin importing coffee from Latin America, hence its name ('Brezilya Kurukahve' means Brazilian Coffee Shop).

INTEQ/GETTY IMAGES ©

1. Lamps at the Grand Bazaar (p96) 2. Cushions at Arasta Bazaar (p91) 3. Shoppers browse the Grand Bazaar (p96) 4. Spice Bazaar (p97)

ANASTASIA MARTYSHINA/SHUTTERSTOCK ©

İstanbul's Bazaars

Turks have honed the ancient arts of shopping and bargaining over centuries. In İstanbul, the city's Ottoman-era bazaars are as much monuments as marketplaces, spaces showcasing architecture and atmosphere that are nearly as impressive as the artisan wares offered for sale.

The Grand Bazaar

One of the world's oldest and best-loved shopping malls, the Grand Bazaar (p96), has been luring shoppers into its labyrinthine lanes and hidden *hans* (caravanserais) ever since Mehmet the Conqueror ordered its construction in 1461. Come here to purchase carpets and kilims, bathwares, jewellery and textiles. Be sure to investigate its fabulous fast-food opportunities too.

The Spice Bazaar

Seductively scented and inevitably crammed with shoppers, this building (p97) opposite the Eminönü ferry docks has been selling goods to stock household pantries since the 17th century, when it was the last stop for the camel caravans that travelled the legendary Spice Routes from China, Persia and India. These days it's a great place to source dried fruit and spices.

The Arasta Bazaar

In the shadow of the Blue Mosque, this elongated open arcade of shops (p91) has a laid-back atmosphere that stands in stark contrast to the crowded and noisy Grand and Spice Bazaars. Come for carpets and kilims, bathwares, ceramics and textiles.

Produce Markets

İstanbul is blessed with fabulous fresh produce markets. Consider visiting the following markets:

Kadıköy Produce Market (p110)

Fish Market (Balık Pazarı; p103)

Women's Bazaar (Kadınlar Pazarı; p94)

Çiçek İşleri HOMEWARES

(Map p84; ☑0216-336 2122; www.cicekisleri.com; Moda Caddesi 44, Moda; ⏱10am-7pm; 🚢Kadıköy) Creative jewellery, colourful ceramics, contemporary tea glasses, olive-wood coasters and bold-patterned textiles are among the 'ideas inspired by nature' at this lively, eclectic shop in Kadıköy, featuring homewares and accessories by local designers. A good place to pick up gifts and souvenirs that have Turkish flavour without being touristy.

🏠 Nişantaşı, Bomonti & Harbiye

Feriköy Organic Market FOOD & DRINKS

(Map p108; Lala Şahin/Gökkuşağı Sokak, Feriköy/Bomonti; ⏱7am-5pm Sat; Ⓜ Osmanbey) 🍃 Established in 2006 as Turkey's first '100% ecological bazaar', this bustling Saturday market is still going strong, with hundreds of colourful stalls piled high with certified organic fruit and veg. A stroll through the market offers plenty for photographers to snap and self-caterers to buy, including cheeses, bread, dried fruits and nuts, preserves, yoghurt and olive oil.

Gönül Paksoy CLOTHING

(Map p84; ☑0212-236 0209; www.gonulpaksoy.com; Demet Apt 4a, Akkavak Sokak, Nişantaşı; ⏱10am-7pm Tue-Sat, from 1pm Mon; Ⓜ Osmanbey) Paksoy creates and sells pieces that transcend fashion and step into art. In fact, every piece of clothing she designs is a one-off creation that has been handmade using naturally dyed Turkish fabrics (mainly silk, linen, cotton, cashmere, goat hair and wool).

Kulak Ceramic Atelier CERAMICS

(Map p84; ☑0532 300 5815; www.kulakceramic.com; Muradiye Bayırı Sokak 39, Teşvikiye; ⏱10.30am-7pm Mon-Sat; Ⓜ Osmanbey) Elegant yet just a bit off-kilter, the contemporary ceramic pieces made by Zeynep Saraçoğlu and Pınar Philliskirk have an air of *wabi-sabi* – the ancient Japanese philosophy of finding beauty in imperfection. Watch the craftswomen at work in their light-filled corner studio and pick up some of their distinctive plates, bowls or cups to take home (carefully!) with you.

ℹ️ Information

MEDICAL SERVICES

Though they are expensive, it's probably easiest to visit one of the private hospitals listed if you need medical care when in İstanbul. Their standard of care is generally quite high and you will have no trouble finding staff who speak English. Both accept credit-card payments and will charge around ₺300 for a standard consultation.

American Hospital (Amerikan Hastenesi; ☑0212-444 3777; www.americanhospital istanbul.com; Güzelbahçe Sokak 20, Nişantaşı; ⏱24hr; Ⓜ Osmanbey) Paediatric, dental and many other clinics.

Memorial Şişli Hospital (☑0549 639 3366; www.memorial.com.tr/en; Piyalepaşa Bulvarı, Şişli; ⏱24hr emergency department; Ⓜ Şişli) Emergency department, eye centre and paediatric clinic.

Şişli Hamidiye Eftal Eğitim ve Araşıma Hastanesi (☑0212-373 5000; https://sisli etfaleah.saglik.gov.tr; Etfal Sokak, off Halaskargazi Caddesi; ⏱vaccination clinic 8am-noon & 1.30-4.30pm Mon-Fri; Ⓜ Osmanbey) Public

---

ℹ️ MUSEUM PASS İSTANBUL

If, like most visitors, you plan to spend at least three days in İstanbul and cram as many museum visits as possible into your stay, purchasing a Museum Pass İstanbul (www.muze.gov.tr/museumpass) may be worth considering. Valid for 120 hours (five days) from the first museum you visit, the pass costs ₺220 and allows one entrance to each of Topkapı Palace and Harem, Aya İrini, the İstanbul Archaeology Museums, the Museum of Turkish and Islamic Arts, the Museum of Great Palace Mosaics, the Kariye Mosque (Chora Church), Galata Mevlevi House Museum, Fethiye Museum, Rumeli Hisarı and the İstanbul Museum of the History of Science and Technology in Islam. Purchased individually, admission fees to these sights would total considerably more than the price of the pass. Having a pass sometimes allows you to bypass ticket queues, too.

As well as giving entry to these government-operated museums, the pass also provides discounts on entry to privately run museums including the Pera Museum and the Rahmi M Koç Museum.

The pass can be purchased through some hotels and from the ticket offices of museums including Aya İrini, Topkapı Palace, the İstanbul Archaeology Museums, the Museum of Turkish and Islamic Arts, the Museum of Great Palace Mosaics, the Kariye Mosque (Chora Church) and Rumeli Hisarı.

hospital with a vaccination clinic providing rabies shots.

MONEY

ATMs are widespread. Credit cards accepted at most shops, hotels and upmarket restaurants.

POST

Post Office (Map p84; Kadırga Limanı Caddesi 79) Located in Kadırga, between the Bazaar District and Sultanahmet.

SAFE TRAVEL-

➡ Political tensions within Turkey led to a violent, ultimately unsuccessful military coup d'état in 2016. There have also been terrorist incidents including bomb attacks in areas and facilities frequented by tourists. Visitors should stay alert at all times.

➡ Before and during your visit, be sure to monitor your government's online travel advisories.

➡ Always employ common sense when exploring city neighbourhoods. Be particularly careful near the historic city walls, as these harbour vagrants and people with substance-abuse problems – don't walk here alone or after dark.

Pedestrian Safety

As a pedestrian, always give way to vehicles; the sovereignty of the pedestrian is recognised in law but not out on the street. Footpaths (sidewalks) and road surfaces are often in a poorly maintained state and some shops have basements that are accessed from the footpath via steep steps without barriers – watch where you are walking!

Theft

Theft is not generally a big problem and robbery (mugging) is comparatively rare, but don't let İstanbul's relative safety lull you. Take normal precautions. Areas in which to be particularly careful include Aksaray/Laleli (the city's red-light district), the Grand Bazaar (pickpocket central) and the streets off İstiklal Caddesi in Beyoğlu.

TOURIST INFORMATION

The Ministry of Culture & Tourism (www.turizm.gov.tr) currently operates three tourist information offices or booths in the city and has booths at both international airports.

Tourist Office – Sirkeci Train Station (Map p88; 📞 0212-511 5888; Sirkeci Gar, Ankara Caddesi, Sirkeci; ⏰ 9am-8pm; Ⓜ Sirkeci, 🚊 Sirkeci) In a dedicated office accessed from the street.

Tourist Office – Sultanahmet (Map p88; 📞 0212-518 1802; Hippodrome; ⏰ 9am-8.30pm; 🚊 Sultanahmet) Helpful and centrally located. ATMs and public toilets are found behind the office to the south.

ⓘ TELEPHONE CODES

If you are in European İstanbul and wish to call a number in Asian İstanbul, you must dial 0216 before the number. If you are in Asian İstanbul and wish to call a number in European İstanbul, use 0212. Do not use a prefix (that is, don't use the 0212/6) if you are calling a number on the same shore.

Tourist Office – Taksim (Map p100; 📞 0212-233 0592; AKM Yanı Devlet Opera ve Balesi Müdürlüğü, Mete Caddesi, Taksim; ⏰ 9am-5pm; Ⓜ Taksim)

ⓘ Getting There & Away

It's the national capital in all but name, so getting to İstanbul is easy. There are currently two international airports, one *otogar* (bus station) from which national and international services arrive and depart, plus a limited number of international rail connections.

Flights, cars and tours can be booked online at www.lonelyplanet.com/bookings.

AIR

İstanbul Airport

The city's newly opened but not yet completed main airport, **İstanbul Airport** (📞 444 1442, Whatsapp 0549 563 3434; www.istairport.com/en; Terminal Caddesi 1, Arnavutköy), is located in Arnavutköy, on the European side of the city near the Black Sea. The international terminal (Dış Hatlar) and domestic terminal (İç Hatlar) are currently operating at a reduced capacity; when completed in 2028 the airport should be able to host more than 100 airlines and 200 million passengers annually.

The airport has car-rental desks, ATMs, exchange offices and stands of mobile-phone companies.

Left luggage A booth to your right as you exit customs offers luggage storage and charges between ₺53 and ₺72 per suitcase or backpack per 24 hours depending on the size; it's open around the clock.

Tourist information There's a small **office** (📞 0212-891 6205; ⏰ 9am-11pm) in the international arrivals hall that provides maps and advice.

Sabiha Gökçen International Airport

The city's second international airport, **Sabiha Gökçen International Airport** (SAW, Sabiha Gökçen Havalimanı; 📞 0216-588 8888; www.sabihagokcen.aero/homepage; Pendik), is at Pendik/Kurtköy on the Asian side of the city.

It has ATMs, car-rental desks, stands of mobile-phone companies, exchange offices, a mini-market and a PTT (post office) in the international arrivals hall.

Left luggage A booth in the international arrivals hall offers luggage storage.

Tourist information There's a small **office** (☑ 0216-588 8794; ☺ 9am-9pm) in the international arrivals hall that provides maps and advice.

BUS

The **Esenler Otogarı** (Büyük İstanbul Otogarı, Big İstanbul Bus Station; ☑ 0212-658 0505; Ⓜ Otogar) is the city's main bus station for both intercity and international routes. Often called simply 'the Otogar' (Bus Station), it's located at Esenler in the municipality of Bayrampaşa, about 10km west of Sultanahmet. The metro service between Aksaray and the largely decommissioned Atatürk International Airport stops here (Otogar stop). From the Otogar you can take the metro to Zeytinburnu (₺5) and then easily connect with a tram (₺5) to Sultanahmet or Kabataş/Taksim; both of these trips will be cheaper if you purchase and recharge an İstanbulkart (travel card; ₺10, including ₺4 credit) from the machines at the metro entrance. If you're going to Beyoğlu, bus 830 leaves from the centre of the Otogar every 15 minutes between 6am and 9.50pm and takes approximately one hour to reach Taksim Meydanı (Taksim Sq). You'll need an İstanbulkart. A taxi will cost approximately ₺45 to Sultanahmet and ₺50 to Taksim.

There's a second, much smaller, otogar at Alibeyköy, where buses from central Anatolia (including Ankara and Cappadocia) stop en route to Esenler. From here passengers can hop on the new T5 Golden Horn tram line which stops at Eyüp, Balat and Fener and finishes at Cibali (three kilometres west of Eminönü). The tramline's final link, between Cibali and Eminönü, is planned to be finished in 2022.

The city's third otogar is in Ataşehir, on the Asian side at the junction of the O-2 and O-4 motorways. From Ataşehir, *servises* transfer passengers to Asian suburbs, including Kadıköy and Üsküdar.

TRAIN

There are two international sleeper train services to/from İstanbul: the İstanbul–Sofya Ekspresi to Sofia in Bulgaria and the Bosfor Ekspresi to Bucharest in Romania.

At the time of writing the İstanbul–Sofya Ekspresi was departing Halkalı station on the European side of the city at 9.40pm daily in high season (approximately June to September) and 10.40pm daily in the low season (approximately October to May); the trip from Halkalı takes 10 to 11 hours and ticket prices start at €27.90. The

Marmaray (direction Gebze, every 15 minutes) links Sirkeci Station and Halkalı. Passengers can change in Sofia for Belgrade in Serbia.

The Bosfor Ekspresi operates in high season (June to October) only; its carriages are attached to the İstanbul–Sofya Ekspresi until it crosses the Bulgarian border, where the Bosfor Ekspresi branches off at Dimitrovgrad, heading north to Bucharest. The journey from Halkalı to Bucharest takes 21 to 22 hours and ticket prices start at €31.40.

Note that services, timetables and ticket costs change regularly.

Travellers wanting to make their way to Iran can take the high-speed train to Ankara and then connect with the weekly Trans-Asya service to Tabriz and Tehran; the trip from Ankara takes 2½ days.

A fast-train service operates up to eight times daily between Ankara and İstanbul. This takes 4½ hours and ticket prices start at ₺71. The most convenient place to board the train is at Söğütlüçeşme station in Kadıköy, which is easily accessed from Sirkeci Station via the Marmaray (direction Gebze, every 15 minutes).

❶ Getting Around

➡ *Jetons* (ticket tokens) can be purchased from ticket machines or offices at tram stops, *iskelesi* (ferry docks) and funicular and metro stations, but it's much cheaper and easier to use an İstanbulkart.

➡ You must have an İstanbulkart to use a bus.

➡ Pay the driver when you take a dolmuş (shared minibus); fares vary according to destination and length of trip.

➡ Ticket prices are usually the same on public and private ferry services; İstanbulkarts can be used on some private ferries, but not all.

➡ İstanbulkarts cannot be used to pay for Bosphorus ferry tours.

TO/FROM İSTANBUL AIRPORT

Havaist (Havataş; ☑ 444 2656; http://havatas.com) buses depart from the downstairs level of the arrivals hall to destinations including Sultanahmet (₺18, every 30 to 45 minutes from 5am to 4.15am, 60 to 100 minutes depending on traffic) and Taksim (₺18, every 15 to 30 minutes from 5.10am to 4.30am, 40 to 80 minutes depending on traffic). The Sultanahmet bus service also stops at Eminönü. At Taksim, the bus stops in front of the Point Hotel, close to Taksim Meydanı. Note that signage on the buses and at stops sometimes reads 'Havaş' rather than 'Havataş'. You'll need an İstanbulkart to use the bus – these are available from machines near the bus stands.

Many hotels offer hotel shuttle services to/from the airport.

ⓘ İSTANBULKARTS

İstanbul's public-transport system is excellent, and one of its major strengths is the İstanbulkart, a rechargeable travel card similar to London's Oyster Card, Hong Kong's Octopus Card and Paris' Navigo.

İstanbulkarts are simple to operate. As you enter a bus or pass through the turnstile at a ferry dock, tram stop or metro station, swipe your card for entry and the fare will automatically be deducted from your balance. The cards offer a considerable discount on fares (₺2.60, as opposed to the usual ₺5, with additional transfers within a two-hour journey window: ₺1.85 for the first transfer, ₺1.40 for the second, ₺0.90 for the third). They can also be used to pay for fares for more than one traveller (one swipe per person per ride).

The cards can be purchased from machines at metro, ferry and funicular stations for a nonrefundable charge of ₺10 (including ₺4 credit) and can be loaded with amounts between ₺5 and ₺300 at kiosks or at machines at ferry docks, metro and bus stations.

A taxi from the airport to Sultanahmet costs around ₺135 and takes approximately 50 minutes. To get to Beyoğlu you'll be looking at ₺130 and 40 minutes.

TO/FROM SABIHA GÖKÇEN INTERNATIONAL AIRPORT

Havaist buses (₺18) travel from the airport to Abdülhak Hamit Caddesi in front of the Point Hotel near Taksim Meydanı between 4am and 1am. There are also services to Kadıköy (₺14). If you're heading towards the Old City from Taksim, you can take the funicular from Taksim to Kabataş (₺5, or ₺2.60 on an İstanbulkart) followed by the tram from Kabataş to Sultanahmet (₺5, or ₺1.85 on an İstanbulkart). From Kadıköy, ferries travel to Eminönü (₺5, or ₺2.60 on an İstanbulkart).

Note that the M4 metro line from Kadıköy is being extended to Sabiha Gökçen; the completion date is unknown.

Many hotels offer hotel shuttle services to/from the airport.

Taxis from this airport to the city are expensive. To Beyoğlu you'll be looking at around ₺165; to Sultanahmet around ₺175.

BUS

The bus system in İstanbul is extremely efficient, though traffic congestion in the city means that bus trips can be very long. The introduction of Metrobüs lines (where buses are given dedicated traffic lanes) aims to relieve this problem, but these tend to service residential suburbs out of the city centre and are thus of limited benefit to travellers. The major bus stands are underneath Taksim Meydanı and at Beşiktaş, Kabataş, Eminönü, Kadıköy and Üsküdar, with most services running between 6am and 11pm. Destinations and main stops on city bus routes are shown on a sign on the right (kerb) side of the bus (otobüs),

or on the electronic display at its front. You must have an İstanbulkart before boarding.

The most useful bus lines for travellers are those running along both sides of the Bosphorus and the Golden Horn, those in the western districts and those between Üsküdar and Kadıköy.

FERRY

The most enjoyable way to get around town is by ferry. Crossing between the Asian and European shores, up and down the Golden Horn and Bosphorus, and over to the Adalar (Princes' Islands), these vessels are as efficient as they are popular with locals. Some are operated by the government-owned İstanbul Şehir Hatları (p116); others by private companies, including **Dentur Avrasya** (☑ 0216-444 6336; www.denturavrasya.com), **Turyol** (☑ 0212-251 4421; www.turyol.com) and **Mavi Marmara** (☑ 0850-480 6767; www.mavimarmara.net). Timetables are posted at *iskelesi* (ferry docks).

On the European side, the major ferry docks are at the mouth of the Golden Horn (Eminönü and Karaköy) and at Beşiktaş.

The ferries run to two annual timetables: winter (mid-September to May) and summer (June to mid-September).

Ferry schedules vary, with popular routes usually functioning between 7am and 9pm or 10pm. The possibility of future 24-hour services has been flagged – check www.sehithatlari.istanbul for updates.

Tickets are cheap (usually ₺5) and it's possible to use an İstanbulkart on most routes.

There are also *deniz otobüsü* (sea bus) and *hızlı feribot* (fast ferry) services, but these ply routes that are of less interest to the traveller and are also more expensive than the conventional ferries. For more information, check **İDO** (İstanbul Deniz Otobüsleri; ☑ 0850-222 4436; www.ido.com.tr).

Ferries ply the following useful two-way routes:

+ Beşiktaş–Kadıköy
+ Beşiktaş–Üsküdar
+ Eminönü–Anadolu Kavağı (Bosphorus cruise)
+ Eminönü–Rumeli Kavağı (Bosphorus commuter line)
+ Beşiktaş–Eminönü–Kadıköy–Kınalıada–Burgazada–Heybeliada–Büyükada–Bostancı (Princes' Islands ferry)
+ Eminönü–Kadıköy
+ Eminönü–Üsküdar
+ Karaköy–Kadıköy
+ Karaköy–Üsküdar
+ Üsküdar–Karaköy–Kasımpaşa–Fener–Balat–Hasköy–Ayvansaray–Sütlüce–Eyüp (Golden Horn Ferry)

There are also limited services to, from and between the Bosphorus suburbs. İDO operates car ferries between Eminönü and the Harem İskelesi (Ferry Dock; Map p84).

FUNICULAR & CABLE CAR

There are two funiculars (funıküleri) and two cable cars (teleferic) in the city. All are short trips and İstanbulkarts can be used.

A funicular called the Tünel carries passengers between Karaköy, at the base of the Galata Bridge (Galata Köprüsü), to Tünel Meydanı, at one end of İstiklal Caddesi. The service operates every five minutes between 7am and 10.45pm and a ride costs ₺5 (₺2.60 on an İstanbulkart).

The second funicular carries passengers from Kabataş, at the end of the tramline, to Taksim Meydanı, where it connects to the metro. The service operates every five minutes from 6am to midnight and a ride costs ₺5 (₺2.60 on an İstanbulkart).

A cable car runs between the waterside at Eyüp and the Pierre Loti Café (p132) every 10 minutes from 8am to 11pm; İstanbulkart transfer discounts don't apply. Another travels between Maçka (near Taksim) and the İstanbul Technical University in Taşkışla (8am to 7pm). Rides costs ₺5 (₺2.60 on an İstanbulkart).

METRO

Metro services depart every five minutes between 6am and midnight. Some lines function throughout the night on Friday and Saturday nights. Jetons (ticket tokens) cost ₺5 but trips are considerably cheaper if you use an İstanbulkart. Tickets are double the usual price between 12.30am and 5.30am on the weekend all-night services and more expensive on long trips on the Marmaray – the cost depends on the length of the trip.

One line (the M1A) connects Yenikapı, southwest of Sultanahmet, with the largely decommissioned Atatürk International Airport. This stops at 16 stations, including Aksaray and the Otogar, along the way.

Another line (the M2) connects Yenikapı with Taksim, stopping at three stations along the way: Vezneciler, near the Grand Bazaar; on the bridge across the Golden Horn (Haliç); and at Şişhane, near Tünel Meydanı in Beyoğlu. From Taksim it travels northeast to Hacıosman via nine stations. A branch line, the M6, connects one of these stops, Levent, with Boğaziçi Üniversitesi near the Bosphorus.

A fourth line, known as the Marmaray, connects Halkalı, west of the Old City, with Ayrılık Çeşmesi, on the city's Asian side. This travels via a tunnel under the Sea of Marmara, stopping at Yenikapı, Sirkeci and Üsküdar en route and connecting with the M4 metro running between Kadıköy and Tavşantepe.

TAXI

İstanbul is full of yellow taxis. There are also Turquoise taxis, which are newer, more comfortable and slightly more expensive. Some drivers are lunatics, others are con artists; most are neither. If you're caught with the first category and you're about to go into meltdown, say 'yavaş!' (slow down!). Drivers in the con-artist category tend to prey on tourists. All taxis have digital meters and must run them, but some of these drivers ask for a flat fare, or pretend the meter doesn't work so they can gouge you at the end of the trip. The best way to counter this is to tell them no meter, no ride. Avoid the taxis waiting for fares near Aya Sofya Meydanı – we have received reports of rip-offs.

Taxi fares are very reasonable and rates are the same during both day and night. It costs around ₺18 to travel between Beyoğlu and Sultanahmet.

Few taxis have seat belts. If you take a taxi from the European side of the city to the Asian side over one of the Bosphorus bridges, it is your responsibility to cover the toll (₺7). The driver will add this to your fare. There is no toll when crossing from Asia to Europe.

Uber has operated in the city since 2014, but at the time of writing was banned. The local rideshare company is BiTaksi (www.bitaksi.com/en).

TRAM

An excellent tramvay (tramway) service runs from Bağcılar, in the city's west, to Zeytinburnu (where it connects with the metro from the airport) and on to Sultanahmet and Eminönü. It then crosses the Galata Bridge to Karaköy (to connect with the Tünel) and Kabataş (to connect with the funicular to Taksim Meydanı). A second service runs from Cevizlibağ, closer to Sultanahmet on the same line, through to Kabataş. Both services run every five minutes from 6am to midnight. The fare is ₺5; jetons are available from machines on every tram stop and İstanbulkarts can be used.

A new tram line (the T5) connects Cibali (three kilometres west of Eminönü) with the Alibeyköy otogar (bus station) running via the western Golden Horn suburbs of Fener, Balat and Eyüp. The final section connecting Cibali and Eminönü is due to open in 2022.

A small antique tram travels the length of İstiklal Caddesi in Beyoğlu from a stop near Tünel Meydanı to Taksim Meydanı (7am to 10.20pm). Electronic tickets (₺5) can be purchased from the ticket office at the Tünel funicular, and İstanbulkarts can be used.

Another small tram line follows a loop through Kadıköy and the neighbouring suburb of Moda every 10 minutes between 6.55am and 9.20pm. *Jetons* cost ₺5 and İstanbulkarts can be used.

AROUND İSTANBUL

Princes' Islands

Most İstanbullus refer to the Princes' Islands as 'The Islands' (Adalar). Lying 20km southeast of the city in the Sea of Marmara, the islands are a popular destination for a day escape from the city but are oppressively crowded between May and October, when visitors can number up to 50,000 per day on weekends. Five of the nine islands in the group are populated; most visitors head to the two largest, Büyükada and Heybeliada.

Dedicating half a day to each will give you enough time to get a taste of island life, but won't allow much time for exploration. If you are keen to do some walking and/or swimming, you'll be best off limiting yourself to one island – Büyükada is the popular choice.

The islands are best visited in the warmer months. Many restaurants and most hotels are closed between November and early April, and ferry services are occasionally cancelled due to poor weather, which can result in visitors being stranded overnight without accommodation.

Adalardan (www.adalardan.net) is a Turkish-language website that includes up-to-date ferry timetables. Other information can be out of date.

🛈 Getting There & Away

On summer weekends, you should board ferries at least half an hour before the departure time to ensure that you get a seat. Ferries sail towards the Sea of Marmara, treating passengers to fine views of Topkapı Palace, Aya Sofya and the Blue Mosque, Kız Kulesi, Haydarpaşa train station and the distinctive minaret-style clock towers of Marmara University on the journey. The ferries stop at two, three or four islands in the group depending on the ferry company: the first island is Kınalıada (30 minutes), then Burgazada (15 minutes), Heybeliada (15 minutes), the second-largest island, and Büyükada (10 minutes), the largest island in the group.

Be sure to check the websites of all companies as schedules and routes change regularly.

İstanbul Şehir Hatları (p116) At least eight ferries sail each day from Eminönü, leaving between 6.50am and 11pm. These depart from the Adalar İskelesi (Adalar Ferry Dock). The most useful departure times for day-trippers are 8am, 9am and 10.10am Monday to Saturday, 8.30am, 9.10am and 10.10am Sunday. There are also a few services starting at Kabataş, the most useful of which leaves at 8.45am. The trip costs ₺7 one way (₺5.20 with an İstanbulkart) and takes 95 minutes. The last ferries leave Büyükada at 7.30pm and 8.30pm, picking up passengers in Heybeliada, Kınalıada and Burgazada en route.

Dentur Avrasya (p143)/**Mavi Marmara** (p143) Operate small ferries (adult ₺10 one way, child under 6 free; 12 daily) that depart from Beşiktaş and stop to take on extra passengers at the dock behind the gas station at Kabataş before heading to Heybeliada and Büyükada; additional services start from Kabataş. The journey between Kabataş and Büyükada takes 1¼ hours; the last service from Büyükada departs at 7.30pm weekdays, 9pm weekends. Also operates four services per day from Sirkeci (adult ₺10 one way, child under 6 free), two departing in the morning and two in the early afternoon. The journey takes one hour and the last ferry leaves Büyükada at 4.30pm.

Turyol (p143) Operates up to eight services per day from Eminönü, stopping to take on extra passengers at Karaköy and Kadıköy (₺10 one way), and heads to Kınalıada, Heybeliada and Büyükada. The first service departs Eminönü at 9.40am on weekdays and 8.40am on weekends; the last ferry departs Büyükada at 7pm weekdays, 8pm weekends.

🛈 Getting Around

One of the wonderful things about the Princes' Islands is that they are car-free zones. The main forms of transport are motorised carts, bicycles and electric vehicles.

THE HISTORY OF THE FAYTON

The name *fayton* comes from the mythical Phaeton, son of the sun god Helios. Long used as a form of transport on the Princes' Islands, which are free of cars, these horse-drawn carriages were a popular tourist attraction, taking visitors around the islands on scenic tours. However, growing consternation about the welfare of *fayton* horses prompted calls to ban their use both on the Princes' Islands and elsewhere in Turkey. Animal-welfare activists lauded the 2019 decisions of municipal governments in the cities of İzmir and Antalya to ban their use and turned their passionate attention to a campaign to do the same on the islands. Groups including the Turkish Animal Rights Federation (HAYTAP) and the Confederation of Animal Rights (HAYKONFED) claimed that dozens of horses died on the islands each year due to injury and exhaustion, while others died from starvation in the tourist-free winter months, when their owners abandoned them in the islands' forests so as not to pay for their feed. Calling for *faytons* to be replaced with electric or solar-powered carriages, the activists gathered considerable support (even President Erdoğan supported a ban), but the local municipality pushed back, citing the importance of the *fayton* industry to the local economy. In an attempt to reach a compromise, İstanbul's mayor Ekrem İmamoğlu pledged in 2019 that a centre would be established to take care of the horses' health, care and treatment, but activists were unconvinced. Later that year, *faytons* were finally relegated to the past and were replaced in 2020 by a small fleet of four- and 14-seat electric vehicles.

Büyükada

The largest island in the Adalar group, Büyükada (Great Island) is impressive viewed from the ferry: gingerbread villas climb up the slopes of the hill and the bulbous twin cupolas of the Splendid Palas Hotel provide an unmistakable landmark. Home to notable exiles throughout history – including the Byzantine empress Eirene in the 9th century and Russian revolutionary Leon Trotsky in the 20th century – the island's streets are dotted with handsome 19th-century timber villas and its hills are covered with heavily wooded pine forests laced with walking tracks and picnic spots. There are also a number of relatively clean beaches that attract droves of summer visitors.

You'll disembark the ferry at the island's attractive Ottoman Revival–style *iskele* (ferry dock) building designed by Mihran Azaryan and constructed in 1915. The Museum of the Princes' Islands, Church and Monastery of St George, forests and beaches are a pleasant, although often uphill, walk or a short electric vehicle ride away.

Büyükada has some good swimming beaches, but you'll need to pay for the privilege of using them. Try Nakibey, Yörükali and Viranbağ, where you'll pay between ₺40 and ₺60 per day per person (this will include use of a sun lounge and umbrella).

Museum of the Princes' Islands   MUSEUM
(Adalar Müzesi, Aya Nikola Hangar Müze; ☑0216-382 6430; www.adalarmuzesi.org; Yılmaz Türk Caddesi; adult/student ₺10/5, Wed free; ⊘9am-5.30pm Tue-Sun) Relegated to an isolated site next to Aya Nikola Beach on the southeastern side of the island, this excellent museum is often overlooked by visitors but we highly recommend making the effort to get here. Multimedia exhibits focus on the history and culture of the Adalar and cover every aspect of island life, including geology, flora, religious heritage, food, architecture, music, festivals and literature. Interpretative panels and videos are in both Turkish and English, and there are objects galore to admire.

Church & Monastery of St George   MONASTERY
(Aya Yorgi Kilise ve Manastırı) There's not a lot to see at this Greek Orthodox monastery complex located on a 203m-high hill known as Yücetepe, but the panoramic views from the monastery terrace make the hour-long trek worthwhile. A small church is the only building of note, so most visitors spend their time at the pleasant **Yücetepe Kır Gazinosu** (☑0216-382 1333; böreği ₺12-20, mains ₺20-25; ⊘9am-10pm) restaurant. Its outdoor tables have views to İstanbul and the nearby islands of Yassıada and Sivriada. You'll need to be dressed modestly to enter the church.

ℹ Getting Around

Bicycles are available for rent in several of the town's shops (per hour/day approximately ₺10/20), and shops on the market street can provide picnic supplies. The electric vehicle stand is to the left of the clock tower.

Heybeliada

Heybeliada (Heybeli for short) is the prettiest island in the Adalar group, replete with ornate 19th-century timber villas and offering gorgeous sea views from myriad viewpoints. It's extremely popular with day trippers from İstanbul, who flock here on weekends to walk in the pine groves and swim from the tiny, and usually crowded, beaches. The island's major landmarks are the hilltop Hagia Triada Monastery, which is perched above a picturesque line of poplar trees in a spot that has been occupied by a Greek monastery since Byzantine times, and the Deniz Lisesi (Turkish Naval Academy), which was established in 1824 and whose late 19th-century buildings you'll see to the left of the ferry dock as you arrive.

Hagia Triada Monastery   CHURCH
(Aya Triada Manastırı; ☑ 0216-351 8563; www.the ologicalschoolhalki.com; Ümit Tepesi 5; ⊙ daily by appointment) Perched above a picturesque

line of poplar trees in a spot that has been occupied by a Greek monastery since Byzantine times, this 1896 complex of buildings housed a Greek Orthodox theological school until 1971, when it was closed on the government's orders; the Ecumenical Orthodox Patriarchate is waging an ongoing campaign to have it reopened. There's a small 17th-century church with an ornate altar on the site, as well as a library housing many old and rare manuscripts.

İnönü Evi Müzesi   MUSEUM
(İnönü House Museum; ☑ 0216-351 8449; www. ismetinonu.org.tr/heybeliada-ismet-inonu-evi; Refah Şehitleri Caddesi 67; ⊙ 10am-5pm Tue-Sun) Turkey's second president, İsmet İnönü, purchased this four-storey villa in 1934, four years before he assumed the presidency after Atatürk's death. He and his family spent summers here until his death in 1973. Still furnished with original pieces, the villa is now open to the public as a house museum.

ℹ Getting Around

Bicycles are available for rent in several of the town's shops. Prices change according to demand, quality of bicycle and the season; expect to pay anywhere from ₺10 to ₺40 per day.

İSTANBUL PRINCES' ISLANDS

Thrace & Marmara

Best Places to Eat

→ Muhitt (p170)
→ Kilye Suvla Lokanta (p167)
→ Mustafanın Kayfesi (p177)
→ Sardalye (p169)
→ Biyer Kafe Dukkan (p177)

Best Places to Stay

→ Anemos Hotel (p176)
→ Hotel Casa Villa (p166)
→ Gallipoli Houses (p166)
→ Set Özer Hotel (p169)
→ Meydani Butik Hotel (p176)

Why Go?

Grand narratives have unfolded across this region's rolling hills and serrated coast for millennia, leaving an extraordinary archaeological site (Troy), sublime Ottoman architecture (Edirne), historical battlefields (Gallipoli), and a fascinating and beautiful island (Gökçeada). Alexander the Great crossed the Hellespont here on his victorious march to Persia, and the Achaeans (Greeks) and Trojans fought the war immortalised by Homer in the Iliad. Mehmet II conquered Constantinople from the Ottoman capital of Edirne, and Allied forces landed on the forested and cobalt-fringed Gallipoli (Gelibolu) Peninsula in 1915, triggering a nine-month stand-off with Turkish troops that would help to define the modern nations of Turkey, Australia and New Zealand. History continues to echo at attractions like the Museum of Troy and the poignant Sons of Çanakkale exhibition, but there is a contemporary verve in the student bars and hip cafes of Çanakkale and the emerging wine-making scene of Thrace.

When to Go

Edirne

°C/°F **Temp**   **Rainfall** Inches/mm

	J	F	M	A	M	J	J	A	S	O	N	D

Apr & May
Multicoloured wildflowers carpet hillsides on the Gallipoli Peninsula.

May & Jun
Organic black cherries and semi-deserted beaches on Gökçeada island.

Aug Locals party on Çanakkale's waterfront during the Troia Festival.

Thrace & Marmara Highlights

1 **Selimiye Mosque** (p150) Visiting this exquisite World Heritage–listed building in the former Ottoman capital of Edirne.

2 **Thrace Wine Route** (p156) Sampling local wine and food at vineyards among stunning scenery.

3 **Gökçeada** (p175) Investigating the fascinating Greek heritage and windswept landscape of this Aegean island.

4 **Gallipoli (Gelibolu) Peninsula** (p157) Walking in the footsteps of WWI soldiers and taking time to contemplate the horrors of war.

5 **Çanakkale** (p168) Lazing away an afternoon while admiring the view over the Dardanelles at a waterfront *çay bahçesi* (tea garden).

6 **Museum of Troy** (p174) Exploring this superb museum telling the story of one of history's most fabled sites.

Edirne

⏹ 0284 / POP 167,000

Capital of the Ottoman empire before Mehmet II conquered Constantinople and moved his court there, Edirne is blessed with imperial building stock, a notable culinary heritage and a lingering and much-cherished sense of civic grandeur. Close to the Greek and Bulgarian borders, the city has a European flavour that is best appreciated in summer, when locals party on the banks of the Tunca and Meriç Rivers.

History

Emperor Hadrian made Hadrianopolis (later Adrianople) the main centre of Roman Thrace in the early 2nd century AD. In the mid-14th century, the nascent Ottoman state began to grow in size and power, and in 1363 its army crossed the Dardanelles, skirted Constantinople and captured Adrianople, renaming it Edirne and making it the third capital of the Ottoman Empire.

The city functioned in this role until 1453, when Constantinople was conquered and became the new capital. Subsequent sultans continued to acknowledge Edirne's historical importance by maintaining its industries and preserving its buildings. It was briefly occupied by imperial Russian troops in 1829, during the Greek War of Independence, and in 1878, during the Russo-Turkish War, but remained relatively unscathed by these events. Its role as a fortress defending Ottoman Constantinople and eastern Thrace during the Balkan Wars of 1912–13 was more significant, and it suffered heavy losses of life and property at this time.

When the Ottoman Empire collapsed after WWI, the Allies handed Thrace to the Greeks and declared İstanbul an international city. In the summer of 1920, Greek armies occupied Edirne, only to be driven back by forces under the command of Atatürk. The Treaty of Lausanne (1923) ceded Edirne and eastern Thrace to the Turks.

◉ Sights

◉ City Centre

★ Selimiye Mosque   MOSQUE

(Selimiye Camii; Mimar Sinan Caddesi) Designed by Ottoman architect Mimar Koca Sinan (1497–1588), whose best-known works adorn İstanbul's skyline, this exquisite World Heritage-listed mosque is Edirne's most cherished building. Built between 1569 and 1575 by order of Sultan Selim II at Edirne's highest point, the mosque features four 71m-high minarets and was positioned in the centre of an extensive *külliye* (mosque complex), which included a *medrese* (Islamic school of higher studies), *darül Hadis* (Hadith school) and *arasta* (arcade of shops).

The main entrance is through the western courtyard, home to a lovely marble *şadırvan* (ablution fountain). Inside, the broad, lofty dome is supported by eight unobtrusive pillars, arches and external buttresses, creating a surprisingly spacious interior.

Selimiye Foundation Museum   MUSEUM

(Selimiye Vakıf Müzesi; ⏹ 0284-212 1133; ◷ 9am-5pm Tue-Sun) FREE This museum is housed in a handsome building in the Selimiye Mosque's *külliye* (in a *medrese* in the southeastern corner of the courtyard). It showcases a collection of art and artefacts drawn from mosques and religious buildings in and around Edirne.

Edirne Turkish
& Islamic Art Museum   MUSEUM

(Edirne Türk-İslam Eserleri Müzesi; ⏹ 0284-225 5748; ₺7; ◷ 9am-5pm) The small rooms of the elegant *darül Hadis* in the northeastern corner of the Selimiye Mosque's courtyard house an eclectic collection of Ottoman-era artefacts, including calligraphy, weaponry, glass, woodwork, ceramics, costumes and jewellery. Some of the rooms feature mannequins in ethnographic-style displays; our favourite is the Circumcision Room.

Edirne Archaeology
& Ethnography Museum   MUSEUM

(Edirne Arkeoloji ve Etnografya Müzesi; ⏹ 0284-225 1120; Kadır Paşa Mektep Sokak 7; ₺7; ◷ 9am-6.30pm mid-Apr–Sep, to 5.30pm Oct–mid Apr) This museum has two sections: one archaeological and the other ethnographic. Archaeological highlights include Thracian funerary steles featuring horsemen. The ethnographic section showcases carpets, embroidery, textiles, calligraphy and jewellery; don't miss the wooden objects decorated in the Edirnekâri style, a lacquering technique developed locally during the Ottoman era. The museum is located behind the Selimiye Mosque.

Old Mosque   MOSQUE

(Eski Camii; Muaffıklarhane Sokak) Though not as prominent on Edirne's skyline as the Selimiye and Üç Şerefeli mosques, the Eski (Old) Mosque is an important landmark in

KIRKPINAR OIL-WRESTLING FESTIVAL

The testosterone-charged **Tarihi Kırkpınar Yağlı Güreş Festivali** (Historic Kırkpınar Oil-Wrestling Festival; www.kirkpinar.org) is famous throughout Turkey and attracts enormous crowds to Edirne for three days in late June or early July every year.

The crowds come to cheer on muscular men skimpily clad in *kispet* (tight leather shorts) and lathered in olive oil, who attempt to wrestle their opponents to the ground or to lift them above their shoulders. It may sound theatrical, but this is a serious, ultra-macho sport, Turkish style.

According to local legend, the festival's origins go back to 1363, when the Ottoman sultan Orhan Gazi sent his brother Süleyman Paşa along with 40 men to conquer the Byzantine fortress at Domuz. The soldiers were all keen wrestlers, and after their victory they challenged each other to bouts. Two of them were so evenly matched that they fought for days without any clear result, until both of them finally dropped dead. When their bodies were buried under a nearby fig tree, a spring mysteriously appeared. The site was given the name Kırkpınar ('40 Springs'), in the wrestlers' honour.

The annual three-day contest has been held in Sarayiçi on the outskirts of Edirne since the birth of the republic, and is now preceded by four days of wrestling-themed festivities. Wrestlers, who are classed not by weight but by height, age and experience, compete in 13 categories – from *minik* (toddler) to *baş* (first class) – and dozens of matches take place simultaneously in the Sarayiçi stadium. Bouts are now capped at 30 or 40 minutes, after which they enter 'sudden death' one-fall-wins overtime. When all the fights are decided, prizes are awarded for conduct and technique, as well as the coveted and hotly contested head-wrestler title.

Entry to the first day of the wrestling is free; tickets (₺70) are required for the next two. There's a ticket box at the venue, or you can purchase tickets from Biletix (www.biletix.com). Note that accommodation in and around the city over this week fills up fast.

the city and has a large and loyal local congregation. Built between 1403 and 1414, it is the oldest of the city's imperial mosques and features a square, fortress-like form and an arcaded portico topped with a series of small domes. Inside, there are huge calligraphic inscriptions on the walls.

The mosque originally had an extensive *külliye*, but today only its handsome *bedesten* (covered bazaar) remains. This comprises 36 strongrooms covered by 14 domes in two rows of seven. The **bedesten** (☉ sunrise-sunset) was the centre of commercial activity in Edirne in the 15th century and the strongrooms were needed to secure valuable goods. Today its stores sell merchandise that is considerably less impressive.

Üç Şerefeli Mosque   MOSQUE
(Üç Şerefeli Cami; Hükümet Caddesi) Edirne's *merkez* (town centre) is visually dominated by this mosque, which was built by order of Sultan Murat II between 1437 and 1447 and has four strikingly different minarets. Its name refers to the *üç şerefeli* (three balconies) on the tallest minaret; the second tallest has two balconies and the remaining two have one balcony each.

The mosque has a wide and beautifully decorated interior dome mounted on a hexagonal drum and supported by two walls and two massive hexagonal pillars. In a style emulated by later Ottoman architects, the partly covered courtyard features a portico with small, beautifully decorated domes.

Kaleiçi   HISTORIC SITE
Roughly translated, *kaleiçi* means 'inside the castle'. In Edirne it is used to describe the old streets to the south of Talat Paşa Caddesi and west of Saraçlar Caddesi. Dating from the medieval period, this is the heart of the old city and it retains a number of ornately decorated timber houses dating from the 18th, 19th and early 20th centuries, as well as a couple of handsome stone civic buildings.

When exploring, look out for the **Kırkpınar Evi** (Kırkpınar House; ☎ 0284-212 8622; www.kirkpinar.org; Maarif Caddesi; ☉ 10am-noon & 2-6pm) **FREE** opposite Polis Parkı (Police Park). Its collection of memorabilia associated with oil wrestling is drab, but the building itself is a good example of Edirne's traditional houses. Some of these have undergone recent restoration (the Mihran Hanım Konağı

Edirne

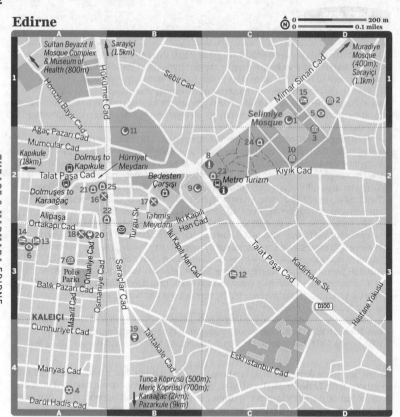

in Gazipaşa Caddesi is a good example), but many are in a sad state of disrepair. Other interesting buildings include the police station in Maarif Caddesi.

Grand Synagogue of Edirne SYNAGOGUE
(Maarif Caddesi 75; ⊙9am-5pm Tue-Sun) FREE
Reopened in 2016 after a 36-year closure and a five-year US$2.5 million restoration project, Edirne's Grand Synagogue is the sole reminder of when a community of more than 20,000 Sephardic Jews lived in the city. Built in 1906 to replace 13 smaller synagogues destroyed in the Great Fire of Edirne in 1903, the elegant building features a delicately hued arched roof and beautifully tiled floors.

When the synagogue was first constructed, it could house up to 1200 worshippers. Its vibrant yellow exterior now shines amid the fading wooden houses and boxy apartment buildings of Edirne's former Jewish Quarter. The city's Jewish population now

numbers in single figures, but the synagogue has been consecrated for religious purposes in addition to being considered a museum.

Muradiye Mosque MOSQUE
(Muradiye Camii; Mimar Sinan Caddesi) Built for Sultan Murat II between 1426 and 1436, this mosque interestingly once housed a Mevlevi (whirling dervish) lodge. The mosque's T-shaped plan has twin *eyvans* (vaulted halls), an unusual cupola, fine İznik tiles covering the interior walls and striking calligraphy on the exterior. It's an easy 15-minute walk northeast of Selimiye Mosque.

The small cemetery on the east side contains the grave of Şeyhülislâm Musa Kâzım Efendi, the Ottoman Empire's last chief Islamic judge, who fled the British occupation of İstanbul after WWI and died here in 1920.

Edirne

◉ North of the Centre

Sultan Beyazıt II Mosque Complex MOSQUE
(Beyazıt II Camii ve Külliyesi; Beyazıt Caddesi, Yıldırım Beyazıt Mahallesi) Standing in splendid isolation on the banks of the Tunca River, this complex was commissioned by Sultan Beyazıt II and built between 1484 and 1488. The mosque's design lies midway between two other Edirne mosques: its prayer hall has one large dome, similar to the Selimiye, but it also has a courtyard and fountain like the Üç Şerefeli. The *külliye* includes a *tabhane* (travellers hostel), *tımarhane* (asylum), *tip medresesi* (medical school) and *darüşşifa* (hospital).

The complex is a 10-minute taxi ride (₺25) from the centre or a longish but pleasant walk down Horozlu Bayır Sokak and across the Yalnıgöz and Sultan Beyazıt II Bridges. The Yalnıgöz (Lonely Arch, or Lone Eye) dates from 1570 and was designed by Mimar Sinan; the Beyazıt II dates from 1488. Alternatively, dolmuşes (minibuses; ₺2.50) to Yenimaret ('Y.Maret') leaving from opposite the tourist office pass the complex.

Museum of Health MUSEUM
(Sağlık Müzesi; ☎ 0284-224 0922; https://saglik muzesi.trakya.edu.tr; Sultan Beyazıt II Mosque Complex, Beyazıt Caddesi, Yıldırım Beyazıt Mahallesi; ₺5; ☉ 9am-5.30pm) The extremely beautiful *darüşşifa* and *tip medresesi* in the Sultan Beyazıt II mosque complex now house this museum tracing the history of Islamic medicine. Overseen by Trakya Üniversitesi, the museum highlights innovative treatments developed and utilised in the hospital and medical school here from 1488 to 1909. Mannequins dressed as Ottoman-era doctors, patients and medical students are used in scenes illustrating various medical procedures, and interpretative panels explain the connection between the hospital's physical design and treatments.

Sarayiçi HISTORIC SITE
It was here, in the 15th century, that Sultan Murat II built the Eski Sarayı (Old Palace). Little remains of this grand structure, which was blown up just before the Russo-Turkish War of 1877–78 to prevent the Russians capturing weapons stored inside. Fortunately, the kitchens where Ottoman palace cuisine was developed have been rebuilt and today an area that was once the sultans' private hunting reserve is home to a modern stadium where the famous Kırkpınar oil-wrestling festival (p151) is held.

Near the stadium, which is flanked by bronze sculptures of wrestling *başpehlivan* (champions), stands the Adalet Kasrı (Justice Hall; 1561), a stone tower with a conical roof that dates from the time of Süleyman the Magnificent (r 1520–66). In front of it are two square columns: on the Seng-i Hürmet (Stone of Respect) to the right, people would place petitions to the sultan, while the Seng-i İbret (Stone of Warning) on the left displayed the heads of high-court officers who had managed to anger the sultan.

WORTH A TRIP

SANCAKLAR MOSQUE

Cutting-edge architects are rarely given commissions to design religious buildings in modern-day Turkey, and as a result most contemporary mosques are uninspired pastiches of Ottoman-era structures. The extraordinary **Sancaklar Camii** (Sancaklar Mosque) near Büyükçekmece Lake in Thrace is a notable exception to this rule. Designed by Emre Arolat Architects and built between 2011 and 2012, its most striking feature is a subterranean interior that manages to be theatrical and deeply contemplative at the same time.

Other notable features of the mosque include a rectangular minaret, a minimalist *minber* (pulpit) and *mihrab* (niche indicating the direction of Mecca), a feature wall with illuminated calligraphy, and a terraced prayer space that follows the contours of the site.

To get here, take the O-3 (tolled) and E80 from İstanbul. Before reaching Büyükçekmece, exit towards Alkent. Turn right, pass through the Alkent 200 residences and make your way to the Toskana Vadisi Evleri housing development; the mosque is on the edge of this, opposite the Toskana Çarsısı (Market).

Behind the Adalet Kasrı is the small Fatih Köprüsü (Conqueror Bridge; 1452). Across it and on the right is a sombre Balkan Wars memorial; straight ahead and to the left are the scattered ruins of the Eski Sarayı.

To get here, walk north along Hükümet Caddesi and cross the Tunca River on Saraçhane Köprüsü (Saddler's Bridge; 1451); or head north on Mimar Sinan Caddesi and Saray Yolu, and cross the river on Kanumi/Saray Köprüsü (Kanumi/Palace Bridge), which was designed by Mimar Sinan in 1560. Alternatively, it's a scenic 1km walk along the road to the north of the river from the Sultan Beyazıt II Mosque complex.

🛏 Sleeping

Most of Edirne's budget and midrange hotels are on or near Maarif Caddesi.

Limon Hostel HOSTEL $
(📞 0545 271 0120; www.facebook.com/limonhostel; Türkocağı Arka Sokak 14; dm/s/d €10/15/20; 🛜) Simple rooms are enlivened by colourful decor and lots of light at this friendly hostel a short walk from good cafes and restaurants. The six-bed dorms have bunk beds and there are a few private rooms, too. Shared bathrooms are basic but clean. No heating or cooling, no lockers and no breakfast.

Sarı Pansiyon PENSION $
(📞 0284-212 4080; www.saripansiyon.com; Mehmet Karagöz Sokak 17; s/d without bathroom ₺70/120; @🛜) Named for its daffodil-yellow exterior, this unassuming place offers simple rooms with single beds and satellite TV.

Shared bathrooms are clean, with 24-hour hot water. The location is convenient but is opposite a school, so it can be noisy in the morning. Though the owner doesn't speak English, he's a whizz at using Google Translate to communicate.

Hotel Edirne Palace HOTEL $$
(📞 0284-214 7474; www.hoteledirnepalace.com; Vavlı Cami Sokak 4; s/d/tr €34/53/67; 🅿 ❄ @ 🛜) Tucked into the quiet backstreets below the Old Mosque, this modern business hotel offers comfortable, bright and impeccably clean rooms with a good range of amenities. The staff are extremely helpful, breakfast is better than average and there's free on-site parking. It's definitely the best sleeping option in the city centre.

Taşodalar Otel BOUTIQUE HOTEL $$$
(📞 0284-212 3529; www.tasodalar.com; Selimiye Arkası Hamam Sokak 3; s/d €50/90; ❄ @) The location next to Selimiye Mosque and the 14th-century Sultan Selim Saray Hamam is the most obvious reason to stay at this 15th-century Ottoman house. The shared spaces have an air of elegance, and the surprisingly spacious rooms are packed with antiques. The tea garden is pleasant and shaded, and an easy-going vibe is enhanced by the friendly manager.

🍴 Eating

A wide assortment of eateries lie along Saraçlar and Maarif Caddesis. Most of the riverside restaurants south of the centre are open only in summer and are often booked solid at weekends.

Balkan Piliç
TURKISH $

(☎0284-225 2155; Saraçlar Caddesi 14; portions ₺10-20; ⏰11am-4pm Mon-Sat) The *piliç* (chicken) roasting in the window signals the house speciality at this extremely popular *esnaf lokanta* (eatery serving ready-made food). Order a *porsyon* (portion) with a side order of *pilav* (plain rice or rice cooked with bulgur or lentils). Alternatively, choose from the daily changing array of meat and vegetable stews in the bain-marie.

Niyazi Usta
KEBAP $

(☎0284-213 3372; www.cigerciniyaziusta.com.tr; Alipaşa Ortakapı Caddesi 5/2; portions/half-portions ₺25/15; ⏰9am-9pm) This bright, modern and very friendly joint is perhaps the best place in town to try a *porsyon* of *tava ciğer* (thinly sliced calf's liver deep fried and eaten with crispy fried red chillies). Wash it down with a glass of *ayran* (yoghurt drink) or *şalgam* (sour turnip juice).

Köfteci Osman
TURKISH $$

(Kuyumcular Sokak; ciğer & köfte ₺30; ⏰11am-10pm) Recommended by locals for its tasty *tava ciğer* and *köfte* (meatballs), Osman has a convenient location a short walk from the city's main pedestrian street. Efficient waiters ensure tables turn over quickly and there are a few other branches scattered around central Edirne.

🍷 Drinking & Nightlife

In fine weather, the social scene in Edirne moves to the banks of the Tunca and Meriç Rivers, a 20- to 25-minute walk from the tourist office on Hürriyet Meydanı. To join the party, follow Saraçlar Caddesi past the stadium and cross the Tunca Köprüsü, an Ottoman stone humpback bridge dating back to 1615, and then the longer and extremely graceful Meriç Köprüsü, built in 1847.

Kahverengi
BAR

(☎0284-214 4210; Orhaniye Caddesi 14; ⏰10am-3am) Its laid-back ambience, pleasant outdoor deck and bargain snack-and-beer combo deals make Kahverengi popular with a youthful local clientele. Efes beer is the tipple of choice, but there are also imported beers and robust cocktails on offer. Pretty good music, too. In the adjacent laneway, a couple of other cafes and bars are also worth a look.

Çalgılı Meyhane
PUB

(☎0284-213 8945; Saraçlar Caddesi; ⏰9pm-late) A boozy atmosphere, friendly staff and live *halk meziği* (folk music) five days per week are the attractions at this traditional Turkish tavern. Basic *meyhane* (pub) food is available, but it's fine to stick with drinks only; a huge tankard of ice-cold Efes costs a mere ₺20. Be sure to tip the musicians before you leave.

🛍 Shopping

Ali Paşa Covered Bazaar
MARKET

(⏰7am-sunset) Mimar Sinan designed this long and highly atmospheric bazaar in 1569. Inside, Turkuaz (☎0284-214 1171; Ali Paşa Çarşısı 125) is one of the best spots in the city to buy *meyve sabunu* (fruit-shaped soap).

Keçecizade
FOOD & DRINKS

(☎0284-212 1261; www.kececizade.com; Saraçlar Caddesi 50; ⏰9am-8pm) Edirne's residents are particularly partial to sweet treats, as is evident by the huge number of *şekerlemes* (sweet shops) scattered through the city. Keçecizade is one of two popular local chains specialising in *lokum* (Turkish delight) and *badem ezmesi* (marzipan), and is a good place to sample both. There's another branch (☎0284-225 2681; Belediye Dükkanları/Eski Camii Karşısı 4; ⏰9am-8pm) opposite the Old Mosque.

ℹ Information

Tourist Office (☎0284-213 9208; edirne tourisminformation@gmail.com; Talat Paşa Caddesi; ⏰8.30am-5.30pm) Very helpful, with English-language brochures and a city map.

ℹ Getting There & Away

BUS & DOLMUŞ

Edirne's otogar (bus station) is 9km southeast of the centre on the access road to the E80. Buses 1, 3, 3A and 3BA travel between the otogar and *merkez*. A ticket costs ₺4 and can be purchased on board the bus. A taxi between the otogar and the city centre costs around ₺50.

Çanakkale (₺77, four hours) At least four buses daily on Truva (www.truvaturizm.com).

İstanbul (₺61, 2¾ hours) Frequent buses to the Büyük Otogar in Esenler on Metro and Nilüfer. Demand is high, so book ahead.

Kapıkule (₺4, 25 minutes) Dolmuşes run to this Bulgarian border crossing, 18km northwest, from a stop near the Şekerbank branch on Talat Paşa Caddesi.

THRACE WINE ROUTE

Vines have been cultivated in Thrace (Trakya) since ancient times. In his epic poem the *Iliad*, Homer wrote about the honey-sweet black wine produced here. Generations of local farmers have capitalised on the region's rich soil, flat geography and benign climate to grow grapes for wine production.

Inspired by Italy's Strade del Vino (Wine Roads) network, the Thrace Wine Route aims to entice visitors to Thracian vineyards, to enjoy local gastronomy, investigate regional heritage and admire the area's stunning scenery. The route passes through mountains, forests and a variety of micro-climates surrounded by three seas (the Sea of Marmara, the Aegean Sea and the Black Sea).

Guided tours (www.trakyabagrotasi.com) of vineyards are offered from the first 'bud breaks' in late April to the harvest in October. Book ahead for tours, vineyard restaurants and on-site accommodation. The highly regarded Arcadia Vineyards (☑0533 514 1490; www.arcadiavineyards.com; Köyü Lüleburgaz; ☺by appointment), an hour's drive southeast of Edirne, is worth a detour en route to/from İstanbul or the Gallipoli Peninsula.

Many vineyards along the wine route have restaurants and cafes where local wine and food are matched. Both Arcadia and Barbare (☑0212-257 0700; www.barbarewines. com; ☺by appointment) have worthwhile restaurants, and other vineyards offer summer dining. Booking ahead at vineyard restaurants is recommended.

Pazarkule The nearest Greek border post is 9km southwest of Edirne. Catch a dolmuş to Karaağac (₺4, 15 minutes) from the stop on the southern side of Talat Paşa Caddesi and tell the driver that you want to go to Pazarkule. Shuttles to/from the otogar also depart from here.

Sofia, Bulgaria (₺92, 5½ to 6½ hours) Five services daily on **Metro Turizm** (www.metro turizm.com.tr; Talat Paşa Caddesi; ☺10am-7pm). Also stop off at Plovdiv (₺81, 4½ hours). Booking a day ahead is recommended to confirm the Edirne departure location.

Tekirdağ

☑0282 / POP 183,000

Overlooking an attractive bay on the northern shore of the Sea of Marmara, Tekirdağ features a bustling waterfront area complete with parks, playgrounds and *çay bahçesi*. Though definitely not worth a trip in itself, the waterfront and a scattering of timber houses dating from the 18th century make the town a reasonable pit stop en route to/from Greece or the Gallipoli Peninsula. Nearby are the vineyards of the Thrace Wine Route, and the city also hosts a few good museums.

◉ Sights

Tekirdağ Archaeological & Ethnographic Museum MUSEUM

(Tekirdağ Arkeoloji ve Etnografya Müzesi; ☑0282-261 2082; Rakoczi Caddesi 1; ☺9am-5pm Tue-Sun) FREE Housed in the Tekirdağ Vali

Konağı (Governor's Mansion), a fine Ottoman Revival–style building dating from 1927, this modest museum gives a fascinating glimpse into the history of Thrace. The most striking exhibit is the display of marble furniture and silver plates from the Naip tumulus (burial mound) dating back to the late 4th century BC; this would have formed a celebratory setting for the serving of wine.

Rákóczi Museum MUSEUM

(Rakoczi Müzesi; ☑0282-263 8577; Hikmet Çevik Sokak 21; ₺5; ☺9am-noon & 1-5pm Tue-Sun) This house museum is a shrine to Prince Ferenc (Francis) II Rákóczi (1676–1735), who led the first Hungarian uprising against the Habsburgs between 1703 and 1711. Forced into exile, the Transylvanian was given asylum by Sultan Ahmet III in 1720 and lived in this pretty 18th-century timber *konak* (mansion) for a number of years. The *konak's* interior fittings are good-quality reproductions, as the originals were returned to Kassa in Hungary (now Košice in Slovakia). Displays include portraits, weapons and letters.

⊨ Sleeping & Eating

Yat Hotel HOTEL $$

(☑0282-261 1054; www.yathotel.com; Yalı Caddesi 21; d ₺300-420; P❉☎) This 1970s-era block opposite the waterfront claims three-star status and has had a recent renovation to boost these claims. Front rooms can be noisy, but the quieter and slightly cheaper options at the rear are smaller and darker. Handily close to good restaurants.

Özcanlar
KÖFTE $$
(☏ 0282-263 4088; www.ozcanlarkofte.com; Liman Karşısı 68, Atatürk Bulvarı; köfte ₺20-35; ☉10am-10pm) The most popular of various *köfte* (meatball) restaurants overlooking the waterfront, Özcanlar has been serving up a limited range of soups, meat dishes and local desserts since 1953. Tables on the outdoor terrace fill fast, as the cafeteria-style dining room can be noisy.

❶ Getting There & Away

The otogar is located 1km northeast of the main waterfront promenade. Arriving by bus from İstanbul (₺30, 2½ hours) or Edirne (₺20, two hours), it's an easy walk downhill on Çiftlikönü Caddesi to the waterfront. Buses to/from Eceabat (₺55 three hours) and Çanakkale (₺50, 3½ hours) travel via both the otogar and the waterfront and can be flagged down along Atatürk Caddesi.

Dolmuşes travel throughout the town and its outlying suburbs. Tickets cost ₺4 and can be purchased from the driver.

Gallipoli Peninsula

☑ 0286
Today, the Gallipoli (Gelibolu) Peninsula battlefields are protected landscapes covered in pine forests and fringed by idyllic beaches and coves. However, the bloody battles fought here in 1915 are still alive in Turkish and foreign memories and hold important places in the Turkish, Australian and New Zealand national narratives. Australians and New Zealanders view the peninsula, now protected as the Gallipoli Campaign Historic Site, as a place of pilgrimage, and visit in their tens of thousands each year; they are outnumbered by Turks who, drawn by the legend of the courageous 57th regiment and its commander, Mustafa Kemal (the future Atatürk), also travel here in ever-increasing numbers to pay their respects.

History

Less than 1500m wide at its narrowest point, the Strait of Çanakkale (Çanakkale Boğazı), better known to English-speakers as the Dardanelles or the Hellespont, has always offered the best opportunity for travellers – and armies – to cross between Europe and Asia Minor.

King Xerxes I of Persia forded the strait with a bridge of boats in 481 BC, as did Alexander the Great a century and a half later. In Byzantine times, it was the first line of defence for Constantinople, but by 1402 the strait was under the control of the Ottoman Sultan Beyazıt I (r 1390–1402), which allowed his armies to conquer the Balkans. Beyazıt's great-grandson Mehmet the Conqueror fortified the strait as part of his grand plan to conquer Constantinople (1453), building eight separate fortresses. The strait remained fortified after he defeated the Byzantines, signalling to foreign powers that this strategic sea passage was firmly in Ottoman hands.

The Ottomans remained neutral at the outbreak of WWI, but in October 1914 they joined the Central Powers and closed the Dardanelles, blocking the Allies' major supply route between Britain, France and their ally Russia. In response, the First Lord of the British Admiralty, Winston Churchill, decided that it was vitally important that the Allies take control of both the strait and the Bosphorus, which meant capturing İstanbul. His Allied partners agreed, and in March 1915 a strong Franco-British fleet attempted to force the Dardanelles. It was defeated on 18 March in what the Turks commemorate as the Çanakkale Naval Victory (Çanakkale Deniz Zaferi).

Undaunted, the Allies devised another strategy to capture the strait. On 25 April, British, Australian, New Zealand and Indian troops landed on the Gallipoli Peninsula; in a diversionary manoeuvre, French troops landed at Kum Kale near Çanakkale. The landings on the peninsula were a disaster for the Allies, with the British 29th Division suffering horrendous losses at Cape Hellas and the Anzac troops landing at a relatively inaccessible beach north of their planned landing point near Gaba Tepe (Kabatepe). Rather than overcoming the Turkish defences and swiftly making their way across the peninsula to the strait (the planned objective), the Allies were hemmed in by their enemy, forced to dig trenches for protection and stage bloody assaults to try and improve their position. After nine months of ferocious combat but little headway, the Allied forces withdrew in December 1915 and January 1916.

The outcome at Gallipoli was partly due to bad luck and leadership on the Allied side, and partly due to reinforcements to the

Turkish side brought in by General Liman von Sanders. But a crucial element in the defeat was that the Allied troops landed in a sector where they faced Lieutenant Colonel Mustafa Kemal. The future Atatürk had managed to guess the Allied battle plan correctly when his commanders did not, and he stalled the invasion in spite of bitter fighting that wiped out his regiment. Kemal commanded in full view of his troops throughout the campaign, miraculously escaping death several times. Legend has it that at one point a piece of shrapnel hit him in the chest but was stopped by his pocket watch. His brilliant performance made him a folk hero and paved the way for his promotion to *paşa* (general).

The Gallipoli campaign – in Turkish, the Çanakkale Savaşı (Battle of Çanakkale) – resulted in a total of more than half a million casualties, of which 130,000 were deaths. The British Empire saw the loss of some 36,000 lives, including 8700 Australians and 2700 New Zealanders. French casualties numbered 47,000 (making up over half the entire French contingent); 8800 Frenchmen died. Half of the 500,000 Ottoman troops were decimated, with almost 86,700 killed.

⊙ Sights

The **Gallipoli Campaign Historic Site** protects 40 Allied war cemeteries at Gallipoli, and at least 20 Turkish ones. The principal battles took place on the peninsula's western shore, around Anzac Cove (Anzac Koyu), 12km northwest of Eceabat, and in the hills east of the cove. If you wish to identify a particular grave when you are here, the Commonwealth War Graves Commission website (www.cwgc.org) is a useful resource.

There are several different signage systems in use: Turkish highway signs; national-park administration signs; and wooden signs posted by the Commonwealth War Graves Commission. This can lead to confusion because the foreign and Turkish troops used different names for the battlefields, and the park signs don't necessarily agree with those erected by the highway department. We've used both English and Turkish names.

⊙ Northern Peninsula

About 3km north of Eceabat, the road to Kabatepe heads west into the park.

Çanakkale Epic Promotion Centre

If visiting Gallipoli independently, it's a good idea to start your tour at the **Çanakkale Epic Promotion Centre** (Çanakkale Destanı Tanıtım Merkezi; ☑ 0286-810 0050; http://canakkaledestani.milliparklar.gov.tr; simulation experience & museum adult/child ₺15/free, museum only adult/child ₺5/free; ⊙ 9am-4pm), roughly 1km east of the village of Kabatepe. It comprises a two-floor museum and 11 gallery rooms in which high-tech 3D simulation equipment takes the viewer on a historical journey through the Gallipoli naval and land campaigns, taking a predominantly Turkish point of view. Individual headsets allow visitors to choose their presentation language. Note that the simulations are extremely loud, and are not suitable for young children. Bookings advisable.

Kabatepe Village

The small harbour here was probably the object of the Allied landing on 25 April 1915. In the predawn dark it is possible that uncharted currents swept the Allies' landing craft northwards to the steep cliffs of Arıburnu – a bit of bad luck that may have sealed the campaign's fate from the start. Today there's little in Kabatepe except for a camping ground, a cafe and a dock for ferries to Gökçeada island. Just north of the promontory is the stretch of sand known as **Brighton Beach**, a favourite swimming spot for Anzac troops during the campaign. Today, it's the only officially sanctioned swimming spot on the peninsula.

Anzac Cove

A short drive north along the coastal road from Brighton Beach takes you to **Beach (Hell Spit) Cemetery**. Before it, a rough track cuts inland to Lone Pine (1.5km) and, across the road from the car park at the cemetery, another track heads inland to **Shrapnel Valley Cemetery** and **Plugge's Plateau Cemetery**.

Following the road for another 400m from the turn-off, or taking the footpath from Beach Cemetery past the WWII bunker, brings you to **Anzac Cove**. This now extremely narrow stretch of sand beneath and just south of the Arıburnu cliffs was where the ill-fated Allied landing began on 25 April 1915. Ordered to advance inland, the Allied forces at first gained some ground but later in the day met with fierce resistance from the Ottoman forces under the leadership of Mustafa Kemal, who had foreseen where

LOCAL KNOWLEDGE

WALKING THE BATTLEFIELDS

The best way to explore the battlefields is undoubtedly in the footsteps of the original combatants. Walking the hills and gullies of this landscape offers a glimpse into the physical challenges that faced troops in 1915. It also allows you to enjoy the wonderful views and landscape of the national park.

The Australian Goverrnment's Department of Veterans Affairs website (www.anzac site.gov.au) includes details of a one-day walk exploring the main area held by Anzac troops during the campaign. This starts in North Beach, includes sites such as Anzac Cove and Lone Pine, and ends on the high ground near the Nek and Walker's Ridge. Walk instructions, downloadable audio commentary and plenty of historical information is available on the website. For a New Zealand perspective, see www.ngatapuwae.govt.nz for audio guides, maps and an excellent downloadable smartphone app that really brings to life the history of the battlefields.

Crowded House Tours (p163) offers several walking tours. Expert guides lead a number of trails including a one-day tour of the battlefields of the Anzac sector; a half-day 'New Zealand Trail' following the advance of NZ troops to Chunuk Bair; and a full-day walk around the Helles sector following the paths of British troops. Guides will try to accommodate special interests, including visiting particular graves. The cost depends on how many walkers are in the group and includes lunch and transport to/from the start and finish points from Eceabat and Çanakkale.

Walkers should be sure to bring sturdy shoes, as the terrain can be steep and difficult in parts. Hats and sunblock are essential in the warmer months; a rain jacket is useful at other times of the year. Don't forget water and food.

they would land and disobeyed an order to send his troops further south to Cape Helles.

In August of the same year, a major offensive was staged in an attempt to advance beyond the beach up to the ridges of Chunuk Bair and Sarı Bair (Yellow Slope). It resulted in the battles at Lone Pine and the Nek, the bloodiest of the campaign, but little progress was made.

Another 300m along is the **Arıburnu Sahil Anıtı** (Arıburnu Coastal Memorial), a moving Turkish monument inscribed with Atatürk's famous words of peace and reconciliation, spoken in 1934:

'To us there is no difference between the Johnnies and the Mehmets...You, the mothers, who sent your sons from faraway countries, wipe away your tears; your sons are now lying in our bosom...After having lost their lives in this land, they have become our sons as well.' After restoration in 2017, it was reinstated in its original form.

Just beyond the memorial is **Arıburnu Cemetery** and, 750m further north, **Canterbury Cemetery**. Between them is the **Anzac Commemorative Site** (Anzac Tören Alanı) at North Beach, where dawn services are held on Anzac Day (25 April). This is where the much-photographed Anzac monument is located. From it, look up towards the cliffs and you can easily make out the

image in the sandy cliff face nicknamed 'the Sphinx' by young diggers (Aussie infantrymen) who had arrived from Australia via Egypt.

Less than 1km further along the seaside road, on the right-hand side, are the cemeteries at **No 2 Outpost**, set back inland from the road, and **New Zealand No 2 Outpost**. The **Embarkation Pier Cemetery** is 200m beyond the New Zealand No 2 Outpost on the left.

Towards Lone Pine

Returning to the Çanakkale Epic Promotion Centre, around 1km east of Kabatepe, you should then follow the signs to Lone Pine, 3.5km uphill.

En route, the first monument you'll come to is **Mehmetçiğe Derin Saygı Anıtı**, on the right-hand side of the road about 1km from the junction. It's dedicated to 'Mehmetçik' (Little Mehmet, the Turkish 'tommy' or 'digger'), who carried a Kiwi soldier to safety.

Another 1200m brings you to the **Kanlısırt Kitabesi** (Bloody Ridge Inscription), a memorial that describes the battle of Lone Pine from the Turkish viewpoint.

Lone Pine

Lone Pine (Kanlısırt), 400m uphill from Kanlısırt Kitabesi, is perhaps the most moving of all the Anzac cemeteries. Australian forces

Gallipoli (Gelibolu) Peninsula

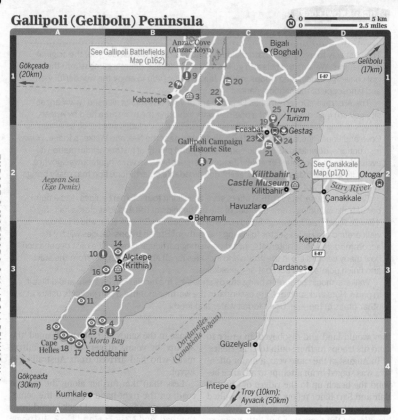

See Gallipoli Battlefields Map (p162)

See Çanakkale Map (p170)

captured the Turkish positions here on the afternoon of 6 August 1915. During the battle, which was staged in an area the size of a soccer field, more than 4000 men died and thousands more were injured. The trees that once shaded the cemetery were swept away by a forest fire in 1994, leaving only one: a lone pine planted from the seed of the original solitary tree that stood here at the beginning of the battle and gave the battlefield its name.

Explore the tombstones, which carry touching epitaphs. The cemetery includes the grave of the youngest soldier to die here, a boy of just 14. You can view the remains of trenches just behind the parking area.

From here, it's another 3km up the one-way road to the New Zealand Memorial at Chunuk Bair.

Johnston's Jolly to Quinn's Post

Progressing up the hill from Lone Pine, the ferocity of the battles becomes more apparent; at some points the trenches are only a few metres apart. The order to attack meant certain death to those who followed it, and virtually all did as they were ordered on both sides.

The road marks what was the thin strip of no-man's land between the two sides' trenches, as it continues to the cemeteries Johnston's Jolly (Kırmızı Sırt), 200m on the right beyond Lone Pine, Courtney's & Steele's Post, roughly the same distance again, and Quinn's Post, 100m uphill.

57 Alay & Kesikdere Cemeteries

One kilometre uphill from Lone Pine is the cemetery (57 Alay Şehitliği) and monument for the Ottoman 57th Regiment, which was led by Mustafa Kemal and was almost completely wiped out on 25 April while halting the Anzac attempt to advance to the high ground of Chunuk Bair.

The statue of an old man showing his granddaughter the battle sites represents

Gallipoli (Gelibolu) Peninsula

Hüseyin Kaçmaz, who fought in the Balkan Wars, the Gallipoli campaign and at the fateful Battle of Dumlupınar during the War of Independence. He died in 1994 aged 111, the last surviving Turkish Gallipoli veteran.

Down some steps from here, the **Kesikdere Cemetery** contains the remains of another 1115 Turkish soldiers from the 57th and other regiments.

Sergeant Mehmet Monument & The Nek

About 100m uphill past the 57th Alay Cemetery, a road goes west to the **Sergeant Mehmet Monument**, dedicated to the Turkish sergeant who fought with rocks and his fists after he ran out of ammunition, and the **Nek**. It was at the Nek on the morning of 7 August 1915 that the 8th (Victorian) and 10th (Western Australian) Regiments of the third Light Horse Brigade vaulted out of their trenches into withering fire and were cut down before they reached the enemy line, an episode immortalised in Peter Weir's 1981 film *Gallipoli*.

Baby 700 Cemetery & Mesudiye Topu

About 200m uphill on the right from the access road to the Nek is the **Baby 700 Cemetery** and the Ottoman cannon called the **Mesudiye Topu**. Named after its height above sea level in feet, Baby 700 was the limit of the initial attack, and the graves here are mostly dated 25 April.

Düztepe & Talat Göktepe Monuments

The **Düztepe Monument**, uphill from the Baby 700 Cemetery, marks the spot where

the Ottoman 10th Regiment held the line. Views of the Dardanelles and the surrounding countryside are superb. About 1km further on is a **monument** to a more recent casualty of Gallipoli: Talat Göktepe, chief director of the Çanakkale Forestry District, who died fighting the devastating forest fire of 1994.

Chunuk Bair & Around

At the top of the hill, some 500m past the Talat Göktepe Monument, a right turn at the T-junction takes you east to the **Suyatağı Anıtı** (Watercourse Monument). Having stayed awake for four days and nights, Mustafa Kemal spent the night of 9 August here, directing part of the counterattack to the Allied offensive.

Back at the T-junction, turn left for Chunuk Bair (known as Conk Bayiri in Turkish), the first objective of the Allied landing in April 1915, and now the site of the **Chunuk Bair New Zealand Cemetery & Memorial** (Conkbayırı Yeni Zelanda Mezarlığı ve Anıtı).

As the Anzac troops made their way up the scrub-covered slopes on 25 April, Mustafa Kemal brought up the 57th Infantry Regiment and gave them his famous order: 'I am not ordering you to attack, I am ordering you to die. In the time it takes us to die, other troops and commanders will arrive to take our places.'

Chunuk Bair was also at the heart of the struggle for the peninsula from 6 to 10 August 1915, when some 16,000 men died on this ridge. The Allied attack from 6 to 7 August, which included the New Zealand

Gallipoli Battlefields

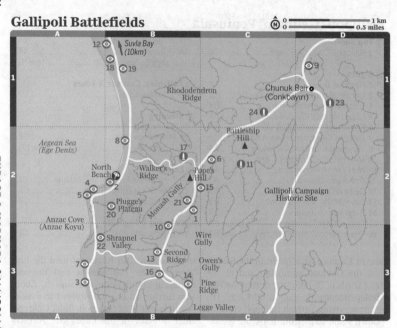

Gallipoli Battlefields

Mounted Rifle Brigade and a Maori contingent, was deadly, but the attack on the following day was of a ferocity which, according to Mustafa Kemal, 'could scarcely be described'.

◎ Southern Peninsula

From Kabatepe, it's about 12km to the village of Alçıtepe, formerly known as Krithia. A few metres north of the village's main intersection is the **Salim Mutlu War Museum** (Salim Mutlu Müzesi; ₺2; ◎8am-8pm), a hodgepodge of rusty finds from the battlefields, giving a sense of just how much artillery was fired. At the main intersection, a sign points right to the Turkish **Sargı Yeri Cemetery**, approximately 1.5km away, with its enormous statue of 'Mehmet' and solid **Nuri Yamut Monument**. Take the first left for the **Twelve Tree Copse Cemetery**, 2km away, and the **Pink Farm Cemetery**, 3km away.

From Pink Farm, the road passes the **Lancashire Landing Cemetery**. Turn right 1km before **Seddülbahir village** for the **Cape**

Helles British Memorial, a commanding stone obelisk honouring the 20,000-plus Britons and Australians who perished in this area and have no known graves. The initial Allied attack was two-pronged: in addition to the landing at Anzac Cove in the north, there was a landing on 'V' Beach at the tip of the peninsula. Yahya Çavuş Şehitliği (Sergeant Yahya Cemetery) remembers the Turkish officer who led the resistance to the Allied landing here, and who caused heavy casualties. 'V' Beach Cemetery is visible 500m downhill.

North of Seddülbahir, the road divides; the left fork leads to the Skew Bridge Cemetery, followed by the Redoubt Cemetery. Turn right and head east, following signs for Abide or Çanakkale Şehitleri Anıtı at Morto Bay, and you'll pass the French War Memorial & Cemetery. French troops, including a North African regiment, successfully attacked Kumkale on the Asian shore in March 1915, then re-embarked and landed in support of their British comrades-in-arms at Cape Helles, where they were virtually wiped out. The rarely visited French cemetery is extremely moving, with rows of metal crosses and five white-concrete ossuaries each containing the bones of 3000 soldiers.

The Çanakkale Şehitleri Anıtı (Çanakkale Martyrs' Memorial), also known as the Abide (Monument), is a gigantic stone structure that commemorates all the Turkish soldiers who fought and died at Gallipoli.

☞ Tours

Kenan Çelik TOURS
(☑0286-217 7468, 0532 738 6675; www.kcelik.com; half-/full-day small-group tours €120/150) One of Turkey's foremost experts on the Gallipoli campaign, Kenan Çelik has retired from his position as lecturer in English language and literature at Çanakkale Onsekiz Mart University and now conducts private tours of the battlefields. He offers full-day tours concentrating on significant Anzac or Turkish sites, and can also cover Suvla Bay and Cape Helles.

There's an extra charge of €50/100 if transport is required.

Crowded House Tours TOURS
(☑0286-814 1565; www.crowdedhousegallipoli.com; Zubeyde Hanim Meydani 28) Based at spacious premises right on the Eceabat waterfront, this is the most professional of the tour companies operating on the Gallipoli

Peninsula and is heartily recommended, especially if you can join a tour led by the affable and extremely knowledgeable Bülent 'Bill' Yılmaz Korkmaz. Its core offering is a half-day tour of the main Anzac battlefields and cemeteries (€25).

Other options include a morning tour of Cape Helles (€35), a morning snorkelling excursion around a WWI shipwreck at Anzac Cove (€20), an afternoon tour by boat of the Anzac landing sites (₺55), and two-day Gallipoli and Troy packages from İstanbul (€110 without accommodation).

Bülent Korkmaz also leads walking tours of the battlefields.

TJ's Tours TOURS
(☑0286-814 3121; www.anzacgallipolitours.com; TJ's Hotel, Cumhuriyet Caddesi 5/A; ◷9am-7pm Mon-Sat, 1-6pm Sun) Very experienced tour company offering a variety of options including daily departures from Eceabat to the Gallipoli battlefields (per person €39) and Troy (per person €39). Also half-day snorkelling excursions to see a WWI landing craft (per person €30) and scuba diving around battleships (per person €75). Note the snorkelling involves a 150m swim from the beach to the site.

Hassle Free Travel Agency TOURS
(☑0286-213 5969; www.anzachouse.com; Cumhuriyet Meydanı 59) Operating from its base at Anzac House Hostel in Çanakkale, this long-standing company offers a half-day tour of the Anzac battlefields and cemeteries (€40 including lunch) and a package including a boat trip to the Anzac landing beaches, a snorkel at Anzac Cove and a visit to the Gallipoli Simulation Centre (€50). It also offers Gallipoli and Troy tours with onward transport to İstanbul or Selçuk/Ephesus.

⭐ Festivals & Events

Çanakkale Naval Victory Day CULTURAL
The Turkish WWI naval victory in the Dardanelles is commemorated in Çanakkale on 18 March. Politicians' speeches and plenty of flag-waving are the main features of the commemoration.

Anzac Day CULTURAL
(◷25 Apr) A sombre mood prevails at the dawn service marking the anniversary of the WWI landing of the Australian and New Zealand Army Corps (Anzacs) at Gallipoli, which attracts up to ten thousand travellers from Australia and New Zealand each year.

Gallipoli Battlefields

Pilgrimage is the oldest – and often the most rewarding – form of travel. In Turkey there are a number of ancient pilgrimage destinations, but only one dates from modern times and draws both local and international visitors: the pine-scented peninsula where the bloody Gallipoli campaign of WWI unfolded.

Cemeteries

There were almost 130,000 Turkish and Allied deaths at Gallipoli and the battlefields are home to more than 60 meticulously maintained cemeteries. Places for contemplation and commemoration include the Allied cemeteries at Beach (Hell Spit), Arıburnu (Anzac Cove), Lone Pine, Chunuk Bair and V Beach; and the Turkish 57 Alay (57th Regiment) and Kesikdere cemeteries.

Memorials

Gallipoli is a place where bravery and sacrifice are honoured and where the narratives of modern nations have been forged. The most famous memorial on the peninsula is the Arıburnu Sahil Anıtı (Arıburnu Coastal Memorial), which records Atatürk's famous words of peace and reconciliation between the 'Johnnies' and the 'Mehmets'. Other memorials include the stone obelisk at Cape Helles that commemorates the 20,000-plus Britons and Australians who perished on the southern peninsula and have no known graves.

Landing Beaches

Few places are so closely associated with national identity as Anzac Cove, where Australian and New Zealand troops landed on 25 April 1915. Today, the annual Anzac Day dawn service is held at nearby North Beach. Casualties at Anzac Cove were relatively minor, as opposed to those incurred on the five beaches at Cape Helles – most notably V and W Beaches – where thousands of deaths occurred.

1. Mehmetçiğe Derin Saygı Anıtı (p159) memorial by Tankut Öktem 2. Arıburnu Cemetery (p159) 3. Anzac Cove (p158) 4. Cape Helles British Memorial (p162) by Sir John James Burnet

SALVATOR BARKIZ/GETTY IMAGES ©

NEJDET DUZEN/SHUTTERSTOCK ©

🛌 Sleeping & Eating

★ Gallipoli Houses   BOUTIQUE HOTEL $$$

(☏ 0286-814 2650; www.thegallipolihouses.com; Kocadere; s €50-70, d €60-80; ☺ mid-Mar–mid-Nov; P ❄ ☎) Located in a farming village within the Gallipoli Historical National Park, this is an excellent option when visiting the peninsula. Many of the lovely rooms have outdoor areas perfect for relaxing after visiting the battlefields and the well-travelled owners are excellent hosts. There's usually a minimum stay of two nights and children under the age of 10 are not accommodated.

Rooms are spacious and comfortable, and there is a pleasant bar area where guests can enjoy a drink and chat before dinner (€17.50). Eric, the Belgian co-host, and his Turkish wife, Ozlem, are equally at ease preparing home-cooked Turkish cuisine as tailoring a battlefields itinerary. Lunch boxes are also available.

Doyuranlar Aile Çay ve Gözleme   TURKISH $

(☏ 0286-814 1652; mains ₺10-15; ☺ from 7.30am; ☎) The village women in charge of this roadside eatery and *çay bahçesi* midway between Eceabat and Kabatepe serve up huge breakfast platters, *köfte* and *menemen* (eggs scrambled with white cheese, tomatoes and peppers). Regulars opt for the house speciality: crisp and delicious *gözleme* (stuffed flatbreads) washed down with a glass of *ayran*.

ⓘ Information

Visit Gallipoli (www.anzacportal.dva.gov.au) Full of useful information.

ⓘ Getting There & Away

The most convenient bases for visiting the battlefields are Eceabat on the western shore of the Dardanelles, and Çanakkale on the eastern shore, accessed via car ferry (25 minutes) from Eceabat.

Many tour companies offer one-day tours from İstanbul that involve 10 to 12 hours of travel time in a minibus. We do not recommend these as they are exhausting and we have received reports of drivers exceeding speed limits and driving dangerously so as to minimise time on the road.

ⓘ Getting Around

With your own transport you can easily tour the northern battlefields in a day. Cars can be rented in Çanakkale and Eceabat. Trying to do both the northern and southern parts of the peninsula is possible within one day, provided you get a very early start. Without your own transport, a guided tour is the most time-efficient means of exploring the area.

A taxi between Kabatepe and Eceabat will cost approximately ₺80.

DOLMUŞ

The only regular public-transport options on the peninsula are the dolmuş between Eceabat and Kilitbahir (₺4, every 45 minutes) and the dolmuş between Eceabat and Kabatepe (₺7, 15 minutes). The latter meets ferries from Gökçeada year-round and makes more frequent runs in the summer months. There are usually a couple of dolmuşes each day from Kilitbahir to Seddülbahir and Alçıtepe, but the timetable changes frequently.

Eceabat

☏ 0286 / POP 6000

Eceabat (ancient Maydos) is an unremarkable waterfront town on the southern shore of the Dardanelles. It is notable only for its proximity to the main Gallipoli battlefields and for its ferry link to Çanakkale. Ferries dock by the main square (Cumhuriyet Meydanı), which is ringed by hotels, restaurants, ATMs, a post office, bus-company offices, and dolmuş and taxi stands.

🛌 Sleeping

TJ's Hotel   HOTEL $

(☏ 0286-814 3121; www.tjshotel.com; Cumhuriyet Caddesi 5/A; per person €12-25; ❄ ☎) A convenient location one block from the harbour makes TJ's a favourite with groups visiting Gallipoli from İstanbul. Shared twin and triple rooms have private bathrooms and larger rooms – some with balconies – are very popular with Anzac Day TV crews from Australia. Turkish-Australian owner TJ is an experienced guide and runs excellent tours of the battlefields (p163).

★ Hotel Casa Villa   BOUTIQUE HOTEL $$

(☏ 0286-814 1320; www.otelcasavilla.com; Çamburnu Sokak 75; r ₺300; P ❄ ☎) Casa Villa maximises its hilltop location above Eceabat with excellent views from elegantly decorated rooms; plenty of outdoor furniture makes it easy to enjoy the ocean and town vistas. Breakfast – served in a sunny glass conservatory – is one of western Turkey's best; treats such as freshly cooked *sigara böreği* (deep-fried pastries with cheese) and omelettes are offered most mornings.

KİLİTBAHİR

Kilitbahir (Lock of the Sea), a tiny fishing harbour 4.5km south from Eceabat on the Gallipoli Peninsula, is dominated by a massive fortress that was opened as an excellent museum in 2019. A huge image of a soldier stands on the hill nearby, with text that reads: *'Dur yolcu. Bilmeden gelip bastyöyn bu toprak bir devrin battyöy yerdir'* ('Traveller halt! The soil you tread once witnessed the end of an era').

Sprawling **Kilitbahir Castle Museum** (Kilitbahir Kale Müzesi; admission ₺15, audio guides ₺5; ⏱9am-5pm Sep-Apr, to 7pm May-Aug) was originally built by Mehmet the Conqueror in 1452 and given a grand seven-storey interior tower a century later by Süleyman the Magnificent. It and Çimenlik Kalesi in Çanakkale ensured the Ottomans retained control of the Dardenelles. It's now a museum focussing on Ottoman and maritime history. Don't miss ascending the interior tower for views of the storied waterway. A studio with VR headsets allows less mobile travellers to still experience the castle's interior and exhibitions.

Getting There & Away

Gestaş operates a ferry service to/from Çanakkale (per person/car ₺3/62, 20 minutes) every 30 to 60 minutes between 7am and 11.30pm. There are dolmuşes every 45 minutes (₺4, 10 minutes) from Eceabat.

Hotel Crowded House HOTEL **$$**
(☑0286-810 0041; www.hotelcrowdedhouse.com; Hüseyin Avni Sokak 4; s/d/tr €23/34/42; ❄🖳) Conveniently located near the ferry port, Crowded House offers basic rooms with comfortable beds and clean bathrooms, plus a simple breakfast.

✖ Eating & Drinking

A pleasant option is to catch a dolmuş to nearby Kilitbahir and dine in the simple seafood eateries huddled around the port's compact fishing harbour.

Liman Balık Restaurant SEAFOOD **$$**
(Liman Fish Restaurant; ☑0286-814 2755; www.limanrestaurant.net; İstiklal Caddesi 67; mezes ₺12-20, mains ₺25-50; ⏱noon-10pm; 🖳) Next to the water (*'liman'* means 'harbour'), this laid-back place is particularly pleasant on summer nights, when seats on the outdoor terrace are highly prized (book ahead). The food, service and wine list are unexpectedly impressive. Choose mezes from the refrigerated cabinet and be sure to inspect the catch of the day before ordering your fish.

★ Kilye Suvla Lokanta TURKISH **$$$**
(☑0286-814 1000; www.suvla.com.tr; Suvla Winery, Çınarlıdere Mevkii 11; mains ₺40-84, pizza ₺42-55; ⏱lokanta noon-3pm, tasting room & concept store 8.30am-5.30pm; ✍) Suvla's 60 hectares of certified organic vineyards are located near Kabatepe on the opposite side of the peninsula, but its winery, complete with an ultra-stylish garden restaurant, tasting room

and produce store, is on Eceabat's outskirts. Worth a dedicated visit, its menu features simple modern twists on Turkish classics such as *köfte,* plus fresh salads, pastas and Turkish-style pizzas.

Suvla produces wines in five categories, ranging from its base tipples, the Kabatepe *kırmızı* (a red wine), *beyaz* (white) and blush, to a mightily impressive grand reserve cabernet sauvignon and Roussane Marsanne. All can be sampled in the winery's tasting room (tastings ₺35 to ₺80) or in the restaurant, which features a huge glass wall looking into an ageing room that's full of oak barrels.

The winery is at the end of a road off Atatürk Caddesi, in the southwestern corner of town.

Boomerang Bar BAR
(Cumhuriyet Caddesi 102; ⏱4pm-late) Run by Mersut, a rakı (aniseed brandy)–loving local who revels in his role as host, the Boomerang is a kitschy Aussie- and Kiwi-themed beach shack that somehow makes the perfect place for a beer after touring the Gallipoli battlefields. It's at the town's northern entrance. Free camping is unofficially available on a nearby stretch of rocky beach.

❶ Getting There & Away

BOAT

Gestaş (☑444 0752; www.gdu.com.tr) ferries cross the Dardanelles between Eceabat and Çanakkale in both directions (per person/car

₺4.50/67, 25 minutes) every hour on the hour between 7am and midnight, and roughly every two hours after that. The ticket box is right next to where passengers embark.

Bus tickets can be purchased from the **Truva Turizm** (☑ 0286-814 1110; www.truvaturizm. com; Cumhuriyet Meydanı; ☺ 8am-10pm) office opposite the port or from the Metro office in Çanakkale.

BUS

Long-haul buses stop in Cumhuriyet Meydanı, in front of the ferry port. Bus services run to İstanbul: those to the Büyük Otogar in Esenler leave regularly (₺88, five hours); those to Ataşehir Otogar near Kadıköy on the Asian side are less frequent. Truva Turizm offers the best service.

❶ Getting Around

Dolmuşes run to Kilitbahir every 45 minutes (₺47, 10 minutes). In summer, regular dolmuşes run to Kabatepe ferry dock (₺7, 15 minutes); in winter they only take the ferries. If asked, the dolmuş will drop you at the Çanakkale Epic Promotion Centre, 750m southeast of the bottom of the road up to Lone Pine and Chunuk Bair.

Çanakkale

☑ 0286 / POP 133,000

If you thought Çanakkale was worth visiting only as a launching point for Gallipoli's battlefields, think again. The Çanakkale Onsekiz Mart University endows this small city with a sizeable student population that loves to eat, drink and party in the atmospheric cobbled lanes around the *saat kulesi* (clock tower; 1897) and along the sweeping *kordon* (waterfront promenade).

The undisputed hub of the region, Çanakkale is replete with mythological associations. It was from the ancient town of Abydos immediately north that Leander swam across the Hellespont every night to see his love, Hero; and it was in the Dardanelles that Helle, the daughter of Athamas, was drowned in the legend of the Golden Fleece, giving the waterway its ancient name. Close by are the remnants of ancient Troy, immortalised by Homer in his epic poem the *Iliad*. Opened in late 2018, the Museum of Troy is an essential destination.

◉ Sights

Dardanelles Straits

Naval Command Museum MUSEUM
(Çanakkale Boğaz Komutanlığı Deniz Müzesi; ☑ 0286-213 1730; Çimenlik Sokak; ₺10;

☺ 9am-noon & 1.30-5pm Tue-Sun) At the southern end of the *kordon,* a park lies dotted with guns, cannons and military artefacts. Near the park entrance is this small military museum containing exhibits on the Gallipoli battles and some war relics. Museum ticket-holders can also board the replica of the Nusrat mine-layer, which played a significant role in the Çanakkale Naval Victory, and visit Çimenlik Kalesi (built by order of Mehmet the Conqueror in 1452) located behind the park.

Kent Müzesi MUSEUM
(City Museum; ☑ 0286-214 3417; www.canakkale kentmuzesi.com; Fetvane Sokak 31; ☺ 10am-7pm Tue-Sun Apr-Aug, to 5pm Sep-May) **FREE** The lives of Çanakkale's residents since Ottoman times are the focus of this small museum, which has drawn on oral histories for the content of many of its display panels. There are photographs, newspaper articles and a few artefacts on show. Ask for the English-translation texts to get the most out of the exhibitions.

Çanakkale'nin Evlatları MUSEUM
(Sons of Çanakkale; www.canakkaleninevlatlari. com; ☺ 10.30am-7pm) **FREE** Located right on Çanakkale's waterfront, this compact installation combines black and white battle footage and contemporary interviews to tell the story of the 1915 Gallipoli campaign from both sides. Interactive maps also offer excellent insights into the conflict; the exhibition's bilingual website is a valuable online resource if your want to learn more.

Trojan Horse MONUMENT
Wolfgang Petersen's 2004 movie *Troy* had a big impact on the Çanakkale region, including boosting visitor numbers to the archaeological site and endowing the northern stretch of the waterfront promenade with this wooden horse, which was used in the film shoot. There are information displays and a model of the ancient city underneath.

Yalı Hamam HAMAM
(Çarşı Caddesi 46; full treatments ₺80; ☺ men 6am-11pm, women 8.30am-7pm) Women may not feel comfortable in this 17th-century hamam, as it is a mixed facility and the attendants are all male. That said, it's clean, the *göbektaşı* (raised platform used for massage) is piping hot and the massage will please those who like a bit of a pummel.

🎊 Festivals & Events

Troia Festival
CULTURAL

(Troia Festivali; ☉ mid-Aug) Parades, concerts and exhibitions take over the *kordon* and big-name Turkish music acts perform at free concerts in Cumhuriyet Meydanı for five days.

Hellespont & Dardanelles Swim
SPORTS

(www.swimhellespont.com; ☉ 30 Aug) On Turkey's Victory Day, the Dardanelles Strait is closed to maritime traffic for 1½ hours when swimmers race the 4.5km from Eceabat to Çanakkale.

🛏 Sleeping

Anzac House Hostel
HOSTEL $

(☑ 0286-213 5969; www.anzachouse.com; Cumhuriyet Meydanı 59; dm €6.50, s/d/tr without bathroom €10/17/22.50; ❇ 🛜) Operated by the Hassle Free Travel Agency, Çanakkale's only backpacker hostel offers basic but clean dorms and private rooms, but is woefully short on character and facilities (no lockers or reading lights). Dorms sleep between six and 16 and are hot in summer; shared bathrooms are barracks-style and don't always have hot water. No breakfast.

There are four cramped and horribly claustrophobic rooms without external light – make sure you don't get stuck in one of these.

⭐ Set Özer Hotel
HOTEL $$

(☑ 0286-213 0292; www.setozerhotel.com; Kemalyeri Sokak 14; r from ₺300; ❇ 🛜) Opened in 2019, the classy and good-value Set Özer Hotel combines a central location near good cafes and restaurants with a bold design aesthetic. Standard rooms are relatively compact, but the quirky addition of retro Turkish advertising art enlivens the experience. Breakfasts are enjoyed in a stylish inner courtyard that's a total surprise when entering from the street.

Anzac Hotel
HOTEL $$

(☑ 0286-217 7777; www.anzachotel.com; Saat Kulesi Meydanı 8; s/d/tr €30/35/40; P ❇ 🛜) An extremely professional management team ensures that this keenly priced hotel opposite the clock tower is well maintained and has high levels of service. Rooms are a good size, include tea- and coffee-making facilities and have double-glazed windows. The small bar on the mezzanine shows the movies *Gallipoli* and *Troy* nightly. Parking costs €3 per night.

Hotel Kervansaray
BOUTIQUE HOTEL $$

(☑ 0286-217 8192; www.otelkervansaray.com; Fetvane Sokak 13; s/d from €40/50; ❇ 🛜) In an Ottoman house once owned in the early 20th century by a judge, the Kervansaray is one of Çanakkale's more historic accommodation options. The smell of yesteryear may permeate the older rooms, but the dowdiness is kind of fun. Rooms in the newer section have bathtubs instead of showers. The garden en route to the rooms is a little oasis.

Grand Anzac Hotel
HOTEL $$

(☑ 0286-216 0016; www.grandanzachotel.com; Kemalyeri Sokak 11; s/d/tr from €30/40/50; P ❇ 🛜) Operated by the Anzac Hotel crew, this hotel offers slightly larger rooms than its sister establishment; soundproofing between them could be better. There's a cafeteria on the ground floor where breakfast and dinner is served. Parking costs €3 per night.

Hotel des Etrangers
BOUTIQUE HOTEL $$$

(☑ 0286-214 2424; www.hoteldesetrangers.com. tr; Yalı Caddesi 25-27; r from €65; ❇ 🛜) This historic hotel is an atmospheric sleeping choice offering eight rooms with whitewashed wooden floors, inlaid timber ceilings and tasteful country-style furniture. The four rooms at the front are larger and have small balconies overlooking the harbour and bustling Yalı Caddesi. Note that windows aren't double glazed and the location can be noisy. Heinrich Schliemann, who led the first excavation of Troy, once stayed here.

🍴 Eating

⭐ Sardalye
SEAFOOD $

(Küçük Hamam Sokak 24b; fish sandwiches ₺10-20, fish & salad ₺30-45; ☉ 11am-10pm Mon-Fri, 9am-10pm Sat, 9am-6pm Sun) On the corner of the Aynalı Çarşı, this no-frills place named in honour of a plentiful local fish (*sardalya* means sardine) serves everything from superfresh *balık ekmek* (fish sandwiches) to tasty plates of *midye tava* (fried mussels) or deep-fried fish. Sit at the counter on the street and chat with the locals between tasty mouthfuls, or order to go.

Cevahir Ev Yemekleri
TURKISH $

(☑ 0286-213 1600; www.facebook.com/cevahirevyemekleri; Fetvane Sokak 15; mixed plates ₺17-25; ☉ 8.30am-10.30pm) Cheap and cheerful is the motto at this popular *ev yemekleri* (eatery serving home-cooked food) close to the clock tower. Choose from bean, vegetable

Çanakkale

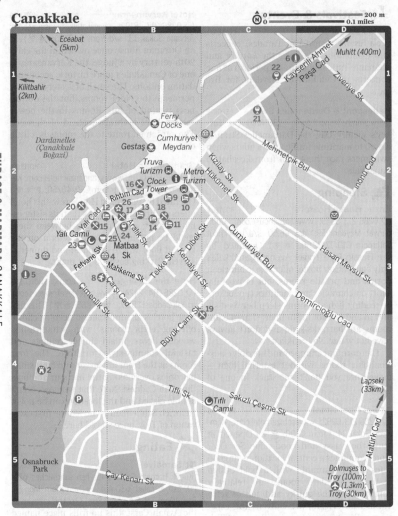

and meat dishes from the bain-marie. Plates come in *küçük* (small), *orta* (medium) or *büyük* (large) sizes. No alcohol.

Babalık Peynir Helvası SWEETS **$**
(☎ 0286-217 3610; Yalı Caddesi 47; per kg ₺30; ⊕ 8am-7pm) *Peynir helvası* (a dessert of flour or semolina, butter and sugar) is the showcase dish at this family-owned business. Try it with a scoop of vanilla ice cream (₺10) as an essential mid-afternoon snack.

Çonk Coffee CAFE **$**
(Kemalyeri Sokak 3; tostu ₺10-15; ⊕ 7am-10pm) A display of old radios, cameras and

photographs adorns the walls of this small and extremely friendly cafe, which serves Turkish and espresso coffee, hot dogs, sandwiches and the city's best *tostu* (toasted sandwiches). Brilliant freshly squeezed orange juice too. The owner is originally from Turkey's Black Sea region and speaks good English.

★ Muhitt CAFE **$$**
(☎ 0286-214 3514; Gazi Bulvarı 58; fixed menu per person ₺35-45; ⊕ 8.30am-5pm; ☒) Make your way to the northern end of Çanakkale's waterfront *kordon* for this relaxed and stylish cafe offering excellent all-day breakfasts.

Çanakkale

Either select individual dishes off the menu, or settle in for one of the fixed price menus with a table-covering array of fresh cheeses, jams and other assorted goodies. Look forward to at least an hour of leisurely feasting.

Yalova SEAFOOD $$
(📋0286-217 1045; www.yalovarestaurant.com; Gümrük Sokak 7; mezes ₺15-45, mains ₺25-65; ⊙12.30pm-1am) Locals have been coming here for slap-up meals since 1940. A two-storey place on the *kordon*, it serves seafood that often comes straight off the fishing boats moored out the front. Head upstairs to choose from the meze and fish displays, and be sure to quaff some locally produced Suvla wine with your meal.

Cafe du Port INTERNATIONAL $$
(📋0286-217 2908; Yalı Caddesi 12; mains ₺35-60; ⊙8am-11pm) The restaurant at Hotel Limani is popular for good reason. The glass-fronted building on the *kordon* is stylish and inviting; the chefs are the most versatile in Çanakkale; and the service is brilliant. Specialities include steaks, salads, pastas, and whatever else inspires the manager during his regular İstanbul sojourns. If nothing else, settle in for an end-of-day mojito.

🍷 Drinking & Entertainment

★**Kahverengi Roastery** CAFE
(Çarşı Caddesi 8; ⊙8.30am-11pm) Often bathed in sunshine, this hip cafe and roastery serves up excellent coffees, including very good lattes and flat whites. Secure a table outside or sit inside and admire the heritage interior and retro floor tiles. Don't be surprised if you return the following morning for another session of Çanakkale's best coffee.

★**Yalı Hanı** TEA GARDEN
(Fetvane Sokak 26; ⊙8am-10pm, closed Dec-Feb) Hidden in the wisteria-covered courtyard of a late 19th-century caravanserai is this atmospheric hybrid *çay bahçesi* and bar that doubles as a performance and film-festival venue. It's a favourite haunt of boho types, who linger over glasses of wine and earnest conversation after checking out the art exhibitions that are often held in the upstairs space.

Mekan Sestra PUB
(📋0544 242 1517; www.facebook.com/mekan sestra; Fetvane Sokak 19; ⊙11am-late) One of Çanakkale's newest eating and drinking spots is also one of its most versatile. Downstairs, lured by frosty brews, international street food and cocktails, the spacious beer garden is popular with a good percentage of the city's student population, while Mekan Sestra's smaller upstairs space is used for regular live gigs by up and coming Turkish bands and DJs.

Helles Cafe BAR
(Kayserili Ahmet Paşa Caddesi 29a; ⊙8am-2am) Turkish craft beer in Çanakkale – who'd have thought? The Helles Cafe increases its friendly ambience and al fresco appeal along the *kordon* by serving craft brews from the Gara Guzu brewery in the southwestern city

of Muğla. Beers include a hoppy amber ale and a Belgian-tinged blonde ale, both decent tipples if Efes is tasting a little bland.

Akava Lounge
BAR

(www.akava.com.tr; Kayserili Ahmet Paşa Caddesi 24a; ⊗8.30am-2am) Regulars crowd in for cocktails served amid colourful street art and wall murals, and the international menu features pizza, pasta, steaks, salads and Mexican dishes. There's a bigger-than-usual range of beers on tap, and even a few flavourful and interesting international bottled brews.

Joker Bar
LIVE MUSIC

(www.jokerbarcanakkale.com; Matbaa Sokak 3; concerts from ₺30; ⊗noon-1am) Local students crowd in for gigs that usually kick off around 8pm on Friday and Saturday nights. Nearby laneways are also packed with other pubs, cafes and restaurants. It's an ever-changing scene, so check out what's new and popular.

🛍 Shopping

Kepenek Keramik
CERAMICS

(www.kepenekkeramik.com; Yalı Hanı 28/30, Fetvane Sokak; ⊗10am-6pm) Çanakkale has a long history of ceramics manufacturing, and the designs at Kepenek are often interesting updates on this established tradition. Highlights of the store's well-priced range include robust terracotta kitchenware enlivened with vibrant and colourful glazes, and rustic and compact figurines that make excellent gifts and souvenirs. The little Trojan horses – complete with wheels – are particularly cool.

ℹ Information

Tourist Office (☑0284-217 1187; İskele Meydanı 67; ⊗8.30am-5.30pm Mon-Fri, 9.30am-12.30pm & 1.30-4pm Sat & Sun) Strategically located between the ferry pier and the clock tower, this office can supply city maps, information about Gallipoli battlefields and dolmuş timetables.

ℹ Getting There & Away

BOAT
Ferry services are all handled by **Gestaş** (☑444 0752; www.gdu.com.tr), which has a modern and spacious ticket office and waiting room in Çanakkale.

Most ferries depart from the main ferry dock.
Bozcaada (₺25, passenger ferry only) Daily Tuesday to Sunday summer only.

Eceabat (per person/car ₺4.50/67, 25 minutes) Departs every hour on the hour between 7am and midnight, and every one to two hours after that.

Kilitbahir (per person/car ₺3/62, 20 minutes) Departs every 30 to 60 minutes between 6am and 11.45pm.

BUS
The easiest way to get to/from Çanakkale on public transport is by bus. The city's **otogar** (Bursa Yolu 4km) is around 7km east of the centre, just off the highway to Bursa, but many buses pick up and drop off at the ferry dock. If not, local bus 9 (₺4) trundles down the hill to the city centre; buy a ticket from the newsstand at the otogar. **Metro Turizm** (☑0286-213 1260; www.metroturizm.com.tr) and **Truva Turizm** (☑0286-212 2222; www.truvaturizm.com; İskele Meydanı 69) offer the most frequent service schedules, but other companies also service the city. Both Metro and Truva offer passengers a free *servis* (shuttle bus) between the otogar and *iskele* (dock).

Ankara (₺135, 10 hours) Ten daily on Metro and Pamukkale.

Bursa (₺60 4½ hours) Three daily on Metro.

Edirne (₺60, 4½ hours) At least two daily on both Truva and Metro.

İstanbul (₺89, six hours) Services to Büyük Otogar in Esenler on the city's European side (Metro and Truva) and to Ataşehir Otogar near Kadıköy on the Asian side (Truva).

İzmir (₺72, 5¾ hours) Via Ayvalık (₺50, 3¼ hours) At least one service daily on both Truva and Metro.

DOLMUŞ
Dolmuşes to Troy (₺10, 35 minutes) leave hourly on the half-hour between 9.30am and 5pm from a station at the northern end of the bridge over the Sarı River in Çanakkale and drop passengers at the archaeological site's car park. During summer, the first dolmuş departs Çanakkale at 7.30am and the last departure back from Troy leaves at 8.15pm.

Troy
☑0286

While not the most dramatic of Turkey's ancient sites, Troy is testament to the importance of myth to the human experience. Some imagination is needed to reconstruct the city's former splendour, but a decent guide will quickly bring to life the place that set the scene for Homer's *Iliad*. Opened in late 2018, the Museum of Troy is one of Turkey's finest museums and an essential destination before visiting the actual site.

Troy

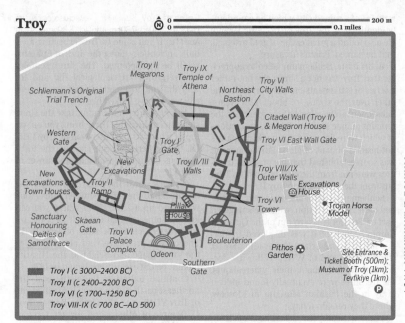

Troy is a popular destination for week-ending school parties; try to visit mid-week. While it can be visited as a long day trip from Istanbul, a more leisurely visit incorporating an overnight stay in nearby Çanak-kale is recommended.

History

This area was first inhabited during the early Bronze Age (late 4th millennium BC). The walled cities called Troy I to Troy V (3000–1700 BC) had cultures similar to that of the Bronze Age, but Troy VI (1700–1250 BC) took on a different, Mycenae-influenced character, doubling in size and trading prosperously with the region's Greek colonies. By the time of Troy VI, the city probably covered the entire plateau, making it one of the largest towns in the Aegean region. An earthquake brought down the city walls in 1350 BC, but these were rebuilt. There is evidence of widespread fire and slaughter around 1250 BC (Troy VII), which leads many historians to believe that this is when the Trojan War occurred. What is known of the economic and political history of the Aegean region in this period suggests that the real cause of the war was intense commercial rivalry between Troy and the mercantile Mycenaean kingdom, the prize being control

of the Dardanelles and lucrative trade with the Black Sea.

The city was abandoned by the end of the 2nd millennium BC but was reoccupied by Greek settlers from Lemnos in the 8th century BC (Troy VIII, 700–85 BC). In 188 BC, it was identified by the Romans as the fabled city of Homer and recognised as the mother city of Rome (Ilium Novum), and was granted exemption from taxes. The city prospered under Roman rule and survived a severe earthquake in the early 6th century. Abandoned once again in the 9th century, it was reoccupied in the later Byzantine period and not finally deserted until well into the Ottoman period.

Discovering Troy

Up until the 19th century, many historians doubted whether ancient Troy had ever existed. One man who was convinced of its existence – to an almost obsessive level – was the German businessman Heinrich Schliemann (1822–90), who in 1870 received permission from the Ottoman government to excavate a hill near the village of Hisarlık, which archaeologists had previously identified as a possible site for the city.

Schliemann was more of an eager treasure hunter than a methodical archaeologist and he quickly tore open the site, uncovering the remains of a ruined city, which he confidently identified as the Troy of Homeric legend. He also found a great cache of gold artefacts that he named 'Priam's Treasure'.

In his haste, Schliemann failed to appreciate that Troy was not a single city but rather a series of settlements built one on top of the other over the course of about 2500 years. Subsequent archaeologists have identified the remains of nine separate Troys, large sections of which were damaged during Schliemann's hot-headed pursuit of glory. Furthermore, it was soon established that his precious treasures were not from the time of Homer's Troy, but from the much earlier Troy II.

Schliemann's dubious approach continued after the excavation, when he smuggled part of 'Priam's Treasure' out of the Ottoman Empire. Much of it was displayed in Berlin, where it was seized by invading Soviet troops at the end of WWII. Following decades of denials about their whereabouts, the treasures were eventually found hidden away in the Pushkin Museum in Moscow, where they remain today.

Located nearby in the village of Tevfikiye, the superb Museum of Troy opened in late 2018 during the 'Year of Troy' (www.2018troia.com), the 20th anniversary of the site's inclusion on Unesco's World Heritage list. It is hoped that one day the treasures in Moscow's Pushkin Museum will be returned to Turkey for display in the museum.

◉ Sights

★ Museum of Troy   MUSEUM
(Troya Müzesi; www.troya2018.com; Tevfikiye; ₺42; ⊘8.30am-7pm mid-Apr-Sep, 8.30am-5.30pm Oct–mid-Apr) The Museum of Troy's rust-coloured cube, rising from sunbaked earth, is a spectacular multi-floor showcase of the archeological layers of the historic site and also the legendary romance of the Trojan Wars as described by Homer in the *Iliad*. A series of ramps, interactive displays and excellent signage in Turkish and English allows visitors to discover four thousand years of history. Highlights include 24 delicate examples of gold jewellery dating back to around 2400 BCE and a spectacular Greek sarcophagus.

Allow at least three hours to explore the museum and definitely visit *before* continuing to the archeological site around 750m away. Stretching to the coast, the views from the museum's top floor terrace are very good.

Ruins of Troy   ARCHAEOLOGICAL SITE
(₺42; ⊘8.30am-7.30pm Apr-Oct, 8.30am-5.30pm Nov-Mar) If you come to Troy expecting a rebuilt ancient city along the lines of Ephesus, you'll be disappointed. The site resembles an overgrown archaeological dig and it's very difficult to imagine what the ancient city would have looked like.

As you approach the ruins, take the stone steps up on the right. These bring you out on top of what was the outer wall of Troy VIII/IX, from where you can gaze on the fortifications of the east wall gate and tower of Troy VI.

Go back down the steps and follow the boardwalk to the right, between thick stone walls and up a knoll, from where you can look at some original (as well as some reconstructed) red-brick walls of Troy II/III. The curved protective roof above them is the same shape and height as the Hisarlık mound before excavations began in 1874.

Continue following the path, past the northeast bastion of the heavily fortified city of Troy VI, the site of a Graeco-Roman Troy IX Temple of Athena and further walls of Troy II/III. You can make out the stone foundations of a megaron (building with porch) from the same era.

Next, beyond traces of the wall of Early/Middle Troy (Troy I south gate) are more remains of megarons of Troy II, which were inhabited by a literal 'upper class' while the poor huddled on the plains.

The path then sweeps past the original trial trench established by Heinrich Schliemann; this cuts straight through all the layers of the city. Signs point out the nine city strata in the trench's 15m-high sides.

Just round the corner is a stretch of wall from what is believed to have been the two-storey-high Troy VI Palace Complex, followed by traces from Troy VIII/IX of a sanctuary to unknown deities. Later, a new sanctuary was built on the same site, apparently honouring the deities of Samothrace. Eventually, the path passes in front of the Roman Odeon, where concerts were held and, to the right, the Bouleuterion (Council Chamber), bringing you back to where you started.

☞ Tours

Uran Savaş   TOURS
(✆0542 263 4839; uransavas17@hotmail.com) Local guide Uran Savaş is based at the Troia Pension. He speaks excellent English and conducts private tours of the archaeological site (€50) and museum (€50).

🛌 Sleeping

Troia Pension
PENSION **$$**

(☑ 0286-283 0571; www.troiapension.com; Truva Mola Noktası, Tevfikiye; campsites/campervan sites without breakfast €15, s/d €30/50; ☒ 🛜) Located across the road from the Museum of Troy, this welcoming place sits behind a cafe. Run by tour guide Uran Savaş, it offers four twin rooms and powered sites for visitors with tents or campervans. There are squeaky-clean showers and toilets as well as a facility for changing toilet water in vans. Meals are available in the cafe.

ℹ️ Getting There & Away

Dolmuşes to Troy (₺10, 35 minutes, hourly) leave on the half-hour between 9.30am and 5pm from a station at the northern end of the bridge over the Sarı River in Çanakkale and drop passengers at the archaeological site's car park. Ask first to be let off at the Museum of Troy from where it is a 750m walk to the archaeological site.

During summer, the first dolmuş departs Çanakkale at 7.30am and the last departure back from Troy leaves at 8.15pm. The tourist information office can provide a handy flyer with the latest timings.

It costs ₺10 to park at carparks at Museum of Troy and the site itself.

Gökçeada

📞 0286 / POP 8640

'Heavenly Island' is a spectacular Aegean outpost 20km from the Gallipoli Peninsula. On weekends and holidays during the summer months, it is popular with residents of İstanbul and İzmir, who are drawn by its unspoiled landscape, sandy beaches and Greek-influenced culture. At other times it is a tranquil, windswept place where visitors are rare and the surroundings are truly bucolic.

It's a mystery to us why Gökçeada isn't more popular as a base for those visiting the nearby Gallipoli battlefields. A ferry links the island with Kabatepe at the heart of the Gallipoli Peninsula, carries both cars and passengers and takes only 75 minutes. There is a small but alluring range of accommodation options on offer and plenty of opportunities for swimming, windsurfing, trekking and cultural tourism.

History

Gökçeada was once a predominantly Greek (Rum) island known as Imbros or İmroz. During WWI, it was an important base for the Gallipoli campaign; indeed, Allied commander General Ian Hamilton stationed himself at the village of Aydıncık (then Kefalos) on the island's southeastern coast. Along with its smaller island neighbour to the south, Bozcaada, Gökçeada was ceded to the new Turkish Republic in 1923 as part of the Treaty of Lausanne but was exempted from the population exchange, retaining a predominantly Greek population. However, in 1946 Turkish authorities installed the first wave of Turkish settlers from the Black Sea region, starting a clear but unstated process of 'Turkification' that reached its height in the 1960s and 1970s when up to 6000 ethnic Turks from the mainland – many from the east – were relocated here. Greek schools were forcibly closed, many Greek churches were desecrated and 90% of the island's cultivatable land was appropriated from Greek residents, most of whom had no choice but to leave. In 1970, the island was renamed Gökçeada by the Turkish government. These days, there are approximately 200 Greek residents, most of whom are elderly.

👁 Sights

The main sights of interest are the area's villages. Heading west from Gökçeada town, better known as Merkez (Centre), you'll pass Zeytinli (Aya Theodoros) after 3km, Tepeköy (Agridia), another 7km on, and Dereköy (Shinudy), another 5km west. All were built on hillsides overlooking the island's central valley to avoid pirate raids. Many of the stone houses in these villages are deserted and falling into disrepair. However, thanks to a few enthusiastic and entrepreneurial residents of Greek heritage in Zeytinli and Tepeköy, the villages are discovering the benefits of small-scale tourism and some former residents and their families are returning.

🏖 Beaches

The sand beach at **Aydıncık** is the best on the island. It is adjacent to **Tuz Gölü** (Salt Lake), a favourite shelter for pink flamingos between November and March. The lake is rich in sulphur and reputed to be good for the skin. Further west there are good beaches at **Kapıkaya** and **Uğurlu**.

🏊 Activities

Aydıncık and Tuz Gölü are popular for windsurfing and kitesurfing. Cycling is also popular, and noticeboards in Merkez detail

Gökçeada

routes – some hilly – around the island. Mountain bikes, which are in pretty good order, can be hired in Merkez.

Sleeping

Most accommodation is centred around Kaleköy and Merkez, and there are also characterful options in Greek villages such as Zeytinli and Tepeköy. In summer it's not unusual for locals to approach and offer you a spare room in their house *(ev pansiyonu)* for considerably less than the prices charged by pensions and hotels. Many establishments close during the low season.

Merkez

Taylan Hotel HOTEL $
(☑ 0286-887 2451; omertaylanada@hotmail.com; Atatürk Caddesi; s/d ₺100/150; ❄ 🤶) On the main street in Merkez, this place has seen better days, but it's clean, the management is friendly (though not bilingual) and there's a bustling downstairs restaurant.

★**Meydani Butik Hotel** BOUTIQUE HOTEL $$$
(☑ 0286-888 0010; Atatürk Caddesi 33; d €70; P ❄ 🤶) A welcome addition to the Merkez accommodation scene, this swish 2019 opening features very comfortable rooms right in the heart of Gökçeada's biggest town. Lots of restaurants are a short walk away and transport to other parts of the island is convenient. Breakfast is offered in the associated bakery located downstairs. Look forward to delicious aromas occasionally wafting upstairs.

Kaleköy & Eski Bademli

★**Anemos Hotel** BOUTIQUE HOTEL $$$
(☑ 0286-887 3729; www.anemos.com.tr; Yukarı Kaleköy 98, Yukarı Kaleköy; r basic/standard/superior ₺400/500/600; ❄ 🤶 ❄) *Anemos* means 'wind' in Turkish, and this hotel certainly brought the winds of change to Gökçeada. It's responsible for introducing the concept of the boutique hotel and has attracted clients from the mainland who would previously have headed to style-setting Bodrum for their vacations. Ground-floor basic rooms are smallish, standards are spacious, and superiors are large (some have private terraces). All are well appointed.

Dimitri Ada Evi BOUTIQUE HOTEL $$$
(☑ 0532 485 0938; www.dimitriadaevi.com; Eski Bademli; r ₺550) Cascading down a hillside in Eski Bademli, this hotel's boutique charm includes colourful if slightly rustic rooms, and a characterful ambience courtesy of the friendly family owners. Rugs and antiques create a cosy vibe, and the astounding views from the terrace of Dimitri Ada Evi's restaurant (open July to September) include the imposing profile of the Greek island of Samothraki.

Zeytinli & Tepeköy

Pansyon Agridia PENSION $$
(☑ 0286-887 2138; www.pansiyonagridia.com; Tepeköy; s/d €30/40) Owner Dimitris Assanakis is extremely proud of his whitewashed pension perched on Tepeköy's highest point.

There are three simply decorated rooms with good beds; a double and twin share a bathroom and the second twin has an en suite. All can be hot in summer, but the balcony with its magnificent view over the valley well and truly compensates.

Delicious, largely organic breakfasts are made with eggs, fruit, vegetables and spring water from the village. Dimitris can also advise on nearby walks of one to three hours, which take in excellent swimming beaches, natural springs and deserted Greek villages.

Zeytindali Hotel BOUTIQUE HOTEL $$$
(☑0286-887 3707; Zeytinliköy 168, Zeytinli; s/d ₺400/600; ☺May-Oct; ❋🞱) Two rebuilt Greek stone houses at the top of Zeytinli's old village showcase island style and comfort. The 16 rooms – each named after a Greek god – have satellite TVs and views of the village or the sea; wi-fi is only available in the lobby and on the terrace. The ground-floor restaurant is popular with day trippers.

Eating

You'll find a good range of restaurants in Merkez, and the best options for seafood with a view are the eateries in Kaleköy, such as **Yakamoz** (☑0286-887 2057; www.gokceadayakamoz.com; Yukarı Kaleköy; mains ₺35-60; ☺11am-3pm & 6-10pm) and around the compact fishing harbour. Village dining in Zeytinli and Tepeköy is also highly enjoyable.

The seafood restaurants at Kaleköy serve beer, rakı (aniseed brandy) and wine. During summer, you can have a good time combining wine and live music at venues in Merkez and the Greek village of Tepeköy.

Merkez

★Biyer Kafe Dukkan TURKISH $
(☑0286-887 2117; Nadir Nadi Sokak 4; portions ₺15-30; ☺9am-11pm Tue-Sun; 🖉) Welcome to Gökçeada's best homestyle cooking. There's no fixed menu, but you can guarantee everything will be delicious. The younger waitstaff often speak good English, so just accompany them to the kitchen to see what's good. Lamb and seasonal veggies are bound to feature; it's also a tempting spot to pop in for coffee and cake later at night.

Balbadem Cafe CAFE $
(Yesilada Sokak 8; snacks & mains ₺15-30; ☺7am-11pm) Framed by grape arbours, our favourite cafe in Merkez is concealed in an old stone house a short walk from the main square. Colourful tables fill Balbadem's shaded verandah; there's an excellent range of teas and coffees; and don't be surprised if the friendly posse of local cats patiently lines up while you're tucking into the *köy kahvaltı* (village-style breakfast; ₺35).

Kaleköy

★Mustafanın Kayfesi CAFE $$
(☑0286-887 2063; breakfast plates ₺40; ☺9am-9pm) Look for the free-standing bell tower of the Ayia Marina church to find this welcoming cafe, which is tucked into the adjacent garden. The village-style breakfast is delicious, and the Turkish coffee is the best on the island. In the late afternoon, a nargile (water pipe) and coffee combo really hits the spot.

Tepeköy

Barba Yorgo Taverna TURKISH $$
(☑0286-887 4247; www.barbayorgo.com; mains ₺40-60; ☺noon-3pm & 6-11pm May-Sep) A good time is assured at this atmospheric village restaurant overlooking vineyards and the 1780 Ayios Yioryios church. The menu includes goat stew, wonderfully tender octopus and platefuls of meze, all washed down with carafes of the house-made wine. Baba Yorgo produces a knock-your-socks-off retsina, an eminently quaffable red blend and a more sophisticated organic cabernet sauvignon.

Shopping

Gökçeada is one of only nine Turkish Cittaslow (www.cittaslowturkiye.org) cities and is committed to producing organic foodstuffs. At the forefront of this endeavour is local organic farm Elta-Ada (www.elta-ada.com.tr); find its products in a few restaurants and delicatessens in Merkez. Shops around Merkez's main square sell local products including artisan-made soap, olive oil, jams, honey and *dibek* coffee. The best of these is **Ada Rüzgarı** (☑0286-887 2496; www.adaruzgari.com; Suluoğlu İş Merkezi 24b; ☺8am-10pm).

ℹ️ Information

Facilities such as a bank, ATMs and a post office are found 6km inland at Merkez, where most of the island's population lives.

Tourist Office (📞 0286-887 3005; www. gokceadarehberim.com; Cumhuriyet Meydanı; ⊙9am-2pm & 3-7pm) In a timber kiosk next to the main dolmuş stop in Merkez. Opening hours can be haphazard.

ℹ️ Getting There & Away

Ferry departures change according to the season; check the **Gestaş** (📞 0286-444 0752; www.gdu.com.tr) website or with your hotel.

Ferries cross between Kabatepe and Gökçeada (per person/car ₺6/64, 75 minutes). Services run three times daily each way from September to May, five times daily in June and July, and more regularly in August.

ℹ️ Getting Around

CAR

Note that the only petrol station is 2km from Merkez on the Kuzulimanı road. There are three car-hire companies on the island,

including **Gökçeada-Rent-A-Car** (📞 0532 667 9384; www.gokceadarentacar.com; Nadir Nadi Sokak 15), in Merkez, which charges around ₺250 per day for a small car. Scooters and 4WD ATV vehicles are also available.

DOLMUŞ

Ferries dock at Kuzulimanı, from where you can take a dolmuş to Merkez (₺6, 15 minutes, eight per day). Change at Merkez to continue to Kaleköy, 5km further north (₺4, 25 minutes). Some of the Kaleköy dolmuşes stop in Yeni Bademli and Yukarı Kaleköy en route.

TAXI

It costs around ₺500 to hire a taxi for half a day and tour the island. The following are approximate costs for short trips:

Kuzulimanı–Merkez ₺40, 10 minutes

Kuzulimanı–Kaleköy ₺55, 20 minutes

Kuzulimanı–Yukarı Kaleköy ₺70, 25 minutes

Merkez–Kaleköy ₺25, five minutes

Merkez–Zeytinli ₺35, 10 minutes

Merkez–Tepeköy ₺50, 20 minutes

Merkez–Aydıncık ₺45, 15 minutes

İzmir & the North Aegean

Best Places to Eat

➡ Ayşa (p210)

➡ Asma Yaprağı (p220)

➡ Bumba Breakfast Club (p220)

➡ Çeşka Anne Mutfağı (p217)

➡ Ayna (p196)

Best Places to Stay

➡ Assos Alarga (p186)

➡ Taş Konak (p200)

➡ Latife Hanım Konağı (p181)

➡ Nar Konak (p186)

➡ Assosyal Otel (p186)

Why Go?

An extraordinary number of attractions are waiting to be discovered along the short stretch of coast between the Dardanelles and the Çeşme Peninsula. There are sandy beaches aplenty, and innumerable scenic viewpoints from where the Greek islands of Lesbos and Chios appear to float on the sparkling Aegean Sea.

There are also plenty of reminders of the region's importance in antiquity, most notably the extraordinary Acropolis and Asklepion at Bergama (Pergamum), the evocative ruins of Teos and the spectacularly sited Temple of Athena at Behramkale (Assos).

But as wonderful as these beaches and ruins are – not to mention the compelling attractions on offer in the urbane city of İzmir – most people who visit this part of the country say their most lasting memories are of the bittersweet traces of Greek heritage that have influenced the local cuisine and architecture and enriched the lives of its inhabitants.

When to Go

İzmir

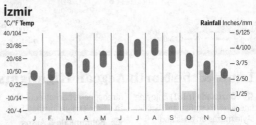

Apr Alaçatı hosts a foodie celebration of Aegean *ot* (wild greens).

Jun The International İzmir Festival brings music to the region.

Sep Bozcaada celebrates the grape harvest at its wine festival.

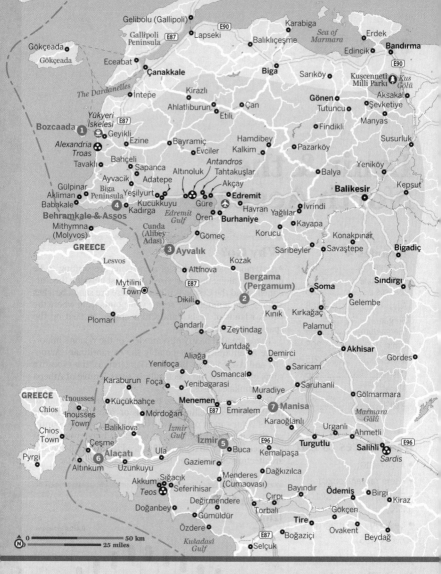

İzmir & the North Aegean Highlights

❶ Bozcaada (p181) Enjoying fine wine, fresh fish and Greek-style mezes on an island escape.

❷ Bergama (Pergamum) (p196) Exploring one of Turkey's most magnificent ancient sites.

❸ Ayvalık's Old Town (p188) Wandering the atmospheric backstreets of this Greek neighbourhood.

❹ Behramkale & Assos (p185) Admiring the glorious sea views from the Temple of Athena.

❺ İzmir (p203) Losing yourself in the labyrinthine lanes of the historic Kemeraltı Market.

❻ Alaçatı (p219) Partying with the glitterati in the glamour town of the Çeşme Peninsula.

❼ Manisa (p215) Marvelling at the beauty of the 16th-century Muradiye Mosque.

Bozcaada

📞 0286 / POP 3020

Windswept Bozcaada (Tenedos in Greek) is a hugely popular weekend and summer destination for residents of İstanbul, Çanakkale and İzmir. A showcase of rustic Aegean style, it's more down to earth than Alaçatı and Bodrum but is still crowded and expensive in the high season. Most of the action occurs in Merkez (or Bozcaada Town), which has an atmospheric historic Greek quarter full of brightly painted houses that have been converted into boutique hotels, B&Bs, tavernas and bars.

The island is small – just under 40 sq km – with sandy beaches and picturesque vineyards. These supply the grapes for Bozcaada's boutique wineries, whose vintages can be sampled at cellar doors and in the many Greek-style tavernas in Merkez.

Many businesses shut down outside the high season (mid-June to mid-September); between November and March the island is as quiet as a graveyard. Information about the island is available at www.bozcaadarehberi.com and www.gobozcaada.com.

⦿ Sights

The best swimming beaches are on the southern side of the island and include **Akvaryum** (Aquarium), **Ayazma** and **Sulubahçe**. All are jam-packed during summer. Ayazma is by far the most popular and best equipped (umbrellas and deckchair hire ₺10 per day), boasting several tavernas. It's also the location of the small Greek Orthodox **Aya Paraskevi Monastery** (Ayazma Monastery). **Çayır Beach** on the northern side of the island is a popular windsurfing and kitesurfing destination.

Bozcaada Castle   CASTLE
(Bozcaada Kalesi; ₺6; ⊙9am-8pm) It is generally thought that Bozcaada's colossal fortress dates to Byzantine times, but it has been significantly rebuilt by the Venetians, Genoese and Ottomans. Over the dry moat and within the double walls are traces of a mosque, ammunition stores, a barracks, an infirmary and Roman pillars. It sits right next to the ferry terminal.

Bozcaada Museum   MUSEUM
(Bozcaada Yerel Tarih Araştırma Merkezi; 📞0532-215 6033; www.bozcaadamuzesi.net; Lale Sokak 7; adult/student & child ₺10/5; ⊙10am-8pm late

Apr-late Oct) Located 100m west of the ferry terminal in the old Greek district, this small museum and local-history research centre is a treasure trove of island curios: maps, prints, photographs, seashells and day-to-day artefacts.

Church of St Mary   CHURCH
(Meryem Ana Kilisesi, Teodoku Eastern Orthodox Church; 20 Eylül Caddesi 42a) This 19th-century church in the old Greek neighbourhood to the west of the fortress is one of only two remaining Greek Orthodox churches on the island (there were originally more than 30). Its distinctive bell tower was built in 1865. The church opens for mass on Sunday mornings at 8am but is closed at other times.

🛏 Sleeping

It's sensible to book your accommodation in advance, especially between June and September. Most hotels and pensions are in Merkez, with many options in the old Greek quarter around the Church of St Mary. Light sleepers be warned, this quarter is noisy well into the wee hours; for a quieter option consider the Turkish quarter on the hill behind the castle. Many businesses only open for the high season.

Kale Pansiyon   PENSION $$
(Castle Pension; 📞0286-697 8840; www.kalepansiyon.net; İnönü Caddesi 69; basement d ₺220, d/tr ₺320/380; ⊙mid-Jun–mid-Sep; ❄🛜) Reached via a steep climb from the old Greek quarter, and with commanding views over the town, the family-run 'Castle' offers simple but clean rooms; those in the basement are darker but cheaper. There's a friendly host and a lovely garden to have breakfast in. Of its two pink-coloured houses, the one on the right has better bathrooms. There's a minor discount for cash payments.

⭐**Latife Hanım Konağı**   BOUTIQUE HOTEL $$$
(Madam Latife Mansion; 📞0286-690 0030; www.latifehanimkonagi.com; Atatürk Caddesi 23; d/ste ₺400/1100; ❄🛜) The island's most stylish hotel occupies a meticulously restored century-old house near the Church of St Mary in the Greek quarter. Standard rooms are tastefully decorated with white bedspreads and kilims (traditional rugs), but are small. Views from the 2nd-floor roof terrace, where breakfast is served, are commanding. The hotel has a private beach elsewhere on the island. Excellent value.

Bozcaada

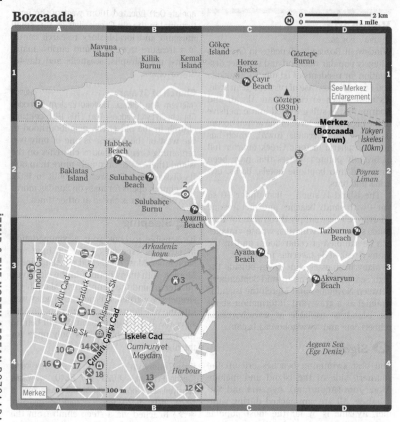

N 0 ——— 2 km
0 ——— 1 mile

Bozcaada

Sights
1	Amadeus Vineyard	C1
2	Aya Paraskevi Monastery	B2
3	Bozcaada Castle	B3
4	Bozcaada Museum	A4
5	Church of St Mary	A4
6	Corvus Vineyard	D2

Sleeping
7	Bademlik Otel	A3
8	Kaikias Otel	B3
9	Kale Pansiyon	A3
10	Latife Hanım Konağı	A4

Eating
11	Boboz	A4
12	Boruzan	B4
13	Çiçek Pastanesi	B4
14	Hasan Tefik	A4

Drinking & Nightlife
15	Kahverengi	A4
16	Tenedeion Winehouse	A4

Shopping
17	Çamlıbağ Şarapları	A4
18	Corvus	A4

Kaikias Otel BOUTIQUE HOTEL **$$$**
(☎0532 363 2697; www.kaikias.com; Eskici Sokak 1; d ₺550-650, ste ₺1000; ☷mid-Jun–mid-Sep; ❇🛜) Overlooking a tiny square near the castle, this 20-room hotel in two buildings has attractive, sometimes quirky, decor and a variety of room types. The standard rooms are cramped – opt for a VIP room or suite if possible. The terrace right on the water is a major drawcard, but the in-house cafe means that noise is a given.

Bademlik Otel
B&B $$$

(☑0535 825 6812; www.bademlikotel.com; Asmalı Fırın Sokak 19; d ₺450; P❋🐾) Opened in 2015, this designer B&B in the Turkish quarter near the castle offers five rooms with white walls, minimal furniture and pretty but cramped tiled bathrooms. Breakfast is served on the attractive front terrace.

✗ Eating

Local specialities you can sample while you visit include *kurabiye* (biscuits) made with *bademli* (almonds) and *sakızlı* (mastic); *oğlak kapama* (goat meat stewed with lettuce and fennel); and *domates reçeli* (tomato jam).

Many of the island's eateries and cafes are open during the high season only. Others open their doors only at weekends and on Wednesdays, when a **produce market** is held in Hamam Sokak between the *iskele* (dock) and the Alaybey Mosque.

Boboz
SANDWICHES $

(☑0542 692 6269; Çınarlı Çarşı Caddesi 57; sandwiches ₺20-30; ☺10am-11pm; ☑) A good value alternative to Bozcaada's more expensive cafes and restaurants, Boboz specialises in tasty gourmet sandwiches. Seafood, meat and vegetarian options are on offer, all crammed with healthy fillings. Our favourite is the Ecnebi (No 3, the 'Stranger') with roast beef, caramelised onions, walnuts and cream cheese. Either takeaway or enjoy with a cold beer on-site.

Çiçek Pastanesi
CAFE $

(☑0286-690 0053; Cumhuriyet Meydanı 17; snacks from ₺5; ☺7am-11pm) Its location in a pretty square near the Alaybey Mosque is only one of the attractions of this friendly cafe and bakery, which was established in 1959. There are indoor tables, but the choice seating is outside under the trees. The *poğaças* (savoury pastries) and biscuits are delicious (try the *tenedos kurabiye* or the *acıbadem kurabiye,* which are made with almonds).

Hasan Tefik
SEAFOOD $$

(☑0532 385 1652; www.hasantefik.com; Alsancak Sokak 2; mezes ₺20-35, fish per kg; ☺noon-2am May-Oct) Standing out from most other Bozcaada restaurants with its wider range of interesting mezes, Hasan Tefik is definitely worth seeking out. Menu highlights include a spicy octopus *güveç*, and

interesting black and white photographs of Bozcaada's fishing fleet are shaded by a grape arbour. The tiny but feisty kitten we met on our visit is probably running the show now.

Boruzan
SEAFOOD $$

(☑0286-697 8414; www.boruzanrestoran.com; Liman İçi; mezes ₺15-25, mains ₺30-50; ☺9am-1am) Our favourite of the fish restaurants by the *liman* (harbour), blue-and-white Boruzan offers a wide range of mezes made with produce from the restaurant's own vegetable patch, as well as simple seafood dishes such as *kalamar tava* (grilled squid). Keep your eyes open for the branch that opens in summer at Ayazma Beach.

☕ Drinking & Nightlife

Many of the island's cafes and bars are open for the high season only.

Kahverengi
CAFE

(coffee from ₺8; ☺8.30am-midnight; 🐾) Cosmopolitan coffee style comes to Bozcaada at this laneway cafe and roastery. Excellent lattes and flat whites are served in cute earthenware cups; other options for the travelling caffeine aficionado include Chemex and cold brew. The shaded outdoor tables are the most relaxing of the available options, and there's also a small onsite shop selling local jams and other artisan produce.

Tenedeion Winehouse
WINE BAR

(☑0286-697 8055; www.facebook.com/tenedion; Atatürk Caddesi 11; tasting flight ₺30; ☺11am-midnight) Secure a comfy cushion outside under Tenedeion's street art–style mural and enjoy a tasting of nine different wines from the island's Çamlıbağ winery. Standouts among their offerings include the cabernet sauvigon and the Vasilaki, a flinty white wine native to the island. Just maybe the best way to ease into a Bozcaada twilight.

ℹ Information

There's a row of ATMs near the PTT on Çınar Çeşme Caddesi in Merkez.

ℹ Getting There & Away

BOAT

Gestaş (☑444 0752; www.gdu.com.tr) ferries run daily to Bozcaada from Yükyeri İskelesi (return per person/car ₺11/115, 35 minutes),

LOCAL KNOWLEDGE

BOZCAADA'S WINERIES

Bozcaada has been one of Turkey's great wine-growing regions since ancient times, when enormous quantities of wine were used to fuel the debauchery at festivals for the wine god Dionysus. Nobody is quite sure why, but some magical alchemy of the island's climate, topography and soil make-up perfectly suits the growing of grapes. Among the island's best-known winemakers are:

Corvus Vineyard (☑0286-697 8181; www.corvus.com.tr; ⊘11am-7pm) The island's best-known winery, owned by Turkish architect Reşit Soley, is a short drive from Merkez, on the road to Akvaryum Beach. Tasting glasses and bottles of award-winning drops such as Corpus Reserve and Corvus Blend Number 5 are available (wine by glass from ₺20).

Amadeus Vineyard (☑0533 371 0470; info@amadeuswine.com; ⊘11am-7pm May-Sep) Austrian winemaker Oliver Gareis is the driving force behind the Gareis family's vineyard and winery on Bozcaada, and his vintages are winning fans across the country. Pop into the winery for a tasting (five small glasses ₺30), or to purchase bottles from the cellar door. Oliver is a convivial and engaging host and his cabernets are particularly impressive.

Çamlıbağ Şarapları (☑0286-697 8055; Emniyet Sokak 24; ⊘8am-7pm) The first Turkish-owned winery to be founded on the island (in 1925), Yunatcılar markets its wines under the Çamlıbağ label. Its quaffable vintages of local varietals, including Kuntra and Karalahna, can be tasted (₺20) at this showroom near Cumhuriyet Meydanı.

Corvus (☑0286-697 8181; Çınarlı Çarşı Caddesi 53; ⊘10am-6pm mid-Sep–mid-Jun, to 9.30pm mid-Jun–mid-Sep) The island's best-known winery has a retail outlet just off Cumhuriyet Caddesi in Merkez.

The four major indigenous grape varietals are Vasilaki and Cavus for the production of white wine and Kuntra and Karalahana for red. Generally speaking, the cabernet sauvignon and cabernet shiraz wines produced here are the most impressive.

The annual **Bozcaada Wine Festival** takes place over the first weekend of September, during the grape harvest.

4km west of Geyikli, south of Troy. Out of the high season, it operates three to four times daily. In the high season, there are many more services. Check the Gestaş website for the most up-to-date timetable, as these change frequently. Also ask at the bus companies in İstanbul when booking transport south from the city's Büyük Otogar to Geyikli's Yükyeri İskele.

In the high season – usually June to August – Gestaş passenger-only hydrofoils sail from Çanakkale daily at 9am and return from Bozcaada at 7pm (one way ₺25). Double-check departure times at the Gestas office on Çanakkale's waterfront the day before travelling.

BUS

In summer, Metro, Truva, Pamukkale and other companies run services between İstanbul's Büyük Otogar and Geyikli's Yükyeri İskelesi (₺125, 8¾ hours), from where ferries travel to the island. Make sure that your bus will connect with a ferry – it's usually best to travel overnight and connect with the morning ferry.

Outside summer, buses usually only travel as far as Ezine, from where you'll need to take a taxi or dolmuş to the *iskele;* it's a 20km (₺10) trip.

ⓘ Getting Around

Hourly dolmuşes leave from near the *iskele* in Bozcaada town and travel to Ayazma Beach (₺6). In summer more frequent dolmuşes also serve Ayazma via Sulubahçe Beach, and there's a service to Polente Feneri (Polente Lighthouse) on the westernmost point for watching sunsets.

A taxi from Bozcaada town to Ayazma costs about ₺60.

Mountain bikes can be rented from **Akyüz** (☑0545 541 9515; Çınarlı Çarşı Caddesi; ⊘mid-Jun–mid-Sep), located around the corner from the Cumhuriyet Meydanı.

Behramkale & Assos

📞 0286

The hilltop *köyü* (village) of Behramkale is home to the ancient remains of the Greek settlement of Assos. These include a spectacularly sited Temple of Athena, a theatre and a necropolis. Below the village is a *liman* with a small pebble beach; the locals call this part of the village the İskele Mevkii (Wharf Area). Here, the old stone buildings and warehouses have been transformed into hotels and fish restaurants.

Try to avoid visiting on weekends and public holidays from the beginning of April to the end of August, when tourists pour in by the coachload. And definitely avoid coming here between December and February, when temperatures plummet and the wind chill is merciless.

There are few facilities other than an ATM and pharmacy in the upper village.

History

The Mysian city of Assos was founded in the 8th century BC by colonists from Lesbos, who built its great temple to Athena in 540 BC. The city enjoyed considerable prosperity under the rule of Hermeias, a former student of Plato who encouraged philosophers to live in Assos. Aristotle himself lived here from 348 to 345 BC and ended up marrying Hermeias' niece, Pythia. Assos' glory days came to an abrupt end with the arrival of the Persians, who crucified Hermeias and forced Plato to flee.

Alexander the Great drove the Persians out, but Assos' importance was challenged by the ascendancy of Alexandria Troas to the north. From 241 to 133 BC, the city was ruled by the kings of Pergamum.

St Paul visited Assos briefly during his third missionary journey, walking here from Alexandria Troas to meet St Luke before boarding a boat for Lesbos. In late Byzantine times the city dwindled to a village, a state that it retains today.

👁 Sights

Behramkale's main sight, the Temple of Athena, is located at the highest point of the Assos Archaeological Site, which stretches from the temple down to the lower road that leads to the İskele Mevkii. The theatre and some scant remains of the ancient agora are located by the roadside.

Temple of Athena RUINS

(₺18; ⊙ 8am-5pm Oct-May, to 7pm Apr-Sep) Built in 540 BC on top of a 238m-high hill overlooking the Gulf of Edremit, this temple with its squat Doric columns has undergone a reconstruction that hurts more than helps. However, the setting with its view out to the Greek island of Lesbos is spectacular and well worth the admission fee. Erected by settlers from Lesbos, the temple once boasted a decorative frieze that is now part of the collection of the İstanbul Archaeology Museum.

Ask at your accommodation about a planned walking trail linking the Temple of Athena with the theatre.

Theatre RUINS

(archaeological site & Temple of Athena ₺18) FREE A heavily restored theatre and the remains of the ancient city walls can be seen below the agora; the theatre is accessed via a gate on the winding road leading down to the harbour. The surrounding fields are scattered with sarcophagi (from the Greek, 'flesh-eaters') from the ancient necropolis. According to Pliny the Elder, the sarcophagi were carved from stone that was caustic and that 'ate' the flesh off the deceased in 40 days. The theatre site opens intermittently.

Hüdavendigâr Mosque MOSQUE

Next to the entrance to the Temple of Athena, this poorly maintained 14th-century mosque is a simple structure – a dome on squinches set on top of a square room – that was constructed with materials from a 6th-century-AD church and is one of just two remaining Ottoman mosques of its kind in Turkey (the other is in Bursa, and Hüdavendigar is in fact a poetic name for that city).

🛏 Sleeping

Boutique options are in Behramkale, and resort-style places are down by the water. In high season, virtually all the hotels around the harbour insist on *yarım pansiyon* (half board).

🛏 Village

Tekin Pansiyon PENSION $$

(📞 0286-721 7099; https://assos-tekin-pansiyon.business.site; Behramkale; s/d €20/30; ❄ 🛜) This simple but clean place in the upper village fulfills the basic pension requirements, and even though the eight rooms face away

WORTH A TRIP

BIGA PENINSULA

Postcard-perfect Aegean scenery and deserted ancient ruins make this coastal route between Bozcaada and Behramkale (Assos) one of the most enjoyable drives in the region. There are also some relatively isolated beaches along the route which, while not entirely off the beaten track, are seldom as crowded as others further south.

Ten kilometres southeast of **Geyikli** lie the ruins of **Alexandria Troas** FREE, scattered around the village of Dalyan. After the death of Alexander the Great in 323 BC, his general Antigonus took control of this land, founding the city of Antigoneia in 311 BC.

Some 32km south is **Gülpınar** (pop 1333), a small farming village once the ancient city of Chryse (or Krysa), famous for its 2nd-century-BC Ionic temple to Apollo. Known as the **Apollon Smintheion** (Apollon Smintheus; ☑ 0286-742 8822; ₺10; ☉ 8am-5pm mid-Sep–mid-Jun, to 7.30pm mid-Jun–mid-Sep), the ruins are signposted 300m down a side road to the right as you enter the village.

From Gülpınar, a road heads 9km west past an enormous and unsightly residential development to **Babakale** (ancient Lekton), the westernmost point of mainland Turkey. It's a sleepy place that seems almost overawed by its 18th-century **fortress**, the last Ottoman castle built in present-day Turkey.

Travelling through the peninsula by public transport is difficult; you're much better off exploring by car, motorcycle or bicycle. There are six daily dolmuş services between Gülpınar/Babakale (₺15/18) and Ayvacık, but few others.

from Behramkale's panoramic views, the little tables in the open verandah overlook village goings-on. No English is spoken.

★ **Nar Konak**　　　　BOUTIQUE HOTEL **$$$**
(☑ 0533 480 9393; www.assosnarkonak.com; Behramkale Köyü 62, Behramkale; r €90-120; ☉ Mar-Dec; ❉ ☎) There can't be too many hotels in the world where St Paul preached, but Gizem and Juan's charming guesthouse has a huge rock in its flower-filled garden that apparently served as the apostle's pulpit. Five pretty rooms feature crocheted bedspreads and colourful rugs; the best (Daphne) has a terrace with Acropolis views. There is a terrace bar and a comfortable lounge.

★ **Assos Alarga**　　　　BOUTIQUE HOTEL **$$$**
(☑ 0537 663 1338, 0286-721 7260; www.assosalarga.com; Behramkale; r €90-120, ste €130-180; ⓟ ❉ ☎ ☎ ☎) Located in the quiet end of the village just below the Temple of Athena, this lovely hotel has just five rooms, guaranteeing stellar service from Ece, the affable owner. The setting is wonderful, with plenty of trees, an attractive pool area and panoramic views over the mountains from all rooms. Note that the least expensive room, Viya, doesn't have wi-fi.

★ **Assosyal Otel**　　　　BOUTIQUE HOTEL **$$$**
(☑ 0532 666 0759; www.assosyalotel.com; Alan Meydanı 8, Behramkale; s/d/f €80/90/110; ❉ ☎) Why stay in a pension when there is a stunning option like this on offer? This 16-room

hotel is full of contemporary art, serves a lavish and delicious breakfast and has a series of terraces with mountain views. Occupying a vine-clad stone house that has been given a modern makeover, its rooms are cramped but comfortable nonetheless.

🛏 Harbour

Yıldız Otel　　　　PENSION **$**
(☑ 0286-721 7025; muzafferozden17@gmail.com; İskele Mevkii; s/d €35/55; ❉) Yıldız (the Star) offers rooms with brightly coloured walls, small double beds with clean white linen, fridge and decent bathrooms. Those off the welcoming terrace restaurant and lounge aren't ideal – request one of the front rooms with a harbour view instead.

Dr No Antik Pansiyon　　　　PENSION **$$**
(☑ 0286-721 7397; www.assosdrnoantikpansiyon.com; İskele Mevkii; s €15-22, d €30-43; ❉ ☎) No sign of an evil conspiracy at this very basic but friendly pension, which offers six cramped rooms over the restaurant of the same name. It's the best budget option down at the harbour.

Assos Kervansaray Hotel　　　　HOTEL **$$$**
(☑ 0286-721 7093; www.assoskervansaray.com; İskele Mevkii; d/tr €100/140; ⓟ ❉ ☎ ☎) Housed in a 19th-century acorn warehouse that has been subjected to an endearingly eccentric renovation, the Kervansaray offers 40 rooms; 16 have a sea view. This is a great

choice for families as there's an on-site fish restaurant on the waterside terrace, a small pebble beach, a pool table and two outdoor pools (one for children).

✕ Eating & Drinking

Don't expect to eat well here. The fish restaurants on the harbour are unpleasantly crowded and barely acceptable in quality. They're expensive, too – be sure to check the cost of fish and bottles of wine before ordering. Other options are cheaper but no better. We suggest eating in your hotel if possible.

Mavi Kapi   TURKISH **$$**
(Behramkale; mains ₺20-50; ⊙1-11pm; 🖉) Homestyle cooking combines with sunset views at the friendly 'Blue Door Cafe'. Tables on the upper terrace are very popular, but the downstairs garden is still a fine place to enjoy the concise menu incorporating succulent *köfte* meatballs, eggplant and yoghurt dips and pasta dishes. Plenty of vegetarian dishes make it a versatile choice.

Unique Cafe   CAFE
(Behramkale; ⊙10am-11pm) Located high on Behramkale's slopes near the Temple of Athena, this cool and compact cafe and bar has excellent views over surrounding valleys and across to the Greek island of Lesbos. Jazz bubbles away in the stone-lined interior and there's a concise snacks menu to partner wine and beer.

❶ Getting There & Away

There are two daily dolmuşes to/from Çanakkale (₺30, 1½ hours). Alternatively, regular dolmuşes travel between Çanakkale and Ayvacık (₺20, half-hourly), from where dolmuşes travel to/from Behramkale (₺10, five to seven daily). Services operate between 8am and 7pm.

To get to Küçükkuyu, Gülpınar or Babakale by dolmuş, you'll need to travel via Ayvacık.

A taxi costs ₺50 to/from Ayvacık and ₺100 to/from Küçükkuyu.

❶ Getting Around

From May to mid-October, a dolmuş links the harbour and village every 30 minutes during the day (₺3). A taxi costs ₺15. The steep walk takes around 30 minutes. The dolmuş stand at the harbour is next to the Rıhtım Büfe on the main road.

There is little to no parking at the harbour, and the road ends in a bottleneck that can be extremely stressful for drivers should they get trapped in it. There is a large paid car park on the winding road leading downhill – park there rather than risking getting stuck further down.

Bay of Edremit

If you're travelling down the E87 from Çanakkale to İzmir, or from Behramkale (Assos) to Ayvalık, you will follow the coastal route (aka the 550 Hwy) along the shore of this bay, which is very close to the Greek island of Lesbos. The coastal towns along its edge are popular holiday destinations and are full of ugly modern hotels and shopping malls, but the once-Greek villages in the hinterland – including Yeşilyurt and Adatepe – are relatively unspoiled, filled with pretty stone houses and surrounded by dense pine forest and ancient olive groves.

Olives are the region's most famous industry and olive products, including oil and soap, are available at the many farmers markets that are held in the major centres; the best are in Edremit (Friday) and Altınoluk (Tuesday and Saturday).

⊙ Sights

The area around the appealing village of Adatepe is great for walking, with waterfalls, plunge pools for swimming and a Roman bridge near the waterfalls at Başdeğirmen.

Adatepe Olive-Oil Museum   MUSEUM
(Adatepe Zeytinyağı Müzesi; 🖉0286-752 1303; www.adatepedukkan.com; İzmir-Çanakkale Yolu, Küçükkuyu; ⊙9am-6pm) **FREE** Housed in an old olive-oil factory, this unassuming but interesting museum explains the process of making olive oil and illustrates the product's many uses. There's a cafe downstairs, as well as an excellent shop selling every olive-oil product imaginable. Try the falafel wraps and the homemade kombucha (fermented tea).

Antandros   ARCHAEOLOGICAL SITE
(🖉0266-395 0493; Altınoluk; ⊙10am-4pm) **FREE** Located on the coastal slope of Mt Ida, the Greek city of Antandros was established in the 7th century BC and was famous for its dockyards and harbours. The city lost its strategic importance over the centuries and eventually disappeared altogether, only to be partially rediscovered in recent times. This Roman-era villa is one of the sites that is being excavated by archaeologists from İzmir's Ege Üniversitesi (Aegean University),

and its rooms adorned with frescoes and mosaic floors are open to visitors.

The villa is in a forested glade off the main coastal highway, just east of Altınoluk. Signage isn't all that clear, so you'll need to keep your eyes peeled. There's a small car park next to the site, and a caretaker who is responsible for security.

Alibey Kudar
Etnografya Galerisi MUSEUM
(Alibey Kudar Ethnographic Gallery; ☑0266-387 3340; www.etnografya-galerisi.com; Tahtakuşlar; adult/student & child ₺4/2; ⊘8am-7pm) The jumble of objects at this privately operated museum below the village of Tahtakuşlar provides an insight into the history of the local Turkmen population – many of the Alevi faith – whose descendants moved to this part of Turkey in the 15th century. There's everything from a yurt to textiles, with strange exhibits on Shamanistic culture around the world also thrown into the mix.

To get here from the coastal highway, follow the brown signpost and head 2.5km north into the hills.

🛏 Sleeping & Eating

The villages of Adatepe and Yeşilyurt are full of country-house hotels; there are also a few in the village of Çamlıbel.

Hünnap Han BOUTIQUE HOTEL $$$
(☑0286-752 6581; www.hunnaphan.com; Adatepe; d/tr ₺500/7400, ste ₺800; P❄🅿︎🛜🏊︎) Named after the 200-year-old *hünnap* (jujube) tree in its garden, this group of three restored stone houses in the village of Adatepe offers 22 rooms, mountain and sea views, a restaurant and an attractive pool area.

Zeytin Bağı TURKISH $$$
(☑0266-387 3761; www.zeytinbagi.com; Çamlıbel; starters ₺20, mains ₺45-60; ⊘8am-midnight) Owner/chef Erhan Şeker is rightly proud of his hybrid restaurant, hotel and cookery school overlooking the Bay of Edremit, and he loves to introduce guests from around the globe to the joys of local Aegean produce. You'll dine on local specialities in an elegant indoor dining space or panoramic garden terrace, and can stay overnight in simple but pretty guest rooms (single/double/family ₺350/450/550).

Staying overnight is highly recommended because the Zeytin Bağı organic breakfast spread (included in room price, ₺50 otherwise) is famous throughout the country for its freshness, variety and deliciousness. If you sign up for the full-day cooking class in spring and autumn (US$50 including meal), you may even be able to emulate it at home.

ⓘ Getting There & Away

Turkish Airlines and Pegasus Airlines both fly between İstanbul (Sabiha Gökçen) and Koca Seyit airport in Edremit. Shuttle buses then travel to Küçükkuyu (₺45) and Altınoluk (₺25).

From Küçükkuyu, taxis cost ₺125 to Yeşilyurt, ₺30 to Adatepe and ₺100 to Behramkale (Assos).

BUS & DOLMUŞ
Buses stop at Küçükkuyu's otogar on the main highway every hour en route to Çanakkale (₺35), İzmir (₺45) and İstanbul (₺154).

Dolmuşes travel between Ayvacık and Küçükkuyu six times daily between 8.45am and 6.30pm (₺10); a taxi between the two towns costs ₺70.

Ayvalık
☑0266 / POP 71, 060 (INCL CUNDA)
On first glance, Ayvalık may seem unremarkable, a port town similar to many others in this region. But wander a few streets back from the waterfront and you'll discover an old Greek village in spirited abandon. Colourful shuttered doors conceal boutique hotels in restored stone houses, mosques converted from Greek Orthodox churches welcome the faithful to prayer and historic cafes full of locals line hidden squares. Put simply, it's got Aegean ambience in spades.

The region's olive-oil production is centred on Ayvalık, and there are plenty of shops selling the end product. The broken chimneys in the town centre belonged to now-abandoned olive-oil factories; these days local production occurs on the edge of town.

◉ Sights

There are a number of good sandy beaches a few kilometres south of the city. The oddly named **Sarımsaklı Plaj** (Garlic Beach) is the most popular and is almost always crowded in summer. **Badavut Plaj** (Badavut Beach) to the west is quieter.

★**Old Town** HISTORIC SITE
Ayvalık's old town is a joy to explore. A maze of cobbled streets east of the *liman,* it is full of market squares, atmospheric cafes,

Ayvalık

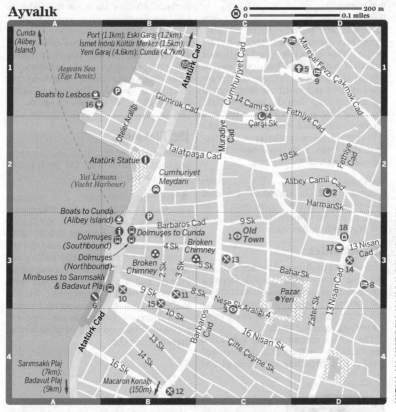

N 0 ——— 200 m
0 ——— 0.1 miles

IZMIR & THE NORTH AEGEAN AYVALIK

Ayvalık

Greek Orthodox churches and pretty stone houses built by Greek residents during the Ottoman era. Be sure to wander along Barbaros Caddesi, home to historic businesses such as the **Karamanlar Unlu Mamülleri** (Barbaros Caddesi; ⊘ 6am-4pm) bakery, and also visit the atmosphere-drenched Şeytan Kahvesi (p194), aka 'the Devil's Coffeehouse', on Alibey Cami Caddesi.

Taksiyarhis
Memorial Museum CHURCH
(Taksiyarhis Anıt Müzesi; ☑0266-327 2734; Mareşal Fevzi Çakmak Caddesi; ₺5; ⊙9am-5pm Tue-Sun) This erstwhile Greek Orthodox cathedral, built in 1844 but never used as a place of worship, was completely renovated in 2013 and positively shimmers in the midday sun. Note the *catedra* (bishop's seat) decorated with pelicans and a crown, the wonderful pulpit and the 18th-century icons in the apse. The cathedral is huge, with three aisles and a free-standing belfry.

Köy Pazarı MARKET
(⊙6am-1pm Thu) On Thursdays, a 'village market' is held in this square next to the main *pazar yeri* (marketplace), which is also filled with market stalls.

Activities

Cruise boats head around the bay's islands, including Cunda (Alibey; p195), stopping here and there for swimming, sunbathing and walking. These generally depart at 11am and return by 6.30pm and cost around €60 per person, including lunch.

The waters around Ayvalık are famed among divers for their rare deep-sea red coral at sites including Deli Mehmet and Kerbela. Another boon for the industry was the discovery of a wrecked jet in 2009. Dive companies in Ayvalık can organise trips to see these places and their attendant marine life, including moray eels, grouper, octopus and sea horses. An experienced and recommended local dive company is **Ayvalik 3 Sea Diving Center** (☑0544 292 5214; www.ayvalik3sea.com; Ayvalık Limanı).

🛏 Sleeping

There are plenty of atmospheric boutique and budget options in the Old Town, but no top-end choices of note.

★**Taksiyarhis Pansiyon** PENSION $$
(☑0266-312 1494; www.taksiyarhispansiyon.com; Maraşal Çakmak Caddesi 71; dm €12, s/d €22/43, s/d without bathroom €18/36; ❄🐾) This 200-year-old Greek house behind the cathedral is full of old Turkish textiles and objets d'art. Facilities include a communal kitchen and a vine-shaded terrace with sweeping views. Rooms are rustic chic and the small dormitory sleeping up to six is quite charming. Bathrooms are clean and plentiful. Wi-fi is on the ground floor only; breakfast costs ₺20.

LOCAL KNOWLEDGE

GHOSTS FROM THE PAST

The early 1920s hold mixed memories for Ayvalık. Pride over its role in the Turkish War of Independence – it was here that the first shots were fired – is tempered by what happened afterwards. The Ottoman Greeks, who made up the majority of the population in Ayvalık, were forced to abandon the land of their ancestors and relocate to the Greek island of Lesbos, while some Turks from that island were, in turn, forced to start new lives in Ayvalık. Despite the enormous distress this must have caused, the Ayvalık–Lesvos exchange is nonetheless regarded as one of the least damaging episodes of the period because of the proximity of the two communities, which enabled people from both sides to continue visiting their former homes – mixed though their emotions must have been during those trips. Furthermore, both communities were involved in the production of olive oil, and so would have found much that was familiar in the other.

Today, whispers from the past are everywhere here. Some elderly locals can speak Greek and many of the town's former Greek Orthodox churches remain standing, though converted into mosques. In 1923, the former Ayios Yannis (St John's) church became the **Saatlı Camii** (Clock Mosque; Çarşı Sokak), named for its clock tower and now minaret. The former Ayios Yioryios (St George's) is today the **Çınarlı Camii** (Yeni Hamam Sokak), named after the *çınar* (plane trees) that grew here. The grand Greek cathedral was never converted but has now been turned into the Taksiyarhis Memorial Museum.

Madra House
PENSION **$$**

(☑ 0533 911 1076; www.madrahouse.com; 13 Nisan Caddesi, Aralığı 29; per person ₺150; ❄ 🛜) Australian-Turkish couple Diana and Genghis opened this charming pension in 2016, offering seven attractively decorated rooms (one with a balcony and commanding sea views), a lounge with pot-belly stove and a large terraced garden. The house itself is a lovely example of the Greek houses built here in the late 19th century, with original features galore. Great value.

Çeşmeli Han
B&B **$$**

(☎ 0266-312 8084; www.cesmelihan.com; Mareşal Fevzi Çakmak Caddesi 87; d/tr ₺340/400; ☉ May-Oct; ❄ ❄ 🛜) The gorgeous courtyard garden and upstairs terrace with panoramic view are the major draw at this family-run B&B, which has seven cramped rooms with exposed-brick walls, tiled floors and spotless bathrooms. Guests rave about the lavish home-cooked breakfast.

🍴 Eating

There are plenty of good cheap eats to be enjoyed in Ayvalık, but there are few restaurants of note – it's best to head to Cunda (p195) to eat in the evening. There are markets on Thursday (town centre) and Sunday (on Atatürk Caddesi next to the İsmet İnönü Kültür Merkez building).

Minta Bahçe
CAFE **$**

(Barbaros Caddesi 55; mezes & portions ₺15-30; ☉ 8am-10pm; 🛜 ☝) Tucked away in the middle of Ayvalık's Pazar Yeri, the shaded garden at this family-owned *lokanta* (restaurant serving ready-made food) is a good place for seasonal *meze* and prepared dishes. There's no formal menu, so you'll be led to the kitchen to make your selection. Vegetarian choices abound and it's a good breakfast option when checking out Ayvalık's good Thursday morning market.

Café Caramel
CAFE **$**

(☑ 0266-312 8520; Barbaros Caddesi 9 Sokak; börek ₺10, cakes ₺15; ☉ 9am-8pm Mon-Sat May-Sep, to 6pm Oct-Apr) This eccentrically decorated and very popular cafe in the old town offers a nostalgic jazz soundtrack, extensive dessert menu (cakes, soufflés, tiramisu), homemade soda and savoury snacks

FAST FOOD – AYVALIK STYLE

Ayvalık may have made its name as an olive-oil producer, but these days it's better known throughout Turkey for a rather less-refined culinary offering: Ayvalık *tost* (toast). The town's take on fast food is essentially a toasted white-bread sandwich crammed with all manner of ingredients, including cheese, *sucuk* (spicy veal or beef sausage), salami, pickles and tomatoes. These fillings are then lathered in ketchup and mayonnaise (unless you specifically request otherwise). The faint-hearted can opt just for one or two ingredients, but this is most decidedly frowned upon.

The *tostu* are available at cafes and stalls throughout town; **Avşar Büfe** (Atatürk Caddesi; dishes ₺12-18; ☉ 24hr May-Sep, 7am-3am Oct-Apr) and the surrounding eateries with communal tables and benches are good places to try it.

including böreks (filled pastries). Sit inside or in the atmospheric laneway.

Tamam Meyhane
TURKISH **$$**

(☑ 0546 545 1010; www.tamammeyhane.com; Sokak 1, Barbaros Caddesi 19; set menu ₺85; ☉ 7pm-late; ☝) Framed by an overflowing grape arbour, Taman Meyhane's slim laneway space is a perfect spot to while away a few hours enjoying the fixed menu of 15 different vegetarian, meat and seafood *meze*. Service can be on the leisurely side, but with a nightly soundtrack of live music and Turkish folk songs, you'll probably be in no rush anyway.

Pino
CAFE **$$**

(13 Nisan Caddesi; mains ₺25-40; ☉ 8am-9pm daily Apr-Sep, closed Mon Oct-Mar) Named after its English-speaking owner Pinar (Pino to her friends), this friendly cafe in an old stone house opened in 2016 and is a good choice for a coffee or light lunch. There's banquette seating inside and a few tables on the street. The menu includes burgers, bruschetta, pastas and quiche. No alcohol, but freshly squeezed juice is on offer.

FODRGUN/GETTY IMAGES ©

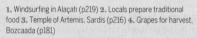

1. Windsurfing in Alaçatı (p219) 2. Locals prepare traditional
food 3. Temple of Artemis, Sardis (p216) 4. Grapes for harvest,
Bozcaada (p181)

İzmir & the North Aegean Highlights

Travellers are spoiled for choice in this region and, at the risk of sounding cliché, there really is something for everyone here. Its ancient cities bring history alive, the beaches are seldom as frenetic as elsewhere, the food and wine are among the country's best and the ghosts of times past are ever present.

Ruins

The ancient city of Pergamum (now Bergama) is at the top of everyone's list of places to visit, and Assos in Behramkale is as dramatically situated as you'll find anywhere. But don't miss the wealth of ruins at lesser-known sites such as Teos on the Biga Peninsula or Sardis east of İzmir.

Beaches

The beaches at Bozcaada are rightfully celebrated and easily accessible. But go the extra kilometre to take the plunge at Badavut Plaj, south of Ayvalık. And if you prefer to be on rather than in the water, head for Alaçatı Surf Paradise, the centre for windsurfing in Turkey.

Memories

The north Aegean has been colonised for millennia and is one of the most ethnically diverse regions in Turkey. Reminders of the region's multilayered past are seen, felt and sometimes even heard – especially in places such as Ayvalık, where many Greeks made their home before independence, and in İzmir with its community of Sephardic Jews.

Food & Drink

Those rich, multi-ethnic influences are especially palpable in the region's cuisine, which has taken much from the Greek, Cretan and Jewish styles of cooking. There are well-regarded wineries on Bozcaada and southwest of İzmir.

☕ Drinking & Nightlife

★ Şeytan Kahvesı
CAFE

(Palabahçe Kahvehanesi; Alibey Cami Caddesi; ⏰6am-8pm Oct-May, to 11pm Jun-Sep) One of the town's best-loved and most historic cafes, Şeytan Kahvesi (the Devil's Coffeehouse) was named after the current owner's grandfather, who certainly had an interesting name to live up to. Its street-side terrace is a hugely atmospheric people-watching spot – order a Turkish coffee or glass of *koruk suyu* (freshly pressed unfermented fresh grape juice, available from June to November).

The devilish connotations don't stop with the cafe's name – it was a location for the popular Turkish television series *İki Yaka Bir İsmail* (Two Continents, One İsmail), the story of a philanderer who keeps two women in two different ports, one Turkish and one Greek.

Leyla Gastro Pub
BAR

(☎0543 516 2524; Talatpaşa Caddesi 7; ⏰10am-1am; 🛜) Negotiate the backstreets around Ayvalık's waterfront to the best place to enjoy sunset. The town's bright young things crowd in for cold beer, good cocktails and surprising snacks like decent burgers and tacos, and there's always good music on high rotation. Check out Leyla's Facebook and Instagram pages for advice of occasional live gigs.

Şatan Sofrası
CAFE

(Satan's Supper; Balıkesir/Ayvalık Şeytan Tepesi; ⏰9am-9pm Oct-May, closes later Jun-Sep) Commanding spectacular views over the islands in the bay, this outdoor cafe on a hill 8km south of the centre is most crowded at sunset, when spots in the restaurant car park (₺10) are hotly contested. Coffee, tea and ice cream are the popular menu choices.

🛍 Shopping

★ Çöp(m)adam
ARTS & CRAFTS

(☎0266-312 1360; www.copmadam.com; off 13 Nisan Caddesi; ⏰8.30am-5.30pm Mon-Sat Oct-May, 9.30am-6.30pm Mon-Sat Jun-Sep) 🌿 A social enterprise helping unemployed women earn a living by creating fashionable items from throwaway materials, the 'Garbage Lady' saves at least six tons of waste from going to landfill annually, and sells more than 4000 items. This workshop and retail outlet is near Şeytan Kahvesı in the old town and stocks cards, aprons, bags, toys and tea towels.

ℹ Getting There & Away

BOAT

Boats to Mytilini (Midilli in Turkish) in Lesbos, Greece, depart from the port building at the northern end of Atatürk Caddesi. Look for the 'TC Ayvalık Deniz Hudut Kapısı' sign. There are at least three weekly services (one way/return €20/30); the trip takes 1½ hours. From June to August, boats sail daily. Note that times do change and you must make a reservation (in person or by telephone) 24 hours before departure. When you pick up your tickets, bring your passport.

For information and tickets, contact **Jale Tour** (☎0266-331 3170; www.jaletur.com; Gümrük Binası Karşısı, Atatürk Caddesi; ⏰10am-7pm Mon-Sat) or **Turyol** (☎0266-331 6700; www.turyolonline.com; Güzide İş Karşısı, Atatürk Caddesi 296/2; ⏰10am-7pm Mon-Sat); both have offices opposite the port building.

BUS

There are two bus stations in Ayvalık: the Yeni Garaj (New Garage) on the main İzmir–Çanakkale highway and the Eski Garaj (Old Garage) on Atatürk Caddesi in the centre of town. Most inter-city bus services use the Yeni Garaj, from where the following buses arrive and depart:

Çanakkale (₺50, 3½ hours, 170km) Regular services, sometimes on İstanbul-bound buses.

İstanbul (₺110, eight hours, 560km) Usually via Çanakkale.

İzmir (₺35, two hours, 160km) Regular services.

CAR

The inland route to Bergama, via Kozak, is much more scenic and only marginally slower than the coast road, winding through idyllic pine-clad hills. Backtrack north for 10km towards Edremit, then turn east.

DOLMUŞ

Bergama Hourly services to Bergama's otogar (₺20) pick up passengers from outside the Garaj Büfe opposite the Eski Garaj and also from stops along Atatürk Caddesi.

Cunda Frequent dolmuşes (₺5) travel two routes between Ayvalık and Cunda: the Yeni Yol (New Rd) service goes to/from Cunda's harbour and the Eski Yol (Old Rd) goes to Cunda from the beaches. The main stops in Ayvalık are in front of the tourist information booth on Atatürk Caddesi – northbound services leave from the town side, southbound from the sea side.

Edremit Frequent services travel to/from the Eski Garaj between 7am and 8.15pm (₺18).

ⓘ Getting Around

Navigating Ayvalık old town's fiendishly narrow lanes can be an extremely stressful experience. You're much better off parking at one of the car parks along the waterfront. These generally charge around ₺20 per day.

A taxi from the Yeni Garaj to the town centre costs around ₺45. Taxis between the rank in the town centre and Cunda can cost as much as ₺60.

DOLMUŞ

Dolmuşes service the town centre, stopping to put down and pick up passengers along a series of short set routes. You can catch most of them at the stops near the Migros Supermarket and tourist information kiosk south of Cumhuriyet Meydanı. Fares are typically ₺5.

Regular domuşes run between the Yeni Garaj and Cumhuriyet Meydanı (₺5). They also pick up regularly from Cumhuriyet Meydanı and from the stop opposite the tourist information kiosk before continuing to Sarımsaklı and Badavut beaches.

Cunda (Alibey Island)

☑ 0266

Named after a hero of the Turkish War of Independence, Alibey Island (Alibey Adası), known to locals as Cunda Island (Cunda Adası) or just Cunda, faces Ayvalık across the water. Linked to the mainland by a causeway (it can be reached by car, ferry or dolmuş), it's generally regarded as a quieter extension of Ayvalık itself, with residents of both communities regularly shuttling back and forth between the two.

The ferry docks at a small quay lined with fish restaurants. Behind these sit a small, distinguished-looking town made up of old (and in parts rather dilapidated) Greek stone houses. As with Ayvalık, the people here were compelled into a population exchange in the early 1920s, in this instance with Muslims from Giritli (Crete).

To the east of the ferry pier is the town's main square. Behind the square is a small tourist market with stalls selling jewellery and other trinkets.

◉ Sights & Activities

The prettiest parts of the island are to the west, where there are good beaches for sunbathing and swimming, and north, much of which is taken up by the **Pateriça Nature Reserve**. This has good walking routes and, on the north shore, the ruins of the Greek **Ayışığı Manastırı** (Moonlight Monastery).

Rahmi M Koç Museum   MUSEUM

(☑ 0266-327 2734; www.rmk-museum.org.tr/en; Şeref Sokak 6a; ₺7; ◷ 10am-5pm Tue-Sun Oct-Mar, to 7pm Tue-Sun Apr-Sep) Housed in the magnificently restored Taksiyarhis Church (Church of the Archangels), a Greek Orthodox church built in 1873 and now painted in a distinctive shade of yellow, this is a sibling museum to İstanbul's excellent Rahmi M Koç Museum and has a collection that is similarly strong on exhibits concerned with transportation and engineering.

🛏 Sleeping

Cunda Inn   BOUTIQUE HOTEL $$

(☑ 0552 350 6366; www.cundainn.com; 15 Eylül Caddesi 24, Sokak 6; r €55-60; ⓟ ❄ 🛜) Built and opened in 2019, the Cunda Inn channels a heritage village vibe amid the rustic but stylish decor of its spacious rooms. Breakfast includes fresh *börek* pastries from a nearby bakery, and there's a pleasant courtyard and garden area. Convivial owner Mehmet has worked for international companies around the world, and is a chatty and cosmopolitan host.

Cunda Fora   BOUTIQUE HOTEL $$$

(☑ 0266-327 3031; www.cundafora.com; 1 Sokak 7, off Mevlana Caddesi; r ₺750; ⓟ ❄ 🛜) Hugely popular with honeymooning couples, this relatively new hotel is located just off the main road back from the harbour, so it's quieter than most of the places near the waterfront. There's a charming rear verandah with water views, an in-house hamam (complimentary for guests) and comfortable rooms with attractive decor and top-quality amenities. Breakfast is a highlight.

Taş Bahçe   BOUTIQUE HOTEL $$$

(☑ 0266-327 2290; www.tasbahcebutikotel.com; 15 Eylül Caddesi 33; d ₺450-500; ⓟ ❄ 🛜) The lovely 'Stone Garden' occupies two newly built townhouses that look centuries old. It's on the main road into town about 400m from the seafront, but the windows in the 10 rooms have double glazing, ensuring island tranquillity. There's a lounge-library and a lovely garden where breakfast is served. Deluxe rooms have views.

✕ Eating & Drinking

★ Lâl Girit Mutfağı   GREEK $$

(Ruby Cretan Cuisine; ☑ 0266-327 2834; Altay Pansiyon Yanı 20; mezes ₺20-30, mains ₺50; ◷ noon-midnight Sep-Jun, 8pm-1am Jul & Aug) Owner and chef Emine was taught to cook

Girit (Cretan) dishes by her grandmother, and the results are simply inspired. Expect her to emerge from the kitchen to explain what's in the meze selection (there's always a huge variety). You can be sure that your choice will be fresh, unusual and delectable. Slow-cooked lamb is the only main dish on offer.

Cunda Bahçecik
BREAKFAST $$

(☑ 0532 163 4843; www.cundabahcecik.com; 15 Eylul Caddesi 11; breakfast ₺35-40; ⊙ 9am-3pm) Having a second breakfast for lunch is a perfectly valid dining choice, especially when it's the array of small plates on offer at this specialist breakfast garden cafe. Highlights enjoyed in the shaded garden include the *menemem* (Turkish-style scrambled eggs) and the *kaymak* (clotted cream) with honey. Have another glass of tea to extend your stay into a second hour.

Şef Mehmet'in Balik Evi
SEAFOOD $$

(☑ 0553 397 0843; www.sefmehmetinbalikevi.com; Mektep Sokak; mezes ₺15-40; ⊙ noon-2am) Decked out in blue and white, this friendly eatery with ocean views is a good option at the quieter eastern end of Cunda's harbourfront strip. Diligent waiters work hard to deliver the freshest of seafood, and there's a top selection of mezes. Our particular highlight was the grilled octopus.

★ Ayna
TURKISH $$$

(☑ 0266-327 2725; www.aynacunda.net; Çarşı Caddesi 22; soup ₺15, starters ₺35-50, mains ₺50-70; ⊙ 10am-midnight Tue-Sun Feb-Dec; ※❀) ✎ We love everything about this extremely chic eatery behind Taş Kahve at the *liman*. Owned by the Kürsat olive-oil mill, it offers a delicious seasonal menu featuring *börek* stuffed with wild herbs, vegetables cooked in olive oil and home-style soups and mains. The cakes, pastries and desserts are delicious, too. Pop in for lunch; book for dinner.

Taş Kahve
BAR

(☑ 0266-327 1166; www.taskahve.com.tr; Sahil Boyu 20; tea ₺3, beer ₺20; ⊙ 7am-midnight) It's worth the trip to the island just to sip tea and talk fishing in this cavernous venue adorned with stained-glass windows and period black-and-white photos. Its front terrace positively heaves with people in summer.

Vino Şarap Evi
WINE BAR

(Wine House; ☑ 0535-737 3384; www.vinosarapevicunda.com; Cumhuriyet Caddesi 8; ⊙ noon-2am) Lingering over a glass of wine at one of the laneway tables at this convivial wine bar close to the harbour is a popular local pastime. Choose from local and international drops, including a quaffable house-made one. Many patrons stay for a simple pasta dinner.

❶ Getting There & Away

Frequent dolmuşes (₺5) travel two routes between Cunda and Ayvalık: the Yeni Yol (New Rd) service goes to/from Cunda's harbour and the Eski Yol (Old Rd) goes to/from the beaches.

A taxi between the island and central Ayvalık will cost around ₺60.

Parking on the waterfront is charged between 8am and midnight (₺10) and you will be fined if you don't have a ticket. A better and more secure option is the large car park (₺10) opposite the Taş Bahçe hotel.

Bergama (Pergamum)

☑ 0232 / POP 103,200

The laid-back market town of Bergama is the modern successor to the once-powerful ancient city of Pergamum. Unlike Ephesus, which heaves with tourists year-round, Pergamum is for the most part a site of quiet classical splendour. Its ruins – especially the Asklepion and Acropolis – are so extraordinary that they were inscribed on Unesco's World Heritage list in June 2014, the 999th site in the world (and the 14th in Turkey) to be so honoured.

History

Pergamum owed its prosperity to Lysimachus, one of Alexander the Great's generals, who took control of much of the Aegean region when Alexander's far-flung empire fell apart after his death in 323 BC. In the battles over the spoils, Lysimachus captured a great treasure, estimated at more than 9000 gold talents, which he entrusted to his commander in Pergamum, Philetaerus, before going off to fight Seleucus for control of Asia Minor. But Lysimachus lost the battle and was killed in 281 BC. Philetaerus then set himself up as governor.

Philetaerus, a eunuch, was succeeded by his nephew and heir Eumenes I (r 263–241 BC), who was in turn followed by his adopted son, Attalus I (r 241–197 BC). Attalus

Bergama (Pergamum)

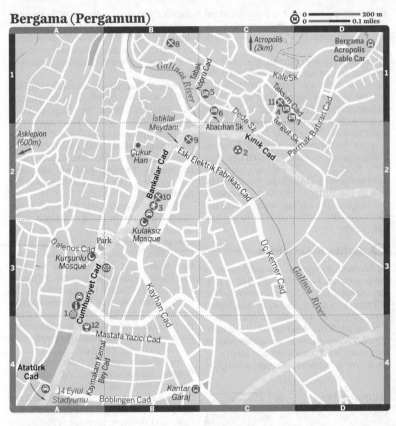

Bergama (Pergamum)

◉ Sights

✦ Activities, Courses & Tours

🛏 Sleeping

declared himself king, expanding his power and forging an alliance with Rome.

During the reign of Attalus' son, Eumenes II (r 197–159 BC), Pergamum reached its golden age. He founded a library that would in time rival that of Alexandria, Egypt, then the world's greatest repository of knowledge. This was partly due to the large-scale production here of *pergamena* (parchment),

the writing material made from stretched animal skin and more durable than papyrus.

Eumenes also added the Altar of Zeus to the buildings already crowning the Acropolis, built the 'middle city' on terraces halfway down the hill, and expanded and beautified the Asklepion. Much of what he and the other kings built hasn't survived the ravages of the centuries (or the acquisitive enthusiasm of Western museums, notably the Pergamon Museum in Berlin), but what remains is impressive, dramatically sited and well worth visiting.

Eumenes' brother Attalus II (r 160–138 BC) kept up the good work, but under the short rule of his son, Attalus III (r 138–133 BC), the kingdom began to fall apart. With no heir, Attalus III bequeathed his kingdom to Rome, and Pergamum became the Roman province of Asia in 129 BC.

Along with İzmir, Sardis and Ephesus, Pergamum is one of the the Seven Churches of the Revelation (or Apocalypse), the major churches of early Christianity mentioned by St John the Divine in the New Testament's last chapter. The phrase 'where Satan has his throne' (Rev 2:13) may refer to the Red Hall (p200).

◎ Sights & Activities

★ **Bergama Acropolis**　　ARCHAEOLOGICAL SITE
(Bergama Akropol; Akropol Caddesi 2; ₺42; ⊙ 8am-7pm mid-Apr–Sep, to 6.30pm Oct–mid-Apr) One of Turkey's most impressive archaeological sites, Bergama's acropolis is dramatically sited on a hill to the northeast of the town centre. There's plenty to see in this ancient settlement, with ruins large and small scattered over the upper and lower cities. Chief

Acropolis

Ⓝ
0 ——— 200 m
0 ——— 0.1 miles

among these are the Temple of Trajan, the vertigo-inducing 10,000-seat Hellenistic theatre, the Altar of Zeus (sadly denuded of its magnificent frieze, which now resides in Berlin) and the whimsical mosaic floors in Building Z.

There are two ways to access the site. You can drive to the upper car park (parking ₺5) or instead follow the signposts along Akropol Caddesi to the lower station of the **Bergama Acropolis Cable Car** (Bergama Akropolis Teleferik; ☑ 0232-631 0805; return ₺35; ⊙ 8am-7pm mid-Apr–Sep, 8.30am-5.30pm Oct–mid-Apr). There's a paid car park here, too (again ₺5). The cable-car ride takes five minutes.

From the **Upper City**, a line of rather faded blue dots marks a suggested route around the main structures – you might instead consider hiring the audio guide for ₺10. These structures include the **library** that helped put Pergamum on the map and the colossal marble-columned **Temple of Trajan** (or Trajaneum), built during the reigns of the emperors Trajan and Hadrian and used to worship them as well as Zeus. It's the only Roman structure surviving on the Acropolis, and its foundations were used as cisterns during the Middle Ages.

Immediately downhill from the temple, descend through the vaulted tunnel-like temple foundations to the impressive and unusual **Hellenistic theatre**. Its builders decided to take advantage of the spectacular view (and conserve precious space on top of the hill) by building the theatre into the hillside. In general, Hellenistic theatres are wider and rounder than this, but at Pergamum the hillside location made rounding impossible and so it was increased in height instead.

At the northern end of the theatre terrace is the ruined **Temple of Dionysus**, while to the south is the **Altar of Zeus** (also known as the Great Altar), which was originally covered with magnificent friezes depicting the battle between the Olympian gods and their subterranean foes. However, 19th-century German excavators were allowed to remove most of this famous building to Berlin, leaving only the base behind.

Piles of rubble on top of the acropolis are marked as five separate palaces, including that of **Eumenes II**, and you can also see fragments of the once-magnificent defensive walls as well as **barracks** and **arsenal**.

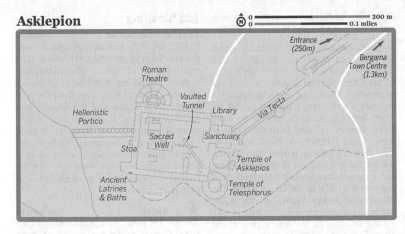

N | 0 ——————— 200 m
0 ——————— 0.1 miles

Entrance (250m)

Bergama Town Centre (1.3km)

Roman Theatre

Vaulted Tunnel

Library

Via Tecta

Hellenistic Portico

Sacred Well

Sanctuary

Stoa

Temple of Asklepios

Ancient Latrines & Baths

Temple of Telesphorus

To escape the crowds and get a good view of the theatre and Temple of Trajan, walk downhill behind the Altar of Zeus, or turn left at the bottom of the theatre steps, and follow the sign to the **antik yol** (ancient street) past the **Upper Agora** and the **bath-gymnasium**. Within what was once a sprawling residential area of the **Middle City** is modern **Building Z** (2004), protecting part of a peristyle court and some fantastic floor mosaics. Look for the grotesque masks with wild animals, the child Dionysus with Silenus supping from a cup and the remnants of tinted stucco on the walls. You'll then pass more baths, gymnasia and the sumptuous **Palace of Attalus I** before reaching the **Lower Agora**.

Asklepion RUINS
(Prof Dr Frieldhelm Korte Caddesi 1; ☏37; ☺8am-7pm Apr-Sep, to 6.30pm Oct-Mar) The Asklepion may not be as dramatic as the Acropolis, but in some ways it is even more extraordinary. One of the most important healing centres of the Roman world, it had baths, temples, a theatre, a library, treatment centres and latrines in its heyday. Remnants of many of these structures have been preserved on site, and what we see now is quite similar to how the centre would have appeared in the time of Emperor Hadrian (117–138 BC).

Said to have been founded by Archias, a local who had been cured at the Asklepion of Epidaurus (Greece), Pergamum's Asklepion offered many different treatments, including mud baths, the use of herbs and ointments, enemas and sunbathing. Diagnosis was often by dream analysis.

The centre came to the fore under Galen (AD 129–216), who was born here and studied in Alexandria, Greece and Asia Minor before setting up shop as physician to Pergamum's gladiators. Recognised as perhaps the greatest early physician, Galen added considerably to the knowledge of the circulatory and nervous systems, and also systematised medical theory. Under his influence, the medical school at Pergamum became renowned throughout the ancient world. His work was the basis for Western medicine well into the 16th century.

The Roman **Via Tecta**, a colonnaded sacred way, leads from the entrance to the **sanctuary**, where you'll see the base of a column carved with snakes, the symbol of Asclepios, the god of medicine. Just as the snake sheds its skin and gains a 'new life', so the patients at the Asclepion were supposed to 'shed' their illnesses. Signs mark a circular **Temple of Asklepios**, a **library** and, beyond it, a heavily restored **Roman theatre**.

There are **latrines** over a channel in the southwest corner of the main courtyard and a **sacred well** in its centre. From here, pass along the vaulted tunnel to the **treatment centre**, a temple to another god of medicine called Telesphorus. Patients slept in the round temple hoping that Telesphorus would send a cure or diagnosis in a dream. The names of Telesphorus' two daughters, Hygeia and Panacea, have passed into medical terminology.

Soft drinks and snacks are available from an on-site snack bar.

To get here, turn into Galenos Caddesi between the small park and the Kurşunlu Mosque on Cumhuriyet Caddesi (look for a street sign pointing the way to the Asklepion and 'Katlı Otopark'), and head 2km uphill.

Bergama Archaeology Museum · MUSEUM

(Bergama Müze Müdürlüğü; ☑0232-483 5117; Cumhuriyet Caddesi 6; ₺7; ⊘8am-7pm Apr-Oct, 8.30am-4.30pm Nov-Mar) Boasting a small but impressive collection of artefacts, Bergama's museum is well worth a visit. On exhibit are reliefs from the Acropolis, including a wonderful Roman-era relief from the Demeter Terrace, and a Hellenistic frieze and architrave from the Athena Terrace. Also impressive are the many statues from the Asklepion and a mosaic floor featuring Medusa's head that was originally in the Lower Agora. The ethnography gallery focuses on the crafts, costumes and customs of the Ottoman period.

Look out, too, for the scale replica of the Altar of Zeus (the original is in the Pergamon Museum in Berlin) and the many objects (ceramic, glazed terracotta, iron, marble and glass) salvaged from the excavations in both the Acropolis and Asklepion. Of the exhibits in the ethnography gallery, the extraordinary collection of dresses of the Bergama region – influenced by the nomadic Yürük (Turkomen) peoples – is most impressive.

Red Hall · RUINS

(Kızıl Avlu; Kınık Caddesi; ₺7; ⊘8am-6.30pm Apr-Sep, to 4.30pm Oct-Mar) The cathedral-sized Red Hall, sometimes called the Red Basilica, is thought to have been built by the Romans as a temple to the Egyptian gods Serapis and Isis in the 2nd century AD. It's an imposing-looking structure with two domed rotundas; visitors can enter the southern rotunda but not the main temple (currently being restored) or the northern rotunda. The southern rotunda was used for religious and cult rituals – look for the huge niche where a cult statue would have sat.

Originally, this must have been an awe-inspiring place. In his Book of Revelation, St John the Divine wrote that this was one of the Seven Churches of the Apocalypse, singling it out as the 'throne of the devil'. In fact, the building is so big that the early Christians didn't convert it into a church, but in the 5th century AD built a basilica inside it instead.

Hacı Hekim Hamamı · HAMAM

(☑0232-631 0102; Bankalar Caddesi 42; hamam ₺35, scrub & massage ₺50; ⊘men 6am-11pm, women 8.30am-7pm) This 16th-century hamam just north of the Kulaksız Mosque has separate entrances for men and women. The women's entrance is around the side.

🛏 Sleeping

Odyssey Guesthouse · PENSION $

(☑0232-631 3501; www.odysseyguesthouse.com; Abacıhan Sokak 13; dm ₺50, s with/without bathroom ₺100/70, d with/without bathroom ₺140/110; ⊘closed Jan–mid-Feb; ❋ 🛜) Superb views of all three archaeological sites from the roof terrace are a highlight of this friendly and well-run pension. There are nine simple rooms spread over two buildings, a book exchange and a communal kitchen; the copy of Homer's *Odyssey* in every room is a nice touch. Breakfast costs ₺20 and the English-speaking owner provides plenty of local information.

★ Taş Konak · HISTORIC HOTEL $$

(☑0507 776 1940; www.bergamataskonak.com; Taksim Caddesi 25; s/d from €35/45; P❋ 🛜) Located amid the backstreets of Bergama's hillside old town, Taş Konak's stone-walled heritage style is infused with warmth by the friendly family owners. A compact terrace provides excellent views of the imposing outline of the Red Hall, and generous breakfasts are packed with local ingredients. There's a handy off-street car park a short stroll away if you're travelling by car.

Aristonicus Boutique Hotel · BOUTIQUE HOTEL $$

(☑0232-632 4141; www.facebook.com/pg/aristonicushotel; Taksim Caddesi 37; s/d/tw/tr & q €27/45/55/63; P❋ 🛜) Offering good value, this operation has converted two old stone houses into an attractive hotel offering six immaculately presented rooms with satellite TV, kettle and minibar. The singles are tiny and some of the doubles have slightly cramped bathrooms, but the comfort levels are generally more than acceptable. Breakfast is served in a small shady courtyard.

The hotel sometimes closes for the winter period.

Hera Hotel · BOUTIQUE HOTEL $$$

(☑0232-631 0634; www.hotelhera.com; Tabak Köprü Caddesi 38; s/d/tr from €33/50/68; P❋ 🛜) Here at the Hera, a pair of 200-year-old Greek houses have been cobbled into sophisticated accommodation. Each of the 10 rooms, which are named after mythological Greek deities, feature timber ceilings, parquet floors and kilims. The best rooms are Zeus and Hera; both have views and Zeus' bathroom is particularly large. There's a garden and panoramic breakfast terrace.

🍴 Eating & Drinking

Bergama's bustling Monday market is in the streets near the hospital. It's great for fresh fruit and veg. There are plenty of cheap eateries along Bankalar Caddesi and on İstiklal Meydanı in the town centre.

On warm nights, locals flock to the tea- and coffeehouses around the Ottoman Bazaar and to the bars and *çay bahçesi* on İzmir Caddesi just south of the stadium to meet up with friends. A party atmosphere with plenty of music prevails. For a cold beer, head to the compact strip of beer gardens along Cumhuriyet Caddesi.

Bergama Sofrası   TURKISH $
(☑ 0232-631 5131; Bankalar Caddesi 44; soup ₺10, portions ₺14-18; ☉ 9am-9pm) One of a number of *lokantas* that can be found on the town's main drag, this friendly place next to the hamam has indoor and outdoor seating, clean surfaces and an open kitchen. The spicy *köfte* is the speciality. The usual *lokanta* rule applies – eat here at lunch when the food is still fresh.

Arzu   PIDE $
(☑ 0232-612 8700; İstiklal Meydanı 35; soups ₺8-12, pides ₺15-20 İskender kebap ₺30; ☉ 6am-midnight) Located on a busy corner, this ultrafriendly *pideci* (pide place) is probably the most popular eatery in town. The pides (Turkish-style pizzas) are excellent – try the unusual *biberli maydanozlu* (green pepper and parsley) topping. There are also soups and kebaps on offer.

Akropolis Restauarant   TURKISH $$
(mains ₺30-50; ☉ 5-10pm) Either dine inside the restaurant's heritage dining room or amid the leafy garden. There's no surprises to the menu, but the concise array of kebabs, salads and mezes is delivered with warmth, and it's a fine place for a frosty Efes beer at the end of the day. Caution: must like cats.

Kybele   TURKISH $$
(☑ 0232-632 3935; Les Pergamon Hotel, Taksim Caddesi 35; mezes ₺10-20, mains ₺30-45; ☉ 7-10pm) Formerly a fine-dining restaurant, Kybele is now a more informal garden eatery with excellent views across Bergama. The bar serves up good cocktails, pasta and salads complement the selection of kebabs and meze dishes, and there's also occasional live music in the leafy surroundings.

Zıkkım Birahanesi   PUB
(Cumhuriyet Caddesi; ☉ 10.30am-1am) With shady garden seating just off the main road, this cool beer garden makes a welcome mid-town pit stop. It's one of three dishevelled *birahanesi* (beer houses) in this stretch of Cumhuriyet Caddesi.

ℹ Information

Tourist Office (☑ 0232-631 2851; bergama-turizm@kultur.gov.tr; Cumhuriyet Caddesi 11; ☉ 8.30am-noon & 1.30-5.30pm Mon-Fri) This extremely helpful office is on the ground floor of the Hükümet Konağı (Provincial Government) building just north of the museum.

ℹ Getting There & Away

BUS & DOLMUŞ

Bergama's *yeni* (new) *otogar* (Tepeköy) lies 7km from the centre, at the junction of the İzmir–Çanakkale highway and the main road into town. At the time of writing it was woefully under-utilised and virtually all intercity buses departed from the more centrally-located Kantar Garaj.

Bus services include the following:

Ankara (₺120, 8½ hours, 480km, nightly)

Çanakkale (₺55, 4½ hours, 220km)

İzmir (₺25, two hours, 110km, every 30 minutes)

Regular dolmuşes to Ayvalık (₺20) and Çandarlı (₺8) leave from the **Kantar Garaj**.

TRAIN

İzmir's efficient İzban rail travels to Aliağa (₺3 on an İzmirm Kart), from where bus no 835 and dolmuşes (₺6) continue to Bergama. You'll need an İzmirm Kart (p214) to use the bus.

ℹ Getting Around

A cable car (p198) links the Acropolis with the lower car park on Akropol Caddesi.

A 'city tour' from the centre to the Asklepion, Red Hall and the Acropolis, with 30 minutes at the first two sights and an hour at the latter, will cost around ₺200. Taxis wait near the Archaeology Museum, Kulaksız Mosque and at the otogar. Individual fares from the taxi rank on the corner of Atatürk Bulvarı and 99 Merdivenler Caddesi are ₺35 to the Asklepion and ₺45 to the Acropolis.

Between 6am and 10pm, half-hourly dolmuşes do a loop through town (₺3.50).

Çandarlı

☑ 0232 / POP 6160

The small resort town of Çandarlı (ancient Pitane) sits on a peninsula jutting into the Aegean, 33km southwest of Bergama. It's dominated by the small but stately 15th-century restored Venetian Çandarlı Castle and has a small and slender sandy beach.

Local tourism fills most of the pensions in high summer. Out of season, Çandarlı is pretty much a ghost town.

Shops and the PTT are in the centre, 200m behind the seafront. The castle, pensions and restaurants line the seashore. Market day is Friday.

◉ Sights

Çandarlı Castle CASTLE
(Çandarlı Kilesi; ⊙24hr) **FREE** This 15th-century Ottoman castle was built by order of the Grand Vizier Çandarlı Halil Pasha the Younger.

❶ Getting There & Away

Frequent buses run between Çandarlı and İzmir (₺20, 1½ hours) via Dikili (₺5, 20 minutes). At least six dolmuşes run daily to/from Bergama (₺10, 30 minutes).

Eski Foça

📞0232 / POP 28,600
Called Eski Foça (Old Foça) to distinguish it from its newer (and rather dull) neighbour, Yeni Foça, this happy-go-lucky holiday town straddles both the Büyük Deniz (Big Sea) and the picturesque Küçük Deniz (Small Sea). The Ottoman-Greek houses fronting the Küçük Deniz are among the finest on the Aegean coast, with doors that open onto a storybook esplanade where locals and visitors play, promenade and dine al fresco. The ruined structure on the small promontory between the Büyük Deniz and Küçük Deniz bays has been built and rebuilt over millennia, and traces of ancient shrines to Cybele and a Temple to Athena are being slowly excavated.

Once the site of ancient Phocaea, more recently Foça was an Ottoman-Greek fishing and trading port. It's now a prosperous, middle-class resort, with holiday villas gathered on the outskirts and a thin, dusty beach with some swimming platforms. There are some better beaches to the north heading towards Yeni Foça.

◉ Sights & Activities

A ruined theatre, the remains of an aqueduct near the otogar and traces of two shrines to the goddess Cybele on the promontory are what's left of the ancient settlement. Some 7km east of town on the way to the İzmir highway and on the left-hand side of the road lies an *anıt mezarı* (monumental tomb) from the 4th century BC.

Between May and late September, boats leave daily at about 11am from both the Küçük Deniz and Büyük Deniz for day trips around the outlying islands. Trips include various swim stops en route and return about 5pm. Most drop anchor at Siren Rocks and typically cost ₺120, including lunch. Shorter trips around the harbour are around ₺15.

Belediye Hamamı HAMAM
(📞0232-812 1959; 115 Sokak 22; hamam ₺30, scrub & massage ₺100; ⊙8am-midnight) The full works costs ₺100 at this tourist-friendly mixed hamam above the Büyük Deniz.

🛏 Sleeping

Menendi Otel HOTEL $$
(📞0232-812 1717; www.menendiotel.com; Reha Midilli Caddesi 104; r €55; ❄🅿🛜) A new opening set amid a line of restaurants, the Menendi's spotless rooms feature crisp, neutral decor enlivened with nautical touches. Ask for a room at the back to negate the minimal chance of noise, and look forward to breakfast in the downstairs cafe. If you're driving a car, there's a handy council-owned car park a short walk away.

Ayshe Pansiyon PENSION $$
(📞0232-812 2111; www.ayshepansiyon.com; Reha Midilli Caddesi 104; f €50-65; ❄🛜) Rustic wood-hewn furniture and quirky style combine at this family-owned pension with absolute front-row views of Foça's harbour. Rooms are airy and light and combine modern decor with heritage touches. Breakfast enjoyed in the morning sun is highly rated and the friendly proprietors can recommend local boat trips. Ayshe's cute feline host is equally welcoming.

Siren Pansiyon PENSION $$
(📞0232-812 2660, 0532 287 6127; www.sirenpansiyon.com; 161 Sokak 13; s/d/tr ₺180/250/300; ⊙www.sirenpansiyon.com; 🛜) This friendly family-run pension is very popular with budget travellers. Located in a quiet pocket just off the seafront promenade, it has 13 rooms, the best of which are upstairs (opt for the rear double with garden view or the terrace triple). The rooftop terrace with sea view is a great spot to relax.

Lola 38 Hotel BOUTIQUE HOTEL $$$
(📞0232-812 3826; www.lola38hotel.com; Reha Midilli Caddesi 140; r ₺400-500, ste ₺600; 🅿❄🛜) First, the warning: Lola's deluxe rooms with their lurid colour scheme and generally

over-the-top decor won't be to all tastes. But now the good news: the garden rooms behind this converted Greek stone house at the quiet end of the Küçük Deniz are comfortable, attractive and beautifully maintained. No child guests under 10.

✗ Eating & Drinking

Nazmi Usta Girit Dondurmaları ICE CREAM $
(Reha Midilli Caddesi 82; per scoop ₺4; ⊕9am-1am) Ice cream and the seaside go together like Fred and Ginger or Posh and Becks, and this is the best place in Foça to order a cone. Nazmi Usta is an acclaimed *dondurma* (ice cream) maker, and his fruit and nut flavours go down a treat with locals and visitors of every age.

Harika Köfte Evi KÖFTE $
(☑0232-812 5409; 91 Sokak 2; soups ₺12, köfte ₺20-25, piyaz ₺6; ⊕8am-midnight) In addition to four types of *köfte* – reputedly the best in town – the 'Wonderful Köfte House' serves various types of *çorba* (soup) and *tavuk şiş* (roast skewered chicken kebap).

Volkan'ın Yeri Aheste SEAFOOD $$
(197 Sokak 1/16; mezes ₺15-40; ⊕noon-midnight) Very popular at the time of writing, it's definitely worth booking ahead for this spot specialising in seafood meze-style shared plates. Highlights are the tender octopus *carpaccio* and the seafood *güveç*. Pop in during lunch and secure a table for later in the evening when the rakı (aniseed brandy) really begins to flow.

Letafet TURKISH $$
(☑0232-812 1191; 197 Sokak 3; mezes ₺8-29, mains ₺30-80; ⊕noon-1am) This popular *meyhane* (tavern) and *şarap evi* (wine house) is hidden behind a stone wall in the old town, but the giveaway is the loud music and the clink of cutlery. Diners enjoy classic Turkish cuisine at reasonable prices, and are serenaded by live musicians every night except Monday. Music usually kicks off around 9pm.

Kavala Cafe & Winehouse CAFE
(☑0232-812 2920; www.kavalacafewinehouse.com; Reha Mıdıllı Caddesi 47; ⊕10am-11pm) Enjoying a sunset drink on the waterside terrace of this restored stone house at the very end of Reha Midilli Caddesi is a Foça highlight. There's a decent selection of bottled beer, an even better one of rakı, and decent espresso coffee. Wines are mainly Turkish varietals, with a few from the up and coming area around Urla.

ℹ Information

Tourist Office (☑0232-812 1222; kocoglu harun@hotmail.com; Foça Girişi 1; ⊕8.30am-noon & 1-5.30pm Mon-Fri, 10am-7pm Sat Jun-Sep) Only open during the major summer holiday period, this small office can supply maps and advice.

ℹ Getting There & Away

Between 6.30am and 9.15pm (11pm in summer), half-hourly buses run to İzmir (₺18, 1½ hours, 86km), passing through Menemen (₺9), where there are connections to Manisa.

Three to five city buses run daily to/from Yeni Foça (₺6, 30 minutes, 22km). They pass pretty little coves, beaches and camping grounds along the way.

İzmir

☑0232 / POP 2.93 MILLION

Turkey's third-largest city is proudly liberal and deeply cultured. Garlanded around the azure-blue Bay of İzmir, it has been an important Aegean port since ancient times, when it was the Greek city of Smyrna, and its seafront *kordon* (promenade) is as fetching and lively as any in the world.

The city's rich and fascinating heritage reflects the fact that it has been the home of Greeks, Armenians, Jews, Levantines and Turks over the centuries. While not as multicultural these days, it still has resident Jewish and Levantine communities and its unique and delicious cuisine attests to this.

Foreign visitors here are largely limited to business travellers and tourists en route to Ephesus. The reason for this is a mystery to us, as the city is home to compelling attractions, including one of Turkey's most fascinating bazaars, an impressive museum of history and art, and a local lifestyle as laid-back as it is welcoming.

History

İzmir was once Smyrna, a city founded by colonists from Greece some time in the early part of the 1st millennium BC. Over the next 1000 years it would grow in importance as it came under the influence of successive regional powers: first Lydia, then Greece and finally Rome. By the 2nd century AD, it was, along with Ephesus and Pergamum, one of the three most important cities in the Roman province of Asia. Its fortunes declined under Byzantine rule, as the focus of government turned north to

İzmir

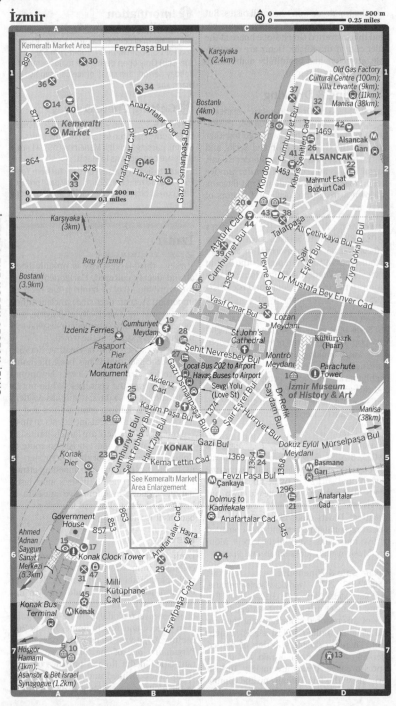

Kemeraltı Market Area

Fevzi Paşa Bul

Karşıyaka
(2.4km)

Bostanlı
(4km)

Anafartalar Cad

Kemeraltı
Market

Gazi Osmanpaşa Bul

Havra Sk

Old Gas Factory
Cultural Centre (100m);
Villa Levante (9km);
(11km);
Manisa (38km);

Kordon

Cumhuriyet Bul

Alsancak
Garı

ALSANCAK

Kıbrıs Şehitleri Cad

Mahmut Esat
Bozkurt Cad

Karşıyaka
(3km)

Bay of İzmir

Bostanlı
(3.9km)

Atatürk Cad

Cumhuriyet Bul

Talatpaşa

Ali Çetinkaya Bul

Şair Eşref Bul

Ziya Gökalp Bul

Plevne Cad

Dr Mustafa Bey Enver Cad

Vasıf Çınar Bul

Lozan
Meydanı

İzdeniz Ferries

Cumhuriyet
Meydanı

Pasaport
Pier

Atatürk
Monument

St John's
Cathedral

Şehit Nevresbey Bul

Montrö
Meydanı

Kültürpark
(Fuar)

Parachute
Tower

Local Bus 202 to Airport

Havaş Buses to Airport

Gazi Osmanpaşa Bul

Akdeniz
Cad

Sevgi Yolu
(Love St)

Şair Eşref Hürriyet Bul

İzmir Museum
of History & Art

Manisa
(38km)

Kazım Paşa Bul

Halit Ziya Bul

Gazi Bul

Dokuz Eylül
Meydanı

Mürselpaşa Bul

Konak
Pier

Cumhuriyet Bul

Şehit Fethibey Bul

KONAK

Kema Lettin Cad

Fevzi Paşa Bul

Çankaya

Dr Refik
Saydam Bul

Basmane
Garı

See Kemeraltı Market
Area Enlargement

Dolmuş to
Kadifekale

Anafartalar Cad

Anafartalar
Cad

Ahmed
Adnan
Saygun
Sanat
Merkezi
(5.3km)

Government
House

Konak Clock Tower

Milli
Kütüphane
Cad

Konak Bus
Terminal

Konak

Anafartalar Cad

Havra Sk

Eşrefpaşa Cad

Hoşgör
Hamamı
(1km);
Asansör & Bet Israel
Synagogue (1.2km)

Constantinople. Things only began to look up again when the Ottomans took control in 1415, after which Smyrna rapidly became Turkey's most sophisticated and successful commercial city.

After the collapse of the Ottoman Empire at the end of WWI, the Greeks invaded. They were eventually expelled following fierce fighting, which, along with a devastating fire, destroyed most of the Greek and Armenian neighbourhoods in the city – tens of thousands of residents perished. The day that Atatürk and his troops recaptured Smyrna (9 September 1922) marked the moment of victory in the Turkish War of Independence.

◉ Sights

★**Kemeraltı Market**   MARKET
(Kemeraltı Çarşısı; Konak; ⊘8am-7pm Mon-Sat; Ⓜ Çankaya, Konak) A labyrinthine bazaar stretching from Konak Sq through to the ancient Agora, Kemeraltı dates back to the 17th century and is home to shops, eateries, artisans' workshops, mosques, coffeehouses,

tea gardens and synagogues. Spending a day exploring its crowded and colourful streets, historic places of worship, hidden courtyards and grand caravanserais reveals the real İzmir. Highlights include the cafes between the Hisar Mosque and the Kızlarağası Han, which serve the city's famous *fincanda pişen Türk kahvesi* (Turkish coffee boiled in the cup).

The bazaar's main drag is Anafartalar Caddesi – use this and the historic Hisar, Şadırvan and Kestanepazarı Mosques as navigational aids. You're bound to get lost – even locals do – but losing your way and coming across unexpected treasures is part of the bazaar's attraction. Look out for the **Kızlarağası Hanı** (Cevahir Bedesteni; off 895 Sokak, Kemeraltı Market, Konak; ⊘8am-5pm; Ⓜ Çankaya, Konak), built in 1744, an Ottoman *bedesten* (warehouse) and *kervansaray* (caravanserai) similar to the İç (Inner) Bedesten in İstanbul's famous Grand Bazaar. Other highlights include the produce market in Havra (Synagogue) Sokak within the city's historic Jewish enclave. To spend

İzmir

İZMIR'S SEPHARDIC SYNAGOGUES

When the Jews were expelled from Spain and Portugal by King Ferdinand and Queen Isabella in 1492, many settled in cities of the Ottoman Empire, in particular Constantinople (İstanbul), Salonika (now Thessaloniki in Greece) and Smyrna (today's İzmir). For several centuries they were the predominant power in commerce and trade; indeed, the sultan is said to have commented that Ferdinand's action made his own land poorer and the empire richer. Jews, who followed the Sephardic tradition and spoke a medieval Spanish language called Ladino, enjoyed a tolerance under the Muslim Ottomans unknown in Christian Europe. For instance, unlike in the West, there were no restrictions on the professions Jews could practice.

In Ottoman times, Jews were concentrated in the **Mezarlıkbaşı** quarter or around **Havra Sokağı** (Synagogue Street, 929 Sokak; Ⓜ Çankaya), both of which are located in or around Kemeraltı Market. Here they built some three dozen synagogues in traditional Spanish style, eight of which remain in varying conditions. The İzmir Project is a locally driven initiative trying to save these synagogues and create a living cultural monument to the city's rich Sephardic Jewish heritage; four of the synagogues – the **Şalom**, **Algazi**, **La Sinyora (The Lady)** and **Bikur Holim** – date from the 17th and 18th centuries and still function; one, the **Bet Hillel**, was the former house of a well-known rabbi and has recently been restored; and another, the 13th-century **Etz Hayim (Tree of Life)**, is in the process of being restored. All of the synagogues have an unusual 'triple arrangement' of the Torah ark. In Mezarlıkbaşı, there are four remaining *cortijos* (*yahudhane* in Turkish), distinctive Sephardic Jewish family compounds with a courtyard and fountain.

Also worth visiting is **Karataş**, an area about 3km south of the centre of town, where many members of the city's Jewish community once lived. Here you'll find **Bet Israel** (☑ 0232-421 4709; Mihat Paşa Caddesi 265; ₺20; ⊙ 10am-3pm Sun-Fri; ☐ 10, 21), the city's largest synagogue, built in 1907, and the **Asansör** (off Mithatpaşa Caddesi; ☐ 10, 21) **FREE**, a lift (elevator) built in the same year by a Jewish banker to facilitate trade between Karataş and the coastline – the alternative is 155 steps. At the foot of the lift, a plaque marks a typical old İzmir house where Darío Moreno (1921–68), the late Jewish singer of 'Canım İzmir' (My Dear İzmir), lived. Sadly, the city's Jewish community now has only 1500 members.

It is possible to visit the synagogues either independently (€10 per person), or on a fully guided half-day tour of the city's Jewish sites (€70 per person). For both options, applications to visit and tour bookings must be made at least 24 hours in advance for security reasons at www.izmirjewishheritage.com.

For more information about the synagogues also see www.izmirjewishheritage.com and www.wmf.org/project/central-izmir-synagogues.

a food-focused day within and around the bazaar, consider signing up for the Only in İzmir guided culinary walk (p208) operated by the well-regarded Culinary Backstreets outfit.

Note that it is not safe to wander through Kemeraltı at night, particularly in the area around Havra Sokağı.

★ **Kordon** WATERFRONT
(☐ 12, 253, 811, Ⓜ Konak) It's difficult to imagine life in İzmir without its iconic seafront *kordon,* which stretches north from Cumhuriyet Meydanı to Alsancak and south from Konak Pier to Konak Meydanı. A triumph

of urban renewal, these two stretches are grassed, have bicycle and walking paths, and are lined on their eastern edge with bars, cafes and restaurants. Locals flock here at the end of the day to meet with friends, relax on the grass and watch the picture-perfect sunsets.

A number of museums and attractions are located on the *kordon,* including the **Zübeyde Hanım Museum Ship** (Zübeyde Hanım Müze Gemisi; Pasaport Pier, Konak; ⊙ 10am-6pm Tue-Wed & Fri-Sun; ☑) **FREE**, the **Arkas Art Centre** (Arkas Sanat Merkezi; ☑ 0232-464 6600; www.arkassanatmerkezi.com; 1380 Sk 1, Alsancak; ⊙ 10am-6pm Tue, Wed & Fri-Sun, to 8pm

Thu) **FREE** and the **Atatürk Museum** (Atatürk Müzesi; ☑0232-464 8085; Atatürk Caddesi 248, Alsancak; ⊙8.30am-5pm Tue-Sun) **FREE**. There are also **bicycles** (☑0232-433 5155; www.bisim.com.tr; per hr ₺3; ⊙6am-11pm; ☐169) for hire, and **horse-drawn carriages** sometimes offering short tours on weekends.

Konak Meydanı
SQUARE

(off Mustafa Kemal Sahil/Atatürk Bulvari, Konak; Ⓜ Konak) On a pedestrianised stretch of Cumhuriyet Bulvarı, this wide plaza, named after the prominent Ottoman-era Government House, built in 1872, to the east, marks the heart of the city. It's the site of the late Ottoman Konak Clock Tower and the lovely **Yalı Mosque** (Waterside Mosque, Konak Mosque), built in 1755, which is covered in Kütahya tiles.

Jutting into the sea to the north is the 1890 **Konak Pier** (Konak İskelesi), which was designed by Gustave Eiffel and was recently converted into a shopping mall.

★İzmir Museum of History & Art
MUSEUM

(İzmir Tarih ve Sanat Müzesi; ☑0232-445 6818; near Montrö Meydanı entrance, Kültürpark; ₺6; ⊙8am-7pm mid-Apr–Sep, 8.30am-6pm Oct–mid-Apr; ☐12, 253, Ⓜ Basmane) This museum is overlooked by many visitors to the city, who do themselves a great disservice in the process. Spread over three pavilions, it is one of the richest repositories of ancient artefacts in the country and its Sculpture pavilion – crammed with masterpieces from ancient Smyrna, Teos, Miletos and Pergamon – is simply sensational. The Precious Objects and Ceramics pavilions contain jewellery, coins and pots, all displayed in a somewhat dated fashion but with informative labelling in English.

Highlights include the coin collection in the **Precious Objects pavilion**, which includes some of the coins minted at Sardis during the reign of King Croesus. These date from the very early 7th century BC and were made of electrum, an alloy of gold and silver with traces of other elements. The jewellery in this pavilion is also impressive.

The **Sculpture pavilion** is so full of treasures that it is hard to single out only a few. Don't miss the friezes from the Temple of Dionysos at Teos and from the theatres and other buildings at Miletos – the frieze from the theatre at Miletos is particularly stunning. Also upstairs and of particular note are the sculptural fragments from the Belevi

Mausoleum near Ephesus, which date from the 3rd century BC.

Downstairs, look out for the Roman-era statue of the river god Kaistros from Ephesus (2nd century AD), the amazingly lifelike Hellenistic three-figure stele from Tralleis (Aydın) and the high reliefs of Demeter and Poseidon from İzmir's Agora.

Church of St Polycarp
CHURCH

(Sen Polikarp Kilisesi; ☑0232-484 8436; Necati Bey Bulvarı 2, İsmet Kaptan; ⊙3-5pm Mon-Sat; Ⓜ Çankaya) Built in the early 17th century, this Catholic church is the oldest still-functioning Christian house of worship in the city. Its survival during the 1922 fire, which razed all neighbouring buildings to the ground, was nothing short of miraculous. Inside, the walls are covered in frescoes that were restored and added to in the 19th century by local architect Raymond Charles Père, who depicted himself in the fresco of St Polycarp's martyrdom (he's the mustachioed chap with the bound hands).

The church is named in honour of the city's patron saint, who was converted to Christianity by St John the Evangelist and became Bishop of Smyrna. He was burned at the stake by the Romans in AD 155 after refusing to renounce Christ and his feast day is observed on 26 January.

Ring the white door on Necati Bey Bulvarı 2 to gain entrance.

Agora
RUINS

(Agora Caddesi; ₺12; ⊙8am-7pm mid-Apr–Sep, 8.30am-6.30pm Oct–mid-Apr; Ⓜ Çankaya) Dating from the end of the 4th century BC, Smyrna's ancient agora was ruined in an earthquake in AD 178 but soon rebuilt by order of the Roman emperor Marcus Aurelius. The reconstructed Corinthian colonnade and Faustina Gate are eye-catching, but the vaulted chambers and cisterns in the basements of the two stoas (basilicas) are even more interesting, giving visitors a good idea of how this rectangular-shaped, multilevel marketplace would have looked in its heyday. Archaeological investigations are still underway.

A Muslim cemetery was later built on the agora and many of the old tombstones remain on site. The ticket office is located on the south side, just off Gazi Osmanpaşa Bulvarı.

Archaeology Museum
MUSEUM

(Arkeoloji Müzesi; ☑0232-489 0796; www.izmir muzesi.gov.tr; Halil Rifat Paşa Caddesi 4, Bahri

Baba Parkı; ₺12; ☉ 8am-6.30pm mid-Apr–Sep, 8.30am-5pm Oct–mid-Apr; Ⓜ Konak) The city's Archaeology Museum has some gems in its collection, including a late-Hellenistic-period bronze statue of a runner found in the Aegean Sea near the ancient city of Kyme, near Aliağa. The museum is a short walk up the hill from Konak Sq.

Ethnography Museum MUSEUM

(Etnografya Müzesi; ☑ 0232-489 0796; Halil Rıfat Paşa Caddesi 3, Bahri Baba Parkı; ☉ 9am-noon & 1-5pm; Ⓜ Konak) **FREE** Housed in a splendid stone building that once functioned as a hospital, this museum showcases the arts, crafts and customs of İzmir. Dioramas, displays, photos and information panels focus on local traditions and though the dioramas are dated and dusty, many of the objects are fascinating. Subjects include everything from camel wrestling, pottery and tin-plating to felt-making, embroidery and *nazar boncuks* (traditional glass amulets used to fend off the evil eye).

City Museum & Archive MUSEUM

(Ahmet Piriştina Kent Arşivi ve Müzesi, Apikam; ☑ 0232-293 3900; www.apikam.org.tr; Şair Eşref Bulvarı 1, Çankaya; ☉ 9.30am-4.30pm Mon-Sat; Ⓜ Çankaya) **FREE** Housed in a fire station built by the British in 1923, this small museum mounts changing displays on İzmir's history. It is named after Ahmet Piriştina, a former mayor of the city who spearheaded the urban redevelopment of the port and *kordon,* the construction of İzmir's metro and the creation of many new parks.

Kadifekale FORTRESS

(Velvet Castle; Rakım Elkutlu Caddesi) Legend has it that in the 4th century Alexander the Great chose this site on Mt Pagos as the location for Smyrna's acropolis. Nothing remains of the Greek settlement, but parts of the fortifications date back to the Roman era, as do the yet-to-be-excavated remains of a hillside theatre. These days there's not much to see on site, but the view of the Gulf of İzmir is pretty good. To get here take a **dolmuş** (Anafartalar Caddesi; one way ₺4).

When here, you'll see women from Turkey's southeast baking bread in makeshift ovens and weaving colourful textiles that they happily sell to visitors. There is some talk of excavating the Roman theatre and extending the site all the way down to the

Agora, but no concrete project or timeline has been announced.

İzmir Mask Museum MUSEUM

(İzmir Mask Müzesi; ☑ 0232-465 3107; www.izmirmaskmuzesi.com; 1448/Cumbalı Sokak 22, Alsancak; ☉ 9am-5pm Tue-Sat; ☐ 12, 253) **FREE** Tucked away in an old house on a street filled with bars, this little museum spread over three floors has an esoteric collection of ceremonial and decorative masks from around the world as well as masks of notable Turks, including Atatürk; his successor as president, İsmet İnönü; and poet Nâzım Hikmet.

🏃 Activities & Tours

★ **Only in İzmir Culinary Walk** WALKING

(www.culinarybackstreets.com; per person US$125) The many unusual and delicious culinary treats of İzmir are investigated on this 5½-hour guided walk in and around the Kemeraltı district, which offers fascinating information about the city's history and culture as well as giving all participants the opportunity to eat and drink to their fullest capacity (and then some). Wear sensible shoes and skip breakfast on the day.

Pürovel Spa & Sport SPA

(☑ 0232-414 0000; www.swissotel.com/hotels/izmir; Swissôtel Büyük Efes, Gazi Osmanpaşa Bulvarı 1, Alsancak; daily pool & gym pass ₺195; ☉ 6am-11pm; Ⓜ Çankaya) One of the best spa and fitness centers in the country, this facility in the upmarket Swissôtel Büyük Efes offers a gym, tennis court, indoor and outdoor swimming pools, pilates and yoga studio, Jacuzzi, hamam, sauna and steam bath. It also offers beauty and relaxation treatments including massage (₺300 to ₺485).

🎊 Festivals & Events

İzmir European Jazz Festival MUSIC

(☑ 0232-482 0090; www.iksev.org/en/caz-festivali; ☉ Mar) Held each year, this popular festival is organised by the Izmir Foundation for Culture, Arts and Education (İKSEV), and hosts a high-profile lineup of European and local jazz performers. Venues include the İKSEV Salonu and the Ahmed Adnan Saygun Sanat Merkezi (AASSM).

International İzmir Festival · MUSIC

(Uluslararası İzmir Festivali; ☑0232-482 0090; www.iksev.org/en; ⊘ late May-early Jun) Usually held in early summer, this annual festival is organised by the İzmir Foundation for Culture, Arts and Education (İKSEV) and focuses on classical music. Venues include the Ahmed Adnan Saygun Sanat Merkezi (AASSM) in İzmir, as well as at the Celsus Kütüphanesi and Büyük Tiyatro at Ephesus.

🛏 Sleeping

İzmir's waterfront is dominated by large high-end business hotels, while most midrange and budget options are located in Alsancak or Basmane. All accommodation prices skyrocket during the trade fairs, especially the Marble Fair in March. It's always sensible to book accommodation in advance of your stay. Note that most of the city's hotels allow smoking in rooms. Fortunately, the larger establishments usually have dedicated smoke-free floors.

🛏 Bazaar & Basmane

Just southwest of Basmane train station, 1296 Sokak is known as 'Oteller Sokak' (Hotel Street) due to its plethora of budget and midrange hotels, most of which are in restored Ottoman houses. Think twice before staying in any of the Anafartalar Caddesi or Kemeraltı hotels, as these locations are not particularly safe or pleasant at night.

Hotel Baylan Basmane · HOTEL $

(☑0232-483 0152; www.hotelbaylan.com; 1299 Sokak 8, Basmane; s/d/tr from €20/25/30; P❋@🛜; Ⓜ Basmane) A sound three-star choice, the Baylan has a loyal business clientele so you'll need to book in advance to snaffle a room. One of the cleanest and most professionally run hotels in the city, it has free on-site parking and a variety of room types, including deluxe rooms with private terraces, cramped twins and some singles with light-well windows only.

Met Boutique Hotel · BOUTIQUE HOTEL $

(☑0232-483 0111; www.metotel.com; Gazi Bulvari 124, Basmane; s/d/ste €30/47/80; ❋🛜; Ⓜ Basmane) It certainly doesn't deliver on its claim to boutique status, being more of a business hotel, but the good-value Met is worth considering nonetheless. Offering 38 well-presented rooms with kettles, satellite TVs and good beds, its most compelling draws are its central location and stylish foyer cafe. Front rooms can be noisy, as they overlook busy Gazi Bulvarı.

🛏 Alsancak & Seafront

The city's best hostels are in the eating and entertainment hot spot of Alsancak. Most midrange and top-end choices are on or close to the *kordon*, with the best being near Cumhuriyet Meydanı.

InHouse Hostel · HOSTEL $

(☑0232-404 0014; www.inhousehostel.com; 1460 Sokak 75, Alsancak; dm €8.50-11, d €20-45; ❋@🛜; 🚍12, 253, 🚉Alsancak) Opened in 2015, this hostel offers 56 beds in private rooms and in cramped dorms sleeping between three and 10. Dorms have under-bed lockers, hard bunk beds and clean but limited shared bathrooms. There's 24-hour reception, a kitchen for common use, a small foyer lounge and an entertainment program predominantly consisting of nightly pub crawls. The Alsancak location is excellent.

Otel Kilim · HOTEL $

(☑0232-484 5340; www.kilimotel.com.tr; Atatürk Caddesi, Pasaport; s/d/tr ₺200/300/350; P❋@🛜; Ⓜ Çankaya) The decor at this multistorey hotel in the Pasaport section of the *kordon* is old-fashioned (sometimes hilariously so) but rooms are well priced, comfortable, clean and well-equipped with kettle, work desk and reading lights. Deluxe rooms face the sea but none have balconies. There's a cafe and fish restaurant on the ground floor, and plenty of free parking is available.

Shantihome · HOSTEL $

(☑0546 235 0805; www.shantihome.org; 1464 Sokak 15, Alsancak; dm €9-11, d/f without bathroom €20/40; 🛜; 🚍12, 253, 🚉Alsancak) You'll feel as if you've teleported to Rishikesh c 1968 when staying in this hostel run by chilled-out, English-speaking host Veli. Located in an atmospheric street in Alsancak, it offers small dorms with power points and reading lights but no lockers (Veli told us that the world needs more love and trust). Bathroom facilities are stretched. Guests love the daily vegetarian breakfasts (donation requested).

★ **Swissôtel Büyük Efes** HOTEL $$

(☎0232-414 0000; www.swissotel.com/hotels/izmir; Gazi Osmanpaşa Bulvarı 1, Alsancak; r standard/executive from €90/130; P❖❀@🔊🗙🏊; Ⓜ Çankaya) Guests here have been known not to leave the premises at all during their city stay. Frankly, we're not at all surprised. Rooms are comfortable and well appointed, but it's the hotel's gorgeous garden and impressive facilities that are the real attraction. These include indoor and outdoor swimming pools, tennis court, spa, gym and rooftop bar with panoramic bay views.

The garden is filled with important works of art including pieces by Antony Gormley and Fernando Botero, and eating and drinking options include the rooftop Equinox Restaurant and the Aquarium Restaurant in the garden. The breakfast buffet (€10) served in Cafe Swiss on the ground floor is both lavish and delicious.

Zeniva Hotel HOTEL $$

(☎0232-422 4046; www.zenivahotel.com; Kizilay Caddesi 1, Alsancak; r €50-70; ❖❀🔊; Ⓜ Çankaya) Modern and spacious rooms blend business and boutique style at this recent opening a short walk from the city's waterfront. Breakfast is worth lingering over – especially the fresh honeycomb – and the surrounding neighbourhood combines a quieter residential vibe with a few good cafes and restaurants. Dining recommendations from the friendly team at reception are usually spot on.

Key Hotel HOTEL $$

(☎0232-482 1111; www.keyhotel.com; Mimar Kemalettin Caddesi 1, Konak; r €120-180, ste €210-410; P❖❀@🔊; Ⓜ Çankaya) This sleek offering near Konak Pier occupies a former bank building; the original vault is now a glass-topped atrium. Popular with visiting dignitaries and as a conference and wedding venue, it offers 31 luxe rooms with high-tech fitout, work desks, rain showers and king-size beds. The huge top-floor grand suite with panoramic terrace is spectacular.

🏨 **Bornova**

Villa Levante BOUTIQUE HOTEL $$

(☎0232-343 1888; www.villalevante.com.tr; 80 Sokak 25; d/ste from €65/80; P❖🔊; Ⓜ Bornova) Located in leafy Bornova, 9km outside the city centre, this is İzmir's only boutique hotel. An 1831 Levantine villa that has been tastefully renovated, it offers six standard rooms and five suites, all with chandelier, wooden floor, lofty ceiling, comfortable bed, satellite TV and work desk. There's also a popular restaurant in the rear garden (mains ₺40 to ₺75).

🍴 **Eating**

Most restaurants on the *kordon* specialise in seafood and have terraces overlooking the bay. The best cheap eats are available in and around the Kemeraltı Market, and the best cafes are in Alsancak.

Léone CAFE $

(☎0232-464 3400; www.leone-tr.com; Vasıf Çınar Bulvarı 29a, Alsancak; pastries ₺10-15, cakes ₺20, tartines ₺20-22; ⊙8am-8.30pm, closed Sun summer; 🔊; ☐12, 253) A Parisian-style *divertissement* in the heart of the city, this stylish cafe on Lozan Meydanı is wildly popular with Alsancak's ladies-who-lunch. Coffee is excellent and the croissants and gateaux are simply sensational. At lunch, *tartines* (filled baguettes) and *croque monsieurs* (baked ham, cheese and béchamel sandwiches) are the popular choices. The refreshing *limonata* (lemonade) is just maybe İzmir's best.

Sevinç CAFE $

(☎0232-421 7590; www.sevincpastanesi.com.tr; Ali Çetinkaya Bulvarı 31, Alsancak; cakes ₺15-18, pastries ₺6-12; ⊙7am-midnight; ☐12, 253) Romantic rendezvous, reunions and regular catch-ups – the terrace at this long-established cafe has been hosting all three for six decades. It's an excellent spot to relax after a saunter along the *kordon*.

Köfteci Salih Arslan KÖFTE $

(☎0232-446 4296; 879 Sokak 16a, Kemeraltı Market, Konak; portions köfte ₺25, piyaz ₺7; ⊙11am-4pm Mon-Sat; Ⓜ Konak, Çankaya) In the Kestane Pazarı (Chestnut Market) section of Kemeraltı, this simple place has been serving tender and tasty Macedonian/Albanian–style *köfte* with *piyaz* (white-bean salad) since 1970 and has built a devoted local following in the process. Beware the fiendishly hot sun-dried chillies served on the side!

★ **Ayşa** TURKISH $$

(☎0232-484 1525; Abacıoğlu Han, Anafartalar Caddesi 228, Kemeraltı Market, Konak; meze plates ₺20-25, portions from ₺20; ⊙8am-6pm Mon-Sat; ❀🍴; Ⓜ Konak, Çankaya) Serving Bosnian food that is remarkably similar to Turkish home cooking, this stylish *lokanta* in the pretty Abacıoğlu Han offers both indoor

İZMIRI FAST FOOD

Culinary tourism is big business these days, and Turkey is a popular destination for foodies wanting to knock some big-ticket items off their culinary bucket list – baklava in Gaziantep, *hamsi* (anchovies) on the Black Sea etc. In recent years, a growing number of these enthusiasts have been heading to İzmir, lured by reports of its fascinating Sephardic-influenced fast food. When in the city, be sure to try the following:

Boyo (pl: *boyoz*) A fried pastry made with flour, sunflower oil and a small amount of tahini; traditionally enjoyed with hard-boiled eggs and a glass of *sübye* (drink made from melon seeds and sugar water). Try one at **Dostlar Fırını** (📞 0232-421 9202; www. alsancakdostlarfirini.com; Kıbrıs Şehitleri Caddesi 120; boyoz ₺1.25-1.50, hard-boiled egg ₺1.25; ⏰ 6.30am-7pm; 🚌 12, 253, 811) in Alsancak.

Gevrek The local version of a *simit* (chewy bread ring dipped in water and molasses syrup and encrusted with sesame seeds), made with fewer sesame seeds and less salt. Sold by street vendors across the city.

Kumru Sandwiches made with soft bread, aged *kaşar* cheese from Kars, sausage from Urfa and local tomato paste; the name means 'collared dove', and derives from the shape of the sandwich. Note that the version with white cheese, fresh tomato and green pepper sold by some street vendors is not authentic; instead, head to **Kumrucu Apo** (1318 Sokak 12; sandwiches from ₺8; Ⓜ Konak, Çankaya) in the Kemeraltı Market (p205).

Şambali A cake made with almond-studded semolina, yoghurt and sugar. After being cooked, it's doused with sweet syrup and lathered with *kaymak* (clotted cream). The best place to try one of these is **Meşhur Hisarönü Şambalicisi** (901 Sokak; şambali ₺5; ⏰ 9am-7pm Mon-Sat; 📞; Ⓜ Konak, Çankaya) in the Kemeraltı Market.

Söğüş Poached tongue, cheek and brain served cold in bread with chopped onion, parsley, mint, tomato, cumin and hot chilli flakes. Served at a number of stands in the Kemeraltı Market; not for the faint-hearted.

and outdoor seating. Choose from the DIY meze display and secure a piece of *börek* if it's available. Main dishes are displayed in the bain-marie and include both meat and vegetable choices.

Bizim Mütfak
TURKISH $$

(📞 0232-484 9917; 914 Sokak 12, Kemeraltı Market, Konak; soup ₺25, portion ₺20-35; ⏰ 7.30am-4.30pm Mon-Sat; Ⓜ Konak, Çankaya) The blue-and-white checked tablecloths give this popular *lokanta* in the courtyard of the Mirkelam Han near the Hisar Mosque a Greek-island vibe, but the food is resolutely İzmiri, with a focus on unusual soups (trotter, rabbit, duck or fish) and local specialities including İzmir *köfte* (baked spicy meatballs). It opened in 1950 and has a passionately devoted clientele.

Can Döner
KEBAP $$

(📞 0232-484 1313; www.candoner.com; Millüküphane Caddesi 6b, Kemeraltı; İskender kebap ₺33; ⏰ 11am-6.30pm; 🚫; Ⓜ Konak) Kemeraltı's best-loved *kebapçı* (kebab eatery) is located near Konak Sq and serves an excellent İskender kebap (döner served on fresh pide and topped with tomato sauce and browned butter). Eat inside or at one of the street-side tables.

Meşhur Tavacı Recep Usta
ANATOLIAN $$$

(📞 0232-463 8797; http://tavacirecepusta.com. tr; Atatürk Caddesi 364, Alsancak; kebaps ₺70-89; ⏰ noon-10.30pm Mon-Thu, from 10am Fri-Sun; 🚌 12, 253) Serving tasty dishes harking from Diyarbakır in the country's southeast, this is a popular venue for celebratory and family dinners, and is also known for its set weekend brunch (₺70 per person). Order a main course and you'll receive complimentary mezes, salad, *lavaş* bread and dessert. The house speciality is *lık kaburga dolma* (stuffed lamb ribs, ₺178 for two people).

Veli Usta Balık Pişiricisi
SEAFOOD $$$

(📞 0232-464 2705; www.balikpisiricisiveliusta. com; Atatürk Caddesi 212a, Alsancak; mezes ₺10-45, mains from ₺45; ⏰ noon-11pm; 🚌 12, 253) In İzmir, three ingredients make for the perfect meal: *balık* (fish), *roca* (rocket) and rakı. This friendly terrace restaurant on the *kordon* is a great spot to sample all three, and is hugely popular with locals. Be sure to order the rolled sole, grouper or dory (described as *şiş* on the menu), which is the signature dish.

Drinking & Nightlife

Alsancak is the city's nightlife hub, particularly in the clubs and bars on the side streets running between Kıbrıs Şehitleri Caddesi and Cumhuriyet Caddesi – head to 1452, 1453 and 1482 Sokaks.

To enjoy a traditional Turkish coffee, make your way to Kahveciler Sokak (Coffeemaker's St) behind the Hisar Mosque in the Kemeraltı Market. The cafes here all serve the local speciality of *fincanda pişen Türk kahvesi* (Turkish coffee cooked in the cup rather than in the usual long-handled copper coffee pan).

La Puerta   BAR
(☑ 0232-422 4457; www.facebook.com/lapuertaizmir; 1469 Sokak 71, Alsancak; ⊗ 10am-1am; ☎; Ⓜ Alsancak) La Puerta's spacious inner courtyard is a popular spot for early evening beers and cocktails later at night. The friendly bar staff can advise on the best of Turkish craft beers – look out for brews from Gara Guzu and Feliz Kulpa. The international menu of bar snacks and meals includes Indian, Middle Eastern and Mexican flavours.

No 9 Cafe & Bar   CAFE
(İrfan Boyuer Sokak 9, Alsancak; ⊗ 11am-late; ☎; ▣ 12, 253) One of our favourite spots amid the laneways of the Alsancak neighbourhood, No 9's interior is packed with old radios, vintage telephones and other assorted detritus of the last few decades. The bar features an exceedingly laid-back ambience, and happy-hour beers and a good wine list partner well with a surprising soundtrack of vintage Turkish jazz and indie pop.

Kahveci Ömer Usta   COFFEE
(☑ 0232-425 4706; www.kahveciomerusta.com; 905 Sokak 15, Kemeraltı Market, Konak; ⊗ 9am-8pm; Ⓜ Çankaya, Konak) One of the popular cafes behind the Hisar Mosque in the Kemeraltı Market, Kahveci Ömer Usta specialises in *fincanda pişen Türk kahvesi*.

Sunset Cafe   BAR
(☑ 0232-463 6549; Ali Çetinkaya Bulvari 2a, Alsancak; ⊗ 7am-2am; ▣ 12, 253) On the edge of the boulevard, the Sunset makes a great end-of-day watering hole, with tables on the pavement and a relaxed, youthful crowd.

Kovan   BAR
(☑ 0232-463 2393; 1482 Muzaffer İzgü/Sokak 6, Alsancak; ⊗ 8am-2am; ▣ 12, 253) Those who are young and fond of partying in İzmir tend to be regulars here. A barn-like space with an open-air courtyard at the rear, it literally heaves with patrons on Friday and Saturday nights. The draws are an inclusive vibe, cheap beer, bar food (pizza, fries, samosas) and loud music supplied by in-house DJs.

Entertainment

İzmir Milli Kütüphane   PERFORMING ARTS
(☑ 0232-484 2002; www.izmirmillikutuphane.com; Millikütüphane Caddesi 39, Konak; Ⓜ Konak) This handsome 1912 Ottoman Revival building is the home base of the İzmir Devlet Opera Ve Balesi (İzmir State Opera & Ballet Company).

Old Gas Factory
Cultural Centre   ARTS CENTRE
(Tarihi Havagazı Fabrikası Kültür Merkezi; ☑ 0232-293 1091; www.izmir.bel.tr/tr/Projeler/1382/4; Liman Caddesi, Alsancak; ⊗ hours vary; ▣ 12, 253) These two mid-19th-century Ottoman Gas Company warehouses have been converted into a cultural centre where occasional art exhibitions and workshops are staged. It's located 500m east of Alsancak's 19th-century train station.

🛍 Shopping

Şekercibaşı Ali Galip   FOOD & DRINKS
(☑ 0232-483 7778; www.aligalip.com; Anafartalar Caddesi 10, Konak; ⊗ 8.30am-7pm Mon-Sat; Ⓜ Konak) It first opened for business in 1901, and this much-loved sweet shop is still the first port of call for many shoppers when visiting Kemeraltı. It sells *lokum* (Turkish delight), chocolate and *helva* (sweet made from sesame seeds) that are made at the shop's İzmir factory.

Altan Manisalı   FOOD & DRINKS
(☑ 0232-425 5346; www.manisali.com; Havra/929 Sokağı 13, Kemeraltı Market, Konak; ⊗ 8.30am-7pm; Ⓜ Çankaya) Selling particularly delicious *helva*, tahini and *pekmez* (syrup made from grape juice) since 1885, this is one of the most famous food stores in the market. Members of the same family operate nearby Beşe, which sells the same produce and is equally historic and loved.

Information

Tourist Office (☑ 0232-483 6216; 1344 Sokak 2, Konak; ⊗ 8.30am-5.30pm Mon-Fri;

Ⓜ Konak) Housed on the ground floor of the ornate art-nouveau İzmir Valiliği İl Turizm Müdürlüğü (Culture and Tourism Directorate) building near Konak Pier; can provide a city map. English-speaking staff.

❶ Getting There & Away

AIR

Many domestic and European flights arrive at İzmir's modern and efficient Adnan Menderes Airport (www.adnanmenderesairport.com). Some of the airlines offer shuttle-bus services from the airport to regional destinations.

Anadolu Jet (www.anadolujet.com) Flies between İzmir and Ankara, and İzmir and İstanbul (Sabiha Gökçen).

easyJet (www.easyjet.com) Flies between İzmir and the UK (London Gatwick).

Pegasus Airlines (www.flypgs.com) Domestic flights between İzmir and İstanbul (Grand and Sabiha Gökçen), Trabzon, Erzincan, Ankara, Hatay, Kayseri and Adana.

Qatar Airways (www.qatarairways.com) Flies between İzmir and Qatar (Doha).

Sun Express (www.sunexpress.com) Flies between İzmir and İstanbul (Sabiha Gökçen), Adana, Van, Antalya, Diyarbakır and Gaziantep, as well as seasonal European destinations.

Turkish Airlines (☑ 484 1220; www.thy.com; Halit Ziya Bulvarı 65) Flies between İzmir and İstanbul (Grand and Sabiha Gökçen).

BUS

İzmir's mammoth but efficient **otogar** (www.izotas.com.tr; Kemalpaşa Caddesi) lies 6.5km east of the city centre. For travel on Friday or Saturday to coastal towns located north of İzmir, buy your ticket a day in advance; in high season, two days in advance. Tickets can also be purchased from the bus companies' offices in the city centre; most of these are located in Dokuz Eylül Meydanı in Basmane.

Inter-regional buses and their ticket offices are found on the lower level of the otogar; regional buses (eg Selçuk, Bergama, Manisa and Sardis) leave from the upper level (buy tickets on the bus). City buses and dolmuşes leave from a courtyard in front of the lower level.

Short-distance buses (eg the Çeşme Peninsula) leave from a smaller local bus stand in Üçkuyular, 6.5km southwest of Konak, but pick up and drop off at the otogar as well.

TRAIN

Most intercity services arrive at/depart from **Basmane station** (Basmane Gar). For northern or eastern Turkey, change at Ankara or Konya.

There is one daily train to Ankara (₺44, 14 hours), leaving Basmane at 6.05pm and travelling via Eskişehir (₺52, 12 hours).

There are six daily trains between Alsancak and Manisa (₺7, 1¾ hours). Six daily trains travel to Selçuk from Basmane station (₺7, 1½ hours) between 9.08am and 7.43pm.

The city's commuter rail system, İzban, runs to Cumaovası, south of the city, where passengers can connect with services to Tepeköy near

İZMIR & THE NORTH AEGEAN İZMIR

SERVICES FROM İZMIR OTOGAR

DESTINATION	FARE (₺)	DURATION (HR)	DISTANCE (KM)	FREQUENCY	VIA
Ankara	99	8	550	hourly	Afyon
Antalya	94	7	450	hourly	Aydın
Bergama	20	2	110	half-hourly	Menemen
Bodrum	44	3	286	hourly	Milas
Bursa	61	5	300	hourly	Balıkesir
Çanakkale	77	6	340	hourly	Ayvalık
Çeşme	23	1¾	116	hourly	Alaçatı
Denizli	47	3	250	half-hourly	Aydın
Eski Foça	15	1½	86	half-hourly	Menemen
İstanbul	120	8	575	hourly	Bursa
Konya	99	10½	575	6 daily	Afyon
Kuşadası	30	1¼	95	hourly	Selçuk
Manisa	15	1	45	frequent	Sarnıc
Marmaris	60	4	320	hourly	Aydın
Salihli	20	1½	90	half-hourly	Sardis
Selçuk	18	1	80	frequent	Belevi

Selçuk. Trips cost ₺3 on an İzmir Kart. There are plans to extend the service from Cumaovası to Selçuk in the future.

İzban rail travels to Aliağa (₺3 on a İzmirm Kart), from where bus 835 and dolmuşes continue to Bergama (₺6). There are plans to extend the İzban service north to Bergama in the future.

ⓘ Getting Around

İzmir has two travel cards, which cover bus, metro, İzban and ferry trips. These are available and can be recharged at stations, piers and shops with the İzmirm Kart sign.

İzmirm Kart (City Card) You pay a ₺6 deposit when you buy the card and then top it up with credit. When you use the card, ₺3 is debited from it, then every journey you make for the next 90 minutes is free.

Üç-Beş (Three-Five) This card with two/three/ five credits, each valid for a single journey, costs ₺7/10/14. It can be hard to access.

TO/FROM ADNAN MENDERES AIRPORT

İzmir's Adnan Menderes Airport is 15km south of the city centre on the way to Ephesus and Kuşadası.

Havaş (www.havas.net; one way ₺11) buses (one hour) are the fastest and most comfortable way to travel between the airport and the city centre. They leave hourly from Gazi Osmanpaşa Bulvarı outside the Swissôtel Büyük Efes between 3.30am and 11.30pm; and from domestic arrivals to the same hotel between 8.40am and 3.30am. Havaş Buses also travel from the airport to Çeşme, Kuşadası and Aydın.

Local **bus 202** (₺5.20) runs between both arrivals terminals and Cumhuriyet Meydanı via Üçkuyular bus station; the trip costs ₺6 on an İzmirm Kart. The buses leave from outside the Swissôtel Büyük Efes at 2am, 4am and then on the hour until midnight. From the airport, they leave at 1am, 3am, 5am and then on the hour until midnight.

Bus 204 (₺6 on an İzmirm Kart) travels between the airport terminals and the Bornova metro hourly between 5.40am and 3.40am.

The city's commuter rail system, İzban, runs between the airport and Alsancak in the city centre (₺6 on an İzmirm Kart).

A taxi between the airport and Cumhuriyet Meydanı costs around ₺90.

TO/FROM İZMIR OTOGAR

Passengers on intercity buses operated by the larger bus companies can usually take advantage of the free *servis* (shuttle bus) between the otogar and bus company offices in Dokuz Eylül Meydanı in the city centre. Alternatively, use local bus 302, which travels between the otogar and Konak (₺3 on an İzmirm Kart).

A taxi between the city centre and the otogar costs around ₺70.

To get to Üçkuyular bus station, take the metro (Fahrettin Altay stop, ₺3 on an İzmirm Kart). Alternatively, use local bus 302, which travels between the otogar and Konak (₺3 on an İzmirm Kart).

BICYCLE

İzmir has a cycle-share hiring scheme called Bisim (p207), with a couple of dozen docking stations, mostly along the seafront and *kordon*.

BOAT

İzdeniz (🖀 0232-330 8922; www.izdeniz.com. tr; ⏰ 7.15am-11.30pm) operates regular ferry services (₺3 on an İzmirm Kart) from Konak to Karşıyaka and Bostanlı on the opposite side of the bay, and less frequent services to the same destinations from Pasaport and Alsancak.

BUS & DOLMUŞ

Buses are operated by **ESHOT** (🖀 0232-3200 320; www.eshot.gov.tr). Check the website for route information. The city's main local **bus terminal** is at Konak, close to the metro.

Dolmuşes (p208) from the city centre to Kadifekale depart when full from the stop opposite the multistorey car park in Anafartalar Caddesi – look for the sign with a big D and the word Kadifekale.

CAR

Large international car-hire franchises have 24-hour desks at the airport, and some have offices in town.

You'll pay to park your car in the city. There are convenient car parks in front of Konak Pier, at the Kültürpark and at the Alsancak Municipal Carpark. These charge around ₺10 for one to three hours and ₺35 for 12 to 24 hours.

METRO & TRAIN

İzmir Metro (www.izmirmetro.com.tr; fare ₺3; ⏰ 6am-12.20am) is clean, quick and cheap. There are currently 17 stations running from Fahrettin Altay to Evka-3 via Konak, Çankaya, Basmane and Ege Universitesi (Aegean University). Trips cost ₺3 on an İzmirm Kart.

The city's commuter rail system is called İzban. The northern line runs from Aliağa, near Bergama, to **Alsancak** (Alsancak Garı; 🖀 0232-464 7795); the southern line runs from Alsancak to Cumaovası, south of the city, where passengers can connect with services to Tepeköy near Selçuk. The latter stops at the airport en route. Trips cost ₺3 on a İzmirm Kart.

TAXI

You can hail a taxi on the street or pick up one from a taxi stand or outside one of the big hotels, including one near Swissôtel Büyük Efes. Fares start at ₺5 then cost ₺4 per kilometre.

Manisa

☑ 0236 / POP 380,000

In ancient times, Manisa was known as Magnesia ad Sipylum and was a strategically important city. It prospered during the Byzantine period but reached its apogee under the Ottomans, when it became the place where the *şehzades* (crown princes) were trained for their imperial destinies. Many of the buildings in the historic centre date from the nine-year period when Süleyman the Magnificent and his mother Ayşe Hafsa Sultan lived here. The main reasons to visit are to see the glorious Muradiye Mosque and to attend the annual Mesir Macunu Festivalı, which is inscribed on Unesco's list of intangible cultural heritage.

◉ Sights & Activities

★ Muradiye Mosque   MOSQUE

(Murat Caddesi) The architectural genius of Mimar Sinan is well and truly on show at this exquisite mosque, which was commissioned by Sultan Murat III and constructed between 1583 and 1585. After admiring its twin minarets and front portico, enter through the ornately decorated door – a triumph of inlaid wood and marble – and you'll be confronted by one of the most beautiful of all Ottoman mosque interiors, with a profusion of İznik tiling and delicate stained glass. The interior owes much to the work of Sedefkar Mehmed Aga, architect of İstanbul's Blue Mosque, who was one of the two architects who supervised the mosque's completion – its tiled *mihrab* (niche indicating the direction of Mecca) is particularly beautiful.

There's a pleasant garden courtyard in front of the mosque that has clean public toilets (₺1).

Sultan Mosque   MOSQUE

(İzmir Caddesi) Commissioned by Ayşe Hafsa Sultan, the wife of Sultan Selim I and mother of Süleyman the Magnificent, this mosque was built in 1522 and is part of a complex that originally consisted of a *medrese* (seminary), *bimarhane* (mental hospital), *mektep* (primary school) and hamam. The hamam is still functioning, the *bimarhane* houses the Medical History Museum and the *mektep* houses a cafe.

Medical History Museum   MUSEUM

(Hafsa Sultan Şifahanesi Tıp Tarihi Müzesi; ☑ 0236-201 1070; ☺10am-10pm) **FREE** Tracing the history of medicine across the globe, this ambitious museum in the grounds of the Sultan Mosque occupies a handsome *bimarhane* that was commissioned by Süleyman the Magnificent in 1539. Run by Celal Bayar Üniversitesi, its exhibitions are fascinating but sometimes quite gruesome. There's a pleasant cafe in the courtyard.

Tarihi Sultan Hamam   HAMAM

(☑0236-231 2051; 2505 Sokak 1; DIY bath ₺50, bath service ₺120-160; ☺men 7am-11pm, women 11am-6pm) This 16th-century hamam is part of the original Sultan Mosque complex. It has separate baths for men and women; women should call ahead to make an appointment.

✲✦ Festivals & Events

Mesir Macunu Festivalı   CULTURAL

(Mesir Festival; www.manisakulturturizm.gov.tr; ☺Mar/Apr) Those visiting Manisa in spring may be lucky enough to catch the Mesir Macunu Festivalı, a week-long festival in celebration of *Mesir macunu* (Mesir paste), a sugar-and-spice confection that has passionate fans and equally passionate detractors throughout the country. The festival usually occurs in late March or April.

▭ Sleeping & Eating

Looks Hotel   HOTEL $$

(☑0236-231 7070; www.lookshotel.com.tr; Atatürk Bulvarı 28; r ₺250, ste ₺400; ❇ ☏ 🛜) Overlooking Eski Emekler Park in the old part of town, this business hotel opened in 2015 and offers comfortable, well-sized rooms with hard beds, kettles and work desks. There's a pub on the ground floor.

Gülcemal   KEBAP $

(☑0236-231 5342; www.gulcemalkebap.com; 1603 Sokak, off Cumhuriyet Meydanı; Manisa kebap ₺20; ☺8am-7pm) This is the best place to sample the town's speciality of Manisa kebap (cylindrical *köfte* served on pide and topped with tomato sauce and yoghurt).

➊ Getting There & Away

The easiest way to get here from İzmir is by bus (₺21, one hour, every 15 minutes). Don't alight at the first (blue) otogar – known as the Eski (Old) Garaj – as to get to the old section of town you must go to the Yeni (New) Garaj and then take a dolmuş. These leave from the western side of the otogar next to the fast-food stands. Dolmuş 1 (₺60) will take you to the Vilayet or Valiligi (Town Hall) on Mustafa Kemal Paşa Caddesi.

WORTH A TRIP

SARDIS

Sardis (₺12; ⊙8am-5pm, to 7pm Apr-Sep) was once the capital of the powerful Lydian kingdom that dominated much of the Aegean before the Persians arrived. It is also the site of one of the Seven Churches of Revelation (or Apocalypse) mentioned in the New Testament. From 560 BC to 546/7 BC, the city was ruled by king Croesus. During his reign, local metallurgists discovered the secret of separating gold from silver, and produced both gold and silver coins of a hitherto unknown purity. This made Sardis rich and Croesus' name became synonymous with wealth itself. For this reason, Sardis is often described as the place where modern currency was invented.

The city's ruins lie at the eastern end of the village of **Sartmustafa** (or Sart), some 80km east of İzmir.

Entry is via an 18m-long paved **Roman road**, past a well-preserved **Byzantine latrine** and a row of almost 30 **Byzantine shops** that belonged to Jewish merchants and artisans in the 4th century AD (Jews settled here as early as 547 BC). Turn left at the end of the Roman road to enter the **synagogue** (*havra*), impressive because of its size and beautiful decoration. The southern shrine housed the Torah.

Next to the synagogue is the **palestra**, which was probably built in the early 3rd century AD and abandoned after a Sassanian invasion in 616.

Right at the end is a striking two-storey building called the **Marble Court of the Hall of the Imperial Cult**, which, though heavily restored, gives an idea of the former grandeur of the building.

Continuing excavations on the way to the village to the south have uncovered a stretch of the Lydian city wall and a Roman villa with painted walls right on top of an earlier Lydian residence. A sign points south to the **Temple of Artemis**, just over 1km away. Today only a few columns of the once-magnificent but never-completed building still stand. Nevertheless, the temple's plan is clearly visible and very impressive. Nearby is an early Christian **church** dating from the 4th century AD.

Getting There & Around

Buses to Salihli (₺22, 1½ hours, 90km) leave from İzmir's otogar every 30 minutes and pass Sartmustafa en route. You can also catch dolmuşes (minibuses that stop anywhere along their prescribed route) to Sartmustafa (₺5, 15 minutes, 9km) from behind the Salihli otogar. Buses travelling between Salihli and Manisa (₺18, one hour) can be hailed along the highway, making it possible – just – to visit both Manisa and Sardis in the same day.

From here, the mosques and museums are only a short walk away.

From the Yeni Garaj, buses to Salihli pass Sardis (₺120, one hour, every half-hour).

Çeşme

📋 0232 / POP 29,180

Unlike many resort towns in this region, Çeşme has retained a local population and flavour. Only 8km from the Greek island of Chios (Sakız), the town has a long seafront perfect for promenading, a magnificent castle built by the Genoese and a bustling *merkez* (commercial centre) with plenty of shops and cheap eateries. Popular with weekending İzmiris and with those who balk at the high prices and style overload at nearby Alaçatı, it's an excellent base for exploring the region.

◉ Sights & Activities

Çeşme is surrounded by beaches. **Diamond Beach** (Pırlantı Plajı) is good for kitesurfing and windsurfing, and ultrapopular **Altınkum** has sandy coves and is good for swimming. Both are south of the city centre and can be easily accessed by dolmuş.

Çeşme Museum FORTRESS
(Çeşme Müzesi, Çeşme Kalesi; 1015 Sokak; ₺14; ⊙8am-6pm) Çeşme's majestic Genoese-built fortress dates from 1508 and was later repaired by order of Sultan Beyazıt II, son of Sultan Mehmet the Conqueror, in order to defend the coast from attack by pirates. Impressively restored, it now houses the town's museum. Rooms in the Umur Bey tower and around the bailey (inner enclosure) house archaeological and historical exhibits, and the terraced bailey is filled with historic

gravestones and stelae. The battlements offer excellent views of the town and harbour.

The archaeological finds come from nearby Erythrae (now Ildırı), as well as from the Bağlararası Bronze Age harbour settlement (tools, a curious stone phallus) and the Roman era (superb gold diadems). Two rooms in the tower house a comprehensive exhibit about Russian Empress Catherine the Great and the Russian-Ottoman naval battle of 5 July 1770, which occurred in Çeşme Bay. A decisive engagement of the Russo-Turkish War of 1768–74, the Russians were triumphant and the Ottoman fleet wiped out.

Ayios Haralambos Church CHURCH
(Ayios Haralambos Kilisesi; İnkılap Caddesi) North of Çeşme Fortress, this imposing but decommissioned 19th-century Greek Orthodox church, fully restored in 2012, is used for temporary exhibitions.

Boat Trips
From late May to September, *gülets* (traditional Turkish wooden yachts) operated by companies including **Çeşme Lady Bente** (☑0536 310 0560; cruise incl buffet lunch ₺100) offer boat trips to nearby Donkey Island, Green Bay, Blue Bay, Paradise Island and Aquarium Bay, where you can swim and snorkel. The cruises usually cost around ₺100 per passenger, including lunch, and involve plenty of partying on board. Boats depart 10am to 10.30am and return in the late afternoon.

🛏 Sleeping

Note that hotels on or close to the waterfront can be noisy on warm nights. Everything is fully booked in summer – book well in advance of your visit.

Mai Hotel HOTEL $$
(☑0232-712 8845; www.maiotelcesme.net; 3025 Sokak 35; r €55-70; P 🅿 ❄ 🛜) A garden courtyard and just maybe Çeşme's friendliest family hosts are highlights at this relaxed hotel a short walk from Çeşme's pedestrian main street. Some of the rooms are on the compact side, but they're all spotless and recently decorated. Breakfast is a leisurely affair, and convenient off-street parking can be arranged if you're exploring the North Aegean by car.

Yalçın Otel HOTEL $$
(☑0232-712 6981; www.yalcinotel.com; 1002 Sokak 14; s/d/tr ₺120/300/400; P ❄ 🛜) Ebullient Bülent Ulucan runs this great little

hotel on the hillside overlooking the marina. Its 18 rooms are clean and reasonably comfortable (some with renovated bathrooms), but the major draws here are the extremely friendly atmosphere, two harbour-facing terraces, a shared lounge (free tea) and a compact garden.

Dantela Butik Otel B&B $$$
(☑0232-712 0389; www.dantelabutikotel.com; 3054 Sokak 4; r ₺400-450; ❄ 🛜) Right on the waterfront and close to the entertainment action, this B&B above the Penguen Restaurant is run by the same ultrafriendly owners. The seven rooms have pretty, very feminine decor – opt for one upstairs (front rooms have harbour views, rear rooms are larger). A lavish breakfast is served on the restaurant terrace. Expect noise in summer.

🍴 Eating & Drinking

Fish restaurants with terraces are dotted along the waterfront, but none are noteworthy. Most locals eat on or around İnkılap Caddesi (2001 Sokak). Some of the restaurants along the marina turn into live music venues during summer.

★ Çeşka Anne Mutfağı TURKISH $
(portions ₺10-25; ⊙11am-9pm) Operated by a local women's cooperative, this humble spot a short stroll from Çeşme's busy main street specialises in homestyle cooking. The ever-changing menu is strictly seasonal and local, and dishes could include *cağla badem arapsaçı bakla* (green beans with unripe almond and wild fennel). Topped with garlic, yoghurt and red-pepper flakes, the 200 year-old recipe actually originated in Crete.

Tokmak Hasan'ın Yeri TURKISH $
(☑0232-712 0519; 1015 Sokak/Çarşı Caddesi 11; soups ₺12-20, portions ₺15-30, döners ₺20-30; ⊙7am-11pm; ❄) Winning the prize for the biggest and best döner in town (order an İskender), this long-established and friendly *lokanta* is hugely popular with locals, who flock here at lunchtime. Enter through the passage lined with souvenir shops, and arrive early to snaffle your choice from the huge and uniformly tasty spread displayed in the bain-maries. Also does *paket* (takeaway).

Rumeli BAKERY $
(☑0232-712 6759; www.rumelipastanesi.com.tr; İnkılap Caddesi/2001 Sokak 46, Merkez; ice cream per scoop ₺3.50; ⊙8am-2am) Occupying a

Çeşme

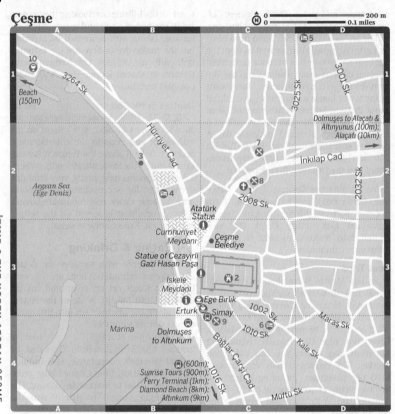

IZMIR & THE NORTH AEGEAN ÇEŞME

Çeşme

converted Ottoman stone house and opened in 1945, this *pastane* (patisserie) is known throughout the region for its house-made *dondurma* (ice cream). It also makes milk-based puddings, biscuits, jams and preserves.

Kirmizi   BAR
(3264 Sokak 2; ⏰ 11am-late; 🌐) Kirmizi translates to 'red' in Turkish and there's no

mistaking the colourful decor of this bar's corner location. It's a good spot to watch the day-trip boats arrive back into harbour around 6pm, and after-dark DJs and a pool table are other attractions. On summer weekends, big barbecues out the front provide grilled meat and seafood as dinnertime snacks.

❶ Getting There & Away

TO/FROM ADNAN MENDERES AIRPORT
Simay (☑ 0532 151 2835; www.simayturizm. com; 1015 Sokak/Hulusi Öztin Çarşısı Caddesi 3) runs a shuttle-bus service between Çeşme and İzmir's Adnan Menderes Airport (€20 per passenger). Shuttles leave 10 times per day between 5am and midnight.

BOAT
Erturk (☑ 0232-712 6768; www.erturk.com.tr; 1015 Sokak/Hulusi Öztin Çarşısı Caddesi 6-7; ☷9am-8pm), **Ege Bırlık** (☑ 0232-712 3040; www.egebirlik.eu; 1015 Sokak/Hulusi Öztin Çarşısı Caddesi 3) and **Sunrise Tours** (☑ 0232-712 9797; www.chiossunrisetours.com.tr; Atadağ Caddesi 2, Çeşme Liman) all offer services to Chios in Greece; slow ferries (50 minutes) take both passengers and cars; fast catamarans (20 minutes) take passengers only. Same-day return fares hover around €25 on the slow ferry and €28 for the fast ferry and ticket prices include a €2 port tax. Cars cost around €100.

The ferries sail at least twice a day between July and September and three times per week from October to June (usually Wednesday or Friday, and Saturday and Sunday). It's not necessary to purchase your ticket in advance unless you have a car. You'll need a passport.

BUS & DOLMUŞ
You'll need to change in İzmir if travelling between Çeşme and major destinations. Çeşme's otogar is a kilometre south of Cumhuriyet Meydanı, and bus companies have offices there. Most dolmuşes leave from the otogar and stop at various points in town (look for the signs with a large 'D').

There are morning and evening services to İstanbul (10 hours) with Metro (₺130) and Ulusoy (₺130); in summer other companies offer additional services. Çeşme Seyahat runs services every 15 to 40 minutes to both İzmir's main otogar (₺23, 1¾ hours) and the city's smaller Üçkuyular bus station (₺20, 1½ hours).

Dolmuşes to Alaçatı (₺6) depart from the otogar every 10 minutes from 7.30am to 7.30pm, then every 30 minutes from 7.30pm to 9pm, at 10pm and at 11pm, picking up passengers at a more convenient stop at the eastern end corner of İnkılap Caddesi (1015 Sokak) and travelling via Altınyunus (₺5).

Dolmuşes to Altınkum beach (₺6) leave from a stop just south of the Tourist Office (look for the sign with the big 'D').

Alaçatı
☑ 0232 / POP 10.060
A mere two decades ago, this rather unassuming erstwhile Greek village some 10km southeast of Çeşme was known predominantly for its excellent olive oil and world-class windsurfing. But thanks to some forward-thinking hoteliers, who transformed many of its dilapidated *taş evleri* (stone houses) into high-end boutique accommodation, Alaçatı has become one of Turkey's hottest destinations for the free-spending middle class. A walk along Kemalpaşa Caddesi in Merkez (the centre) showcases the town's main attractions: world-class boutique hotels, restaurants specialising in Aegean cuisine, sleek cafes and high-end boutiques catering to glamour pusses of both sexes. In the high season (May to September), it's a crowded, often-chaotic and always-chic place to spend a few days.

🛏 Sleeping

Çiprika Pansiyon PENSION $
(☑ 0232-716 7303; www.ciprika.com; 3045 Sokak 1, Merkez; r ₺120; ❋🕿) This humble pension is one of a few budget options in the town, offering seven decently sized but frayed stone rooms. The main drawcard is the huge shaded corner garden.

★**Taş Otel** BOUTIQUE HOTEL $$$
(Stone Hotel; ☑ 0232-716 7772; www.tasotel. com; Kemalpaşa Caddesi 132, Merkez; s €90-110, d €110-135; ❋@🕿🌊🐾) This is Alaçatı's first boutique hotel, and the tranquil oasis comprising seven simple but charming rooms, a gorgeous library/lounge, and a walled garden with large pool is still one of town's best places to stay. Breakfast and afternoon tea (complimentary) are delicious. Also available is an adjacent standalone stone villa with a kitchenette and private swimming pool.

Yucca HOSTEL $$$
(☑ 0232-716 7871; www.yuccaalacati.com; 18000 Sokak 35, Liman Mevkii; s/d €80/100; 🕿) Fancy staying in a carefully styled getaway designed around a lush garden near Alaçatı's main surf beach? This designer hostel offers 12 simple rooms and a garden with hammocks, sun lounges, bar and restaurant. There's a party vibe (especially on weekends) and helpful hosts.

İncirli Ev BOUTIQUE HOTEL $$$
(Fig Tree House; ☑ 0232-716 0353; www.incirliev. com; cnr 3076 & 3074 Sokaks, Merkez; r €80-140; ❋🕿) The quiet but still-central location isn't the only draw at this boutique option. The eight rooms in the century-old property

WINDSURFING IN ALAÇATI

Alaçatı was 'discovered' as a windsurfer's paradise in the 1970s by a handful of intrepid German campers. Its strong, consistent northerly winds – blowing at up to 25 knots – make it a big hit with the surfing community. The main windsurfing beach is Alaçatı Surf Paradise (Alaçatı Sörf Cenneti).

Sadly, the beach has suffered here in recent years. The construction of a marina cannibalised 1km of the beach, reducing it to 2km and leading to fears for the surfers' safety with boats motoring past. The road there is now lined with large houses, which are part of the ongoing Port Alaçatı residential development, but for now windsurfing and kitesurfing continues largely unhindered.

ASPC (Alaçatı Surf Paradise Club; ☑ 0232-716 6611; www.alacati.info; Liman Mevkii) This Turkish-German operation offers well-regarded windsurfing courses and hires high-quality equipment, charging €135 to €185 for a three-day package (board, wetsuit, harness and shoes). Basic, sport and pro boards are available. A starter course consisting of five hours (10 hours for three students or more) across three days costs €225. Sea-kayak and mountain-bike hire is also available.

Myga Surf Company (☑ 0232-716 6468; www.myga.com.tr; Liman Mevkii) This outfit has a range of equipment, charging from ₺190 for a one-day package. A five-hour starter course (7½ hours for two students, 10 hours for three or more), which can be spread across a few days, costs ₺1090.

are attractive and comfortable, and owners Sabahat and Osman are extremely welcoming. Guests love the lavish breakfast and complimentary afternoon tea served under the old *incir* (fig) in the garden, which gives the hotel its name.

Bey Evi   BOUTIQUE HOTEL **$$$**
(☑ 0232-716 8085; www.beyevi.com.tr/en; Kemalpaşa Caddesi 126, Merkez; r standard/deluxe €215/250, ste €275; ❋ ☜ ☲) It's difficult to tag this popular hotel. The decor, size and personal service place it in the boutique category, but the variety of accommodation and the swish pool area with bar and pizzeria are reminiscent of a resort. Rooms are attractive and well equipped – opt for a spacious deluxe room or suite if possible.

✖ Eating & Drinking

★ Bumba Breakfast Club   TURKISH **$$**
(☑ 0506 938 3311; www.facebook.com/bumba breakfastclub; 2000 Sokak 35, Merkez; breakfast ₺60, mezes ₺25-30, mains ₺35-70; ☉ 9am-midnight) Bumba's table-covering breakfasts are packed with local and seasonal herbs, cheeses and fruit. Highlights of 15 small plates could include yoghurt with mulberries or delicate honey and tahini. After 4pm, the energetic young owners transform Bumba into a bustling *meyhane* with loads of *meze* and rakı-fuelled fun. Look out for the family of tortoises sometimes patrolling the restaurant's floor.

Roka Bahçe   TURKISH **$$**
(☑ 0232-716 9659; Kemalpaşa Caddesi 107, Merkez; mezes ₺20-32, mains ₺35-60; ☉ 6pm-3am) This stylish courtyard restaurant on the main eating and shopping strip offers unusual Aegean dishes including braised goat with chard and thistles, *tire köfte* (small meatballs in a casserole) and calamari stuffed with Aegean greens. Bookings essential.

★ Asma Yaprağı   TURKISH **$$$**
(☑ 0538 912 1290; www.asmayapragi.com.tr; 1005 Sokak 50, Merkez; mezes ₺15-25, mains ₺75; ☉ breakfast from 9.30am, lunch from 1pm, dinner from 8pm) A meal at the 'Vine Leaf' is an essential experience for gastronomes. Seating is in an atmospheric courtyard between April and November, and inside between December and March. Once seated, you'll wait in turn to visit the kitchen and choose from the excellent mezes and mains. Sadly, the wine list is limited and service can be shambolic. Reservations essential.

Ferdi Baba   SEAFOOD **$$$**
(☑ 0232-568 6034; www.ferdibababalik.com; Liman Caddesi, Yat Limanı; fish per kg; ☉ 10am-midnight) This is without doubt the best restaurant down on the Alaçatı marina. It serves all of the standards, and is known for the freshness of its mezes and the quality of its fish (priced by weight). There's another branch on Kemalpaşa Caddesi in Merkez.

Agrilia MEDITERRANEAN $$$
(☑ 0232-716 8594; Kemalpaşa Caddesi 86, Merkez; starters ₺30-55, pastas ₺45-55, mains ₺60-90; ⊙ 7pm-midnight daily Jul-Sep, 7pm-midnight Fri, 1pm-midnight Sat & Sun Oct-Jun) This long-running alternative to traditional Turkish fare recently moved into new and very swish digs within the Alavya hotel compound. Chef-owner Melih Tekşen creates Mod Med dishes but relies heavily on local Aegean produce to create his seasonally driven flavours. Regulars love the steaks and art-directed cocktails.

Zeplin BAR
(2012 Sokak 2, Merkez) With its wood-lined interior and unfussy sprawl of outdoor tables, Zeplin is an unpretentious alternative to other Alaçatı bars paying just a little too much attention to their social media activity. Chilled big bottles of Bomonti beer and zingy spritzes are preferred by most punters, but Zeplin's also well-regarded for its whisky selection. Good music too, including occasional live gigs.

Traktör BAR
(☑ 0232-716 0679; cnr 1005 & 1101 Sokaks, Merkez) Hip staff, a courtyard garden, good coffee, cold beer and live jazz music – the recipe for a perfect bar-cafe! Traktör is one of the best watering holes in town, and is blessedly free of the attitude overload at many nearby establishments. It's near the Pazaryeri Mosque.

❶ Getting There & Around

You can hire cars and scooters at **Radiance Rent A Car** (☑ 0232-716 8514; www.isiltirentacar. com; Atatürk Bulvarı 55a; scooter/car per day from ₺120/230). ASPC hires mountain bikes.

BUS & DOLMUŞ

Çeşme Seyahat (www.cesmeseyahat.com) runs regular direct departures to İzmir (₺25, 90 minutes). For other major destinations you'll need to transit either through Çeşme or İzmir.

Dolmuşes run between Alacatı and Çeşme's otogar (₺5, 10 minutes, 10km) every 10 minutes between 7.30am and 7.30pm and less frequently from 7.30pm to 11pm. Between mid-May and September, dolmuşes run to/from Alaçatı Surf Paradise (₺4), which is 4km south of town on the western side of the *liman*.

Sığacık

☑ 0232

Sığacık is a small village clustered around a crumbling 16th-century Genoese castle and an ugly marina. There's little to do here except stroll the waterfront, watch the fishers returning with their famous catch of *kalamar* (squid) and *barbunya* (red mullet), head to nearby beaches or explore the ruins at Teos, 2km north.

◉ Sights

★ **Teos** ARCHAEOLOGICAL SITE
(☑ 0232-745 1413; www.teosarkeoloji.com; ₺6; ⊙ 7am-7pm) The evocative ruins of this ancient city, which was one of the 12 cities of

İZMİR & THE NORTH AEGEAN SIĞACIK

WORTH A TRIP

URLA WINE SCENE

The rural area surrounding the Aegean town of Urla is one of Turkey's emerging wine-growing regions. Archeological evidence shows a history of viticulture dating back 4000 years, but it's only in the past decade or so that Turkish winemakers have reinvigorated the industry after damage by the *phylloxera* virus in the 1900s. A few decades later, the 1923 Greek–Turkish population exchanges and the Turkish War of Independence significantly altered the demographic of this coastal region, and winemaking largely became obsolete.

In 2006, **Urlice Vineyards** (Urlice Şarapçılık; ☑ 0232-754 6859; www.urlice.com; 7 Sokak 1168, Urla; pizza ₺45-65, wine by the glass/bottle ₺35/135; ⊙ 11am-9pm Mon-Sat) was a pioneer in the new wave of Urla viticulture, and its vineyard restaurant now combines excellent cabernet sauvignon, merlot and shiraz varietals with wood-fired pizza. The region is an easy day trip from either İzmir, Alaçatı or Çeşme, but the **Urla Bağevi** (☑ 0530 829 0175; www.urlabagevi.com; Sokak 9005, Yağcılar; d €90) offers boutique accommodation in the quiet rural village of Yağcılar. See www.urlabagyolu.net for touring maps and details of seven different vineyards.

Public transport to Urla from İzmir involves a combination of metro and minibus so it's recommended the area is explored with your own transport.

the Ionian League, are spread over a low hilly isthmus now used as farmland. A flourishing seaport with two fine harbours in Greek and Roman times, Teos was known for its wines, theatre and Temple of Dionysis; the ruins of the latter two can be explored on site and other features are being unearthed in ongoing excavations being conducted by the University of Ankara.

There are five major sites here, all of which can be reached via recently constructed paths: the rectangular **bouleuterion** (assembly or senate house), **agora temple**, **theatre**, columned **Temple of Dionysis** (the largest temple of Dionysis erected in the ancient world) and **ancient harbour**. Informative interpretative panels in Turkish and English are provided.

There are no eating or drinking options at the site, but Teos Park, a forestry department picnic grove, is located 1km away, on the road to Akkum. A shady restaurant operates here in summer, and there's a year-round shop where you can buy snacks and cold drinks to enjoy beneath the pine trees overlooking the Aegean.

Sleeping & Eating

Beyaz Ev PENSION $$
(☑0532-598 1760; www.sigacikpansiyon.net; 162 Sokak 19; s/d ₺250/400; ❄☎) The three-room 'White House' is a popular and friendly pension located slightly inland but with a huge terrace overlooking the seafront. Rooms are spacious and bright, and the suite has a sitting area and kitchenette.

Teos Lodge HOTEL $$$
(☑0232-745 7463; 126 Sokak 26; r ₺450-550, ste ₺650; P❄☎) Upgraded from a pension in recent years, this friendly hotel near the marina has simple rooms equipped with a kettle; some have sea views. Its main drawcard is an in-house restaurant with a lovely terrace overlooking the water.

Liman SEAFOOD $$
(☑0232-745 7011; www.sigaciklimanrestaurant. com; off Liman Caddesi; mezes ₺15-40, mains ₺30-70; ◷9am-midnight) Right on the marina,

Liman is known throughout the region for its fresh fish and mezes. Seating is on the terrace or in the huge dining room, which overlooks the marina through large plate-glass windows.

ⓘ Getting There & Away

For direct bus services, you must travel from İzmir. Alternatively, take the bus from Çeşme to İzmir as far as Güzelbahçe (where the university campus is) and change there to bus 730, which travels between İzmir's Üçkuyular bus station and Seferihisar between 6am and 11.25pm (₺12, 70 minutes, half-hourly). From Seferihisar, blue-and-yellow dolmuşes run half-hourly to Akkum (₺5) and Sığacık (₺5).

Akkum
☑0232
This waterfront settlement is popular with domestic tourists, who come here to swim or windsurf at the two sandy beaches and live it up in swish beach resorts. Büyük Akkum is the main beach and has the best facilities. Küçük Akkum is usually quieter.

The archaeological site at Teos is a 3km drive or walk away.

Euphoria Aegean Resort & Spa RESORT $$$
(☑0232-750 5100; www.euphoriahotels.com/tr; Akkum Caddesi 20; d ₺800, ste ₺1300; P❄@☎☀) Occupying a promontory above Akkum's main beach, this huge resort has spacious, well-equipped rooms, a beach club and a huge array of spa and leisure facilities. A five-day minimum stay applies in summer.

ⓘ Getting There & Away

Blue-and-yellow dolmuşes travel between the Büyük Plaj (Main or Big Beach) and Seferihisar (₺5, 20 minutes), stopping at Sığacık (₺5) en route.

A taxi from Sığacık to Akkum will cost about ₺30; a return trip to Teos (including waiting time) will cost around ₺90.

Ephesus, Bodrum & the South Aegean

Best Places to Eat

➜ Limon (p266)

➜ Orfoz (p263)

➜ Kaplan Dağ Restoran (p241)

➜ Culinarium (p276)

➜ Bistrot 4 (p267)

Best Places to Stay

➜ Nişanyan Hotel (p243)

➜ Bonjuk Bay (p280)

➜ Liman Hotel (p245)

➜ Big Blue Otel (p281)

➜ Agora Pansiyon (p254)

Why Go?

Home to two of the seven Ancient Wonders of the World, civilisation on Turkey's idyllic south Aegean coast looks back thousands of years. The region's embarrassment of ruins include majestic Ephesus, the celebrated capital of Roman Asia Minor, while nearby, the ancient ports of Priene and Miletus, and temples at Euromos and Didyma offer an evocative picture of the past.

Blessed with a sparkling coastline of dramatic bays and gorgeous cove beaches, the south Aegean becomes a magnet for millions of tourists in summer. Marmaris and Kuşadası attract the masses, while Bodrum is Turkey's most exclusive seaside getaway, boasting lanes of whitewashed townhouses and a landmark 15th-century castle. For more elemental pleasures, head to the remote Bozburun or Datça Peninsulas, home to rugged terrain and lonely fishing villages, while the impressive Dilek National Park has challenging hiking trails and a glorious undeveloped shoreline.

When to Go
Selçuk

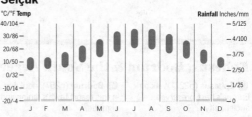

May & Jun Tour ancient sites while it's sunny but not oppressively hot or crowded.

Jul & Aug Party with Turks and foreigners till dawn in Bodrum and Marmaris.

Sep Enjoy the coast's beaches while the sea is still warm and costs are lower.

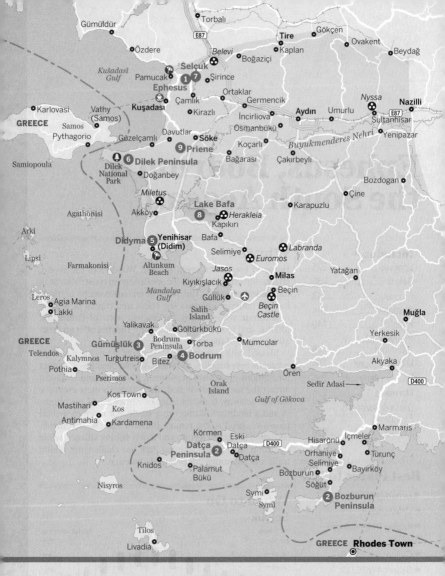

Ephesus, Bodrum & the South Aegean Highlights

1 Ephesus (p227) Walking Europe's best-preserved ancient city.

2 Datça & Bozburun (p274) Feeling miles from anywhere on these rugged peninsulas.

3 Gümüşlük (p266) Enjoying sea views over fresh fish.

4 Bodrum (p257) Indulging in this resort town's dining and nightlife.

5 Didyma (p252) Gaping in wonder at the columns of the Temple of Apollo.

6 Dilek Peninsula (p248) Finding pristine Aegean beaches and exploring mountain paths.

7 Selçuk (p236) Touring the sights of this traditional Turkish town.

8 Lake Bafa (p253) Toasting sunset from a hilltop littered with ruins.

9 Priene (p249) Surveying rolling fields where the sea once lay from this ancient port.

History

Understanding the south Aegean coast's history requires visualising bays and peninsulas where they no longer exist – otherwise, the stories of the key ancient cities of Ephesus, Priene and Miletus, all now several kilometres inland, make no sense. Before the lazy Büyük Menderes River silted up, these were economically and strategically significant port cities, fully integrated into the wider Greco-Roman world back when the Mediterranean Sea was dubbed the 'Roman lake'. Geographical changes, however, saw the coast's centres of power and commerce move to accommodate the subcontinent's evolving contours.

Mycenaeans and Hittites were among the region's earliest recorded peoples (from 1200 BC). More important, however, were the later Ionians, who fled here from Greece; they founded Ephesus, Priene and Miletus. South of Ionia was mountainous Caria – site of the great King Mausolus' tomb, the Mausoleum of Halicarnassus (now Bodrum). Along with Ephesus' Temple of Artemis, it was one of the Seven Wonders of the Ancient World.

Under the Romans, Ephesus prospered, becoming the capital of Asia Minor, while the Temple of Artemis and Didyma's Temple of Apollo were spectacular pilgrimage sites. As Christianity spread, pagans, Jews and Christians coexisted peacefully in the big towns. Most famously, St John reputedly brought Mary, the mother of Jesus, to Ephesus, where tradition attests part of his gospel was written.

During subsequent Byzantine rule, the coastal communities maintained their traditional social, cultural and economic links with the nearby Greek islands.

In the late 11th and 12th centuries, overland Seljuk expansion coincided with Crusaders on the move to the Holy Land. In 1402, the Knights Hospitaller (who then controlled much of the Greek Dodecanese islands) built a grand castle in Halicarnassus with stones from the ancient mausoleum and renamed the town Petronium. After Süleyman the Magnificent's 1522 conquest of Rhodes, Petronium was ceded to the Ottomans (thus the Turkicised name 'Bodrum'). Although the coast would be Turkish-controlled thereafter, it remained significantly populated by Greeks called Rum; their traditional knowledge of sailing, shipping and shipbuilding would prove

crucial to the empire's maritime commerce and naval success.

After Turkey's War of Independence, the 1923 Treaty of Lausanne decreed the tumultuous Greek-Turkish population exchanges – terminating three millennia of Greek coastal civilisation with one stroke of the pen.

Despite the peaceful holiday atmosphere here today, this frontier's strategic significance remains as vital now as always – Greek and Turkish fighter pilots regularly engage in mock dogfights over the coast. The two countries' long-standing 'Aegean Dispute' over territorial waters, sovereign territory and airspace almost caused a war in January 1996, when Turkish commandos briefly stormed the uninhabited Greek islet of Imia (Kardak in Turkish), causing frantic diplomatic activity in Western capitals.

Today, tensions remain over the Aegean and periodically flashpoints arise. President Erdoğan has frequently issued provocative claims to Greek territory, stoking nationalist sentiment within Turkey. Greece has also accused Turkey of failing to deal with the flow of refugees and migrants fleeing to its islands from the latter's coast; on one day alone (29 August 2019), 650 people (mainly from Syria and Afghanistan) arrived in Lesbos.

Ephesus

🎧 0232

The Greco-Roman world truly comes alive at Ephesus, a Unesco World Heritage Site. After more than a century and a half of excavation, the city's recovered and renovated structures have made Ephesus Europe's most complete classical metropolis – and that's with 80% of the city yet to be unearthed!

As capital of Roman Asia Minor, Ephesus was a vibrant city of over 250,000 inhabitants, the fourth largest in the empire after Rome, Alexandria and Antioch. Adding in traders, sailors and pilgrims to the Temple of Artemis, these numbers were even higher, meaning that in Ephesus one could encounter the full diversity of the Mediterranean world and its peoples. So important and wealthy was Ephesus that its Temple of Artemis, on the western edge of present-day Selçuk, was the biggest on earth, and one of the Seven Wonders of the Ancient World.

Close by are two other important Christian sites: Mary's House, where the Virgin Mary is said to have lived, and the Grotto of the Seven Sleepers.

History

Early Legend

According to legend, 10th-century-BC Dorian incursions forced Androclus, Ionian prince of Athens, to seek a safer settlement. First, however, he consulted the famed Delphic oracle, which foresaw 'the fish, the fire and the boar' as markers of the new Ionian city.

After crossing the Aegean, Androclus and his crew rested on the Anatolian shore and cooked a freshly caught fish – so fresh, in fact, that it jumped out of the pan. The toppled coals set the nearby forest ablaze, smoking out a wild boar that Androclus chased down and killed; on that very spot, he resolved to build Ephesus. Other sources say Ephesus was founded by a tribe of Amazons. Parts of both legends are depicted on a frieze on the Temple of Hadrian (p234).

Worship of Artemis

Androclus and his Ionian followers had been preceded on the coast by the Lelegians, one of the aboriginal peoples of the Aegean littoral who worshipped the Anatolian maternal fertility goddess Cybele. The Ionians fused local ritual with their own, making their Artemis, the beautiful twin sister of Apollo, a unique fertility goddess here. Despite the 7th-century-BC flood that damaged the temple, and the Cimmerian invaders who razed the entire city around 650 BC, the Artemis cult continued, and the determined population rebuilt their temple after each setback.

Croesus & the Persians

Ephesus' massive wealth, accumulated from maritime trade and the pilgrims to the Temple of Artemis (or Artemision), aroused the envy of Croesus, King of Lydia, who attacked in around 560 BC. The autocratic king relocated the populace inland, where the new Ephesus was built (near the temple's southern edge). However, Croesus also respected the cult, funding the temple's reconstruction over the next decade to 550 BC.

Everyday life continued as the Ephesians paid tribute to Lydia and, later, to Persian invaders under Cyrus. Ephesus revolted in 498 BC, sparking the Greco-Persian War, which briefly drove out the eastern invaders, and Ephesus joined Athens and Sparta in the Delian League. However, in the later Ionian War, Ephesus picked the losing side and was again ruled by Persia.

In 356 BC, the year Alexander the Great was born, a young notoriety seeker,

Herostratus, burned down the Temple of Artemis, to ensure his name would live on forever. The disgusted Ephesian elders executed Herostratus and declared that anyone who mentioned his name would also be killed. A new temple, bigger and better than anything before, was immediately envisioned. In 334 BC, an admiring Alexander the Great offered to pay for the construction provided the temple was dedicated to him. But the Ephesians, who were fiercely protective of their goddess, declined, cunningly pointing out that it was unfitting for one divinity to erect a temple in honour of another. When completed, the Artemision was recognised as one of the Seven Wonders of the Ancient World.

Lysimachus & the Romans

Upon Alexander's death, one of his generals named Lysimachus took Ionia. However, by then silt from the River Cayster (Küçük Menderes in Turkish, which translates as 'Little Meander') had already started to block Ephesus' harbour, and Lysimachus moved the population eastward to today's site, strategically set between two hills and protected by walls 10km long and 5.6m thick. When the Ephesians revolted again, Lysimachus' Seleucid rivals invaded, leading to a messy period of conquest and reconquest that only ended when Ephesus was handed to the Romans in 133 BC.

Augustus' decision to make Ephesus capital of Asia Minor in 27 BC proved a windfall for the city; its population grew to around 250,000, drawing immigrants, merchants and imperial patronage. The annual festival of Artemis (now Diana to the Romans) became a month-long spring party drawing thousands from across the empire. Yet Ephesus also attracted Christian settlers, including St John, who supposedly settled here with the Virgin Mary after the death of Jesus and wrote his gospel here. St Paul also lived in Ephesus for three years (probably in the AD 60s) during three visits.

Decline & Fall

Despite Attalus II of Pergamum's rebuilding the harbour and Nero's proconsul's dredging it in AD 54, the harbour continued to silt up. A century later, Emperor Hadrian tried diverting the Cayster, but silt eventually pushed the sea back as far as today's Pamucak. Malarial swamps developed, the port was lost, and Ephesus' increasingly Christian population meant diminished funds for the Artemis/Diana cult. In 263, Germanic Goths sacked Ephesus, burning the temple yet again. Sackings by the Arabs in the 7th century hastened the decline.

Nevertheless, Ephesus' association with two disciples of Christ (not to mention his mother), and its status as one of the Seven Churches of Asia mentioned in the Book of Revelation, inspired pious Byzantine emperors to hold on to what they could. The 4th-century emperor Constantine the Great rebuilt many public buildings, with additional works overseen by Flavius Arcadius (r 395–408). And 6th-century Emperor Justinian I built a basilica (p237) dedicated to St John on Ayasuluk Hill in today's Selçuk.

The fortress settlement there later became known as Agios Theologos ('Divine Theologian' in Greek) – hence the later Turkicised name, Ayasuluk. Amusingly, medieval Crusaders versed in the classics were surprised to find a forlorn village here, rather than the epic ancient city they had anticipated.

Modern archaeological research in Ephesus dates to 1863, when British architect John Turtle Wood, sponsored by the British Museum, began to search for the Artemision, parts of which he uncovered six years later. The story continues to unfold more than a century and a half later.

Sights

A visit to **Ephesus** (Efes; main site adult/child ₺60/free, Terraced Houses ₺30, parking ₺10; ⊙8am-7.30pm Apr-Oct, to 5.30pm Nov-Mar) takes at least two hours – add 20 minutes if visiting the Terraced Houses (p233). Visit in the early morning or late afternoon to avoid crowds and the bright midday sun (between 9.30am and 1.30pm is busiest). The softer morning light is best for photographing the ruins, but the site is generally quietest after 3pm, when the tour groups depart. If you can, avoid public holidays altogether. Take a hat, sunglasses, sunscreen and plenty of water, or you will have to pick them up in the overpriced shops and cafes at the entrances.

Ephesus' two gates are 3km apart. The most popular entrance is the Upper Gate (also known as the Magnesian Gate), which allows you to walk down the Curetes Way with the Library of Celsius below you and exit through the Lower Gate. However, the Lower Gate is quieter, as it receives fewer crowds from the cruise ships and tour

ⓘ EPHESUS TIPS

Tips for getting the most out of your visit.

➡ In the hot summer months, take a good hat with you, as there is very little shade on site.

➡ Toilets are located at the entry gates only – there are no toilets once you are inside.

➡ The Terraced Houses are a must-see (though they cost extra)!

➡ Stay in Selçuk at least two nights as there is much to see in the area besides Ephesus, including the lively Saturday market.

buses, and is easier to reach by public transport. Either way, if you end up entering and exiting through the same gate, retracing your steps is not a huge hardship and you will get to see the site twice.

◉ Lower Ephesus

Church of St Mary   RUINS
(Double Church; car park) Northwest of the Lower Gate, a signposted path leads to the ruins of the Church of St Mary, also called the Double Church. The original building was a Hall of the Muses, a place for lectures, teaching and debates. Destroyed by fire, it was rebuilt as a church in the 4th century – the first one named after the Virgin Mary.

Later it served as the site of the Council of Ephesus (AD 431), which condemned the Nestorian heresy which refused to refer to Mary as the 'Mother of God'. Over the centuries several other churches were built here, somewhat obscuring the original layout. The rubble at the exit from the church area is a pile of **milestones** that once indicated distances to and from Ephesus.

Gymnasium of Vedius   RUINS
On a side road between the Lower Gate car park and the Selçuk road, this ruined 2nd-century-AD structure has exercise fields, baths, a lavatory, covered exercise rooms, a swimming pool and a ceremonial hall. Unfortunately, it cannot be visited.

Stadium   RUINS
Outside the Lower Gate, the stadium dates from the 2nd century AD. The Byzantines removed most of its finely cut stones to

Ephesus

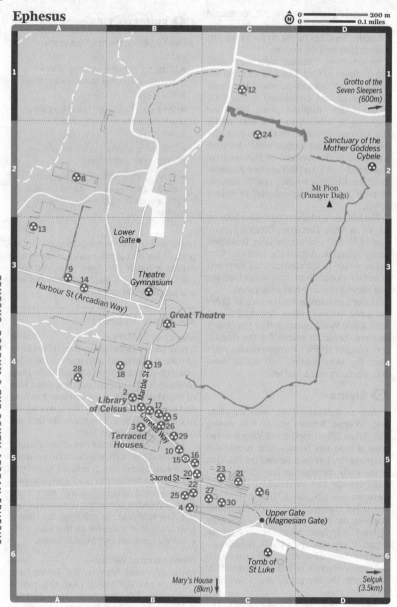

N | 0 ————— 200 m
0 ————— 0.1 miles

Grotto of the Seven Sleepers (600m)

Sanctuary of the Mother Goddess Cybele

Mt Pion (Panayır Dağı)

12

24

13

Lower Gate

Theatre Gymnasium

9 14

Harbour St (Arcadian Way)

8

Great Theatre

1

28

18

19

Marble St

Library of Celsus 2 11

17 7

Curetes Way

3 26 5

29

Terraced Houses

10

15 16

20

Sacred St 22

23 21

25 27 30 6

4

Upper Gate (Magnesian Gate)

Tomb of St Luke

Mary's House (8km)

Selçuk (3.5km)

build the fortress and the Basilica of St John on Ayasuluk Hill. This 'quarrying' of precut building stone from older, often earthquake-ruined structures was a constant feature of Ephesian history. The stadium is not open to the public.

Harbour Street RUINS
(Arcadian Way) The 530m-long Harbour St was built by Byzantine Emperor Arcadius (r 395-408) to link the Great Theatre and the Middle Harbour Gate in a late attempt to revive the fading city. At the time, it was Ephesus'

Ephesus

most lavish thoroughfare, with the poshest shops of imported goods, and illuminated at night by 50 lamps on its colonnades – the only city outside Rome and Antioch to have street lighting. Look for the high column of the propylon (entry gate) at the end of the street to see how far inland the sea reached in ancient times.

Columns of the Evangelists   RUINS

The middle of Harbour St (Arcadian Way) is marked by the shafts of Corinthian columns that once supported statues of the four Evangelists erected in the 6th century AD.

Harbour Baths   RUINS

These baths, part of a complex that included a gymnasium and a sports area, were erected at the end of the 1st century AD but were badly damaged by an earthquake in 262 and not completed until the 4th century.

★ Great Theatre   RUINS

Originally built under Hellenistic King Lysimachus, the Great Theatre was reconstructed by the Romans between AD 41 and 117 and it is thought St Paul preached here. However, they incorporated original design elements, including the ingenious shape of the *cavea* (seating area), part of which was under cover. Seating rows are pitched slightly steeper as they ascend, meaning that upper-row spectators still enjoyed good views and acoustics – useful, considering that the theatre could hold an estimated 25,000 people.

Indeed, Ephesus' estimated peak population (250,000) is supported by the archaeologists' method of estimation: simply multiply theatre capacity by 10. Climb the stairs for a glimpse of the Aegean from the upper seats. Renovation work is ongoing to stabilise the structure. The theatre is still used for live musical performances and has a seating capacity of 8000.

Marble Street   RUINS

This street, paved with marble slabs slightly raised to aid drainage, formed part of the Sacred Way linking the city centre with the Temple of Artemis. Ruts indicate that vehicles used the thoroughfare frequently; manholes provided access to drains. The holes in the walls on either side of the street were caused by Crusaders who ripped out lamps for the metal. Look for the footprint, the head of a woman and the rectangular shape (cheque? credit card?) etched in one of the pavement slabs. It indicates the way to the brothel.

Lower Agora   RUINS

(Commercial Agora) This 110-sq-m one-time market had a massive colonnade. The shops in the colonnades traded in food and textiles; the agora's proximity to the harbour suggests that the goods were imported.

Temple of Serapis   RUINS

This massive structure, reached by a flight of marble steps in the southwest corner of the Lower Agora, may have contained a temple to the Greco-Egyptian god of grain. Egypt was one of the granaries of ancient Rome and Alexandria and Ephesus had close commercial links.

Ephesus

A DAY IN THE LIFE OF THE ANCIENT CITY

Visiting Ephesus might seem disorienting, but meandering through the city that was once the fourth largest in the Roman Empire is a highlight of any trip to Turkey. The illustration shows Ephesus in its heyday – but since barely 20% of Ephesus has been excavated, there's much more lurking underfoot than is possible to depict here. Keep an eye out for archaeologists digging away – exciting new discoveries continue to be made every year.

A typical Ephesian day might begin with a municipal debate at the **1 Odeon**. These deliberations could then be pondered further while strolling the **2 Curetes Way** to the **3 Latrines**, perhaps marvelling on the way at imperial greatness in the sculpted form of Emperor Trajan standing atop a globe, by the Trajan fountain. The Ephesian might then have a look at the merchandise on offer down at the **4 Lower Agora**, before heading back to the **5 Terraced Houses** for a leisurely lunch at home. Afterwards, they might read the classics at the **5 Library of Celsus**, or engage in other sorts of activities at the **6 Brothel**. The good citizen might then worship the gods at the **7 Temple of Hadrian**, before settling in for a dramatic performance at Ephesus' magnificent **8 Great Theatre**.

FACT FILE

➡ Ephesus was famous for its female artists, such as Timarata, who painted images of the city's patron goddess, Artemis.

➡ The Great Theatre could hold up to 25,000 spectators.

➡ According to ancient Greek legend, Ephesus was founded by Amazons, the mythical female warriors.

➡ Among Ephesus' 'native sons' was the great pre-Socratic philosopher, Heraclitus.

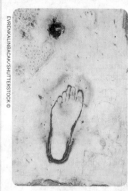

Brothel
As in other places in the ancient world, a visit to the brothel was considered rather normal for men. Visitors would undertake progressive stages of cleansing after entering, and finally arrive in the marble interior, which was decorated with statues of Venus, the goddess of love. A foot imprint on the pavement in Marble St indicates the way.

Harbour

Harbour Road

Halls of Veralanu

Temple of Hadrian
The exquisitely detailed archways and columns of this imposing temple, dedicated to the Emperor Hadrian in 138 AD, made it one of the most impressive structures in the city.

Library of Celsus
Generations of great thinkers studied at this architecturally advanced library, built in the 2nd century AD. The third-largest library in the ancient world (after Alexandria and Pergamum), it was designed to protect its 12,000 scrolls from extremes of temperature and moisture.

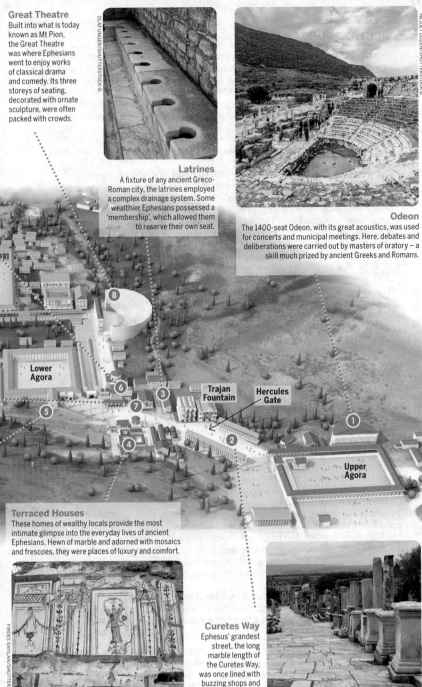

Great Theatre
Built into what is today known as Mt Pion, the Great Theatre was where Ephesians went to enjoy works of classical drama and comedy. Its three storeys of seating, decorated with ornate sculpture, were often packed with crowds.

Latrines
A fixture of any ancient Greco-Roman city, the latrines employed a complex drainage system. Some wealthier Ephesians possessed a 'membership', which allowed them to reserve their own seat.

Odeon
The 1400-seat Odeon, with its great acoustics, was used for concerts and municipal meetings. Here, debates and deliberations were carried out by masters of oratory – a skill much prized by ancient Greeks and Romans.

Lower Agora

Trajan Fountain

Hercules Gate

Upper Agora

Terraced Houses
These homes of wealthy locals provide the most intimate glimpse into the everyday lives of ancient Ephesians. Hewn of marble and adorned with mosaics and frescoes, they were places of luxury and comfort.

Curetes Way
Ephesus' grandest street, the long marble length of the Curetes Way, was once lined with buzzing shops and statues of local luminaries, emperors and deities.

SIGHTS AROUND EPHESUS

Atop the foundations of **Mary's House** (Meryem Ana Evi; ☑ 0232-894 1012; Meryemana; admission ₺25, parking ₺10; ⊙ 8am-6pm, mass 10.30am Sun, 6pm Sun-Fri Apr-Oct, 5pm daily Nov-Mar) on the slopes of Bülbül Dağı (Mt Coressos), said by some to be where the Virgin Mary lived, a chapel now receives busloads of pilgrims and tourists. There may not be space to see much inside the tiny chapel because of all the visitors lighting candles in front of the altar but note the small **fresco** on exiting and the larger orange bricks at the base of the exterior wall, which indicate the **original foundation**.

A **'wishing wall'** below the chapel is covered in bits of white cloth, paper, plastic or anything else at hand that the faithful have tied to a frame while making a wish. Taps here dispense potable spring water.

The house foundations, discovered in 1881 by French priest Julien Gouyet, are from the 6th century AD (though certain elements are older). Although legend had long attested that the Apostle John brought the Virgin Mary to Ephesus near the end of her life (AD 37–48), it took until the 19th century for the site to become a place of pilgrimage. Gouyet claimed to have found Mary's house based on the visions of a bedridden German nun, Anne Catherine Emmerich (1774–1824), and four popes have visited since then (most recently, Benedict XVI in 2006). Although the Vatican has not taken an official position on the case, the late John Paul II beatified Emmerich in 2004.

Multilingual information panels line the walkway leading to the house, and brochures and booklets are available. *The Holy Virgin's House: The True Story of Its Discovery* by P Eugene Poulin is available from the bookshop opposite the cafe.

Appropriate dress and behaviour is required when visiting this site, which many of the Christian faithful consider sacred.

Meryemana, the site of Mary's House, is 8km from Ephesus' Upper Gate and 9.5km from the Lower Gate. Dolmuşes don't go there; taxis from Selçuk's bus station are ₺50/85 single/return (including a 30-minute wait).

The road to/from Ephesus' Lower Gate passes the **Grotto of the Seven Sleepers** (Yedi Uyuyanlar Mağarası) on Panayır Dağı (Mt Pion), where seven young legendary Christians, persecuted by Emperor Decius in AD 250, are thought to be buried. Walk 200m south from the car park to see the ruins, following the hill path to the right. The grotto is clearly visible through a wire fence, though much must be left to the imagination.

The story goes that, having refused to recant their Christian beliefs, the seven young men gave their possessions to the poor and went to pray in this hilltop cave. They soon fell asleep, and Decius had the cave sealed. When the men were awoken centuries later by a landowner seeking to use the cave, they felt they had slept but a day, and warily sent someone into pagan Ephesus. The dazed young emissary was just as surprised to find Christian churches there as the Ephesians were to find someone presenting 200-year-old coins. The local bishop, Stephen, met the Seven Sleepers, who later died and were buried in their cave around 450.

The bishop quickly proclaimed the miracle, immediately creating a Byzantine place of pilgrimage that would last for over 1000 years. The legend became famous as far away as France and England, and there's even a Koranic variation attracting Muslim pilgrims.

Excavation, begun in 1927, has unearthed hundreds of 4th- and 5th-century terracotta oil lamps, decorated with Christian and, in some cases, pagan symbols. They indicate that the scores of rock-carved graves in this necropolis were important to many people for many centuries.

The Grotto of the Seven Sleepers is a couple of kilometres east of the Lower Gate and best visited after touring Meryemana and Ephesus. Frequent dolmuşes link Selçuk with Çamlık (₺5, 20 minutes), which is 8.5km to the southeast.

★ **Library of Celsus**　　　　　　　　RUINS
This magnificent library dating from the early 2nd century AD, the best-known monument in Ephesus, has been extensively restored. Originally built as part of a complex, the library looks bigger than it actually is: the convex facade base heightens the central elements, while the middle columns and capitals are larger than those at the ends. Facade niches hold replica statues

of the Four Virtues. From left to right, they are Sophia (Wisdom), Arete (Goodness), Ennoia (Thought) and Episteme (Knowledge).

The originals are in Vienna's Ephesus Museum; the Austrian Archaeological Foundation restored the Library of Celsus in the 1970s. As a Greek and Latin inscription on the front staircase attests, Consul Gaius Julius Aquila built the library in AD 110 to honour his deceased father, Gaius Julius Celsus Polemaeanus, the governor of Asia Minor from 105 to 107, who was buried under the building's western side. Capable of holding 12,000 scrolls in its wall niches, the Celsus was the third-largest library in the ancient world after those at Alexandria and Pergamum. The valuable texts were protected from temperature and humidity extremes by a 1m gap between the inner and outer walls.

The library's monumental facade lay in ruins for many centuries, but was reconstructed in the 1970s.

◉ Along the Curetes Way

Curetes Way RUINS
Named for the demigods who helped Lena give birth to Artemis and Apollo, the Curetes Way was Ephesus' main thoroughfare, 210m long and lined with statuary, religious and civic buildings, rows of shops selling incense, silk and other goods, workshops and even restaurants. Walking this street is the best way to understand Ephesian daily life.

Circular depressions and linear grooves are sporadically gouged into the marble to keep pedestrians from slipping on the slick surface. This was important not only during winter rains, but also during the searing summer heat; shopkeepers would regularly douse the slippery marble street with water from the fountains to cool them down.

Flowering trees once shaded the street and shops which also lowered the temperature. Right under where they stood, there are occasional stone abutments adorned with 12 circular depressions – boards for games of chance that ancient Ephesians would play for fun and even bet on: the contest was known in Latin as Ludus Duodecim Scriptorum (Game of 12 Markings), the predecessor of backgammon.

There's a rather patchwork look to the street's marble blocks – many are not in their original places, due to ancient and modern retrofitting. An intriguing element in some blocks are the tiny, carved Greek-language initials; they denoted the name of the specific builder responsible for the relevant section. This helped labourers collect their pay, as it proved they had been put into place.

Several structures along the way have occasional oval depressions in the walls – these held the oil lamps that lent a magical glow to the city's main thoroughfare by night. The larger holes in the marble were for torches.

Gate of Hadrian RUINS
This monumental arch, which links the Curetes Way with Marble St, is thought to have been dedicated to Hadrian when he visited Ephesus.

Brothel RUINS
This site, demurely called the 'Love House' on signboards, is eagerly anticipated by visitors, but its rather dishevelled state makes envisioning licentious goings-on a challenge. Indeed, some experts believe that visiting sailors and merchants simply used it as a guesthouse and bath, which of course would not necessarily exclude prostitution services on demand. The priapic statue of Bes in the Ephesus Museum (p237) in Selçuk was found in a well here. Whatever the brothel's fundamental purpose, its administrators reputedly required visitors to this windowless structure to undergo various degrees of cleansing before entering the inner areas, which were adorned with little statues of Venus and mosaics of the four seasons (Winter and Autumn still visible). Rumours also abound about the possible existence of a secret underground tunnel connecting the brothel to the Library of Celsus opposite.

★ Terraced Houses RUINS
(₺20) The roofed complex here contains seven well-preserved Roman homes built on three terraces, which are well worth the extra visiting fee. As you ascend the stairs through the enclosure, detailed signs explain each structure's evolving use during different periods. Extensive use of glass flooring allows you to step all over history. Even if you aren't a history buff, the colourful mosaics, painted frescoes and marble provide breathtaking insight into the lost world of Ephesus and its aristocracy.

In dwelling 2, keep an eye out for handwritten wall graffiti including everything from pictures of gladiators and animals to love poems and shopping lists. Dwelling 3 has depictions of the Nine Muses, Sappho and Apollo and, in the spacious inner courtyard, renowned philosophers of the period. Dwelling 6 contains a huge 185-sq-m marble hall as well as remarkable hot and cold baths, dating from the 3rd century AD.

The whole residential area was originally a graveyard – the Romans built the terraces for their homes over this and other Hellenistic structures.

Temple of Hadrian RUINS

One of Ephesus' star attractions and second only to the Library of Celsus, this ornate, Corinthian-style temple honours Trajan's successor and originally had a wooden roof when completed in AD 138. Note its main arch; supported by a central keystone, this architectural marvel remains perfectly balanced, with no need for mortar. The temple's designers also covered it with intricate decorative details and patterns: Tyche, goddess of chance, adorns the first arch, while Medusa wards off evil spirits on the second.

Sailors and traders in particular invoked Tyche, who was also the patroness of Ephesus, to protect them on their long journeys. After the first arch, in the upper-left corner is a relief of a man on a horse chasing a boar – a representation of Ephesus' legendary founder Androclus. On the right-hand arch are a band of Amazons, other possible founders. At shoulder height are Greek 'key' designs that represent the nearby Büyük Menderes River.

Latrines RUINS

This square structure has toilet 'seats' along the back walls with a roof above. Although some wealthy citizens had private home bathrooms, they also used the public toilets; some even paid a membership fee to claim a specific seat. Turning into the structure's entrance, you'll note a small aperture; here stood the clerk, who collected fees from visitors. While the whole experience was indeed a public one, the flowing Roman toga would have provided a modicum of privacy.

The rest of the room was open to the sky, with a floor covered in mosaics (visible though the wooden boards you walk on). 'Toilet paper' in ancient times was a natural sponge on a stick soaked in a vinegar solution.

Trajan Fountain RUINS

This honorary fountain from the early 2nd century AD was once dominated by a huge statue of the great soldier-emperor Trajan (r AD 98–117), grasping a pennant and standing on a globe; the inscription reads, 'I have conquered it all, and it's now under my foot.' Today, only the globe and a single foot nearby survive. The fountain's water flowed under the statue, spilling onto and cleaning the Curetes Way. Note the superb mosaics on the opposite side.

Baths of Scholasticia RUINS

Marble steps located behind the Trajan Fountain lead up Bath St to this large hamam. In one niche is a headless statue of Scholasticia, who repaired the baths in the 4th century AD.

Hercules Gate GATE

Marking the upper boundary of the Curetes Way, this two-storey gate with reliefs of Hercules on both main pillars was constructed in the 4th century AD. One of its functions was to stop wagons from entering the pedestrian thoroughfare.

◉ Upper Ephesus

Hydreion RUINS

This rectangular fountain with four columns sits next to the Memmius Monument.

Memmius Monument RUINS

This monument from the 1st century AD is dedicated to Caius Memmius, nephew of the dictator Sulla who sacked Ephesus in 84 BC. Pillars with dancing figures rest on a colossal square base.

Pollio Fountain RUINS

Backing onto the Upper Agora, this fountain honouring the builder of a nearby aqueduct hints at the lavish nature of ancient Ephesus' fountains, most of which were Roman and filled the city with the relaxing sound of rushing water.

Temple of Domitian RUINS

This ruined temple recalls Domitian (r AD 81–96), the tyrant as evil as Nero who banished St John to Patmos (where the evangelist wrote the Book of Revelation), and who executed his own nephew for showing interest in Christianity. The unpopular ruler demanded the structure be raised in his honour, but the temple and its statue were promptly demolished when news of his assassination reached Ephesus. The head of the statue is now in the Ephesus Museum in Selçuk.

Asclepion RUINS

A side road called Sacred St running along the western edge of the Upper Agora led to the Asclepion, the medical centre of Ephesus. Protected by the god Asclepius and his daughter Hygieia, doctors used the Rod of Asclepius snake symbol to indicate their presence; look nearby for the block of marble with such a symbol as well as a pharmaceutical cup. The serpent was used as a medical symbol because of the snake's ability to shed its skin and renew itself. At the same time the ancients also knew that snake venom had curative powers. Ephesus was famous for its medical school.

Prytaneum
RUINS

(City Hall) Two of six original Doric columns mark the entrance to the ruined Prytaneum, one of the most important civic structures in Ephesus. It contained the Temple of Hestia, and was also where religious and civil officials received official guests.

Here and elsewhere in Ephesus, note the differences between the Ionian Greeks' heavily ornamented, spiralling **columns**, and their smooth, unadorned Roman counterparts. Both coexist in tandem across the site, due to ancient recycling and modern relocations. A similar difference is notable in **arches**: the genius of single-material, harmoniously balanced Ionian Greek arches, and the pragmatic use of mortar by the Romans.

Temple of Hestia
RUINS

The Prytaneum hosted this shrine, where the city's eternal flame was tended by vestal virgins, and was fronted by a giant statue of Artemis, now in the Ephesus Museum in Selçuk. The fertility goddess was portrayed with huge breasts and arms extended in welcome, though her hands (probably crafted from gold) are long gone. Many of the statues of deities, emperors and other luminaries here originally had precious gemstones for eyes – another indicator of Ephesian wealth.

Odeon
RUINS

Built around AD 150, this once-lavish 1400-seat theatre boasts marble seats with lions' paws and other carved ornamentation. It was used primarily for lectures and musical performances but, given its location next to the Upper Agora, it almost certainly also functioned as a 450-seat **bouleuterion** (council chamber) for matters concerning city government. It is still used for musical performances. Ephesus had one of the ancient world's most advanced aqueduct systems, and there are signs of this in **terracotta piping** for water along the way to the building. The holes that appear intermittently at the top were used to unblock the pipes.

Upper Agora
RUINS

(State Agora) This large square measuring 58m by 170m, and used for legislation and local political talk, was flanked by grand columns and filled with polished marble. More or less in the middle was the small

Temple of Isis
– testament to the cultural and trade connections between Ephesus and Alexandria in Egypt. The agora's columns would later be reused for a Christian **basilica** on the agora's northeastern edge, which was a typically Byzantine three-nave structure with a wooden roof. From here, there are several archways in the distance, once food-storage houses.

Baths of Varius
RUINS

Baths were situated at the main entrances to ancient cities so that visitors could be disinfected and wash before entering. These 2nd-century ones stand at the entrance to Upper Ephesus beside the Magnesian Gate erected under Emperor Vespasian in the 1st century AD. Greco-Roman baths also served a social function as a meeting and massage destination. This is one of four bath complexes at Ephesus.

Tours

If signing up for a tour, make sure your guide is licensed and well informed, and understand exactly how much time you'll get on-site, compared to how much time will be spent on detours to carpet and other shops. Also check whether your tour includes entrance to the Terraced Houses – this is a highlight and mustn't be missed.

Random guides lurk at the entrances, asking about ₺200 for two hours (the official rate is over ₺300). The garbled and uninformative multilingual audio guides (₺20) available at the gates are not recommended. Many of the ruins in Ephesus have good English-language signage.

Selçuk-based operators such as Enchanting Tours (p239), Alaturka Turkey (p239) and No Frills Ephesus Tours (p239) offer recommended tours.

❶ Getting There & Away

Unless they hold a travel agent's license, hotels are not allowed to take guests to Ephesus, so most visitors will need to take a taxi or a car or join a tour. Selçuk is roughly a 3.5km walk from both entrances, with the Temple of Artemis and shade provided by mulberry trees en route to the Lower Gate. Biking here is possible (a cycle lane is under construction).

Dolmuşes serve the Lower Gate (₺2.50) every half-hour in summer, hourly in winter. Alternatively, dolmuşes between Selçuk and Kuşadası drop off and pick up at the turn-off for the Lower Gate, about a 20-minute walk from the site.

A taxi to/from either gate costs about ₺25.

Selçuk

0232 / POP 37,800

Were it not for nearby Ephesus, Selçuk might be just another Turkish farming town with a weekly produce market and ploughs rusting away on side streets. That said, the gateway to Ephesus does have plenty of its own attractions, many topped with a picture-perfect stork's nest: Roman/Byzantine aqueduct arches, a lone pillar remaining from one of the Seven Wonders of the Ancient World, and the hilltop

Byzantine ruins of the Basilica of St John and Ayasuluk Fortress.

Like all small places catering to short-term visitors, there is plenty of competition in the local tourism trade, which can result in both good deals for visitors and less-than-welcome pressure. Yet all in all, Selçuk remains a likeable, down-to-earth place, mixing a traditional country feel with a tourist buzz and family-run pensions offering a taste of Turkish hospitality and home cooking. It's a relaxing place to cool your heels for a spell.

Selçuk

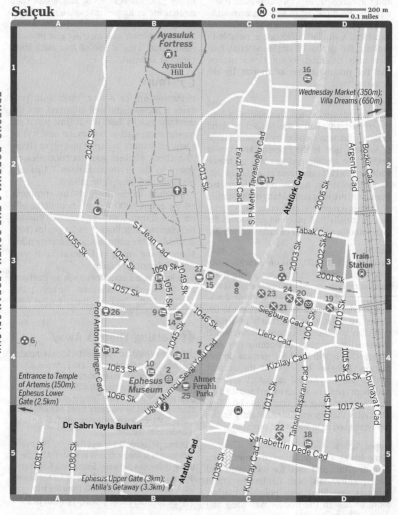

EPHESUS, BODRUM & THE SOUTH AEGEAN SELÇUK

◉ Sights

★Ephesus Museum   MUSEUM

(📞0232-892 6010; Uğur Mumcu Sevgi Yolu Caddesi; ₺15; ⊙8am-9pm mid-Apr–Oct, 8.30am-6.30pm Nov–mid-Apr) An essential stop on every Ephesus itinerary, this small museum contains artefacts from the ancient city, including scales, jewellery and cosmetic boxes as well as coins, funerary goods and ancient statuary. Highlights include the famous phallic terracotta effigy of Bes in room 2, the huge statue of a resting warrior in room 4 and the two extraordinary multibreasted marble statues of Artemis in room 7. The timelines on the walls are extremely useful for placing objects within their historical context.

Finds from a gladiators' cemetery are displayed here too, with commentary on their weaponry, training regimes and occupational hazards. Also notable are the ivory frieze from one of the Terraced Houses in room 2, which depicts the Emperor Trajan and the Roman army in a victorious campaign against the Dacians; and the frieze from the Temple of Hadrian in gallery 8, which is devoted to the Imperial Cult. The latter shows four heroic Amazons with their breasts cut off – early Greek writers attributed Ephesus' founding to them.

The museum is probably best visited after touring Ephesus itself, so that you'll be able to imagine how the objects would have looked in their original context.

İsa Bey Camii   MOSQUE

(St Jean Caddesi) At the southern base of Ayasuluk Hill, this imposing mosque was built in a post-Seljuk/pre-Ottoman transitional style, when Selçuk was capital of the Aydın Emirate. An inscription in Arabic above the main entrance states that it was built in 1375. It is open to visitors (except at prayer times).

Roman & Byzantine Aqueduct   RUINS

Running eastward from the southern base of Ayasuluk Hill, the remains of this long and quite tall Roman and Byzantine aqueduct are festively adorned with the huge nests of migrating storks, who stand guard from March through September.

Basilica of St John   CHURCH

(Aziz Yahya Kilisesi; St Jean Caddesi; incl Ayasuluk Fortress ₺15; ⊙8am-7pm Apr-Oct, 8.30am-5.30pm Nov-Mar) Despite a century of restoration, the once-great basilica built by Byzantine Emperor Justinian (r 527–565) remains a skeleton of its former self. Nonetheless, it is an atmospheric site with excellent views, and the best place in the area for a sunset photo. The information panels and scale model highlight the building's original grandeur, as do the marble steps and monumental gate.

Over time, earthquakes and attackers ruined Justinian's splendid church dedicated to the Apostle John, who reportedly visited Ephesus twice. His first visit (AD 37–48) was with the Virgin Mary; the

Selçuk

LOCAL KNOWLEDGE

STORKS IN SELÇUK

White storks can be spotted across Turkey, from the Black Sea to central Anatolia, but travellers are most likely to encounter them in Selçuk. This giant bird, which stands at over 1m tall and has a wingspan of 2m, migrates between the savannahs of southern Africa and West Asia, arriving in Selçuk in mid-March – a journey which crosses the Sahara and can take 50 days. You'll see the huge nests of the species, which can weigh up to 250kg, dotted around town, often perched on top of classical monuments including the sole remaining pillar of the Temple of Artemis and the town's Roman & Byzantine Aqueduct.

Locals have covered power lines with protective cabling to safeguard storks from electrocution, a main cause of death, and erected platforms to aid nesting. Male storks often choose the same nest each year to raise their young; the female usually lays four eggs, though clutches up to seven do occur. Stork nests are so large that other bird species (from house sparrows to little owls) are able to find a corner to 'squat' inside the host nest.

second (AD 95) was when he is thought to have written his gospel on this very hill. These legends, and the existence of a 4th-century tomb supposedly containing the saint's relics, inspired Justinian to build the basilica here and it drew thousands of pilgrims until the late Byzantine period. The **tomb of St John**, marked by a marble slab in the sanctuary, is surrounded by the cruciform outlines of Justinian's basilica. Note the 12 **pillars** that supported the dome with Christian symbols etched onto them and a full-immersion **baptistery** which dates from the 4th century.

★ **Ayasuluk Fortress**   FORTRESS
(Ayasuluk Kalesi; St Jean Caddesi; incl Basilica of St John ₺15; ⊘8am-7pm Apr-Oct, 8.30am-5.30pm Nov-Mar) Selçuk's crowning achievement is accessed on the same ticket as the Basilica of St John, once the citadel's principal structure. Earlier and extensive excavations here, concluded in 1998 after a quarter century, proved that there were castles on Ayasuluk Hill going back beyond the original Ephesian settlement to the Neolithic age. The fortress' partially restored remains, about 350m north of the church, date from Byzantine, Seljuk and Ottoman times and are an essential visit.

Enter via the so-called **Gate of Persecution** and walk uphill beyond the church to the fortress. Well-signposted ruins through the West Gate include a **hamam**, several **cisterns** and the reconstructed **Castle Mosque**, with a discernible mihrab (prayer niche facing toward Mecca) and walls of alternating layers of brick and stone. Since 2010, more than 100m of the western **walls** and **towers** have been restored using original materials.

One section of the fortress, the partially restored **Castle Palace** (or Inner Fortress) made headlines when excavated in 2009 as it had last been mentioned by British traveller John Covell in 1670. Built for a ruling Ottoman family, the structure was probably created by the same architects as the nearby İsa Bey Camii.

Recent excavations of the palace have also uncovered the remains of three houses south of the mosque, an area comprised of 15 bedrooms now dubbed the **Southern Terrace Houses**. There is written record that the great Ottoman traveller Evliya Çelebi stayed here in the late 17th century.

Temple of Artemis   RUINS
(Temple of Artemision, Artemis Tapınağı; off Dr Sabrı Yayla Bulvarı; ⊘8am-7pm Apr-Oct, 8.30am-6pm Nov-Mar) **FREE** In an empty field to the west of the centre, this lone reconstructed pillar is all that remains of the massive Temple of Artemis (or Artemision), built entirely from marble, one of the Seven Wonders of the Ancient World. Today it's often topped by a stork's nest. At its zenith, the temple counted 127 columns; today, the only way to get any sense of its grandeur is to visit Didyma's better-preserved Temple of Apollo (which had a 'mere' 122 columns).

The temple was damaged by flooding – the surrounds are still frequently covered with water in spring – and various invaders during its 1000-year lifespan. But it was always rebuilt – a sign of the great love and attachment Ephesians felt for their fertility goddess (Diana to the Romans), whose cult brought tremendous wealth to the city from pilgrims and benefactors who included the greatest kings and emperors of their day. The Artemis statue here was made of cedar wood. From the south, there is a good view of the lonely pillar with İsa Bey Camii and Ayasuluk Hill beyond.

Saturday Market   MARKET
(Şahabettin Dede Caddesi; ☺9am-5pm Sat winter, 8am-7pm summer) Both sightseers and self-caterers will enjoy this lively weekend market east of the bus station. Like the smaller **Wednesday market** (3018 Sokak; ☺9am-5pm Wed Nov-Apr, 8am-7pm May-Oct) to the northeast, it offer fruits, veg and cheeses from village farms in the surrounding area.

☞ Tours

★No Frills Ephesus Tours   TOURS
(☏0232-892 8828, 0545 892 8828; www.ephesus.co; St Jean Caddesi 3a; half-/full-day tour from €40/55; ☺9am Apr-Oct) Noticing how carpet-selling tactics were irritating time-poor independent travellers, Mehmet Esenkaya and his Australian wife Christine launched these small-group tours led by entertaining, well-informed guides, without any shopping side trips. Half-day tours include the Temple of Artemis and Ephesus; full-day ones add the Ephesus Museum and Mary's House. The Basilica of St John, Terraced Houses and Şirince cost €10 extra each.

Enchanting Tours   TOURS
(☏0535 245 3548, 0232-892 6654; www.enchantingtoursturkey.com; Hotel Bella, St John Caddesi 3b; ☺8am-7.30pm) Based at the Hotel Bella in Selçuk, this outfit offers full-day tours of Ephesus as well as Mary's House, the Temple of Artemis, Basilica of St John or Şirince. Half-day four-hour private tours of just Ephesus with a licensed guide cost ₺350; it's double that for a full day, including the Terraced Houses.

Alaturka Turkey   TOURS
(☏0232-892 9052; www.alaturkaturkey.com/ephesus-tours; Uğur Mumcu Sevgi Yolu Caddesi 16; ☺9am-7pm) Highly professional outfit offering a wide range of tours and transfers, including a full-day tour of Ephesus (€39). Tours include most (but not all) entrance fees. Its office is next to the Ephesus Museum.

🛏 Sleeping

★Homeros Pension   PENSION $
(☏0507 715 7848, 0232-892 3995; www.homerospension.com; 1048 Sokak 3; tw/d/tr €23/24/32; ❉⑤) This long-time, family-run favourite offers 10 rooms in two buildings. The decor involves heavy use of colourful hanging

textiles, vibrant colours and handcrafted furniture (made by affable owner Derviş, a carpenter and antiques collector): this ain't no minimalist hip hotel. Both houses boast roof terraces. The six rooms in the newer (main) building are the nicest. Three of the rooms are economy ones with shared bathroom; private bathrooms are cramped.

Atilla's Getaway   HOSTEL $
(☏0232-892 3847; www.atillasgetaway.com; Acarlar Köyü; camping €9, dm €10-16, d €24-40 tr €60-80; ❉⑤≋) A mecca for travellers, this well-run and fun place to stay is named after its affable Turkish-Australian owner and is justifiably popular. Guests get the run of a lovely twin pool area, garden filled with fruit trees, pool table, table tennis and volleyball court. There are family-style dinners (₺40) every evening and a sangria happy hour (6pm to 7pm). The roadside complex is 3km south of Selçuk, linked by free shuttles and a dolmuş every 20 minutes (₺2.50); a 50-minute walk through the hills to/from Ephesus' Upper Gate. The bungalows with shared facilities are fairly basic, but there are 20 comfortable, modern en-suite rooms and two decent dorms.

Vardar Pension   PENSION $
(www.vardar-pension.com; Şahabettin Dede Caddesi 9; s/d from ₺90/120; ❉⑤) In the heart of town, a short walk from the train station and otogar, the Vardar is a super-dependable pension run by a very hospitable family. Rooms are clean and orderly, some with shared bathrooms, and there's a roof terrace with fortress views.

Barım Pension   PENSION $
(☏0232-892 6923; www.barimpension.com; 1045 Sokak 42; s/d ₺90/125; ❉⑤) This long-running pension stands out for its unusual wrought-iron furnishings, crafted by two friendly metalworking brothers who run Barım with their wives. The pension occupies a characterful 140-year-old stone house, with a leafy back garden for breakfast. The 10 rooms have charm, but are slightly worn around the edges. Owners Adnan and Recep are keen cyclists and can organise bike rental and suggest local routes.

Boomerang Guesthouse   GUESTHOUSE $$
(☏0232-892 4879, 0534 055 4761; www.ephesusboomerangguesthouse.com; 1047 Sokak 10; dm/s/d/f €10/40/55/80, s/d without bathroom €20/30; ❉@⑤) Very welcoming Turkish/Australian-Chinese operation with a lovely

stone courtyard for socialising with other travellers, and a popular bar-restaurant. The best of the 10 rooms have balconies (Nos 13 and 14); all have kettles and fridges, but some bathrooms are not en suite. The basement dorm has 12 single beds, shares two bathrooms and has fans rather than air-con.

Villa Dreams
PENSION $$

(☑ 0545 379 5210, 0232-892 3514; www.ephesus villadreams.com; 3046 Sokak 15; r €50-80; ❀ 🛜 ❄) Villa Dreams offers great views, an outdoor swimming pool and a communal kitchen. It has 10 modern standard rooms and two big family rooms with shiny wood floors and balconies. The rooftop terrace affords fantastic castle views. Located 1.5km east of the centre, but there's a free shuttle six times a day. Each room has a balcony, with eight looking to the Ayasuluk Fortress and three to the garden (where some turtles lounge around their own pool). Ask the staff to point out the three castles visible from the bar of the roof terrace.

Hotel Bella
HOTEL $$

(☑ 0232-892 3944; www.hotelbella.com; St Jean Caddesi 7; s €38-52, d €46-60, tr €67, f €72; ❀ 🛜) Offers 11 well-designed rooms (some small) with Ottoman flourishes in the decor. There's a small library and antiques and artefacts decorate the rooftop lounge and restaurant. It's opposite the Basilica of St John and fortress. Free rides to/from Ephesus are a bonus.

Nazar Hotel
HOTEL $$

(☑ 0232-892 2222; www.nazarhotel.com; Şehit Polis Metin Tavaslıoğlu Caddesi 34; d/tr/f from €38/77/92; ❀ @ 🛜 ❄) Beneath Ayasuluk Fortress, the Turkish/French-run Nazar stands out for its excellent service. Nothing is too much trouble for host İlker and meals on the roof terrace are home-cooked feasts with views of the fortress. The 13 rooms are functional rather than fancy; four have balconies.

Casa Callinos
HOTEL $$

(☑ 0232-892 4030; www.casacallinos.com; 1062 Sokak 2a; d/tr from €40/60; ❀ 🛜) Opposite the Temple of Artemis, this little hotel offers excellent value. Cobbled together from three buildings, it counts eight rooms, two of which look to the street and the rest to a tranquil courtyard. Furnishings veer towards the fussy but the use of brick and wood in the guestrooms is a plus. Good-sized bathrooms.

★ Celsus Butik Otel
BOUTIQUE HOTEL $$$

(☑ 0232-892 3030; www.celsushotel.com; 1051 Sokak 7; r €55-95; ❀ 🛜 ❄) A very well managed hotel with delightful rooms in many different categories (some with hot tubs, and one even has a private sauna) set around a small pool and walled garden. Breakfast is served in a pretty side garden and is generous and nutritious. Located on a quiet street a short walk from the Basilica of St John and town centre.

★ Ayasoluk Hotel
BOUTIQUE HOTEL $$$

(☑ 0232-892 3334, 0541 565 3545; www.ayaso lukhotel.com; 1051 Sokak 12; r €60-140; ❀ 🛜 ❄) With elegant decor, a good range of facilities (swimming pool, bar) and friendly staff, Ayasoluk is a great choice in the historic centre. Rooms have extremely comfortable beds, bathrooms with rain showers and satellite TVs, and the pool terrace commands sweeping views. Also home to one of the best restaurants in town.

Hotel Kalehan
HOTEL $$$

(☑ 0232-892 6154, 0532 272 6584; www.kalehan. com; Atatürk Caddesi 57; s/d/tr €50/75/100; ❀ 🛜 ❄) A fine historic hotel, the 'Castle Caravanserai' has a really classy ambience thanks to the antiques, fireplace, black-and-white photos, books to browse and dark wood furniture. Rooms are beautifully presented and the bar-restaurant is a pleasant spot to relax after a day at the ruins, with a commendable selection of Turkish wines on offer. Located 600m north of the centre.

🍴 Eating

Ramazan Usta Gaziantep Kebap
KEBAB $

(☑ 0232-892 8383; Siegburg Caddesi 11; kebaps ₺16-24; ⏰ 5-11pm Sun, Mon & Thu, 6pm-midnight Tue & Sat, 5pm-midnight Wed) A pocket-sized outpost of Turkey's southeast located in a pedestrianised street near the aqueduct, Master Ramazan's kebapçı (kebap eatery) serves the best meat dishes in town for some of the cheapest prices. It even serves beer.

Sişçi Yaşar'ın Yeri
KÖFTE $

(☑ 0232-892 3487; Atatürk Caddesi; mains from ₺14; ⏰ 10am-10pm; 🛜) Under vines next to a 14th-century mosque, 'Yaşar's Place' is good for a simple lunch of izgara (grills): köfte and çöp şiş (şiş kebap served rolled in a thin pita with onions and parsley).

Tat Restaurant
TURKISH $

(☑ 0538 200 2511, 0232-892 1916; Cengiz Topel Caddesi 9; mains ₺15-38; ⏰ 10am-midnight; 🛜) Touristy Tat's food won't set the world on fire – although the güveç (stew) and other fiercely sizzling dishes could start a blaze. But it is a pleasant spot with seating on a

WORTH A TRIP

TİRE & KAPLAN

The farming town of Tire, 40km northeast of Selçuk, lies on the fields beneath the Bozdağlar Mountains. Its popular Tuesday market provides a slice-of-life view of rural Turkey, sprawling across the town centre and filling whole streets with the aroma of freshly picked herbs and grilling *kokoreç* (seasoned lamb or mutton intestines). A smaller market takes place on Friday.

Tire clings on to its traditional felt-making industry, with several *keçeci* (felt makers) still working on blends of teased wool on Lütfü Paşa Caddesi, the cobbled lane running uphill from the small **Leyse Camii** (1543).

To reach here from the main square/roundabout, walk south along Atatürk Caddesi and turn left (east) into Akyol Caddesi opposite Ziraat Bankası. Lütfü Paşa Caddesi is on the right-hand (north) side.

Up a steep and winding 5km road from Tire, is Kaplan. This mountain village with the über-cool name of 'Tiger' attracts visitors as much for its restaurant as its stunning scenery. The **Kaplan Dağ Restoran** (☑ 0507 745 7372, 0232-512 6652; mezes from ₺10, mains ₺20-45; ۞ 12.30-9.30pm Tue-Sun; 🛜🍴) offers superbly prepared local dishes with lashings of olive oil and wild herbs. Seasonal mezes like fish in soya oil and stuffed zucchini flowers are offered, and mains include Tire-style *köfte* (meatballs) and *şiş* kebaps (roast skewered meat). Book ahead on Tuesdays and weekends.

Getting There & Away

Dolmuşes serve Tire from Selçuk (₺10, 45 minutes) every 40 minutes. A taxi costs about ₺110. A taxi to Kaplan from Tire and back – the only way to get here – will cost ₺60. Ring driver **Mehmet Yıldırımer** (☑ 0531 883 2655) who is available 24/7.

pedestrianised walkway. The menu takes in kebaps, seafood and seven types of meze including fried zucchini and hummus.

Old House　　　　　　　　　　TURKISH $$
(Eski Ev; ☑ 0232-892 9357; 1005 Sokak 1a; mezes ₺8-15, mains ₺24-60; ۞ noon-11pm; 🛜) Welcoming, atmospheric little restaurant where you can feast in a covered patio or tiny street terrace on mezes like stuffed peppers, then graduate to meaty mains like chicken satay or a perfectly grilled *adana kebap* (₺28). Local wine by the glass is ₺20.

Boomerang Garden Restaurant　　CHINESE $$
(☑ 0534 055 4761, 0232-892 4879; 1047 Sokak 10; mezes ₺6, mains ₺18-48; ۞ 8am-midnight; 🛜🍴) Delightful courtyard restaurant (and bar) perfect for all your rice and noodle fixes; head straight here, the chef is Chinese. But don't limit yourself, if you want Turkish – from kebaps to cheese *köfte* – or even vegetarian fare, Candy (Çağıran) can oblige. Always a warm welcome.

Ejder Restaurant　　　　　　　TURKISH $$
(☑ 0542 892 3296, 0232-892 3296; Cengiz Topel Caddesi 9e; mezes ₺8-12, mains ₺14-35; ۞ 11am-11pm) Next to the aqueduct, this outdoor restaurant on a pedestrianised walkway has lots of choices including the generous *tavuk şiş* (roast

skewered chicken). The owners, Mehmet, Rahime and their son Akan, are proud to show off their guestbook, which includes photos from the Clinton family's visit in 1999.

★**Ayasoluk Restaurant**　　INTERNATIONAL $$$
(☑ 0232-892 3334; www.ayasolukhotel.com; 1051 Sokak 12; dinner ₺120; ۞ 5-10pm; 🛜) One of the best dining experiences in town, this hotel's rooftop restaurant has a panoramic view of the fortress and distant mountains, particularly evocative at sunset. Strong on both meat (try the lamb shank) and fish (the grilled sea bass is perfect), dinner is a set menu costing ₺120. There's fine Turkish wine, and Selçuk's best (only?) selection of craft beers.

🍸 Drinking & Nightlife

While seaside Kuşadası offers an unbridled nightlife, Selçuk's desultory bar/cafe scene exists mainly to get males out of home to watch televised football matches. Selçuk's liveliest bars are found on the cobbled pedestrian streets south of the Byzantine aqueduct.

★**Kallinos Kafe**　　　　　　　　CAFE
(1045 Sokak 6; ۞ 9am-midnight; 🛜) The coolest cafe in town is the haunt of students and Selçuk's fashionable youth, serving fine

espresso combos, cold coffee brews, teas and tasty sweet treats such as cheese cake. Hosts occasional art exhibitions too. No booze.

Destina BAR

(☑ 0532 423 8223; Prof Anton Kallinger Caddesi 26; ☺ 9am-1am; ☎) Destina's little front garden overlooking the greenery around the Temple of Artemis is perfect for a late-afternoon *çay* or sunset beer.

ℹ Information

Selçuk State Hospital (Selçuk Devlet Hastanesi; ☑ 0232-892 7036; www.selcukdh.saglik. gov.tr; Dr Sabri Yayla Bulvarı) Across the main road south of the Ephesus Museum.

Tourist Office (☑ 0232-892 6945; Uğur Mumcu Sevgi Yolu Caddesi; ☺ 8.30am-12.30pm & 1.30-5.30pm Mon-Fri) Hopeless, don't even bother as staff are completely disinterested.

SAFE TRAVEL

Look out for conniving 'coin-men' prowling the major tourist sites: these guys are hoping that naive tourists will part with a couple hundred euros or dollars for their fake ancient coins.The fraudsters are most often found around Ayasuluk Fortress, the Temple of Artemis and the gates of Ephesus.

ℹ Getting There & Away

TO/FROM İZMIR AIRPORT

There are a number of options for getting to or from İzmir Adnan Menderes Airport.

Shuttle Havaş (www.havas.net) runs a shuttle bus to/from Kuşadası (₺32, 16 daily) that stops in front of Selçuk's hospital en route; this runs around the clock.

Taxi Expect to pay around ₺160.

Train The simplest and cheapest public-transport option to the airport is the 1½ hour train journey (₺8). You can check the latest timetables and fares at www.tcddtasimacilik. gov.tr. There are eight daily departures but as services are not always punctual, allow extra time. Trains are air conditioned but passengers are not assigned a seat. Also note that the train's airport stop is a 15- to 20-minute walk from the departures terminal.

BUS & DOLMUŞ

Buses depart from the **otogar** (Atatürk Caddesi). Companies include Pamukkale (www.pamukkale.com.tr), Kamil Koç (www. kamilkoc.com.tr), Efe Tur (www.efetur.com.tr) and Nevşehir Seyahat (www.nevsehirseyahat. com.tr).

TRAIN

There are eight trains per day to/from İzmir's Basmane Garı (₺8, 1½ hours) between 7.42am and 7.30pm, via the airport. These travel on to Denizli. Check times at www.tcddtasi macilik.gov.tr.

Electric suburban trains operated by IZBAN (www.izban.com.tr) operate roughly every 75 minutes between İzmir Alsancak station and Selçuk; a change is needed at Tepeköy.

ℹ Getting Around

Walking is the best way to explore Selçuk. Bicycles are also available from hotels and guesthouses, including Barım Pension (p239) and Boomerang Guesthouse (p239), and a cycle lane is being built to Ephesus. A taxi across town costs about ₺12.

SERVICES FROM SELÇUK OTOGAR

DESTINATION	FARE (₺)	DURATION (HR)	FREQUENCY
Ankara	112-126	8	5-6 daily
Bodrum	30	3	4 daily summer; change in Kuşadası & Aydın winter
Bursa	68	6	6 daily
Denizli	35	3	2 daily
Fethiye	77	5½	daily (summer only)
İstanbul	120-140	9	8-10 daily
İzmir	12	1	dolmuşes every 30-40 min
Kuşadası	7	25min	dolmuşes every 30 min
Nevşehir (for Cappadocia)	120	12	daily
Pamukkale	50	3	daily (direct); or change in Denizli

Şirince

☑ 0232 / POP 640

Nine kilometres southeast of the gateway town of Selçuk, and at the end of a long narrow road that winds its way up into the hills passing orchards and vines, sits Şirince, a perfect collection of stone-and-stucco houses with red-tiled roofs.

Şirince's bucolic setting and long wine-making tradition have made it popular, and it's become something approaching a tourist trap during summer. It's much more tranquil by night, and off-season.

History

Şirince was originally settled when Ephesus was abandoned but what you see today mostly dates from the 19th century. The story goes that a group of freed Greek slaves settled here in the 15th century and called the village Çirkince (Foulness) to deter others from following them. This altered to Kirkinje by the 19th century, and, following the exodus of the Greeks in the population exchange of the 1920s, its name was changed to the more honest Şirince (Pleasantness).

Şirince was repopulated by Turks from northern Greece; they built a mosque, but retained the local alcohol trade, and today you can sample their unique fruit wines (made from raspberry, strawberry, peach, black mulberry and apple) in local restaurants and cafes. Grape-based *şarap* (wine) is also available.

◎ Sights

Church of St Demetrius   CHURCH

This 18th-century church, at the northern end of the village, is up the steps to the right as you enter Şirince along the Selçuk road. It served as a mosque after 1923 but is now abandoned and open to the elements. Have a look at what remains of its frescoed vaulted ceiling and choir loft, iconostasis and marble floor.

Church of St John the Baptist   CHURCH

(⊙ 9am-6pm) This is the more important of Şirince's two churches and dates back to 1805. Neglected for decades by modern Turkey and held together (just barely) by an American charitable society, the church and its faded Byzantine wall frescoes have been partly renovated, though the interior is very spartan. Occasional art and craft exhibitions are held here.

🛏 Sleeping

Kırkınca Pansiyon   HERITAGE HOTEL **$$**

(☑ 0232-898 3133, 0232-898 3069; www.kirkinca. com; r ₺250-500; ❊ 🖘) Kırkınca constitutes a trio of restored 250-year-old houses with a selection of elegantly appointed rooms with flowery names. Some have four-poster beds and fireplaces, and Lale (Tulip) even has a mini-hamam. The main building's shaded roof terrace offers great views.

Şirince Doğa Pansiyon   PENSION **$$**

(☑ 0555 358 2121, 0530 922 4858; www.sirince dogapansiyon.com; s ₺160-180, d ₺190-280; 🖘) 'Nature' pension offers eight delightfully rustic rooms, with stone fireplaces and rugs. The three rooms at the top are more traditional – the one called Naz is delightful – the five below slightly more modern. A keen walker, owner Mustafa can organise hiking trips in the area. Located along a lane above the quieter southern end of Şirince.

★ Nişanyan Hotel   BOUTIQUE HOTEL **$$$**

(☑ 0533 304 0933, 0232-898 3208; www.nisan yan.com; d €100-180; 🖘 ▧) This stunner of a boutique hotel in the hills to the south offers a number of choices. The main inn, set in a 19th-century renovated house, counts five rooms individually decorated with antiques and frescoes, and there's a library, an excellent restaurant and a real hamam. On the extended grounds above are cottages, stone houses and a 12m-high tower folly.

🍴 Eating & Drinking

Pervin Teyze   TURKISH **$**

(☑ 0232-898 3083, 0532 284 2831; gözleme from ₺12, mezes & mains ₺10-30; ⊙ 8am-10pm) This ramshackle terrace restaurant serves simple dishes including great *gözleme* (stuffed flatbreads) made by village ladies, with choices changing according to the season and availability. Located above the Church of St John the Baptist.

Şirincem Restaurant   ANATOLIAN **$$**

(☑ 0232-898 3180, 0537 831 8297; www.sirincem pansiyon.com; mezes ₺5-10, mains ₺10-35; ⊙ 8am-midnight; 🖉) A rustic restaurant under shady foliage up the steps from the main road into town and owned by a friendly fruit-farming family. Offers a good range of mezes, vegetarian and meat dishes, and Anatolian wines as well as *kahvaltı* (breakfast).

Yorgo Şarapevi
WINE BAR

(☏ 0555 824 2684; ⏱ 9am-11pm Jun-Sep, to 7pm Oct-May) Simple place that nevertheless has a fine collection of wine, with everything from fruit wines (₺25 to ₺40 a bottle) to real red and white grape *şarap* (wine) starting at around ₺50 a bottle.

❶ Getting There & Away

Dolmuşes (₺4) leave Selçuk for Şirince every 20 minutes (15 minutes at the weekend) in summer, half-hourly in winter. Parking at the village entrance costs ₺10.

Kuşadası

☏ 0256 / POP 92,000

Kuşadası is a popular package-tour destination and, as the coastal gateway to Ephesus, Turkey's busiest cruise port. Lacking the sights and ambience of Bodrum and the mix of Marmaris, Kuşadası remains a runner-up on the Aegean party scene, but the pubs, discos and multilingual touts certainly create a memorably ribald atmosphere, particularly in the lively downtown area of Kaleiçi. So if you prefer to mix your Ephesus visit with nightlife and sea views rather than the rural ambience of Selçuk, then Kuşadası could be worth considering, offering some good seafood restaurants and a lively bazaar.

◉ Sights & Activities

Travel agencies such as Barel Travel (p248) and Meander Travel (p247) offer trips to Ephesus (half-/full day from €40/60); the full-day tour can also include visits to Priene, Miletus and Didyma.

★ Kuşadası Castle
FORTRESS

(Güvercin Adası; ⏱ 8am-11pm May-Aug, 9am-9pm Sep-Apr) **FREE** Kuşadası's small, picturesque Byzantine fortress stands on the causeway-connected **Güvercin Adası** (Pigeon Island) and has recently been renovated. It's now part of a popular and well-kept public park. A path winds around the island past excellent information boards and a small lighthouse, providing fine views of Kuşadası. Inside the fortress there's a skeleton of a 14.5m fin whale and a few models of sailing boats.

Kaleiçi Camii
MOSQUE

(off Barbaros Bulavarı) The 'Old Town Mosque', built by Grand Vizier Öküz Mehmed Paşa in the 17th century, is the most impressive mosque in Kuşadası and can accommodate 550 worshipers.

Kadınlar Denizi
BEACH

(Ladies Beach) Kuşadası's most famous beach is Kadınlar Denizi (literally 'Ladies Sea'), south of town and served by dolmuşes running along the coastal road. Kadınlar Denizi is slim and crowded with big hotels, but beachgoers love it for its hustle and bustle. The coast further south of Kadınlar Denizi has several more stretches of sand.

Kuşadası Town Beach
BEACH

Kuşadası town's small artificial beach is nice enough, but gets very crowded in summer with tourists from the big nearby hotels.

Aqua Fantasy
WATER PARK

(☏ 0232-850 8500; www.aquafantasy.com; Ephesus Beach, Sultaniye Köyü; adult/child/under 3yr €25/18/free; ⏱ 10am-6.30pm May-Oct) Waterpark which sprawls across 18 hectares of land just in from the beach, and has 31 slides, a wave pool and a 400m 'Lazy River'. Also has a hotel and spa centre complex for longer stays. It's 9km north of Kuşadası.

☞ Tours

Boats moored at the causeway leading to Kuşadası Castle or at the marina offer one-hour sunset cruises for ₺10 and, between April and October, day trips around the coast (from ₺70 including lunch and soft drinks). Usual stops include Soğuksu Bay, Klaros Island and Baradan Beach.

Full day trips (from ₺95) to gorgeous Dilek Peninsula-Büyük Menderes National Park (p248) are preferable, as it has stunning cove beaches and lovely swimming in pristine water. Operators include **Ali Kaptan 2** (☏ 0535 438 0801, 0535 515 6821; www.kusadasitekneturu.com), **Matador** (☏ 0532 461 3889; www.facebook.com/matadorboattrip) and **Aydın Kaptan 53** (☏ 0534 317 2623, 0532 206 4545).

🛏 Sleeping

Kuşadası centre has pensions and business hotels, while package-tour resorts and luxury hotels are generally on the outlying coasts. For a good night's sleep, avoid the hotels on or around Atatürk Bulvarı as these are located in the thick of the extremely loud and 24-hour summer party scene.

Sezgin Hotel Guest House
GUESTHOUSE **$**

(☏ 0256-614 4225; www.facebook.com/sezgin hotelguesthouse; Arslanlar Caddesi 68; dm ₺100, s ₺100-150, d ₺150-200, tr ₺200-300; ❋ @ 🛜 ⛱) Uphill from the action on Bar St, Sezgin is a dependable choice. Its 20 bright and spacious rooms have modern bathrooms, satellite TVs, fridges and hairdryers and there's a five-bed mixed dorm. The reception and corridors are less appealing, but the rear courtyard has a chill-out area and pool overlooked by orange trees. The friendly and very well-travelled owner Sezgin dispenses information and can set up boat trips for guests.

★ Liman Hotel
HOTEL $$

(☏0256-614 7770; www.limanhotel.com; cnr Kıbrıs & Güvercinada Caddesi; s/d/tr €35/45/55; ❄🅿🛜) Run by the ever-hospitable Hasan 'Mr Happy' Değirmenci, the Harbour Hotel has been a hit with independent travellers for decades. The 14 rooms (accessed by lift!) are simple but comfortable, and have satellite TV, kettle and balcony (six are sea-facing). The real pleasure of staying here is the sociable vibe, especially on the rooftop terrace.

There's a lobby lounge and a help desk offering assistance with everything from bus tickets to local excursions. Breakfast is served on the roof terrace, as the cruise liners glint in the docks below. The terrace is also the venue for drinks and nightly barbecues from mid-April to October.

Ephesian Hotel Guesthouse
GUESTHOUSE $$

(☏0553 428 4335, 0256-614 6084; www.ephesianhotel.com; Aslanlar Caddesi 9; s/d/tr/f €20/32/40/48; ❄@🛜) This agreeable family-run budget pension in an old Greek house is within spitting distance of Bar St. The 16 rooms are smallish but tastefully decorated and all have balconies (some with sea views) and there's a stunning roof terrace. Helpful owner Ceyhan has many good local tips for his guests.

Anzac Golden Bed Pension
PENSION $$

(☏0530 340 6948; www.anzacgoldenbed.com; Uğurlu Sokak 1, Çıkmazı 4; r €24-35; ❄🛜) Perched on the hilltop old quarter, this pension was renovated and updated in 2019. Affable Australian owner Sandra Galloway has eight rooms (some small, four have balconies, book 304 or 305 for the best views) decorated with tasteful furnishings and a superb rooftop garden terrace, where sweeping views can be enjoyed over breakfast.

Villa Konak
BOUTIQUE HOTEL $$$

(☏0256-614 6318; www.villakonakhotel.com; Yıldırım Caddesi 55; standard r €60, deluxe r €60-75, f €120; ⊙closed late Oct-early Apr; ❄🛜🏊) The lovely garden and pool area is a real highlight at this small homely hotel, which has very tasteful rooms all decorated with parquet floors, Ottoman knick-knacks, rugs and period furniture. Located in a quiet old quarter far above the harbour. No children under six.

Ilayda Avant Garde
HOTEL $$$

(☏0256-614 7608; www.ilaydaavantgarde.com; Atatürk Bulvarı 42; r/ste from €85/160; ❄🛜🏊) Jet-setting beach bums will feel at home in this minimalist-on-holiday aesthetic with art deco touches. The 85 cool, neat rooms are slightly small but restful, with parquet floors and multicoloured furnishings behind double glazing. Amenities include a lobby bar on the 2nd floor and a rooftop pool and bar-restaurant.

✕ Eating

Waterfront dining is atmospheric but can be expensive, there are dozens of seafood places around the fish market. Fish is sold by weight so verify prices before ordering. If ambience isn't important, head inland for cheaper kebap shops. A popular street food is *midye dolması* (mussels stuffed with rice).

Fish Market
SEAFOOD $

(Balık Halı; Atatürk Bulvarı; fish sandwiches ₺6-10; ⊙9am-midnight) Eateries around the fountain in the modern square at the fish market do *balık ekmeği* (fish bread), consisting of fish or calamari in sliced bread with salad. You can also buy fish here and ask nearby restaurants to cook it; restaurants should charge about ₺12 to ₺15 per kilo for this service.

Yuvam
TURKISH $

(☏0256-614 9460, 0256-614 2928; 7 Eylül Sokak 4; mains ₺12-20; ⊙10am-6pm) For a filling, authentic meal, this daytime *lokanta* (eatery serving ready-made food) in the heart of the Old Town is great. Serves up some freshly prepared home cooking at moderate prices.

Ferah
SEAFOOD $$

(☏0256-614 1281, 0536 321 2547; İskele Yanı Güvercin Parkı İçi; mezes ₺8-12, seafood portions ₺22-45; ⊙8.30am-2am) Next to the little park and city tea garden, this is one of Kuşadası's more popular waterfront fish eateries, with great sunset sea views and good quality seafood and mezes.

★ Kazım Usta
SEAFOOD $$$

(☏0256-614 1226; Liman Caddesi 4; mezes ₺10-35, mains ₺30-60; ⊙11am-midnight) Kuşadası's top (and priciest) fish restaurant commands a prime harbourfront location and serves dishes ranging from octopus casserole to a

Kuşadası

200 m
0.1 miles

Istiklal Cad

Gençlik Cad

Ülgen Sk

Toplani Sk

Candan Tarhan Bul

Dolmuşes for Selçuk via Pamucak

Sevgi Sk

50 Yıl Cad

Bahçearası Sk

Tavaslı Sk

Adnan Menderes Bul

Demiroğlu Sk

Dolmuşes for Söke & Dilek National Park

Ataturk Bul

Ismet İnönü Bul

Kuşadası Town Beach (400m); Setur Marina (500m); Loft (550m); Aqua Fantasy (10km)

Ismet İnönü Bul

Bus Company Offices

(800m)

Kemal Arıkan Cad

Oğe Sk

KALEİÇİ

Sağlık Cad

Bozkurt Sk

Kahramanlar Cad

Zafer Sk

Sevgi Sk

Kışla Sk

Bahar Sk

Tuna Sk

17

Bar St (Barlar Sk)

Hacı İbrahim Camii

Cephane Sk

Ataturk Bul

Monumental Arch

Barbaros Hayrettin Bul

Yıldırım Cad

14

Çetin Sk

Okurlak Sk

Deniz Sk

Arslanlar Cad

7

6

11

12

15

Bazaar

9

Kıbrıs Cad

Anıt Sk

İleri Sk

Kuşadası Cruise Terminal

Scala Nuova

13

Ferry to Samos

5

18

Güvercinada Cad

Bezirgan Sk

İmam Sk

Aydınlık Sk

Doğru Sk

Kemer Sk

Atatürk Monument

Sülün Sk

Samos (Greece)

Yılancı Burnu Yolu

Güvercinada Cad

Kadınlar Denizi (2km)

4

3

Kuşadası Castle

1

Kuşadası

wide choice of fish (including red mullet and sea bream). Meze options include yoghurt with smoked aubergine. It closes earlier in winter.

⏛ Drinking & Entertainment

Narya Cafe   TEAHOUSE
(İskele Yanı, Bülent Ecevit Parkı; ☺8.30am-11pm) The outdoor tables at this hybrid cafe and *çay bahçesi* (tea garden) in a small park on the water's edge have a million-dollar view and are sensational spots to enjoy a tea, coffee or soft drink, particularly at sunset. It goes under various names – look for the Cafe Salvador and Narya Cafe signs.

Bar St   PUB
(Barlar Sokak) On this cacophonous strip, tattoo and piercing parlours line up alongside shamrocks, sex shops and gaudy bars, soundtracked by karaoke, televised football and loquacious touts. At the northern end, the long-standing **Jimmy's Irish Bar** and, opposite, **Kitty O'Shea** fulfil just a portion of the leprechaun quota; halfway down, **Kuşadası Club & Bar** is a popular hang-out for young locals.

★ Orient Bar   LIVE MUSIC
(☎0256-612 8838; www.orientkusadasi.com; Kışla Sokak 14; ☺11am-4am) On a narrow street in the Kaleiçi, this perennial favourite in an atmospheric old stone house and courtyard is where you can listen to the nightly acoustic guitarist or settle in for a cosy chat beneath the vine trellis.

Adı Meyhane   LIVE MUSIC
(☎0256-614 3496; www.facebook.com/adimey hanekusadasi; Bahar Sokak 18; ☺4pm-4am) In the heart of Kaleiçi, marked by low beams, stone walls and hung instruments, this tavern-like bar is popular with Turks and visitors alike; serves food and hosts good live Turkish folk music.

ℹ Information

Özel Kuşadası Hastanesi (☎0256-613 1616; www.kusadasihastanesi.com; Ant Sokak; ☺24hr) Excellent, English-speaking private hospital 3km north of the centre (just off Turgut Özal Bulvarı, aka the Selçuk road).

Tourist Office (☎0256-614 1103; Liman Caddesi; ☺8am-noon & 1.30-5pm Mon-Fri) Near the cruise-ship dock, staff give out maps and brochures but speak little English.

ℹ Getting There & Away

TO/FROM İZMIR AIRPORT

There are a number of ways to get to or from İzmir Adnan Menderes Airport.

Bus Take a dolmuş to Selçuk and change. Allow 2½ hours for the journey.

Shuttle Havaş runs 16 daily shuttle bus services to/from the otogar. **Last Minute Travel** (☎0256-614 6332; Otogar) and **Sözgen Turizm** (☎0256-612 4949; www.izmirhavali maniservisi.com; Otogar) are also reliable. Rates are ₺30 to ₺40.

Taxi About ₺300.

BOAT

Meander Travel (☎0256-612 8888; www. meandertravel.com; Mahmut Esat Bozkurt Caddesi 14b; ☺7am-11pm Apr-Oct, 9am-6pm Mon-Sat Nov-Mar) operates a ferry to the Greek island of Samos. The daily service operates from April to October, with boats departing Kuşadası between 8.30am and 9.30am and Samos at 5pm or 6pm. Tickets for the 1½-hour

DİLEK PENINSULA

The spectacular 277-sq-km **Dilek Peninsula-Büyük Menderes National Park** (Dilek Yarımadası-Büyük Menderes Deltası Milli Parkı; www.dilekyarimadasi.com; per person/car ₺5/18; ⏰7am-7pm Jun-Sep, 8am-5pm Oct-May, last entry 1hr before close) reserve on the Dilek Peninsula has walking trails, stunning vistas, azure coves for swimming, deep-green forests inhabited by wild boar and fallow deer and more than 250 species of bird (including cormorants, ospreys and flamingos). It encompasses an important wetland zone and a lovely old Greek village. The national park is easily accessible from nearby Kuşadası.

Beyond the entrance, where there's good information in the **visitor centre**, four semicircular bays with sand or pebble beaches lie below the road, which has great views from designated pullover points. The road tapers off at a high-security military compound covering the peninsula's end, from which soldiers can train their binoculars on the tourists frolicking on Samos.

The first cove, **İçmeler Köyü** (1km from the entrance), has a sandy beach, but it is the busiest and not the cleanest; look to the north and there are sweeping views of Kuşadası's urban sprawl. About 4km further on, **Aydınlık Köyü** is a quieter, 800m-long pebble strand backed by pines, and is busy enough to warrant a lifeguard station, though it is not always staffed.

About 1km further along, the signposted **kanyon** (canyon) appears on the left. Boards here give information and maps of the park. A 15km walk down a forest path, the old Greek settlement of **Doğanbey** has beautiful stone houses, restored by affluent newcomers, cafe-restaurants and a guesthouse or two. A few kilometres west of Doğanbey, the fishing village and ancient Hellenistic port of **Karine** has a waterfront fish restaurant. The path's first 6km are open to all, but after that you need a permit or to be led by a licensed guide. There is also a 25km cycle track to Doğanbey from Güzelçamlı, just east of the park entrance.

Dilek's third bay, **Kavaklı Burun Köyü** (1km past the canyon entrance), has a half-moon-shaped pebble beach. The final beach open to the public, pebbly **Karasu Köyü** (11km from the entrance), is the most placid, and enjoys delightful views of mountainous Samos rising from the sea. If you're lucky, you might see a dolphin or even a rare Mediterranean monk seal.

All four beaches have free wood-slatted chairs, which are quickly taken, and umbrellas and fold-out chairs to rent.

About 200m southeast of the park entrance, a brown sign points to **Zeus Mağarası** (Zeus Cave), a show cave with azure-blue water that is refreshingly cold in summer and warm in winter.

Getting There & Away

Between late May and early October, dolmuşes run every 20 to 40 minutes from Kuşadası to the national park (₺8, 50 minutes), but only as far as the third bay (Kavaklı Burun Köyü). Off season, if your dolmuş is empty, the driver may just stop at the park gate. Regular dolmuşes also run from Söke to Doğanbey (via Priene) in summer. With your own wheels, you can drive to Doğanbey, 30km southwest of Söke; look for the turn-off on the road from Priene to Miletus.

crossing cost €31 for a single, €36 for a same-day return and €47 for an open return, including port tax. Arrive one hour before departure for immigration formalities. If you are returning to Kuşadası, check your Turkish visa is multiple-entry.

Barel Travel (☎0256-614 4463; www.barel travel.com; Scala Nuova Shopping Center, Güvercinada Caddesi; ⏰7.30am-10pm Apr-Oct, 9am-5pm Nov-Mar) also runs ferries to Samos for exactly the same rates. Boats depart Kuşadası at 9am, returning at 6pm from April to October.

BUS & DOLMUŞ

Kuşadası's **otogar** (Garaj Caddesi) is at the southern end of Süleyman Demirel Bulvarı, on the bypass highway, with *servises* (free shuttles) running to/from the bus companies' offices, which are (mostly) on İsmet İnönü Bulvarı. Dolmuşes depart from centrally located Candan Tarhan Bulvarı and from the otogar.

Bodrum (₺38, 2½ hours) Pamukkale has two daily services in summer; otherwise take a dolmuş to Söke, from where they run half-hourly.

Bursa (₺79, 6½ hours) Two daily services.

İzmir (₺19, 1½ hours) Half-hourly buses in summer, hourly in winter.

Pamukkale (₺55, 3½ hours) Once a day via Selçuk and Aydın.

Selçuk (₺6, 20 minutes) Dolmuşes from the roundabout at the southern end of Candan Tarhan Bulvarı every 20 to 30 minutes via Pamucak and the turn-off for Ephesus Lower Gate.

Söke (₺7, 40 minutes) Dolmuşes from the same roundabout every 20 to 30 minutes.

❶ Getting Around

Şehiriçi minibuses (No 5, ₺2.50) run every few minutes in summer (every 15 to 20 minutes in winter) from the otogar to the centre and along the coast to Kadınlar Denizi.

There are taxi ranks all over town, including on Güvercinada Caddesi, Adnan Menderes Bulvarı and İsmet İnönü Bulvarı, generally with their prices for longer journeys on display. Fares for long trips are cited in euros and include €50 return to Ephesus, €65 including Mary's House. Other long-haul trips include Didyma and Miletus (€80). Short hops around town cost from ₺12.

Kirazlı

☑ 0232, 0256 / POP 1010

Some 10km east of Kuşadası, on a back road, the white houses and terracotta roofs of traditional Turkey rise from a bowl in the hills at Kirazlı, the 'Place of Cherries'.

With around 1000 inhabitants, Kirazlı has retained its agricultural ways, but the arrival of tourists and foreign home-buyers has caused a rethink; Kirazlı now plays up its organic produce, sold at a **Sunday farmers market**. Another draw is the Yedi Bilgeler Vineyards, which can be visited.

Yedi Bilgeler Vineyards WINERY
(☑ 0530 068 9662, 0232-894 8257; www.yedi bilgeler.com; Gökcealan Köyü; ⊙ 8.30am-11pm) This impressive vineyard 6.5km north of Kirazlı also boasts a fine boutique hotel and restaurant. Award-winning wines produced here are named after the 'Seven Sages', 6th-century-BC philosophers based in nearby Ephesus, Miletus and Priene. Tour the vineyards and fabulous *şarap mahzeni* (wine cellar) where you can taste and buy the Bias Cabernet, Anaxagoras Chardonnay and Lasos Rose Shiraz (prices start at ₺50 a bottle).

Accommodation (r €78-170) consists of six rooms named after grape varietals in the purpose-built main building and many more in a modern wing overlooking a swimming pool. Self-catering suites are large (up to 80 sq metres) but we love the Malbec double room in the main building with vineyard views.

Expect fine dining in the winery's lovely **restaurant**. Meals (mains ₺30 to ₺65) are served in a large, atmospheric dining room made cosy by a hearth and overlooked by a mural of the wine god Dionysus. A breezy terrace offers outside seating in warm weather. There's live music most weekends.

❶ Getting There & Away

Dolmuşes link Kirazlı and Gökcealan with Kuşadası (₺5, 20 minutes).

Priene, Miletus & Didyma

Visiting the ancient settlements of Priene, Miletus and Didyma, which run more or less in a line 80km south of Kuşadası, is easily done in a full day by car or guided tour. A tour is worth considering – the sites are not as excavated or well signposted as Ephesus, so having a professional guide will help bring them to life. Travel agencies in Selçuk and Kuşadası offer the 'PMD' (Priene, Miletus and Didyma) tour for €50 to €60, including transport, lunch, an hour at each site and possibly one or two add-ons such as Söke market and/or the beach at Altınkum. Tours usually require at least four participants. Ascertain in advance where you'll go and for how long; make sure the tour includes the Miletus Museum (p251).

Visiting Priene, Miletus and Didyma all in a day by public transport is tricky. Regular dolmuşes connect Söke with all three, but they can be infrequent off-season and you might have to return to Söke between two of them. Nonetheless, with luck and a few changes in Söke, it may be possible to visit all three in a day in summer.

Priene

Priene (₺6; ⊙ 8am-7pm Apr-Oct, 8.30am-5pm Nov-Mar) enjoys a commanding position just below Mt Mykale, giving it a real natural grandeur. This Greco-Roman site is delightful to explore, with pine trees providing shade while its isolated location deters the crowds. Like Ephesus, Priene was once a sophisticated port city with two harbours. But

Priene

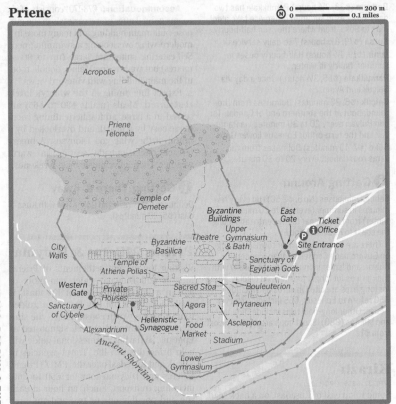

Acropolis

Priene
Teloneia

Temple of
Demeter

Byzantine
Buildings

East
Gate

Ticket
Office

City
Walls

Byzantine
Basilica

Theatre

Upper
Gymnasium
& Bath

Site Entrance

Temple of
Athena Polias

Sanctuary of
Egyptian Gods

Western
Gate

Private
Houses

Sacred Stoa

Bouleuterion

Sanctuary
of Cybele

Agora

Prytaneum

Alexandrium

Hellenistic
Synagogue

Food
Market

Asclepion

Ancient Shoreline

Stadium

Lower
Gymnasium

all that went pear-shaped when the changing course of the Büyük Menderes River silted them both up. Today it's very peaceful, its elevated position giving stunning vistas across patchwork fields.

Priene was important by 300 BC (when the League of Ionian Cities held congresses and festivals here), peaking between then and 45 BC. Still, it was smaller than nearby Miletus, and the Romans made fewer modifications to its Hellenistic buildings, which has preserved its unique 'Greek' look. By the 2nd century AD, however, the silt had won the battle in this port city once famed for its shipbuilding industry and sailing tradition, and most of the population relocated to Miletus. Amid the rubble, a tiny Greek village called Samson existed until 1923, when the Greeks were expelled and the remaining Turks moved to the neighbouring village of Güllübahçe.

Digging, led by British and German archaeologists, only started here in the late 19th century. Plenty of marble statues and other antiquities ended up in their museums – in some cases, traded by sultans for such things as trains and modern farming equipment.

Beyond the ticket booth (ask for a copy of the free *Priene Visitor Information and Tour* map), walk along the paved pathway and turn right up the steep stone steps. Note that Priene's streets meet at right angles – a system invented by the Miletus architect Hippodamus (498–408 BC). As at Ephesus, Priene's marble streets have gouged lines and notches to prevent slipping.

On a high bluff backed by stark mountain and overlooking what was once the sea (see the information panels to comprehend the extent of the silting) stands the ruined **Temple of Athena Polias**, dating from the 4th century BC. Priene's biggest and most influential structure (it became the model for Ionic architecture), it was designed by Pytheos of Priene, who also designed the

Mausoleum of Halicarnassus (now Bodrum). An original inscription, now in the British Museum, states that Alexander the Great funded the temple.

Unlike Hippodamus, whom Aristotle recalled as being rather the free spirit (he never cut his hair and wore the same clothes year-round), Pytheos was a stickler for detail. He saw his Classical Ionian temple design as solving the imperfections he perceived in preceding Doric design. Today's five re-erected columns give some sense of the temple's original look, though many others lie in unruly heaps around it.

Priene's **theatre** (capacity 6500) is among the best-preserved Hellenistic theatres anywhere. Whistle to test the acoustics, and slip your fingers between the lion's-paw indentations on the finely carved *prohedria* (marble seats for VIPs) in the front row.

Nearby lie the ruins of a **Byzantine basilica** from the 5th century AD (note the fine stone pulpit and steps to the apse) and **Roman Baths** (which were 45m long and had four rooms of differing temperatures). Also see the nearby **bouleuterion**, which could seat up to 640 interlocutors; from here a narrow path leads down to the ruined medical centre, the **Asclepion** (once thought to be a temple to Zeus Olympios). To the west are remains of **private houses** (some of them with two storeys) and a **Hellenistic synagogue**; to the south are the **gymnasium**, **stadium** and **agora**.

You can follow the remains of the **city wall**, once 2.5km long and 6m high with 16 towers, back to the car park via the main **East Gate**.

There are toilets in the car park and in the village of Güllübahçe below that abut a ruined Byzantine aqueduct.

Dolmuşes run from Söke to Güllübahçe (₺4, 20 minutes) every 20 minutes, stopping 250m from Priene, by the Byzantine aqueduct cafes. They run hourly in winter.

Miletus

Ancient Miletus in the valley of the Büyük Menderes River was once a great port city. Its mixed Hellenistic-Roman ruins are impressive, though due to erosion and overgrazing there's little shelter from the sun and you'll have to pick your way across rocky scrubland. Highlights include the Great Theatre and the fascinating **Miletus Museum** (Milet Müzesi; ₺5; ⊙8am-7pm Apr-Oct, 8.30am-5pm Nov-Mar), which also exhibits findings from

nearby Priene. Make the museum your first port of call in order to pick up the informative (and free) *Miletus Circular Tour* map.

Although Miletus' distant origins remain unclear, it's likely that Minoan Cretans came in the Bronze Age (the word Miletus is of Cretan origin). Ionian Greeks consolidated themselves from 1000 BC, and Miletus became a leading centre of Greek thought and culture over the following centuries; most significantly, the Milesian School of Philosophy (from the 6th century BC) featured such great thinkers as Thales, Anaximander and Anaximenes. Their observations of nature emphasised rational answers rather than mythical explanations, putting them among the world's first scientists.

Like the other coastal cities in the region, Miletus was fought over by Athens and Persia, and finally taken in 334 BC by Alexander the Great, who ushered in the city's golden age. Rome took over exactly two centuries later, and a small Christian congregation developed after St Paul's visits at the end of his third missionary journey around AD 57. In Byzantine times Miletus was an archbishopric. Unlike other coastal cities, enough of its port was free from silt build-ups for the Seljuks to use it for maritime trade through the 14th century. The Ottomans abandoned the city when its harbour finally silted up, and the Büyük Menderes River has since pushed Miletus 10km inland.

You'll notice almost immediately that the streets of Miletus have a right-angle grid plan – the brainchild of local architect Hippodamus. Approaching the site from the car park, the **Great Theatre** dominates. Miletus' commercial and administrative centre from 700 BC to AD 700, the 5000-seat Hellenistic theatre had majestic sea views. The Romans reconstructed it in the 1st century AD to seat 15,000 spectators.

Exit the theatre through the *vomitorium* (an exit tunnel) on the right to reach the rest of the site. Above the theatre, **Byzantine castle** ramparts provide views to the east of the former port called **Lion Harbour** after the leonine statues that guarded its entrance. South of the harbour are the northern and southern **agoras**, and between them, the **bouleterion**.

Adjoining the northern agora to the east is the **Delphinium** dedicated to Apollo; it's the oldest shrine in Miletus. It marked the start of a 15km-long processional way to the temple and oracle at Didyma. As if by magic,

Miletus (Milet)

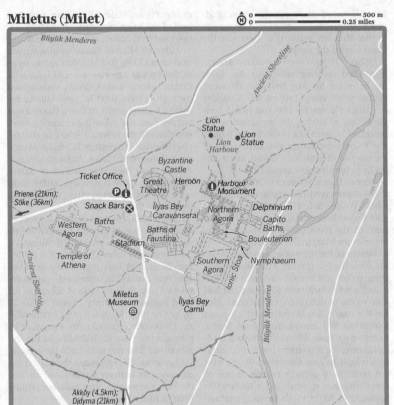

0   500 m
0   0.25 miles

Büyük Menderes

Ancient Shoreline

Lion Statue

Lion Statue

Lion Harbour

Byzantine Castle

Ticket Office

Great Theatre

Heroön

Harbour Monument

Priene (21km);
Söke (36km)

Snack Bars

İlyas Bey Caravanserai

Northern Agora

Delphinium

Capito Baths

Western Agora

Baths

Baths of Faustina

Stadium

Bouleuterion

Temple of Athena

Ancient Shoreline

Southern Agora

Ionic Stoa

Nymphaeum

Miletus Museum

İlyas Bey Camii

Büyük Menderes

Akköy (4.5km);
Didyma (21km)

the laurel trees that Greeks considered sacred to Apollo still cast their shade near the Milesian temple ruins.

Southwest of the southern agora, the **Baths of Faustina**, constructed for Marcus Aurelius' wife, are worth visiting; the massive walls and inner floors of the two spacious structures still survive. The designers' ingenious plan used *hypocausts* (an underfloor system of hot-water pipes) and *tubuli* (terracotta wall flues), which kept the interior of the *caldarium* very hot. Next to it was a refreshing *frigidarium* (cold bath).

Southwest of the baths is the **stadium** and the Miletus Museum. To the southeast is the post-Seljuk **İlyas Bey Camii** (1404), renovated in 2012 with an intricate doorway.

There are cafes near the entrance, including one flanking a 14th-century caravanserai.

Dolmuşes linking Söke (₺8, 40 minutes) with Didyma (₺5, 25 minutes) via Miletus run hourly in summer and every two hours in winter.

Didyma (Didim)

☑ 0256 / POP 61,700

The ancient religious centre of Didyma, with its Temple of Apollo, was a marvel of the ancient world. Not only was it stunning architecturally, it was a beacon for the faithful because of its celebrated oracle (who would, sadly, come to an unhappy end with the advance of Christianity). Today, however, Didyma's huge and impressive temple compound feels hemmed in by holiday sprawl, with souvenir shops and tourist restaurants clustered around the site and package hotels close by.

◎ Sights

Temple of Apollo RUINS
(admission ₺18, audio guide ₺10; ⊙ 8.30am-7pm mid-May–mid-Sep, to 5pm mid-Sep–mid-May) Didyma (now Didim) was a important religious centre, the site of the Oracle of Apollo. The astonishing Temple of Apollo here was once the ancient world's second largest; with

122 columns, only five fewer than Ephesus' Temple of Artemis. Since the latter has only one column standing today, visiting Didyma really helps travellers visualise the lost grandeur of Artemis' temple, too. Though the site is largely in ruins, its scale is still breathtaking and two original pillars remain in situ.

In Greek, Didyma means 'twin' (here, referring to the twin siblings Apollo and Artemis). Didyma's Oracle of Apollo had an importance second only to the Oracle of Delphi. Although destroyed by Persians in the early 5th century BC, Alexander the Great revitalised it in 334 BC and, about 30 years later, Seleucid rulers planned to make it the world's largest temple. However, it was never completed and Ephesus' Temple of Artemis took first prize instead.

In AD 303 the oracle allegedly supported Emperor Diocletian's harsh persecution of Christians – the last such crackdown, since Constantine the Great soon thereafter made Christianity the state church of the Roman Empire. Oops. The now-unpopular oracle was silenced by Emperor Theodosius I (r 379–395), who closed other pagan temples such as the Delphic Oracle.

Entering from the ticket booth, clamber up the temple's 13 wide **steps** to marvel at the massively thick and towering **columns**.

Behind the temple porch, in a room called the **chresmographeion**, oracular poems were inscribed on a great doorway and presented to petitioners. Covered ramps by the porch lead down to an interior building called the **cella** (or naos in Greek), where the oracle prophesied after drinking from the sacred spring; reach it by way of two vaulted and sloped passages.

Just east of the temple is the **purification well** and **circular altar** where clients of the oracle offered their sacrifices. You can't miss the huge **Medusa head** nearby that once took pride of place in the frieze of the architrave over the outer row of columns. Further east is the sacred way lined with ornate **statues** (relocated to the British Museum in 1858) that led to Miletus.

There's little or no shade, so bring a hat and sunscreen.

🛏 Sleeping & Eating

⭐ Medusa House   PENSION $$
(📞0536 767 6734, 0256-811 0063; www.medusa house.com; Atatürk Bulvarı 246; s/d €40/60; 🖤) Just a few steps from the Temple of Apollo, this lovingly restored 150-year-old Greek stone home, and a more recently built annexe, offers 10 pleasant rooms in a flowery garden to the back and the front. The six rooms in the old house have wooden ceilings and fireplaces but those in the out-building are larger and more modern.

The Turkish-German couple who manage the pension maintain contacts with descendants of the original Greek owners. They have set up a small 'House of Turkish-Greek Friendship', which exhibits artefacts and traces the history of the house and village.

Tapınak Cafe   CAFE $
(Özgürlük Caddesi 75; snacks ₺15-30; ⏰8am-11.30pm; 🖤) Overlooking the temple, this friendly modern cafe offers a simple snack menu of sandwiches, salads and cakes. It also has an espresso machine for that perfect latte and whips up good milkshakes. Alcohol is available should you need a cool beer after touring the temple.

ℹ Getting There & Away

Frequent dolmuşes run from Söke to Didyma (₺7, 40 minutes) and Altınkum (₺9, 1¼ hours). Services are less frequent in winter.

Lake Bafa

📞0252 / POP BAFA: 1640

Landlocked, but 50% saltwater, 70-sq-km Lake Bafa constitutes the last trace of the Aegean's former inland reach. It's a peaceful place, ringed by traditional villages such as **Kapıkırı** on the lake's far eastern shore. Bygone Byzantine hermitages and churches abound in the Bafa hills, and the region is a rich natural habitat boasting sights from orchids (up to 20 species) to owls, butterflies and chameleons. In particular, some 350 avian species are represented, including eagles, pink flamingos, pelicans and spoonbills.

The ruins of Herakleia (p254) are found throughout Kapıkırı, which is populated by roving chickens, donkeys and old women hawking trinkets and crafts. The ruins leave much to the imagination; it's the rustic 'other-worldly' scene and the lakeside setting that comprise most of the experience.

The upper village, where most of the ruins are, is called 'town side' and lower Kapıkırı is 'island side'.

◎ Sights & Activities

Pension owners organise boat and fishing trips (from ₺160) and half-day hikes to 6000-year-old Neolithic caves (from €150), with the possibility of spending a night camping in the hills. Many can also help with birdwatching, botany, cultural and photography tours; contact **Latmos Travel** (☑0252-543 5445, 0532 416 3996; www.latmos-travel.com; Agora Pansiyon, Kapıkırı) for details.

Herakleia
RUINS

(Kapıkırı) FREE The ruins of the ancient Carian port city Herakleia are scattered throughout Kapıkırı. In the upper village, the large **Temple of Athena**, just west of the central **agora**, occupies a promontory overlooking the lake. Only three of its walls remain, but the perfectly cut blocks (no mortar) are impressive. Other signposted paths lead eastwards to the **bouleuterion** in a private garden, a uniquely Roman **bathhouse** and the unrestored **theatre**, with barely a few seating rows remaining (it once sat up to 4000 spectators).

The Hellenistic **city walls** (circa 300 BC) extend for 6.5km. For sublime lake views, follow the road down past the rock-hewn **Temple of Endymion** and the ruined **Byzantine castle**, which overlooks the rock tombs of the **necropolis**. From the beach and its ruined **Byzantine church**, note the island just opposite – its base conceals ancient building foundations. Once joined to the mainland, the island is only accessible by boat nowadays, even at low tide.

🛏 Sleeping & Eating

The lake is popular with German tourists, and many pension owners speak German better than English. Staying in idyllic Kapıkırı commands high prices.

Most pension restaurants are open to nonguests. Lake Bafa's unusual saltwater/freshwater composition – it's as salty as the Black Sea – means they serve both sea and lake fish caught in the same waters. A local speciality is smoked eel. Market day down in Bafa village is Friday.

★ Agora Pansiyon
PENSION $$$

(☑0532 416 3996, 0252-543 5445; www.agora pansiyon.com; Kapıkırı; s/d B&B €50/65, incl half board €65/100, apt €35-48; ❉ 🛜) Nestled between gardens and a shaded terrace with hammocks, this delightful pension has rooms and wooden cabins decorated with folk art and kilims (flatweave rugs), plus a real hamam. The two brothers who run the place, Mithat and Oktay Serçin, are affable hosts, lead tours and are fonts of information. Mum's cooking is legendary.

If you're looking for an even more rustic village experience, stay at one of the three beamed village houses up the hill that sleep two to four people. One of them dates back 130 years, but they have all the mod-cons including up-to-date kitchens and bathrooms. Agora rents bicycles for ₺20 a day.

Selene's Pension
PENSION $$$

(☑0542 316 4550, 0252-543 5221; www.selenes pansion.com; Kapıkırı; d incl half board €75-100, house €60; ❉ 🛜) Kapıkırı's largest pension with 15 rooms and wooden cabins is like a mini village on the road down to the beach. Double 101 and triple 102 have sweeping views of the lake, as does the enclosed terrace restaurant. There is also a house which can sleep four and has cooking facilities. The gardens below the Temple of Athena are a delight.

Karia Pansiyon
PENSION $$$

(☑0543 846 5400, 0252-543 5490; www.karia pension.com; Kapıkırı; s/d incl half board €60/80, campsites per person €5; ❉ 🛜) This fine lodge offers some of the best lake views in town from its large terrace restaurant and homely rooms climbing the rocky hillside. There's also a bungalow (€95) for up to four people, and space for campers. Short hikes or overnight treks are offered.

❶ Getting There & Away

Buses and dolmuşes will drop you on the highway in Bafa village (formerly called Çamıçı) at the turn-off for Kapıkırı. It's 10km north from there to Kapıkırı; two dolmuşes (₺5) serve the route in the morning and one in the afternoon and a taxi costs ₺22. If you stay for a few days, your pension may provide a free pick-up.

Milas & Around

☑0252 / POP MILAS: 60.600

Mylasa (now Milas) was ancient Caria's royal capital, except during the reign of Mausolus from Halicarnassus (present-day Bodrum). While this agricultural town is most interesting for its Tuesday farmers market, the surrounding area contains several unique archaeological sites.

◉ Sights

Milas' best sights are within a 25km radius. Ruins in town include **Baltalı Kapı** (Axe Gate), a well-preserved Roman gate with a carving of a *labrys* (Greek-style double-bitted axe) on the north side. It is also called Zeus Gate. Up a steep path from Gümüşkesen Caddesi is the 2nd-century-AD chambered Roman tomb called **Gümüşkesen** (Silver Purse), possibly modelled on the Mausoleum of Halicarnassus.

Euromos
RUINS

(ŧ6; ⊙ 8am-7pm May-Sep, to 5pm Oct-Apr) Founded in the 6th century BC, Euromos peaked between 200 BC and AD 200 under Hellenistic and then Roman rule. Its indigenous deity had earlier been synthesised with Zeus, and indeed the partially restored Corinthian **Temple of Zeus Lepsynus** is testimony to that. Inscriptions on the west columns record donations by prominent citizens; look to the south side for a **carving of a labrys** (double-bitted axe), Zeus' symbol, flanked by two ears, suggesting that an oracle was in residence.

Excavations are ongoing here. The temple is between Bafa (formerly Çamıçı) and Milas, signposted from the highway just south of Selimiye village. To get here, take a bus or dolmuş running between Milas and Söke and ask to get off at the ruins, which lie about 200m north of the highway.

Labranda
RUINS

(⊙ 8am-7pm May-Sep, to 5pm Oct-Apr) **FREE** This remote hillside site occupies the area that supplied drinking water to Mylasa (Milas) and is one of the most interesting sites in Caria. Never a city but a religious centre linked by a **sacred way** with Mylasa, Labranda worshipped a local deity since at least the 6th century BC, subsequently becoming a sanctuary dedicated to Zeus. The great **Temple of Zeus Labrayndus** honours the god's warlike, 'Axe-Bearing' aspect. Festivals and athletic games occurred at Labranda, which possibly possessed an oracle.

To reach the temple, walk west from the guardian's kiosk at the main entrance, past the distinctive **Doric House** and up a magnificent **stairway** with 24 steps. The **temple** and other religious buildings stand on a series of steep artificial terraces.

Labranda is 15km northeast of Milas via rural lanes. Milas taxis charge ŧ130, including 40 minutes of waiting.

Beçin Castle
RUINS

(Beçin Kalesi; ŧ6; ⊙ 8am-7pm mid-Apr–Oct, to 5pm Nov–mid-Apr) At the beginning of Beçin village, about 6km south of Milas on the road to Ören, a steep signposted road climbs to Beçin Castle. Originally a Byzantine fortress, it was remodelled by the short-lived Menteşe

beylik (principality) in the 14th century. The castle, crowning a 210m-high rocky outcropping, offers great views of Milas below from its walls.

The ruins of more Menteşe-era structures can be seen across the valley and up another hill, including the **Kızılhan** (Red Caravanserai), **Bey Konağı** (Bey's Residence), **Orhan Mosque**, the **Büyük Haman** (Great Bathhouse) and the wonderfully restored **Ahmet Gazi Madrasah**. You can borrow an English-language guidebook from the ticket booth. Half-hourly dolmuşes run between Milas and Beçin village (ŧ3).

Iasos
RUINS

FREE The seaside village of Kıyıkışlacık is surrounded by ancient Iasos, a Carian city that was once an island and prospered from its excellent harbour, rich fishing grounds and red-tinted marble quarried in the nearby hills. A member of the ancient Delian League, Iasos participated in the Peloponnesian Wars, but later weakened and was sacked by the Spartans. Nevertheless, it was definitely a Byzantine bishopric from the 5th to the 9th centuries, before being finally abandoned in the 15th century.

Today, the walled **acropolis-fortress** stands high above the fishing harbour. Across the isthmus linking the village with Iasos are the excellent remains of a **bouleuterion**, with four stairs dividing the seat rows, a huge **agora**, the scant remains of a **theatre** and, to the south, a **Roman stoa** from the 2nd century AD dedicated to Artemis Astias. Unfortunately, the site is badly signposted and very confusing.

❶ Getting There & Away

Milas' otogar is a kilometre north of the centre, on the highway near the Labranda turn-off, and well connected to the central otogar, from where **dolmuşes** (Köy Tabakhane Garajı; Mayıs Bulvarı) serve local destinations.

Bodrum Peninsula

☏ 0252 / POP 167,300

The Bodrum Peninsula, named after the seaside resort town near its centre, offers a mix of exclusive resorts and laid-back coastal villages where you can enjoy good swimming and upmarket restaurants. Despite the glaringly visible inroads of modern tourism (huge villa complexes dot once-forested hillsides) tradition and tranquillity are partially preserved by local open-air vegetable

EPHESUS, BODRUM & THE SOUTH AEGEAN BODRUM PENINSULA

markets and the rugged coastline. The area has an efficient and inexpensive dolmuş network, making it easy to hop between Bodrum and the outlying coves.

ⓘ Information

Consult www.theguidebodrum.com and www.facebook.com/TheBodrumEcho.

ⓘ Getting There & Away

AIR

Milas-Bodrum Airport (BJV; ☎ 0252 523 0101), 36km northeast from Bodrum town, receives flights from all over Europe, mostly charters and budget airlines such as EasyJet and TUI in summer. Anadolu Jet, Pegasus Airlines and Turkish Airlines all serve İstanbul and/or Ankara. There are even connections to Moscow, Qatar and Kuwait in peak season.

BOAT

Visit operators' offices or phone to check their website departure info, which isn't always reliable. Check, too, if your ferry uses Bodrum's old port near the castle or the newer cruise port south of town. Drivers in particular should book in advance; this can often be done online. **Bodrum Express Lines** (Map p258; ☎ 0252-316 1087; www.bodrumexpresslines.com; Kale Caddesi 18; ⊙ 8am-11pm May-Sep, to 8pm Oct-Apr) serves Kos (single/same-day return/open return/car €17/20/25/75, one hour) daily between April and October, with reduced services the rest of year. **Bodrum Ferryboat Association** (Bodrum Feribot İşletmeciliği; Map p258; ☎ 0252-316 0882; www.bodrumferryboat.com; Kale Caddesi 22; ⊙ 8am-7pm May-Sep, to 6pm Oct-Apr) serves Datça and Greek islands including:

Datça (single/return/car €60/110/175, 1½ hours) Three times daily June to September, two sailings daily in October and two or three sailings weekly November to May. The ferry docks at Körmen on the peninsula's northern coast, and the fare includes the 15-minute shuttle to Datça town.

Kalymnos (one way/same-day return/open return €20/25/35, one hour) From Turgutreis two to three weekly, late-May to mid-October.

Kos (one way/same-day return/open return/car €17/19/30/50, 45 minutes) Up to four sailings daily from May to September. From mid-June to October, **Yeşil Marmaris** (Map p257; ☎ 0252-313 5045; www.kosferry.com) offers fast daily Bodrum–Kos catamarans (one way/same-day return/ open return €22/26/38, 20 minutes) from the cruise port.

Patnos (one way/same-day return/open return €42/42/70, 1½ hours) One sailing weekly at 8.30am on Wednesday from June to September.

Rhodes (one way/same-day return/open return €42/42/70, two hours) Fast catamaran sailings on Friday and Sunday at 8.30am between June and September. Yeşil Marmaris also operates services to Rhodes (one way/same-day return/open return €42/42/84).

Symi (one way/same-day return/open return €42/42/70, 1½ hours) Two sailings per week between June and September on Thursday and Saturday. Yeşil Marmaris offers Sunday sailings to Symi (one way/return €42/84, 1¾ hours).

BUS

All the major bus companies serve **Bodrum Yeni Otogar** (Bodrum New Bus Station; Bodrum-Milas Yolu; http://bodrumotogar.com/en/), six kilometres northwest from Bodrum Town. Half-hourly dolmuşes depart from the Yeni Otogar to **Bodrum Eski Otogar** (Map p258; off Artemis Caddesi) in Bodrum Town. Buy a Muğlakart (transport card) from the otogar's machines (or use a contactless debit/credit card) to pay for the dolmuş. For local transport, most dolmuş services heading to villages on the Bodrum Peninsula start from Bodrum Eski Otogar. Download the Muğlakart app for up-to-date local transport schedules.

ⓘ Getting Around

Numerous companies in Bodrum and at the airport rent out cars, motorbikes and scooters, including **Avis** (☎ 0252-316 2333; www.avis.com; Neyzen Tevfik Caddesi 66a; ⊙ 9am-7pm), which is also in Turgutreis, and Bodrum-based **Neyzen Travel** (☎ 0252-316 7204; www.neyzen.com.tr; Kıbrıs Şehitler Caddesi 34).

From Bodrum's Yeni otogar, dolmuşes whiz around the peninsula every 10 minutes (half-hourly in winter) and display their destinations in their windows. You can get to most villages for ₺4 to ₺7, with services running from 8am to 11pm (round the clock June to September). From Bodrum to Yalıkavak takes about 30 minutes and costs ₺7.

There are services between Turgutreis and Akyarlar, Gümüşlük, Yalıkavak, Gündoğan and Göltürkbükü, and between Yalıkavak and Gümüşlük.

TO/FROM THE AIRPORT

Havaş (www.havas.net) and **Muttaş** (☎ 0542 683 4800; www.muttas.com.tr) shuttle between the airport and Bodrum's Yeni Otogar (₺18, 40 minutes) almost every 30 minutes between midnight and 10pm.

Atlasjet provides a free shuttle, leaving Turgutreis three hours before departures and stopping in Bitez, Gümbet, Bodrum otogar and Konacık en route to the airport. Both services also meet arrivals.

Otherwise a taxi (₺130) is your only option.

Bodrum Peninsula

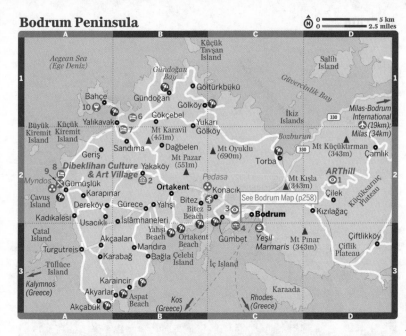

N 0 _____ 5 km
0 _____ 2.5 miles

Bodrum Peninsula

◎ Top Sights
1 ARThill	D2
2 Dibeklihan Culture & Art Village	B2

◎ Sights
3 Myndos Gate	C2
4 Windmills	C3

✦ Activities, Courses & Tours
5 Yoga Center Bodrum	C2

🛌 Sleeping
6 4 Reasons	B1
7 Sandima 37	B2
8 Victoria's	A2

✕ Eating
Bistrot 4	(see 6)
9 Limon	A2

◉ Drinking & Nightlife
10 Xuma Beach Club	A1

Bodrum Town

☎ 0252 / POP 39,600

Although more than a million tourists flock to its beaches, boutique hotels, trendy restaurants and clubs each summer, the town of Bodrum (ancient Halicarnassus) never seems to lose its cool. More than any other Turkish seaside getaway, it has an enigmatic elegance, from the town's crowning castle and glittering marina to its flower-filled cafes and quirky backstreets. Even in the most hectic days of high summer, you can still find little corners of serenity in the town.

Urban planners have sought to preserve Bodrum's essential Aegean character, which was influenced by the Cretans who moved here during the population exchange of the 1920s. Today, laws restrict buildings' heights, and the whitewashed houses with bright-blue trim evoke a lost era. The evocative castle and the ancient ruins around town also help keep Bodrum a discerning step above the rest.

Only in the past few decades has Bodrum come to be associated with paradisiacal beaches and glittering summertime opulence. Previously, it was a simple fishing and sponging village, and old-timers can still remember when everything was in a different place or didn't exist at all. Long before the palmed promenades and upmarket seafood restaurants, Bodrum wasn't even desirable. Indeed, for a while it was the place where

Bodrum

dissidents against the new Turkish republic were sent into exile.

All that started to change after one of the inmates took over the prison. Writer **Cevat Şakir Kabaağaçlı** (aka the 'Fisherman of Halicarnassus') was exiled to sleepy Bodrum in 1925 for his political articles, and quickly fell in love with the place. After serving his sentence, he proceeded to introduce a whole generation of Turkish intellectuals, writers and artists to Bodrum's charms in the mid-1940s.

From then on, there was no going back: by the mid-1980s, well-heeled foreigners started to arrive and today Bodrum is a favourite getaway for everyone from European package tourists to Turkey's elite. But it was Kabaağaçlı's early influence, giving the town its arty identity, that saved it from the ignominious fate of other Turkish fishing-villages-turned-resorts.

⊙ Sights

★ Bodrum Castle
CASTLE

(Bodrum Kalesi; Map p258; ☐ 0252-316 1095; www.bodrum-museum.com; İskele Meydanı; ₺48; ⊙ 8.30am-5pm) Bodrum's magnificent waterfront castle, built by the Knights Hospitaller, dates back to the 15th century. It houses the

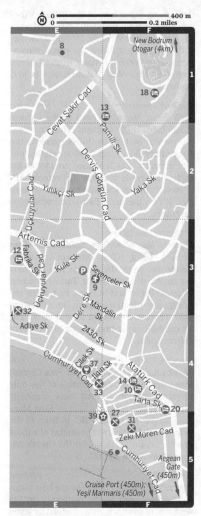

Bodrum

◎ Top Sights
1 Bodrum Castle	C4
2 Mausoleum	B2

◎ Sights
3 Ancient Theatre	A1
4 Bodrum Maritime Museum	D3
5 Ottoman Cemetery	A4

⊕ Activities, Courses & Tours
6 Ezgi Boats	F5
7 My Way Boat Trip	C3
8 Neyzen Travel & Yachting	E1
9 Tarihi Bardakçı Hamamı	E3
Yağmur	(see 6)

⊟ Sleeping
10 7 Art Fesleğen Hotel	F4
11 Antique Theatre Hotel	A2
12 Artunç Hotel	E3
13 El Vino Hotel	F1
14 Eskici Hostel	F4
15 Ha lâ Bodrum	A3
16 Kaya Apart & Pansiyon	D3
17 Marina Vista	A3
18 Regnum Escana Villas & Boutique Hotel	F1
19 Su Otel	C2
20 Uyku Pansiyon	F4

⊗ Eating
21 Avlu	D3
22 Bodrum Denizciler Derneği	C4
23 Cremeria Milano Bodrum	A3
24 Fish Market	D3
25 Fruit & Vegetable Market	D2
26 Gemibaşı	A3
27 Iki Sandal	F5
28 Kalamare	D3
29 La Pasión	D3
30 Nazik Ana	C3
31 Orfoz	F5
32 Otantik Ocakbaşı	E3
33 Ox	E4

⊜ Drinking & Nightlife
34 Dada Salon	C4
35 İxir	A3
36 Marina Yacht Club	A3
37 White House	E4

⊛ Entertainment
38 Kule Rock City	D4
39 Mavi Bar	F5

excellent **Museum of Underwater Archaeology** (Sualtı Arkeoloji Müzesi), arguably the most important museum of its type in the world. However, at the time of research, the castle and museum were only partially open, with a lengthy €25 million restoration ongoing.

Based on Rhodes, the Knights Hospitaller built the castle during Tamerlane's Mongol invasion of Anatolia in 1402, which weakened the Ottomans and gave the order an opportunity to establish a foothold here. They used marble and stones from Mausolus' famed Mausoleum, which had collapsed in an earthquake, and changed the city's name from Halicarnassus to Petronium, recalling St Peter. By 1437, they had finished building, although they added new defensive features (moats, walls, cisterns etc) right up until 1522, when Süleyman the Magnificent captured Rhodes. The Knights were forced to cede the castle, and the victorious Muslim sultan promptly turned the chapel into a mosque, complete with new minaret. For centuries, the castle was never tested, but French shelling in WWI toppled the minaret (re-erected in 1997).

Bodrum Maritime Museum
MUSEUM

(Bodrum Deniz Müzesi; Map p258; ☑ 0252-316 3310; www.bodrumdenizmuzesi.org; Eskiçi Besdesten Binası; adult/reduced ₺10/5; ☺ 9.30am-10pm Tue-Sun Jun-Oct, to 6pm Tue-Sun Nov-May) This small but well-formed museum spread over two floors examines Bodrum's maritime past through finely crafted scale models of boats and an excellent video on traditional 'Bodrum-type' boat building. Much is made of Bodrum's role as a sponge-diving centre and local writer Cevat Şakir Kabaağaçlı – the much-loved 'Fisherman of Halicarnassus'.

★ Mausoleum
RUINS

(Mausoleion; Map p258; Turgutreis Caddesi; ₺12; ☺ 8.30am-6.30pm Tue-Sun Apr-Oct, to 5pm Tue-Sun Nov-Mar) One of the Seven Wonders of the Ancient World, the Mausoleum (originally 44.8m high) was the greatest achievement of Carian King Mausolus (r 376–353 BC), who moved his capital from Mylasa to Halicarnassus. Today very little remains: pre-Mausolean stairways and tombs; the narrow entry to Mausolus' tomb chamber; original drainage systems; precinct wall bits; and some large fluted marble column drums.

Before his death, the king planned his own tomb, to be designed by Pytheos, the architect of Priene's Temple of Athena. When he died, his wife (and sister), Artemisia, oversaw the completion of the enormous, white-marble colonnaded tomb topped by a 24-step pyramid and a quadriga, a four-horse chariot carrying Mausolus. In the late 15th century, the Knights Hospitaller found the mausoleum in ruins, perhaps destroyed by an earthquake, and between 1494 and 1522, almost all of it was reused as building blocks for the castle or burned for the lime content to strengthen the walls. Luckily, the more impressive ancient friezes were incorporated into the castle walls, while original statues of Mausolus and Artemisia ended up in the British Museum.

The site has relaxing gardens, with excavations to the west and a covered arcade to the east – the latter contains a copy of the famous frieze now in the British Museum. Four original fragments displayed were discovered more recently. Models, drawings and documents indicate the grand dimensions of the original mausoleum. A scale model of Mausolus' Halicarnassus is also on display.

Ancient Theatre
RUINS

(Antik Teatro; Map p258; Kıbrıs Şehitler Caddesi; ☺ 8am-7pm) FREE Ancient Halicarnassus' theatre was built in the hillside rock in the 4th century BC to seat 5000 spectators but that capacity was increased to 13,000 for gladiatorial contests in the 3rd century AD. It hosts concerts and other events in summer. It's on the main four-lane highway to Turgutreis.

Ottoman Cemetery
CEMETERY

(Osmanlı; Map p258; Şafak Sokak; ☺ 9am-6pm Tue-Sun) FREE This Ottoman cemetery stands just above the marina, and contains the tombs of two famous Turkish seamen (Mustafa Pacha and his son). Part of the enclosure also functioned as an Ottoman shipyard. There are excellent coastal views and art exhibitions are housed in a 18th-century defence tower.

Myndos Gate
GATE

(Myndos Kapısı; Map p257; Cafer Paşa Caddesi) These are the restored remains of the only surviving gate from what were originally 7km-long walls probably built by King Mausolus in the 4th century BC. In front of the twin-towered gate are the remains of a moat in which many of Alexander the Great's soldiers drowned in 334 BC.

Windmills
VIEWPOINT

(Map p257; Haremtan Sokak) For the best vistas of Bodrum, head to the peninsula on the west side of town which is crowned by seven old windmills.

🏃 Activities & Tours

Travel agents all over town offer tours and activities. Excursions include Ephesus, 2½ hours' drive away, for about €60 (€70 including one or two stops en route such as Euromos and/or Miletus); taxis charge from about €160 for up to five people.

Excursion boats moored in both bays offer day trips (usually 10am to 5pm) around the peninsula's beaches and bays, charging from ₺50 including five or so stops and lunch. Karaada (Black Island), with hot-spring waters gushing from a cave, is a popular destination where you can swim and loll in supposedly healthful orange mud.

Recommended operators include **Bodex Travel & Yachting Agency** (☑0252-313 2843, 0533 638 1264; www.bodextravel.com; Ataturk Caddesi 74), **Ezgi Boats** (Map p258; ☑0542 345 4392; Cumhuriyet Caddesi; ⊙10am-6pm) and **Yağmur** (Map p258; ☑0533 341 1450; Cumhuriyet Caddesi) – or contact **My Way Boat Trip** (Map p258; ☑0507 442 1240; www.mywayboattrip.wixsite.com/mywayboattrip; Bodrum marina; day charter incl lunch €650; ⊙Apr-Oct) to charter your own boat.

Yoga Center Bodrum　　　　　　　YOGA
(Map p257; ☑0532 343 2309; www.yogacenterbodrum.com; Yıldırım Beyazıt Caddesi 21/2; class per hr ₺50) Professional yoga studio with daily hatha and yin yoga classes for all levels. Also offers teacher training programs. Located 2.7km northwest of Myndos Gate, just off the D330 highway.

Neyzen Travel & Yachting　　BOATING
(Map p258; ☑0252-316 7204; www.neyzen.com.tr; Kıbrıs Şehitleri Caddesi 34) This company offers excellent *gület* (traditional Turkish wooden yacht) excursions around the Turkish coastline (and neighbouring Greek islands). Trips include a week-long tour of the Gulf of Gökova taking in Sedir Island, English Harbour and Kisebuku (from €740 per person, including all meals and drinks).

Tarihi Bardakçı Hamamı　　　HAMAM
(Map p258; ☑0536 687 3743; Dere Sokak 32; hamam ₺40, oil massage or scrub & foam massage ₺45; ⊙8am-midnight) Going since 1749, Bodrum's oldest hamam offers mixed bathing, marble surrounds and good massages.

🛏 Sleeping

In high summer, accommodation fills up fast. Hotels near the marina and Bar St get the most noise from the clubs and bars. If arriving by bus, you may be harassed by touts offering 'budget accommodation'. It's your call, but we ignore them.

★7 Art Fesleğen Hotel　　　HOTEL $
(Map p258; ☑0252 316 5334; www.feslegenhotel.com; Papatya Sokak 26; d/tr €55/80; ❄🕸🛜) Just a stone's throw from the shore on the eastern side of town, this cute little hip-ish hotel has a dash of style, good cleanliness standards and reasonable rates. Most rooms have a balcony or terrace looking over the (tiny) pool or towards the sea. Staff are eager to please.

Uyku Pansiyon　　　　　　PENSION $
(Map p258; ☑0252 316 4663; www.uyku-pansiyon.thebodrumhotels.com/tr; Akasya Sokak 50; s/d/tr €26/32/42; ❄🕸) This spotless little pension, run by a hospitable team, has a handy location just off the prom with a fine roof terrace and a selection of inviting rooms. Breakfast is generous and tasty.

Artunç Hotel　　　　　　PENSION $
(Map p258; ☑0532 236 3541, 0252-316 1550; www.artuncotel.com; Fabrika Sokak 32; r €60-80; ❄🕸🛜🏊) Enjoying a quiet, convenient location, this recently renovated little blue-and-white hotel boasts a contemporary feel including pale floors and modish furniture. Check out the owner's collection of bright-red model Ferraris in the reception area, and you'll enjoy the hammocks located poolside under lemon trees.

Kaya Apart & Pansiyon　　　PENSION $
(Map p258; ☑0535 737 7060; www.kayapansiyon.com.tr; Eski Hükümet Sokak 10; s/d ₺195/270; ⊙Apr-Oct; ❄🕸) The very central Kaya has 12 clean, simple rooms plus a studio apartment with safe and TV; six rooms boast a balcony as well. There is a roof terrace with a castle view for breakfast, a flowering courtyard with a bar for lounging, and helpful owners Mustafa and Selda can arrange activities.

Eskici Hostel　　　　　　HOSTEL $
(Map p258; ☑0535 573 3203, 0252-316 8072; www.facebook.com/eskicihostel; Papatya Sokak 24; dm €11-14, d & tw €42, tr €55; ❄🕸🏊) If you're keen to party, head here for the social vibe, organised pub crawls and boat trips. On the flip side, cleanliness is lacking (and staff can be too). Eskici has a small pool in its downstairs garden, a rooftop bar with castle and sea views, and an array of private rooms and mixed dorms (most with air-con and bathroom).

★Ha lâ Bodrum　　　　　B&B $$
(Map p258; ☑0532 368 1411; www.halabodrum.com; Davalcu Ali Sokak 17; r €60-120; ❄🕸) Offering lashings of character and style, this 550-year-old stone house is filled with authentic Ottoman furnishings and objets d'art. It offers five rooms with beds made with antique cotton and silk linen and the two-hectare garden filled with lemon trees and bougainvillea is an enchanting spot to while away summer evenings over cocktails and dinner. It's very close to the marina.

★**El Vino Hotel**   BOUTIQUE HOTEL **$$**
(Map p258; ☑0252-313 8770; www.elvinobodrum.
com; Pamili Sokak; r/ste from €120/180; ❈ 🛜 ⛱) Staff really go the extra mile to assist guests at this long-standing favourite set back from the shore. Classy rooms are dotted around stone buildings in an enormous leafy garden. There are two pools (including a shallow rooftop one) and an outdoor Jacuzzi. Be sure to enjoy a meal in the terrific rooftop restaurant too.

Marina Vista   RESORT **$$**
(Map p258; ☑0252-313 0356, 0549 792 9613; www.hotelmarinavista.com; Neyzen Tevfik Caddesi 168; d/ste ₺775/1100; ❈ 🛜 ⛱) From the impressive woodcarving in reception and the enormous pool in the courtyard to the terrace restaurant overlooking the marina and bar with leather stools, this mini-chain hotel with 92 rooms is a relaxing waterfront option in Bodrum. A spa, gym, sauna and children's activities are also on offer.

Su Otel   BOUTIQUE HOTEL **$$**
(Map p258; ☑0252-316 6906; www.bodrumsu
hotel.com; Sokak 1201, off Turgutreis Caddesi; s/d/ste from €70/100/140; ❈ @ 🛜 ⛱) With an exterior epitomising Bodrum's white-and-sky-blue aesthetic, the relaxing 'Water Hotel' has 25 rooms and suites, most with balconies giving on to a courtyard pool, a restaurant open to the skies and a bar. The suites have kitchenettes and hamam-style bathrooms.

Antique Theatre Hotel   HOTEL **$$**
(Atik Tiyatro Oteli; Map p258; ☑0252-316 6053; www.antiquetheatrehotel.com; Kıbrıs Şehitler Caddesi 169; r €110-130, ste €150-190; ❈ 🛜 ⛱) Next to the town's amphitheatre, this welcoming place enjoys great castle and sea views, and has a big outdoor pool and pretty gardens. Original artwork and antiques adorn the 18 bright rooms, which each have an individual character. Alas, it's on a very busy road.

Regnum Escana Villas & Boutique Hotel   LUXURY HOTEL **$$$**
(Map p258; ☑0252-316 3738; www.regnumescana.
com; Sulu Hasan Caddesi 33; r/villa from €165/790; ❈ 🛜 ⛱) The disadvantage of this sumptuous hillside hotel is it's on the north side of the busy highway behind Bodrum, but the elevated views and space more than compensate. The 10 rooms are huge, even the basic 'superior' rooms are 45 sq metres and beautifully appointed, while villas offer the ultimate in space and comfort. A taxi from the marina is ₺20.

 Eating

Bodrum's waterfront has pricey restaurants with multilingual menus (not always bad), but also discreet backstreet contenders, fast-food stalls and some excellent fish-market restaurants. Generally, eateries on the western bay are more upscale, while the eastern bay has more informal fare. Kebap stands are also found in the market hall, where the Friday **fruit and veg market** (Map p258; Külcü Sokak; ⏱7am-2pm Fri) takes place.

Cremeria Milano Bodrum   ICE CREAM **$**
(Map p258; Neyzen Tevfik Caddesi 78; ice-cream scoop ₺10; ⏱9am-midnight Apr-Nov) Offers the best ice cream in town, with authentic flavours including walnut and coconut. Also serves good espresso coffee.

Bodrum Denizciler Derneği   CAFE **$**
(Bodrum Mariners Association; Map p258; ☑0252-316 1490, 0542 316 4835; İskele Meydanı 44; snacks & mains ₺6-24; ⏱7am-midnight) This mariners' club cafe attracts locals from *çay*-drinking sea dogs to young landlubbers nursing bottles of Efes Malt. Burgers, sausage and chips, *tost* (toasted sandwiches) and *kahvaltı* (breakfast) are served with a front-row view of the yachts and tour boats. Very friendly.

Nazik Ana   TURKISH **$**
(Map p258; ☑0252-313 1891; www.nazikanares
taurant.com; Eski Hükümet Sokak 5; mezes ₺9-12, portion ₺14-18, pides ₺15-25; ⏱8.30am-11pm; ❈) This simple, back-alley place has a no-nonsense, rustic feel with bench seating and stone walls. Offers hot and cold prepared dishes, viewable *lokanta*-style at the front counter, good pides (Turkish-style pizzas) and *köfte*. One of Bodrum's most authentic and friendly eating experiences.

★**Otantik Ocakbaşı**   TURKISH **$$**
(Map p258; Atatürk Caddesi 46; mezes ₺14, mains ₺27-65) Terrific *ocakbaşı* (grill house), famed for its traditional kebabs (try an İskender or *köfte*), with reasonable rates and huge portions. Staff are super-eager to help you select dishes, though English can be a little lacking. It also serves decent pides, steaks and some pasta dishes, but really it's all about the grilled meat here.

Kalamare   SEAFOOD **$$**
(Map p258; ☑0252-316 7076; www.facebook.com/
kalamare48; Sanat Okulu Sokak 9; mezes ₺10-15, mains ₺25-60; ⏱noon-midnight) Though a bit cramped and inland, this distressed-looking

place, with whitewashed tables and pastel-coloured walls, is certainly worth investigating (though be prepared to wait in high season). Serving octopus, calamari, sea bass et al (as well as meat dishes), Kalamare attracts a cool, young crowd.

Avlu
TURKISH $$

(Map p258; ☑0538 670 3687; www.avlubistro.com; Sanat Okulu Sokak 14; mains ₺28-60; ◷3pm-midnight) The 'Courtyard' is a bistro in an old stone house on a cobbled lane that offers outdoor dining, opt for the intimate dining rooms spread over two minute floors. It has a good wine selection and serves mostly Turkish dishes plus some international options like crispy sea bass with guacamole sauce.

Gemibaşı
SEAFOOD $$

(Map p258; ☑0252-316 1220; www.gemibasi.com/restaurant; Neyzen Tevfik Caddesi 132; mezes ₺7.50-17.50, mains ₺35-60; ◷noon-midnight) Located opposite the marina, this trad *meyhane* (tavern) serves fresh mezes and fish to a rakı-raddled clientele. It's renowned for its seafood. Book ahead to score a table on the street-side terrace.

Fish Market
SEAFOOD $$

(Map p258; off Cevat Şakir Caddesi; ◷10am-midnight) Bodrum's fish market (sometimes called *manavlar* for the fruit stands at the entrance to this small network of back alleys) offers a direct dining experience: you choose between myriad fresh fish and seafood on ice at fishmongers' tables and, having paid there, bring them to any adjoining restaurant to have it all cooked for ₺15.

If in doubt, waiters can help you decide – options run from top-end catches to cheaper farmed fish. It should cost about ₺15 to ₺20 for enough farmed sea bass or bream for one, but few fishmongers will go that low and many will try to sell you a whole kilo (around ₺35). Sea fish costs from about ₺90 per kilo.

The plain restaurants spill across the small streets, which get incredibly crowded and have little atmosphere, save maybe for the people-watching. If you can't decide which one, pick the busiest-looking place – locals are fiercely loyal to their favourites.

★ Iki Sandal
TURKISH $$$

(Map p258; ☑0252 367 1444; www.ikisandal.com; Cumhuriyet Caddesi 183; mezes ₺12-55, mains ₺40-95; ◷11am-2am; ☞☑) One of the most creative restaurants in town, this

place occupies a lovely old stone house and has a front terrace with harbour views. A lot of care has gone into the menu, which features healthy, unusual starters like *topik* (an Armemian dish of caramelised onions, blackcurrants, pine nuts and chickpeas) and a smashed cucumber salad that's made from an Ottoman-era recipe.

★ Orfoz
SEAFOOD $$$

(Map p258; ☑0544 316 4285, 0252-316 4285; www.orfoz.net; Zeki Müren Caddesi 13; set menus from ₺150, incl wine from ₺200; ◷7pm-12.30am mid-Jun–mid-Sep, 6pm-midnight Tue-Sun Mar-mid Jun & mid-Sep–Nov) Often cited as one of Turkey's best fish restaurants, this gem has views over Bodrum's eastern shore from its front terrace. Serves delectable seafood such as oysters with parmesan, smoked eel, sea snails with wine sauce, clams, scallops, sea urchins and blue crab. Excellent selection of Turkish wines. Reservations are essential.

La Pasión
SPANISH $$$

(Restaurante Español; Map p258; ☑0252-313 4594, 0530 643 8444; www.lapasionbodrum.com; Uslu Sokak 8; tapas ₺28-66, mains ₺44-120; ◷noon-midnight) With a lovely courtyard setting, this refined Spanish restaurant down a cobbled side street is perfect for tapas, excellent paella (₺120 to ₺180 for two) or Iberian classics like *zarzuela* (fisherman's stew). The restaurant occupies an old Greek stone house, with tables set under fig trees.

Ox
BURGERS $$$

(Map p258; ☑0532 356 7652; Cumhuriyet Caddesi 155; burgers ₺38-62; ◷noon-midnight; ☞) An upmarket and highly fashionable meat feast of a place with street-side tables and a fine menu that majors in gourmet burgers (in 120g or 180g portions), served with toppings including everything from blue cheese to bacon. Optional sides include wonderful double truffle fries (₺35).

🍷 Drinking

Bodrum's varied nightlife scene caters to its diverse clientele. The Turkish jet set fill the clubs on the harbour, while foreign visitors frequent the loud waterfront bars and clubs of Bar St (Dr Alim Bey Caddesi and Cumhuriyet Caddesi). In high summer, Bodrum becomes a 24/7 town, with many nightspots partying until dawn; more bars and clubs pop up on the peninsula's beaches and coves.

★ Dada Salon
COCKTAIL BAR

(Map p258; ☑0252-316 0038; www.dadasalon.com.tr; Dr Alim Bey Sokak 44; ☺9pm-5am; ☎) Occupying an old sponge warehouse, this bohemian speakeasy is owned by Okan Bayulgen, a well-known TV, film and theatre actor. An intimate venue for cabaret, theatre and live-music acts, it occupies three floors and has two bars, one on the ground floor and another on the roof terrace. Gay friendly.

İxir
COCKTAIL BAR

(Map p258; Neyzen Tevfik Caddesi 136; ☺noon-2am; ☎) Fine new cocktail bar established by two mixologists from İstanbul, one of whom is Mehmet Şahin (formerly of Lucca). Mocktails and good Anatolian wines are available by the glass, too.

Marina Yacht Club
BAR

(Map p258; www.english.marinayachtclub.com; Neyzen Tevfik Caddesi 5; ☺9am-2am) This big, breezy waterfront nightspot has four bars and offers live music (more MOR than cutting edge) and shows most nights year-round. In winter, the inside section by the port gates is more popular.

White House
CLUB

(Map p258; ☑0532 334 9642; www.facebook.com/WhiteHouseBodrum; Cumhuriyet Caddesi 147; ☺10am-5am mid-Apr–mid-Oct) This ever-popular beachfront bar-club hosts DJs playing chart hits and pretty commercial house music.

☆ Entertainment

Both the castle and ancient theatre host opera, ballet and rock performances; for upcoming event schedules and tickets, visit Biletix Ticketmaster (www.biletix.com).

Kule Rock City
LIVE MUSIC

(Map p258; ☑0555 824 8834, 0252-313 2850; www.kulebar.com; Dr Alim Bey Caddesi 55b; ☺11am-6am) This rock bar and club is grungy by Bodrum's standards, although there are still plenty of beautiful people on the outside decking. Two-for-one drink promotions are sometimes offered. Decor is quirky: there are great old motorbikes and sharks' heads on the walls.

Mavi Bar
LIVE MUSIC

(Map p258; ☑0252-316 3932; Cumhuriyet Caddesi 175; ☺6pm-5am) This tiny white-and-blue venue stages live music (Turkish rock, folk and jazz) most nights. It's busiest after 1am. It's waterside, right by the harbour.

❶ Information

Bodrum State Hospital (Bodrum Devlet Hastanesi; ☑0252-313 1420; www.bodrumdh.saglik.gov.tr; Elmadağ Caddesi 18; ☺24hr) Efficient and has some English-speaking staff. Consult the website www.theguidebodrum.com for updated cultural information and restaurant and bar reviews.

Tourist Office (Map p258; ☑0252-316 1091; Kale Meydanı 48; ☺8am-noon & 1-5.30pm Mon-Fri) Not that useful but near the castle; note it closes on weekends.

❶ Getting There & Around

Bus services depart from Bodrum's Yeni otogar (p256). The **ferry terminal** (Map p258) is at the south end of the harbour.

There's an intracity dolmuş service (₺3.50), which frequently gets stuck in traffic. Central Bodrum's roads are busy, slow and mostly follow a one-way clockwise system – missing your turn means repeating the whole process.

Taxis are quite affordable, a short hop across town is around ₺15. **Köşem Taxi**

SERVICES FROM BODRUM YENI OTOGAR

DESTINATION	FARE (₺)	DURATION (HR)	DISTANCE (KM)	FREQUENCY (PER DAY)
Ankara	109	12	689	8
Antalya	74	8	496	3
Denizli	43	5	250	13
İstanbul	129	12	851	8-12
İzmir	39	3½	286	hourly
Konya	109	12	626	4
Kuşadası	35	3	151	2
Muğla	18	2	110	hourly
Söke	22	2½	125	hourly

(📱 0542 326 3312; Atatürk Caddesi) is honest and reliable. There are taxi stands at **Cevat Şakir Caddesi** (Map p258), **Türkkuyusu Caddesi** (Map p258) and at the **centre** (Map p258) and **west** (Map p258) ends of Neyzen Tevfik Caddesi.

Otoparks (car parks) around town cost from ₺8 for one hour, ₺30 for a day; there's an **otopark** (Dere Sokak) in the east of town.

For a reliable motorbike or scooter, contact **Bodrum Motosiklet Scooter** (📱 0252-316 4442; www.bodrummotosikletkiralama.com; Demiröz Sokak 40; ⊙ 9am-6pm Mon-Sat), with rates from ₺75 a day.

Bitez

📱 0252 / POP 9970

Bitez is one of Turkey's less frenetic beach resorts, with an easy-going ambience and an attractive seafront promenade that snakes along its horseshoe-shaped bay. A kilometre or two inland, Bitez village is framed by lovely orchards and doesn't go into total hibernation in winter.

For some cultural edification, visit the ruins of **Pedasa**, signposted just before the turnoff to Bitez village on the D330 linking Bodrum with Turgutreis. A relic of the lost Lelegian civilisation that predated the Carians, this small site features defensive wall foundations and a number of chamber graves.

🏃 Activities

In summer, **Siesta Daily Boat Cruises** (📱 0535 920 5242; trips incl lunch & tea ₺65-100) offers day trips from the beach departing at 10am and returning around 6pm.

★ Aquapro Dive Center   DIVING (📱 0532 394 9165; www.aquapro-turkey.com; Bitez Mahallesi; open-water course €480, two fun dives incl all gear €50; ⊙ 8am-10pm May-Oct) Professionally-run PADI dive school offering courses and fun dives on wrecks in the bays around Bitez. Equipment is in good order and the 21m dive boat is very decent. The instructor-owners are native English and Turkish speakers.

🛏 Sleeping

The most attractive accommodation in Bitez is (not surprisingly) by the beach.

Ambrosia   RESORT $ (📱 0252-363 792; www.hotelambrosia.com.tr; Yalı Caddesi; s/d from ₺320/350; ❄🛜🏊) Rated four stars, this large beachside resort

hotel boasts an impressive pool set in a landscaped garden, while the bar-library just off the lobby is an oasis out of the sun. Ambrosia's rooms, done up in blue and light pine, are quite large, most with sea views.

Garden Life   RESORT $$ (📱 0252-313 1111; www.bitezgarden.com; Bergamut Caddesi 52; s/d incl full board & drinks €95/130; ❄🛜🏊) In the orchards surrounding Bitez on the coast road from Gümbet, various pools (a total of four), bars, a private beach and 176 pleasant rooms in cool whites and blues are all set in Garden Life's eponymous greenery.

🍴 Eating

Bitez has a few good eateries working year-round. On weekends, seafront restaurants' brunch buffets have become a local tradition.

Asmali Bitez Meyhane   TURKISH $$ (📱 0252 363 0349; www.facebook.com/asmali. mey.bitez; Şah Caddesi; mezes ₺10-20, mains ₺20-60; ⊙ noon-late May-Oct) This tasteful restaurant packs far more of a local flavour than most tourist-geared places in Bitez. There's a lovely courtyard setting for summer evening dining, with fine seafood (try the sea bream) and authentic meat dishes. Expect terrific live Turkish folk music three nights a week. It's a block inland from the beach.

Lemon Tree   MEDITERRANEAN $$ (📱 0252-363 9543; Sahil Yolu 28, Mart Kedileri; mains ₺27-65; ⊙ 8am-late; 🛜) Right on the beach promenade next to the small Yalı Mosque, this hugely popular place marked by breezy white-and-green decor lets you eat, drink and enjoy at shaded tables or on its lounge chairs on the sand. There's an appetising blend of Turkish and Mediterranean fare (try the house 'Lemon Tree chicken' – a light take on sweet-and-sour chicken).

Black Cat   TURKISH $$ (📱 0252-363 7969; Şah Caddesi 8/7; mezes ₺12, mains ₺25-40; ⊙ 8am-11pm; 🛜) An intimate, good-value restaurant, decorated with holidaying children's pictures of cats, serving light meals by day and heartier fare at night. House specials include *özel kebap*, featuring aubergine piled with meat and yoghurt. Find it one block inland from the beach.

Gümüşlük

📞 0252 / POP 3700

Gümüşlük is a jewel: a gorgeous bay of cobalt waters, its shoreline ringed by tottering old fishermen's houses. Its beauty has not gone unnoticed however by metropolitan Turks, and many properties have now been converted into simple yet stylish eateries and upscale guesthouses. Nevertheless, a distinctly boho vibe endures (particularly in the evening when the tourist coaches have departed).

It's said that famed Carian King Mausolus built Myndos (which largely awaits excavation) due to its strategic position and harbour – indeed, the sea just north of Rabbit Island is very deep. Look straight across these waters beyond **Sergeant Island** (Çavuş Adası) to see two specks of rock, the Kardak Islands (Imia in Greek). Contested sovereignty of these islands almost sparked a war between Greece and Turkey in January 1996, following gratuitous flag-planting exchanges and a more serious but brief Turkish commando occupation. Today, the area is strictly off limits.

👁 Sights & Activities

Unlike the many fishing villages hijacked by modern tourism, Gümüşlük has thankfully been spared excessive concrete development because it lies around the ruins of ancient Carian **Myndos**, a protected archaeological zone. Just offshore, **Rabbit Island** (Tavşan Adası) can be reached on foot at low tide.

Victoria's offers horse riding (from ₺75 per hour), pony rides (₺30) and lessons from an English-speaking coach.

🛏 Sleeping

Gümüşlük is relatively expensive, but family-run pensions still exist, as do vacation rentals. In all cases, book ahead.

★ Oda Bodrum Gümüşlük HOTEL $
(📞 0252-394 4111; www.odabodrum.com; Atatürk Caddesi 54; r €65-95; ❄🛜) A modern, recently-built hotel with clean, inviting though small rooms that have a contemporary feel. There's room service and staff are helpful. Located on the approach road to Gümüşlük, 750m inland from the shore.

Victoria's FARMSTAY $$
(Map p257; 📞 0532 137 0111, 0252-394 3264; www.victoriasclub.net; 1396 Sokak 4, Çukurbük; s/d from €80/100; ❄🛜🏊) Around 2km north of Gümüşlük, this pastoral hideaway nestles between a farmyard and a private beach, though recent villa construction on nearby hills has mired the scene. Accommodation is in well-equipped, though ageing, stilted cabins overlooking the stables, and packages including horse riding are available.

Otel Gümüşlük HOTEL $$
(📞 0252-394 4828, 0544 645 2661; www.otelgumusluk.com; Yalı Mevkii 28; r from €100; ❄🛜🏊) Set back from the shore, this two-storey, ranch-style hotel is open year-round and has spacious, slightly dated rooms around a huge pool. It's a three-minute walk to the dolmuş stop and the hotel also offers apartment rental in the village. Off-season, rates plunge by around 50%.

Zemda Hotel HOTEL $$
(📞 0252-424 0579; s/d from €85/125; ❄🛜🏊) At the bay's southern end, this tranquil getaway has 28 rooms in a Mediterranean mix of colours and sun-bleached white. The bar-restaurant is sandwiched between the large pool and beach.

🍴 Eating & Drinking

Gümüşlük's atmospheric little beach restaurants and cafes are excellent for eating, drinking or just whiling away the time.

Self-caterers can greet the incoming fisherfolk on the docks (8am to 10am) to relieve them of some of their burden, otherwise destined for local restaurants.

Ali Riza'nin Yeri SEAFOOD $$
(📞 0505 652 8987, 0252-394 3047; www.facebook.com/AlirizaOzyanik; Gümüşlük Yalısı; mezes from ₺10, mains ₺30-55; ⏰8am-midnight) Established in 1972, this waterfront classic is run by a local fishing clan whose boats float nearby. With eight different types of rakı (aniseed liquor) to choose from, the business of feasting on seafood is taken extremely seriously here.

★ Limon SEAFOOD $$$
(Map p257; 📞 0252-394 4044, 0544 740 6260; www.limongumusluk.com; Kardak Sokak 7; mezes ₺15-40, mains ₺40-75; ⏰9.30am-midnight Apr–mid-Oct; 🅿) A rustic escape in the hills

above Gümüşlük, Limon sprawls across garden terraces and a whitewashed farmhouse, with stunning views over a ruined Roman bath and Byzantine chapel ruins to the glistening Aegean. There's a real earthy, authentic flavour to the food here: organic salads, exquisite mezes like *mücveru* (zucchini cakes with yoghurt) and mains including *kuzu incik* (lamb shank with aubergine purée). There's also espresso or Turkish coffee, special teas, homemade cakes and lemonade and hand-picked, vodka-soaked petals in the *gelincik* (poppy) cocktail. You'll find live music here some nights. It's along the main road to Yalıkavak.

Mimoza   SEAFOOD **$$$**
(☑ 0252-394 3139; www.mimoza-bodrum.com; Gümüşlük Yalı; mezes ₺15-45, mains ₺40-90; ⊙ 11am-2am Apr-Oct) Visually this place is simply stunning, with whitewashed shabby-chic tables placed right by the water's edge (and even in the shallows), and lots of arty decor. Although the cuisine is good (lots of seafood), there's no real menu so pricing is very casual, and sure to be very costly. On north side of the bay; book well ahead.

★**Club Gümüşlük**   BAR
(www.clubgumusluk.com; ⊙ 9am-2am Apr-Oct; 🛜) This hip new addition to the Gümüşlük scene enjoys a shorefront location, and there's ample space for loafing and lounging with a coffee during the day and enjoying a cocktail or chilled Turkish white wine at night. There's a full menu. Club Gümüşlük also hosts music sessions, film screenings and art exhibitions.

Jazz Cafe   BAR
(☑ 0252-394 3977; www.gumusluk.com/en/r/jazz-cafe; Çayıraltı Halk Plajı 21) This come-as-you-are beach bar, founded by jazz greats Cengiz Sanli and Mete Gurman in 2008, hosts live jazz and blues on weekend nights.

Yalıkavak

☑ 0252 / POP 15,200

A former fishing and sponge-diving village, Yalıkavak has changed beyond all recognition and is now home to one of Turkey's largest and swankiest marinas (home to myriad super yachts) and ringed by holiday-home sprawl. It's a popular resort with

well-heeled Turks, with some attractive bays to the north.

🛏 Sleeping

★**Sandima 37**   APARTMENT **$$$**
(Map p257; ☑ 0252-385 5337, 0530 330 0637; www.sandima37suites.com; Atatürk Caddesi 37; ste €240-415; 🌸🛜🏊) On the hillside road into town, Sandima 37's stylish suites boast lovely attention to detail and are set around a lush garden with sweeping views of the marina and surrounding headlands. The restored stone cottage by the pool with its own spa bath has the most ambience. Staff are welcoming and full of restaurant recommendations and advice.

4 Reasons   BOUTIQUE HOTEL **$$$**
(Map p257; ☑ 0252-385 3212; www.4reasons hotel.com; Bakan Caddesi 2; s/d/tr/q from €175/195/265/320; 🌸@🛜🏊) A hip hillside retreat featuring 20 self-described 'nubohemian' rooms with designer touches, exposed brick and fine locally sourced marble fixtures. The garden is a venue for bocce, massage, yoga and Pilates, and the poolside bistro serves Aegean flavours with sunset views of Yalıkavak Bay.

🍴 Eating & Drinking

Yalıkavak runs pretty much year-round and day trippers will always find at least a few restaurants open. Geriş Altı, the western district towards Gümüşlük, is the place for the day's fishing catch.

Le Café   ITALIAN **$$**
(☑ 0532 362 3909, 0252-385 5305; www.lecafe bodrum.com; İskele Caddesi 33; mains ₺20-40; ⊙ 8.30am-11.30pm; 🛜) This Indian-owned restaurant is everything to everyone, serving up pizza, pasta and the house speciality, chicken parmigiana, with as much aplomb as it does pakoras, samosas and tikka masala. Davendra is both an expert chef and a charming host. The waterfront location is sublime.

★**Bistrot 4**   MEDITERRANEAN **$$$**
(Map p257; ☑ 0252-385 3212; www.4reasonshotel. com; mezes ₺9-40, mains ₺49-92; ⊙ 8am-midnight May-Oct; 🛜) This stylish hotel resto in the hills behind town offers a lovely setting for a memorable meal. The creative menu features mezes like smokey trout with arugula, lemon, red onion and capers (₺14), while mains include lamb tagine with pears

EPHESUS, BODRUM & THE SOUTH AEGEAN BODRUM PENINSULA

(₺89). The raki aniseed brandy) and wine lists are excellent. No children under 12.

Yalı Kıyı
SEAFOOD $$$

(☑0530 920 1113, 0252-385 4143; www.yalikiyiba lik.com; Iskele Meydanı 37a; mezes ₺10-15, mains ₺30-65; ☺8.30am-midnight; ☎) This seafood restaurant is as popular for its waterfront location with its incomparable views westward as its fresh fish dishes and mezes.

Xuma Beach Club
CLUB

(Map p257; ☑0541 531 1111; www.xuma.com.tr; Küdür Caddesi 81; entrance ₺100; ☺Jun-Sep) This beach club enjoys a stellar location on a lovely cove with wonderful swimming in gin-clear water north of Yalıkavak. Ambience is chilled in the day, and clubby later. Gets *very* busy on weekends, when staff can struggle to cope.

Gündoğan

☑0252 / POP 7780

Placid Gündoğan Bay, the deepest on the the Bodrum Peninsula, offers a sandy beach with good swimming right in the centre and stays relatively sedate at night. Most of its part- or full-time occupants in the villas climbing halfway up the hills on both sides are well-off retirees from İstanbul or Ankara who, despite their secularist proclivities, have not been able to get the local imam to turn down the volume at the mosque – about the only noise that could jolt you out of bed here.

Settlement here probably began around AD 1100, though an earlier Roman town, Vara, had existed nearby. In 1961, the village's original Greek name (Farilya) was changed to Gündoğan.

🛏 Sleeping & Eating

★ Villa Rustica Hotel
HOTEL $$

(☑0252-387 7052; www.villarusticahotel.com; Uğur Öztop Caddesi 85; r €75-90; ❀🅿❄) A small family-run place a short stroll from the shore with welcoming hosts and 28 comfortable, spotless rooms set around a pool. Breakfast, featuring many local dishes, really will set you up for the day. There's a restaurant and poolside bar.

Costa Farilya
RESORT $$$

(☑0252-387 8487; www.costafarilya.com; Yalı Mevkii 62; r €115-350; ❀🅿❄) Accommodation in this self-proclaimed 'special class hotel' is in modern grey blocks, some formed of crushed stone behind metal grilling. Rooms are muted, with hardwood floors, a grey-and-white colour scheme, low-slung beds and dramatic views across the bay from those with balconies. Rates can drop to €70 or so in the low season.

Plaj Cafe Restoran
SEAFOOD $$

(Terzi Mustafa'nin Yeri; ☑0252-387 7089, 0535 925 0912; www.terzimustafaninyeri.com; Atatürk Caddesi 10; mezes from ₺10, mains from ₺35; ☺8am-midnight) This long-running favourite is run by a fishing family and serves a good range of mezes and mains, marine and otherwise. There's no noise save for the wind, the waves and the caged birds chirping. Grilled fish is the house speciality. Locals call it the 'Beach Cafe' or 'Tailor Mustafa's Place'.

Göltürkbükü

☑0252 / POP 4970

The reputation of Göltürkbükü as Aegean Turkey's poshest beach getaway is kept alive by the celebrities, politicians and business moguls who flock here each summer. Better beaches exist elsewhere on the peninsula, but Göltürkbükü has a solution to that: ingeniously permitting floating platforms to be anchored just off its shoreline, each replete with designer sun loungers and boasting full service from adjoining landside restaurants.

Even in a place where women go to the beach in high heels, tongue-in-cheek reminders of social divisions remain; the tiny wooden bridge between the two halves of the main beach is jokingly said to divide the 'European side' from the 'Asian side' – a reference to İstanbul and local land prices.

Türkbükü bay forms the north side of the resort. Mere mortals not on a billionaire's budget should head to the southern cove of Gölköy, where prices are more affordable and the vibe is a notch less ostentatious.

🛏 Sleeping

Göltürkbükü's accommodation is unsurprisingly pricey, but off season rates can be quite affordable. Note that the summer clubs keep things loud until late.

Daphnis Hotel
HOTEL $

(☑0252 357 7088; www.daphnishotel.com; Akdeniz Caddesi 37, Gölköy; r/apt from €55/70; ❀🅿) Vaguely akin to a Göltürkbükü hostel, this beachfront place has a plethora of tiny

EPHESUS, BODRUM & THE SOUTH AEGEAN BODRUM PENINSULA

(though perfectly formed, and designed) rooms bang on Gölköy beach, and some apartments a couple of blocks away. There's a lovely garden to chill in with dreamy bay views, and a fine bar-resto.

★ Faros Hotel Bodrum HOTEL $$
(⌨0252-357 8118; www.farosbodrum.com; Yalı Mevki, Gölköy; r/ste from €110/185; ✳❄☎) Seriously stylish and fine value considering the location, all low-rise accommodation at this contemporary hotel is grouped around a pool and Bali-style tropical garden. Rooms have an understated elegance, finished in earthy greys and creams, while suites have colossal Jacuzzi-baths. There's a good beachside restaurant, or you can recline in style on one of Gölköy's largest bathing platforms (300 sq metres).

No:81 Hotel BOUTIQUE HOTEL $$$
(⌨0530 266 8490, 0252-377 6105; www.no81 hotel.com; Mimoza Sokak 10, Türkbükü; r from €275; ✺mid-May–Oct; ✳❄☎) Popular with İstanbul's movers and shakers, No:81 is an ongoing party during summer, with a wooden deck for lounging, pool and beach bars, and a club extending over the water. The 49 rooms and suites have arty elements such as Plexiglas chairs and original paintings on the walls. Warm welcome, friendly service.

Maçakızı LUXURY HOTEL $$$
(⌨0533 642 5976, 0252-311 2400; www.macakizi. com; Narçiçeği Sokak, Türkbükü; r incl half board from €525; ✳❄☎) Ground zero for Göltürkbükü's chic summer crowd and the last hotel on the inner bay, this monument to the high life combines a resort feel with boutique trimmings and minimalist decor. Rooms, all with balcony or terrace, are huge and some have glassed-in showers with sea views. There's a sociable restaurant, a lively bar and a huge hamam and spa.

✗ Eating

Deluxe hotels have excellent though pricey restaurants, while others are clustered by the waterfront. Book ahead.

Flamm TURKISH $$$
(⌨0252-357 7600; https://flammbodrum.com; 30 Sokak 3, Gölköy; mains ₺45-95; ☎) With a prime beachside plot, this Ibiza-style hotel restaurant has elegant tables for dining (seafood is popular, though pricey) and chillout zones for sipping cocktails (₺60

to ₺70). Draws one of Göltürkbükü's most beautiful crowds. Or just order a cappuccino (₺20) and take it all in.

Miam INTERNATIONAL $$$
(⌨0252-377 5612; Atatürk Caddesi 51a, Türkbükü; mezes ₺12-30, mains ₺40-75; ⊙8.30am-midnight; ☎) Always busy, this waterfront restaurant is a good place to take a break from seafood; options include deli and cheese plates, lamb chops and lamb shank. Morphs into more of a lounge bar scene later in the night, with DJs.

Garo's SEAFOOD $$$
(⌨0252-377 6171; www.garosturkbuku.com; 83 Sokak 9, Türkbükü; mezes from ₺15, mains ₺40-80; ⊙9am-midnight) Local favourite Garo's is pricey, but popular for its mezes. The owner-chef serves seafood like *dağ kekikli kalamar izgara* (mountain thyme grilled calamari) and fine meat dishes at white-and-blue tablecloths under dangling lights and open Aegean skies.

Torba
⌨0252 / POP 3250

Despite being just 7km northeast of Bodrum, Torba has stayed quieter and more family-oriented than most other places on the peninsula. It has a nice beach, but lacks the seclusion of places on the peninsula's more distant corners and has a more workaday feel.

🛏 Sleeping & Eating

Accommodation here runs the gamut from package tourist mega-resorts to eccentric 'art hotels'. The resorts are awash in eateries, though you'll find kebap houses in the village and fish restaurants on the beach.

★ Casa Dell'Arte
Residence BOUTIQUE HOTEL $$$
(⌨0252-367 1848; www.casadellartebodrum. com; İsmet İnönü Caddesi 64-66; ste €320-650; ✳❄☎) Staying at this exquisite 'house of art and leisure' with a dozen different suites, owned by a cultured Turkish family, is like visiting the home of an eminent curator. Modern art and antiques decorate the flowing interior and sculptures stand around the pool. Luxuries such as an outdoor Jacuzzi in the garden, 18m pool, a spa complete with treatments, and a clay tennis court only add to this unique property's appeal.

Gonca Balık SEAFOOD $$$
(☑0252-367 1796; Mutlu Sokak 15; mezes ₺12-20, fish from ₺30; ⊘9am-11.30pm; 🛜) With cheery orange and blue tables strung along the sand and looking to the ebbing waves, this friendly place is Torba's spot for a meal of mezes and fresh fish.

Eastern Peninsula

☑0252

The bays southeast of Bodrum are less well known than those to the west, in some cases because hotels have swallowed them whole. Inland, the villages and lanes are quiet and rustic, but save for one excellent art centre, the area is a little lacking in sights and appeal.

Accommodation on the east side of the peninsula tends to be rather exclusive. Resorts have a full range of sit-down restaurants and more informal cafes.

Regularly scheduled *dolmuşes* run along the Yalıçiftlik-Bodrum Yolu, the road running down the coast southwest of the D330, and pull into the resorts along the way.

◉ Sights

★ ARThill ARTS CENTRE
(Map p257; ☑0532 208 7781; www.enderguzey. com; Yalı; ⊘11am-7pm Tue-Sun) Painter and sculptor Ender Guzey established this unique space in a remote hillside location east of Bodrum, showcasing contemporary art and (occasional) music performances in a landmark modernist structure. The quality of exhibits here is superb. It's quite tricky to find, 15km east of Bodrum, and cannot be accessed by public transport.

Marmaris

☑0252 / POP 38,500

A popular resort town that swells to over a quarter-million people during summer, Marmaris is loud, brash and in your face in peak season. During the hot months, it's one of the few places along the coast where you might leave feeling more stressed out than when you arrived.

That said, if it's a last night out, a *gület* cruise along the coast or a ferry to Greece you're after, then this tourist haven is pretty much the Full Monty. Bar St offers unparalleled decadence, while from the *kordon* (seafront), charter boats will whisk you to the Turquoise Coast.

Marmaris does boast a fine coastal cycle path and a pretty harbour crowned by a castle and lined with wood-hulled yachts. And it even has history. It was from here that Britain's Admiral Horatio Nelson organised his fleet for the attack on the French at Abukir in northern Egypt in 1798.

◉ Sights & Activities

Marmaris Castle & Museum CASTLE
(Marmaris Kalesi ve Müzesi; 30 Sokak; ₺14; ⊘8am-6.30pm Apr-Oct, to 5pm Nov-Mar) Marmaris' hilltop castle (1522) was Süleyman the Magnificent's rallying point for 200,000 troops, used to recapture Rhodes from the Knights Hospitaller. The castle hosts small but well-organised **Marmaris Museum**, which exhibits amphorae, tombstones, figurines, oil lamps and other finds from surrounding archaeological sites, including from Knidos and Datça. Saunter along the castle's **walls** and **ramparts** and gaze down on the bustling marina. There are excellent information boards in English and Turkish.

Among the museum's highlights are the **Apollo Altar** frieze from Knidos, the **Datça stele** and amphorae retrieved from shipwrecks in Marmaris Bay.

Old Town HISTORIC SITE
The hilly streets around Marmaris Castle, atmospheric lanes that feel far removed from the yacht-filled marina, contain the city's last remaining traditional buildings.

Jinan Garden GARDENS
(Atatürk Caddesi) This Zen-style garden, complete with a pagoda and soothing water, commemorates Marmaris' Chinese twin city, Jinan in Shandong province. There's also a restaurant here.

Beaches
Marmaris' narrow, shingle **town beaches** allow decent swimming, but much better are **İçmeler** and **Turunç** (10km and 20km southwest, respectively). From late April to October, **water taxis** serve İçmeler (₺20, 30 minutes, half-hourly) and Turunç (₺25, 50 minutes, hourly).

From Marmaris otogar (p274), frequent dolmuşes – every 20 minutes or so at least – also whizz to İçmeler (₺3.50, 25 minutes), while dolmuşes to Turunç (₺5.50, 45 minutes) leave roughly every hour. Both can be caught from any dolmuş stand along Ulusal Egemenlik Bulvarı and Atatürk Caddesi.

Marmaris

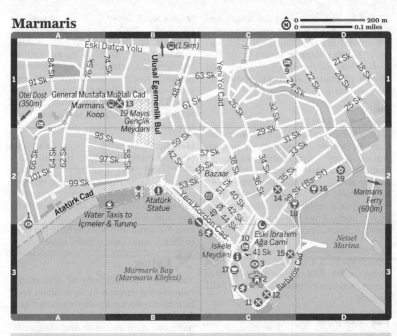

Marmaris

Sights
1 Jinan Garden...A2
2 Marmaris Castle & Museum.................C3
3 Old Town...C3

Activities, Courses & Tours
4 Black Pearl..B2
5 Marmaris Blue Paradise........................C3
6 Professional Diving Centre...................B2
7 Yeşil Marmaris..C3

Sleeping
8 Maltepe Pansiyon....................................A1
9 Marina Apart Otel...................................C1
10 Mets Boutique Hotel..............................C3

Eating
11 Aquarium Kitchen
    Cafe...C3
12 Fellini...C3
13 Köfteci Ramiz...B1
14 Meryemana Mantı Evi............................C2
15 Ney..C3

Drinking & Nightlife
16 Bar St...D2
17 Fredonia Coffee......................................C3
18 Greenhouse...C2

Entertainment
19 Davy Jones's Locker...............................D2

A good cycle path connects Marmaris with İçmeler.

There are also dolmuşes to the beach at **Günlücek Park**, a forest-park reserve 3.5km southeast of Marmaris.

Boat Trips

Marmaris Bay day trips (₺60 to ₺120 including simple lunch, soft drinks and pickup) offer eye-opening views and inviting swimming holes. Dozens of boats offer these trips (usually from May to October), but **Black Pearl** (☑ 0538 633 0863, 0535 549 2605; www.facebook.com/blackpearl.marmaris;

Atatürk Caddesi; boat trips from ₺60) is reliable, as is **Marmaris Blue Paradise** (☑ 0536 347 6957; www.facebook.com/marmarisblueparadise; Yeni Kordon Caddesi; from ₺60). Before signing up, confirm all details (exact boat, itinerary, lunch etc). Be aware that the vast majority of these trips include loud pumping music, pack as many as a hundred people on board and offer various live 'entertainments' put on by the crew. If this isn't your cup of tea, it's best to give them a wide berth.

Hiring a yacht with a group of friends or with random new ones, offers the pleasure of a blue cruise down the coast. Cruises offered by Yeşil Marmaris (p256) are recommended; as for the rest, compare prices, ask around and negotiate. Yeşil offers seven- to 10-day itineraries taking in the Turquoise Coast or the Datça Peninsula and Rhodes. Dalyan is a popular destination for shorter trips.

Diving

Several dive boats on Yeni Kordon Caddesi offer excursions and courses from May through October. As with the numerous cruises, many boats operate, so choose carefully; equipment, insurance, lunch and pick-up are normally included. Since diving is potentially more life-endangering than lounging on a yacht, ask whether the company is licensed by PADI or the Turkish Underwater Sports Federation.

Professional Diving Centre   DIVING
(☑0533 456 5888; www.prodivingcentre.com; Yeni Kordon Caddesi; PADI open water €350) Offers recreational dive excursions as well as PADI courses.

🛏 Sleeping

Marmaris is package-tourist orientated. The western edge of town is home to most of the sleeping options but good central options are limited.

Maltepe Pansiyon   PENSION $
(☑0252-412 1629; www.maltepepansiyon.com; 66 Sokak 9; s/d/tr/q ₺60/120/170/230; ✳🛜) This 22-room pension has been a backpacker's favourite for decades, and though rooms are small and perhaps in need of updating, the shady garden is a great place to chill and chat with fellow travellers. Friendly manager Mehmet (Memo) goes out of his way to help. A self-catering kitchen is available, as are cheaper rooms with shared bathroom.

Otel Dost   HOTEL $$
(☑0252-412 1343; www.oteldost.com; General Mustafa Muğlalı Caddesi 74; s/d/tr/apt €35/50/65/110; ✳🛜🏊) Turkish-British couple İbrahim and Natalie offer 18 well-equipped modern rooms (Suite 206 is the choicest) and a vine-covered terrace for breakfast. Across the road is a pool and **snack bar**. The owners will help out with tours, transfers, rental cars and ferry tickets. Book direct for the best rates.

Marina Apart Otel   APARTMENT $$
(☑0252-412 2030; www.marinaapartotel.com; Mustafa Kemal Paşa Sokak 24; d/q €45/65; ✳@🛜🏊) The 10 hotel rooms and 40 self-catering apartments for up to four people are sparsely furnished but quite good value, each with kitchenette, sofa and balcony. There's a **cafe-bar** in reception and a neighbouring bakery for provisions. Rates include breakfast.

Mets Boutique Hotel   BOUTIQUE HOTEL $$$
(www.metsboutiquehotel.com; 26 Sokak 42; r €54-90; ✳🛜) Old town hotel a few steps from the harbourfront with seven renovated rooms that have a contemporary feel, exposed beams and fine linen – those with sweeping bay views command a higher rate. For those who want to be in the thick of things; expect some street noise.

🍴 Eating

Marmaris has hundreds of restaurants, many aimed squarely at the summer tourist masses, offering a range of international fare. Head inland, away from the promenade, for more authentic and cheaper local food. Beware of the few unscrupulous harbourside restaurants that offer a free bottle of wine with meals, and then recoup their outlay by charging for bread, service and so on.

Meryemana Mantı Evi   TURKISH $
(Virgin Mary Mantı House; ☑0252-412 7855, 0542 662 4863; 35 Sokak 5b; mains ₺9-16; ⊙7.30am-11pm; 🛜) Bustling, non-touristy *lokanta* ideal for authentic, fine-value *gözleme* as well as ready-made prepared *etli yemek* (meat dishes) and *sebzeli yemek* (vegetable dishes). It's a good place to try some Turkish classics.

Köfteci Ramiz   KÖFTE $
(☑0532 441 3651; www.kofteciramiz.com; General Mustafa Muğlalı Caddesi 5a; mains ₺15-33; ⊙9am-midnight) At lunchtime, local suits queue for this long-established *köfte* chain's salad bar (₺9), not to mention the succulent *köfte*, kebaps and other grills. Meal deals abound. Founded by two brothers from Macedonia, it's been here since 1928.

★Ney   TURKISH $$
(☑0252-412 0217; 26 Sokak 24; mezes ₺11, mains ₺20-35; ⊙noon-midnight) Tucked away up

some steps from the western end of the marina is this tiny but delightful restaurant in a 250-year-old Greek stone house with Bugül at the stove. Decorated with seashells and wind chimes, it offers delicious home cooking including inventive mezes and meaty casseroles. Specials are chalked up outside.

★**Kervan Ocakbaşı** GRILL **$$**
(Mareşal Fevzi Çakmak Caddesi; mezes ₺8-17, mains ₺26-50; 🕿🅿) In a suburban location 1km inland from the beach, this is where locals direct you when you need a real meat feast. There's a pleasant street terrace where you can enjoy *pides* (₺12 to ₺17), kebaps, or the house specialty mixed grill (₺50). Waiters speak limited English, but it's fine value and alcohol is sold. There's a little play area for kids too.

Fellini ITALIAN **$$**
(☑0252-413 0826; Barbaros Caddesi 71; mains ₺28-60; ☺8am-1am) With the floodlit castle directly behind and the waterfront directly ahead, this Italian-cum-international restaurant certainly has a fine location. On offer are thin-crust pizzas, pasta, seafood, steaks and kebaps.

Aquarium Kitchen Cafe INTERNATIONAL **$$$**
(☑0252-413 1522; www.facebook.com/aquarium kitchencafemarmaris; Barbaros Caddesi 55; snacks ₺28-42, mains from ₺35; ☺9.30am-2am; 🕿) One of the more creative eateries on the waterfront, offering filling grills and grilled fish. The lunch menu features lighter meals, including steak sandwiches and quesadillas.

🍷 Drinking & Entertainment

Marmaris by night offers more neon than Vegas, and almost as many drunks certain they're just one shot away from the big score. Away from the infamous debauchery of Bar St, there are quieter spots for drinks and harbour views, including the more tranquil waterfront bar-restaurants lining Barbaros Caddesi and the marina.

★**Fredonia Coffee** CAFE
(www.facebook.com/fredoniacoffee; Barbaros Caddesi 1; ☺8.30am-1am; 🕿) Fredonia boasts a prime spot on the prom, and from its lovely front terrace you can gaze over the azure waters of Marmaris bay. Offers a full range of espresso coffees (from ₺7) using a Cimbali machine, mochas and hot

chocolates, cold brews (₺15) and, of course, Turkish coffee. Baristas are chatty and there's fine selection of cakes and snacks to choose from too.

Bar St BAR
(39 Sokak) This raucous stretch of licentiousness is dominated by big and brassy bar-club complexes that spill out onto the street. If you like laser beams, dance music, liquored-up louts and tequilas by the half-dozen, this is for you.The major action takes place between Eski İbrahim Ağa Cami and the Netsel Marina footbridge. Most bars open from 7pm to 4am. As the night wears on, the street becomes a veritable cacophony, as each place tries to drown out its neighbours by cranking up the volume. Beers cost from ₺15, shooters around ₺10 and cocktails ₺20 to ₺30. Happy hours, free shots and buy-one-get-one-free incentives are offered, but there's no guarantee that 'name-brand' spirits will be authentic.

Heading east from the Eski İbrahim Ağa Cami, you first come to a strip of Türkü Bars and *meyhanes* (taverns) playing live Turkish folk and *fasıl* (Ottoman classical music); worth a stop to see how Turks unwind over a few milky glasses of *rakı*. These peter out around the marina office and the Ibiza beats and fluorescent shooters begin.

Davy Jones's Locker LIVE MUSIC
(☑0252-412 1510; www.davyjonesslocker1992. com; 39 Sokak 156; ☺8pm-3am) This two-floor place on the far side of Bar St is one of Marmaris' few rock bars, with '90s American and British music especially well-represented. Davy Jones hosts live bands in summer.

ℹ Information

British Honorary Consulate (☑0252-412 6488; www.gov.uk/government/world/organi sations/british-honorary-consulate-marmaris; Barbaros Caddesi 13; ☺2-4pm Mon & Fri, 9am-12.30pm Tue & Thu) In the same building as Yeşil Marmaris.

Tourist Office (☑0252-412 1035; İskele Meydanı 2; ☺8am-noon & 1-5pm Mon-Fri mid-Sep–May, daily Jun–mid-Sep) The exceptionally helpful staff here dispense solid information and give out free maps.

ⓘ Getting There & Away

TO/FROM DALAMAN AIRPORT

Havaş (☎0850 222 0487; www.havas.net) runs a six to seven daily shuttle buses between Dalaman airport and Marmaris otogar (₺25, 1½ hours). Otherwise, **Marmaris Koop** (☎0252-413 5542; www.marmariskoop.com; General Mustafa Muğlalı Caddesi) has hourly buses from the otogar to Dalaman town (₺15, 1½ hours), from where you can catch a taxi to the airport.

A taxi to Dalaman airport costs €35, contact the reliable **Seagull Transfers** (☎0252-417 2008; www.seagulltransfers.com/en; Turgutreis Caddesi 19b, İçmeler).

BOAT

From late April to October, one or two daily catamarans serve Rhodes (one hour), departing from the main port around 1.5km southeast of Marmaris, at 9.15am and 5pm. Tickets, including port tax, cost one-way (or same-day return) adult/child 7-12 years/under 6 years €40/28/5; open return tickets cost adult €70-75, child 7-12 years €50-55, child under 6 years €5-10. Return services from Rhodes leave at the same times. There are also sporadic departures between March and May. Greek catamaran companies also serve this route, but are generally 10% more expensive.

Travel agencies, including **Yeşil Marmaris** (☎0252-412 1033, 0533 430 7179; www.yesilmarmarislines.com; Barbaros Caddesi 13; ⊙9am-11.30pm) in town and **Marmaris Ferry** (☎0252-413 0230; www.marmarisferry.com; Mustafa Munir Elgin Bulvarı; ⊙8am-7pm) at the port sell tickets. Book ahead at least one day in advance and bring your passport. Be at the dock one hour before departure for immigration formalities. Some agencies provide free hotel pickup for same-day return passengers.

BUS

Marmaris' small **otogar** (Mustafa Münir Elgin Bulvarı) is 3km north of the centre. From the otogar, any dolmuş labelled 'iç şehir' heads into the centre at the waterfront. Bus-company offices line General Mustafa Muğlalı Caddesi (between 19 Mayıs Gençlik Meydanı and 84 Sokak) in the city centre; some companies provide a *servis* (free shuttle-bus) between here and the otogar. Destinations include:

Antalya (₺70, 6¼ hours) Two services daily with Kamil Koç.

Bodrum Catch a dolmuş to Muğla (₺14, one hour) and then the bus to Bodrum (₺22, two hours).

Fethiye (₺26, three hours) Hourly Marmaris Koop buses via Dalaman town and Göcek.

İstanbul (₺160, 13 hours) Nine to 12 services daily with Kamil Koç and Pamukkale, among others.

İzmir (₺50, four hours) Hourly with Kamil Koç and Pamukkale, among others.

ⓘ Getting Around

Marmaris has an excellent cycle path connecting the town with İçmeler beach. The town boasts a municipal bicycle hire scheme, with bikes available at points along the prom, however as you have to register with a credit card, it's a hassle for tourists. For a quality mountain bike, contact **Best Motor** (www.bestmotor.com.tr; 158 Sokak; ⊙9am-10pm), which also has scooters and cars for hire.

Frequent dolmuşes (₺2.50) run between the otogar and the centre of town and the bay via Ulusal Egemenlik Bulvarı. Most then carry on heading west along Atatürk Caddesi, out to the main hotel area.

Datça & Bozburun Peninsulas
☑ 0252

If it is a less frenetic experience you're after, head for the rugged peninsulas that jut out from Marmaris and stretch for over 100km into the Aegean Sea. The western arm is called the Datça (sometimes called Reşadiye) Peninsula; its southern branch is called the Bozburun (or Loryma) Peninsula.

This is spectacular, raw Turkish coastline. Aside from the joy of sailing near the peninsula's pine-clad coasts and anchoring in some of its hundreds of secluded coves, visitors come to explore fishing villages, mountain towns, wee hamlets and epic ruins, such as Knidos at the tip of the Datça Peninsula.

Datça
☑ 0252 / POP 14,100

Some 70km from the regional centre of Marmaris, down a winding road dotted with both traditional windmills and 21st-century wind turbines, Datça is the peninsula's major harbour town. Given its seaside location, it's surprisingly workaday but that lends it a certain laid-back authenticity.

Datça makes a pleasant base for seeing the area, with a string of waterside restaurants that spill onto the beach once the weather turns warm.

The one real sight is the stunning little historic village of Eski Datça (Old Datça), just 2.5km to the north.

KNIDOS

The ruins of **Knidos** (₺12; ⊙ 8.30am-7pm Apr-Oct, to 5pm Nov-Mar) (kuh-nee-dos), a once-prosperous Dorian port city dating to 400 BC, lies scattered across the western tip of the Datça Peninsula. Steep terraced hillsides, planted with olive, almond and fruit trees, rise above two idyllic bays where yachts drop anchor and a lighthouse perches dramatically on a headland. You may even see Mediterranean monk seals swimming offshore here.

The Datça Peninsula's unpredictable winds meant that ships often had to wait for favourable winds at Knidos (also known by the Latinised name, Cnidus); this boosted the boat repair business, hospitality and general trade. St Paul, en route to Rome for trial in AD 50 or 60, was one of many maritime passengers forced to wait out the storm here.

Although few of the ancient buildings are easily recognisable, the city paths are well-preserved. Don't miss the round **temple of Aphrodite Euploia**, which once contained the world's first free-standing statue of a woman. The 8000-seat Hellenistic **lower theatre** and the **sundial** from the 4th century BC comprise other ancient attractions, as do the remnants of a Doric **stoa** with a cross-stone balancing precariously on top and some fine carvings in what was once a **Byzantine church**.

The on-site **restaurant** at Knidos is only open in summer – it's worth a stop more for the great views than the overpriced food.

Knidos is a one-hour drive from Datça, along a winding and scenic road. Hiring a car or scooter allows you to detour onto the back roads on the peninsula's southern coast. **Datça Koop** (☑ 0252-712 3101; near Cumhuriyet Meydanı) will take up to three people to Knidos and back, with one hour's waiting time, for ₺200.

From June to mid-September, Palamutbükü dolmuşes (₺12) leave from the Datça otogar for Knidos at 11am and 4pm, returning at 2.20pm and 8.30pm.

Datça harbour excursion boats also visit Knidos in summer, leaving around 10am and returning by 7pm and cost from ₺60 including lunch and soft drinks.

Datça has three small beaches: **Kumluk Plajı** (Sandy Beach), not the cleanest but tucked behind the main street; **Hastanealtı Plajı** (literally 'Below the Hospital Beach'), a bigger and more attractive strand hugging the northern shore; and **Taşlık Plajı** (Stony Beach) at the harbour's end to the south. Behind it is is a large **natural pool** fed by underground hot springs.

🏃 Activities & Tours

Excursions boats and travel agencies including **Bora Es Tour** (☑ 0252-712 2040, 0532 311 3274; Yat Limanı) offer day trips from Datça harbour (from ₺60, including lunch and soft drinks), which often take in the ruins at Knidos.

🛏 Sleeping

Datca Beyazev Hotel   HOTEL **$$**
(White House Hotel; ☑ 0252-712 8822; www.datcabeyazev.com; 85 Sokak; r €45-65; ❄ 🅿 🛜) Spotless modern rooms, fine value and a peaceful location are the main draw at this small new hotel, around 1km north of the centre of town. English is limited, but

breakfast is certainly not – expect quite a spread.

Tunç Pansiyon   PENSION **$$**
(☑ 0252-712 3036; www.tuncpansiyon.com; İskele Mahallesi; s/d/apt ₺120/165/250; ❄ @ 🛜) Owner Metin is a friendly soul who goes the extra mile to welcome guests and offers advice about sightseeing, including organising excursions to Knidos. Rooms are quite basic but spotless, many with balconies, and there's a fabulous rooftop deck.

★ Villa Tokur   BOUTIQUE HOTEL **$$$**
(☑ 0252-712 8728; www.hoteltokur.com; Koru Mevkii; d/ste €90/120; ❄ 🛜 🏊) This Turkish-German-owned hilltop hotel has lovely grounds overlooking the sea, a large swimming pool and offers a choice of stylishly furnished and very comfortable rooms. It's a 10-minute walk uphill from Taşlık Plajı and feels more like a home than a hotel thanks to the welcoming hosts (Müslüm owns a tribal art and rug store in town).

Konak Tuncel Efe
HOTEL $$$

(☑0252-712 4488; www.konaktuncelefe.com; Atatürk Caddesi 55; s/d from €70/90; ❈@🛜) İznik tiles and exposed walls abound in this purpose-built building, with a feeling of age created in the 20 rooms by a mix of modern and vintage furniture. The lobby has a bar, scattered sofas and tables piled with books, while some rooms have commanding bay views.

Kumluk Otel
HOTEL $$$

(☑0252-712 2880; www.kumlukotel.com; Atatürk Caddesi 39; r/ste ₺370/540; ❈🛜) The Kumluk offers 25 surprisingly modern rooms with long mirrors, glass-fronted fridges and flat-screen TVs. The decor attractively mixes white with flashes of primary colours and there's a lovely terrace in the hotel's adjoining shore-side restaurant for breakfast.

✖ Eating

Rumeli
TURKISH $

(☑0534 611 0564; 86 Sokak 3; mains ₺15-28; ◷10.30am-midnight) Family-owned place where all food is freshly prepared daily, located in simple premises: look out for the purple-and-white gingham tablecloths on a small lane. Strong on meat, including offal. Prices are very moderate.

Zekeriya Sofrası
TURKISH $

(☑0252-712 4303, 0532 468 9997; Atatürk Caddesi 70; dishes ₺10-15; ◷8am-11pm; ☑) The pre-prepared and made-to-order dishes in this bright eatery on the main drag allow a great-value sampling of Anatolian home cooking. All sorts of meat and vegetable creations are prepared daily, some recipes from as far afield as Şanlıurfa, where the owner's family hails from. No alcohol.

★ Café Inn
CAFE $$

(☑0534 1169, 0252-712 9408; Atatürk Caddesi 51; mains ₺28-70; ◷9am-11.30pm; 🛜) With its nose poking into the surf from Kumluk Plajı, this chilled hang-out with mismatched furniture serves a decent cappuccino and dishes from a full range of *dolmades* (stuffed grape leaves) to linguine with smoked aubergine (₺30) and good salads. House wine is ₺24 by the glass.

Küçük Ev
SEAFOOD $$

(☑0533 550 0578, 0252-712 3266; www.kucukevrestaurant.com; Yat Limanı; mezes from ₺8, mains ₺23-55; ◷8am-11pm; 🛜) Founded in 1979, this harbourside eatery called the 'Little House' serves Mediterranean and

seafood dishes like *ahtapot güveç* (octopus casserole). Also offers a good choice for vegetarians, try the *mercimek köfte* (lentil balls with mint and spices).

★ Culinarium
MEDITERRANEAN $$$

(☑0252-712 9770, 0539 970 1207; www.culinarium-datca.com; 64 Sokak 20; mains ₺50-90; ◷7pm-midnight Mar-Nov; 🛜) In new intimate premises a couple of blocks inland from the shore (though there are harbour views from the dining room), head here for a truly gourmet experience. The Turkish-German owners prepare everything with real care and attention and offer a limited menu: favourite dishes are zucchini flowers stuffed with fish and prawns and John Dory. Reserve well ahead.

🍷 Drinking & Nightlife

★ Coffee Grinder
CAFE

(www.thecoffeegrinder.com.tr; Ali Osman Çetiner Caddesi 9d; ◷8am-11.45pm; 🛜) Datça's best cafe enjoys a lovely position at the north end of the beach prom, and serves the full gamut of perfectly prepared coffee options: cold brew, flat white, espresso and french press. Beans are imported from as far away as Guatemala and Ethiopia. Snacks and breakfast are available.

Roll Coffee House
BAR

(☑0252-712 2266; Atatürk Caddesi 94a; ◷10am-3am; 🛜) This tiny (misnamed) beer house stocks around 90 different types of brew from around the world. Perched high above the marina, Roll is in the hands of owner Hüseyin, as welcoming a host as you'll find anywhere in Turkey.

Eclipse Music Bar
BAR

(☑0532 424 2896, 0252-712 8321; Atatürk Caddesi 89; ◷3pm-3am May-Oct; 🛜) Eclipse's outside deck is a great spot for a sunset beer while inside, beneath exposed beams, pop-art superheroes overlook the dancefloor. Live music on Saturday evening; check out its Facebook page.

ℹ Getting There & Away

BOAT

Bodrum Ferries link Datça with Bodrum three times a day between June and September (three weekly in late May, twice a day in October). Buy tickets (one way/return ₺60/110, car/bicycle one way ₺175/10) and confirm times at the **Bodrum Ferryboat Association** (☑0252-316 0882, 0252-712 2323; www.bodrumferryboat.com; Turgut Özal Meydanı;

⊙9am-8pm) in central Datça. Arrive at the office 45 minutes before departure for the *servis* (shuttle bus) to Körmen harbour at Karaköy (5km northwest of Datça). If staying in Eski Datça, with prior notice the *servis* can pick you up on the main road.

Rhodes & Symi Regular ferries were not running from Datça to Greece at the time of research. Greek ferries usually make day trips from the islands to Datça on summer Saturdays; Greece-bound passengers can return with them. In summer, operators such as **Seher Tour** (✆0252-712 2473, 0532 364 5178; www.sehertour.com; Atatürk Caddesi 88e) offers day trips to Symi, charging about €100 per passenger with a minimum of six to eight passengers.

BUS

Regular summer dolmuşes (₺16, 1¾ hours, every 30 minutes to an hour between 6am and 10pm) connect Datça with Marmaris from a dusty **otogar** (Çevre Yolu), which is 1km north of the harbour. There's also a daily connection to Mugla at 8am (₺26, three hours). Pamukkale operates one daily bus to Marmaris at 1pm (₺28) and has a **ticket office** (✆0252-712 3101; Atatürk Caddesi) in town. For connections to anywhere in Western Turkey, head to Marmaris.

Eski Datça

✆ 0252 / POP 650

Tiny 'Old Datça', capital of an Ottoman district stretching into what is now Greece, is much more atmospheric than its newer counterpart, Datça, just to the south. Its cobbled lanes wend beckoningly between stone houses draped with bougainvillea, providing a blissful escape into the untroubled coast of yesteryear. Eski Datça is home to a handful of terrific cafe-restaurants and the odd boutique hotel.

🛏 Sleeping & Eating

★**Kaya GuestHouse**　　　GUESTHOUSE $$$
(✆0252-712 0045; www.kayaguesthouse.com; Sardunya Sokak 3; r €75-95; ﹡🛜🌊) A welcoming, well-run rural retreat with a peaceful village location, stone buildings, a leafy garden and a lovely pool area. Rooms are stylishly furnished and spacious and breakfast is a real highlight, with lots of healthy options.

★**Eski Datça Evleri**　　　BUNGALOW $$$
(Old Datça Houses; ✆0252-712 2129; www.eski datcaevleri.com; s/d/tr from €85/130/175; ﹡🛜) Three bungalows built in traditional fashion, with thick stone walls keeping the heat from their white interiors. Inside are hamam-style bathrooms and small kitchens, while the courtyard cafe is a rustic hang-out. Fig is closest to the centre; Almond and Olive are 100m up the hill. Rates drop in the shoulder season.

Olive Farm Guesthouse　　　INN $$$
(✆0252-712 4151; http://guesthouse.olivefarm. com.tr; Güller Dağı Çiftliği, Reşadiye; s €65-80, d ₺80-130; ⊙May-Oct; ﹡🛜🌊) This stylish country retreat has pastel-hued rooms and suites with bright bedding, rustic furnishings and its own branded olive-based toiletries. The mix of children's playroom, garden hammocks and artistic decoration creates the feel of a farm designed by Antoni Gaudí. Find it in Reşadiye, 2km north of Eski Datça.

Datça Sofrası　　　TURKISH $$
(✆0252-712 4188; Eski Datça; mezes ₺10-18, mains ₺15-40; ⊙9am-midnight) This terrace restaurant beneath a vine-clad arbour serves good mezes and grilled-meat dishes, including house speciality *bademli köfte* (meatballs with local almonds). Daily specials are chalked up on a board outside.

Taş Konak Eski Datça　　　MEDITERRANEAN $$$
(✆0252-712 9454; www.taskonakeskidatca.com; Mustafa Kemal Caddesi; mains ₺25-75; ⊙8am-11pm; 🛜) A fine hotel cafe-restaurant with lovely terrace for al fresco dining. The chef is Italian, so this is the perfect spot for a bowl of pasta (or espresso); the Turkish food is also excellent.

🛍 Shopping

Olive Farm Mill Store　　　FOOD & DRINKS
(✆0252-712 8377; www.olivefarm.com.tr; Güller Dağı Çiftliği, Reşadiye; ⊙8.30am-9pm) Set amidst seemingly endless olive groves, this farm shop offers tastings of its olives and first-press oil, jams and vinegars distilled from anything you can think of – fig, orange, carob etc. It does an excellent line of olive oil–based toiletries and cosmetics. In Reşadiye, 2km north of Eski Datça.

ℹ Getting There & Away

In summer, dolmuşes run every 30 minutes to/from Datça (₺2.50), 2.5km south. Eski Datça is 100m from the main road, so you can get off the dolmuş from Marmaris at the turn-off and walk.

Selimiye

📞 0252 / POP 1470

Boat-building is the traditional industry in these parts and the coastal village of Selimiye is still a tad scruffy around the edges, despite the growing importance of tourism. There's no real beach, though the waterfront promenade, lined with restaurants and bars, is attractive enough.

Between June and September, boats offer day cruises around the bay, stopping at beaches for swimming, from about ₺60 including lunch and drinks. Or you can hire out a paddle board to explore the shore.

🛏 Sleeping

Hydas Pansiyon   PENSION $$
(📞 0505 316 7562; www.facebook.com/HydasPansiyon; s/d ₺220/250; ❄ 🌐) Just a step or two from the promenade, this simple pension is efficiently run by Ozan and Cenk and has comfortable, well-scrubbed rooms with good linen and modern bathrooms. The breakfasts, in true Turkish village fashion, are superb and very generous; the rooftop bar is a fun place to hang.

Jenny's House   PENSION $$$
(📞 0252-446 4289, 0507 667 8155; www.jennyshouse.co.uk; Selimiye Köyü Mahallesi; s/d ₺400/450; ❄ 🌐 🐾) Across the road from the harbour, this charming pension has rooms around a lush garden. A couple of rooms give on to the pool in the centre, but we prefer the two doubles on the 1st floor with a large shared balcony. Affable Briton Jenny offers afternoon tea, with homemade cakes and jam, and her Turkish brother-in-law Salih can help with holiday rentals.

🍴 Eating & Drinking

Paprika   DESSERTS $
(📞 0252-446 4369; Buruncuk Mevkii 80; desserts ₺10-16; ⏰ 8am-1am Apr-Oct) This tiny white cottage facing the marina might have some thinking they'd arrived in Macarıstan (Hungary). Not quite... This all-Turkish establishment focuses on desserts, with some 30 different calorific and inventive ones served up daily. Oh, and it also offers fine coffee and an espresso machine.

Falcon   TURKISH $$
(📞 0252-446 4105, 0537 598 3819; Selimiye Köyü Mahallesi; mains ₺12-35) For fair prices and hearty food, the Falcon is perfect: a stone oven pumps out delicious pide (₺13 to ₺20) or opt for sizzling lamb and chicken dishes. The Falcon has never stopped talking about the day in 1999 when a Greek boat disgorged Princes William and Harry – who promptly sat down and had a meal. And they have posted newspaper cuttings to prove it.

ℹ Getting There & Away

Dolmuşes (roughly every hour) between Marmaris (₺12, one hour) and Bozburun stop in Selimiye in summer. They pull over on the main road at the village's northern end.

Bozburun

📞 0252 / POP 2210

Bozburun (Grey Cape), a 30km drive down the Bozburun (or Loryma) Peninsula from the Marmaris–Datça road, retains its rustic farming, fishing and *gület*-building roots, though tourism (mostly from visiting yachts) has arrived too. It's an agreeable spot far from the masses, with a pretty promenade that snakes around the shore, but there are no real beaches. You can, however, swim in deep blue waters from jettys and platforms (just watch out for sea urchins). Local charter boats venture into the idyllic surrounding bays. Market day is Tuesday.

🛏 Sleeping & Eating

Yilmaz Pansiyon & Apart   PENSION $$
(📞 0537 046 2410, 0252-456 2167; www.yilmazpansion.com; İskele Mahallesi 391; s/d/apt from ₺160/180/260; ❄ 🌐) A friendly pension with six simple but cheerful rooms in an older building and 11 two-bedroom self-catering apartments – No 3 is a favourite – with kitchens and balconies in a newer one. All rates include breakfast served on a vine-covered terrace just metres from the sea and there's a shoreside deck for sunbathing. It's just southeast of the marina.

Pembe Yunus   PENSION $$
(Pink Dolphin; 📞 0536 250 2227, 0252-456 2154; www.bozburunpembeyunus.com; Cumhuriyet Caddesi 131; s/d incl half board from ₺170/270; ❄ 🌐) Located 800m southeast of the

OFF THE BEATEN TRACK

CARIAN TRAIL

The longest of Turkey's 20-odd long-distance hiking trails, the **Carian Trail** (Karia Yolu; www.cariantrail.com), meanders 820km from the Milas area south to the Datça and Bozburun Peninsulas, crossing through much of the ancient kingdom of Caria. It passes by many important archaeological sites and offers an opportunity to see the emerald hills and azure coves of the Aegean at a slow pace, hiking beyond the tourist trail to secret corners such as Lake Bafa's Neolithic **cave paintings**. You can walk short sections of the route; find the Carian Trail guidebook (€19), 1:100,000-scale map and more information on the trail's website as well as at **Culture Routes in Turkey** (www.cultureroutesinturkey.com).

Self-guided hiking along the Carian Trail is possible, contact **Self Guided Turkey** (www.selfguided-tr.com); for €635 you get seven nights half board in the Bozburum peninsula, 24-hour support along the way, luggage transfers, a guidebook and transport to/from Dalaman Airport. Other Carian Trail hikes are available, including 15-day adventures.

marina, the 'Pink Dolphin' is a friendly place, with white interiors, bleached wooden floors, mosquito nets and shared terraces (room 12) or little balconies (room 5) enjoying vast sea views. Dinner is enjoyed at the water's edge, and the hotel has a boat for trips to the Greek island of Symi across the bay.

Dolphin Boutique Hotel HOTEL **$$$**
(☎0252-456 2408; www.dolphinpension.com; r €75-95; ❄📶) On the slim promenade 900m south of the marina, this well-run place is owned by a welcoming local family. There's a selection of spacious rooms with wonderful bay views. It's very peaceful here, and the in-house restaurant is a pleasure to dine in.

Sabrinas Haus BOUTIQUE HOTEL **$$$**
(☎0252-456 2045; www.sabrinashaus.com; d incl half board €450-1300; ⏲May-Oct; ❄📶🏊) Truly a sybaritic escape, Sabrinas Haus enjoys a stunning location on a remote shoreline. There are 17 individually designed rooms and suites (think whitewashed wood floors, antiques and four-poster beds) in a beautiful mature garden. However beware the hotel's policy of charging extras for many items (tea, drinking water etc).

The infinity pool, seafront deck and thatched bar at the end of a pier are all super; the spa offers myriad massages and treatments; and activities include cruises to Symi on the hotel's own 88ft gület (wooden sailing boat). Note that there is a minimum two-night stay (three nights June to September), and children under 14 aren't allowed.

Fisherman House SEAFOOD **$$**
(☎0252-456 2730; Kordon Caddesi; mezes ₺8-20, mains ₺25-50) Fresh fish at honest prices is served at this place run by Serkan (a fisherman who owns the Yilmaz Pansiyon to the south of the marina); the grilled calamari is superb. He'll also advise about what to do around town.

ℹ Getting There & Away

Five daily dolmuşes serve Marmaris (₺12, 1½ hours) via Selimiye, with three extra services in summer.

Bozburun Transfer (☎0252-456 2603, 0535 749 0113; www.marmaristransfer.biz; Atatürk Caddesi 10; 1-3 people ₺325, 4-7 people ₺450) does transfers to/from Dalaman International Airport (2½ hours).

Akyaka

☎0252 / POP 2890

The laid-back village of Akyaka (White Shore) lies tucked between pine-clad mountains and a grey-sand beach at the far end of the Gulf of Gökova. It's especially popular with well-heeled Turkish tourists and kitesurfers.

At the mouth of the Azmak River, Akyaka was the second town in Turkey to join the Cittaslow (Slow City) movement and has resisted unsightly development, with half-timbered houses built and restored in 'Ula-Muğla' Ottoman style. Confusingly, Akyaka is sometimes also called Gökova, which is an older township located several kilometres inland. The road from Muğla crosses the Sakar Pass (Sakar Geçidi; 670m), offering breathtaking views of the sea.

⊙ Sights & Activities

Blue Flag **Akyaka Beach** in the centre is good for swimming, while south of town **Akçapınar Beach** is one of Turkey's **kitesurfing** hotspots, regularly hosting competitions – the main season is late April to November when conditions are often perfect for beginners. **Çinar Beach**, 2km to the northwest, has deep water for snorkelling.

In summer, the fishing cooperative offers **boat tours** (₺60 to ₺100 including lunch) to local beaches, bays and **Cleopatra Island**, which has bright golden sand and Hellenistic and Roman ruins. Year-round boat trips glide up the lovely **Azmak River** (₺12, half-hour) over waving strands of green waterweed.

Kiteboard Gokova
KITESURFING
(✆0535 399 3154; www.kiteboardgokova.com; Akçapınar Beach; 3-day course group/private €320/380; ⊙8am-8pm Apr-Oct) Established school offering excellent IKO (International Kiteboarding Organization) courses with experienced instructors; all gear is included in the rates. Kite rentals are also available.

Kitebase Gökova
KITESURFING
(✆0535 795 1737; www.kitebasegokova.com; Akçapınar Beach; courses from €280; ⊙8am-10pm Apr-Oct) Instructors speak fluent Turkish, English and German at this beach-based school, which was set up in 2012. Beginner and advanced courses are well structured, and quality Airush rental gear is available for hire.

Delta Bisiklet Akyaka
CYCLING
(✆0544 800 4011; www.deltabisiklet.com; Karanfil Sokak 28a; bikes per hr/day from ₺7/30; ⊙8am-10pm) Professional outfit which hires out road and mountain bikes, three-wheelers and tandems. Can also recommend trails along the coast or into the hills.

Gökova Rüzgar Sports Center
WATER SPORTS
(✆0252-243 4217; www.kiteboardturkey.com; Hamdi Yücel Gürsoy Sokak 2; kiteboard per day ₺240, 8hr course €375; ⊙9am-8pm Apr-Nov) Hires out equipment and gives lessons for sea kayaking, canoeing and stand-up paddle boarding on Akyaka Beach in front of the landmark Yücelen Hotel.

🛏 Sleeping

Numerous holiday apartments are available for rent in Akyaka. Contact **Captain's Travel Agency** (✆0252-243 5398, 0532 326 6094; www.akyakateknetur.com; Liman Sokak;

⊛🛜) or **Tomsan Okaliptus** (✆0252-243 4370; www.tomsanokaliptus.com; Türkoğlu Sokak 8; from €40; ⊛🛜🌊).

Akyaka Kamp
CAMPGROUND $
(✆0551 448 7034, 0252-243 5156; www.akyakakamp.com; Akyaka Beach; campsites per tent/caravan ₺40/50, d/tr/q bungalow without breakfast ₺175/225/250, stone cottage without breakfast ₺380; ⊛🛜) Above the western end of Akyaka Beach, this campground has tent pitches, bungalows and stone cottages accommodating up to five on a hill overlooking the beach as well as a lovely cafe-bar.

★ Bonjuk Bay
CAMPGROUND $$
(✆0537 810 2705; www.bonjukbay.com; Bonjuk Cove; from €30; ⊛🛜) 🌿 This remote back-to-nature escape offers a unique experience. Occupying a secluded private cove, Bonjuk Bay draws an in-the-know crowd of creative guests, who are accommodated under safari-style canvas expanses, simple lotus tents or in stone cottages. Yoga sessions, free-diving lessons, musical performances, DJ-driven parties and random creative happenings are very much the Bonjuk scene. Space (24 max) is very limited.

Bonjuk's organic farm and garden provides delicious sustenance for rustic, healthy meals, and there's a cool lounge area, lovely dining room and ample space for chilling. The cove is also home to a community of (docile) sandbar sharks, as well as the odd ray and seal, so snorkelling is very rewarding. Non-guests are not really encouraged to visit, but should call ahead and are charged a ₺150 access fee to swim in the bay. Located 28km south of Akyaka or 25km north of Marmaris, access is via a dirt road.

Nova Aparts
APARTMENT $$
(✆0252-243 5354; www.nova-aparts-tr.book. direct; Sefa Sokak 4; apt ₺140-200; ⊛🛜) Steps from the seafront and river, these tidy apartments offer fine value given the location, many with garden views from their wooden balconies. They're on the small side but very clean and there's parking.

Yelken Hotel
HOTEL $$
(✆0532 648 6046; www.facebook.com/yelkenhotelakyaka; Cumhuriyet Caddesi 10; d/tr/q ₺280/330/380; ⊛🛜🌊) Frequent name changes aside, this small hotel is a dependable choice, its rooms all boasting wood floors and balconies. Two of them look to the street, with the rest gazing at the pool and back garden.

THE GULF OF GÖKOVA

An azure body of water situated between the jaw-like outline of the Bodrum and Datça peninsulas, the **Gulf of Gökova** forms a spectacular stretch of coastline. There's very little development along the southern section of the gulf, home to dozens of idyllic coves, many of which are only accessible by boat (book a *gület* cruise from Bodrum or Marmaris).

The gulf has rich marine life, and NGOs including the Mediterranean Conservation Society (Akdeniz Koruma Derneği) coordinate environmental protection. Six zones are off-limits to fishers, and rangers have been employed to monitor these areas, where numbers of key species including the golden grouper have significantly increased. Gökova is also home to very rare Mediterranean monk seals (which can be occasionally glimpsed from the ruins of Knidos) and loggerhead sea turtles.

Perhaps the gulf's most celebrated species is the **sandbar shark**, a year-round resident. This bulky shark, which can grow to 2.5m, congregates in bays including tiny, remote Bonjuk cove, accessed from Bonjuk Bay, which forms the Med's most important nursery ground for this fish. A docile bottom-dweller, the sandbar shark is not considered dangerous to swimmers. For more information, consult the Mediterranean Conservation Society's website (www.akdenizkoruma.org.tr/en).

Turkuaz Apart Otel
HOTEL **$$**

(🍽0537 257 9112, 0252-243 4389; www.turkuazak yaka.com; Kermetur Karşısı; d/apt without breakfast ₺220/280; ❄🛜) Turkuaz offers 20 fairly comfortable, spacious and spotless rooms and self-catering apartments accommodating up to four people. It's housed in a neo-Ottoman structure with wooden balconies.

★ Big Blue Otel
HOTEL **$$$**

(🍽0252-243 4544; Sanat Sokak 6; d/ste from €60/105; ❄🛜) Six rooms hard by the sea with a real Med feel courtesy of the azure blue and white theme. Ground-floor rooms are spacious and have terraces, while three middle rooms have balconies and stunning sea views (choose No 5 with two windows). The penthouse King Studio has both sea and forest views, a huge balcony and a bonus rear window.

All rooms have top-quality mattress, bed clothes and fridges, and the seaside restaurant-cafe is delightfully situated. However breakfast is basic and needs improving.

Yücelen Hotel
RESORT **$$$**

(🍽0252-243 5108; www.gokovayucelen.com; Hamdi Yücel Gürsoy Sokak 4; s/d from €75/100; ❄🛜🏊) Accommodation in this vast beachside complex is in Ottoman-style blocks, reached across bridges over a network of soothing streams. The rooms have parquet or tile floors, stylish wooden furniture and all have balconies. There are three pools (one indoor) and fitness facilities.

✗ Eating

Balık ekmeği (fish sandwiches) are sold all over town from ₺10. Fish restaurants line the north bank of the Azmak.

Wednesday is market day in Akyaka, while on Saturday it's in Gökova village, 4km to the southeast.

★ West Cafe & Bistro
CAFE **$$**

(🍽0252-645 2794; https://westcafe.business. site; İnişdibi Caddesi 56; mains ₺25-70; 🛜🍽) A kilometre east of town on the road to Gökova, this peaceful, refined garden restaurant offers a wide choice of food, from Turkish staples to Mexican, vegetarian and vegan choices, all executed beautifully. West Cafe is famous for its breakfasts, plus there's good coffee and a decent wine selection.

❶ Getting There & Away

Dolmuşes serve Muğla (₺5, 30 minutes) half-hourly (hourly in winter) and Marmaris (₺6, 45 minutes) twice daily (mid-May to mid-October). Otherwise, for points north and west (eg Muğla and Bodrum), walk to the highway junction 2km uphill from the beach. You can pick up frequent buses headed south from Gökova village, 4km to the southeast.

Muğla

🍽0252 / POP 72,800

Muğla (*moo*-lah) is a rarity for a Turkish provincial capital – compact and relaxed, with plane tree–lined boulevards and narrow streets that lead to a historic quarter.

EPHESUS, BODRUM & THE SOUTH AEGEAN MUĞLA

The whitewashed Ottoman houses are particularly well preserved and there's an array of chilled *çay bahçesi* filled with friendly students from the nearby university. Muğla makes for a pleasant (and easy) reintroduction to Turkish urban life after a spell on the beach.

◉ Sights & Activities

Old Town
HISTORIC SITE

From Cumhuriyet Meydanı, the main square and roundabout with Atatürk's statue as focal point, walk north along Kurşunlu Caddesi to **Kurşunlu Cami** ('Lead-Covered Mosque'; 1493) to reach Muğla's old quarter. The pink-and-white **mosque's** minaret and courtyard were added in 1900. Beyond here, the **bazaar's** narrow lanes are jammed with artisans' shops, confectioners and tea houses.

Muğla's 18th- and 19th-century **Ottoman houses** and its **Ulu Cami** (1344) are further north; the mosque was built by Menteşe emirs though alterations made in the 19th century have rendered its pre-Ottoman design almost unrecognisable. Nearby is the Greek-built **clocktower** *(saatli kule)* dating from 1905 which sounds a church-like bell on the hour. To the west, the Ottoman **Sekibaşı Hamamı**, renovated in 2010, hosts occasional art exhibits; its intricate architecture alone, with branching side rooms and central marble bath-table, make it worth a peek.

Zahire Pazarı
HISTORIC BUILDING

(Grain Market; Zahire Pazarı; ⊙9am-11pm) This carefully restored market in the shadow of the Pazar Cami (Bazaar Mosque) features lazy cafes spilling across a leafy cloistered courtyard dotted with traditional craft shops; the city subsidises their rent to maintain traditions such as marbled paper *(ebru)*, hand-woven items and intricate painted boxes. Even if you're not shopping, come for an atmospheric drink.

Muğla Museum
MUSEUM

(✆0252-214 6948; Postane Sokak; ⊙9am-noon & 1-5pm Tue-Sun) **FREE** Muğla's excellent museum contains a small collection of prehistoric finds as well as Greek and Roman antiquities displayed in rooms around an open courtyard filled with statuary. Don't miss the riveting **Gladiator Room**, with mock-ups, weapons, stone carvings and excellent information panels about the lives of these professional combatants. There's also a room containing traditional arts and crafts of the region.

⌂ Sleeping & Eating

Petek Hotel
BUSINESS HOTEL $$

(✆0252-214 3995; www.petekhotel.com; Cumhuriyet Caddesı 27; d/ste ₺160/190; ❉ ♠) Though the three-star, 64-room Petek is a bit characterless and faces a busy and rather noisy boulevard southeast of Cumhuriyet Meydanı, it is comfortable and very professionally run. Good in-house restaurant, 24-hour room service and a rooftop bar.

Baba Geyikli Pub Bistro
BURGERS $$

(✆0507 691 0415; Saatli Kule Caddesi 10-12; mains ₺12-27; ⊙noon-1am) Housed in a the stunningly restored Bıcılar Han caravanserai, this lively place serves hamburgers, kebaps and chicken dishes, along with fine cocktails (from ₺28). The central courtyard, decked out with metalwork sculptures and wall murals, is a boon in the warmer months. Gigs take place here (from 9pm) on Friday and Saturday.

ⓘ Information

Tourist Office (✆0252-214 1261; Cumhuriyet Caddesi 22a; ⊙8am-noon & 1-5pm Mon-Fri) About 600m southeast of Cumhuriyet Meydanı. English is spoken and free maps are available.

ⓘ Getting There & Away

Muğla's otogar is on Atatürk Bulvarı some 750m southwest of the main square via Zübeyde Hanım Bulvarı. Buses, including services by **Kamil Koç** (✆0252-444 0562; Otogar), **Metro** (✆0252-212 0805; Otogar) and **Pamukkale** (✆0252-213 0811; www.pamukkale.com.tr; Kurşunlu Caddesi 28; ⊙7am-8pm), and dolmuşes serve Antalya (₺72, five hours, daily), Bodrum (₺18, two hours, hourly), Denizli (₺40, 2½ hours, hourly) and Marmaris (₺12, 1¼ hours, half-hourly). If heading east along the coast, change at Marmaris.

Western Anatolia

Best Places to Eat

➡ Kebapçı İskender (p295)

➡ Big Apple Restaurant (p314)

➡ Mezze (p298)

➡ Sagalassos Lodge & Spa (p315)

Best Places to Stay

➡ Kitap Evi (p293)

➡ Fulya Pension (p313)

➡ Armistis Hote (p296)l (p296)

➡ Limnades Hotel (p287)

➡ Melrose House (p305)

Why Go?

This is the place to drop off the tourist radar. Except for the shimmering white travertines of Pamukkale, which pack in the tourists, western Anatolia is the big chunk of Turkey most travellers miss. Vast classical cities such as Sagalassos, Afrodisias and Laodicea are served up without the crowds, lakeside Eğirdir is a laid-back base for biking, boating and heading off to hike the St Paul Trail's forest-clad tracks, while the Phrygian Valley's rock-cut ruins reveal the Iron Age sphere of King Midas and co.

For urban exploits after exploring this agricultural heartland head to Bursa, the original Ottoman capital, where grand mosques, sprawling bazaars and imperial mausoleums await. Then dose up on a more contemporary scene in student-central Eskişehir, where cafe-culture rules the roost and the brand new OMM (Odunpazarı Modern Museum) is dedicated to modern art.

When to Go
Bursa

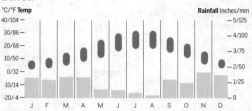

Jan & Feb Skiers and snowboarders head to Uludağ for fun on the slopes.

May & Jun Join in the rose harvest around mountain-ringed Lake Eğirdir.

Oct Pension prices drop and the tour buses peter out, but Pamukkale's travertines remain magnificent.

Western Anatolia Highlights

1 Pamukkale
(p302) Wading through turquoise-blue pools on the snow-white calcite travertines beneath the ruins of ancient Hierapolis.

2 Sagalassos
(p314) Gazing at the fully restored nymphaeum amid the lonely heights of this ruined mountain city.

3 Bursa (p288)
Winding your way through bazaars then watching the dervishes whirl in the first Ottoman capital.

4 Afrodisias
(p309) Channelling your inner Roman gladiator within this ancient site's vast stadium.

5 Eğirdir (p311)
Pulling on your hiking boots to trek part of the St Paul Trail from this idyllic lake town.

6 Uludağ (p294)
Riding the world's longest cable car up this ski resort's slopes.

7 Eskişehir (p296)
Checking out the serious coffee scene before brushing up on contemporary art in inner Anatolia's liveliest city.

İznik

📞 0224 / POP 43,330

Turks are proud of İznik's Ottoman tile-making tradition, and the city's Byzantine incarnation as Nicaea once played a significant role through its church councils in shaping Christianity. Today, İznik is a somewhat dusty and run-down collection of tile shops, teahouses and handicraft stalls, though its ruined fortifications and lakeside setting make a visit worthwhile. Easily accessed from İstanbul via a ferry across the Sea of Marmara to Yalova, İznik is a good candidate for a break from the big city.

◉ Sights & Activities

City Walls & Gates   RUINS

İznik's once-imposing Roman walls, renovated by the Byzantines, no longer dominate but parts of their 5km circumference remain impressive. Four main gates still transect the walls, while remains of 12 minor gates and 114 towers also stand.

The most impressive chunk of fortifications, still soaring between 10m and 13m in height, can be seen in the southeastern section between **Lefke Gate** (Kılıçaslan Caddesi) and the southern **Yenişehir Gate** (Atatürk Caddesi). Lefke Gate itself is interesting for its three Byzantine gateways.

İstanbul Gate (Atatürk Caddesi), the ancient city's northern entrance, is the most impressive. Note the decorative features of carved stone heads facing outwards. **Göl Gate** (Kılıçaslan Caddesi) has little left of its entranceway, nor does the minor **Saray Gate** (Vakıf Sokak), but it's photogenically situated over a quiet country lane set between

---

LOCAL KNOWLEDGE

SHOPPING FOR İZNIK TILES

Shops all over town sell multicoloured tiles, as well as other ceramics and handicrafts. Good places to start looking are the small workshops along **Salim Demircan Sokak**; the workshop belonging to the **İznik Foundation** (İznik Vakıf Çinileri; www.iznik.com/en; Vakıf Sokak; ⊗ 8am-6pm Mon-Fri); and shopping complexes such as **Nilüfer Haltun** (Kılıçaslan Caddesi; ⊗ 9am-7.30pm), which also has cafes and teahouses. Shop around, and note there is room for bargaining at all.

---

olive groves and poplars. It's named this because Sultan Orhan (r 1326–61) had a palace *(saray)* nearby. İznik's ruined **Roman Theatre** (Tiyatro Sokak) is on the route between Atatürk Caddesi and the Saray Gate.

Aya Sofya   MOSQUE

(Orhanlı Camii; Atatürk Caddesi) **FREE** Originally a great Justinian church, Aya Sofya (Church of the Divine Wisdom) is now a mosque surrounded by a rose garden. The building encompasses ruins of three different structures. A mosaic floor and a mural of Jesus, Mary and John the Baptist survive from the original church.

Yeşil Cami   MOSQUE

(Green Mosque; Müze Caddesi) Built between 1378 and 1387 under Sultan Murat I, Yeşil Cami has Seljuk Turkish proportions, influenced by the Seljuk homeland of Iran. The minaret's green-and-blue-glazed zigzag tiles foreshadowed the famous local tile-making industry. The minaret is the highlight here; the mosque's interior is quite plain.

İznik Museum   MUSEUM

(İznik Müzesi; 📞 0224-757 1027; Müze Sokak; ₺5; ⊗ 9am-1pm & 2-6pm Tue-Sun) İznik's museum is housed in a soup kitchen that Sultan Murat I built for his mother, Nilüfer Hatun, in 1388. Born a Byzantine princess, Nilüfer was given to Sultan Orhan to cement a diplomatic alliance. The museum has been shut for restoration for a few years. Come here to see its lofty halls displaying original İznik tiles of milky bluish-white and rich 'İznik red' hues.

II Murat Hamamı   HAMAM

(📞 0505 744 3259; Maltepe Sokak; soak & scrub adult/child ₺20/15, massage ₺15; ⊗ men 6am-midnight daily, women 1-5pm Mon & Thu) Clean and kid-friendly, this 15th-century hamam was constructed during the reign of Sultan Murat II. The huge pile of wood outside will give you the confidence that this is an authentic wood-fired affair. One of our favourite hamams in Turkey.

🛏 Sleeping

Kaynarca Pansiyon   PENSION $

(📞 0224-757 1753; https://kaynarca-pansiyon.business.site; Gündem Sokak 1; s/d/tr ₺70/140/210; 🛜) Guests receive a warm welcome at this centrally located pension with very plain but tidy rooms up narrow flights of

İznik

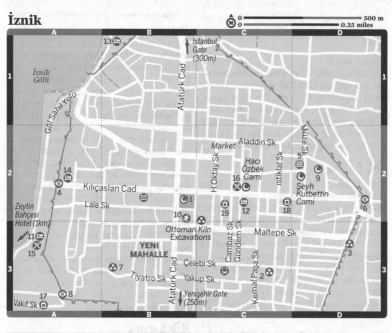

İznik Gölü

İstanbul Gate (300m)

Yenişehir Gate (250m)

İznik

◎ Sights

1 Aya Sofya	B2
2 Church of the Koimesis	C3
3 City Walls & Gates	D3
4 Göl Gate	A2
5 İznik Museum	D2
6 Lefke Gate	D2
7 Roman Theatre	B3
8 Saray Gate	A3
9 Yeşil Cami	D2

◎ Activities, Courses & Tours

10 II Murat Hamamı	B2

⬛ Sleeping

11 Çamlık Motel	A3
12 Kaynarca Pansiyon	C2
13 Limnades Hotel	B1
14 Seyir Butik Pansiyon	A2

⊗ Eating

15 Çamlık Restaurant	A3
16 Karadeniz	C2
Seyir Cafe	(see 14)

🛍 Shopping

17 İznik Foundation	A3
18 Nilüfer Haltun	C2
19 Salım Demircan Sokak	C2

stairs. You're right in the heart of İznik's bustle here, good for shopping and cheap eating options, but not so fantastic for light sleepers.

★**Limnades Hotel**　　BOUTIQUE HOTEL **$$**
(✆0224-757 5724; www.limnadeshotel.com; Göl Sahil Caddesi 38; s/d ₺200/300, ste ₺350-500; 🅿❅🅪🌊) İznik's jazziest place to bed down is this white-and-blue villa fronted by a long terrace with a pool and surrounded by gardens. Inside, furniture in candy pinks, violets and blues, colourful wall murals and flouncy white canopy veils draped over beds create

a riotous decor mishmash that all somehow works in its own quirky way. Suites have Jacuzzis and lake-view balconies.

Seyir Butik Pansiyon　　PENSION **$$**
(✆0224-757 7799; www.seyirbutik.com; Kılıçaslan Caddesi 5; s/d/f ₺150/172/318; ❅🌊) Wrought-iron balconies, colourful flower boxes and rooms full of countryside style featuring warm wood details, floral bed linen and contemporary bathrooms all combine at this small family-friendly pension a hop, skip and jump from the lake. The generously proportioned family rooms come with

lake-view balconies, and downstairs in the shady garden cafe, there's a children's play area.

Çamlık Motel GUESTHOUSE $$
(☑ 0224-757 1362; www.iznik-camlikmotel.com; Göl Sahil Yolu; s/d ₺140/230; 圖 ☗) Run by the English-speaking Cumhur, the 'Pine Grove' has neat-as-a-pin, decent-sized rooms with crisp white bedding and good bathrooms. Get a front room if possible because they come with narrow balconies overlooking the lake.

✕ Eating

Seyir Cafe CAFE $
(www.seyircafem.com; Kılıçaslan Caddesi 5; mains ₺8-20; ⊙ 8.30am-11pm; 🖬) The shady garden of the Seyir Butik Pansiyon (p287) has tables surrounded by roses and kitschy classical statuettes. It's a tranquil spot for a lunch of juicy *gözleme* (stuffed flatbreads) or a filling bowl of *mantı* (Turkish ravioli), and a top choice for travelling families, with playground equipment on site to keep the kids busy while you have an after-lunch çay.

Karadeniz PIDE $
(Kılıçaslan Caddesi 149; mains ₺14-20; ⊙ 11am-9pm) 'Black Sea' dishes up *lahmacun* (Arabic-style pizza; ₺5 to ₺6) and pide (Turkish-style pizza). If you've already explored Turkey's world of pide and are looking for something different to the standard cheese and *sucuk* (spicy veal sausage) toppings, try the *kuşbaşılı* (finely chopped beef, pepper and tomato) version.

Çamlık Restaurant SEAFOOD $$
(Göl Sahil Yolu; meze ₺6, mains ₺25-35; ⊙ 11.30am-11pm) The licensed restaurant at the Çamlık Motel is a local favourite for grilled lake fish enjoyed with views of the water. When the weather's fine, enjoy a meze and a drink in the lakeside garden, or angle for a table by the window in the yawning interior. Either way, the beer is cold and the rakı (aniseed brandy) pleasantly robust.

ⓘ Getting There & Away

İznik Otogar (İznik Bus Station; Çelebi Sokak) Half-hourly dolmuşes (minibuses with a prescribed route) shuttle from 6am to 9pm to Bursa (₺15, 1½ hours). Coming from Bursa, catch them from platform 91 at Bursa's otogar (bus station). There are also hourly dolmuş departures to Yalova (₺15, one hour), 62km northwest of İznik. From Yalova, regular İDO ferries (www.ido.com.tr) link to İstanbul Yenikapı (₺34, 1¼ hours) and Pendik.

Bursa

☑ 0224 / POP 1.9 MILLION

Industrial sprawl makes a mockery of its moniker '*Yeşil Bursa*' ('Green Bursa'), but the big city bustle doesn't detract from Bursa's historic allure. Awarded Unesco World Heritage status in 2014 for being the birthplace of the Ottoman Empire, the city is built around the mosques, mausoleums and monuments from its grand epoch as the Ottoman capital. After admiring architectural finery and getting lost amid the push and shove of the bazaar crowds, it's time to partake in Bursa's culinary contribution to the world. This is the home of İskender kebap (or Bursa kebap; döner kebap on fresh pide topped with tomato sauce and browned butter) and trust us, you haven't tasted how good it can be until you've had the real deal here. Afterwards, balance out the butter-soaked decadence with some fresh air and a zoom up to Uludağ (Turkey's premier ski resort) on the world's longest cable car.

◉ Sights

◉ Central Bursa (Osmangazi)

Bursa Citadel CASTLE
(Hisar; Map p290; Orhan Gazi Caddesi) FREE
Some ramparts and walls still survive on the steep cliff that is the site of Bursa's citadel and its oldest neighbourhood, Tophane. Walk up Orhan Gazi (Yiğitler) Caddesi to reach the *hisar* (fortress). On the summit, a park contains the **Tombs of Sultans Osman & Orhan** (Osman Gazi ve Orhan Gazi Türbeleri; Map p292; Timurtaş Paşa Park; by donation), the Ottoman Empire's founders. Osman Gazi's tomb is the more richly decorated. Although it was ruined in the 1855 earthquake, Sultan Abdül Aziz rebuilt the mausoleum in baroque style in 1863.

The six-storey **clock tower** (Map p292; Timurtaş Paşa Park), the last of four that also served as fire alarms, stands in a square with a cafe where families and couples gaze out over the valley and snap photos.

★ Ulu Cami MOSQUE
(Grand Mosque; Map p290; Atatürk Caddesi) This enormous Seljuk-style mosque (1399) is central Bursa's dominating feature. Sultan Beyazıt I built it in a monumental compromise – having pledged to build 20 mosques after defeating the Crusaders in the Battle

SHADOW PUPPETS

Originally a Central Asian Turkic tradition, Karagöz shadow-puppet theatre developed in Bursa and spread throughout the Ottoman Empire. Puppets are made of camel hide, treated with oil to turn translucent and are then painted. They are manipulated by puppeteers behind a white cloth screen onto which their images are cast by backlighting.

Legend attests that Karagöz the Hunchback, foreman of Bursa's enormous mosque Ulu Cami, distracted the workforce with the humorous antics he carried out with 'straight man' Hacivat. An infuriated sultan executed the comic slackers, whose joking became immortalised in Bursa's Karagöz shadow puppetry. Director Ezel Akay revived this legend in 2006's comic film *Killing the Shadows* (original title *Hacivat Karagöz Neden Öldürüldü?*).

Puppeteer Şinasi Çelikkol has championed Karagöz puppetry. His **Karagöz Antique Shop** (Map p290; ☑0224-221 8727; www.karagozshop.net; Eski Aynalı Çarşı 12; ⊘9.30am-7pm) is a lively place to see the puppets and watch an impromptu performance. Ask about his ethnographic museum in the nearby village of Misi. He also founded Bursa's **Karagöz Museum** (Karagöz Müzesi; ☑0224-232 3360; Çekirge Caddesi 59; ⊘9.30am-5.30pm Tue-Sun, performances 11am Wed) **FREE**, opposite the Karagöz monument. The collection includes magnificent Turkish, Uzbek, Russian and Romanian puppets and puppet-making tools. Performances often take place at 11am on Wednesday mornings at the museum. Check with Şinasi Çelikkol at his shop for current show times.

of Nicopolis, he settled for one mosque with 20 small domes. Two massive minarets augment the domes, while the giant square pillars and portals within are similarly impressive. The *minber* (pulpit) boasts fine wood carvings, and the walls feature intricate calligraphy.

Kapalı Çarşı MARKET
(Map p290; Kapalı Çarşı Caddesi; ⊘8.30am-8pm Mon-Sat, 10.30am-6pm Sun) Bursa's sprawling Kapalı Çarşı (Covered Market) complex is made up of several historic buildings strung out along Kapalı Çarşı Caddesi, the market's main thoroughfare.

They include the 14th-century **Bedesten** (Vaulted Market; Map p290; ⊘8.30am-8pm Mon-Sat, 10.30am-6pm Sun), built by Sultan Beyazıt I (reconstructed after an 1855 earthquake), and the **Eski Aynalı Çarşı** (Old Mirrored Market; Map p290; ⊘8.30am-8pm Mon-Sat, 10.30am-6pm Sun), which began its life as the Orhanbey Hamamı in 1335. Note its domed ceiling with skylights. Several shops in the Eski Aynalı Çarşı sell traditional handicrafts including Karagöz shadow puppets.

Koza Han HISTORIC BUILDING
(Cocoon Caravanserai; Map p290; Uzun Çarşı Caddesi) The finely restored Koza Han, with its leafy inner courtyard filled with cafes, is the most popular place to break your market explorations. The surrounding chambers where traders once bunked down for the night are now home to expensive silk shops.

The *han* (caravanserai) was built in 1490 and its small courtyard mosque (1491) honours Yıldırım Beyazıt.

⊙ Yeşil

★**Yeşil Cami** MOSQUE
(Map p290; Yeşil Caddesi) Built for Mehmet I, the Yeşil (Green) Cami was completed in 1422 and represents a departure from the previous, Persian-influenced Seljuk architecture that dominated Bursa. Exemplifying Ottoman styling, it contains a harmonious facade and beautiful carved marble work around the central doorway. The mosque was named for the interior walls' greenish-blue tiles.

Yeşil Türbe TOMB
(Green Tomb; Map p290; Yeşil Caddesi; ⊘8am-noon & 1-5pm) **FREE** The mausoleum of 5th Ottoman sultan Mehmed I Çelebi (and several of his children) stands in a cypress-trimmed park opposite the Yeşil Cami. During his short rule (1413–21), he reunited a fractured empire following the Mongols' 1402 invasion. Despite its name, the *türbe* (tomb) is not green; it has blue Kütahya tiles outside that post-date the 1855 earthquake. The structure has a sublime, simple beauty, the original interior tiles exemplifying 15th-century decor.

Turkish & Islamic Arts Museum MUSEUM
(Map p290; Yeşil Caddesi; ₺5; ⊘8.30am-noon & 1-7pm Tue-Sun) Housed in the former *medrese*

WESTERN ANATOLIA BURSA

Central Bursa & Yeşil

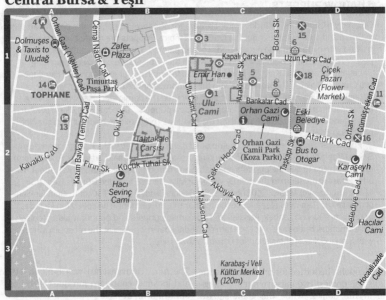

Central Bursa & Yeşil

(seminary) of the Yeşil Cami (p289), this museum contains 14th- to 16th-century İznik ceramics, jewellery, embroidery, calligraphy, dervish artefacts and Karagöz puppets.

◉ Muradiye

★ **Muradiye Complex**   HISTORIC SITE
(Map p292; 2 Murat Caddesi) **FREE** This Ottoman-era complex incorporates a stately *medrese* (1426) and the equally handsome **Sultan Murat II (Muradiye) Cami**, also built in 1426, but its most

interesting elements are the 12 imperial *türbes* in the cemetery. A number of these **tombs** are exquisitely decorated with tiles, painted calligraphy and inlaid woodcarving. Don't miss the 14th-century **tomb of Cem Sultan** (the third son of Mehmet the Conqueror) and 16th-century **tombs of Şehzades Mahmud and Ahmed**, the sons of Beyazıt II. Like other Islamic dynasties, the Ottomans did not practice primogeniture – any royal son could claim power upon his father's death, which, unsurprisingly, resulted in

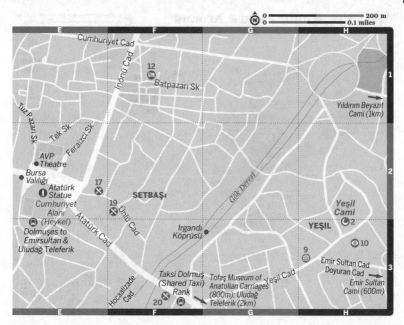

numerous bloodbaths. The tombs preserve this macabre legacy: all the *şehzades* (imperial sons) interred here were killed by close relatives. While many of the tombs are ornate, the **tomb of Sultan Murat II** (r 1421–51), an ascetic and part-time dervish as well as father to Mehmet II (Mehmet the Conqueror), is simple and stark.

The 15th-century **Muradiye Medresesi** was a tuberculosis clinic in the 1950s and still houses a medical centre. It's not open to visit. Similarly, the **Sultan Murat II Hamamı** (Map p292; Kaplıca Caddesi), which catered to the *medrese* students, is now a government building. A taxi from the city centre will charge around ₺15 to get here.

Ulumay Museum of Ottoman Folk Costumes & Jewellery   MUSEUM

(Osmanlı Halk Kıyafetleri ve Takıları Müzesi; Map p292; ☑ 0224-222 7575; 2 Murat Caddesi; ₺5; ⊙ 8.30am-6.30pm Tue-Sun) Originally the Şair Ahmet Paşa *medrese* (1475), this museum exhibits around 70 costumes and more than 350 different pieces of jewellery.

Hüsnü Züber Evi   HISTORIC BUILDING

(Map p292; Uzunyol Sokak 3; by donation; ⊙ 10am-noon & 1-5pm Tue-Sun) Knock to gain entry to this restored 19th-century Ottoman

house, located uphill behind Sultan Murat II Hamamı. The collection inside includes ornate musical instruments and intricately carved and painted Anatolian wooden spoons. Beyond lie winding alleys, shops and crumbling Ottoman houses.

Archaeology Museum   MUSEUM

(Arkeoloji Müzesi; Map p292; Kültür Parkı; ⊙ 8am-noon & 1-5pm Tue-Sun) **FREE** This museum's small collection ranges from beautiful Roman pottery and figurines to stone tools and artefacts dating back to the Paleolithic era.

⊙ Çekirge

Murat I (Hüdavendigâr) Cami   MOSQUE

(I Murat Caddesi, Çekirge) This unusual mosque from 1366 features a barrel-vaulted Ottoman T-square design, and includes ground-floor *zaviye* (dervish hostel) rooms. The only visible part of the 2nd-floor facade gallery, originally a *medrese*, is the sultan's *loge* (box), above the mosque's rear.

Sarcophagus of Murat I   TOMB

(I Murat Caddesi; ⊙ 8am-10pm) Sultan Murat I (r 1359–89), most famous for the Battle of Kosovo that claimed his life, is interred in this huge sarcophagus opposite the

WESTERN ANATOLIA BURSA

Muradiye, Kültür Parkı & Around

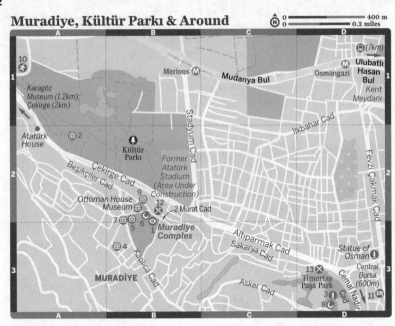

Muradiye, Kültür Parkı & Around

Hudavendigar Mosque. Murat's remains were brought from Kosovo by his son, Beyazıt I.

 Activities & Tours

Karagöz Travel Agency   TOURS
(Map p290; ☑ 0224-223 8583; www.karagoz travel.com; Eski Aynalı Çarşı 4, Kapalı Çarşı Caddesi) English-speaking Uğur runs half-day and full-day tours of Bursa's sights as well as trips further afield that explore nearby towns and villages. These include a tour of Mudanya and Tirilye, and visits to the village of Cumalikizik and mountain nomad villages on the slopes of Uludağ.

Eski Kaplıca   HAMAM
(☑ 0224-233 9309; Eski Kaplıca Sokak; scrub & soak ₺140, massages ₺35; ☺ 7am-10pm) The bath is hewn of marble and the hot rooms have plunge pools at this restored 14th-century hamam, run by the adjacent Kervansaray Termal Hotel on the eastern side of Çekirge. In good news for couples, the ₺140 hamam price is charged for up to two people. Pretty annoying if you're a solo traveller though.

Yeni Kaplıca   HAMAM
(Map p292; ☑ 0224-236 6955; www.yenikaplica. com.tr; Mudanya Caddesi 10; scrub & soak men/ women ₺45/35, massages ₺45; ☺ 5am-11pm) The 'new thermal bath' is actually the city's

oldest, founded by 6th-century Emperor Justinian I, and renovated in 1522 by Süleyman the Magnificent's grand vizier, Rüstem Paşa. There are women-only *kaynarca* (thermal) baths here, and family-oriented baths at the neighbouring Karamustafa Hotel. Yeni Kaplıca is west of Kültür Parkı, signposted downhill from Çekirge Caddesi near Atatürk House.

🛏 Sleeping

City-centre hotels cater mainly to business travellers, leading to higher prices. A few boutique options have opened in heritage buildings. Good budget-style hotels generally have prices that hover just into the low-midrange bracket. Hunt for cheaper sleeps in the streets east of Tahtakale Çarşısı.

For a quieter scene, head uphill (4.5km northwest of Ulu Cami) to the spa suburb of Çekirge.

🛏 Central Bursa (Osmangazi)

Hotel Efehan   BUSINESS HOTEL $
(Map p290; ☑ 0224-225 2260; www.efehan.com.tr; Gümüşçeken Caddesi 34; s/d ₺100/160; ❈ 🛜) The central Efehan offers value, good service and fresh standard rooms, including a dozen family-sized options. The top-floor breakfast hall and bar have city views, but avoid the room up top, which is oddly shaped and poky. Decent English is usually spoken at reception.

★ İpek Yolu   BOUTIQUE HOTEL $$
(Map p290; ☑ 0224-222 5009; www.ipekyolu butikhotel.com; Batpazarı Sokak 12; s/d ₺180/280; ❈🛜) In a quiet but central neighbourhood, several Ottoman-era buildings have been repurposed as a classy boutique hotel. The spacious inner courtyard is perfect for breakfast and for relaxing at the end of the day, while the antique-filled rooms are elegant and stylish. It's a short walk to Bursa's main square and sights.

Safran Otel   BOUTIQUE HOTEL $$
(Map p290; ☑ 0224-224 7216; www.safranotel.com; Kale Sokak 4; s/d ₺260/380; ❈🛜) The Safran occupies an elegant restored Ottoman house in the historic Tophane district, just through the citadel's main gate. Although the building includes a Byzantine wall, the 10 rooms are thoroughly modern affairs. Room 5 is spacious with a good street view and 9 has a large bathroom.

Bursa City Hotel   HOTEL $$
(Map p292; ☑ 0224-221 1875; www.bursacityhotel.com; Durak Caddesi 15; s/d ₺90/180; ❈ 🛜) Run by friendly English- and German-speaking Taner, this hotel sits amid the buzz of Bursa's rabbit warren of markets. Despite the central location, the well-kept, simple rooms are quiet after dark and eating options abound within metres. The architectural splendour of Ulu Cami (p288) is a short stroll away through plenty of shopping opportunities.

★ Kitap Evi   BOUTIQUE HOTEL $$$
(Map p290; ☑ 0224-225 4160; www.kitapevi.com.tr; Burç Üstü 21; s/d from €65/75; ❈🛜) Tucked inside the citadel battlements far above Bursa's minarets and domes, this Ottoman mansion and one-time book bazaar offers 13 individually styled rooms and larger suites (one suite boasts a marble-lined hamam). There's also a gorgeous rear courtyard with fountain where drinks and meals are served. We applaud the free pick-up/drop-off from the BUDO/İDO seaports or Bursa otogar.

🛏 Çekirge

Kadi Konağı   HOTEL $$
(☑ 0224-235 6030; www.kadikonagihotel.com; Cami Aralığı Sokak 2; s/d/tr €30/40/50; ❈🛜) This small family-owned hotel is a great alternative to Çekirge's larger spa hotels. Rooms are relatively compact but stylish and well kept, and there's an on-site hamam that can be booked and used free of charge. Ask for a room with a balcony, and definitely make the short walk to nearby tea gardens for brilliant views of Bursa's impetuous sprawl.

Gönlüferah 1890   HISTORIC HOTEL $$
(☑ 0224-232 1890; www.gonluferah.com; 1 Murat Caddesi; d from ₺360; ❈🛜❈) Dating from 1890, the hilltop Gönlüferah has been a hotel since the early 20th century, and in that time has hosted many a famous guest. It looks the part, with thick carpets and portraits of Bursa's Ottoman forefathers. Rooms range from 'economic' and 'standard', with city or mountain views, to 'Prince' and 'Sultan'.

Cheaper rooms are small, particularly the bathrooms, but continue the opulent tone through plush headboards, dangling lights and minibars featuring wine and spirits.

WORTH A TRIP

BURSA'S GREAT MOUNTAIN

Close to Bursa and İstanbul, Uludağ (Great Mountain; 2543m) is Turkey's favourite ski resort. The resort is 33km from Bursa, and its *teleferik* (cable car) – an attraction in itself – transports visitors and snow-sports fans all the way to the mountain's hotel area and ski slopes.

At 8.2km, the **Uludağ Teleferik** (Uludağ Cable Car; ☑ 444 6345; www.bursateleferik.com. tr/en; Teferrüç İstasyonu 88; adult/student one way ₺35/25, return ₺38/27; ☉10am-6pm) took the mantle as the world's longest cable car when it reopened in mid-2016. The system begins at Teferrüç (236m) before travelling via Kadıyayla (1231m), and continuing to Sarıalan (1635m). At Sarıalan, passengers can disembark and explore teahouses, cook-your-own barbecue restaurants and wooded walking trails before continuing to the terminus station, Oteller (1810m) where Uludağ's hotels and snow-sports infrastructure are located. The entire ascent takes 22 minutes.

In summer you're here for the cable car views and clean, cool air; the resort is dead outside the December-to-March ski season.

Getting There & Away

To the teleferik station Dolmuşes (minibuses with a prescribed route) and buses S/1 and S/2 run from Heykel to the Teferrüç *teleferik* station (₺3, 15 minutes), from where you can ascend by cable car. From the İDO ferry port at Mudanya, bus F/3 travels directly to Teferrüç (₺6, one hour).

To Sarıalan and Oteller Dolmuşes (₺14, one hour) run to the ski resort several times daily in summer (more frequently in winter) from Tophane in Bursa by road via Kadıyayla and Sarıalan. Taxis from Tophane cost about ₺130; in winter you will likely find someone to share the ride with or be able to negotiate the price down. Motorists must pay ₺15 to enter the park at the Uludağ National Park gate, 11km from the resort.

Eating

As well as its nationwide fame as birthplace of the İskender kebap (or Bursa kebap; döner kebap on fresh pide topped with tomato sauce and browned butter), Bursa has a couple of sweet treats to sample. Both *kestane şekeri* (candied chestnuts) and *dondurmalı irmik halvası* (ice cream with warm semolina halva) are sugary specialities of the city.

Head to Sakarya Caddesi to join the locals at its street-side *meyhanes* (taverns), *Türkü evi* (Turkish music bars) and hipster cafes.

Baycan Bey'in Meşhur Kahvesi DESSERTS $

(Map p290; Fidanhan 40, Uzun Çarşı Caddesi; portion ₺7.50; ☉10am-8pm) Swerve off Uzun Çarşı Caddesi into the Fidanhan, built by Sultan Mehmet I's Grand Vizier Mahmut Paşa. This tree-shaded *han* is a tranquil respite from the bustle outside. At the far wall you'll find this cafe, which serves up the delicious and completely addictive Bursa speciality of *dondurmalı irmik halvası* (ice cream with warm semolina halva).

Pervane ANATOLIAN $

(Map p292; 2 Murat Caddesi 28; mains ₺15-25; ☉10.30am-10pm) Come here for lunch after exploring the Muradiye Complex (p290) across the road and dig into homemade Anatolian favourites of *mantı* (Turkish ravioli), *mücver* (vegetable fritters) or *cevizli erişte* (buttery pasta with cheese and walnuts). Sit in the eclectic interior amid 1950s armchairs and pot plants, or outside on the terrace with views over the busy streets below.

Also good for a mid-afternoon cake stop or weekend brunch.

Mahfel CAFE $

(Map p290; Namazgah Caddesi 2; ice cream scoop from ₺8; ☉8am-11pm) With seating overlooking either the ravine or the street-front courtyard, Bursa's oldest cafe is still going strong and thrums with customers day and night. It's known for its *dondurma* (ice cream). Order *bir porsiyon* (one portion) to dig into a veritable sundae.

It's a handy refreshment stop if you're walking from Cumhuriyet Alanı (Republic Sq) up the (gentle) hill to Yeşil Cami and Yeşil Türbe in the Yıldırım neighbourhood.

★ **Kebapçı İskender**   KEBAB **$$**
(Map p290; Ünlü Caddesi 7; İskender portion ₺38; ⊙11am-9pm) If you eat one meal in Bursa, have it here. This refuge for serious carnivores is famous nationwide and is one of two Bursa restaurants claiming to be where the legendary İskender kebap was created in 1867. The other restaurant making the claim is **İskender** (Map p290; Atatürk Caddesi 60; İskender portion ₺37; ⊙11am-5pm).

The wood-panelled interior with tiled pillars and stained-glass windows creates a suitably traditional ambience in which to taste the renowned dish. There's no menu; simply order *bir* (one) or *bir buçuk* (1½) portions.

This is the main branch of a dozen eponymous restaurants around Bursa; the **branch** (Map p290; İc Koza Han; İskender portion ₺38; ⊙11am-9pm) next to the Koza Han (p289) has an atmospheric vaulted setting.

Sakarya Caddesi
Fish Restaurants   SEAFOOD **$$**
(Map p292; off Altıparmak Caddesi; mains ₺25-60; ⊙11am-11pm) In the former Jewish quarter, about a 10-minute walk from Ulu Cami (p288), cobbled Sakarya Caddesi is a busy lane of fish restaurants. Crowds wander between the al-fresco tables, joined by waiters carrying trays of rakı, and the occasional accordion-wielding *fasıl* (gypsy music) band.

Of the two dozen eateries, the best is **Arap Şükrü**, named after its founder, an Independence War hero whose descendents still run it. If it is full, dining next door will likely be equally enjoyable. Be warned that your bill may be higher than you anticipate; many establishments add a cover charge for live music.

ⓘ Getting There & Away

BOAT
The best way to travel between Bursa and İstanbul is by seabus (p296).

BUS
Bursa Terminal (☏0850-850 9916; Yeni Yalova Yolu 8km, Alaşarköy Mahallesi) Bursa's otogar is 11km north of the centre on the Yalova road. Bus-company ticket offices are found throughout the centre, including next to Çakır Ağa Hamamı on Atatürk Caddesi.

City buses leave from the stands at the front of the otogar next to the taxi stand.

City Centre Bus 38 (₺3.50, 45 minutes). Heading to the otogar, wait at the stop on Atatürk Caddesi opposite the *eski belediye* (old town hall). A taxi costs ₺40.

Çekirge Bus 96 (₺3.50, one hour). A taxi is around ₺50.

A tram line is currently being built between the otogar and the city centre, which will make transport to/from town faster and more convenient.

ⓘ Getting Around

Bursa's transport website (www.burulas.com.tr) has plenty of information (in Turkish) about transport in and around Bursa.

Buy a Bursakart (rechargeable transport card; ₺10 including ₺4 credit) if you want to use Bursa's metro, city bus and tram network. Cards and top-up credit are available from automatic machines (with English instructions) at metro stops and other major transport stops.

SERVICES FROM BURSA OTOGAR

DESTINATION	FARE (₺)	DURATION (HR)	FREQUENCY
Afyon	40-55	4-5	hourly morning, 2 afternoon, 6 evening
Ankara	75-89	5¼-6½	every 30 minutes
Bandırma	20-25	1½-2	hourly
Çanakkale	45-60	3¾-4¼	hourly
Denizli	90-108	8½-9	3 morning, 4 afternoon, 4 evening
Eskişehir	35-45	2½	every 30 minutes
İstanbul	60	3-4½	every 30 minutes
İzmir	65-70	5½-6	every 30 minutes
İznik	15	1½	every 30 minutes
Kütahya	35-40	2½-3¾	3 morning, 3 afternoon, 4 evening

BUS

City buses have their destinations and stops visible. Journeys cost between ₺1.75 and ₺3.50. You pay by tapping your Bursakart on the machine beside the driver at the front of the bus. Stops line Atatürk Caddesi opposite Koza Parkı and the *eski belediye*. Bus 1/C is useful, running around the city centre from Heykel to Çekirge via Atatürk Caddesi.

DOLMUŞ

City Centre Taksi dolmuşes (Map p290) (shared taxis), their destinations indicated by an illuminated rooftop sign, are the same price as city buses but faster and more frequent, especially to Çekirge. The most useful route around the city centre runs anticlockwise from Cumhuriyet Alanı (Heykel) up İnönü Caddesi to Kent Meydanı and along Çekirge Caddesi to Çekirge, returning via Altıparmak, Cemal Nadir and Atatürk Caddesi. Drivers pick up and drop off all along the route. There is also a rank on the eastern side of the Setbaşı road bridge, from where *taksi dolmuşes* follow a similar route to Çekirge.

METRO & TRAM

The metro (₺2.55) runs every eight to 12 minutes between 6am and midnight. The closest station to the city centre is Şehreküstü, near the Kapalı Çarşı, and around 500m north of Atatürk Caddesi.

Tram rides cost ₺1.40. You need a Bursakart.

Green Tram This heritage-style tram runs from Zafer Plaza, along Cumhuriyet Caddesi and east to Çınarönü.

Red tram Runs a circular route edging the city centre, running along Atatürk Caddesi, past the Ulu Cami and Cumhuriyet Alanı (Heykel), up to and along Haşim İscam Caddesi and around to the Kültür Parkı.

A third tram line out to the otogar is being constructed.

Mudanya

☑ 0224 / POP 93,700

Mudanya is a lively seaside town most known for its İstanbul ferry. Strategically set on the Sea of Marmara, it is where the Armistice of Moudania was signed by Italy, France, Britain and Turkey on 11 October 1922 (Greece reluctantly signed three days later). Under the agreement, all lands from Edirne eastward, including İstanbul and the Dardanelles, became Turkish. The whitewashed 19th-century dwelling where the treaty was signed houses a **museum** (Mudanya Armistice House Museum; Mütareke Meydanı; ₺5; ⊙ 8-11am & 1-6pm Tue-Sun) of historic Armistice-related photos.

★**Armistis Hotel** BOUTIQUE HOTEL **$$**
(☑ 0224-544 6680; www.armistishotel.com.tr; Ünlü Sokak 7; s/d ₺200/240; ❋ ☎) With a brilliant location one block from the waterfront, the Armistis is a charming boutique collection of 16 rooms in a restored Ottoman heritage building. Attention to detail in the rooms is excellent – look forward to superior bed linen and high-end bathroom products – and a cosmopolitan and international vibe is enhanced by the multilingual team at reception.

🛈 Getting There & Away

BUDO (Bursa Deniz Otobüsleri, Bursa Sea Buses; https://budo.burulas.com.tr) ferries link İstanbul Eminönü with Mudanya (₺40, two hours, six to eight ferries daily). BUDO also operates a summer Mudanya–Tekirdağ service. There is a helpful ticket and information booth near the ferry terminal for good advice on the best options to get to Bursa.

To Bursa Yellow bus 1/M runs from Mudanya BUDO ferry terminal to Bursa's Emek metro station (₺4, 25 minutes, three times per hour between 7am and 10pm). From there you can continue to Şehreküstü metro station, the closest station to the city centre, just north of Kapalı Çarşı. You will need a Bursakart (₺6) to use both the 1/M bus and the Bursa metro. Purchase and/or top up your card at an orange ticket machine at the BUDO information booth.

Alternatively catch a Bursa-bound dolmuş (₺4, every 30 minutes) from the dolmuş stand on İpar Sokak, one block inland from the BUDO terminal. These also drop you at Bursa's Emek metro station.

For other destinations, catch bus F/1 from the ferry terminal to the Bursa otogar (₺4, hourly).

From Bursa to Mudanya Catch the 1/M bus (₺4, 25 minutes, three every hour between 6.30am and 11pm) from the signed BUDO bus stand next to Emek metro station or a Mudanya-bound dolmuş from the dolmuş car park next to Organize Sanayi metro station (two stops before Emek).

İDO (İstanbul Deniz Otobüsleri, İstanbul Sea Buses; www.ido.com.tr) Ferries link İstanbul Yenikapı and Kadıköy with Güzelyalı (₺39, 2¼ hours), 4km east of Mudanya ferry terminal. Bus 1/G links Güzelyalı to Bursa's Emek metro station, from where you can connect to central Bursa.

Eskişehir

☑ 0222 / POP 720,100

With its massive university population, Eskişehir is one of Turkey's liveliest and most youthful cities. An oasis of liberalism in austere middle Anatolia, its progressive spirit is associated with mayor Yılmaz Büyükerşen, who realised the potential of the city's Porsuk River, adding walking bridges and a sand beach while building pedestrian thoroughfares and a smoothly efficient tram system. In summer you can even explore the Porsuk by gondola or boat.

The cumulative result is a liveable city with a roaring nightlife, thriving coffee scene, plenty of green spaces and a small old quarter. To be fair, as far as sights go there isn't a lot to see, though the 2019 opening of the Odunpazarı Modern Museum has now marked Eskişehir as a must-do destination for contemporary art. And if you've been travelling in Turkey for a while and are desperately in need of a flat white, don't miss a stop here.

◉ Sights

★Odunpazarı Modern Museum   GALLERY
(OMM; www.omm.art; Atatürk Bulvarı 37; adult/student ₺20/12; ⊙10am-6pm Tue, Thu-Sat, to 8pm Wed, 11am-6pm Sun) This ambitious art museum, with its highly contemporary woodslat facade riffing on Eskişehir's history as a major wood-market town, opened in 2019. Founded to showcase construction magnate Erol Tabanca's significant modern art collection, the galleries focus on works by Turkish artists such as Burhan Doğançay, Azade Köker and Taner Ceylan. It also features international names such as Japanese artist Tanabe Chikuunsai IV, whose huge installation, which twists from wall to floor in one gallery, was created specifically for the museum.

★Odunpazarı   AREA
(Ottoman Quarter) Eskişehir's protected heritage district is crammed with cobblestone alleyways of timber-framed konaks (mansions) with overhanging upper stories. Many of the creaky pastel-shaded houses contain small museums, craft shops and cafes and on weekends day-tripping Turks head here to stroll the lanes, browse the stalls and sit in the shady cafes supping çay. This was Eskişehir's first Turkish district, and it features Ottoman and even Seljuk structures. Odun means 'firewood' (the area was once a firewood bazaar).

To get to Odunpazarı from central Eskişehir, catch the EStram to the Atatürk Lisesi stop, or it's around a 2.5km walk southeast of the Porsuk River.

Kurşunlu Külliyesi Complex   HISTORIC SITE
(Mücellit Sokak, Odunpazarı; ⊙8am-10pm) FREE This religious complex, once used as a Mevlevi lodge by Eskişehir's Sufi community, was built between 1517 and 1525 by a leading master of classical Ottoman architecture, Acem Ali (although internal structures were built and rebuilt in following centuries).

Inside, the Kurşunlu Mosque, with its kurşunlu (leaden) dome, is centre stage. Head inside to see the prayer hall's painted mihrab (niche indicating the direction of Mecca).

Archaeological Museum   MUSEUM
(Atatürk Bulvarı; ₺6; ⊙8am-6.30pm) This modern museum showcases artefacts from the Chalcolithic era to Ottoman times. Downstairs is devoted to bigger pieces such as sarcophagi, milestones and floor mosaics. Upstairs, exhibits walk you through the region's history using finds from local archaeological sites with particularly beautiful collections of Bronze Age and Roman goddess idols on display. The statuary dotting the garden outside is well worth a browse and the attached cafe (www.facebook.com/muzedecafe; Müze Sokak; mains ₺12-42; ⊙8am-midnight) is a popular spot for lunch or a çay stop. Last ticket sales are 4.30pm from November to March.

🛏 Sleeping

İbis Hotel   BUSINESS HOTEL $$
(📞0222-211 7700; www.ibishotel.com; Siloönü Sokak 5; r weekdays/weekends ₺169/199; 🅿❄🛜) Resembling a salmon-coloured Flatiron Building, the İbis has six floors of slightly dated but good-sized rooms jazzed up with orange accents and light-coloured wood. Corner rooms are the most spacious. It's just steps to both the train station and Espark tram station, and the service is smooth like the saxophone-shaped beer tap in the muzak-infused bar.

Abacı Konak Otel   HERITAGE HOTEL $$
(📞0222-333 0333; www.abaciotel.com; Türkmen Hoca Sokak 29; s/d ₺180/270; ❄🛜) With its pastel-toned konaks clustered around a flowering, fountain-filled courtyard, Abacı Konak is like your own personal Ottoman quarter. In the rooms, the original dark wood ceilings and creaky floors have been preserved and enhanced by subtle vintage furnishings. Bathrooms are on the small side though and could do with an update.

Senna City Hotel
HOTEL **$$**

(☑ 0222-333 0505; www.sennacity.com; Adalar Sokak 1; r ₺210-310; ❋ 🕾) The bright, spacious rooms, decked out in shades of grey, and its location, right amid the river cafe district, make Senna City a top choice if you want to check out Eskişehir's youthful vibe. The breakfast buffet is excellent and staff are on the ball. The closest tram stop is Çarşı.

Arus Hotel
HOTEL **$$**

(☑ 0222-233 0101; www.arusotel.com; Oğuz Sokak 1; s ₺150, d ₺200-250; ❋ 🕾) Within easy walking distance from both the train station and Espark tram stop, as well as bars, cafes and restaurants, the central Arus offers small, modern beige-toned rooms and one of the city's best breakfast buffets.

OMM Inn
DESIGN HOTEL **$$$**

(☑ 0222-220 0646; www.omminn.com; Turkmen Hoca Sokak 15; r from €75; P ❋ 🕾) Next door to the Odunpazarı Modern Museum (p297), Eskişehir's newest hotel is this style-focused boutique option. Part contemporary new build and part restored Ottoman building, the OMM shrugs off the typical Turkish aesthetic in its 12 very spacious rooms, instead using sleek minimalist design with all the mod cons and comforts.

🍴 Eating

Eskişehir's vast restaurant scene caters to its university students. Cheap eats abound, with numerous snack bars tempting people in with meal deals.

Kırım Tatar Kültür Çibörek Evi
ANATOLIAN **$**

(Şemsettin Sokak 15, Odunpazarı; portion ₺10; ⊙ 10am-10pm) *Çibörek* (deep-fried turnovers filled with mincemeat) is the local version of the Crimean Tartar *chebureki*. During the 18th and 19th centuries, Crimean Tartars emigrated in substantial numbers here and as well as absorbing the community, the city adopted this as its favourite snack. A portion of three of these oily, puffed-up pastries makes for a filling – though not particularly healthy – lunch. Look for the green house, a few metres further down the lane after the main entrance into the Kurşunlu Külliyesi Complex (p297).

★Mezze
SEAFOOD **$$**

(☑ 0222-230 3009; www.mezzebalik.com; Nazım Hikmet Sokak 2, Kızılcıklı Mahmut Pehlivan Caddesi; mezes ₺14-20, mains ₺28-65; ⊙ 4pm-1am) Aegean-style feasting in deep Anatolia. The shared plates and seafood here brings to mind lazy lunches along Turkey's western coastline. Choose your fish, then sit back on the white terrace with your rakı while savouring a selection of flavourful meze dishes.

Ask up front for the approximate cost of the various fish to avoid surprises at the end of your meal.

Dublin Cafe
BISTRO **$$**

(www.facebook.com/dublineskisehir; Siloönü Sokak 5; mains ₺24-59; ⊙ 11am-2am; 🕾) Most of Eskişehir's bar-restaurants churn out mediocre pizza, burgers and grilled meat plates by the bucket-load, but Dublin's versions of international favourites and Turkish grill staples are a step above everyone else's. In warm weather its grassy inner courtyard is the place to be, while during cooler months the outer halo of undercover seating is sheltered and welcoming.

The beer menu goes beyond Efes and Bomonti with Leffe and other European beers available, service is excellent and when we last stopped by the music was some of the best we've heard anywhere in Anatolia.

🍷 Drinking & Entertainment

Fuelled by its student population, Eskişehir has a lively after-dark scene. Vural Sokak, known as Barlar Sokak (Bar Street), is a well-oiled lane where shot bars, theme bars, DJ bars, *meyhanes* (Turkish taverns) and clubs jostle for attention. For travellers needing a break from Turkey's instant coffee obsession, Eskişehir's cafes serve up the best espresso-based coffees in the country.

★Black Cat Coffee & Roastery
COFFEE

(www.facebook.com/pages/Black-Cat-Coffee; Baydemir Sokak 2; ⊙ 10am-11.30pm) The best cup of coffee you'll get in Turkey. This is serious coffee-nerd territory complete with a vintage-meets-contemporary interior vibe and baristas who really know what they're doing. Order up your flat white or cortado, sit out at the pavement tables watching the world go by, and enjoy caffeine bliss.

Travelers Cafe
PUB

(www.travelerscafe.com.tr; Porsuk Bulvarı 7; ⊙ 8am-2am) Grandstand views of the Poruk River and loads of travel memorabilia from around the planet are fine reasons to come here, but the addition of some of Eskişehir's cheapest and coldest brews and budget meals make it loads of fun and a thoroughly unpretentious destination to meet a few friendly locals and Turkish students.

Eskişehir Municipal Symphony Orchestra
LIVE MUSIC

(Eskişehir Büyükşehir Belediyesi Senfoni Orkestrası; ☑ 0222-211 5500; http://senfoni.eskisehir.bel.tr; İsmail Gaspıralı Caddesi 1) Eskişehir's symphony orchestra is one of Turkey's best, and offers weekly concerts for an enthusiastic local audience. It also provides backup for operas and ballets. Works performed here run the gamut from classical masterpieces to modern musicals, plus kids' shows. The orchestra tours widely abroad and cooperates with visiting musicians, too.

❶ Getting There & Away

BUS

Eskişehir Otogar (Sivrihisar 2 Caddesi) is 3km east of the central city. It's linked to central Eskişehir by tram routes 1 and 4 and city buses. A taxi from the centre costs around ₺20.

Regular buses serve the following:

Afyon (₺33-45, three hours, four morning and four afternoon)

Ankara (₺35-48, 2¾ to four hours, hourly at least)

Bursa (₺30-45, 2½ to 3½ hours, hourly at least)

İstanbul (₺70-80, 5½ to six hours, every one to two hours)

Kütahya (₺15-20, 1¼ hours, every one to two hours)

TRAIN

Eskişehir Train Station (Eskişehir YHT Gar; http://tcdd.gov.tr; İstasyon Caddesi) is northwest of the centre near Espark tram stop. If you don't have heavy luggage it's within walking distance of city centre accommodation.

High-speed (YHT) trains run to/from the following:

Ankara (₺31, 1½ hours, 14 daily)

İstanbul (₺46, three hours, 11 daily) Söğütlüçeşme is the most useful İstanbul station to get off at.

Konya (₺39.50, 1¾ hours, 10.43am, 4.02pm and 9.58pm)

There are also daily regular train services to:

Denizli (*Pamukkale Ekspresi;* ₺36, 8½ hours, 10.25am)

İzmir (*İzmir Mavi Treni;* ₺39, 11½ hours, 10.06pm)

❶ Getting Around

Prepaid single-use tickets (₺3.50) for trams and buses are available at green kiosks by larger tram stops (including the otogar) and *bakkals* (small grocery stores) displaying the green-and-yellow circular Es Karti sign. Dolmuş journeys cost ₺2 and you pay the driver.

Trams on the ESTram network run between 6am and midnight; the normal waiting time is about 10 minutes. Tram 1, which runs from the otogar and through the central city stops of Çarşı, İsmit İnönü and Espark (the nearest tram stop to the train station), is the most useful tram route for visitors. Trams display their final destination at the front, but it can be confusing to identify which tram is which at certain crossover stops, so ask if unsure.

Taxis are plentiful, and there are electronic signal buttons on some street-corner posts that you can press to hail one.

Phrygian Valley

Anatolia's mysterious ancient Phrygians once inhabited this rock-hewn valley (Frig Vadisi), which runs haphazardly past Eskişehir, Kütahya and Afyon. Although an increasingly popular hiking destination, it is still relatively untouched and offers spectacular Phrygian relics. The rugged terrain is exhilarating and highly photogenic. The Afyon-area ruins are the best preserved and the Eskişehir-area ruins also impress; Kütahya's are less abundant.

◉ Sights

Most sites are along dirt tracks and some can be very hard to find, even when you're right beside them. Navigation is slowly getting better as local municipalities are paving a 'Tourist Route' through the region.

◉ Eskişehir Ruins

As you travel from Seyitgazi to Afyon through **Yazılıkaya Vadisi** (Inscribed Rock Valley), turn south after 3km, down a road marked with a brown sign pointing to Midas Şehri. Further along this rough road a sign leads you right for 2km to the **Doğankale** (Falcon Castle) and **Deveboyukale** (Camel Height Castle), both riddled with formerly inhabited caves.

Further south, another rough track leads 1km to the **Mezar Anıtı** (Monumental Tomb), and a restored, rock-carved tomb. Continuing south again, you will find another temple-like tomb, **Küçük Yazılıkaya** (Little Inscribed Rock).

Midas Şehri (Midas City; ◷ 8am-6.30pm) FREE is at Yazılıkaya village, several kilometres from Küçük Yazılıkaya and 32km south of Seyitgazi. This is the most

WESTERN ANATOLIA AFYON

important, and most impressive, Phrygian site in the area. The site guardian usually has good brochures with a map of the Yazılıkaya site that will aid your exploring – though the paths here can be confusing even with this aid. The major monument is the **Midas Türbe** (Midas Tomb) with its carved 17m-high relief. Surrounding the tomb you'll spot Phrygian-alphabet inscriptions.

A path behind the tomb leading to a tunnel passes a **smaller tomb**, unfinished and high in the rock. Continue upwards to the high mound, where an **acropolis** once stood. The stepped **altar stone**, possibly used for sacrifices, remains, along with traces of walls and roads. Interestingly the first evidence of water collection comes from here – carved holes were found with slatted steps that trapped rainwater for the dry season.

⊙ Afyon Ruins

Afyon-area ruins include examples from Phrygian up to Turkish times. Start your exploration in Doğer, around 50km north of Afyon. Head north on the D665 en route to Eskişehir, and turn left at Gazlıgöl after 22km. Doğer village's **han** dates to 1434 (if it is locked, ask for the key at the municipal building opposite). From here, tracks lead to lily-covered **Emre Gölü** (Lake Emre), which is overlooked by a small stone building once used by dervishes and a rock formation with a rough staircase, the **Kirkmerdiven Kayalıkları** (Rocky Place with 40 Stairs). The track then continues 4km to **Bayramaliler** and Üçlerkayası, which feature rock

formations called *peribacalar* (fairy chimneys), resembling Cappadocia's.

After Bayramaliler, **Göynüş Vadisi** (Göynüş Valley) is a 2km walk from the Eskişehir–Afyon road; it has fine Phrygian rock tombs decorated with lions.

At Ayazini village – turn right off the D665 around 9km north of Gazlıgöl – there once stood a rock settlement, **Metropolis**, also reminiscent of Cappadocia. The apse and dome of its Byzantine **church** are hewn from the rock face, and several rock-cut **tombs** have carvings of lions, suns and moons.

Around Alanyurt, east of Ayazini, more caves exist at **Selimiye**, and there are further fairy chimneys to discover at Kurtyurdu, Karakaya, Seydiler and İscehisar, including the bunker-like rock **Seydiler Kalesi** (Seydiler Castle).

❶ Getting There & Away

The easiest way to explore the ruins is by rental car; try **Europcar** (☑0222-231 0182; www.europcar.com.tr; Kızılcıklı Mahmut Pehlivan Caddesi 22/B; 1 day rental from €35; ☉8.30am-7pm) in Eskişehir. Between October and April, heavy rain sometimes renders the area's back roads impassable.

Visiting the ruins by public transport is difficult, but there are dolmuşes to the villages from Afyon otogar. Regular buses and dolmuşes on the main roads between Eskişehir, Kütahya and Afyon will also pick up from the roadside, so if you start early, it may be possible to visit a few sites in a day.

From Afyon, dolmuşes serve Ayazini (on the Afyon–Eskişehir road). From the church drop-off, walk 500m to find the Metropolis rock settlement. To continue to Doğer, take the dolmuş back towards Afyon, but disembark at Gazlıgöl and pick up a dolmuş heading northwest.

Afyon

☑0272 / POP 299.670

This provincial city sprawls out below craggy castle remnants that perch atop a vertiginous rock. Everyone from the Hittites to Ottomans have stomped through, but the local claim to fame is that Atatürk briefly made this his headquarters before routing the Greeks in the 1922 Battle of Dumlupınar during the War of Independence. Despite this long history, Central Afyon (Afyonkarahisar) comes across as a rather humdrum place at first glance, but it's hiding a couple of surprises up its sleeve. Puff your way up to the castle for eagle-eye views, admire the fine carving details inside the Ulu Cami and then ramble through the Ottoman quarter alleys of timber-framed houses decked out in sweet-shop pastel hues for a fun afternoon.

👁 Sights

Ulu Cami
MOSQUE

(Grand Mosque; Ulu Cami Cadessi; ⊙10am-6pm) Among the most important surviving Seljuk mosques in Turkey, the Ulu Cami (1273) is supported by 40 fat, soaring wooden columns with intricate stalactite capitals and features a flat-beamed roof. Outside, local green tiles decorate the minaret.

The mosque should be open for visiting daily between 10am and 6pm (excluding prayer times), but occasionally it's locked. To make sure you can gain access, arrive just after prayers have finished. It's located right under the castle in the old town.

Afyon Castle
CASTLE

(Afyon Kalesi; Kale Sokak; FREE) This *kale* or *hisar* overlooks Afyon from a craggy rock. The strenuous approach up a steep but well-maintained set of stairs passes Ottoman guard towers on what was once a formidable defensive structure. Hittite King Mursilis II built the first castle here, c 1350 BC. Since then, various rulers have restored the original *kara hisar* (black fortress) – most recently the Turkish government, with unorthodox white masonry. The path is signposted opposite the Ulu Cami.

Old Town
AREA

The hilly cobbled streets that radiate out around the Ulu Cami are chock-a-block with a liquorice allsorts selection of colourful Ottoman timber-framed houses, some serving as teahouses and restaurants. Sunset is the best time to explore this area, when the shadows lengthen and families are strolling around their neighbourhood. Unlike some overly restored old-town neighbourhoods in Turkey, Afyon's heritage area combines renovation and renewal with its original grittier ambience.

🛏 Sleeping & Eating

Hotel Soydan
HOTEL $$

(☑0272-215 2323; www.soydanhotel.com; Karagözoğlu Sokak 2; s/d from ₺120/200; 🕸🛜) Amid the bustling heart of Afyon, the Soydan is a solid, typical provincial hotel choice. The 36 rooms are all comfortable, but see if you can score one of the more spacious rooms that overlook both Afyon's main drag, Birlik Caddesi, and the castle.

İkbal
ANATOLIAN $$

(Millet Caddesi 19/A; mains ₺15-40; 🍴) In business since 1922, the original owner of this *lokanta* cooked for Atatürk on his 1934 Afyon visit. Adventurous eaters should opt for the *ciğer sarma* (liver and rice, wrapped in caul fat) and there's a decent selection for upping your vegetable content including *taze fasulye* (green beans) and *patlıcan biber kızartma* (fried aubergine and peppers).

ℹ Getting There & Around

Afyon Otogar (off Afyon–Çevre Yolu) is, annoyingly, 6km west of the central city. To get into town a taxi will cost you ₺30. Dolmuşes (₺2, every 20 minutes) run from in front of the otogar and down Birlik Caddesi, the main road.

Denizli

This prosperous, spread-out city is the jumping-off point for heading to Pamukkale and the overgrown and lesser-visited ruins of Laodicea and Afrodisias. Most travellers don't stay. Instead, it's used as a transport hub by travellers heading into the surrounding countryside.

ℹ Getting There & Away

AIR

Denizli Çardak Airport (Denizli Çardak Havalimanı, DNZ; https://cardak.dhmi.gov.tr; Denizli–Afyon Yolu, Çardak) is around 60km east of Denizli so isn't particularly convenient. Turkish Airlines (www.turkishairlines.com) has daily connections to Denizli from İstanbul. Pegasus Airlines (www.flypgs.com) arrives from İstanbul's Sabiha Gökçen airport.

Airport buses are operated by **Baytur** (☑444 2807; www.bayturbilet.com). It has bus services to and from central Denizli (₺25, 45 minutes) for all scheduled flights. Various tour companies in Pamukkale operate airport shuttles (€10, one hour). It's easiest to book an airport transfer through your hotel.

BUS

Denizli Otogar (İzmir Bulvarı) is a supermodern, well organised regional hub with departures heading around the country. Long-distance buses depart from the ground floor. Local dolmuş transport, including to Pamukkale, departs from the basement level. Head down the escalator to platform 76 for the Pamukkale dolmuş.

TRAIN

Denizli Train Station (Denizli Garı; http://tcdd.gov.tr; İzmir Bulvarı) is opposite Denizli

Otogar, making it exceedingly easy to transfer between your train and the dolmuş service to Pamukkale.

The *Pamukkale Ekspresi* (₺36, 8½ hours) travels daily between Denizli and Eskişehir. Heading to Denizli it leaves Eskişehir train station at 10.25am. From Denizli it departs at 7.50am.

There are also six trains daily between İzmir and Denizli (₺28.50, 4¾ hours). These local trains are sometimes cancelled due to line upgrade work so check the current situation at the train station.

Pamukkale

☎ 0258 / POP 2020

Pamukkale has been made eternally famous by the gleaming white calcite travertines (terraces) overrunning with warm, mineral-rich waters on the mountain above the village – the so-called 'Cotton Castle' (*pamuk* means 'cotton' in Turkish). Just above the travertines lie the rambling ruins of Hierapolis, once a Roman and Byzantine spa city.

Unesco World Heritage status has brought measures to protect the glistening bluffs and put paid to the days of freely traipsing around, but walking down the travertines remains one of Turkey's singular experiences.

While the photogenic travertines get busloads of day-trippers passing through for a quick soak and selfie op, staying overnight allows you to visit the site at sunset and dodge some of the crowds. This also allows time for a day trip to the beautiful and little-visited ancient ruins of Afrodisias and Laodicea and to appreciate the village of Pamukkale itself.

◉ Sights

★ **Travertines** NATURE RESERVE
(adult/child incl Hierapolis ₺50/free; ⊙ 8am-9pm mid-Apr–Sep, 8.30am-5pm Oct–mid-Apr) The World Heritage–listed saucer-shaped travertines of Pamukkale wind sideways down the powder-white mountain above the village, providing a stunning contrast to the clear blue sky and green plains below. To protect

---

LOCAL KNOWLEDGE

NAVIGATING PAMUKKALE

Pamukkale is a dedicated tourist town around Cumhuriyet Meydanı, but in quieter parts of the village life is still soundtracked by clucking chickens and birdsong. Pamukkale's double attractions – the shimmering white travertines and the adjacent ruins of ancient Hierapolis – are a package deal. Both are accessed on the same ticket and comprise their own national park, located on a whitewashed hill right above Pamukkale village.

Of the site's three entrances, the **south gate** (⊙ 6am-9pm) is most practical. It is about 2.5km from Pamukkale, on the hill near Hierapolis' main sights, meaning you see both Hierapolis and the travertines while walking downwards, exiting through the middle gate and finishing in the village. This is the gate most tour groups use.

To dodge the crowds, use the **north gate** (⊙ 8am-8pm) about 3km away, allowing you to enter Hierapolis via the necropolis and Frontinus St and, likewise, walk downhill to the village. Both gates are uphill from Pamukkale. You can access the north gate by dolmuş (minibus with a prescribed route). Otherwise, grab a taxi or a free lift provided by your accommodation rather than walking; Hierapolis and the travertines comprise a large site, so save your energy.

The **middle gate** (⊙ 8am-8pm Apr-Oct, to 5pm Nov-Mar), on the edge of Pamukkale itself, is at the base of the terraced mountain, meaning you walk uphill over the travertines to Hierapolis and either take the same route back to the village – not a logical route, but it does offer two looks at the travertines – or exit via the north gate and flag down the dolmuş to Pamukkale as it goes past. If you are just after a little R&R in the pools, this is the quickest and easiest entrance.

Note the various opening times of the entrance gates; you can exit when you like. Tickets are only good for one entry so you must see the site in one go. Nevertheless, you can stay inside as long as you like, and for most people a single visit is enough; pensions are generally happy to make a picnic lunch so you can take your time and enjoy an all-day visit. Additional fees apply for the Hierapolis Archaeology Museum (p304) and Antique Pool (p305).

the unique calcite surface that overruns with warm, mineral-rich waters, guards oblige you to go barefoot (or in socks or shower shoes), so if you're planning to walk down to the village via the travertines, be prepared to carry your shoes with you.

Although the ridges look rough, in reality the constant water flow keeps the ground mostly smooth, even gooey in places, and the risk of slipping is greater than that of cutting your feet. To walk straight down without stopping takes about 30 minutes. The constant downward motion can be hard on the knees.

Although the terrace pools are not particularly deep, you can get fully submerged in the thermal water. There is a gushing channel of warm water at the top of the path down through the travertines, where representatives of many nations sit and give their legs a good soak. If you do not have a bathing suit or shorts, or otherwise do not wish to get too wet, note that although there are usually many dry sections leading down, the amount of pools (up to calf-height) you have to wade through depends on the time of year. Also note that midday to 4pm means crowds and sharp sunlight reflecting off the dazzling white surface; early morning or sunset is better.

★ **Hierapolis** ARCHAEOLOGICAL SITE
(adult/child incl travertines ₺50/free; ⊙ 8am-9pm)
This ancient spa city's location atop Pamukkale's tourist-magnet travertines is quite spectacular. Founded as a curative centre around 190 BC by Eumenes II of Pergamum, it prospered under both the Romans and Byzantines, when large Jewish and Orthodox Christian communities comprised most of the population. Recurrent earthquakes brought disaster, and Hierapolis was finally abandoned after an AD 1334 tremor. When visiting, don't miss the Roman Theatre, the agora and the on-site museum. From mid-October to March, last tickets are 5pm.

➡ **Byzantine Gate to the Martyrium of St Philip the Apostle**
Entering at the south gate, walk through the 5th-century **Byzantine gate**, built of travertine blocks and marble among other materials, and pass the Doric columns of the 1st-century **gymnasium**. An important building in health-oriented Hierapolis, it collapsed in a 7th-century earthquake. Continue straight on for the foundations of the **Temple of Apollo**. As at Didyma and

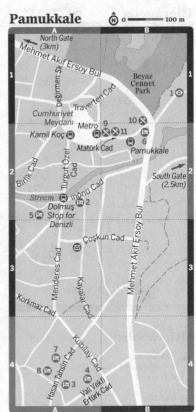

Pamukkale

⊙ **Sights**
1 Middle Gate...B1

🛌 **Sleeping**
2 Beyaz Kale Pension................................A2
3 Hotel Dört Mevsim..............................A4
4 Melrose House.....................................A4
5 Melrose Viewpoint..............................A2
6 Mustafa Hotel......................................B2
7 Venus Hotel..A4
8 Venus Suite Hotel...............................A4

🍴 **Eating**
9 Kayaş..B2
10 Mehmet's Heaven.............................B1
11 White House.......................................B2

Delphi, eunuch priests tended the temple's oracle. Its alleged power derived from an adjoining spring, the Plutonium (named after the underworld god Pluto). Apparently

Hierapolis

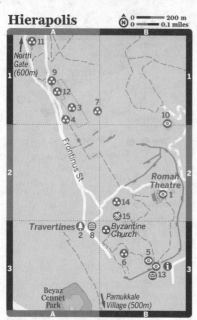

N 0 ——— 200 m
0 ——— 0.1 miles

Hierapolis

only the priests understood the secret of holding one's breath around the toxic fumes that billowed up from Hades, immediately killing the small animals and birds they sacrificed.

The spectacular **Roman Theatre**, built in stages by emperors Hadrian and Septimius Severus, could seat more than 12,000 spectators. The stage mostly survives, along

with some decorative panels and the front-row VIP 'box' seats.

From the theatre, tracks lead uphill and to the left towards the less-visited but fascinating **Martyrium of St Philip the Apostle**, an intricate octagonal structure on terrain where St Philip was supposedly martyred.

➜ Hellenistic Theatre to Frontinus Street

From the Martyrium, a rough path that gives fantastic views of the site and the plains beyond leads west across the hillside to the completely ruined **Hellenistic Theatre**, above the 2nd-century **agora**. One of the largest ever discovered, the agora was surrounded by marble porticoes with Ionic columns on three sides, and enclosed by a basilica on the fourth.

From the theatre, follow the steep overgrown diagonal path towards the poplars to reach the agora (alternatively, backtrack to the Martyrium of St Philip the Apostle for an easier path down). Walking downhill through the agora, you will re-emerge on the ridgeline main path. Turn right on colonnaded **Frontinus Street**, where some original paving and columns remain. Monumental archways once bounded both ends of what was the city's main commercial thoroughfare. The ruined **Arch of Domitian** is at the southern end; just before this is Hierapolis' large **latrine** building.

➜ Necropolis

Beyond the Arch of Domitian are the ruined **Roman Baths**, and further past these, an Appian Way–style paved road leads to the north gate passing through an extraordinary **necropolis**, which extends up the hills. The tombs range from circular tumulus-style to ornate double-storey sarcophagi.

➜ Hierapolis Archaeology Museum

Housed in former Roman baths, this excellent **museum** (adult/child ₺7/free; ⊙8.30am–6.45pm) exhibits spectacular sarcophagi from nearby archaeological site Laodicea (p308) and elsewhere; small finds include jewellery, oil lamps and stamp seals from Hierapolis (p303) and around; and in the third room, with its massive vaulted ceiling and entrance watched by a sphinx, there are friezes and Roman-era statuary from the Roman theatre. Left of the entrance are impressive capitals from Hierapolis' agora and other parts of the site. Closing is 4.45pm from November to March.

🏃 Activities

Ballooning and paragliding are growing in popularity in the skies over Pamukkale, and offer a bird's-eye view of Hierapolis and the travertines. Shop around; ask to see operators' credentials and check they are fully insured, for your personal safety as much as the good of your wallet. Ballooning in particular may only operate during the peak tourist season.

Antique Pool   SWIMMING
(Hierapolis; adult/child under 6yr/6-12yr ₺50/free/20; ⊗8am-8.30pm) There has been a pool at this spa site since ancient times. Bring a swimsuit and experience the modern version, which features a mostly shallow pool where guests can relax while lounging against submerged sections of ancient marble columns. The waters, which are abundant in minerals and a more-than-balmy 36°C, have long been thought to have restorative powers.

Entrance is free to the poolside area, which includes two cafes and a tree-shaded picnic area. You only pay a fee to enter the water. In summer the spa is busiest from 11am to 4pm. Outside of peak summer, the Antique Pool site has earlier closing hours: at 5.30pm from mid-September to March, and at 7.30pm from April to May.

🛏️ Sleeping

Pamukkale's pensions and small hotels are split between the bustling centre and the rustic lanes on the village's south side. Stiff competition translates into good service. Most places offer free transport to the Hierapolis gates; the better ones also offer a pool, a restaurant and tour-booking services. Book ahead in July and August. Outside of summer, room rates drop substantially.

Mustafa Hotel   PENSION $
(☑0258-272 2240; mustafamotel@hotmail.com; Atatürk Caddesi 22; s/d/tr ₺100/120/140; ❄️🛜) Simple spotless rooms, a rooftop licensed restaurant and a location slap in the heart of the village make Mustafa Pamukkale's most popular budget digs.

★Melrose House   HOTEL $$
(☑0258-272 2250; www.melrosehousehotel.com; Vali Vekfi Ertürk Caddesi 8; s/d/tr/q/f €25/28/37/47/55; ❄️🛜🏊) The closest thing to a boutique hotel in Pamukkale, Melrose House has 17 spacious, modern rooms (some with balconies) including a family room

and two suites with circular beds. Decor throughout is eclectic, mixing bright sateen bedspreads with pillars, wallpaper and exposed stonework. The poolside restaurant is a peaceful place to linger. Owners Mehmet and Ummu are a helpful and refreshingly impartial source of local info.

Beyaz Kale Pension   PENSION $$
(☑0258-272 2064; www.beyazkalepension.com; Oguzkaan Caddesi 4; s/d/f €25/30/60; ❄️🛜🏊) Everything is so clean here it shines. This friendly and very homely pension has 10 white-and-cream rooms over two floors, all big, bright and spotless with simple but good-sized bathrooms. The garden has a small pool and the roof terrace restaurant serves some of the best local pension fare (set menus ₺40) in town. The family room sleeps six.

Melrose Viewpoint   HOTEL $$
(Melrose Suites; ☑0544 498 9114; www.melroseviewpoint.com; Çay Sokak 7; s/d/tr/f from €22/26/36/46; P❄️🛜🏊) This blue mid-rise is run by the same friendly family that owns Melrose House, so service is top-notch. Spacious rooms come with turquoise and bronze decor, kettles, satellite TV and good-sized bathrooms. Some have balconies with views over to the travertines. The internal courtyard has an attractive pool area and the restaurant (mains ₺25 to ₺47) serves home-cooked flavours.

Hotel Dört Mevsim   PENSION $$
(☑0258-272 2009; www.hoteldortmevsim.com; Hasan Tahsin Caddesi 27; s/d/tr/q ₺120/180/240/300, campsite per person ₺30; P❄️🛜🏊) The family that runs this simple pension is hugely welcoming. The white and maroon rooms are basic and the very small bathrooms are a bit smelly, but the tranquil setting, with a shaded poolside terrace where you can relax with a beer or dig into homemade food, is a winner.

Venus Suite Hotel   HOTEL $$$
(☑0258-272 2270; www.venushotel.net; Sümbül Sokak 7; d €60-65; ❄️🛜🏊) This annexe of the **Venus Hotel** (☑0258-272 2152; Hasan Tahsin Caddesi; r €50-55; ❄️🛜🏊) offers spacious, comfortable rooms with decorative İznik-style tiles. Rooms overlook the street or rear courtyard with its swimming pool and licensed restaurant. Dinner (menus from ₺40) and buffet breakfast are catered for on a generous scale. Staff happily provide guests complimentary shuttles to the top gate at Hierapolis.

1. Sculpture detail, Afrodisias (p309) 2. Hierapolis (p303)
3. Laodicea (p308) 4. Sagalassos (p314)

IGOR STRAMYK/SHUTTERSTOCK ©

Western Anatolia Highlights

Ancient ruins scatter this region where civilisations once prospered. On street corners and windblown plateaus, weathered inscriptions and chipped statues tell the stories of the Phrygians, Greeks, Romans, Ottomans and others. Wonderfully, because most of Western Anatolia's ruins are off the tourist circuit, at some sites it might be just you, the Anatolian wind and a ticket salesman who is keen to chat. Arrive early or late to have vast theatres and civic squares to yourself.

Hierapolis

The ruins of Hierapolis, a multicultural spa city in Roman and Byzantine times, stand in decaying splendour atop Pamukkale's famous snow-white mountain of travertine rock formations.

Afrodisias

Splendiferous Afrodisias boasts two of western Turkey's most photogenic relics. The tetrapylon (monumental gateway) welcomed travellers when Afrodisias was the provincial capital of Roman Caria, and the 30,000-seat stadium still echoes with the roars of gladiators and spectators.

Sagalassos

The Roman ruins of Sagalassos, which was also a major Pisidian city, are scattered in an unbeatably poetic location at an altitude of 1500m in the Taurus Mountains.

Laodicea

Entered along a colonnaded street, Laodicea was a prosperous city on two trade routes and home to one of the Seven Churches of Asia (mentioned in the Book of Revelation).

İznik

İznik's Roman walls and Byzantine churches recall its heyday when the first Ecumenical Council, which shaped Christianity, met here.

WORTH A TRIP

LAODICEA

Laodicea (Laodikya; Pamukkale–Denizli Yolu; ₺15; ⊙8am-7pm) was once a commercial city straddling two major trade routes, famed for its black wool, banking and medicines. Cicero lived here for a time and it was also home to a large Jewish population. Enter the site up colonnaded **Syria St** from where you reach a **2nd-century temple** with a glass-floor showing toppled pillars beneath. Nearby is Laodicea's **basilica church**, one of the 'seven churches of Asia' mentioned in the Book of Revelation, which holds beautifully restored mosaic flooring.

From here paths wind across the hill to the remains of the **north theatre** and the **west theatre**, both with good views of Pamukkale's travertines. Note that excavation and restoration work is continuing in the far north and west portions of the site and some areas can't be entered. Afterwards, backtrack to Syria St to see its **agoras** and **bath ruins**. With more time up your sleeve, head south from Syria St to the **stadium** and **south baths complex**. Make sure to wear good walking shoes as the southern portion of the site is very overgrown in places.

Laodicea is 8km from Pamukkale and easily reached using the Pamukkale–Denizli dolmuş (minibus with a prescribed route; ₺4). The site entry is a 1km walk from the signposted turn-off. When you're finished, simply walk back down to the highway and flag the dolmuş down as it goes by.

Closing time is 5pm from October through to mid-April.

✖ Eating & Drinking

Pamukkale's restaurants are mostly unremarkable and overpriced – your accommodation will likely offer better fare. There are a few laid-back bars, and most restaurants and accommodation places also serve beer and wine.

★ White House   TURKISH $$

(Atatürk Caddesi 7; meze ₺10-25, mains ₺36-59; ⊙11am-10pm; 🔊🅿) Bucking the trend of Pamukkale's ho-hum food, White House packs its dishes with flavour. The *sigara boreği* (deep-fried cigar-shaped pastries, often stuffed with cheese) are crammed with dill as well as white cheese, and the *yaprak sarma* (stuffed vine leaves) are some of the fattest and tastiest we've had anywhere in Turkey. Mains range from *pirzola* (lamb cutlets) to pasta.

Eat either within the Aegean-influenced white-and-blue interior or, in warmer months, in the back garden.

Kayaş   TURKISH $$

(Atatürk Caddesi 3; mains ₺25-45; ⊙11am-11pm; 🔊🅿) This central bar-restaurant with a vine-covered terrace and big TV (for football matches, generally) is the best spot in town for a beer, but it also serves a Turkish menu featuring *şiş* kebaps (roast skewered meat), *karnıyarık* (stuffed aubergines) and a better-than-normal selection of vegetarian dishes such as *güveç mantarlı*

(mushroom casserole) and a grilled vegetable plate.

Mehmet's Heaven   TURKISH $$

(Atatürk Caddesi 25; meze ₺15-20, mains ₺15-45; ⊙8am-10pm; 🔊🅿) Long-established Mehmet's has a back terrace with excellent travertine views and some of the friendliest service in town. The Turkish fare – *köfte* (meatballs), grilled meat plates and plenty of vegetable meze dishes – is nothing to write home about, but snagging a terrace table and watching sunset over the travertines with a beer can't be beaten.

ℹ Information

SAFE TRAVEL

Pamukkale's travel agencies have a bad reputation; stories of poor service and fly-by-night operations abound. They are best avoided apart from booking a day trip to Afrodisias. Definitely do not book tours and activities in other parts of Turkey, such as Cappadocia. Many agencies share offices with the bus companies, so when buying bus tickets make sure you are dealing directly with the bus operator or its appointed agent.

Travellers are sometimes taken off the dolmuş from Denizli and taken to a pension to receive the hard sell. Asian travellers in particular have been targeted with this and other scams. If this happens, leave and go to your first choice of accommodation.

ℹ Getting There & Away

Long-distance bus services arrive at and depart from Denizli. Dolmuşes run every 20 minutes between Pamukkale and Denizli's otogar (₺4.50, 20 minutes) between 6.30am and 11pm. Denizli city buses (₺2.50, between 6.30am and 7pm) also run the same route, but you need to buy a Denizli transport card to use them, so the dolmuş is more convenient for a short stay.

Bus companies **Metro** (www.metroturizm. com.tr; Cumhuriyet Meydanı; ◷9am-9pm), **Kamil Koç** (www.kamilkoc.com.tr; Cumhuriyet Meydanı; ◷9am-8pm) and **Pamukkale** (www. pamukkale.com.tr; Atatürk Caddesi 9; ◷8am-8pm) have ticket-booking offices in the village centre, though you'll have to catch the dolmuş to Denizli otogar to pick up the bus.

ℹ Getting Around

The Denizli–Pamukkale dolmuş carries on to Karahayıt so can drop you at Hierapolis' northern gate (₺3). Flag it down anywhere along Kübilay or Menderes Caddesis as it zips through town or at Cumhuriyet Meydanı. Tell the driver you want to be dropped at 'kuzey kapısı'.

Taxis to Hierapolis' south gate cost around ₺25 from Pamukkale. Some Pamukkale accommodation operators will also drop you there at no charge.

Afrodisias

The remoteness of Afrodisias (₺20; ◷8am-6.30pm), out in the Anatolian hinterland among Roman poplars, green fields and warbling birds, safeguards its serenity from the masses. Afrodisias may not have fine individual ruins to match those of Turkey's famous archaeological site Ephesus, but it wins for sheer scale, and its on-site museum is impressive too, housing many of the site's treasures. The site is relatively untended, with some side paths disappearing into thickets and bramble, and with luck you could have it almost to yourself, creating the exotic sensation of discovering lost ruins.

◉ Sights

From the car park, a tractor will tow you 500m to the entrance in a connected carriage. Take the circular site tour first, then dry your sweat over a drink, saving the cooler indoor **museum** for last. You have two route choices; the anticlockwise route is less affected by the occasional mid-morning package-tour groups.

Turn right beside the museum for the grand **house** with Ionic and Corinthian pillars on the left. Further on the left, the elaborate **tetrapylon** (monumental gateway) once greeted pilgrims coming to the Temple of Aphrodite. The impressive monument has been reconstructed using 85% of its original blocks.

The **tomb** of Professor Kenan T Erim is on the lawn here. A Turkish professor from New York University, the trailblazing archaeologist oversaw excavations here from 1961 to 1990.

Continue down the steps on the straight footpath, and turn right across the grassy field for the 270m-long **stadium**. One of the biggest and best-preserved classical stadiums, this massively long structure has 30,000 overgrown seats. Some were reserved for individuals or guilds, and the eastern end was a gladiatorial arena. Standing in the dark and sloping tunnel and looking out onto the huge field, you can imagine the fear, exhilaration and sheer adrenaline the ancient warriors would have felt, striding

---

DON'T MISS

AFRODISIAS MUSEUM

To understand the magnitude of this site, see the approximately 70 (of the once-existing 190) reliefs in the elegant museum. They occupy opposing sides of the main interior hall. The unique combination of friezes acknowledges a Greek culture and mythology underpinning the worldly achievements of the pragmatic Romans. So, along with the statues illustrating mythical heroes are representations of robust emperors. Note how subjugated nations are always portrayed in female form: Trajan rips open the shirt of chaste Dacia, whilst Claudius delivers a death blow to the slumped figure of Britannia.

Other marbles here include Aphrodite's 2nd-century cult statue, and busts of great writers and thinkers. One, labelled simply 'a philosopher', may be the great 3rd-century AD peripatetic philosopher Alexander of Afrodisias. See, too, sculptures of Caius Julius Zoilos, Octavian's freed slave who became a wealthy local benefactor, and the interactive screen, which shows how Afrodisias would have looked in its heyday.

Afrodisias

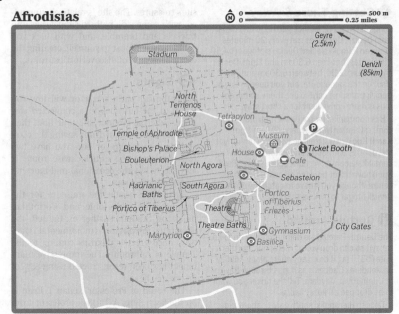

Geyre
(2.5km)

Denizli
(85km)

towards imminent death amid a raucous crowd demanding blood.

The erstwhile **Temple of Aphrodite**, once dedicated to the goddess of love, was converted to a basilica around AD 500. Its cella was removed, its columns shifted to form a nave, and an apse was added, making it hard to now visualise the original structure. Nearby, the **Bishop's Palace** is a grand house that previously accommodated Roman governors. Just beyond, the left fork in the path leads to the beautiful marble **bouleuterion** (council chamber), preserved almost undamaged for 1000 years by mud.

Return to the fork and follow the sign to the *tiyatro* (theatre). The path leads past the **north agora** and through the early 2nd-century AD **Hadrianic baths** to the **south agora**, with a long, excavated pool, and the grand **Portico of Tiberius**.

Stone stairs up the earthen, prehistoric mound lead to the white marble **theatre**, a 7000-capacity auditorium complete with stage and individually labelled seats. Just southeast was the large **theatre baths** complex.

The path now leads downhill to the **Sebasteion**: originally a temple to the deified Roman emperors, it was visually spectacular, with a three-storey-high double colonnade decorated with **friezes** of Greek myths

and imperial exploits. In the same area, the impressive many-faced friezes come from the Portico of Tiberius.

❶ Getting There & Away

Afrodisias is 55km southeast of Nazilli and 101km from Denizli. Visiting by public transport from Pamukkale is tricky, as you have to change dolmuşes numerous times. A guided tour or transfer (transport only) is easier; book with travel agencies around Cumhuriyet Meydanı (or your hotel) in Pamukkale. Group transfers/guided tours cost about ₺60/150 per person, though this fluctuates depending on the number of participants and by operator. Generally, agencies will not undertake the journey with less than six people; between June and September, there are normally enough travellers to guarantee departures. Most operators leave around 9.30am and return by 4pm, giving you 2½ hours at the site.

A private return transfer should cost ₺400.

Lake District

Tucked away within the forested hills and mountains of inner Anatolia, the lake region has an escapist, even otherworldly feel. At its heart is Eğirdir (*ey*-eer-deer), a placid town overlooked by mountains including Sivri (1749m), Davraz (2653m) and Barla (2800m).

This area offers year-round action, including the rose harvest in May and June, the lavender harvest in July, the apple harvest in autumn and skiing in winter. History-loving hikers can explore the St Paul Trail and ascend to the lofty ruins of Sagalassos, perched among the rocky peaks of the Taurus Mountains. But you may find it is the kind hospitality of the locals, unaffected by mass tourism, that makes visiting most worthwhile.

ℹ Getting Around

The lake district is a great area in which to hire a car. If you don't have your own transport, the Eğirdir Outdoor Centre organises day trips to sights such as Sagalassos and Lake Kovada National Park. Outside of the main late-May to September tourism season though, you most likely won't be able to find fellow travellers to make up the numbers for the trips to run. Dolmuşes run between Isparta and Eğirdir, Isparta and Ağluson (the nearest town to Sagalassos), and Isparta and Yalvaç.

Example return taxi fares from Eğirdir to various sights: Lake Kovada National Park (₺200); Yazılı Canyon Nature Park (₺300); Sagalassos (₺300); and Antiocheia-in-Pisidia (₺300).

Eğirdir

📞 0246 / POP 32,440

Ringed by steep mountains and on the edge of Eğirdir Gölü (Lake Eğirdir), Eğirdir offers a relaxing respite from Anatolia's heat and dust. A major stop on the long-distance St Paul trekking trail, this small town, with its causeway stretching across the water to tiny Yeşilada (Green Island), is all about outdoor activities with hiking, mountain biking and boat trips high on the agenda. Its simple family-run pensions, offering hearty home-cooked meals, add to Eğirdir's attraction as a base for exploring regional sites.

◉ Sights & Activities

From the peninsula's northern shore by the castle to its tip at Yeşilada, you'll find several small beaches, many with food stalls and *çay ocakları* (tea stoves). Out of town, at Yazla (less than 1km down the Isparta road) lies sandy **Belediye Beach**. Several kilometres further north is pebbly **Altınkum Beach**. In summer dolmuşes run every 15 minutes (₺2) from the otogar.

Further north again, 11km towards Barla, is long, sandy **Bedre Beach**. Cycle or catch a taxi (₺30). Eğirdir Outdoor Centre offers mountain-bike rental.

Pınar Pazarı   MARKET

(Pınar; ⊙Sun Aug-Oct) On Sundays between August and October, you can buy apples, cheese, yoghurt or even a goat at this village market run by the Yörük Turks, who descend from their mountain redoubts to hawk their wares and stock up for winter. In the old days, wily Yörük mothers would use these public events to negotiate marriages for their children. Pınar is 7km southeast of Eğirdir, served by dolmuş (₺2.25).

★**Eğirdir**
Outdoor Centre   ADVENTURE SPORTS

(📞0246-311 6688; www.facebook.com/Egirdir -Outdoor-Centre; day trips to Sagalassos, Lake Kovada or Çandır Kanyon per person ₺130; ⊙8am-8pm mid-May–mid-Oct) This activities centre, run by outdoor enthusiast İbrahim Ağartan and family, should be your first port of call in Eğirdir. It offers free information, mountain-bike hire (per hour/day ₺7.50/80),

---

LOCAL KNOWLEDGE

LAKE EĞİRDİR BOAT TRIPS

Some of Eğirdir's best swimming spots are accessible only by boat trips, which also allow you to relax, try some fishing, and generally bliss out on the lake's breezy blue waters.

Boat trips – run from 15 June to 15 September – have traditionally provided a second income for fishers and pension owners. Arrange a trip through your pension or Eğirdir Outdoor Centre, which charges ₺130 per person for a six-hour excursion. The trip involves visiting hidden coves, swimming, sunbathing and a barbecue lunch of freshly caught fish, and you'll gain an insight into a local fisher's life.

Fishing trips (per person ₺30) can also be booked through the Eğirdir Outdoor Centre. Count on an early start (between 5am and 7am), two to three hours on the water, and a hands-on, sunrise experience helping a local fisher haul in the nets. It can be chilly on the lake so wrap up warmly. Fishing trips are not offered from 15 March to 15 June, to allow the lake's fish to breed.

Eğirdir

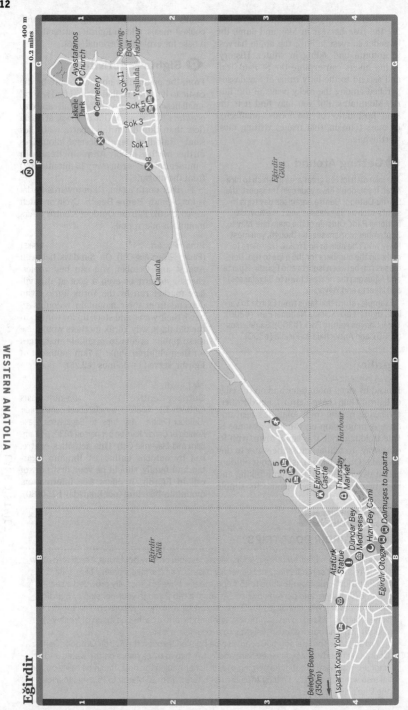

Eğirdir Gölü

Eğirdir Gölü

Canada

G
Ayastafanos Church
Rowing-Boat Harbour
Cemetery
Sok 11
Yeşilada
İskele Park
Sok 5
6
4
9
Sok 3
Sok 1
8

C
1
3 5
2
Eğirdir Castle
Thursday Market
Eğirdir Cami
Dündar Bey Medresesi
Hızır Bey Cami
Dolmuşes to Isparta
Atatürk Statue
Eğirdir Otogar

A
7
Isparta Konay Yolu
Beledıye Beach (350m)

Harbour

0   400 m
0   0.2 miles

Eğirdir

day trips to local sights like Sagalassos and Lake Kovada (minimum three people), boat trips (p311), transport for independent travellers to St Paul Trail stops, and tours, from fishing to snowshoeing. During the harvest seasons, it specialises in rose (May) and lavender (July) tours, taking visitors out into the fields.

Hikers can hire camping equipment here (tent, sleeping bag, mat, rucksack and stove for ₺75) and obtain excellent recommendations and self-guided maps for biking and walking trails around the area. If you're a keen kayaker or windsurfer, ask here to borrow equipment from the local training centres for a nominal fee.

The centre also has a laundry (₺20), a cafe (p314) and acts as a book exchange. Out of season, if the shop is shut, head to Charly's Pension for information on all services.

Sivri Dağı Trail   HIKING
(Akpınar Köyü) Mt Sivri (1749m) makes a good day walk from Eğirdir. The 6km return trek to the peak from the hill village of Akpınar takes about 3½ hours. Organise transport to/from Akpınar, 5km from Eğirdir, through your accommodation or Eğirdir Outdoor Centre (p311).

🛏 Sleeping

Çetin Pansiyon   PENSION $
(☎0246-311 2154; 3 Sokak 12; d/tr ₺100/130; 🖥) Near the castle, Çetin has six basic rooms up a narrow staircase, some with views across the lake. The room at the top has a rudimentary kitchenette. Breakfast is an additional ₺20.

★ Fulya Pension   PENSION $$
(☎0543-486 4918; www.fulyapension.com; Camiyanı Sokak 5; s/d/tr/q €45/50/70/80; 🌡🖥)

Along with Charly's next door, the Fulya is Eğirdir's vortex of traveller action, run by multilingual İbrahim who also runs the Eğirdir Outdoor Centre (p311). Rooms are sunny, spacious and comfortable; some have lake views and heritage stone walls. The rooftop breakfast room and terrace has sweeping views of both the lake and surrounding mountains, and the breakfast feast includes proper coffee.

★ Göl Pension   PENSION $$
(☎0246-311 2370; www.golpension.com; Yeşilada; d/tr/q ₺250/300/500; ⊙Apr-Oct; 🌡🖥) Run by the delightful Davras sisters, 'Lake' Pension has a true welcoming ambience and six sparkling clean, comfortable rooms with decent-sized bathrooms, some with balconies. The two attic rooms with sloped ceilings share a big private terrace and can be joined together – useful for travelling families or groups of friends. It usually opens for the season from late April.

Charly's Pension   PENSION $$
(☎0246-311 4611; www.charlyspension.com; 5 Sokak 2; dm/s/d €10/30/35, campsite per person €10; 🌡🖥) Behind the castle, İbrahim Ağartan and family offer simple rooms and a homely atmosphere with a back terrace overlooking the lakefront. This is the heart of Eğirdir's hiker-backpacker scene and the terrace is the place to linger over an evening beer while İbrahim organises activities and dispenses information to make the most of your time.

Nis Otel   BOUTIQUE HOTEL $$
(Eskiciler Konağı; ☎0246-333 2016; Kaynak Sokak 19; d €55; 🌡🖥) This restored stone and wood mansion has rooms that subtly combine heritage features and modern decor, and the beautiful shared public spaces are dotted with antiques and colourful Turkish rugs. In fine weather, breakfast and meals are served on a spacious outdoor deck. Don't expect lake views; a new construction directly in front of the building has destroyed its vistas.

Choo Choo Pension   PENSION $$
(☎0530 404 2383, 0246-311 4926; www.choochoopension.com; Yeşilada; d/tr/q €50/70/90; 🌡🖥) This island pension is run by an old fishing clan, which also runs Halikarnas restaurant, straight out front facing the lake. The eight good-sized rooms, all named after European painters and decorated with their prints, are bright, modern and renovated,

WESTERN ANATOLIA LAKE DISTRICT

ST PAUL TRAIL

Almost two millennia ago, the apostle Paul trekked northwards from Perge (near the coast and Antalya) through the Anatolian wilds to today's Yalvaç, near Eğirdir. The winding 500km route – from sea level to a 2200m peak – passes crumbling ancient ruins. Although some hikers today start the trail from the south, you will have more options and help available by starting in Eğirdir, which is a good base for both the northern and southern sections of the 500km trail.

For trail information check out Culture Routes in Turkey (http://culture routesinturkey.com) and its 'Trekking in Turkey' mobile app, which features the St Paul Trail. Kate Clow's *St Paul Trail* guidebook is the indispensable guide to the trail. It can be bought on the Trekking in Turkey website (www. trekkinginturkey.com) and is available at Eğirdir Outdoor Centre (p311).

with new beds. Four have balconies. Homemade *börek* (filled pastries) feature in the lakeside breakfast.

✖ Eating & Drinking

Eğirdir Outdoor Centre   CAFE $

(mains ₺20-25; ⊙10am-8pm; 🖉) Eğirdir's main organisation and information point for outdoor activities also serves up home-style Turkish fare (including vegetarian options), snacks and quick meals of *tost* (toasted sandwiches). Cappuccino and espresso are on the menu too.

★ Big Apple Restaurant   SEAFOOD $$

(Yeşilada; mains ₺30-45; ⊙11.30am-10.30pm) Our favourite Yeşilada seafood place has perfectly grilled fish, excellent calamari and lush meze. Order your *levrek* (sea bass) or *çupra* (gilt-head sea bream), throw in a garlic-heavy rocket salad and some *dolmas* (vegetables stuffed with rice or meat) and you've got one of the town's best seafood meals. Don't forget the rakı if you're going full local.

Poyraz   SEAFOOD $$

(Yeşilada; meze ₺13, mains ₺15-35; ⊙11am-10pm) Eat on the waterfront, where fishers pull in their nets, or in the less atmospheric interior

across the road. Poyraz offers seafood dishes of trout, perch and calamari as well as *köfte* and grilled chop plates. Grab meze dishes of *acılı ezme* (spicy tomato and onion paste) and aubergine salad to go with your main. No alcohol available.

Akpınar Yörük Çadiri   TEAHOUSE

(Akpınar Köyü; ⊙11am-10pm) For panoramic lake views head to this mountain-top teahouse in Akpınar village, 5km uphill from Eğirdir. Order your tea by the pot as the locals do (for two/three people ₺10/15) and relax on the shaded deck. There are also cold drinks and simple meals of *gözleme* (stuffed flatbreads; ₺10) available. Akpınar is a bracing walk or a ₺35 taxi ride.

❶ Getting There & Away

Eğirdir Otogar (Eğirdir Bus Station) has a few direct long-distance services daily. Most are run by Isparta Petrol bus company (www. ispartapetrol.com.tr).

Antalya (₺38, three hours, two morning, two afternoon and one evening)

Aydın (₺45-65, six hours, three morning, one afternoon and one evening) For Selçuk.

Denizli (₺40-45, four hours, three morning, one afternoon and one evening) For Pamukkale.

İstanbul (₺125, 10 hours, one evening)

İzmir (₺62-75, 7½ hours, two morning, one afternoon and one evening)

Konya (₺55-59, four hours, one morning, three afternoon and five evening)

The frequency of long-haul buses is greater from nearby Isparta. Dolmuşes (₺8, 40 minutes) leave every 15 minutes from a bus stand at the back of Eğirdir otogar. The dolmuşes terminate at Isparta's *köy garaj* (bus station), which has ticket offices for the major bus companies. These companies provide free onward *servis* (shuttle bus) transport to Isparta otogar, 5km away on the other side of the city centre, where long-haul buses depart from.

Sagalassos

To visit the sprawling ruins of Sagalassos, high amid the jagged peaks of Ak Dağ (White Mountain), is to approach myth: the ancient ruined city set in stark mountains seems to illuminate the Sagalassian perception of a sacred harmony between nature, architecture and the great gods of antiquity.

Sagalassos is one of the Mediterranean's largest archaeological projects, but it is rarely troubled by tour buses or crowds; sometimes the visiting archaeologists or sheep wandering the slopes outnumber tourists. This is a place for getting perspective, for feeling the raw Anatolian wind on your face, and of course for seeing some very impressive ancient ruins. While you can rush through in about two hours, take the time to linger and properly appreciate this mountaintop site.

Although repeatedly devastated by earthquakes, the ancient city was never pillaged and reconstruction is slowly moving ahead.

Sights

At the **ticket booth** (₺12; ⊙ 9am-6.30pm), request the *anahtar* (key) to the oft-closed Neon Library. From the entrance you can turn up to the right, starting from the top and working your way downhill (a somewhat steeper approach), or proceed from the bottom and work your way up and around.

Following the latter, clockwise route, you'll see the marble **colonnaded street** that marked the city's southern entrance from the lowland valleys. The lack of wheel indentations suggests that it was mainly used by pedestrians. It is the spine and central axis of Sagalassos, stretching upwards through it.

From the bottom, it would have appeared that the city's terraced fountains were one triple-tiered tower of water – an impressive optical illusion. Passing through the **Tiberian gate**, see the **lower agora** and the massive reconstructed **Roman baths** complex to the right. At the agora's rear (back up the metal staircase), the **Hadrianic nymphaeum** stands flanked by the mountainside. The well-preserved former fountain here contains elaborate sculptures of mythic (and mostly headless) nereids and muses. A ruined **Odeon** sits just beyond.

The main path now winds up to the **upper agora**, once the main civic area and political centre. Thanks to restoration, it boasts Sagalassos' most impressive attraction: the **Antonine Nymphaeum**, a huge fountain complex some 9m high and 28m wide. Originally wrought from seven different kinds of stone, the fountain was ornately decorated with Medusa heads and fish motifs. Although it collapsed in an earthquake in AD 590, the rubble lay clustered, aiding modern restorers. The impressive result is a massive structure supported by rows of thick columns (including bright blue marble ones in the centre), through which huge sheets of water gush into a lengthy receptacle. The

fountain is bedecked by statues, including a large marble Dionysus replica (the original is in nearby Burdur Museum).

The agora's western edge is flanked by the **bouleuterion**; some of its seating remains intact. Rising over the fountain in the northwest corner is a 14m-high **heroon** (hero's monument). In 333 BC Alexander the Great had a statue of himself erected here (now also in Burdur Museum). Peer over the agora's southern edge to spot the **macellon** (food market), dedicated to Emperor Marcus Aurelius, with its trademark Corinthian columns. Note the **tholos** in the middle; the deep fountain was used to sell live fish.

From here, turn right and up into the hills for the late-Hellenistic **Doric fountainhouse**, its piping now reattached to its original Roman-era source. Behind it is Sagalassos' only restored covered building, the **Neon Library**, which features a fine mosaic floor. In the darkness at the rear, an original Greek inscription commemorates Flavius Severianus Neon, a noble who funded the library in AD 120. The back podium contained curving and rectangular niches for storing reading material. The library was modified over the following centuries, with the striking mosaic of Achilles' departure for Troy commissioned during the brief reign of Emperor Julian (361–363), whose unsuccessful attempt to restore paganism to the Orthodox empire augured his demise.

Finally, atop the hill is Sagalassos' 9000-seat **Roman theatre** – one of Turkey's most complete, despite earthquake damage to the seating rows. Just above its top steps, walk parallel with the theatre through its eerie tunnel, where performers and contestants once entered (note that it is dark, strewn with debris and has a very low exit point). The bluff east of here offers stunning panoramic views over the city, mountains and plains.

Sleeping & Eating

★ **Sagalassos Lodge & Spa**   HOTEL $$$
(☏ 0248-731 3232; www.sagalassoslodge.com; Kıraç Mahallesi, Yaylakent 1 Sokak 1; d/tr €74/94; ❉ 🛜 🏊) Surrounded by pine trees, the Sagalassos Lodge & Spa is located on the road between Ağlasun and the ruins of Sagalassos. Modern, spacious rooms feature balconies and big bathrooms. The bar has great views and outside a sun-kissed pool beckons. There's a spa with hamam, and bikes are available for independent exploration.

Outside guests are welcome at the excellent **restaurant** (mains ₺15-35; ⊙ 11am-3pm & 6-10pm; P ✐).

❶ Getting There & Away

A return taxi from Eğirdir costs about ₺300. Eğirdir Outdoor Centre (p311) links up independent travellers to reduce costs and runs trips for ₺130 per person.

Dolmuşes run by Ağlasun Minibus Kooperatifi (www.aglasunkoop.com) travel between Isparta and Ağlasun, 7km south of Sagalassos. From Isparta they leave from the *köy garaj* (₺10, one hour, hourly 7.30am to 7.30pm, and at 11.30pm). From Ağlasun they make the return run hourly between 7.15am and 3.15pm and then at 4.30pm, 5.30pm, 6.30pm and 9.30pm. Ağlasun Minibus Kooperatifi also runs a couple of dolmuşes to and from Antalya daily (₺22, 2½ hours).

From Ağlasun, a steep and winding road climbs 7km to Sagalassos. There is also a 3km path. A return taxi costs ₺50, including waiting time at Sagalassos of an hour or so; your dolmuş driver from Isparta may be persuaded to do the same for a similar fee.

Yazılı Canyon Nature Park

Deep in the Taurus Mountains, roughly 65km south of Eğirdir, this forested **gorge** (Yazılı Kanyon Tabiat Parkı; parking motorbike/car ₺9/18) separates the Lake District (ancient Pisidia) and the Antalya region (Pamphylia) and their unique climatic zones. From the riverside picnicking spot, where a simple restaurant serves fresh fish (meal ₺20), follow a path upstream for 3km through the glorious Çandır Kanyon to alpine waterfalls. There are shady bathing spots filled with cathartically cold water. It gets busy in summer, but otherwise is tranquil.

The Eğirdir Outdoor Centre (p311) organises day trips here.

Antiocheia-in-Pisidia

Antiocheia-in-Pisidia (Yalvaç; ₺6; ⊙ 8am-7pm) is a largely unexcavated ancient Pisidian city, about 2km from Yalvaç. St Paul of Tarsus visited several times (as recorded in the Bible's Acts of the Apostles). Located on the strategic borderland of ancient Phrygia and Pisidia, it became an important Byzantine city, but was abandoned in the 8th century after Arab attacks.

After the gate, a Roman road leads up past triumphal arch foundations, then turns right to the theatre. Further uphill, on a flat area surrounded by a semicircular rock wall, is the main shrine. Originally dedicated to the Anatolian mother goddess Cybele, and later to the moon god Men, it became an imperial Roman cult temple of Augustus. On the left you will see the nymphaeum, once a spring.

Several Antiocheian aqueduct arches are visible across the fields. Downhill from the nymphaeum, ruined Roman baths feature several excavated large chambers, and a largely intact original ceiling. The foundations of St Paul's Basilica also remain.

Antalya & the Turquoise Coast

Why Go?

The ancient Lycians were on to something when they based their empire on the stunning Teke Peninsula, the chunk of Mediterranean paradise between Antalya and Fethiye. This is Turkey at its most staggeringly beautiful: sandy sweeps of shore hug a coastline lapped by jade waters and backed by forest-blanketed slopes. The Turquoise Coast is prime sun-and-sea territory, but step off the beach and you'll find ancient cities such as Xanthos, Tlos and Arykanda perched precariously atop hills, and ornate tombs carved into cliffs at Pınara and Myra. Hike between ruins on a section of the 500km-long Lycian Way and you'll be richly rewarded with scenery worth the sweat.

If you just want the beach, though, you're in the right place. For starters, there's Patara's stunning stretch of sand, the pristine shoreline linking Olympos and Çıralı, and photogenic Kaputaş. And, of course, there are ancient sites just around the corner from all three.

Best Places to Eat

➡ İzela Restaurant (p333)

➡ Kalamaki Restaurant (p345)

➡ Mozaik Bahce (p328)

➡ Zeytinlik (p345)

➡ Yöruk Restaurant (p359)

Best Places to Stay

➡ Hotel Villa Mahal (p345)

➡ Owlsland (p347)

➡ Hideaway Hotel (p350)

➡ Mehtap Pansiyon (p354)

➡ Turan Hill Lounge (p336)

When to Go
Antalya

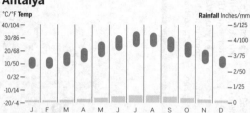

Mar & Apr Prime walking time. Stride across rugged hills alive with spring flowers.

May Sneak in before peak season and set sail on the Med. September's also good.

Jun–Aug Summer silly season: Antalya, Kaş, Fethiye and Dalyan are bustling and festive.

Antalya & the Turquoise Coast Highlights

1 Kekova Island (p353) Kayaking over the sunken city of Simena.

2 Kayaköy (p332) Discovering the Greek ghost town abandoned a century ago.

3 Patara (p339) Brushing up on history at the ruins before an afternoon on the beach.

4 Lycian Way (p341) Hiking some of the trail, from holiday havens such as Kaş.

5 Blue Voyages (p326) Setting sail from Fethiye on a *gület* (traditional wooden yacht).

6 Kaleiçi (p359) Wandering the labyrinthine streets of Antalya's historic district.

7 Dalyan (p319) Admiring rock tombs in this peaceful town.

8 Chimaera (p358) Hiking up Mt Olympos to see the eternal flame.

9 Kalkan (p341) Dining out in Mediterranean Turkey's most glamorous resort.

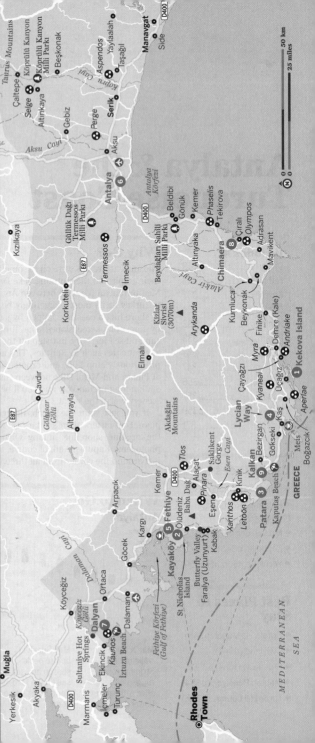

Dalyan

📞 0252 / POP 6350

This charming little town enjoys a stunning location on the banks of the Dalyan River with one of Turkey's best stretches of sand, İztuzu Beach, a short boat ride away. Tourism has certainly made an impact here – bringing an armada of excursion boats from Marmaris and Fethiye during summer – but Dalyan's easy-going character definitely still endures. Though the town's little high street is lined with cafes, restaurants and bars, there's no raucous nightlife to contend with and its riverside promenade is a delight to stroll.

As well as the atmospheric ruins of Kaunos on its doorstep, Dalyan is an excellent base for exploring Köyceğiz Gölü (Lake Köyceğiz) and a turtle rehabilitation centre at İztuzu. As the evening approaches, pull up a pew riverside to admire Dalyan's most famous feature: the mighty Kings' Tombs of ancient Caria. Hewn into the cliffs, they take on a golden glow as the sun sets.

⊙ Sights

★ Kings' Tombs   TOMB

Dalyan's famous Carian rock tombs are carved into cliffs across the Dalyan River, southwest of the centre. You can get good views of the tombs by walking south from town along Maraş Caddesi to the western end of Kaunos Sokak. Alternatively, board one of the private rowing boats moored next to Saki restaurant in Dalyan (₺15 return); it will take you across the river to the teensy settlement of Çandır, from where it's a five-minute walk to the tombs.

Kaunos   ARCHAEOLOGICAL SITE

(₺14; ⊙ 8am-7pm Apr-Oct, to 5pm Nov-Mar) Founded in the 9th century BC, Kaunos (also spelled Caunus) was an important Carian city by 400 BC. On the border with Lycia, its culture reflected aspects of both empires.

On the left as you enter, the theatre is well preserved; on the hill above are remnants of an acropolis and fabulous views over the surrounding countryside. Straight ahead when you enter are impressive ruins of a Roman bath and a 6th-century church, while down the slope is the port agora.

There are good information panels on-site in English and Turkish. To get here, board one of the boats moored next to Saki restaurant in Dalyan (₺15 return). It will

take you across the river to Çandır, from where you can walk uphill to Kaunos in 20 minutes.

★ İztuzu Beach   BEACH

(İztuzu Kumsalı) An excellent swimming beach, İztuzu (Turtle) Beach is one of the Mediterranean nesting sites of the loggerhead turtle, and special rules to protect it are enforced. Although the beach is open to the public during the day, night-time visits (8pm to 8am) are prohibited from May to September. A line of wooden stakes on the beach indicates the nest sites, and visitors are asked to keep behind them to avoid disturbing the nests.

This 4.5km-long strip of sand is 10km south of Dalyan's centre and is accessible via the Dalyan River and road. Most people arrive by boat but minibuses (₺11 return; 25 minutes) run between the beach and Cumhuriyet Meydanı in Dalyan every half-hour in season (four services daily in winter).

Sea Turtle Research, Rescue & Rehabilitation Centre   WILDLIFE RESERVE

(Deniz Kaplumbağaları Araştırma, Kutarma ve Rehabilitasyon Merkezi, DEKAMER; 📞 0252-289 0077; www.dekamer.org.tr; İztuzu Beach; donations welcome; ⊙ 10am-6pm) 🅿 FREE At the southern end of İztuzu Beach is the headquarters of this turtle rescue centre, established in 2009 largely through the influence of Englishwoman June Haimoff, who campaigned for years to save this beach from development. You'll find good information displays about turtles and a short film to watch. This centre has saved many loggerhead and green turtles, and you'll see 30kg to 40kg turtles injured by fishing hooks, nets and boat propellers being treated.

🏃 Activities & Tours

★ Kaunos Tours   ADVENTURE SPORTS

(📞 0252-284 2816; www.kaunostours.com; Sarısu Sokak 1a) At the eastern end of the main square, Kaunos Tours offers any number of organised activities, both on and off the water. These include canyoning (€30), sea kayaking (€32), a village life tour (€22) and a luxury *gület* (traditional wooden yacht) sailing cruise around a dozen islands in the Göcek area (€42). Prices include lunch.

Dalyan Kooperatifi   BOATING

(📞 0541 505 0777) The Dalyan Kooperatifi, whose members moor on the river southwest of Dalyan's main square, offer many

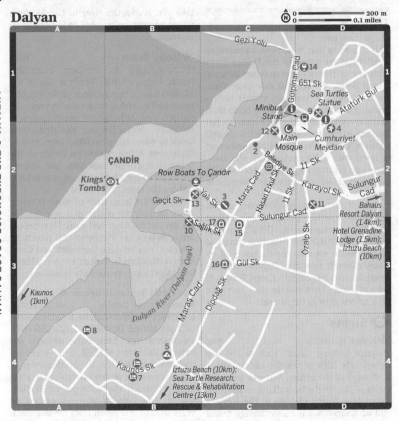

Dalyan

◎ Top Sights

✛ Activities, Courses & Tours

🛏 Sleeping

✗ Eating

◑ Drinking & Nightlife

🛍 Shopping

local trips. Boats leave the quayside at 10am or 10.30am heading to Lake Köyceğiz, Sultaniye Hot Springs and İztuzu Beach. Full-day tours, including lunch, cost ₺65 per person and return around 6pm.

The shorter four-hour afternoon tour, leaving at 2pm, costs ₺45.

Boats belonging to the cooperative also operate a river dolmuş service between Dalyan and İztuzu Beach, charging ₺20 for the return trip. In high summer boats head out every 20 minutes from 10am to 2pm and return between 1pm and 7pm (5pm or 6pm in shoulder season). Avoid any trips advertising themselves as 'turtle-spotting' tours, which inappropriately lure turtles out during daylight using bait. Only join tours on boats with propeller guards to protect the turtles; these can be identified by a flag bearing the Kaptan June Sea Turtle Conservation Foundation's logo.

If you can drum up a team of like-minded folk, you can hire a passenger boat that holds from eight to 12 people. A two-hour tour just to Kaunos costs ₺300 for the boat. Clearly negotiate a price per boat or per person, as captains have been known to claim misunderstandings to drive the price up. Tours also cross the lake to Köyceğiz' Monday market (₺40, 10.30am to 4pm, with three hours in Köyceğiz) and follow the coast west from İztuzu Beach to Ekincik beach and caves (₺90 including lunch, 10am to 4pm).

Sultaniye Hot Springs HOT SPRINGS
(Sultaniye Kaplıcaları; ☑ 0507 853 8333; ₺5; ☺ 8am-11pm) For some good (and dirty) fun, head for the Sultaniye Hot Springs, on the southwest shore of Lake Köyceğiz, which are accessible from both Köyceğiz and Dalyan. These bubbling hot mud pools (temperatures can reach 39°C) contain mildly radioactive mineral waters that are rich in chloride, sodium, hydrogen sulphide and bromide. They get very busy in high season, however. To get here from Dalyan, take a boat tour or a dolmuş boat (₺15, 30 minutes), which leave when full (every half-hour or so in summer, every hour otherwise) from the riverfront.

Ethos Dalyan Dive Centre DIVING
(☑ 0555 412 5438, 0252-284 2332; www.dalyan dive.com; Yalı Sokak 5) This professional outfit offers snorkelling and diving trips. Day-long excursions, including two dives and lunch (€60), are offered to sites including the wreck of the *Kurt* (a 40m *gület*) and Stingray Bay.

🛏 Sleeping

Try to score a riverside hotel if you can. Main drag Maraş Caddesi and the adjoining Kaunos Sokak are happy hunting grounds for pensions. The majority of Dalyan's accommodation only opens between April and late October.

Dalyan Camping CAMPGROUND $
(☑ 0252-284 5316, 0506 882 9173; www.dalyan camping.net; Kaunos Sokak 4; campsites per person ₺40, bungalows incl breakfast ₺120-160; ☺ May-Oct; P⊝❀❄) This well-shaded site offers rustic bungalows in three sizes, with stone floors and basic furniture, as well as space to set up your tent. Smaller bungalows are more like huts. There's a kitchen and washing machines for guest use, and the spa jetty-terrace attached to the barbecue restaurant looks over to the Kings' Tombs. No children under 12.

★ Hotel Arp Dalyan HOTEL $$
(☑ 0252-284 5076; www.arpdalyan.com; Kaunos Sokak 14; s/d/f from ₺300/350/600; ❀❄❄) There's a wide choice of rooms at this delightful little riverside hotel, from the compact to very spacious, all presented beautifully with contemporary furnishings and spotlessly clean. The young owners are ever-helpful, speak fluent English and like a little joke with their guests. Breakfast on the terrace restaurant, overlooking the river and rock tombs, is an utterly memorable experience.

★ Kilim Hotel BOUTIQUE HOTEL $$
(☑ 0532 573 9577, 0252-284 2253; www.kilimhotel. com; Kaunos Sokak 11; s/d/f €45/60/70; ❀❄❄) Turkish-British owners and musicians Becky and Emrah have created a fine place to relax and perhaps socialise with others while enjoying an evening of acoustic music. From the rugs adorning the walls to the rooftop physiotherapy, massages, shiatsu and holistic treatments, a feeling of culture pervades the tranquil getaway. Rooms are huge, airy and stylish.

Kamarca House Hotel BOUTIQUE HOTEL $$
(☑ 0252-284 4517; www.kamarcahotel.com; Tepearası Köyü; r €280; ⊝❀❄❄) If you're seeking luxury amid absolute tranquillity, head for this 'gourmet hotel' in the countryside. Rooms and suites are wonderfully decorated in a tactile mix of natural wood and stone, antique furnishings and original artwork. Hostess Kamer's cooking is legendary; she ran a restaurant in the USA. Located in Tepearası village, 8km from Dalyan en route to Köyceğiz.

Midas Pension PENSION $$
(☑ 0252-284 2195; www.midasdalyan.com; Kaunos Sokak 32; r ₺300-350; ❀❄) Family-friendly riverside pension complete with waterside deck-cum-dock shaded by trees. The 10 whitewashed rooms, five in the main house

and five in the garden, are small but cosy and clean, and hosts Selçuk and Saadet Nur are most welcoming.

★ **Bahaus Resort Dalyan** HOTEL $$$
(🖥0533 688 2988, 0252-284 5050; www.bahaus resort.com; İztuzu Yolu 25; r/ste from €65/95; ❄🛜🏊) Perfect for those who like an active holiday, this lovely place is spread over an enormous farm-like property with 18 boutiquey rooms. Food at breakfast is locally sourced, barbecues regularly take place, free bikes are offered to guests and the complex has a gym, pool tables, table tennis, fussball, a volleyball field and mini football playing area. It's about 1km from central Dalyan, along the road to İztuzu Beach, and connected to both by dolmuş.

✖ Eating & Drinking

Dalyan's restaurant scene swings between good quality and tourist-oriented places making generally poor versions of international staples, with most eateries found on main square Cumhuriyet Caddesi and Maraş Caddesi. For local eateries, head to the warren of side streets between Cumhuriyet Caddesi and Karayol Sokak to the south. Saturday is market day – great for fresh local produce.

There is a host of cafes and bars along Maraş Caddesi, and a few riverside options too.

Çağrı PIDE $
(Gülpınar Caddesi; pide/mains ₺10/25; ⊗11am-10pm) This cheap and cheerful pide (Turkish-style pizza) place is often packed with happy local customers. There are also kebaps and *lokanta* (ready-made) dishes in the bain-marie.

Dalyan İz CAFE $$
(🖥0542 451 5451; www.dalyaniz.com; Özalp Sokak 1; cakes/dishes from ₺15/20; ⊗9am-6pm Tue-Sun; 🛜) A sweet garden cafe that's popular thanks to its healthy, home-cooked flavours including fine breakfasts, salads (try a 'Mix Iz' with lettuce, rocket, spring onions and green peppers; ₺31) and ever-changing array of homemade baking. Tables are shaded beneath fig and rubber trees, and there's often mellow jazz on the playlist.

★ **Saki** TURKISH $$$
(🖥0252-284 5212; Geçit Sokak; mains ₺38-85; 🛜🍽) Some of the best cooking in town, with a lovely river-facing terrace setting. There's no menu; choose from the glass cabinet of

homemade mezes (₺16 to ₺60) as well as perfectly executed meat and fish dishes. Vegetarians and vegans are well catered for, as well as those eating gluten-free. Try a bottle of Gara Gazu ('Black Sheep') craft beer while you're here.

Kordon SEAFOOD $$$
(🖥0252-284 2261; Çarşi İçi 2; mezes ₺13-25, mains ₺45-80; ⊗11am-10pm; 🛜🍽) Kordon is renowned for fish and seafood and has a riverside garden with a commanding position near where the excursion boats moor. Dishes are priced high (sea bass or calamari are both ₺60), thanks to the prime location. Ichthyophobes can choose from a large selection of steaks and grills, with plenty for vegetarians.

Jazz Bar Dalyan BAR
(🖥0507 063 4614; www.jazzbardalyan.com; Gülpınar Caddesi; ⊗9pm-late; 🛜) With a fine array of cocktails on offer (try a gin fizz), this cool neon-lit place has a garden for enjoying the river views and live music nightly (Friday and Saturday only from mid-October to mid-April).

🛍 Shopping

Unique Art JEWELLERY
(🖥0546 545 1719; www.theuniqueart.com; Maraş Caddesi 42; ⊗8.30am-midnight Apr-Nov) Jeweller Kenan sells fine pieces and gifts from across Turkey in his shop-cum-gallery. Choose between coral earrings from İstanbul, rings from İzmir, textiles, ceramics, and soap made with olive oil and cinnamon from eastern Anatolia. Kenan's work has a vintage style with Ottoman motifs, and the jewellery comes with a lifetime guarantee.

DLBS Handmade CLOTHING
(Davran Caddesi 4a; ⊗9am-midnight) Classy boutique selling lovely tie-dyed sarongs, shirts, skirts and bed covers in soft muted colours.

Gallery İz ART
(🖥0542 451 5451; Dipdağ Sokak 12a; ⊗9.30am-10.30pm) Aiming to introduce customers to Turkish culture, Gallery İz has a wonderful assortment of Turkish artwork. Formerly Dalyan İz, and in a new location.

ℹ Getting There & Away

Dolmuşes (minibuses that stop anywhere along their prescribed route) use a stop in Cumhuriyet Meydanı, near the main mosque. There are no direct minibuses from here to Dalaman (the nearest airport). First take a minibus to Ortaca

(₺4, every 25 minutes in high season, every hour in low season, 14km) and change there. From Ortaca otogar (bus station), regular buses go to Köyceğiz (₺6, 25 minutes, 22km), Dalaman (₺4, 15 minutes, 9km) and Fethiye (₺12, 1¼ hours, 75km). A taxi to Dalaman airport is ₺120.

From May to September, there are daily dolmuşes from Dalyan to Köyceğiz, Marmaris and Fethiye at 10am.

Travel agencies, including Kaunos Tours (p319), offer car rental.

Fethiye

📱 0252 / POP 112,800

In 1958 an earthquake levelled the seaside city of Fethiye (feh-tee-yeh), sparing only the remains of the ancient city of Telmessos. Today it's once again a prosperous hub of the western Mediterranean, and a major base for *gület* cruises. Despite its booming growth, Fethiye is fairly low-key for its size, due mostly to the transitory nature of the *gület* business, which brings travellers flocking here between April and October. A pretty promenade rings the shoreline which is a delight to stroll in the early evening.

Fethiye's natural harbour is perhaps the region's finest, tucked into the southern reaches of a broad bay scattered with pretty islands, including Şövalye Adası, glimpsed briefly in the James Bond film *Skyfall*. Fethiye also makes a good base for visiting Ölüdeniz, one of Turkey's seaside hot spots, and many interesting sites in the surrounding countryside, including the ghost town of Kayaköy just over the hill.

◉ Sights

There isn't much left to see of ancient Telmessos. Dotted around town are Lycian stone sarcophagi dating from around 450 BC and broken into by tomb robbers centuries ago. One excellent **Lycian sarcophagus** (Atatürk Caddesi) is just east of the *belediye* (city hall). Another good example is the **sarcophagus** in the middle of Kaya Caddesi; on the neighbouring patch of waste ground are more tombs in a worse state of repair.

Fethiye Museum MUSEUM
(📱 0252-614 1150; 505 Sokak; ⊙ 9am-7pm mid-Apr–mid-Oct, 8am-5pm mid-Oct–mid-Apr) FREE
Focusing on Lycian finds from Telmessos as well as the ancient settlements of Tlos and Kaunos, this small museum exhibits pottery, jewellery, small statuary and votive stones (including the important Grave Stelae and

the Stelae of Promise). Its most prized significant possession, however, is the so-called **Trilingual Stele** from Letoön, dating from 338 BC, which was used partly to decipher the Lycian language with the help of ancient Greek and Aramaic. All exhibits are labelled in English and Turkish.

Tomb of Amyntas TOMB
(117 Sokak; ₺7; ⊙ 8.30am-7.30pm) Fethiye's most recognisable sight is the mammoth Tomb of Amyntas, an Ionic temple facade carved into a sheer rock face in 350 BC, in honour of 'Amyntas son of Hermapias'. Located south of the centre, it is best visited at sunset. Other smaller rock tombs lie about 500m to the east. Unfortunately there's a lot of graffiti evident at the site.

Roman Theatre RUINS
FREE In the centre of Fethiye, just behind the harbour, is Telmessos' 6000-seat Roman theatre dating from the 2nd century BC. Neglected for years, it's undergoing serious restoration.

Crusader Fortress FORTRESS
On the hillside above (and south of) Fethiye and along the road to Kayaköy, you can't miss the ruined tower of a Crusader fortress, built by the Knights of St John at the start of the 15th century on earlier (perhaps Lycian, Greek and Roman) foundations.

Çalış Beach BEACH
About 5km north of Fethiye's centre is Çalış, a narrow stretch of gravel beach lined with concrete hotels as well as pubs and chip shops patronised by British expats. Part of the James Bond film *Skyfall* was shot here. Dolmuşes depart for Çalış (₺2.50, 10 minutes) from Fethiye's minibus station (beside the mosque) every five to 10 minutes.

🏃 Activities

Ocean Yachting Travel Agency OUTDOORS
(📱 0252-612 4807; www.gofethiye.com; Fevzi Çakmak Caddesi; 3-night cruise €175-220; ⊙ 8am-8pm) Ocean Yachting sells a bundle of local tours and activities, including paragliding (€110), day-long rafting trips (from €45), jeep safaris to Saklıkent Gorge and Tlos (€45), Dalyan tours (€50), and the 12-island boat trip (€45). It also offers cruise choices under the brand V-GO Yachting & Travel and is a good option for chartering an entire *gület*.

Fethiye

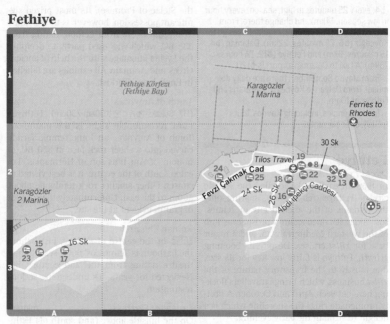

Fethiye

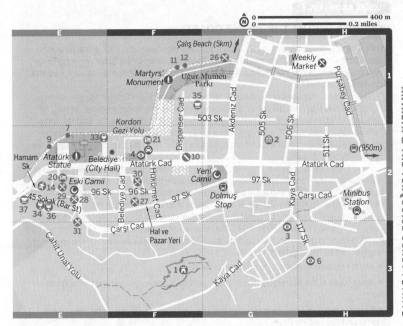

European Diving Centre   DIVING
(☑ 0252-614 9771; www.europeandivingcentre.com; 2nd fl, Demirci İş Hanı 26, Dispanser Caddesi 27) Daily diving trips and the full gamut of Professional Association of Diving Instructors (PADI) dive courses, including Open Water (€320), Divemaster and Instructor level.

Old Turkish Bath   HAMAM
(Tarihi Fethiye Hamamı; ☑ 0252-614 9318; Hamam Sokak 4, Paspatur; bath, scrub & massage ₺100; ⊘ 7am-midnight) Low-key and small, the Old Turkish Bath in Paspatur, the oldest section of Fethiye, dates to the 16th century. There are separate sections for men and women (and a mixed section for couples). Extra services include aromatherapy massages.

☞ Tours

Fethiye is a major base for travellers wanting to explore the surrounding countryside and coastline.

Some boat tours are little more than booze-cruises that cram passengers aboard and blast out loud music for the entire time on the water. If this isn't your scene, make sure you check beforehand. In general, the busier double-decker boats usually charge

around ₺60 for a day-long boat trip, while tours on less-crowded sailboats start at ₺80.

Day tours also visit Butterfly Valley (per person ₺60), with a shuttle to Ölüdeniz; Dalyan (per person ₺100), including a shuttle and a tour of the lake, mud baths at Sultaniye, tombs at Kaunos and beach at İztusu; and Saklıkent Gorge (per person around ₺75), including the ruins at Tlos and a trout lunch.

12-Island Tour Excursion Boats   BOATING
(⊘ 9.30am-6.30pm mid-Apr–Oct) Many visitors not joining the longer blue voyages opt for the 12-Island Tour, a day-long boat trip around Fethiye Körfezi (Fethiye Bay). The boats usually stop at five or six islands and cruise by the rest, but either way it's a great way to experience the coastline. Most companies offer return hotel transfers and include lunch in their rates.

Hotels and travel agencies sell tickets or you can deal directly with the boat companies along the waterfront parade at the marina. The normal tour visits Yassıcalar (Flat Island) for a stop and a swim, then Tersane Adası (Shipyard Island) for a dip and a visit to the ruins, followed by Akvaryum Koyu (Aquarium Bay) for lunch, a swim

CRUISES ON THE TURQUOISE COAST

For many travellers, a cruise on a *gület* (traditional wooden yacht) along the Turquoise Coast is the highlight of their trip to Turkey. Turkish authors Cevat Şakir and Azra Erhat first coined the phrase *mavi yolculuk* (blue voyage) in their writings about exploring this dramatic coastline.

There are many possible routes and departure points. From Fethiye the classic three night/four day trips usually call in at Ölüdeniz and Butterfly Valley and stop at Kaş, Kalkan and/or Kekova, with the final night at Gökkaya Bay, opposite the eastern end of Kekova. Boat trips from Demre via Kekova to Olympos are another option. Marmaris-based operators also offer trips which sail south and east along the Turquoise Coast via spots including Dalyan.

Food is usually included in the price, but you sometimes have to pay for water and soft drinks and always for alcohol. All boats are equipped with showers, toilets and smallish but comfortable double and triple cabins (usually between six and eight of them). Most people sleep on mattresses on deck as the boats are not air-conditioned.

Blue voyage prices vary by season – in summer three night/four day trips from Fethiye typically range from €220 to €340. We receive feedback from travellers who have had disappointing experiences with badly organised or dishonest operators. Here are some suggestions to avoid getting fleeced:

➡ Ask for recommendations from other travellers.

➡ Avoid touts at the bus stations and go straight to agencies (especially those listed here).

➡ Bargain, but don't necessarily go for the cheapest option, because the crew might skimp on food and services.

➡ Check out your boat if you are on-site and ask to see the guest list.

➡ Ask whether your captain and crew speak English.

➡ Ask for details of the itinerary and whether the weather and sailing conditions will allow you to stick to it.

➡ Don't go for gimmicks such as free water sports; they often prove to be empty promises.

➡ Bring your own snorkel and mask (those provided often leak).

➡ Confirm whether the boat ever actually uses the sails (though most don't, in any case) rather than relying on a diesel engine.

➡ Avoid buying your ticket in İstanbul, as pensions, travel agents and tour operators there take a healthy cut.

➡ Book well ahead – both in high season (July and August), when spaces are in great demand, and low season, when far fewer boats take to the water.

The following Fethiye-based outfits have a good reputation. Marmaris-based operator Yeşil Marmaris (p274) also runs recommended trips.

Alaturka (☑ 0252-612 5423; www.alaturkacruises.com; Fevzi Çakmak Caddesi 29b; 3-night cruise from €245) This company's blue voyages between Fethiye and Olympos are consistently recommended by readers. It also offers many other routes, including Kaş to Olympos (from €225) and Marmaris to Fethiye (from €270).

Before Lunch Cruises (☑ 0535 636 0076; www.beforelunch.com; Kordon Gezi Yolu; 3-night cruise €350) Run by a reputable company that follows its own unique itinerary, incorporating Göcek Bay and the Gulf of Fethiye. These ecofriendly tours include two optional morning walks. More expensive than most, but gets fine feedback. Cash only.

V-GO Yachting & Travel (☑ 0252-612 2113; www.bluecruisesturkey.com; 3-night cruise from €196; ☺ 8.30am-11.30pm) Has a good reputation and offers tempting private charter options.

and a snorkel. **Cennet Koyu** (Paradise Bay) is next for a plunge, followed by **Kleopatra Hamamı** (Cleopatra's Bath) and finally **Kızılada** (Red Island) with its beach and mud baths.

Two reliable companies based along the waterfront promenade are **Kardeşler** (☑0542 326 2314, 0252-612 4241; www.kardeslerboats.com; Kordon Gezi Yolu; tour incl lunch from ₺70) and **Hanedan** (☑0252-614 1937; www.hanedan2.com; Kordon Gezi Yolu; tour incl lunch ₺75).

🛏 Sleeping

The bulk of accommodation options are up the hill behind the Karagözler 1 marina, or further west behind the Karagözler 2 marina. Many pensions will organise transport from the otogar, but there are also frequent dolmuşes to/from Karagözler 2.

Most holiday villas and apartments are at Çalış Beach, in the nearby resorts of Hisarönü and Ovacık, and in the village of Kayaköy.

★ Tan Pansiyon
PENSION $

(☑0252-614 1584, 0546 711 4559; www.tanpansiyonfethiye.com; 30 Sokak 41; s ₺80-100, d ₺100-140, f ₺150-200; ❄🖥) By the marina, this welcoming budget place has nine small, spartan rooms (with tiny bathrooms) which contrast with the large roof terrace overlooking the bay. It's all sparkling clean and quiet, with a kitchen for guest use. Run by the charming Öztürk family who can help out with travel planning and local excursions.

★ El Camino Pub & Hostel
HOSTEL $

(☑0252 612 1415; www.facebook.com/elcamino hostelpub; İpekçi Caddesi 9; dm/d €12/25; ❄🖥) A well-run hillside hostel, with four-bed dorms (fitted with reliable air-con) and attractive private rooms, some with fine bay views from their balconies. There's a roof terrace for breakfasts, which doubles as a pub, and a washing machine is available for guests.

★ Minu Hotel
HOTEL $$

(☑0252-612 2050; www.minuhotel.com; 40 Sokak 4; s/d €35/48; ❄🖥) All white-on-white minimalism in the rooms and friendly, highly efficient service, the Minu is a fantastic central Fethiye find. Breakfast is a feast and the beds are among the comfiest in town. Be aware though, it's amid the main eating and nightlife area (the music dies down at midnight) so early-to-bedders may want to give it a miss.

Duygu Pension
PENSION $$

(☑0535 796 6701, 0252-614 3563; www.duygupen sion.com; 16 Sokak 54; s/d/tr €25/30/32; ❄🖥) Popular with hikers and independent travellers, this warm and welcoming family-run pension near the Karagözler 2 marina has 11 homely rooms brightened by colourful wall stencils and frilly touches, while the rooftop terrace has spellbinding sea views. Birol is your man and a great source of information. Connected with the centre via a busy dolmuş route.

Orka Boutique Hotel
BOUTIQUE HOTEL $$

(☑0252-614 5010; www.orkaboutique.com; Kordon Boyu Başlangıç Mevkii 1; s/d from ₺180/230; 🅿❄🖥) With watery views from its pleasant ground-floor bar-restaurant, the Orka is all floor-to-ceiling windows and swish contemporary styling in cool pastels and lashings of white. The seafront rooms are the ones to bag (or else your mammoth windows are wasted on a panorama of a taxi stand).

Yıldırım Guest House
PENSION $$

(☑0252-614 4627; www.yildirimguesthouse. com; Fevzi Çakmak Caddesi 53; dm/s/d/tr ₺50/150/175/250; 🅿❄🖥) In a strip of four pensions, 'Lightning' is popular with hikers going the Lycian Way and distinguishes itself through its services (manager Omer is very helpful) rather than its infrastructure. There are six-bed female and mixed dorms, a four-bed male dorm and simple, spotless rooms.

Villa Daffodil
HOTEL $$

(☑0252-614 9595; www.villadaffodil.com; Fevzi Çakmak Caddesi 139; s/d from €38/52; ❄🖥) Staff are super-helpful and service spot-on at this decent-value option, with views of the sea or forested hills from its rooms and suites. Rooms opening onto the walkway to the pool are better, as a low-ceilinged and worn staircase leads to some internal rooms (eg 304 to 307). The rear pool area is perfect for lounging after a day's sightseeing.

Ferah Pension
PENSION $$

(☑0532 265 0772, 0252-614 2816; www.ferah pension.com; 16 Sokak 23; dm/s/d/tr/q €15/30/35/55/75; ❄🖥) A hospitable pension with an inner terrace dripping in vines and bedecked by flowerpots, with a teensy pool. Rooms are basic and some are very compact; try to score one with a harbour view.

Hotel Unique
BOUTIQUE HOTEL $$$

(☑0252-612 1145; www.hoteluniqueturkey.com; 30 Sokak 43a; r from €75; ❄🖥) This fine hotel offers a contemporary seaside take on Ottoman-village chic. The service and attention to detail are impressive, with wooden beams, floors and hand-carved doors from Black Sea houses in the rooms, and pebbles from the beach in the bathroom floors.

Yacht Classic Hotel   BOUTIQUE HOTEL $$$

(☏ 0252-612 5067; www.yachtclassichotel.com; Fevzi Çakmak Caddesi 1; s €100-175, d €125-220, ste/villas from €250/350; ✳ 🕸 ☷) Recently renovated, this luxe hotel is a symphony in soothing pastels and cream with lovely bathrooms and a tasteful contemporary ambience. Guests get to enjoy the large pool terrace overlooking the harbour and what could be the most stylish hotel hamam on the Med.

La Farine Hotel   BOUTIQUE HOTEL $$$

(☏ 0532 564 6816; www.lafarinehotel.com; Fevzi Çakmak Caddesi 33; r/ste from €60/90; ✳ 🕸) By the marina, this stylish hotel has 15 rooms (eight with bay views, which are worth the extra as some others with 'mountain view' actually face a wall), all with sleek modern decor, and a couple of swanky suites. Also home to a good patisserie.

✖ Eating

The bulk of accommodation options are up the hill behind the Karagözler 1 marina, or further west behind the Karagözler 2 marina. Many pensions will organise transport from the otogar, but there are also frequent dolmuşes to/from Karagözler 2.

Most holiday villas and apartments are at Çalış Beach, in the nearby resorts of Hisarönü and Ovacık, and in the village of Kayaköy.

Fish Kebap Boats   SEAFOOD $

(Kordon Gezi Yolu; fish kebaps ₺8; ☉ 11am-10pm) A few small boats moored off Uğur Mumcu Parkı offer *balık ekmek* (fish sandwiches) and fish and chips (₺15), with seating on their bobbing decks. They offer a cheap way to sample the local fish, but are better for lunch, as their small kitchens may not exactly be squeaky clean after a busy day.

★ Mozaik Bahce   TURKISH $$

(☏ 0252-614 4653; www.facebook.com/mozaik bahce; 91 Sokak 2a; mains ₺22-45; ☉ 8am-11pm Mon-Sat) Intimate backstreet restaurant that can be relied on for really authentic and beautifully crafted dishes from the southeastern city of Antakya (Hatay), so a Syrian influence is evident. Try the hummus, Arab kebaps, salads and mezes. No bookings and very popular; be prepared to wait for a table.

★ Paşa Kebab   TURKISH $$

(☏ 0252-614 9807; www.pasakebap.com; Çarşı Caddesi 42; pides ₺12-19.50, kebaps ₺36-65; ☉ 11am-1am; 🕸) Nearly always bustling, and with a menu that's something of a novella, Paşa does a fine line in Turkish staples. If you're hungry, try a mixed kebap (₺65) which will feed two and features an Adana kebap, lamb and chicken *şiş*, roasted peppers and tomato, sumac onion and bulgur wheat. Book ahead.

Hilmi   SEAFOOD $$

(☏ 0252-614 2232; www.hilmi.com.tr; Hal ve Pazar Yeri; mezes from ₺8, mains from ₺28; ☉ 11am-1am Jun-Sep, to 11pm Nov-May) Established in 1935, this inviting, always busy little eatery allows you to experience the buzz of the Fish Market without purchasing from the fishmongers. The delightful mezes and mains include calamari, octopus, prawns with garlic butter and chilli. Locals favour rakı (aniseed brandy) with their fish and seafood, though there's also a decent wine list of Turkish and international bottles.

Ruzanna Food & Etc   CAFE $$

(Fevzi Çakmak Caddesi 19; snacks & mains ₺14-75; ☉ 24hr; ✳ 🕸) Opposite the marina, this little slice of foodie paradise has some of the best cakes (from ₺12) and pastries in town. It also has superb coffee and juices, very friendly staff and attractive modern premises with stylish seating. There's a full bar. Check it out on Facebook.

Meğri Lokantası   TURKISH $$

(☏ 0252-614 4046; Çarşı Caddesi 26; dishes ₺12-60; ☉ 9.30am-11.30pm; 🌱) Looking for us at lunchtime in Fethiye? We're usually here. Head inside and mix and match a plate (large mixed plate ₺22) from the glass counter display of hearty, home-style vegetable and meat dishes.

Fish Market   SEAFOOD $$

(Balık Pazarı, Balık Halı; Hal ve Pazar Yeri, btwn Hükümet & Belediye Caddesis; ☉ 11am-10pm) This circle of fishmongers ringed by restaurants is Fethiye's most atmospheric eating experience: buy fresh fish (per kilo ₺18 to ₺55) or shellfish, take it to a restaurant to have them cook it, and watch the fishmongers competing for attention with the waiter-touts, flower sellers and roaming *fasıl* (gypsy music) buskers.

The fishmongers are much of a piscatory muchness, but you could try **Pehlivan Baş**. It may try to steer you towards a restaurant it works with, but you are, of course, under no obligation. There is also little to distinguish the restaurants, which typically charge ₺10 for mezes and ₺8 to ₺10 per head to cook the fish, with an olive oil and garlic sauce, lemon, rocket and çay thrown in. Make sure unordered mezes aren't placed on your table – you'll be charged for them. **Reis Balık** (☑0532 472 5989, 0252-612 5368; www.reisrestaurant.com) and **Cem & Can** are both good choices. A small **vegetable market and produce shops** selling cheese and honey adjoin the market's central covered courtyard.

Meğri Restaurant INTERNATIONAL **$$**
(☑0252-614 4046; www.megrirestaurant.com; 40 Sokak 10; mezes & salads ₺9-20, mains ₺24-55; ☑) Meğri Restaurant (not to be confused with nearby Meğri Lokantasi) offers a more varied menu than many competitors, including plenty for veggies. Try the risotto with chicken and saffron or dip into the huge meze selection. Seating is under awnings on the Paspatur walkway.

Drinking & Nightlife

Bars, clubs and *meyhanes* (taverns) spill onto the pedestrianised 45 Sokak in the old town. Known as Barlar Sokak (Bar St), this tacky strip is home turf for the drunk and disorderly. On Kordon Gezi Yolu, near the Atatürk statue, several bars and restaurants are ideal for a waterfront sundowner.

If caffeine is more your scene, you'll find a growing number of specialist cafes scattered around town.

⭐**Keçi Coffee Roastery** CAFE
(www.facebook.com/kecicoffeeroastery; 504 Sokak; ⊙10am-10pm; 🛜) Fethiye's best specialist coffee shop, with imported beans that are roasted on the premises. There's a choice of specials (brews and drips include Chemex and Aeropress) as well as good old-fashioned Turkish coffee and espresso. There's plenty of space to lounge around on sofas and armchairs, and enjoy a dose of air-con in the hot summer months.

Pukka Coffee & Cake CAFE
(Fevzi Çakmak Caddesi 2; ⊙9am-midnight; 🛜) With bay views from its front terrace and an attractive air-conditioned interior, Pukka is a good bet for a flat white, latte or piece of cheesecake. Geeky barista-ista options including V60, Aeropress, syphon and Chemex are available.

Address BAR
(☑0252-614 4453; Kordon Gezi Yolu; ⊙4pm-late) The name says it all: Address' roomy waterfront garden is kilometre zero for everyone from çay-sipping locals to beer-drinking foreign residents watching the football on big screens. Fit in with both groups by ordering an Efes beer and a nargile (water pipe).

Kum Saati Bar BAR
(☑0252-614 4867; 45 Sokak; ⊙11am-late) A popular joint on Fethiye's most raucous street after dark, the 'Hour Glass' keeps good time throughout the day as a bar and has several screens showing football. Turns into more of a club with music and dancing after midnight.

Car Cemetery BAR
(☑0535 218 8153; Haman Sokak 33; ⊙10am-3am Mon-Sat) With bumpers protruding above its doors, this wacky, car-themed British boozer-cum-club stages live music at weekends when its popularity with locals and tourists alike guarantees standing (or falling-down) room only.

🛍 Shopping

Old Orient Carpet & Kilim Bazaar CARPETS
(☑0532 510 6108; c.c_since.1993@hotmail.com; 45 Sokak 5; ⊙9am-midnight mid-Apr–Oct, to 6pm Nov–mid-Apr) This shop is where the discerning buy their carpets and kilims, following the sage advice of carpet seller Celal Coşkun. Hoping to preserve the dying art of carpet making, Celal also offers classes in making and repairing carpets.

ℹ Getting There & Away

Airport buses operated by **Havaş** (☑0555 985 1165; www.havas.net) offer links between Dalaman International Airport and Fethiye otogar (₺23, one hour).

BOAT
Ferries sail to Rhodes in Greece once or twice daily between June and September (one way/ same day return/open return €40/45/55, 1½ hours) from Fethiye pier, opposite the tourist office. They operate every Monday, Wednesday, Thursday and Friday in May and October, and roughly weekly during April. Boats depart at 8.30am (and sometimes 4.30pm) from Fethiye and leave from Rhodes at 4.30pm (plus a few additional services at 9am).

Cruising the Turquoise Coast

A 'blue cruise' is sightseeing with swags of style. Board a *gület* (Turkish yacht) to experience the Turquoise Coast's scenery in all its glory, from lazy days filled with swimming and sunbathing to sunset toasts in one of the prettiest corners of the Mediterranean.

Casting Off

Fethiye is the most popular departure point for average landlubbers who want a taste of on-the-sea life. More experienced yachties (and those chartering an entire boat rather than a cabin) often head for Göcek or Kaş.

Day One

Gülets head out from Fethiye and skim the lush green coastline to Ölüdeniz before cruising on to the cliff-hemmed beach at Butterfly Valley. The first day usually ends at St Nicholas Island, where there's plenty of time for swimming, snorkelling and – if you want your land legs back – exploring the island's ancient ruins.

Day Two

A full day of soaking up some sun on-board, with opportunities aplenty for swimming. On day two you usually cruise by the dinky harbour towns of Kalkan and Kaş and moor near the Liman Ağzı peninsula.

Day Three

Mixing history into the sunshine and salt spray, day three sails past tiny Üçağız to Kekova Island's famous sunken-city remnants, before visiting Kaleköy to clamber up the hilltop to the fortress ruins of ancient Simena.

Day Four

On this day you head east along the coast, with plentiful swimming stops to savour the scenery. Çayağzı (the ancient harbour of Andriake), just south of Demre, is the usual disembarking point.

1. Kalkan (p341) 2. Kaleköy (p353) 3. Ölüdeniz (p334)
4. Beach at Butterfly Valley (p335)

Tickets are available near the pier from Ocean Yachting Travel Agency (p323) and **Tilos Travel** (☑ 0252-614 3434, 0533 498 2254; www.tilostravel.com; Fevzi Cakmak Caddesi 35b; ☺ 8am-8pm).

BUS & DOLMUŞ

Fethiye's small but busy **otogar** (Fethiye Bus Station; İnönü Bulvarı) is 2.5km east of the town centre.

Buses and dolmuşes (minibuses) taking the coastal route to Antalya (₺45, six hours) leave around every hour in high season, stopping at Kınık (for Xanthos; ₺12, one hour), Kalkan (₺18, 1½ hours), Kaş (₺22, two hours) and the Olympos turn-off (₺40, 4¾ hours). There are 15 daily summer bus services (less November to March) on the much quicker inland road direct to Antalya (₺36 to ₺53, 3½ hours).

Heading north to Marmaris (₺24, two hours), dolmuşes leave every 30 minutes between 7.45am and 10.45pm.

You can also catch the dolmuşes direct to Ölüdeniz, Faralya and Kabak, and Kayaköy at the bus stop on the main road outside the otogar, in front of the Carrefour supermarket.

Many dolmuşes heading for destinations in the local vicinity depart from a **station** (off Çarşı Caddesi), 1km east of the centre, near the petrol station, but handily stop at a **dolmuş stand** (Akdeniz Caddesi) in the town centre, near the new mosque and opposite the TTNet shop. Destinations include Ovacık (₺4), Hisarönü (₺4), Kayaköy (₺5.50), Ölüdeniz (₺6), Faralya and Kabak (₺6) and Saklıkent (₺12).

ⓘ Getting Around

If you're basing yourself in the Muğla region (covering Bodrum to Fethiye) for a while and planning to use a lot of local transport, the **Muğla kentkart** (rechargeable transport card) gives you discounted ticket prices on both the in-town dolmuşes and any town-council-run minibuses which ply the routes out of town to nearby destinations. In the Fethiye area, for example, the transport routes to Ölüdeniz and Kayaköy as well as to Marmaris are covered. The card costs ₺5 plus credit and can be bought at stores and supermarkets.

Some readers have also successfully downloaded and used a Kentkart app on their smartphones.

Dolmuşes (₺3) ply the one-way system along Atatürk Caddesi and up Çarşı Caddesi to the otogar, as well as along Fevzi Çakmak Caddesi to/from the Karagözler 2 pensions and hotels, west of the centre. There are also dolmuşes to Çalış Beach.

A **taxi** (off Atatürk Caddesi) from the otogar to Karagözler 2 costs about ₺28 and takes 15 minutes. The journey to Dalaman International Airport takes one hour and costs €30.

Head to the Karagözler 1 section of Fevzi Çakmak Caddesi for car-rental outfits, including **Levent Rent a Car** (☑ 0252-614 8096; www.leventrentacar.net; Fevzi Çakmak Caddesi 37b; car rental per day from €21; ☺ 9am-8pm) which also hires out scooters from €8 per day.

Kayaköy

☑ 0252 / POP 2400

About 9km south of Fethiye is Kayaköy (ancient Karmylassos), an eerie ghost town of 4000-odd abandoned stone houses and other structures that once made up the Greek town of Levissi. Today this timeless village, set in a lush valley with some vineyards nearby, forms a memorial to Turkish-Greek peace and cooperation. In the evening, when the ruined village's churches are spotlit, Kayaköy is truly surreal.

History

Levissi was deserted by its mostly Greek inhabitants in the general exchange of populations supervised by the League of Nations in 1923 after the Turkish War of Independence. Most Greek Muslims came to Turkey and most Ottoman Christians moved from coastal Turkey to Greece. The abandoned town was the inspiration for Eskibahçe, the setting of Louis de Bernières' 2004 novel, *Birds Without Wings*.

As there were far more Ottoman Christians than Greek Muslims, many Turkish towns were left unoccupied after the population exchange. Greeks did come to Kayaköy from Thessaloniki, but they were settled in the modern village in the valley below, where the accommodation and restaurants are now. The original Kayaköy, or Kaya as it is known locally, was later damaged by an earthquake in 1957.

With the tourism boom of the 1980s, a development company wanted to restore Kayaköy's stone houses and turn the town into a holiday village. Scenting money, the local inhabitants were delighted, but Turkish artists and architects were alarmed and saw to it that the Ministry of Culture declared Kayaköy a historic monument, safe from unregulated development.

◎ Sights

★ **Kayaköy (Levissi)**
Abandoned Village   RUINS
(₺7; ☺ 9am-7pm Apr-Oct, 8am-5pm Nov-Mar)
The tumbledown ruins of Levissi are highly

atmospheric. The roofless, dilapidated stone houses sit on the slopes like sentinels over the modern village below.

Not much is intact, except the two churches. The 17th-century **Kataponagia Church**, with an ossuary containing the mouldering remains of the long-dead in its churchyard, is on the lower part of the slope, while the **Taxiarkis Church** is near the top of the hill. Both retain some of their painted decoration and black-and-white pebble mosaic floors.

Near the latter is a ruined **castle**, while the hilltop **tower** above Kataponagia Church has commanding views of the valley.

🛏️ Sleeping & Eating

Kayaköy Jungle Camping   CAMPGROUND **$**
(☑ 0554 311 3425; www.facebook.com/kayakoy junglehouseandcamp; tent/hut ₺70/140; 🖥️) Inexpensive Kayaköy budget base with attractive simple wooden huts and a campsite. There's a friendly vibe, with Turks and travellers mixing well, camp fires at night and a clean bathroom block.

★ **Günay's Garden**   RESORT **$$$**
(☑ 0534 360 6545, 0252-618 0073; www. gunaysgarden.com; 2-/3-bed villas per week €1100/1200; ❄️🖥️🏊) This fine boutique resort consists of self-catering villas hidden within lush gardens and set around a shimmering pool. Some of the villas have both front and back balconies, and all have generous terraces with ample sunloungers. The views of the abandoned village are evocative.

★ **Villa Rhapsody**   GUESTHOUSE **$$$**
(☑ 0532 337 8285, 0252-618 0042; www.villarhap sody.com; s/d/tr €44/62/80; ⊗ Apr–Oct; ❄️🖥️🏊) This welcoming place has 16 comfortable rooms with balconies overlooking a delightful walled garden and poolside bar. Atilla and Jeanne, the Turkish and Dutch owners, are full of advice about local hikes, activities and restaurants, and breakfast is a feast. It's 200m west of the village, at the beginning of the road to Gemiler beach and St Nicholas Island.

★ **Cin Bal Kebap Salonu**   BARBECUE **$$**
(☑ 0252-618 0066; www.cinbal.com; mains ₺30–45; ⊗ 11am–midnight) Established in 1989, Cin Bal specialises in lamb *tandir* (clay oven) dishes and kebaps, with seating inside and in its grapevine-covered garden courtyard. Most people choose from the choice cuts, then DIY barbecue on a little charcoal table

LOCAL KNOWLEDGE

DAY HIKES FROM KAYAKÖY

The Kayaköy to Ölüdeniz extension of the Lycian Way (p341) trek takes in serene forest scenery and jaw-droppingly beautiful coastal panoramas. For keen walkers who don't have time for a longer trek, it's a fantastic half-day hike. The signposted trailhead starts within Kayaköy's abandoned village ruins and is waymarked the entire length. The 8km walk takes two to 2½ hours.

You can also walk over the hill and through pine woods to Fethiye (5km, 1½ hours), or west to Kabak and St Nicholas Island (7km, two hours). On all of these walks, you can catch a dolmuş (minibus) back.

grill, which waitstaff set up for you. Otherwise, leave it to the experts. It's just off the Hisarönü road. Cash only.

★ **İzela Restaurant**   MEDITERRANEAN **$$$**
(☑ 0252-618 0073, 0534 360 6545; www.gu naysgarden.com; mezes from ₺20, mains from ₺45; ⊗ 7.30am–11.30pm; 🖥️🍴) This lovely restaurant is located in the lush grounds of Günay's Garden, with its poolside bar for aperitifs. It specialises in Mediterranean cuisine, with more than a tip of the hat to modern Turkish, and serves generous dishes from seafood and steaks to sumptuous meze selections. Free local pick-ups and drop-offs included.

Lebessos Wine   MEDITERRANEAN **$$$**
(☑ 0536 484 7290; mains ₺40–90; ⊗ 11am–11.30pm; 🖥️) This 400-year-old stone building houses a stunning wine house and restaurant, with a cellar containing hundreds of bottles of Turkey's finest. Expect a wonderful meze selection and expert guidance from a sommelier who will offer free tastings. Book to avoid disappointment. It's near the ruins on the Hisarönü road. Call for a free pick-up.

ℹ️ Getting There & Away

Dolmuşes run to Fethiye (₺5.50, 20 minutes) every half-hour from May to October and every couple of hours in low season. A taxi from Fethiye costs around ₺50, a little less from Ölüdeniz. All dolmuşes on their way to/from Kayaköy pass through Hisarönü, from where dolmuşes leave every five minutes for Ölüdeniz (20 minutes in low season).

Ölüdeniz

🎵 0252 / POP 4900

With its sheltered (and protected) lagoon beside a lush national park, a long spit of sandy beach and Baba Dağ (Mt Baba) casting its shadow across the sea, Ölüdeniz (*eu*-leu-den-eez), 15km south of Fethiye, is a dream sprung from a glossy brochure. Problem is, like most beautiful destinations, it has become a victim of its own package-tourism success – in high summer the motionless charms of the 'Dead Sea' are swamped by the Paradise Lost of the tacky adjoining town.

If you're looking for an easy-going day on the beach, though, you can't really go wrong here. Similarly, if you've always wanted to throw yourself off a mountain, Ölüdeniz is one of Turkey's top destinations for tandem paragliding. Nearby is the starting point for the wonderful Lycian Way walking trail, which runs high above the fun and frolics.

◉ Sights & Activities

A string of beach clubs running along the lagoon, including **Sugar Beach** (📞 0252-617 0048; www.thesugarbeachclub.com; Ölüdeniz Caddesi 63; bungalow s/d/tr/q €60/70/83/95; ☺ May-Oct; 🅿🌀❄🛜) and **Seahorse** (📞 0252-617 0888; www.seahorsebeachclub.com; Ölüdeniz Caddesi; r s/d from €80/90, caravan €90-120; 🅿🌀❄🛜), offer access to their beaches and use of their facilities, including sunloungers, parasols, showers, canoes and paddle boats, for varying charges. Some offer all-inclusive

---

DON'T MISS

ÖLÜDENIZ PARAGLIDING

. . . .

The descent from 1960m Baba Dağ (Mt Baba) can take up to 40 minutes, with amazing views over the Blue Lagoon, Butterfly Valley and, on a clear day, as far as Rhodes.

Operators include **Pegas Tur** (📞 0252-617 0051; Çetin Motel, Ölüdeniz Caddesi; ☺ 8am-11pm) and **Gravity Tandem Paragliding** (📞 0252-617 0379; www.flygravity.com; Denizpark Caddesi; ☺ 9am-10pm). All charge around ₺500, with another ₺200 or so to pay for photos or video. Whichever company you choose, ensure it has insurance and the pilot has the appropriate qualifications. Parasailing on the beach is also possible.

---

day entry, also including lunch, drinks and snacks, for around €40 per person. Sections of shoreline also offer public access for swimming.

Ölüdeniz Beach & Lagoon   BEACH
(Ölüdeniz Caddesi; lagoon adult/child ₺7/3.50, bicycle/car parking ₺7/25; ☺ 8am-8pm) The beach is why most people visit Ölüdeniz. While the decent strip of pebble shore edging the holiday resort is free, the famed lagoon beach is a protected national park (Ölüdeniz Tabiat Parkı) that you pay to enter. Both the public beach and lagoon get heavily crowded in summer, but, with the mountains soaring above you, it's still a lovely place to while away a few hours. There are showers, toilets and cafes; sunshades (₺15), loungers (₺15) and paddle boats can be rented.

Boat Excursions   BOATING
(per person incl lunch ₺50-80; ☺ 11am-6pm) Throughout summer, boats set out from Ölüdeniz beach to explore the surrounding coast. The day-long boat tours typically include the Blue Cave, Butterfly Valley, St Nicholas Island, Camel Beach, Akvaryum Koyu (Aquarium Bay), and a cold-water spring. Ask the tourist office for more information or book direct with the boats moored on the beach. Many boats blare out cheesy party tunes to 'entertain' their guests.

🛏 Sleeping & Eating

Mozaik Hotel   APARTMENT $$$
(📞 0252-617 0496; https://mozaik-hotel.business. site; 238 Sokak 1; r/apt from €80/120; ❄🛜🏊) Perfect for families, this modern, beautifully designed complex has well-maintained, spotlessly clean rooms and apartments overlooking a huge pool area. Expect all mod cons, including large flatscreens; some units have hot tubs and swim-up access. Located about 800m inland from the beach.

Oyster Residences   BOUTIQUE HOTEL $$$
(📞 0252-617 0765; www.oysterresidences.com; 224 Sokak 1; s/d/tr from €150/160/220; ☺ May-Oct; ❄🛜🏊) Inspired by old Fethiye-style houses, this boutique pad has 26 bright and airy rooms over three floors, done up in a kind of neotropical style. Accommodation opens on to lush gardens that creep all the way to the beach. Rates drop below €100 in the off-season.

İnci Restaurant TURKISH $$

(📞0536 967 6716; Jandarma Sokak; mains ₺25-50; ⏰11am-midnight Jun-Oct, 11am-10pm Nov-May; 📶) One of Ölüdeniz' more authentic eateries, 'Pearl' Restaurant serves Turkish classics, *ev yemekleri* (home cooking), international dishes and daily specials. It offers good-value set menus, kebaps, and lighter lunch fare such as *gözleme* (stuffed flatbread).

★ Buzz Beach Bar INTERNATIONAL $$$

(📞0252-617 0526; www.buzzbeachbar.com; Belcekız 1 Sokak; mains ₺28-85; ⏰8am-2am; 📶) For elevated views over Mediterranean Turkey's best beach, head to the upper deck of this stylish place. Offers a wide menu, including falafel (₺35), burgers, pasta (from ₺42) and seafood. This is also a top spot for a sunset cocktail (₺40 to ₺45) – try a negroni or pink gin spritz.

ⓘ Getting There & Away

In high season, dolmuşes leave Fethiye (₺7.50, 35 minutes) for Ölüdeniz roughly every five minutes, passing through Ovacık and Hisarönü. In low season, they go every 20 minutes by day and hourly at night. A taxi to Fethiye costs about ₺80.

Butterfly Valley & Faralya

Tucked away on the Yedi Burun (Seven Capes) coast 12km from Ölüdeniz is the village of Faralya, also called Uzunyurt. Below it is the paradise-found Butterfly Valley, a deep gorge with a fine beach at its mouth. This sublime spot has been a legendary hang-out since the 1970s, a mecca for bohemian Turks and travellers. The existential, back-to-nature vibe has inevitably changed, but it's still a sublime setting, even if it's very much on the agenda of day-tripping boats from nearby Ölüdeniz. But they don't hang around long.

There are some lovely walks through the valley, home to the unique Jersey tiger butterfly, from which the beach takes its name. Access is only by boat from Ölüdeniz, or on foot via a very steep path that winds its way down a cliff from Faralya.

⌷ Sleeping

There is a basic accommodation in Butterfly Valley, and numerous pensions above the valley in Faralya.

⌷ Butterfly Valley

Butterfly Valley CAMPGROUND $$
(Kelebekler Vadisi; 📞0555 632 0237; www.yenike lebeklervadisi.org; per person incl half board tents/bungalows/teepee ₺150/180/325; ⏰Mar-Oct; ✳) This unique spot, on a truly spectacular cove beach, isn't the hippy hang-out of years back, but there's still an earthy vibe evident. Accommodation is simple, yet not that cheap: tents for rent (bed linen and mattresses provided), 29 simple bungalows (with electricity, and some with en-suites) and upmarket teepees (with air-con!). There are ample places to eat and drink and socialise with other guests.

⌷ Faralya

Butterfly Guesthouse PENSION $
(📞0533 140 8000, 0252-642 1042; www.butter flyguesthouse.com; s/d ₺110/140, without bathroom ₺90/120; ✳📶) Here Önur, Gülser and daughter Eliz offer an experience of local life in a whitewashed house on a village lane, among the twittering birds and roosters. There are five simple rooms in the main house, three sharing a bathroom, and a spacious and modern room in the garden of citrus and olives.

Melisa Pansiyon PENSION $$
(📞0252-642 1012, 0535 881 9051; www.melisa pension.com; campsites per person ₺25, s/d/tr/q/f ₺140/210/285/320/450, roof terrace s/d/tr ₺90/150/195; ✳📶) This simple, very welcoming Turkish-Austrian pension has well-maintained and cheerful rooms, a pretty garden (campers welcome), fully stocked guests' kitchen and a vine-bedecked terrace overlooking the valley. Owner Mehmet speaks English and is a good source of local information. Guests can wake up to stunning views on the trellised roof terrace, which is equipped with a cushioned *köşk* (kiosk) and toilet.

★ Die Wassermühle LUXURY HOTEL $$$

(The Watermill; 📞0252-642 1245; www.natur-rei sen.de; Hisar Sokak 4; r/ste incl half board from €110/120; ⏰mid-Apr–Oct; 📶✳) A lovely German-owned rustic timber-and-stone lodge almost hidden on a wooded slope. Both the suites (with kitchenettes) and standard rooms are spacious and use all-natural materials. Views from the restaurant and spring-water pool terraces are commanding. The owners prepare 'healthy, organic and regional' cuisine for their guests – dinner is served family-style and takes in five or six dishes, a veritable banquet.

❶ Getting There & Away

Water taxis connect Ölüdeniz with Butterfly Valley (₺30 return, 11am to 6pm) five times daily between May and October; services are sporadic in winter. Many organised boat trips from Fethiye and Ölüdeniz stop by too.

To Faralya, hourly minibuses (every two hours November to April) run to/from Fethiye (₺10, one hour) via Ölüdeniz (₺6, 25 minutes). The road up here from Ölüdeniz is as memorable for its views as for its knuckle-whitening corners. A taxi from Fethiye should cost about ₺100.

Kabak

📞 0252 / POP 170

Six kilometres south of Faralya – and worlds away from everywhere else – Kabak calls to camping and hiking enthusiasts, yoga devotees and all fans of untapped beauty. Once this region's best-kept secret and a haven for Turkish alternative lifestylers, the cat (not to mention the downward dog) is firmly out of the bag: the pine-tree-flanked valley above the beach now counts over a dozen camps and a growing number of upmarket lodges. Nonetheless, Kabak remains one of the Fethiye area's most tranquil spots and anyone craving a slice of back-to-nature bliss will adore a stay here. Whether you walk or take a high-suspension vehicle down the steep track to Kabak Valley (Gemile Beach), you'll be rewarded with a spectacular beach flanked by two long cliffs.

🛏 Sleeping & Eating

Accommodation down in Kabak Valley consists of camping or tented platforms and bungalows. Nearly all include half board in the price, as there are no stand-alone restaurants on Gemile Beach, only up in Kabak village, on the road to/from Faralya. Most camps open from mid-April to October and most can organise transport down if you phone, email or text ahead.

Above Kabak Valley, near the dolmuş stop on the main road, are a couple of restaurants. In summer, a small grocery shop by Gemile Beach sells basic supplies.

★ **Turan Hill Lounge**   BUNGALOW $$
(📞 0532 710 1077, 0252-642 1227; www.turan camping.com; incl half board per person own/deluxe tent ₺95/100, bungalows without bathroom s/d ₺190/220, houses s/d from ₺290/330; ❋ 🛜 ☷)
The epitome of Turkish glamping, Turan Hill opened in 1987 and Turan, Ece and Ahmet's place remains a trendsetter; growing out of its hippyish roots to become a stylish luxe-camping getaway. There's a choice of tented platforms, rustic semi-open bungalows and incredibly cute houses brimming with colourful character.

It also has lovely views and lots of mellow lounging areas. Yoga courses and daily classes take place on the enormous platform in the valley below.

Reflections Camp   BUNGALOW $$
(📞 0252-642 1020; www.reflectionscamp.com; incl half board per person own/camp tent ₺80/90, bungalow ₺150-300; 🛜) 🍴 The friendly crew here has an ethos of simple, sustainable living. Reflections is a comfortable place with some of Kabak's best sea views from its inviting terrace, and bungalows constructed from compacted-earth bags, bamboo and wood. Views from the secluded campsite are nothing short of awesome.

★ **Avalon**   BOUTIQUE HOTEL $$$
(📞 0252-642 1022; www.kabakbeach.com; r €140; ❋ 🛜 ☷) Avalon is an intimate hideaway, sitting on the Lycian Way above the secluded bay at Kabak. Beautiful wooden cabins, each with balcony, offer stunning bay views. There's a small spa and the inhouse restaurant offers great local cuisine with a focus on healthy eating. Rates drop considerably outside high season.

Olive Garden   BUNGALOW $$$
(📞 0252-642 1083, 0536 439 8648; www.olive gardenkabak.com; incl half board s/d ₺300/550; ❋ 🛜 ☷) The Olive Garden is conveniently located down a side track just 100m from the village. Wooden bungalows are surrounded by gorgeous views, with an infinity pool jutting into the void high above the aquamarine shallows. Owner Fatih is a former chef and the food here is superb. Many of the ingredients come from his family's fruit trees, olive groves and vegetable gardens.

Mamma's Restaurant   CAFE $
(📞 0252-642 1071; mains ₺10-18; ⏰ 8am-9pm) Mamma dishes up simple, hearty food,

including *gözleme* (stuffed flatbread; ₺7) and her own homemade *ayran* (yoghurt drink; ₺3) from her front patio near the dolmuş stop in Kabak village. She also has a couple of simple and tidy rooms to rent that are popular with walkers.

❶ Getting There & Away

The road from Faralya carries on for another 6km until it reaches tiny Kabak village. Between June and October hourly minibuses trundle to/from Hisarönü (₺7, 40 minutes, 20km) via Ölüdeniz and Faralya. There are three daily services in winter. A taxi from Fethiye should cost about ₺110.

From the dolmuş stop on the main road, next to Last Stop Cafe at the far end of the village, a 4WD vehicle is usually on hand to transfer people down to the camps (₺50 for one to eight people), or you can take the 20-minute walking path leading down into the valley. Phone 0538 888 0298 to be picked up.

Tlos

On a rocky outcrop high above a pastoral plain, **Tlos** (₺5; ⊗9am-7pm mid-Apr–Oct, 8am-5pm Nov–mid-Apr.) was one of the most important cities of ancient Lycia. So effective was its elevated position that the well-guarded city remained inhabited until the early 19th century. As you climb the winding path to the ruins, look for the **acropolis** topped with an Ottoman fortress. Below the ticket kiosk are the ruins of the **stadium**, its central pool suggesting it was used for social and ritual activities as well as sports and games.

Beneath the fortress are **rock tombs**, including that of the warrior Bellerophon, of Chimaera fame. It has a temple-like facade carved into the rock face and to the left a fine bas-relief of our hero riding Pegasus, the winged horse.

The site's **theatre**, 150m across the road from the ticket office, is in excellent condition, with most of its marble seating intact; the stage wall has been rebuilt. Opposite the theatre are ruins of **ancient baths** (note the apothecary symbol – snake and staff – carved on an outer wall on the south side) and basilica.

From Fethiye, minibuses travel to Saklıkent Gorge via Tlos (₺9, 45 minutes) every 20 minutes. Some services travel directly to Saklıkent, in which case you can get off at the junction in the village of Güneşli, from where the site is a 4.5km hike (uphill all the way).

Saklıkent Gorge

☑ 0252

Some 12km after the turn-off to Tlos heading south, this spectacular gorge is really just a fissure in the Akdağlar, the mountains towering to the northeast. Some 18km long, and up to 200m high, the gorge is too narrow in places for even sunlight to squeeze through. Luckily *you* can, but prepare yourself for some very cold water year-round – even in summer.

You approach the gorge along a wooden boardwalk towering above the river. On wooden platforms suspended above the water, you can relax, drink tea and eat fresh trout while watching other tourists slip and slide their way across the river, hanging onto a rope and then dropping into the gorge proper. Good footwear is essential, though plastic shoes and helmets can be rented (₺8).

Saklıkent Gorge Club   CAMPGROUND **$$**
(☑ 0533 438 4101, 0252-659 0074; www.gorge club.com.tr; camp sites €10, tree house dm/s/d €16/30/48, bungalows s/d from €38/60; ❄ ⍨ ⌨) This rustic, backpacker-oriented camp has basic but very real tree houses, camp sites and some snazzier bungalows for those who don't want to rough it. The camp has a pool, bar and restaurant. With the exception of camping, rates include half board.

The restaurant (mains ₺18 to ₺40) serves trout and kebaps in a leafy riverside setting.

❶ Getting There & Away

Minibuses run every 20 minutes between Fethiye and Saklıkent (₺11, one hour). The last one back is at 10pm between May and October, and 7pm from November to April. In summer, a daily minibus runs from Patara to Saklıkent (₺13, one hour) at 11am, returning at 4pm.

Pınara

Some 46km southeast of Fethiye along the D400 is the turn-off for **Pınara** (₺5; ⊗9am-7pm May-Oct, to 5pm Nov-Apr) and its spectacular ruins. Pınara was one of the six highest-ranking cities in ancient Lycia, but although the site is vast, the actual ruins are not the region's most impressive. Instead, it's the splendour and isolation that makes it worth visiting. Rising high above the site is a sheer column of rock honeycombed with rock tombs; other tombs are within the ruined city itself.

The Royal Tomb, has fine reliefs, including several showing walled Lycian cities. With its photogenic mountain backdrop, Pınara's theatre is in good condition, but its odeon and temple to Aphrodite (with heart-shaped columns) are ruined. On the latter's steps, note the graffiti carved by its builders: an enormous (and anatomically correct) phallus.

Half-hourly dolmuşes from Fethiye (₺7, one hour) drop you at the Pınara turn-off, which is 5.5km from the site. In summer, taxis wait at the turn-off, charging ₺40 to ferry you to the site, wait and bring you back.

Xanthos

Up on a rock outcrop at Kınık, 63km southeast of Fethiye, are the ruins of ancient Xanthos (☑0242-247 7660; ₺14; ☺8.30am-7pm mid-Apr–Sep, 8.30am-5pm Oct–mid-Apr, ticket office shuts 30min before closure), once the capital and grandest city of Lycia, with a fine Roman theatre and pillar tombs.

From Kınık you pass the old city gates and the plinth where the fabulous Nereid Monument (now in London's British Museum) once stood.

Further up, opposite the car park, is the Roman theatre, agora and ticket office. Follow the colonnaded street to find some well-preserved mosaics, the Dancers' Sarcophagus and Lion Sarcophagus, and some rock tombs.

For all its grandeur, Xanthos had a chequered history of wars and destruction. At least twice, when besieged by clearly

superior enemy forces, the city's population committed mass suicide.

As many of the finest sculptures (eg the Harpies Monument) and inscriptions were carted off to London by Charles Fellows in 1842, most of the inscriptions and decorations you see today are copies of the originals.

❶ Getting There & Away

Any of the regular (about every hour) dolmuşes between Fethiye and Kaş can drop you at the Xanthos turn-off on the highway (₺10, one hour), from where it's a 1.5km walk to the site, or in the village of Kınık, which is closer.

Letoön

Sharing a place with the Lycian capital Xanthos on Unesco's World Heritage list since 1988, Letoön (₺12; ☺9am-7pm mid-Apr–Sep, 8am-5pm Oct–mid-Apr) is home to some of the finest ruins on the Lycian Way. Located about 17km south of the Pınara turn-off, this former religious centre is often considered a double site with Xanthos, but Letoön has its own romantic charm.

Letoön takes its name and importance from a large shrine to Leto, who, according to legend, was Zeus' lover and bore him Apollo and Artemis. Unimpressed, Zeus' wife Hera commanded that Leto spend eternity wandering from country to country. According to local folklore, she passed much time in Lycia and became the national deity. The federation of Lycian cities then built this very impressive religious sanctuary to house her statue.

The core of Letoön's ruins consists of three temples standing side by side and dedicated to Apollo (the Doric one on the left), Artemis (the Ionian in the middle) and Leto (the Ionian on the right and now partially reconstructed). On the floor in the middle of the Apollo temple is a mosaic (a replica; the original is in Fethiye Museum) showing a lyre, a bow and arrow, and a floral centre.

The permanently flooded nymphaeum (ornamental fountain with statues) is inhabited by frogs, which, in folklore, are said to be the shepherds who refused Leto a drink from the fountain and were punished for their lack of hospitality. The atmospheric structure is appropriate, as worship of Leto was associated with water.

Just to the north of the main temple complex is a large Hellenistic theatre dating from the 2nd century BC.

LOCAL KNOWLEDGE

WALKING BETWEEN LETOÖN & XANTHOS

The road between Letoön and Xanthos is an easy 5km section of the Lycian Way (p341) walking trail. Head out of Letoön and turn right at the turn-off to Kumluova village. Head straight up this road for about 1km until you get to Lycian Way signposted crossroads. Take the road signed for Xanthos and follow it until you reach Kınık village and the entrance road for the ruins.

ANCIENT LYCIA 101

The Lycian kingdom stretched roughly from Antalya to Dalyan, encompassing the bump of coastal terrain known as the Teke Peninsula. The enigmatic people who inhabited this area, the Lycians, date back to at least the 12th century BC, but first appear in writing when Homer's *Iliad* records their presence during an attack on Troy. It is thought they may have been descended from the Lukkans, a tribe allied with the ancient Hittites.

Lycian History

By the 6th century BC the Lycians had come under the control of the Persian Empire. Thus began a changing of the guard that occurred as regularly as today's ritual at Buckingham Palace. The Persians gave in to the Athenians, who were defeated in turn by Alexander the Great, the Ptolemaic Kingdom in Egypt and then Rhodes.

Lycia was granted independence by Rome in 168 BC and it immediately established the Lycian League, a loose confederation of 23 fiercely independent city states. Six of the largest – Xanthos, Patara, Pınara, Tlos, Myra and Olympos – held three votes each; the others just one or two. The Lycian League is often cited as the first protodemocratic union in history, and the *bouleuterion* (council chamber) among the ruins of Ancient Patara has been dubbed the world's first parliament.

Partly as a result of this union, peace held for over a century, but in 42 BC the league made the unwise decision not to pay tribute to Brutus, the murderer of Caesar, whom Lycia had supported during the civil war. Brutus' forces besieged Xanthos and the city state's outnumbered population, determined not to surrender, committed mass suicide.

Lycia recovered under the Roman Empire, but in AD 43 all of Lycia was amalgamated into the neighbouring province of Pamphylia, a union that lasted until the 4th century, when Pamphylia became part of Byzantium.

Ancient Legacy

Lycia left behind very little in the way of material culture or written documents. A matrilineal people, they spoke their own unique language – which has still not been fully decoded. What Lycia did bequeath to posterity, however, were some of the most stunning funerary monuments from ancient times. Cliff tombs, 'house' tombs, sepulchres and sarcophagi – the Teke Peninsula's mountains and valleys are littered with them, and most are easily accessible on foot or by car.

❶ Getting There & Away

Minibuses run from Fethiye via Eşen to Kumluova (₺10, one hour) every half-hour or so. They can drop you off at the (signposted) Letoön turn-off, from where it's an easy 1km walk to the site.

If driving from Fethiye and the north, turn right off the highway at the 'Letoön/Kumluova/Karadere' signpost. Go 4km, bear right, turn left after another 3.5km at the T-junction then right after 100m and proceed 1km – all signposted – to the site.

Patara

☑ 0242 / POP 850

Patara, on the coast 8km south of Xanthos, can claim Turkey's longest uninterrupted beach as well as a swag of atmospheric Lycian ruins. Just inland, 1.5km from the beach and ruins, is the laid-back village of Gelemiş. This is the perfect spot to mix ruin rambling with some dedicated sun worship.

Once a stop on the hippy trail, Gelemiş remains relatively unspoiled – a miracle given its obvious charms. Yes, there's been a mini tourism boom, but at heart the village remains a farming community, as the surrounding city of polytunnels attests. There are no huge resort hotels, and virtually all visitors are independent travellers, many returning year after year to the same family-owned pensions.

◉ Sights & Activities

Patara is on the Lycian Way (p341) and two day-walks lead to Patara Aqueduct, either along the coast (12km, 4½ hours) or inland (10km, four hours). You can catch a bus back to Gelemiş from the aqueduct (₺5). A shorter 7km circuit leads through the village (turn right at the Golden Pension) to the forest, over the dunes to the beach and back past the ruins.

Ancient Patara
ARCHAEOLOGICAL SITE

(incl Patara Beach ₺24; ⊙8am-7pm mid-Apr–Sep, 8am-5.30pm Oct–mid-Apr) Patara's grand monuments lie scattered along the road to the beach. The main section of ruins is dominated by the dilapidated 5000-seat theatre. Next door is the bouleuterion, ancient Patara's 'parliament', where it is believed members of the Lycian League met. It has been thoroughly restored, following a two-year, ₺8.5-million reconstruction. The colonnaded street, with re-erected columns, runs north from here. This would have been Patara's grandest boulevard, lined by shops and with the agora at its southern end.

Away from the main ruins there are plenty more remnants of Patara's long history to fossick through. From the ticket booth, along the Gelemiş–Patara Beach road, you first pass the 2nd-century triple-arched triumphal Arch of Modestus, with a necropolis containing a number of Lycian tombs nearby. As you head along the road, next is a Harbour Baths complex and the remains of a Byzantine basilica before you arrive at the central section of ruins.

From the colonnaded street, a dirt track leads to a lighthouse built by Emperor Nero that lays claim to being one of the three oldest lighthouses in the world. This is the area of the ancient harbour, once on a par with Ephesus and now a reedy wetland. It is also home to the enormous Granary of Hadrian, used to store cereals and olive oil, and a Corinthian-style temple tomb.

Patara's place in history is well documented. It was the birthplace of St Nicholas, the 4th-century Byzantine bishop of Myra who later passed into legend as Santa Claus. Before that, Patara was celebrated for its temple and oracle of Apollo, of which little remains. It was Lycia's major port – which explains the large storage granary still standing – and boasted three churches and five bathhouses in Roman times. According to Acts 21:1-2, Saints Paul and Luke changed boats here while on their third mission from Rhodes to Phoenicia. The inscribed tablets flanking the entrance to the *bouleuterion* give fascinating insights into daily life here in millennia past.

Patara Beach
BEACH

(incl Patara ruins ₺24; Plaji Pass for 10 visits ₺30) Backed by large sand dunes, this splendid, 18km-long sandy beach is one of Turkey's best. Due to its length, you can find a quiet spot even in the height of summer. Sunshades (₺10) and loungers (₺10) can be rented and there's a cafe for when you get peckish. Depending on the season, parts of the beach are off limits as it is an important nesting ground for sea turtles. It closes at dusk and camping is prohibited.

You can get here either by following the road for 1km past the Patara ruins to the busy main section of the beach, or by turning right at the Golden Pension in Gelemiş and following a somewhat rough road which heads for the sand-dunes area along the western side of the beach, where it's far quieter. Between May and October, half-hourly minibuses (₺3) run from the highway through the village to the beach. If you plan to visit a few times, buy a multi-visit Plaji Pass long-stay ticket allowing 10 entries over 10 days. In summer, ask your pension owner about accompanying the students who count the turtles' eggs at night.

Patara Horse Riding
HORSE RIDING

(⌁0242-843 5298; www.patarahorseriding.com) Based at the Patara Ranch Hotel, it offers three-hour rides (₺100) through the Patara dunes and along the beach, or on the Lycian Way. It uses 'Western' saddles with soft suede seats.

Kirca Travel
CANOEING

(⌁0242-843 5298; www.kircatravel.com; Mehmet Apartments) Kirca specialises in six-hour canoeing trips on the Xanthos River (₺120 including lunch), but also offers horse riding, day hikes and trips to Pamukkale.

🛏 Sleeping

As you come into Gelemiş, the main road and the hillside on your left contain hotels and pensions. A turn to the right at the Golden Pension takes you to the village centre, across the valley and up the other side to more accommodation. Many places offer self-catering apartments.

★ Akay Pension
PENSION $$

(⌁0242-843 5055, 0532 410 2195; www.patara akaypension.com; s/d/tr/apt €28/40/50/70; ❄🛜❄) It's the hard-working, hospitable owners Kazim and Ayşe, who really make this fine place, which has a comfy Ottoman-style lounge and well-maintained, attractive rooms with good air-con and minibars, modern bathrooms and balconies overlooking citrus groves. There's a pair of two-bedroom apartments for families, too. Ayşe's cooking is legendary; sample at least one set meal (from ₺30) while here.

★ **Patara View Point Hotel** HOTEL $$
(☑ 0242-843 5184; www.pataraviewpoint.com; s/d/tr €45/55/60; ❀@🛈❄) A fine English-Turkish-owned hotel with a lovely pool, 27 sea- or mountain-facing rooms, a cosy library and an Ottoman-style terrace. Owner Muzaffer is a history buff and you'll find 350-plus antiques here and old farm implements outside, including a 2000-year-old olive press, an ancient beehive and a replica Lycian tomb (for his dog). The owners also offer four modern and spacious apartments (€450 per week in high season), and lead excellent highly informative tours.

Flower Pension PENSION $$
(☑ 0242-843 5164; www.pataraflowerpension. com; s/d/tr/apt €30/40/50/60; ❀🛈❄) The Flower has bright, simply decorated rooms with balconies overlooking the lovely garden, two self-catering studios and two apartments with well-equipped kitchens and two bedrooms. Fine village-style Turkish food (dinner from ₺30) is available. There are discounts for longer stays.

Golden Lighthouse Hotel HOTEL $$
(☑ 0242-843 5107; www.pataragoldenlighthouse. com; s/d/tr €42/50/58; ❀🛈❄) Tucked away in a tranquil spot at the rear of the village, this small hotel has rooms overlooking a large pool and garden. The owners really go out of their way to get to know their guests, many of whom won't holiday anywhere else. Breakfast is a large buffet spread on a shaded terrace. Rooms are quite Spartan, but spacious and spotless.

✗ Eating & Drinking

You'll get the best local food in the many pensions which prepare home-cooked meals for both guests and nonguests. In the village centre, just downhill from Golden Pension you'll find a handful of fairly average cafe-restaurants. Savoury and sweet *gözleme* (₺6 to ₺12) are popular.

Durak lokantasi TURKISH $
(☑ 0542 302 8100; mains from ₺17; ⊙9am-midnight) The best of the village restaurants, this simple-looking place run by Ibrahim offers hearty dishes like stuffed peppers, courgette fritters and a famous rice pudding. No booze, but you can bring your own.

THE LYCIAN WAY

Acclaimed as one of the world's top-10 long-distance walks, the **Lycian Way** follows signposted paths around the Teke Peninsula from Fethiye to Antalya. The 500km route leads through pine and cedar forests beneath mountains rising almost 3000m, past villages, stunning coastal views and an embarrassment of ruins at Lycian cities. For those who don't have plenty of time to trek the entire trail, it can easily be walked in individual sections.

Beanies CAFE
(⊙10am-midnight; 🛈) A lovely little village cafe on one side of the Sim Bar, serving flat whites, cappuccinos, Turkish and filter coffee to the caffeine needy. Also teas and shakes. Feeling naughty? Order an espresso martini.

Medusa Bar BAR
(☑ 0242-843 5193; ⊙9am-3am; 🛈) With cushioned benches and walls hung with old photos and posters, laid-back Medusa plays blues, jazz and rock until the wee hours. Owner Pamir is a genial soul and happy to chat about Patara's attractions.

❶ Getting There & Away

Any bus heading between Kaş and Fethiye can drop you on the highway, 3.5km from Gelemiş village. Between May and October, local dolmuşes run to the village and on to the beach every 30 to 40 minutes from the highway drop-off point (₺3). If you're arriving early or late in the year, ring your pension in Gelemiş to check.

Gelemiş has roughly hourly dolmuşes in summer to Kalkan (₺7, 30 minutes) and Kaş (₺11, one hour) and a daily departure to Saklıkent Gorge (₺10, 45 minutes) at 11am. There are fewer services during winter.

Year-round, you can catch minibuses and buses at the turn-off on the main road to Fethiye (₺14, 1½ hours) and Antalya (₺30, 3¾ hours).

Kalkan

☑ 0242 / POP 3650
A thriving Greek fishing village called Kalamaki until the 1920s, today Kalkan is an upmarket resort town built largely on a hillside that tumbles down to an almost-perfect bay. If you're in search of a perfectly mixed cocktail followed by dinner in a seafood

restaurant and a night in a boutique hotel, you've come to the right place. Yes, Kalkan's natural beauty has certainly not gone unnoticed, and an ever-increasing sprawl of holiday homes around the town has spoilt the bay's idyllic scene somewhat.

⊙ Sights & Activities

Most people use Kalkan as a base to visit the Lycian ruins, or engage in the many local activities. Apart from the beach (Yat Limanı) near the marina, and Kaputaş, a perfect little sandy cove about 7km east of Kalkan en route to Kaş, watery activities include scuba diving and snorkelling trips, kayaking and beach clubs.

Anıl Boat   BOATING
(☑0533 351 7520; www.facebook.com/anilboat kalkanturkey; Kalkan Harbour) Kalkan is an excellent place for a day-long boat trip. One possibility is Ali Eğriboyun's Anıl Boat, which costs from €30 per person (or about €300 for the whole boat, accommodating up to eight people), including lunch. There are ample cushions for chilling on deck, food is supplied, and the crew are very friendly indeed.

Aristos Watersports   WATER SPORTS
(☑0537 600 9827; www.kalkanwatersports. com; İskele Sokak) This established Turkish-Australian operation offers adrenaline-pumping watery fun, including speedboat trips, wakeboarding and waterskiing, inflatable rides and SUP.

Dolphin Scuba Team   DIVING
(☑0542 627 9757; www.dolphinscubateam.com; İskele Sokak; day €40, PADI discover scuba €50) There are a couple of wrecks and a fair amount of sea life to the west of Kalkan harbour. Dolphin Scuba has a 13m dive boat and good hire equipment, and offers recreational diving and the full gamut of PADI courses. Any nondiving friends and family who want some snorkelling action are welcome along while you dive (€15).

🛌 Sleeping

Kleo Pansiyon   PENSION $$
(www.kleopension.com; off Kocakaya Caddesi; s/d €50/57; P❋❀❂) Friendly Nafiz and Nermin run this low-key old-town pension, with kitschy but comfortable and spacious rooms featuring fridge, tea and coffee, and steps descending to the bed. Breakfast and pre-ordered dinner (mains ₺30 to ₺35) are served on the roof terrace with harbour views.

🏃 Road Trip
The Lycian Coast

DURATION/DISTANCE 7 DAYS/363KM
GREAT FOR HISTORY & CULTURE, OUTDOORS
BEST TIME TO GO MAY, JUNE, SEPTEMBER

This drive takes in the best of the ancient kingdom of Lycia, encompassing many ancient sites, some terrific beaches and Turkey's most dramatic coastline.

Fethiye to Patara
Begin the drive in the town of ❶ Fethiye (p323), its superb bay lined with *gülets* (traditional wooden yachts). Follow the D400 highway into the hills east of town for an hour until you reach the spectacularly-sited Lycian ruins of ❷ Tlos (p337), perched on a rocky summit overlooking a patchwork of fields. Climb up to the acropolis, and consider this settlement dates back to the 15th century BC, before taking in the ancient theatre and stadium area (its swimming pool measured 72m!). Next up, it's a short hop to the ❸ Saklıkent Gorge (p337), which you can explore on foot via a wooden boardwalk, or even organise a rafting or canyoning excursion. From Saklıkent, it's a 30km drive south to the sleepy village of ❹ Gelemiş, which has excellent guesthouses and restaurants.

In the morning, explore the superb adjacent archaeological site of ❺ Patara (p340), admiring the restored *bouleuterion* which functioned as Lycia's parliament building. Then enjoy a day on the sweeping sands of Patara Beach, which is backed by huge dunes.

Patara to Kalkan
Depart for a quick tour of the nearby ruins of ❻ Xanthos (p338) and ❼ Letoön (p338), before heading east along the D400 highway. Just above the idyllic town of Kalkan, this coastal route comes into its own, providing breathtaking views of an azure Mediterranean. Lunch in ❽ Kalkan (p341) and spend the afternoon exploring its boutiques and lanes of old Greek houses and in the evening feast on seafood.

Kalkan to Kaş
Continuing east the next day, you'll pass the lovely cove of ❾ Kaputaş, backed

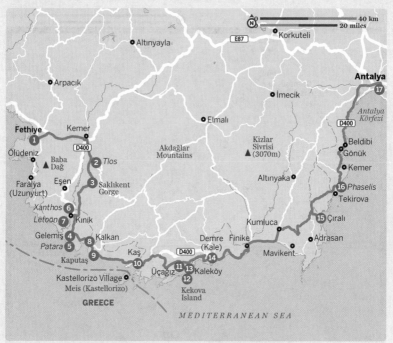

by high cliffs and the perfect spot for a dip, and then the highway clings to the coastline for 20km, with the big blue to your right and towering mountains on your left. **10 Kaş** (p347) is your next stop, a historic port nestled beneath looming hills which seem to isolate it from the rest of the world. There's plenty of interest here for a couple of nights, with a plethora of cafes and restaurants, bars and live-music venues. Water taxis will whisk you to beaches and islands, and there's also Turkey's best scuba diving offshore. Even in bustling Kas, reminders of the ancient past are never far away, and at night illuminated Lycian rock tombs gaze down on the heady tourist scene below.

Kaş to Çıralı

The next day involves an early start as there's a lot to pack in. The first port of call is the beguiling coast around **11 Üçağız** (p352), a tiny settlement reached via a detour off the D400. Now it's time to get off the road for a few hours. Park up in Üçağız and either join a tour or charter a boat to the nearby watery delights of **12 Kekova** (p353) and its Batık Şehir (Sunken City), and **13 Kaleköy** (p353), where you can scramble up to the ruined

castle. Back on dry land, get reacquainted with your car and continue northeast through dry scrubland to the dusty town of **14 Demre** (p354), home to the impressive Lycian ruins of Myra (p355), and Church of St Nicholas.

From Demre, it's 78km (around 90 minutes) along the D400 to the beach at **15 Çıralı** (p357). The first section of this drive is astonishing, as the road parallels the coastal mountains, slaloming around hairpins before turning inland and cutting through pine forests to the Çıralı turn-off.

Çıralı to Antalya

After a couple of nights in Çıralı, hit the road again, travelling north along the D400. Pause for an hour or two (perhaps for a picnic) to take in gorgeous **16 Phaselis** (p357), where there are three perfect little cove beaches and some more ruins to enjoy. Finally, it's a fast road to the metropolis of **17 Antalya** (p359), your final destination. This large city has a fascinating historic quarter called Kaleiçi, which is replete with Roman, Seljuk and Ottoman monuments. There's no vehicle access to Kaleiçi, so park and explore the district on foot.

Kalkan

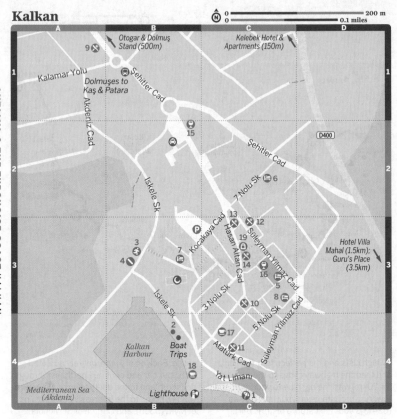

Kalkan

◎ Sights
1 Public Beach C4

✦ Activities, Courses & Tours
2 Anıl Boat B4
3 Aristos Watersports B3
4 Dolphin Scuba Team B3

🛏 Sleeping
5 Courtyard Hotel C3
6 Gül Pansiyon C2
7 Kleo Pansiyon B3
8 White House Pension C3

✕ Eating
9 Hünkar Ocakbaşı A1

10 Kalamaki Restaurant C3
11 Korsan C4
12 Salonika C3
13 Small House C3
14 Zeytinlik C3

🍷 Drinking & Nightlife
15 Bezirgan's Pub B2
16 Botanik Garden Bar C3
17 Cafe Del Mar C4
18 Fener Cafe &
   Brasserie B4

🛍 Shopping
19 Just Silver C3

Gül Pansiyon   PENSION $$
(☏ 0242-844 3099; www.kalkangulpansiyon.com;
7 Nolu Sokak 10; s/d/apt €40/50/60; ❄ ⓢ) The
'Rose' has a rooftop with million-dollar

views, small but tidy rooms with balconies,
and three apartments with kitchenettes
and washing machines. Try to bag one of
the rooms on the 3rd floor for the views

and the light. There are discounts outside of peak summer, when it's a popular base for hikers.

Kelebek Hotel & Apartments APARTMENT $$
(☑ 0242-844 3770; www.butterflyholidays.co.uk; Karayolları Sokak 4; apt/r from €32/36; P ➡ ❄ 🛜 ≋) North of the centre, just off the D400, this family-run hotel offers good value for self-caterers. The rooms, fronted by a large swimming pool, are clean, if slightly frayed around the edges, but the eight one- and two-bedroom self-catering apartments in a separate block are a great deal. It also offers villas (from €520 per week).

★ Courtyard Hotel BOUTIQUE HOTEL $$$
(☑ 0242-844 3738, 0532 443 0012; www.court yardkalkan.com; Süleyman Yilmaz Caddesi 24-26; r €130; P ➡ ❄ 🛜) Cobbled out of a couple of 19th-century village houses, this sympathetically-restored property is an old-town delight. With six rooms retaining their original fireplaces, wooden ceilings and floors, the Courtyard has lashings of Ottoman character and shares a garden with the White House Pension. Halıl and Marion are delightful hosts.

★ Hotel Villa Mahal LUXURY HOTEL $$$
(☑ 0533 766 8622, 0242-844 3268; www.villama hal.com; Kışla Caddesi; s/d/tr from €240/290/360; ❄ 🛜 ≋) One of Turkey's most stylish hotels lies atop a cliff on the eastern side of Kalkan Bay. The rooms, individually designed in whiter-than-white minimalism with colourful Mediterranean splashes, have panoramic sea views. The 19m infinity freshwater pool is spectacularly suspended on the edge of the void, while stone steps descend to seafront bathing platforms shaded by olive trees.

White House Pension PENSION $$$
(☑ 0242-844 3738, 0532 443 0012; www.kalkan whitehouse.co.uk; 5 Nolu Sokak 19; s/d from €42/60; ❄ 🛜) Situated on a quiet corner at the top of the old-town hill, this attentively run pension has 10 compact, breezy rooms – four with balconies – in a spotless family home. The real winner here, though, is the view from the terrace and friendly owners Halıl and Marion.

✖ Eating

While the restaurants and bars on the harbour have considerable appeal, there are also interesting options inland. Running through the old town, Süleyman Yilmaz Caddesi has taken off with its little restaurants, bars and meyhanes (taverns). In season, book ahead no matter where you plan to eat.

Small House TURKISH $$
(Küçük Ev; ☑ 0242-844 2817; Hasan Altan Caddesi 18; mains ₺28-75) Quirky family-run restaurant in a tiny little dining room (it sits about 12) where Turkish dishes (superb mezes, stews and seafood) are prepared with love and skill. Walls are covered in messages left by contented diners. There's also a balcony table (which you'll have to book many months ahead) with great views down Kalkan's main drag.

Hünkar Ocakbaşı KEBAP $$
(☑ 0242-844 2077; Şehitler Caddesi 38e; mains ₺18-50; 🛜) This authentic ocakbaşı (grill house) serves all the traditional kebap favourites and has a large terrace to enjoy them on. It also does pide as well as five kinds of güveç (casserole), including a vegetarian one. No alcohol though.

Guru's Place ANATOLIAN $$
(☑ 0536 331 1016, 0242-844 3848; D400; mezes ₺12-15, mains ₺20-42; ⊗ 8am-11pm; 🍴) Affable Hüseyin and his family, who have been in the area for four centuries, have been running this scenically located seaside restaurant (4km south of town) for 20 years. Food is authentic and fresh, coming from their own garden. The small menu is mostly focused on daily specials and Turkish classics such as kuzu incik (lamb shank).

Cooking classes are also offered (€45 per person) which involve shopping for local ingredients then a slap-up meal.

★ Kalamaki Restaurant MODERN TURKISH $$$
(☑ 0242-844 1555; Hasan Altan Caddesi 47a; mains ₺50-95; ⊗ 11am-10pm; 🛜🍴) A modern venue with a very stylish minimalist pub on the terrace and a restaurant upstairs, serving superb Turkish dishes with a European twist. Try the ballı tavuk (grilled chicken with sauce made from apricot, hazelnuts, shallots and cinnamon) or the vegetarian şiş kebap (roasted on a skewer). Host Tayfur takes it all in his stride – even when celebs like Gordon Ramsay come a-calling.

★ Zeytinlik MODERN TURKISH $$$
(Olive Garden; ☑ 0242-844 3408; 1st fl, Hasan Altan Caddesi 17; mains ₺36-85; 🛜🍴) This fine British-Turkish restaurant serves some of the most authentic, creative local dishes around; it states 'we don't do fusion food'. You'll find excellent vegetarian choices, and

meaty winners like house speciality *baharath kuzu* (lamb and onion stew flavoured with cinnamon and cardamom; ₺70). The roof terrace setting is great too.

Korsan   SEAFOOD $$$

(☑ 0242-844 3076; www.korsankalkan.com; Atatürk Caddesi; mains ₺36-109; ☺ 10am-midnight; ☺ ☑) This restaurant is among the finest seafood experiences in Kalkan, with a fine harbour-facing streetside terrace and also rooftop dining for dishes like sea bream with spicy mash and sauteed vegetables (₺90). A feast of delicious vegetarian meze dishes is ₺65 and serves two. Sip a homemade lemonade or select a bottle of Turkish wine from the vaults.

Salonika   TURKISH $$$

(☑ 0242-844 2422; www.salonika.co; Süleyman Yilmaz Caddesi; mains ₺35-95; ☺ 11am-11pm; ☺ ☑) With tables on the lane and exposed stone walls inside, this white building with blue trim calls itself a *meyhane* (tavern), but the atmosphere is romantic rather than ribald. Occasional live music accompanies the mezes, salads, pides, Turkish casseroles (₺59 to ₺92), grills and fish.

🍷 Drinking & Nightlife

There are bars dotted around town, including a strip of strobe-blazing places around the municipal parking lot.

Botanik Garden Bar   BAR

(☑ 0535 470 9099; Süleyman Yilmaz Caddesi; ☺ noon-3am; ☎) For a flavour of 20th-century Kalkan, when things were far more mellow, head to this garden bar under a canopy of mature trees for cocktails or wine. Perch at the bar, swing in a hammock, lounge in a sofa or climb a tree house.

Cafe Del Mar   CAFE

(☑ 0242-844 1068; Hasan Altan Caddesi 61a; cakes & desserts ₺12-15; ☺ 8.30am-1am; ☎) An Aladdin's cave of a place brimming with antiques and curios, hanging lanterns, sea shells and curvy metalwork furniture. It's most popular as a cafe, with an excellent range of coffees (including Baileys and frappés) and teas, as well as great homemade cakes. Also offers good cocktails (happy hour 8pm to 10pm); the owner Benjamin is a chatty character.

Bezirgan's Pub   PUB

(Hasan Altan Caddesi; ☺ noon-midnight; ☎) This open-fronted bar decorated with photos of Hollywood icons is like an Irish pub spliced

with a beach bar. Sit outside or head inside for Guinness on tap and football on the TV.

Fener Cafe & Brasserie   CAFE

(The Lighthouse; ☑ 0242-844 3752; Yat Limanı; ☺ 8am-1am) The closest thing Kalkan has to a tea garden, this place wraps around Kalkan's tiny *fener* (lighthouse). Sip a latte or swig a beer from a waveside table.

🛍 Shopping

Just Silver   JEWELLERY

(☑ 0242-844 3136; Hasan Altan Caddesi 28; ☺ 10am-11pm) Designing and selling ear, nose, neck, finger and toe baubles for 30 years, Kalkan's best-known shop offers silver and gold-plated jewellery in traditional and modern styles.

ℹ Information

Consult the Facebook page of the Kalkan Turkish Local News (www.facebook.com/ktlncommunity) for all things Kalkan.

ℹ Getting There & Away

Kalkan otogar (Şehitler Caddesi) is serviced by Pamukkale, Ulusoy, Varan and Kamil Koç companies, with services including three evening buses to İstanbul (₺160 to ₺178, 13 hours) and five daily buses to İzmir (₺85, seven hours).

Buses to Fethiye (₺20, 1½ hours) leave from the otogar every hour.

Kalkan is on the Kaş–Kınık local dolmuş route with regular dolmuşes heading west to Patara (₺8, 25 minutes) and Kınık (for Xanthos; ₺9, 35 minutes) and east to Kaş (₺9, 35 minutes) via Kaputaş beach (₺3.50, 15 minutes). These buses can be caught at the dolmuş stand on Şehitler Caddesi as well as at the otogar.

Contact **Brave Tours** (☑ 0242-844 1166; Şehitler Caddesi 47; per day from €17; ☺ 8am-9.30pm) or **Kalkan Sun Travel** (☑ 0242-844 2244; www.kalkansuntravel.net; Şehitler Caddesi 41; per day from €16; ☺ 8am-10pm) for car rental at fair rates.

Bezirgan

☑ 0242

In an elevated valley 17km northeast of Kalkan by road sits the beautiful village of Bezirgan, a timeless example of Turkish rural life. Towering some 725m above the fruit orchards and fields of wheat, barley, chickpeas, almonds and sticky sesame are the ruins of the Lycian hilltop citadel of Pirha. In the colder months there is a distant backdrop of snowcapped peaks.

A 9km (three-hour) section of the Lycian Way climbs from Kalkan, emerging at the distinctive **grain stores** at the western end of the village. You can also walk from here to İslamlar (about 10km), either by road or over the mountain on the old mill track, once used by locals taking their corn to İslamlar's mills.

★ **Owlsland**   GUESTHOUSE **$$$**
(Erol's Pansiyon; ☑ 0242-837 5214; www.owlsland. com; Bezirgan; per person €45, incl half board €65; ❄ ⬤) This 150-year-old farmhouse is idyllically surrounded by fruit trees and run by charming Turkish-Scottish couple, Erol and Pauline. The three cosy rooms, previously a kitchen, a stable and Erol's grandparents' bedroom, contain most of their original features and are decorated with old farm implements. The upstairs room with balcony, traditional decor and wood burner is especially nice.

Erol, a trained chef, turns out traditional Turkish dishes made with locally grown produce and Pauline makes her own cakes and jams.

ⓘ Getting There & Away

Bezirgan is signposted five minutes' walk off the Lycian Way, between Kalkan and Kaş.

From Antalya, there are several daily direct buses (₺42, 4½ hours) to Bezirgan via Elmali with Bati Antalya.

If you're under your own steam, consult the excellent directions on the Owlsland website. Basically, you'll need to head north from Kalkan, cross over the D400 linking Fethiye and Kaş, and follow the signs for Elmalı.

Kaş

☑ 0242 / POP 8400
It may not sport the region's finest beaches but its central Teke Peninsula location, mellow atmosphere and menu of adventure activities have made Kaş – pronounced (roughly) 'cash' – an ideal base for forays into the surrounding area. For divers, this is Turkey's hub for underwater exploits, with excellent wreck-diving just offshore. A plethora of boat trips, kayaking tours and hikes are also easily arranged from here.

The 6km-long Çukurbağ Peninsula extends west of the pretty old quarter, town square and harbour. At the start of it, you'll find a well-preserved ancient theatre, which is about all that's left of ancient Antiphellos, the original Lycian town. Above Kaş, several Lycian rock tombs in the mountain wall can be seen even at night, when they're illuminated.

Lying just offshore, dominating the harbour view, is the geopolitical oddity of the Greek island of Meis (Kastellorizo), which can be visited on a day trip.

⊙ Sights

Antiphellos Theatre   RUINS
(Hastane Caddesi; ⊙ 8am-7pm May-Oct, to 5pm Nov-Apr) **FREE** Antiphellos was a small settlement and the port for Phellos, the much larger Lycian town further north in the hills. The small Hellenistic theatre, 500m west of Kaş' main square, could seat 4000 spectators and is in good condition. It was built in the 1st century BC and restored 300 years later, probably after the great 141 AD earthquake. There's a good view of Kaş from the top tier of seating.

Liman Ağzı   BEACH
If you're after a full day on the beach, the best idea is to hop on one of the **water taxis** (return ₺25) in Kaş harbour and head for one of these three beaches on the peninsula opposite at Liman Ağzı. All three have **cafes**, you can rent sunloungers and sunshades, and the cove has calm water. You can also hike here (3km) on a pleasant section of the Lycian Way footpath, which begins at Büyük Çakıl Plajı.

Büyük Çakıl Plajı   BEACH
(Big Pebble Beach; Hükümet Caddesi) For swimming, head for 'Big Pebble Beach', a relatively clean beach 1.5km southeast of Kaş town centre. Although it's largely pebble-based, there's a few metres of sand at one end. There are shaded cafes for refreshments, which also rent out sunloungers and sunshades.

🕴 Activities & Tours

Kaş is the centre for diving in the Mediterranean, with wrecks and a lot of underwater sea life. It's also an excellent base for exploring the Turquoise Coast, and local travel agencies offer a huge range of day tours and adventure activities. Kaş is also a stop along the Lycian Way (p341), with stunning hiking trails around town.

Boat trips to Kekova are a fine day out and include swimming stops as well as time to see several interesting ruins. There are also very popular kayaking excursions to Kekova, and longer trips to the area incorporating

Kaş

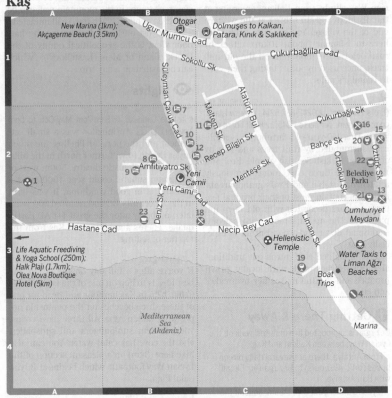

New Marina (1km);
Akçagerme Beach (3.5km)

Otogar

Uğur Mumcu Cad

Dolmuşes to Kalkan,
Patara, Kınık & Saklıkent

Çukurbağlılar Cad

Sokollu Sk

Süleyman Çavuş Cad

Atatürk Bul

Çukurbağlı Sk

Bahçe Sk

Meltem Sk

Recep Bilgin Sk

Menteşe Sk

Ortaokul Sk

Öztürk Sk

Belediye
Parkı

Amfitiyatro Sk

Yeni
Camii

Yeni Camı Cad

Deniz Sk

Hastane Cad

Necip Bey Cad

Limanı Sk

Cumhuriyet
Meydanı

Hellenistic
Temple

Water Taxis to
Liman Ağzı
Beaches

Boat
Trips

Life Aquatic Freediving
& Yoga School (250m);
Halk Plajı (1.7km);
Olea Nova Boutique
Hotel (5km)

Mediterranean
Sea
(Akdeniz)

Marina

the Lycian ruins of Aperlae. A great idea is to charter a boat from the marina; rates start around €180 per day.

★ Dragoman
OUTDOORS

(☎0242-836 3614; www.dragoman-turkey.com; Uzun Çarşı Sokak 15; 1-/6-dive pack €26/148, sea-kayaking day tours €29-50; ☺9am-9pm) This dynamic outdoor activities centre has built a reputation for its 5-star PADI dive shop with professional and knowledgeable dive instructors. Other activities include sea kayaking day and multiday tours exploring the coast around Kekova and further afield, terrific hiking (day trips from €35, five-day treks €325), mountain-biking trips, SUP and several excellent snorkelling excursions (from €15).

★ Bougainville Travel
OUTDOORS

(☎0242-836 3737; www.bougainville-turkey. com; İbrahim Serin Caddesi 10) This reputable English-Turkish tour operator has much

experience in organising any number of activities and tours, including canyoning (€50), mountain biking (€40), tandem paragliding (€80 for flights lasting 20 to 30 minutes), scuba diving (€23 for one dive including equipment, €30 for a sample dive) and sea kayaking (€35).

Seven Capes
OUTDOORS

(☎0537 403 3779; www.sevencapes.com) One of the best ways to see the Med up close is in a sea kayak or on a stand-up paddleboard (SUP). This experienced British-Turkish outfit offers daily kayak and SUP tours (from ₺110), plus excellent walking trips around the south Aegean. SUPs can be rented for €32 per day.

Xanthos Travel
OUTDOORS

(☎0242-836 3292; www.xanthostravel.com; İbrahim Serin Caddesi 5a; Kekova day tours €35) As well as Xanthos' popular Kekova boat tours, it runs sea-kayaking excursions that get you

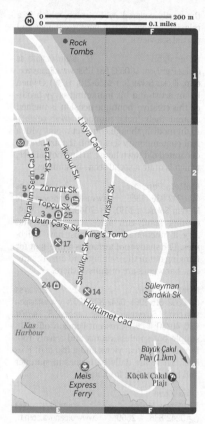

Kaş

up close with the sunken city ruins (€30 to €45) and diving trips. For landlubbers, there are jeep safaris to the mountain village of Gömbe and Yeşil Gölü (Green Lake) in the Akdağlar range (€35), mountain biking, trekking, canyoning, horse riding and paragliding.

**Life Aquatic Freediving
and Yoga School** DIVING
(☎0532 400 88 36; www.lifeaquatickas.com; Hastane Caddesi 3) Set yourself (and your lungs) a real challenge at this SSI freediving school. Also offers good yoga classes (€12 for 90 minutes) and SUP rental.

Subaqua Diving Centre DIVING
(☎0532 221 0129; www.subaquadive.com; Limanı Sokak) Professional dive centre offering PADI courses, including an Open Water diver (€250) and Rebreather (€600). One fun dive is €25.

🍃 Courses

Culinary Kaş COOKING
(☎0530 322 0187; www.culinarykas.com; full day €45) Excellent Turkish cooking courses, including a meze workshop where you prepare five dishes (€35). Courses are run by Ayse, a fluent English speaker, who also leads gastronomy tours.

✦✦ Festivals & Events

Kaş Caz Festival MUSIC
(www.kascazfestivali.com; Kaş Marina; ⊗Sep) Three-day festival featuring Turkish and international jazz artists. DJs and bands also perform.

Kaş Lycia Festival CULTURAL
The annual Kaş Lycia Festival runs for a week in late June. It features prominent folk-dancing troupes and musicians – and an international swimming race – and works

to foster an improved relationship between Greece and Turkey. Events also take place in Kalkan.

🛏 Sleeping

Can Mocamp
HOSTEL, CAMPGROUND $

(☎0537 545 6032; www.canmocamp.com; Uğur Mumcu Caddesi 23; dm/tent/hut/bungalow €15/22/30/45; ✳🛜) By the marina, this long-running bohemian campsite now has a couple of decent dorms: a four-bed female option and a six-bed mixed. There's a good vibe and it's a fine place to mix with both Turkish and international travellers. Also home to a bistro bar and dive school. Bathrooms are pretty basic and camping is a little pricey.

Anı Pension
PENSION $

(☎0533 326 4201, 0242-836 1791; www.motelani. com; Süleyman Çavuş Caddesi 12; dm/s/d €14/27/32; ✳@🛜) With a seven-bed dorm (no lockers) and kitchen for guests, the Anı is worth considering, though cleanliness could be a little better. Decent-sized rooms all have balconies and the roof terrace is a hub where you can kick back.

Santosa Pension
PENSION $

(☎0242-836 1714, 0535 846 3584; Suleyman Çavuş Caddesi 4; s/d/tr ₺120/150/180; ✳🛜) A quiet, homely choice with a diminutive terrace and tidy, small rooms that have balconies and cheerful floral stencilling on the walls.

Hideaway Hotel
HOTEL $$

(☎0546 836 1887; www.hotelhideaway.com; Anfitiyatro Sokak 7; s €46, d €58-70; ✳🛜🏊) This lovely hotel has large, airy rooms (some with sea views) with a fresh white-on-white minimalist feel and gleaming modern bathrooms. There's a pool for cooling off and a roof terrace that's the venue for morning yoga and sundowners at the bar with Meis views. Run by the unstoppable Ahmet, a font of local information. There are excellent room discounts outside the July to September peak season.

Ateş Pension
PENSION $$

(☎0242-836 1393, 0532 492 0680; www.ates pensionkas.com; Anfitiyatro Sokak 3; dm/s/d/ tr/f €14/30/35/45/50; Ⓟ🚻✳🛜) Offering four-bed dorms and private rooms in two buildings, 'Hot Pension' is a cut above Kaş' other pensions, with snug duvets and modern bathrooms. Owners Recep and Ayşe are superfriendly hosts and serve Turkish feasts (₺30) and breakfasts of 55 items on

the partly covered roof terrace, which is a relaxing lounge with a book exchange and partial sea views.

8 Pansiyon
BOUTIQUE HOTEL $$

(Sekiz Pansiyon; ☎0533 631 1153; www.8pansiyon. com; İlkokul Sokak 9; r ₺150-210; ✳🛜) Owned by an artist and his marketing-savvy brother, this creative 'boutique pension' is themed around their lucky number: *sekiz* (eight). Eight modish, though compact rooms with a real contemporary feel climb the artistically decorated old town house to the roof terrace, which is quite a social scene in summer.

Meltem Pension
PENSION $$

(☎0242-836 1855; www.meltempansiyon.com; Meltem Sokak; s ₺110, d ₺170-190; ✳🛜) Welcoming family-run place with bright and airy, if functional, rooms; most have balconies. The shady roof terrace is a fine spot for hanging out in the evening, and during summer barbecues are organised there.

Hilal Pansiyon
PENSION $$

(☎0532 615 1061, 0242-836 1207; www.hilalpen sion.com; Süleyman Çavuş Caddesi 8; s/d/tr €30/40/50; ✳🛜) 'Crescent Pension' offers 18 simple but spotless rooms and a leafy roof terrace with great views and a fridge of Efes beer. There are daily barbecues in summer and bikes are free for guests.

Olea Nova Boutique Hotel
BOUTIQUE HOTEL $$$

(☎0242-836 2660; www.oleanova.com.tr; Demokrasi Caddesi 43; r/f/ste from €130/240/330; ✳🛜🏊) Set amid olive groves and villas, with panoramic sea views, this swish boutique hotel is just the ticket for those seeking a peaceful break. Rooms and suites are all pristine white minimalism, while the kidney-shaped pool, adjoining bar-restaurant and private beach are slothing central. Located 5km west of town.

🍴 Eating

Havana Balık Evi
SEAFOOD $

(☎0242-836 4111; Öztürk Sokak 7; mains ₺12-35; ⊙8am-midnight; 🍴) Cheap and cheerful seafood place renowned for *balık ekmek* (₺12), the simple fish sandwich that is a staple in coastal Turkey. There are also hearty bowls of *balık güveç* (fish casserole) and *hamsi tava* (pan-fried Turkish anchovies).

★ Oburus Momus
VEGETARIAN $$

(☎0507 704 2032; www.facebook.com/oburus momus; Necip Bey Caddesi 22; mains ₺30-44;

WORTH A TRIP

MEIS

Visiting the teensy Greek island of Meis (Kastellorizo) is a popular day trip from Kaş. The **Meis Express Ferry** (adult €25, child under 12yr €20, under 7yr free) sails twice daily (May to October) at 10am and 6pm and once daily at 10am the rest of the year. It returns at 4pm and 11pm in summer and at 3pm in winter. The voyage takes 20 minutes. Meis is a simple fishing village of cute pastel-coloured houses with a sprinkling of restaurants, a superb bakery, a duty-free shop selling Greek wine and pork, some excellent hikes over the hill and a decent museum. From Meis' harbour it's also easy to arrange boat trips to swim inside the fabulously surreal blue cave along the island's coast.

It's possible to spend the night in Meis, or continue onwards into Greece proper. There are ferries to Rhodes (3¾ hours) twice a week and a high-speed catamaran (2½ hours) in summer. Meis even has a tiny landing strip from where you can fly to Rhodes (40 minutes). On Meis, your best source of information is **Papoutsis Travel** (☑ +30 224 604 9356, +30 693 721 2530; www.facebook.com/papoutsisyachting; ⊘ 8am-7pm).

Tickets for Meis can be bought from the **Meis Express office** (☑ 0242-836 1725; www.meisexpress.com; Cumhuriyet Meydanı; ⊘ 8.30am-7pm) or any travel agency. If you haven't booked your ticket the day before, make sure you arrive a half-hour before sailing.

⊘ 2-10.30pm; 🛜 ☑) Tucked away from the centre, this terrific vegetarian/vegan restaurant serves up fine international (Indian curries, falafel, pad thai, vegan desserts) and local dishes to an adorning clientele (book ahead). Presentation is superb and the premises are modern and inviting, with a slim street terrace. Craft beers, sangria and good juices are available.

⭐**Hünkâr Ocakbaşı** TURKISH $$
(☑ 0242-836 3660; Çukurbağlı Sokak 7e; mains ₺24-75; ⊘ 11am-11.30pm) Buzzing *ocakbaşı* (grill house) with a streetside terrace that serves a mighty fine range of meats. Classics like Adana kebap (₺32) have a wonderful charcoal flavour, served on a board with chewy domed flatbread and a couple of grilled vegetables. Wraps are just ₺20. No booze served, but they might bring you a beer in a mug if you ask nicely.

Bi Lokma ANATOLIAN $$
(☑ 0242-836 3942; www.bilokma.com.tr; Hükümet Caddesi 2; mains ₺22-40; ⊘ 10am-10.30pm; ☑) Also known as 'Mama's Kitchen', this place has green tables in a terraced garden high above the harbour. The 'mama' in question is Sabo, whose daughters have taken the culinary baton, turning out traditional Turkish soul food, including excellent meze (like pumpkin salad and lentil balls) and its famous house *mantı* (Turkish ravioli).

Köşk ANATOLIAN $$
(☑ 0242-836 3857; Gürsoy Sokak 13; mains ₺24-50; ⊘ 1pm-midnight) In a lovely little square off a cobbled street just up from the water, Köşk occupies a rustic, 150-year-old house with two terraces and seating in the open courtyard. Forgo the mains and feast instead on the gorgeous meze dishes, which draw from both Mediterranean and Anatolian influences.

Bella Vita ITALIAN $$$
(☑ 0531 724 5846; 1st fl, Cumhuriyet Meydanı 10; mezes ₺21-45, mains ₺28-69; ⊘ noon-11.30pm; 🛜) Overlooking the main square, Kaş' most popular Italian pumps out fine pizza, a wide array of pasta dishes (such as vegetable ravioli; ₺32) and a few seafood, fish (try the oven-baked sea bass; ₺48) and meat mains. Look it up on Facebook.

🍷 Drinking & Nightlife

⭐**Linckia Roastery Cafe** CAFE
(www.facebook.com/linckia77; Necip Bey Caddesi 36c; ⊘ 10am-11pm; 🛜) One glance at the gleaming La Marzocco machine (cost in Turkey €20,000!) in this spacious cafe and it's clear Linckia is totally serious. Drip coffee (from ₺20) is from as far afield as El Salvador and Indonesia, while the perfectly balanced house espresso is ₺12. Cakes (from ₺18) and meals (try a stir-fry) are prepared by the Chinese owner.

Kaş Türk Kahvecisi CAFE
(Öztürk Sokak 8a; ⊘ 8.30am-1am; 🛜) A hole-in-the-wall specialist cafe with the full gamut of caffeine options, including cold brews and filtered coffee using beans from across the globe. Turkish coffee using cloves and

cardamom are intriguing too. Down a little lane off Öztürk Sokak, there's courtyard seating; see Facebook.

Happy Bar
BAR

(Bahçe Sokak; ⊙5pm-4am; 🛜) Declaring itself an 'alternative style cafe bar' this tiny little place has a handful of tables where you can enjoy a cheeky German beer or cocktail while tuning into well-selected funk and soul.

Echo Cafe & Bar
BAR

(📞0242-836 2047; www.echobarkas.com; Limanı Sokak; ⊙4pm-4am; 🛜) Hip and stylish, this venue has Kaş high society sipping fruit daiquiris to both live and canned jazz and acoustic sounds. There's a historic building where live acts perform and a harbour-facing front terrace. Entrance is normally free, but on busy weekend nights a cover of ₺40 to ₺50 is sometimes charged.

Hideaway Bar & Cafe
BAR

(📞0242-836 3369; Cumhuriyet Meydanı 16a; ⊙4pm-3am) Garden cafe and bar, accessed by a nondescript doorway on the main square, and a relaxed spot for evening drinks. Only a stone's throw from the hustle and yet a world away.

🔒 Shopping

★Turqueria
ANTIQUES, ART

(📞0242-836 1631; nauticakas@superonline.com; Uzun Çarşı Sokak 21; ⊙9am-midnight Apr-Nov, by appointment Dec-Mar) Run by Orhan and Martina, a charming Turkish-German couple and long-time residents in Kaş, Turqueria is an Aladdin's cave of treasures that include old advertisements, paintings, camel-skin *karagöz* shadow puppets, and curios like cast-iron divers' helmets.

Gallery Anatolia
CERAMICS

(📞0242-836 1954, 0533 342 3533; www.gallery-anatolia.com; Hükümet Caddesi 2; ⊙9am-11pm mid-Apr–mid-Nov, by appointment mid-Nov–mid-Apr) This upmarket gallery overlooking the marina has locally designed ceramic and porcelain pieces, including crockery.

❶ Getting There & Away

The Meis Express (p351) ferry sails twice daily (May to October) at 10am and 6pm and once daily at 10am the rest of the year. The voyage takes 20 minutes. Take your passport to the ticket office the day before to book.

From the **otogar** (Atatürk Bulvarı), 350m north of the centre, there are three to four daily

services to İstanbul (₺175 to ₺193, 15 hours) and two daily buses to İzmir (₺90, eight hours).

A brand new otogar was being constructed in the hills high above Kaş, 5km east on the D400, however it was not operational at the time of research.

Batı Antalya (www.batiantalyatur.com.tr) dolmuşes head approximately every hour to Antalya (₺38, four hours) via Demre (₺9, one hour) and the Olympos turn-off (₺24, 2½ hours). The same company has departures to Fethiye (₺25, 2½ hours) roughly hourly between 7am and 6pm.

In summer, local Öz Kaş dolmuşes to Kalkan (₺7, 35 minutes) leave every 20 to 40 minutes from the otogar between 7.30am and 9.30pm; this same service continues on to Patara (₺11, 45 minutes) and Kınık (for Xanthos; ₺13, one hour). There are fewer departures from November to April. There's also one dolmuş daily to Saklıkent Gorge (₺16, one hour) at 10.10am. It makes the return journey from Saklıkent at 4pm.

Üçağız & Kekova

📞0242 / POP 420

Declared off limits to development, Üçağız (ooch-*eye*-iz) is a quaint fishing and farming village in an idyllic setting on a bay amid islands and peninsulas. The squiggle of lanes behind the harbour remains a watercolour-worthy scene of rustic cottages, though as a lot of tour buses pass through, independent travellers can expect some hustle from local touts.

Üçağız is a regular stop on the *gület* yacht circuit and the jumping-off point for visiting the sunken city at Kekova and the secluded settlement of Kaleköy. In the evening, when tour buses have left, Üçağız snaps back into snooze mode.

To the west, on the Sıçak Peninsula, is **Aperlae**, an isolated and evocative ancient Lycian city on the Lycian Way.

🛏 Sleeping

Üçağız' pensions all offer free boat services to the beaches and swimming platforms on and around Kekova Island. They are also excellent bases for hiking sections of the Lycian Way (p341). Apart from Likya Pension, most pensions are on the waterfront.

★Boynuzağacı Pension
PENSION $$

(📞0542 327 1075; https://boynuz-agac-cafe-pension.business.site; Sokak 33; r/f €50/55; ❇🛜) The 'Carob Tree' is located in a lane inland from the harbour and run by a super-hospitable family who are originally from

EXPLORING THE KEKOVA AREA

Given the difficulty of getting to the Kekova area by public transport, most people end up taking a boat tour from Kaş or Kalkan, which starts with a bus ride to Üçağız, where you'll board the boat.

After a visit to **Kekova Island** and its Batık Şehir (Sunken City) you'll have lunch on the boat and then head on to Kaleköy, passing a couple of submerged (and very photo-worthy) Lycian tombs just offshore where you can snorkel or kayak. There's usually about an hour to explore Kaleköy and climb up to the hilltop fortress.

Tours from Kaş, which cost around €25 per person, generally leave at 10am and return around 6pm. You can also organise a **tour** by negotiating with boat captains at Üçağız harbour. Hikers can pick up a boat ride from Üçağız to Aperlae and walk back.

The closest you can get to the Kekova sunken city ruins is on the sea-kayaking tours (from €40 per person) run by Kaş operators such as Bougainville Travel (p348) and Dragoman (p348) and also offered locally by pensions in both Üçağız and Kaleköy.

İstanbul. They offer three lovely, spotless rooms with sky-blue and white decor above their little cafe, two of which share a balcony. Electric bikes are available for guests.

★ **Onur Pension**　　　　　　PENSION $$
(📞 0242-874 2071, 0532 762 9319; www.onur pension.com; s/d/tr from €35/50/65; ⏰ Feb-Oct; 🌐 🛜) Turkish-Dutch–owned pension right on the harbour, with eight small, simple and tidy rooms, including four with full sea views and cute attic rooms. All have en-suites. Helpful owner Onur, a trekking guide, marked local hiking routes and offers pointers.

Cennet Pension　　　　　　PENSION $$
(📞 0242-874 2250, 0533 462 8554; kekova14@ mynet.com;　s/d/tr/f　€45/55/70/85;　🌐 🛜) 'Paradise' indeed: gregarious Mehmet and friendly wife Zuhra have eight large, bright and spotlessly clean rooms set back from the waterfront, with a self-catering kitchen and killer views across the harbour from the terrace. We love the garden full of fruit trees (mulberry, plum, orange, lemon, banana, apricot and more) and Zuhra's home cooking (fish dinner ₺60).

Likya Pension　　　　　　PENSION $$
(📞 0242-874 2251, 0531 596 8408; www.kekova likyapansiyon.com; s/d/tr from €35/45/60; 🌐 🛜) This peaceful oasis snuggles in a lush garden of fruit trees, on an alleyway just up from the harbour, with sea views from the breakfast terrace. Eight cosy rooms in three buildings brim with rustic charm. Guests can use the kitchen and laundry, and owner Halil can organise canoeing, diving, car rental and boat transfers for hikers.

✗ Eating

★ **Boynuzağacı Cafe**　　　　　CAFE $$
(📞 0542 327 1075; https://boynuz-agac-cafe-pen sion.business.site; Sokak 33; snacks/mains from ₺10/35; ⏰ 8am-11pm; 🌐 🛜) A delightful little cafe that consists of a tiny air-conditioned room and a slim terrace. A lot of care and attention goes into preparing the meals (try the pizza) here, and cakes and pastries are made with carob molasses instead of refined sugar. Espressos and cappuccinos available.

İbrahim Restaurant　　　　TURKISH $$
(📞 0533 363 9206, 0242-874 2062; mains ₺22-50; ⏰ 11am-10pm; 🛜) The village's original restaurant is perennially popular for its decent kebap and seafood mains, as well as *köfte*, *güveç* and a great selection of mezes (₺7.50). The harbour-front location is another plus.

ℹ Getting There & Away

There is no bus service from Kaş, but tour companies in Kaş will let you hitch a lift on their daily boat-tour transfers to Üçağız if they have a spare seat (around ₺20). These generally leave Kaş around 10am.

One dolmuş leaves Antalya for Üçağız daily at 2.45pm (₺32, four hours). It stops in Demre en route at 5.30pm (₺7, 30 minutes). From Üçağız, the dolmuş leaves at 7am. Pensions can organise transfers from Antalya International Airport (€75), Dalaman International Airport (€80), Demre (€20) and Kaş (€30).

Kaleköy

📞 0242 / POP 150

The watery paradise of Kaleköy is one of the western Mediterranean's truly delightful spots, home to the ruins of ancient **Simena** and an impressive **Crusader fortress** (₺14; ⊙8am-7pm mid-Apr–Oct, to 5pm Nov–mid-Apr) perched above the hamlet looking out to sea. However, in high season an endless armada of tour boats descends on the place, and trinket vendors line the steps up to the castle, so expect plenty of company.

Within the fortress, the ancient world's tiniest **theatre** is cut into the rock, and nearby you'll find ruins of several temples and public baths. From the top you can look down upon a field of **Lycian tombs**, and the old **city walls** are visible on the outskirts.

🛏 Sleeping & Eating

In summer, many of the village houses climbing the rocky slope beneath the fortress open their doors as pensions of varying quality. You pay a premium to stay in this special and secluded location, so expect some rustic eccentricity despite the top-end prices. Half a dozen restaurants along the Kaleköy seafront serve freshly caught seafood with a view. Double-check prices of fish before you order as overcharging is not unknown. Most places are closed in the winter, but the village has a shop and the pensions can provide meals.

Paradise Teras   PENSION $$
(☑0537 354 6329, 0535 794 9186; r ₺260; ❄🌐) Three rooms here are worthy of Cappadocia, being organically built into the cliff with the toilet slotted into a crevice in one. The remaining two rooms in a stone house (and the terrace) gaze down on Kaleköy's stunning bay. The restaurant does pizza, Turkish food and homemade goat's-milk ice cream. Look it up on Facebook.

⭐**Mehtap Pansiyon**   PENSION $$$
(☑0535 592 1236, 0242-874 2146; www.mehtap pansiyon.com; s/d/tr €85/95/110; ❄🌐) The 10-room Mehtap has million-dollar views over the harbour and submerged Lycian tombs from its bougainvillea-draped terraces. Four rooms are in a 200-year-old stone house, another four are in a Lycian building dating back over two millennia and the other two occupy a pair of purpose-built wood cottages. Saffet and his father, İrfan, are warm and knowledgeable hosts. Saffet's wife, Nazike, grows her own vegetables and is an excellent cook (set meal ₺40).

Simena Pansiyon   PENSION $$$
(☑0532 779 0476, 0242-874 2025; www.simena pansiyon.com; r €80; ❄❄🌐) This gorgeous

150-year-old Greek stone house (look out for the lovely mosaic on the verandah) has four rooms with double beds, wardrobes and simple en-suites. All share a wide verandah.

I Am Here   ICE CREAM $
Everywhere sells ice cream in Kaleköy, but locals swear this is the best. There's a lovely terrace to enjoy it on, with bay views.

Ankh   CAFE $$
(☑0242-874 2171; www.ankhpansion.com; mains from ₺35, ice cream ₺12; ⊙11am-10pm; 🌐) This waterside pension cafe has been making its own peach, banana and hazelnut ice cream for 25 years. Sea bass and calamari are also on the menu and the terrace has spectacular views.

ⓘ Getting There & Away

Kaleköy is accessible from Üçağız by boat (₺40, 10 minutes; free with accommodation) or on foot (45 minutes) via a 4km section of the Lycian Way trail, which takes you through a boatyard and up to the fortress. Car access is poor, best for 4WD only.

Demre

☑0242 / POP 17,900
Officially 'Kale' but called by its old name 'Demre' by just about everyone, this sprawling, dusty town was once the Lycian (and later Roman) city of Myra. By the 4th century it was important enough to have its own bishop – most notably St Nicholas, who went on to catch the Western world's imagination in his starring role as Santa Claus. In AD 60, St Paul put Myra on the liturgical map by changing boats at its port, Andriake, while on his way to Rome (or so Acts 27:4-6 tells us).

Once situated on the sea, Demre moved inland as precious alluvium – deposits of clay, silt, sand and gravel – flowed from the Demre stream. The resultant fertile soil is the foundation of the town's wealth, and it remains a major centre for the growing and distribution of fruit and vegetables.

◉ Sights

Church of St Nicholas   CHURCH
(Noel Baba; Müze Caddesi; ₺20; ⊙8.30am-7pm Apr-Oct, 8.30am-5.30pm Nov-Mar) Demre's Church of St Nicholas, where the eponymous saint was laid upon his death in AD 343, is a star attraction for pilgrims and tourists (particularly Russians). Although

St Nicholas is no longer in situ (Italian merchants smashed open the sarcophagus in 1087 and supposedly carted his bones to Bari), the church features interesting Byzantine frescoes and mosaic floors. Expect crowds and a lot of trinket sellers.

The church was made a basilica when it was restored in 1043. Later restorations in 1862 were sponsored by Tsar Nicholas I of Russia (St Nicholas is the patron saint of Russia) and changed the church by constructing a vaulted ceiling and a belfry. More recent work by Turkish archaeologists is aiming to protect it from deterioration.

There are a couple of statues of the saint – one of them the height of kitsch as Santa Claus – in the square in front of the church. Souvenir shops opposite the church sell faux icons to Russian tourists; St Nick's feast day (6 December) is a very big event here.

Myra ARCHAEOLOGICAL SITE
(₺20; ☺8am-7pm mid-Apr–Oct, 8am-5pm Nov–mid-Apr) If you only have time to see one striking honeycomb of Lycian rock tombs, choose the memorable ruins of ancient Myra. Located about 2km inland from Demre's main square, they are among the finest in Lycia. There's a well-preserved 10,000-capacity **Roman theatre** here, which includes several theatrical masks carved on stones lying in the nearby area.

The so-called **Painted Tomb** near the river necropolis portrays a man and his family in relief both inside and out.

Alakent Caddesi leads 2km north from the square (3km from the highway) to the tombs; it's a 25-minute walk or ₺15 taxi ride.

Andriake RUINS
(₺7; ☺9am-7pm Apr-Oct, to 5pm Nov-Mar) The ruins of ancient Andriake are strewn over a wide area of an approach road to Çayağzı beach, 10km southwest of Demre. The entire site, which sprawls along the edge of a great flood plain, has recently been the subject of large investment and there are good information boards and well-constructed stone paths. Unfortunately the famous **granary** built by Hadrian in AD 139 has been reconstructed insensitively with a modern roof, and it's difficult to imagine the original building.

In 2009, the ruins of the first synagogue found in ancient Lycia were uncovered here. The new on-site **Museum of Lycian Civilizations** has good displays. Platforms and hides overlooking the river delta offer fine birding.

Çayağzı's final claim to fame is as one possible disembarkation (or embarkation) point of the famous blue yacht voyages (p326). Dolmuşes run sporadically out to Çayağzı from Demre; your best bet is probably a taxi (₺25).

OFF THE BEATEN TRACK

ARYKANDA

Built over five terraces, **Arykanda** (₺6; ☺8am-7pm mid-Apr–mid-Oct, to 5pm mid-Oct–mid-Apr) is one of the most dramatically situated ruins in Turkey. The city's most outstanding feature is its 10m-tall two-storey **baths complex**, standing next to the **gymnasium** on the lowest terrace. Following a path to the next terrace, you'll come to a large colonnaded **agora**. Its northern arches lead into an **odeon**. Above is a fine 2nd-century **theatre** and **stadium**. Another agora, a *bouleuterion* (council chamber) and cistern are found on the upper terraces.

One of the oldest sites on the Teke Peninsula, Arykanda was part of the Lycian League from its inception in the 2nd century BC, but was never a member of the 'Big Six' group of cities that commanded three votes each. This may have been due to its profligate and freewheeling ways as much as anything else. Arykanda was apparently the party town of Lycia and forever deeply in debt. Along with the rest of Lycia, it was annexed by Rome in AD 43 and survived as a Byzantine settlement until the 9th century, when it was abandoned.

If you're driving from the coast, there's an exit off the D400 at the unremarkable provincial centre of Finike, leading north for another 30km to Arykanda.

Hourly dolmuşes (minibuses) headed for Elmalı (₺12) from Finike will drop you off at the foot of the hill leading to the site entrance, from where it's a steep 3km walk to the ruins. A taxi will cost about ₺170 from Demre, 29km southwest of Finike, including two hours of waiting time.

🛌 Sleeping

⭐ Hoyran Wedre
Country House   BOUTIQUE HOTEL $$$
(☑ 0532 291 5762, 0242-875 1125; www.hoyran.
com; s/d from €100/120; ☺ Apr-Oct; ❄ 🛜 🏊) A
destination hotel if ever there was one, this
complex of stone buildings is a rural oasis
up in the Taurus Mountains, with astounding views across the countryside. There are
20 rooms and suites done in traditional
fashion (wattle-and-daub plastered walls)
with antique furniture and wooden balcony
or stone terrace. There are many fine hikes
in the area.

We love the nearby Lycian acropolis (which
owner Süleyman can guide you through), the
pool shaped like a traditional cistern, the set
meals (lunch/dinner €14/21) prepared entirely from locally grown produce (though some
rooms have kitchens if you prefer to self-
cater) and the afternoon tea.

It's 18km west of Demre, and 3km south
of Davazlar village, off the D400.

❶ Getting There & Away

Buses and dolmuşes travel half-hourly to/from
Kaş (₺10, one hour, 45km) and Antalya (₺32, 2½
hours) via the Olympos and Çıralı turn-offs (₺23,
1½ hours). The otogar is 200m southwest of the
main square. Eynihal Caddesi, the street running
south from the Church of St Nicholas, passes it.

Olympos

☑ 0242 / POP 570

An important Lycian city in the 2nd century
BC, Olympos is more famous these days for
being a backpacking beach resort. It's right
next to (and shares the same beach with)
Çıralı, which is more family oriented and
developed.

Staying in an Olympos 'tree house' (most
are actually log cabins) or at one of the
dozen-or-so camps that line the 5km road
along the valley down to the ruins and beach
has long been the stuff of travel legend. The
former hippy-trail hot spot has gentrified
considerably in past years, however.

Love it or hate it, Olympos still offers
good value and an up-for-it party atmosphere in a lovely setting. The nearest ATMs
are in Çıralı, a 1km walk away.

◉ Sights & Activities

Most people visit the wonderful beach that
fronts the ruins, but there are numerous
other activities available, including boat
cruises (full day with lunch €15 to €25), canyoning (full day €35), sea kayaking (half day
€20), paragliding (€75), mountain biking,
rock climbing and even scuba diving. Some
of the best and most difficult rock climbing
is at Hörguc, a wall opposite Olympos.

All camps organise nightly transport to
view the Chimaera (around ₺40).

Olympos Beach   BEACH
For most visitors, the superb 4km-long sand-
and-shale beach is the main attraction. Entrance is free from the Çıralı end, whereas at
the Olympos end you have to access it from
the Olympos ruins and thus pay.

Olympos Ruins   ARCHAEOLOGICAL SITE
(☑ 0242-247 7660; incl Olympos Beach ₺20,
parking ₺4; ☺ 8am-7pm mid-Apr–Oct, 8am-6pm
Nov–mid-Apr) The rambling ruins of ancient
Olympos are scattered beside the trickling
Ulupınar Stream and set inside a deep,
shaded valley that runs directly to the sea.
If you plan to visit a few times, you will save
money by buying a long-stay ticket allowing
10 entries over 10 days.

Olympos devoutly worshipped Hephaes-
tus (Vulcan), the god of fire, which may
have been inspired by the Chimaera (p358),
an eternal flame that still burns from the
ground in nearby Çıralı. The city went into
decline in the 1st century BC. The arrival of
the Romans, at the end of the 1st century
AD, brought about the city's rejuvenation,
but pirate attacks during the 3rd century
caused its importance to wane. In the Middle Ages, the Venetians and Genoese built
fortresses along the coast, but by the 15th
century the site had been abandoned.

Dark Travel   TOURS
(☑ 0507 007 6600, 0242-892 1311; www.darktravel.
com; Yazırköyü; ☺ 8am-9.30pm) This tour operator, located next to Şaban Pension, also
offers diving, sea kayaking, rafting and canyoning in Köprülü Kanyon, daily boat trips
(from ₺60) and blue voyages. Also nightly
excursions to Chimaera (₺40 including entrance, torch and transport).

Olympos
Adventure Center   ADVENTURE SPORTS
(☑ 0532 686 1799; www.olymposadventurecenter.
com; Kadır's Tree Houses; climbing trips 3hr/full day
from €45/70; ☺ 8am-10pm) Adventure-sport
specialist offering activities including diving, canyoning and sea kayaking. Rock
climbers head here for a huge range of trips
and courses.

🍴 Sleeping & Eating

Rates at many camps include half-board (breakfast and dinner). Outside peak summer months expect good discounts.

While many tree houses (small, rustic bungalows, sometimes slightly raised off the ground) have shared bathrooms, most camps now boast bungalows with en suite and air-conditioning. Not all tree houses have reliable locks, so store valuables at reception.

Bayrams   BUNGALOW $
(📞 0536 990 7749, 0242-892 1243; www.bayrams. com; Yazırköyü; dm ₺50, tree house ₺140, bungalow with bathroom & air-con ₺170; 🌐 @ 🛜) Come to this large operation to socialise and party at the lively bar. The accommodation itself is basic but doable, with narrow paths leading between small wooden cabins; the dorm has air-con. You'll find cushioned garden platforms for playing backgammon or puffing away on a nargile (water pipe).

⭐ Şaban Pension   BUNGALOW $$
(📞 0242-892 1265; www.sabanpansion.com; Yazırköyü; incl half-board dm €12, bungalows s/d/tr €26/35/48, tree houses without bathroom s/d €24/28; 🌐 🛜) This is the place to lounge in a hammock in the orchard or on a platform by the stream enjoying sociable owner Meral's home cooking (including lots for vegetarians). Accommodation is in charming cabins and tree houses; the 12-bed dorm has air-con. Şaban isn't a party spot; it's a tranquil getaway where relaxed conversations strike up around the bonfire at night.

Olympos Camlik Pension   HOSTEL $$
(📞 0242-892 1257; www.olimposcamlik.com; cabins €22-36; 🌐 🛜) Family-run with a choice of stilted (genuine!) tree houses, cabins and

ample hammocks and cushioned spaces for chilling in a leafy compound. Food is varied and healthy and there's a bar with a good variety of beers and cocktails. Located 1.5km inland from the beach.

Pehlivan Pansiyon   CAFE $
(📞 0242-892 1113; mains ₺12-22; ⊙ 11am-10pm; 🛜) 'Hero' pension's delicious *gözleme* are rolled and cooked by headscarf-clad ladies. Alcohol, and, in summer, sandwiches and grills are served, with cushions on wooden platforms for reclining. Find it just before the inland entrance to the Olympos ruins.

ℹ️ Getting There & Away

From the Olympos Junction, dolmuşes (₺6, 20 minutes) depart every half-hour between 8am and 8pm from May to October. Returning, minibuses leave Olympos at 9am then every hour until 7pm. From October to April they generally run two-hourly, with the last minibus usually departing Olympos at 6pm.

Çıralı
📞 0242

Çıralı (cher-*ah*-luh) is one of the best beaches in Turkey, a sweeping 4km-long expanse of sand and shingle backed by coastal dunes and pines. Development has been restricted here, so there are no concrete hotels spoiling the natural scene, only a mountain backdrop to admire. The beach is an important nesting ground for sea turtles; you'll see markers indicating nesting sites along the shore.

Behind the beach is a relaxed, family-friendly hamlet of mostly upscale pensions, hotels and campgrounds. Nightlife is minimal, save the odd bar. It's a quieter

ANTALYA & THE TURQUOISE COAST ÇIRALI

WORTH A TRIP

EXPLORING AROUND PHASELIS

About 16km north of the exits for Olympos and Çıralı from the D400 is the romantically sited ancient Lycian port of Phaselis (₺36; ⊙ 8am-7pm Apr-Oct, to 5pm Nov-Mar, ticket office shuts 30min before closure) are arranged around three small, perfectly formed bays. Some 9km inland, a cable car called the Olympos Teleferik (📞 0242-242 2252; www.olymposteleferik.com; adult/child 7-12yr €33/16.50; ⊙ 9.30am-6pm May & Jun, 9am-7pm Jul-Sep, to 6pm Oct, 10am-5pm Nov-Mar, to 5.30pm Apr) climbs almost to the top of 2365m-high Tahtalı Dağ (Wooded Mountain), the centrepiece of Olympos Beydağları National Park (Olimpos Beydağları Sahil Milli Parkı).

Frequent buses on the highway from Antalya (₺12, one hour) and Kemer (₺6, 20 minutes) pass both the exits for Phaselis and the Olympos Teleferik.

The cable-car company runs hourly shuttle buses from the highway exit to the *teleferik* station between 10am and 5pm.

alternative to the backpackers' haunt 1km down the beach at Olympos. And it's close to the magical and mystical Chimaera.

Sights & Activities

Boat trips around the coast are worthwhile. Several *gülets* moored on the beach offer excursions (10am to 5pm, ₺80 including lunch) which stop at different spots for swimming and snorkelling. You may see turtles, which boat crews should not be encouraged to feed.

Several places offer yoga, including Myland Nature Hotel, where nonguests can join the morning class for ₺40. Otherwise the hike to Chimaera is essential while you're here.

★ Chimaera   HISTORIC SITE

(₺6; 24hr) Known in Turkish as Yanartaş, or 'Burning Rock', the Chimaera is a cluster of small flames that naturally blaze on the rocky slopes of Mt Olympos. At night it looks like hell itself has come to pay a visit, and it's not difficult to see why ancient peoples attributed these extraordinary flames to the breath of a monster – part lion, part goat and part snake – that had terrorised Lycia.

The mythical hero Bellerophon supposedly killed the Chimaera by mounting the winged horse Pegasus and pouring molten lead into the monster's mouth. Today, gas still seeps from the earth and bursts into flame upon contact with the air. The exact composition of the gas is unknown, though it is thought to contain methane. Although a flame can be extinguished by covering it, it will reignite close by into a new and separate flame. At night the 20 or 30 flames in the main area are visible at sea.

The best time to visit is after dinner. From Çıralı, follow the Chimaera signs 3.5km on the main road along the hillside until you reach a valley and walk up to a car park. From there it's another 20- to 30-minute climb up a stepped path to the site; bring or rent a torch (flashlight). From Olympos, most camps organise transport every night after dinner.

Marshmallows can be purchased in Cirali and then roasted over the flames.

Sleeping

Sima Peace Pension   BUNGALOW $$

(0242-825 7245, 0532 238 1177; www.facebook.com/simapeace; off Yanartaş Yolu; s/d from €30/50; ※🛜) For a feel of old-school Çıralı,

when it was more of a bohemian escape, check into this quirky place. You'll love its hammocks, swing chairs, rocking horse and views across the fields, with rustic bungalows surrounded by fruit trees and quaint, basic rooms. Assisted by Coco the parrot, owner Aynur's cooking is legendary (dinner €10). Around 150m inland from the beach.

Dostlar Evi   PENSION $$

(0242-825 7236; mevlutdarbas@hotmail.com; s/d/tr/q €45/60/75/80, dinner ₺40; ※🛜) Around 400m inland from the beach, along the road to the Chimaera, Mevlüt and family run this pastoral farm stay with accommodation in farmhouses and bungalows. The food comes straight from their plots and you will surely leave a *dostlar* (friend). Look it up on Facebook.

★ Caretta Caretta Pension   PENSION $$$

(0242-825 7330, 0545 825 7330; www.carettacaretta.com.tr; s/d/f/villa €48/58/88/95; ※🛜) Perfect for a peaceful holiday, the family owners here look after guests well and prepare delicious breakfasts. Dotted around a verdant garden, the rooms, lovely cabins and spacious villas are very nicely presented and kept really clean. Located just off the shore, at the northern end of the beach. Bikes are available to explore.

★ Odile Hotel   HOTEL $$$

(0242-825 7163; www.hotelodile.com; Sahil Yolu; s/d €70/80, bungalows with kitchenette s/d/tr/q €100/120/150/180; P🅿️※🛜🏊) On this beachside estate-like property, spacious and modern bungalows are set around a pool with terraces looking at the mountains, within a well-maintained garden. Just behind the main complex, surrounding another pool and child's pool, are larger 'luxe' bungalows made of lovely scented cedar which are perfect for self-caterers.

Hotel Canada   HOTEL $$$

(0538 647 9522, 0242-825 7233; www.canadahotel.net; s/d from €50/60, 4-person bungalows from €100; ※🛜🏊) This is a beautiful place, offering the quintessential Çıralı experience: warmth, friendliness and homemade honey. The main house rooms are comfortable and the garden is filled with hammocks, citrus trees and 11 bungalows. Canadian Carrie and foodie husband Şaban also offer excellent set meals. It's 750m from the beach; grab a free bike and pedal on down.

✕ Eating & Drinking

★ **Yörük Restaurant**   TURKISH $$

(📞 0536 864 8648; Köprü Başı Mevkii; gözlemes
₺10-12, pides ₺10-14, mains ₺16-30; ⊙ 11am-10pm;
📶 ✎) Just after the bridge into Çıralı, this
is the best place for Turkish food: behind a
counter heaving with mezes and seafood,
the open kitchen turns out elongated pide,
light and fluffy *gözleme, mantı,* kebaps
and grills. Well priced and welcoming, with
space for children to roam.

★ **San Simon**   PIZZA $$$

(📞 0506 328 0051; www.facebook.com/sansimon
restobar; mains ₺32-70; ⊙ noon-1am; 📶) On the
north side of the river, modish San Simon
is the coolest place in town serving pizza
and Turkish dishes on a wonderful terrace.
There's a loungey vibe in summer, with electronic music and laughter filling the night
air. Good wine and cocktail lists.

★ **Yedi**   CAFE

(⊙ 9am-midnight; 📶) The best cafe in town, a
hip little joint with expertly prepared espresso options created by a knowledgeable baris-
ta; plus cakes and pastries. Alt-Turkish tunes
are on the playlist, and it sells a few bits of
jewellery and clothing too. It's just over the
bridge on the west side of the riverbank; see
Facebook.

❶ Getting There & Away

Transport to Çıralı (₺6, 20 minutes) from the
Çıralı Junction on the coastal highway is irreg-
ular; dolmuşes often don't depart until they are
full, so you may wait some time. On average,
there are departures every 40 minutes in summer, and two morning and one afternoon service
in winter. When they reach Çıralı, dolmuşes usually head along the beach road then turn inland
and pass the Chimaera turn-off, before returning
to the village along the edge of the hillside.

Antalya

📞 0242 / POP 1.31 MILLION

Once seen simply as the gateway to the
Turkish Riviera, Antalya today is very much
a destination in its own right. Situated right
on the Gulf of Antalya (Antalya Körfezi), the
largest city on Turkey's western Mediterranean coastline is both classically beautiful and
stylishly modern. If you're on a beach holiday
in the area it's well worth dropping by the city
to experience a slice of metropolitan Turkish
life, for there's a real buzz about Antalya, particularly during the long hot summer months.

The city's core is the wonderfully preserved historic district of Kaleiçi (literally
'within the castle'), which offers atmospheric accommodation in the finely restored
Ottoman houses on its winding lanes. The
old city wraps around a splendid Roman-era
harbour with clifftop views of hazy-blue
mountain silhouettes that are worth raising
a toast to. Just outside of the centre are two
beaches and one of Turkey's finest museums.

History

Antalya was originally named Attaleia, after
its 2nd-century founder, Attalus II of Pergamum. His nephew, Attalus III, ceded the
town to Rome in 133 BC. When the Roman
emperor Hadrian visited the city more than
two centuries later, in AD 130, he entered the
city through a triumphal arch (now known
as Hadrian's Gate) built in his honour.

There followed a succession of new 'land-
lords': the Byzantines took over from the
Romans, followed by the Seljuk Turks in the
early 13th century. The latter gave Antalya
both a new name and an icon – the Yivli
Minare (Fluted Minaret).

The city became part of the Ottoman
Empire in 1391. After WWI, the empire collapsed and Antalya was ceded to Italy. In
1921 it was liberated by Atatürk's army and
made the capital of Antalya Province.

◉ Sights

★ **Kaleiçi**   HISTORIC SITE

Antalya's historic district is a sight in itself
and you could happily spend half a day
strolling the narrow lanes here while admiring the mix of finely restored and creakily
dilapidated Ottoman-era architecture.

The district begins at the main gate, **Kale
Kapısı** (Fortress Gate), which is marked by
the old stone **Saat Kulesi** (Clock Tower)
and statue of Attalus II, the city's founder.
To the north is the **İki Kapılar Hanı** (Old
Bazaar; ⊙ 10am-10pm), a sprawling covered
bazaar dating to the late 15th century. Walk
south along Uzun Çarşı Sokak, the street
that starts opposite the clock tower. Immediately on the left is the 18th-century **Tekeli
Mehmet Paşa Camii** (Paşa Camii Sokak), a
mosque built by the Beylerbey (Governor
of Governors), Tekeli Mehmet Paşa, and
repaired extensively in 1886 and 1926. It's
currently being renovated but note the
beautiful Arabic calligraphy in the coloured
tiles above the windows and along the base
of the dome.

Antalya

(5.7km)

Antalya Museum (1.8km);
Havaş Bus Stop (3.6km);
7 Mehmet Restaurant (3.7km);
Konyaaltı Plajı (6km);
Tiritcizade Restoran
(6.7km)

Cumhuriyet Cad

Cumhuriyet
Meydanı

Atatürk
Statue

İskele
Cad

İskele Cad

Kalekapısı

Tombs

İmaret Sk 1

Paşa Camii Sk

Sur Sk

Uzun Çarşı Sk

Karanlık
Sk

İmaret Sk

İzmir li Ali Efendi Sk

Kaleiçi

Balık Pazarı Sk

Paşa Camii Sk

Mescit Sk

Civelek Sk

Hamit Efendi Sk

Hesapçı Sk

Koçatepe Sk

Kandiller Geçidi

Akarçeşme Sk

Marina

Mermerli Sk

Mermerli Banyo Sk

Kordon Sk

Zafer Sk

Müze Sk

Kurtuluş Sk

Viewpoint

Kaledibi Sk

Hıdırlık Sk

Camii Sk

Fırın Sk

Kadırpaşa Sk

Seferoğlu

Yeni Kapı Sk

Hesapçı Geçidi

Hesapçı Sk

Fırın Sk

Zeytin Çıkmazı

Zeytin Geçidi
Sk

Tabakhane Sk

Hıdırlık Sk

Gulf of Antalya
(Antalya Körfezi)

İnönü Cad

İsmet Paşa Cad

İsmet
Paşa

Fevzi
Çakmak Cad

Wander further into this protected
zone, where many of the gracious old Ottoman houses have been restored and
converted into pensions, boutique hotels
and shops. To the east, at the top of Hes-
apçi Sokak, is the monumental Hadrian's

Gate (Hadriyanüs Kapısı; Atatürk Caddesi), also
known as Üçkapılar or the 'Three Gates',
erected for the Roman emperor's visit to
Antalya in 130 AD.

The Roman Harbour (İskele Caddesi) at
the base of the slope was Antalya's lifeline

elevator (Asansör) descends the cliff to the harbour from the western end of Cumhuriyet Meydanı.

At the southwestern edge of Kaleiçi, on the corner of large, attractive, flower-filled **Karaalioğlu Parkı** (Atatürk Caddesi) rises **Hıdırlık Kalesi**, a 14m-high tower dating to the 1st or 2nd century AD. It was built as a mausoleum and later, due to its excellent position above the bay, played an important role in the city's defences as a watchtower and lighthouse.

Yivli Minare   HISTORIC SITE
(Fluted Minaret; Cumhuriyet Caddesi) This handsome and distinctive 'fluted' minaret, erected by Seljuk Sultan Aladdin Keykubad I in the early 13th century, is Antalya's symbol. The adjacent mosque (1373) is still in use today.

Mawlawi Lodge Museum   MUSEUM
(Antalya Mevlevihanesi; Yivli Minare complex, off İskele Caddesi; ☺8am-6pm) **FREE** Tucked away within the Yivli Minare complex, this fascinating domed structure dates back to 1377 and was beautifully restored in 2018. Its original use is uncertain but it was certainly a monastery for whirling dervishes during Ottoman times. There are excellent exhibits (in English and Turkish) about the life and times of the poet and Sufi spiritual leader Rumi, and you can view rooms used by the dervishes and displays about traditional musical instruments.

Sultan Alaadın Camii   MOSQUE
(Seferoğlu Sokak) This gem of a mosque is squirrelled away in the back alleys of Kaleiçi. It began life as the Greek Orthodox Panhagia Church in 1834 and was converted to a mosque in 1958. Uniquely in Antalya, the prayer hall's original painted ceiling, with its intricate star motifs, has been preserved.

There are no official opening times, but the mosque is usually open in the afternoon after midday prayer. When you see the gate open, you can visit.

Yenikapı Greek Church   CHURCH
(Hagios Alypios; ☑0242-244 6894; www.spcc turkey.com; Yeni Kapı Sokak) This small 19th-century church, renovated in 2007, has a beautiful interior with frescoes and hand-carved decorations. Orthodox services still take place here.

from the 2nd century BC until late in the 20th century, when a new port was constructed about 12km to the west, at the far end of Konyaaltı Plajı. The harbour was restored during the 1980s and is now a marina for yachts and excursion boats. An

Antalya

Suna & İnan Kıraç
Kaleiçi Museum   MUSEUM
(☎0242-243 4274; Kocatepe Sokak 25; ⊙9am-
6pm Thu-Tue) FREE This small ethnography
museum is housed in a lovingly restored
Antalya mansion. The 2nd floor contains a
series of life-size dioramas depicting some
of the most important rituals and customs
of Ottoman Antalya. More impressive is the
collection of Çanakkale ceramics housed
in the former Greek Orthodox church of
Aya Yorgi (St George), just behind the main
house, which has been fully restored and is
worth a look in itself.

Antalya Culture & Arts   CULTURAL CENTRE
(Antalya Kültür Sanat; ☎0242-242 0257; www.
antalyakultursanat.org.tr; Şehit Binbaşı Cengiz
Toytunç Caddesi 60; adult/student/child under 14yr
₺20/10/free; ⊙11am-7pm Tue, Wed & Fri-Sun, to
9pm Thu) This contemporary cultural centre
has a lively program of exhibitions covering

artists from local heroes to Picasso and Warhol. There's a cafe and small store here.

★**Antalya Museum**   MUSEUM
(☎0242-238 5688; Konyaaltı Caddesi; ₺30;
⊙8.30am-7pm mid-Apr–Oct, to 6pm Nov–mid-Apr)
Do not miss this comprehensive museum
with exhibitions covering everything from
the Stone and Bronze Ages to Byzantium.
The Hall of Regional Excavations exhibits
finds from ancient cities in Lycia (such as
Patara and Xanthos) and Phrygia, while the
Hall of Gods displays beautiful and evocative statues of 15 Olympian gods, many in
excellent condition. Most of the statues were
found at Perge, including the sublime Three
Graces and the towering Dancing Woman
dominating the first room.

The sarcophagi, including one for a
third-century dog from Termessos, are also
stunning. Upstairs are coins and other gold
artefacts recovered from Aspendos, Side

and various Byzantine and Ottoman sites, including the so-called Elmalı Treasure of almost 2000 Lycian coins.

Exhibits have good English explanations, and there's a cafe and bookstore. The museum is about 2km west of the Kaleiçi district, accessible on the *antik/nostalji tramvay* (tram) from Kale Kapısı. The tram heads along Cumhuriyet and Konyaaltı Caddesis to the museum (Müze stop).

Konyaaltı Plajı
BEACH

For a good dose of beach culture, head west from the centre to Konyaaltı, accessed by taking the *antik tram* to its final stop (Müze) and then walking further west and down the snaking road.

Lara Plajı
BEACH

South of the centre, Lara is sandier than Konyaaltı to the west. Dolmuşes run here down Atatürk and Fevzi Çakmak Caddesis.

Activities & Tours

Excursion boats tie up in Kaleiçi's Roman Harbour (p360). One-, two- and six-hour trips are offered (€10/15/30 at the top end; your accommodation can likely get you a better deal). The latter includes lunch and stops such as Kemer, the Gulf of Antalya islands and some beaches for a swim. In addition, ferries (₺10) run from the harbour to Kemer marina at 9am, noon and 5pm, returning at 10.30am, 1.30pm and 6.30pm (less frequently in winter).

For ferry times and information, visit www.antalyaulasim.com.tr.

Sefa Hamamı
HAMAM

(☏0532 526 9407, 0242-241 2321; www.sefa hamam.com; Kocatepe Sokak 32; steam bath ₺40, full hamam ₺180; ☉12.30-8pm Mon-Sat) This atmospheric hamam retains much of its 13th-century Seljuk architecture. Men and women bathe separately, with mixed bathing also available. You can reserve a massage online but it's cash only. Full hamam includes soak, soap, scrub and steam.

Nirvana Travel Service
TOURS

(☏0242-244 3893, 0532 521 6053; www.nirvana tour.com; İskele Caddesi 38/4) Offers a huge range of excursions including Land Rover tours up the Taurus Mountains (€40) and full-day outings to Side via Perge, Aspendos and Manavgat Waterfalls (€45 to €55).

Pamukkale trips and a three-day tour to Cappadocia are also offered. A minimum of four people required for day tours.

Sleeping

The most atmospheric – and central – place to stay is the old town of Kaleiçi, a virtually vehicle-free district that has everything you need. Kaleiçi's winding streets can be confusing to navigate, although signs pointing the way to most pensions are posted on street corners.

Many pensions and hotels close from October to April; those that remain open offer discounts. Parking and airport pick-ups can generally be organised with advance notice.

Sabah Pansiyon
PENSION $

(☏0555 365 8376, 0242-247 5345; www.sabah -pansiyon-tr.book.direct; Hesapçı Sokak 60; s/d/tr €18/28/40, 2-bedroom apt from €80; ☀❄☎☎) A dependable pension in a historic house that's run by staff switched on to travellers' needs. Rooms vary in size but all are simple and clean, though bathrooms need updating. The courtyard is prime territory for meeting other guests and its on-site restaurant Yemenli (p366) turns out decent Turkish classics.

If you're looking for self-catering facilities, check out its complex of modern, spacious apartments nearby that can accommodate up to five people.

Lazer Pension
PENSION $

(☏0242-242 7194; www.lazerpansiyon.com; Hesapçı Sokak 61; s/d/tr €19/35/50; ☀❄☎) This worth-considering budget option has spacious though dated rooms, an upstairs terrace and a courtyard decorated with pot plants. Cleanliness is good and staff are amiable.

White Garden Pansion
PENSION $$

(☏0242-241 9115; www.white-garden-pansion. antalyahotel.org; Hesapçı Geçidi 9; s/d ₺220/280; ❄@☎☎) Combining quirky Ottoman character, modern rooms with an old-world veneer, and excellent service from Metin and team, this is a good choice for a Kaleiçi base. The building itself is a fine restoration and the courtyard is particularly charming with its large pool. The breakfast also gets top marks.

ANTALYA & THE TURQUOISE COAST ANTALYA

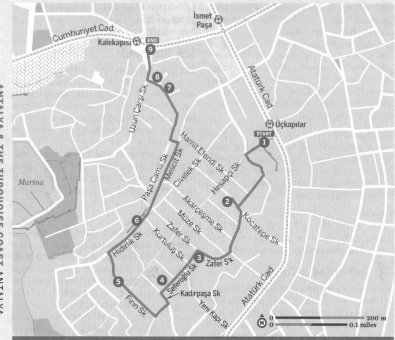

City Walk
Kaleiçi's Architecture Through the Ages

START HADRIAN'S GATE
END KALE KAPISI
LENGTH 1.5KM; TWO HOURS

Begin by strolling through the arches of **1** **Hadrian's Gate** (p360) and taking the first narrow alley to your left into Kaleiçi's quiet residential district. You'll see some good examples of Ottoman mansions. Note the characteristic protruding shuttered *cumba* (oriel) windows, where the women of the house would host guests – being able to see out but not be seen themselves.

Turn right onto Kocatepe Sokak to visit the **2** **Suna & İnan Kıraç Kaleiçi Museum** (p362). Backtrack and continue along the lane until you arrive at a pretty square with a trickling fountain. Turn right here onto Zafer Sokak then left onto Seferoğlu Sokak to reach **3** **Sultan Alaadın Camii** (p361). At the far end of the ruined **4** **Kesik Minare** (p361), where restoration work is ongoing, turn left again onto Kadırpaşa Sokak, noting the fine Ottoman mansion with a beautiful stone-pebble entrance.

You'll notice that nearly all of the houses are built of stone – a fire in 1895 destroyed much of the original timber housing. Turn right onto pretty **5** **Fırın Sokak** with its mix of restored mansions now used as pensions and dilapidated houses awaiting attention, and then right onto Hıdırlık Sokak.

As you walk up the road you'll see the crumbling remains of the **6** **Roman- and Byzantine-era walls** that once encircled the town. Follow the road up until you come to a lonely, incisor-like wall chunk marking a split in the road. Take the left-hand road and follow tourist shop–lined Mescit and Paşa Camii Sokaks; look out for another large chunk of the **7** **old city walls** with derelict examples of complete timber-framed Ottoman houses incorporated.

End your walk by visiting 17th-century **8** **Tekeli Mehmet Paşa Camii** (p359) before exiting the old town at **9** **Kale Kapısı** (p359), marked by the old stone *saat kulesi* (clock tower) and a statue of Attalus II, the city's founder.

Hotel Hadrianus
HOTEL **$$**

(☑0242-244 0030; www.hadrianushotel.com; Zeytin Çıkmazı 4; s/d/tr €40/50/70; ☺❋☎) Named after the Roman emperor (the city's first bona fide tourist), this good-value 11-room hotel is set in a 750-sq-metre garden: a veritable oasis in Kaleiçi, filled with birdsong in the morning and the setting for breakfast. Rooms all have a flatscreen TV with satellite channels and contain reproduction antique furnishings; those at the top are larger.

Mavi & Anı Pansiyon
PENSION **$$**

(☑0242-247 0056; www.maviani.com; Tabakhane Sokak 13-23; s/d €30/45; ❋☎) In the heart of Kaleiçi, this restored Ottoman house has a fabulously peaceful garden, common areas decorated with old Anatolian furniture and bric-a-brac, and characterful rooms. The only let-down are the basic showers. If you want something more contemporary, it also has four apartments, with kitchen facilities and access to a pool, nearby.

Hotel Blue Sea Garden
HOTEL **$$**

(☑0242-248 8213, 0537 691 4164; www.hotel blueseagarden.com; Hesapçı Sokak 65; s/d/tr/ste €30/50/65/75; ☺❋☎❋) Blue Sea Garden's trump card is its fine pool and decidedly lovely outdoor area. Rooms are functional and a little plain, though kept clean and tidy. The in-house restaurant is an appealing place to while away an evening. Rates drop considerably in the off-season.

The 'boutique' annexe around the corner has a poky economy room and pleasant standard rooms with exposed stone and brick walls. Guests have breakfast at Blue Sea Garden and can use the pool.

★Arkk Homes
APARTMENT **$$$**

(☑0242-255 0055; www.arkkhomes.com; 1293 Sokak 10; apt €85-160; ❋☎) Just outside Kaleiçi, a few steps from Hadrian's Gate, this sleek address is perfect for families or those in search of space and style. All units (some with two bedrooms) boast modish furnishings, some have fine sea views, and even the studios are a gigantic 60 sq m. Facilities include fully equipped kitchens, dining tables and washing machines.

Tekeli Konakları
HERITAGE HOTEL **$$$**

(☑0242-244 5465, 0545 662 2117; www.tekeli.com. tr; Dizdar Hasan Sokak; r from €69; ☺❋☎❋)

Historic hotel comprising eight rooms in a complex of lemon-yellow Ottoman buildings. Rooms feature stained glass, bathrooms with all-over İznik tiles, beds on raised platforms in Ottoman style and even a display cabinet with Ottoman porcelain and tapestries. Staff are hospitable and kind and it's good value for the location, a short walk from the harbour.

Tuvana Hotel
BOUTIQUE HOTEL **$$$**

(☑0242-247 6015; www.tuvanahotel.com; Karanlık Sokak 18; r €93-153; ❋☎❋) In lush gardens, this compound of Ottoman houses has been stylishly converted into a refined city hotel with 47 rooms and suites, four with balconies. Its plush rooms have a historic feel, with varnished floorboards, rugs and wall hangings, plus mod cons such as DVD players and safes. Attention to detail is superb and there are three on-site restaurants: Seraser (p366), Il Vicino and Pio.

✖ Eating

Cafes and restaurants are tucked in and around the Kaleiçi area, colonising the cobbled lanes with their outdoor tables. For cheap eats, walk east to the **Dönerciler Çarşısı** (Market of Döner Makers; İnönü Caddesi; mains ₺12-30; ⊙11am-11pm), or north to the rooftop kebap places across the main drag from Kale Kapısı. Cafes line the western side of Atatürk Caddesi north of Yeni Kapı Sokak, fuelling the promenading students.

★Can Can Pide ve Kebap Salonu
TURKISH **$**

(☑0242-243 2548; Arık Caddesi 4; pides from ₺10, mains from ₺12; ⊙7am-midnight Mon-Sat) For authentic local food at cheap prices, Can Can (jan jan) certainly has lots of *can* (soul) with street tables and locals buying *güveç* (stews) well into the evening. Choose between *çorba* (soup), thin and crispy *kıymalı* pide (Turkish pizza with meat topping), Adana *dürüm* (kebap rolled in flatbread) and *mantı* (Turkish ravioli).

Tarıhı Balık Pazarı Unlu Mamülleri
BAKERY **$**

(Balık Pazarı Sokak; pastries ₺3-5) This excellent little bakery churns out a mind-boggling array of sweet and savoury baked goods. Great *kıymalı* (meat) and *sosis* (sausage) *börek* pastry cigars, fine spinach *gözleme* (stuffed flatbreads) and sugar-dusted treats. Accompany with *ayran* (yoghurt drink) from the fridge and grab a stool outside.

ÇaY-Tea's
CAFE $$

(📱 0542 233 4464; www.facebook.com/cayteas lunchroom; Hıdırlık Sokak 3; meals from ₺20; ⏰ 9am-11pm; 🕾) Çay, coffee, milkshakes and juices are served with ribbon-wrapped shortbread at this eclectic Dutch-Turkish cafe, where vintage furniture spills into the street and a wine cellar houses an inviting country kitchen-style space. The menu is great light-lunch territory with sandwiches, omelettes, crepes, vegan specialities and homemade cakes.

Tiritcizade Restoran
TURKISH $$

(📱 0242-229 2900; www.tiritcizade.com.tr; Atatürk Bulvarı 247; mains ₺22-36; ⏰ noon-10.30pm; ❄🕾) Terrific Turkish food, including many beautifully presented lamb dishes from the Anatolian city of Konya. There's an air-con interior and also outdoor seating. No booze but *ayran* is just ₺4. Located 5km west of the Antalya Museum.

Yemenli
TURKISH $$

(📱 0242-247 5345; Hesapçı Sokak 60; mains ₺20-45; ⏰ noon-11pm; 🕾) Tried-and-true Turkish favourites are served up by the team behind Sabah Pansiyon (and named after their Yemen-born grandfather) with tables spilling out onto the street right in front of the hotel. There's an extensive wine list.

LeMan Kültür
CAFE $$

(📱 0242-243 7474; www.lmk.com.tr; Atatürk Caddesi 44; mains ₺15-25; ⏰ 9am-midnight; 🕾) This gorgeous garden cafe south of Hadrian's Gate is rammed all summer long with Antalya's bright young things. Great for coffee, snacks and flirting.

7 Mehmet Restaurant
TURKISH $$

(📱 0242-238 5200; www.7mehmet.com; Atatürk Kültür Parkı 201; mezes ₺10-18, mains ₺24-65; ⏰ 11am-11pm Oct-May, to 1am Sat & Sun Jun-Sep) Antalya's most famous eatery is a couple of kilometres west of the centre, with its spacious indoor and stylish outdoor dining areas occupying a hill overlooking Konyaaltı Beach and the city. Yedi Mehmet's menu of grilled mains, fish and mezes is unsurprising but of high quality, attracting businesspeople and other discerning diners.

Hasanağa Restaurant
TURKISH $$

(📱 0242-247 1313; Mescit Sokak 15; mains ₺25-40; ⏰ 11am-10pm) Expect to find the garden

at this restaurant and *şarap odası* (wine room) chock-a-block on the nights when traditional Turkish musicians and folk dancers entertain from 8pm onwards. The kitchen does produce seasonal salads, but it's most famous for *pirzola* (grilled lamb cutlets).

Seraser
MEDITERRANEAN $$$

(📱 0242-247 6015; www.seraserrestaurant.com; Tuvana Hotel, Karanlık Sokak 18; mains ₺45-120; ⏰ noon-11pm) International dishes including homemade pasta and fillet steak with gorgonzola sauce (₺95) in Ottoman surrounds, featuring pasha-style chairs, a glass-bead chandelier and lovely outdoor seating. The Turkish coffee crème brûlée is legendary. Lunchtime dining is more casual, and there's live jazz some nights.

Balikci Meyhanesi Kaleici
TURKISH $$$

(📱 0555 630 8466; https://kaleicibalikcimey hanesi.business.site; Hıdırlık Sokak 17; mezes ₺16, fish mezes ₺25-50, mains ₺30-75; ⏰ noon-1am May-Oct, to midnight Nov-Apr; 🕾) On a hot summer night, streetside tables at this (mainly) seafood restaurant on the main drag are the perfect location for a memorable meal with marine-blue-and-white seating beneath an old stone-walled townhouse. Turkish musicians play traditional tunes most nights.

Vanilla
INTERNATIONAL $$$

(📱 0242-247 6013; www.vanillaantalya.com; Hesapçı Sokak 33; starters ₺27-122, mains ₺36-119; ⏰ noon-10.15pm; ❄🍴) Modern British-owned restaurant that boasts an eclectic, global menu featuring starters such as dynamite prawns (₺42) and classic mains like rib-eye steak (₺119). Located in the beating heart of Kaleiçi and perfect for those needing a kebap break.

Arma Restaurant
SEAFOOD $$$

(📱 0242-244 9710; www.clubarma.com.tr; İskele Caddesi 75; mezes ₺35-70, mains ₺50-120; ⏰ 11am-11pm; 🕾🍴) Housed in a former oil depot on the rocks overlooking the harbour, this upmarket *balık evi* (fish restaurant) specialises in mezes and seafood from sea bass to shrimp. On a balmy evening, the fabulous terrace with its five-star view is one of the city's most romantic dining experiences. Try the grilled grouper with julienne vegetables, potatoes and rocket (₺90).

🍷 Drinking & Entertainment

Buzzy beer gardens with million-dollar views and live-music venues with everything from rock to *türkü* (Turkish folk music), Kaleiçi has much to offer after dark. The old town is highly atmospheric at night, with *meyhanes* (taverns), bars and cafes filling the cobbled streets with tables and the strains of live music.

★**Luna Garden** CAFE
(www.lunagarden.com.tr; Kocatepe Sokak 4; ◉9am-1pm; ☎) This huge garden cafe on the eastern side of Kaleiçi is rammed to the rafters in the evening with young holidaying Turks sipping tea and coffee, flirting and texting under a leafy canopy of evergreen trees and lanterns. Waitstaff zip about on blades and snacks like pide are served. No alcohol.

★**Castle Café** CAFE
(☑0242-248 6594; Hıdırlık Sokak 48; ◉8am-midnight) This perch on the cliff edge is a superb choice at sunset, attracting a crowd of young Turks with its affordable drinks. Service can be slow, but the terrace's jaw-dropping views of the beaches and mountains west of town more than compensate, as does the well-priced menu (mains ₺18 to ₺40) featuring fish and chips and burgers. Access is either from the path just opposite the Hıdırlık Kalesi or through the back – down stairs and along the side of an old building – from Hıdırlık Sokak.

Dem-Lik BAR
(☑0242-247 1930; Zafer Sokak 6; ◉noon-midnight Sun-Thu, to 1am Fri & Sat; ☎) This chilled-out garden bar-cafe, with tables scattered along stone walls and beneath shady fruit trees, is where Antalya's university crowd reshapes the world over ice-cold beers, while listening to Turkish troubadours perform live jazz, reggae, folk and more (on Wednesday, Friday and Saturday evenings). There's a menu of cheap pasta and other international dishes as well.

Kale Bar BAR
(☑0242-248 6591; Mermerli Sokak 2; ◉11am-midnight; ☎) For the most spectacular harbour and sea views in Kaleiçi, head to this patio bar at the CH Hotels Türkevi. Beers start at ₺22 and cocktails are priced north of ₺32.

🛍 Shopping

The Kaleiçi district is jam-packed with shops and stalls that are firmly pegged for the tourist market. The northwest section of the old city is basically one big bazaar of T-shirts and souvenirs rolling down the hilly alleyways to the harbour. If you're looking for something a little less plastic-fantastic to take home, head to the İki Kapılar Hanı.

Yaz JEWELLERY, FASHION
(☑0533 556 3339; Zafer Sokak 31; ◉10am-7.30pm Mon-Sat) Graphic designer Ebru's tiny concept store sells Turkish design, perfume, cushions, jewellery (₺30 to ₺600) and quirky T-shirts (₺50 to ₺120). Chat with him over a coffee (from ₺7) or piece of cake.

ℹ Information

Antalya Guide (www.antalyaguide.org) A comprehensive website with info on everything Antalya-related, from climate to cultural events.

Tourist Office (☑0242-247 7660 ext 133; ◉8.30am-5.30pm) This office off Cumhuriyet Caddesi is very little help but has a few city maps and brochures. Minimal English spoken.

ℹ Getting There & Away

AIR

Antalya's busy **international airport** (Antalya Havalimanı; ☑0242-444 7423; www.aytport.com; Serik Caddesi) is 10km east of the city centre on the D400 highway. In the arrivals hall there's a tourist information desk, and a number of car-hire agency counters.

Low-cost carriers operate plentiful direct flights to European cities, Middle Eastern and Gulf destinations including Beirut and Sharjah, and many Russian cities.

Turkish Airlines (www.turkishairlines.com), **Pegasus Airlines** (www.flypgs.com) and **Sun Express** (www.sunexpress.com) operate extensive domestic networks from Antalya, serving many Turkish cities, including daily flights to/from İstanbul.

BUS

Antalya's **otogar** (Antalya Bus Station; Adnan Selekler Caddesi; ◉24hr), about 4km north of the city centre, just off highway D650, consists of two large terminals fronted by a park. Looking at the otogar from the main highway or its parking lot, the **Şehirlerarası Terminalı** (Intercity Terminal), which serves long-distance destinations, is on the right. The **İlçeler Terminali** (Domestic Terminal), serving nearby destinations such as Side and Alanya, is on the left.

The **AntRay tram** is the quickest way into town. Follow the signs from the bus station to the underpass which brings you to Otogar

SERVICES FROM ANTALYA OTOGAR

DESTINATION	FARE (₺)	DURATION (HR)	FREQUENCY
Adana	85-125	11-12	16 daily
Alanya	25-30	3	every 20min
Anka	70-95	8	18 daily
Çanakkale	130-149	12	8 daily
Denizli (Pamukkale)	45-53	4	15 daily
Eğirdir	32	3½	hourly to Isparta (transfer there)
Fethiye	36-52	3½	12 daily
Göreme	100-105	9-10	5 daily
İstanbul	136-160	11-13	very regular, over 30 daily
İzmir	77-99	7-8	hourly
Kaş	38	3½	every 30min
Kemer	12	45min	every 15min
Konya	50-70	5-6	17 daily
Marmaris	60-75	6	3-5 daily
Olympos/Çıralı	14	1½	every 30min
Side/Manavgat	15	1½	every 20min in season

tram stop. It's a 20-minute ride (eight stops) to the central İsmet Paşa stop just outside Kaleiçi.

Buses (cnr Ali Çetinkaya & Cebesoy Caddesi) also link the centre of town with the otogar.

❶ Getting Around

For bus and tram times and information, visit www.antalyaulasim.com.tr

To ride any public transport, you must buy an **Antalyakart** (rechargeable transport card). They can be purchased at many kiosks and newsagents near tram stops or on the bus. It costs ₺5, plus credit. Tram journeys cost ₺2.40 and bus journeys from ₺2.60.

Taxis (Kesik Minare Sokak) around the centre cost about ₺15. It's around ₺30 to the otogar from Kaleiçi.

TO/FROM THE AIRPORT

Antalya's **AntRay tram** connects the airport and the centre of town. From the airport (Havalimanı) tram stop it's 12 stops (around 40 minutes) to İsmet Paşa tram stop, the closest stop to Kaleiçi.

Antalyakarts are available for purchase at the airport tram stop. A taxi will cost ₺80 to ₺90.

There is also an hourly **Havaş** (☑ 0242-330 3800; www.havas.net; Atatürk Bulvarı; ☺ 1.30am-10pm) shuttle, which runs from the 5M Migros shopping centre near Konyaaltı Plajı (about 45 minutes; ₺12). Coming into the city, it stops at the otogar before following the ring road to 5M Migros.

TRAM

Antalya's sleek, double-track **AntRay tram** red line runs from the northwestern part of the city via the otogar into the centre and then heads east via the airport and Aksu (for Perge). For travellers, it's the simplest way of getting in and out of town from the transport hubs, plus it provides a cheap and efficient option of visiting Perge. Trams run every five to 10 minutes. There's also a second purple line under construction (the route will be of little interest to travellers though).

Antalya's original 6km-long single-track *antik* or *nostalji tramvay* (tram) has 10 stops. It runs every half-hour between 7am and 11pm. The tram stops at Kale Kapısı at 12 and 42 minutes past the hour, and heads along Cumhuriyet and Konyaaltı Caddesis to Antalya Museum (Müze stop).

The two tram lines are not linked, but the İsmet Paşa stop on the AntRay is a short walk from the central Kale Kapısı stop on the *antik tramvay*.

Around Antalya

Antalya is an excellent base for excursions to the ancient sites of Termessos, Perge and Aspendos. The latter two sites are east of the city, just off the D400. Since Antalya's 2017 AntRay line extension, a trip to Perge is now as simple as hopping on the tram. Both sites can also easily be visited from the town of Side. Termessos is in the mountains northwest of Antalya, off the inland road to Fethiye.

◎ Sights

Perge ARCHAEOLOGICAL SITE
(Atatürk Caddesi, Aksu; ₺35; ⊙8am-7pm mid-Apr–mid-Oct, to 5pm mid-Oct–mid-Apr; 🚊 Aksu)
Some 17km east of Antalya, Perge was one of the most important towns of ancient Pamphylia. Inside the site, walk through the massive **Roman Gate** with its four arches. To the left is the southern **nymphaeum** and well-preserved **baths**, and to the right, the large square-shaped **agora**. Beyond the **Hellenistic Gate**, with its two huge towers, is the fine **colonnaded street**, where there's an impressive collection of columns. Allow two hours to fully tour the site, which has very little shade.

The water source for the narrow concave channel running down the centre of the colonnaded street was the northern **nymphaeum**, which dates to the 2nd century AD. From here it's possible to follow a short path to the ridge of the hill with the **acropolis** where there are stupendous views over the ruins.

Perge's 12,000-seat **theatre** and impressive **stadium** are located along the access road just after the main site entrance and car park.

Perge experienced two golden ages: during the Hellenistic period in the 2nd and 3rd centuries BC and under the Romans in the 2nd and 3rd centuries AD (from which most of the ruins here date). Turkish archaeologists first began excavations here in 1946 and a selection of the statues discovered – many in magnificent condition – can be seen at the Antalya Museum (p362). Excavations and restoration work continue on-site.

Antalya's AntRay tram extends east to Aksu. From İsmet Paşa tram stop in central Antalya, it's 14 stops to Aksu. From the tram stop, it's an easy 2km walk to the ruins. Many Antalya travel agencies run combined excursions to Perge and Aspendos. A half-day taxi tour will be about €45 for the two sites.

★ Aspendos ARCHAEOLOGICAL SITE
(Aspendos Yolu, Belkıs; admission ₺25, parking ₺5; ⊙8am-7pm mid-Apr–mid-Oct, to 5pm mid-Oct–mid-Apr) People come in droves to this ancient site near the modern-day village of Belkıs for one reason: to view the awesome **theatre**, considered the best-preserved Roman theatre of the ancient world. It was built during Aspendos' golden age in the reign of Emperor Marcus Aurelius (161–80 AD), and was used as a caravanserai by the Seljuks during the 13th century. The history of the city, though, goes all the way back to the Hittite Empire (800 BC).

After touring the area in the early 1930s, Atatürk declared Aspendos too fine an example of classical architecture to stay unused. Following a restoration that didn't please many historians, the 15,000-seat theatre became a venue once again. Operas, concerts and events, including the Aspendos Opera & Ballet Festival (p370) and Antalya's **film festival** (Antalya Film Festivalı; www.antalyaff.com/en; ⊙late Oct), are staged here. The acoustics are excellent and the atmosphere at night is sublime.

Apart from the theatre, the ancient city ruins are extensive and include a **stadium**, **agora** and 3rd-century **basilica**, although there is little left intact. To reach them, follow the trail to the right of the theatre entrance. Further on are the remains of the city's **aqueduct**.

Aspendos lies 47km east of Antalya and 3km north of Belkıs. If driving, immediately on your right as you exit the D400 for Aspendos is a restored Seljuk-era switchback **bridge** with seven arches spanning the Köprü River. It dates from the 13th century but was built on an earlier Roman bridge.

Perge

ANTALYA & THE TURQUOISE COAST AROUND ANTALYA

Most folk visit Aspendos on a tour from Antalya or Side. Otherwise catch any dolmuş that runs between Antalya and Side along the D400 and get off at the Aspendos turn-off, from where you can walk (45 minutes) or hitch the remaining 4km to the site. Taxis waiting at the highway junction will take you to the site for (an outrageous) ₺20.

Termessos ARCHAEOLOGICAL SITE
(₺7; ⊘ 8.30am-7pm mid-Apr–mid-Oct, to 5pm mid-Oct–mid-Apr) Hidden high in a rugged mountain valley, 34km northwest of Antalya, lies the ruined but still massive ancient city of Termessos. Neither Greek nor Lycian, the inhabitants were Pisidian, fierce and prone to warring. They successfully fought off Alexander the Great in 333 BC, and the Romans (perhaps wisely) accepted Termessos' wishes to remain independent and an ally in 70 BC. It's a fairly tough 150m hike over rocky terrain to the upper city, so good footwear is essential.

In the car park, at the end of the Termessos access road (King's Rd), you come across the **lower city ruins**. The portal on the hillock to the west was once the entrance to the **Artemis-Hadrian Temple** and **Hadrian Propylaeum**. From here follow the steep path south; you'll see remains of the **lower city walls** on both sides and pass through the **city gate** before reaching, in about 20 minutes, the lower **gymnasium** and **baths** on your left.

A short distance uphill from the lower city ruins are the remnants of Termessos' **upper city walls** and a **colonnaded street**. Just above is the upper **agora** and its five large cisterns, an ideal spot to explore slowly and to catch some shade.

On the eastern side of the upper agora is the **theatre**, which enjoys a positively jaw-dropping position atop a peak, surrounded by a mountain range; you can see Antalya on a clear day. Walk southwest from the theatre to view the cut-limestone **bouleuterion**, but use caution when scrambling across the crumbled **Temple of Artemis** and **Temple of Zeus** to the south.

Termessos' southern **necropolis** is at the very top of the valley, 3km (one hour's walk) up from the car park at the site entrance.

The site is spread out and requires much scrambling over loose rocks and up steep, though well-marked, paths. Allow a minimum of two hours to explore and bring plenty of drinking water.

Taxi tours from Antalya cost around €50, or you could take an organised excursion for less. A cheaper option is to catch a bus from Antalya otogar bound for Korkuteli (₺12) and alight at the entrance to Güllükdağı Termessos National Park. Taxis waiting here in the warmer months will run you up the 9km-long King's Rd to the ruins and back. The fare should be about ₺30, but you will have to negotiate.

✦✦ Festivals & Events

**Aspendos Opera
& Ballet Festival** PERFORMING ARTS
(Aspendos Opera ve Bale Festivalı; www.facebook.com/aspendosfestival; ⊘ Aug/Sep) This event is held in Aspendos's Roman theatre, either in June or in late August and September (depending on the year). Tickets can be bought online, from kiosks opposite the theatre and set up beside Antalya Museum and Side Museum, as well as from travel agents in Antalya and Side.

Selge & Köprülü Kanyon

The ruins of ancient Selge are strewn about the Taurus-top village of Altınkaya, 12km above spectacular Köprülü Kanyon and within a national park with peaks up to 2500m. The road climbs from the Köprü

Termessos ⓝ
0 ————— 400 m
0 ————— 0.2 miles

Artemis-Hadrian Temple &
Hadrian Propylaeum

Northern
Necropolis

Cistern — Hadrian's
Gate

Rock
Tomb

Lower City
Walls

Colonnaded
Street

City Gate

Tomb of
Alcetas Osbaras

Stoa

Gymnasium & Baths

Upper City Walls

Corinthian
Temple

Agora

Termessian House

Theatre

Upper Gymnasium

Attalos Stoa

Heroon

Upper
Agora

Bouleuterion

Temple of Artemis

Temple of Zeus

Southern
Necropolis

River through increasingly dramatic scenery of rock formations and olive groves backed by snow-capped peaks.

◉ Sights

Selge RUINS

FREE About 350m of ancient Selge's city wall still exists, but its most striking monument is its huge **theatre**, restored in the 3rd century AD. Close by is the **agora**. As you wander through the village and its ruins, consider that Selge once counted a population of more than 20,000. Today the site is unexcavated and largely overgrown.

Because of the city's elevated position, its walls and surrounding ravines, approaching undetected wasn't a simple task and Selge was able to ward off most invaders. Nevertheless, the Romans eventually took hold of the territory, which survived into the Byzantine era.

At the foot of the ascent from the Köprü River to Selge, you'll discover two Roman-era bridges. The first (and smaller) is the **Bürüm Bridge** and the second, the dramatically arched **Oluk Bridge**, spanning 14m across a deep canyon of the ancient Eurymedon (now Köprü) River. It has been in service since the Romans put it here in the 2nd century AD.

The villagers sometimes block the road about 1km before Selge (within sight of the theatre) for agricultural reasons. You can park there and continue on foot.

🏃 Activities

Rafting

There are more than two-dozen companies offering rafting trips in the canyon, including **Antalya Rafting** (📞0532 604 0092, 0242-311 4845; www.antalya-rafting.net), **Gökcesu Rafting** (📞0242-765 3384, 0533 522 3205; www.gokcesu.net) and independent local guides such as **Adem Bahar** (📞0535 762 8116; Altınkaya).

Hiking

Around the Oluk Bridge, you'll find villagers keen to guide you on hikes up from Köprülü Kanyon along the original Roman road for about ₺100 or so. It's about two hours up and 1½ hours down. An excellent qualified guide who knows the area inside out is Adem Bahar. He also organises rafting trips.

You can also arrange guided mountain treks for groups to Mt Bozburun (2504m) and other points in the Kuyucak Dağları

(Kuyucak Range) for about €30 per group per day. There is a three-day walk through the Köprülü Kanyon on the St Paul's Trail.

ℹ Getting There & Away

Many travel agencies in Antalya include Köprülü Kanyon Milli Parkı and Selge in their tours. Unless you have your own transport, this is your best option.

If you do have a vehicle, however, you can visit in half a day, though it deserves a lot more time. The turn-off to Selge and Köprülü Kanyon is about 5km east of the Aspendos road (51km from Antalya) along highway D400. Another 30km up into the mountains, the road divides, with the left fork marked for Karabük and the right for Beşkonak. If you take the Karabük road along the river's west bank, you'll pass most of the rafting companies and the pensions. About 11km from the turn-off is the graceful old Oluk Bridge, from where the paved road marked for Altınkaya climbs 12km to the village and the Selge ruins.

If you follow the river's east bank via Beşkonak, it is 6.5km from the fork in the road to the canyon and the narrow Oluk Bridge, which you can just squeeze a car over.

Side

📞0242 / POP 12,700

Down at Side harbour, the re-created colonnade of the Temple of Athena marches towards the blue sea, while at the top of Side old town's gentle hill, the 2nd-century theatre still lords it up over the surrounding countryside. Between these two ancient relics, the lanes of this once-docile fishing village have long since given themselves over to souvenir peddlers and restaurant touts hustling for business. Despite the constant stream of visitors, the liberal scattering of glorious Roman and Hellenistic ruins sitting incongruously between shops means you can just about imagine (if you scrunch up your eyes) the tourists picking over togas rather than T-shirts.

◉ Sights & Activities

Boat tours (€15-30) departing from the harbour include beaches, dolphin sightings, Manavgat waterfall and market, and a look at the Temples of Apollo and Athena from the water.

★ Temples of Apollo & Athena RUINS
(Side Harbour) **FREE** This compact site is one of the most romantic on the Mediterranean

Side

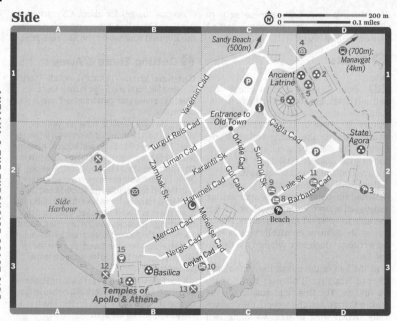

Sandy Beach (500m)

4

(700m); Manavgat (4km)

Ancient Latrine 2

6 5

Entrance to Old Town

Çağla Cad

State Agora

Yasemin Cad

Turgut Reis Cad

Liman Cad

Orkide Cad

Sümbül Sk

14

Zambak Sk

Karanfil Sk

Gül Cad

Lale Sk 11

9

Side Harbour

Hanımeli Cad

8 Barbaros Cad

3

7

Menekşe Cad

Beach

Mercan Cad

Nergis Cad

Ceylan Cad

15

10

12

1 Basilica

13

Temples of Apollo & Athena

coast. Apollo and Athena were Side's deities, although Apollo eventually became more important. The Temple of Athena dates from the 2nd century BC, and a half-dozen columns have been placed upright in their original spots with a frieze of Medusa heads.

Theatre RUINS
(Çağla Caddesi; ₺36; ⊙ 8am-7pm late Apr-late Oct, to 5pm late Oct-late Apr) Built in the 2nd century AD, Side's spectacular theatre could seat up to 20,000 spectators and rivals the nearby theatre of Aspendos for sheer drama.

Look at the wall of the *skene* (stage building) for reliefs of figures and faces, including those of Comedy and Tragedy. During the town's September festival it's the venue for performances.

Side Museum MUSEUM
(₺18; ⊙ 8.30am-7pm May-Oct, to 5pm Nov-Apr) Contained within a 5th-century bathhouse, Side's museum has an impressive (if small) collection of statues, sarcophagi, reliefs and coins in air-conditioned rooms. Explanations are in English and Turkish.

Agora
RUINS

Just east of Side's theatre and across the road from the museum are these agora remains, which once functioned as the ancient town's slave market.

Temple of Tyche
RUINS

The ruined, circular-shaped Temple of Tyche is dedicated to the goddess of fortune. Right next door is an arresting ancient latrine with two-dozen marble seats.

Eastern Beach
BEACH

If you walk down Barbaros Caddesi, passing by the large State Agora ruin, you'll come to the lovely Eastern Beach, which is a prime spot of sand on which to throw down your beach towel. You can rent sunloungers and sunshades here for about ₺10 per day.

Sandy Beach
BEACH

Side's main beach is north of the centre, and backed by rows of resort hotels. Follow the main road out of town (Side Caddesi) and turn left at Şarmaşık Sokak opposite the otogar. There is regular dolmuş transport to the beach from near Side Theatre.

✯ Festivals & Events

Side Festival
CULTURAL

(☉early Sep) The Side International Culture and Art Festival features classical music, ballet and dance performances in Side's ancient theatre and Temple of Apollo. All events start at 9.30pm and are free.

🛏 Sleeping

★ Beach House Hotel
HOTEL $$

(☎0242-753 1607; www.beachhouse-hotel.com; Barbaros Caddesi; s/d/f €23/46/56; ❄@🛜🏊) Formerly the celebrated Pamphylia Hotel (once a magnet for celebrities including Rudolph Nureyev and Jean-Paul Sartre), the Beach House's prime seafront location and welcoming Turkish-Australian owners make it fine value. Most rooms face the Med and all have balconies. We love the roof terrace (with plunge pool), library and garden complete with Byzantine ruins.

Hotel Poseidon
MOTEL $$

(☎0242-753 2687; www.poseidonmotel.com; Lale Sokak 11; s/d €40/50; ❄🛜) Offers 20 small, motel-style rooms around a garden, a short stroll from the beach. Cem, the English- and German-speaking owner distinguishes his property through personal service and advice. Rooms are simple with

tiled floors, TV and fridge; those downstairs are more spacious.

Hotel Sevil
HOTEL $$

(☎0242-753 2041; www.sevilhotel.com; Ceylan Caddesi; s/d €40/55; ❄🛜) Set around a courtyard with mulberry trees and palms, this midrange option has a chilled vibe with friendly management. The 15 rooms all have balconies (some with sea views, others looking over the Temple of Apollo) and feature wood panelling. The excellent buffet breakfast gets good reports.

Kaktüs Boutique Hotel
BOUTIQUE HOTEL $$$

(☎0543 716 9090; www.kaktusboutiquehotelside. business.site; Barbaros Caddesi; r €50-65; ❄🛜) This inviting little family-owned hotel has smart, renovated rooms, some with sea views, enlivened with jolly-coloured furnishings and art, though bathrooms are small. There's a pretty terrace for your Turkish breakfast and snacks.

🍴 Eating & Drinking

If you're staying out of town, most restaurants will arrange free transport. Liman Caddesi is lined with touristy bars and restaurants with German signage. More chichi waterside spots are found at the harbour end of this thoroughfare.

Atmospheric watering holes are scattered across Side old town.

Balık & Köfte Ekmek
SANDWICHES $

(Balıkçı Rasim; Side Harbour; sandwiches/meals from ₺10/20; ☉9am-midnight) A thrifty haven for travellers watching their lira, this converted fishing boat serves up good-value fish and köfte (meatball) sandwiches. Meze platters and fish soup of the day are also available.

Calypso
INTERNATIONAL $$$

(☎0530 546 1295; www.calypsoside.com; Barbaros Caddesi 52; starters ₺35-60, mains ₺40-115; ☉9am-2am; 🛜) Raising the stakes in Side, this modish, high-end newcomer has a superb ocean-facing terrace and a nice contemporary vibe. Best for Western food, including pistachio saddle of lamb (₺80), pasta, seafood, rice dishes (including paella) and salads. Doubles as a lounge bar, with live music in season.

Karma
INTERNATIONAL $$$

(Turgut Reis Caddesi; mains ₺35-90; ☉11am-11pm; 🛜) Karma has an unbeatable garden fronting a patch of iridescent blue ocean (lit by submerged turquoise lights). The emphasis here is on meat – try the chateaubriand for a memorable meal – but there's also sushi and seafood. Call and they'll pick you up from your hotel then trundle you through Side in a golf buggy to your table.

Apollonik's BAR
(☑ 0242-753 1070; www.facebook.com/apollonik cafeside; Liman Yolu; ⊙ 9.30am-late) Right beside the Temples of Apollo and Athena, Side's oldest bar remains its most popular local hang-out and a favourite sunset spot. It does classically-themed cocktails, salads, burgers and sandwiches at reasonable rates. Sit on the terrace overlooking the harbour, or inside snuggled up on the cushion-strewn *sedir* (bench) seating.

ⓘ Information

Tourist Office (☑ 0242-753 1367; ⊙ 8am-9.30pm Mon-Sat late Apr-late Oct, to 5pm late Oct-late Apr) Wheelchairs are available here for touring the ruins.

ⓘ Getting There & Away

The **otogar** (Side Bus Station; Side Caddesi) is just east of the old town. In summer, a shuttle (₺2) transports visitors between the otogar and the old-town gate but it's also an easy – and scenic – walk past crumbled ruins into the centre.

Frequent dolmuşes connect Side's otogar with the Manavgat otogar (₺3), 4km to the northeast, from where buses go to Antalya (₺16, 1½ hours) and Alanya (₺16, 1½ hours). For destinations in western Turkey, including İzmir, Konya and Fethiye, get a connection in Antalya.

Coming into Side, most buses drop you at either the Manavgat otogar or the petrol station at the Side *kavşağı* (junction) on the highway, from where a free *servis* (shuttle bus) will transfer you to Side.

Vehicular entrance to the old town, where most accommodation is located, is restricted: you can only enter and exit between midnight and 10am. Outside those hours, get ready to lug your toothbrush from one of the two *otoparks* (car parks) at the entrance to the old town.

Parking at the entrance to the old town costs ₺15 for up to six hours.

A taxi from Side to Manavgat otogar should cost about ₺25 and take around 10 minutes; taxi drivers at the old-town gate will initially ask for more.

Eastern Mediterranean

Best Places to Eat

➡ Avlu Restaurant (p399)

➡ Paşalimanı Bistro (p394)

➡ İskele Sofrası (p380)

➡ Deniz Kızı Balık Lokantası (p383)

➡ Narlıkuyu Balık Restaurant (p388)

Best Places to Stay

➡ Villa Turka (p379)

➡ Elif Hatun Konağı (p391)

➡ Jasmin Konak Otel (p398)

➡ Rain Hotel (p389)

➡ Arsuz Otel (p398)

Why Go?

Turkey's eastern slice of Mediterranean coastline has long lived in the shadow of its more fashionable neighbour to the west. And why not? That's razzle-dazzle and this is 'real' Turkey, where enormous vegetable farms and fruit orchards work overtime between the mountains and stunning coastline, and timeless hillside villages peek down on large industrial cities with nary a tourist in sight. Here you'll be rewarded with modern, secular and very friendly locals as well as all the requisite fun things to see and do: ancient Hittite settlements, Crusade castles, trekking. To some visitors, though, it is the abundance of important Christian sites, places where the Apostles actually preached the Gospel and made converts to the new religion, that make this a chosen destination. Others will be fascinated by the peninsula that faces southward to Syria, an area offering one of Turkey's most fascinating mixes of cultures, religions, languages and foods.

When to Go
Antakya

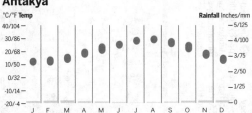

Apr & May Spring after the rain and before the crowds is an ideal time.

Jul & Aug Thermometers shoot sky-high and Turkish families hit the beaches.

Oct Autumn is ideal for exploring Antakya's old town in between cafe stops for syrupy *künefe*.

Eastern Mediterranean Highlights

1 Hatay Archaeology Museum (p395) Marvelling at Roman and Byzantine artistry surrounded by arguably the finest mosaics in the world.

2 Kızkalesi Castle (p388) Pootling through the Mediterranean shallows to this romantically situated island castle.

3 Anemurium (p382) Re-enacting past glories at this isolated Byzantine city.

4 Caves of Heaven and Hell (p387) Descending into the massive Chasm of Heaven.

5 Karatepe (p395) Stepping back into Hittite history amid this site's stone reliefs and statuary.

6 Tarsus (p390) Soaking up the ramshackle atmosphere of bygone days in the compact old town where St Paul was born.

7 Arsuz (p398) Taking a break from the ruins with a little R&R at this delightful seaside retreat.

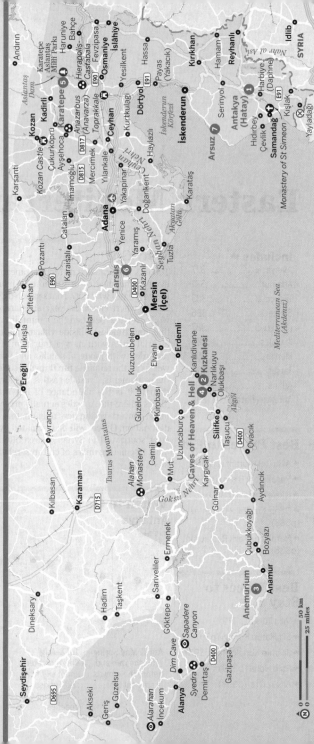

Alanya

📞 0242 / POP 167,100

A former seaside bastion for a succession of Mediterranean powers, Alanya has boomed in recent decades and is a densely populated tourist haven for both international and domestic sunseekers. Aside from taking a boat cruise or a stroll along the waterfront, many visitors only shuffle between their hotel's pool and all-inclusive buffet restaurant, perhaps dropping into a raucous nightclub after dark. Indeed, at night the downtown area can resemble 'Vegas by the Sea'.

But look up from the bars and tattoo parlours for a minute, and you'll find Alanya has abundant charms. Looming high above the promontory, to the south of the modern centre, is an impressive fortress complex with the remains of a fine Seljuk castle, some atmospheric ruins and a sprinkling of traditional red-tile-roofed houses rimming the alleys that climb up the hillside. Alanya is a tale of two cities if ever there was one.

⊙ Sights

Red Tower　　　　　HISTORIC BUILDING
(Kızılkule; İskele Caddesi; ₺7, combined ticket with Tersane & Armoury ₺10; ⊙8.30am-7pm Apr-Oct, to 5.30pm Nov-Mar) This striking five-storey octagonal defence tower, measuring nearly 30m in diameter, more than 30m in height and with a central cistern within for water storage, looms over the harbour at the lower end of İskele Caddesi. Constructed in 1226 by Seljuk sultan Alaeddin Keykubad I (who also built Alanya Castle), it was the first structure erected after the Armenian-controlled town surrendered to the sultan, and is now the city's symbol. Climb the 70-odd steps to the roof; the views are amazing.

Tersane　　　　　HISTORIC BUILDING
(Shipyard; ₺7, combined ticket with Red Tower & Armoury ₺10; ⊙8.30am-7pm Apr-Oct, to 5.30pm Nov-Mar) A wooden walkway runs south along the old harbour's east wall from the Red Tower to the Tersane, the only Seljuk-built shipyard remaining in Turkey. Antique ceramic shards litter the stones, indicating the succession of civilisations that have built here – with the waves sloshing through its five restored vaulted chambers, it's highly atmospheric. From here the walkway continues further along the shoreline to a small **armoury** (Tophane; ₺7, combined ticket with Red Tower & Tersane

₺10; ⊙8.30am-7pm Apr-Oct, to 5.30pm Nov-Mar), which would have served as a coastal watchtower during the Seljuk era. It is currently under renovation.

Ehmedek　　　　　AREA
As you walk up to Alanya Castle, the road passes a turn-off for the village of Ehmedek, which was the Turkish quarter during Ottoman and Seljuk times. Today a number of old wooden houses still cluster around three-towered **Ehmedek Castle** (Ehmedek Kalesi; admission ₺20; ⊙8.30am-7pm Apr-Oct, to 5.30pm Nov-Mar), built in 1227, and the boxlike 16th-century **Süleymaniye Camii** (Ehmedek Sokak), the oldest mosque in Alanya. Also here is a former Ottoman **bedesten** (vaulted covered market) and the **Akşebe Türbesi** (Akşebe Tomb), a distinctive 13th-century mausoleum.

There's also an **Ömürlü Kemal Atli Cultural Centre** (Ömürlü Kemal Atli Kültür Evi; Kocabas Sokak; ⊙9.30am-6.30pm Tue-Sun) FREE, re-creating comfortable life in Ottoman times on two floors. Don't miss the views from the delightful balcony.

★ Alanya Castle　　　　　FORTRESS
(Alanya Kalesı; 📞0242-511 3304; www.muze. gov.tr; Kaleyolu Caddesi) FREE Surmounting Alanya's rocky peninsula is its awesome, Seljuk-era castle, girdled by 6km of walls and awaiting Unesco World Heritage listing. Climb to it through the steep streets of the Tophane district to get a sense of its scale, enjoying a wonderful **viewpoint** (⊙9.30am-12.30pm & 2-6.30pm) across the city and Cilician mountains. Right at the top is the **İç Kale** (Inner Fortress; ₺20; ⊙8.30am-7pm Apr-Oct, to 5.30pm Nov-Mar), within which are plentiful ruins including some 400 cisterns, the shell of a small 11th-century Byzantine church and a platform over a vertiginous drop to the sea.

If you're not up to the steep 3.5km climb, catch **bus 4** (off Bonstancıpınarı Caddesi) from the dolmuş station behind the Grand Bazaar (₺2.50, hourly from 9am to 7pm, half-hourly in summer) or opposite the regional tourist office (10 minutes past the hour and, in summer, also 15 minutes before the hour). Taxis are around ₺25. Alternatively, catch the new **Alanya Teleferik** (www.alanyateleferik.com.tr/en; adult/child one-way ₺22/14, return ₺28/17; ⊙9.30am-11pm), a cable car that ferries passengers between the lower station near Cleopatra's Beach and the upper station in the castle's Ehmedek section.

Alanya

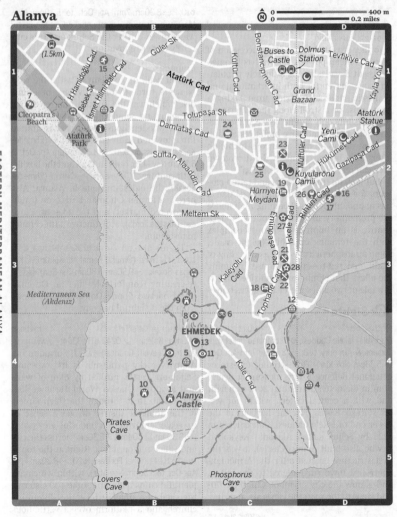

Alanya Archaeological Museum
MUSEUM

(Alanya Arkeoloji Müzesi; İsmet Hilmi Balcı Caddesi 2; ₺6; ⊙8.30am-7.30pm Apr-Oct, 8am-5pm Nov-Mar) Refurbished in 2012, Alanya's small but excellently curated museum is worth a visit to see artefacts, including tools, jugs, jewellery, letters and coins, from the succession of cultures that have called the surrounding area home. Its prize pieces include a fine 52cm bronze of Hercules from the 2nd century AD and a kind of deed in Phoenician dating to 625 BC.

Cleopatra's Beach
BEACH

(Kleopatra Plajı) Sandy and quite secluded in low season, and with fine views of the fortress, Cleopatra's Beach is the city's best. Alanya's main beaches are also decent enough, although east of the centre they're fronted by a busy main road. The teleferik (p377) will deposit you practically on Cleopatra's Beach from the castle.

🏃 Activities & Tours

Every day at around 10.30am, boats leave from near Rıhtım Caddesi for a five- or six-hour voyage around the promontory, visiting

Alanya

EASTERN MEDITERRANEAN ALANYA

several caves, as well as Cleopatra's Beach. If you're after a relaxing day at sea, try the small but perfectly formed **Delfin Boat** (☑0530-203 6934; kaya-ali-2014@hotmail.com; per person incl lunch €25; ⊙10.30am-4pm). Some boats, made up to look like pirate ships, such as **Hüseyin Kaptan** (☑0536-739 7393; incl drinks €35; ⊙from 9pm), are essentially floating parties – complete with foam-filled dance floors. Other cruises include one-hour sunset jaunts around the harbour (from ₺40).

Alanya Aquapark　　　　WATER PARK
(☑0242-519 3674, 0543 834 7005; www.alanya aquapark.net; Atatürk Caddesi 99 & İsmet Hilmi Balcı Caddesi 62; adult/child ₺55/25; ⊙9am-6pm; 🎑) Kids had enough of castles and ruins? This large water park, near Alanya's centre, has plenty of wet and wild fun with pools and 15 slides appropriate for both little ones and their minders. There's a nice area with sunloungers for wiped-out grown-ups, too.

🛏 Sleeping

Temiz Otel　　　　　　HOTEL $$
(☑0242-519 1559, 0242-513 1016; www.temizotel. com.tr; İskele Caddesi 8; s/d ₺140/250; 🅿❄🛜) If you want to be slam in the centre of the action, the five-storey Temiz has 32 decently sized, if bland, rooms. Those at the front have balconies (like 407), but light sleepers should ask for a room at the back as the thumping noise from the bars goes on into the wee hours. There's a lift.

★ **Villa Turka**　　　　BOUTIQUE HOTEL $$$
(☑0530 547 4641, 0242-513 7999; www.hotel villaturka.com; Kargı Sokak 7, Tophane; r/ste €75/130; 🅿❄🛜❄) Our favourite boutique hotel in Alanya, the Villa Turka is housed in a 200-year-old Ottoman mansion lovingly restored to showcase its original wooden ceilings and tiled floors. There are 10 rooms here, featuring quality bed linen, honey-toned cedar decor and antiques, while views take in the nearby Red Tower and the distant Taurus Mountains.

Lemon Villa　　　　BOUTIQUE HOTEL $$$
(☑0553 91 6864, 0242-513 4461; www.lemonvilla. com; Tophane Caddesi 20, Tophane; r/ste/apt from €60/120/150; 🅿❄🛜❄) The nine stone-walled rooms at this restored Ottoman house are full of authentic details, with ornate wooden ceiling panels, hanging lamps and original fireplaces. The two suites at the top, reached by lift, are particularly sumptuous, with suitably grand sea views to top it off.

🍴 Eating

The restaurant trade is fierce enough in Alanya to guarantee you'll be accosted repeatedly by touts as you walk by. Many places serve food aimed at European tourists, but there are more traditional Turkish *lokantalar* (eateries serving ready-made food) to be found.

Mini Mutfak
TURKISH $

(📞0242-513 6136; Bostancıpınarı Caddesi 3a; mains ₺12-20; ⊗11am-9pm) The 'Mini Kitchen' is a rare and refreshing thing in central Alanya: a traditional Turkish *lokanta* (eatery serving ready-made food) with unfussy, home-cooked food made by people who make you feel genuinely welcome. Lamb kebabs, slow-cooked white beans, cabbage rolls, zucchini fritters... It wouldn't raise excitement to the same degree elsewhere in Turkey, but here it's a godsend.

★ İskele Sofrası
TURKISH $$

(📞0532 782 4647, 0533 717 3520; Tophane Caddesi 2b, www.facebook.com/fatherandsonplace; mezes ₺13, mains ₺34-95; ⊗10am-midnight; 🍴) Three generations of the friendly Öz family run this restaurant, uphill from the harbour. There are never less than 10 mezes on at once – perhaps *girit ezmesi,* an unforgettable mash-up of feta-like cheese, walnuts and olive oil. All the usual grills and loads of seafood headline the menu, but special lamb hotpots (*kuzu güveçt*) can be cooked with a day's notice. The terrace, with harbour views, is a delight, and perfect with a cold beer.

Kaleiçi Meyhanesi Alanya
SEAFOOD $$$

(📞0546 639 4263; www.facebook.com/kaleici meyhanesialanya; İskele Caddesi 80; meze ₺13-15, mains ₺38-74; ⊗4pm-1am) Perched just above the harbour, the 'Inner Town Alanya Tavern' is more restaurant than boozer, with at least 30 types of meze to choose from by the entrance and an enormous selection of fish and shellfish. It's one of the few large restaurants on the waterfront that we'd recommend.

Drinking & Entertainment

Along Rıhtım Caddesi you'll find discos with themes ranging from Hawaiian and Irish to Nordic and Casablanca.

Ottoman Türk Kahvesi
CAFE

(📞0242-511 6556, 0505 082 5688; www.facebook. com/cesbesalanya; Damlataş Caddesi 13; ⊗9am-3am) Inside a 100-year-old stone villa surrounded by lush gardens, Ottoman Turkish House is an atmospheric cafe, serving coffee and drinks (soft and hard) and dispensing nargiles (water pipes). Though very close to the centre it somehow feels off the beaten track.

Robin Hood
CLUB

(📞0539 459 0266, 0242-511 2023; www.facebook. com/robinhodbar; Rihtim Caddesi 12; ⊗9pm-3am) The first two floors of this all-singin', all-dancin', all-flashin' monstrosity – the biggest, most pulsating club in Alanya – are decked out in (you guessed it) a Sherwood Forest theme. Above that is the Latino Club, which is usually the one making all the noise.

Ehl-i-Keyf Cafe
CAFE

(📞0555 495 6208, 0555 227 4957; www.ehlikeyf nargile.com; Damlataş Caddesi 32; ⊗9am-2am) The shaded back courtyard of this restored Ottoman residence is a trendy hang-out for Alanya's bright young things, and a great antidote to the more touristy bars and cafes around town. Enjoy a relaxing combo of tea, nargile and backgammon, or a freshly squeezed juice. Note that only alcohol-free beer is served.

Çello Cafe Bar
LIVE MUSIC

(📞0242-511 4290; www.facebook.com/celloalanya; İskele Caddesi 36; ⊗3pm-4pm Sun, from 3pm Mon & Sat, from 8pm Tue-Thu, from from 6pm Fri) This rollicking, friendly Turkish bar features live 'protest and folk music' and is a top spot for an acoustic-fuelled night of rakı (aniseed brandy) and beers. Locals crowd in before the bands start (at 9.30pm), escaping the booming manufactured beats in the superclubs by the harbour.

Sky Lounge Bar
LIVE MUSIC

(📞0533 725 0790; www.skyloungebar.com; İskele Caddesi 80; ⊗8pm-4am) Music and decent beer are the draws at this slick, multistorey venue by the harbour. The main action is on the 6th floor with soft chill-out music early on and a mix of club and house later on. Live music too at 10pm most nights.

❶ Information

Alanya has two tourist offices: a **regional one** (📞0242-513 1240; Damlataş Caddesi 81; ⊗8.30am-12.30pm & 1.30-5.30pm Mon-Fri) on the west side of town near the Alanya Archaeological Museum, and a more central (and helpful) **city tourist office** (www.visitalanya.com; Bostancıpınarı Caddesi 4; ⊗9am-5pm Mon-Sat) on the east side just next to the Kuyularönü Camii.

❶ Getting There & Away

The **otogar** (Alanya Otogarı) is on the coastal highway (Atatürk Caddesi), 3km west of the centre. Most services are less frequent in the off season, but buses generally leave hourly for Antalya (₺25, 2½ hours) and 11 times daily to Adana (₺80, nine hours). The three daily buses to Konya (₺60, five hours) take the Akseki–Beyşehir route.

THE ARMENIAN KINGDOM OF CILICIA

During the early 11th century, the Seljuk Turks swept westwards from Iran, wresting control of much of Anatolia from a weakened Byzantium and pushing into the Armenian highlands. Thousands of Armenians fled south, taking refuge in the rugged Taurus Mountains and along the Mediterranean coast, where in 1080 they founded the kingdom of Cilicia (Lesser Armenia) under the young Prince Reuben.

While Lesser Armenia struggled against foreign invaders and the subsequent loss of its statehood, the Cilician Armenians lived in wealth and prosperity. Geographically, they were in the ideal place for trade and their feudal class structure. Cilicia became a country of barons, knights and serfs, with the court at Sis (today's Kozan) even adopting Western-style clothing. Latin and French became the national languages. During the Crusades, the Christian armies used the kingdom's castles as safe havens on their way to the Holy Land.

This period of Armenian history is regarded as the most exciting for science and culture, as schools and monasteries flourished, teaching theology, philosophy, medicine and mathematics. It was also the golden age of Armenian ecclesiastical manuscript painting, noted for its lavish decoration and Western influences.

The Cilician kingdom thrived for nearly 300 years before it fell to the Mamluks of Egypt. The last Armenian ruler, Leo V, spent his final years wandering Europe trying to raise support to recapture his kingdom before dying in Paris in 1393.

If you're travelling down the coast from Side, most buses from Manavgat otogar conveniently drop you off at the central **dolmuş station** (off Bonstancıpınarı Caddesi) behind the Grand Bazaar.

ⓘ Getting Around

Dolmuşes (minibuses) to the otogar (₺3) can be picked up at the dolmuş station near the mosque behind the Grand Bazaar, north of Atatürk Caddesi. From the otogar, walk out towards the coast road and the dolmuş stand is on the right.

City buses 101 and 102 run the same route (₺3). A taxi to the otogar from the centre costs ₺20 and takes about 10 minutes.

Bus 4 (off Bonstancıpınarı Caddesi; ₺2.50) runs from the dolmuş station to Alanya Castle every half-hour in summer (hourly rest of year).

A cable car (p377) now links the Ehmedek district of Alanya Castle with the Damlataş district (off Güzelyalı Caddesi).

Around Alanya

There are several notable attractions on or just north of the D400 on either side of Alanya. About 30km before Alanya and just after Incekum beach is a turning for a road leading north for 9km to Alarahan (www.turkishhan.org/alara.htm; Merkez Sokak 191, Çakallar; ⊙9am-5pm) FREE, a 13th-century *han* (caravanserai). At the head of the valley a kilometre away are the 13th-century ruins of Alara Castle (Alara Kalesi; www.facebook.com/alaracastle; Merkez Sokak 196, Çakallar).

Southeast from Alanya, a turn-off near the 11km marker leads northward for 7km to Dim Cave (Dim Mağarası; ☎0242-518 2275, 0532 372 4185; www.dimcave.com.tr; Kestel; adult/child ₺18/10; ⊙9am-7pm Apr-Oct, to 5.30pm Nov-Mar), a subterranean fairyland of spectacular stalactite and stalagmite. A turning another 13km on the D400 leads to the seldom-visited ancient site of Syedra (www.kultur.gov.tr/EN-114120/syedra.html) FREE. From a turning at 27km, another road runs 18km northeast to beautiful Sapadere Canyon (Sapadere Kanyonu; ☎0532 651 6017, 0242-543 1212; www.sapaderekanyonu.com; adult/child ₺10/5; ⊙9am-7pm Apr-Oct, to 5.30pm Nov-Mar). Access for walkers through the gorge is along a 750m-long path.

This region was ancient Cilicia Tracheia (Rugged Cilicia), a somewhat forbidding part of the world because of the mountains and the fearsome pirates who preyed on ships from the hidden coves.

Anamur

☎0324 / POP 38,589

Surrounded by hillside banana plantations and mammoth polytunnels hiding strawberry crops, Anamur is a prosperous farming town with a laid-back resort as an adjunct. The waterfront İskele district, with its pleasant strip of sand, springs into action on summer weekends when locals head to the coast to cool off. The beach's eastern end is capped by the storybook bulk of Mamure Castle, while to the west of town is the massive Byzantine city of Anemurium, with tumbledown ruins galore.

Whether it's the ruins or relaxed beach life that brings you here, don't leave town without sampling the local *muzlar* (bananas), which are shorter and sweeter than imported varieties and on sale everywhere.

Anamur lies north of the D400. About 2.5km southeast of the main roundabout is the İskele beachfront area. Anemurium is 8.5km to the west, while Mamure Castle is 7km east.

Sights

★ Anemurium

Ancient City   ARCHAEOLOGICAL SITE
(Anemurium Antik Kenti; ₺6; ◎8am-7pm Apr-Oct, to 5pm Nov-Mar) Anemurium's sprawling and eerily quiet ruins stretch for 500m down to a pebble beach, with mammoth city walls scaling the mountainside above. From the huge **necropolis** area with 350 tombs, walk south past a 4th-century **basilica**; look behind it for a mosaic of a leopard and a kid flanking a palm tree. Above the church is one of two **aqueducts**. The best-preserved structure in Anemurium is the 3rd-century **baths complex**, with a **palaesta** (training area) with mosaic floor.

Also worth seeking out is the **theatre** dating from the 4th century AD and, opposite, the best preserved **odeon** in Turkey, with 900 seats and a tiled floor and dating to the 2nd century AD.

Although founded by the Phoenicians in the 4th century BC, Anemurium suffered a number of devastating setbacks, including an attack in AD 52 by a vicious Cilician tribe, and most of the visible ruins date from the late Roman, Byzantine and medieval periods. Archaeologists have also uncovered evidence that an earthquake destroyed the city in about 580.

Anamur is 8.5km to the west of the centre. Approaching from Anamur or down from the Cilician mountains, a sign points south towards the ruins of Anemurium Antik Kenti. The road then bumps along for 3km to the *gişe* (ticket kiosk); it's another 500m to the car park.

Mamure Castle   CASTLE
(Mamure Kalesi; ₺6; ◎8am-7pm Apr-Oct, to 5pm Nov-Mar) This tremendous castle, with its crenellated walls, 36 towers and part of its moat still intact, is the biggest and best-preserved fortification on the Turkish Mediterranean coast. The rear of the castle sits on the beach, where sea turtles come in summer to lay their eggs, while its front end almost reaches the D400 highway.

At the time of writing, the castle was undergoing an extensive (and long overdue) restoration, which should hopefully be completed by the time you visit.

🛏 Sleeping

Hotel Nice   HOTEL $$
(☑0324-816 6595, 0555 388 9593; www.facebook.com/anamurnice; İnönü Caddesi 55; s/d ₺120/240; P❀🤖) Somehow managing to be both multistorey beachside hotel and family home, this is a friendly option in Anamur. The eight rooms are simple but very comfortable, and breakfast usually includes freshly cooked *sigara böreği* (fried filo and cheese pastries). Room 202 is a good choice.

Hotel Luna Piena   HOTEL $$
(☑0324-814 9045; www.hotellunapiena.com; Süleyman Bal Sokak 14; s/d ₺130/230; P❀🤖) Just paces from the beach, this block-shaped beige hotel offers 32 rooms with parquet floors, balconies with full sea views, spacious showers and a preference for sparkling white decor. Room 505 is a large suite with sea views; 507 has a balcony. Reception is on the 1st floor and there is a lift.

🍴 Eating & Drinking

Olta Balık Evi   SEAFOOD $$
(☑0542 268 06 20, 0324-814 2500; İskele Meydan; mains ₺15-35) On the main square in İskele just up from the pier, the family-run Olta is the fish restaurant of choice in Anamur.

İskele Sofrası   TURKISH $$
(☑0532 156 4340; Sokak 1709; mains ₺12-35; ◎10am-midnight) Just one block back from the beach, this popular family place (no booze) turns out top-notch mezes and generous grills – order the *beyti* kebap (minced lamb with garlic). Good fish dishes and Anamur's best pide (Turkish-style pizza) round out the menu.

Masalim   TEA GARDEN
(İnönü Caddesi; ◎7am-midnight) We really like this friendly sand-between-your-toes tea garden smack-dab on the seafront. Run by a couple of friendly sisters, its highlights include cheap eats and a couple of kilim-bedecked day beds. Fire up a nargile session,

or order a cold beer and listen to the bouncy Turkish pop music cascading over nearby waves.

ⓘ Getting There & Away

Anamur's otogar is at the intersection of the D400 highway and 19 Mayıs Caddesi. Frequent buses depart daily to Alanya (₺40, three hours, 130km), Taşucu/Silifke (₺30, two hours, 140km) and Adana (₺80, 5½ hours, 305km).

ⓘ Getting Around

Town buses to İskele depart from a small stand behind the otogar (₺2, every 30 minutes). You have to buy a ticket before boarding the bus: the small *bakkal* (grocery shop) across the road from the bus stand sells them, or the driver will stop at a shop that does. A taxi between İskele and the otogar costs around ₺25.

If you're heading to Anemurium, flag down a dolmuş to Ören (₺2, half-hourly) from outside the Yağmur Market, opposite the mosque in front of the otogar. The driver will drop you off at the Anemurium turn-off on the main highway, from where it's a 2.5km walk. Expect to pay close to ₺100 for a taxi to Anemurium and back, with an hour's waiting time.

Frequent dolmuşes headed for Bozyazı (₺2) will drop you off outside Mamure Castle, or it's about a 3.5km walk along the beach from İskele. Walk east to the end of İnönü Caddesi and across the bridge where the fishing boats dock in the river, then take the dirt track down to the beach and walk towards the battlements.

Taşucu

📞 0324 / POP 9600

It may be the working port of Silifke, 11km to the northeast, but a lovely strip of beach and well-maintained seafront promenade make Taşucu (tah-*shoo*-joo) a destination in its own right. This is an extremely low-key holiday resort that is also a favourite stop for birdwatchers who want to combine some swimming and sunbathing with visits to the nearby wetlands of the Göksu Delta. The lush salt marshes, lakes and sand dunes of the delta shelter some 330 bird species.

Taşucu is also an important transport hub, with ferries for both walk-on passengers and cars travelling to/from Girne in Northern Cyprus. The beach is fronted by Sahil Caddesi, which stretches eastward from the ferry pier and has several good pensions. Around the harbour, excursion boats depart for day trips (per person ₺40) along the coastline and to nearby islands.

🛏 Sleeping & Eating

Taşucu Motel PENSION $$

(📞 0324-741 2417; www.tasucumotel.net; Sahil Caddesi 25a; d/tr ₺300/400; 🅿 ❄ 🛜) The spic-and-span Taşucu has 14 big, airy rooms with great seafront views and a chilled-out roof terrace for relaxing. Room 3 has a small balcony. It's on the main beach road, directly opposite the harbour promenade.

Holmi Marina Otel HOTEL $$

(📞 0545 948 3806, 0324-741 5378; www.holmihotel.com; Sahil Caddesi 23; s/d ₺200/250; ❄ 🛜) The rooftop terrace at this 15-room pension on the main harbour-front road is particularly nice on a hot day. Around half the rooms have sea views, and two rooms have their own kitchens. All the rooms – though on the smallish side – have benefited from renovation and now boast shiny modern bathrooms.

Meltem Apart Otel Pansiyon PENSION $$

(📞 0533 360 0726, 0324-741 4391; www.meltempansiyon.net; Sahil Caddesi 75; s/d/tr ₺100/200; ❄ 🛜) Superfriendly and right on the beach, this family-run apartment hotel-pension is a homely choice. Eight of the 20 modest rooms face the sea. The rest of the rooms have balconies facing the street. Breakfast (₺15 extra) is served on the delightful seafront patio out back.

Dilek Lokantası PIDE $

(📞 0324-741 4625; İsmet İnönü Caddesi 68; mains ₺17-30; ⏰ 24hr) This cheerful kebap place right in the middle of the main drag along the seafront never shuts, and its hearty portions of döner (spit-roasted lamb slices) and *dürüm* (döner sandwiches) are popular with locals and travellers alike. Don't miss the *tantuni dürüm* (sandwich of beef, peppers, garlic and onion; ₺7).

★ Deniz Kızı Balık Lokantası SEAFOOD $$

(📞 0324-741 4194; İsmet İnönü Caddesi 62c; mains ₺35-75; ⏰ noon-11pm) The kind of fish restaurant you hope for when visiting the Med, the 'Mermaid' does superfresh fish, simply and with real generosity of spirit. Housed in a lovely, solid stone building by the waterfront, with two floors and a rooftop deck strung with shells, it does a wonderful *balık buğulama* (fish stewed with tomatoes, peppercorn and parsley; ₺60). The pastries are top-notch, too.

1. Yılankale (p391) 2. Pit of Hell (p388) 3. Temple of Zeus Olbius, Uzuncaburç (p387) 4. Stone facade at Karatepe (p395)

FOTOPANORAMA360/SHUTTERSTOCK ©

Antiquities of the Eastern Med

Want to explore rugged crumbling ruins without the crowds? The eastern Mediterranean is chock-a-block full of vast archaeological sites, important early Christian shrines and craggy clifftop castles that are all the more fun to explore because of their half-forgotten feel.

Anemurium Ancient City

This sprawling swath of ruins tumbles down the cliffside to the beach. Soak up the heady atmosphere of long-lost grandeur while surveying the city from high on the citadel walls or clambering through the once lavish Roman baths.

Caves of Heaven & Hell

The underworld has come a-calling. Stand over Hell's abyss and inside the wide, yawning mouth of Heaven and check visiting the abode of the gods off your list.

Yılankale

If you can only visit one castle in the eastern Mediterranean, pick this wondrous pile of ramparts and towers clinging onto a hilltop east of Adana. It's a sweat-inducing scramble to get up to the highest tower, but the views are worth it.

Karatepe

Giant slabs of inscribed reliefs guarded by glaring-eye sphinxes and lions are among the well-preserved remains of this 8th-century-BC Hittite town whose greatest king was Azitawata.

Uzuncaburç

Roman and Hellenistic ruins, including the columns of the Temple of Zeus Olbius, are clustered within this village in the Mediterranean hinterland.

TOP CHRISTIAN SITES

➡ Memorial Church of St Peter (p397)
➡ Tarsus (p390)
➡ Alahan Monastery (p386)
➡ Cave Church of St Thecla (p387)

ALAHAN MONASTERY

Tentatively listed for World Heritage status, this remarkable **monastery** (Alahan Manatırı; near Geçimli; ₺6; ⊘9am-7pm Apr-Oct, 8am-5pm Nov-Mar) perches on a terraced slope high above the Göksu Valley, northwest of Silifke. Above the entrance is a cave church chiselled into the cliff face. A grand entry adorned with richly carved reliefs of angels and demons leads into the ruins of the western Church of the Evangelists with its re-erected Corinthian columns. The better preserved 6th-century Eastern Church is considered to be one of most ambitious early examples of domed-basilica architecture.

Although today the location amid the pine-forested slopes of the Taurus Mountains has a middle-of-nowhere feel, during the Byzantine age the monastery sat near Claudiopolis (today's Mut) on a vital trade and communications route, and archaeologists believe Alahan was probably one of Turkey's most important religious centres during the 5th and 6th centuries.

To get here, take the inland (D715) highway from Silifke to Mut (1¼ hours, 75km) and then continue north for another 24km to the village of Geçimli, where a signposted turn-off to the monastery, on the right, leads for 2km up a steep incline.

Baba Restaurant SEAFOOD **$$**
(☑0324-741 5991; İsmet İnönü Caddesi 43; mains ₺35-70; ⊘noon-11pm) The waterfront terrace at Baba, which is regarded as the area's best restaurant, is a beautiful place to sip a cold beer or slurp imported Italian gelato. It's the excellent food that really lures diners though, especially the tempting cart of mezes.

ⓘ Getting There & Away

BOAT

AB Kıbrıs Denizcilik (☑0324-741 4033, 0535 443 3070; www.kibrisdenizcilik.com; İsmet İnönü Caddesi 58) runs *feribotlar* (car ferries) from Taşucu to Girne in Northern Cyprus on Sunday, Tuesday and Thursday (passenger one way/return ₺190/405, with car one way/return ₺540/1105). Boats are boarded at midnight and depart from the harbour at 2am, arriving in Girne at 8.30am. You must be at the harbour to clear immigration at 10.30pm. For the return leg, ferries leave Girne every Monday, Wednesday and Friday, also at midnight.

The same company also runs a fast, 2½-hour boat along the same route, leaving Taşucu at noon on Wednesday and Saturday, and Girne the same time on Tuesday and Friday. It's ₺225/475 per adult one way/return.

BUS

Buses heading northeast to Silifke can drop you (if you let them know ahead) on the main highway just past the turn-off for the road down to the harbour. It's an easy five-minute walk to the waterfront and the hotels from there.

There are dolmuşes every half-hour between Taşucu and Silifke otogar (₺3), where you can make most long-distance bus connections. The dolmuş route trundles the length of the waterfront, and they can be flagged down anywhere along Sahil Caddesi and İsmet İnönü Caddesi.

Silifke

☑0324 / POP 60,600

Silifke is a riverside country town with a long history. A striking castle towers above the mineral-rich blue-green Göksu River, dubbed the Calycadnus in ancient times. In the vicinity are other archaeological and natural sights begging for a visit.

Seleucia ad Calycadnum, as Silifke was once known, was founded by Seleucus I Nicator in the 3rd century BC. He was one of Alexander the Great's most able generals and founder of the Seleucid dynasty that ruled Syria after Alexander's death.

The town's other claim to fame is that Emperor Frederick Barbarossa (r 1152–90) drowned in the river about 7km north of town while leading his troops on the Third Crusade. It was apparently the weight of his armour that brought him down.

There are a couple of perfectly serviceable hotels in central Silifke, although most visitors choose to overnight in nearby Taşucu, by the sea. You'll find lots of *kebapçi* and places selling *tantuni* (chopped beef sautéed with onions, garlic and peppers, wrapped in a flatbread called *lavaş ekmek*) along Özcan Seyhan Caddesi. Try the *Silifke yoğurdu* while here: a local yoghurt celebrated and enjoyed throughout Turkey.

Sights

Cave Church of St Thecla
CHURCH

(Azize Tekla Mağara Kilisesi; Aya Tekla Sokak; ⊙8am-7pm Apr-Oct, to 5pm Nov-Mar) FREE This Christian site is dedicated to St Thecla, one of St Paul's early devotees. Thecla is said to have spent her later years here trying to convert the locals of Seleucia to Paul's teachings. She ruffled the feathers of local healers, who decided to kill her, but on their arrival at her cave she vanished into thin air. The very atmospheric (though modest) church carved out of the cave where she lived is an important pilgrimage site, especially among the Orthodox Christians.

In the late 5th century a large basilica was built on the grassy knoll above the cave, but only an incisor-like chunk of the apse is still standing. There are also the remains of the basilica's cistern to the northwest.

The church is signposted off the D400 highway, 3km southwest of Silifke. Any dolmuş travelling between Taşucu and Silifke can drop you at the turn-off, from where it's a 1km walk to the site.

ⓘ Information

Tourist Office (☎0324-714 1151; Veli Gürten Bozbey Caddesi 6; ⊙8am-noon & 1-5pm) Just north of Atatürk Caddesi, you'll find lots of literature and dedicated staff here.

ⓘ Getting There & Away

Buses from **Silifke's otogar** (İnönü Caddesi) depart hourly for Adana (₺35, three hours, 165km). Other frequent services include Mersin (₺25, two hours, 95km), Alanya (₺65, 5½ hours, 265km) and Antalya (₺80, eight hours, 395km).

Dolmuşes to Taşucu (Cavit Erdem Caddesi) cost ₺3 and depart every 10 minutes from a stand on the south bank of the Göksu; they pass by the otogar on their way out of town. A taxi to Taşucu costs about ₺35.

Dolmuşes to Uzuncaburç cost ₺12 and leave from Celal Bayar Caddesi, diagonally opposite the Silifke tourist office at 8am, 10.30am and 3pm, returning from Uzuncaburç at 11am, 2pm and 6pm.

Narlıkuyu

☑0324 / POP 2530

Lovely little Narlıkuyu, on a cove 5km southwest of Kızkalesi, is renowned for its fish restaurants, but the other-worldly mountain caves nearby also can't be overlooked. In addition, the delightful Mediterranean cove the town is wrapped around is a favourite of loggerhead turtles. Inside the village's tiny museum, housed in a pint-sized 4th-century Roman bath, you'll find a wonderful mosaic of the 'Three Graces' and daughters of Zeus: Aglaia, Thalia and Euphrosyne.

Narlıkuyu's pretty little harbour is ringed with seafood restaurants, while breakfast cafes are strung along the climb from the main road to the Caves of Heaven and Hell.

Sights

★ Caves of Heaven and Hell
CAVE

(₺18; ⊙8am-7pm Apr-Oct, to 5pm Nov-Mar) Near Narlıkuyu, a road winds north for 2km to several caves – sinkholes carved out by a subterranean river and places of great

---

OFF THE BEATEN TRACK

UZUNCABURÇ RUINS

The remnants of Roman Diocaesarea sit within the village of **Uzuncaburç** (₺6; ⊙8am-7pm Apr-Oct, to 3pm Nov-Mar), 30km northeast of Silifke. Originally this was the Hellenistic city of Olba, home to a zealous cult that worshipped Zeus Olbius.

The impressive **Temple of Zeus Olbius**, with two dozen erect columns, lies to the left of the one-time **colonnaded street**. Beside the temple are various sarcophagi bearing reliefs. Other important Roman structures include a **nymphaeum** (2nd century AD), an arched **city gate** and the **Temple of Tyche** (1st century AD).

Just before the massive **monumental arch** serving as the entrance to the main site is a small 2500-seat **Roman theatre** built under Marcus Aurelius in the 2nd century AD.

To view a Hellenistic structure built before the Romans sacked Olba, head north through the village, where you'll pass a massive, five-storey **watch tower** with a **Roman road** behind it. Another 600m down into the valley leads to a long, roadside **necropolis** of rock-cut tombs and more sarcophagi.

On the road to Uzuncaburç, 8km out of Silifke at **Demircili** – ancient Imbriogon – you'll pass several superb examples of Roman **monumental tombs** that resemble houses.

mythological significance. The walk from Narlıkuyu junction to the main entrance gate is quite steep. Enterprising locals usually offer taxi services up the hill for ₺10 (one way).

The mammoth underground **Chasm of Heaven** (Cennet Mağarası) – 250m long, 110m wide and 70m deep – is reached by 450-odd steps to the left of the ticket booth. Right in front of the cave mouth (and at the 300th step) are the tiny but beautiful remains of the 5th-century Byzantine **Chapel of the Virgin Mary**, used for a short time in the 19th century as a mosque. Once inside the cave, the stairs can be very wet and slippery and there are no handrails, so wear decent shoes and walk carefully. At the furthest end of the colossal grotto is the **Cave of Typhon** (Tayfun Mağarası), a damp, jagged-edged, devilish theatre. Locals believe this to be a gateway to the eternal furnace, and the 1st-century AD historian Strabo mentions it in his *Geography*. According to legend, the cave's underground river connects with the hellish River Styx – this seems plausible when you hear the underground current thundering away below.

Back on terra firma, follow the path from the ticket office further up the hill to the **Pit of Hell** (Cehennem Mağarası) with its almost vertical walls that you view by stepping out onto a heart-stopping platform extending over the 130m-deep pit. This charred hole is supposedly where Zeus imprisoned the 100-headed, fire-breathing monster Typhon after defeating him in battle.

✖ Eating

★ **Narlıkuyu**
Balık Restaurant SEAFOOD $$$
(☏ 0324-723 3286; meals around ₺70; ⊗ 8am-11pm) Spanning a lovely terrace on one arm of Narlıkuyu's little cove, this seafood restaurant is a delight. Seafood meals come complete with huge piles of salads and scrumptious meze, including pickled *kaya koruğu,* a wild vegetable growing on rocks by the shore. There's no menu, but a fish meal with all the extras is about ₺50.

❶ Getting There & Away

Frequent dolmuşes run between Kızkalesi and Silifke via Narlıkuyu (₺3). Get off here to walk 2km up the steep hill to the Caves of Heaven and Hell.

Kızkalesi

☏ 0324 / POP 1660

The coastal village of Kızkalesi boasts a lovely swathe of beach bookended by two perfect castles: one on the mainland, the other perching photogenically on an island just offshore. The town itself is less interesting visually – a grid of rather grim-looking concrete-slab apartment blocks that look like they were slapped up in five minutes. Kızkalesi really springs into action from June to September when locals make a beeline for the beach on steaming-hot weekends. For archaeology and history buffs, though, the village is a popular base as a springboard for the virtual open-air museum of ruins scattered across the Olba Plateau. There are also other places to the southwest and northeast of Kızkalesi that are of genuine historical interest and importance, which include everything from an idyllic seaside village with an important mosaic to a descent into the very bowels of the earth.

◎ Sights

★ **Kızkalesi Castle** CASTLE
(Maiden's Castle; incl Corycus Castle ₺6; ⊗ 8am-8pm Apr-Oct, to 6pm Nov-Mar) **FREE** Rising from an island 250m offshore, impossibly romantic Kızkalesi Castle (also called the Sea Castle) is like a suspended dream. Check out the **mosaics** of birds and trees in the central courtyard, where there are the remains of two chapels side by side, and the vaulted **gallery** with 13 arches. Walk along the castle **walls** and climb one of the four **towers** (the square one at the southeast corner has the best views).

Corycus Castle CASTLE
(Korykos Kalesi; incl Kızkalesi Castle ₺6; ⊗ 9am-8pm Apr-Oct, 8am-5pm Nov-Mar) At the northern end of Kızkalesi beach, Corycus Castle (sometimes called the 'Land Castle') was rebuilt with Roman material by the Byzantines, briefly occupied by the Armenian kingdom of Cilicia and once connected to Kızkalesi by a causeway. Walk carefully up the worn stairway to the east, where a ruined tower affords a fine view of Kızkalesi Castle rising up from the sea.

Elaiussa Sebaste ARCHAEOLOGICAL SITE
FREE Some 4km northeast of Kızkalesi and just off the D400 are the extensive remains of ancient Elaiussa Sebaste, a city dating back to the early Roman period and perhaps

even to the time of the Hittites. Important structures on the western side of the D400 include a 2300-seat hilltop **theatre**, the remains of a 2nd-century **Byzantine basilica** and Roman **agora** with fabulous fish and dolphin mosaics, and a total-immersion cruciform-shaped **baptistery**.

Adamkayalar
TOMB

Tricky to get to, but well worth the effort, is Adamkayalar (Men Rock Cliff), 17 Roman-era reliefs carved on a cliff face about 8km north of Kızkalesi. They are part of a 1st-century-AD necropolis and immortalise warriors wielding axes, swords and lances, and citizens, sometimes accompanied by their wives and children. Two of the reliefs have inscriptions. High up on a cliff face overlooking breathtaking Devil's Canyon (Şeytan Deresi), it's a slightly difficult (and dangerous) scramble to get there.

★ Kanlıdivane
ARCHAEOLOGICAL SITE

(₺6; ⊙8am-7pm Apr-Oct, to 5pm Nov-Mar) About 8.5km northeast of Kızkalesi at Kumkuyu is the 33-54, the road leading 3km to the ruins of Kanlıdivane, the ancient city of Kanytelis.

Central to Kanlıdivane (Crazy Place of Blood) is a 60m-deep chasm where criminals were said to be thrown to wild animals. Peering down, you'll see reliefs on the cliff walls of a six-member family (southwest) and a Roman soldier (northwest). Ruins ring the pit, including a 17m-high Hellenistic tower, four **Byzantine churches** and a **necropolis** with a 2nd-century **temple tomb**.

🛏 Sleeping & Eating

★ Rain Hotel
HOTEL $$

(☑ 0324-523 2782, 0535 321 5416; www.rainhotel. com; Ahmet Erol Caddesi 13; s/d/tr €25/40/52; [P][✳][�]) With a warm and friendly vibe, the Rain is a perennially popular choice, with 18 spotless and spacious rooms, a few with small balconies. The homely downstairs lounge is a good place to kick back and meet other travellers, and the affable owner Mehmet Öztop can organise pretty much any activity or tour for guests. Free sunloungers and beach umbrellas.

Has Hotel
HOTEL $$

(☑ 0551 386 3324, 0324-523 2367; www.hashotel. net; Ahmet Erol Caddesi 40; s/d/tr €25/40/52; [✳][�]) The Has has a front-row seat on the sea, and the 26 colourful rooms are cool and comfortable. All of the rooms, spread over six floors, have balconies except those at the top. For a true seaside experience, though, grab a room facing the sea (such as 301 and 401). The breezy front terrace is another bonus, as is the new lift.

Zeugma
KEBAP $

(☑ 0541 327 46 88; www.zeugmakizkalesi.com; Silifke Caddesi; mains ₺25-40; ⊙9am-4am) The best in a row of welcoming pide/*mangal* (barbecue) places on the main strip, Zeugma does spot-on *mercimek çorbası* (lentil soup), served with bread, herbs, pickled chillies, lemon and a drizzle of chilli oil), *lahmacun* (Arabic-style pizza; ₺18 to ₺22) and kebaps (₺10 to ₺12). Tending his wood-fired oven, the perspiring *fırıncı* (baker) is the reason the bread's so good.

★ Rain Garden Restaurant
TURKISH $$

(☑ 0535 321 5416; www.rainhotel.com; Avcılar Sokak 14; mains ₺20-50; ⊙8am-midnight) This much-welcome new addition to Kızkalesi's beachfront is in an attractive old building in the shade of an enormous 50-year-old rubber tree. The rainbow-coloured fan lights complement the cheery menu of tasty, good-value international favourites as well as what might be the finest *sıkma börek* (pastry filled with cheese or meat) in the eastern Mediterranean.

There's a wonderful wood-burning stove baking bread to die for, and Continental/full Turkish breakfast is ₺28/35. The upstairs terrace overlooking Kızkalesi Castle is a delight. Great outdoor bar, too.

There are also four retro-style rooms (single/double/triple €40/70/85) on the 1st floor with full-frontal views of the sea and romantic Kızkalesi Castle.

ⓘ Getting There & Away

Frequent buses, departing from the D400, link Kızkalesi with Silifke (₺6, 30 minutes, 24km) and Mersin (₺11, 1½ hours, 60km). Regular dolmuşes link Narlıkuyu and Kızkalesi (₺3). To get to Adamkayalar you'll need a taxi or to be willing to walk.

Mersin

☑ 0324 / POP 974,100

Mersin was earmarked a half-century ago as the seaside outlet for Adana and its rich agricultural hinterland. Today it is the largest port in Turkey and for the most part a sprawling, workaday place in which most travellers don't linger. But Mersin, with its official name of İçel (also the name of the province of which it is capital), does have some attractions, despite the neglect: two decent museums and great food are but two of them. If you scrunch up your eyes, some of the streets near the sea at the eastern end of Atatürk Park almost have a Marseilles feel to them, and there are definitely worse ways to while away an afternoon than a lazy seafood lunch on one of the excursion boats lining the harbour.

Mersin Archaeological Museum
MUSEUM

(Mersin Arkeoloji Müzesi; ☑ 0324-231 9618; www. kulturportali.gov.tr/turkiye/mersin/gezilecekyer/ mersin-muzesi; Adnan Menderes Bulvarı 54; ᵗ6; ⊗9am-7pm Apr-Oct, 8.30am-5pm Nov-Mar) FREE This purpose-built museum, which opened in 2017, is one of the best in provincial Turkey and will help you to put much of what you've seen along the coast in perspective. In eight halls over two floors it exhibits finds from nearby tumuli (burial mounds) like Yumuktepe and sites including Kanlıdivane and Elaiussa Sebaste near Kızkalesi, a great statue of Dionysus and curious odds and ends, such as a Roman-era glass theatre 'token', Hellenistic figurines and Hittite artefacts around 3500 years old.

❶ Getting There & Away

BUS

Mersin's new **otogar** (Mersin Otogarı; ☑ 0324-238 1648; Mersinli Ahmet Caddesi 1) is on the city's northern outskirts, 10km from the centre. To get to the centre, leave by the main exit, walk up to the main road (Akbelen Bulvarı) and catch a city bus travelling south (ᵗ3). Buses from town to the otogar leave from outside the train station, as well as from a stop opposite the Mersin Oteli.

From the otogar, frequent buses run to Adana (ᵗ20, one hour, 75km), Silifke (ᵗ25, two hours, 95km) via Kızkalesi (ᵗ12, one hour), and Alanya (ᵗ85, 8½ hours, 375km). There are also dolmuşes every 30 minutes to Tarsus (ᵗ5).

TRAIN

There are frequent rail services to Tarsus (ᵗ5, 20 minutes) and Adana (ᵗ8.50, one hour) throughout the day between 5.45am and 10.30pm from the **train station** (Mersin Garı; ☑ 0324-231 12 67; Çakmak Caddesi; ⊗5.30am-9.30pm). Trains to İskenderun (ᵗ20, 3¼ hours) depart at 6.30am and 4.30pm only.

Tarsus
☑ 0324 / POP 262,050

Should Tarsus' most famous son, St Paul, return two millennia after his birth, he would hardly recognise the place through the sprawl of concrete apartment blocks. For pilgrims and history buffs, the scattering of early Christian sites here is reason enough to linger, but stroll through the historic city core, with its twisting narrow lanes rimmed by ancient houses slouching in various states of dilapidation, and you'll really discover the town's timeless appeal.

◉ Sights

Old Town
HISTORIC SITE

(Antik Şehir) The compact Old City lies between Adana Bulvarı and Hal Caddesi. It includes a wonderful 60m-long stretch of **Roman road** and a labyrinth of alleyways hemmed by **Tarsus Historical Houses**, many crumbling, but one now housing the **Elif Hatun Konağı** boutique hotel.

Just southeast are several historic mosques, including the **Eski Cami** (Old Mosque), a medieval structure that was originally a church dedicated to St Paul. Adjacent looms the barely recognisable brickwork of a huge old **Roman bath**.

Just south is the late-19th-century **Makam Cami** (Official Mosque), and to the southwest across Adana Bulvarı is believed to be the tomb of the **Prophet Daniel**. To the south is the 16th-century **Ulu Cami** (Great Mosque), sporting a curious 19th-century minaret moonlighting as a clock tower. Nearby is the 19th-century **Kırkkaşık Bedesten** (Forty Spoons Bazaar), still used as a covered bazaar today.

St Paul's Well
HISTORIC SITE

(St Paul Kuyusu; Hal Caddesi; ᵗ6; ⊗8am-7pm Apr-Oct, to 5pm Nov-Mar) Just on the edge of the Old City is St Paul's well, where the holy man did slake his thirst some two millennia ago. In the leafy courtyard the ruins of Paul's house – his supposed birthplace – can be viewed underneath sheets of Plexiglas.

Church of St Paul
CHURCH

(St Paul Kilisesi; www.kulturportali.gov.tr/turkiye/ mersin/gezilecekyer/st-paul-anit-muzesi; Abdı İpekçi Caddesi/2731 Sokak; ᵗ6; ⊗8am-7pm Apr-Oct, to 5pm Nov-Mar) South of the Old City, what is also called the St Paul Memorial Museum (St Paul Anıt Müzesi) was originally built in 1850 as a Greek Orthodox church to commemorate the saint. It was utilised as a warehouse as recently as 1993, when the Ministry of Culture began a restoration. It was opened up for services again in 2001. There are simple frescoes of Jesus and the Evangelists on the ceiling inside, and there's a bell tower on the northwest corner.

🛏 Sleeping & Eating

Elif Hatun Konağı   BOUTIQUE HOTEL $$
(☑0324-666 0003; www.elifhatunkonagi.com. tr; 3416 Sokak 28; s/d ₺120/230; P❄🛜) This long-awaited addition to Tarsus' meagre accommodation options is a stunning boutique hotel converted from a traditional 250-year-old Tarsus house in the centre of the Old City. Eight of the 12 rooms have stone walls, antique furniture, velvet drapes and İznik tiles and are named after wives and consorts of the Ottoman sultans.

St Paul's Cafe & Restaurant   CAFE $
(☑0535 712 8024, 0324-622 3126; Eski Evler Sokağı/2710 Sokak; mains ₺15-25; ⊙8am-11pm) Our favourite place for a nibble and a sip is this rabbit warren of a creaky old house just down from St Paul's well. The 20-odd dishes on offer include *mantı* (Turkish ravioli), various köfte and *lahmacun*, the service is warm and the decor, well, rural with farm implements and riding accoutrements strewn throughout.

ℹ Getting There & Away

Tarsus' **otogar** (Tarsus Otogarı; Ankara Bulvarı) is 3.5km east of the centre. A taxi there will cost ₺15 and a city bus is ₺3. Frequent small buses and dolmuşes connect Tarsus with Mersin (₺6, 29km) and Adana (₺7, 42km). They always pick up and drop off passengers from just beside Cleopatra's Gate and also along Adana Bulvarı.

The **train station** (Tarsus Garı; Yavuz Donat Bulvarı), with regular services to Mersin (₺5) and Adana (₺6) throughout the day between 6.15am and 11pm, is northwest of centre at the end of Hilmi Seçkin Caddesi. Trains to İskenderun (₺18, 2¾ hours) depart at just after 7am and just after 5pm only.

Adana

☑0322 / POP 1.72 MILLION

With a pedigree stretching back to the ancient Hittites and beyond, Adana is an energetic, modern place with just a handful of sights, some pretty good cafes, restaurants and bars and excellent transport links. Turkey's fifth-largest city makes a good base for exploring the little-visited historic sites and ruins to the southwest, and if you've been travelling lazily along the Med, the urban buzz may be just the city-slicker injection you need.

The city is more or less cut in two by the D400 highway. North of the road (called Turan Cemal Beriker Bulvarı in town and running west to east and over Seyhan Bridge) are well-heeled, leafy residential districts. South of the trendy high-rise apartments and pavement bars and cafes, things get more cluttered and housing starts to sprawl. The Seyhan River delimits the city centre to the east.

◉ Sights & Activities

Adana Museum   MUSEUM
(Adana Müzesi; ☑0322-454 3857; www.kultur. gov.tr/EN-113882/adana-archaeological-museum. html; Ahmet Cevdet Yağ Bulvarı 7; ₺10; ⊙9am-7pm Tue-Sun Apr-Oct, 8.30am-5pm Tue-Sun Nov-Mar) Now housed in an enormous purpose-built complex on the site of a former textile factory about 4km west of the centre, Turkey's largest museum might also be its finest. It is especially rich in statuary from the Cilician Gates, north of Tarsus, which was the main passage through the Taurus Mountains and an important transit point as far back as Roman times. Note especially the 2nd-century

---

WORTH A TRIP

YILANKALE

Yılankale (Snake Castle) FREE, an impressive castle rising boldly from a rocky ridge in the middle of modern-day corn fields, is a fantastic example of medieval Armenian architecture. Built in the mid-13th century, when this area was part of the Armenian kingdom of Cilicia, it took its name from a serpent once entwined in the coat of arms above the entrance. From the car park there's a well-laid path for 100m then a rough trail.

Reaching the castle's highest point requires a steep climb over the rocks, through two arches and a gatehouse with a relief of a rampant above it. Further on are cisterns, vaulted chambers and the remains of a small chapel. Standing high above the wheat fields, though, you'll feel on top of the world. Yılankale is 38km east of Adana and just over 2km south of the D400 highway.

Adana

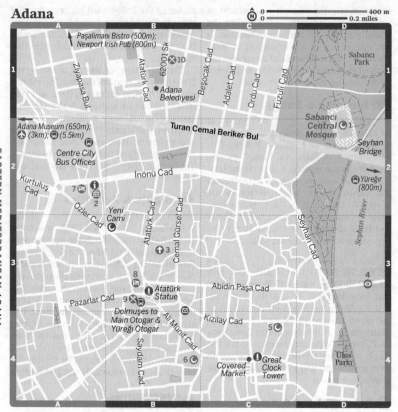

Adana

◎ Top Sights

◎ Sights

✪ Activities, Courses & Tours

⊟ Sleeping

⊗ Eating

Achilles sarcophagus, decorated with scenes from the Iliad, and the sphinx from Silifke.

★ **Sabancı Central Mosque**   MOSQUE
(Sabancı Merkez Camii; Turan Cemal Beriker Bulvarı) The most imposing mosque in Adana is the six-minaret Sabancı Merkez Camii, rising gracefully from the left bank of the Seyhan River. The largest mosque between İstanbul and Saudi Arabia, it was built by the late industrial magnate Sakıp Sabancı (1933–2004), a philanthropist and founder of the second-richest family dynasty in Turkey, and is covered top to tail in marble and gold leaf. With a 54m-high central dome, it can accommodate an estimated 28,500 worshippers.

Stone Bridge
BRIDGE

(Taşköprü; Abidin Paşa Caddesi) This Roman-era stone bridge over the Seyhan River at the eastern end of Abidin Paşa Caddesi was probably built under Hadrian (r AD 117–138) and repaired in the 6th and 9th centuries. Its 300m-long span had 21 arches – seven of which are now underwater – and carried vehicles up until 2007.

Ulu Cami
MOSQUE

(Great Mosque; Kızılay Caddesi) The beautiful early 16th-century Ulu Cami is reminiscent of the Mamluk mosques of Cairo, with black-and-white banded marble and elaborate window surrounds. The complex includes a *medrese* (seminary) and a *türbe* (mausoleum) housing remains of the poet Ziya Paşa. The tiles in the *mihrab* (niche indicating the direction of Mecca) came from Kütahya and İznik.

Just south is the delightful 15th-century **Ramazanoğlu Mansion** (Ramazanoğlu Konağı).

Yağ Camii
MOSQUE

(Oil Mosque; Ali Münif Caddesi) The Yağ Camii, with its imposing portal and typical Seljuk-style architecture, started life as a Crusader church dedicated to St James but was converted into a mosque in 1501. It got its name from an oil bazaar that once stood in front of it.

St Paul's Catholic Church
CHURCH

(San Pol Bebekli Kilise; Çakmak Caddesi) Built in 1870 by the Armenian community, this church is still in service today as a Roman Catholic place of worship.

Kuruköprü Memorial Museum
MUSEUM

(Kuruköprü Anıt Müzesi; ☑ 0322-454 3857; www. adanamuzesi.gov.tr/Tr/Kurukopru_Muzesi_Adana_Evi.aspx; Ziyapaşa Bulvarı 118; ⊙9am-7pm Tue-Sun Apr-Oct, to 4.30pm Tue-Sun Nov-Mar) FREE Just off İnönü Caddesi, what was until recently the city's ethnography museum has now reopened as an art gallery with some ethnographic exhibits, including a traditional Adana house. It's housed in a former Orthodox church built in 1845 that later did time as a mosque before being converted into a museum in 1983.

Mestan Hamamı
HAMAM

(Merry Bath; ☑ 0322-351 5189; Pazarlar Caddesi 3; bath ₺25, scrub ₺19, half-hour massage ₺40; ⊙6am-11pm) The Mestan Hamamı, a very friendly bath right in the centre of town, is a great place to experience a soak, scrub and massage.

🛏 Sleeping

Branches of major international hotel chains augment the good-value independent hotels to be found in downtown Adana.

Otel Mercan
HOTEL $

(☑ 0322-351 2603, 0322-351 9397; www.otelmercan.com; 5 Ocak Meydanı; s/d/ste ₺70/120/140; ❄ 🛜) One of the friendliest hotels in Adana, the Mercan is right in the middle of the city centre. It's an old building with a new front and retains some original features like a bit of stained glass here and there. The lobby is more recently renovated than the rather 35 prosaic rooms, but they're still perfectly comfortable. Note that there's no lift.

★ Hotel Mavi Sürmeli
BUSINESS HOTEL $$

(☑ 0322-363 3437; www.mavisurmeli.com.tr; İnönü Caddesi 97; s/d/ste ₺160/220/400; 🅿❄🛜) The slickest top-end hotel in Adana, the Mavi is centrally located and a truly luxurious choice at a very affordable price. Its 117 rooms are spacious enough for contact sports, and there's a cavalcade of outlets, including the Turunç bar on the ground floor.

🍴 Eating & Drinking

Famous worldwide is Adana kebap: minced beef or lamb mixed with powdered red pepper grilled on a skewer. It is served with sliced onions dusted with the slightly acidic spice sumac and barbecued tomatoes. Look for bars and pubs in the residential and shopping streets north of Turan Cemal Beriker Bulvarı.

Şen Lokantası
TURKISH $

(☑ 0322-453 8291, 0322-457 0960; 62001 Sokak 16a; mains ₺15-35; ⊙10am-5pm Mon-Sat; 🥢) Heading north on Atatürk Caddesi, turn right into 62002 Sokak and then left into 62001 Sokak to find this relaxed neighbourhood *lokanta* popular with desk jockeys from nearby offices and featuring loads of vegetarian options. The best place to sit is on the terrace shaded by a grape arbour. Excellent (and unusual) desserts.

★ Öz Asmaaltı
KEBAP $$

(☑ 0322-351 4028, 0322-351 1775; www.ozasmaalti.com; Pazarlar Caddesi 9; Adana kebap meals with meze ₺30; ⊙10am-10pm) This local favourite may look like just another Adana *kebap-döner salonu*, but the mains and meze are a cut above. This is an excellent place to try Adana kebap, and you'll get meze, salad and perhaps *kadayıf* (dough soaked in syrup and topped with clotted cream) with your meal.

★ **Paşalimanı Bistro**   BISTRO $$$
(☑ 0322-458 3555; www.pasalimani.com.tr; Şinasi Efendi Caddesi 16; mains ₺34-56; ☺ 10am-midnight Mon-Thu, to 1am Fri & Sat) Our favourite new place to eat in Adana is this stylish bistro just north of Atatürk Parkı in the well-heeled Kurtuluş district. In addition to the enlightened Turkish favourites, it offers a surfeit of pasta dishes, Viyana (that's Wiener) schnitzel and fish and chips.

Seating is in the uber-designed modern interior dining room or the lovely front terrace. Warm welcome and the service is excellent.

Newport Irish Pub   IRISH PUB
(☑ 0322-456 0914; www.facebook.com/pages/Newport-Irish-Pub/156610815288796; Şinasi Efendi Caddesi, 64019 Sokak 4; ☺ 9am-1am) An Irish pub in name (and some decor) only, the Newport is nonetheless a pleasant option for an evening restorative after wandering the upmarket shopping streets north of Atatürk Parkı. The open-plan layout and corner location are good for people-watching, and there's food available throughout the day (mains ₺20 to ₺30).

❶ Getting There & Away

Adana's airport (Şakirpaşa Havaalanı) is 4km west of the centre on the D400. The otogar is 2km further west on the north side of the D400. The **train station** (Adana Garı) is at the northern end of Ziyapaşa Bulvarı, 1.5km north of İnönü Caddesi.

BUS

Adana's large otogar has direct bus and/or dolmuş services to just about everywhere in Turkey. Note that dolmuşes to Kadirli (₺20, two hours, 108km) and Kozan (₺18, one hour, 72km) leave from the **Yüreğir bus station** (Yüreğir Otogarı; Kozan Caddesi), on the right bank of the Seyhan River. There's a string of bus offices along the northern end of Ziyapaşa Bulvarı where you can book trips and buy tickets.

TRAIN

There are trains almost twice an hour between 6.15am and 10.30pm to Mersin (₺8.50, one hour) via Tarsus (₺7, 40 minutes). Trains to İskenderun (₺15, 2¼ hours) depart at 7.43am and 5.47pm only.

Long-haul services include the Toros Ekspresi (7.45pm, ₺21, six hours), which links Adana with Konya daily, and the Erciyes Ekspresi (4.30pm, ₺19, 5½ hours), which serves Kayseri.

❶ Getting Around

A taxi from the airport into town costs ₺20, and from the otogar into town it's about ₺30. A taxi from the city centre to the Yüreğir otogar will cost ₺10. There are also **dolmuşes** (Saydam Caddesi) to both bus stations,

SERVICES FROM ADANA OTOGAR

DESTINATION	FARE (₺)	DURATION (HR)	DISTANCE (KM)	FREQUENCY (PER DAY)
Adıyaman (for Nemrut Dağı)	55	5	335	frequent
Alanya	80	9	440	frequent
Ankara	70	8	475	hourly
Antakya	30	3	190	hourly
Antalya	90	11	565	frequent
Diyarbakır	80	8	535	frequent
Gaziantep	40	3	220	hourly
İstanbul	130	12	920	frequent
Kayseri	50	5½	355	frequent
Konya	75	6	335	frequent
Kozan	18	1¼	72	2
Şanlıurfa	60	5	360	frequent
Silifke	35	3	165	frequent
Van	170	13	910	up to 8

KARATEPE-ASLANTAŞ OPEN-AIR MUSEUM

Archaeology buffs should make a beeline for the **Karatepe-Aslantaş Open-Air Museum** (Karatepe-Aslantaş Açık Hava Müzesi; ₺6; ⊙10am-7pm Apr-Oct, 8am-5pm Nov-Mar), within the national park of the same name. The ruins date from the 8th century BC, when this was an important town for the late-Hittite kings of Cilicia, the greatest of whom was named Azitawata. Today the remains on display consist of statuary, stone reliefs and inscribed tablets – some of which have played a critical role in helping archaeologists decipher the hieroglyphic Hittite language.

The first group of Karatepe's statuary is displayed at the Southern (Palace) Gate, with views across the forested hilltop overlooking Lake Ceyhan (Ceyhan Gölü), an artificial lake used for hydroelectric power and recreation. From here, traces of the 1km-long walls that defended the town are still evident. Under the protective shelter are carved representations of lions and sphinxes and rows of fine stone reliefs, including one showing a relaxed feast at Azitawata's court, complete with sacrificial bull, musicians, monkeys and performing bears.

A kilometre-long circular path leads to the Northern (Lower) Gate with Karatepe's best stone carvings, including reliefs of a galley with oarsmen, warriors doing battle with lions, a woman suckling a child under a tree and the Hittite sun god. The sphinx statues guarding the reliefs are extremely well preserved.

Karatepe's small but excellent three-room museum beside the main gate displays items unearthed by excavations here and has plenty of information panels explaining the site's significance. There is also a scale model of the site, which helps put everything into perspective.

Karatepe is a tricky site to reach without your own transport. If you're driving from Kozan follow route 817 south for 18km to Çukurköprü and then head east for another 18km to Kadirli, from where a secondary road leads for 22km to the site. It's easier to reach Karatepe along route 80-76 from Osmaniye, 26km to the southeast, which is served by dolmuş from Adana (₺20, 1½ hours, 95km) and İskenderun (₺25, 1½ hours, 105km). If carless, your best bet is to organise a taxi from Osmaniye, where you'll find a taxi rank beside the otogar. A return trip to Karatepe (two hours) with an hour's stop at the ruined Hellenistic city of Hierapolis-Castabala will cost about ₺150.

Antakya (Hatay)

☑ 0326 / POP 341,200

Built on the site of ancient Antiocheia ad Orontem (Antioch), Antakya, officially known as Hatay, is a prosperous and modern city near the Syrian border. Under the Romans, an important Christian community grew out of the already large Jewish population that was at one time led by St Paul. Today Antakya is home to a mixture of faiths – Sunni, Alevi and Orthodox Christian – and has a cosmopolitan and civilised air. Locals call their hometown Barış Şehri (City of Peace), and that's just what it is. In this ecumenical city, you'll find at least five different religions and sects represented within a couple of blocks of one another.

The Arab influence permeates local life, food and language; indeed, the city only became part of Turkey in 1939 after centuries conjoined in some form or another to Syria. Most visitors come to Antakya for its archaeology museum or as pilgrims to the Church of St Peter. Be sure to take time to stroll along the Asi (Orontes) River and through the bazaars and back lanes of a city we rate as an underrated jewel of the Turkish Mediterranean.

◉ Sights

★**Hatay Archaeology Museum** MUSEUM
(Hatay Arkeoloji Müzesi; ☑ 0326-225 1060; www.kulturportali.gov.tr/turkiye/hatay/gezilecekyer/arkeoloji-muzesi149365; Antakya Reyhanlı Yolu 117; ₺20; ⊙9m-6.30pm Apr-Oct, 8am-4.30pm Nov-Mar) This incomparable museum contains one of the world's finest collections of Roman and Byzantine mosaics, covering a period from the 1st century AD to the 5th century. Many were recovered almost intact from Tarsus or Harbiye (Daphne in ancient times), 9km to the south. The entire collection from the old museum in the centre of

Antakya (Hatay)

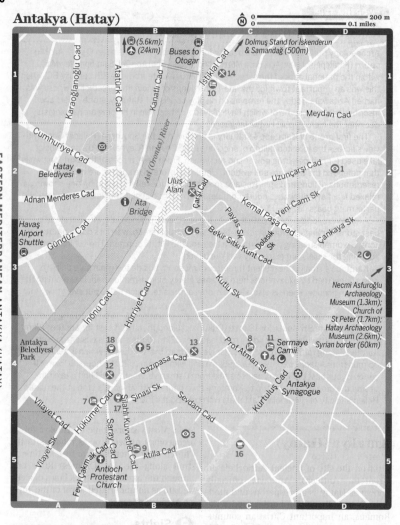

Antakya (Hatay)

Antakya has been moved to purpose-built premises just out of town on the D430 to Reyhanlı.

The museum is positively enormous, spread over 19 halls and at present difficult to navigate. Among the museum's highlight pieces (most found in Room 7) are the full-body mosaic of **Oceanus & Thetis** (2nd century) and the **Buffet Mosaic** (3rd century), with its depictions of dishes of chicken, fish, eggs and bread. **Thalassa & the Nude Fishermen** (5th century) shows children riding whales and dolphins, while the fabulous 3rd-century mosaics of **Narcissus & Echo** and the **Drunken Dionysus** depict stories from mythology. Among the museum's quirkier mosaics are the happy hunchback with an oversized phallus; the black fisherman; an obese infant Hercules strangling two snakes; and our favourite: the mysterious portrayal of a raven, a scorpion, a dog, a snake, a centipede, a rat and a pitchfork attacking a *nazar* (evil eye) while a horned dwarf with a gigantic trailing phallus obliviously plays the pipes.

Along with mosaics, the museum also showcases artefacts recovered from various mounds and tumuli (burial mounds) in the area, including a Hittite mound near Dörtyol, 16km north of İskenderun, and a Palaeolithic-era cave called Üçağızlı Mağarası near Samandağ. Taking pride of place in the collection (Room 15) is the so-called **Antakya Sarcophagus** (Antakya Lahdı), a spectacularly carved marble tomb from the 3rd century with an unfinished reclining figure on the lid.

Necmi Asfuroğlu Archaeology Museum
MUSEUM

(Museum Hotel; www.themuseumhotelantakya.com/the-museu; Kurtuluş Caddesi; ₺40; h8.30am-7pm) Start any construction project in Turkey and you might be in for a surprise. Hotel developers had to throw their original plans out the window when excavation work at this site, near the turn-off to the Church of St Peter, revealed major archaeological finds including the world's largest single-piece floor mosaic. The resulting museum is cleverly integrated into the hotel's lower levels with suspended bridges allowing access to view the multiple Hellenistic, Roman and Byzantine floor mosaics as well as a Roman baths complex.

Memorial Church of St Peter
CHURCH

(St Pierre Anıt Kilisesi; ☑0326-225 1568; Senpiyer Caddesi; ₺20; ☺8.30am-6.30pm Apr-Oct, to 4.30pm Nov-Mar) This early Christian church cut into the slopes of Mt Haç (or Staurin, the 'Mountain of the Cross') is thought to be the earliest place where the newly converted followers of Jesus Christ met and prayed secretly. Peter lived in Antioch between AD 47 and 54 and almost certainly preached here. Tradition has it that this cave was the property of St Luke the Evangelist, who was born in Antioch, and that he donated it to the burgeoning Christian congregation.

When the First Crusaders took Antioch in 1098, they constructed the wall at the front and the narthex, the narrow vestibule along the west (left) side of the church. To the right of the altar faint traces of an early fresco can be seen, and some of the simple mosaic floor from the 4th or 5th century survives. The water dripping in the corner is said to have curative powers. It was declared a pilgrimage site in 1983 by Pope Paul VI.

Just 2.5km northeast of the city, St Peter's church is accessible on foot in about half an hour along Kurtuluş Caddesi.

Old Town
HISTORIC SITE

(Antik Şehir) The squiggle of lanes between Kurtuluş Caddesi and Hürriyet Caddesi is an atmospheric huddle of Antakya's remaining old houses, with carved lintels, wooden overhangs and hidden courtyards within the compounds. Slightly north, around the 7th-century **Habibi Neccar Camii** (Mosque of Habib-i Neccar; Kurtuluş Caddesi), you'll find more preserved examples of Antakya architecture. The priests at the Catholic church believe St Peter would have lived in this area when he first arrived in Antakya in AD 47 as it was then the Jewish neighbourhood.

➡ Bazaar
A sprawling market fills the back streets north of Kemal Paşa Caddesi. The easier way to see it is to follow Uzunçarşı Caddesi (Long Market Street), the main shopping street, from the river.

➡ Ulu Cami
(Great Mosque; Uzunçarşı Caddesi 11) This mosque, in the heart of the Old Town, was built by the Mamluks of Egypt in 1268 and is one of the city's oldest places of worship. It has a peaceful garden with citrus trees and a pretty little fountain.

WORTH A TRIP

ARSUZ

For a little R&R between exploring the dusty remains of the Armenian Kingdom of Cilicia, head for Arsuz (Uluçınar), a delightful fishing town jutting out into the sea, 33km southwest of İskenderun. Relaxing highlights include swimming (available 10 months of the year), gazing at the distant mountains, or trying your luck fishing in the nearby river.

The accommodation of choice is at the **Arsuz Otel** (☑0326-643 2444; www.arsuzotel.com; Atatürk Bulvarı 2; s/d €60/75; P❋☎☀), a rambling 'olde worlde' (though really less than 60 years old) hotel with two wings fronting the sea, with its own beach and 50 spacious and airy rooms.

To get here from Antakya, catch a dolmuş to İskenderun, which drops you at the bus stands on İskenderun's main highway from where dolmuşes run to Arsuz (₺6, 30 minutes) throughout the day.

➡ **St Luke Catholic Church**

(Aziz Luka Katolik Kilisesi; www.anadolukato likkilisesi.org/antakya/en; Prof Atman Sokak; ◷10am-noon & 3-5pm, mass 8.30am daily, plus 6pm Sun Apr-Oct, 5pm Nov-Mar) The Italian-ministered Roman Catholic church was built in 1846 and occupies two houses in the city's old quarter, with the chapel in the former living room of one house dating only from the 1970s.

St Peter Orthodox Church CHURCH

(Senpiyer Ortodoks Kilisesi; Gazipaşa Caddesi 9; ◷divine liturgy 8.30am & 6pm) Most of the city's 1200-strong Christian population worships at this fine Orthodox church dating to 1860. Rebuilt with Russian assistance after a devastating earthquake in 1900, the church is fronted by a lovely courtyard up some steps from the street, and contains some beautiful icons, an ancient stone lectern and valuable church plate. Enter from Hürriyet Caddesi 53.

🛌 Sleeping

St Luke House GUESTHOUSE $

(Aziz Luka Evi; ☑0326-215 6703; www.anadoluka tolikkilisesi.org/antakya; Prof Atman Sokak; per person €10; ❋☎) A positively delightful place to stay (if you can get in), this guesthouse run by the local Catholic church next door has

eight tidy double rooms wrapped around a leafy (and suitably reflective) courtyard. Guests are invited (though not required) to attend daily Mass in the church opposite.

Mozaik Otel HOTEL $

(Mosaic Hotel; ☑0533 746 6567, 0326-215 5020; www.mozaikotel.com; İstiklal Caddesi 18; s/d ₺100/145; ❋☎) The rooms at this budget option are surprisingly peaceful, despite its great central position near the bazaar. Service lets the side down though, being rather haphazard and less than friendly, but the 24 rooms are decorated with folksy bedspreads and mosaic reproductions. There's an excellent restaurant next door.

⭐ **Liwan Hotel** BOUTIQUE HOTEL $$

(☑0326-215 7777; www.theliwanhotel.com; Silahlı Kuvvetler Caddesi 5; s/d ₺275/375; P❋☎) This 1920s eclectic building was once owned by the president of Syria and contains 24 tastefully furnished (though smallish) rooms across four floors; there's a lift. Room 104 looks to the main street and has a small balcony. For those who adore old-timer hotels, there's bucketloads of atmosphere to lap up here.

Antik Beyazıt Hotel BOUTIQUE HOTEL $$

(☑0533 380 8474, 0326-216 2900; www.antik beyazitoteli.com; Hükümet Caddesi 4; s/d ₺190/300; ❋☎) Housed in a pretty French Levantine colonial house dating from 1903, Antakya's first boutique hotel is looking a bit frayed, though it's as friendly as ever and the antique furnishings and tiles, oriental carpets and ornate chandelier in the lobby still evoke a more elegant past. The 25 rooms are fairly basic; the ones on the 1st floor have the most character.

Jasmin Konak Otel BOUTIQUE HOTEL $$$

(☑0553 588 8884, 0326-223 9090; www.jasmin konak.com; Dr Ataman Demir Caddesi 18; s/d/tr ₺200/400/550; ❋☎) This stunning boutique hotel up a narrow cobbled lane in the Zenginler (Rich People's) district counts 10 very different rooms but each one boasting stone walls, period furnishings and the scent of jasmine. The leafy central courtyard is a cool oasis and the welcome always warm.

🍴 Eating

Kral Künefe SWEETS $

(☑0326-214 7517; Çarşı Caddesi 7; künefe ₺7; ◷8am-1am) In the shadow of Ulu Cami's minaret, the 'King Künefe' is the friendliest place in town to try Antakya's favourite dessert, the eponymous *künefe* (layers of *ka-dayıf* cemented together with sweet cheese, doused in syrup and served hot with a sprinkling of pistachio).

Anadolu Restaurant
TURKISH $

(☏0326-215 3335; www.anadolurestaurant.com; Hürriyet Caddesi 30a; mains ₺15-26; ☺9am-midnight) Popular with families, Antakya's culinary anchor serves a long list of fine mezes on gold-coloured tablecloths in a covered garden where the trees push through the roof. Meat dishes include Anadolu kebap (small pieces of lamb, tomatoes and onions grilled on skewers) and the special *kağıt* kebap (₺22), which is wrapped and cooked in 'paper'. Try the *oruk*, a croquette of spicy minced beef encased in bulgur-wheat flour and fried.

★ Avlu Restaurant
TURKISH $$

(☏0326-216 1312; www.avlurestaurant.com; Kahraman Sokak 39; mains ₺16-50; ☺9am-midnight) Popular with Antakya's glitterati and the expense-account brigade, the 'Courtyard' is more about being seen and seeing than about food, though the meze (₺12 to ₺20) and grills are more than acceptable. Try to get a seat in one of the upper-level balconies looking down on the eponymous courtyard and all the action. Service is a bit cavalier.

Hatay Sultan Sofrası
ANATOLIAN $$

(☏0326-213 8759; www.sultansofrasi.com; İstiklal Caddesi 20a; mains ₺25-35; ☺9am-9pm) Antakya's premier spot for affordable tasty meals, this bustling place is just the ticket to dive into Hatay's fusion of Middle Eastern and Turkish cuisine. The articulate manager loves to guide diners through the menu, and will help you pick from the diverse array of mezes and spicy local kebap options. Leave room to order *künefe* for dessert.

🍸 Drinking & Nightlife

Cabaret
BAR

(☏0326-215 5540; Hürriyet Caddesi 26; ☺8am-1am Mon-Sat) This local student hang-out with brick walls and shuttered windows is an atmospheric spot for a tea, coffee or something stronger. There's occasional live music, cheap snacks aplenty, and tucked around the back is an even cosier private courtyard. A happening place. Sandwiches (₺7.5 to ₺15), döners (₺9 to ₺16) and burgers (₺10 to ₺15) available, too.

Barudi Bar
BAR

(☏0530 746 6569; www.barudicafebar.com; Silahlı Kuvvetler Caddesi; ☺1pm-late) The Barudi Bar is one of Antakya's best-kept secrets, with its hideaway inner courtyard, decent range of imported beers and impressive list of cocktails. It also does simple dishes like salads (₺17 to ₺22) and pasta (₺20 to ₺25).

Affan Kahvesi
COFFEE

(☏0326-215 1248; www.affankahvesi.com; Kurtuluş Caddesi 42; ☺8am-midnight) This authentic coffeehouse, in a building dating back to 1911, has old-world ambience in spades. Pull up a wooden chair inside (don't forget to marvel at the gorgeous tiled floor), or head out back to the shady courtyard, to drink an Antakya coffee. It's famed for its *Haytalı* dessert: a shocking-pink layered pudding of ice cream and rose water.

❶ Getting There & Away

Antakya's **Hatay Airport** (Hatay Havaalanı; ☏0326-235 1300; www.airportia.com/turkey/hatay-airport) is 27km north of the city. Both **Pegasus Airlines** (www.flypgs.com) and **Turkish Airlines** (www.turkishairlines.com) have regular flights to/from İstanbul starting from about ₺175. A taxi from the airport is around ₺100, and **Havaş** (☏0555-985 1101; www.havas.net; Gündüz Caddesi; per person ₺14) runs a regular airport shuttle bus to/from central Antakya.

Antakya's **intercity otogar** (Antakya Otogarı; D817 Hwy) is 6.5km to the northwest of the centre. Direct buses go to Ankara, Antalya, İstanbul, İzmir, Kayseri and Konya, usually travelling via Adana (₺30, 3½ hours, 190km). There are also frequent services to Gaziantep (₺35, four hours, 262km) and Şanlıurfa (₺50, seven hours, 400km).

Minibuses and dolmuşes for İskenderun (₺15, one hour, 58km) and Samandağ (₺10, 40 minutes, 28km) leave from near the Shell petrol station along Yavuz Sultan Selim Caddesi, at the top of İstiklal Caddesi.

❶ Getting Around

A taxi between the city centre and the otogar will cost ₺25. Many of the big bus companies run free *serviş* (shuttle bus) transfers into central Antakya. Ask on arrival. Buses 5, 9 and 16 (₺2.50) run from just outside the otogar to the western bank of the Asi (Orontes) River, which is central to hotels. They depart from here for the **otogar** (İzzet Güçlü Caddesi) as well.

Central Anatolia

Why Go?

Somewhere between the cracks in the Hittite ruins, the fissures in the Phyrgian burial mounds and the scratches in the Seljuk caravanserais, the mythical, mighty Turks raced across this highland steppe with big ideas and bigger swords. Alexander the Great cut that eponymous knot in Gordion where King Midas displayed his deft golden touch. Julius Caesar came, saw and conquered, and in Konya, the whirling dervishes first spun. This central sweep of Turkey was also where Atatürk forged his secular revolution along dusty Roman roads that all lead to Ankara, an underrated capital city and geopolitical centre. Further north through the nation's fruit bowl, in Safranbolu and Amasya, 'Ottomania' is still in full swing; here wealthy weekenders come to capture a glimmer of a bygone age amid bendy-beamed mansions. Central Anatolia is the meeting point between the fabled past and the present – a sojourn here will enlighten and enchant.

Best Places to Eat

➡ Atış Cafe (p418)

➡ Somatçi (p438)

➡ Amaseia Mutfağı (p429)

➡ Lezzetçi (p433)

Best Places to Stay

➡ Selvili Köşk (p417)

➡ Angora House Hotel (p407)

➡ Uluhan Otel (p429)

➡ Dadibra Konak (p417)

➡ Gönül Sefası (p429)

When to Go
Ankara

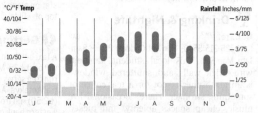

°C/°F Temp		Rainfall Inches/mm
40/104 —		— 5/125
30/86 —		— 4/100
20/68 —		— 3/75
10/50 —		— 2/50
0/32 —		— 1/25
-10/14 —		
-20/-4 —		— 0
J F M A M J J A S O N D		

May & Jun Fruit harvest: time to feast on cherries and apricots.

Jul & Aug Join summer's crowds of Turkish tourists in the Ottoman towns of Safranbolu and Amasya.

Dec Konya's Mevlâna Festival is a Sufi spectacular of extraordinary human spirit.

Ankara

☎ 0312 / POP 4.9 MILLION

Turkey's 'other' city may not have showy Ottoman palaces or regal facades but Ankara thrums to a vivacious, youthful beat unmarred by the tug of history. Drawing comparisons with İstanbul is pointless – the flat, modest surroundings are hardly the stuff of national poetry – but the civic success of this dynamic city is assured thanks to student panache and foreign-embassy intrigue.

The country's capital has made remarkable progress from a dusty Anatolian backwater to today's sophisticated arena for international affairs. Turkey's economic success is reflected in the booming restaurant scene around Kavaklıdere and the ripped-jean politik of Kızılay's sidewalk cafes, frequented by hip students, old-timers and businesspeople alike. And while the vibrant street life is enough of a reason to visit, Ankara also boasts two extraordinary monuments central to the Turkish story – the beautifully conceived Museum of Anatolian Civilisations and the Anıt Kabir, a colossal tribute to Atatürk, modern Turkey's founder.

History

Although Hittite remains dating back to before 1200 BC have been found in Ankara, the town really prospered as a Phrygian settlement on the north–south and east–west trade routes. Later it was taken by Alexander the Great, claimed by the Seleucids and finally occupied by the Galatians around 250 BC. Augustus Caesar annexed it to Rome as Ankyra.

The Byzantines held the town for centuries, with intermittent raids by the Persians and Arabs. When the Seljuk Turks came to Anatolia, they grabbed the city, but held it with difficulty. Later, the Ottoman sultan Yıldırım Beyazıt was captured near here by Central Asian conqueror Tamerlane and subsequently died in captivity. Spurned as a jinxed endeavour, the city slowly slumped into a backwater, prized for nothing but its goats.

That all changed when Atatürk chose Angora, as the city was known until 1930, to be his base in the struggle for independence. When he set up his provisional government here in 1920, the city was just a small, dusty settlement of some 30,000 people. After his victory in the War of Independence, Atatürk declared it the new Turkish capital, and set about developing it. From 1919 to 1927, Atatürk never set foot in İstanbul, preferring to work at making Ankara top dog.

◉ Sights

★ **Anıt Kabir** MAUSOLEUM

(Atatürk Mausoleum & Museum; Map p404; www.anitkabir.org; Anıt Caddesi; audio guide ₺4; ⊙9am-5pm mid-May–Oct, to 4pm Nov–mid-May) FREE

The monumental mausoleum of Mustafa Kemal Atatürk (1881–1938), the founder of modern Turkey, sits high above the city with its abundance of marble and air of veneration. The tomb itself actually makes up only a small part of this complex, which consists of **museums** and a **ceremonial courtyard**. For many Turks a visit is virtually a pilgrimage, and it's not unusual to see people visibly moved. Allow at least two hours in order to visit the whole site.

The main entrance to the complex is via the **Lion Road**, a 262m walkway lined with 24 lion statues – Hittite symbols of power used to represent the strength of the Turkish nation. The path leads to a massive courtyard, framed by colonnaded walkways, with steps leading up to the huge tomb on the left.

To the right of the tomb, the extensive **museum** displays Atatürk memorabilia, personal effects, gifts from famous admirers, and re-creations of his childhood home and school. Just as revealing as all the rich artefacts are his simple rowing machine and huge **multilingual library**, which includes tomes he wrote. Downstairs, extensive exhibits about the War of Independence and the formation of the republic move from battlefield murals with sound effects to over-detailed explanations of post-1923 reforms. At the end, a **gift shop** sells Atatürk items of all shapes and sizes.

As you approach the **tomb** itself, look left and right at the gilded inscriptions, which are quotations from Atatürk's speech celebrating the republic's 10th anniversary in 1932. Remove your hat as you enter, and bend your neck to view the ceiling of the lofty hall, lined in marble and sparingly decorated with 15th- and 16th-century Ottoman mosaics. At the northern end stands an immense marble **cenotaph**, cut from a single piece of stone weighing 40 tonnes. The actual tomb is in a chamber beneath it.

The memorial straddles a hill in a park about 2km west of Kızılay and 1.2km south of Anadolu metro station (the closest Ankaray-line station to the entrance). A free shuttle regularly zips up and down the hill from the entrance; alternatively, it's a pleasant walk to the mausoleum.

Central Anatolia Highlights

❶ Safranbolu
(p415) Turning back the clocks while wandering amid Eski Çarşı's cobblestones and timber-framed houses.

❷ Ankara (p401) Brushing up on Turkey's mind-boggling roots at the Museum of Anatolian Civilisations, the country's premier museum.

❸ Konya (p434) Paying homage to Rumi at the Mevlâna Museum then exploring the city's glut of Seljuk and Ottoman architectural finery.

❹ Hattuşa (p421) Hitting the Hittite hills in the heartland of Anatolia's first great empire.

❺ Amasya (p426) Pondering Pontic tombs that poke out from craggy cliffs above a riverside rim of restored mansions.

❻ Tokat (p430) Meandering crooked back alleys to search out *medreses* (seminaries), mosques and museums.

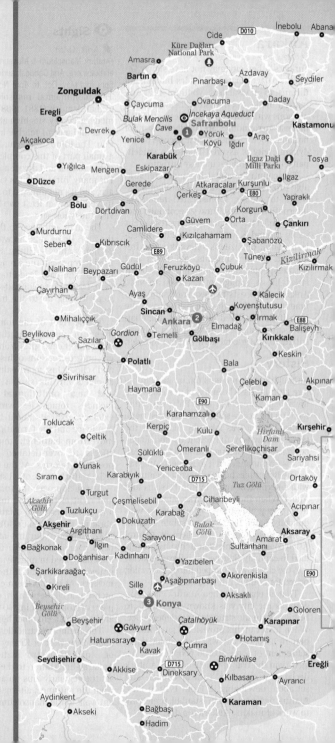

Ankara

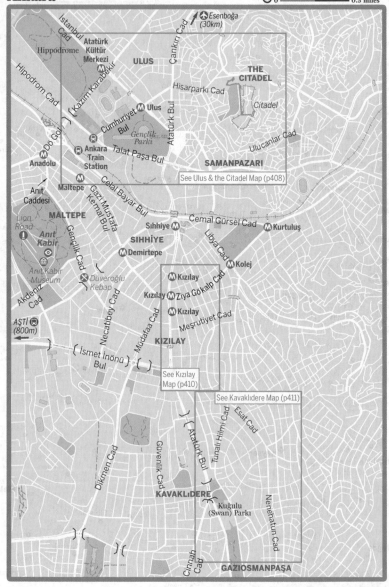

★ **Museum of Anatolian Civilisations** MUSEUM

(Anadolu Medeniyetleri Müzesi; Map p408; ☎0312-324 3160; www.anadolumedeniyetlerimuzesi.gov.tr; Gözcü Sokak 2; ₺30; ☺8.30am-7pm mid-Apr–Sep, to 5.15pm Oct–mid-Apr) The best place in the country to get to grips with the complex weave of Turkey's history, the exhibits here house artefacts cherry-picked from just about every significant archaeological site in Anatolia.

The central hall houses reliefs and statuary, while the surrounding halls take you on a journey of staggering history from

Neolithic and Chalcolithic, through the Bronze Age Assyrian and Hittite eras, to the Iron Age's Phrygian and Urartian periods.

The exhibits are chronologically arranged starting with the Palaeolithic and Neolithic displays to the right of the entrance, then continue in an anticlockwise direction. Do the full loop before visiting the central hall and then backtrack to head downstairs where there are displays of Roman artefacts unearthed at excavations in and around Ankara.

Items discovered at one of the most important Neolithic sites in the world – Çatalhöyük (p440), southeast of Konya – are displayed in the first hall, including the most famous mother goddess sculptures and the wall mural thought by some experts to be the world's first town map.

Some of the most interesting exhibits are in the early Bronze Age section where the fascinating finds unearthed during excavations of the Assyrian trading colony Kültepe (near Kayseri, in Cappadocia) are displayed. These include cuneiform tablets that date to the beginning of the 2nd millennium BC, disk-shaped idols and cult objects.

The Hittite collection follows, with Hattuşa's (p421) haul of cuneiform tablets (including the famed letter of friendship sent by Naptera, wife of Pharaoh Ramses II, to Puduhepa, wife to Hittite king Hattusili III) and striking figures of bulls and stags.

Most of the objects from the Phrygian capital Gordion (p414), including incredible inlaid wooden furniture, are displayed in the last hall. The exhibits also include limestone blocks with still-indecipherable inscriptions resembling the Greek alphabet, and lion- and ram-head ritual vessels that show the high quality of Phrygian metalwork.

Urartian artefacts are displayed at the end of the final hall. Spurred by rich metal deposits, the Urartians were Anatolia's foremost metalworkers, as the knives, horsebits, votive plates and shields on display demonstrate. This last hall also contains neo-Hittite artefacts and terracotta figures of gods in human form, some revealing their divine powers by growing scorpion tails.

The central hall contains a staggering amount of intricately carved stone slabs, principally from the sites of Arslantepe (p549), near Malatya, Alacahöyük (p425), near Hattuşa, and Kargamış, south of Gaziantep.

★**Erimtan Archaeology & Arts Museum** MUSEUM
(Map p408; ☑0312-311 0401; www.erimtanmuseum.org; Gözcü Sokak 10; adult/child ₺10/5; ☺10am-6pm Tue-Sun) Ankara's newest museum houses the astounding collection of mostly Roman (but also Bronze Age, Hittite and Byzantine) artefacts collected over the years by Turkish businessman and archaeology enthusiast Yüksel Erimtan. Exhibits are creatively curated with an eye for storytelling and feature state-of-the-art multimedia displays. There are some fabulously beautiful ceramic and jewellery pieces here as well as a vast coin collection, cuneiform tablets from Kültepe and an ornate Urartian belt.

The cafe downstairs has a tranquil garden setting and serves excellent coffee.

The basement floor hosts temporary exhibitions and also a program of cultural events. Check the website to see what's on while you're in town.

Rahmi M Koç Industrial Museum MUSEUM
(Map p408; ☑0312-309 6800; www.rmk-museum.org.tr; Depo Sokak 1; adult/child ₺10/5; ☺10am-5pm Tue-Fri, to 6pm Sat & Sun) The surprisingly absorbing Rahmi M Koç Industrial Museum, located inside the beautifully restored Çengelhan caravanserai building, has three floors covering subjects as diverse as transport, science, music, computing, Atatürk and carpets. If you were born before about 1985, be prepared to feel old as childhood memories such as ZX Spectrum computers and cassette tapes are worthy of museum exhibit status here.

Citadel AREA
(Ankara Kalesi; Map p408; Gözcü Sokak) The imposing *hisar* (citadel) is the most interesting part of Ankara to poke about in. This well-preserved quarter of thick walls and winding streets took its present shape in the 9th century AD, when the Byzantine emperor Michael II constructed the outer ramparts. The inner walls date from the 7th century.

Parmak Kapısı (Finger Gate) is the main gate. From here, meander the main alleyway to **Alaettin Cami** (Alitaş Sokak), the citadel mosque that dates from the 12th century. I To your right a steep flight of stairs leads to the **Şark Kulesi** (Eastern Tower), with panoramic city views. If you look to the north from here you'll see the **Ak Kale** (White Fort). It is out of bounds to visitors, though there are more good views from near its hilltop perch if you follow the alleyway leading up to the tower.

ANKARA'S ROMAN REMNANTS

Temple of Augustus & Rome (Map p408; Hacı Bayram Veli Caddesi) Except for a couple of imposing, inscribed walls, not much remains of this temple (AD 25) built to honour the Roman emperor Augustus.

Roman Baths (Roma Hamaları; Map p408; Çankırı Caddesi; ₺5; ⊙8.30am-5pm) At the sprawling 3rd-century Roman Baths ruins, the layout is still clearly visible; look for the standard Roman *apoditerium* (dressing room), *frigidarium* (cold room), *tepidarium* (warm room) and *caldarium* (hot room). A Byzantine tomb and Phrygian remains have also been found here. Make sure you wear sturdy shoes as the site is very overgrown in parts.

Roman Theatre (Map p408; Hisarparkı Caddesi) From Hisarparkı Caddesi, you can view the sparse remains of a Roman theatre from around 200 to 100 BC.

Column of Julian (Jülyanus Sütunu; Map p408; Çam Sokak) Erected in honour of Roman emperor Julian the Apostate's visit to Ankara, the Column of Julian sits in a square ringed by government buildings.

Some local families still live inside the citadel walls and the houses often incorporate broken column drums, bits of marble statuary and inscribed lintels into their walls. For a long time the neighbourhood here was extremely run-down but the past few years have seen the area gentrified somewhat, although once you duck off the main route there are still many narrow, ramshackle alleys to explore.

Arslanhane Cami
MOSQUE
(Map p408; Kale Sokak) This Seljuk-era mosque is one of Ankara's most beautiful. It has an interior of chunky wooden columns topped by Roman capitals, an intricately carved *minber* (pulpit) and a large, ornately tiled *mihrab* (niche indicating the direction of Mecca).

Hacı Bayram Cami
MOSQUE
(Map p408; Hacı Bayram Veli Caddesi) Ankara's most revered mosque is Hacı Bayram Cami. Hacı Bayram Veli was a Muslim 'saint' who founded the Bayramiye dervish order around 1400. Ankara was the order's centre and Hacı Bayram Veli is still revered by pious Muslims. The mosque was built in the 15th century, with tiling added in the 18th century. The surrounding neighbourhood has been spruced up in recent years with the mosque sitting in a manicured square, surrounded by cafes and shops selling religious paraphernalia. There are great views over to the *hisar* area from here.

Vakıf Eserleri Müzesi
MUSEUM
(Ankara Museum of Religious Foundation Works; Map p408; Atatürk Bulvarı; ⊙9am-5pm Tue-Sun) **FREE** The tradition of carpets being gifted to mosques has helped preserve many of

Turkey's finest specimens. This extensive collection – which once graced the floors of mosques throughout the country – was put on display to the public in 2007. A must for anyone interested in Turkish textiles, the exhibits also include a fascinating Ottoman manuscript collection, tile work, metalwork and intricately carved wood panels.

All of it is superbly displayed with detailed information panels in English (labelling for individual items though is generally only in Turkish) explaining the history of Turkish crafts.

Ethnography Museum
MUSEUM
(Etnografya Müzesi; Map p408; Türkocağı Sokak, Samanpazarı; ₺12; ⊙8.30am-6.45pm) Housed inside the building (built 1927) that served as Atatürk's mausoleum until the Anıt Kabir (p401) was built, the Ethnography Museum has a small but well-curated collection that showcases Turkey's artistic heritage. In the entrance hall, Atatürk's mausoleum space is preserved with photographs of his funeral displayed on the walls.

The left-hand hall leading off the entrance contains Seljuk ceramics, Anatolian jewellery and a particularly beautiful collection of Ottoman woodwork including intricately carved *minbars* and mosque doors.

The right-hand hall exhibits daily-life dioramas complete with mannequins.

Painting & Sculpture Museum
MUSEUM
(Resim ve Heykel Müzesi; Map p408; Türkocağı Sokak, Samanpazarı; ⊙9am-6pm Tue-Sun) **FREE** The Painting & Sculpture Museum showcases the cream of Turkish artists. Ranging from angular war scenes to society portraits, the pieces demonstrate that 19th- and

20th-century artistic developments in Turkey paralleled those in Europe, with increasingly abstract form.

Cer Modern
GALLERY

(Map p408; ☑ 0312-310 0000; www.cermodern. org; Altınsoy Caddesi 3; adult/child ₺20/free; ☺ 10am-8pm Tue-Sun) Located in an old train depot, this huge artists' park and gallery exhibits modern and challenging art from across Europe, plus there's an excellent cafe and shop. Cultural events are also staged here.

🛏 Sleeping

🛏 Ulus & the Citadel

Grand Sera Otel
HOTEL $

(Map p408; ☑ 0312-310 8999; www.grandseraotel. com; Denizciler Caddesi 16, Ulus; s/d ₺100/140; ❈ 🄰 🛜) One of the best budget deals in town with good-sized, freshly decorated rooms that have big bathrooms, home to generously sized showers. Front rooms come with little balconies though back rooms are the quieter choice. On the downside, they really need to buy a better vacuum cleaner but everything else is kept clean and shiny.

Otel Mithat
HOTEL $

(Map p408; ☑ 0312-311 5410; www.otelmithat. com.tr; Tavus Sokak 2, Ulus; s/d ₺90/130; ❈ 🛜) With groovy carpeting and sleek neutral bed linen, the Mithat's rooms are fresh and modern. The teensy bathrooms do let the side down but this is a minor complaint about what is, overall, a solid budget choice. Nonsmokers will be pleased that, unlike most Ankara hotels in this price range, the Mithat takes its no-smoking policy seriously.

⭐ Angora House Hotel
BOUTIQUE HOTEL $$

(Map p408; ☑ 0312-309 8380; www.angorahouse. com.tr; Kale Kapısı Sokak 16, Ankara Kalesi; s/d/ tr €30/55/66; ❸ ❈ 🛜) Be utterly charmed by this restored Ottoman house set within the citadel neighbourhood. The six rooms are infused with old-world atmosphere and simply decorated with dark wood accents. One of the best breakfast feasts – served outside in the courtyard – in Turkey awaits you in the morning and staff are delightfully helpful.

Buğday Hotel
HOTEL $$

(Map p408; ☑ 0312-311 7700; www.bugday.com. tr; İstiklal Caddesi 18, Ulus; r ₺220; 🄿 ❈ 🛜) Just one block away from Ulus metro station, the Buğday has spacious, well-kept rooms decked out in white and red with good amenities (kettles, satellite TV with plenty of English channels). Staff are keen to please and there's a bar and restaurant.

Divan Çukurhan
HISTORIC HOTEL $$$

(Map p408; ☑ 0312-306 6400; www.divan. com.tr; Depo Sokak 3, Ankara Kalesi; r/ste from €86/130; ❈ 🛜) Soak up the historic ambience of staying in the 16th-century Çukurhan caravanserai. Set around a dramatic glass-ceilinged interior courtyard, each individually themed room blends ornate decadence with sassy contemporary style. Ankara's best bet for those who want to be dazzled by oodles of sumptuous luxury and sleek service.

Ankara Hotel
BUSINESS HOTEL $$$

(Map p408; ☑ 0312-508 1010; www.theankara hotel.com; Celal Bayar Bulvarı 78, Maltepe; r €70; 🄿 ❈ 🛜) This contemporary hotel opened next door to Ankara train station in 2018. There's a bar-cafe in the vast foyer and the minimalist-style rooms are decked out with blond-wood accents, floor-to-ceiling windows and ridiculously big flat-screen TVs. Outside of peak times, you can often bag a room for half the going rates. Check online for deals.

🛏 Kızılay & Kavaklıdere

⭐ Deeps Hostel
HOSTEL $

(Map p410; ☑ 0312-213 6338; www.deepshostel ankara.com; Ataç 2 Sokak 46, Kızılay; dm/d without bathroom or breakfast ₺50/115; ❸ 🛜) At Ankara's best backpacker choice, friendly owner Şeyda has created a colourful, light-filled hostel with spacious dorms and small private rooms with squeaky-clean, modern shared bathrooms. It's all topped off by masses of advice and information, a fully equipped kitchen, laundry facilities and a cute communal area downstairs where you can swap your Turkish travel tales.

Gordion Hotel
BOUTIQUE HOTEL $$

(Map p411; ☑ 0312-427 8080; www.gordion hotel.com; Büklüm Sokak 59; s/d/ste from ₺200/260/450; ❈ 🛜 🄲) This independent hotel in the middle of the Kavaklıdere neighbourhood is a fabulously cultured inner-city residence with stately rooms, a basement swimming pool, Vakko textiles in the lobby, centuries-old art engravings, a conservatory restaurant and an extensive DVD library. At current rates it's an out-and-out bargain.

Ulus & the Citadel

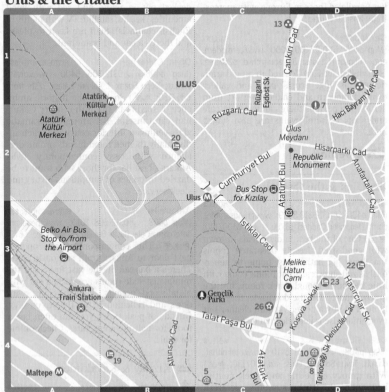

Ulus & the Citadel

◎ Top Sights
1 Erimtan Archaeology & Arts Museum	E3
2 Museum of Anatolian Civilisations	E3

◎ Sights
3 Alaettin Cami	E2
4 Arslanhane Cami	F3
5 Cer Modern	C4
6 Citadel	E2
7 Column of Julian	D2
8 Ethnography Museum	D4
9 Hacı Bayram Cami	D1
10 Painting & Sculpture Museum	D4
11 Parmak Kapısı	E3
12 Rahmi M Koç Industrial Museum	E3
13 Roman Baths	C1
14 Roman Theatre	E2
15 Şark Kulesi	F2
16 Temple of Augustus & Rome	D1
17 Vakıf Eserleri Müzesi	C4

◎ Sleeping
18 Angora House Hotel	E3
19 Ankara Hotel	B4
20 Buğday Hotel	B2
21 Divan Çukurhan	E3
22 Grand Sera Otel	D3
23 Otel Mithat	D3

◎ Eating
24 Antik Cafe	E3
Kınacızade Konağı	(see 18)

◎ Drinking & Nightlife
25 Kirit Cafe	E3

◎ Entertainment
26 Ankara State Opera House	C4

◎ Shopping
27 Hamamönü District	E4
28 Hisar Area	E3

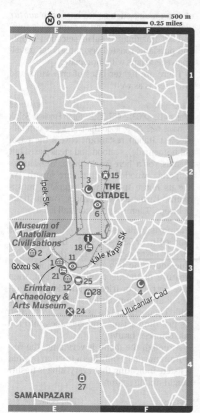

✖ Ulus & the Citadel

Antik Cafe
ANATOLIAN **$**

(Map p408; Koyunpazarı Sokak, Ankara Kalesi; mains ₺10-20; ⊗8.30am-9pm; 🍴) Tuck into some of the fattest, juiciest *gözleme* (stuffed flat-breads) in town or a filling bowl of *mantı* (Turkish ravioli) at this friendly little cafe at the bottom of the citadel hill. Either eat street-side, under the vine trellis, watching the tour groups trudge up the cobblestones, or inside with its simple traditional decor.

Kınacızade Konağı
TURKISH **$$**

(Map p408; ☎0312-324 5714; Kale Kapısı Sokak 28, Ankara Kalesi; mains ₺10-40; ⊗9am-9pm Mon-Sat; 🍴) This Ottoman house, smack in the middle of the citadel neighbourhood, serves up a range of typical Turkish dishes from *gözleme* to *güveç* (meat and vegetable stew). The shady courtyard, enclosed by picturesque timber-framed facades in various states of higgledy-piggledy disrepair, is a delightful place to while away time over a lazy lunch.

✖ Maltepe

Düveroğlu Kebap
PIDE **$**

(Map p404; ☎0312-229 7938; www.duveroglu.com. tr; Gençlik Caddesi 28b, Anıttepe; mains ₺10-38; ⊗11am-10pm) In business since 1963, this is the original outlet of Ankara's most famous name in pide (Turkish-style pizza) and kebap. It's renowned for its *sarımsaklı Antep lahmacun* (garlic-drenched Arabic-style pizza, a speciality of Gaziantep), which makes for a cheap and seriously tasty lunch. Just don't breathe on anyone afterwards.

✖ Kızılay

Ata Aspava
KEBAB **$$**

(Map p410; ☎0312-419 9027; Karanfıl Sokak 19; mains ₺29-45; ⊗10am-10pm) If we're in the mood for *urfa kebap* (a mild version of the Adana kebap served with onion and black pepper) or İskender kebap (or Bursa kebap; döner kebap on fresh pide topped with tomato sauce and browned butter) in Ankara, this is where we head. It's nothing fancy, just a typical Turkish grill restaurant with solid service, great complimentary salads and some seriously well-cooked meat.

Big Baker
BURGERS **$$**

(Map p410; ☎0312-419 3777; www.bigbaker.com. tr; Yüksel Caddesi 17a; mains ₺21-31; ⊗8am-10pm; 🍴) Gourmet burgers have hit Ankara and this place is one of the best in town to sink your teeth into one. There are Mexican-style,

Hotel Eyüboğlu
BUSINESS HOTEL **$$**

(Map p410; ☎0312-417 6400; www.eyuboglu hotel.com; Karanfıl Sokak 73; s/d ₺180/250; 🅿🛜) Probably the best-run hotel in Kızılay with on-the-ball staff who go out of their way to help. No-nonsense, neutral-toned rooms have beds so comfortable you'll happily smack the snooze button for an extra few minutes. Some rooms are bigger than others so ask to see a few.

✖ Eating

Most downtown Ulus options are basic. In Kızılay it's all about street-side eating and cafe-hopping. Much of the food on offer though is a fairly identikit mix of snacky or fast-food-type meals and finding a decent restaurant can be harder than it might first appear.

In Kavaklıdere the scene is European and sophisticated, catering primarily to the embassy set.

Kızılay

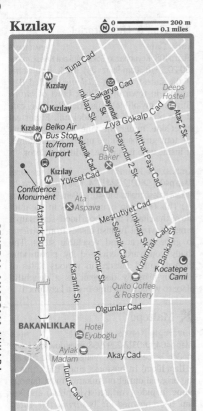

goat's cheese, and BBQ burger options or for a truly Turkish take on the humble burger try the *köz patlıcanlı*, which comes with roasted aubergine and peppers.

Kavaklıdere

Mangal
KEBAB $

(Map p411; ☑0312-466 2460; www.mangalkebap. com; Bestekar Sokak 78; mains ₺15-33; ☺9am-10pm) Swamped with local families on the weekends, Mangal is a neighbourhood star that has been churning out mountains of pide and kebaps for 20 years. If you're looking for a simple meal of *tavuk şiş* (chicken kebap) or Adana kebap, you can't go wrong here.

Café des Cafés
CAFE $$

(Map p411; ☑0312-428 0176; Tunalı Hilmi Caddesi 83; mains ₺24-51; ☺8.30am-11pm) Quirky vintage styling and comfy sofas make Café des Cafés one of our favourite Kavaklıdere pit stops. The menu is bistro-style cooking

offering mains such as sea bass with *zaatar* (wild thyme, sumac and sesame spice mix) and an imaginative salad selection (apple and purslane, roasted vegetable) that travelling vegetarians will appreciate.

There are lighter bites of croissants and bruschettas as well.

Mezzaluna
ITALIAN $$

(Map p411; ☑0312-467 5818; Turan Emeksiz Sokak 1; mains ₺29-75; ☺noon-11pm; 🖛) The capital's classiest Italian restaurant covers the pasta (all homemade), seafood and steak bases but trust us, you're here for the pizza. Mezzaluna's thin-crust, wood-fired pizzas are superb. We like its house special with eggplant, mushrooms, Parmesan and proper Parma ham. Delicious. There's a good cocktail list too.

Marmaris Balıkçısı
SEAFOOD $$

(Map p411; ☑0312-427 2212; Bestekar Sokak 88/14a; mains ₺25-52; ☺11am-11pm) At this blue-and-white fish restaurant, pluck your creature of the deep off its ice bed, then have it grilled or fried up and doused in olive oil and lemon. Order sides of salad and grilled peppers and do as the Turks do when it's fish dinner time and get stuck into the rakı (aniseed brandy).

Although the menu is very long, the restaurant normally only has a fraction of what is listed, indicating that everything is freshly caught and in season.

La Gioia
INTERNATIONAL $$$

(Map p411; www.lagioia.com.tr; Tahran Caddesi 2; mains ₺41-98; ☺10am-11.45pm; 🖛🖛) The see-and-be-seen crowd packs out the front terrace on sunny days, tucking into European-style mains of grilled steak with sage risotto and gorgonzola sauce and chicken parmigiana or gossiping over salads of beetroot and goat's cheese or artichoke and quinoa. There's an excellent wine list and plenty of cocktails on offer if you just want to people-watch with a drink.

The main dining room is a giant conservatory-style affair, but the outdoor tables are the ones to bag.

🍷 Drinking & Nightlife

Kızılay is ripe for a night out with Ankara's student population. Good spots include Olgunlar Caddesi, Tunus Caddesi and Bayındır Sokak (between Sakarya and Tuna Caddesis). Many places offer live Turkish pop or rock music after around 9pm and plentiful cheap beer deals. Solo female travellers should feel OK in most of them.

Quito Coffee & Roastery　　COFFEE
(Map p410; Selanik Caddesi 82; ⊘8am-11pm; 🛜) Simply the best coffee in Kızılay. Head here for your flat white, Chemex, Aero-Press or cold brew needs. The interior is all chic wood and open shelves contemporary-style, and there's a small outdoor terrace too.

Louise Brasserie　　BAR
(Map p411; ☑0312-447 5100; www.louise.com.tr; Filistin Sokak 37; ⊘9am-1am; 🛜) No we don't know why this bar-restaurant is decked out in plantation-colonial style either, but Ankara's chi-chi set laps it up. As well as a full bar list, there are quirky cocktails like the Rossella (hibiscus, tequila, rose petals, cloves and Cointreau) and the Bite of Mastik (Mastic liqueur, Aperol and orange juice).

The outdoor terrace is the place to be on a summer evening. There's a full food menu as well.

Kirit Cafe　　CAFE
(Map p408; Koyunpazarı Sokak, Ankara Kalesi; ⊘10am-8pm) With a fun felt shop on the ground floor and quirky local art gracing the walls of the cafe upstairs, this place is a lovely find. Great for a çay or coffee stop after exploring the cobblestone alleyways of the citadel area. There's a menu of burgers, pasta and cheesecake if you're peckish.

Hayyami　　WINE BAR
(Map p411; ☑0312-466 1052; Bestekar Sokak 82b; ⊘noon-4am) Named after the renowned Sufi philosopher, this thriving wine house/restaurant attracts a hobnobbing crowd to its lowered courtyard. It boasts a long and diverse wine selection and there's a menu of tapas-style dishes and sharing platters to complement your tipple.

Aylak Madam　　CAFE
(Map p410; ☑0312-419 7412; Karanfil Sokak 2; ⊘10am-late; 🛜) A cool French bistro-cafe in Kızılay with a mean weekend brunch (from 10am to 2.30pm), plus sandwiches, head-kicking cappuccinos, and a jazz-fusion soundtrack. Postgraduates and writers hang out here, hunched over their laptops or with pens tapping against half-finished manuscripts.

⭐ Entertainment

6.45　　LIVE MUSIC
(Map p411; www.645kk.com; Tunus Caddesi 66; concerts ₺40-50; ⊘concerts from 10pm) One of the best places in town to see local bands.

6.45 has a regular mix of musicians along with tribute bands playing classic rock, and dance parties focused on tunes from the '70s and '80s. Check the website for upcoming events and to buy tickets.

Ruhi Bey　　LIVE MUSIC
(Map p411; www.ruhibeymeyhane.com; Budak Sokak 5/1; ⊘7pm-5am) Every Friday and Saturday night, the bar of this *meyhane* (tavern) restaurant hosts local musicians; rock, acoustic,

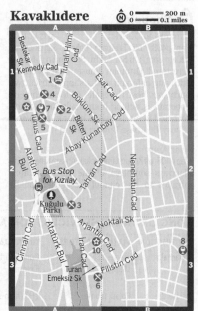

Kavaklıdere

🔵 **Sleeping**

❌ **Eating**

🟢 **Drinking & Nightlife**

⭐ **Entertainment**

electronica and more traditional music have all been on the set list here.

Ankara State Opera House PERFORMING ARTS (Opera Sahnesi; Map p408; ☑0312-324 6801; www.dobgm.gov.tr; Atatürk Bulvarı 20) This venue plays host to all the large productions staged by the Ankara State Opera and Ballet. The season generally runs from September to June and it's worthwhile trying to catch a performance if you're in town at that time.

🛍 Shopping

Hamamönü District ARTS & CRAFTS (Map p408; off Talatpaşa Bulvarı, Samanpazarı; ⊙10am-8pm) On Sarıkadın Sokağı, in this area of restored Ottoman houses that's become a thriving cafe and crafts shop district, two courtyards host the stalls of local women's cooperatives, selling homemade knitted and crocheted items as well as other gifts. Swerve off busy Talatpaşa Bulvarı to find it.

Hisar Area ARTS & CRAFTS (Map p408; off Koyunpazarı Sokak, Ankara Kalesi) The alleyways southeast of the Parmak Kapısı entrance to the citadel were traditionally the centre for trading in angora wool. Walk downhill on Koyunpazarı Sokak to dive into the neighbourhood to explore. You'll come across copper beaters, carpet and antique stores, small galleries and craft shops.

ⓘ Information

MEDICAL SERVICES

Pharmacists take it in turns to open around the clock; look out for the *nobetçi* (open 24 hours) sign. **Bayındır Hospital** (☑0312-428 0808; www.bayindirhastanesi.com.tr; Atatürk Bulvarı 201, Çankaya; ⊙24hr) is an up-to-date private hospital.

TOURIST INFORMATION

Tourist Office (Map p408; ☑0312-310 3044; Kale Kapısı Sokak; ⊙10am-5pm) Inside the Citadel. Gives out a decent free map of town and a pamphlet on Ankara's sights. There are also (usually unstaffed) branches at the AŞTİ otogar and at the train station.

ⓘ Getting There & Away

AIR

Ankara Esenboğa Airport (Ankara Esenboğa Havalimanı, ESB; ☑0312-590 4000; www.esenbogaairport.com; Özal Bulvarı, Balıkhisar)

LONG-DISTANCE SERVICES FROM ANKARA TRAIN STATION

DESTINATION	VIA (MAJOR STOPS)	TRAIN NAME	FARE (₺)	DURATION (HR)	FREQUENCY
Diyarbakır	Kayseri, Sivas, Malatya	Güney Kurtalan Ekspresi	42	20¼	11am Mon, Wed, Thu, Fri & Sat
Eskişehir	Polatlı (some services)	YHT (high-speed)	31	1½	14 departures daily
İstanbul	Eskişehir	YHT (high-speed)	71	4½	8 departures daily
İstanbul	Eskişehir	Ankara Ekspresi	65	7½	10pm daily
İzmir	Eskişehir, Kütahya, Manisa	İzmir Mavi Treni	52	14½	7pm daily
Kars	Kayseri, Sivas, Erzurum	Doğu Ekspresi	48	24¼	6pm daily
Kars	Kayseri, Sivas, Erzurum	Turistik Doğu Ekspresi	400	31	4.55pm daily
Konya	Polatlı (some services)	YHT (high-speed)	31	1¾	7 departures daily
Tatvan	Kayseri, Sivas, Malatya	Vangölü Ekspresi	48	23¾	11am Tue & Sun
Tehran (Iran)	Tatvan, Van, Tabriz	Trans Asya Treni	41	57	2.25pm Wed

The high-speed (YHT) trains to İstanbul stop at four İstanbul stations. The most useful one for travellers to get off at is İstanbul Söğütlüçeşme. From there you can either transfer to the Marmaray Line to head to Sirkeci, or catch a bus or walk 1.5km to Kadıköy İskelesi (ferry station) to catch a ferry to Eminönü.

SERVICES FROM ANKARA (AŞTİ) OTOGAR

DESTINATION	FARE (₺)	DURATION (HR)	FREQUENCY
Antalya	80-95	7-8	every 1 to 1½ hours
Denizli (for Pamukkale)	85-105	7-8½	every 30 minutes morning, every 2 hours afternoon & evening
Eskişehir	35-45	3	every 30 minutes morning & afternoon, hourly evening
İstanbul	70-95	6½-7½	every 30 minutes
İzmir	80-105	7½-9½	hourly at least morning & afternoon, 6 evening
Kastamonu	45	4-5	every 1½ to 2 hours
Konya	45-50	4	hourly at least
Nevşehir (for Cappadocia)	70	4½-5	3 morning, 5 afternoon, 2 evening
Safranbolu	45	3	4 morning, 5 afternoon, 4 evening
Sungurlu (for Hattuşa)	40	2½-3	every 1 to 1½ hours morning & afternoon

is 33km north of the city. In recent years many more international routes have opened up making it a viable alternative to İstanbul.

Turkish Airlines (www.turkishairlines.com) has regular direct flights to many domestic airports including Adana, Antalya, Dalaman, İstanbul, İzmir, Kars, Mardin, Şanlıurfa, Trabzon and Van. It has an **office** (☑ 0312-465 6363; www.anadolujet. com; Atatürk Bulvarı 211; ☺ 9am-8pm) in the city centre. Pegasus Airlines (www.flypgs.com) flies regularly to Antalya, İstanbul, İzmir and Bodrum.

For international destinations, Turkish Airlines and Pegasus Airlines both fly to northern Cyprus; Turkish Airlines also has direct services to Paris, Stuttgart and Tbilisi; Pegasus offers direct flights to Amman, Copenhagen, Dusseldorf and Kiev; Iran Air (www.iranair.de) and Mahan Air (www.mahan.aero/en) fly to Tehran; Sun Express (www.sunexpress.com.tr) has departures to various German cities; and Qatar Airways (www.qatarairways.com) flies to Doha.

BUS

AŞTİ Otogar (Ankara Şehirlerarası Terminali İşletmesi, Ankara Bus Station; Mevlâna Bulvarı), Ankara's gigantic otogar, is at the western end of the Ankaray underground train line, 4.5km west of Kızılay. Every Turkish city or town of any size has direct buses to Ankara. Because there are so many buses to many parts of the country, you can often turn up, buy a ticket and be on your way in less than an hour. Don't try this during public holidays, though.

The *emanet* (left-luggage room) on the lower level charges ₺5.50 to ₺7.50 per item stored; you'll need to show your passport.

TRAIN

Ankara train station (Ankara Garı; www.tcddtasimacilik.gov.tr; Celal Bayar Bulvarı) offers both high-speed (YHT) train services heading

to Eskişehir, İstanbul and Konya (Celal Buyar Bulvarı entrance) and regular trains across the country (Cumhuriyet Bulvarı entrance). The two sides are linked by an overpass inside the station.

Ticket queues can be long so it's best to buy tickets the day before travel or online at www.tcddtasimacilik.gov.tr.

❶ Getting Around

If you're going to be kicking around the city for a couple of days it's worth getting an **Ankara Kart** (rechargeable transport card; available at all metro station ticket counters and many kiosks around town), which gives you discounted fares of ₺2.50 on both the metro and bus systems.

TO/FROM THE AIRPORT

Belko Air airport buses (☑ 444 9312; www.belkoair.com; arrivals fl, AŞTİ otogar) link the airport with the city centre and AŞTİ otogar (bus station; ₺15, one hour). Departures to/from the airport are every 30 minutes between 5am and midnight daily. After midnight buses leave hourly.

From the airport, buses leave from in front of the passenger arrivals gate H (domestic arrivals); international arrivals should walk left on leaving the airport terminal.

Heading to the airport, buses depart from the ground-floor arrivals terminal of the AŞTİ otogar, and then pick up passengers at Belko Air's **Kızılay stop** (Map p410; Atatürk Bulvarı, Gama İş Merkezi Bldg) roughly 10 minutes after and from a **stop** (Map p408; Talat Paşa Bulvarı) in front of Ankara train station (roughly 20 minutes after) on the way to the airport.

A taxi between the airport and the city costs between ₺85 and ₺100 and (depending on traffic) takes around 40 minutes.

TO/FROM THE OTOGAR (BUS STATION)

The easiest way to get into town is on the Ankaray metro line, which has a station at the AŞTİ otogar (p413). Get off at Kızılay for midrange hotels. Change at Kızılay (to the metro line) for Ulus and cheaper hotels.

A taxi costs about ₺35 to the city centre and usually takes around 15 minutes.

TO/FROM THE TRAIN STATION

Ankara train station (p413) is about 1km southwest of Ulus Meydanı and 2km northwest of Kızılay.

From Ulus metro station (Ankaray Line), it's a straight 200m walk up Cumhuriyet Bulvarı to the station.

From Maltepe metro station (Metro 1 Line), turn right along Gazi Mustafa Kemal Bulvarı at the metro exit and walk around 20m down the street to the *alt geçidi* (pedestrian underpass), which exits in front of the train station.

In 2019, a new 'gar' (train station) metro station was being built directly across the road from the train station on Celal Bayar Bulvarı.

Many dolmuşes and buses head west along Celal Bayar Bulvarı to Ulus.

BUS

Ankara has a good city-bus and dolmuş (minibus with a prescribed route) network. Signs on the front and side of the vehicles are often better guides than route numbers. City buses chug frequently between **Ulus** (Map p408) and Kızılay and Kızılay and **Kavaklıdere** (Map p411) from stops along Atatürk Bulvarı.

Those marked 'gar' go to the train station and those marked 'AŞTİ' to the otogar (bus station).

Single-use ₺3 tickets are available anywhere displaying an EGO Bilet sign (most easily purchased from metro station ticket booths), or buy an Ankara Kart (p413).

METRO

Ankara's underground train network is the easiest way to get between Ulus and Kızılay and the otogar. There are two main lines useful for visitors.

The Ankaray line runs between AŞTİ otogar (p413) in the west through Maltepe and Kızılay (Kızılay's official station name is '15 Temmuz Kızılay Milli İrade') to Dikimevi in the east.

The M1 Metro line runs from Kızılay ('15 Temmuz Kızılay Milli İrade') northwest via Sıhhiye and Ulus to Batıkent.

The two lines interconnect at Kızılay. Trains run from 6.15am to 11.45pm daily.

A one-way fare costs ₺3, or ₺2.50 with the Ankara Kart (p413). Tickets are available at all stations.

A new metro line is currently being built that will connect Ankara train station to the network.

Around Ankara

Gordion

The capital of ancient Phrygia, with some 3000 years of settlement behind it, Gordion's ruins lie 106km southwest of Ankara in the village of Yassıhöyük.

Gordion was occupied by the Phrygians as early as the 9th century BC, and soon afterwards became their capital. Although destroyed during the Cimmerian invasion, it was rebuilt before being conquered by the Lydians and then the Persians. Alexander the Great came through here and famously cut the Gordian knot in 333 BC, but by 278 BC the Galatian occupation had effectively destroyed the city.

The flat patchwork of fields around Yassıhöyük are dotted with the humps of tumuli (burial mounds) marking the graves of the Phrygian kings. Of some 90 identified tumuli, 35 have been excavated. You can enter the largest tomb, and also view the Gordion citadel mound where digs revealed five main levels of civilisation from the Bronze Age to Galatian times.

Gordion Museum
MUSEUM

(Yassıhöyük; incl Midas Tumulus ₺6; ⊙8.30am-7pm) In the museum opposite the Midas Tumulus, Macedonian and Babylonian coins show Gordion's position at the centre of Anatolian trade, communications and military activities, as do the bronze figurines and glass-bead jewellery from the Syro-Levantine region of Mesopotamia.

Midas Tumulus
TOMB

(Yassıhöyük; incl Gordion Museum ₺6; ⊙8.30am-7pm) In 1957 Austrian archaeologist Alfred Koerte discovered Gordion, and with it the intact tomb of a Phrygian king, probably buried some time between 740 and 718 BC. The tomb is actually a gabled 'cottage' of cedar surrounded by juniper logs, buried inside a tumulus 53m high and 300m in diameter. It's the oldest wooden structure ever found in Anatolia, and perhaps even in the world. The tunnel leading into the depths of the tumulus is a modern addition.

Inside the tomb archaeologists found the body of a man between 61 and 65 years of age, 1.59m tall, surrounded by burial objects, including tables, bronze situlas (containers) and bowls said to be part of the funerary burial feast. Despite the name, the occupant remains unknown though some archaeologists posit that it was the burial site of Midas' father, King Gordius.

Citadel Mound
RUINS

(Yassıhöyük) **FREE** Just beyond Yassıhöyük village – 2km west of the museum – is the weatherbeaten 10th-century-BC fortified citadel area. Excavations here have yielded a wealth of data on Gordion's many civilisations. The site is a mass of jumbled, half-buried walls; thankfully, excellent English information panels dotted along the trail around the ruins help you decipher the site.

Although the ruins themselves are scant, the bucolic views of green fields interrupted by round tumuli make it well worth a visit.

The lofty main gate on the western side of the acropolis was approached by a 6m-wide ramp. Within the fortified enclosure were four *megara* (square halls) from which the king and his priests and ministers ruled the empire.

❶ Getting There & Away

Gordion is most easily reached with your own wheels, but if you don't fancy hiring a car for the trip, the simplest way to visit is a train/taxi combo. From Ankara train station there are 15 high-speed (YHT) trains to Polatlı (₺16, 40 minutes) daily. Heading back to Ankara, there are 14 services daily. Polatlı YHT train station is 2km outside of Polatlı town and Yassıhöyük is a further 18km away. Taxis from the station charge ₺150 for the return journey to Yassıhöyük including waiting time.

You could also jump on local bus 212 at Polatlı train station, which regularly chugs between the station and Polatlı and then get a taxi in the centre of Polatlı, but the taxi fare to Yassıhöyük will most likely be the same.

From Polatlı you could also head on to Eskişehir, Konya or İstanbul by train, but note that there is no left-luggage facility at the station so your bags will have to come with you on the taxi trip to Yassıhöyük.

Safranbolu

☎ 0370 / POP 67.040

Safranbolu's old town, known as Eski Çarşı, is a vision of red-tiled roofs and meandering alleys chock-a-block full of candy stores and cobblers. Having first found fame with traders as an isolated source of the precious spice saffron, Safranbolu now attracts people seeking to recapture the heady scent of yesteryear within the muddle of timber-framed mansions converted into quirky boutique hotels. Yes it is completely twee and trussed up for tourists, but it's so damn pretty you probably won't care.

Spending the night here is all about soaking up the enchanting Ottoman scene – all creaky wooden floors, exuberantly carved ceilings and traditional cupboard-bathrooms. A day at the old hamam or browsing the market shops and revelling in the cobblestone quaintness is about as strenuous as it gets. On summer weekends you'll be sharing ye olde-worlde bliss with the crowds, so come on a weekday for a mellower experience.

◎ Sights

⭐ **Eski Çarşı**
ARCHITECTURE

The real joy of Safranbolu is simply wandering the cobblestone alleys. Everywhere you look in Eski Çarşı (Safranbolu's old town) is a feast for the eyes. Virtually every house in the neighbourhood is an original, and what little modern development there is has been held in check. Many of the finest historic houses have been restored, and as time goes on, more and more are being saved from deterioration and turned into hotels, shops or museums.

Köprülü Mehmet Paşa Cami
MOSQUE

(İzzet Paşa Sokak) This beefy, helmet-roofed building beside the Shoe-Maker's Bazaar (p418) dates to 1661. The metal sundial in the courtyard was added in the mid-19th century.

Cinci Hanı
HISTORIC BUILDING

(Saraçlar Sokak; ⏰9am-9pm) **FREE** Eski Çarşı's most famous and imposing structure is this brooding 17th-century caravanserai that has hotel rooms on the 2nd floor and a cafe-restaurant plus souvenir shops on the ground floor. You can climb up to the rooftop for red-tiled-roof panoramas over the town. On Saturdays a market takes place in the square behind it.

İzzet Paşa Cami
MOSQUE

(İzzet Paşa Sokak) This is one of the largest mosques constructed during the Ottoman Empire. It was built by the grand vizier in 1796 and restored in 1903. Its design was influenced by European architecture.

Metalworker's Bazaar
MARKET

(Demirciler Arastası; Debbag Pazarı Sokak) You'll hear the clang of hammers before you get here. This fascinating area is where the traditional metalworkers of Safranbolu still ply their trade and you can see them at work shaping farm implements and household

Safranbolu – Eski Çarşı

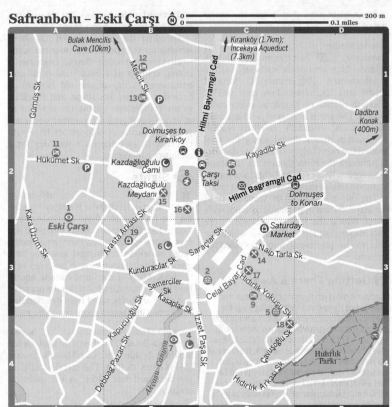

Safranbolu - Eski Çarşı

◉ Top Sights
1 Eski Çarşı..A2

◉ Sights
2 Cinci Hanı......................................C3
3 Hıdırlık Tepe..................................D4
4 İzzet Paşa Cami.............................B4
5 Kaymakamlar Museum....................C3
6 Köprülü Mehmet Paşa
Cami..B3
7 Metalworker's Bazaar.....................B4

◉ Activities, Courses & Tours
8 Cinci Hamam.................................B2

◉ Sleeping
9 Bastoncu Konak.............................C3

10 Efe Guesthouse.............................C2
11 Gülevi...A2
12 Kadıoğlu Şehzade
Konakları....................................B1
13 Selvili Köşk..................................B1

◉ Eating
14 Atış Cafe......................................C3
15 Çızgi Cafe....................................B2
16 Hanım Sultan................................B2
17 Safranbolu
Sofrası.......................................C3
18 Taşev...C4

◉ Shopping
19 Shoe-Maker's
Bazaar.......................................B3

goods. Towards the back of the bazaar you'll also find shops selling antiques and metalworkers making intricately engraved handcrafted trays and plates.

Kaymakamlar Museum MUSEUM
(Kaymakamlar Müze Evi; Hıdırlık Yokuşu Sokak; adult/child ₺5/4; ⏰9am-5.30pm) This typical Safranbolu home has all the classic features

CENTRAL ANATOLIA SAFRANBOLU

of Ottoman houses. Once owned by a lieutenant colonel, it still feels like an address of note as you climb the stairs looking up to the wooden ceiling decoration. Tableaux (featuring some rather weary mannequins) re-create scenes such as bathing in a cupboard and a wedding feast. There's a peaceful cafe in the garden outside.

Hıdırlık Tepe VIEWPOINT
(Hıdırlık Yokuşu Sokak; ₺1.50; ⊙8am-8pm) For the best vantage point over town head up to the top of Hıdırlık *tepe* (hill) where you'll find a park and cafe as well as excellent views.

İncekaya Aqueduct MONUMENT
(Su Kemeri) FREE Originally built in Byzantine times but restored in the 1790s by İzzet Mehmet Paşa, İncekaya ('thin rock') Aqueduct is just over 7km north of Safranbolu. You can't walk across it due to safety concerns, but just before the aqueduct an entrance leads down into the **Tokatlı Canyon** (Tokatlı Kanyonu; ₺4; ⊙8.30am-6.30pm) where there are excellent views looking back up to the arched stone structure from the wooden walkway. Nearby is the highly popular **Crystal Terrace** (Kristal Teras; ₺5.50; ⊙8.30am-6.30pm) – a glass viewing platform looking over the gorge, but not the aqueduct.

A taxi from Safranbolu costs ₺60 return including waiting time.

🏃 Activities

Cinci Hamam HAMAM
(☑0370-712 2103; Kazdağlıoğulu Meydanı; soak & scrub ₺45, full hamam with massage ₺82; ⊙men 6am-11pm, women 9am-10pm) One of the most renowned bathhouses in all of Turkey, with separate baths for men and women. If you're going to get scrubbed down to rosy-pink skin just once on your Turkey travels, this is the place to do it.

🛏 Sleeping

Efe Guesthouse GUESTHOUSE $
(☑0370-725 2688; Kayadibi Sokak 8; s/d/tr ₺110/160/175; 🖢) This place dishes up Safranbolu's Ottoman charm at backpacker prices. Snug, neat-as-a-pin rooms come with beamed walls and small bathrooms, while up top the terrace restaurant has views over town.

Bastoncu Konak GUESTHOUSE $
(☑0533 206 3725; Hıdırlık Yokuşu Sokak 4; r ₺150; 🖢) Bastoncu has four simple rooms on the upper floor of a 350-year-old building (entered through a ·souvenir shop). You want

either Room 104 or Room 101, as those are the two with all the original wooden wall panelling and ceilings. Breakfast is an extra ₺50.

★Selvili Köşk BOUTIQUE HOTEL $$
(☑0370-712 8646; www.selvilikosk.com; Mescit Sokak 23; s/d ₺130/200; 🖢) From the engraved banisters to the carved ceilings, this welcoming hotel, run by Hakan and Nihal, offers a step-back-in-time experience for lovers of ambience over amenities. Dazzling carpets cover every inch of floor and are layered over the *sedirs* (low bench seats), while local embroidered linens grace the beds in sun-drenched rooms. Grab Room 6 for a true Ottoman mansion experience with its wooden cupboard panelling running across the walls. Note that this room comes with a *gusülhane* (cupboard bathroom) so the less agile may want to give it a miss.

★Dadibra Konak BOUTIQUE HOTEL $$
(☑0370-712 1020; www.dadibrakonak.com; Altuğ Sokak 21; s/d/tr ₺180/300/350; 🖢) A contemporary take on Safranbolu's Ottoman aesthetic. Colourful, tassel-strewn textiles jazz up large beam-walled rooms, while downstairs the lounge/breakfast salon, with its chunky wood pillars and exposed stone walls, has shelves spilling over with cacti and succulents, and quirky cowbell mobiles strung from the ceiling. It's all topped off by a shady garden bursting with pink and purple blooms.

Kadıoğlu Şehzade Konakları HOTEL $$
(☑0370-712 5657; www.kadioglusehzade.com; Mescit Sokak 24; s/d ₺100/220; 🖢) Although a bigger hotel than many of Safranbolu's other offerings, the friendly, on-the-ball staff here create a homely atmosphere. Common areas are crammed full of local character with Turkish carpets, old photos and cabinets full of curios. Rooms are a bit plainer but good-sized (for Safranbolu); some have beamed-wall details and dark-wood-panel features.

Gülevi BOUTIQUE HOTEL $$$
(☑0370-725 4645; www.canbulat.com.tr; Hükümet Sokak 46; s €60-75, d €80-100, ste from €120; 🖢) Architect-design couple İbrahim and Gül have crafted what might be Safranbolu's most striking reinterpretation of the Ottoman aesthetic. 'Rose House' is an affordable masterpiece where urban luxury mingles seamlessly with traditional Ottoman design. Amid a shaded, grassy garden, the rooms (spread over three houses) are all soft colours, wood panelling and Turkmen carpets, set off by flamboyant artistic touches.

✕ Eating & Drinking

Eski Çarşı has plenty of small cafes offering menus dishing up Safranbolu's local cuisine (much of which hails from the Black Sea region). Also be sure to try all the flavours of the locally produced soda, Bağlar Gazozu, an institution since 1936.

There are plenty of cafes in Eski Çarşı. The nicest place for a wine is Taşev.

★ Atış Cafe   ANATOLIAN $
(Celal Bayer Caddesi; mains ₺17-35; ☺10am-10pm; 🕿🍴) Safranbolu has cute cafes dishing up regional cuisine aplenty, but Atış is our favourite for its solid home-style cooking. Dig into traditional dishes of *etli keşkek* (slow-cooked porridge of wheat, chickpeas and meat), *peruhi* (pasta parcels drenched in a butter sauce) and *bükme* (pastry filled with meat and spinach) on the itsy terrace or inside in the cosy floral-styled salon.

Safranbolu Sofrası   ANATOLIAN $
(Celal Bayer Caddesi; mains ₺18-30; ☺10.30am-10pm) This little place's cheerful, friendly service sets it apart. Tuck into freshly made *etli yaprak sarma* (stuffed vine leaves with meat) or try the Black Sea delicacy of *kuymak* (cheese and cornmeal fondue). Snag a front terrace table for excellent people-watching potential as the tour groups troop up to Kaymakamlar Museum.

Hanım Sultan   ANATOLIAN $
(Akın Sokak 6; mains ₺10-35; ☺11am-8.30pm) Squirrelled away down a little alleyway, this place rustles up rustic, wholesome cooking from simple plates of *gözleme* to local specialities such as *hingel mantı* (a fatter, more dumpling-style version of Turkish ravioli) for a hearty lunch.

Çızgi Cafe   ANATOLIAN $$
(☏0370-717 7840; Arasta Arkası Sokak; mains ₺15-45; ☺9.30am-11pm; 🕿) With outdoor seating on the square above and in the alleyway, plus cubby-hole dining inside, Çızgi has snagged prime territory. Order the *rum mantı* (Turkish ravioli served in a soy-sauce broth), which we think is the best in town, then kick back with a çay or nargile (water pipe) and watch the world go by.

Taşev   TURKISH $$
(☏0370-725 5300; www.tasevsanatvesarapevi.com; Hıdırlık Yokuşu Sokak 14; mains ₺25-60; ☺10am-11pm Tue-Sun; 🕿🍴) This is Safranbolu's bona fide contemporary dining option and it delivers with thick steaks and creamy pasta dishes. The Turkish cheese platter is a must for cheese lovers. Service is warm and waitstaff will helpfully explain menu items and help you choose from the extensive wine list.

🔒 Shopping

Shoe-Maker's Bazaar   MARKET
(Yemeniciler Arastası; Arasta Arkası Sokak; ☺9.30am-7pm) The restored Yemeniciler Arastası is the best place to start looking for crafts, although the makers of the light, flat-heeled shoes who used to work here have long since moved out. The cubbyhole stores are mostly home to textile shops. Be aware that prices tend to be high.

ℹ Information

Eski Çarşı has a bank and a couple of stand-alone ATMs on Kazdağlıoğulu Meydanı.

Tourist Office (☏0370-712 3863; www.safranboluturizmdanismaburosu.gov.tr; Hilmi Bayramgil Caddesi; ☺9am-5.30pm) One of Turkey's most helpful tourist information offices. Informed, multilingual staff can provide loads of tips and advice, and will even help with booking bus tickets.

ℹ Getting There & Away

If you're driving, exit the Ankara–İstanbul highway at Gerede and head north, following the signs for Karabük/Safranbolu.

Safranbolu Otogar (Safranbolu Bus Station; Adnan Menderes Bulvarı) is in upper Safranbolu (known as Kıranköy), 3km up the hill from Eski Çarşı. Regular dolmuşes (₺3, every 10 to 15 minutes) pass by the otogar. Flag them down from beside the pedestrian overpass directly in front of the otogar. They deposit you in central Kıranköy at the **dolmuş stand** (Adnan Menderes Bulvarı), from where you switch to another dolmuş that trundles down the hill to Eski Çarşı. Some hotels will do bus station pick-ups if you ask when booking.

Several bus companies share an office in central Kıranköy. Take the small side street with the sign 'Şehirlerarası Otobüs Bilet Satış Büroları', three blocks down Sadrı Artunç Caddesi, to find them. You can buy onward bus tickets here, and all the companies provide a free *servis* (shuttle bus) to the otogar.

Destinations with regular bus departures include the following:

Ankara (₺45, three to four hours, four morning, four afternoon, four evening)

Bartın (₺20, 1½ hours, hourly at quarter-past the hour)

İstanbul (₺100, seven to eight hours, every one to two hours)

Kastamonu (₺30, two hours, two morning, two afternoon, two evening)

Nevşehir (for Cappadocia, ₺100, 8½ hours, 10.30am)

For Amasra take a bus to Bartin and change there.

❶ Getting Around

Dolmuşes ply the route from Eski Çarşı's main square, over the hills and into central Kıranköy every 15 minutes (₺3). From the last stop, at Kıranköy dolmuş stand you can catch another minibus to Karabük, which passes by Safranbolu Otogar on its route. You only have to pay the bus fare once if you're going all the way.

A **taxi** (📞 0370-725 2595; Hilmi Bayramgil Caddesi) from Eski Çarşı to Kıranköy will cost around ₺22.

Yörük Köyü

Along the Kastamonu road, 15km east of Safranbolu, Yörük Köyü (Nomad Village) is a beautiful settlement of crumbling old houses once inhabited by the dervish Bektaşı sect. The government forced the nomads to settle here so it could tax them, and once they'd put down roots these new villagers grew rich from their baking prowess. There's little to do but wander the cobblestone alleys rimmed by traditional timber-framed *konaks* (mansions) and soak up the slumberous lost-in-time atmosphere. Visit on a weekday morning and it's likely you'll have Yörük Köyü's squiggly lanes all to yourself.

Sipahioğlu Konağı   HISTORIC BUILDING
(📞 0536 479 1050; Cemal İpekci Sokağı; ₺2; ⊙ approx 10am-5pm) Turkey has a glut of Ottoman houses thrown open to the public, but this one's in a league of its own. It's actually half of one enormous mansion that was divided in two by the builder's warring sons – the other half is Kasım Sipahioğlu Konağı – and you tour the sides separately. Sipahioğlu Konağı's interiors are immaculate with ornate, niche-studded wall panelling, a living room with an intricate *hazerpare* (radiating medallion design) ceiling and vibrant floral paintings decorating cornices and fireplaces.

Kasım Sipahioğlu Konağı   HISTORIC BUILDING
(Cemal İpekci Sokağı; ₺2; ⊙ approx 10am-5pm) Although the interiors here aren't as interesting as in neighbouring Sipahioğlu Konağı, it's well worth paying another ₺2 to see, as owner Filiz Teyze (Aunty Filiz) often shows

you around herself and she's quite the character. There is an excellent example of a traditional *gusülhane* (cupboard bathroom) upstairs and great rooftop views from the attic.

❶ Getting There & Away

There is no direct bus service from Safranbolu to Yörük Köyü, but **dolmuşes** (Hilmi Bayramgil Caddesi) to the nearby village of Konarı (₺5, 8.20am, 10.30am, 12.45pm, 2pm, 5pm and 7pm, fewer services on weekends) can drop you at the Yörük Köyü turn-off on the main road. From there it's a 1km walk to the village (though the drivers will often deviate off their course to take you right up to the village).

Çarşı Taksi charges ₺70 return, including waiting time, to Yörük Köyü from Safranbolu.

Kastamonu

📞 0366 / POP 148,930

At first glance Kastamonu doesn't seem to be anything other than a busy mid-sized town of little obvious tourist appeal, but veer into the helter-skelter of alleyways off bustling Cumhuriyet Caddesi and you'll discover decaying remnants of former glory at every turn. A wealth of Ottoman mansions slowly slumping and sliding into picturesque abandon line Kastamonu's lanes while market streets throng with locals on a bargain hunt. It's a glimpse of provincial Turkey yet to be trussed up for the tourists, while just out of town, Kasaba's intricately carved and painted wooden mosque provides enough of a reason to spend the night.

◎ Sights

★**Mahmud Bey Cami**   MOSQUE
(Kasaba Köyü; ⊙ 9am-5pm) **FREE** Amid rolling hills and fertile fields, the hamlet of Kasaba, 17km northwest of Kastamonu, is a pretty but unlikely place to find one of Turkey's finest surviving wooden mosques. Dating to 1366, the interior of Mahmud Bey Cami is a feast of intricate craftwork with painted wooden columns, a wooden gallery and finely painted ceiling rafters. You can climb some rough ladders to the gallery's third storey for closer views of the ornate beam-ends and interlocking motifs topping the pillars.

A return taxi from Kastamonu, with waiting time, costs around ₺80.

Nasrullah Meydanı   SQUARE
(off Cumhuriyet Caddesi) Leading off from Nasrullah Bridge, Kastamonu's main square centres on the Ottoman **Nasrullah Cami**

SERVICES FROM KASTAMONU OTOGAR

DESTINATION	FARE (₺)	DURATION (HR)	FREQUENCY
Amasya	75	4¼	3.30pm & 6.30pm
Ankara	45	4½-5	at least every 2 hours
İstanbul	100-110	8½-10	every 1 to 2 hours
Safranbolu	30	1½-2	4 morning, 2 afternoon, 3 evening
Samsun	75	4½	3 afternoon
Sinop	50	2½-3	1 morning, 2 afternoon, 1 evening

(1506). Poet Mehmet Akif Ersoy delivered speeches in this mosque during the War of Independence. The former seminary of **Münire Medresesi** at the rear houses craft shops. West of the square are old market buildings, including the decrepit **Aşirefendi Hanı** and the restored 15th-century **İsmail Bey Hanı**, now a hotel (⌨ 0366-214 2737; www.kursunluhan.com; Aktarlar Çarsısı; s/d ₺180/280; ☏).

Archaeology Museum   MUSEUM
(⌨ 0366-214 1070; Cumhuriyet Caddesi; ☉ 8.30am-12.30pm & 1.30-5.30pm Tue-Sun) **FREE** South of Nasrullah Bridge, this small museum has well-displayed exhibits and detailed information panels in English. The central hall is devoted to Kastamonu's role in Atatürk's sartorial revolution, while the left-hand room houses Hellenic and Roman finds. Upstairs are Hittite and Bronze Age exhibits from regional excavations.

🛏 Sleeping & Eating

⭐ **Uğurlu Konakları**   BOUTIQUE HOTEL **$$**
(⌨ 0366-212 8202; www.kastamonukonak lari.com; Şeyh Şaban Veli Caddesi 47-51; s/d/tr ₺150/250/330; ☏) A short walk from Kastamonu centre and the castle, this hotel comprises two Ottoman houses faithfully restored, with Indian carpets, red-brown trimmings and lashings of dark wood. Rooms in the front house are more appealing, leading off from atmospheric communal salons. There's a private garden outside. One room is fitted-out for disabled access. It's very popular and worth booking ahead.

Otel Mütevelli   BUSINESS HOTEL **$$**
(⌨ 0366-212 2020; www.mutevelli.com.tr; Cumhuriyet Caddesi 46; s/d/tr ₺160/250/300; ☏) This modern mid-rise does a buzzing trade with Turks in town on business and its popularity is well-earned. Bright rooms come with good amenities (including plenty of English channels on the TVs, kettles and good-sized, contemporary bathrooms), the

breakfast spread is top-notch and the location – just steps away from Nasrullah Meydanı – can't be beaten.

Münire Sultan Sofrası   ANATOLIAN **$**
(Nasrullah Meydanı; mains ₺10-22; ☉ noon-10pm) Tucked inside the Münire Medresesi complex, we like this place for its local specialities such as *banduma* (chicken and filo pastry drenched in butter and chopped walnuts) and *ecevit çorbası* (rice and yoghurt soup). Also big thumbs up for doing half portions; great for solo travellers. Order a glass of *eğşi* (sour plum drink) to wash it all down.

ⓘ Getting There & Away

Kastamonu Otogar (Kastamonu Bus Station; Kazım Karabekir Caddesi) is in the suburbs, 6km out of the centre. To get into town, catch a taxi (₺25) or hop on a city bus (₺2.25) from the bus stand marked 'Şehir Merkezi' in the bus parking lot next to the otogar. The buses all head down Cumhuriyet Caddesi and will drop you opposite Nasrullah Bridge.

Both Metro and Kamil Koç bus companies have offices for booking onward journeys in the centre of town on Cumhuriyet Caddesi, near Nasrullah Bridge.

Boğazkale & Hattuşa

⌨ 0364 / POP 1300

The village of Boğazkale has geese, cows and wheelbarrow-racing children wandering its narrow alleys; farmyards with Hittite and Byzantine gates; and a constant sense that a once-great city is just over the brow. Most visitors come solely to visit Hattuşa and Yazılıkaya, which can be accessed on foot if it's not too hot, but there is more to explore. Surrounded by valleys with Hittite caves, eagles' nests, butterflies and a Neolithic fort, the area around Hattuşa is ripe for hiking. Head 4km east of Yazılıkaya and climb **Yazılıkaya Dağı** to watch the sun set, or head to the **swimming hole** (locally known as *hoşur*) on the Budaközü River to cool off after Hittite rambles. Late in the day, the silence in Boğazkale is broken only by the occasional car kicking up dust on the main street, and the rural solitude may tempt you to stay an extra night.

◎ Sights

★ Boğazkale Museum   MUSEUM

(Sungurlu Asfalt Caddesi; ₺6; ⊙8am-6.45pm) Excellent information boards provide a thorough grounding in both Hittite history and culture while the pieces on display – all unearthed at Hattuşa – have been thoughtfully and artistically curated to aid visitor understanding. The pride of the collection are the two original sphinx statues that once stood guard at Hattuşa's Sphinx gate, atop the fortified mound above the postern gate of Yer Kapı. They were only returned to Boğazkale in 2011, having previously been on display in Berlin and İstanbul. It's one of the best little provincial museums in Turkey and a must for anyone interested in the Hittites.

Last tickets are sold at 4.45pm between November and March.

★ Hattuşa   ARCHAEOLOGICAL SITE

(₺10; ⊙8am-6.30pm) In the Bronze Age, the Hittite kingdom encompassed an area that stretched west to the Aegean Sea and south into Syria with its command centre here in the Hittite capital of Hattuşa. This mountainous, isolated site had a population of 15,000. Today the remnants of its defensive walls, with their ceremonial gateways and concealed postern tunnel, which wrap around the scattered ruins, are the most impressive remaining feature. If you're walking, a full circuit around the site with stops takes around three hours.

➡ Lower City & Temple

This vast complex, dating from the 14th century BC and destroyed around 1200 BC, is the closest archaeological site to the entrance gate and the best preserved of Hattuşa's Hittite temple ruins, but even so you'll still need plenty of imagination.

As you walk down the wide processional street, the administrative quarters of the temple are to your left. The well-worn cube of green nephrite rock here is thought to have played a significant role in the Hittite religion. The main temple, to your right, was surrounded by storerooms thought to be three storeys high. In the early 20th century, huge clay storage jars and thousands of cuneiform tablets were found in these rooms. Look for the threshold stones at the base of

some of the doorways to see the hole for the hinge-post and the arc worn by the door's movement. The temple is believed to have been a ritual altar for the deities Teshup and Hepatu; the large stone base of one of their statues remains.

➡ Sarı Kale

(Yellow Fortress) About 250m south of the lower city and temple ruins the road forks; take the right fork and follow the winding road up the hillside. On your left in the midst of the old city you can see several ruined structures. The rock-top ruins of the Sarı Kale may be a Phrygian fort on Hittite foundations.

➡ Yenıce Kale

Upon the top of this rock outcrop are the remains of the Yenıce Kale, which may have been a royal residence or small temple. You can climb to the summit from the east side.

➡ Aslanlı Kapı

(Lion's Gate) At Aslanlı Kapı, two stone lions (one rather poorly reconstructed) protect the city from evil spirits. This is one of at least six gates in Hattuşa's 4000-year-old defensive walls, though it may never have been completed. You can see the best-preserved parts of Hattuşa's fortifications from here, stretching southeast to Yer Kapı and from there to Kral Kapı. The walls illustrate the Hittites' engineering ingenuity, which enabled them to either build in sympathy with the terrain or transform the landscape, depending on what was required. Natural

---

❶ VISITING HATTUŞA

➡ The ruins are an easy, and extremely pretty, walk from Boğazkale.

➡ Arrive early in the morning to tour the ruins before the 21st century intrudes in the form of tour buses.

➡ Enter the lower city and temple ruins from the trail uphill from Hattuşa's ticket office, opposite the remains of a house on the slope.

➡ The circuit is a hilly 5km loop; if you want to walk, wear sturdy shoes and take enough water.

➡ There is very little shade so don't forget a hat and sunblock.

➡ The ticket office complex at the entrance has toilets and a cafe. There are no other facilities on-site.

Boğazkale & Hattuşa

outcrops were appropriated as part of the walls, and massive ramparts were built to create artificial fortresses.

➡ Yer Kapı

(Earth Gate) Hattuşa's star attraction is this postern gate complex with an artificial mound pierced by a 70m-long tunnel. The Hittites built the tunnel using a corbelled arch (two flat faces of stones leaning towards one another), as the 'true' arch was not invented until later. Primitive or not, the arch of Yer Kapı has done its job for millennia, and you can still pass down the stony tunnel as Hittite soldiers did, emerging from the postern. Afterwards, re-enter the city via one of the **monumental stairways** up the wide stone glacis and pass through the **Sphinx Gate**, once defended by four great sphinxes. Of the original statues, one is still in situ, two are in the Boğazkale Museum and the other has been lost. The two replica sphinxes gracing the inner gate here used to call the Boğazkale Museum home before the originals were returned in 2011.

There are wonderful views over the upper city temple district from here.

➡ Kral Kapı

(King's Gate) Kral Kapı is named after the regal-looking figure in the relief carving. The kingly character, a Hittite warrior god protecting the city, is (quite obviously) a copy; the original was removed to Ankara's Museum of Anatolian Civilisations (p404) for safekeeping.

➡ Nişantaş

At Nişantaş a rock with a faintly visible Hittite inscription cut into it narrates the deeds of Suppiluliuma II (1215–1200 BC), the final Hittite king.

➡ Güney Kale

(Southern Fortress) Immediately opposite Nişantaş, a path leads up to the excavated Güney Kale with a fine (fenced-off) hieroglyphics chamber with human figure reliefs.

➡ Büyük Kale

(Great Fortress) Although most of the Büyük Kale site has been excavated, many of the older layers of development have been re-covered to protect them, so what you see today can be hard to decipher. This fortress held the royal palace and the Hittite state archives.

Yazılıkaya   ROCK ART

(Yazılıkaya Yolu; ⊙8am-7pm) **FREE** Yazılıkaya means 'Inscribed Rock', and that's exactly what you'll find in these outdoor rock galleries, around 2km from Hattuşa. There are two galleries: the larger one, to the left, was the Hittite empire's holiest religious sanctuary; the narrower one, to the right, has the best-preserved carvings. Together they form the largest known Hittite rock sanctuary, sufficiently preserved to make you wish you could have seen the carvings when they were new.

In the larger gallery, Chamber A, there are the faded reliefs of numerous goddesses and pointy-hatted gods marching in procession. Heads and feet are shown in profile, but the torso is shown front on, a common feature of Hittite relief art. The lines of men and women lead to some large reliefs depicting a godly meeting. Teshup stands on two deified mountains (depicted as men) alongside his wife Hepatu, who is standing on the back of a panther. Behind her, their son and (possibly) two daughters are respectively carried by a smaller panther and a double-headed eagle. The largest relief, on the opposite wall, depicts the complex's bearded founder, King Tudhaliya IV, standing on two mountains. The rock ledges were probably used for offerings or sacrifices and the basins for libations.

On the way into Chamber B, you should supposedly ask permission of the winged, lion-headed guard depicted by the entrance before entering. The narrow gallery is thought to be a memorial chapel for Tudhaliya IV, dedicated by his son Suppiluliuma II. The large limestone block could have been the base of a statue of the king. Buried until a century ago and better protected from the elements, the carvings include a procession of 12 scimitar-wielding underworld gods. On the opposite wall, the detailed relief of Nergal depicts the underworld deity as a sword; the four lion heads on the handle (two pointing towards the blade, one to the left and the other to the right) double as the deity's knees and shoulders.

☞ Tours

Hattuşas Taxi CULTURAL
(☑ 0535 389 1089; www.hattusastaxi.com; Hattuşa, Yazılıkaya & Alacahöyük day tour per person ₺150)
Murat Bektaş is a mine of Hittite information and runs excellent tours in Hattuşa and around the surrounding area. If you can't get a group of at least three together for his well-priced full-day tour, he charges ₺300 for a tour of Hattuşa and Yazılıkaya, and ₺200 for Alacahöyük. Highly recommended.

🛏 Sleeping & Eating

Hittite Houses GUESTHOUSE $
(☑ 0364-452 2004; www.hattusas.com; Sungurlu Asfalt Caddesi; s/d/f ₺80/140/190; P😑🛜)

Behind a mocked-up Hittite wall facade, this hotel's modern, light-filled rooms (some with balconies) are a bargain, while the tranquil garden out front is a great place to wind down after a day's exploring. It's run by the knowledgeable owners of the Aşıkoğlu Hotel opposite, so guests have access to all the services there.

Aşıkoğlu Hotel & Pension GUESTHOUSE $$
(☑ 0364-452 2004; www.hattusas.com; Sungurlu Asfalt Caddesi; s ₺40-120, d ₺80-220, tr ₺260, campsite or caravan per person ₺40; P😑🛜)
Deniz and family serve up oodles of helpful local advice and friendly service at this welcoming hotel that's just the ticket for resting your head after visiting Hattuşa. Midrange rooms are large, spick and span and simply furnished, while a budget wing with small rooms (and tiny bathrooms) gives backpackers a cheap-and-cheerful option. The restaurant is Boğazkale's best eating choice.

Set menus cost ₺50 and there's decent wood-fired pide for ₺20 to ₺30. If you ring ahead the hotel can organise taxi pick-ups from Sungurlu otogar (bus station) or Yozgat otogar. As the rooms are unheated, during winter most guests prefer to bed down in Hittite Houses, the family's annexe-hotel across the road. Campers can use the next-door shady apple garden. Shared bathroom facilities are available.

Hitit Natural Park CAFE $
(Yazılıkaya Caddesi; gözleme ₺15, campsite or caravan per person ₺40; ⊙10am-8pm Apr-Nov)
In a prime position for lunch on the route between Yazılıkaya and Hattuşa, this garden cafe dishes up gözleme, tost (toasted sandwiches) and other Turkish light bites with seating in the wooden cabin or outside in wooden cabanas. There's also a shady campground set between cherry and pine trees, with shared toilets and showers, and campervan spaces (with electricity).

ℹ Information

There is a bank with an ATM in the village centre.

ℹ Getting There & Away

Boğazkale is accessed via either Sungurlu (31km northwest) or Yozgat (41km southeast).

There are two **dolmuşes** daily from Sungurlu at 7.30am and 5.30pm (₺5). They make the return journey from Boğazkale at 7am and 5pm. Due to this dire public transport situation, most people take a taxi. The going rate for a taxi between Sungurlu and Boğazkale is ₺60 to ₺80. Be aware that some taxi drivers at Sungurlu

THE HITTITES OF HATTUŞA

While the name may evoke images of skin-clad barbarians, the Hittites were a sophisticated people who commanded a vast Middle Eastern empire, conquered Babylon and challenged the Egyptian pharaohs more than 3000 years ago. Apart from a few written references in the Bible and Babylonian tablets, there were few clues to their existence until 1834 when a French traveller, Charles Texier, stumbled upon the ruins of the Hittite capital of Hattuşa.

In 1905 excavations turned up notable works of art and the Hittite state archives, written in cuneiform on thousands of clay tablets. From these tablets, historians and archaeologists were able to construct a history of the Hittite empire.

The original Indo-European Hittites swept into Anatolia around 2000 BC, conquering the local Hatti, from whom they borrowed their culture and name. They established themselves at Hattuşa, the Hatti capital, and in the course of a millennium enlarged and beautified the city. From 1660 to 1190 BC Hattuşa was the capital of first a Hittite kingdom and then empire that, at its height, shared Syria with Egypt and extended as far as Europe.

The Hittites worshipped over a thousand different deities; the most important were Teshup, the storm or weather god, and Hepatu, the sun goddess. The cuneiform tablets revealed a well-ordered society with more than 200 laws. The death sentence was prescribed for bestiality, while thieves got off more lightly provided they paid their victims compensation. Although it defeated Egypt in 1298 BC, the empire declined in the following centuries, undone by internal squabbles and new threats such as the invasion into Anatolia of the 'sea peoples'. Hattuşa was torched and its inhabitants dispersed. Only a few outlying city states survived until they, too, were swallowed by the Assyrians.

otogar (bus station) will try to insist on using their meter for the journey (resulting in a fare of over ₺150). You'll get the fairest price by preordering a taxi to pick you up from the otogar through Aşıkoğlu Hotel (p423) in Boğazkale.

If you're coming from Cappadocia the quickest access point to Boğazkale is via Yozgat. A Kamil Koç bus service to Yozgat leaves Göreme at 1.20pm daily (₺78, three hours). From Yozgat there is no public transport at all to Boğazkale so you need to take a taxi. Taxis should charge around ₺130 to ₺140, but again, some will insist on running the meter. To save hassle, ask Aşıkoğlu Hotel to organise a taxi to pick you up at Yozgat otogar.

ⓘ Getting Around

The Hattuşa entry gate is 1km from the Aşıkoğlu Hotel and Boğazkale Museum at the start of the village.

To get around Hattuşa and Yazılıkaya without your own transport you'll need to walk or hire a taxi. From the site entrance and ticket kiosk, the road looping around the site is 5km (not including Yazılıkaya, which is a further 2km away). The walk itself takes at least an hour and a half, plus time spent exploring the ruins, so figure on spending a good three hours here.

Boğazkale's two taxi drivers, Murat Bektaş and Sıddık Özel (☑ 0534 891 0653), can provide transport around the Hattuşa site as well as to outlying attractions and towns. Murat is also an excellent tour guide.

Alacahöyük

The tiny farming hamlet of Alacahöyük (25km north of Boğazkale and 45km south of Çorum) rims an archaeological site that dates back to the Chalcolithic era. It's most famous though for finds excavated here from the Bronze Age when it was first an important Hattian civilisation city-state and then later, a Hittite city. The excavation area and on-site museum make a good stop between Boğazkale and Çorum and the drive here itself, between rolling fields planted with wheat and beetroot, is a picturesque slice of rural Turkey. Come in spring for poppies and other wildflowers blooming between the ruins. There's a cafe/souvenir shop directly opposite the archaeological site's entrance, good for a cup of tea before hitting the road again.

◎ Sights

Alacahöyük
Excavation Area ARCHAEOLOGICAL SITE
(incl museum ₺6; ⊘ 8am-6.45pm) One of Turkey's most important Bronze Age sites (though settlement here actually stretches from the Chalcolithic through to the Iron Age), Alacahöyük's excavation area comprises a monumental gate with two sphinxes, a temple complex, a set of early Bronze Age royal shaft graves and a fortified postern gate with a tunnel passage you can still walk through.

The site is entered through the **Sphinx Gate** with two eyeless sphinxes guarding the door. The detailed reliefs bordering the gate are copies; the originals are in Ankara's Museum of Anatolian Civilisations (p404). They portray musicians, a sword swallower, animals for sacrifice and the Hittite king and queen – all part of festivities and ceremonies dedicated to the Hittite storm god Teshup, shown here as a bull. Once through the gate, the main excavations on the right-hand side are of a Hittite palace/temple complex.

To the left of the monumental gate, protected under plastic covers, are the pre-Hittite (Hattian civilisation-era) **royal shaft graves**. Dating to 2500 to 2000 BC, each skeleton was buried individually along with a variety of personal belongings and several oxen skulls, which archaeologists presume to be the leftovers of a funereal meal.

On the far left of the back of the excavation area is the ancient city's **postern gate**, a man-made stone and earthen mound with a vaulted tunnel running through it. Walk through and look down at the surrounding farm fields below to see how the Alacahöyük site was built up over the millennia.

Last tickets are 4.45pm from November to March.

Alacahöyük Museum   MUSEUM
(incl excavation area ₺6; ⊙8am-6.45pm) This little museum does a good job of explaining Alacahöyük's history and significance despite comprising only two rooms. One room is dedicated to small finds excavated at the site – most of the larger finds are on display in Ankara's Museum of Anatolian Civilisations – including idol figurines and a delicately beautiful deer statuette, while a second room details the history of archaeological work here.

ℹ Getting There & Away

There's no public transport between Alacahöyük and Boğazkale, so the best way to reach the site is by taxi (₺200 for a return fare, including waiting time) or with your own transport.

If you're really keen, you could take a bus or dolmuş from Çorum to Alaca and another from Alaca to Alacahöyük (one or two services per day on weekdays, none at weekends).

Çorum

📞 0364 / POP 294,800

Çorum's one claim to fame is that it is chickpea capital of Turkey. The town is stuffed with *leblebiciler* (chickpea roasters) and sacks upon sacks of the chalky little pulses, sorted according to fine distinctions obvious only to a chickpea dealer. It's a prosperous, busy but unremarkable provincial capital set on an alluvial plain on a branch of the Çorum River, but for non-chickpea fanatics there is one reason to stop. The Çorum Museum gives visitors a thorough grounding in the area's pre-Hittite and Hittite past so is an excellent preparation for Hattuşa.

Although Çorum can also serve as a base for exploring the region's ruins, unless you fancy a slice of its provincial town life head on to overnight in the more atmospheric, tiny village of Boğazkale, next to Hattuşa.

◉ Sights

Çorum Museum   MUSEUM
(Cengiz Topel Caddesi; ₺10;   ⊙8am-7pm) Çorum's museum is well worth a stop particularly if you're interested in Turkey's Chalcolithic, Bronze Age and Iron Age eras. Pieces have been cherry-picked from archaeological sites across the local region and there are excellent information panels in English throughout. Highlights include the stunning sword of Hittite king Tudhaliya from Hattuşa (p421), an intricate and tiny gold statuette of the Hittite fields god from Alacahöyük, and Hittite cult vessels decorated with bull and goat heads from Şapinuva.

In the same building (and included in the entrance fee), is the less impressive **Ethnographic Museum** containing the usual selection of mannequins making pots, drinking çay and so forth.

The museum is on the main road in the centre of town.

⊨ Sleeping

Grand Park Hotel   HOTEL **$**
(📞 0364-225 4131; www.grandpark.com.tr; İnönü Caddesi 60; s/d ₺110/160; ❀🐾) A typical Turkish provincial town hotel with good-sized rooms featuring beige-bland furniture and small but functional bathrooms. The friendly staff and lightning-bolt-fast wi-fi are a bonus.

Anitta Hotel   BUSINESS HOTEL **$$**
(📞 0364-666 0999; www.anittahotel.com; İnönü Caddesi 80; s/d ₺240/325; P❀❀🐾🏊) The snazziest hotel for miles. No it probably isn't the five stars it seems to have awarded itself, but this is a genuinely comfortable place to stay with further bonuses of super-keen staff and buckets of facilities including bar,

hamam (free for guests), pool and rooftop restaurant. Spacious rooms are white-on-cream minimalism with good-sized bathrooms; two have disabled access.

ⓘ Information

Tourist Information Booth (İnönü Caddesi; ⊙8.30am-12.30pm & 1.30-5pm) If you're heading to Hattuşa and surrounding sites after visiting Çorum, pop in here to pick up the good booklet on local sights (available in English, German and Japanese).

ⓘ Getting There & Away

Çorum otogar (Çorum Bus Station) is 3km out of the centre. Nearly all bus companies provide a free *servis* into town. A taxi costs around ₺17. If you just want to go into Çorum to visit the museum before heading onward, the otogar's *emanet* (left-luggage office) costs ₺10 per piece. Regular buses go to:

Ankara (₺40 to ₺50, four hours, every one to two hours)

Kayseri (₺55 to ₺65, 4¾ hours, one morning, two afternoon, five evening)

Samsun (₺30 to ₺35, 2¼-three hours, every one to 1½ hours)

Just behind the otogar, and connected to it, the **İlçe terminal** (Regional Bus Station) has dolmuş services to nearby towns including the following:

Alaca (₺8, 45 minutes, every one to two hours)

Amasya (₺20, 1½ hours, every 1½ to two hours 8am to 6pm)

Sungurlu (₺13, one hour, hourly)

Amasya

☑ 0358 / POP 149,080

Amasya is a tale of two shores. On the north of the Yeşilırmak River, rows of half-timbered Ottoman houses sit squeezed together like chocolate cakes in a patisserie window. To the south, the newer, more modern Turkey tries to get on with things in an outward-looking ode to the succession of empires that reigned in this narrow, rocky valley. Towering above the minarets and the *medreses* (seminaries) are pockmarks of Pontic tombs, etched into the high-rise bluff and guarded by a lofty citadel. Amasya's setting may evoke high drama but life here unfolds as slowly as the train takes apples out of town via a mountain tunnel. In local folklore, these tunnels were dug by Ferhat, a tragic star-crossed figure who was in love with Sirin, the sister of a sultan queen.

◉ Sights

◉ North of the River

The **Hatuniye Mahallesi** is Amasya's wonderful neighbourhood of restored Ottoman houses, interspersed with good modern reproductions, which lines the north bank of the river. After dark the riverfront buildings, and the castle and rock tombs on the hill behind, are lit up like an architectural Christmas tree with rather unsubtle blue and red up-lighting.

★**Tombs of the Pontic Kings**　　TOMB
(Kral Kaya Mezarları; ₺5; ⊙8.30am-6.30pm) Looming above the northern bank of the river is a sheer rock face with the conspicuous rock-cut Tombs of the Pontic Kings. The tombs, chiselled deep into the limestone as early as the 4th century BC, were used for cult worship of the deified rulers. Up close, they aren't that impressive, and some are covered in graffiti and have a distinct whiff of urine. They're much more striking when viewed, as a whole, from the southern bank of the river.

There are more than 20 (empty) tombs in the valley but there are four that you can walk up to. Climb the wooden steps from the souvenir stalls to the ticket office. Watch where you're stepping; the steps are poorly maintained and some are broken in places. Just past the office the path divides. Turn right to head to the **Tombs of Mythridates I, Ariobarzan & Mythridates II**, the first three kings of the kingdom of Pontus. There are impressive panoramas of the Amasya valley from up here. Turning left from the ticket office brings you first to the remnants of the **Baths of the Maidens Palace**, built in the 14th century. Afterwards, continue on through a rock-hewn tunnel to arrive at the **Tombs of Mythridates III & Pharnaces I**, the fourth and fifth kings.

At night the entire caboodle is lit up in a memorably garish fashion.

Hazeranlar Konağı　　HISTORIC BUILDING
(Hazeranlar Sokak; ₺5; ⊙8.30am-5pm Tue-Sun) The Hazeranlar Konağı, constructed in 1865 and restored in 1979, was built by Hasan Talat, the accountant of governor-poet Ziya Paşa, for his sister, Hazeran Hanım. The restored rooms are furnished in period style, with a refined feel to their chandeliers and carved wood. The **Directorate of Fine Arts gallery** in the basement has changing exhibitions.

Amasya

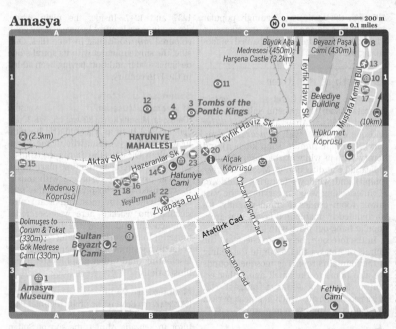

N ⌃ 0 ————— 200 m
0 ————— 0.1 miles

Amasya

⊚ Top Sights

⊚ Sights

✪ Activities, Courses & Tours

⊟ Sleeping

⊗ Eating

⊝ Drinking & Nightlife

Harşena Castle   CASTLE

(Harşena Kalesi; ₺5; ⊙8am-7pm) Perched precariously atop rocky Mt Harşena, Amasya's *kale* (castle) offers magnificent views down the valley. The much-repaired walls date from Pontic times, perhaps around King Mithridates' reign, but a fort stood here from the early Bronze Age. Destroyed and rebuilt by several empires, it once had eight defensive layers descending 300m to the Yeşılırmak River and a tunnel with 150 steps cut into the mountain.

To reach the castle turn left when you get to the **Büyük Ağa Medresesi** (Teyfik Havız Sokak) and follow the road for about 1km to a street on the left marked 'Kale'. It's 1.7km up the mountainside to the entrance.

If you're travelling with little ones in tow, keep a close eye on them; there are plenty of sheer drops and very few safety barriers.

Although the castle is exceedingly popular with families during the day, travellers are advised not to go up unaccompanied on foot during the evening.

👁 South of the River

★ Sultan Beyazıt II Cami   MOSQUE

(Ziyapaşa Bulvarı) The graceful Sultan Beyazıt II Cami (1486) is Amasya's largest *külliye* (mosque complex), with a *medrese* (seminary), fountain, *imaret* (soup kitchen) and library. With its white marble *mihrab* (niche indicating the direction of Mecca), *minber* (pulpit) and windows featuring *kündeka-ri* (interlocking wooden carvings), the vast prayer room exudes a grand serenity. It's surrounded by manicured lawns that are a popular hang-out place with locals.

In the forecourt, be sure to check out the murals of Amasya that decorate the ceiling of the fountain's roof. The mosque grounds are also home to the small and rather eccentric **Minyatür Amasya Müzesi** (₺2; ☺9am–noon & 1-7pm), which is a near perfect re-creation of Amasya in miniature.

★ Amasya Museum   MUSEUM

(☑0358-218 4513; Atatürk Caddesi; ₺6; ☺9.30am–6.45pm Tue-Sun) Amasya's museum packs in treasures from the Chalcolithic era up to the Byzantine age in its ground-floor galleries. Look out for the famous bronze statuette of Hittite storm god Teshup, which was unearthed locally. Upstairs, in the ethnographic section, a separate room holds the museum's highlight: a collection of mummies dating from the 14th-century İlkhan period. The bodies, mummified without removing the organs, were discovered beneath the Burmalı Minare Cami. They're not very suitable for squeamish or young eyes.

Gök Medrese Cami   MOSQUE

(Mosque of the Sky-Blue Seminary; Atatürk Caddesi) The Gök Medrese Cami was built from 1266 to 1267 for Seyfettin Torumtay, the Seljuk governor of Amasya. The *eyvan* (vaulted recess) serving as its main portal is unique in Anatolia, while the *kümbet* (domed tomb) was once covered in *gök* (sky-blue) tiles, hence the name. A full restoration of the mosque began in 2017 and was still ongoing during our last visit, though was nearing its final phase so check if it's open again when you're in town.

Burmalı Minare Cami   MOSQUE

(Twisted Minaret Mosque; Özkan Yalçın Caddesi) This Seljuk-era mosque was built between 1237 and 1247. Inside, the plain white, domed interior is offset by a very jazzy gold-coloured *mihrab* framed by blue tiles. Outside, the single minaret with its spiral stone design is a later addition, having been added in the 17th century.

Sabuncuoğlu History of Medicine Museum   MUSEUM

(Darüşşifa; Mustafa Kemal Bulvarı; ₺5; ☺8.30am–5pm Tue-Sun) Built as a psychiatric hospital in 1309 by Ilduş Hatun, wife of the İlkhanid Sultan Olcaytu, the Darüşşifa (Bimarhane) may have been the first place to try to treat psychiatric disorders with music. It was used as a hospital until the 18th century. One of the most important physicians who worked here was Serefedin Sabuncuoğlu and today the hospital is a museum to his work displaying some rather terrifying surgical equipment along with fascinating (and rather graphic) treatment illustrations.

Mehmet Paşa Cami   MOSQUE

(Mustafa Kemal Bulvarı) The pretty Mehmet Paşa Cami was built in 1486 by Lala Mehmet Paşa, tutor to Şehzade Ahmet, the son of Sultan Beyazıt II. It's rather simple inside but worth a look for the intricately carved *minber* and stained-glass-window details. The complex originally included the builder's tomb, an *imaret* (soup kitchen), *tabhane* (hospital), hamam and *handan* (inn).

🏃 Activities

Yıldız Hamamı   HAMAM

(Star Hamam; Hazeranlar Sokak; scrub & soak ₺21; ☺men 6-10am & 4-11pm, women 10am-4pm) Built by a Seljuk commander in the 13th century and restored in the 16th century, the Yıldız is a good hamam option on Amasya's north bank of the river.

Mustafa Bey Hamamı   HAMAM

(☑0358-218 3461; Mustafa Kemal Bulvarı; scrub & soak ₺23; ☺men 6-10am & 4-11pm, women 10am-4pm) Built in 1436, the Ottoman Mustafa Bey Hamamı is a suitably historic building to have a scrub-down in.

🛏 Sleeping

Şükrübey Konağı   GUESTHOUSE $

(☑0358-212 6285, 0507 298 2625; www.sukrubeykonagi.com.tr; Hazeranlar Sokak 55; s/d ₺80/170; 🛜) A sweet family choice. Presided over by a welcoming host, Şükrübey has simple, cosy rooms set around a courtyard. If you can snag one of the two that have narrow balconies overlooking the Yeşilırmak River, you're getting one of the best deals in town.

★**Uluhan Otel** BOUTIQUE HOTEL **$$**
(☑0358-212 7575; www.oteluluhan.com; Teyfik Haviz Sokak 15; s/d/tr ₺160/240/280, ste from ₺350; ❉ 🅪) Amasya's slickest operation by far, the Uluhan's two restored Ottoman buildings are home to good-sized rooms decked out in classic European style with carved wood ceilings and shiny modern bathrooms. Suites in the riverfront building have balconies, while most other rooms have views down onto the tranquil courtyard where guests sun themselves or relax with a drink.

★**Gönül Sefası** GUESTHOUSE **$$**
(☑0543 655 2032, 0358-218 0059; www.gonulsefasi.com; Yalıboyu Sokak 24; s/d/tr ₺140/220/260; 🅪) Antique farming equipment decorates the vine-shaded courtyard while Ottoman curios fill every nook in the little restaurant, adding lots of local character to this friendly family-run hotel. The large rooms, with comfy beds, are kept elegantly simple. Grab one of the two hosting teensy balconies over the Yeşilırmak River to make the most of this delightfully dinky place.

İlk Pansiyon GUESTHOUSE **$$**
(☑0358-218 6277; www.facebook.com/ilkpansiyon; Mustafapaşa Kemal Bulvarı; s/d ₺120/250; 🅪) This creaky old mansion, brimming with bric-a-brac, has rooms with traditional mattress-on-floor beds and original painted ceilings. Bathrooms are simple and could do with an update, but if you prefer character over amenities you can't help but be charmed by its old-fashioned style. There's a lovely plant-filled courtyard for breakfasting. It's down a tiny alley, signposted off the main drag.

Hasırcı Konakları GUESTHOUSE **$$**
(☑0358-218 0059; Hazeranlar Sokak 53; s/d ₺120/250; 🅪) The family that owns this six-room riverfront guesthouse is a genuinely welcoming bunch that goes out of their way to help. Rooms are spotless and very spacious (with good-sized bathrooms), but don't expect any character as they've been renovated in a bland modern fashion devoid of any style. Two rooms at the back have riverfront balconies.

✖ **Eating & Drinking**

★**Amaseia Mutfağı** ANATOLIAN **$**
(Hazeranlar Sokak; mains ₺15-35; ⊙11.30am-11pm) Head up the creaky stairs to the dining room of this old Ottoman house to dig into regional flavours of *etli bamya* (lady fingers and meat stew), *toyga çorbası* (a minty yoghurt, wheat and chickpea soup) and *mantı* (Turkish ravioli). If you're lucky, grab one of the tables on the tiny balcony for excellent riverfront views.

The menu offers typical Turkish grills as well but it's its local dishes you should be ordering.

Anadolu Mantı Evi ANATOLIAN **$**
(☑0358-212 3030; Hazeranlar Sokak 57a; mains ₺18-26; ⊙11am-10pm) Every version of *mantı* (Turkish ravioli) you know, and plenty that you may have never seen before – from bowls of the little dumplings drenched in walnut crumbs to a deep-fried version. Dine in the cheerful flower-filled courtyard or in the intimate blue-toned rooms overlooking the river.

They'll ask you if you want *şaramşık* (garlic) in your yoghurt sauce when you order; the answer is yes.

Sehzade Balık Ekmek TURKISH **$**
(Ziyapaşa Bulvarı; sandwiches ₺8-10; ⊙11am-11pm) *Balık ekmek* (fish sandwiches), *köfte ekmek* (meatball sandwiches) and *gözleme* served up on a boat moored on the Yeşilırmak. Skip it for dinner – when students are wooed in by incredibly loud Turkish rock music – but this is great stuff for a cheap lunch.

Amasya's food culture is intrinsically linked to the flavours of the Black Sea, so the *hamsi* (Black Sea anchovies) fish sandwich option is the local choice.

Sehr-i Zade Konağı Hotel Cafe CAFE
(Teyfik Haviz Sokak; ⊙10.30am-11pm) Amasya's best spot to park yourself up and sink a few beers. From the entrance, head out back, then up the stairs to the riverfront terrace to sit back and while away a couple of hours with an Efes in hand or *çay* (don't bother with the coffee: the lattes and cappuccinos are out of a packet).

ⓘ **Getting There & Away**

Amasya Otogar (Amasya Bus Station; Boğazköy) is inconveniently 10km northeast of the central city, on the main highway. All bus companies provide free *servises* to and from their respective booking offices in the centre. Taxis cost around ₺30.

Bus company offices including Kâmil Koç, Metro and Tokat Yildizi congregate around the *meydan* (town square).

The most convenient way to get to Tokat or Çorum is by dolmuş. Dolmuşes to Tokat (₺15,

1¾ hours, hourly between 8.30am and 7.30pm) leave from an **office-kiosk** (Atatürk Caddesi) opposite the Gök Medrese Cami.

Dolmuşes to Çorum (₺20, 1½ hours, hourly 8am to 10am, then noon, 1.30pm, 2.15pm, 4pm, 5.15pm and 6pm) are run by Lüks Hitit company and leave from its **office** (Atatürk Caddesi), directly behind the Amasya Park Mall, next to the Gök Medrese Cami.

From the otogar there are regular services to the following:

Ankara (₺60, five to six hours, four morning, hourly afternoon, two evening)

Kayseri (₺80, six to seven hours, three morning, four afternoon, two evening)

Samsun (₺25, 1¾ to 2½ hours, every one to 1½ hours)

Tokat (₺30, two hours, every one to two hours)

Tokat

📞 0356 / POP 201,300

Locals claim you can hear the steps of civilisations creeping up behind you in Tokat, where history buffs gorge themselves on the mosques, mansions, hamams and *hans* (caravanserais) in this ancient town at the heart of Anatolia.

The town's history features an inevitable roll call of Anatolian conquerors. The Hittites and Phrygians, the Medes and the Persians, the empire of Alexander the Great, the kingdom of Pontus, the Romans, the Byzantines, the Danışmend Turks, the Seljuks and the Mongol İlkhanids all once marched through this trading entrepôt.

Physically on the rise due to seven centuries of sodden silt, Tokat's architectural treats guarantee the town won't sink into obscurity any time soon. You can easily spend a day here exploring the mazy riddle of back alleys, visiting the excellent museum and getting knuckled by Tokat's notorious masseurs.

◎ Sights & Activities

The neighbourhood of squiggling lanes lined with old half-timbered Ottoman houses, behind the Taş Han and running west to Sulusokak Caddesi, is fun to explore. Sulusokak Caddesi runs west from the north side of Cumhuriyet Meydanı on GOP Bulvarı. It is home to many of Tokat's most interesting historic buildings. This road was the main thoroughfare through town before the perpendicular Samsun–Sivas road was improved in the 1960s.

Taş Han   HISTORIC BUILDING
(GOP Bulvarı; ⊙8am-8pm) **FREE** The 17th-century Taş Han is an Ottoman caravanserai and workshop. The shops within its arched arcades sell a mixture of hand-painted *yazmas* (headscarves) and other textiles, copper ware and knick-knacks. The courtyard is home to the **Divan Cafe** (⊙8am-11pm), which makes a good *Türk kahvesi* (Turkish coffee) stop while you're exploring.

★**Ulu Cami**   MOSQUE
(Cami Kabir Sokak) Tokat's historic neighbourhood of slouching Ottoman houses, nestled at the foot of the castle hill, hides this gem of a mosque with floral motifs crawling up the arched stone columns and a colourful painted wood-panel ceiling in dazzling orange and blue. To find it, take the lane off GOP Bulvarı just before the Taş Han and head up the hill.

Ali Paşa Cami   MOSQUE
(Ali Paşa Mosque; Sulusokak Caddesi) Classically Ottoman in architecture, Tokat's Ali Paşa Cami has been finely restored with its vast prayer hall under a grand central dome. It was built between 1566 and 1572. The mosque is just off GOP Bulvarı, behind the main square.

★**Tokat Museum**   MUSEUM
(Sulusokak Caddesi; ⊙8am-noon & 1-5pm Tue-Sun) **FREE** Tokat's impressive museum is housed within the beautifully restored Arastalı Bedesten (covered market). The collection packs in intricately decorated Bronze Age and Hittite artefacts, Phrygian ceramics, Hellenic jewellery, Roman tombs, and icons and relics from Tokat's churches (including a Greek Orthodox representation of John the Baptist with his head on a platter), all with plenty of English information to help you make sense of the vast amount of history on display here. It's easily one of central Anatolia's best museums.

Yağıbasan Medresesi   HISTORIC BUILDING
(Sulusokak Caddesi) This spectacular *medrese* (seminary) across the road from Tokat Museum was built in 1152 and was one of Anatolia's first open-domed *medreses*. Although the years-long restoration of the building had finally been completed in 2019, it had not yet been opened to the public at the time of research. It's well worth walking behind the building to snap a photo of its huge metal dome with the craggy contours of Tokat's castle cliff in the background.

Ali Paşa Hamam
HAMAM

(☑0356-214 4453; GOP Bulvarı; scrub & soak ₺28, massage ₺15; ⏱men 5am-11pm, women 9am-6pm) These baths, under domes studded with glass bulbs to admit natural light, were built in 1572 for Ali Paşa, one of the sons of Süleyman the Magnificent. It's professionally run, has separate bathing areas for men and women, and is known for its rather brutal traditional massages.

🛏 Sleeping

Çamlıca Otel
HOTEL $

(☑0356-214 1269; 79 GOP Bulvarı; s/d ₺80/150; 🛜) Look, don't expect anything flashy because then the small beige rooms are bound to disappoint, but this central cheapie is a comfortable, friendly and safe place to bed down for the night.

Tokat Dedeman
BUSINESS HOTEL $$

(☑0356-228 6600; www.dedeman.com; Orhangazi Caddesi 15; s/d €40/50; P🅿❄🛜🏊) The Dedeman arrived in town in 2017 and is by far the most comfortable place to sleep in Tokat. It's incredibly good value with spacious, contemporary rooms, a vast breakfast buffet, lobby bar, pool and gym. The only downside is that it's riverside, a 3km (flat) walk into the centre. Room rates are often cheaper if business is quiet.

Tokat Royal Otel
HOTEL $$

(☑0356-213 0314; www.tokatroyalotel.com; GOP Bulvarı 165; s/d ₺90/180; ❄🛜) New on the Tokat hotel scene, the Royal is in a great position, opposite the Taş Han. Good-value, large rooms are bright and fresh thanks to lots of white. Some come with little sitting areas for even more room to spread out.

🍴 Eating

★Chef Un's Çi Börek – Mantı
TURKISH $

(Mihatpaşa Caddesi; dishes ₺8-15; ⏱8am-8pm; 🛜) With its blue-and-white decor, Chef Un's has a vibe more Turkish Med than Anatolian heartland. And you know the *mantı* (Turkish ravioli) has got to be good when Turks are crammed in at lunchtime slurping down bowls of the stuff. It does *börek* (filled pastries) as well, and good soup, but the *mantı* is what it's known for.

Plevne Restaurant
TURKISH $

(Sulusokak Caddesi; mains ₺12-25; ⏱8am-10pm; 🍴) We've eaten a lot of pide in our time and we'll stick our neck out to say Plevne dishes up some of the best in Turkey. Order the *karaşık* (mixed toppings) for a supreme feast. Service is super friendly and the black-and-white decor with red strip-lighting running along the walls adds a cheerfully weird element to your meal.

Ocakbaşı Mis Kebap
KEBAB $$

(Hükümet Caddesi; mains ₺22-33; ⏱10am-11pm) Ask a local where the best *tokat kebaps* (garlicky lamb, potato and eggplant kebap), and pretty much any other kind of kebap, can be found and there's a good chance they'll send you to this bustling restaurant. The monster-sized *tokat kebap* (₺55) is a must if you're not dining solo.

ⓘ Getting There & Away

Tokat Otogar (Tokat Bus Station; Gültekin Topçam Bulvarı) is about 1.7km northeast of the main square. Bus companies should provide a *servis* to ferry you to/from town, but they can take a while to turn up. If you don't want to wait, a taxi will cost about ₺15.

Several bus companies have ticket offices around Cumhuriyet Meydanı. Bus-company offices in the centre will also provide a free *servis* to the otogar. Local bus companies Tokat Yıldızı (www.tokatyildizi.com) and Tokat Seyahat offer the most departures.

Services include the following:

Amasya (₺30, 1¾ hours, every one to two hours)

Ankara (₺90, seven hours, one morning, hourly afternoon, three evening)

İstanbul (₺150, 11 to 13 hours, one morning, hourly evening)

Kayseri (₺60, five hours, every one to 1½ hours)

Samsun (₺50, three hours, three morning, every one to two hours afternoon and evening)

Sivas (₺25 to ₺30, two hours, hourly)

Local dolmuşes leave from the separate **İlçe ve Köy Terminal** (Regional Bus Station; Meydan Caddesi), east from the Taş Han, though restoration was underway in this area so the station may move.

Sivas

☑0346 / POP 377,560

With a colourful, sometimes tragic history and some of the finest Seljuk buildings ever erected, Sivas is a good stopover en route to the wild east. The city lies at the heart of Turkey politically as well as geographically, thanks to its role in the run-up to the War of Independence. The Congress building resounded with plans, strategies and principles as Atatürk and his adherents discussed

Sivas

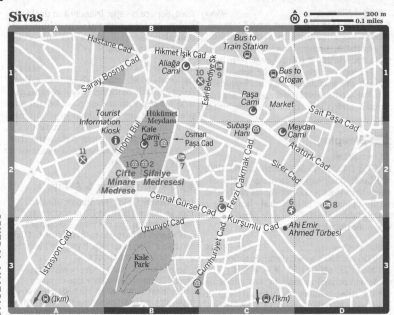

Sivas

◎ Top Sights
1 Çifte Minare Medrese	B2
2 Şifaiye Medresesi	B2

◎ Sights
3 Bürüciye Medresesi	B2
4 Gök Medrese	B3
5 Ulu Cami	C2

✈ Activities, Courses & Tours
6 Kurşunlu Hamam	C2

🛏 Sleeping
7 Buruciye Otel	B2
8 Otel Çakır	D2
9 Sultan Otel	C1

🍴 Eating
10 Lezzetçi	C1
11 Sema Hanımın Yeri	A2

their great goal of liberation. At night, as the red flags on the *meydan* (town square) compete for attention with the spotlit minarets nearby, İnönü Bulvarı might be central Anatolia's slickest thoroughfare outside Ankara. The occasional horse and cart gallops down the boulevard, past the neon lights, like a ghost of Anatolia's past.

◉ Sights & Activities

★ **Şifaiye Medresesi**   HISTORIC BUILDING
(Hükümet Meydanı) **FREE** Dating to 1218, this was one of the most important medical schools built by the Seljuks and was once Anatolia's foremost hospital.

The decoration features stylised sun/lion and moon/bull motifs, blue Azeri tile work and a poem in Arabic composed by the sultan. Today the courtyard is chock-a-block with cafe tables while the surrounding *eyvans* (vaulted halls) are home to souvenir stalls. Look to the right as you enter the courtyard to see the porch that was walled up as a tomb for Sultan İzzettin Keykavus I, who commissioned the building before he died of tuberculosis. Come in the early evening as the sun sets and swallows swoop between the minarets of the neighbouring mosques and you could imagine yourself in Iran.

★ **Çifte Minare Medrese**   HISTORIC BUILDING
(Seminary of the Twin Minarets; Hükümet Meydanı) **FREE** Commissioned by the Mongol-İlkhanid vizier Şemsettin Güveyni after defeating the Seljuks at the battle of Kosedağ, the Çifte Minare Medrese (1271) has a *çifte* (pair) of mighty red-brick and blue-tile minarets. In fact, that's about all that is left standing of this *medrese,* along with the elaborate portal front facade. Stand on the

path between the Çifte and Şifaiye Medresesi to see the difference made by half a century and a shift in power.

Bürüciye Medresesi
HISTORIC BUILDING

(Hükümet Meydanı; ⊙ cafe 9am-10pm Jun-Aug) **FREE** The Bürüciye Medresesi's monumental Seljuk gateway is a fitting entry to this *medrese*, built to teach 'positive sciences' in 1271. Inside, in a modest salon to the left of the entrance, is the tiled tomb of the building's sponsor, Iranian businessman Muzaffer Bürücerdi. The courtyard interior is often used for exhibitions and during the summer months it's used as a cafe. During the evening it's a good place to sit back with a çay.

Ulu Cami
MOSQUE

(Great Mosque; Cemal Gürsel Caddesi) The Ulu Cami (1197) is Sivas' oldest significant building, and one of Anatolia's oldest mosques. Built by the Danışmends, it's a large, low room with a forest of 50 columns. The superfat brick minaret was added in 1213 and if you look at it from the southern side of the road you'll notice it has a very distinct tilt. Inside, 11 handmade stone bands surround the main prayer area and the ornate *mihrab* was discovered during renovations in 1955.

Gök Medrese
HISTORIC BUILDING

(Sky-Blue Seminary; Cumhuriyet Caddesi) Having been shuttered for years, the Gök Medrese was nearing the end of an extensive restoration project on our last visit. Built in 1271 at the behest of Sahib-i Ata, the grand vizier or Sultan Giyasettin Keyhüsrev III, its exuberantly decorated marble portal, twin blue-tile and red-brick minarets (which were still covered in scaffolding while we were in town) and carved circular corner buttresses are a fabulous example of Seljuk-era architecture.

Kurşunlu Hamam
HAMAM

(☑ men 0346-222 1378, women 0346-221 4790; Kurşunlu Caddesi; soak & scrub ₺25, massage ₺18; ⊙ men 7am-11pm, women 9am-6pm) Built in 1576 this huge, multiple-domed structure had the indignity of being put to work as a salt warehouse for 30 years before it was restored to its former glory and put back into service as a hamam. There are separate men's and women's sections.

🛏 Sleeping & Eating

Otel Çakır
HOTEL $

(☑ 0346-222 4526; www.cakiroteli.com; Kurşunlu Caddesi; s/d ₺90/140; 🗑) As long as you don't expect any frills, the Çakır is a fine place to bed down for the night. The poky rooms are clean and tidy and the friendly manager speaks a smattering of English.

★ Buruciye Otel
HOTEL $$

(☑ 0346-222 4020; www.buruciyeotel.com.tr; Hoca İmam Caddesi 18; s/d ₺145/240; 🅿 😊 ❄ 🗑) You're not going to get a more central hotel than this, just steps from the main square and with views of the Çifte Minare Medrese's minarets from some rooms. The Buruciye is excellent value with comfortable, classically styled rooms, home to mod-con home comforts (big flat-screen TVs, kettles, spacious showers), plus friendly, helpful staff.

Sultan Otel
HOTEL $$

(☑ 0346-221 2986; www.sultanotel.com.tr; Eski Belediye Sokak 18; s/d ₺130/180; 😊 ❄ 🗑) This boutique-style hotel has 27 rooms brushed up with swanky fixtures and furnishings in soft sage and neutral tones, while the bathrooms are sparkling and modern. Some are a wee bit on the small side though. It's all squeaky-clean and professionally run, with a rooftop bar-restaurant to add to the mix.

Sema Hanımın Yeri
ANATOLIAN $

(☑ 0346-223 9496; Reşat Şemsettin Sokak; mains ₺12-20; ⊙ 8am-11pm) The welcoming Madame Sema serves home-cooked food such as *içli köfte* (meatballs stuffed with spices and nuts) in this small restaurant tucked down a backstreet off İnönü Caddesi.

★ Lezzetçi
KEBAB $$

(☑ 0346-224 2747; Aliağa Camii Sokak 12; mains ₺15-40; ⊙ 8am-midnight; 🗑) This poshed-up pide and kebap restaurant, complete with exposed-brick walls and modern chandelier lighting, does food as good as its decor. Have the *beyti kebap* (spicy ground meat baked in a thin layer of bread) or feast on the *sivas kebapı* (lamb, aubergine and peppers, similar to a *tokat kebap*; half/full portion for two people ₺40/65).

ⓘ Getting There & Away

BUS

Bus services from **Sivas Otogar** (Sivas Bus Station; Kayseri Caddesi) aren't all that frequent. The most regular services from the otogar include the following:

Amasya (₺40 to ₺50, 3¼-four hours, every one to two hours)

Ankara (₺60 to ₺80, six-7½ hours, two morning, every one to two hours afternoon and evening)

Kayseri (₺30 to ₺40, three hours, hourly)

Malatya (₺50, 3½ hours, 8am, 10am, noon, 2.30pm and 5.30pm; services are run by Hekimhan Net bus company)

DİVRİĞİ'S ULU CAMİ & DARÜŞŞİFASI

The quadruplet of 780-year-old stone doorways on Divriği's **Ulu Cami and Darüşşifası** (Grand Mosque & Hospital; Ulu Cami Sokak; ⊙8am-5pm) **FREE** complex are so intricately carved that some say their artisanship proves the existence of god. Although the sleepy settlement of Divriği seems an obscure place for one of Turkey's finest old religious structures, this was once the capital of a Seljuk *beylik* (principality), ruled over by the local emir Ahmet Şah and his wife, Melike Turan Melik, who founded the adjoining institutions in 1228.

The Ulu Cami is currently undergoing a major restoration project, repairing its roof to protect the building from water damage. Nobody can enter the building during this time and the facade is covered in scaffolding. Restoration work is planned to finish by 2021. Check in Sivas before making the long drive out here.

Dolmuş (minibus) services from Sivas leave from the terminal beside Sivas otogar at 9am, noon, 3pm and 5pm (₺25, 2½ hours). From Divriği back to Sivas they leave at 8.30am, noon and 4.30pm. All stop in Kangal.

Drivers should note that there's no through road to Erzincan from Divriği, forcing you to head northwest to Zara and the highway before you can start driving east.

Samsun (₺60 to ₺70, 5¼-6½ hours, three morning, four afternoon, hourly evening)

Tokat (₺25 to ₺30, two hours, hourly)

Many bus companies provide a free *servis* (shuttle bus) into the city centre. A taxi costs ₺15. City buses (₺2 plus ₺3 for Kentkart rechargeable transport card) run between the otogar and the central city, via Atatürk Caddesi.

TRAIN

Sivas Train Station (Sivas Garı; ☑ 0346-221 7000; www.tcddtasimacilik.gov.tr; İstasyon Caddesi) is a major rail junction for both east–west and north–south lines, though the times the trains pull into town makes taking the train from here not very appealing. The main daily express service is the Doğu Ekspresi between Ankara and Kars. The Van Gölü Ekspresi between Ankara and Tatvan stops here twice a week and the Güney Kurtalan Ekspresi between Ankara and Diyarbakır, five times weekly.

There are also local services to Divriği.

A bus runs to the train station from Hikmet İşik Caddesi.

Konya

☑ 0332 / POP 1.4 MILLION

An economic powerhouse that is religiously inspired and a busy university city that's as conservative as they come: Konya treads a delicate path between its historical significance as the hometown of the whirling dervish orders and a bastion of Seljuk culture, and its modern importance as an industrial boom town. The city derives considerable charm from this juxtaposition of old and new. Ancient mosques and the maze-like market district rub up against contemporary Konya around Alaaddin Tepesi, where hip-looking university students talk religion and politics in the tea gardens. If you are passing through this region, say from the coast to Cappadocia, then make time to explore one of Turkey's most compelling cities.

⊙ Sights

★**Mevlâna Museum**　　　MUSEUM
(☑ 0332-351 1215; Aslanlı Kışla Caddesi; audio guide ₺10; ⊙9am-6.30pm May-Sep, to 5pm Oct-Apr) **FREE** For Muslims and non-Muslims alike, the main reason to come to Konya is to visit this former lodge of the whirling dervishes and home to the tomb of Celaleddin Rumi (later known as Mevlâna), who we have to thank for giving the world the whirling dervishes. This is one of the biggest pilgrimage centres in Turkey, and the building's fluted dome of turquoise tiles is one of Turkey's most distinctive sights.

For Muslims, this is a very holy place, and more than 1.5 million people visit it a year, most of them Turkish. You will see many people praying for Rumi's help. When entering the mausoleum everyone must wear the plastic shoe-coverings provided, women should cover their head and no one should wear singlets or shorts.

After walking through a pretty garden you pass through the **Dervişan Kapısı** (Gate of the Dervishes) and enter a courtyard with an ablutions fountain in the centre.

At the entrance to the **mausoleum**, the Ottoman silver door bears the inscription, 'Those who enter here incomplete will come out perfect'. Once inside the mausoleum, look out for the big bronze Nisan tası (April bowl) on the left. April rainwater, vital to the farmers of this region, is still considered sacred and was collected in this 13th-century bowl. The tip of Mevlâna's turban was dipped in the water and offered to those in need of healing. Also on the left are six sarcophagi belonging to Bahaeddin Veled's supporters who followed him from Afghanistan.

Continue through to the part of the room directly under the fluted dome. Here you can see Mevlâna's Tomb (the largest), flanked by that of his son Sultan Veled and those of other eminent dervishes. They are all covered in velvet shrouds heavy with gold embroidery, but those of Mevlâna and Veled bear huge turbans, symbols of spiritual authority; the number of wraps denotes the level of spiritual importance. Bahaeddin Veled's wooden tomb stands on one end, leading devotees to say Mevlâna was so holy that even his father stands to show respect. There are 66 sarcophagi on the platform, not all visible.

Mevlâna's tomb dates from Seljuk times. The mosque and *semahane*, the hall where whirling ceremonies were held, were added later by Ottoman sultans (Mehmet the Conqueror was a Mevlevi adherent and Süleyman the Magnificent made charitable donations to the order). Selim I, conqueror of Egypt, donated the Mamluk crystal lamps.

The semahane to the left of the sepulchral chamber contains exhibits such as the original copy of the *Mathnawi*, Mevlâna's cape and other clothing, a 9th-century gazelle-skin Christian manuscript and a copy of the Koran so tiny that its author went blind writing it. In the middle of the room is a display case holding a casket that contains strands of Mohammed's beard. The small mosque in front of the *semahane* is reserved for prayers but as you exit the building, look to the left of the *mihrab* for a *seccade* (prayer carpet) bearing a picture of the Kaaba at Mecca. Made in Iran of silk and wool, it's extremely fine, with some three million knots (144 per sq cm).

CENTRAL ANATOLIA KONYA

DON'T MISS

WATCHING THE WHIRLING DERVISHES

The Mevlevi worship ceremony *(sema)*, is a ritual dance representing union with the divine; it's what gives the dervishes their famous whirl, and appears on Unesco's third Proclamation of Masterpieces of the Oral and Intangible Heritage of Humanity. Watching a *sema* can be an evocative, romantic, unforgettable experience. There are many dervish orders worldwide that perform similar rituals, but the original Turkish version is the smoothest and purest, more of an elegant, trancelike dance than the raw energy seen elsewhere.

The dervishes dress in long white robes with full skirts that represent their shrouds. Their voluminous black cloaks symbolise their worldly tombs, their conical felt hats their tombstones.

The ceremony begins when the *hafız*, a scholar who has committed the entire Koran to memory, intones a prayer for Mevlâna and a verse from the Koran. A kettledrum booms out, followed by the plaintive sound of the *ney* (reed flute). Then the *şeyh* (master) bows and leads the dervishes in a circle around the hall. After three circuits, the dervishes drop their black cloaks to symbolise their deliverance from worldly attachments. Then one by one, arms folded on their breasts, they spin out onto the floor as they relinquish the earthly life to be reborn in mystical union with the divine.

By holding their right arms up, they receive the blessings of heaven, which are communicated to earth by holding their left arms turned down. As they whirl, they form a 'constellation' of revolving bodies, which itself slowly rotates. The *şeyh* walks among them to check that each dervish is performing the ritual properly.

The dance is repeated over and over again. Finally, the *hafız* again chants passages from the Koran, thus sealing the mystical union with the divine.

It's worthwhile planning your Konya trip to be here when the *sema* ceremony is performed:

Mevlâna Culture Centre (Whirling Dervish Performance; www.emav.org; Aslanlı Kışla Caddesi; ₺15; ☉7pm Sat) This venue hosts a whirling dervish *sema* every Saturday night year-round. There's no pre-booking; just turn up about 30 minutes beforehand.

Mevlâna Museum Rose Garden (Mevlâna Museum Gardens, Aslanlı Kışla Caddesi; ☉8.45pm Thu Jun-Sep) FREE During summer there is a wonderfully intimate Thursday night *sema* performance, outdoors in the garden of the Mevlâna Museum.

Konya

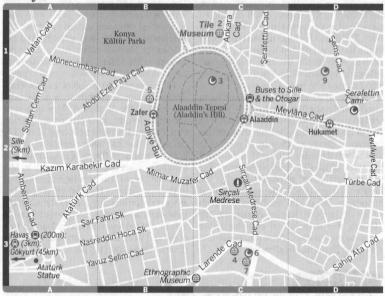

The **matbah** (kitchen) of the lodge is in the southwest corner of the courtyard. It is decorated as it would have been in Mevlâna's day, with mannequins dressed as dervishes. Look out for the wooden practice board, used by novice dervishes to learn to whirl. The **dervish cells** (where the dervishes lived) run along the northern and western sides of the courtyard. Inside the cells are a host of ethnographic displays relating to dervish life. In particular, one room contains personal items belonging to Şems of Tabriz including his hat and a manuscript of the *Mâkâlât*, his most famous work.

The complex can get oppressively busy, and seeing any of the contents of the museum display cases can be a pushing and shoving, head-ducking affair. Come early on a weekday if you want to see all the items in peace. On the other hand, the atmosphere on busy days is almost addictive and more than makes up for not being able to properly examine the museum pieces.

Beside the museum is the **Selimiye Cami** (Mevlâna Caddesi).

Şems-i Tebrizi Cami
MOSQUE

(Şems Caddesi) An important pilgrimage place, this mosque contains the elegant 14th-century tomb of Rumi's spiritual mentor, Şemsi Tebrizi (Şems of Tabriz). It's in a park just northwest of Hükümet Meydanı.

★ Tile Museum
MUSEUM

(Karatay Medresesi Çini Müzesi; ☑ 0332-351 1914; Ankara Caddesi; ₺6; ☺ 9am-6.40pm) Gorgeously restored, the interior central dome and walls of this former Seljuk theological school (1251) showcase some finely preserved blue-and-white Seljuk tile work. There is also an outstanding collection of ceramics on display including exhibits of the octagonal Seljuk tiles unearthed during excavations at Kubad Abad Palace on Lake Beyşehir. Emir Celaleddin Karatay, a Seljuk general, vizier and statesman who built the *medrese,* is buried in one of the corner rooms.

Museum of Wooden Artefacts & Stone Carving
MUSEUM

(Tas ve Ahsap Eserler Müzesi; ☑ 0332-351 3204; Adliye Bulvarı; ₺6; ☺ 9am-6.40pm) The İnce Minare Medresesi (Seminary of the Slender Minaret), now a museum, was built in 1264 for Seljuk vizier Sahip Ata. Inside, many of the carvings feature motifs similar to those used in tiles and ceramics. The Seljuks didn't heed Islam's traditional prohibition against human and animal images: there are images of birds (the Seljuk double-headed eagle, for example), humans, lions and leopards. The octagonal **minaret** in turquoise relief outside is over 600 years old and gave the seminary its popular name. If it looks short, this is because the top was sliced off by lightning.

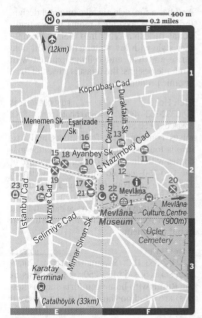

Alaaddin Cami   MOSQUE

(Alaaddin Tepesi) Konya's most important religious building after the Mevlâna shrine, this Seljuk mosque bestrides Alaaddin Tepesi. Built for Alaeddin Keykubad I, Sultan of Rum from 1219 to 1231, the rambling 13th-century building was designed by a Damascene architect in Arab style. Over the centuries it was embellished, refurbished, ruined and restored. The grand original entrance on the northern side incorporates decoration from earlier Byzantine and Roman buildings. Surrounding the mosque is **Alaaddin Tepesi**, the town's favourite flower garden and park. There are several pleasant tea shops and cafes here.

The mosque and some of the surrounding area on Alaaddin Tepesi have been undergoing a huge restoration for the past few years so expect some scaffolding.

Sahib-i Ata Külliyesi   MOSQUE

(Larende Caddesi) Behind its requisite grand entrance is the Sahib-i Ata Külliyesi, originally constructed during the reign of Alaaddin Keykavus. Destroyed by fire in 1871, it was rebuilt in 13th-century style. The *mihrab* is a fine example of blue Seljuk tile work.

Sahib-i Ata Vakıf Müzesi   MUSEUM

(Sırçalı Medrese Caddesi; ⊙ 9am-12.30pm & 1-5pm Tue-Sun) **FREE** This old dervish lodge, with its red-brick and blue-tiled interior, is home to the Sahib-i Ata Vakıf Müzesi, with an interesting collection of religious artefacts.

Archaeological Museum   MUSEUM

(☑ 0332-351 3207; Larende Caddesi; ₺5; ⊙ 9am-12.30pm & 1.30-5pm) The rather dusty Archaeological Museum houses interesting finds from Çatalhöyük (p440), including the skeleton of a baby girl, clutching jewellery made of stone and bone, and a geometric wall painting discovered on-site in 2011 and transplanted to the museum in 2016. Other artefacts range across the millennia, from Chalcolithic terracotta jars to Hittite hieroglyphs, an Assyrian oil lamp shaped like a bunch of grapes, and bronze and stone Roman sarcophagi, one narrating the labours of Hercules in high-relief carvings. There's an official ticket price but last time we were here, they were letting visitors in for free.

🎊 Festivals & Events

Mevlâna Festival RELIGIOUS
(Mevlâna Culture Centre) The annual Mevlâna Festival runs for a fortnight, culminating on 17 December, the anniversary of Mevlâna's 'wedding night' with Allah. Tickets (and accommodation) should be booked well in advance; contact the tourist office for assistance. If you can't get a ticket, other venues around town host dancers during the festival, although they are not of the same quality.

🛏 Sleeping

Hotel Yasin HOTEL **$**
(✆0332-351 1624; www.otelyasin.com; Yusuf Ağa Sokak 21; s/d ₺50/100; 🛜) In the heart of the souk, this place has more than just price going for it. Backpackers will find decently maintained, amply proportioned, light-filled rooms and friendly management.

Otel Derya HOTEL **$**
(✆0332-352 0154; Ayanbey Sokak 18; s/d ₺100/160; ❄🛜) Bring on the sparkles. The lobby is the epitome of Turkish-glitz complete with crystal-studded wall decor and plastic-fantastic palm central feature. Luckily all the glitter doesn't follow you into the rooms, which are decked out in a more moderate colour scheme of lime green and white.

Mevlâna Sema Otel HOTEL **$**
(✆0332-350 4623; Mevlâna Caddesi 67; s/d ₺80/140; ❄🛜) The lobby area has had a swish makeover but unfortunately the update has yet to move on to the small rooms, which are looking worn these days. Nevertheless, the Sema is a safe and exceedingly well-located bet. Ask for a rear-facing room to avoid the din of the main road.

★ Derviş Otel BOUTIQUE HOTEL **$$**
(✆0542 375 6261; www.dervishotel.com; Güngör Sokak 7; s/tr €40/90, d €50-60; ❄❄🛜) This airy, light-filled, 200-year-old house has been converted into a rather wonderful boutique hotel. All seven spacious rooms have soft colour schemes with local carpets covering the wooden floors, comfortable beds and modern bathrooms to boot. With enthusiastic management providing truly personal service, this is a top-notch alternative to Konya's more anonymous hotels.

Araf Hotel BOUTIQUE HOTEL **$$**
(✆0332-350 4444; www.arafhotel.com; Nacı Fikrit Sokak 3; s ₺160-190, d ₺190-245; ❄🛜) As colourful as a pack of pick 'n' mix sweets, the Araf has a fun, eclectic take on hotel design. Individually decorated rooms weave traditional Turkish accents into their contemporary style with art, statement walls in bold cerise and teal, and ceilings painted with İznik tile designs. Breakfast is a feast of local organic produce.

Hich Hotel BOUTIQUE HOTEL **$$**
(✆0332-353 4424; www.hichhotel.com; Celal Sokak 6; r €50-80; ❄❄🛜) This design hotel mixes contemporary furnishings and luxurious touches such as espresso coffee machines with the elegant original structure of the two 150-year-old buildings it occupies. There are gorgeous floor tiles and stained-glass window features in abundance. Outside is a sunny garden terrace cafe and you can spin your way to the Mevlâna Museum in but a moment.

Hotel Rumi HOTEL **$$**
(✆0332-353 1121; www.rumihotel.com; Durakfakih Sokak 5; s/d ₺160/250; ❄🛜) Rooms at the Rumi (with home comforts such as kettles) are a tad on the small side and styled plainly in beige, but staff seem to delight in offering genuine service and the top-level breakfast room has killer views over to the Mevlâna Museum. It's an oasis of calm in central Konya.

🍴 Eating & Drinking

Central Konya has plentiful cheap canteens and a handful of notable restaurants focusing on regional cuisine. Two specialities are *fırın kebap*, slices of (hopefully) tender, oven-roasted mutton served on puffy bread, and *etli ekmek* (the region's version of pide; literally 'bread with meat').

Şifa Lokantası TURKISH **$**
(✆0332-352 0519; Mevlâna Caddesi 29; mains ₺14-36; ⏱10am-9.30pm; ❄) Old-timer on the Konya scene, Şifa has had a rather smart makeover. As well as tasty pide and typical kebaps, check out the menu for Konya specialities including a delicious *tirit* (a traditional wedding dish of bread, lamb and peppers topped with yoghurt and browned butter).

There are usually a few good vegetarian dishes on offer too.

★ Somatçi ANATOLIAN **$$**
(✆0332-352 4200; www.somatci.com; Celal Sokak 39; mains ₺18-35; ⏱9am-10pm Tue-Sun; ❄) Rekindling old recipes from the Seljuk and Ottoman age, this restaurant uses the finest ingredients and cooks everything with panache. Dig into more unusual dishes such

SULTANHANI

The highway between Konya and Aksaray crosses quintessential Anatolian steppe: flat grasslands as far as the eye can see with only the occasional tumbleweed and a few mountains in the distance breaking the monotony. The Seljuks built a string of *hans* (caravanserais) along this Silk Road route and, 110km from Konya, 42km from Aksaray, the dreary village of Sultanhanı is home to one of the most stunning *hans* still standing.

The largest caravanserai in Anatolia, the Sultanhanı (Atatürk Caddesi; ₺5; ⊙8am-7pm) was constructed in 1229, during the reign of the Seljuk sultan Alaaddin Keykubad I, and restored in 1278 after a fire (when it became Turkey's largest *han*). Through the wonderful carved entrance in the 50m-long east wall, there is a raised *mescit* (prayer room) in the middle of the open courtyard, which is ringed with rooms used for sleeping, dining and cooking.

Monday to Friday there are hourly dolmuşes (minibuses with a prescribed route) from Aksaray's Eski Garaj (p481) to Sultanhanı between 7.30am and 6.30pm. From Sultanhanı's tiny otogar (500m down the road from the caravanserai), dolmuşes make the return run on the hour between 7am and 5pm. There are fewer services on weekends.

Coming from Konya, any bus heading to Aksaray can drop you off in Sultanhanı. Heading back in that direction, walk back out to the highway to flag down a bus.

as *kayısılı kuzu gerdan* (chicken in apricot sauce) and *incirli et* (beef and dried figs). Staff are happy to advise on dishes and the setting inside a restored building is spot on.

Vegetarians are well looked after here with plenty of choice.

Konya Mutfağı ANATOLIAN $$
(☑0332-350 4141; Mevlâna Caddesi 71; mains ₺18-32; ⊙11.30am-11pm) Run by the *belediye* (town council), this restaurant offers up the regional tastes of Konya. It's a great place to sample *patlıcan közleme kebabı* (roasted eggplant, peppers and tomatoes topped with grilled lamb) and *tırıt* (a traditional wedding dish of bread, lamb and peppers topped with yoghurt and browned butter). Then cleanse your palate with a tamarind sherbet.

Deva 1 Restaurant KEBAB $$
(☑0332-350 0519; Mevlâna Caddesi; mains ₺20-56; ⊙11.30am-10pm) Our favourite place in town for *fırın kebap* (a Konya speciality; slices of tender, fairly greasy, oven-roasted mutton served on puffy bread). The meat here is always succulent and cooked to perfection. Staff are a friendly bunch.

HI Cafe CAFE
(Mevlâna Caddesi; ⊙10.30am-8pm) In a serious sign of Konya moving with the times, this funky cafe serves up cappuccinos, French press and frappés a hop-skip-jump from the Mevlâna Museum entrance. Very contemporary presentation – all chunky wooden boards and icing-sugar-dusted

complimentary treats – and endearingly sweet service top off the coffee experience. We love it.

ℹ Information

SAFE TRAVEL

Konya has a longstanding reputation for religious conservatism. Not that this should inconvenience you, but take special care not to upset the pious and make sure you're not an annoyance. If you visit during Ramazan, be aware that many restaurants will be closed during the daylight fasting hours; as a courtesy to those who are fasting, don't eat or drink in public during the day. Non-Muslim women seem to encounter more hassle in this bastion of propriety than in many other Turkish cities, and dressing conservatively will help you avoid problems. Men can wander around in shorts without encountering any tension, but may prefer to wear something longer to fit in with local customs.

Male travellers have reported being propositioned in the Tarihi Mahkeme Hamamı.

TOURIST OFFICES

Tourist Office (☑0332-353 4020; off Aslanı Kışla Caddesi; ⊙9am-5pm Mon-Sat) This helpful, exceedingly enthusiastic tourist office has free city maps and bundles of brochures covering historic sites in and around Konya. Can also organise guides and has information on the whirling dervish shows.

ℹ Getting There & Away

BUS

Konya Otogar (Konya Bus Station; Dr Halil Ürün Caddesi) is about 7km north of Alaaddin

Tepesi. There are bus company ticket offices on Mevlâna Caddesi and around Alaaddin Tepesi.

The **Karatay Terminal** (Eski Garaj; Pırıeasat Caddesi), 1km southwest of the Mevlâna Museum, has dolmuş services to local villages.

TRAIN

Konya train station (Konya YHT Garı; www.tcddtasimacilik.gov.tr; Alay Caddesi) is about 3km southwest of the centre. Konya is on Turkey's high-speed (YHT) train network. In 2017, engineering work began on a new high-speed line between Konya and Antalya.

Ankara (₺31, 1¾ hours, seven daily)

İstanbul (Söğütlüçeşme is the most useful İstanbul station to get off at; ₺86, 4¼ hours, three daily)

Eskişehir (₺39.50, 1¾ hours, three daily)

There are also regular train services to Adana on the daily Toros Ekspresi (₺21, 5¾ hours, 2.30pm) and İzmir on the daily Konya Mavi Treni (₺44, 12 hours, 7.30pm)

ⓘ Getting Around

In order to use Konya's city buses, trams and dolmuşes you can either tap a contact-less credit/debit card on the fare machine or buy a Konya ElKart (rechargeable transport card; ₺1) from the signed metal booths adjoining any of the larger tram and bus stops. Fares, which cover two journeys, are ₺3.40.

BUS

Innumerable dolmuşes and city buses ply Mevlâna Caddesi. The main **bus stop** (for buses heading towards the otogar and into the suburbs) is at the intersection of Mevlâna Caddesi and Adliye Bulvarı.

TRAM

Trams run 24 hours a day with only one per hour after midnight. There are two tram lines. The main line runs from Selçuk Üniversite, via the otogar into the centre of town, terminating at Alaaddin. The second line starts at Zafer (on the western side of Alaaddin Tepisi), stops at Alaaddin, and then runs east along Mevlâna Caddesi, past the Mevlâna Museum and Mevlâna Culture Centre, terminating at Adliye tram stop.

Around Konya

Çatalhöyük

Rising 20m above the surrounding flat Konya plains, the East Mound at Çatalhöyük (Küçük Köy; ⊙8am-5pm) FREE is one of the most important, and largest, Neolithic settlements on earth. About 9500 years ago, up to 8000 people lived here, and the mound comprises 13 levels of buildings, each containing around 1000 structures. Little remains of the ancient centre other than the two excavation areas, which draw archaeologists from all over the world.

If you visit between June and September, when the digs mostly take place, you might find an expert to chat to. At other times, the museum does a good job of explaining the site and the excavations, which began in 1961 under British archaeologist James Mellaart and have continued with the involvement of the local community. Mellaart's controversial theories about mother-goddess worship here caused the Turkish government to close the site for 30 years.

Near the museum entrance stands the experimental house, a reconstructed mud-brick hut used to test various theories about Neolithic culture. People at Çatalhöyük lived in tightly packed dwellings that were connected by ladders between the roofs instead of streets, and were filled in and built over when they started to wear out. Skeletons were found buried under the floors and most of the houses may have doubled as shrines. The settlement was highly organised, but there are no obvious signs of any central government system.

From the museum you can then walk across the mound to the dome-covered north shelter where excavation work has uncovered the remains of several buildings with their outlines still visible. A short trail then leads to the south shelter. With 21m of archaeological deposits, many of the site's most famous discoveries were made here. The lowest level of excavation, begun by Mellaart, is the deepest at Çatalhöyük and holds deposits left more than 9000 years ago. There are information panels on the viewing platforms of both excavation areas that help you decipher the site.

ⓘ Getting There & Away

To get here by public transport from Konya, 33km northwest, get the Karkın minibus, which leaves the Karatay Terminal (also called Eski Garaj) at 7am, 9.30am and 4.50pm on weekdays. Get off at the village of Küçük Köy (₺8, 45 minutes) and walk to the site on the village edge, or you may be able to persuade the driver to take you the whole way. Going back, minibuses leave Küçük Köy at 7.15am, 3pm and 7pm. Getting there by bus at the weekend is much harder: there are buses at 9am and midday on Saturdays and none on Sundays.

A taxi from Konya to the site and back, including waiting time, will cost about ₺150.

Cappadocia

Best Places to Eat

➜ Dibek (p450)

➜ Ziggy Cafe (p469)

➜ Pumpkin Cafe (p451)

➜ Cappadocia Home Cooking (p474)

➜ Tık Tık Kadın Emeği (p468)

Best Places to Stay

➜ Sota Cappadocia (p467)

➜ Koza Cave Hotel (p449)

➜ Kale Konak (p455)

➜ Kelebek Hotel (p449)

➜ Hezen Cave Hotel (p465)

Why Go?

As if plucked from a whimsical fairy tale and set down upon the stark Anatolian plains, Cappadocia is a geological oddity of honeycombed hills and towering boulders of other-worldly beauty. The fantastical topography is matched by the human history. People have long used the region's soft stone, seeking shelter underground and leaving the countryside scattered with fascinating cavern architecture. The fresco-adorned rock-cut churches of Göreme Open-Air Museum and the subterranean refuges of Derinkuyu and Kaymaklı are the most famous sights, while simply bedding down in one of Cappadocia's cave hotels is an experience in 21st-century cave living.

Whether you're wooed here by the hiking potential, the history or the bragging rights of becoming a modern troglodyte for a night, it's the lunarscape panoramas that you'll remember. This region's accordion-ridged valleys, shaded in a palette of dusky orange and cream, are an epiphany of a landscape – the stuff of psychedelic daydreams.

When to Go
Kayseri

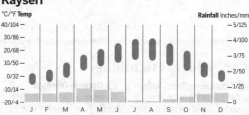

May High season begins. Valley moonscapes at their most colourful. Pack an umbrella.

Jul Pull on your hiking boots; the prime time to tackle the Ala Dağlar.

Dec–Feb Room rates drop. Valley vistas dusted with snow. Ski season at Erciyes Dağı (Mt Erciyes).

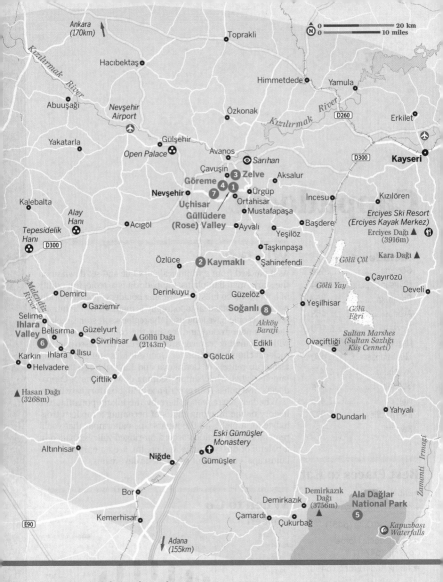

Cappadocia Highlights

❶ Güllüdere (Rose) Valley (p445) Seeking out hidden churches amid pigeon-house-riddled cliffs and rock spires.

❷ Kaymaklı Underground City (p463) Delving downwards into a labyrinth of tunnels.

❸ Zelve (p457) Imagining village life amid knobbly cliffs of abandoned caverns.

❹ Göreme Open-Air Museum (p444) Examining fresco finery inside these cave-cut churches.

❺ Ala Dağlar National Park (p476) Hitting the trails to experience the Taurus Mountains' visceral beauty.

❻ Ihlara Valley (p478) Strolling between verdant fields and cliffs speckled with rock-cut chapels.

❼ Uçhisar (p454) Gazing over a surreal panorama of rippling rock from the castle.

❽ Soğanlı (p474) Exploring this monastic clutch of churches hewn out of conical rocks.

History

The Hittites settled Cappadocia (Kapadok-ya) from 1800 BC to 1200 BC, after which smaller kingdoms held power. Then came the Persians, followed by the Romans, who established the capital of Caesarea (today's Kayseri). During the Roman and Byzantine periods, Cappadocia became a refuge for early Christians and, from the 4th to 11th centuries, Christianity flourished here; most churches, monasteries and underground cities date from this period. Later, under Seljuk and Ottoman rule, Christians were treated with tolerance.

Cappadocia progressively lost its importance in Anatolia. Its rich past was all but forgotten until a French priest travelled here and revealed the rock-hewn churches to the wider world in 1907. The tourist boom in the 1980s kick-started a new era and now Cappadocia is one of Turkey's most famous and popular destinations.

❶ Safe Travel

Most buses arriving in Cappadocia from the west terminate in Nevşehir. There are some direct services to Göreme and Avanos from İstanbul and towns on the Mediterranean coast but unless your ticket states these names then your final destination is Nevşehir. From here you'll need to take local transport onward to the villages. Be aware that tour companies based at Nevşehir otogar (bus station) have a bad reputation for attempting to get tourists onto their private shuttle buses and then proceeding to hard-sell them tours and accommodation in Nevşehir. We suggest that you avoid any dealings with the tour agents here.

Walking in central Cappadocia's valleys is a wonderful experience and should not be missed, but solo travellers who do not want to hire a guide should buddy up before venturing into the more isolated areas as there have been several attacks on female tourists in the valleys in recent years. It's also advisable to avoid the valleys and the unlit roads between villages in the evenings.

That said, compared to many other popular traveller destinations across the world, Cappadocia remains an incredibly safe place for solo female travellers. As with any destination, common sense should prevail. Solo travellers should be wary of accepting invitations to go out into the valleys with new acquaintances and all hikers with mobile phones should program their hotel's number into it and take it while walking as a sensible precaution in case they get lost or have an accident.

❶ Getting There & Away

AIR

Two airports serve central Cappadocia: **Kayseri Airport** (Kayseri Erkilet Havalimanı, ASR; ☑ 0352-337 5244; Mustafa Kemal Paşa Bulvarı) and **Nevşehir Airport** (Nevşehir Kapadokya Havalimanı, NAV; ☑ 0384-421 4455; https://kapadokya.dhmi.gov.tr; Nevşehir Kapadokya Havaalanı Yolu, Gülşehir). Both have several flights daily to/from İstanbul. The main operators are Turkish Airlines (www.turkishairlines.com) and Pegasus Airlines (www.flypgs.com).

BUS

Most buses from İstanbul and other western Turkey destinations travel to Cappadocia overnight. The vast majority of services terminate at **Nevşehir Otogar** (Nevşehir Bus Station; Aksaray–Nevşehir Yolu) though a decent number of buses from the main coastal destinations (most run by Kâmil Koç and Süha bus companies) do direct services to both Göreme and Avanos. If you're not on a direct service (or are heading to Ortahisar, Uçhisar or Ürgüp) you have to transfer onto a local bus or dolmuş (minibus with a prescribed route) at the otogar to get to the villages.

TRAIN

The are train stations at Niğde (p476) and Kayseri (p484).

❶ Getting Around

TO/FROM THE AIRPORT

Very reasonably priced airport shuttle-bus services operate between both Cappadocia airports and the various villages. They must be pre-booked. If you have booked your accommodation the easiest solution is to ask your hotel to arrange an airport-shuttle pickup for you, though be aware that some hotels beef up the price of shuttle transfers ridiculously. You can also book directly with the shuttle-bus services.

There are a few companies to choose from but **Helios Transfer** (☑ 0384-271 2257; www.heliostransfer.com; Adnan Menderes Caddesi 25a; per passenger to/from Nevşehir/Kayseri airport ₺40/50; ☺ for bookings 9am-6pm) and **Cappadocia Express** (☑ 0384-271 3070; www.cappadociatransport.com; per passenger to/from Nevşehir Airport ₺30, to/from Kayseri Airport ₺40; ☺ for bookings 9am-6pm) seem to be the pick of the bunch, with services operating for all flights coming into and going out of both airports. Both will pick up from and drop off to hotels in Avanos, Çavuşin, Göreme, Nevşehir, Ortahisar, Uçhisar and Ürgüp.

CAR & MOTORCYCLE

Cappadocia is great for self-drive visits. Away from the immediate area around Göreme and Ürgüp, roads are often empty and their condition is reasonable. Signposting of sights and towns is, in most cases, excellent. On the downside, parking is a serious issue in Göreme during high season and pulling up outside some cave hotels can be tricky.

LOCAL TRANSPORT

Dolmuşes (minibuses with a prescribed route; ₺4 to ₺6 depending on where you get on and off) travel between Ürgüp and Avanos via Ortahisar, the Göreme Open-Air Museum, Göreme, Çavuşin, Paşabağı and Zelve. The services leave Ürgüp otogar (bus station) hourly between 8am and 7pm. Going in the opposite direction, starting from Avanos, the dolmuşes operate hourly between 8am and 8pm. You can hop on and off anywhere along the route.

There are several other dolmuş services between villages.

The Ihlara Valley in southwest Cappadocia can be visited on a day tour from Göreme. If you want to visit it independently, plan to spend the night, as bus changes in Nevşehir and Aksaray prolong travelling time.

TAXI

Taxis are a reasonably priced option for moving between villages, particularly during the evening when public transport stops. Meters operate but for longer taxi day trips – eg to Soğanlı or Ihlara – a quoted flat rate is the norm.

Göreme

☑ 0384 / POP 2100

Surrounded by epic sweeps of golden, moonscape valley, this remarkable honey-coloured village hollowed out of the hills has long since grown beyond its farming-hamlet roots. The hub of Cappadocia's tourism industry, Göreme has wriggling hillside alleys studded with boutique cave-hotels offering sublime views, while the small 'downtown' strip bustles with restaurants and tacky souvenir stores. These days most visitors come simply for the famed hot-air-ballooning vistas, but the encompassing countryside's surreal beauty is much better revealed on the ground. In summer the village may be packed solid with visitors, but wander in any direction out of town and you'll still find storybook landscapes and little-visited rock-cut churches at every turn.

◎ Sights

★ **Göreme Open-Air Museum** HISTORIC SITE
(Göreme Açık Hava Müzesi; **☑** 0384-213 4260; Müze Caddesi; ₺54; ⊙ 8am-7.15pm) This Unesco World Heritage site is an essential stop on any Cappadocian itinerary. First thought to be a Byzantine monastic settlement that housed some 20 monks, then a pilgrimage site from the 17th century, this splendid cluster of monastic Byzantine artistry with its rock-cut churches, chapels and monasteries is 1km uphill from Göreme's centre.

The site's highlight – the Dark Church – has an additional entrance fee. Note that the ticket office closes at 4.30pm October to April.

From the museum ticket booth, follow the cobbled path until you reach the 11th-century **Chapel of St Basil** (Aziz Basil Şapeli), dedicated to Kayseri-born St Basil, one of Cappadocia's most important saints. In the main room, St Basil is pictured on the left; a Maltese cross is on the right, along with St George and St Theodore slaying a (faded) dragon, symbolising paganism. On the right of the apse, Mary holds baby Jesus with a cross in his halo. Nearby is the **Chapel of St Barbara** (Azize Barbara Şapeli). Some art historians theorise that Byzantine soldiers carved out this 11th-century church, dedicated to their patron saint, who is depicted on the left as you enter. Look up at the ceiling and note the red ochre motifs – the middle one could represent the Ascension; above the St George representation on the far wall, the strange creature could be a dragon and the two crosses the beast's usual slayers.

Past the Chapel of St Barbara the lane loops down to the columned and nine-domed **Apple Church** (Elmalı Kilise), which contains well-preserved, colourful, professionally painted frescoes of biblical scenes as well as simple red-ochre daubs. The Ascension is pictured above the door while Christ Pantocrator is depicted on the church's central dome. The church's name is thought to derive from an apple tree that grew nearby or from a misinterpretation of the globe held by the Archangel Gabriel, in the third dome.

Heading uphill you come to the **Snake Church** (Yılanlı Kilise), also called the Church of St Onuphrius, where St George's ubiquitous dragon-foe is still having a bad day. To add insult to fatal injury, the church got its current moniker when locals mistook the pictured dragon for a snake. The hermetic hermaphrodite St Onuphrius is depicted on the right, holding a genitalia-covering palm leaf. Straight ahead, the small figure next to Jesus is one of the church's financiers.

The small **Pantocrator Chapel** and **Nameless Chapel** (İzimsiz Şapel) with their simple red-ochre geometric decorations and Maltese crosses are a little further along the path as well as a series of caves thought to have served as **refectory** and **kitchen** areas with a rock-cut table in one cavern.

On the highest point of the path, head up the tunnel to the stunning, fresco-filled **Dark Church** (Karanlık Kilise; ₺18), the most famous of the museum's churches. It takes its name from the fact that it originally had very few windows. Luckily, this lack of light preserved the vivid colour of the frescoes, which show, among other things, Christ Pantocrator, the Nativity, the Transfiguration, the Betrayal by Judas and the Crucifixion. The church was restored at great expense and the entrance fee is intended to limit visitor numbers to further preserve the frescoes.

Just past the Dark Church, the little **Chapel of St Catherine** (Azize Katarina Şapeli) contains frescoes of St George, St Catherine and the Deesis (a seated Christ flanked by the Virgin and John the Baptist).

The **Rahibeler Monastery** is at the bottom of the hill, just before you get back to the museum entrance area. It was originally several storeys high and it's posited by historians that a small community of nuns resided here during the 11th century. All that remains is a large plain dining hall and, up some steps, a small chapel with unremarkable frescoes, but the entire craggy structure is now cordoned off due to rock falls.

When you exit the Open-Air Museum, don't forget to cross the road to visit the **Buckle Church** (Tokalı Kilise), 50m down the hill towards Göreme and covered by the same ticket. This is one of Göreme's biggest and finest churches, with an underground chapel and fabulous restored frescoes painted in a narrative (rather than liturgical) cycle. Entry is via the barrel-vaulted chamber of the 10th-century 'old' chapel, with frescoes portraying the life of Christ. Behind it, the 'new' church, built less than 100 years later, is also alive with frescoes on a similar theme. The holes in the floor once contained tombs, taken by departing Greek Christians during Turkey's population exchange.

Note that photography is not allowed inside any of the churches.

ⓘ VISITING GÖREME OPEN-AIR MUSEUM

➡ Arrive early in the morning or near closing to bypass the crowds.

➡ Avoid weekends if possible; it's crammed here then.

➡ Don't skimp on the additional fee and miss the Dark Church (Karanlık Kilise) – it's the highlight of a visit here.

➡ The museum is an easy, though uphill, 1km walk from town.

➡ Beware the sun – this is an 'open-air' museum.

★ **Güllüdere (Rose) Valley**   AREA

The trails that loop around Güllüdere Vadısı (Rose Valley) are easily accessible to all levels of walkers and provide some of the finest fairy-chimney-strewn vistas in Cappadocia. As well as this, though, they hide fabulous, little-visited rock-cut churches boasting vibrant fresco fragments and intricate carvings hewn into the stone. If you only have time to hike through one valley in Cappadocia, this is the one to choose.

Follow the signs from the Güllüdere Valley trailhead to the **Kolonlu Kilise** (Columned Church), chiselled out of a nondescript rock facade. Take the trail through the orchard and then cross the tiny bridge over the gully to enter the church's gloomy lower chamber. Climb up the staircase and you'll find a white stone nave studded with sturdy columns carved out of the rock.

Backtrack through the orchard and follow the main trail to the **Haçlı Kilise** (Church of the Cross), where the **Cross Church Cafe** with its shady terraces just below the entrance provides the perfect excuse for a break. The church, accessed by a rickety wooden staircase, has frescoes dating to the 9th century on its apse and a spectacular large cross carved into its ceiling.

Head north from the Haçlı Kilise and, when the trail branches, take the right-hand path to reach the **Üç Haçlı Kilise** (Church of the Three Crosses), with its stunning ceiling relief and damaged frescoes featuring an enthroned Jesus.

El Nazar Kilise   CHURCH

(Church of the Evil Eye; Zemi Valley; ₺5; ☉8am-5pm 16 Apr–14 Dec) Carved from a ubiquitous cone-like rock formation, the 10th-century El Nazar Kilise has been well restored with

Göreme

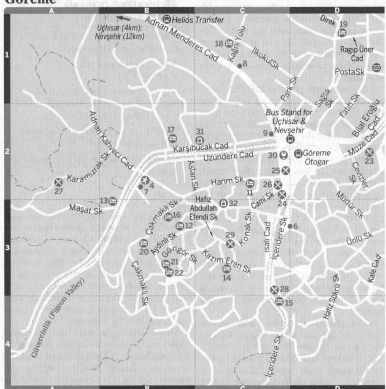

its snug interior a riot of colourful frescoes. To find it, take the signposted Zemi Valley trailhead off Müze Caddesi.

Aynalı Kilise
CHURCH

(Mirror Church; Müze Caddesi; ₺5; ⊗9am-5pm) From the Open-Air Museum entrance, a 1km walk uphill along Müze Caddesi brings you to the signposted trail leading down to the Aynalı Kilise. The main chapel is adorned with interesting red-ochre geometric decorations, but the real highlight here is shimmying through the network of narrow tunnels interconnecting a series of rooms within the rock face. The on-site guardian provides torches for visitors.

Saklı Kilise
CHURCH

(Hidden Church) A yellow sign points the way off Müze Caddesi to the Saklı Kilise, only rediscovered in 1956. When you reach the top of the hill, follow the track to the left and look out for steps leading downhill to the right.

Sunset View Hill
VIEWPOINT

You get one of the best panoramas across Göreme by walking up the steep hill through alleyways to this wooden platform suspended on the edge of the cliff high above the village. From here you can follow a rough track along the ridge for sweeping views of the village on your left and vistas of the wind- and water-sculpted rock formations of Görkündere Valley to your right.

Despite the moniker, we don't recommend coming here for sunset in summer when it can get ridiculously crowded and the road leading up to the viewpoint is crammed with cars. Note for sunrise hot-air-balloon views, there's a ₺3 entrance fee. During the day there are far fewer people about, it's free and the views are just as good.

🏃 Activities

★ Mehmet Güngör
HIKING

(📱0532 382 2069; www.walkingmehmet.net; 3/5/7hr €60/80/100) Mehmet Güngör's

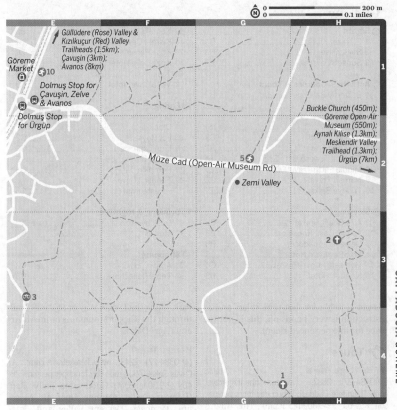

nickname, 'Walking Mehmet', says it all. Göreme's most experienced local walking guide has an encyclopedic knowledge of the surrounding valley trails and can put together hiking itineraries to suit all interests and levels of fitness. Highly recommended.

Fatma's Turkish Cooking Class   COOKING

(☑ 0384-271 2597, 0534 242 0852; İçeridere Sokak; per person ₺200) These cooking classes – operated out of the Çingitaş family's hostel (p448) – will have you rustling up the hearty dishes of the Anatolian plains like a pro. Book a day in advance for a half-day class that takes you through the Turkish staples of lentil soup, stuffed vine leaves, stuffed aubergines and the Cappadocian pudding *aside*, made from dough and *pekmez* (grape syrup). Book through Cafe Şafak (p450).

Cappadocia Bike   MOUNTAIN BIKING

(☑ 0505 656 1064; www.cappadociabike.com; 3-4hr bike tours per person incl transport to/ from hotel €40) Enthusiastic cyclist Niyazi showcases Cappadocia's weird and wacky landscape by bike. Tours do a loop from Göreme through Paşabağı and Devrent Valleys, Ürgüp and Kızılçukur Valley. Bikes are B'TWIN 24-speed mountain bikes, and helmets are provided.

Kelebek Turkish Bath Spa   HAMAM

(☑ 0384-271 2531; Kelebek Hotel, Yavuz Sokak; soak & scrub €35, 30min massage €35; ☉ by appointment) Unwind after the chimney-spotting and treat yourself to Cappadocia's most luxurious hamam experience with a full range of spa-style added extras. Reservations essential.

Dalton Brothers   HORSE RIDING

(☑ 0532 275 6869; www.cappadociahorseriding. com; Müze Caddesi; 2/4hr €45/75) Ekrem Ilhan – Göreme's resident horse whisperer – trains Cappadocia's wild horses from Erciyes Dağı (Mt Erciyes) and runs this trekking stable from where you can set out to explore Cappadocia from the saddle. Many of the horses

Göreme

are not suitable for first-time riders and as instruction is very hands-off, this is not the place for inexperienced riders.

Tours

★ Heritage Travel   TOURS
(☎0384-271 2687; www.turkishheritagetravel. com; Uzundere Caddesi; group day tours per person €55-65; ⊙9.30am-5.30pm) This highly recommended local agency offers day-tour itineraries that differ from most Cappadocia operators, including an 'Undiscovered Cappadocia' trip that visits Soğanlı and Mustafapaşa's St Nicholas Monastery and a 'Heritage Cappadocia' tour that goes to Zelve and Özkonak Underground City. Group tour sizes are limited to 12 people.

Among its many other local activities, it's known for its traditional cooking classes (€65), which take place in a valley. Heritage also specialises in tailor-made Turkey itineraries with a particular strength in setting up custom private tours of southeast Anatolia.

Middle Earth Travel   ADVENTURE
(☎0384-271 2559; www.middleearthtravel.com; Adnan Menderes Caddesi; day hike per person 4/3/2 people from €50/60/70, bike tour per person 4/3/2 people €90/100/120) This adventure travel specialist offers a range of day hikes and daily bike tours exploring the Cappadocia area as well as multiday biking itineraries and treks through Ala Dağlar National Park, along the Lycian Way or St Paul's Trail, through the Kaçkar Mountains or up Mt Ararat (Ağri Dağı).

Hereke Travel   TOURS
(☎0384-271 2243; www.hereketravel.com; Ali Çavuş Sokak 7/A; group day tours per person €28-40; ⊙9.30am-6pm) Good-value daily 'Red' (Uçhisar Castle, Göreme Open-Air Museum, Paşabağı, Devrent Valley and Ortahisar Castle), 'Green' (Ihlara Valley and an underground city) and 'Blue' (Soğanlı and surrounding sights; four people minimum) tours. Also arranges tours out to Tuz Gölü (Salt Lake) west of Aksaray, and private tours to Nemrut Dağı (Mt Nemrut).

Sleeping

★ Homestay Cave Hostel   HOSTEL $
(☎0534 242 0852; www.homestaycavehostel.com; İçeridere Sokak; dm €16, r €39; ☎) Who needs to pay wads of cash to stay in a Cappadocian cave? Beeline to the friendly Çingitaş family's hostel to sleep in a spacious 10-bed cave-dorm (one mixed, one female-only), where each bed is equipped with privacy curtain, reading lamp, power point and locker. Shared bathrooms are spotless, and there's a kitchen and a roof terrace for lounging around.

Ali's Guest House   HOSTEL $
(☎0384-271 2434; www.alisguesthouse.com; Harım Sokak 13; dm/d/tr ₺40/120/160; ☏☎)

We've whinged about Göreme's backpacker digs trussing themselves up to cater for the boutique crowd, so a big thumbs up to Ali's as it's aimed squarely at the budget end of the market. There are two snug cave-dorms sharing small, clean bathrooms, and three cosy private rooms upstairs. The outdoor courtyard is a pot-plant-strewn communal haven.

Köse Pension
PENSION $

(📞0384-271 2294, Ahmet 0554 205 0008; www.kosepension.com; Ragıp Üner Caddesi; dm €10, r €30-35; ☺🛜🛏) Ably managed by Ahmet and long-term staffer Yunus, this friendly backpacker favourite provides simple private rooms with bathroom, good-sized four-bed dorms and a spacious (summer-only) rooftop 12-bed dorm. The swimming pool is a bonus after a hot hike and they were about to open a garden-bar area when we were last in town.

Kismet Cave House
GUESTHOUSE $$

(📞0384-271 2416; www.kismetcavehouse.com; Kağnı Yolu 9; r €40-80, f €80-100; ☺🛜) Kismet's fate is assured. Guests consistently rave about the intimate experience here, created by welcoming, well-travelled host Faruk. Rooms (some in actual fairy chimneys) and communal areas are full of local antiques, carved wood features, colourful rugs and quirky artwork, while the roof terrace is home to cosy cushion-scattered nooks.

Kemal's Guest House
GUESTHOUSE $$

(📞0384-271 2234; www.kemalsguesthouse.com; Ayzazefedi Sokak 4; s/d/tr €38/48/58; ☺✳🛜) Comfortable stone rooms, a sun-dappled garden and old-fashioned hospitality in spades; this is a home away from home with plenty of repeat guests. Kemal is a terrific cook (dinner feasts €15), and Dutch wife Barbara leads guests to hike Cappadocia's trails. Sun yourself on the roof terrace with its views across to Uçhisar, and thumb your nose at your 'boutique' friends.

Vista Cave Hotel
BOUTIQUE HOTEL $$

(📞0384-271 3088; www.vistacavehotel.com; Aydınlı Sokak 15; d €40-90, tr €115; ☺✳🛜) Vista by name, vista by nature: 180-degree views over the village and out to the valleys from the terrace make breakfast an occasion. Stone-cut rooms with balconies are elegant and bright, while cave-cut ones come with carved ceiling motifs and traditional Ottoman styling. Hosts Şenol and Yvette dish out local advice, and complimentary home-baked goodies are a winner.

Taşkonak
GUESTHOUSE $$

(📞0384-270 2680; www.taskonak.com; Güngör Sokak 23; r/ste ₺250/400; ☺🛜) This hideaway has got the cave character and killer views from the terrace but has room rates below many of its hillside neighbours. Standard stone rooms are snug and simple, while spacious cave suites below come with snazzy contemporary bathrooms (bag Room 3 for the roll-top bath and double shower).

★Koza Cave Hotel
BOUTIQUE HOTEL $$$

(📞0384-271 2466; www.kozacavehotel.com; Çakmaklı Sokak 49; d €165-200, ste €220-350; ☺✳🛜) 🌿 Koza is a masterclass in stylish sustainable tourism. Passionate owner Derviş spent decades living in Holland and has incorporated Dutch eco-sensibility into every cave crevice. Grey water is reused, and upcycled antiques and local wood furniture, handcrafted by Derviş himself, are used in abundance in the 10 spacious cave-and-stone rooms and suites that brim with sophisticated and idiosyncratic style.

Multiple terraces, strewn with pot plants, with couch corners to slouch on and a roof terrace boasting views that tumble over Göreme and out to the valleys, top off a seamlessly brilliant hotel stay. This is eco-chic done the right way. You may never want to leave. Highly recommended.

★Kelebek Hotel
BOUTIQUE HOTEL $$$

(📞0384-271 2531; www.kelebekhotel.com; Yavuz Sokak 31; s/d €68/85, ste from €120, fairy chimney s/d without bathroom €44/55; 🅿☺✳🛜) Local guru Ali Yavuz leads a charming team at one of Göreme's original boutique hotels, which has seen a travel industry virtually spring from beneath its stunning terraces. Exuding Anatolian inspiration at every turn, the rooms are spread over a labyrinth of stairs and balconies interconnecting two gorgeous stone houses, each with a fairy chimney protruding skyward.

With an in-house hamam, a swimming-pool deck complete with bar and hammocks, and a village-garden project offering guests a slice of the Cappadocia of old – with cooking classes and complimentary valley breakfasts – Kelebek continues to innovate. It's no wonder people leave smitten.

Aydınlı Cave House
BOUTIQUE HOTEL $$$

(📞0384-271 2263; www.thecavehotel.com; Aydınlı Sokak 12; r €80-90, f €140, ste from €100; ☺✳🛜) Proprietor Mustafa has masterfully converted his family home into a haven for honeymooners and those requiring swags of swanky rock-cut style. Leading off terraces scattered with old farming utensils, salons once used for drying fruit and making wine are now swoon-worthy cave rooms, while a secret tunnel under the road leads to a hamam and garden annexe of stone-cut rooms.

ErenBey Cave Hotel
BOUTIQUE HOTEL $$$

(☑ 0384-271 2131; www.erenbeycavehotel.com; Kazım Eren Sokak 19; d €70-90, f/ste €100/150; ❄✳🌐) The Eren family converted their generations-old homestead into nine exceedingly spacious rooms that play up their quirky cave shapes with aplomb and offer buckets of idiosyncratic design. The terrace is a restful spot for a quiet afternoon and Room 9, with its rock-carved four-pillared bed, bathtub-with-a-view and private balcony is the stuff of romantic getaway dreams.

Design Cappadocia
BOUTIQUE HOTEL $$$

(☑ 0384-271 3344; www.designcappadocia.com; Maşat Sokak 2; s/d from €75/95; 🅿❄✳🌐) Brothers Mustafa and Hasan head up an on-the-ball, friendly team at this classy boutique option. Smoothly minimalist style highlights the cave-cut character of spacious rooms, which come with some of the biggest cave-bathrooms in town. The petunia-strewn roof terrace offers sunrise balloon views, breakfast comes with good filter coffee and – bonus – there's no hill to climb to get to bed.

🍴 Eating

Nazar Börek
TURKISH $

(☑ 0532 685 4272, 0384-271 2201; Karamızrak Sokak; mains ₺10-30, village-food set menu ₺40; ⏰9am-11pm; 🌐🅿) Rafik and family have converted their family home on the edge of Güvercinlik Valley, surrounded by fairy chimneys, into one of the town's most scenic places to dine. Come for excellent-value meals of *gözleme* (stuffed flatbreads), grilled meat mains, the speciality *sosyete böregi* (stuffed spiral pastries served with yoghurt and tomato sauce) and a daily-changing traditional-village-food set menu.

Vegetables come straight from the family's garden out front, the terrace views stretch all the way to Erciyes Dağı (Mt Erciyes), and multilingual Rafik dishes up plentiful local information and hiking advice as well as your meal.

To find it, take the first left-hand turn on Adnan Kahveci Caddesi and follow the cobbled lane into the valley (about 800m from the centre of town). Rafik will pick up guests from town if you ring him beforehand.

Fırın Express
PIDE $

(☑ 0384-271 2266; Camı Sokak; pide ₺10-20; ⏰10am-10pm; 🌐🅿) Simply the best pide (Turkish-style pizza) in town is found in this local haunt. The cavernous wood oven fires up meat and vegetarian options and anything doused with egg. For a bargain feed we suggest the *patlıcan* (aubergine) or *ıspınaklı kaşarlı* (spinach and cheese) pide and adding an *ayran* (yoghurt drink) to wash it down with.

Cafe Şafak
CAFE $

(Müze Caddesi; dishes ₺10-29; ⏰10am-10pm; 🌐) Fatma and son Ali serve good-value Turkish favourites of *gözleme*, *menemen* (scrambled eggs with peppers, tomatoes and sometimes cheese) and simple grilled meat plates at this cafe, smack in the middle of town. Ali trained as a barista in coffee-hipster Melbourne so this is one of Göreme's top spots for espresso and flat whites too.

⭐ Dibek
ANATOLIAN $$

(☑ 0384-271 2209; www.dibektraditionalcook.com; Camı Sokak 1; mains ₺28-70, tasting menu ₺80; ⏰11am-11pm Mon-Sat; 🌐) Diners sprawl on cushions and take a taste-bud tour of village food at this family restaurant. Take our advice and order the *tadım* (tasting) menu plus a *testı kebapı* (meat and vegetable stew slow-cooked in a sealed terracotta pot; the best in town). The *bamya* (okra) will convert even the ambivalent to the joys of this most divisive of vegetables.

Don't leave without having the moreish *tel kadayf* (dough soaked in syrup and topped with walnuts and tahini) and trying the homemade sour cherry liqueur for a lush digestif.

In 2019, wine-buff owner Mehmet converted the rooftop of this 475-year-old building into a slick wine bar, which also serves cheese and antipasto platters as well as a more European-style menu (mains ₺50 to ₺150). Head upstairs after your village feast to sip wine overlooking Göreme village.

⭐ Topdeck Cave Restaurant
ANATOLIAN $$

(☑ 0384-271 2474; www.facebook.com/topdeckcave; Hafız Abdullah Efendi Sokak 15; mixed meze plates ₺35-54, mains ₺36-62; ⏰5.30-11pm Mon-Thu, to midnight Fri-Sun; 🅿) If it feels as though you're dining in a family home, it's because you are. Talented chef Mustafa (aka Topdeck) and his gracious clan have transformed an atmospheric cave room in their house into an intimate restaurant where diners dig into hearty helpings of Anatolian cooking with a spicy twist.

WALKING IN THE VALLEYS AROUND GÖREME

Göreme village is surrounded by Cappadocia's most magnificent valleys, which are easily explored on foot; each needs about one to three hours. Most are interconnected, so you could easily combine several in a day, especially with the help of the area's many dolmuşes (minibuses with a prescribed route). Don't forget a bottle of water and sunscreen.

Some of the most interesting and accessible valleys:

Bağlıdere (White) Valley From Uçhisar to Göreme.

Görkündere (Love) Valley Trailheads off Zemi Valley and from Sunset View Hill in Göreme; particularly spectacular rock formations.

Güllüdere (Rose) Valley Trailheads just north of Göreme and at Çavuşin; superb churches and panoramic views.

Güvercinlik (Pigeon) Valley Connecting Göreme and Uçhisar; colourful dovecotes.

İçeridere Valley Running south from İçeridere Sokak in Göreme.

Kılıçlar (Swords) Valley Running north off Müze Caddesi on the way to the Göreme Open-Air Museum.

Kızılçukur (Red) Valley Running between the Güllüdere and Meskendir Valleys; trailheads from Kızılçukur viewpoint (opposite the Ortahisar turn-off); great views and vibrant dovecotes.

Meskendir Valley Trailhead next to Kaya Camping, running north off Müze Caddesi past the Göreme Open-Air Museum; tunnels and dovecotes.

Zemi Valley Trailhead running south off Müze Caddesi.

A word of warning: although many of the valleys now have trailhead signposts and signage has been put up at strategic points along the paths of Güllüdere and Kızılçukur Valleys, many of the trails remain only basically marked and there's no detailed map of the area available. It's quite easy to get lost if you don't stick to the trails.

Choose a mixed meze plate and Topdeck's signature chicken and herb *sigara böreği* (deep-fried cigar-shaped pastries) for a flavour-packed blowout your stomach will thank you for. Reservations recommended.

Fat Boys INTERNATIONAL **$$**
(☑ 0535 386 4484; Belediye Caddesi; mains ₺17-65; ☉ noon-late; 🅿🛜🍴) This restaurant-bar is a relaxed and friendly evening hang-out. We love kicking back on the terrace's cushions, munching spring rolls and watching the world go by with an Efes (500ml ₺22) in hand. The menu stars are its generously portioned Turkish classics, but there are also global pub-grub offerings of burgers, Aussie-style pies and fajitas plus interesting vegetarian options.

The well-stocked bar and nargile (water pipe) choice mean there are plenty of reasons to linger after your meal, plus there's an outdoor-table terrace and a cafe corner serving espresso-based coffee.

★ Pumpkin Cafe ANATOLIAN **$$$**
(☑ 0542 808 5050; İçeridere Sokak 7; set menu incl soft drinks, tea & coffee ₺120, vegetarian ₺100;

☉ 6-11pm; 🍴) With its wooden balcony and snug stone-cut room decorated with whimsically carved-out pumpkins (what else), this cute-as-a-button restaurant is one of the cosiest dining picks in Göreme. The four-course set menu (with a choice of lamb shank, beef, chicken or vegetarian main) is a feast and it's topped off by some of the friendliest, most on-the-ball service in town.

🍷 Drinking & Nightlife

★ Dusk by Koza COCKTAIL BAR
(☑ 0531 688 1909; www.facebook.com/duskby koza; Koza Cave Hotel, Çakmaklı Sokak 49; ☉ 4-10pm May-Sep; 🛜) Sip sunset cocktails while taking in the best view in town. Tamer and Lisa have created Göreme's most chilled-out, intimate summer drinking spot on the top two terraces at Koza Cave Hotel (p449). The cocktails (₺60 to ₺65) play with local flavours from a Turkish delight mojito to a fig old-fashioned, and there's craft beer (₺30) including the excellent Frederik IPA.

A tapas-style menu of small bites was in the works when we were last there so you

DON'T MISS

CAPPADOCIA FROM ABOVE

These days, Cappadocia is more famous for its hot-air ballooning than its surreal landscapes. Flight conditions are especially favourable here with balloons operating most mornings throughout the year. Seeing this area's remarkable landscape from above is a truly magical experience and many travellers judge it to be the highlight of their trip. Transport between your hotel and the balloon launch site is included in the hefty price, as is a sparkling-wine toast.

Flights take place just after dawn. Unfortunately, due to demand, even the reputable companies now offer a second, later-morning flight as well. Winds can become unreliable and potentially dangerous later in the morning, so you should always book the dawn flight. Ballooning is incredibly popular and the large bus-tour companies block-book in advance to guarantee a place. Because of this, during high season, the balloons are often fully booked. Independent travellers should book as far in advance as possible; we recommend booking three to four months ahead, if you can.

There's a fair amount of hot air among the operators about who is and isn't inexperienced, ill-equipped and under-insured. Be aware that, despite the aura of luxury that surrounds the hot-air ballooning industry, this is an adventure activity and is not without its risks. There have been several fatal ballooning accidents here over the past decade. It's your responsibility to check the credentials of your chosen operator carefully. Don't pick the cheapest operator if it means they might be taking shortcuts with safety or overfilling the balloon baskets (which, if nothing else, will mean you won't be able to see the views you've paid a princely sum for).

It's important to note that the balloons travel with the wind and that the companies can't ensure a particular flight path on a particular day. All companies try to fly over the fairy chimneys but sometimes – albeit rarely – the wind doesn't allow this. Occasionally (particularly in November and April) unfavourable weather means all flights are cancelled for safety reasons; if this happens you'll have your payment refunded or – if you're lucky and they're not fully booked – you might be offered a flight on the next day. Although this may be disappointing, it is preferable to flying in dangerous conditions.

All passengers should take a warm jumper or jacket and should wear trousers and flat shoes. Children under six will not be taken up by reputable companies.

The following agencies have good credentials:

Butterfly Balloons (☏0384-271 3010; www.butterflyballoons.com; Uzundere Caddesi 29; 1hr flight from €180; ⊗9.30am-6pm) This seamless operation has an excellent reputation, with highly skilled and professional pilots. Standard flights take up to 16 passengers.

Turkiye Balloons (☏0384-271 3222; www.turkiyeballoons.com; Bilal Eroğlu Caddesi 8; 1hr standard flight €190; ⊗9.30am-6pm) Most of Turkiye's balloon pilots have over 10 years' experience flying for various companies. Standard flights take up to 20 passengers.

Voyager Balloons (☏0384-271 3030; www.voyagerballoons.com; Kapadokya Caddesi 84; 1hr standard flight €190; ⊗5am-7pm) Recommended for its multilingual pilots and professional service. Standard flights use either 20- or 28-passenger baskets.

may soon be able to munch on popcorn chicken, meze dips and feta-smothered fries while you soak up the views.

Note, as the bar is outdoors, it doesn't open when it rains.

Mosaik WINE BAR
(☏0384-271 2119; https://mozaik-restaurant.business.site; Belediye Caddesi 31; ⊗noon-11pm; ☎) Behind Mosaik's sleek wood bar is the best selection of Turkish wines in the village, and at ₺25 for a very generous pour, you'll be tempted to linger for more than

one. The menu is made for grazing, with smoked-meat and cheese platters plus veggie options such as stuffed zucchini flowers, while caffeine fans are kept happy with on-the-money flat whites.

 Shopping

Tribal Collections CARPETS
(☏0384-271 2760; www.tribalcollections.net; Köşe Cıkmazı Sokak 1; ⊗9am-9pm) As well as being the proprietor of this mighty fine rug shop, owner Ruth is well known for her highly recommended carpet educationals (think of

it as Carpets 101), which explain the history and artistry of these coveted textiles.

Argos CERAMICS
(Karşıbucak Caddesi; ⊘10am-8pm) A classy selection of handmade ceramics, both modern and traditionally inspired, with a lot of unusual pieces that you won't see at Cappadocia's other ceramic shops, as well as interesting stone pieces.

ℹ Information

There are stand-alone clusters of ATM booths on and around Belediye Caddesi and Uzundere Caddesi but no bank. Some of the town's travel agencies will exchange money, but the best exchange rates are found at the **post office** (PTT; Posta Sokak; ⊘9am-12.30pm & 1.30-5pm Mon-Fri).

ℹ Getting There & Away

Most direct services to/from **Göreme Otogar** (Göreme Bus Station; Belediye Caddesi) are run by Kâmil Koç and Süha bus companies and are mostly to destinations on the Mediterranean coast and a couple of direct İstanbul services.

Many other bus services coming in from western Turkey terminate at Nevşehir Otogar (p461). From Nevşehir otogar car park you can either catch an Avanos dolmuş (₺6, 30 minutes, every two hours from 8.45am to 5.45pm plus 7.50pm), which travels to Avanos via Göreme, or hop on city bus 1 from the car park, which will drop you at a bus stand opposite Migros Supermarket where you can catch the half-hourly Göreme dolmuş (let the city-bus driver know you're going to Göreme; they'll

tell you when to get off). The majority of buses coming in from the east terminate at Kayseri.

You can buy tickets for all the services starting from Nevşehir and Kayseri at Göreme otogar's bus company offices, but you have to make your own way there.

ℹ Getting Around

Nomad Travel (☑ 0533 553 4346, 0384-271 2169; www.nomadtravel.com.tr; Belediye Caddesi; group day tours per person €28-55; ⊘9am-8pm) is one of several places in town to hire mountain bikes, scooters and motorbikes as well as cars.

The better rental car companies have offices in Ürgüp. Since there are no petrol stations in Göreme and your rental car comes with a near-empty tank, head to one of the garages on the main road near Ortahisar to fill up.

Hiring a taxi for the day to do a tour is a good alternative to a private tour (and with three people works out as basically the same cost as a group tour but with more flexibility). A day taxi tour following the typical group 'Red' tour itinerary (Göreme Open-Air Museum, Uçhisar Castle, Devrent Valley, Paşabağı, Avanos) plus Kaymaklı Underground City costs between €80 and €100.

Two recommended Göreme taxi drivers for tours are Ali Uludağ (☑ 0532 543 2714), who speaks excellent English, and Ufuk Polat (☑ 0532 608 0652). A taxi to Ürgüp (around 15 minutes) costs about ₺45, to Ortahisar ₺25.

BUS

Göreme has good connections to the other Cappadocian villages. The Ürgüp–Avanos dolmuş (₺4 to ₺6 depending on where you get off) picks up and drops off passengers on its way through town in both directions. To **Ürgüp** (Müze

CAPPADOCIA GÖREME

SERVICES FROM GÖREME OTOGAR

DESTINATION	FARE (₺)	DURATION (HR)	FREQUENCY
Antalya	80-85	10	3 morning, 1 afternoon, 3 evening
Bodrum	99	14	1 evening
Bursa	80	10	1 evening
Dalaman	100-104	12	2 evening
Denizli (for Pamukkale)	85-95	10½-12½	1 afternoon, 5 evening
Eğirdir	69	7½	1 morning, 1 afternoon, 1 evening
Fethiye	95-100	11¾	2 evening
İstanbul	130	12	3 evening
İzmir	100	12	1 morning, 3 evening
Konya	40-45	3½	3 morning, 2 afternoon, 5 evening
Marmaris	110-115	12	2 evening
Sivas	50	4	2 morning
Trabzon	115	14	1 evening

LOCAL KNOWLEDGE

AVOIDING THE CROWDS

Cappadocia is busy. It's more a tourists-only-go-to-four-places problem than an over-tourism one though. There are plenty of ways to not just avoid the crowds but feel like you're the only visitor for miles.

➡ Cappadocia's lunar-like valleys (p451) are what made it famous, but these days only a smidge of travellers bother to explore them. Sure you can get good aerial shots of the valleys from above in a hot-air balloon, and jeep and ATV tours skirt the edges of the area, but if you really want to be wowed by this surreal, alien landscape, put your hiking shoes on and head off to explore.

➡ For rock-cut churches without tour buses, both Gülşehir's Church of St Jean (p461) and Niğde's Eski Gümüşler Monastery (p476) have incredible frescoes and you're likely to be the only visitor.

➡ Both Zelve (p457) and Soğanlı (p474) receive only a handful of the visitors the Göreme Open-Air Museum gets.

➡ The Ihlara Valley (p477) is only busy on the middle section between Belisırma and the Ihlara Vadısı Turistik Tesisleri (Ihlara Valley Tourist Facility) because that's the only section the day-tour groups walk. The most beautiful section though is Selime to Belisırma and you'd be lucky to meet two other hikers along that stretch.

Caddesi) it stops in Göreme at 25 minutes past the hour between 8am and 8pm and to **Avanos** (Bilal Eroğlu Caddesi), via Paşabağı and Zelve Open-Air Museum, at 15 minutes past the hour between 8am and 7pm. There's no bus stand for the latter; just wait in front of the Kapadokya Shop opposite the Ürgüp bus stand.

The hourly direct bus to Avanos (from Nevşehir) also passes through town around 20 minutes past the hour. Pick that up at the Ürgüp bus stand.

The Göreme Belediye Bus Corp has a regular dolmuş service from Göreme **otogar** (Belediye Caddesi) to Nevşehir (₺3.50) via Uçhisar (₺3) every 30 minutes between 7.30am and 10pm. To get to Derinkuyu and Kaymaklı Underground Cities by public transport, take this bus and change at Nevşehir's central dolmuş stand.

To get to Nevşehir otogar, take the same Göreme Belediye Bus Corp dolmuş and get off at the bus stand in front of Migros Supermarket in Nevşehir. From here you can flag down any Nevşehir city bus marked 'Terminal' to the bus station.

Uçhisar

📞 0384 / POP 3630

Pretty little Uçhisar has undergone rapid development since its heady Club Med days. The French love affair with the clifftop village continues each summer as Gallic tourists unpack their *joie de vivre* in trendy hotels at the foot of Uçhisar Castle. The royal rectangular crag, visible from nearby Göreme, is the dramatic centrepiece of a stylish Cappadocian aesthetic, albeit at

times a touch manufactured. Unfortunately, some ill-judged large hotel construction has spoilt some of the village's dreamlike fairy-chimney vistas, while for reasons that remain unfathomable the town council has kept itself busy lately by ripping out the town square's beautiful tree-filled park and replacing it with swaths of concrete. Both of these things somewhat distract from Uçhisar's famously surreal setting.

⊙ Sights

Uçhisar Castle FORTRESS
(Uçhisar Kalesi; adult/child ₺9/4.50; ⊙7am-7pm)
This tall volcanic-rock outcrop is one of Cappadocia's most prominent landmarks and visible for miles around. Riddled with tunnels, it was used for centuries by villagers as a place of refuge when enemy armies overtook the surrounding plains. Wind your way up the stairs to its peak for panoramic views over the rock valleys of the Cappadocian countryside.

🛌 Sleeping

Uçhisar Pension PENSION $
(📞 0384-219 2662; Göreme Caddesi; r ₺140, cave r ₺300; 🐕) Mustafa and Gül dispense lashings of old-fashioned Turkish hospitality in their cosy pension. Simple rooms are spick and span with white-washed walls, cheerful floral bedspreads and small but squeaky-clean bathrooms. Downstairs, the roomy cave suites are decorated traditionally. In summer, swing from the rooftop hammock

and pinch yourself for your luck on finding million-dollar views for budget prices.

Cozy Villa Cappadocia GUESTHOUSE $$
(📞0535 650 8350; www.cozyvillacappadocia.com; 6 Guven Sokak 11; s €45, d €50-65, f €65-70, s/d without bathroom €15/25; 🅿🛜) If you're not bothered about cave character or valley views, this charming guesthouse in Uçhisar's modern village neighbourhood, run by well-travelled dynamo Buket and Paco, is a true home away from home. Good-sized rooms, are light-filled and decorated in a mix of traditional and modern, while a budget room under the eaves keeps backpackers happy. Regular discounts online.

Kilim Pension GUESTHOUSE $$
(📞0384-219 2774; www.sisik.com; Göreme Caddesi; s/d/tr/f ₺200/350/400/400; 🛜) The pride of fun-loving, multilingual 'Şişik', Kilim Pension has a glorious vine-draped terrace and spacious rooms with swish bathrooms as a bonus. Upstairs rooms have more character and lovely views to wake up to. The complimentary chaperoned hikes into the valleys are highly recommended.

⭐**Kale Konak** BOUTIQUE HOTEL $$$
(📞0384-219 2828; www.kalekonak.com; Kale Sokak 9; r €108-130, ste €150; 🛜) Take a handful of minimalist retreat-chic, blend it with touches of artistic flair and balance it all out with wads of Ottoman style and you get this effortlessly elegant hotel. Spacious cave rooms lead out through underground passageways to comfortable reading corners, communal areas strewn with fat cushions, and shady terraces in the shadow of Uçhisar's craggy *kale* (fortress).

The marble hamam tops off what has to be Uçhisar's most super sophisticated place to stay; the epitome of casual luxury.

🍴 Eating & Drinking

Kadıneli TURKISH $
(📞0384-219 2010; www.facebook.com/uchis arkalkinmavedayanismadernegi; Belediye Meydanı; mains ₺6-15; ⏰8.30am-7.30pm; 🍴) 🌿 Lunch on *gözleme*, *yaprak sarma* (stuffed vine leaves) and other staple Turkish dishes, served up at this good-value restaurant run by the Avanos women's cooperative. For a more substantial meal, ask what the dish of the day is. Entry is through an arch next to the Kadıneli shop.

Saklı Konak ANATOLIAN $$
(📞0384-219 3066; www.saklikonakhotel.com; 2 Karlık Sokak 3; mains ₺25-55; ⏰2-10pm; 🛜) At this cosy upstairs restaurant, dishes are cooked by local women traditionally in the *tandır* (clay oven), and ingredients are sourced from the neighbour's gardens. The *testı kebapı* (meat and vegetable stew slow-cooked in a sealed terracotta pot) is the signature dish; reserve beforehand to be sure of getting one as they often run out.

Mouton Rouge TURKISH $$
(📞0384-219 3000; www.facebook.com/lemou tonrouge; Belediye Meydanı; meze ₺10-20, mains ₺25-60; ⏰10am-midnight; 🛜🍴) The shady courtyard, with its comfy wicker seating, is a relaxed place to while away an afternoon, tucking into meze plates of spicy *muhammara* (dip of walnuts, bread, red peppers and lemon juice; also known as *acuka* or *civizli biber*), *sigara böreği* (deep-fried cigar-shaped pastries, often stuffed with cheese) and *içli köfte* (ground lamb and onion with a bulgur coating).

Reserved TURKISH $$$
(📞0384-219 2523; Adnan Menderes Caddesi 50; meze ₺18-52, mains ₺50-82; ⏰noon-midnight Tue-Sun; 🅿🛜🍴) Contemporary Turkish dining in a gorgeous stone building. Smaller plates are the menu stars. Main courses are bland so avoid these to instead feast on creative meze dips of pistachio, basil and cheese or freekeh, strained yoghurt and mint, good salads and – if you're feeling daring – *kokoreç* (seasoned lamb or mutton intestines wrapped around a skewer and grilled over charcoal).

🛍 Shopping

Kadıneli ARTS & CRAFTS
(Belediye Meydanı; ⏰8.30am-7pm) 🌿 Funky, colourful felt bags, cute knitted children's toys, crocheted jewellery and scarves, and local foodie products such as *mantı* (Turkish ravioli) pasta and preserves, all made by Avanos' women's cooperative.

Kocabağ Winery Shop WINE
(www.kocabag.com; Adnan Menderes Caddesi; ⏰10am-7pm) This rather swish outlet for Cappadocia's Kocabağ Winery is the best place in town for a spot of wine tasting. Just outside, a small selection of vines displays the different grape varieties for interested connoisseurs, while the shop stocks all of Kocabağ's wines and offers free tastings.

ℹ Getting There & Away

Dolmuşes to Nevşehir (₺3, 20 minutes) leave from opposite the *belediye* (town hall) on the main square every half-hour between 7am and 7pm.

The Nevşehir–Avanos bus (hourly) and the Nevşehir–Göreme dolmuş (every 30 minutes) both also pass through Uçhisar and drop off and pick up passengers on the corner of Atatürk and Hacı Alibey Caddesis at the bottom of the village.

A taxi to Göreme takes about 10 minutes and costs around ₺25.

Çavuşin

Midway between Göreme and Avanos is little Çavuşin, dominated by a cliff where a cluster of abandoned houses spills down the slope in a crumbling stone jumble. The main hive of activity is the clutch of souvenir stands at the cliff base, which spring into action when the midday tour buses roll into town. When the last bus has left for the day, Çavuşin hits the snooze button and resumes its slumber.

◉ Sights

Çavuşin has trailheads into the main valley area encompassing Güllüdere (Rose), Kızılçukur (Red) and Meskendir Valleys. You can even go as far as the Kızılçukur viewpoint (p464), then walk to the Nevşehir–Ürgüp road and catch a dolmuş back to your base.

Çavuşin Old Village Ruins　　　RUINS
FREE Carved into Çavuşin's craggy cliff face is a labyrinthine complex of abandoned houses that you can wander through by climbing up the short cliff path that leads upwards from the village's tiny old mosque. The timeless ambience has been lost somewhat due to the hotel that has been slapped right in the middle of the ruins, but there's still plenty to explore and the views from the summit are excellent.

If you're walking through the valleys from Göreme, head through Çavuşin's cemetery into the village and turn right at the new mosque. From here it's a short stroll to the old mosque and the cliff path. If you're coming by dolmuş, get off at Çavuşin Kilisesi on the highway, and walk up the main road through the village until you get to the new mosque.

Church of St John the Baptist　　CHURCH
FREE Right at the top of Çavuşin's village ruins rock outcrop is the Church of St John the Baptist, one of the oldest churches in Cappadocia. While the interior frescoes are severely damaged and faded, the still-standing columns inside the cavern are impressive

and the views across the countryside from the church entry are sublime.

Tarihi Ev　　　ARCHITECTURE
(◷approx 10am-5pm) **FREE** Mehmet Ali has thrown open the door of his old family home (which they moved out of in the 1970s) so that visitors can get a taste of what Cappadocian village life was once like. Rooms, chiselled into the cliff and backed by agricultural plots that the family still tends, have been decorated traditionally, and the agile can clamber (stairs and then rope to pull yourself up) into the old bedroom upstairs.

To get here follow the path that leads behind the old mosque at the foot of Çavuşin's old village ruins. Entrance is free but visitors are encouraged to buy some of the organic produce (snack packs of raisins, roasted green wheat) the family makes.

☞ Tours

Mephisto Voyage　　　ADVENTURE
(☎0384-532 7070; www.mephistovoyage.com; Mehmet Yılmaz Caddesi; ◷9am-6pm) Based at the İn Stone House, this group has been operating for over 15 years and offers multiday trekking, horse riding and biking packages in Cappadocia and the Taurus Mountains. It also gets big kudos for being the only operator in Cappadocia that offers hiking tours specifically designed for wheelchair users using the Joëlette system.

⌂ Sleeping

★ Azure Cave Suites　　BOUTIQUE HOTEL $$
(☎0384-532 7111; www.azurecavesuites.com; r €60, ste €100-200; P🅿❀🛜) This romantic warren of caves, at the top of Çavuşin hill, offers vistas across the countryside and a contemporary decorative touch that gives a distinctly fresh approach to Cappadocia's cave aesthetic. We're particularly enamoured with the garden-house annexe for its communal lounge, Room 11's hot tub with millionaire views, and the secret tunnel to three modern-minimalist-meets-cave-opulence royal suites. You'll need sturdy legs if you want to walk anywhere but it's worth it.

İn Stone House　　　GUESTHOUSE $$
(☎0384-532 7070; www.pensionincappadocia.com; Mehmet Yılmaz Caddesi; r €30-60, f €60; P🛜) This longtime Çavuşin hotel, near the main square, has come a long way since its pension roots. It still has a couple of simple, small budget rooms, but the majority of rooms have been seriously spruced up with wood and stone accents and new

bathrooms. Downstairs, deluxe rooms come with loads of traditional stone features and lovely decorative touches.

You get built-in travel advice here courtesy of in-house Mephisto Voyage.

 Eating

Seyyah Han TURKISH $$$
(☑ 0384-532 7214; Maltepi Sokağı; mains ₺35-70; ☉ 10am-10pm Tue-Sun; 🖉) Get a window table in the stone-cut dining room for views that stretch over to Göreme. For meze, order the spicier-than-usual *acılı ezme* (spicy tomato and onion paste) and dill-loaded whipped yoghurt dip. Lamb dishes are the speciality but we're more a fan of the *tavuk sarma* (chicken stuffed with cheese and spinach) and *dana kaburga* (beef ribs).

For such a meaty menu, full points for including a small selection of vegetarian mains plus plenty of vegetarian meze choices.

ⓘ Getting There & Away

Çavuşin is on the route of both the hourly Nevşehir–Avanos and Ürgüp–Avanos dolmuşes. Walk down to the highway and flag them down as they go by.

Paşabağı

The road between Çavuşin and Avanos passes a turn-off to the Zelve Open-Air Museum. **Paşabağı Valley** (Zelve Yolu), halfway along the road to Zelve, has a three-headed rock formation and some of Cappadocia's most famous examples of basalt-topped fairy chimneys. Monks once inhabited the valley and you can climb inside one chimney to a monk's quarters, decorated with Hellenic crosses. Wooden steps lead to a chapel where three iconoclastic paintings escaped the vandals; the central one depicts the Virgin holding baby Jesus.

Paşabağı is on the typical Cappadocia tour route and gets crammed with tour buses from around 10am, so if you want to miss the crowds try to get here first thing in the morning. Plans were afoot to charge an entrance fee to the valley (a planned combined ticket with Zelve). Fencing now surrounds the site and a large tourist complex building with cafes and tacky souvenir stalls aplenty is now the only way you can enter. Tickets were still not being charged when we were last there.

For independent travellers, Paşabağı is easily reached as it's on the Ürgüp–Avanos dolmuş route. Going to Avanos, it reaches the valley at around 20 to 25 minutes past the hour. Heading in the opposite direction for Göreme and Ürgüp, you can flag it down on the road when it trundles past at approximately 20 minutes past the hour.

Zelve

Halfway between Çavuşin and Avanos, three valleys of crumbling cave-habitations and churches converge at **Zelve Open-Air Museum** (Zelve Açık Hava Müzesi; Zelve Yolu; ₺15; ☉ 8am-6.15pm). Zelve was a monastic retreat from the 9th to the 13th century and then a village. Today its sinewy valley walls, topped with knobbly rock antennae, are a wonderfully picturesque place for poking around.

The valleys were inhabited until 1952, when they were deemed too dangerous to live in and the villagers were resettled a few kilometres away in Aktepe, also known as Yeni Zelve (New Zelve). An excellent walking trail loops around the valleys allowing access to the various caverns, although erosion continues to eat into the valley structures and certain areas are cordoned off due to rockfalls. **Valley One** is home to the old *değirmen* (mill), with a grindstone, and to the impressive **Üzümlü Kilise** (Grape Church) and neighbouring **Balıklı Kilise** (Fish Church) with fish figuring in one of the primitive paintings. In **Valley Three** is a small, unadorned rock-cut mosque.

There are plenty of small stalls selling *gözleme* and fresh-pressed orange juice lining the Zelve car park.

The Ürgüp–Avanos dolmuş stops at Zelve. If you're heading onward to Avanos after your visit, the dolmuş swings by Zelve car park at roughly 25 minutes past the hour; going the other way, towards Göreme and Ürgüp, it passes by around 15 minutes past the hour. It's an easy 1.5km flat walk along the road from Zelve to Paşabağı.

Note that the Zelve ticket office closes at 4.15pm from October to mid-April.

Devrent Valley

Look: it's a camel! The rock formations in **Devrent Valley** (Ürgüp-Avanos Yolu) **FREE**, nicknamed 'Imagination Valley' locally, are some of the best formed and most thickly clustered in Cappadocia. Most of the rosy rock cones are topped by flattish, darker stones of harder rock that sheltered the cones from the rain until all the surrounding rock was eaten away. This process is known to geologists as differential erosion but you can just call it kooky.

Tour guides here love pointing out the weird rock shapes. See if you can spot the dolphin, seals, Napoleon's hat, kissing birds, Virgin Mary and various reptilian forms. The camel is easily seen. For others, you may need to put on your imagination hat.

Devrent Valley lies on the direct (east) road between Avanos and Ürgüp. There's no public transport along this route but if it's not too hot and you don't mind a roadside walk, it's easy enough to get here on foot from Zelve. From the Zelve site entrance, go about 200m back down the access road to where the road forks and take the right-hand road marked for Ürgüp. After about 2km you'll come to the village of Aktepe (Yeni Zelve). Bear right and follow the Ürgüp road uphill for another 2km.

To cut down on walking time, the Ürgüp–Avanos dolmuş can drop you off at Aktepe. You can get çay and cold drinks from the souvenir stand at Devrent Valley, but you'll have to head on to Zelve, Ürgüp or Avanos for lunch.

Avanos

📞 0384 / POP 13,530 / ELEV 910M

The Kızılırmak (Red River) is the slow-paced pulse of this provincial town and the unusual source of its livelihood: the distinctive red clay that, mixed with a white, mountain mud variety, is spun to produce the region's famed pottery. Typically painted in turquoise or the earthy browns and yellows favoured by the Hittites, the beautiful pieces are traditionally thrown by men and painted by women.

Aside from the regulation tour groups (which, quicker than an eye-blink, get bussed into the pottery workshops and then bussed out again), Avanos is relatively devoid of foreign visitors, though on weekends it heaves with day-tripping locals from Kayseri here to stroll the riverbank. That leaves you alone midweek to meander the alleys that snake up the hillside, lined with gently decaying grand Greek-Ottoman houses, but riverside is still the place to ponder the sunset as you sip your umpteenth çay.

○ Sights

Head up the hillside through the arch, from the main square (opposite the mosque), to explore Avanos' old village district.

Güray Ceramic Museum   MUSEUM
(www.guraymuze.com; Dereyamanlı Sokak 44; ₺10; ⊙9am-7pm) Touted as the only underground ceramics museum in the world, this vast series of modern tunnelled-out caves, underneath the Güray Ceramic showroom, displays a private collection of ceramic art featuring pieces from as far back as the Chalcolithic era. To get here from Avanos centre, cross the river at Taş Köprü bridge (at Atatürk Caddesi's western end), take the first right-hand turn onto Kapadokya Caddesi and follow the signs for 1km.

Avanos Market   MARKET
(off Mithat Dülge Caddesi; ⊙9am-5pm Fri) Avanos market is the best, and biggest, local produce market in the region. It's foodie central with market traders selling fresh honeycomb, slabs of homemade butter and a huge array of seasonal fruit and vegetables. It bustles with shoppers all day but is best in the morning. It's held every Friday on the south bank of the Kızılırmak River, near Taş Köprü bridge.

Chez Galip Hair Museum   MUSEUM
(www.chezgalip.com; 110 Sokak 24; ₺2; ⊙8.30am-6pm) This pottery gallery, in the alley opposite the post office, is home to Cappadocia's infamous hair museum. Yes, that's right: it's a museum dedicated to locks of hair that past female visitors have left here for posterity – roughly 16,000 samples of hair hang down from the walls and ceiling of the back caves here. You'll find it either kookily hilarious or kind of (OK, a lot) creepy. Feel free to add your own contribution. Scissors are provided. Snip. Snip.

Özkonak Underground City   HISTORIC SITE
(Özkonak Yeraltı Şehri; Özkonak village; ₺15; ⊙8am-6.15pm) About 15km north of Avanos, the village of Özkonak hosts a smaller version of the underground cities of Kaymaklı and Derinkuyu, with the same wine reservoirs and rolling stone doors. Although Özkonak is neither as dramatic nor as impressive as the larger cities, it is much less crowded. On weekdays you can often have it all to yourself.

The easiest way to get here is by dolmuş from Avanos (₺2, 30 minutes, hourly between 8am and 5pm). Be aware that services can be erratic due to a lack of customers so it's best to check times locally for the current

HOW TO MAKE A FAIRY-CHIMNEY LANDSCAPE

The *peribacalar* (fairy chimneys) that have made Cappadocia so famous began their life when a series of megalithic volcanic eruptions was unleashed over this region about 12 million years ago. A common misconception is that the culprits for this reign of fire were the now-dormant volcanic peaks of Erciyes Dağı (Mt Erciyes) and Hasan Dağı (Mt Hasan) that still lord it over Cappadocia's landscape. These volcanoes were formed much later, however. The true perpetrators have long since been levelled by erosion, leaving only slight evidence of their once mighty power.

During this active volcanic period – which lasted several million years – violent eruptions occurred across the region, spewing volcanic ash that hardened into multiple layers of rock geologically known as tuff (consolidated volcanic ash). These layers were then slowly but surely whittled away by the grinding effects of wind, water and ice.

This natural erosion is the sculptor responsible for the weird and wacky Cappadocian landscape. Where areas of a harder rock layer sit above a softer rock layer, the soft rock directly underneath is protected while the rest gets winnowed away, creating the bizarre isolated pinnacles nicknamed 'fairy chimneys'. Depending on your perspective, they look like giant phalluses or outsized mushrooms. The villagers call them simply *kalelar* (castles).

schedule. There are no services on the weekend. Ask to be let off at the *yeraltı şehri* (underground city); the bus stops at the petrol station, a 500m stroll from the entrance.

Tours

Kirkit Voyage TOURS
(☏0384-511 3259; www.kirkit.com; Atatürk Caddesi 50; ⊙9am-6pm) This company has an excellent reputation and friendly multilingual staff. As well as the usual guided tours, it can arrange walking, biking, canoeing, horse-riding and snowshoeing trips and can arrange airport transfers (reservation essential). The highly recommended guided horse-riding treks range from €40 for two hours to €80 for a full day including proper riding equipment and lunch.

Sleeping

★Kirkit Hotel BOUTIQUE HOTEL $$
(☏0384-511 3148; www.kirkithotel.com; Genç Ağa Sokak; s/d/tr/f €25/40/45/50; ☎) This rambling stone house, right in the centre of town, is an Avanos institution. Rooms, made cosy and colourful with kilims (pileless woven rugs), intricately carved cupboards and *suzanis* (Uzbek bedspreads), are set around a courtyard brimming with plants and quirky antiques. Looked after by incredibly knowledgeable and helpful management, Kirkit is a great Cappadocia base.

Venessa Pansiyon PENSION $$
(☏0384-511 3840; 800 Sokak 20; s/d ₺150/180; ☎) Owned by enthusiastic local history expert Mükremin Tokmak, the Venessa is a homey Avanos option with simple, bright rooms full of local kilims and traditional

yastık (cushions). A cosy rooftop terrace has views and bundles of local character, and the pension also has its own small Cappadocian art exhibition and museum, which nonguests are welcome to visit.

Sofa Hotel BOUTIQUE HOTEL $$
(☏0384-511 5186; www.sofahotel.com; Gedik Sokak 9; d €40-70; ☎) A higgledy-piggledy wonderland for adults struck by wanderlust, Sofa is the creation of artist Hoja, who has spent a fair chunk of his life redesigning the Ottoman houses that make up the hotel. Rooms merge eclectic-chic and traditional decoration with plenty of wood-beam accents and colourful textiles.

Eating & Drinking

★Neman Cafem ANATOLIAN $
(☏0533 746 7664; www.facebook.com/nemankafe; Atatürk Caddesi 54; mantı ₺18; ⊙10am-11pm; ☎) You could easily blink and miss this tiny cafe as you're walking down the main road, but if you've picked up a *mantı* (Turkish ravioli) addiction on your Turkey travels make sure you don't. As well as typical *mantı*, it dishes up the local Avanos version (flat pasta strips and mincemeat served in a rich tomato and yoghurt sauce). Delicious.

Kapadokya Urfa Sofrası TURKISH $$
(Atatürk Caddesi; pide ₺15-20, mains ₺38-50; ⊙10.30am-10pm; ☎🅿) Our pick of Avanos' kebap joints is this welcoming place in the centre of town. Its pide is good for a cheap, tasty lunch but we recommend the *beyti sarma* (spicy ground meat baked in a thin layer of bread). Non-meat eaters also get a look-in with a couple of vegetable casserole options.

Bizim Ev TURKISH $$
(☏0384-511 5525; Baklacı Sokak 1; mains ₺20-45; ⏱11am-11pm; ☕) The cave wine cellar could tempt you into a few lost hours, but if you make it upstairs, the terrace is the place for atmospheric Avanos dining. Typical local dishes such as *testı kebapı* rule the menu, and full hat-tip for a decent selection of vegetarian mains.

Tafana STEAK $$$
(☏0384-511 4862; www.tafanasteakhouse.com; Atatürk Caddesi 31; mains ₺30-110; ⏱11am-11pm) Not going to lie: we're here for the cheapest thing on the menu. The Tafana burger (₺30) may just be the best burger in Turkey. It's by far the best in Cappadocia so if you're in a comfort-food mood make a beeline here. Most of the rest of the menu is dedicated to steak, some of it at eye-watering prices.

Lemon Coffeehouse CAFE
(900 Sokak 6; ⏱10am-10pm Tue-Sun) On a stinking-hot summer day, climb up the stairs on Atatürk Caddesi to this stone house for a thirst-quenching homemade lemonade or fruit smoothie. Prime seating is on the tiny river-facing balcony. Good for a cheap lunch of *tost* (toasted sandwiches) or a mid-afternoon pick-me-up slice of cake.

🛍 Shopping

Most visitors come to Avanos to see the pottery artisans at work. Tour groups are shuffled into the warehouses lining the main roads outside of town. The smaller, independent pottery workshops in the centre are more relaxed and offer better prices, and most will happily show you how to throw a pot.

İkizler Atölyesi CERAMICS
(☏0384-511 5094; www.ikizleratolyesi.com; 301 Sokak; ⏱9am-6pm) Our favourite Avanos ceramic workshop is a bit of a local secret. Twins Levent and Mehmet create quirky contemporary ceramics that often riff on Anatolian themes and motifs but are quite unlike anything else in town.

Le Palais du Urdu CERAMICS
(off Camii Sokak; ⏱10am-6pm) This Avanos artisan haunt is a combined drum-making and pottery studio. It's just off the main square, to your right if you're facing the hill.

ℹ Getting There & Away

You can book long-distance buses at Avanos' small **otogar** (Avanos Bus Station; Kapadokya Caddesi), a 10-minute walk across the Kızılırmak River from the centre. Avanos has most of the same direct bus services as Göreme (p453). For more variety of services and more destinations, head to Nevşehir Otogar (p443).

Nine of the Avanos–Nevşehir dolmuş services daily go all the way to Nevşehir Otogar (current timetables for the otogar services are pinned up at Avanos Otogar). Avanos Otogar also has dolmuş services to Kayseri (₺20, one hour, hourly 7am to 11am and 1pm to 6pm).

ℹ Getting Around

Dolmuşes from Avanos to Nevşehir (₺5) leave roughly every 20 minutes between 7am and 7pm. Services departing on the hour travel via Çavuşin, Göreme and Uçhisar (₺4); other departures take the direct route.

Dolmuşes to Ürgüp (₺6) leave hourly between 7am and 8pm, travelling via Zelve, Paşabağı, Çavuşin, Göreme and Göreme Open-Air Museum (₺4 to ₺6 depending on where you get off).

Both of these dolmuş services drop off and pick up passengers along Atatürk Caddesi.

Monday to Friday there is supposed to be a dolmuş service to Özkonak Underground City (p458) hourly between 8am and 5pm. In reality, the only guaranteed services seem to be at 9am, midday and 4pm; ask locally to check current times. The **dolmuşes** (Atatürk Caddesi) leave from behind the post office near the main square.

Kirkit Voyage (p459) hires out mountain bikes for ₺50 per day.

There are several taxi stands dotted around the centre including **Avanos Taksi** (☏0544 582 2361; Atatürk Caddesi; ⏱24hr).

Nevşehir
☏0384 / POP 110,100 / ELEV 1260M
Poor old Nevşehir. Surrounded by the stunning countryside of Cappadocia, this provincial capital of bland mid-rise apartment buildings has never offered travellers an incentive to linger. Things may be looking up though; an underground city was discovered when the town council began clearing away the old neighbourhood around Nevşehir castle. Continuing excavations have since revealed a vast tunnel network and a frescoed church that may date back to as early as the 5th century. The underground city is pegged to open to the public in the near future, so check locally for the latest information.

ℹ Getting There & Away
Nevşehir is the main regional transport hub for the central Cappadocian villages.

AIR
Nevşehir Airport (Nevşehir Kapadokya Havalimanı, NAV; ☏0384-421 4455; https://

SERVICES FROM NEVŞEHİR OTOGAR

DESTINATION	FARE (₺)	DURATION (HR)	FREQUENCY
Adana	65	4	2 morning, 2 afternoon, 2 evening
Aksaray	20-25	1	every 1-2 hours until 10.30pm
Ankara	60-70	4-5	every 1-2 hours until 8pm
Antalya	100-110	8-9½	2 morning, 1 afternoon, 7 evening
Denizli	90-110	9½-10	1 afternoon, 5 evening
Fethiye	100-120	10½	1 afternoon, 3 evening
Gaziantep	90	7¼	1 morning, 1 afternoon, 1 evening
İstanbul	140	10¼-12	3 morning, 2 afternoon, 4 evening
Kayseri	18-20	1½	at least hourly
Konya	60	3½	every 1-1½ hours until 11.30pm
Şanlıurfa	100	9¾	1 morning, 1 evening

kapadokya.dhmi.gov.tr; Nevşehir Kapadokya Havaalanı Yolu, Gülşehir) is 30km northwest of town, past Gülşehir. Turkish Airlines (www.turkishairlines.com) operates several flights daily to İstanbul from here. Airport shuttle buses (p443) run between the airport and the villages of central Cappadocia. They must be pre-booked.

BUS

Nevşehir Otogar (Aksaray–Nevşehir Yolu) is 2.5km southwest of the city. Many bus services from İstanbul and other towns in western and southern Turkey terminate here.

Heading to the Cappadocian villages, direct dolmuş services leave from the otogar car park:

Avanos via Göreme (₺6, weekdays every two hours from 8.45am to 4.45pm plus 5.45pm and 7.50pm; weekends 7.45am, 8.55am, then every two hours from 10.45am to 4.45pm, plus 5.45pm and 7.50pm)

Ürgüp (₺8, 8.10am, 9.15am, 11.15am, 1.15pm, 2.15pm, 3.15pm, 5.15pm, 6.30pm, 8pm, 9pm, 10.40pm and 1am)

If those times don't work, hop on Nevşehir city bus 1 (₺2.25, 20 minutes, every 10 minutes), which leaves from the otogar car park and will drop you at the **bus stand** (Kayseri Caddesi) opposite Migros supermarket – all the dolmuşes to Avanos, Göreme, Ortahisar, Uçhisar and Ürgüp stop here.

Coming to the otogar from the Cappadocian villages, get off the village dolmuş at the **bus stand** (Kayseri Caddesi) in front of Migros supermarket and flag down Nevşehir city bus 1 (marked 'Terminal') as it goes by.

Central Nevşehir has excellent transport links to the surrounding Cappadocian villages from its **dolmuş stand** (Osmanlı Caddesi) on Osmanlı Caddesi in the city centre. It's unsigned – look for the row of benches opposite the Business

Han Hotel. From here local dolmuşes run to the following:

Avanos (₺6, every 20 minutes from 7am to 7pm)
Göreme (₺3.50, every 30 minutes from 7.30am to 10pm)
Kaymaklı/Derinkuyu Underground Cities (₺5/8, every 30 minutes between 9am and 6.30pm)
Niğde (₺12, hourly between 9am and 6pm)
Ortahisar (₺5, hourly from 8am to 6pm)
Uçhisar (₺3, every 30 minutes from 7.30am to 7.30pm)
Ürgüp (₺6, every 15 minutes from 7am to 8pm)

Dolmuşes to Hacıbektaş leave from the Hacıbektaş office, on Lale Caddesi, just around the corner. Many village dolmuşes have fewer services on Sundays.

Gülşehir

📞 0384 / POP 12,030

This small town, 19km north of Nevşehir, has two rocky attractions on its outskirts. They may not be as famous as their central Cappadocian cousins, but don't believe for a second that this means they're second-rate. Hiding just off the road to Gülşehir is one of the region's most fabulous fresco-filled churches, while a couple of kilometres further along the road to Nevşehir is a large Byzantine monastery complex.

★ **Church of St Jean**   CHURCH
(Karşı Kilise; Kırşehir-Nevşehir Yolu; ₺6; ⊙ 8am-5pm) On the main highway into Gülşehir, just before the turn-off to the centre (another 500m further) is a signposted trail leading to the incredible 13th-century Church of St Jean. This two-levelled, rock-cut church

GOING UNDERGROUND

Thought to have been first carved out by the Hittites, the vast network of underground cities in this region was first mentioned by the ancient Greek historian Xenophon in his *Anabasis* (written in the 4th century BC).

During the 6th and 7th centuries, Byzantine Christians extended the cities and used them as a means by which to escape persecution. If Persian or Arab armies were approaching, a series of beacons would be lit in warning – the message could travel from Jerusalem to Constantinople in hours. When it reached Cappadocia, the Christians would relocate to the underground cities, hiding in the subterranean vaults for months at a time.

One of the defense mechanisms developed by the cities' inhabitants was to disguise the air shafts as wells. Attackers might throw poison into these 'wells', thinking they were contaminating the water supply. Smoke from residents' fires was absorbed by the soft tuff rock and dispersed in the shafts – leaving the prowling attackers none the wiser.

The shafts, which descend almost 100m in some of the cities, also served another purpose. As new rooms were constructed, debris would be excavated into the shafts, which would then be cleared and deepened so work could begin on the next floor. Some of the cities are remarkable in scale – it is thought that Derinkuyu and Kaymaklı housed about 10,000 and 3000 people respectively.

Around 37 underground cities have already been opened. There are at least 100 more, though the full extent of these subterranean refuges may never be known. One currently being excavated in Nevşehir may be about to flip the commonly accepted theory of how the cities were used on its head, as archaeologists say there is evidence that city was used as a permanent habitation rather than a temporary shelter.

Touring the cities is like tackling an assault course for history buffs. Narrow walkways lead you into the depths of the earth, through stables with handles used to tether animals, churches with altars and baptism pools, granaries with grindstones and blackened kitchens with ovens. While it's a fascinating experience these aren't sites for the claustrophobic and during the May to September high season be prepared for unpleasantly crowded conditions at Derinkuyu and Kaymaklı. Go early in the morning to beat the tour groups and avoid weekends if at all possible.

Following are four of the most interesting cities to visit but there are others, including the underground cities in the village of Güzelyurt (p479), and at Özkonak (p458) near Avanos.

is home to marvellous frescoes, including scenes depicting the Annunciation, the Descent from the Cross, the Last Supper, the Betrayal by Judas and the Last Judgement (rarely depicted in Cappadocian churches), which were all painstakingly restored to their original glory in 1995.

Open Palace MONASTERY
(Açık Saray; Kırşehir–Nevşehir Yolu; ⊙ 8am-5pm) FREE This fine rock-cut monastery complex has a cluster of churches, refectories, dormitories and a kitchen, all carved out of fairy chimneys and dating from the 6th and 7th centuries. It's signposted off the main Gülşehir–Nevşehir road, about 4km before Gülşehir's town centre. Right at the back of the complex is the site's much photographed mushroom-shaped rock – walk to the end of the path where the willow trees begin, jump the small stream and take the signposted trail.

❶ Getting There & Away

Dolmuşes to Gülşehir (₺3.50, 25 minutes, every 30 minutes) from Nevşehir depart from an unsigned dolmuş stand on Lale Caddesi, directly after the intersection with Osmanlı Caddesi. Ask to be let off at the Açık Saray or Karşı Kilise to save a walk back from town. Returning, just flag the bus down from the side of the highway. You can also flag down dolmuşes heading onward to Hacıbektaş from the highway.

Hacıbektaş

🖉 0384 / POP 5050

Hacıbektaş could be any unremarkable, small Anatolian town if it weren't for the beautiful dervish *dergah* (lodge) and museum set right in the main square. A visit here is a glimpse at the history and culture of the Bektaşi Alevi religious sect. The annual Hacı Bektaş Veli pilgrimage and festival is a fascinating experience if you're here at that time.

Kaymaklı Underground City (₺42; ⊙8am-6.15pm) Kaymaklı's large, well-lit caverns and not-too-steep tunnels make this Cappadocia's most photogenic underground city. The subterranean labyrinth is carved eight levels deep into the earth (only four levels can be visited). There are plenty of carved details including huge round stone doors and a mind-boggling ventilation shaft you can look into about halfway down.

Derinkuyu Underground City (₺42; ⊙8am-6.15pm) Located 10km south of Kaymaklı, this maze of narrow tunnels (some steep) leading to cavernous rooms competes with Kaymaklı for Cappadocia's most popular underground site. You get to descend down seven levels here making it the deepest. When you get all the way to the bottom, look up the ventilation shaft to see just how far down you are. If you have any doubts about being prone to claustrophobia, this is one to avoid.

Gaziemir Underground City (₺10; ⊙8am-6pm) Some 18km east of Güzelyurt, just off the road to Derinkuyu, is Gaziemir underground city. Churches, a winery with wine barrels, food depots, hamams and *tandır* (clay-oven) fireplaces can be seen. Camel bones and loopholes in the rock for tethering animals suggest that it also served as a subterranean caravanserai.

Özlüce Underground City (⊙9am-6.30pm) FREE Turn right as you enter Kaymaklı village from the north and you'll be heading for the small village of Özlüce, 7km further away. The underground city here is very small and not deep; a good option for those with claustrophobia to see an underground city, knowing they're never too far from the exit.

Getting There & Away

Although you can visit one of the cities as part of a day tour, it's also easy to see them on your own. From Nevşehir, Derinkuyu Koop runs dolmuşes (minibuses with a prescribed route) to Derinkuyu (₺8, 40 minutes, 7.35am, 8.15am and then every 30 minutes between 9am and 6.30pm), which also stop in Kaymaklı (₺5, 30 minutes). Derinkuyu otogar (bus station) is next door to the underground city. There are also separate Kaymaklı dolmuşes every 30 minutes. The bus stop in Kaymaklı is in front of the underground city entrance. Both these services leave Nevşehir from its central village dolmuş stand on Osmanlı Caddesi, which all the dolmuşes to and from the villages pass by; tell the dolmuş driver you're heading to Derinkuyu or Kaymaklı and they'll let you know when to get off.

You'll need a taxi or a hire car to take you to Özlüce from Kaymaklı or to visit Gaziemir.

CAPPADOCIA HACIBEKTAŞ

Hacıbektaş Veli Museum   MUSEUM

(Hacıbektaş Veli Müzesi; Atatürk Caddesi; ⊙8am-6pm) FREE Right in Hacıbektaş' centre is this tranquil dervish *dergah* (lodge), now a museum as well as a place of pilgrimage for those of the Bektaşi faith. Several rooms are arranged as they might have been when the Bektaşi order lived here, with dioramas of dervish life and beautiful exhibits of clothing, musical instruments and jewellery. The **Meydan Evi** (meeting house), where initiation ceremonies were performed, has an intricate wooden dove-tailed ceiling, its cross-beams symbolising the nine levels of heaven.

Amid the rose gardens of the museum's inner courtyard is the **Pir Evi** (House of the Masters), which contains the **Mausoleum of Haci Bektaş Veli**. Walk down the stairs, passing the tiny cell where dervishes would retreat to pray, to enter the Kırklar Meydanı (where dervish ceremonies took place), its walls decorated with colourful floral and geometric motifs. Haci Bektaş Veli's tomb is in a separate room to the right.

Across the rose gardens from the Pir Evi is the **Mausoleum of Balım Sultan** (another important religious leader), with a 700-year-old mulberry tree – its aged branches propped up by wooden posts – just outside.

Hacıbektaş

Archaeological Museum   MUSEUM

(Atatürk Caddesi; ⊙9am-5pm Tue-Sun) FREE This surprisingly good museum on the main road contains a large collection of ceramics from the Chalcolithic era up to the Iron Age, including pieces from the nearby Saluca Karahöyük archaeological site, which has yielded finds dating back to the early Bronze Age. There's plenty of information in English on offer too, explaining the different archaeological periods of Anatolia as a whole. The last room is devoted to the ethnography section with displays of costumes and household objects.

ℹ️ Getting There & Away

From Nevşehir, the Hacıbektaş office on Lale Caddesi, one block north of the intersection with Osmanlı Caddesi, has departures to Hacıbektaş (₺3.50, 40 minutes) at 7.30am, 8.45am and then hourly from 10.30am to 6.30pm. All dolmuşes head on from Hacıbektaş to Kırşehir (₺7, 1½ hours).

Catch the returning dolmuş from Hacıbektaş otogar (7.30am and then hourly from 10.30am to 6.30pm). Note that on the return journey you will often be charged the full ₺7 fare from Kırşehir. There are also seven daily departures for Ankara.

Ortahisar

📞 0384 / POP 3600

Known for the jagged castle that gives the town its name, Ortahisar is the epitome of Cappadocia's agricultural soul. Wander downwards from the central square and you'll discover cobbled streets rimmed by worn stone-house ruins leading out to a gorge of pigeon-house-speckled rock. Head upwards (towards the highway) and you'll see the cave complexes where Turkey's citrus-fruit supply still overwinters.

Overlooked for years by travellers, the secret is now firmly out. The past couple of years have seen a flurry of boutique and larger hotel openings here as visitors searching for the Cappadocia-of-old begin to discover Ortahisar's beguiling, Arcadian beauty. Despite the sudden influx, Ortahisar's rustic nature is still very much in place. Donkey carts rattle down the lanes regularly, elderly men mooch all day outside teashops and, if you're here in April when the citrus storage caves are thrown open, the scent of lemons permeates the town.

◉ Sights & Activities

Pigeon-house-studded **Ortahisar Valley** is easiest accessed from the bottom of Tahir Bey Sokak. There's also easy access into the **Uzengi Valley** (home to some incredible pigeon-house views) from the southeast end of the village. For trailheads into the more famous Kızılçukur (Red), Güllüdere (Rose) and Meskendir Valleys, head to the Kızılçukur Viewpoint.

★ **Kızılçukur Viewpoint**   VIEWPOINT
(Panoramik Viewpoint; off Nevşehir-Ürgüp Yolu; cars ₺10) One of the best views of Kızılçukur

Valley's fang-like rock cones and wavy cliff ridges is from this lookout point, signposted off the highway, opposite the Ortahisar turn-off road. For hikers there are trailheads into the main valley area from here, allowing you to do a circular loop of Kızılçukur and Güllüdere Valley or finish in Göreme or Çavuşin. Rustic cafes at the viewpoint provide refreshments for those who just want to admire the valley vista.

The Ürgüp–Avanos, Ürgüp–Nevşehir and Ortahisar–Ürgüp dolmuşes can all drop you at the turn-off, from where it's about 2km to the viewpoint. From late afternoon to sunset the viewpoint gets crammed with tour groups. Head here in the morning to avoid the crowds.

Hallacdere Monastery   MONASTERY
(off Nevşehir-Ürgup Yolu) FREE The facade of this rock-cut complex has some of the most colourful geometric pigeon-house decorations in Cappadocia while inside there are unusual ornamental features. Look for the animal heads on the column capitals in the main church and the human figure sculpted onto the wall in the left-hand chamber. The monastery has become a favourite stop on jeep-safari excursions, which tend to arrive in packs and blare loud music. Get here before 11am to have it to yourself.

Access is signposted from the main Ortahisar–Ürgüp highway about 1km northeast of the Ortahisar turn-off.

Ortahisar Castle   CASTLE
(Cami Sokak; ₺3; ◷ 9am-6pm) Slap in the middle of Ortahisar's town centre, this 18m-high rock outcrop was used as a fortress in Byzantine times. It was reopened after a restoration project stabilised the crumbling edifice, and you can now climb the precarious metal ladders and stairways to the viewing terrace halfway up and admire the glorious view. Head up in the late afternoon for the best photography light.

Pancarlı Kilise   CHURCH
(Beetroot Church; ₺5; ◷ 9am-4.30pm Apr-Oct) This rarely visited 11th-century church is snuggled amid a particularly photogenic vista of orange-hued rock. The small nave has a dazzling interior of well-preserved frescoes, while the surrounding cliff face is pockmarked with a warren of rooms that once served as living areas for hermit monks. To find it, head southeast from Ortahisar Castle, following Hacı Telegraf Sokak down the hill. Cross the bridge across the gully and take the eastern (signposted) farm track for 3km.

SAVING CAPPADOCIA

Like many regions that have witnessed a tourism boom, Cappadocia walks a tightrope between hanging onto its authentic soul (which attracted travellers here in the first place) and responding to the push for progress. The showstopping landscapes and ancient rock-cut shelters have transformed this area's economy from subsistence agriculture to one of the world's most unique tourism destinations.

Its popularity with travellers has not been without problems. The hot-air-ballooning industry's rush to cater for increasing numbers has led to the bulldozing of sections of valley to make way for multiple take-off sites. The popularity of jeep and ATV tours into the valleys has caused needless erosion. Hotel construction has boomed – with a handful of entrepreneurs more interested in cashing in than in preserving Cappadocia's rich natural heritage.

In recent years the tide slowly started turning, with laws banning ATVs and jeeps from going into some valley areas and the demolition of some hotels that had been built illegally in protected areas. However, in October 2019, in a move that horrified many locals, the government removed national park status from the region. Much of the Cappadocian community fears this could open up vast swaths of the area – previously protected as part of Göreme National Park – to development. The next few years may prove critical in preserving Cappadocia's unique topography and cultural heritage.

Cemal Ranch   HORSE RIDING
(☑ 0532 291 0211; www.cemalranch.com; off Nevşehir-Ürgüp Yolu; incl transport to/from hotel 1/2hr ₺150/250, 4/6hr incl lunch ₺450/650) Cemal Ranch offers riding excursions in the surrounding countryside. Sunset and sunrise two-hour tours head through Red and Rose Valleys. Longer horse treks (for experienced riders) explore more secluded Üzengi and Pancarlık Valleys and include lunch. The ranch is signposted off the main highway, opposite the Ortahisar turn-off, along the road to Kızılçukur Viewpoint.

🛌 Sleeping

Elaa Cave Hotel   BOUTIQUE HOTEL $$
(☑ 0384-343 2650; www.elaacavehotel.com; Tahir Bey Sokak 4; r €50-60; ☜) Chickens wander the alley outside but through Elaa's gate that rural Anatolian aesthetic gets a Turkish-modern makeover. Vibrant colours sit alongside intricately carved wood panels, fine carpets and quirky art in six snug cave rooms, while the chic roof terrace is loomed over by Ortahisar's rock-castle.

Breakfast feasts are presided over by the ever-smiling Necla, while owners Cemal and Ruth dish out local knowledge.

★ Hezen Cave Hotel   BOUTIQUE HOTEL $$$
(☑ 0384-343 3005; www.hezenhotel.com; Tahir Bey Sokak 87; r/ste from €92/137; ☺ Mar-Nov; P ✽ ☜) From the foyer's statement-piece ceiling of recycled *hezen* (telegraph poles) to the gourmet breakfasts on the terrace with 360-degree village views, every detail at this gorgeous design hotel has been thought

through. A riot of quirky colours enlivens doors, window frames and fixtures, adding a shot of contemporary chic to cave rooms that exude effortless cool.

Extra touches such as the honesty bar, washing machines for guest use, a small but well-put-together menu for evenings when you can't be bothered going out, and the hotel's complimentary drop-off and pick-up service to local restaurants top off an experience where you wonder if you've wandered into a VIP's daydream. Don't pinch us. We don't want to wake up.

Lamihan   BOUTIQUE HOTEL $$$
(☑ 0384-343 3316; www.lamihan.com; Cami Sokak 15; r €55-70; P ☜) Owner Hayriye has transformed this 300-year-old mansion into Ortahisar's most interesting place to stay. Higgledy-piggledy courtyards graced by pansies, herb gardens and hammocks lead to four rooms (three of them high-ceilinged caves) that hold onto many original features, including stone fireplaces and grape presses. At sunset, head to the rooftop, with its 180-degree vistas over the village and valleys beyond.

Anitya Cave House   APARTMENT $$$
(☑ 0535 494 6814, 0535 448 3845; www.anitya cavehouse.com; Hacı Telegraf Sokak; d/tr/q from €80/90/100; ☜) Travelling families, or those who simply prefer a more independent experience than hotels offer, will adore these three spacious studios (two of them cave studios) with terrace views out to the valley's pigeon-house cliffs and Erciyes Dağı (Mt Erciyes) beyond. All come fitted out with full

kitchen, large lounge area with local artisan work, separate bedroom and contemporary bathroom.

Eating

Uğurlu Restaurant TURKISH $
(☑0384-343 2050; Meydan; mains ₺10-25; ☉10am-10pm) Friendly Uğurlu dishes up really good thin-crust pide along with cheap and filling *kiremit* (clay-dish baked) dishes and kebaps. Dine either on the front terrace or in the basic canteen-style interior.

★No 10 Restaurant TURKISH $$
(☑0384-343 2525; Cami Sokak 10; mains ₺25-70; ☉noon-11pm; ☎☑) Upmarket, contemporary dining, with modern tweaks to Turkish classics and a fun approach to dish presentation, is the name of the game here. Order the Erciyes kebap (a mountain-shaped mound of chips, grilled beef and peppers smothered in a rich sauce) or the Castle chicken – balsamic-sauce-drenched chicken served under a *lavaş* (flatbread) castle-hat, a tribute to Ortahisar's castle.

Full marks for its good vegetarian mains, a pasta selection and excellent meze-style plates for when you just want a light lunch. Dine on the outdoor terraces in summer or inside the cosy lounge-bar.

❶ Information

There are stand-alone ATMs in the town centre.

❶ Getting There & Away

Dolmuşes leave from the main square to Ürgüp (₺4, every 30 minutes from 8am to 5.30pm Monday to Saturday) and Nevşehir (₺5, hourly from 8am to 5pm Monday to Saturday). There are fewer services on Sundays. Heading to Göreme, you have to walk 1km uphill to the main Nevşehir–Ürgüp highway, where you can catch passing Ürgüp–Avanos dolmuşes from the bus stand.

Hisar Taksi has a stand in the main square. It's around ₺25 to Göreme and ₺35 to Ürgüp.

Ürgüp

☑0384 / POP 20,300
When Ürgüp's Greek population was evicted in 1923 the town's wealth of fine stone-cut houses was left teetering into gentle dilapidation until tourism began to take off. Now, more than 90 years later, these remnants of another era have found a new lease of life as some of Cappadocia's most luxurious boutique hotels. Ürgüp is the rural retreat for those who don't fancy being too rural, with its bustling, modern downtown area a direct foil to the old village back lanes still clinging to the hillside rim. There's not a lot to do in town itself. Instead, Ürgüp has cleverly positioned itself as the connoisseur's base for exploring the geographical heart of Cappadocia, with boutique-hotel frippery at your fingertips.

◉ Sights & Activities

Three Graces
Fairy Chimneys NATURAL FEATURE
(Üç Güzeller; Nevşehir-Ürgüp Yolu) FREE These three black-capped fairy-chimney formations (also known as 'the three beauties'), overlooking the rolling countryside just outside of town, are Ürgüp's best-known landmark. It's a prime spot to capture a sunset photo. The site is 1km along the main road, heading towards Ortahisar, from the roundabout at the top of Tevfik Fikret Caddesi.

If you want to view the fairy chimneys from a lower angle, a steep path leads down into the valley from the wooden walkway. There's also an easier access trail just off the highway, about 20m along the road heading back towards Ürgüp.

Turasan Winery WINERY
(☑0384-341 4961; Tevfik Fikret Caddesi; wine tasting ₺30; ☉8.30am-6pm) The abundant sunshine and fertile volcanic soil of Cappadocia produce delicious sweet grapes, and several wineries carry on the Ottoman Greek winemaking tradition. You can sample some of the local produce here; there's a free tasting of two small samples (one red, one white) then a paid tasting of three larger ones.

★Old Village AREA
The back alleys of Ürgüp are home to many examples of the traditional stone architecture of this region. In particular, in the northern section of the old village walk up Dere Sokak, with its road-archway topped with a tiny mosque. Or take a wander through the southern section, heading up Barbaros Hayrettin Sokak for its decoratively carved doorways, and then continuing on, walking through the back alleys where the old village houses rub up against the hill.

☞ Tours

Argeus Tourism & Travel TOURS
(☑0384-341 4688; www.argeus.com.tr; İstiklal Caddesi 47; private day tours per person 4/3/2 people from €85/105/145) Private Cappadocia day tours include the 'Dream' tour (Mustafapaşa, Keşlik Monastery and Soğanlı) and the 'Shop, Cook, Eat and Hike' tour, which

takes in a cooking lesson at a local village home and a hike in Red Valley. Argeus also organises mountain-biking trips, seven- to 15-day packages across Turkey, flights and car hire.

It runs a reputable airport shuttle service for flights arriving in Kayseri and Nevşehir. Book in advance.

Honeycomb Travel   TOURS
(☑ 0384-341 4322; www.cavekonak.com; Şehir Hamamı Karşısı; group day tours per person ₺200-300; ☺ 9am-7pm) Run by the friendly folk at Hotel Cave Konak, Honeycomb offers good-value 'Red' (Göreme Open-Air Museum, Paşabağı, Avanos), 'Green' (Ihlara Valley and Derinkuyu Underground City) and 'Blue' (Mustafapaşa, Soğanlı) group tours. It can also arrange private day tours combining valley hikes and historic sights and a variety of other activities.

🛏 Sleeping

Hotel Elvan   PENSION $
(☑ 0384-341 4191; www.hotelelvan.com; Barbaros Hayrettin Sokak 11; r ₺100-160; ☎) Bah – who needs boutique style when you have pensions like the Elvan, where Hasan and family dish out oodles of homespun hospitality. Set around an internal courtyard brimming with colourful pot plants, the standard rooms are sparkling clean and bright. On the ground floor, stone-arch deluxe rooms have snazzy onyx-stone bathrooms and TVs.

Canyon Cave Hotel   BOUTIQUE HOTEL $$
(☑ 0384-341 4113; www.canyoncavehotel.com; Sair Mahfi Baba 3 Sokak 9; r €50-80, apt €70, f €80-100; P☺☎) Host Murat İşnel creates a fun, sociable atmosphere at his nine-room hilltop pad with its rooftop bar overlooking the entire sweep of Ürgüp's craggy cliffs. Set around a courtyard abloom with roses and lavender, rooms (both half- and full cave) are generously sized and simply furnished. Breakfast is a slap-up feast featuring cafetière coffee and homemade cake.

If you need more space, the well-equipped one-bedroom apartment, with knock-out views from its balcony, is a winner.

Hotel Cave Konak   GUESTHOUSE $$
(☑ 0384-341 4322; www.cavekonak.com; Şehir Hamamı Karşısı; d ₺250-300, tr/q ₺400/550; P☎) If you don't fancy tackling Ürgüp's hills to get to bed, this rambling Greek mansion is right in the centre of town.

Stone-arch rooms are large and come with snazzy big bathrooms decked out in beautiful onyx-travertine, while cave rooms below brim with original carved details. Travelling families are well looked after here with good-value, exceptionally spacious room options.

★**Sota Cappadocia**   DESIGN HOTEL $$$
(☑ 0384-341 5885; www.sotacappadocia.com; Burhan Kale Sokak 12; r €120-130, ste €150; ☺☎) ✿ Ürgüp's hippest hotel. Nil Tuncer, with help from acclaimed interior decorator Oytun Berktan, has stamped the nine rooms with a minimalist design as much at home in New York as within the swirling natural coloured caves. Dramatic black accenting, repurposed *gözleme*-pans as statement wall art, hanging lamps salvaged from a Russian tanker – Sota's swaggering style shakes up the Cappadocia scene. This place has serious substance too, with exceptional attention paid to all the little details. Guests can borrow iPads and stacks of books to chill out on the sun-lounger-scattered terraces, there's a well-stocked bar, and breakfast includes espresso and artisan breads. Even better, this little hotel has got sustainability credentials with grey-water reuse in place and eco-pellets (rather than coal) being used for the central heating.

★**Esbelli Evi**   BOUTIQUE HOTEL $$$
(☑ 0384-341 3395; www.esbelli.com; Esbelli Sokak 8; r €80-270; ☺ Mar-Oct; P☺✴☎) Jazz in the bathroom, whisky by the tub, secret tunnels to secluded walled gardens draped in vines – this is one of Cappadocia's most individual boutique hotels. A lawyer who never practised, Süha Ersöz instead (thank God!) purchased the 12 surrounding properties over two decades and created a highly cultured yet decidedly unpretentious hotel that stands out on exclusive Esbelli Hill.

The detailed rooms feel more like first-class holiday apartments for visiting dignitaries, from the state-of-the-art family suite with fully decked-out kids' room to the raised beds and provincial kitchens in the enormous cave suites. The breakfast spread is organic and delicious, while an enchanting evening on the terrace is an education in local history, humility and grace.

Serinn House   DESIGN HOTEL $$$
(☑ 0384-341 6076; www.serinnhouse.com; Esbelli Sokak 36; d from €80; ☺☎) This intimate hideaway seamlessly merges İstanbul's European aesthetic with Turkish provincial life and is run with aplomb by charming host

Ürgüp

Eren Serpen. Just five spacious rooms (four of them caves) employ a chic minimalist style ethos, featuring Archimedes lamps, signature chairs and hip block-colour rugs, to bring a thoroughly 21st-century swagger to Cappadocia cave living.

🍴 Eating & Drinking

★ **Tık Tık Kadın Emeği** ANATOLIAN **$**
(📞 0384-341 3373; İstiklal Caddesi 13; mains ₺10-20; ⏱ 11am-7pm; 🛜) 🍴 This local women's cooperative serves up true homespun village flavours with *mantı*, *içli köfte* (ground lamb and onion with a bulgur coating, often served as a hot meze) and stuffed vine leaves on the menu. If you're here for lunch, you'll also often be able to watch the women making the intricate *mantı* pasta for the day.

Mavi Cafe TURKISH **$**
(📞 0384-341 3848; Dağıstanlı Sokak 54; mains per portion ₺10-16; ⏱ 9am-10pm; 🛜🍴) This *lokanta* (eatery serving ready-made food) run

by a friendly couple is deservedly popular. Choose from the six to eight daily-changing dish selection on the counter (you buy by the portion; half-portions are possible) and feast on wholesome dishes such as spinach and bulgur bake, *kuru fasulye* (haricot beans cooked in a spicy tomato sauce) and *börek* (filled pastry) stuffed with chicken and herbs.

Zeytin Cafe TURKISH **$**
(📞 0384-341 7399; Atatürk Bulvarı; dishes ₺10-22; ⏱ 10am-10pm; 🍴) This thoroughly welcoming cafe dishes up Turkish staples along with a host of good veggie dishes including bulgur-filled peppers, *bamya* (okra) stew and *kiremitte mantar* (baked mushrooms with cheese).

Han Çırağan Restaurant TURKISH **$$**
(📞 0384-341 2566; Cumhuriyet Meydanı; mains ₺22.50-66; ⏱ 10am-1am Mon-Fri, to 2am Sat & Sun; 🛜🍴) The menu here is a meander through Turkish favourites with a modern twist

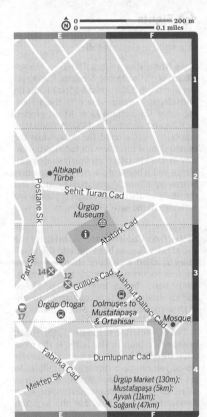

from *tandır* (clay oven) cooked lamb to the destroy-your-waistline-but-worth-it and totally addictive *paçanga böreği* (fried pastries stuffed with cured beef and cheese). After dinner, retire to the vine-trellis-covered bar downstairs with its excellent wine list.

★ **Ziggy Cafe**   MEZZE $$$
(☑0384-341 7107; www.ziggycafe.com; Tevfik Fikret Caddesi 24; meze set menu ₺90, mains ₺45-80; ⊗noon-11pm; ☑) Ziggy's has nailed the essence of casual-yet-classy dining. The *pastırmalı börek* (pastry filled with preserved beef) and lush *yaprak ciğer* (lamb liver fillets) are stand-out stars of the finest meze menu in Cappadocia, created by chef Ali Ozkan. In summer, the two-tiered terrace fills with a hip clientele enjoying cocktails while in winter the stone-arched interior is a cosy retreat.

Don't miss a browse in the treasure-trove **atelier** downstairs, which sells beautiful handmade jewellery and quirky giftware.

Mack Bear Coffee   CAFE
(Atatürk Bulvarı; ⊗9am-10pm; �) Since this Antalya-based cafe brand opened in Ürgüp in 2018 it's become the town's favourite meeting point. It has a Starbucks vibe for both the espresso-based coffees (fine and drinkable, but not the greatest flat white or macchiato you're going to have in your life) and seating (plenty of comfy couches) along with friendly baristas and a great rooftop terrace.

Efendi Şarap Evi   WINE BAR
(☑0384-341 4024; Tevfik Fikret Caddesi 12; 8-wine tasting tray ₺45, glass/bottle of wine from ₺18/75; ⊗11am-8pm) The shaded porch here is one of the nicest places in Cappadocia to partake in a spot of wine tasting. Tastings consist of eight wines and you can order meze-style snacks or a cheese platter to accompany them. Afterwards, buy your favourites by the bottle or glass and keep kicking back on the porch.

ⓘ Getting There & Away

Although bus companies retain offices at **Ürgüp Otogar** (Ürgüp Bus Station; Güllüce Caddesi) where you can buy tickets, there are no longer any direct long-distance services from Ürgüp.

You either have to go to Göreme otogar (p453) to pick up a service or to Nevşehir otogar (p461). From the otogar, dolmuşes travel to the following:

Avanos (via the Ortahisar turn-off, Göreme Open-Air Museum, Göreme village, Çavuşin and Zelve; ₺6, 40 minutes, hourly between 8am and 7pm)

Kayseri (₺17, one hour, hourly between 7am and 8pm)

Nevşehir (₺6, 25 minutes, every 15 minutes from 7am to 7pm and then at least hourly until midnight)

Twelve of the above Nevşehir services carry on the extra 2.5km outside of Nevşehir city to Nevşehir otogar (₺8, roughly every two hours between 7am and midnight). A schedule posted outside Ürgüp otogar lists current times. This same service picks up from Nevşehir otogar on the same schedule of roughly every two hours.

From the **car park** (Güllüce Caddesi), next door to the otogar, there are dolmuşes to Mustafapaşa (₺3, 10 minutes, every 30 minutes between 8am and 8.30pm) and Ortahisar (₺4, 20 minutes, every 30 minutes between 8am and 6pm; fewer services on Sunday).

There are also a couple of services daily to Ayvalı and Taşkınpaşa. They depart from the car park that connects Dumlupınar Caddesi to the main otogar.

Mustafapaşa

📞 0384 / POP 1600

This quiet Cappadocian village is shifting slowly from yesteryear and during weekdays is injected with a jolt of youthful energy as students from Nevşehir University arrive to study at the campus here. Still known widely by its pre-WWI Greek name of Sinasos, Mustafapaşa is home to some of the region's loveliest examples of typical Greek stone-carved-mansion architecture, serving as a reminder of its prosperous past when wealthy Greek-Ottoman merchants made up a sizeable portion of the community. When you've finished admiring the faded grandeur, the minor rock-cut churches amid the outlying valleys allow a decent dose of natural scenery.

You enter Mustafapaşa at an enlarged intersection, the Sinasos Meydanı. Follow the road downhill and you'll come to Cumhuriyet Meydanı, the centre of the village, which sports the ubiquitous bust of Atatürk, the Ayios Kostantinos-Eleni church and several cafes.

☉ Sights

To the west of Mustafapaşa there are 4km to 8km walks in Gomeda Valley.

Ayios Kostantinos-Eleni Kilise CHURCH
(Church of SS Constantine & Helena; Cumhuriyet Meydanı; ₺5; ☉ 8.30am-noon & 1-5pm) Right on Mustafapaşa's main square is the imposing Ayios Kostantinos-Eleni Kilise, erected in 1729 and restored in 1850. A fine stone grapevine runs around the door, while the ruined domed interior with faded 19th-century frescoes has a picturesquely shabby ambience and is home to a series of information boards explaining Mustafapaşa's history and the story of the Greece-Turkey population exchange in the early 20th century.

Monastery Valley PARK
Follow Zafer Caddesi to the old bridge at the end of the village to head out into this small valley studded with fairy chimneys. There are four rock-carved chapels and one monastery here, though most are kept locked and are disappointing in comparison to other Cappadocian churches. Still, it makes for a lovely walk.

The **St Nicholas Monastery** (₺5; ☉ open by request), rebuilt in the 1870s, is the most interesting and even though it's usually closed you can peer through the railings to get a good look at the exterior. The tourist office, above the teahouse next to the Ayios Kostantinos-Eleni Kilise, has the key. You can sometimes convince staff there to unlock it for you, though they're more willing to do it for groups than solo travellers.

From the monastery, take the right-hand fork off the main path to arrive at the **St John the Baptist Church**, hollowed out of rock cone. Scramble up the trail and squeeze through the broken rock to see the very dilapidated and graffiti-covered interior with its broken columns and scraps of colourful frescoes.

🛏 Sleeping & Eating

Pacha Hotel GUESTHOUSE $$
(📞 0384-353 5331; www.pachahotel.com; Kale Sokak; s/d/tr €30/45/55; 🖥) This sprawling Ottoman-Greek house boasts neat-as-a-pin rooms and a tasty upstairs restaurant (dinner €12) full of local bric-a-brac. The vine-covered courtyard provides sun-seeker bliss on lazy summer afternoons, while the cave rooms downstairs (with separate lounge area with bed) are a bargain find for travelling families.

SOĞANLI ROAD TRIP

If you only rent a car, or hire a taxi for a day, once on your trip, the day you visit Soğanlı could be the time to do it. Not only is Soğanlı impossible to reach by public transport, the drive there is beautiful. The open countryside makes a change from central Cappadocia's canyons and you can stop in sleepy country villages that give an idea of what Göreme was like 30 years ago. Here are our top stops along the way:

Cemil Church (☑ to reach the guardian 0535 045 1160; ⊗ open on request) **FREE** Signposted from the main Soğanlı road, some 6km south of Mustafapaşa, is the town of Cemil, where chickens rule the cobblestone paths, overlooked by abandoned Greek mansions on the hillside that are teetering into disrepair. Follow the alleyway through the village to the picturesque blue-columned Cemil Church with its fresco fragments (all extremely defaced). To make sure the church is open (they tend to keep the door locked these days), ring the guardian before you arrive.

Keşlik Monastery (₺10; ⊗ 9am-6.30pm Apr-Nov) This rock-cut Byzantine complex, 10km south of Mustafapaşa, is a labyrinth of a place where hundreds of monks lived. The main 13th-century monastery chapel has blackened frescoes, which friendly site guardian Cabir Coşkuner will explain to you. The maze of monk living quarters underneath include a refectory and kitchen. Next door is the rock cone harbouring the 9th-century Stephanos Church with a vibrant, well-preserved cross-form ceiling fresco that extends all along the vault.

Taşkınpaşa Mosque **FREE** Some 7km south of Keşlik Monastery, tractors bounce along hilly, cobbled streets in Taşkınpaşa, which is named after its 600-year-old Seljuk mosque. The original, 14th-century pulpit is now in Ankara's Ethnographical Museum. Outside, Taşkın Paşa himself is buried in one of the two Seljuk tombs; traders stayed under the arches during the caravanserai days. On the way back to the main road you will see a *medrese* (seminary) with an ornate door frame.

Sobesos (⊗ 8.30am-5.30pm) **FREE** At the ancient city of Sobesos, signposted from Şahinefendi village, the various sections of the Roman baths can easily be distinguished. The late 4th-century Byzantine Church ruins behind hold some fine Roman and Byzantine mosaics and graves.

Upper Greek House HOTEL **$$$**
(☑ 0384-353 5352; www.uppergreekhouse.com; Zafer Sokak; d ₺400-500; 🖥) Right at the top of Mustafapaşa's hill, this quiet retreat has big and airy stone-arch rooms – decorated with simple elegance and a bit of sparkly bedspread pizzazz – opening onto large terraces or the shady courtyard downstairs.

Hanımeli
Kapadokya Restaurant ANATOLIAN **$$**
(☑ 0384-353 5203; Yılmaz Sokak 14; set menus per person ₺35-75; ⊗ 11am-10pm) Set on the Karagöz family's rooftop, this friendly place rustles up hearty home-cooking feasts. Local mezes are followed by your choice of wholesome mains – have the *testı kebap;* it's particularly good here. If you manage to demolish that lot, you're doing better than we did and there's still dessert to go.

Old Greek House TURKISH **$$**
(☑ 0384-353 5306; www.oldgreekhouse.com; Şahin Caddesi; meze ₺15-25, mains ₺35-75; ⊗ noon-11pm; 🖥☑) The atmospheric hall of this 250-year-old Greek Mansion, with its ceiling draped in vines, is Mustafapaşa's main venue to dig into Turkish flavours. The food isn't going to wow your socks off (stick to the meze rather than ordering the mains), but it's all fresh and filling and service is top-notch. Head upstairs after dining to peek at the ornate salons.

🛈 Getting There & Away

Dolmuşes to Ürgüp leave from the main square (₺3, every 30 minutes between 8am and 6.30pm and then hourly 7pm to 10pm). A taxi costs ₺25.

Ayvalı
☑ 0384 / POP 648
This lovely little village in a valley south of Ürgüp is a snapshot of the Cappadocia of old. It's a sleepy place surrounded by farming plots with a meander of cobbled alleyways rimmed by wonky stone houses. Tourists are virtually unsighted...for now.

Cappadocian Frescoes 101

The frescoes of Cappadocia's rock-cut churches are, to be exact, *seccos* (whereby tempera paints are applied to dry plaster). Most of the frescoes here date from the 10th to the 12th centuries.

Christ Pantocrator

Christ 'the All-Powerful: typically painted on the church dome, depicting Jesus holding a book in one hand and giving a blessing with his other.

Nativity

Jesus' birth in Bethlehem. The Nativity in Eski Gümüşler Monastery is particularly striking.

Transfiguration

Portrayal of the miracle of Christ's metamorphosis in front of his disciples. A good depiction of this scene is in the Tokalı Kilise.

Anastasis

The 'Resurrection': Christ pictured with prophets, freeing souls from hell. The Karanlık Kilise has a superb example.

Deesis

Similar to 'Christ Pantocrator', Deesis scenes show a seated Christ flanked by the Virgin Mary and St John the Baptist.

Last Judgement

'Judgement Day': when righteous souls will ascend to heaven. The depiction in the Church of St Jean in Gülşehir is vividly well preserved.

1. Last Judgement fresco, Church of St Jean (p461), Gülşehir 2. Deesis fresco, Dark Church (p445), Göreme 3. Fresco of the Nativity, Eski Gümüşler Monastery (p476)

KNOW YOUR FRESCO SAINTS

St George Legend says this epic dragon slaughter took place upon Erciyes Dağı.

St Basil the Great Archbishop of Caesarea, credited with beginning monasticism in Cappadocia.

St Gregory the Theologian Friend of St Basil and Archbishop of Constantinople.

St Barbara Early Syrian Christian convert, martyred by being beheaded by her father.

Aravan Evi
GUESTHOUSE $$$

(☑ 0384-354 5838; www.aravan.com; d/tr €70/100; ☎) Looking for a slice of rural life without sacrificing modern comforts? A stay at this charming guesthouse, with its simply decorated, bright rooms, is a welcoming time-out from the bustle of life. The gorgeous terrace restaurant (open to nonguests; reservations essential) is a flavourful trip through Cappadocian dishes and specialises in *tandır* (clay oven) cooking.

★ Cappadocia Home Cooking
ANATOLIAN $$$

(☑ 0384-354 5907; www.cappadociahomecooking. com; cooking class & meal per person €50, meal only per person €25; ⊙ noon-9pm) Tolga and his family have swung open the doors to their home – surrounded by their organic garden and overlooking Ayvalı's deep gorge – to offer a taste of true home-style Cappadocian cooking. They offer meals and highly recommended cooking classes with hands-on appeal, guided by Tolga's tiny dynamo of a mother, Hava. It's a foodie haven. Reservations are essential. It's on the Ayvalı main road. Tolga can arrange transport to/from Ayvalı from your base in Cappadocia. It also has a couple of rooms for guests who want a homestay-style experience.

❶ Getting There & Away

If you don't have your own transport, getting to Ayvalı is a bit tricky. From Ürgüp, dolmuşes depart for Ayvalı at 8.30am, 2pm and 5pm (₺3, 20 minutes). Returning from Ayvalı to Ürgüp the dolmuses leave at 8am, 9.30am and 3pm.

Soğanlı

☑ 0352 / POP 500

A series of rock-cut churches hide within the sheer cliffs of Soğanlı's two secluded valleys. The barren setting of rippling rock has in the past led some guides to tell tourists a few fibs, so first off let's get one thing straight: no scene in *Star Wars* was ever filmed in Soğanlı, or anywhere else in Turkey. It may not be a movie star, but the Byzantine remnants within the Aşağı Soğanlı (Lower) and Yukarı Soğanlı (Upper) Valleys, 36km south of Mustafapaşa, are reason enough to visit. A morning exploring the frescoed walls of these cave chapels may inspire you to write your own script.

The ticket office for the site is next to Hidden Apple Garden restaurant. At stalls in the site car park, local women sell the dolls for which Soğanlı is supposedly famous.

◉ Sights

Soğanlı's valleys were first used by the Romans as necropolises and later by the Byzantines for monastic purposes.

The most interesting churches are in the Yukarı Soğanlı (the right-hand turn on entering the site) and the entire site can be easily circuited on foot in about two hours. All the churches are signposted, but be careful and wear decent walking shoes as the crumbly tuff slopes you walk up to access them can be slippery.

The Aşağı Soğanlı is accessed by taking the left-hand road from the entrance.

Tokalı Kilise
CHURCH

(Buckle Church) On the main road into Soğanlı, about 800m before the ticket office, signs point to the Tokalı Kilise on the right, reached by a steep flight of worn steps.

Gök Kilise
CHURCH

(Sky Church) The Gök Kilise is just to the left of the Tokalı Kilise. It has twin naves separated by columns and ending in apses. The double frieze of saints is badly worn.

Karabaş Kilisesi
CHURCH

(Black Hat Church) In Soğanlı's Yukarı Valley the first church on your right is the Karabaş Kilisesi, which is covered in paintings showing the life of Christ, with Gabriel and various saints. A pigeon in the fresco reflects the importance of pigeons to the monks, who wooed them with dovecotes cut into the rock.

Yılanlı Kilise
CHURCH

(Church of St George, Snake Church) The Yılanlı Kilise sits in the furthest corner of the Yukarı Valley, its frescoes deliberately painted over with black paint, probably to protect them. The hole in the roof of one chamber, surrounded by blackened rock, shows that fires were lit there.

Kubbeli Kilise
CHURCH

(Domed Church) Turn left at the Yılanlı Kilise, cross the Yukarı Valley floor and climb the far hillside to find the Kubbeli Kilise. The Kubbeli is unusual because of its Eastern-style cupola cut clean out of the rock.

Saklı Kilise
CHURCH

(Hidden Church) Nestling in the Yukarı Valley hillside, very near the Kubbeli Kilise, is the Saklı Kilise, which, as its name suggests, is indeed completely obscured from view until you get close.

Geyikli Kilise CHURCH

(Deer Church) In the Aşağı Valley, the Geyikli Kilise has a monks' refectory and a still-visible fresco on the wall of St Eustace with a deer (from which the church's name is derived).

Tahtalı Kilise CHURCH

(Church of St Barbara) The Tahtalı Kilise sits at the furthest end of the Aşağı Valley. It has well-preserved Byzantine and Seljuk decorative patterns.

🛏 Sleeping & Eating

Emek Pansion PENSION $$

(📞0532 375 6538, 0352-653 1029; http://jhonneston1952.wix.com/emek; dm incl half board €30; ⊘May-Sep) We love this place for its authentic Cappadocian charm. The cave rooms (with shared bathroom) sleep up to six on *sedir*-style beds, layered with carpets and cut into the rock. The terrace cafe above, brimming with antiques, is a relaxing place to while away a few hours whether you stay the night or not. It's opposite **Soğanlı Restaurant** (📞0352-653 1016; mains ₺15-20; ⊘9am-7pm; 🍴), after the site ticket office.

Hidden Apple Garden TURKISH $

(Soğanlı Kapadokya Restaurant; 📞0352-653 1045, 0538 578 4583; mains ₺15-20; ⊘8.30am-7.30pm) Head down the stairs just before the Soğanlı ticket office to find this tranquil garden where Yılmaz Ablak and family dish up rustic meals under the apple trees. We could spend all day eating his wife's *acılı ezme*

(spicy tomato and onion paste), but leave room for the simple yet tasty *kiremit* (clay-dish baked) mains served with lashings of hospitality. A slap-up feast of warm village bread, served with homemade butter and cheese, and local honey, a side of thick-cut chips or salad plus a main dish will set you back around ₺45 per person.

Campers can pitch their tent in the garden for free. There are clean toilets and a shower on-site.

❶ Getting There & Away

If driving, turn off the main road from Mustafapaşa to Yeşilhisar and proceed 4km to Soğanlı village. It's impossible to get to Soğanlı by public transport. From Kayseri's Batı Otogar (p483) you can get as far as Yeşilhisar (₺6, every 30 minutes from 7am to 9pm) but you'd then have to negotiate for a taxi to take you the last 15km. From Ürgüp, there are four dolmuşes daily to Taşkınpaşa but no onward transport options. It's easier to hire a car/taxi or sign up for a day tour.

Niğde

📞0388 / POP 224.300

Backed by the snow-capped Ala Dağlar mountain range, Niğde, 85km south of Nevşehir, is a busy agricultural centre with a small clutch of historic buildings dating back to its foundation by the Seljuks. Unless you have a soft spot for provincial towns, you most likely won't want to stay but may have to if you want to visit the fabulous Eski

CAPPADOCIA NİĞDE

WORTH A TRIP

SULTAN MARSHES

An afternoon spent strolling the boardwalks, set between tall reeds, at **Sultan Marshes** (Sultansazlığı Milli Parkı; Ovaciftliği; adult/student ₺6/3; ⊘24hr) might not sound like your cup of birdseed but there's something undeniably fascinating about this giant patch of Ramsar-listed wetland set between Soğanlı and Ala Dağlar. Entry into the national park is at the teensy village of Ovaciftliği where there's a small bird museum, a wildlife viewing tower and access to the boardwalk route, which loops for a few kilometres around the marshes.

For nonbirders the major attraction are the photo opportunities of Erciyes Daği (Mt Erciyes) with its snow-capped craggy bulk looming over the endless swaying reed beds. Among the twitching fraternity though, this area is rightly famous and keen birders descend year-round to spot the 301 species that breed or overwinter here. Even those just out for a marsh boardwalk stroll will see aquatic birds such as Eurasian coots and maybe a turtle paddling about beside the reeds. To get completely amid the wetlands though, you're going to need a boat.

The affable owners at **Sultan Pansion** (📞0352-658 5549; www.sultanbirding.com; Ovaçiftliği, Sultansazlığı; d ₺200; 🅿❄🛜), directly opposite the park entrance, operate well-regarded boat trips (half hour/three hours ₺100/500) from their hotel, which backs onto the marshes themselves. If you want to overnight, this is your only accommodation option. The tidy rooms are simple but comfortable and the restaurant is decent.

Gümüşler Monastery, 10km northeast. You may also pass through en route to the basecamp villages for trekking in the Ala Dağlar National Park.

Sights

★ Eski Gümüşler Monastery   MONASTERY

(Gümüşler; ₺7; ⊙ 8.30am-6.30pm) Some of Cappadocia's best-preserved and most captivating frescoes are hidden within this rarely visited rock-hewn monastery that was only rediscovered in 1963. The lofty main church is covered with colourful Byzantine frescoes, painted between the 7th and 11th centuries. Of particular interest is the striking Virgin and Child to the left of the apse, which depicts Mary giving a Mona Lisa smile – it's said to be the only smiling Mary in existence.

Last tickets are 5pm October to March.

Although the frescoes are the monastery's most famous feature, the warren of rooms here are fun to explore too. You enter the complex via a rock-cut passage, which opens onto a large courtyard with reservoirs for wine and oil, and rock-cut dwellings, crypts, a kitchen and a refectory. A small hole in the ground acts as a vent for a 9m-deep shaft leading to two levels of subterranean rooms. You can descend through the chambers or climb to an upstairs bedroom.

Eski Gümüşler Monastery sprawls along the base of a cliff about 10km northeast of Niğde. To get there, Gümüşler Belediyesi dolmuşes (₺3, 20 minutes) depart every hour from Niğde's Eski Otogar. As you enter Gümüşler, don't worry when the bus passes a couple of signs pointing to the monastery – it eventually passes right by it. To catch a bus back to Niğde, wait at the bus stand across the road from the monastery entrance. The bus back to Niğde comes past at roughly 10 minutes to the hour and 20 minutes past the hour.

Niğde Museum   MUSEUM

(Niğde Müzesi; ☑ 0388-232 3397; Dışarı Caddesi; ₺7; ⊙ 8am-4.30pm) Niğde Museum houses a well-presented selection of finds from the Assyrian city of Acemhöyük near Aksaray, through the Hittite and Phrygian Ages to sculptures from Tyana (now Kemerhisar), the former Roman centre and Hittite capital 19km southwest of Niğde. There's also a collection of 10th-century mummies (four baby mummies, and the mummy of a blonde nun discovered in the 1960s in the Ihlara Valley).

From October to mid-April the museum opens at 8.30am and last tickets are at 5pm.

🛏 Sleeping

Hotel Şahiner   HOTEL $

(☑ 0388-232 2121; www.hotelsahiner.com; Giray Sokak 4; s/d ₺105/140; ❈ ☎) Sure, it doesn't have much character, but professional staff and decent-sized, clean rooms with comfortable beds make the Şahiner a solid and safe choice if you need to stay the night in Niğde. It's in an alleyway off Bankalar Caddesi, right in the centre of town.

❶ Getting There & Away

BUS

Niğde Otogar (Adana Yolu) is 4km out of town on the main highway. There are hourly buses run by Derinkuyu Koop to Nevşehir (₺12, 1½ hours), via Derinkuyu and Kaymaklı and their underground city sites. The otogar also has buses to the following:

Adana (₺35, two hours, every one to two hours)

Ankara (₺60, 4½ hours, six daily)

İstanbul (₺120, 11 hours, five daily)

Kayseri (₺25, 1½ hours, every one to two hours)

Konya (₺45 to ₺55, 3½ hours, 10 daily)

Eski Otogar (Old Bus Station; Emin Erişingil Bulvarı) is right in the centre of town. It has dolmuşes to Gümüşler Monastery (₺3, 20 minutes, half-hourly) and Çamardı (₺15, 1½ hours, hourly) as well as frequent services to other outlying villages.

TRAIN

Niğde Train Station is in the town centre, right at the end of İstasyon Caddesi. The daily Erciyes Ekspresi between Adana (₺17.50, 3½ hours, 9.08am) and Kayseri (₺14, two hours, 8.14pm) stops here.

Ala Dağlar National Park

The Ala Dağlar National Park (Ala Dağlar Milli Parkı) protects the rugged middle range of the Taurus Mountains between Kayseri, Niğde and Adana. It's famous throughout the country for its extraordinary trekking routes that snake through craggy limestone ranges and across a high plateau dotted with lakes. For bird enthusiasts a trip to the Ala Dağlar is all about spotting the elusive Caspian snowcock, which makes its home in the high reaches of the Taurus.

The most popular walks start at the small settlements of Çukurbağ and Demirkazık, 40km east of Niğde. Çukurbağ is also the best base from which to plan any Ala Dağlar adventures thanks to clued-up pension owners who can organise a range of activities.

You can also reach the mountains via Yahyalı, 80km south of Kayseri. From here it's another 60km to the impressive **Kapuzbaşı waterfalls** (best seen between March and May) on the Zamantı River.

🏃 Activities

It's best to trek between June and late September; at other times weather conditions can be particularly hazardous, especially since there are few villages and little support other than some mountaineers' huts. Bring warm gear and prepare for extreme conditions.

There are a variety of walks in the mountains. The most famous is the five-day trek across the Ala Dağlar range beginning in Demirkazık, traversing the Karayalak Valley and the beautiful Yedigöller (Seven Lakes Plateau; 3500m), and ending at the Kapuzbaşı waterfalls. There are plenty of shorter options and day-hike opportunities as well.

Although solo trekkers do sometimes venture into the mountains, unless you're experienced and prepared you should consider paying for a guide or joining a tour. Be aware that the sheepdogs guarding their flocks in this remote area can be ferocious – another good reason to have a local guide with you.

All trekking arrangements, including guide and equipment hire, can be made through the guesthouses in Çukurbağ. Costs depend on number of hikers/days; a five-day hike for three people including guide, mules (to carry luggage), muleteer, food and all equipment hire costs around €500 per person. If you prefer to trek as part of an organised tour, Middle Earth Travel (p448) is a good first port of call in Göreme. The agency offers excursions in the Ala Dağlar, with prices starting at €320/520 (three-/five-day itinerary) per person for a minimum of four people. Other agencies such as **Sobek Travel** (☑ 0388-232 1507; www.ozsafak.net) based in Niğde, and **Terra Anatolia** (☑ 0242-244 8945; www.terra-anatolia.com), based in Antalya, can also organise Ala Dağlar trekking tours.

🛏 Sleeping

Özşafak Pension PENSION **$$**
(☑ 0536 230 3120, 0388-724 7049; www.ozsafak. net; Çukurbağ Village; r per person incl half board €30, campsites per person €10) This delightfully homey pension is run by enthusiastic English-speaking local guide Başar, who can organise all your trekking or birdwatching activities. Rooms are super simple but clean,

with beds piled high with snugly thick duvets. There are majestic mountain views from the pension's balcony and both breakfast and dinner are feasts of fresh, hearty local fare. It's right on the main road's intersection to Çukurbağ village. All the dolmuş drivers can drop you off here if you let them know.

Şafak Pension & Camping PENSION **$$**
(☑ 0388-724 7039; www.safaktravel.com; Çurkurbağ Village; r per person incl half board €30, campsites per person €10) Run by friendly, multilingual local guide Hasan, who can organise pretty much any activity, Şafak offers simple, clean rooms with hot water, heating and comfortable beds. Campsites have electricity and their own bathroom facilities, and the terrace and garden command magnificent views of Mt Demirkazık. It's on the main-road intersection with the Çurkurbağ village turn-off.

Taurus Guesthouse PENSION **$$**
(☑ 0545 881 5729; www.taurusguesthouse.com; Çukurbağ Village; s/d/tr/q ₺150/200/250/300) Set behind a shady garden, this pension right in the heart of Çukurbağ is run by a friendly family. It offers good-sized, neat-as-a-pin rooms with modern bathrooms, excellent home-cooked meals and can organise all your hiking, cycling and horse-riding needs. Very little English is spoken so it won't suit everyone.

ℹ Information

Çukurbağ has basic shops for supplies but no banking facilities so bring all the cash you will need.

ℹ Getting There & Away

From Niğde, take a Çamardı-bound dolmuş (₺15, 1½ hours, hourly between 7am and 5pm from Monday to Saturday, fewer services on Sunday) and ask to be let off at Çukurbağ junction and village (it's 5km before Çamardı). From Çamardı there are 10 services to Niğde between 6am and 5.30pm from Monday to Saturday and three services on Sunday.

Ihlara Valley

☑ 0382
Southeast of Aksaray, the Ihlara Valley scythes through the stubbly fields. Once called Peristrema, the valley was a favourite retreat of Byzantine monks, who cut churches into the base of its towering cliffs. Today it is home to one of the prettiest strolls in the world.

Ihlara Valley

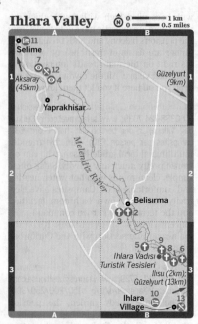

Following the Melendiz River – hemmed in by jagged cliffs – as it snakes between painted churches, piles of boulders and a sea of greenery ringing with birdsong and croaking frogs – is an unforgettable experience. The most dramatic scenery is along the Selime to Belisırma trail section, while the vast amount of the churches are between Belisırma and the Ihlara Vadısı Turistik Tesisleri entrance. Come in May when spring wildflowers carpet the valley floor to see

Ihlara at its most beguiling. The best times to visit are Monday to Friday when fewer people are about.

◉ Sights

Hiking the full **Ihlara Valley** (Ihlara Vadısı; incl Selime Monastery ₺36; ⊙8am-6.30pm) trail between Ihlara village and Selime is a wonderfully bucolic day out. Most visitors come on a tour and only walk the short stretch with most of the churches, entering via the 360 steps of the **Ihlara Vadısı Turistik Tesisleri** (Ihlara Valley Tourist Facility) ticket booth and exiting at Belisırma. This means the rest of the path is blissfully serene, with farmers tilling their fields and shepherds grazing their flocks the only people you're likely to meet.

Other entrances are at **Ihlara village**, **Belisırma** and **Selime**. Including stops to visit the churches along the way, it takes about an hour to walk from Ihlara village to the Ihlara Vadısı Turistik Tesisleri stairs, 1½ hours to walk from there to Belisırma, and another hour to walk from Belisırma to Selime.

If you're planning to walk the entire trail, it's best to start early in the day, particularly in summer, when you'll need to take shelter from the fierce sun. Along the valley floor, signs mark the different churches.

Travel agencies in Göreme, Avanos and Ürgüp offer tours incorporating Ihlara for between €35 and €50 per person.

Kokar Kilise   CHURCH
(Fragrant Church) This church has some fabulous frescoes – the Nativity and the Crucifixion for starters – dating from the 9th and 11th centuries.

Ağaçaltı Kilise   CHURCH
(Daniel Pantonassa Church) This cruciform-plan church is most famous for its incredibly well-preserved fresco ceiling depicting the Ascension.

Sümbüllü Kilise   CHURCH
(Hyacinth Church) Some frescoes remain, but this church is mostly noteworthy for its simple but elegant facade.

Yılanlı Kilise   CHURCH
(Snake Church) Many of the frescoes are damaged, but it's possible to make out the one outlining the punishments for sinners, especially the three-headed snake with a sinner in each mouth and the nipple-clamped women (ouch) who didn't breastfeed their young.

Kırk Dam Altı Kilise
CHURCH

(St George's Church) Although badly graffitied, the frescoes are still gloriously vibrant, and above the entrance you can see St George on a white horse, slaying a three-headed snake.

Direkli Kilise
CHURCH

(Belisırma village) This cross-shaped church has four columns, with lovely partially preserved frescoes of saints. The large adjoining chamber originally had two storeys, as you can see from what's left of the steps and the holes in the walls from the supporting beams. It's in Belisırma village, off the main Ihlara Valley trail; a sign near the Belisırma trailhead ticket booth points the way to the entry.

Bahattın'ın Samanlığı Kilise
CHURCH

(Bahattın's Granary; Belisırma village) Sitting on Belisırma village's cliff face, next door to the Direkli Kilise, this tiny church contains defaced but still vivid frescoes depicting scenes from the life of Christ. It's named after a local who used to store grain here.

Selime Monastery
MONASTERY

(Selime village; incl Ihlara Valley ₺36; ⊙8am-6pm) This monastery is an astonishing rock-cut structure incorporating a vast kitchen with a soaring chimney, three churches, stables with rock-carved feed troughs and other evidence of the troglodyte lifestyle.

🛏 Sleeping & Eating

If you want to walk all of the gorge and don't have your own transport you'll have to stay overnight. There are modest accommodation options handily placed at both ends of the gorge (in Ihlara village and Selime). Note that most accommodation is closed from December to March.

Both Selime and Ihlara village have riverside restaurants and midway along the gorge, below Belisırma village, a cluster of low-key restaurants feed hungry hikers, with dining on platforms right upon the river. Trout is the local speciality here.

🛏 Ihlara Village

Akar Pansion & Restaurant
PENSION $$

(📞0382-453 7018; www.ihlara-akarmotel.com; s/d ₺150/200; 🖥) The best option in Ihlara Valley, Akar's large rooms have cheerfully bright linen and are kept decently clean and well maintained. Grab one of the rooms in the new building with private balconies. Helpful English-speaking staff can fill you in on Ihlara queries, the restaurant serves tasty local dishes (₺15 to ₺30) and the attached shop sells picnic ingredients.

Star Restaurant & Pension
TURKISH $

(📞0382-453 7020; mains ₺15-30; ⊙10am-9pm; 🖥🖥) Right beside the river, this friendly, family-run place has a wonderful shady terrace and is just the spot for lunch and chilling out with a beer after a hike. Local trout is the speciality, but there are meaty casseroles and vegetarian options too. It also has 10 simple rooms upstairs (single/double ₺100/200) and a small, grassy camping area (campsites ₺30).

🛏 Selime

Çatlak Hotel
HOTEL $

(📞0382-454 5006; www.catlakturizm.com.tr; s/d ₺75/150; 🖥) Despite the gaudy 1970s-style decor, Çatlak has good-sized rooms and smiley staff.

Çatlağın Yeri Restaurant
TURKISH $$

(📞0382-454 5006; mains ₺15-35; ⊙10.30am-10pm) Across the road from Selime's Ihlara Valley trailhead, this large riverside restaurant with friendly staff dishes up plenty of *köfte*, fresh local trout and *güveç* options. Camping is available on the grounds.

ℹ Information

There is an ATM in Ihlara village.

ℹ Getting There & Away

On weekdays six dolmuşes per day make the run between Aksaray and Ihlara village, travelling down the valley via Selime and Belisırma. Dolmuşes leave Aksaray at 7.30am, 10am, noon, 2pm, 4pm and 6pm. They leave Ihlara village for the return run at 6.45am, 8am, 9am, 11am, 1pm and 4pm (₺6, 45 minutes). On weekends there are fewer services. To get to Güzelyurt ask the driver to drop you at the Selime T-junction, where you can wait for a Güzelyurt dolmuş.

Güzelyurt

📞0382 / POP 11,761 / ELEV 1485M

This hillside tumble of crumbling stone houses, with back alleys presided over by strutting cockerels and the odd stray cow, leads down to a valley studded with the remnants of rock-cut churches. Surrounded by rolling hills, a lakeside monastery, and with the silhouette of Hasan Dağı (Mt Hasan) glowering over the horizon, the gentle-paced rhythm of life here is a refreshing glimpse of rural Cappadocia. Known as Karballa (Gelveri) in Ottoman times, up until the population exchanges of 1924 the town was inhabited by 1000 Ottoman Greek families and 50 Turkish Muslim families. Afterwards the Greeks of Gelveri went to Nea Karvali in Greece, while Turkish families from Kozan and Kastoria in Greece moved here. The relationship between the two countries is now celebrated in an annual Turks & Greeks Friendship Festival in July.

◉ Sights

Yüksek Kilise & Manastır MONASTERY
(High Church & Monastery) FREE This religious complex is perched high on a rock overlooking Güzelyurt lake, some 2km south of a signposted turn-off on the Ihlara road 1km west of Güzelyurt. The walled compound containing the plain church and monastery is graffitied inside and looks more impressive from afar but has sweeping views of the lake and mountains.

Monastery Valley HISTORIC SITE
(₺7; ◷8am-6.30pm) The 4.5km Monastery Valley is full of rock-cut churches and dwellings cut into the cliff walls. Exploring it makes for a scenic stroll. From Güzelyurt's main square, take the signposted right-hand turn and follow the street down about 400m to the ticket booth.

Beside the ticket office is **Güzelyurt Underground City**. The complex is great for adventurous travellers – covering several levels and including a section where you descend to the next level through a hole in the floor.

The impressive facade of the **Büyük Kilise Cami** (Mosque of the Great Church) is the first major building after the ticket office. Built as the Church of St Gregory of Nazianzus in AD 385, it was restored in 1835 and turned into a mosque following the population exchange in 1924. St Gregory (330–90) grew up locally and became a theologian, patriarch and one of the four Fathers of the Greek Church. Check out the wooden sermon desk that was reputedly a gift from a Russian tsar.

Opposite the Büyük Kilise Cami, a set of stairs leads up to the tranquil **Sivişli Kilisesi** (Church of the Panagia), with damaged but still colourful frescoes decorating the apse and domed ceiling. There are fantastic views over Güzelyurt if you climb up to the ridge from here.

Some 2km after the ticket office you enter a gorge hemmed in by high cliffs. The **Kalburlu Kilisesi** (Church with a Screen) with its superb chiselled entrance is the first rock-outcrop building in the group. Almost adjoining it is the **Kömürlü Kilisesi** (Coal Church), which has carvings including

an elaborate lintel above the entrance and some Maltese crosses. In winter last tickets are sold at 5.30pm.

Kızıl Kilise CHURCH
(Red Church) FREE Against a backdrop of stark, sweeping fields, the red masonry of the Kızıl Kilise stands out for miles. One of Cappadocia's oldest churches, it was built in the 5th or 6th century and dedicated to St Gregory of Nazianzus. It's 8km out of Güzelyurt on the Niğde road, just past the village of Sivrihisar.

⌇ Sleeping

Osmanoğlu Hotel GUESTHOUSE $$
(☏0533 736 3165, 0382-451 2767; osmanogluko
nak@hotmail.com; Necdet Sağlam Caddesi; s/d
₺350/400) Mother and son duo, Nuriye and Semih, provide lashings of Cappadocian hospitality at this charming guesthouse on Güzelyurt's main road. Large stone-arched rooms brim with local character with rustic textiles and traditional *sedir* seating rimming the windows. Downstairs there are cosy cave rooms but claustrophobes should beware: these are proper caves with no windows.

❶ Getting There & Away

From Aksaray, dolmuşes leave from the bus stop across the road from the Eski Garaj for Güzelyurt (₺8, one hour) at 7.30am, 9.45am, 11.30am, 1.30pm, 3.30pm, 5.30pm and 6.30pm. Returning dolmuşes travel from Güzelyurt to Aksaray at 6.30am, 7.30am and then every two hours, with the last at 5.30pm. On weekends there are fewer services. Going either way, dolmuşes can drop you at the T-junction near Selime, from where you can wait for an Ihlara Valley–bound dolmuş.

Aksaray

☏0382 / POP 295,350

Sitting in the shadow of Hasan Dağı (Mt Hasan), Aksaray is a prosperous provincial city with a bland modern town centre that is perked up substantially by carefully tended roadside rose beds. Apart from the town council's applaudable attention to municipal gardening, Aksaray doesn't have much to hold your interest but as it's a jumping-off point for the Ihlara Valley you may find yourself snared here for a couple of hours. If so, the Ulu Cami is a reminder of the beauty of Seljuk architecture while a mooch through the throng in the centre, where the odd horse and cart still rattles down the main road holding up traffic, is an unequivocally Anatolian experience.

◉ Sights

Aksaray Museum   MUSEUM
(Aksaray Müzesi; Atatürk Bulvarı; ⊘9am-4.30pm)
FREE Well, you certainly won't have problems finding this massive museum en route from the otogar along the main road to Aksaray centre. The revamped displays covering early Cappadocian human history have excellent English information boards, but the prize exhibit is the small collection of mummies unearthed in the Ihlara Valley.

Ulu Cami   MOSQUE
(Grand Mosque; Bankalar Caddesi) The Ulu Cami has decoration characteristic of the post–Seljuk Beylik period. A little of the original yellow stone remains in the grand doorway.

Eğri Minare   MONUMENT
(Crooked Minaret; Nevşehir Caddesi) Built in 1236 and leaning at an angle of 27 degrees, the curious Eğri Minare in the older part of Aksaray is, inevitably, known to locals as the 'Turkish Tower of Pisa'.

🛏 Sleeping & Eating

Head up Atatürk Bulvarı to take your pick from the plentiful choice of bright and modern *ızgara* (grill) restaurants that line the road.

Ahsaray Otel   BUSINESS HOTEL $$
(☏0382-216 1600; www.otelahsaray.com; Karayolu Caddesi 1; s/d ₺150/300; P❋⊛🐾) By far Aksaray's best choice, even if its location – near the otogar, a 2km walk into the centre – is a bit annoying. The friendly English-speaking manager here goes out of his way to help travellers while the spacious business-style rooms come with kettles, flat-screen TVs, big comfy beds, and bathrooms decked out with hilarious gold-coloured fittings.

❶ Getting There & Away

Aksaray Otogar (Aksaray Bus Station; Konya Caddesi/Atatürk Bulvarı) is 5km southwest of the city centre. City buses make the regular trundle from the otogar into the centre of town. A taxi to the centre will cost around ₺20. There are regular services to the following:

Ankara (₺40, 3½ to four hours, hourly)

Göreme (₺30, 1½ hours, 6am, 6.45am, 7am, 7.30am, 5pm and 7pm)

Konya (via Sultanhanı, ₺35, two to 2½ hours, every 30 minutes to 1½ hours)

Nevşehir (₺25, one hour, roughly hourly until 7pm)

Niğde (₺30, 1½ hours, every one to two hours until 8pm)

Eski Garaj (Old Bus Station; Atatürk Bulvarı), a group of bus stands in a car park opposite the Migros supermarket in the centre, has dolmuşes to Güzelyurt (₺8, one hour), the Ihlara Valley (₺5, 45 minutes) and Sultanhanı (₺5, 45 minutes).

Kayseri

📞0352 / POP 1.3 MILLION / ELEV 1067M

Mixing Seljuk tombs, mosques and modern developments, Kayseri is both Turkey's most Islamic city after Konya and one of the economic powerhouses nicknamed the 'Anatolian tigers'. Most travellers whizz through town on their way from the airport to Cappadocia's villages, only seeing the shabby high-rises and ugly industrial factories on Kayseri's outskirts. The city centre of this Turkish boom town, though, is full of surprises. An afternoon pottering within the narrow bazaar streets and poking about the Seljuk and Ottoman monuments – all loomed over by mighty Erciyes Dağı (Mt Erciyes) – is an interesting contrast to exploring the more famous fairy-chimney vistas to the city's west.

◉ Sights

Kayseri Castle   CASTLE
(Kayseri Kalesi; Cumhuriyet Meydanı) The monumental black-basalt walls of Kayseri castle were first constructed under Roman emperor Gordian III and rebuilt by the Byzantine emperor Justinian 300 years later. The imposing edifice you see today though is mostly the work of 13th-century Seljuk sultan Alaattin Keykubat. The outer fortifications stamp their way down Park and Talas Caddesis. At the time of research, the inner castle was undergoing a mammoth restoration project.

➔ Archaeological Museum
(Kayseri Kale; ₺6; ⊘8am-5.30pm Tue-Sun)
Kayseri's small archaeological museum is a minor magpie's nest, featuring finds from nearby Kültepe (ancient Kanesh, chief city of the Hatti people and the first Hittite capital). Other exhibits include a stunning sarcophagus illustrating Hercules' labours and a fascinatingly creepy exhibit of child mummies. In 2019 the museum was closed in readiness for all the artefacts to be moved to their new home inside the restored Kayseri Castle.

Mahperi Hunat
Hatun Complex   HISTORIC BUILDING
(Talas Caddesi) **FREE** The austere and stately Mahperi Hunat Hatun complex is one of

Kayseri

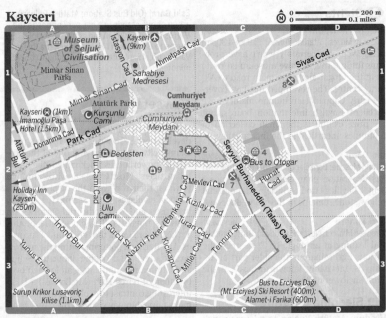

Kayseri

Kayseri's finest Seljuk monuments, built in the 13th century during the reign of Sultan Alaattin Keykubat. It comprises the **Hunat Hatun Medresesi**, with its shady courtyard now used as a cafe with the surrounding student cells home to various artisan shops, the **Mahperi Hunat Hatun Cami** (mosque) and a still-functioning **hamam**.

★**Museum of Seljuk Civilisation** MUSEUM (Selçuklu Uygarlığı Müzesi; Mimar Sinan Parkı; ₺2; ⏰9am-5pm Tue-Sun) This excellent museum is set in the restored Çifte Medrese, a 13th-century twin hospital and seminary built at the bequest of Seljuk sultan Keyhüsrev I and his sister Gevher Nesibe Sultan. It's thought to be one of the world's first medical training schools. The strikingly serene architecture is

offset by beautiful exhibits of Seljuk artistry, culture and history, complemented by up-to-the-minute multimedia displays. Our one grumble is that not enough of the information panels have English translations.

Surup Krikor Lusavoriç Kilise CHURCH (Church of St Gregory the Illuminator; Necip Fazıl Bulvarı; donation appreciated) FREE The 19th-century Surup Krikor Lusavoriç Kilise is one of Anatolia's few remaining Armenian churches. Its domed interior, complete with dilapidated frescoes and three gilded altars, provides a glimpse of the prominence of Kayseri's once vibrant Armenian community. For entry, head around the back wall of the church, ring the doorbell and the guardian – one of the five Armenians left in the city – will let you in. The church is located 2km straight down Necip Fazıl Bulvarı, off Osman Kavuncu Bulvarı.

🛏 Sleeping

Hotel Büyük
HOTEL **$**

(☑0352-232 2892; www.kayseribuyukotel.com; İnönü Bulvarı 55; s/d/tr ₺100/160/240; 🛜) One of the best of Kayseri's many budget hotels, the Büyük has plain but clean rooms that all come with flat-screen TVs and kettles. Traffic noise can be a bit of an issue so light sleepers should look elsewhere. Manager Fatih tries hard to please.

★ Holiday Inn Kayseri
BUSINESS HOTEL **$$**

(☑0352-315 3000; www.hikayseri.com; Osman Kavuncu Caddesi, Kenarcık Sokak 2; r from €42; 🅿🌀🛜) Holiday Inn opened its Kayseri branch in 2017 and it hasn't put a foot wrong. Bang in the central city, the modern, comfortable, super-quiet rooms come with great amenities and good-sized bathrooms. It's even solved Kayseri's smoky-room problem by creating a separate smoking floor.

İmamoğlu Paşa Hotel
HOTEL **$$**

(☑0352-336 9090; www.imamoglupasaotel.com.tr; Kocasinan Bulvarı 24; s/d €25/45; 🌀🛜) Contemporary rooms come with wide-screen satellite TVs, rain showers, kettles, some of the most comfortable beds in town and minibars (yes, there's beer). You'll want a room on the 5th floor or higher for views of Erciyes Dağı (Mt Erciyes). It's on the road opposite the train station, next door to the police station.

Radisson Blu
BUSINESS HOTEL **$$$**

(☑0352-315 5050; www.radissonblu.com; Sivas Caddesi 24; r from €75; 🅿🌀🛜🏊) A sign of Kayseri's rise in stock, the Radisson is a cool, contemporary customer with huge rooms, accented by soft greys and funky acid-yellows, complete with all mod cons and floor-to-ceiling windows with great city views. The **Roof Lounge** (🕑6pm-midnight; 🛜), open to nonguests, is the best spot in town for a sundowner while contemplating stunning Erciyes Dağı (Mt Erciyes) vistas.

🍴 Eating

İnci Balıkçılık
SEAFOOD **$**

(☑0352-222 9928; Sivas Caddesi 12/B; mains ₺10-40; 🕑10am-10pm) Walk through the fishmongers by the door to this rather brilliant fish restaurant on the terrace out back. As well as cheap, filling and large *balık ekmek* (fish sandwiches), which make for a tasty lunch, the seafood mains are great value and come loaded with salads. Service is spot on.

★ Alamet-i Farika
ANATOLIAN **$$**

(☑0532-232 1080; Deliklitaş Caddesi 8; mains ₺15-50; 🕑10am-9pm) The interior is European-style elegance, but the food is top-notch Anatolian. Tuck into the *mantı*, devour the meaty speciality *çentik kebap* (grilled meat served atop potatoes with a yoghurt and tomato sauce) and save room for the naughtily sweet desserts. Finish up with Turkish coffee, served in dainty teacups with a shot glass of lemonade on the side.

To find it head straight down Talas Caddesi for 1.5km (past the cemetery) until you get to Hüma Hastanesi (a hospital) and the mosque. Take the right-hand turn into Deliklitaş Caddesi straight after the mosque and the restaurant is on the first block.

Elmacıoğlu İskender Merkez
KEBAB **$$**

(☑0352-222 6965; 1st & 2nd fl, Millet Caddesi 5; mains ₺27-48; 🕑10.30am-10pm; 🌀) Bring on the calories. Skip the diet for the day and ascend the lift to the top-floor dining hall with views over the citadel to order the house speciality, İskender kebap (döner kebap on fresh pide topped with tomato sauce and browned butter). Your waistline won't thank us, but your taste buds will.

🛍 Shopping

Kapalı Çarşı
MARKET

(Vaulted Bazaar; Cumhuriyet Meydanı; 🕑10am-8pm) Set at the intersection of age-old trade routes, Kayseri has long been an important commercial centre. Its Kapalı Çarşı was one of the largest bazaars built by the Ottomans. Restored in the 1870s and again in the 1980s, it remains the heart of the city and is well worth a wander.

ℹ Getting There & Away

AIR

Kayseri Airport (p443) is 6km north of the centre. There are regular flights to İstanbul with Turkish Airlines (www.turkishairlines.com) and Pegasus Airlines (www.flypgs.com). Pegasus and Sun Express (www.sunexpress.com) run direct flights to Antalya and İzmir.

BUS

Kayseri Otogar (Kayseri Bus Station; ☑0352-336 4373; Osman Kavuncu Bulvarı) is 9km west of the centre. Nearly all bus companies provide a free *servis* (shuttle bus) into the central city. If there's no *servis*, grab a taxi (₺35), catch a local bus from the otogar entrance car park or take the tram (both ₺2.50).

Batı Otogar (West Bus Station; Osman Kavuncu Bulvarı) is the smaller building next door to

SERVICES FROM KAYSERI OTOGAR

DESTINATION	FARE (₺)	DURATION (HR)	FREQUENCY
Amasya	65-70	6½	3 morning, 5 afternoon, 1 evening
Ankara	45-55	4-5	hourly
Erzurum	80-100	9½	7 evening
Gaziantep	50-55	4½-6	3 morning, 6 afternoon, 5 evening
Göreme	20	1	4 morning, 1 afternoon, 3 evening
Kahramanmaraş	40-45	3½-4½	6 morning, 9 afternoon, 6 evening
Malatya	60	5	8 morning, 3 afternoon, 13 evening
Nevşehir	20	1½	every 1-1½ hours
Sivas	35	3	11 morning, 8 afternoon, 8 evening
Trabzon	100-110	8-11½	2 morning, 1 afternoon, 7 evening

the main otogar. From here there are dolmuşes to the following:

Avanos (₺20, one hour, 8am, 10am, then hourly noon to 7pm)

Göreme (₺20, one hour, 8am, 10am, then hourly noon to 7pm)

Nevşehir (₺20, 1½ hours, hourly 8am to 7pm)

Ürgüp (₺17, one hour, hourly 8am to 8pm)

Alternatively, from the main otogar, hop on one of the Kâmil Koç bus company services that drop off/pick up in Göreme. Note there is no direct dolmuş service from Göreme to Kayseri. Heading to Kayseri, catch the service from Ürgüp.

TRAIN

Kayseri Train Station (Kayseri Garı; www.tcddtasimacilik.gov.tr; Kocasinan Bulvarı) is a stop on several train routes heading east from Ankara including the daily Doğu Ekspresi (between Ankara and Kars); the five-times weekly Güney Kurtalan Ekspresi (between Ankara and Diyarbakır); and the twice-weekly Vangölü Ekspresi (between Ankara and Tatvan). Kayseri arrival and departure times tend to be inconvenient.

The Erciyes Ekspresi (between Kayseri and Adana) departs daily at 7am (₺19, 5½ hours).

To reach the centre from the train station, walk out of the station, cross the big avenue and board any bus heading down Atatürk Bulvarı towards Cumhuriyet Meydanı. Alternatively, you could walk along Altan Caddesi, which isn't as busy as Atatürk Bulvarı.

🛈 Getting Around

TO/FROM THE AIRPORT

A taxi from the central city to the airport costs around ₺35 and takes about 20 minutes, or hop on city bus 102 to Cumhuriyet Meydanı (₺2.50). If you're heading to one of the Cappadocian villages, prebooked shuttle bus services (p443) pick up and drop off passengers at the airport.

TRAM

A state-of-the-art tram system called the **KayseRay** runs through central Kayseri from 6am to 2am daily. It's a very efficient way of getting around and single tickets cost ₺2.50. The nearest tram station to the otogar is Selimiye, a 10-minute walk away. From Selimiye it's 14 tram stops (25 minutes) to the central Cumhuriyet Meydanı tram station opposite Kayseri Castle.

Erciyes Dağı

Erciyes Dağı Ski Resort (Erciyes Kayak Merkez; www.kayserierciyes.com.tr; 1-day ski pass adult/child ₺70/55; ⊙9am-5.30pm Mon-Wed, to 8pm Fri & Sat, to 6pm Sun), on the northeastern side of ruggedly beautiful Erciyes Dağı, has, over the past few years, been undergoing a multimillion-lira revamp intended to establish the mountain as a rival to European ski destinations. The ski runs themselves, and the modern gondola ski-lift system connecting them, are fantastic, with pistes to suit both beginners and hardcore snow bunnies. On weekends in ski season it gets crammed up here so try to come on a weekday if you can.

🛈 Getting There & Away

Erciyes resort is around 80km from Göreme (1½ hours' drive) and 25km (30 minutes) from central Kayseri.

During ski season, Kayseri runs city buses starting at Kayseri Airport (p443) to the ski resort hourly between 7.50am and 11.50am. The buses also pick up from a bus stand in central Kayseri on Talas Caddesi, next to the Ahi Evran Zaviyesi museum, hourly between 8.10am and 12.10pm. Returning to Kayseri, they leave Erciyes hourly between 1pm and 6pm.

Black Sea Coast

Why Go?

The Black Sea (Karadeniz) coast might lack the tourist beaches of the Mediterranean or Aegean, but it has plenty of character and a lush backdrop of terraced tea plantations and orchards fading into a misty mountainous hinterland. Even pretty Amasra, which has the most tangible seaside-holiday vibe in summer, reverts to a quaint port out of season. Big cities like Trabzon and Samsun are interspersed by pint-size fishing villages, while alpine lakes and *yaylalar* (mountainside shepherd pastures) beckon travellers to venture inland.

This is a historic region, scattered with castles, churches, monasteries and mosques that recall the days of the kings of Pontus, the Genoese and the Ottomans. Earlier history dissolves into legend with tales of female Amazon warriors much celebrated at Samsun, while Yason Burnu (Cape Jason) marks a mythical spot where Jason and his Argonauts were miraculously saved from being lost at sea.

Best Places to Eat

➡ Okyanus Balık Evi (p490)

➡ Berweuli (p499)

➡ Derin Balık Lokantası (p494)

➡ Kayadibi Saklıbahçe (p500)

➡ Cemilusta (p499)

Best Places to Stay

➡ Sebile Hanım Konağı (p493)

➡ Hotel İkizevler (p494)

➡ Grand Vuslat (p498)

➡ Taşmektep Otel (p502)

➡ Lonca Hotel (p495)

➡ Denizci Otel (p490)

When to Go
Trabzon

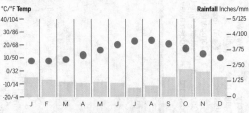

May Springtime revelry kicks off at the traditional International Giresun Aksu Festival.

Jun–Aug Beaches beckon but prices rise dramatically; Trabzon buzzes with summer festivals.

Apr & Sep Time to soak up the lazy-day off-season charms of Amasra and Sinop.

Black Sea Coast Highlights

1 Sumela Monastery (p500) Climbing through pine forests to this cliff-hugging wonder.

2 Amasra (p487) Gazing out across this picture-postcard town with its Byzantine citadel walls.

3 Trabzon (p495) Comparing the bustling central square with the cafe scene hidden away in back lanes.

4 Uzungöl (p500) Seeing beyond the flood of tourists at this gem of a mountain lake.

5 Inebolu (p488) Admiring the plethora of older houses in this delightful coastal town.

6 Zilkale (p503) Exploring upland pastures around this medieval castle.

7 Ünye (p492) Contrasting the mosque-area teahouses with the hip beach-front cafes.

8 Ordu (p494) Riding a cable car for views down upon a city rooftscape.

9 Sinop (p489) Sipping beers atop fortress walls in this historic port.

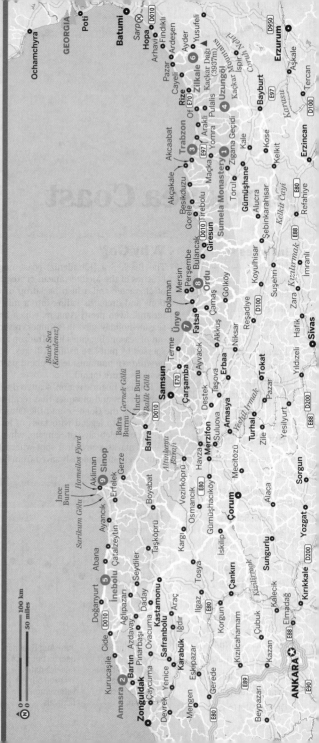

Amasra

☑ 0378 / POP 14,900

The charming historic town of Amasra straddles a small peninsula formed by two pretty
bays, plus a small rocky island to which it's
linked by a Roman bridge. The peninsula section is given definition by some hefty fortress
walls and the bays are fronted by plenty of
fish restaurants. In summer, music bars get
lively, catering mostly to domestic tourists
and weekenders. Midweek, off season, the
vibe is contrastingly sleepy if very friendly.

◉ Sights & Activities

Amasra Castle
WALLS

(Kale, Amasra Kalesi; www.amasra.net/aktivite/
amasra-kalesi; Küçük Liman Caddesi) FREE The
northern section of Amasra is a citadel of
mixed Roman, Byzantine and Genoese heritage with heavy grey-stone walls that are
often woven into today's townscape. The
most dramatic sections are the Küçük Liman trio of gateways guarding the Roman
bridge (Kemere Köprüsü), plus the towering
walls backing Hisar Peçe, a ledge or footpath
that runs east–west along the northern half
of the promontory.

Amasra Museum
MUSEUM

(Müze; ☑ 0378-315 1006; Çamlık Sokak 4; ₺6;
⊙ 8.30am-7pm Apr-Oct, to 5pm Nov-Mar) This
excellent little museum showcases Amasra's
multilayered Roman, Byzantine, Hellenistic and Ottoman history with valuable
statuary, coins and curiosities, including a
5th-century Jesus bread stamp. The explanations have translations, but the English is
sometimes inscrutable.

Boat Trips
BOATING

(Büyük Liman; from ₺15) Several operators offer 45-minute boat trips that potter around
both harbours and pass the countless cormorants and gulls of Rabbit Island. Dolphin
sightings are possible.

🛏 Sleeping

Balkaya Pansiyon
PENSION $

(☑ 0378-315 1434; www.balkayapansiyon.com;
General Mithat Ceylan Caddesi 35; r from ₺50-150;
🌁) Balkaya's 15 neat, whitewashed rooms
are spread over two bland but helpfully
central buildings. Some are very small, and
for wi-fi you'll need to sit in the pastry shop
where you check in, but it's one of Amasra's
cheapest options and friendly owner Turkan
speaks pretty good English.

Kum Butik Otel
HERITAGE HOTEL $$

(☑ 0378-315 1190, 0542-574 8565; www.kumbu
tikotel.com; Turgut Işık Caddesi 92; r ₺350-400;
🌁🛜) Reconstructed from a century-old
wood-fronted house, this atmospheric fam-
ily guesthouse is aimed at those who value
character over space. Two of the five rooms
are especially small, but the upper front op-
tions are bigger and all come with historical
photos, patterned walls and mesmerising
mirror-door designs. Good value out of sea-
son when double prices can reduce to ₺200.

Sardinia Otel
BOUTIQUE HOTEL $$

(☑ 0378-315 2233, 0850-411-1253; www.sar
diniaotel.com; Kucuk Liman Caddesi 20; s/d/tr
₺200/350/450; 🌁🛜) Off season it's hard
to fault the Sardinia for its winning mix of
stylish rooms, a lovely 'secret garden' and an
old-city location with many rooms sporting
balconies that survey the Little Harbour.
June to August, however, that location becomes a curse for light sleepers when pubs
across the road crank up the music very late.

🍴 Eating & Drinking

Sesamos Cafe
CAFE $

(☑ 0378-315 3093; Turgut Işık Caddesi 3; snack-
meals ₺10-15, fish dishes from ₺18; ⊙ 4pm-1am;
🛜) Unwind inexpensively at the waterside
nibbling a freshly grilled fish sandwich (₺10)
or various other snacks on this open-sided
cafe, raised just above the Büyük Liman
sand. It's also great for nursing a beer (from
₺17.50) or for puffing on a nargile (water
pipe; from ₺25)

Mustafa Amca'nin Yeri
SEAFOOD $$

(☑ 0378-315 2606; www.amasracanlibalik.com;
Küçük Liman Caddesi 8; fish portion ₺25-45,
turbot ₺100, salad/meze dishes from ₺8/10;
⊙ noon-midnight; 🛜) Serving quality fresh
fish (*canlı balık*) since 1945, 'Uncle Musta-
fa's Place' has a distinctively characterful
pebble-and-timber 'chalet' facade which
stops just short of kitsch. Service is slick,
there's a decent wine list (glass/bottle from
₺30/105) and both dining room and terrace
offer wonderful sunset views across Little
Harbour.

Cafe 'N Bistro
PUB

(Boztepe; ⊙ 3pm-late) Just across the Roman
Bridge, this friendly little pub pours Tuborg
draft beers from ₺15, has a small range of
Belgian bottled brews (Leffe ₺25) and there's
a vine-draped terrace on the roof with bay
views.

❶ Getting There & Away

Amasra's tiny little **otogar** is tucked behind the museum and deals mostly with minibus shuttles to Bartin (₺6, 20 minutes), the region's main transport hub. The only long distance services from Amasra run to Istanbul (₺115, 8½ hours) at 11am and 10.45pm, to Ankara at 12.30pm (₺80, 5½ hours) plus (June to August only) to Bodrum via Ankara at 4.30pm. All of these are on **Kamil Koç** (☑ 0533-149 1515; www.kamilkoc.com. tr; Atatürk Meydan 1b; ⊙ 8am-12.30am) buses; there's a booking office on Amasra's main square.

A daily Cide Aslan Seyahat bus on the Zonguldak-Bartin-Amasra-Cide route stops outside the PTT (post office) at around 10.15am in both directions reaching Cide (₺) around 12.30pm, in plenty of time to connect with the 2pm Abicim Minibus to İnebolu. Otherwise the only transport east along the coastal route is the dolmuş to Çakraz (roughly hourly).

İnebolu

☑ 0366 / POP 21,740

No town along the Black Sea coast has retained as many of its old timber-topped houses as İnebolu has. This bustling but manageable little place makes an ideal midway break if you're taking the tortuous Amasra–Sinop coastal route.

The central grid of streets retains loads of character, antique houses and Ottoman graves. The beach wins no prizes but there's a very pleasant seaside walk past fish restaurants with sunset views over distant headlands, a kids' play park, mosque and outdoor swimming pool that's remarkably well kept. As Inepolis, the town was a historic port of Pontus known for building a specific type of sailing galley, and today there is still a shipbuilding industry east of the centre.

◉ Sights

Kent Müzesi MUSEUM
(☑ 0366-811 6222; www.inebolu.bel.tr/inebolu-kent-muzesi.asp; Cumhuriyet Caddesi 2; ₺2; ⊙ 8.30am-12.30pm & 1.30-5.30pm Tue-Sun) The most striking feature of this new museum dedicated to the town's history is a *denk* (rowing boat) 'floating' across the glass ceiling, above ethnographic mannequins. The historical displays are fascinating and professionally arranged but are all in Turkish. It's opposite the Yayhapaşa mosque in the atmospheric heart of old İnebolu in an 1882 building that was originally conceived as a *medresa* (Islamic college) before being repurposed as the town hall.

🛏 Sleeping & Eating

Motel Osman Sungur BUNGALOW $
(☑ 0366-811 5060; İsmetpaşa Caddesi; s/d ₺60/110; ⊙ 24hr) Over 30 little cottages and terraced wooden mini houses, designed in traditional red-and-white colours and with fresh pine interiors and small, clean bathrooms. They're set around a spacious garden that's lit at night by what look like gigantic buttercups, backing onto a shingle beach. It's 600m west of İnebolu post office.

Royalife Otel BUSINESS HOTEL $$
(☑ 0366-811 3639; www.royalifeotel.com; Zaferyolu Caddesi 14; s/d/ste ₺150/250/300; ❋ ☎) This fresh, well appointed and unfussy hotel has very comfy beds and good walk-in showers. Four rooms are windowless but the rest are bright and come with balconies facing the sea across the Sinop highway. It's just 300m east of the post office.

Hanimeli ANATOLIAN $$
(İsmetpaşa Caddesi; meals ₺15-35; ⊙ 10am-11pm; ℗) Hanimeli serves fresh fish dishes, local meat stews and *manti* (Turkish ravioli) at simple terrace seating beside the beach, just west of town. There are lovely sunset views and the garden is fragrant with roses.

İne Balık & Et SEAFOOD $$
(☑ 0366-811 4123; Hacı Mehmet Aydın Caddesi 9; mains ₺20-35; ⊙ 10am-8pm) This unpretentious but highly recommended place fries up the day's catch from the family fishmonger's shop right across the lane. Meals are garnished with a simple salad, deliciously dressed in lemon and pomegranate and washed down with *şalgam* (fermented beet & carrot juice). It's in İnebolu's grid of central streets, just four doors west of the museum.

❶ Getting There & Away

The **otogar** (İnebolu Şehirler Arası Otobüs Terminali; Yılmazer Caddesi) is on the west bank of the river, around 1km south of the coast road. From here, several companies offer direct buses to İstanbul at around 9.30am (₺120, 11 hours) and 8.30pm (₺140, 10 hours). For most other destinations, change in Kastamonu to which there are minibuses (₺20, two hours) every 45 minutes until 5.30pm.

For Sinop, the only coastal-route choice starts with the Karadeniz Tur minibus to Ayancik (₺25, two hours) at 3.15pm (Sunday to Friday). It's timed to connect with the onward service to Sinop (₺15, 1¼ hours) which leaves from Ayancik's central square at 5.30pm.

From the D010 slip road directly outside the PTT, Abicim Turizm (📞 0366-886 7272) runs a few minibuses to Doğanyurt. The 9.30am service continues to Cide (₺30, 3½ hours).

Sinop

📞 0368 / POP 53,200

Though Sinop is bursting out of the towering city walls that enclosed it for millennia, the central area retains enough historical mementoes to warrant an hour or two of idle strolling, while the boat-filled harbour and attractive promenade cater merrily to a summer crowd of local tourists. It is the most northerly point in Anatolia and the only southern-facing spot on the coast. The

naturally sheltered port here is unusually safe even in the roughest winter weather, leading to an old-seadog saying: 'the Black Sea has three harbours – July, August and Sinop'.

◉ Sights

Sinop Fortress   FORTRESS
(Sinop Kalesi) FREE Giving definition to much of central Sinop are the very hefty remnants of stone walls. With origins dating back four millennia, these once ran 3km, impregnably ringing the whole city. Several towers still stand, some 25m tall; the most impressive of these overlooks the harbour and can be climbed from Ergül Sokak.

Sinop

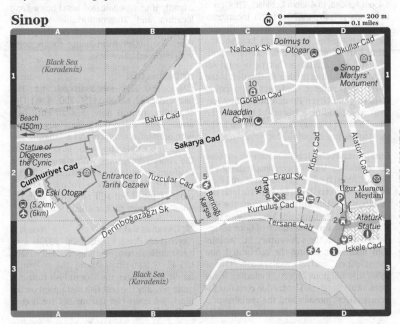

Sinop

◉ Sights

It's topped by a relaxed, open-air **cafe/bar** (www.facebook.com/kaleburccafebar; ⊘ 8am-midnight Apr-Sep, to 5pm Oct-Mar) but you don't have to have a drink to enjoy the fabulous views.

On the western side of the centre, a considerable length of fortress wall encloses the Tarihi Cezaevi, with large bastions also leading down from there to the north coast. Atmospherically collapsing wall sections continue northeast from here along what would have been the coast before the construction of a new reclamation arm.

Tarihi Sinop Cezaevi HISTORIC BUILDING

(Sinop Historical Prison; www.sinopale.org/historical-sinop-prison; Cumhuriyet Caddesi; ₺6; ⊘ 9am-6.45pm Apr-Sep, to 4.45pm Oct-Mar) This once infamous prison (1887 to 1997) incarcerated many famous Turkish writers. Though the extensive site has little in English, the grim, bare blocks and unlit solitary 'punishment' cells are the archetype of a prison nightmare. Adding further fascination is the towering perimeter that was repurposed from original Greco-Roman and Seljuk fortress walls, adding a historical twist to the site. The 16th-century dungeon prison is the most gruesome cell of the lot.

Sinop Archaeological Museum MUSEUM

(Sinop Arkeoloji Müzesi; www.sinopmuzesi.gov.tr; Okullar Caddesi 2; ₺6; ⊘ 8am-7pm Tue-Sun) Highlights of this excellent museum include the fabulous Meydankapı mosaic from the 4th century AD, depicting the four seasons and seven muses; a marble statue of lions savaging a deer from the 4th century BC; various coin hoards, including the celebrated one from Gelincik; and an excellent collection of Byzantine religious objects, including icons from local churches. The garden contains funerary steles, mosaics and the remains of a Temple of Serapis from the 4th century BC.

🏃 Activities

Boat tours around the bay are a popular activity in the city, and a number of operators along Bulent Ecevit Caddesi offer options for short and long trips. Short, 40-minute cruises (per person ₺10) start from the promenade on İskele Caddesi, across the road from the Atatürk Statue; these usually depart once there are more than 12 passengers. Alternatively, in midsummer **Kalyoncular** (☎ 0537-368 8718; Main Harbour) offers a full-day outing to Aklıman Beach (around 90 minutes each way), once around 60 passengers have

signed up, with beer served on board and meals available by pre-arrangement. Call in advance to check the situation – captain Kalyon speaks excellent English.

Turgutlar Hamamı HAMAM

(☎ 0368-261 3464; Tuzcular Caddesi 29; without/with massage ₺10/20; ⊘ noon-11pm, women only on Tue) This 650-year-old hamam is nothing grand but it offers a very real Turkish bath experience that's likely to linger in your memories.

🛏 Sleeping & Eating

Otel 57 HOTEL $

(Elli Yedi; ☎ 0368-261 5462; www.otel57.com; Kurtuluş Caddesi 29; s/d ₺100/170; ❋ 🕾) This friendly if unsophisticated hotel has a great location and 20 comfortably revamped rooms that have a pleasant contemporary vibe. The bigger front-facing rooms come with enclosed balconies.

★ Denizci Otel HOTEL $$

(☎ 0368-260 5934; www.denizciotel.com.tr; Kurtuluş Caddesi 13; s/d from ₺150/200; ❋ 🕾) This charming, central hotel has an encitingly atmospheric foyer that's tastefully packed with orientalist artefacts and a dangling amphora. If possible, choose the large rooms on the upper floors, some with glimpses of the sea from sweet little alcove windows (503 is ideal). On the lower floors, rooms are rather more cramped but still attractive, with the hotel's signature timber finish.

★ Okyanus Balık Evi SEAFOOD $$

(Ocean Fish House; ☎ 0368-261 3950; www.mevsimbalikcilik.com; Kurtuluş Caddesi; mains ₺25-45; ⊘ 11am-10pm) Above the co-owned family fishmonger, the 'Ocean Fish House' is quite possibly the best fish restaurant on the Black Sea coast (for flavour not for decor). As well as grilled or fried whole fish, a superb option is a panful of *iskorpit* (scorpion fish) fillets cooked as a *kavurma*, an utterly delicious reduction of peppers, tomato, garlic and ginger.

Sinop Sofrası ANATOLIAN $$

(Görgün Caddesi; mains ₺25; ⊘ 8am-10pm) This place is hard to beat for really genuine Sinop-style home cooking (*manti, dolmas*, local breakfasts), though the hushed, white-washed interior fails to fully capitalise on its fine setting within an arched chamber of the 13th-century Pervane Medresesi. There's no menu or English spoken, but you can point at photos on the wall. Superb homemade juices.

SERVICES FROM SINOP OTOGAR

DESTINATION	FARE (₺)	DURATION (HR)	DISTANCE (KM)	SERVICES
Ankara	80	7	420	2pm or 10.30pm
Karabük (for Safranbolu & Amasra)	60	5	340	6 daily
Kastamonu	35-50	3½	170	9 daily
Samsun	35	3	168	hourly 6am to 6.30pm plus 9pm
Trabzon	80	8	480	3pm or 9pm

☆ Entertainment

★ Kahveçi Baba   LIVE MUSIC
(☎0368-261 7575; www.instagram.com/per
vanekahvecibaba; Görgün Caddesi; coffee from
₺7.50; ⊙9am-11pm) The very atmospheric
traditional coffeehouse in the rear section of
the Pervane Medresesi is a fine place for soft
drinks and nargile at any time of year. But
from September to May the big attraction is
the nightly concert of mellifluous traditional
music (from 8.30pm, ₺5 cover). Check out its
Instagram feed for a taster.

❶ Getting There & Away

Virtually all intercity buses and minibuses start
from the **otogar** (D0101-13), 5km southwest of
central Sinop, though a few incoming services
will drop arriving passengers at the vastly more
central **Eski Otogar** (Cumhuriyet Caddesi). The
latter is otherwise used only for minibuses to
a handful of nearby villages, including Akliman
and Gerze.

For İnebolu, start with an early morning service to Ayancık (₺15, 1¼ hours, every half hour
from 6am) from Sinop otogar. From the central
square in Ayancık, switch to the daily İnebolu
minibus that departs at 9.15am (₺25, two
hours). To leave Sinop later you could alternatively take one of five daily Sinop–Turkeli minibuses, continuing in dolmuş hops from Turkeli
via Çatalzeytin and Abana, but for the 25km
Çatalzeytin–Abana leg you might need to pay for
a taxi (around ₺90). The last service from Abana
to İnebolu leaves at 6pm.

Samsun

☎0362 / POP 630,000

If you're travelling along the central Black
Sea Coast, you'll almost certainly need to
pass through this sprawling port city. What
Samsun lacks in looks, it makes up for with
memories of its 1919 role in sparking the
Turkish independence struggle and with
straight-faced evocations of its supposed (if
essentially invented) link with the Amazon

women warriors of Greek myth. There's not
much in the way of historical architecture,
but you could admire a few semi-grand older buildings by wandering up Kazımpaşa
Caddesi (nicknamed 'Bank Street') to Büyük
Cami, the central grand mosque, behind
which is an old clock tower and, undergoing a major restoration, a large classic bathhouse complex. The many coastal parks are
also a joy for casual strolling.

◎ Sights

Samsun Kent Müsesi   MUSEUM
(☎0362-234 3454; Cumhuriyet Caddesi; ₺2;
⊙8am-5pm Tue-Sun; ⛟Gar) In a pair of historic wooden houses, this museum appealingly
lays out Samsun's commerce, history and
culture with an audio guide and booklet
in English as well as Turkish. The tobacco
industry is well covered, an antique-style
kitchen displays local cuisine and several
mocked-up workshops demonstrate Samsun crafts. A free booklet as well as a room-
ful of pictures tempts visitors to linger and
visit the region around the city.

Amisos Tepesi   VIEWPOINT
(⛟Baruthane) FREE For extensive views
down between conifers onto a sweep of
coastline, take the five-minute cable-car
ride from Batıpark to this hilltop with its
twin-nippled tumulus. It was here, in 1995,
that archaeologists discovered the Am-
isos treasure, now the main attraction of
Samsun's Archaeology and Ethnography
Museum (closed for reconstruction and extension at the time of writing). Following
the boardwalk you can circle the site in
around 15 minutes. The setting is lovely but
there's minimal explanation and the tunnel entrance to the south tumulus's rock-
hewn tombs is securely gated. Still, selfie
opportunities abound, including one with
an Amazonian statue firing her longbow
at an *I Love Samsun* sign. And the **cafe**
(☎0362-445 0654; mains ₺11-34, desserts ₺7-9;

SERVICES FROM SAMSUN OTOGAR

DESTINATION	FARE (₺)	DURATION (HR)	DISTANCE (KM)	SERVICES
Amasya	22	2½	130	twice hourly
Ankara	70-110	6-7	420	10.30am & frequent 5pm-1am
Giresun	35-50	3½	220	every 90 minutes
Hopa	75-95	8-10	520	5am, 8.30am, 5.30pm & frequent 7pm-2am
Sinop	35	2 (bus), 3 (mini)	154	hourly
Trabzon	50-60	5½	355	frequent 24hrs
Ünye	18-25	1½-2	95	half-hourly minibuses 6.30am-6pm, hourly buses

⊙8am-11.30pm, kitchen closes 10pm) is a delight. Access is by **cable car** (Batıpark; return ₺3; ⊙noon-9.45pm); the station is an obvious short walk from the Baruthane tram stop, crossing a busy highway by footbridge.

🛏 Sleeping & Eating

Otel Necmi   HOTEL **$**
(☎0362-432 7164; www.otelnecmi.com.tr; Tarihi Bedestan Sokak 6; s/d/tr ₺80/145/200; ❉🕸; 🖫Cumhuriyet Meydan) This character-filled budget choice feels like your eccentric uncle's house, with pot plants, minor antiques and big old chairs in reception. The 20 rooms are neither gleaming nor large, and the shared bathrooms are like closets, but owner Mehmet is charming, helpful and speaks a little English.

Sare'n Otel   BUSINESS HOTEL **$$**
(☎0362-435 6808; www.sarenotel.com; Cumhuriyet Caddesi 18a; s/d/tr ₺200/240/300; ❉🕸; 🖫Cumhuriyet Meydan) At off-season walk-in prices (around ₺80 less than peak season), the Sare'n is one of Turkey's greatest bargains. Decent quality fittings, furniture and lamp panels with stylised Ottoman inlay designs complement fine views across the central parkland to ships queuing to enter the port.

Pamuk Kardeşler
Balık Restaurant   SEAFOOD **$$**
(☎0362-445 0433; www.pamukkardesler.com; Batıpark; mains ₺25-45; ⊙11.30am-midnight; 🖫Baruthane) A trinity of seafood restaurants line the sporting marina, around 500m west of the cable-car station in Batıpark. This licensed one is our favourite for its attractive foliage and potted cacti, but all three have their charms.

❶ Getting There & Away

Bus companies have offices at the Cumhuriyet Meydanı end of Cumhuriyet Caddesi. *Servises* (shuttle buses) run between there and the otogar, 3km inland. There's virtually nowhere in Turkey that you can't get a bus to from Samsun.

Heading east, as well as buses there are cheaper if slower Ordu Birlik minibuses to Ordu (₺27, 3½ hours) via central Ünye (₺18, two hours). These can save you going out to the otogar if you catch them from a stop across the D010 highway from the stadium at Tekkeköy Tram Stop, the far eastern end of the tramway line.

Ünye
☑ 0452 / POP 71,350

Central Ünye hugs an east-facing bay with a particularly pretty tree-shaded promenade. Just inland, the old bazaar street of Orta Çarşı links two fine mosques plus a former church that's now used as a hamam. Parallel, one block west, Kazancılar Sokak is Ünye's 'street of coppersmiths'. It retains a few appealing metalwork boutiques, though you'll rarely find smiths a-tapping here these days. From Kazancılar Sokak it's worth climbing cobbled Kadılar Yokuşu Sokak past old stone gateways and the restored historic houses originally built by Ottoman-era judges, before looping back to the right and descending past the museum.

◉ Sights

Ünye Müze Evi   MUSEUM
(Yaşayan Kültürel Miras Müzesi; ☎0452-324 0209; Hacı Emin Caddesi 24; ⊙9am-5pm Tue-Sun) **FREE**
This ambitious little museum occupies a handsome, breezy, 250-year-old Ottoman house, with displays bringing to life the

history, lifestyles and folklore of the different ethnic groups who have made Ünye their home over the centuries.

Ünye Castle
RUINS

(Ünye Kalesi; www.unye.info/unye-kalesi; D850, Güzelkale) **FREE** On a steep, green-sided crag about 7km inland from the town stand the ruins of Ünye Castle, founded by the Pontics and rebuilt by the Byzantines. There's an ancient tomb cut into the rock face below.

🛏 Sleeping & Eating

Otel Güney
HOTEL $

(☎0452-323 8406, 0555-179 8011; www.otelguney.com; Belediye Caddesi 14; s/d ₺70/140/180; ❄ 🛜) A good-value budget option: the 17 compact rooms have been given a cute, fresh makeover and are far more appealing than the hallways and box reception might imply. The delightful manager speaks decent English and there's a rooftop breakfast room with great bay views: guests are welcome to use it throughout the day and even bring in outside drinks and takeaways.

⭐ Sebile Hanım Konağı
BOUTIQUE HOTEL $$

(☎0452-323 7474; www.sebilehanimkonagi.com; Çubukçu Arif Sokak 10; s/d/ste from ₺110/220/350; ❄ 🛜) Dating to 1877, this lovely old mansion has a glorious lobby-cum-dining room, its bare stone walls lavished with antiques. The rooms come with rugs on wooden floors, private baths, fridges and wall fabrics, but sizes vary considerably.

Deluxe rooms are a decent size, some small 'standard' rooms have genuine 1950s furniture and the 'honeymoon suite' has a carved stone fireplace and tiny sauna. You might want to pass on the cheapest options, which are in a low-ceilinged mansard up a spindly spiral staircase, or across the street in the far less atmospheric – if still old – 'Little House'.

Kaptan Balıkçılık
SEAFOOD $

(☎0452-323 2333; Kasaplar Sokak 11b; snacks/mains from ₺10/17; ⏱10am-11pm) This excellent yet inexpensive place for fresh seafood, including *karides güveç* (prawn stew) and fish sandwiches, is a gleaming white contrast to the old-world bustle of the bazaar area outside.

Sarı Konak
BARBECUE $$

(☎0561-351 5252; 1st & 2nd fl, Büyük Cami Caddesi 6a; mains ₺12-35; ⏱10am-8pm) Easily missed as it's upstairs with no sign, this excellent *ocakbaşı* grill house serves assorted meaty morsels on two wooden balconies set with cushioned bench seats. Views look down through the *çinar* (plane tree) leaves onto a delightful square below that's always busy with old men chilling at outdoor tea shops.

BLACK SEA COAST ÜNYE

WORTH A TRIP

THE OLD COAST ROAD

At Bolaman (30km east of Ünye, 8km beyond Fatsa), the D010 to Ordu cuts inland using a 3.8km tunnel, but the old road remains well maintained, winding merrily around a series of rocky coves and through several small port villages. Though essentially rural, there's a good scattering of tea gardens and restaurants throughout the route. A popular stop, 25km northeast from Bolaman, is **Yason Burnu** (Cape Jason; Km16, Rte 52-82), reputed to be the peninsula that magically appeared to help the storm-stricken argonauts in the Golden Fleece myth.

Around 4km further east, **Çaka** is a leafy picnic spot backing a lovely 400m-long strip of narrow creamy-white sand that's regarded as one of the Black Sea's best beaches.

The fishing port of **Perşembe**, 13km further (15km before Ordu), is a slow-paced small Black Sea town on an east-facing bay. Handily right beside the main eastbound minibus stop, the well-maintained if slightly dated **Otel Dede Evi** (☎0452-517 3802; Atatürk Bulvarı 266; s/d/ste ₺100/170/240; ❄ 🛜) has shipshape rooms, the suite (401) offering a large sea-view terrace. Across the road is a little fish market whose haul is cooked up in the outwardly upmarket but fair-value **restaurant** (Atatürk Bulvarı 277; mains ₺25-35; ⏱11am-10pm) behind.

A 'Sahil Yolu' dolmuş runs the whole coastal route between Fatsa and Ordu. It operates every 20 minutes, making this charmingly low-key detour easy for DIY travellers. In Fatsa, vehicles start their run from the office of Yeşil Fatsa, on the main coast road 800m east of Fatsa Otogar.

ℹ️ Getting There & Away

At least every half hour, the Samsun–Fatsa–Ordu minibus passes through town, marked 'Ordu Birlik'. It picks up all along the coast road, including at a stop near the pier (İskele). For Samsun itself, it's faster and more comfortable to take a 'real' bus (₺25, 1½ hours) from the **otogar** (Sahil Yolu, DO10 junction), 2km southeast. Buses to destinations right across Turkey leave from here, several companies having offices just south of the Belediye in the old town and offering *servis* (shuttles) to get you to your bus.

For Perşembe, take the Ordu minibus and change at Fatsa.

Havaş offers a shuttle bus from the otogar to the airports of both Samsun and Giresun.

Ordu

📱 0452 / POP 213,600

Backed by a steep amphitheatre of green mountains, the sprawling but mostly low-rise city of Ordu is a prosperous, appealing place unmatched as the world's hazelnut capital. The curl of seafront has a long, attractive stretch of parkland promenade, though the brown sand is mainly used for quad-bike experiences. Behind, a grid of narrow central shopping lanes have been mostly pedestrianised around a central square whose 1889 stone minaret is overshadowed by the soaring tower of a cable car. Riding that offers fascinating glimpses down onto the mass of tiled rooftops and the nut orchards of Boztepe.

Away from the centre, lanes become more winding and village-like and, especially as you climb northwest into the Taşbaşı area, there is a good scattering of historic houses. Some have been converted to boutique hotels with splendid views across the bay.

👁️ Sights

⭐ **Boztepe Cable Car**   CABLE CAR
(Ordu Teleferik; adult/child return ₺9/5; ⊙ 9am-11.30pm) Ordu's top attraction, this seven-minute *teleferik* (cable-car) ride whisks you 2.3km from the seafront promenade to Boztepe, at an altitude of nearly 500m. The destination is a busy collection of cafes plus a zip-line 'adventure park' amid the pine trees, but views are great and the experience is mostly interesting for the ride itself, staring down onto the city as you fly across the rooftops and swing right by the tip of a minaret.

🛏️ Sleeping & Eating

Hotel Kervansaray   HOTEL $
(✓ 0452-214 1330; Kazım Karabekir Caddesi 1; s/d/tr ₺80/150/210; ❄️ 🛜) The Kervansaray is central, clean and good value, but entirely functional. The most attractive feature is the refurbished 1st-floor Kervansaray Cafe with its fresh, US diner vibe and 1950s car posters.

⭐ **Hotel İkizevler**   BOUTIQUE HOTEL $$
(Twins Hotel; ✓ 0452-225 0081; www.ikizevlerhotel.com.tr; Sıtkıcan Caddesi 44-46; s/d/tr/apt ₺150/270/380/450; ❄️ 🛜; 🚌 67 to 153 Sokak) Wooden floors, antique rugs and huge bathrooms all contribute to the relaxed heritage ambience in this delightful boutique hotel, with 12 rooms of gracious Ottoman style in a pair of restored stately homes. Breakfast is served on the restaurant terrace with splendid sweeping sea views between lilies.

Taşbaşı Butik Otel   BOUTIQUE HOTEL $$
(✓ 0452-223 3530; www.tasbasihotels.com; Kesim Evi Sokak 1; s/d ₺90/160; ❄️ 🛜; 🚌 67 to 153 Sokak) Parisian posters and Turkish film references give further character to this neatly restored mansion in Ordu's characterful former Greek neighbourhood. Views from the spacious upper rooms survey the ridge-backed bay across a foreground of tiled rooftops.

⭐ **Derin Balık Lokantası**   SEAFOOD $$
(✓ 0452 223 4435; Yükçülük Sokak 3; fish mains ₺25-65; 🛜) Derin finds the sweet spot between casual bustle and brasserie-style comfort, with wooden-panelled columns and leaded windows giving semi-classical twists to the contemporary mid-market interior. The fish meals are excellent, the crisp-crusted bread is top notch and even the toilets are immaculate.

Olive   INTERNATIONAL $$
(www.olivecaferesorant.com; DO10; mains from ₺24, steak ₺55-160; ⊙ 8am-2am) Olive is Ordu's top waterside spot, whether you're sipping a macchiato, snacking on fast food or drooling over a New York-style dry-aged steak. The central feature is an eccentric pavilion of pulleys and rope lamps, surrounding which is a light-suffused wraparound veranda with views across the bay.

ℹ️ Getting There & Away

Minibuses for Giresun (₺13, 1¼ hours) start every half-hour from a **stop** (Atatürk Bulvarı 160) half a block east of the *belediye* (town hall). Westbound minibuses to Sinop via Ünye and

Fatsa pick up all along Atatürk Bulvarı: those marked 'Otobandan' go via the main tunnel route, those marked 'Sahil Yolu' take the old road via Perşembe (₺3, 20 minutes) and Yason Burnu (₺7, 45 minutes). For longer distance buses use Ordu's otogar, on the coast road 5km east of centre.

Giresun

☎ 0454 / POP 114,000

If you're shuttling between Trabzon and Ordu, it's well worth stopping for an hour or two to walk through Giresun's fascinating if little-heralded historic backstreets. These cover the lower east flank of the distinctively abrupt central knoll, which is topped by a park that contains the ruins of a fortress that dates back over 4000 years to Giresun's days as the Greek colony of Cerasus (Kerasos). The town's Greek name, meaning something like 'cherry-ville', has led to the idea that cherries were introduced to Europe from here. Today, however, business is focused on hazelnuts, and the town's relaxed central area overlooks the large commercial port from which they are shipped far and wide.

◎ Sights

For a quick walking tour of Giresun's older districts, start up Gazi Caddesi, the pedestrianised shopping street that climbs up from the main square. There are several great cafes hidden in side lanes, notably **Bahçe Cafe** (Sökenişi Sokak 3; coffee ₺10; ☺1-10pm). At the second vehicular cross street turn left, then descend right on the next major road. Approximately opposite the grey-painted library (originally an Armenian church), turn left down an alley called Jandarma Okul Sokak. This takes you to the heart of Giresun's historic zone with fine views up to the castle ruins from between many late 19th-century mansions, some now restored. Descend Dik Sokak ('Steep Lane') past several more antique buildings then turn left by a 'wine house' to reach **Giresun Museum** (Giresun Müzesi; ☎0454-212 1322; www.giresunmuzesi.gov.tr; Sokakbaşı Caddesi 57-62; ☺8am-5pm) FREE, housed in a sturdy, well-preserved stone church. To return to the centre, cross the road and take dolmuş 2 or 4 back towards 'meydan'.

🛏 Sleeping

★**Lonca Hotel** BOUTIQUE HOTEL $$
(☎0454-216 1757; www.loncabutikhotel.com; Kazancılar Sokak 12; s/d ₺120/200; ❈ 🛜) This cosy

Some mountain villages inland from Giresun are very close together as the crow flies but separated by such deep canyons that walking between them can take hours. Thus, to communicate between them a form of coded high-powered wolf-whistles developed into what is nicknamed 'bird language' (*kuş dili*). With the sudden proliferation of mobile phones, this unusual historic quirk has gone into rapid decline, and in 2017 was listed by Unesco as being in danger of disappearance. The best known bird whistlers are from appropriately named Kuşköy village which, since 1997, has held a *Kuşdili* festival (late July). The village is in the Çanakçı area, 26km inland from Görele, itself around half way between Giresun and Trabzon.

little boutique hotel is on the cobbled street that leads steeply up the castle hill's western flank. Rooms are very comfortable for the price with velveteen sofas and immaculate bathrooms. Staff are delightful, but no English is spoken.

ℹ Getting There & Away

The long-distance **bus station** (Aydın Caddesi 10) is situated 4km west of town but, handily, minibuses to both Trabzon and Ordu start from right in the centre.

Though hidden from immediate view, the starting point for Ordu minibuses (₺13, 1¼ hours, twice hourly) is right beside the port gates on the north side of Atatürk Bulvarı.

Trabzon services (₺23, two hours) start from two different spots within 100m of each other along the south side of Atatürk Meydanı/Bulvarı. Prenskale minibuses head to Trabzon's Otogar, **Ulusoy Derya** (☎0454-216 1450; www.ulusoy derya.com; Atatürk Bulvarı 5b; ☺6am-8pm) ones run to Trabzon's Western Minibus Station, both approximately hourly.

Trabzon

☎ 0462 / POP 810,000

Once an important stop on the Silk Route, Trabzon remains the Turkish Black Sea's busiest port and second biggest city. It's an increasingly sophisticated place with a fascinating market area and plenty to explore in Ortahisar district, the former citadel that's

Trabzon

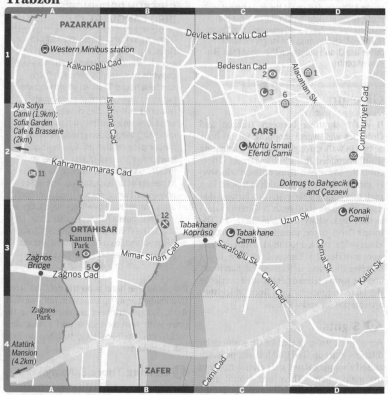

Trabzon

still partly enclosed by city walls. Tourist life is focussed on ever-buzzing Atatürk Alanı, Trabzon's main square, simply known to all as the *meydan* (square). Many agencies here offer tours to the region's popular rural sights, particularly Sumela, Uzungöl and Ayder.

◉ Sights

Pedestrianised shopping street Kunduracılar Caddesi leads from Atatürk Alanı to the Çarşı (Market) quarter within which lie **Çarşı Camii** (Market Mosque; Kemeraltı Sokak), central Trabzon's largest historical mosque,

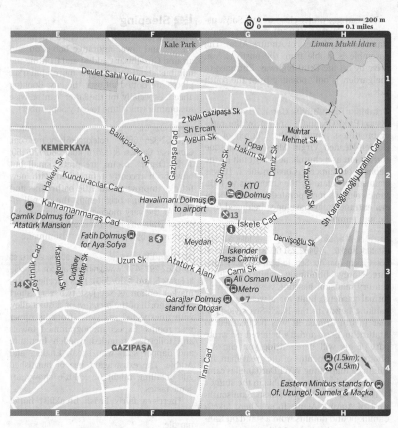

the **Taş Han** (Terziler Sokak 14) and **Alaca Han** (Alacahan Sokak) caravanserais and **Bedesten** (Covered Bazaar; Bedestan Caddesi; ⊙7am-10pm) **FREE**. There's plenty more to explore in the Ortahisar area with its developing river-gorge park and stretches of once-mighty old city wall.

★**Aya Sofya Camii**   MOSQUE
(📞0462-223 3043; Ayasofya Caddesi; ⊙9am-7pm Jun-Aug, to 6pm Apr, May, Sep & Oct, 8am-5pm Nov-Mar) **FREE** Standing in walled gardens amid symphonies of birdsong, 4km west of centre, is this fine 13th-century church-turned-mosque retaining some carved reliefs and colourful Christian-era murals. The bay views are lovely especially at sunset. In addition, there's a 1427 stand-alone bell tower and the remains of a 2nd-century Roman temple that was unearthed in 1997.

The centrepiece, originally called Hagia Sophia (Church of Divine Wisdom), was built between 1238 and 1263, and shows both Georgian and Seljuk design influences, though the wall paintings and mosaic floors follow the prevailing Constantinople style of the time. It was converted to a mosque after the Ottoman conquest in 1461, used as an ammunition-storage depot and hospital by the Russians after 1916, restored in the 1960s and partly reconverted to a mosque in 2013. At the time of research, the main interior was closed but the vaulted western narthex, with its extensively preserved frescoes of various biblical themes, remained accessible. A photo board outside shows you more from the interior.

Set amid column remnants, Ottoman gravestones and an old-world corn-store barn, the site's basic garden cafe is a relaxing place for tea or inexpensive local snacks. Or walk out of the gardens' gate and descend the steps to find the much suaver **Sofia Garden Cafe & Brasserie** (mains ₺27-80, snacks from ₺9; ⊙8.30am-2am; ❋ 🛜).

You can get pretty close to Aya Sofya using a Fatih dolmuş (₺2.50) starting from a stand one block west of Atatürk Alanı. The ensemble is visible from the north as you drive by on the D010 highway. Entrance to the garden is only possible from the south side.

Ortahisar Fatih Büyük Camii MOSQUE
(Kanuni Park) Originally known by the rather breathless name of the 'Church of the Golden-Headed Virgin Mary', this mosque started out as a church, possibly built by the nephew of Emperor Constantine I. It was claimed for Islam by the Ottomans in 1461. Ionic columns incorporated into the northern entrance may have once belonged to a Roman temple.

Atatürk Mansion HISTORIC BUILDING
(Atatürk Köşkü; ☑ 0462-231 0028; Köşk Caddesi; ₺5; ⊙ 8am-7pm Apr-Sep, to 5pm Oct-Mar) This three-storey, blindingly white late-19th-century mansion has fine views and lovely formal gardens. Built for a wealthy Greek banking family in the Black Sea style popular in the Crimea, it was bequeathed to Atatürk in 1924, and it's believed he wrote part of his will here. Inside you can see photos and mementos of the great man, including a map of the WWI Dardanelles campaign scratched into the table in the study.

It is nestled in leafy Soğuksu, 5km southwest of Atatürk Alanı. To get there take a Çamlik-bound dolmuş from a stand on Kahramanmaraş Caddesi (₺2.50).

🏃 Activities

There are numerous local tour companies around Atatürk Alanı that organise full-day packages, generally at the same price as if you book through your hotel. Daily departures are reliable in season to Sumela (including caves and uplands, ₺90), Uzungöl (₺75) and Ayder (₺90). Batumi (Georgia) is also fairly popular but be aware that tours to Pokut (₺120) and Karagöl (₺140), while advertised, rarely get sufficient customers so tend to be cancelled last minute.

Meydan Hamamı HAMAM
(www.meydanhamami.com; Kahramanmaraş Caddesi 3; hamam ₺30, scrub ₺15, massage ₺15; ⊙ men 7am-11pm, women 8am-8pm) Clean and well run, the 'Hamam on the Square' offers saunas, scrubs, bubble washes and massages. There are separate areas for men and women; the women's entrance is around the corner.

🛏 Sleeping

There's a particularly dense cluster of mostly budget and lower midrange hotels on and around Güzelhisar Caddesi and fronting the minibus stand to Of, while more upmarket places are dotted all over the city. Booking ahead, especially for the latter, can be wise in summer (mid-June to early September).

Hotel Özgür HOTEL $
(☑ 0462-326 6616; hotelozgur61@hotmail.com; Güzelhisar Caddesi 8; s/d/tr from ₺80/120/160; 🅿 🛜) Özgür's rooms are pretty small but have been recently refurbished with new fittings improving the little bathrooms and scarlet curtains brightening the overall effect. At the very modest prices charged, it's one of Trabzon's better budget options. Prices increase by up to ₺90 in midsummer.

★ Grand Vuslat BOUTIQUE HOTEL $$
(☑ 0462-291 3434; www.grandvuslat.com; Gençoğlu Sokak 5; s/d ₺310/360) This excellent, upmarket option is set just two very short blocks north of the *meydan* on a quiet alley, with unexpected sea views from its upper rear rooms. Expect monogrammed towels and toiletries, rounded wooden furniture and dapper staff who speak English and Arabic. The extravagant use of burnished gilt detailing might be a little showy for some tastes.

There's a fairly lavish breakfast buffet and an open-air lounge space for smoking nargile.

Zağnospaşa Konakları HERITAGE HOTEL $$
(☑ 0462-300 6300; www.zagnospasakonaklari.com; Zağnos Dereiçi Sokak; s/d/ste from ₺150/300/480; 🅿 ❄ 🛜) Formed of three newly-built mansions in the Ottoman style, this hotel makes the most of a location above the park that divides two impressive sections of Trabzon's fortress wall. The decor is sedate, using plenty of dark wood, and beds are comfortable.

🍴 Eating & Drinking

Kalender ANATOLIAN $
(☑ 0462-323 1011; Zeytinlik Caddesi 16b; dishes ₺9-24, soup ₺7; ⊙ 8.30am-9pm Mon-Sat; ❄) Creating a loveable old-cottage feel, this welcoming cafe-restaurant is a great place to sample a daily changing menu of wholesome and hearty local dishes, often including variants on the Black Sea classic *kuymak* (cheese and cornmeal fondue).

Mixed plates available.

★**Cemilusta** TURKISH **$$**

(☑0462-321 6161; www.cemilusta.com.tr; Atatürk Alanı 6; mains ₺25-45; ☺7am-11pm) Enthusiastic locals don't believe you've really been to Trabzon till you've eaten *Akçaabat köfte* (local meat patties) on Cemilusta's jam-packed *meydan* terrace. The cafe also offers excellent lamb chops, *lahana sarma* (stuffed cabbage rolls), *kuymak* (cheese-heavy 'polenta') and fresh fish. Picture menus are helpful.

The building is an artfully modernised three-storey stone mansion with a modernist take on wagon-wheel chandeliers.

Berweuli FRENCH **$$**

(☑0542-379 3854; https://berweuli-ala-carte-restaurant.business.site; Sarayatik Cami Sokak 20; mains ₺20-40; ☺9.30am-10pm Mon-Thu, to midnight Fri-Sun) This special restaurant serves French-inspired lunches (beef Bourguignon, cassoulet, ratatouille), adding Italian and Ottoman recipes after 6pm. The dining space leads back from a restored historic house into a glass-roofed garden with a pair of olive trees, perched on the top of the Ortahisar fortress parapet.

The name means pomegranate in the Laz language.

★**Bezmigah Cafe & Restaurant** CAFE

(☑0462-544 4444; Bedestan; ☺10am-10pm) If you climb up through the forgettable lower floors of Trabzon's historic covered marketplace (Bedestan), you emerge in this magical, low-lit space of giant square columns and hefty architectural squinches, all lavished with rugs, lanterns, swords, old cameras, samovars and toy cars.

As well as coffees, tea and nargile, there's a limited menu of snacks plus competent, fair-value garnished meals (₺25).

❶ Information

Tourist Office (☑0462-326 4760; www.homeoftrabzon.com; Atatürk Alanı; ☺8am-10pm Jun-Sep, to 5pm Oct-May) The website, free booklet and QR-coded map offered by this helpful tourist office are likely to inspire you to rent a car and drive up into the many beautiful mountain pasturelands in the country behind the city.

❶ Getting There & Away

AIR

Busy **Trabzon Airport** (TZX; Trabzon Havalimanı; www.trabzon.dhmi.gov.tr; off Atatürk Bulvarı) is 5.5km east of the city centre.

BOAT

Some years, a hydrofoil operates between Trabzon and the Russian city of Sochi, most recently through **Olympia Line** (www.olympia-line.ru). When it runs the trip takes 4½ hours and costs around US$130, but the ride can be very uncomfortable. Be aware that most visitors require a visa for Russia.

BUS

Trabzon's **otogar** (D010 Atatürk Bulvarı) is 3km east of the port. Bus companies, most usefully **Metro** (www.metroturizm.com.tr; Limonlu Sokak; ☺9am-6pm) and **Ali Osman Ulusoy** (www.aliosmanulusoy.com.tr; Limonlu Caddesi; ☺9am-9pm), have central booking offices scattered around Atatürk Alanı. Although direct buses are advertised, for Batumi in Georgia you'll often do better taking a bus to Hopa, transferring there to a Sarp minibus and then walking across the border.

Minibus services to Sumela, Üzüngöl and Pazar depart from a series of stands on Çömlekçi Caddesi, the street that parallels the D010 just southeast of the city centre. For Ayder and the Western Kaçkar Mountains, change at Pazar.

Minibuses to Akcaabat and some to Giresun leave from the **Western Minibus Station** (Kalkanoğlu Caddesi) in a rather surreal area of half-demolished buildings. However, Prenskale minibuses to Giresun use the otogar.

BLACK SEA COAST TRABZON

SERVICES FROM TRABZON OTOGAR

DESTINATION	FARE (₺)	DURATION (HR)	FREQUENCY (DAILY)
Erzurum	60	5	10am, noon, 5pm, 6pm, 7pm, 9pm, 1am, 2am
Giresun	23	2	once or twice hourly 6am-7pm, more options from the Western Minibus Station
Hopa	27	2¾	twice hourly 6.30am-8.30pm
Kayseri	130	11	3pm, 6pm, 7.30pm
Rize	14	1¼	three hourly 8am-7pm
Samsun	60	5½-7	at least hourly 7.30am-00.30am
Sinop	80	8½-10½	9.30am, 11.30am, 9pm

ⓘ Getting Around

TO/FROM THE BUS STATION

To reach Atatürk Alanı from the otogar, cross the road in front of the terminal. Any westbound bus or dolmuş marked 'Parkı' or 'Meydan' will head to Atatürk Alanı but some take roundabout routes. The most direct are marked 'Garajlar-Meydan'.

Heading to the otogar, take a Garajlar dolmuş from under the flyover on Limonlu Sokak, just off the southeastern corner of Atatürk Alanı, or one marked **'KTÜ'** (Gençoğlu Sokak) from next to Otel Horon.

Taxis ask ₺20 and can take 15 minutes or longer due to the generally heavy traffic.

DOLMUŞ

Dolmuşes (₺2.50) have numerous starting points. To reach Aya Sofia, take Fatih services from the minibus stand directly southeast of the *meydan* or from an alternative stop (Kahrammanmaras Caddesi 7a) around 100m west of the *meydan.*

For the Atatürk Mansion, take the **Çamlık dolmuş** (Kahrammanmaras Caddesi).

Routes to Bahçecik and Çezaevi start from the southernmost end of Cumhuriyet Caddesi.

Sumela

The extensive ruins of **Sumela Monastery** (Sümela Manastırı; Meryemana; ☑ 0462-326 0748; www.sumela.com; Altindere Vadisi, Maçka; car/motorbike ₺12/6; ⊙ 8am-6pm Apr-Oct, to 4pm Nov-Mar), founded by Greeks in the 4th century, cling improbably to a sheer cliff, high above evergreen forests. This is one of the Black Sea region's unquestionable highlights. Ongoing restoration means you can't go inside until at least 2023, but for many visitors just seeing the exterior from the **'Seyir Noktası' viewpoint** at the **lower car park** is well worth the 40km drive from Trabzon.

Climbing closer takes around 30 strenuous minutes on foot by a 1.2km zigzag footpath (no views) or 10 minutes on the site shuttle-bus (₺5 return) up the 3km road to the **upper car park**. The latter passes a waterfall (700m) and a **monastery viewpoint** (2km) en route. From the upper car park, don't miss a 100m stroll to tiny **Aya Varvara chapel** `FREE`. Inside the chapel, a video displays some of the monastery's murals and behind is another great view surveying the monastery complex through the trees. A **boardwalk path** leads 350m further to a ticket booth beside a restored historic aqueduct. Paying the ₺10 entry fee here allows you to climb some steps and walk 20m to an overlook from which you can look down on an **archaeological site**. That includes a colourfully fresco-festooned church apse, but don't expect to get inside or to see the main complex which, from this point, is hidden around the corner. Visit early or late to avoid the crowds of Turkish tourists.

★ **Kayadibi Saklıbahçe** TURKISH $
(☑ 0462-512 2318; www.kayadibisaklibahce.com; Şehit Ferhat Gedik Tüneli Çıkısı, Maçka; dishes ₺10-24; ⊙ 8am-8.30pm; 📖 451) This 'Hidden Garden', around two thirds of the way to Sumela from Trabzon, serves some of the best Black Sea dishes in the region. Ideally order a mixture of dishes to share (around two per head) including polenta-like cheesy *kuymak*, *karalahana sarması* (mince-stuffed collard leaves) and *pazı kavurma* (slightly spicy sautéed chard, potato and onion mix).

There's an airy, glass-sided main dining hall but the place retains a pleasantly uncommercial village feel and there is plenty of outdoor seating. It's a steep 100m up a lane that climbs off the old D885 road near the southern end of the Şehit Ferhat Gedik Tunnel. From central Maçka it's around 10 minutes' walk north, forking left just after the river bridge.

ⓘ Getting There & Away

Especially if you're travelling alone, a very sensible option is to join a tour from Trabzon. Full-day tours with both Metro (p499) and **Eyce** (☑ 0462-326 7174; www.eycetours.com; Taksim İşhanı Sokak 11, 1st fl) depart every morning and include not just Sumela but also one of the highland meadows and the impressive Karaca Cave, all for ₺90 per person.

By public transport, there is a dolmuş service every 20 minutes from Trabzon's eastern minibus stand to Maçka (₺5, 40 minutes), the nearest town. That's 40km from Trabzon but still 16km short of Sumela. While their signboards often say Sumela, only one or two Maçka services per day actually make the full run (₺25 return). Timetables aren't fixed so enquire the day before.

From Maçka a taxi costs around ₺50 one way but you'll pay an additional ₺40 per hour waiting time.

Uzungöl

☑ 0462 / POP 1500

All across Turkey, tourist posters show Uzungöl as an idyllic Alpine lake fringed with emerald meadows, a handful of tile-roofed cottages and a single mosque with a soaring white minaret. These photos date from circa 2010. In the decade since, virtually all of the main meadowland has become covered with hotels and restaurants and the lake has been edged with a promenade and ring road. With your expectations suitably reduced, however, the scene retains a real beauty, the surrounding mountains recall Switzerland, and the place's popularity makes it relatively easy to reach from the coast.

It's a good, if relatively expensive, base for hikes in the Soğanlı Mountains and to the tiny lakes around Demirkapı in the Haldizen Mountains. Summer weekends get especially busy but most of the restaurants and hotels close down from September to May and in winter snowfall can be heavy.

From Trabzon's Eastern Minibus Stand, **Çaykara Tur** (🖉 Trabzon 0462-321 9949, Uzungöl 0462-656 6141; www.caykaratur.com) minibuses to Uzungöl depart nine times daily between 6.30am and 6.30pm (₺18, 2½ hours). The last return minibuses to Trabzon leave Uzungöl at 6.45pm and 9pm. Buy tickets in advance to guarantee a seat.

Visiting Uzungöl as part of a one-day tour from Trabzon (₺75) makes a lot of sense as the tour adds in visits to some of the higher viewpoints that are otherwise awkward to reach.

Rize

🖉 0464 / POP 123,500

In the heart of Turkey's picturesque tea-growing area, Rize is a modern city centred on a pair of very contrasting squares, one a very pretty little park, the other a soulless expanse of unshaded stone. Directly behind the centre, verdant slopes rise extremely steeply in eccentric hillocks that are lavishly planted with tea bushes. As you'll see from all the giant photos, Rizeans are proud of local-boy-turned-prime-minister Recep Tayyip Erdoğan, who grew up here and now has a university named after him.

◎ Sights

⭐ **Ziraat Botanik Tea Garden**   GARDENS
(Narenciye Sokak 31; tea ₺1.50; ⊘ 24hr) FREE
At the summit of a steep urban hill, this unexpected little paradise is primarily a delightful teahouse beneath a big, fragrant magnolia tree, but there are other fine trees, labelled flowers and shrubs, and a scaled-down version of a tea factory with glass windows for you to peep in and see the machinery. Don't miss the splendid views across the valley to the castle and to the picturesque southern slopes, steeply fused with tea plantations.

Rize Castle   CASTLE
(Rize Kalesi; Piri Reis Caddesi; ⊘ 8am-11pm) FREE
Built by the Byzantines on the steep hill at the back of town, Rize's modest *kale* (castle) has two concentric sections. The upper, inner fortress might date to the 6th century AD; it contains a cafe with sweeping coastal views. To reach the site, head west along Atatürk Caddesi and turn left up Kale Sokak. However, the complex is arguably more impressive, seen from the Ziraat Gardens, or from town when illuminated at night.

🛏 Sleeping & Eating

⭐ **Evvel Zaman**   TURKISH $$
(🖉 0464-212 2188; www.evvelzaman.com.tr; Harem Sokak 2; mains ₺15-25; ⊘ 10am-11pm) This lovingly restored Ottoman house is like a joyously jumbled museum, displaying such an endless selection of ancient copperware, swords, old rugs etc that there's not much space left for seating in some rooms. The short menu offers mainly traditional Black Sea dishes. The Riza speciality *hamsi pilavi* (anchovy pilaf, ₺25) needs to be pre-ordered one day ahead.

Their *köy kahvaltısı* (village breakfast, ₺30) uses the produce from local villages. Or just order tea (₺2.50) and enjoy the atmosphere. It's very close to the museum but entered from the side lane opposite the better marked Pipa's Cafe.

❶ Getting There & Away

For Trabzon (₺14, 1¼ hours), Pazar (₺6, 35 minutes) and Hopa (₺18, 1½ hours) minibuses leave every 20 minutes from a conveniently central series of stands in front of İş Bank. Four daily minibuses to Ayder (₺15, 1½ hours) leave from the same spot (platform 9), departing at 9.30am, 11am, 2pm and 6pm. For big, longer distance buses you'll need the otogar, 2km northwest, reached by dolmuş 5. There are several bus company offices huddled on Cumhuriyet Caddesi between the park and Cumhuriyet Meydanı.

The 14km Ovit Tunnel, which opened in 2018, has dramatically shortened the drive between Rize and Erzurum.

Hopa

🔊 0466 / POP 20,700

Hopa is essentially a place to stop to change minibuses en route to or from Georgia. That said, the town has a new **ethnographic museum** (Kültür Evi; 🔊 0466-351 1068; Kavakdibi Camii Arkası; ⊙ 8am-5pm Tue-Sun; 🚌 Liman) **FREE**, set in a rebuilt traditional house, and there's a trio of excellent cafe-restaurants overlooking a (very modest) promenade (there's no beach).

Acceptable if mostly unremarkable hotels line the main drag, Sahil Caddesi/Turgay Ciner Caddesi, for a kilometre or so north of the river bridge.

Enez Döviz (Cumhuriyet Caddesi; ⊙ 8am-7pm) is a handily central money-changer with excellent rates for US dollars and euros, and passable ones for Azerbaijani manat and Georgian Lari.

ⓘ Getting There & Away

The **minibus stands** for Artvin (₺25, 1¼ hours, hourly till 6pm) and Rize (₺18, 1½ hours, every 20 to 30 minutes) is situated beneath an underpass on the south side of the river bridge that divides Hopa in two. Some 600m northeast up the coast road is the **stand** (🔊 0466-351 5775, 0535-675 5784; Turgay Ciner Caddesi) for the Georgian at Sarp border (₺7, 25 minutes, three hourly). The last service is around 7pm but given the time difference it's unwise to leave it that late as the connecting bus 16 into Batumi stops running at night and you might be landed with a hefty taxi fare.

For longer distance buses including Trabzon (₺27, 2¾ hours, twice hourly) and Erzurum (₺70, five hours, seven daily, last at 4pm), use the main **otogar** (D010, 600m southwest along the coast from the bridge.

Western Kaçkars

The western side of the Kaçkar Mountains (Kaçkar Dağları) is easily accessed from the Black Sea coast through the valleys of the fast-flowing Hala (or Kavron) and Fırtına (or Büyük) rivers. The area is a rainy one (especially April to June), and the steep valley sides are covered in wonderfully luxuriant forest. Above the treeline at about 1900m the upper valleys have many open mountainside pastures with backdrops of craggy, snow-capped peaks. In midsummer the main *yayla* (mountain pasture) villages can get busy with day-trippers and Ayder becomes completely overloaded, but this is also the best time for wonderful walking and hiking in the upland valleys. It's feasible to trek right across to the southern and eastern sides of the Kaçkars if you're well prepared. However, many visitors are more than satisfied with making shorter excursions by car, taking selfies on historic stone river bridges, zip lining, rafting or simply strolling on the magical meadows.

Çamlıhemşin & Around

🔊 0464 / POP 1400 / ELEV 300M

Some 20km inland, the tiny hub town of Çamlıhemşin is a functional, workaday spot crammed into a deep, narrow river valley, but it retains a certain authenticity with a mainly Hemşin population. At the southern end of Çamlıhemşin the road forks: left up the Hala valley to Ayder (17km) or straight ahead up the Fırtına valley towards Çat (28km) via the spectacular castle of Zilkale (13km) and Şenyuva (7km), where you'd turn for the lovely upland meadowland of Pokut (20km, partly unpaved). Both are beautiful routes up densely wooded valleys, passing several elegant Ottoman-era arched stone bridges that frame photogenic river views.

Çamlıhemşin has a post office, supermarket and ATM.

🏃 Activities

Rafting is possible from May to October on a 13km stretch of the Fırtına River downstream from Çamlıhemşin; only about 7km are safely navigable before July. Numerous operators are strung along the Ardeşen–Çamlıhemşin road.

Türkü Tour HIKING
(🔊 0533-341 3430, 0464-651 7230; www.turkutour.com; İnönü Caddesi) Mehmet Demirci, a friendly local entrepreneur and owner of pensions in Ayder and Çamlıhemşin, offers a variety of programmes and possibilities for small groups, including day walks with transport, longer treks including trans-Kaçkar routes, 4WD jeep safaris and wildlife tours.

🛏 Sleeping

⭐ **Taşmektep Otel** BOUTIQUE HOTEL $$
(🔊 0464-651 7010; www.camlihemsintasmektep.com; Halil Şişman Caddesi, Konaklar Mahallesi; s/d/tr from ₺345/370/395; ⊙ mid-May–mid-Nov; 🅿 ❄ 🛜) Transformed by a local NGO from a 1937 stone schoolhouse, this charming boutique hotel has a contemporary country feel with plenty of antiques and

photos illustrating community history. Airy, pine-furnished rooms are spacious, and there's a good buffet breakfast. It's mere centimetres off the main Fırtına Valley road, 1km south of Çamlıhemşin, with a couple of arty little cafes nearby.

Otel Doğa GUESTHOUSE $$
(☑0464-651 7455; www.facebook.com/oteldoga; Şenyuva Yolu; r per person with breakfast/half-board ₺75/95; P ☻ 🛜) Right beside the river on the beautiful Fırtına valley road, 4.5km south of Çamlıhemşin, this friendly, old-fashioned hotel is welcoming and well kept. Good home-cooked local meals are served in the riverside dining room. Nearly all bedrooms have private bathrooms and many have balconies; opt for a corner room.

❶ Getting There & Away

Ayder-bound minibuses from Pazar, which run every 45 minutes in summer (7am to 7pm), make brief stops in Çamlıhemşin (₺8, 45 minutes). Four of these start from Rize. Services are much scarcer out of season. There's a petrol station 2km north of central Çamlıhemşin.

Fırtına Valley & Around

☑0464

Used as a location in the Turkish film *Bal* (Honey), the lushly forested Fırtına Valley is the main gateway to the glorious upper meadowlands of the Western Kaçkars, notably Pokut, (upper) Çat and less visited Elevit, Haçivanak and Amlakit. North of Çamlıhemşin the busy riverside road passes many rafting booths and cross-river zip lines aimed to attract motorists who otherwise zoom towards the heavily over-developed *yayla* resort of Ayder.

Further south, traffic is less frenetic, making it easier to get more of a sense of traditional Hemşin life. Notice early-20th-century mansions built by families enriched by working as pastry chefs in pre-revolutionary Russia. Also spot the winch-wires used for hoisting goods up to remote mountainside homes.

◉ Sights

Graceful arched stone bridges built in early Ottoman times cross the rushing Fırtına River at several selfie-friendly points, notably 5km from Çamlıhemşin (just after Otel Doğa) and at Şenyuva. Popular excursions lead to the magnificently set castle ruins of Zilkale, the popular if less impressive

waterfall **Palovit Şelalesi** and various inaccessible *yaylalar* (mountainside meadow villages), of which **Pokut** has the most panoramic views.

★**Zilkale** CASTLE
(Zil Castle; adult/child & senior ₺3/free; ☉7am-7pm; P) The region's most spectacular man-made attraction is the neatly restored 13th-century shell of Zil Castle, a fine stone tower surrounded by sturdy walls topping a rocky pinnacle above the sheer gorge, 13km south of Çamlıhemşin and 5.5km from Şenyuva.

🛏 Sleeping

Çulina Kendini
Koruyan Mahalle BUNGALOW $$
(☑0533-719 9599; www.kendinikoruyanmahalle.com; per person ₺200) Comfortable if deliberately simple wooden bungalow units without TV or wi-fi, but with superb views. Entirely unique for being accessed via a two-person *teleferik* (cable car). It's an unforgettable if terrifying 80-second ride across a plunging woodland valley starting from a point 2.5km up the Pokut road. There's no other vehicular access. Book ahead.

Pokut Doğa Konuk Evi GUESTHOUSE $$
(☑0532 493 9101, Whatsapp 0539 652 0653; www.pokutdogakonukevi.com/pokuten; Pokut; per person without/with view ₺150/200) The top choice in Pokut, complete with en-suite bathrooms, this wooden mountain house is a marvellous summer perch for surveying the Kaçkars or walking the highlands.

❶ Getting There & Away

During the summer months when the highland villages are inhabited, at least one daily dolmuş (minibus) heads up the Fırtına valley from Çamlıhemşin to Çat, some days continuing to Amlakit (₺40, about 3½ hours via Çat, Elevit, Tirovit and Palovit) and returning the same afternoon. Check locally for the latest timings.

A taxi from Çamlıhemşin costs around ₺100 one way to Çat or about ₺140 to Elevit.

CAR
Brown signs with yellow script indicate routes to the main *yaylalar*. Beyond the trekking-base hamlet of lower Çat (1250m, 28km from Çamlıhemşin), almost all of these are unpaved and, though passable by car on perfectly dry summer days, you'll likely wish for a high-clearance vehicle. Don't attempt them between October and May.

In principle it's possible, and indeed superbly scenic, to make a loop from past Tarzanpark and the Palovit Şelalesi (waterfall), continuing to Amlakit then returning via Elevit and Çat. However, do enquire carefully about road conditions before attempting this as the section north of Amlakit can be exceedingly rough.

Ayder

📋 0464 / POP 500 / ELEV 1380M

The tourism hub of the Kaçkars, little Ayder is an all-hotel 'village' set on a sloping *yayla*, surrounded by steep conifer-clad valley slopes sliced through with two very long cascading streams that approximate to waterfalls. The grassy meadow slope is a picnic area dotted with tall swings that cater to hordes of day-tripping families. Local rules ensure that hotels are built in vaguely traditional style (ie sheathed in wood) to give the settlement a fairly coherent feel, but an old-world village it certainly isn't. In summer, the place is jam packed with crowds of tourists and you'll probably want to press on to one of the higher *yalalar*. However, in spring and autumn the charm returns.

There's an ATM towards the lower (western) end of the village.

◉ Sights

There is a plethora of superb rambles on and from the mountaintop meadows. Nearest to Ayder is **Hüser Yaylası**, barely 2km northeast as the crow flies but around 1000m higher and accessed by some 12km of zigzagging track.

Yukarı Kavron   VILLAGE
(Yukarı Kavrun Yaylası) One of the most popular day-trip driving destinations from Ayder (13km by unpaved track), Yukarı Kavron is a slightly scrappy seasonal *yayla* village in a beautiful upland valley flanked by mountain ridges. In summer the crush of cars can be off-putting, but within a few minutes' walk you can escape the crowds on idyllic hiking trails towards Mt Kaçkar and several mountain lakes.

Ogzalase   CYCLING
(📋 0533-788 9153; www.instagram.com/ogzalase; per person US$30; ⊙mid-May–Oct) Ogzalase offer drive-up, ride-down bicycle trips to the

Hüser mountaintop meadows (12km). It's a fabulous way to combine wonderful views with an adrenaline kick, yet you don't need to be particularly fit. Departures are weather dependent and require a minimum of five people to sign up, though you can discuss private tours with the owners, who speak English. Allow around 3½ hours.

🛏 Sleeping & Eating

Zirve Ahşap Pansiyon   PENSION $
(📋 0537-408 2717, 0464-657 2177; www.ayderzirve. com; Aşağı Ambarlık; per person ₺70; ⊙Apr–mid-Nov; 🛜) This very good budget option has three floors of spick-and-span rooms, all with bathrooms, and some with attractive kilims (woven rugs) on the floors. Views are lacking, but given the remarkably low prices, it's not surprising that the place is often full.

Kuşpuni Dağ Evi   PENSION $$
(📋 0464-657 2052; www.kuspini.com; d/tr ₺300/450; 🛜) This peaceful yet central family-run pension feels more authentic than most with its inviting stove-heated lounge with wooden floors and a few local antiques. Varnished pine rooms have bathrooms with screened showers. Prices reduce by at least ₺100 outside summer.

★ Pilita   ANATOLIAN $
(📋 0553-256 2162; set dinner ₺50-80, mains ₺10-25; ⊙8-10am & 7-11pm; 🛜🍽) This delightful log-cabin restaurant cooks its truly local spread of mountain specialities to order, including *kaydebak* (using seven types of local greens) and *hamimli* (cornbread incorporating local veg). It also does more usual Black Sea foods, espresso coffees and beer. Good spoken English; pre-order dinner by 3pm (or a day in advance for bigger groups).

ℹ Getting There & Away

The **dolmuş stand** (📋 0464-6572141) is across the main road from the Kaplıca. From here there are minibuses to Pazar (₺11, 1¼ hours) every 45 minutes in summer (7am to 7pm) and direct to Rize (at 7am, 8am, noon and 4pm). All pass through Çamlıhemşin (₺7, 30 minutes). Services are much scarcer in out of season.

Northeastern Anatolia

Best Places to Eat

➡ Erzurum Evleri (p509)

➡ Kars Kaz Evi (p521)

➡ Emirşeyh Nedim (p509)

➡ Akca Kale Ada Balık Lokantası (p519)

➡ Olgunlar Cafe (p514)

Best Places to Stay

➡ Black Forest Hotel (p519)

➡ Tehran Boutique Hotel (p528)

➡ Kaçkar Pansiyon (p514)

➡ Uzundere Öğretmenevi (p516)

➡ Kar's Otel (p521)

Why Go?

The northeast is Turkey's best-kept scenic secret, throwing together a smorgasbord of big-ticket landscapes – precipitous gorges, expansive steppe, highland pastures and Alpine mountains. Distances are great and public transport is limited (though perfectly adequate between bigger towns), but roads are remarkably good with minimal traffic, making this a superb region for self-driving tours. Wheels will also help you discover a wealth of half-forgotten Georgian and Armenian churches and spectacularly perched castles.

The most appealing cities are Kars and Erzurum, both with rich historical pedigrees. The Kaçkar Mountains (Kaçkar Dağları) beckon for summer hiking, and, when it's open, the mesmerising cone of Mt Ararat offers a climbing experience of Biblical proportions. Ski resorts at Erzurum and Sarıkamış are growing in popularity while in February and March, the Kars railway and frozen Çıldır Gölü attract domestic tourists seeking the romance of snowy landscapes and sleigh rides on the lake.

When to Go
Erzurum

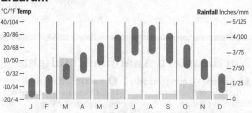

May Steppe blossoms and spring warmth awakens mountain pastures.

Jun–Aug Hike in the Kaçkar Mountains, scale Mt Ararat (if open), and catch summer festivals.

Dec–Mar Ski at Palandöken, or try ice fishing and sleigh rides at Çıldır Gölü. High season in Kars.

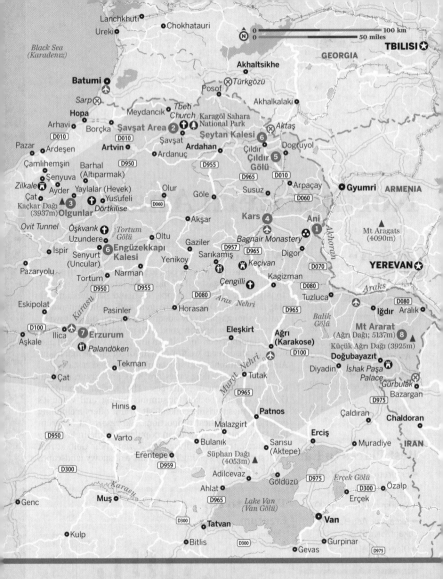

Northeastern Anatolia Highlights

1 Ani (p524) Losing yourself in the ruins of this former Armenian capital.

2 Şavşat Area (p518) Travelling the breathtakingly beautiful Ardahan–Şavşat road.

3 Olgunlar (p513) Making day walks or full Kaçkar Mountain expeditions from this quaint village.

4 Kars (p520) Hanging out in this Russian-influenced city with enjoyable cafes.

5 Çıldır Gölü (p519) Fishing for carp through the winter ice on Turkey's second biggest natural lake after a romantic sleigh ride.

6 Clifftop castles (p516) Marvelling at fortifications

such as Şeytan Kalesi and Engüzekkapı Kalesi.

7 Erzurum (p507) Discovering a medley of Seljuk, Mongol and Ottoman mosques and *medreses*.

8 Mt Ararat (p530) Being mesmerised by the snow-topped cone of Turkey's highest peak (5137m).

Erzurum

📋 0442 / POP 418,000 / ELEV 1890M

One of eastern Turkey's main transport hubs, Erzurum has a main drag lined with Seljuk, Saltuk, Mongol and Ottoman mosques and *medreses* (seminaries), with mountains and steppe forming a fascinatingly discordant backdrop to the jumble of billboards and minarets. Although it's one of Turkey's most piously conservative cities, it is home to two universities with more than 100,000 students who add a relaxed buzz to the summer pavement cafes. And, come winter, the nearby high-octane Palandöken ski resort adds a thriving nightlife.

◉ Sights

★ **Yakutiye Medresesi**   MUSEUM
(Turkish-Islamic Arts & Ethnography Museum; Kent Parkı; ₺6; ⊙8am-7pm Apr-Oct, to 5pm Nov-Mar) Dominating Erzurum's central park, this handsome 1310 *medrese* building features a minaret whose superb mosaic tile work wouldn't look out of place in Central Asia. Inside, hefty stone arches support a stalactite-vaulted ceiling portal that lets in filtered daylight. Duck beneath heavy stone lintels to reach assorted side rooms containing nicely curated exhibits on traditional regional crafts, costumes and local life.

★ **Çifte Minareli Medrese**   ISLAMIC SITE
(Twin Minaret Seminary; Cumhuriyet Caddesi; ⊙9am-5pm) FREE Erzurum's most iconic medieval landmark features twin fluted minarets with detailing in blue glaze on brick. There's a beautifully carved main portal and a distinctive squat spire topping a grand 12-sided domed hall, beneath which the founder of the *medrese* might have been buried. The site no longer functions as an Islamic seminary but its shell of stone interiors, including a porticoed central minigarden, are freely open to visitors. It's across a small park from the castle.

Üç Kümbetler   TOMB
(Three Tombs; off Yenikapı Caddesi) The name means 'three mausoleums' though in fact there are four, or five if you count another some way south across the park. The biggest is believed by some to be the tomb of Emir Saltuk, who established Saltuk Turk rule in Erzurum in the late 11th century.

Erzurum Kalesi   FORTRESS
(Erzurum Castle; off Cumhuriyet Caddesi; ₺6; ⊙8am-5.45pm) Though it's raised just a few metres above the surrounding city centre, Erzurum's castle site nonetheless offers panoramic views of the mountains and townscape. The views are even better if you pay the entry fee and climb the 12th-century minaret, though there's precious little else to see within the sturdy walls.

🏃 Activities

Ejder3200 (www.ejder3200.com; Kartal Sokak, Paladöken; per ride/ten rides ₺12/75; ⊙9am-5pm, last return 6pm) is Turkey's top ski resort. It combines two downhill skiing areas, Palandöken, 5km south of central Erzurum, and a smaller disconnected field at Konaklı, around 20km southwest. Both ski areas have a range of hotels, many with spas and saunas. There are cable cars, chair- and drag-lifts, snowboard and toboggan parks, a ski school and 45km of pistes. The season runs from late November to early April. Weekends are busy, and there's an après-ski scene with bars and discos. The rest of the year, only the main Palandöken gondola operates, and then sometimes weekends only – or not at all.

Medam Turizm (📋0442-235 3538; Esadaş apt 1/4, Ankara Sokak 1; ⊙9am-6.30pm Mon-Fri, 10am-4pm Sat) runs economical day-ski packages from central Erzurum, which include transport to/from the resort, ski passes and lunch.

Winter paragliding is possible in Palandöken (in addition to skiing).

🛏 Sleeping

Kral Otel   HOTEL $
(📋0442-234 6400; Erzincankapı Caddesi 18; s/d ₺80/140; 🕸) The Kral hits you with a striking, ancient-Persia themed lobby. But that's pure folly and receptionists actually sit at an older desk upstairs. Rooms are large, well equipped and the green-wood decor tries hard to look classy. Beds could be firmer and some rooms smell faintly of old cigarette smoke but it's good value for a superbly central location.

★ **Otel Zade**   HOTEL $$
(📋0442-233 1616; www.otelzade.com.tr; İsmet Paşa Caddesi 27; s/d from ₺200/300; 🕸🕸) The Zade's uplit, faux-classical facade is attractively dotted with flower boxes. The very comfortable rooms have slick, contemporary furniture and come kitted out with kettles, minibars and big built-into-the-wall satellite TVs. Even the toiletries are high quality, but staff seem overworked and you might want to pay the upgrade price to get lounging space in a deluxe room.

Erzurum

Erzurum

Hotel Grand Hitit   HOTEL **$$**
(📞0442-233 5001; www.grandhitithotel.com.tr;
Kazım Karabekir Caddesi 26; s/d/tr ₺150/250/320;
🅿🛜) With a low-key contemporary feel, the
Grand Hitit is professionally run and a good
choice for solo women travellers. Pleasant,
fair-sized rooms have well-sprung mattress-
es, sizeable bathrooms, minibars and safes.

🍴 Eating & Drinking

Cumhuriyet Caddesi is crammed with
restaurants and cafes serving everything
from *çiğ köfte* (raw ground lamb mixed
with pounded bulgur, onion, spices and
salt) to *lokum* (Turkish delight). Head to
Kılıçoğlu (Cumhuriyet Caddesi 13; mains ₺10-15;

⊙ 7am-2am; ☎) for baklava, ice cream and espresso coffee.

★**Erzurum Evleri** ANATOLIAN $
(www.tarihierzurumevleri.com; Yüzbaşı Sokak 5; mains ₺15-35, soup ₺10; ⊙ 8am-11pm) More enticing than many a museum, this trio of closely clustered 18th-century houses has been forged into a warren of stone-walled rooms and alcoves so colourfully adorned with rugs and antiques that it charges a ₺3 entry fee to the hordes of photo-snappers who don't order anything. The tasty fare is centred on local Erzurum dishes, including local *böreği* (cheese-stuffed pastries) and a good *tandır kebap* (shredded lamb).

There is live Turkish traditional music nightly from 7pm to 11pm in the main hall or, in good weather, in the rooftop section called Şahane Türkü Evi.

Çagin Cağ Kebap Lokanta KEBAP $
(Orhan Şerifsoy Caddesi; veg/meat mains ₺14/19.50, cağ kebap ₺9.50; ⊙ 7am-11pm, kebaps 11.30am-10pm) Erzurum has dozens of places for *cağ kebap*, but Çagin is a definite cut above the pack. Female friendly, there's smart, hexagonal-themed decor, an English-speaking chef and the very fresh complimentary mixed salad adds mint leaves and corn.

★**Emirşeyh Nedim** KEBAP $$
(www.emirseyh.com.tr; Tebrizkapı Caddesi 172; mains ₺15-45; ⊙ 10.30am-10.30pm) Erzurum's choice meat-eating experience is a two-storey building with carved stone pillars and recessed ceilings festooned with astonishingly rich paintings. With very good food and friendly service, it's a fine choice whether for Emirşeyh *köfte* (meatballs), any of the kebabs or a *karışık ızgara* (mixed grill, ₺89 for two people), all prepared at open ranges.

Çifteler Konağı COFFEE
(Telve Kahve Evi; ☎ 0554-183 0025; Çifte Minareler Sokak 55; coffee ₹10; ⊙ 9am-9pm) Lesser known than some of Erzurum's other 'museum' cafes, this is a quiet, special place for a Turkish coffee in a well-preserved Ottoman-era house, lavished with traditional fabrics, serenaded with spiritual music and adorned with assorted old homewares from copper jugs to radiograms.

ⓘ Information

Tourist Office (www.facebook.com/erzurum tdb; Cumhuriyet Caddesi; ⊙ 8am-noon & 1-5pm) Very helpful, English-speaking tourist office.

ⓘ Getting There & Away

AIR

Erzurum Airport (ERZ; Erzurum Havalimanı; ☎ 0442-327 2834; https://erzurum.dhmi.gov.tr/Sayfalar/default.aspx; Kars Yolu) is 13km northwest of town.

Bendy buses to central Erzurum (₺4, 25 minutes) are timed to fit with each arrival. Going to the airport, they start 90 minutes before each plane's timetabled departure from a **stand** (www.doyumsu.com.tr; İstasyon Sokak) across the square from the train station, where there's a comfortable waiting room. A taxi costs around ₺50.

BUS & DOLMUŞ

The **otogar** (Erzurum Bus Station; Kars Yolu; K4) is 9km northwest of the centre along the airport road. Bus companies including Metro, **Kanberoğlu** (www.kanberoglu.com.tr; Çaykara Caddesi), **Has Bingöl** (Çaykara Caddesi) and **Vangölü** (☎ 0850-650 6565; www.vangoluturizm.com.tr; Çaykara Caddesi; ⊙ 8am-10pm) have central ticket offices on and near the western part of Cumhuriyet Caddesi and most provide a free *servis* (minibus) from their offices to the otogar.

For minibuses, the **Şükrüpaşa Semt Garajı** (off Necip Fazıl Kısakürek Caddesi), built in 2011, was supposed to be the main terminal but the site has proved unpopular and most operators have reverted to using either the otogar or, more frequently, their own offices as departure points.

Ankara (₺120, 11½ hours) 7.30am, 10am plus many 2.30pm to 10.30pm.

Diyarbakır (₺80, six to eight hours) 8am, 11.30am, 1pm, 3.30pm, 4pm, 5pm, 10pm, 11.15pm. Tickets from Has Bingöl.

Doğubayazıt (₺50, four hours) Services at 4.30am, 5am and 9pm are bookable online, but for the daytime services (8am, 11.30am and 2.30pm), buy tickets in person through the Vangölü office.

Iğdır (₺50, 4½ hours) 6.30am, 8.30am, 10am, 6.30pm, 2am and 3.30pm with Iğdırlı Turizm (www.igdirliturizm.com.tr).

İstanbul (₺150, 18 to 20 hours) Many in afternoon and evening.

Kayseri (₺100, nine hours) 10.30am, 2pm, 5.30pm.

Trabzon (₺60, five hours) 8.30am, 9.30am, 2pm, 3.30pm, 5pm, 7pm, 8pm, 11pm, 1.30am.

Van (₺80, six hours) 8.30am, 12.30pm, 5pm, 11pm, 2am, 3.30am through Vangölü.

Various companies have services to Kars (₺30, three hours). Most frequent are those of **Kars Cengiz Turizm** (☎ 0532-505 9067, 0532-647 4157; Ali Ravi Caddesi; G1, G9, K4), running at 7.30am then hourly 9am till 5pm (or every two hours at weekends) from their office 1.3km south of Cumhuriyet Caddesi. Tickets are also sold at the central Vangölü bus office with a free *servis* transporting you to the departure point, but it's generally much faster to get there yourself: many city buses pass in front.

Buses to Yusufeli (₺40, 2½ hours, 9am, 12.30pm and 3.30pm), and those to Hopa (₺70, 5 hours) at 7am, 11.30am, 5.30pm and 7pm via Artvin (₺60, 3½ hours) pick up and drop off passengers at the **Yeşil Artvin Ekspres** (☑ 0442-242 0188; www.yesilartvinekspres. com.tr; Kongre Caddesi 2) office near the **Kongre Binası** (Kongre Caddesi; ☺ 8am-5pm; ☐ K3, G9). Some continue to Rize and there's one bus daily to Ardanuç. You can buy tickets centrally at the Has Bingöl office (p509).

From the otogar, Vangölü has more comfortable Hopa-bound buses at 2pm and 11.15pm.

CAR

Renting a vehicle is almost essential if you are hoping to see much of the Georgian Valleys or to be able to stop and start for the great views along the Erzurum–Yusufuli route. International car-rental firms have branches in Erzurum but local companies are often cheaper. Dozens are

closely packed in around 100m along Milletbahçe Sokak, between Çaykara Caddesi and the Rafo Otel. **GRS** (Tuktu Rent A Car; ☑ 0507-502 4447, 0442-235 3573; Çaykara Caddesi 28; ☺ 9am-10pm) is particularly obliging and has good rates for week-long hires starting from ₺130 per day for a Renault Symbol.

TRAIN

The train station, **Erzurum Gar** (www.tcddtasimacilik.gov.tr; İstasyon Sokak), is around 1.5km north of the Yakutiye Medresesi. The daily **Doğu Ekspresi** train (www.tcddtasimacilik.gov.tr) departs at 2.10pm to Kars (₺17.50, four hours). The overnight service to Ankara (seat/sleeper ₺42/58, 20½ hours) departs at 11.52am, arriving at 8.26am. It stops en route at Sivas (₺24/40.50, 10 hours) and Kayseri (₺30/46.50, 13½ hours).

ⓘ Getting Around

City bus K4 (₺2.50) connects to the otogar from the centre; you can catch it at the southbound **stop** (Hastaneler Caddesi) on Hastaneler Caddesi, just north of Havuzbaşı roundabout. Across

Kaçkar Mountains

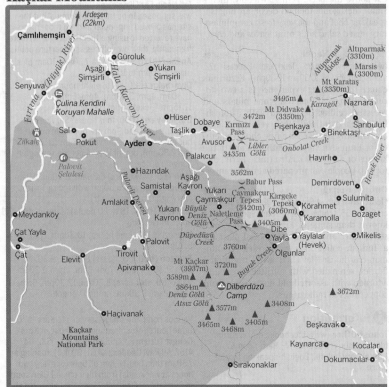

the road is the **stand** (Hastaneler Caddesi) for dolmuş services to Kongre Binası via the train station area. For Palandöken, bus B6 leaves hourly in season from a **stop** (Ali Ravi Caddesi) just south of the Lala Paşa mosque, returning on the hour (8am to 8pm).

Taxis from the **Çaykara stand** (☑ 0442-235 3964; Çaykara Caddesi), close to Atatürk Evi, want around ₺30 to Palandöken, ₺40 (15 minutes) to the otogar.

Eastern Kaçkars

The eastern side of the Kaçkars is generally drier than the western side, meaning better conditions for hiking but a less lush forest cover. It's also far less discovered and the little trailhead villages of Barhal, Yaylalar and Olgunlar remain very modest, rustic settlements. Even the main access town, Yusufeli, has only limited facilities but is nonetheless a likeable base from which to access the region – at least until it gets flooded by a vast dam project in around 2023.

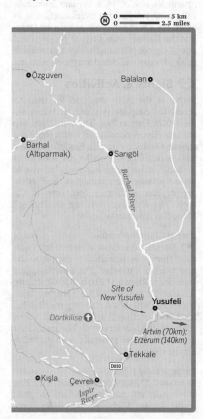

ⓘ Getting There & Around

Yusufeli is the regional hub, connected by a decent road (and a few daily buses) to Erzurum and via a seemingly endless series of tunnels to Artvin, with minibuses approximately hourly.

Driving into the Kaçkars from Yusufeli is a delightful riverside trip, despite a lot of dusty building works after the impressive cragtop castle of **Kisporot**. The winding road is paved but extremely narrow for the section around Sarıgöl, but widens nearer to Barhal (29km). Thereafter the road to Yaylalar (21km from Barhal) is partly unpaved but easy to drive. The last 3.5km to Olgunlar is concreted in parts with fairly steep sections that are treacherous in winter snow. There's a daily dolmuş from Yusufeli to both Barhal and Yaylalar (continuing to Olgunlar on request). Both leave in the early afternoon, returning early next morning.

Yusufeli

☑ 0466 / POP 6400 / ELEV 565M

This likeable, rather old-fashioned valley town is a reasonable place to sleep or stop for lunch en route to the eastern Kaçkars. However, its days are numbered. The towering Yusufeli dam, being built about 12km down the Çoruh River, will completely submerge the town – possibly as early as 2023 or 2025. Construction of a Yeni (New) Yusufeli on the hillside on the west side of the Barhal River is ongoing.

🛏 Sleeping & Eating

Otel Almatur's restaurant has great views and good food. Run-of-the-mill restaurants are dotted along the main street, İnönü Caddesi, with those with terraces above the rushing Barhal River being preferable for their location.

Otel Almatur　　　　　　　　　HOTEL **$$**
(☑ 0466-811 4056; www.almatur.com; Ersis Caddesi 53; s/d/ste ₺125/200/280; ☻❀☂) Well run and attractively appointed, Otel Almatur is Yusufeli's top choice with plenty of comfortable touches and some English spoken. Room sizes vary, the corner rooms being compact but offering views – which are all the more sweeping from the glass-sided 5th-floor restaurant. Sauna use costs ₺20 per person and there's even a pair of mini cinemas in the basement. The hotel is on the west side of the central road bridge.

ÇORUH RIVER DEVELOPMENT PLAN

The Yusufeli dam, under construction about 12km down the Çoruh River from Yusufeli town, is one of at least 15 large dams planned on the Çoruh and its tributaries in a programme to generate huge amounts of hydroelectricity and help Turkey achieve greater energy independence. Several dams are already functioning, and they have made an unsightly mess of large stretches of the otherwise beautiful Çoruh and İspir valleys. One consequence is that the 70km of road between Yusufeli and Artvin now passes through 43 tunnels totalling 27km in length.

❶ Information

Tourist Office (İnönü Caddesi; ⊙ 8am-7pm) On the corner of the main square. Super-friendly but no English spoken.

❶ Getting There & Away

Yusufeli's **otogar** is between the main street and the river, 150m south of the tourist office.

Minibuses to Artvin (₺25, 1¼ hours) leave roughly hourly 6am to 4.30pm. Yeşil Artvin Ekspres (www.yesilartvinekspres.com.tr) buses depart for Erzurum (₺50, 2½ hours) at 7am, 9am and 11am, and to Trabzon (₺80, six hours) via Hopa (₺40, three hours) at 9am. Change at Artvin for more choice. A bus to Kars (₺60, four hours), coming from Artvin, passes the Su Kavuşumu junction on the D950 Artvin–Erzurum road, 10km east of Yusufeli, around 1pm. You can reach Su Kavuşumu by an Artvin-bound dolmuş (₺5) or a taxi (around ₺40).

Tekkale & Dörtkilise

Dörtkilise is one of the most picturesque and atmospheric of all of northeast Turkey's medieval Georgian church ruins. For those with wheels, it makes an easy outing, being just 13km from Yusufeli: drive via Tekkale village passing the dramatically sited castle ruin of Tek Kale Kalesi. A second castle ruin, Peterek Kalesi, is a few kilometres beyond Tekkale towards İspir. Note that the first 6km stretch of the drive from Yusufeli is currently a dusty mess due to heavy construction work related to the future Yusufeli dam.

★ **Dörtkilise**   CHURCH
The enchanting ruins of this 10th-century Georgian basilica are domeless and decaying

but monumentally large, atmospherically mossy and photogenically poised above a remote, sloping meadow. The soaring majesty of its triple-naved form becomes apparent from inside where you'll also see some very faded murals. Around the main church lie three other ruinous monastic buildings: a former seminary (northwest), refectory (west) and two-level burial chapel (southeast).

❶ Getting There & Away

Tekkale village is 7km southwest of Yusufeli. From Tekkale, Dörtkilise is 6km (not 7km as the sign claims) on a road that's partly unpaved, but becomes smoothly asphalted after 3km. If you reach the end of the asphalt you've gone a little too far – turn around and the church becomes apparent. A return taxi from Yusufeli to Dörtkilise costs around ₺100 with limited waiting time.

Barhal (Altıparmak)

📋 0466 / POP 200 / ELEV 1160M
Tiny little Barhal (today officially called Altıparmak) nestles in a verdant mountain valley with two rushing rivers meeting at its heart. It's a hospitable village base for forays into the Kaçkars with a trio of pensions and a good chance of finding advice and trekking guides for day walks and longer expeditions.

◉ Sights & Activities

Barhal is the main trailhead for trekking across the Altıparmak range to Avusor via the 3107m Kırmızı Pass. The walk takes two or three days depending on which route you choose. Guides, along with English-language leaflets detailing day walks, are sometimes available at pensions, but you'd be wise to make advance arrangements and come pre-prepared with your own copy of the book *The Kaçkar: Trekking in Turkey's Black Sea Mountains*.

Barhal Church-Mosque   MOSQUE
(🅿) Barhal's domeless 10th-century Georgian church is remarkably complete and now used as a mosque. The towerless, grey stone form, known as Parkhali to Georgians, is somewhat austere but has a soaring dignity of form with blind arcading on all sides. It's 1.2km northwest of the village centre, 200m off the Naznara road. The imam lives next door and will generally open the building for visitors.

Karagöl Lake Hike   WALKING
At around 2700m, Karagöl is one of a string of beautiful upland lakes far from any road in the Kaçkar Highlands. The whole area

is snowbound in winter but in summer it's possible to walk there in a very scenic but quite strenuous full-day hike starting from Naznara hamlet, 7km northwest of Barhal.

Chapels Walk
WALKING

For views over the village and the jagged peaks beyond, you can walk up to two small ruined chapels across the valley. The walk of around 5km (90 minutes return) starts around 1km from central Barhal, crossing a plank footbridge directly opposite the foot of the access road that leads to the church and Karahan Pension.

📖 Sleeping & Eating

Barhal Pansiyon
PENSION $

(📞 0535 264 6765; www.barhalpansiyon.com; per person ₺60, half-board ₺90; 🅿 📶) Near the entrance of Barhal, when coming from Yusufeli, Barhal Pansiyon's main house looks rather ramshackle but the conjoined L-shaped row of en-suite bungalow units that wrap around it provide clean, good-value pine-walled rooms. Breakfast is delightful and dinners feature multiple dishes.

Karahan Pension
PENSION $$

(📞 0466-826 2071, 0538 351 5023; www.karahan pension.com; per person incl breakfast/half-board ₺100/125; 🕑 Apr-Oct; 🅿 📶) Almost next door to Barhal's church-mosque, 1.2km northwest of the village centre, cosy Karahan has good-quality rooms in a wooden block behind a sprawling family house whose large open veranda is an ideal place to unwind.

The best rooms are the upper-front doubles and family suite, each with balconies. The owner's son Ahmet speaks reasonable English and can offer a wealth of walking suggestions, along with 4WD transfers to get you to the trailheads.

Marsis Kafeterya
CAFE $

(Barhal Village; mains ₺10; 🕑 8am-7pm) Food is likely to be a Hobson's choice – probably *menemen* (scrambled egg and tomato) and a simple salad – but Barhal's little cafe is a loveably rustic family place with the open-sided dining platform spanning the river. It's decked with gourds, old tools and musical instruments and serenaded by gushing water.

ℹ Getting There & Away

Barhal is 29km northwest of Yusufeli. Two or three dolmuşes (minibuses) to Barhal (₺25, 1¼ hours) leave Yusufeli's otogar daily between about 2pm and 4pm when they have enough passengers, returning from Barhal about 6.30am or 7am. Outside those times, you will probably have to hire a taxi (around ₺200).

Yaylalar

📞 0466 / POP 300 / ELEV 1896M

A fine alternative to nearby Olgunlar as a Kaçkar trekking base, Yaylalar (aka Hevek) has a wonderfully bucolic setting in an upland valley with scenic *yaylalar* (mountain pastures) accessible in all directions. There's a spindly ancient footbridge and a few surviving traditional farmhouses, plus a shop and a very well-maintained guesthouse whose English-speaking management can help organise hikes, guides and transfers.

Lovers of peaceful, middle-of-nowhere escapes might well agree with the sign proclaiming Yaylalar 'heaven on earth'.

⭐ Çamyuva Pansiyon
PENSION $$

(📞 0534 361 6959, 0466-832 2001; www.facebook. com/camyuvapansiyon; incl breakfast/half-board per person ₺125/150; 📶) One of the best village *pansiyonlar* in the East Kaçkars, Çamyuva resembles a big Swiss chalet, with comfortable pine-clad rooms (best upstairs), decent en-suite bathrooms and a shared lounge with views across the valley. Across the street are wooden bungalows that sleep four with a stream gurgling underneath – soothing in summer, chilly in winter.

A few rooms with shared bathrooms are around ₺30 per person cheaper. Dinner and breakfast are hearty multi-dish affairs. Owner Naim Altunay speaks some English and can organise trekking guides and supplies. His brother drives the dolmuş to/from Yusufeli and together they own the village food shop, too.

ℹ Getting There & Away

It's a very scenic, winding 21km up the valley of the rushing Hevek River to reach Yaylalar from Barhal.

A **dolmuş** (📞 Ismail 0535 402 5341; 🕑 daily Jul-Sep) runs from Yaylalar to Yusufeli (₺40, 1¾ hours) at around 6am, returning from the Yusufeli otogar (bus station) mid-afternoon according to demand. The same dolmuş serves Olgunlar (₺50, two hours from Yusufeli) on request. Service is usually daily in summer. It's worth calling the driver ahead to save a seat, especially between October and June when the service only runs when there's sufficient custom. Taxis charge around ₺300 from Yusufeli to Yaylalar.

Olgunlar

📞 0466 / POP 60 / ELEV 2130M

The highland hamlet of Olgunlar (Meredet) stands in splendid isolation in an idyllic bowl of grassy mountain ridges serenaded by

CLIMBING MT KAÇKAR

Climbers can make the ascent of Mt Kaçkar (Kaçkar Dağı, 3937m) in three days from Olgunlar by spending two nights at **Dilberdüzü Camp** (☑ Ayhan 0532 560 9798; tent per person half board ₺100-120; ⊗ mid-Jul–late Aug). Essentially it's just a high stream-side meadow, 7.5km up the Büyük Deresi Valley, but in midsummer a caretaker is often on-site (phone ahead to check) and can rent out tents, sleeping bags and mats, plus provide meals reducing the need to carry much equipment. Guides can often be engaged at Dilberdüzü too, or you can arrange one through the Kaçkar Pansiyon in Olgunlar, which can also find mules for porterage if you're taking your own camping gear.

In midsummer the Mt Kaçkar ascent is non-technical but be aware that it's more than a vertical kilometre climb from Dilberdüzü (2860m) to the summit and altitude problems are possible for the non-acclimatised.

babbling brooks and boasting some of Turkey's purest air. Its two pensions provide the closest beds to Mt Kaçkar and the Naleteme Pass, on the hiking route to Yukarı Kavron. A remarkably decent cafe caters helpfully to the trickle of walkers and day trippers.

Activities

In July and August the walking here is sublime. Kaçkar Pansiyon has six different suggestions for one-day loops complete with GPS coordinates. They can also organise guides and horses for longer treks.

Olgunlar also attracts a few fly-fishermen, cross-country skiers (February and March) and chamois hunters (November) but you'll need your own equipment for any of these activities.

Sleeping & Eating

★ **Kaçkar Pansiyon**　　　　PENSION $$
(☑ 0538 306 4564, 0466-832 2047; www.kackar. net; Olgunlar Village; s/d half-board late May-Nov €28/50, Feb-Apr €38/70; ⊗ closed Dec & Jan; P ⊗ ⊗) The region's top choice, this peaceful pine-clad haven has superclean hotel-style rooms, a kitchen for guests' use, and an invitingly comfy stream-view sitting area with library and games to play. Super-friendly owner İsmail speaks French and English.

★ **Olgunlar Cafe**　　　　　TURKISH $
(☑ 0535 203 8105; mains ₺15-32, full breakfast ₺20; ⊗ 7am-8pm mid-Jun–mid-Sep) Well appointed and idyllically located, little Olgunlar Cafe serves up dishes such as trout (₺16), *köfte* (meatballs, ₺30) and *mıhlama* (a local melted cheese dish) with stream-view seating indoors, in a waterside gazebo and round a single table in a raised, glass-sided wooden tower room with 360° panoramas.

It's at the far western end of the hamlet (no road) at the footbridge where the Dilberdüzü trail starts.

❶ Getting There & Away

Olgunlar is 3.5km beyond Yaylalar on a scenic, partly unpaved road. The Yaylalar–Yusufeli dolmuş also serves Olgunlar by advance request (₺50, two hours), departing Olgunlar around 5.30am, returning from Yusufeli bus station mid-afternoon. Outside the summer season, you'll probably require a taxi or transfer.

Georgian Valleys

Much of the far northeast was at some point part of medieval Georgia. One area with a particularly rich collection of romantically ruined castles and Georgian churches lies in the spectacular mountainous country southeast of Yusufeli, where poplars and orchards turn valleys verdant green in stark contrast to the bare, rocky hillsides above.

Driving between Yusufeli and Kars, Erzerum or Sarıkamış, with detours and perhaps an overnight stop at Uzundere, it's easy to visit several impressive church ruins and castles. The Artvin–Erzurum road also goes through a spectacularly grand canyon, passes very close to the impressive Tortum waterfalls and right beside the toe-curling Tortum Lake overview point (though note that neither are anywhere near the city of Tortum).

History

The region stretching from around Tortum (the town not the lake) up to the Turkey–Georgia border area in the north is known to Georgians as Tao-Klarjeti, after the two main Georgian principalities that existed here in medieval times. From the last few centuries BC the region fell mostly within the ambit of the eastern Georgian kingdom of Iveria (or Kartli), but by the 8th century AD it was largely abandoned and deserted as a result of war and invasion. In the 9th century AD, with the Iverian capital Tbilisi now under Arab rule, Tao-Klarjeti was re-settled and revived and, with Byzantine support, developed into the leading centre of Georgian Christian culture. Under the Bagrationi line of kings, who established a capital at Artanuji (now Ardanuç, east of Artvin), an intensive monastic and church-building movement was led by the monk Grigol Khandzteli (Gregory of Khandzta). By the year 1000 this rugged, isolated region just 150km or so long and 120km wide had an estimated 300 Georgian churches, mon-asteries and castles.

❶ Getting There & Away

Public transport is limited but passable enough for reaching Oltu and Uzundere, the latter a stop for Artvin–Erzurum and Yusufeli–Erzurum buses, which also pass alongside Tortum Gölü and through the magnificent 'grand canyon' to its north. For reaching the remote Georgian churches the best option is to hire a car in Erzu-rum or Artvin.

İşhan Kilisesi

Despite a 30m tower-spire, the laboriously restored ancient **İşhan Kilisesi** (Church of the Mother of God) is somewhat hidden amongst trees in Upper İşhan (İşhan Köyü), a green oasis village on an otherwise barren moun-tainside. Founded in the 7th century by an exiled Armenian bishop, it was rebuilt sev-eral times by Georgians, reaching more or less its final form in 1032 as Tao-Klarjeti's most important cathedral. The site is 7km off the D060 (Yusufeli–Gole) highway, turn-ing north 13km east of the Artvin–Erzurum junction near (lower) İşhan.

The cruciform interior features a near-conical dome, arcades of tall horseshoe arches and elaborate fretwork around the windows.

Note that massive roadworks associated with the Yusufeli Dam project will eventu-ally reroute the D60 considerably, taking it through a raised series of viaducts and

Georgian Valleys & Around

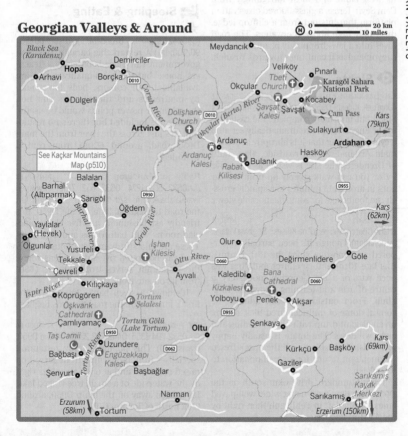

tunnels, and this will likely affect the İşhan access route.

A dolmuş (minibus) leaves Yusufeli some time between 1pm and 3pm for Upper İşhan village, but it doesn't return until next morning so you'll really need your own wheels as there is – as yet – no *pansiyon* hereabouts.

Uzundere

📞 0442 / POP 7300 / ELEV 1105M

Uzundere's newly gentrified town centre has a modest charm and, thanks to its superb-value government-run hotel, it makes a viable base for visiting the region. Nearby you'll find some of northeastern Turkey's most memorable Georgian churches, a climbable castle ruin (Engüzekkapı Kalesi) and Tortum Gölü, an 8km-long, opal-blue lake formed by landslides about three centuries ago.

There are many attractive lake views from the D950 Erzurum–Artvin road, which hugs its west bank, and most intriguingly from Cem Seyir Terası, a glass-floored observation platform that juts out from a clifftop ledge, dizzyingly high above the waters. The road dives into a jaw-droppingly beautiful area of canyonland as it continues towards Yusufeli.

⊙ Sights

Engüzekkapı Kalesi   CASTLE

(Üngüzek Kalesi; D950, Derekapı; ⊙24hr) FREE Small but unusually complete, the castle ruins of Engüzekkapı are dramatically set atop a cylindrical crag that juts abruptly above the main Artvin–Erzurum roadside, 4km south of Uzendere. The site is visible as you drive by, or you can walk steeply up from the car park in around 15 minutes to a spindly crosschasm footbridge for some memorable views.

Taş Camii   MOSQUE

(Haho Church, Meryem Ana Kilisesi; Bağbaşı Village; by donation) Though it's been partially repurposed as a mosque since the 16th century, this late 10th-century church building was once part of a big Georgian monastery, a centre of arts and learning known as Khakhuli. From outside you can admire the conical dome of multicoloured tiles, resting on an elegant drum with blind arcading and eight windows. The imam is usually happy to let visitors inside to see the apse's fresco fragments in return for a small donation to its upkeep.

From Uzundere, drive 6km south on the D950 then 6km west using wide, well-paved lanes forking left in Pehlivanlı then right by the ATM in Bağbaşı.

★Öşkvank Cathedral   CATHEDRAL

(Çamlıyamaç village) Second only to Dörtkilise, Öşkvank is the region's most memorable Georgian church. Large, relatively well preserved and with plenty of very fine relief carvings, it sits in the heart of Çamlıyamaç village. It's 8km off the Erzurum–Artvin road, accessed via a side valley that's full of scenic delights. If you can get in, the interior is breathtaking, with four massive pillars soaring upwards to high arches that support the 12-windowed drum tower and dome.

Tortum Şelalesi   WATERFALL

(off the D950; parking ₺5) FREE Especially in May when it's at full power, this wide, impressive waterfall is well worth the 600m detour off the D950 for those driving between Yusufeli and Erzurum. The parking area leads through to a teahouse-cafe, at the top of which two arcs of stairway lead down great views (and photo opportunities) of the falls from either side.

🛏 Sleeping & Eating

★Uzundere Öğretmenevi   HOTEL $

(📞0442-7912479; Uzundere; s/d/ste ₺67.50/ 90/100; ℗) A remarkable bargain, this new, government-run place is officially a 'teachers' house' but the hotel-quality rooms are available to all comers, beds have quality mattresses and the showers run hot, though more power points would be useful. Breakfast is included but there's no restaurant. It's just across the river from the main D950 road, around 600m from central Uzundere.

Pehlivanlı Pansiyon   PENSION $$

(📞0532 551 1274, 0532 652 7130; www.peh livanlialabalik.com; s/d ₺100/180; ℗🐶🛜) On the road to Bağbaşı, 2km off the D950, this friendly establishment has five clean pineclad rooms with bathrooms and firm beds. These are in a sturdy modern house set behind gazebo-dotted riverside gardens where the restaurant serves trout dinners (₺30) from its on-site trout farm.

It's down a steep bank, 300m after the first Y junction on the road towards Bağbaşı.

★Yedigöler   SEAFOOD $$

(📞0532 794 1356, 0442-792 2378; off the D950; mains ₺30) This popular family restaurant specialises in home-farmed trout served on raised balconies and at open-air tables right by the waterside of a small, tree-ringed lake. It's hidden away off the main D950, around 2km north of Tortum Gölü.

ℹ Getting There & Away

Erzurum–Artvin and Erzurum–Yusufeli buses stop briefly on the main road, just across the river bridge in Uzundere. There are also a few daily dolmuş services between Tortum (the town not the lake) and Bağbaşı (for Taş Camii).

The castle, Engüzekkapı Kalesi, is visible from the Uzundere–Erzurum road but you'll really need wheels if you want to use Uzundere as a base for visiting other regional sights.

Uzundere to Sarıkamış

Driving east from Uzundere, a smooth new four-lane highway sweeps across a 2300m pass before descending steadily towards Oltu, offering up many lovely views into a high, wide valley of patchwork fields and poplar trees, with rocky scarps in the distance. It's worth a brief stop at Oltu to admire the brooding ancient fortress that dominates the centre and to take a quick peek at the restored shopfronts of 50-yil Caddesi, the street that leads to the old mosque. There's also a ruined 19th-century church on the road that leads out of the centre and back towards the eastbound highway.

Continuing east, the scenery continues its grandeur with bright red- and pink-striped mineral outcrops adding colour to the huge vistas. Around 18km northeast of Oltu, Yolboyu is a small junction hamlet behind which a ruined village appears to cover much of a hillside. The Artvin road strikes northeast from here leaving twin fortresses after 3.5km. Meanwhile the eastbound highway continues towards Ardahan: look left 11km after Yolboyu to spy the ruins of the 7th-century Bana Cathedral (Penek) on a mid-distance knoll (if you want to reach the site itself, continue 3km further then double back through Penek village).

A few kilometres beyond Penek, a paved if little-used road heading south winds through a forbidding gorge to Gazilar, a fascinating little castle village set in a vast amphitheatre of mountain-edged fields full of swooping kingfishers. Above, the road curls over a high pass with superb views before crossing into upland steppe, and following the railway east to the ski town and WWI battle-town of Sarıkamış.

Artvin

📞 0466 / POP 24,500 / ELEV 600M

Artvin is curious for its zigzagging layout that climbs precipitously up a steep mountainside. The city is sadly let down by abysmal architecture and the giant scars of dam works in the valley below, but the appeal here comes from the highlands above town, where a famous annual festival features bloodless bull-fighting. Artvin is also a transport gateway to a terrific scenic area that forms a tapestry of rivers, canyons, mountains, forests and *yaylalar,* liberally dotted with castle and church ruins.

✳ Festivals & Events

Kafkasör Kültür, Sanat ve Turizm Festivali CULTURAL
(Caucasus Culture, Arts & Tourism Festival; www.kafkasor.org; Kafkasör Boğa Güreşleri Festival Alanı; ⊙ late Jun/early Jul) FREE This popular, multi-day festival features folk dance, wrestling and, most famously, *boğa güreşleri* (bloodless bull-wrestling). The bulls, matched by equivalent thickness of necks, lock horns and shove at each other until one backs off and is defeated. The festival site is a clearing in the mountainside forest at an altitude of around 1190m, nearly 10km from central Artvin up a long series of switchbacks.

🛏 Sleeping

Otel Sadıkoğlu HOTEL $$
(📞 0466-212 2162; www.sadikogluotel.com; Cumhuriyet Caddesi 8; s/d/tr ₺130/240/280; ❉ 🛜) If you want to be based in downtown Artvin, the Sadıkoğlu is about as central as it gets. It's not an inspiring place but the clean, compact rooms come with wooden furnishings and acceptable bathrooms. Some are oddly shaped.

ℹ Getting There & Away

The **otogar** (D010) is in the valley 5km from central Artvin near the point at which the roads to Erzurum and Ardahan diverge.

Artvin SES and Lüks Artvin buses serve long-haul destinations. Minibuses run roughly hourly to nearby towns:

Hopa (₺25, 1¼ hours) 7am to 7pm
Şavşat (₺25, 1½ hours) 6am to 6pm
Yusufeli (₺25, 1¼ hours) 7.30am to 6pm

For the following, buy tickets from the Yeşil Artvin Ekspres office within the otogar:

Ardahan (₺60, three hours) 11am, 1.30pm
Erzurum (₺60, three hours) 6am, 9.30am, 11am, 2pm, 5.30pm
Kars (₺70, five hours) noon.
Trabzon (₺60, 4½ hours) 7.30am, 8.30am, 10.30am, 11am, 2pm, 4pm, 6pm

DRIVING FROM ARTVIN TO ARDANUÇ

Worth the trip if you're driving, less so by dolmuş, the historic town of Ardanuç (40km from Artvin) may not be much of an attraction these days in itself but it retains a dramatic (if inaccessible) castle and there are several attractions en route from Artvin. From here, you could also continue to Ardahan (75km further).

About 18km east of Artvin on the D010, a well-signed side road climbs 3km very steeply up a narrow but paved lane to Hamamlı village with sweeping views out across the reservoir lake far below. The last (and even steeper) 300m ends at the 10th-century Georgian **Dolişhane Church ruins**, empty inside but fairly intact and with relief carvings of the angels Gabriel and Michael on the south facade. Back on the D010, you cross the reservoir lake on a large bridge after a further 3km. Much of the next 11km to Ardanuç is through tunnels, but several glorious vistas open up in between. Notably, just after the second tunnel, pull over into the parking area to look across the lake towards **Ferhatlı Castle**, whose remaining walls seem to grow almost organically from a crag.

For the last 3km before Ardanuç, the road dives into a dramatic, narrow canyon. Shortly after you emerge, take the sharp, double-back turn to the right that's signed up to **Ardanuç (Gevhernik) Kalesi**. This narrow lane wiggles up towards a fortress ruin that sits impregnably on a towering rocky mesa. Zigzagging 2km up, you drive close to the site. Adventurous spirits might attempt to climb it (from the north edge using a rusty ladder) but this can be dangerous and really the best way to appreciate the site's extraordinary feat of construction is to drive on another 1km and look back from a higher viewpoint, which also surveys the town below and a gloriously wide backdrop of mountains – most spectacular an hour before sunset. It was in this impregnable place that 9th-century Iberian King Ashot I was buried in 830, later to be canonised by the Georgian Church for his battles against the Arabs. It is easy to see how impregnable the fortress must have been: no wonder Ashot I made Ardanuç (then Ardanuji) his capital when establishing his Georgian kingdom in this region in the early 9th century.

If you're continuing towards Ardahan, there's another Georgian ruin to seek out 17km beyond Ardanuç. The 11th-century **Rabat Kilisesi** (Yeni Rabat Church) is abandoned but still largely intact, and exquisitely sited on a grassy platform overlooking an emerald-green valley. The last 1.5km from Bulanık village to the church is along an unpaved road with a precipitous drop at one point – dangerous in wet conditions.

For Ardanuç (₺15, one hour, 7am to 6pm) and some Hopa services, minibuses depart from a stand three quarters of the way up the hill towards the town centre.

Şavşat

📞 0466 / POP 6200 / ELEV 1130M

Şavşat is a bustling little market town around halfway between Artvin and Ardahan. The big attractions hereabouts are the glorious landscapes of soaring green mountainsides, patchworked with grassy meadows and stands of pine, most easily appreciated along the route towards Ardahan. Blink and you might think yourself in Switzerland.

If you're travelling by public transport, a great place to jump off the Ardahan–Artvin minibus is Yavuzköy (altitude around 1700m), 7km east of Şavşat, where you'll find a hilltop viewing platform with 360-degree panoramas. A kilometre beyond, the excellent Black Forest Hotel offers similar views

from its restaurant and comfortable rooms. The whole road to Ardahan is an unforgettable scenic delight and with wheels there's plenty to explore in the side valleys that lead into the Karagöl Sahara National Park.

◉ Sights

Tbeti Church   CHURCH
(Cevizli village) The impressively huge frontage of this shattered 10th-century Georgian church stands at the back of a peaceful highland village accessed by a 10km series of partly asphalted roads amid some very pretty landscapes. As you approach, a carpet of terraced fields rises towards the church, but the ruins are almost invisible between trees until shortly before you arrive. There are a couple of cafes next to the site.

To reach it, take the road signposted to Karagöl from beside Şavşat Kalesi castle, turn almost immediately right onto a new road alongside the river, then left on an unpaved road. Turn left again onto a roughly asphalted older road (away from the next Karagöl sign) then fork right before turning left just before the church. The total distance from Şavşat Kalesi is 10km. There's an alternative route from Şavşat town.

Şavşat Kalesi
CASTLE

(**P**) Founded by Georgians in the 10th century, this castle ruin retains a fairly well-preserved watch tower and curtain wall guarding a river crossing below Şavşat town, 3km towards Artvin beside the main road. Climb 202 steps to reach the information board and the (often closed) gate.

🛏 Sleeping & Eating

⭐ **Black Forest Hotel**
HOTEL $$

(✆0466-5712020; www.blackforesthotelspa. com.tr; Km8, Şavşat-Ardahan Rd, Yavuzköy; s/d ₺240/350) This brand new multi-storey tower crowns a rural ridgetop 9km east of central Şavşat, offering a truly stunning panorama of pastures and peaks. Rooms are well appointed in contemporary style with kettle and excellent beds, and the licensed restaurant is a place to linger. Manager Ceyhun speaks good English and can organise a range of activities and excursions.

⭐ **Laşet Motel**
SEAFOOD $$

(Laşet Tesisleri; ✆0466-571 2136; www.laset.com. tr; Şavşat-Ardahan Rd; mains ₺25-35; ⏰9am-10pm; **P**🛜) Backed by beautiful Alpine scenes reminiscent of Austria, this appealing roadside property specialises in succulent home-reared trout washed down with pewter flagons of fresh spring water, all served on a terrace perched above a mountain stream. There are also eight cosy, pine-fresh hotel rooms (s/d ₺200/300) and the owner's son Bora speaks good English.

It's 10km east of Şavşat beside a bend of the Ardahan-Artvin road. The same family own **Laşet Bungalov Tatil Evleri** (Laşet Bungalov Tatil Köyü; ✆0466-571 2157; www.laset.com. tr; Kocabey village; s/d/tr/q ₺300/400/450/500; **P**🛜), 5km away, where comfortable, well-equipped pine bungalows look out over the village and the hills beyond.

❶ Getting There & Away

Minibuses from Şavşat town run roughly hourly to Artvin (₺25, 1½ hours, 6am to 6pm) plus six times daily on a glorious route to Ardahan (₺25, 1¼ hours) via Yavuzkoy. However, you'll need your own wheels to really appreciate the region's back roads and viewpoints, which cry out for regular photo stops.

Çıldır Gölü & Around
ELEV 1965M

If you're driving between Kars and Ardahan, it's well worth taking the quiet, scenic but well-maintained route around loch-like Çıldır Gölü (Çıldır Lake). It's Turkey's second biggest natural lake (123 sq km), big enough to be impressive but small enough to provide photogenic backdrops and tantalising glimpses of distant headlands. Possible stops include **Doğruyol**, whose older mosque incorporates a 10th-century Georgian church, or nearby **Akçakale**, a hamlet on a pretty bay with small causeway-linked island, family-run fish cafe and rich birdlife. As a tourist site, the lake comes alive in February and March when the frozen surface creates a wonderland for sleigh rides, ice fishing and skidoo rides, plus an annual ice festival.

Confusingly, the friendly if forgettable town of Çıldır is set 5km north of the lake. Driving on towards Ardahan, don't miss catching a glimpse of the fabulous Şeytan Kalesi around 2km after Çıldır.

◉ Sights

⭐ **Şeytan Kalesi**
CASTLE

(Yıldırımtepe) Possibly of Urartian origin, this 'Devil's Castle' was for centuries a Georgian stronghold known as Qajis Tsikhe. It remains one of northeast Turkey's most spectacular fortress ruins, standing on a rocky bluff that's framed on both sides by the plunging Karaçay Canyon. You can catch a distant glimpse from the Ardahan road, about 2km northwest of Çıldır Gölü, where the old and new roads divide.

✺ Festivals & Events

Lake Ice Festival
SPORTS

(Çıldır Kristal Göl Atlı Kiş Şöleni; www.facebook.com/ cildirsancagi; Çıldır Gölü Belediye Sosyal Tesisleri; ⏰early Feb) A day of horse- and sleigh-races on frozen Çıldır Gölü with added ice-fishing contests and skating displays.

🍴 Eating

⭐ **Akca Kale Ada Balık Lokantası**
SEAFOOD $$

(✆0539-6759755; fish/salad ₺30/10; ⏰8am-11pm; 🛜) No need for a menu in this utterly unpretentious family restaurant which sits right at the side of a pretty bay: just order a portion of the superb fried lake fish, served in total simplicity with fresh bread and pomegranate sauce (*nar ekşisi sosu*) to dip it in. Dine in a simple but super-clean timber-ceilinged room or at one of a couple of basic tables under a tree right by the water's edge.

❶ Getting There & Away

Six daily minibuses link Çıldır town to Ardahan (₺15, one hour). There's also a 7am service to Kars (₺25, 1¼ hours). However, driving is the best option if you want to stop off and enjoy the lake's scenery, magical ambience and fish restaurants. From Kars, follow Arpaçay signs. The road along the east and north sides is quiet but well asphalted and very attractive. The south/west coast road is unpaved, but improvements were underway at the time of research. The road to the Aktaş border crossing (Turkey–Georgia) branches north from Çıldır town.

Kars

📞 0474 / POP 102,000 / ELEV 1768M

A useful hub for visiting the magical ruins at Ani (p524), Kars has a distinctive townscape featuring a commanding castle ridge and a considerable number of heavy stone buildings remaining from its years under Russian occupation (1878–1920). The city is a melting pot of cultural influences with many literary connections, notably to Russian writer Alexander Pushkin, esoteric philosopher George Gurdjieff and Turkish author Orhan Pamuk, whose acclaimed novel *Kar* ('Snow') is set here. In winter, temperatures typically drop to -15 or -20°C (in 2015 it hit -35), yet February is high season for Kars tourism: the snow adds photogenic charm to the streets and visitors use the city as a base from which to reach Sarıkamış ski area and to take horse-sleigh rides on frozen lake Çıldır Gölü.

◎ Sights

Kars' town centre is home to some interesting minor sights.

On the main commercial street, Faikbey Caddesi, the Gazi Ahmet Muhtar Paşa Kultur Evi (Faikbey Caddesi; ⊘9am-5pm) FREE is housed in an attractive Ottoman-era house.

Ordu Caddesi, officially renamed Haydar Aliyev Caddesi for the former president of Azerbaijan, is home to buildings with fine Russian-era facades including the Azerbaijani consulate (📞0474-223 6475; www.kars.mfa.gov.az; Ordu Caddesi 36, Kars), the late 19th-century Revenue Office (Ordu Caddesi 45), and the yellow-and-white Old Governor's Mansion (Ordu Caddesi 48). Built in 1883, the latter was where the Treaty of Kars was signed in 1921, defining Turkey's still-current northeastern borders. It faces a sweet little garden surrounded by less showy old buildings.

A short sidestep west of Ordu Caddesi's northern end, the Hotel Cheltikov (📞0474-212 0036; www.hotelcheltikov.com; Şehit Hulusi Aytekin Caddesi 63; s/d/tr ₺240/470/580; 🅿🛜) occupies another classic example of 19th-century stone architecture. Follow the riverside road north to a large marble water fountain and through the Sultan Alparasan Gate to a triangle of pedestrianised square. The most notable old building here is the 16th-century Ottoman Evliya Camii (Saint's Mosque; Aşık Murat Çobanoğlu Caddesi) featuring a free-standing stone minaret and the revered tomb of 11th-century Anatolian Sufi saint Hasan-i Harakani. Across the square, the Harakani Cultural Centre occupies a rebuilt historic structure with stone walls and ogive windows.

★ Kars Castle
FORTRESS

(Kars Kalesi; ⊘8am-midnight) FREE Dating from at least 1153, Kars Castle' s hefty, dark-stone walls crown the craggy ridge that dominates the city-centre's northern edge, fronted by a series of historic mosques. Climbing the ramparts offers a series of sweeping views, especially memorable before sunset, but there is no museum and relatively little to see inside beyond gazing at the panorama from the Kale Cafe.

Kümbet Camii
MOSQUE

(Şehit Öğretmen Vedat Sokak) Below Kars Castle, the imposing, basalt Kümbet Camii was built as a church between 932 and 937 when Kars was (briefly) capital of the Bagratuni kingdom of Armenia. The church was converted to a mosque in 1064, when the Seljuks conquered Kars, then used as a church again in the 19th century by the Russians, who added the porches. Naive reliefs of the 12 apostles still adorn the upper drum tower beneath the conical dome.

Kars Culture & Art Association
MUSEUM

(Kars Kültür Sanat Derneği; 📞0532-291 7226; Bakırcılar Caddesi 39; ⊘call ahead) FREE The address is an unpromising paint shop ('Yeni Akçay Kol. Şir.'). However, if you can find him in, the shop's owner is local historian Vedat Akçayöz who maintains a small library and museum about the Molokan ('milk-drinker') and Doukhobor ('spirit wrestler') spiritual Christian sects.

Kafkaz Cephesi Harp Tarihi Müzesi
MUSEUM

(History Museum of the Caucasian War Front; https://kars.ktb.gov.tr/TR-54869/muzeler.html;

⊗8am-7pm Tue-Sun Jun-Sep, to 5pm Oct-May)
FREE This new museum specialising in early 20th-century history is hosted in the heavy arches of an 1803 bastion, a surviving fragment of vast ramparts that formerly enclosed the city. The most striking display is a recreated WWI-era field hospital with eerily lifelike waxworks. The Halıtpaşa microbus from Eski Otogar passes very close to the site: from the nearest stop, walk up a curl of dead-end lane. Note that the museum is incorrectly marked on most online maps.

🛏 Sleeping

Hotel Temel   HOTEL $
(☎0474-223 1376; Yenipazar Caddesi 9; s/d ₺70/120; 🕸) This highly likeable place is slightly old fashioned and has the odd frayed edge but it is managed with love. Some bathrooms have little half-size baths and there's a nostalgically dated breakfast room. The bigger of two lobby lounges manages a certain belle-époque grandeur.

Konak Hotel   HOTEL $
(☎0474-212 3332; www.karskonakhotel.com; Faikbey Caddesi; s/d/tr ₺100/170/250; 🕸) Handy for the bus offices, the Konak's rooms are pleasant and relatively new, if less smart than you might hope from the cosy little lobby. Overall it's a good-value choice if you get a front room, less so in the windowless back rooms, some of which are very small. Staff are obliging.

Büyük Kale Hotel   HOTEL $$
(Kars Kale Hotel; ☎0474-212 6444; www.karskalehotel.com; Atatürk Caddesi 60; s/d ₺150/250) There are a few minor faults but the top two floors of this helpfully located hotel offer great-value, brand-new rooms with relatively elegant furnishings, good linens, kettles, coffee and excellent walk-in bathrooms. Remarkably, giant-sized room 702 with its fabulous panoramic view of the castle costs no more than a standard double.

Kars-I Şirin   BOUTIQUE HOTEL $$
(☎0474-223 3535; www.karsisirin.com.tr; Ordu Caddesi 61; s/d/tr ₺150/270/320) Tucked quietly behind an older vernacular building, this low-rise 2017 boutique hotel has 23 spacious, comfortable rooms, interestingly shaped and with pleasant brown-toned decor, only slightly let down by mediocre art and a few carpet stains. It's popular with international visitors and staff speak some English.

Hotel Katerina Sarayı   HOTEL $$
(☎0474-223 0636; www.katerinasarayi.com; Celalbaba Caddesi 52; s/d/tr ₺240/340/440; 🅿🕸)

Some showy splashes of gilt can feel a little over-the-top but the smallish rooms are very comfortable and certainly distinctive. The 1879 building was originally a Russian military hospital, and part of its charm is the tranquil riverside setting close to the western foot of the castle crag, around 10 minutes' walk from the centre.

★ Kar's Otel   BOUTIQUE HOTEL $$$
(☎0474-212 1616; www.karsotel.com; Halitpaşa Caddesi 31; s/d/f/ste €90/140/179/210; ❄🕸) This eight-room boutique hotel, in a 19th-century Russian mansion, is a cocoon of luxurious indulgence. Very comfortable, high-ceilinged rooms have king-sized beds and Molton Brown toiletries, and the palatial suite has a marble desk and old fireplace with real fires lit in winter.

🍴 Eating & Drinking

Sini Ev   ANATOLIAN $
(Borsa Sokak 71; mains ₺12-28; ⊗8am-9pm Mon-Sat; 🕸) This friendly, unassuming establishment offers delicious home-style local dishes, fresh daily soups (such as sorrel, lentil or a cool yoghurt-and-herbs creation), stuffed vegetables with or without meat, plus aubergine and köfte kebaps, and some top desserts.

Hanımeli Kars Mutfağı   CAUCASIAN $
(☎0474-212 6131; www.instagram.com/hanimeli karsmutfagi; Faikbey Caddesi 156; mains ₺10-35, goose ₺80; ⊗9am-10.30pm; 🕸) Bringing a rustic, country-kitchen vibe to a formerly bland shop space, Hanımeli specialises in home-style cooking influenced by the broader Caucasian region. Georgian wine is available, both commercially bottled and 'homemade' (₺20 a glass). If you're lucky, the owner may pull out his accordion and sing a song.

Pushkin Cafe & Restaurant   ANATOLIAN $$
(☎0474-212 3535; www.instagram.com/pushkin karsrestaurant; Ataturk Caddesi 28; mains ₺25-75; ⊗9am-11pm) Pushkin's poem *Unknown Country* ushers diners into a Russian-era stone building decorated with samovars where the quality meals focus on lamb and goose dishes plus some Caucasian variants and fresh lake fish (winter only). For dessert try the *Puşkin tatlı* (sponge cake).

Kars Kaz Evi   ANATOLIAN $$$
(☎0474-212 3713; karskazevi@hotmail.com; Atatürk Caddesi 1; mains ₺20-80; ⊗7am-10pm) Widely reckoned Kars' top restaurant, Kaz Evi specialises, as the name suggests, in goose (*kaz*): fried in chunks on rice (₺40),

Kars

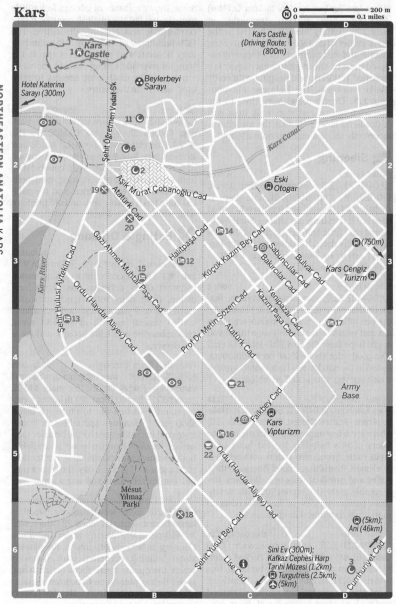

as sautéed foie gras (₺50), or a whole bird cooked in a clay oven (₺320, serves four). Optional side dishes include local Kars curiosities like *haşıl* (yoghurt and bulgur-wheat pilaf with melted butter) and *hangel* (a loose dough with caramelised onions and garlic yoghurt).

Meals come with complimentary side plates of sour pickled veggies and *ezme* (tomato-pepper salsa). The sturdy old-stone building is comfortably appointed with lace curtains, tear-shaped hanging lamps and many a goose image.

Kars

◎ Top Sights
1 Kars Castle	A1

◎ Sights
2 Evliya Camii	B2
3 Fethiye Camii	D6
4 Gazi Ahmet Muhtar Paşa Kultur Evi	C5
5 Kars Culture & Art Association	C3
6 Kümbet Camii	B2
7 Mazlum Ağa Hamam	A2
8 Old Governor's Mansion	B4
9 Revenue Office	B4
10 Taş Köprü	A2
11 Ulu Camii	B2

◎ Sleeping
12 Büyük Kale Hotel	B3
13 Hotel Cheltikov	A4
14 Hotel Temel	C3
15 Kar's Otel	B3
16 Kars-I Şirin	C5
17 Konak Hotel	D4

◎ Eating
18 Hanımeli Kars Mutfağı	B6
19 Kars Kaz Evi	A2
20 Pushkin Cafe & Restaurant	B3

◎ Drinking & Nightlife
21 Pasha Cafe	C4
22 Sugar Beet Cafe	C5

Sugar Beet Cafe   CAFE
(Ordu Caddesi; ⊘8am-midnight) This delightfully quirky cafe has walls roughly decorated with portraits, areas of rug seating and a 'secret garden' section with a small stage for occasional live music.

Pasha Cafe   CAFE
(Gazi Ahmet Muhtar Paşa Caddesi; ⊘7am-midnight) Popular with Kars' under-35 fashionistas, Pasha has a great glass-fronted upstairs gallery, plenty of shaded pavement seating and a gently buzzing atmosphere from morning till night.

❶ Information

Tourist Office (Turizm Danişma; Ali Riza Aslan Caddesi; ⊘8am-10pm Mon-Sat) In the public library. Gives out useful booklets on Kars and Ani.

If you can find a copy, a good investment is Sezai Yazıcı's 2011 bilingual MDG guide map which includes themed routes following Pushkin, Gurdjieff and places related to Orhan Pamuk's novel Snow.

❶ Getting There & Away

AIR
Kars Airport (Kars Harakani Havalimanı; www.dhmi.gov.tr) is 6km south of the town centre.

BUS & DOLMUŞ
You can get to a surprisingly wide selection of long-distance destinations from the miserable **otogar** (Main Kars–Ardahan Rd), 4km northeast of the centre, while **Turgutreis** (📞0532-687 5036; www.turgutreis.com.tr; Aytemiz Caddesi; ⊘8am-6pm) uses its own private **bus station** (Okkan Bulvar) 2km southeast of the centre. If you have plenty of time, use a free servis to/from the city-centre office of the bus company you're

using. These are mostly dotted on and around Faikbey Caddesi, and/or around the Eski Otogar.
Doğu Kars (📞0474-223 2300; www.ozdogukars.com; Faikbey Caddesi 72) services include Trabzon (₺110, seven hours, 1pm), Ankara (₺120, 17 hours, 5pm) and İstanbul (₺150, 22 hours, noon). Similar options are offered by **Kars Kalesi** (off Faikbey Caddesi) and by Turgutreis.

Dolmuşes and minibus services to regional towns leave from the **Eski Otogar** (Eski Garaj; Halitpaşa Caddesi). Destinations include the following:
Ardahan (₺20, 1½ hours, hourly from 8am to 5pm)
Çıldır (₺25, 1¼ hours, 1pm)
Hopa (₺80, 6½ hours, 9.30am with Yesil Artvin; www.yesilartvinekspres.com.tr) via Artvin (₺70, five hours)
Iğdır (₺30, 2½ hours; six to eight daily, 7am to 5pm with Serhat Iğdır)
Posof (₺25, two hours, 1pm)
Sarıkamış (₺10, 45 minutes, every 40 minutes 7am to 6pm)

For Doğubayazıt, you must change in Iğdır.
Most of Kars' bus companies have at least a couple of Erzerum services (₺30, three hours) but the most frequent are with:
Kars Cengiz Turizm (Faikbey Caddesi) Hourly minibuses (every two hours at weekends, 5am to 3pm) from their downtown office.
Doğu Kars (10.30am, 11.30am, noon, 12.30pm, 5pm from the otogar) Start one hour earlier from their city office for the free shuttle.

TRAIN
The **train station** (Kars Garı; www.tcddtasimacilik.gov.tr; İstasyon Sokak) is around 600m southeast of the city centre.

A daily **Doğu Ekspresi** (www.tcddtasimacilik. gov.tr) to Ankara (₺47, 24 hours) via Erzurum (₺16.50, four hours), Sivas (₺29, 14 hours) and Kayseri (₺35, 18 hours) departs at 8am. There's also a tourist special that includes three-hour exploration stops in key places en route.

A beautiful journey, the train can be booked solid in winter when the route is popular for the vistas of snowy landscapes.

The much-delayed passenger service between Kars and Baku (Azerbaijan) via Tbilisi (Georgia) should start in 2022.

Ani

This lonely Unesco World Heritage site of Ani (₺12; ⊘8am-7pm mid-Apr–Sep, to 5pm Oct–mid-Apr; Ⓟ) is an absolute must-see. Dotted behind a vast stretch of fortress wall lie the widely spread wrecks of great stone buildings adrift on a sea of undulating grass. These are landmarks of a ghost city that was, 1000 years ago, the stately Armenian capital. Home to nearly 100,000 people, it once rivalled Constantinople in power and glory. Today's poignant ruins occupy a windswept plateau high above the Arpaçay (Akhurian) Gorge whose river forms the Turkish–Armenian border, and beyond which rises snow-topped Mt Aragats (4090m). With a remarkable lack of crowds, this thought-provoking place leads visitors to ponder upon what went before: the thriving kingdom; the churches' solemn liturgy; and the 11th-century travellers, merchants and nobles bustling about their business in this Silk Road entrepôt.

History

Well served by its natural defences, Ani was selected by the Armenian Bagratid king Ashot III (r 952–77) as the site of his new capital in 961, when he moved here from Kars. Ashot's successors Smbat II (r 977–89) and Gagik I (r 990–1020) presided over Ani's continued prosperity. But internecine feuds and Byzantine encroachment weakened the Armenian state and the Byzantines took over Ani in 1045.

Then in 1064 came the Great Seljuks from Persia, followed by the Kingdom of Georgia and, for a time, local Kurdish emirs. The struggle for the city went on until the Mongols arrived in 1236 and decisively cleared everybody else out. The nomadic Mongols had no use for city life, so cared little when the great earthquake of 1319 toppled much of Ani. The depredations of Central Asian conquerer Tamerlane later that century

hastened the decline; trade routes shifted, Ani lost what revenues it had managed to retain, and the city died. The earthquake-damaged hulks of its great buildings have been slowly crumbling away ever since.

⊙ Sights

Exploring the site in an anticlockwise loop makes sense, as you'll approach the Church of St Prkitch (Redeemer) from its best angle (west). Lighting is generally better in the late afternoon, but morning visits tend to be cooler. Allow at least 2½ hours to explore, three if you're including İç Kale, and double that if adding any significant perusal of the 'Underground City' caves. For inspiration and preparatory reading, consult VirtualANI (www.virtualani.org).

The entrance and **ticket booth** (Arslan Kapısı; ₺12; ⊘site admission 8am-7pm mid-Apr–Sep, to 5pm Oct–mid-Apr) are within the Arslan Kapısı gate.

Arslan Kapısı   GATE
Just inside the Ani ruins is the sturdy Arslan Kapısı (or Aslan Kapısı – Lion Gate). Depending on which guide you believe, it was named after Alp Arslan, the Seljuk sultan who conquered Ani in 1064, or for the *aslan* (lion) relief on the wall inside.

Seljuk Palace   PALACE
(Selcuklu Sarayı) Built into the western tip of Ani's defensive walls, this rectilinear palace has been so painstakingly over-restored that it looks quite out of place, though the portal's star-motif red stonework is handsome. Mind your footing inside – a few holes in the floor drop right through into the tall-vaulted dungeons. To explore these safely, start by descending from a double-back path on the exterior of the south side. The same path, if you don't double back, leads to an intriguing, half-collapsed **cave church**, the most accessible of many around the Ani gorge.

Church of Gagkashen   RUINS
(Gagik 1 Kilisesi) Even though the ruins of this once-enormous church are little more than its circular base and a jumble of column sections within, it is enough to grasp what an astonishing construction it must have been when completed around AD 1000. Based on an original at Zvartnots (Armenia), its ambitious dome collapsed shortly after completion.

Kervansaray   CHURCH
(Church of the Holy Apostles) The Church of the Holy Apostles (Arak Elots Kilisesi) dates

Ani

Ani

◉ Top Sights
1 Ani Cathedral	C3
2 Manuçehr Camii	B3
3 Tigran Honents Church	D3

◉ Sights
4 Arslan Kapısı	C1
5 Cave Church	A1
6 Church of Gagkashen	B1
7 Church of Grigor Pahlavuny	B2
8 Church of St Prkitch	D2
9 Convent of the Virgins	C3
10 İç Kale	A4
11 Kervansaray	B2
12 Kız Kalesi Viewpoint	A4
13 Küçük Hamam	D3
14 Seljuk Palace	A1
15 Silk Road Bridge Supports	C3
16 'Underground City'	A1

from 1031, but after the Seljuks took the city in 1064 they added a gateway with a fine dome and used the building as a caravanserai – hence its name today.

The ruins preserve some decorative carvings, porthole windows, diagonally intersecting arches in the nave, and ceilings sporting geometric patterns of polychromatic stone inlays.

Church of Grigor Pahlavuny   CHURCH
(Abughamrents Kilisesi) A well-preserved central landmark in the heart of the Ani plateau, this rotunda-shaped church with a conical roof was built in about 980 for the wealthy Pahlavuni family.

★ Manuçehr Camii   MOSQUE
Ani's 1072 Manuçehr Camii was built by the Seljuk Turks, using Armenian architects and

ANI'S UNDERGROUND CITY

The cliffs and valleys all around the Ani plateau are riddled with hundreds of caves that guides have collectively dubbed Ani's 'Underground City'. Mostly carved out by humans over the millennia, the caves have served as dwellings, animal shelters, chapels and – the smallest ones – pigeon houses to provide a source of eggs and fertiliser. Visible clusters lie in the gully below the Church of Grigor Pahlavuny and across the valley from the Seljuk Palace.

Anybody can have a poke around the western caves but don't wander down to the Arpaçay Gorge, which is off limits due to border sensitivities. To find the most fascinating caves – multichambered caravanserais, churches with angel frescoes, domed pigeon houses and long tunnels inside the rock – you'll generally need a guide. Celil Ersözoğlu (0532-226 3966; celilani@hotmail.com; rtn to Ani ₺200, with guiding ₺450) is recommended and his underground city explorations will add a couple of extra hours to your time in Ani.

artisans, creating a stylistic blend in what is considered to have been the first Turkish mosque in Anatolia. With a tall octagonal minaret and six surviving vaults, it's relatively well preserved. The refreshingly cool interior features red-and-black stonework with polychrome stone inlays adorning the ceilings.

Convent of the Virgins   CHURCH

(Kusanatz) Out of bounds just above Arpaçay gorge, this complex of ruins is most notable for the dainty, serrated-domed chapel (probably 11th-century) enclosed by a defensive wall. It's best observed from the windows of Manuçehr Camii (p525), with the scant ruins of a probably 9th-century Silk Road bridge in the foreground.

İç Kale   FORTRESS

(Citadel) Covering the large rocky eminence at the southern point of the Ani plateau, İç Kale is a jumble of tumbled stone, with faint vestiges of ancient palaces and walls that date back at least 1500 years – possibly even to Urartian times (8th century BC). Crowning its central hilltop is Ani's oldest church, dating from 622. It is curiously shattered in that the northern half looks fairly intact but the southern section has dropped away entirely.

Lower down to the southwest, but within İç Kale's walls, is a great viewpoint from which to distantly admire a picturesquely perched but out-of-bounds red-stone church that is almost all that remains of Kız Kalesi – a former fortress on a cliff-sided peninsula high above a curl of the Arpaçay Canyon.

★ Ani Cathedral   CATHEDRAL

(Ani Katedrali) Completed in 1010, the grassy-roofed cathedral is the largest building among the Ani ruins. The building's elegantly finished stone walls are relatively plain and partly hidden by scaffolding but the towering interior impresses with its scale, lit by several portholes above slender windows and featuring a blind arcade with slim, soaring columns. The central dome that once crowned the building fell down centuries ago.

★ Tigran Honents Church   CHURCH

(Resimli Kilise) Appealingly sited overlooking a stretch of river gorge, this 13th-century church appears relatively intact, though the current main door is within what was once an internal wall, patched up after the western end of the nave was lost. Built in 1215 by a pious merchant, Tigran Honents, it is dedicated to St Gregory the Illuminator, but sometimes known in Turkish as Resimli Kilise (Church with Pictures) due to the lively, if partly defaced, frescoes depicting scenes from the Bible and Armenian church history.

Church of St Prkitch   CHURCH

(Church of the Redeemer) Walking from the west, Ani's distinctive Church of the Redeemer (1034–36) looks strikingly complete despite the supporting scaffolding. From other angles, however, it's evident that the eastern half has collapsed (due to a 1957 lightning strike) and fencing prevents closer access. The church was built to house a portion of what was believed to be the True Cross of Jesus' crucifixion, brought here from Constantinople; the facade's Armenian inscriptions relay the history.

ℹ Information

It's wise to bring snacks and lots of drinking water. The new **Tourism Centre** beside the car park was not functioning at the time of writing, except to provide toilets, but it has space for proposed cafes. Otherwise the only refreshments available are a desultory selection of soft drinks and crisps sold from a small mobile cafe beside the car park.

ℹ Getting There & Away

The drive from Kars takes around 50 minutes on a smooth, wide road. There is no public transport.

Turgutreis (p523) advertises a daily tour package from Kars (per person ₺90) starting at 9am from their bus station area (p523), but departures depend on customer numbers. Renting your own car typically costs between ₺150 and ₺250 in Kars (plus petrol), though we were offered as little as ₺100 by **Alemdaroğlu** (☑ 0474-212 3958; www.karsalemdaroglu. com; Ordu Caddesi 109; 1-day rental from ₺100; ☉ 8am-8pm) for a same-day car return.

A round-trip taxi from Kars with a Turkish-speaking driver typically costs between ₺200 and ₺250, with about two hours at the site. You'll be on the meter so the longer you stay, the more you'll pay. A good option can be to employ knowledgeable, English-speaking driver-guide Celil Ersözoğlu, who charges a similar rate for the transport, or a larger fee including on-site guiding.

Iğdır

POP 113,000

Pronounced 'Oodr', Iğdır has Mt Ararat (Ağrı Dağı) looming above it to the southeast, a feature that is best appreciated from a distance as you drive into town from the west. It's a friendly little city but there's really not a great deal to do here other than changing buses in transit between Kars, Doğubayazıt and/or Nakhchivan

(Nahçıvan, Naxçıvan), the disconnected exclave of Azerbaijan.

ℹ Getting There & Away

There's a big otogar way out of town with long-distance buses going as far as İstanbul via Erzurum. However, many bus and most dolmuş companies have offices and stops on highway D080 within 200m of Dörtyol (the Fatih/Kars Caddesi crossroads).

Dolmuşes to Doğubayazıt (₺12, 45 minutes) depart every 40 minutes or so between 6am and 6pm. Most leave from outside a small **office** (Iğdır Doğubayazıt Minibüs Yazıhanesi; ☑ 0535-275 8541, 0476-227 0025; Kazım Karabekir Caddesi 46) some 500m southeast of Dörtyol.

Serhat Iğdır (☑ 0476-226 2342; www.serhat igdir.com; Kazım Karabekir Caddesi), 50m southeast of Dörtyol, has midi-buses to Kars (₺25, 2½ hours), running six to eight times daily. Buy tickets before boarding.

TO THE AZERBAIJAN BORDER

From Iğdır, the most convenient way to reach Naxçıvan City in Azerbaijan is using one of the eight-person minivans (AZN20, approx ₺70, three to four hours) that typically pick up passengers from the meydan, starting outside **Iğdırlı Turizm** (☑ 0476-228 6901; www.igdirli turizm.com.tr; Meydan). Such vehicles drop you at your hotel in Naxçıvan City. Alternatively at least three bus companies have bus services (AZN5, approx ₺18, four hours). All leave Iğdır after noon. Most convenient are the 3pm and 5pm services, which pick up from the small

---

OFF THE BEATEN TRACK

NAKHCHIVAN SIDE TRIP

Nakhchivan (Nahçıvan in Turkish, Naxçıvan in Azerbaijani) is one of the most fascinating places you've probably never heard of. This disconnected exclave of Azerbaijan is home to Noah's tomb, the 'Machu Picchu of Eurasia' (Alinja Castle), a Soviet salt mine you can sleep in, and a surreally neat, clean yet historical capital (Naxçıvan City) where all of the countless museums are free. Though part of Azerbaijan it is totally disconnected from the rest of that country. Online visas are now easy to obtain for most nationalities in 24 hours on www.evisa.gov.az (cheaper in 72 hours). To get to the exclave's other highlights you'll need a taxi, or the highly recommended English-speaking tour agent **Nakhchivan Travel** (Natig Travel; ☑ 070-5672506; www.nakhchivantravel.com), which can also organise birdwatching tours and discounts on hotels. A good central accommodation choice in Naxçıvan City is **Hotel Tabriz** (Mehmanxana Təbriz; ☑ 036-5447701; Təbriz meydanı; s/d/tr/ste AZN80/120/160/180; ❄ 🛜 🕸) but **Hotel Qrand** (Grand Hotel Nakhchivan; ☑ 036-544 5930; grandhotel@neqsicahan.az; Cəlil Məmmədquluzadə küç; ℗ ❄ 🛜) is fine and half the price.

If you're travelling between Turkey and Iran, cutting through Nakhchivan is a very viable alternative to the normal route via Bazargan and it also 'notches up another country' on your overland tally. From Naxçıvan City to the Iranian border at Culfa/Jolfa there's a very scenic train ride that departs twice daily and costs the equivalent of just ₺4. The carriages are brand new and, even if you're not going into Iran, the ride is fascinating as you can look into it from the train windows: the railway mostly follows the border with just a narrow river separating the two countries.

Öz Diyarbakır office (☑ Mehmet 0543-478 6828; Kazım Karabekir Caddesi), around 200m southeast of Dörtyol, approximately opposite the Salon Opera cafe.

Note that you need an Azerbaijan visa in advance: apply online through www.evisa.gov. az. Also note that Nakhchivan is a disconnected exclave separated from the rest of Azerbaijan by Armenia with which borders are closed, so to continue to Baku you'll have to fly (or go via Iran).

Doğubayazıt

☑ 0472 / POP 73,000 / ELEV 1550M

Doğubayazıt's setting is superb. To the north, the talismanic Mt Ararat (Ağrı Dağı; 5137m), Turkey's highest mountain, lords it over the landscape. To the southeast, the striking İshak Paşa Palace surveys town from a rocky perch beneath jagged peaks. The town itself – nicknamed 'doggy biscuit' by travellers on the hippie trail – doesn't have too much charm, but it's the obvious base for climbing Mt Ararat (when open to climbers) and its sense of bordertown wildness has a certain appeal. Coming from Erzurum or Kars, you'll quickly notice the distinct atmosphere in this predominantly Kurdish city.

◉ Sights

★ **İshak Paşa Palace** PALACE
(İshak Paşa Sarayı; İshakpaşa Yolu; ₺6; ⊙ 9am-5.45pm Apr-Oct, 8am-3.45pm Nov-Mar, closed some Mondays; 🅿) There are few experiences as magical as watching a blazing sunset from behind this ridgetop stone structure, its dome and minaret silhouetted against a vast landscape that appears to stretch to infinity. Backed by serrated crags, the ruined palace (completed 1784) has been patched up and, while many walls are bare, there are several sections with fine stone reliefs, now partially sheltered by a new glass roof. Even when it's closed, taking the 6km trip up here from central Doğubayazıt is an absolute must.

Combining Ottoman, Seljuk, Georgian, Persian and Armenian design features, the 18th-century palace was built for İshak Paşa, governor of Çıldır and Ahıska, who ended up being banished when the Ottoman authorities realised that he was scheming to set up his own domain.

An elaborate main gateway leads into the first courtyard where, in the far right corner, you can check out the dungeons. In the second courtyard is an elaborate tomb, believed to be that of İshak Paşa, richly decorated with a mixture of Seljuk carvings and Persian relief styles. There are three choices of direction from this area. Straight ahead through a beautifully carved portal are the private quarters, including the harem and the ceremonial hall with its melange of decorative styles. Steps down to the left take you to deep, subterranean granaries and servants' quarters. To the right is the *selamlık* (council quarters), whose highlight is the mosque: remove shoes and push the door to enter and admire plenty of original relief decoration.

On exit, don't miss the chance of walking a little further east to enjoy various exterior views. A new observation platform was under construction at the time of research, on a rise directly behind the palace.

🛏 Sleeping

Murat Camping CAMPGROUND $
(☑ 0542 437 3699; mt.ararat@hotmail.com; İshak-paşa Yolu; per tent ₺15; 🅿 🛜) A traveller favourite for years, Murat's fabled camping area and restaurant has recently moved to an even more memorable spot on a flat-topped hillock staring straight across at İshak Paşa Palace, from which it's just a seven-minute stroll.

★ **Tehran Boutique Hotel** BOUTIQUE HOTEL $$
(☑ 0472-312 0195; www.tehranboutiquehotel.com; Büyük Ağrı Caddesi 72; s/d from ₺150/270; ◉ 🛜) The Tehran's supercomfortable, spacious rooms would trump many an international business hotel. Sports-pitch sized bed, top-quality rain shower, kettle, safe, fridge, desk and sofa all come as standard, alongside monogrammed toiletries. Knowledgeable staff speak great English and can help with information on Ararat climbs and Iran border crossings. A very good breakfast spread is served on the top floor, which has partial glimpses of Ararat, and there's beer, wine and bourbon available at the cute little lobby bar.

Hotel Doğuş HOTEL $$
(☑ 0472-312 6161; www.dogushotel.net; Belediye Caddesi 10; s/d/tr ₺80/150/180; 🛜) The Doğuş provides bright, spotless rooms with rather busy decor but ample space and great walk-in showers in the faux-marble tiled bathrooms. The upper corner doubles have twin-aspect views of both İshak Paşa and Mt Ararat.

✗ Eating & Drinking

★ **Dağkapı Ciğerisi** BARBECUE $
(☑ 0545-749 1037; İnegöl Caddesi 98; mains ₹20; ⊙ 11am-10.30pm) The most colourful restaurant on Doğubayazıt's pedestrianised main street, Dağkapı Ciğerisi is laden with intensely coloured textiles, interspersed by

Doğubayazıt

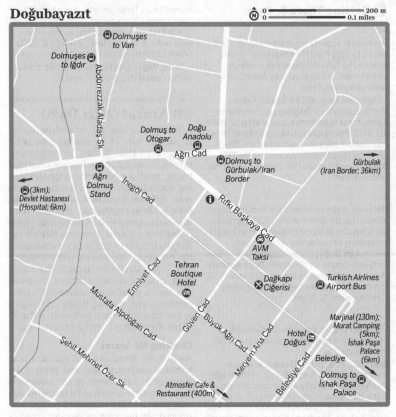

musical instruments and landscape pictures of Mardin and Diyarbakır. Foodwise the focus is on delicious skewered meat, especially offal – with liver a speciality, alongside heart (*yürek*), spleen (*dalak*) and kidney (*böbrek*). There's trotter soup (*paça*) and ram's testicles (*koç yumurtası*) for the adventurous.

Atmosfer Cafe & Restaurant TURKISH **$**
(📞0541-891 9606; Bahçlievler Sokak 38, Radio Tepe; mains ₺12-24; ⏰8.30am-1am) Dine with an amazing view at Atmosfer, a semicircle of glass fronted with two open terraces, all sharing a spectacular 180° panorama that encompasses the whole city, the palace and Mt Ararat (a radio tower slightly marring the foreground). The food (*sac kovurma* and various kebabs) is less special than the setting and the menu's international options are rarely available.

Access is by a hoop of road starting from the southeasternmost end of Mustafa Alpodoğan Caddesi. A couple of possible short cuts are available on foot, though one is very steep.

Marjinal CAFE
(Üzengili Yolu; ⏰10am-9pm) Che Guevara, Marlyn Monroe, Bob Marley and some Bankseyesque figures populate the walls of this spacious, comfortable nargile cafe, lilting with latin and reggae influenced tunes. The clientele is male but the place is not forbidding and some staff are female.

❶ Information

Nişantaş Döviz (📞0472-312 7213; İnegöl Caddesi 140; ⏰8am-6pm Mon-Fri, 9am-3pm Sat, 8am-noon Sun) is one of four nearby moneychangers offering good rates for major currencies. However, Iranian Rials are not accepted: if you're crossing the border, offload Turkish lira or Iranian rials with moneychangers at Bazargan. Changing Turkish lira can be tough elsewhere in Iran, while nobody in Turkey wants to buy rials.

Tourist Information Office (Rıfkı Başkaya Caddesi; ⏰7.30am-noon & 12.30-4pm Mon-Fri) Set up like a mini museum, the tourist office can be helpful but its opening can be unreliable.

❶ Getting There & Away

AIR

The nearest airports are at Iğdır and Ağrı, both served by daily flights to Ankara and İstanbul operated by Turkish Airlines (www.turkish airlines.com) and its subsidiary Anadolu Jet (www.anadolujet.com).

Flights are serviced by a Turkish Airlines shuttle bus to/from Doğubayazıt. For outgoing flights, these leave from a special **stop** (☏ 0472-312 6772; Rıfkı Başkaya Caddesi 3) 2½ to three hours before the scheduled departure. Check up-to-date bus times by phone or at the **THY Office** (İnegöl Caddesi 146; ☉ 9am-6pm) in the centre of town.

BUS

Most long-distance buses start from the otogar, 3km west of the centre on the D100 ring road, but tickets for most destinations can be bought at company offices dotted around the city centre. **Ağrı Doğuş** (İnegöl Caddesi 105; ☉ 9am-7pm) sells tickets for Diyarbakır. **Doğu Anadolu** (Ağrı Caddesi) provides buses to Erzurum (₺50, four hours), departing the otogar at 9.30am, 11am, noon and 12.30pm.

DOLMUŞ

Minibuses to Iğdır, Van, Ağrı and Gürbulak (for Iran) leave from separate stops in central Doğubayazıt:

Iğdır (₺12, 45 minutes) Departs when full from Abdürrezzak Aladaş Sokak, north of Ağrı Caddesi, roughly every 40 minutes till 6pm. Some Hani Baba minibuses also pick up passengers for Iğdır (₺13) at the more central Ağrı dolmuş stand. The drive takes you right around the edge of Ararat's lower slopes but be sure to carry ID for a police checkpoint en route. The Ağrı Doğuş office is at İnegöl Caddesi 105.

Kars Take a dolmuş to Iğdır and change onto the Serhat (p527) service (eight daily Monday to Friday, six daily Saturday and Sunday).

Van (☏ 0472-312 6117; ₺30, three hours) From a side lane behind Kardeşler Simit Saray, just off Abdürrezzak Aladaş Sokak. Departures at 6.30am, 8am, 9am, 11am and 3pm.

Iran (Ağrı Caddesi) Between 6am and around 6pm, dolmuş services   from a point on Ağrı Caddesi run to the border post at Gürbulak (₺8, 30 minutes). Get going before 10am; after that you'll have to wait longer for vehicles to fill up. Once stamped out of Turkey, pay ₺1 for the short share-taxi hop across no-man's land. On the Iran side in Bazargan you can change money and find onward transport. The border is open 24 hours.

❶ Getting Around

A green-and-white **dolmuş** (İshak Paşa Yolu) to İshak Paşa Palace (₺2.50, 15 minutes) and the

Ahmed-I Hani Tomb departs when nearly full from a point 100m east of the *belediye* (city hall). The last return is around 6pm (or 7pm some weekends). A metered **taxi** (☏ 0472-312 0200; Güven Caddesi) will cost around ₺30 one way.

To the otogar, take the yellow-flashed dolmuş from a central stop on Ağrı Caddesi.

Mt Ararat (Ağrı Dağı)

A highlight of any trip to eastern Turkey is catching sight of the soaring cone of Mt Ararat (Ağrı Dağı, 5137m). Eternally snow-capped, it has figured in legends since time began, most notably as the supposed resting place of Noah's ark. The mountain looks quite different from various angles. If you drive between Doğubayazıt and Iğdır you'll traverse the lower western slopes with plenty of fine views. Continue towards Nakhchivan and you'll discover that in fact the mountain has two peaks; the sharply pointed eastern one, Küçük Ağrı (Little Ararat) is no minnow itself, rising to 3925m. Climbing the peaks was once a popular expedition, but permit problems were making things complicated at the time of writing and, even when allowed, the climb is a serious undertaking.

Climbing Mt Ararat

Summitting Ararat is a challenging if non-technical multi-day trek, and permits are required. In 2016, however, the mountain's upper slopes were declared a restricted military zone and the issuing of permits was stopped. At the time of research, permits were still not being issued, though groups had started to make ascents with the authorities apparently turning a semi-official blind eye. This is a dangerous gamble: in past years, some folks climbing unofficially faced prison terms.

Each spring the government decides whether or not to start issuing permits anew, so it is important to get the latest up-to-date information from reliable local sources. In Doğubayazıt, the Tehran Boutique Hotel (p528) is especially clued up; alternatively, you can send enquiries to some of the expert climbers who used to have agencies in Doğubayazıt before 2016, notably **Mustafa Arsin** (☏ 0541 655 3582), **Zafer Onay** (☏ 0551-111 8998; zaferonay@hot mail.com) or Amy Bean, whose **Mount Ararat Trek** (☏ WhatsApp +964-750 027 8028; www. mountararattrek.com) website also has some warnings about using untrained 'guides' and about other potential pitfalls.

Southeastern Anatolia

Best Places to Eat

➜ Ahmet Bey Yöresel Ev Yemekleri (p551)

➜ Cercis Murat Konağı (p554)

➜ Aşiyan Ev Yemekleri (p563)

➜ Metanet Lokantası (p536)

➜ Seyr-İ-Mardin (p554)

Best Places to Stay

➜ Asude Konak (p536)

➜ Kadim Hotel (p554)

➜ Türkmen Konağı (p541)

➜ Aslan Konak Evi (p540)

➜ Hanem Hotel (p550)

Why Go?

From the toppled stone heads of a near-forgotten classical-era kingdom atop Nemrut Dağı (Mt Nemrut) to Göbeklitepe's Neolithic T-shaped pillars, Anatolia's southeast is a place apart from the rest of Turkey – its rock-pitted plateaus more visceral, the city bazaars more workaday than tourist-trinket, its population predominantly Kurdish and the history more kaleidoscopic. This is where hunter-gatherers first began to settle, early city-states like Arslantepe first sprang up and the major trade routes between empires converged. Today the southeast sees far fewer foreign visitors than more brushed-up western Turkey, though domestic tourism in the historic towns of Gaziantep, Mardin and Şanlıurfa is booming. Sadly, both the resumption of hostilities between the PKK (Kurdistan Workers Party) and the Turkish government in 2015, and the ongoing conflict in neighbouring Syria has designated small areas in the region risky for travellers. Always keep up to date with the local situation while travelling here.

When to Go

Gaziantep

Mar See the famed Mardin view of the Mesopotamian plains in springtime's glorious green.

May–Sep The best months to visit the heights of Nemrut Dağı National Park.

Oct Explore domestic-tourism hot spots Gaziantep and Şanlıurfa without the summer crowds.

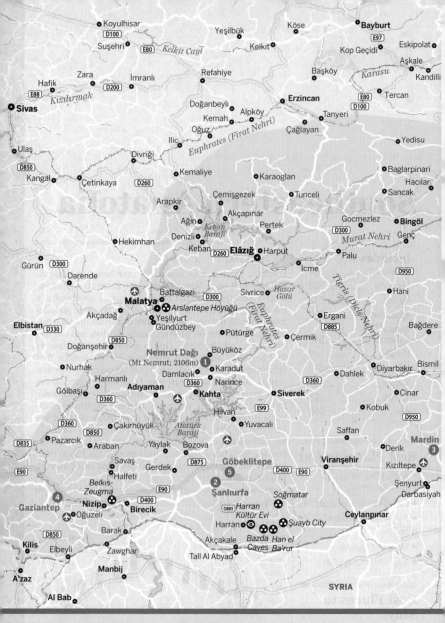

Southeastern Anatolia Highlights

1 **Nemrut Dağı** (p547) Eyeing up the eerie toppled remnants of King Antiochus I's tribute to himself on the summit.

2 **Şanlıurfa** (p538) Feeding greedy fat carp in Balıklıgöl and exploring the skinny alleys of the bazaar before taking in the mind-blowing history of the archaeology museum.

3 **Mardin** (p552) Getting lost by heading downhill amid an alleyway maze of honey-hued heritage buildings.

4 Gaziantep (p534)
Soaking up the intricate beauty of one of the world's most important mosaic collections and then getting stuck into the sticky delights of the city's renowned baklava.

5 Göbeklitepe (p539)
Staring down in wonder at the unearthed megaliths of the world's oldest religious sanctuary.

6 Akdamar Kilisesi (p559)
Marvelling at Armenian artistry at this island church on Lake Van.

Gaziantep

📞 0342 / POP 1.6 MILLION

There's one Turkish word you should learn before visiting Gaziantep: *fıstık* (pistachio). This fast-paced and epicurean city has around 180 pastry shops producing the world's best pistachio baklava. Other culinary treats are also on offer for adventurous foodie travellers.

With the biggest city park this side of the Euphrates and a buzzing cafe culture, Gaziantep oozes panache and self-confidence. It also has one astounding attraction definitely worth travelling across Turkey for – the superb Gaziantep Zeugma Mosaic Museum.

The older parts of the city are being reinvigorated, and the fortress, bazaars, caravanserai and old stone houses have been lovingly restored.

◉ Sights & Activities

★ Gaziantep Zeugma Mosaic Museum
MUSEUM

(www.gaziantepmuzesi.gov.tr; Hacı Sanı Konukoğlu Bulvarı; ₺20; ⊙9am-6.30pm Tue-Sun) This museum does a stellar job of displaying one of the world's most important mosaic collections, most of which was unearthed at the Roman site of **Belkıs-Zeugma** and brought to safety before the Birecik Dam flooded much of the site forever. Its most famous exhibit is the 'Gypsy Girl', which gets its own darkened room – dramatically highlighting the small mosaic's beauty. Equally impressive though are the huge floor mosaics, displayed between columns and wall-fresco segments, also brought from the site.

In particular, don't miss the 'Eros and Psykhe' mosaic downstairs and 'The Kidnapping of Europe' and 'Woman at Breakfast' mosaics upstairs. After viewing the upstairs floor exhibits, take the exterior walkway across to the second building for more mosaics unearthed from the local region.

To walk to the museum, follow the underpass on the left of the railway station, continue under the busy main highway, turn right, and then walk on for about 400m and you'll see the museum on the opposite side of the road. Unfortunately, a fence running along the road's traffic barrier stops you from crossing the road. You need to head another 200m to the tatty pedestrian overpass to cross and then double-back to the museum. A taxi from central Gaziantep should be around ₺18.

Gaziantep Archaeological Museum
MUSEUM

(Kamil Ocak Caddesi; ₺6; ⊙8.30am-noon & 1-5pm Tue-Sun) Gaziantep's archaeological museum houses a solid collection that sweeps from prehistoric fossils right up to the Byzantine era, but really comes alive in the rooms devoted to the late-Hittite local sites of Karkamış (ancient Carchemish) and Zincirli. Upstairs, don't miss the beautiful stele depicting King Antiochus (of Nemrut Dağı fame) shaking hands with the god Mithra. Information panels here are excellent and contain a wealth of knowledge on local archaeological sites and history.

Gaziantep Castle
CASTLE

(Gaziantep Kalesi; Köprübaşı Sokak; adult/student ₺2/free; ⊙8.30am-5.30pm) Thought to have been constructed by the Romans, the citadel was restored by Emperor Justinian in the 6th century and rebuilt extensively by the Seljuks in the 12th and 13th centuries. Inside the fortifications a boardwalk trails between the scant remnants of hamams and kitchens (little more than the foundations remains). On the way up the castle stairs is the **Gaziantep Defence & Heroism Panoramic Museum**, a tribute to the fighters who defended the city against the French in 1920.

Hamam Museum
MUSEUM

(Hamam Müzesi; off Köprübaşı Sokak; adult/student ₺2/free; ⊙8.30am-5.30pm) One of the most interesting of Gaziantep's cache of small, speciality museums, this museum is dedicated to the history and culture of the Turkish bath. Set within the domed space of a 16th-century hamam, exhibits cover everything from hamam slippers and bathing rituals to the important role public bathing played in day-to-day life. Information panels offer plenty of English explanations.

★ Bakırcılar Çarşısı
MARKET

(Coppersmiths' Bazaar; Hamdi Kutler Caddesi; ⊙8.30am-11pm) Gaziantep's labyrinthine bazaar stretches between Hamdi Kutler Caddesi and Kundaracılar Çarşısı Sokak. There are a couple of entrances so just dive in and see where you're spat out. The tiny stores are home to metalworkers, shoemakers, spice hawkers and carpenters. The area includes the restored **Zincirli Bedesten**, with handicraft stores under its vaulted ceiling. To the south, in the **Elmacı Pazarı** area, is the original **Güllüoğlu** (Elmacı Pazarı, off Kundaracılar Çarşısı Sokak; baklava portion ₺14; ⊙8am-6pm; 📷) baklava shop, keeping dentists in business since 1871.

Gaziantep

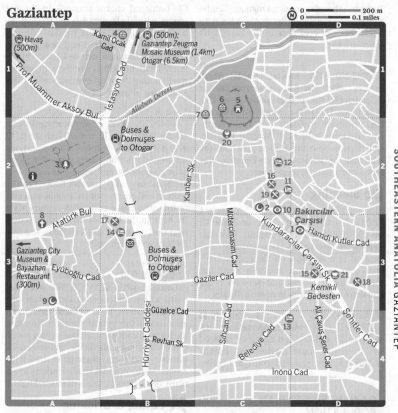

Gaziantep

Gaziantep City Museum MUSEUM
(Gaziantep Kent Müzesi; Atatürk Bulvarı 119; adult/
student ₺2/free; ⊙8.30am-5.30pm) Housed
in the grand old Bayazhan building, this
museum features interactive displays showcasing Gaziantep's culture including the
story of baklava and the city's shoemak-
ing history. Information panels are only in

Turkish, though foreign-language audio guides are available. Afterwards relax with a tea, coffee or cold beer in the Bayazhan's courtyard bar.

Arsan TOURS
(☑ 0342-220 6464; www.arsan.com.tr; Hasırcı Samibey Caddesi; Halfeti & Zeugma group day tour per person €50, Nemrut Dağı tour per person €90; ⊙ 8am-7pm) This well-run local travel agency operates a variety of daily tours in the southeast region including the 'Magical Triangle', which visits both the Halfeti area and the remnants of ancient Belkıs-Zeugma. Car rental can also be arranged here.

🛏 Sleeping

Utkubey Hotel HOTEL $
(☑ 0342-220 0349; Teyfik Uygunlar Sokak 12; s/d ₺90/160; ⊛ 🛜) This friendly spot has well-maintained rooms and a decently quiet location in a lane just off the central city's main drag. Rooms are relatively small but some have castle views, and some floors are non-smoking – a rarity in eastern Turkey.

★ Asude Konak BOUTIQUE HOTEL $$
(☑ 0342-231 2044; www.asudekonak.com; Millet Sokak 20; s ₺140-200, d ₺180-250; ⊛ @ 🛜) You'll feel like you're staying with friends at this lovingly restored courtyard-house.

GAZİANTEP'S SYRIAN POPULATION

With its proximity to Syria, Gaziantep has recently become a haven for refugees fleeing the conflict across the border, and the area around Inönü Caddesi's western end has developed as a 'Little Aleppo'. By 2019, it was estimated that Gaziantep had absorbed around 500,000 Syrian refugees, raising the population of the city by 30%. Although this influx has strained the city's infrastructure dramatically, majorly impacting Gaziantep's housing, water and healthcare resources, the city's local authorities have been widely praised for their efforts to tackle these issues. Their forward-thinking approach, aiming to benefit both citizens and refugees, is involved with upgrading public facilities, building new housing and widely extending public services, and has aided the integration of the Syrian population into the wider Gaziantep community.

Old-fashioned charm abounds in the five rooms with their dark-wood Ottoman in-built wall-cupboards and windows dressed with white embroidered and tasselled curtains. Breakfasts can include *katmer* (pastry layered with nuts and clotted cream) and it's worth opting in for an evening meal – often a lingering al-fresco affair.

Anadolu Evleri BOUTIQUE HOTEL $$
(☑ 0342-220 9525; www.anadoluevleri.com; Köroğlu Sokak; s ₺170, d ₺220-290, ste ₺340; 🅿 ⊙ ⊛ 🛜) These restored stone mansions, set around internal courtyards, offer plenty of 'years-gone-by' ambience. The airy rooms are home to tiled or parquet floors, beamed ceilings and cream-painted inbuilt wall cupboards that evoke early-20th-century style. It's bang in the heart of the bustling centre, near the bazaar, yet still feels quiet and restful behind its high walls.

Şirehan Hotel HERITAGE HOTEL $$
(☑ 0342-221 0011; www.sirehanotel.com; Belediye Caddesi 1; s/d/tr ₺220/300/380; ⊛ 🛜) Bed down where traders once slept when they pulled into town; you can't beat the historic ambience of this old caravanserai. Rimming the internal courtyard, arched-ceiling rooms come with mod cons (kettle, flat-screen TV, minibar) and surprisingly good-sized bathrooms. As the original small windows are in place, don't expect masses of natural light.

🍴 Eating & Drinking

For baklava devotees, Gaziantep is Shangri-La. The city is reckoned to produce the best *fıstıklı* (pistachio) baklava in Turkey, if not in the world. Served ultrafresh, they're impossible to beat, and some baklava shops have reached cult status, such as Güllüoğlu, and the talismanic İmam Çağdaş (Hamdi Kutlar Caddesi; mains ₺9-42, baklava portion ₺9-18; ⊙ 10am-10pm), established in 1887.

★ Metanet Lokantası ANATOLIAN $
(Kozluca Caddesi; beyran ₺20; ⊙ 6am-6pm Mon-Sat, to 1pm Sun) Your lips will tingle and your eyes will tear up as you spoon this oily broth into your mouth. *Beyran* is a mutton and rice soup made viciously red by the liberal addition of *pul biber* (Aleppo red pepper flakes). It's a popular Gaziantep breakfast and lunch dish and Metanet is one of the best places to try it.

Katmerci Murat DESSERTS $
(Atatürk Bulvarı 11; katmer ₺20; ⊙ 7am-9pm; 🖉) The best entertainment of your day could

SERVICES FROM GAZIANTEP OTOGAR

DESTINATION	FARE (₺)	DURATION (HR)	FREQUENCY
Adana	35-40	3-4	every 30 minutes
Antakya	35	4	every 30 minutes
Halfeti	15	1½	every 15 minutes 8am-7pm
Mardin	60	4-5	3 morning
Nevşehir	80-90	7-8	2 morning, 1 afternoon, 3 evening
Şanlıurfa	30	2½	hourly
Van	120	10½-11½	1 afternoon, 4 evening

be watching the graceful actions of Murat's head pastry chef as he transforms a compact ball of dough into a plate of Gaziantep's famed gossamer-light *katmer*. You can diet when you get back home.

Yesemek
ANATOLIAN $$
(Hamdi Kutlar Caddesi; portion from ₺12, mixed plates ₺20-40; ⊙10am-10pm; 🍴) A beacon for travelling vegetarians and vegans with plenty of grain- and pulse-based non-meat options to choose from, this *lokanta* (eatery serving ready-made food) serves up Anatolian home-style cookery. There are always hearty soups, tender meat stew dishes and herb-stuffed bulgur and bean salads all doused in lashings of olive oil.

Bayazhan Restaurant
TURKISH $$
(☎0342-221 0212; www.bayazhan.com.tr; Atatürk Bulvarı 119; mains ₺24-60; ⊙10am-midnight; ❄🍴) Gaziantep's smartest dining is within this caravanserai where suited waiters zip between the courtyard tables delivering trays laden with meze dishes of hummus and sizzling clay-pot-baked Antep cheese, and meaty kebap-based mains. Check out the seasonal menu for regional specialities such as *pirpirim aşı* (purslane soup), *erik tavası* (lamb with green plums) and *ayvalı taraklık* (lamb chops with quince).

Tahmis Kahvesi
COFFEE
(Şehitler Caddesi 25; ⊙10am-10pm) *Türk kahvesi* (Turkish coffee) so thick you could stand a spoon in it. Coffee has been served here since 1635. Today Tahmis Kahvesi occupies both the historic original building and an outdoor terrace across the road (cooled by jets of water mist during hotter months). Try the local *menengiç kahvesi* (a coffee-like drink made from roasted pistachio tree seeds).

Hışvahan
BAR
(☎0342-230 7777; Handan Bey Sokak 23; ⊙11am-midnight) This restored *han* (cara-vanserai), just steps from the castle, has been turned into one of Gaziantep's swankiest bar-restaurants. After a long hot afternoon in the bazaar, chill out here with a cold Efes in hand. There's often live music on weekend evenings.

ℹ️ Getting There & Away

To see surrounding sights, Arsan can arrange car rental.

AIR
Gaziantep Airport (Gaziantep Havalimanı, GZT; https://gaziantep.dhmi.gov.tr; Gaziantep–Kilis Yolu) is 20km southeast of the central city.

Havaş (Nişantaşı Sokak) operates buses to and from the airport (₺13, 40 minutes) from its office just off Prof Muammer Aksoy Bulvarı (behind the Hampton Hilton Hotel). Its buses meet all flights.

BUS & DOLMUŞ
Gaziantep Otogar is 7km from the town centre. Buses to the otogar (₺2.50) leave from bus stands on both Hürriyet Caddesi, north of Gaziler Caddesi, and İstasyon Caddesi. A taxi costs about ₺30.

Around Gaziantep

Halfeti

Halfeti's stone-cut houses trickle down the hillside to the blue-green water of the Birecik Dam where pontoon-restaurants bob. The town used to sit beside the Euphrates River but the dam's construction meant that half of the town, and several archaeological sites, were inundated and part of the population had to be resettled in the bland, purpose-built town of Yeni Halfeti, 9km up the road. The original Halfeti is now known as Eski Halfeti.

Despite the destruction, today Eski Halfeti has recovered its mojo. It's a local favourite day-trip destination for boat tours on the dam passing by Rumkale's fortress – so high on the cliff it escaped being flooded – and the partially sunk village of Savaş with the minaret of its submerged mosque still soaring defiantly above the dam's surface. On summer weekends, Halfeti gets crammed; parking is a serious issue. Come on a weekday for a quieter experience.

🏃 Activities

Tourist boats (₺15 per person) from Halfeti Marina leave approximately every 30 minutes on summer weekends. On weekdays, and outside of the high season, you will probably need to wait longer for the boat to fill up. During summer, don't expect a tranquil boating experience: boats blast Turkish pop and folk tunes and it's common for passengers start dancing on board.

❶ Getting There & Away

Dolmuşes (minibuses with a prescribed route; ₺22) run between Halfeti and Şanlıurfa's otogar (p542) every 30 minutes. Most go all the way to Eski Halfeti but check with the driver before boarding.

Dolmuşes depart for Eski Halfeti (₺15) from the southern platform of Gaziantep's otogar every 15 minutes between 8am and 7pm on weekdays. There are fewer services on weekends.

Şanlıurfa

📋 0414 / POP 573,770 / ELEV 518M

Şanlıurfa (commonly called Urfa and once ancient Edessa) is one of the great spiritual centres, and its history is wrapped up in local lore. Believers say this is where the Prophet Abraham was born, and pilgrims still come to pray in his cave and feed the fat, glossy carp that patrol the waters of Balıklı Göl.

You could easily lose a day here exploring the compact historic centre with its grand domed Dergah Complex, manicured Gölbaşı gardens and the bazaar's tight weave of alleys. But Urfa has more historic attractions up its sleeve. The incredible collection encased in Şanlıurfa Archaeology Museum along with the mosaics inside Haleplibahçe Mosaic Museum have made this city a beacon for travellers trying to make sense of eastern Turkey's staggering history. And just to the northeast is Göbeklitepe, the world-famous Neolithic temple and one of Turkey's newest Unesco World Heritage sites.

◉ Sights

★ Şanlıurfa

Archaeology Museum   MUSEUM

(Haleplibahçe Caddesi; incl Haleplibahçe Mosaic Museum ₺12; ⊙9am-6.30pm Tue-Sat) Şanlıurfa's spectacular archaeology museum is one of the best in Turkey. The region's cultural heritage is displayed across three levels covering a time period that stretches from the Neolithic up to the Ottoman era. The Neolithic halls, exhibiting sculptures and small finds from Göbeklitepe as well as other nearby pre-pottery Neolithic sites, are the highlight. Displays are accompanied by highly detailed information panels that do an excellent job of explaining this area's importance in the earliest years of human history. Come here before visiting Göbeklitepe to aid your understanding of the site.

From November to March the museum shuts at 4.30pm.

Haleplibahçe Mosaic Museum   MUSEUM

(Haleplibahçe Mozaik Müzesi; Haleplibahçe Caddesi; incl Şanlıurfa Archaeology Museum ₺12; ⊙9am-6.30pm Tue-Sat) This domed structure protects the excellent Haleplibahçe (Aleppo Gardens) mosaics, part of a Roman villa complex discovered in 2006 when construction started on a planned theme park as part of an urban renewal project on this site. Instead, archaeologists moved in and began excavating, resulting in a haul of highly detailed Roman-era mosaics that are superbly presented here. Highlights include the Hunted Amazons mosaic, dating from the 5th or 6th century, and the Achilles mosaic, depicting scenes from Achilles' life. The museum closes at 4.30pm from November to March.

★ Gölbaşı   HISTORIC SITE

Legend claims that the Prophet Abraham (father of the three major monotheistic religions) was confronted by Nimrod, the local Assyrian king, while destroying pagan idols. Nimrod had Abraham immolated on a funeral pyre but God turned the fire into water and the burning coals into fish. Abraham was hurled into the air from where the castle stands, landing safely in a bed of roses. Urfa's picturesque Gölbaşı area of fish-filled pools and rose gardens is a symbolic recreation of this story.

Two rectangular pools of water, Balıklı Göl and Ayn-i Zeliha, are filled with supposedly sacred carp, while the area to the east is planted with blooming rose gardens. Local legend has it that anyone catching the carp will go blind.

On the northern side of Balıklı Göl is the elegant **Rızvaniye Vakfı Cami & Medrese-si**, with a much-photographed arcaded wall, while at the western end is the **Halilur Rahman Cami** (Gölbaşı). This 13th-century building, replacing an earlier Byzantine church, marks the site where Abraham fell to the ground. The two pools are fed by a spring at the base of Damlacık hill, on which the castle is built.

Dergah Complex　MOSQUE

Southeast of Gölbaşı is the Dergah mosque complex, Urfa's major pilgrimage destination. From the gate, you enter the colonnaded courtyard in front of the **Mevlid-i Halil Cave** (Hazreti İbrahim Halilullah, Mevlid-i Halil Mağarası; ₺2), which local tradition states is the birthplace of the Prophet Abraham.

The western side of the complex is dominated by the honey-toned, Ottoman-style stone bulk of the **Mevlid-i Halil Cami**. The airy, domed interior contains some lovely tile details and arabesque medallion designs.

According to local lore, the Prophet Abraham's mother hid in the Mevlid-i Halil Cave when pregnant to escape the wrath of King Nimrod who, responding to a prophecy that proclaimed a child soon to be born would destroy his kingdom, had ordered all newborns killed. It's said that Abraham lived here hidden until he was 15 years old. There are separate entrances into the cave for men and women. Women should don a headscarf before entering and everyone should be modestly dressed. Inside pilgrims pray in the cave-cut room.

Kale　CASTLE

(₺5; ⊙8am-8pm) Urfa's fortress on Damlacık hill, from which Abraham was supposedly tossed, has good city views, but there's not much to see at the actual site. On the top, most interesting are the two columns dubbed the Throne of Nemrut after the supposed founder of Urfa, the biblical King Nimrod. We've received reports of women travellers being hassled on the slopes behind the castle, so we recommend visiting during daylight hours and sticking to busy areas.

★Bazaar　MARKET

(off Göl Caddesi; ⊙Mon-Sat) Dive into Urfa's bazaar alleys to find stalls selling everything from sheepskins and pigeons to jeans and handmade shoes. It was largely built by Süleyman the Magnificent in the mid-16th century. One of the most interesting areas is the **bedesten**, with its shops selling silk goods, including colourful local scarves, under a vaulted ceiling. An entrance inside the *bedesten* brings you into the Gümrük Hanı (p542), an old caravanserai with its courtyard now the city's most atmospheric cafe.

★Göbeklitepe　ARCHAEOLOGICAL SITE

(₺30; ⊙9am-6.30pm) Around 11km northeast of Urfa, 'Pot Belly Hill' was first excavated in 1994 by a team led by Professor Klaus Schmidt. Their discovery of a ritual complex dated to the pre-pottery Neolithic era (around 10,000 BC) has turned the previously accepted theory that religion followed the evolution of agriculture on its head.

The small site, protected by a space-age-style dome, contains a complex of circular buildings containing megalithic T-shaped pillars now thought to be the world's first place of worship.

Animal carvings can be seen on the sides of Göbeklitepe's anthropomorphic T-shaped pillars, some of which tower up to 5.5m high. A raised wooden boardwalk leads around the site allowing you to see the pillars below from all sides and study the stylised carvings of foxes and vultures.

In 2018, Göbeklitepe was made a Unesco World Heritage site, though don't expect masses of ruins as you'd see in Turkey's much younger classical-era sites. Göbeklitepe's fame comes from its significant role in furthering our understanding of early human history and culture. The visitor centre at the entrance provides a good introduction to the site with a short – and rather dramatic – video presentation on Göbeklitepe's importance. From near the visitor centre, a regular shuttle bus zips to and from the hilltop archaeological site.

Geomagnetic surveys and ground-penetrating radar systems have identified another 16 ancient megalithic rings buried nearby, and at present only 5% of the entire site has been excavated, with archaeological work here continuing.

A return taxi to Göbeklitepe from Şanlıurfa, including waiting time, is around ₺120.

Tours

Harran-Nemrut Tours　TOURS

(☑0542 761 3065, 0414-215 1575; www.aslankonukevi.com; 1351 Sokak 10; Harran area & Göbeklitepe day tour per person 3/2 people €30/45) A swag of private tours run by Özcan Aslan, a

Şanlıurfa

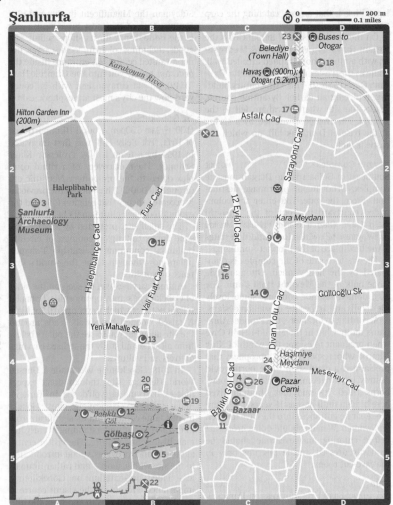

SOUTHEASTERN ANATOLIA ŞANLIURFA

local teacher and owner of Aslan Konak Evi who speaks good English. Tour options for two to four people to nearby sites include a full day visiting Göbeklitepe, Harran, Şuayb City and Soğmatar and a Nemrut Dağı tour (three/two people per person €50/75).

🛏 Sleeping

Central Şanlıurfa has a mix of boutique hotels, guesthouses and mid-rise hotels. Large, new brand-name hotels tend to be a little outside of the historic core. It's a good idea to book accommodation in advance, particularly if you're arriving on a summer weekend

when hordes of domestic tourists descend, as the hotels can get fully booked.

★ **Aslan Konuk Evi** GUESTHOUSE **$**
(📱0542 761 3065; www.aslankonukevi.com; 1351 Sokak 10; dm/d €8/25; ❄🛜) Şanlıurfa's top budget digs is this heritage Urfa building with simple but spacious high-ceilinged rooms arranged around a central vine-draped courtyard. Private rooms come with small bathrooms. The eight-bed dorm shares clean facilities. Good food and cold beer is available in the rooftop terrace restaurant.

Şanlıurfa

Outside guests are welcome for dinner, but you'll need to make a booking in the morning.

★ **Türkmen Konağı** BOUTIQUE HOTEL $$
(☎0414-215 6600; www.turkmenkonagi.com; 1272 Sokak 26; d/tr ₺350/450; ❄🏠) This intimate seven-room mansion – with a history that dates back to the days of Edessa – is a delight. The panoramic views from the rooftop terrace are the best in town, swooping from the castle down to Gölbaşı below. Room-wise, choose either a cosy vaulted room on the ground floor or one of the slightly larger rooms above.

Manici Hotel HERITAGE HOTEL $$
(☎0414-215 9911; www.manici.com.tr; 1252 Sokak 3; s/d/tr ₺150/230/280; P❄🏠) The Manici is in prime position, just steps away from both Gölbaşı and the bazaar area. The 'ye-olde Ottoman splendour' decor of mammoth orientalist paintings and hanging lamps stays on the right side of kitsch and is topped off with contemporary, colourful soft-furnishing touches. Rooms are spacious with modern bathrooms and staff speak some English.

Hilton Garden Inn HOTEL $$
(☎0414-318 5000; https://hiltongardeninn3.hilton.com; 11 Nisan Fuar Caddesi 54; r from ₺330; P❄❄🏠🏊) Good-sized rooms are rather ho-hum bland but they're quiet and comfortable (as you'd expect from a brand-name hotel). The bar with super-cold Bomonti and

Efes and indoor pool are major plus points, and you're just a short stroll from Urfa's museum complex.

Hotel Güven HOTEL $$
(☎0414-215 1700; www.hotelguven.com; Sarayönü Caddesi 78; s/d ₺225/300; ❄🏠) The beige-on-beige room decor (topped off with red carpets) won't rock your world but keen-to-help, English-speaking staff and well-maintained facilities lift the Güven slightly above your standard Turkish provincial business hotel. It's also quiet despite its main road location. When not busy, staff are very quick to drop rates by up to ₺100.

🍴 **Eating & Drinking**

Ikiler Ciğer Salonu KEBAB $
(Faaliyet Alanı; mains ₺16-22; ☉10am-11pm) Grab a street-side stool and tuck into a mini feast of grilled lamb, chicken or *ciğer* (liver), served on *lavaş* (flatbread) with onions and some seriously hot grilled peppers.

Cevahır Han TURKISH $$
(☎0414-215 9377; www.cevahirhan.com; Vali Fuat Caddesi 5; mains ₺22-38; ☉8am-11pm; ❄) This old *han* is the place to come to try Şanlıurfa's local specialities of *borani* (soup of lamb, chickpeas, beetroot and yoghurt) and *çiğ köfte* (raw ground lamb mixed with pounded bulgur, onion, clove, cinnamon, salt and hot black pepper). The rest of the menu deals in mains of kebap and *saç kavurma* (stir-fried cubed meat dishes).

SERVICES FROM ŞANLIURFA OTOGAR

DESTINATION	FARE (₺)	DURATION (HR)	FREQUENCY
Adana	60-70	5-6	hourly
Diyarbakır	35-40	2-3	4 morning, 2 afternoon, 6 evening
Gaziantep	30-35	2-3	hourly
İstanbul	150-170	18½-20	1 morning, 4 afternoon, 5 evening
Mardin	50	3	2 morning, 1 afternoon, 1 evening
Nevşehir	100	9	noon & 7.30pm
Van	120	9	3 evening

Manici Hotel
TURKISH $$

(☑ 0414-215 9911; Balıklı Göl Mevkii; mains ₺24-38; ⊘ noon-2pm & 6-11pm; ❋) A great choice if you fancy a beer with your meal, the restaurant of the Manici Hotel offers traditional Turkish meze and mains in comfortable surroundings. A regal edge to your dining is provided by portraits of Ottoman sultans glaring sternly down at you as you eat.

Gülhan Restaurant
TURKISH $$

(Atatürk Caddesi; mains ₺20-45; ⊘ 11am-10pm; ❋ ☑) Slap in the central city, Gülhan does a roaring trade with generously portioned kebap plates, *lahmacun* (Arabic-style pizza) and local dishes like *borani*. It's known for its *şıllık* (crepes filled with walnuts and syrup), so leave room for dessert. Unlike many other Şanlıurfa kebap-focused restaurants, there are a few choices for vegetarians here.

Çift Mağara
TURKISH $$

(Çift Kubbe Altı Balıklıgöl; mains ₺22-34; ⊘ 10am-11pm; ❋) Climb up the stairs of Şanlıurfa's cliff to reach this higgledy-piggledy restaurant overlooking Gölbaşı with a dining room carved into a rocky bluff and outdoor tables and eating platforms spread out along the stairs as they climb to the summit above. Try the *içli köfte* (ground lamb and onion with a bulgur coating).

Gümrük Hanı
CAFE

(Bedesten; ⊘ 9am-10pm) Thread your way through the vaulted corridors of the bedesten to reach this restored *han* crowded with locals enjoying a cold drink, çay or *Türk kahvesi* (Turkish coffee). It's the most atmospheric spot in Şanlıurfa for a spot of R&R and a good place to try *menengiç kahvesi* (a coffee-like drink made from roasted pistachio tree seeds).

Çay Bahçesi
TEA GARDEN

(Gölbaşı; ⊘ 9am-9pm) The southern side of Gölbaşı, surrounding the Ayn-i Zeliha lake, is crammed with shady tea gardens where families and groups of friends linger on the wooden benches downing cold drinks and umpteen çays. When it's busy, service can be super slow. Try to bag a table overlooking the water.

❶ Getting There & Away

AIR

GAP Şanlıurfa Airport (GAP Şanlıurfa Havalimanı, GNY; Şanlıurfa–Diyarbakır Yolu, Gölgen) is 45km from Urfa on the road to Diyarbakır.

Havaş airport buses meet every flight. Heading to the airport catch them from their bus stop (www.havas.net) next to the Nevali Hotel just off Atatürk Caddesi. They leave two hours before every flight (₺12, 45 minutes). A taxi costs around ₺120.

BUS & DOLMUŞ

Şanlıurfa Otogar is 5km north of town off the road to Diyarbakır. Some buses will drop passengers at a roundabout around 300m from the otogar. City buses to the otogar can be caught on Atatürk Caddesi, but you need to buy an UrfaKart (₺3; available from kiosks and some small grocery stores) first. This allows you two rides.

Dolmuşes (minibuses with a prescribed route) to local destinations leave from the İlçe Terminalı (regional bus station) underneath the otogar. Destinations include the following:

Adıyaman (₺25, two hours, hourly)

Gaziantep (₺25, 2½ hours, hourly)

Halfeti (₺22, 1¾ hours, every 30 minutes)

Harran (₺10, 45 minutes, every 15 minutes between 8am and 6pm)

Harran

☑ 0414 / POP 9000

Harran is reputedly one of the oldest continuously inhabited spots on earth. The book of Genesis mentions Harran and its most famous resident, Abraham, who stayed for a few years in 1900 BC. Modern Harran is a scruffy shadow of its former self with only a handful of examples of its distinctive beehive house architecture still clinging on in the old town area. That fact hasn't hindered Harran's popularity on the local tour bus circuit though. On weekends busloads of Turkish tourists arrive at the Kültür Evi for a half-hour break to romp through its mocked-up beehive house interior and drink çay.

◉ Sights

Harran Kültür Evi   NOTABLE BUILDING

`FREE` This modern beehive house complex is a popular stop for domestic tour buses. Inside, the rooms are decked out in traditional style while the walled courtyard doubles as a cafe, offering cold drinks and çay to visitors. Local guides hang out here and can be a little bit pushy while touting for business.

Kale   CASTLE

`FREE` On the far (east) side of the hill, Harran's crumbling *kale* (castle) stands right by some beehive houses. Fortifications probably already existed here during Hittite times but the current construction dates mainly from after 1059 when the Fatimids took over and restored it. Originally there were four multi-angular corner towers but only two remain. The castle has been closed for restoration for years with no reopening date set so you can only admire its exterior.

Ulu Cami   RUINS

(Grand Mosque) `FREE` The ruins of the 8th-century Ulu Cami, built by Marwan II, last of the Umayyad caliphs, is Harran's most prominent historic site. You'll recognise it by its tall, square and very un-Turkish minaret. It's said to be the oldest mosque in Anatolia. Near here stood the first Islamic university, and on the hillside above it you'll see the low-level ruins of ancient Harran, dating back some 5000 years. The Ulu Cami is undergoing extensive restoration in 2019, which may be ongoing for the next few years. You can still see the site from above during the works.

❶ Getting There & Away

Dolmuşes head to Harran (₺10, one hour, every 15 minutes between 8am and 6pm) from Şanlıurfa otogar. They stop at modern Harran near the post office. From there it's a 10-minute walk to the castle. Check transport times back to Şanlıurfa before you leave, as going the other way dolmuş times are less regular.

Around Harran

The area around Harran has been thoroughly transformed by the GAP project (p555). What was once arid plains is now field upon field of cotton and barley. Amid this landscape are a number of small, little-visited historic sites that make a decent day trip for those with time up their sleeve. Getting around in this area without your own transport is virtually impossible. From Şanlıurfa Harran-Nemrut Tours (p539) runs tours combining a visit to Göbeklitepe with Harran and the outlying sights of Han el Ba'rur, Bazda Caves, Soğmatar and Şuayb City. Taxis in Şanlıurfa charge between ₺400 and ₺450 for the same itinerary.

If you're heading out on this route, pack a picnic lunch and plenty of water. It's also useful to have a pocketful of change for tips along the way. Drivers should note that although the roads have been resealed recently they should still watch out for potholes.

◉ Sights

Bazda Caves   RUINS

`FREE` About 20km east of town, the impressive Bazda Caves (signed 'Bazda Mağaları') are supposed to have been used to build the walls of Harran.

Han el Ba'rur   RUINS

(Göktaş) `FREE` About 6km east of the Bazda Caves are the remains of the Seljuk Han el Ba'rur, a caravanserai built in 1128 to service the local trade caravans.

Şuayb City   RUINS

`FREE` Around 12km northeast of Han el Ba'rur are the extensive remains of Şuayb City, where hefty stone walls and lintels survive above a network of subterranean rooms. One of these contains a mosque on the site of the supposed home of the prophet Jethro. Bring a torch and wear sturdy shoes.

Soğmatar   RUINS

`FREE` About 18km north of Şuayb City, the isolated village of Soğmatar is very atmospheric and is home to the most interesting ruins in the area. Sacrifices were once made to the sun and moon gods here, whose effigies are carved into the side of the ledge. Like Harran, Soğmatar was a centre for the cult worship of Sin, the moon god, from about AD 150 to 200. This open-air altar was the main temple.

Adıyaman

📞 0416 / POP 304,615

This bustling provincial centre may not be much to look at, but its proximity to the sights of Nemrut Dağı National Park and decent choice of accommodation have in recent years made it a popular base for visiting Nemrut Dağı's (Mt Nemrut's) summit. Most travellers breeze through just using it as a place to crash for the night, but the rock tombs of Ancient Perre on the edge of town are well worth adding to your visit.

◉ Sights

Ancient Perre   RUINS
(Perre Antik Kent; Örenli; ₺6; ⊙ 8am-6.30pm)
More than 200 rock tombs pockmark the hillside here, remnants of what was once one of the Commagene Kingdom's major centres. The site retained its importance during the Roman and Byzantine eras before being abandoned. A rambling walkway leads around the necropolis, which contains a diverse mix of tomb styles from simple niches to vast multiroom catacomb vaults. It's 5km north of central Adıyaman.

🛏 Sleeping & Eating

Samos Otel   HOTEL $$
(📞 0416-214 7373; http://hotelsamos.com.tr; Atatürk Bulvarı 328; s ₺100-120, d ₺160-180, tr ₺200-240; ❄🛜🏊) At this central, family-owned hotel, generously proportioned rooms are outfitted in a business-minimalist style with a handful of grandma-chintz artificial flowers and sparkly bed covers thrown in to make you smile. This is a super-friendly Adıyaman choice with staff that do their best to help. Taxi tours to Nemrut Dağı (Mt Nemrut) can be arranged here.

Adıyaman
Hilton Garden Inn   BUSINESS HOTEL $$
(📞 0416-219 1000; https://hiltongardeninn3. hilton.com; 20155 Sokak 1, Atatürk Bulvarı; r from ₺260; 🅿❄🛜🏊) Very popular with the local business crowd, Adıyaman's Hilton is a comfortable choice with spacious modern rooms, a bar, a good restaurant and a pool. Staff speak little English but are very welcoming. It's annoyingly out on the eastern edge of town though, not in the city centre.

Burcu Kebap   KEBAB $
(Sakarya Caddesi; mains ₺20-28; ⊙ 10am-11pm)
This restaurant, just around the corner from Adıyaman Museum (Atatürk Bulvarı;

⊙ 8.30am-noon & 1-5pm Tue-Sun) FREE, serves up solid Turkish kebap staples with good salad and meze sides.

ℹ Getting There & Away

AIR
Adıyaman Airport (Adıyaman Havalimanı, ADF; Boztepe) is 20km east of town. Turkish Airlines (www.turkishairlines.com) has a daily flight to both İstanbul and Ankara.

BUS & DOLMUŞ
Adıyaman Otogar (Adıyaman–Diyarbakır Yolu) is at the eastern edge of town on the road to Kahta. There are frequent dolmuş services to:
Kahta (₺4, 30 minutes, approximately every 20 minutes until 8pm)
Malatya (₺25, two hours, hourly)
Şanlıurfa (₺25, two hours, hourly)

Long-distance bus services include:
Diyarbakır (₺50, three hours, one morning and one evening)
Kayseri (₺100, seven hours, three afternoon)

Kahta

📞 0416 / POP 79,200

Dusty Kahta, with its rows of concrete mid-rises and dishevelled downtown strip, doesn't exactly scream 'holiday' but it's the nearest town to Nemrut Dağı (Mt Nemrut). This is the easiest launchpad to the summit and other sights of Nemrut Dağı National Park, though staying on the mountain itself, around Karadut village, is more scenic.

🛏 Sleeping & Eating

Kommagene Hotel   HOTEL $
(📞 0416-725 9726, 0532 200 3856; www.kom magenehotel.com; Mustafa Kemal Caddesi; s/d €18/24, camping per car/tent €10/5; 🅿❄🛜) Cosy and clean wood-lined rooms with a hodgepodge of furniture and friendly service are the name of the game here. Owner Erfan speaks good English and provides free pickups from Kahta otogar or Adıyaman airport. Free laundry is a welcome bonus. The hotel is geared up for Nemrut Dağı (Mt Nemrut) trips through its travel company Kommagene Tours (📞 0532 200 3856, 0416-725 5385; www.nemrutguide.com; group sunrise/sunset Nemrut tour with 1 night accommodation €65).

⭐ **Neşet'in Yeri**   SEAFOOD $$
(Baraj Yolu Caddesi; meals ₺35-40; ⊙ noon-11pm; 🅿) This wide, leafy terrace restaurant is right beside the blue waters of the Atatürk

Barajı – with views of quacking ducks and fat fish in the water and golden hillsides of wheat fields and grazing goat herds beyond. Come here to dine on succulent oven-baked *alabalık* (trout) served with hot bread and salads and enjoy the best view in town.

ℹ Getting There & Away

Kahta Otogar (Mimar Sinan Caddesi) is in the town centre, just north off Mustafa Kemal Caddesi. Long-distance buses leave from the north side of the terminal building; dolmuşes from the south side. For accurate information about buses, visit the otogar and check for yourself, rather than relying on what some locals may tell you.

Regular long-distance services include:

Ankara (₺120, 12-13 hours, one morning, four afternoon, two evening)

Diyarbakır (₺50, four hours, one morning, one evening)

İstanbul (₺180, 18 hours, one morning, four afternoon)

Kayseri (₺100, seven hours, one morning, two afternoon)

Dolmuşes to Adıyaman (₺4, 30 minutes) go roughly every 20 minutes until 8pm. From Adıyaman you can catch hourly dolmuşes to Malatya and Şanlıurfa.

Don't believe anyone in Kahta who tells you there are no dolmuşes to Karadut. There are two dolmuşes (₺10, 45 minutes) daily at 2pm and 3pm. They leave from the street outside the otogar near Kahta Mangal restaurant. These services will continue on to the hotels and pensions above the village if you let them know. Alternatively, dolmuşes to Gerger leave from the otogar roughly every two hours from about 8am to 6pm and can drop you at the turn-off for Karadut, 2.5km below the village. If you phone ahead, most Karadut accommodation will pick you up from the turn-off for around ₺20.

ℹ Getting Around

Otogar Taksi (☎ 0416-725 6264; Mustafa Kemal Caddesi) has an office in front of the otogar with a helpful chart of its – very reasonable – fares to numerous destinations (eg Karadut ₺90; Nemrut Dağı return ₺140 to ₺160).

Nemrut Dağı National Park

No photos can do justice to the haunting reality of this bare, windy, isolated mountaintop with its strange, gravel-covered, 50m-high burial cone and the presence of those pitilessly staring statues with their partly mutilated, weathered features.

The peak of Nemrut Dağı (*nehm*-root dah-uh; Mt Nemrut) rises to a height of 2106m in the Anti-Taurus Range between Malatya to the north and Kahta to the south. It's set within the 138-sq-km Nemrut Dağı Milli Parkı (Mt Nemrut National Park), which encompasses other monuments from the ancient Commagene kingdom scattered amid a landscape of rolling barley and wheat fields and rhododendron-trimmed river valleys that give way to the barren spine of mountains above.

Visit Nemrut between May and September, when the roads to the summit should be snow-free. They may be passable as early as mid-March and as late as mid-November, but this can't be guaranteed. July and August are the warmest months, but even in high summer it will be chilly and windy on top of the mountain if you come at sunrise or sunset, so you need to pack an extra layer.

History

From 250 BC onwards, this region straddled the border between the Seleucid Empire (the Hellenistic successor to the empire of Alexander the Great) and the Persian-based Parthian Empire.

Under the Seleucid Empire, the governor of Commagene declared his kingdom's independence. In 80 BC, with the Seleucids in disarray and Roman power spreading into Anatolia, a Roman ally named Mithridates I Callinicus proclaimed himself king and set up his capital at Arsameia, near the modern village of Kocahisar.

Mithridates was succeeded by his son Antiochus I Epiphanes, who ruled from about 70 to 38 BC and consolidated his kingdom's security by signing a nonaggression treaty with Rome, turning his kingdom into a Roman buffer against attack from the Parthians. His good relations with both sides allowed him to revel in delusions of grandeur, and it was Antiochus who ordered the building of Nemrut's fabulous temples and funerary mound. This megalomaniacal monarch had two platforms cut in the mountaintop, filled them with colossal statues of himself and the gods (his relatives – or so he thought), and ordered an artificial mountain peak of crushed rock 50m high to be piled between them. Antiochus' own tomb and those of three female relatives are reputed to lie beneath those tonnes of rock.

In the fourth decade of his reign, Antiochus sided with the Parthians in a squabble with

Nemrut Dağı Area

Rome, and in 38 BC the Romans deposed him. The great days of Commagene were thus limited to the 32-year reign of Antiochus.

Before long Nemrut Dağı had been completely forgotten – until 1881, when a German engineer employed by the Ottomans to assess transport routes was astounded to come across the now-famous statues on this remote mountaintop. The American School of Oriental Research began archaeological work here in 1953.

Sights

Karakuş Tümülüsü   RUINS

(P) FREE This large burial mound was built in 36 BC. It's ringed by a handful of remaining columns. An eagle tops a column at the car park, a headless bull tops one on the east side and a faceless lion sits around the west side. Although the remnants are sparse – the limestone blocks were used by the Romans to build the Cendere Bridge – the views are excellent, stretching across surrounding barley fields to the cone-shaped mound atop Nemrut Dağı.

An inscription found here explains that the burial mound holds female relatives of King Mithridates II, successor to Antiochus I who created the Nemrut Dağı mound.

From Kahta, head north on highway D360 for around 6km, where a road forks left

towards Sincik. Taking this left-hand fork, drive for another 1.2km until a second fork left leads 700m to the Karakuş Tümülüsü.

Cendere Bridge   BRIDGE

(Cendere Köprüsü) This magnificent humpback Roman bridge, spanning the Cendere River, was built in the 2nd century AD. The surviving Latin stelae state that the bridge was built in honour of Emperor Septimius Severus. Of the four original Corinthian columns (two at either end), three are still standing. You can walk across the bridge and head down to the wide rocky riverbank where locals paddle in the water.

The bridge is 19km from Kahta on the Sincik road, 10km past the Karakuş Tümülüsü. Coming from Kahta, you'll see it on your left-hand side as you cross the large modern bridge built a little further along the river.

Seljuk Bridge   BRIDGE

(Şeytan Köprüsü) This graceful Seljuk-era bridge is known locally as Şeytan Köprüsü (Devil's Bridge) and is worth a stop for the surrounding scenery. Below it runs the Kahta (Nymphaios) River with a lush thread of rhododendron bushes and poplar trees spanning the riverbank. Above the bridge, atop the jagged rock face, are the fortifications of Yeni Kale (New Fortress; P). The bridge is immediately east of the Kocahisar turn-off on the road towards Nemrut Dağı.

★**Arsameia** RUINS

(Eski Kale) FREE Take the winding path from the road up the hillside to view the remnants of the ancient Commagene capital of Arsameia, passing stelae, stone reliefs and caves on your way to the hilltop. On the summit sits the jumbled toppled masonry of Mithridates I's palace and you'll be rewarded for your sweat by panoramic vistas of the surrounding countryside.

The first monument on your way up the trail (on the left after about 100m) is a large **stele** depicting Mithras (or Apollo), the sun god. Further along are the bases of **two stelae** depicting Mithridates I and Antiochus I, the latter (on the taller stele) holding a sceptre. Behind them you can peer into a deep underground **food-storage chamber**.

Further uphill is a superb **stone relief** portraying Mithridates I shaking hands with the ancient hero Heracles. Adjacent, a **tunnel** descends 158m through the rock to a chamber that was used for religious rites; a lot of loose small stones make the tunnel's steps difficult to negotiate and it's blocked by boulders about halfway down. The long **Greek inscription** above the tunnel entrance describes the founding of Arsameia; the water trough beside it may have been used for religious ablutions.

From the Kocahisar turn-off, another 1.5km south along the road brings you to the signposted Arsameia turn-off heading east. Arsameia is about 1.5km down this road.

★**Nemrut Dağı Summit** RUINS

(incl shuttle bus to/from entrance complex ₺25) Nemrut Dağı's famous statues sit on two terraces flanking Antiochus I's giant gravel-covered, mountaintop burial mound. Their 2m-high heads, toppled from their bodies by earthquakes, now sit silently on the ground in front of their colossal, throned bodies. The **Eastern Terrace** has the better-preserved thrones and bodies; the heads on the **Western Terrace** are in better condition. The statues represent Antiochus and four syncretistic Persian-Greek identities (reflecting Antiochus' own mixed ancestry), plus guardian lions and eagles.

The southern (more popular) approach to the summit, from Karadut or Kahta, brings you to a smart visitor centre complex with a cafe and an expansive terrace with excellent panoramic views. You pay your entrance fee here and then must take a shuttle bus service for the last 2km to the summit car park. From here it's about a 600m uphill walk to the Western or Eastern Terrace. The

northern approach, from the Malatya direction, brings you to an entrance gate and car park within 250m of the Eastern Terrace. It's a 300m walk round either side of the mound from one terrace to the other.

The statues and heads are arranged in the same order on each side: from left to right, lion, eagle, Antiochus, the Commagene Tyche (goddess of fortune and fertility), Zeus-Oromasdes, Apollo-Mithras, Heracles-Artagnes, eagle, lion.

On the backs of the eastern statues are inscriptions in Greek. Low walls at the sides of each terrace once held carved reliefs showing processions of ancient Persian and Greek royalty, Antiochus' 'predecessors'. The site was to be approached by a ceremonial road to what Antiochus termed 'the thrones of the gods', which would be based 'on a foundation that will never be demolished'.

The site is very popular with sunrise tours. There are usually fewer people at sunset but if you want to have the site to yourself, it's well worth coming during daytime when you're very likely to be the only visitor there.

☞ **Tours**

Nemrut tours can be arranged in Kahta (the closest town to the mountain), Şanlıurfa, Malatya and Cappadocia. Private drivers can also be organised in Adıyaman.

From Kahta & Karadut

Historically Kahta has had a reputation as a rip-off town and in recent years its popularity as a jumping-off point for Nemrut tours has faded considerably with just one major tour organiser, Kommagene Tours (p544), left in town. It offers daily group sunrise and sunset tours (between May and October approximately), which include one night's accommodation and breakfast for €65. The tours are well organised and hassle free but generally only have a driver not a guide so don't expect any informed commentary.

If you opt for a sunrise tour you'll leave Kahta about 3am, arriving at Nemrut Dağı for sunrise. After an hour or so you'll go down again via Arsameia, Kocahisar, Cendere Bridge and Karakuş Tümülüsü. Expect to be back in Kahta about 10am. On a sunset tour you'll do the same loop but in the reverse order. You'll leave around 1pm or 2pm and start with the 'subsidiary sights', then go up to the summit, before returning to Kahta (getting back about 8pm or 9pm). Daytime tours can be arranged on a private basis.

All the Karadut pensions and hotels offer return transport up to the summit for ₺100.

Another option is to hire a taxi at Kahta otogar. Otogar Taksi (p545) charges between ₺140 and ₺160 for a return trip to the summit. It has a board in its office displaying all the latest prices.

From Malatya

Malatya offers an alternative way to approach Nemrut Dağı. However, visiting Nemrut from this northern side means you miss out on the other fascinating sights on the southern flanks (reached from Kahta), unless you make special arrangements.

Hassle-free minibus tours to Nemrut Dağı are available from May to October (depending on weather) through English-speaking **Ramazan Karataş** (📞0536 873 0534; ramo4483@hotmail.com). The tour starts from Malatya at noon and gets back around 10am the next day, giving you both sunset and sunrise at the Nemrut summit. You sleep at the simple but pleasant **Güneş Motel Karapinar** (📞0536 287 0639; www. nemrutgunesmotel.com; 🛜) at Yandere village, 14km below the summit on the north side, with dinner and breakfast (not lunch or park fees) included for a total price of €65 per person. Solo travellers may have to pay a little more if there is no one else going.

From Şanlıurfa

Very long day tours (up to about 15 hours) on a private basis from Harran-Nemrut Tours (p539), which charges €75/50 for two/three people per person.

From Cappadocia

Travel companies in Cappadocia offer private tours to Nemrut despite the distance of over 500km each way. Two-day tours cost about €300 per person for two to three people and involve many hours of breakneck driving and an overnight in Adıyaman. If you have enough time, opt for a more leisurely three-day tour – these usually also include Harran and Şanlıurfa. Ask for details on night stops and driving times before committing.

🛏 Sleeping

Karadut village, on the southeast road to the summit, has the most sleeping options. On the mountain's north side there is one pension at Yandere.

Işık Pansiyon PENSION $
(📞0535 865 6059, 0416-737 2010; www.nemrut isikpansiyon.com; Karadut; per person incl half board ₺90; 🅿❄🛜) Right in Karadut village centre, the charming Işık has just four large, bright, well-maintained rooms, kept spick and span and jazzed up with colourful bedding. The welcoming family that owns it speaks a little English and tries hard to help. Excellent home cooking is rustled up for breakfast and dinner. Return transfers to Nemrut's summit are ₺100.

Karadut Pansiyon PENSION $
(📞0416-737 2169, 0535 376 1102; karadutpansi yon@hotmail.com; Karadut; s/d/tr ₺60/120/180, campsite ₺20; 🅿❄🛜) This pension, 1km up the road from Karadut village centre, is run by two amiable brothers and has 12 neat-as-a-pin, simple rooms, some on the snug side. Good meals (₺30 for dinner) are available along with wine or beer on the terrace. The owners can transport you to the summit and back for ₺100.

Nemrut Kervansaray Hotel HOTEL $$
(📞0532 285 3397, 0416-737 2190; www.nemrut kervansarayhotel.com; Karadut; s/d/tr ₺235/270/330; 🅿❄🛜🏊) This tranquil low-rise hotel has the most attractive rooms on the mountain, decked out in white and grey, with comfy beds, satellite TV and contemporary bathrooms. Many have mountain views and six have balconies. The restaurant has wine and cold beer and there's a small swimming pool, though unfortunately it's not kept full when the hotel's not busy.

ℹ Getting There & Around

There are three ways of approaching Nemrut Dağı's summit.

From the south, good paved roads on both the western side (via Arsameia) and eastern side (via Karadut) end at an entrance gate and visitor centre 2km before the beginning of the summit trail. From here you have to take a shuttle bus to the trailhead. It's a 600m walk up from here to the summit terraces.

From the northern side, a good road leads from Malatya, via the D300 and then the Kubbe Geçidi pass and Pazarcık, Tepehan and Yandere villages, to the Güneş Motel. From the motel, it's a further 2.5km to the entrance and parking area 200m from the summit.

CAR

From Kahta it's 46km to the south-side visitor centre and entrance gate via Karakuş Tümülüsü (p546), Cendere Bridge (p546), Kocahisar and

Arsameia (p547). The alternative route, staying on the D360 to Narince then approaching the summit through Karadut, is a few kilometres longer but takes a similar amount of time, around 1¼ hours at a careful pace, not counting stops. Both routes follow decent paved roads all the way. Remember that you'll be driving a good part of the way in low gear, which uses more fuel than normal highway driving.

From Malatya it's a paved road, albeit winding and steep in parts, as far as the Güneş Motel (93km, about two hours). The last 2.5km from here to the entrance and car park is a bit rough in parts but OK with an ordinary car in dry weather.

There is no road at the summit linking the southern and the northern sides, but a reasonable (in dry weather) 20km road does skirt the west side of the mountain from Kocahisar in the southwest to Büyüköz, 13km north of the summit on the road from Malatya. The first 12km from Kocahisar, up to Subaşı village, are surfaced. The final 8km to Büyüköz are unpaved, with some sharp, steep bends, but OK for careful, confident drivers in dry weather. For anyone taking this road in a north–south direction, it's signposted (to Kahta) at the turn-off just north of Büyüköz.

DOLMUŞ & TAXI

Dolmuşes run from Kahta otogar to Karadut at 2pm and 3pm daily (₺10, 45 minutes). From Karadut to Kahta there is one daily service at

7am. All these services will drop off and pick up at the hotels and pensions further up the road from the village towards the summit.

The more regular dolmuş service from Kahta to Gerger (₺20, about every two hours until about 6pm) passes by the Karadut turn-off on the Gerger road, about 2.5km downhill from Karadut village. Many of the Karadut pension owners will pick you up from here for a minimal fee. For a pick-up from Kahta otogar, Karadut hotel and pension owners charge between ₺80 and ₺150. Nearly all of them charge ₺100 for return transport to Nemrut Dağı's summit.

Taxis at Kahta otogar charge ₺90 to Karadut and ₺140 to ₺160 to Nemrut.

Malatya

📞 0422 / POP 453,000 / ELEV 964M

Malatya, Turkey's *kayısı* (apricot) capital, has a habit of growing on you. Sure, its architecture wins no prizes, sights are sparse and the traffic in the congested centre is terrible, but a day spent dawdling amid the busy bazaar alleys after visiting the Chalcolithic settlement mound of Arslantepe and Battalgazi's mosque is a satisfying foil to time spent on the tourist trail.

WORTH A TRIP

ARSLANTEPE

The settlement mound of **Arslantepe** (Arslantepe Mound; ⏰ 8am-4.45pm Tue-Sun) FREE (also called Aslantepe) rises 30m over the surrounding green fields of the tiny village of Orduzu, 5km northeast of Malatya. This 200m-long mound may not look like much but it was here, in the 4th millennium BC, that one of the world's earliest state systems developed.

The mound's main feature is an excavated 4th-millennium-BC palace-and-temple area of mud-brick walls with some surviving wall paintings. Afterwards, climb to the top of the mound for expansive views.

The mound is composed of multiple layers of human settlement stretching from around 4300 BC to AD 400 and although the different superimposed layers within the mound make for a complicated archaeological puzzle, plentiful information panels in English, Italian and Turkish help explain what you're looking at. A wonderful free audio guide (available at the entry office) also does an excellent job of telling the story of the site.

At the site entrance stand replicas of 12th-century BC statues of the neo-Hittite king Tarhunza and two lions; the originals have survived and are now in Ankara's Museum of Anatolian Civilisations (p404).

The settlement's Hittite name in the 2nd millennium BC, Malitiya (Honey Place), lives on in the name of nearby Malatya.

To get to Arslantepe, catch any bus marked Orduzu (₺5 return, 15 minutes) from the large bus stand at the southern side of Buhara Bulvarı near the junction with Dişbudak Sokağı in Malatya. Orduzu buses start their run from here so head to the far eastern end of the bus stand where the stationary buses are waiting. No 400 heads as far as Orduzu's main bus stand beside the village mosque and the signposted turn-off for Arslantepe. It's a 200m walk from there. Nos 401 and 403 pass the site entrance. Buses leave at least every 30 minutes from 6am to 8pm.

Malatya

Malatya

◎ Sights

1 Apricot Market B1
2 Bazaar... B1
3 Malatya Museum.............................. C3

🛏 Sleeping

4 Hanem Hotel..................................... C2
5 Malatya Büyük Otel B1

✖ Eating

6 Ahmet Bey Yöresel Ev Yemekleri.......C3
7 Hacı Baba Sinan Et Lokantası B1

◉ Sights

Bazaar   MARKET
(off Halep Caddesi; ☉approximately 9am-8pm)
Malatya's vibrant city-centre market sprawls
north from Halep Caddesi. Especially fascinating is the lively metalworking section.
Don't leave without spending some time
(and sampling the wares) at the **Apricot
Market** (Kayısı Pazarı; Barbaros Sokak; ☉daily)
within the bazaar.

Malatya Museum   MUSEUM
(Şehit Hamit Fendoğlu Caddesi 33; ₺6; ☉8am-
4.30pm) Malatya's small, old-fashioned museum has a collection of smaller finds from
Arslantepe (p549) including an excellent

haul of metallurgical objects. Other exhibits
cover Chalcolithic and early Bronze Age–
era sites in the nearby area, such as Cafer
Höyük, and artefacts from archaeological
sites now submerged beneath the large Karakaya Reservoir north of Malatya, including
the large 8th-century-BC Urartu inscription
known as the İzoli Yazıtı.

🛏 Sleeping & Eating

Malatya Büyük Otel   HOTEL $
(☏0422-325 2828; www.malatyabuyukotel.com;
Cezmî Kartay Caddesi 1b, Yeni Hamam Mahallesi;
s/d/tr ₺120/170/220; ᴾ❄❐) The best budget
sleep in Malatya, with a prime position close
to the bazaar and overlooking **Yeni Cami**
(New Mosque; İnönü Caddesi). Rooms are definitely on the poky side but are renovated
with modern pine fittings, kettles and sparkling bathrooms. On the downside, staff are
a little lacklustre, but if you're happy doing
your own thing it's a great choice.

★Hanem Hotel   HOTEL $$
(☏0422-324 1818; www.hanemhotel.com.tr; Fuzuli
Caddesi 13; s/d ₺120/190; ᴾ❄❐) By far the
nicest place to bed down in central Malat-
ya. Spacious rooms come with colourful
art and fittings, tea/coffee equipment, and
modern bathrooms with large showers
and plenty of toiletries. There's also a bar,

professional staff and an in-house restaurant. Although in the heart of downtown, the hotel's located on a shopping street that is quiet after dark.

★ **Ahmet Bey**
Yöresel Ev Yemekleri   ANATOLIAN **$$**
(📞0422-321 2000; Beşkonaklar Caddesi 41a; Malatya tabağı ₺40; ⊙10am-8pm) This modest restaurant, run by a charming older couple, dishes up Malatya's foodie specialities, a true taste of Anatolian flavours. You'll have to be rolled out the door after digging into *mumbar* (stuffed lamb intestines), *analı kızlı* (bulgur balls and chickpeas in a tomato stew) and *kiraz yaprağı köftesi* (bulgur-stuffed cherry leaves in a yoghurt sauce).

Order the *Malatya tabağı* (Malatya plate) to try all five dishes on the menu. Prepare to be treated like a long-lost friend and to be firmly encouraged to clear your plate, just like your mum used to do.

Hacı Baba Sinan Et Lokantası   KEBAB **$$**
(📞0422-326 0484; Halfettin Sokağı; mains ₺18-36; ⊙7am-10pm) In business since 1942, Hacı Baba is Malatya's most famous restaurant and has a wall chock-a-block with photos of Turkish celebrities and politicians chowing down on its kebaps to prove it. It's especially famed for its *kuzu tandır kebabı* (tender slow-roasted lamb). Order a natural *ayran* (yoghurt drink) for the perfect accompaniment. Staff are on the ball and eager to help.

❶ Getting There & Away

Malatya Otogar (MAŞTİ; Ankara Caddesi) is 5km west of the centre. Note that the only Diyarbakır services departing during the daytime are the hourly (7am to 7pm) Fırat company midi-buses.

A taxi from the otogar to the central city costs about ₺30. Some bus companies operate free *servises* (shuttle buses) between the otogar and their central city offices. Malatya's tram-bus, which runs down Buhara Bulvarı in the centre,

and city buses 2A, 2D and 152 to İnönü Caddesi, run from the stops across the main road from the otogar. You need to buy a ₺5 *kart* (good for two rides) from the kiosk by the mosque near the bus stops.

Dolmuşes to regional destinations depart from **Köy Garajı** (Local Bus Station; Sanayı Caddesi), a scruffy station 2km north of the central city. There are regular dolmuş services to:

Adıyaman (₺25, two hours, hourly 6.30am to 7.30pm)

Darende (₺16, 1½ hours, hourly 7am to 6pm)

❶ Getting Around

Buy city bus tickets (two journeys for ₺5) from the MOTAŞ kiosk on Fuzuli Caddesi.

City buses to Orduzu (for Arslantepe) and Battalgazi leave from a bus stand on Buhara Bulvarı (Çevre Yol).

Going to the MAŞTİ (Malatya otogar), buses leave from a stand on İnönü Caddesi in front of the Yeni Cami.

Around Malatya

Battalgazi

The remnants of Eski Malatya (Old Malatya) sit 10km north of Malatya at Battalgazi. The walled town was founded by the Romans and had a typically turbulent history, being controlled at various times by (among others) Byzantines, Sassanids, Arabs and Danışmend emirs before the Seljuks arrived in 1105. Afterwards the Ottomans arrived (1399), the armies of Tamerlane (1401), the Mamluks, Dülkadır emirs and the Ottomans again (1515). Although the remains, scattered throughout the modern village, are sparse, the Ulu Cami makes a visit worthwhile.

As you come into the town you'll see some of the ruins of the **Roman walls**, which were finally completed in the 6th century with 95 towers.

There are simple canteens and tea shops dotted around Battalgazi's town square.

SERVICES FROM MALATYA OTOGAR

DESTINATION	FARE (₺)	DURATION (HR)	FREQUENCY
Diyarbakır	50	4	hourly
Erzurum	90	6	1 morning, 2 afternoon, 3 evening
Gaziantep	50	4	every 1 to 1½ hours
İstanbul	160	16-17	hourly afternoon & evening
Kayseri	70	5	every 1 to 2 hours
Sivas	50	4	1 morning, 2 afternoon, 4 evening

❶ Getting There & Away

From Malatya, frequent buses to Battalgazi (₺5 return, 15 minutes) leave from the large bus stand on the southern side of Buhara Bulvarı near the junction with Dişbudak Sokağı. Battalgazi buses start from the far eastern end of the stand. Get off at the bus stand in Battalgazi's main square.

Mardin

📋 0482 / POP 88,500 / ELEV 1325M

Eski (Old) Mardin's labyrinth of meandering lanes cascades down the hillside, scattered with domes and slender minarets and loomed over by a castle. Below, the Mesopotamian plains stretch out to the dusty horizon, lush green in early spring and baked brown once the blistering summer heat hits. The old town's architecture of honey-toned stone houses huddled along higgledy-piggledy alleyways and up and down umpteen staircases, its maze-like bazaar and historic buildings are a joy to explore (wear comfy shoes) and its melting-pot culture of Kurdish, Yezidi, Christian and Syriac heritage is fascinating.

Just don't expect to have the place to yourself. Mardin is short-break destination du jour with holidaying Turks and domestic tourism is booming. Step off the main drag, 1 Caddesi, though and launch yourself into the alleyways and you're much more likely to capture the essence of the Mardin of old.

◉ Sights & Activities

Forty Martyrs Church   CHURCH
(Kırklar Kilisesi; Sağlık Sokak; ◷9am-noon & 1-4pm) **FREE** This church dates back to the 4th century, and was renamed in the 15th century to commemorate Cappadocian martyrs, now remembered in the fine carvings above the entrance. The compact church interior is home to some beautiful paintings and there's a tranquil inner courtyard. Services are held here each Sunday. Photography is not allowed inside the church.

★ Mardin Museum   MUSEUM
(Mardin Müzesi; 1 Caddesi; ₺6; ◷8am-12.30pm & 1.30-5pm Tue-Sun) This superbly restored late-19th-century mansion was once Mardin's Syriac Catholic Patriarchate and sports carved pillars and elegant arcades on the upper floor. Today it houses Mardin's archaeological collection with well-curated exhibits that include finds from the salvage excavations of archaeological sites destroyed by the construction of the Ilısu Dam and a beautifully exhibited collection of idols and cult vessels, many from the Bronze Age site of Girnavaz, in the Beliefs Hall. There is a good cafe on the museum's terrace.

East along 1 Caddesi is the beautiful three-arched facade of the ornately carved **Şahkulubey Mansion**.

★ Bazaar   MARKET
Mardin's rambling commercial hub parallels 1 Caddesi one block down the hill. It's packed with metalworkers, donkey-saddle repairers, woodworkers, stores selling pots and pans, little teahouses and the odd souvenir shop. Donkeys still clop down the cobblestones, vying with motorbikes as the main form of transport within the alley muddle.

Abdüllatif Cami   MOSQUE
(Latifiye Cami) This gracious mosque was built in the 14th century and has been finely restored. Both the external grand gateway, bordered by fine stone carvings, and the internal courtyard gateway, topped with stalactite decoration, are among Mardin's most beautiful examples of mosque architecture from the Artuqid sultan period.

The shady courtyard is centred around a şadırvan (fountain). The minaret is a later addition, built in the 19th century.

Ulu Cami   MOSQUE
This 12th-century Iraqi Seljuk structure suffered badly during the Kurdish rebellion of 1832. Inside it's fairly plain, but the expansive courtyard and delicate reliefs adorning the minaret make a visit worthwhile.

★ Sultan İsa (Zinciriye) Medresesi   HISTORIC BUILDING
FREE Dating from 1385, this *medrese* (seminary) complex's highlight is the imposing recessed doorway, but make sure you wander through the pretty courtyards and visit the small mosque with its ornately carved *mihrab*. Arrive before 4pm if you want to head onto the roof to enjoy the cityscape as the guardian often locks it after then.

Mardin

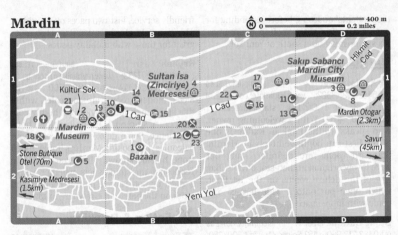

Mardin

◎ Top Sights
1 Bazaar	B2
2 Mardin Museum	A1
3 Sakıp Sabancı Mardin City Museum	D1
4 Sultan İsa (Zinciriye) Medresesi	B1

◎ Sights
5 Abdüllatif Cami	A2
6 Forty Martyrs Church	A1
7 Hatuniye Medresesi	D1
8 Melik Mahmut Cami	D1
9 Old Post Office	C1
10 Şahkulubey Mansion	B1
11 Şehidiye Cami	C1
12 Ulu Cami	B2

⌂ Sleeping
13 Dara Konaği	C1

| | |
|---|---|
| 14 Kadim Hotel | B1 |
| 15 Kaya Ninova | B1 |
| 16 Reyhani Kasrı | C1 |
| 17 Şahmeran Otantik Pansiyon | C1 |

✖ Eating
18 Cercis Murat Konaği	A2
19 Leyli Muse	A1
20 Seyr-İ-Mardin	B1

◉ Drinking & Nightlife
Atilla Çay Bahçesi	(see 13)
21 Kültür Cafe	A1
22 Leylan Cafe & Kitap	C1
23 Mezopotamya Otantik Cafe	B2

Old Post Office HISTORIC BUILDING
(1 Caddesi) Turkey's most impressive post office was built in 1890 and was originally the home of the Şahtana family before becoming Mardin's post office in the 1950s. Today, only a small room in the facade's western tower still deals with official post business and the rest of the building is open for visits. The grand staircase in the courtyard and 1st-floor terrace are a favourite destination for wedding photographers. The 2nd-floor terrace houses a simple cafe with excellent views.

★ Sakıp Sabancı
Mardin City Museum MUSEUM
(Sakıp Sabancı Mardin Kent Müzesi; www.sakip-sabancimardinkentmuzesi.org; Eski Hükümet Caddesi; ₺5; ⊙8am-5pm Tue-Sun) Housed in former army barracks, this superb museum showcases the fascinating history and culture of Mardin. Excellent English-language translations and effective use of audio and video reinforce how cosmopolitan and multicultural the city's past was. Downstairs is used as an art gallery for a rotating series of exhibitions, often including images by iconic Turkish photographers.

Kasımiye Medresesi HISTORIC BUILDING
(off Yeni Yol; ⊙approximately 9am-5.30pm) Built in 1469, two domes stand over the tombs of Kasım Paşa and his sister at this old *medrese* (seminary) complex, but the highlights are the courtyard with arched colonnades and a magnificent carved doorway. Upstairs – get there before 4pm as that's when the guardian usually locks the upstairs section – see

the students' quarters, before ascending for one of Mardin's great rooftop panoramas. It's signposted 800m south of Yeni Yol.

🛏 Sleeping

★ Kadim Hotel
BOUTIQUE HOTEL $$

(📞 0482-212 3322; www.kadimotel.com; 239 Sokak 18, off 1 Caddesi; standard/deluxe r ₺300/350; 🕸🛜) With a welcoming owner, who speaks a little English, Kadim is one of the best-run boutique hotels in Mardin. Standard rooms are definitely snug but have lovely original arched-stone walls. Bag one of the deluxe rooms on the 1st floor, which open out onto a wide terrace and come with more space.

Stone Butique Otel
BOUTIQUE HOTEL $$

(📞 0482-213 9606; 152 Sokak 34; s/d ₺200/250; 🕸🛜) Tucked behind 1 Caddesi (on the alleyway that leads to Mardin Protestant Church), this family-run hotel is a cosy Mardin base. The seven rooms, many with arched ceilings, are modern (with a little Turkish glitz thrown in), while the terrace is the place to pause and take in the rolling views.

Şahmeran Otantik Pansiyon
PENSION $$

(📞 0482-213 2300; 246 Sokak 10, off 1 Caddesi; s/d ₺100/200; 🛜) Named after the mythological 'Queen of the Serpents' from Anatolian folklore, this artsy pension has a laid-back, bohemian vibe. High-vaulted-ceiling rooms with alcove wall features are simply furnished and come with titchy bathrooms, while the stone courtyard below is home to a cafe. Look for the signpost off 1 Caddesi and climb the stairs up to the entrance.

Dara Konaği
BOUTIQUE HOTEL $$

(📞 0482-212 3272; www.darakonagi.com; 39 Sokak 13; s ₺140-170, d ₺240-300; 🕸🛜) Both standard and deluxe rooms in this 800-year-old mansion have high vaulted ceilings and plenty of stone-wall niche details, though the standards are small and have limited natural light. Maintenance of facilities is definitely on the lax side, which is a shame because otherwise it's got oodles of heritage ambience.

Kaya Ninova
BOUTIQUE HOTEL $$$

(📞 0482-212 5015; www.kayaninovaotel.com; 239 Sokak 1; s/d ₺250/400; 🕸🛜) Don't fancy uneven stone-cut staircases to climb on your way to bed? Kaya Ninova is a central choice with business-style modern rooms and a

friendly service, just two paces off 1 Caddesi. There's an elevator between floors too so it's great for those with mobility issues.

Reyhani Kasrı
BOUTIQUE HOTEL $$$

(📞 0482-212 1333; www.reyhanikasri.com.tr; 1 Caddesi 163; s/d/deluxe ₺220/400/500; 🕸🕸🛜) Sleek, modern rooms are concealed within this stone mansion providing a highly contemporary spin on Mardin's boutique hotel experience. Some deluxe rooms come with balconies overlooking Mardin's honey-toned stone hillside sprawl. The terrace bar is a good spot for sundowners whether you're a guest or not. Service here is friendly and more on the ball than elsewhere in town.

🍴 Eating & Drinking

★ Seyr-İ-Mardin
ANATOLIAN $$

(1 Caddesi 249; meze ₺10, mains ₺16-40; ⏱9am-10pm; 🍴) Translating to 'Mardin's Eye', this multi-level cafe, teahouse and restaurant has knock-'em-dead views over the Mesopotamian plains and is always busy. Grab a terrace table and feast on an excellent meze selection or Mardin specialities of *kidre* (slow-cooked lamb casserole) and *tahinli tavuk* (chicken and courgettes in a tahini sauce). There are great choices for vegetarians here.

★ Cercis Murat Konağı
ANATOLIAN $$

(📞 0482-213 6841; 1 Caddesi; mains ₺30-45; ⏱noon-11pm) The Cercis occupies a traditional Syriac Christian home with two finely decorated rooms and a terrace with stunning views. *Mekbuss* (aubergine pickles with walnut), *kitel raha* (Syrian-style meatballs) and *dobo* (lamb with garlic, spices and black pepper) rank among the highlights. Dive into the meze platters (₺40 for two people) for a taste of everything that's good.

Leyli Muse
ANATOLIAN $$

(📞 0482-213 2087; 228 Sokak 7; mains ₺15-50; ⏱10am-midnight; 🍴) This friendly place packs in the atmosphere with a collection of old radios and gramophones inside and a friendly tail-wagging welcome from the restaurant dog on the terrace. The menu concentrates wholly on southeastern Anatolian dishes so it's a good spot to try *mumbar* (stuffed intestines) and *irok* (domes of wheat and rice stuffed with lamb).

Mezopotamya Otantik Cafe
CAFE

(78 Sokak; ⏱9am-10pm) If the eclectic interior of bric-a-brac, chirping canaries, antiques and a random fish tank doesn't charm

HASANKEYF: THE DEATH OF AN ANCIENT TOWN

Hasankeyf is a heartbreaker. An important stop on ancient trade routes, in 2020 this caramel-toned village clinging to a gorge above the Tigris River was submerged forever under the reservoir waters created by the Ilısu Dam despite years of protests against the dam by locals and activists. The blocky town of Yeni (New) Hasankeyf has been completed, high on the opposite hill facing the dam, and the the historic monuments the authorities saw fit to save have been uprooted to sit in Yeni Hasankeyf's culture park complex.

The Ilısu Dam has been one of the most controversial of Turkey's many ongoing dam constructions. Part of the GAP irrigation and hydroelectricity project, the newly created reservoir surface stretches for approximately 400km and has displaced dozens of villages, including the entirety of historic Hasankeyf, while also destroying hundreds of archaeological sites in the area. Archaeologists conducted several salvage excavations in the area in recent years to save what they could before the flooding. Some of the excavation finds are on display in Mardin's museum. Just as important as the loss of cultural heritage is the loss of local livelihood after village farmland was submerged. The Turkish government counters that the dam will spur on the region's agricultural economy and create jobs in a region that has one of the highest unemployment rates in Turkey.

In 2018, Iraq, struggling with drought due to the low levels of the Tigris downriver, successfully lobbied the Turkish government to delay filling the dam but by late 2019 the inundation had begun and the dam waters had submerged Hasankeyf by April 2020.

Hasankeyf's Surviving Relics

The **Zeynel Bey Türbesi** once sat isolated in a field beside the Tigris River. The conical turquoise-tiled türbe (tomb) has been transferred to a purpose-built culture park (Hasankeyf Yeni Kültürel Park) in Yeni Hasankeyf. The tomb was built in the mid-15th century for Zeynel, son of the Akkoyunlu governor, and is a rare survivor from this period.

Noted for its beautiful minaret, the **El-Rizk Cami** (1409) used to sit at the riverfront foot of the trail that led up to Hasankeyf's castle. The mosque has been moved to sit within Yeni Hasankeyf's culture park complex.

There were no plans to save the much-restored, broken arches of the Tigris River's **Eski Köprü** (Old Bridge). They were submerged under the water.

Perched atop a cliff, Hasankeyf's castle survived the rising water. The castle has been reopened to visitors with boat trips to the castle offered from Yeni Hasankeyf.

Getting There & Away

Half-hourly dolmuşes between Midyat and Batman (₺13, 45 minutes) all travel via Hasankeyf.

you, the view of the Mesopotamian plains stretching into the distance from the terrace will. Right across the alley from the Ulu Cami (p552) entrance, this cafe is a friendly, chilled-out spot to rest up after exploring the bazaar back alleys.

Kültür Cafe   CAFE
(Kültür Sokak; ⊙11am-9pm) One of our favourite joints in Mardin. This modern cafe, with a stone-and-wood interior offset by art prints and bookcases, is a relaxing place to while away an hour or two with a *dibek kahvesi* (mortar-ground coffee

beans) or lemonade. Follow the steps up from Mardin Museum (p552) to find it.

Leylan Cafe & Kitap   CAFE
(1 Caddesi; ⊙11am-late) Part cafe, part bookshop and part performance space with occasional live Kurdish music. Also beer, wine and a balcony looking out over Mardin's bustling main drag.

Atilla Çay Bahçesi   TEA GARDEN
(1 Caddesi; ⊙7am-11pm) This simple tea garden has phenomenal views over Old Mardin and the Plains of Mesopotamia.

ℹ Getting There & Around

Taxis are useful for getting to surrounding sights. The main stand is on 1 Caddesi in the car park in front of Mardin Museum.

Mardin Otogar (Mardin–Midyat Yol) is on the main highway, about 7km northeast of Eski Mardin (Old Mardin). A taxi to 1 Caddesi costs around ₺30. Mardin city buses chug between the otogar and 1 Caddesi regularly. Long-distance buses leave from the otogar's road-facing building. Most dolmuşes to nearby destinations leave from the smaller building behind.

There are regular services to:

Cizre (₺30, three hours, five daily) For onward travel to Kurdish Iraq.

Diyarbakır (₺20, 1¼ hours, hourly dolmuşes)

Midyat (₺15, one hour, dolmuşes every 20 minutes)

Şanlıurfa (₺50, three hours, five daily)

Savur (₺15, one hour, around 10 dolmuşes daily)

Heading onward from Mardin, note that it's best to make an early start as services dwindle after 4pm.

Around Mardin

Deyrul Zafaran

The magnificent **Deyrul Zafaran** (Monastery of Mar Hanania; adult/student ₺10/5; ☉9am-noon & 1-6pm) stands about 6km along a good but narrow road in the rocky hills east of Mardin. The monastery was once the seat of the Syriac Orthodox patriarchate but this has now moved to Damascus. In 495 the first monastery was built on a site previously dedicated to the worship of the sun. Destroyed by the Persians in 607, it was rebuilt, only to be looted by Tamerlane six centuries later.

Visits are by guided tour only.

Shortly after you enter the walled enclosure via a portal bearing a Syriac (a dialect of Aramaic) inscription, you'll see the original sanctuary, an eerie underground chamber with a ceiling of huge, closely fitted stones held up as if by magic, without the aid of mortar. This room was allegedly used by sun worshippers, who viewed their god rising through a window at the eastern end. A niche on the southern wall is said to have been for sacrifices.

A guide will then lead you through a pair of 300-year-old doors to the tombs of the patriarchs and metropolitans who have served here.

In the chapel, the patriarch's throne to the left of the altar bears the names of all the patriarchs who have served the monastery since it was re-founded in 792. Past patriarchs are buried seated and facing east, wearing full robes so they're ready and dressed for God. To the right of the altar is the throne of the metropolitan. The present stone altar replaces a wooden one that burnt down about half a century ago. The walls are adorned with wonderful paintings and wall hangings. Services in Aramaic are held here.

In the next rooms you'll see litters used to transport the church dignitaries, and a baptismal font. In a small side room is a 300-year-old wooden throne. The floor mosaic is about 1500 years old.

A flight of stairs leads to very simple guest rooms for those coming for worship. The patriarch's small, simple bedroom and parlour are also up here.

There's no public transport here so you must take a taxi or walk around 90 minutes from Mardin. Taxi drivers in Mardin charge around ₺60 to run you there and back. Try and visit on a weekday or the monastic hush could be disturbed by busloads of Turkish tourists.

Dara

About 30km southeast of Mardin is the village of **Dara** FREE with its ancient Roman garrison city ruins dating back to the 6th century. Dara is where Mesopotamia's first dam and irrigation canals were built. Various sites are scattered throughout the modern village including a series of rock-cut tombs with a catacomb site and two underground cisterns with a cathedral-like ambiance.

Taxis from Mardin charge around ₺180 return for a trip including Dara and Deyrul Zafaran.

Savur

☏0482 / POP 27,300

Savur is like a miniature Mardin, without the crowds. The setting is enchanting, with a weighty citadel surrounded by honey-coloured old houses, lots of greenery and a gushing river running in the valley.

With your own car, drive to **Kıllıt** (Dereiçi) about 7km east of Savur. This Syriac Orthodox village has two restored churches.

🛏 Sleeping & Eating

Hacı Abdullah Bey Konaği PENSION $
(📞 0535 275 2569; savurkonagi@hotmail.com; r per person half board ₺100) Perched on the hilltop, this gorgeous *konak* (mansion) has seven rooms cosily outfitted with kilims (pileless woven rugs), brass beds and antiques. Another pull is the friendly welcome of the Öztürk family. They don't speak much English, but offer a convivial atmosphere and serve traditional meals prepared from fresh ingredients. Bathrooms are shared.

Uğur Alabalık
Tesisleri Perili Bahçe TURKISH $$
(📞 0482-571 2832; mains ₺20-28; ⊙ 8am-9pm) For a leisurely al-fresco meal, head to this shady garden by the gushing river. Relish fresh trout, salads from local organic veggies, and *içli köfte*. Sluice it all down with a glass of local wine or rakı (aniseed brandy).

❶ Getting There & Away

From Mardin otogar, around 10 daily dolmuş services cover the 45km to Savur (₺15, one hour). In winter, services are more restricted.

Midyat
📞 0482 / POP 113,370

The main reason to stop over in Midyat, 65km east of Mardin, is to visit Morgabriel Monastery and the outlying churches of the Tür Abdin.

On first inspection Midyat itself is rather drab with a bland new section, Estel, around 3km from the bustling main drag of the old town (Eski Midyat), with its traffic roundabout as a centrepiece. Scoot off the main road though and you're amid alleys scattered with church steeples that are good for a quick wander. Like Mardin, Midyat's Christian population suffered in the early 20th century, and during the last few decades much of the community has emigrated. There are nine Syriac Orthodox churches in the town, though not all regularly hold services and none are open for casual visits.

👁 Sights

Morgabriel (Deyrul
Umur) Monastery MONASTERY
(off Midyat–Cizre Yolu; ₺5; ⊙ 8.30-11am & 1-4.30pm) About 18km east of Midyat, Morgabriel (Deyrul Umur) Monastery is surrounded by gently rolling hills dotted with olive groves. Though much restored, the monastery dates back to 397. St Gabriel, the namesake of the monastery, is buried here, and the sand beside his tomb is said to cure illness. Entry is by tour (in Turkish). You'll see mosaics and the immense ancient dome built by Theodora, wife of Byzantine emperor Justinian, and visit the church and old kitchen area.

A taxi from Midyat is about ₺100 return including waiting time.

🛏 Sleeping & Eating

Midyat GAP Otel HOTEL $
(📞 0482-464 2425; www.midyatgapotel.com; Atatürk Bulvarı 206; d ₺170; 🅿 ❄ ✳ 📶) It doesn't look like much from the outside, but throw open the doors and you have spacious

---

OFF THE BEATEN TRACK

TOURING THE CHURCHES OF THE TÜR ABDIN PLATEAU

In your own car, or by arranging a taxi in Midyat, it's easy to explore the plateau of Tür Abdin, a traditional homeland of the Syriac Orthodox Church. Dotted around the plateau are historic village churches. All are open for visits though you usually need to knock for entry or occasionally hunt down the church guardian for the key once in the village.

From Midyat, take the road leading due north to Hasankeyf and Batman. After 7km take the turn-off to Barıştepe (Selhê). Follow the road for 3km to the village and **Mor Yakop**, one of the area's most stately and interesting churches.

Afterwards, take the signposted road leading south for 8km to Bağlarbaşı (Arnasê). The high walls of **Mor Kyriakos** sit on the edge of the village. The fortress-style facade and painted stone altar are highlights.

Head west for 8km to the village of Altıntaş (Kiverzê) where you'll spy **Mor Izozoal** perched on a knoll. This well-restored church holds some intricate stone carved decoration. Take the road heading northwest out of Altıntaş for 10km to Anıtlı (Haxê). At the entry to the village you'll see **Meryemana** church. Climb up to the roof to admire its ornate cupola and bell tower.

stone-walled rooms decked out in white with good-sized modern bathrooms. It's on Eski Midyat's main road, three blocks north of the main roundabout.

★ **Shmayaa** BOUTIQUE HOTEL **$$$**
(☑ 0482-464 0696; www.shmayaa.com; 126 Sokak 12; s/d/tr ₺250/400/500; ♠ ❋ ⊛) Parts of Shmayaa's magnificent mansion date back 1600 years, and from 1915 to 1930 the building was used as a military garrison. Those soldiers wouldn't recognise it now. Set within Midyat's old town district, the 15 rooms, some with vaulted ceilings, are dressed in soothing shades of taupe and cream that complement the natural stone tones.

Cihan Et Lokantası TURKISH **$**
(☑ 0482-464 1566; Cizre Caddesi 52; portions ₺12-15; ⊙ 9am-9pm) This is the Midyat favourite for lunchtime *lokanta* meals. Choose from the bain-marie, which usually contains interesting local *güveç* (meat and vegetable stew) options and a spicy version of *taze fasulye* (green beans). The orange-polo-shirted waiters zip through the tables offering friendly and fast service.

❶ Getting There & Away

The rather scrappy **Midyat Otogar** (off Cizre Caddesi) is behind a park, just off the main road (about 200m south of the main roundabout). From here dolmuşes run regularly to:
Batman (₺18, 1½ hours, every 30 minutes)
Cizre (₺20, 1½ hours, hourly)
Hasankeyf (₺13, 45 minutes, every 30 minutes)
Mardin (₺15, 1¼ hours, every 20 minutes)
Silopi (₺25, two hours, hourly)

Tatvan

☑ 0434 / POP 92,700
Tatvan is ideally positioned as a base if you want to climb Nemrut Dağı or take a day trip to Ahlat and Bitlis. Several kilometres long and just a few blocks wide, Tatvan itself is prosaic but is saved from ho-hum blandness by its setting, running along the shore of Lake Van. It is also the western port for Lake Van ferries.

◉ Sights

Nemrut Dağı (Mt Nemrut) MOUNTAIN
Not to be confused with its more famous namesake near Kahta, Lake Van's Nemrut Dağı (3050m) is an inactive volcano with a crater lake, to the north of Tatvan. On the road up to the lake, along the crater rim, there are panoramic views over Lake Van, while the crater lake below is a favourite picnicking spot for local families.

From the crater rim you can hike to the summit (about 45 minutes) – just follow the lip of the crater.

🛌 Sleeping & Eating

Crater Hotel BUSINESS HOTEL **$$**
(☑ 0434-827 3535; http://thecraterhotel.com.tr; Cumhuriyet Caddesi 181; r ₺220; ❋ ⊛) Modern-styled rooms with very comfortable beds and friendly management make the Crater stand out from Tatvan's other hotel offerings. Both the central location and rooftop cafe, with good views of the lake, are added bonuses.

Meltem Büryan KEBAB **$$**
(Cumhuriyet Caddesi; büryan ₺35; ⊙ 8am-5pm) This specialist *büryan* (lamb baked in a pit and served with flatbread) restaurant is your best local lunch bet in Tatvan. *Büryan* is the speciality dish of Bitlis, just to the west, and is typically eaten only for breakfast or lunch.

❶ Getting There & Away

Dolmuşes run regularly to Van (₺30, two hours, hourly) via the lake's southern shore highway. You can flag them down on Cumhuriyet Caddesi. Major bus companies also run this route from Tatvan otogar, at the northern edge of town.

A ferry crosses Lake Van to Van daily (₺11, four hours, 4.30pm).

Dolmuşes to Ahlat (₺5, 30 minutes) leave about hourly from PTT Caddesi, beside Türk Telekom. The dolmuş stand for Bitlis (₺5, 30 minutes, every 10 to 15 minutes) is on Ufuk Caddesi, just up the street. Direct minibuses to Adilcevaz are infrequent; change in Ahlat.

TRAIN

The twice-weekly *Vangölü Ekspresi* (adult/child ₺48/35, 24 hours) runs between Ankara and Tatvan. From Ankara it leaves on Tuesday and Sunday and from Tatvan on Tuesday and Thursday.

Lake Van (South Shore)

After traversing the rock-pitted plateaus and parched plains of southeastern Anatolia, this vast expanse of water surrounded by snowcapped mountains is a scenic diversion. Stretching for 3750 sq km, Lake Van (Van Göllü) was formed when a volcano

(Nemrut Dağı) blocked its natural flow and today this swath of blue is the most conspicuous feature on any map of the region.

Most folk head here to visit **Akdamar Island** and admire the well-preserved biblical reliefs of its medieval Armenian church.

⊙ Sights

★**Akdamar Kilisesi** CHURCH
(Church of the Holy Cross; Akdamar Adası; ₺15; ⊙8am-6pm) Perched on Akdamar Island, 3km out on Lake Van, Akdamar Kilisesi is one of the marvels of Armenian architecture. Built in 921 by the Armenian King of Vaspurkan, Gagik Artzruni, and originally part of a complex that also included a palace and monastery, the church's facade is covered with biblical relief carvings in superb condition that are considered among the masterworks of Armenian art. Inside, the church walls hold faded frescoes.

The facade's biblical scenes include depictions of Adam and Eve, Jonah and the whale (with the head of a dog), David and Goliath, Abraham about to sacrifice Isaac, Daniel in the lions' den and Samson.

A liturgy is held here every September (on the first or second Sunday of the month), presided over by the Armenian Orthodox Archbishop.

Dolmuşes from Van run to Gevaş (₺7) six times per day. Most drivers will arrange for you to be transferred to another dolmuş from Gevaş to Akdamar Harbour (Akdamar İskelesi) for an additional ₺5. Timing-wise though it's usually a better idea to catch one of the hourly dolmuşes heading to Tatvan and ask to be let off at Akdamar Harbour. Make sure you're out on the highway flagging a bus back to Van by 4pm, as soon afterwards the traffic dries up and buses may be full.

Boats to Akdamar Island (per person ₺20) from Akdamar Harbour run as and when visitor numbers warrant the trip (minimum 15 people). From May to September, boats fill up on a regular basis. Weekends are the busiest times with minimal waiting time. During weekdays expect to wait up to one hour. Outside of the summer season, visitor numbers are much lower and you may need to charter your own boat (around ₺250).

⌂ Sleeping & Eating

Akdamar Restaurant
& Camping RESTAURANT **$$**
(☎0542 743 1361; www.akdamarrestaurant.net; Akdamar İskelesi, D300 Hwy; set meals ₺35-40; ⊙Apr-Sep; 🅿🛜) This restaurant and campground is directly opposite the ferry departure point for Akdamar Island. The restaurant has a terrace with lake views and specialises in *kiremet tava* (meat, tomato and peppers cooked in a clay pot) and fried lake fish. It's licensed so grab a beer while you're waiting for a boat to Akdamar to fill up.

If you've got a tent you can camp for free here (you'll be expected to eat in the restaurant). Camper vans can park here and hook up to the electricity for ₺10 per night.

Lake Van (North Shore)

With more time up your sleeve, a driving trip along Lake Van's northern shore offers up better views than the southern side.

To travel around the north shore by public transport, from Tatvan take a dolmuş to Ahlat then hop on another dolmuş to Adilcevaz where you can overnight. The next morning catch another dolmuş to Van.

Ahlat

📞0434 / POP 40,800
On the northern shore of Lake Van (42km east of Tatvan), Ahlat is famous for its splendid Seljuk Turkish tombs and huge graveyard. Founded during the reign of Caliph Omar (AD 581–644), Ahlat became a Seljuk stronghold in the 1060s and when the Seljuk sultan Alp Arslan rode out to meet the Byzantine emperor Romanus Diogenes in battle on the field of Manzikert, Ahlat was his base.

⊙ Sights

Seljuk Cemetery CEMETERY
(Selçuklu Mezarlığı; Bitlis–Van Yolu) **FREE** Ahlat's vast Seljuk cemetery, with stele-like headstones of lichen-covered grey or red volcanic tuff, is the third largest historic Muslim cemetery in the world and Turkey's largest. The headstones span the 11th to 16th centuries and are engraved with intricate geometric patterns, bands of Kufic lettering and floral motifs. Over the centuries earthquakes, wind and water have set the stones at all angles, a striking sight with Nemrut Dağı as a backdrop.

❶ Getting There & Away

From Tatvan, dolmuşes leave for Ahlat (₺6, 30 minutes) from beside the Türk Telekom office and the post office (PTT). Get off at the cemetery on the western outskirts of Ahlat, or you'll have to walk 2km back from the town centre. From Ahlat, there are regular dolmuşes onward to Adilcevaz (₺5, 20 minutes).

Adilcevaz

📞 0434 / POP 30,380

About 25km east of Ahlat is the town of Adilcevaz, once a Urartian town but now dominated by a great Seljuk Turkish **fortress** (1571).

Snowmelt from the year-round snowfields on Süphan Dağı flows down to Adilcevaz, making its surroundings lush and fertile. On the western edge of town is the **Ulu Cami**, built in the 13th century, and still used for daily prayer.

From the centre of town, take a taxi to the **Kef Kalesi**, another Urartian citadel perched higher up in the valley (about ₺60 return).

🛏 Sleeping

Cevizlibağ Otel HOTEL $
(📞 0434-311 3152; www.cevizlibagotel.com; Recep Tayyip Erdoğan Bulvarı 31/1; s/d ₺90/130; 🛜) The best accommodation in town is the Cevizlibağ Otel, handily located midway between the otogar and the town centre and just a short stroll to lakefront tea gardens. The spacious rooms are trimmed in shiny marble with wooden floors and spotless bathrooms.

ℹ Getting There & Away

From Adilcevaz, there are five direct buses to Van (₺20, 2½ hours), but the last one departs around 2pm – make sure you start out early in the day.

Van

📞 0432 / POP 312,250 / ELEV 1727M

In the far southeast, Van is a vibrant urban centre that provides a dose of modern city life after the rigours of the road. The resilient residents here have bounced back and rebuilt their city after 2011's devastating earthquakes, and today the centre buzzes with youthful energy.

Sprawling outward from the shore of Lake Van, where the craggy remains of Van Castle still keep a look out over the blue water, Van is the obvious base for exploring this far corner of Turkey with its Kurdish, Armenian and Urartian heritage. Day trip to Akdamar Kilisesi, explore the lesser-known sites of Çavuştepe and Hoşap, and feast on the famous Van breakfast at Kahvaltı Sokak before getting the train to Iran or heading on to more rural corners of the east.

👁 Sights

Van Castle & Old Van CASTLE
(Van Kalesi ve Eski Van; ₺6; ☺8am-7pm) About 4km west of the centre, Van Castle dominates the view of the city. Visit at sunset for great views across the lake. From the summit the foundations of **Eski Van** – the old city destroyed in WWI – reveal themselves on the southern side of the rock.

Catch a 'Kale' dolmuş (₺2.50) from İskele Caddesi to the castle's northwestern corner for the official entrance and ticket office.

From October to April the castle closes at 5pm.

From the ticket office, a path leads past a cafe area, then across a stone bridge to a stairway leading up the rock, past a ruined mosque and arched-roof building, which used to be a Koranic school, up to the summit.

To reach the ruins of Eski Van, veer to the right from the cafe area and take the path through the willow forest. A few surviving buildings include the restored **Hüsrev Paşa Külliyesi** (1567), the nearby **Kaya Çelebi Cami** (1662), with a striped minaret, the brick minaret of the Seljuk **Ulu Cami**, and the **Kızıl Cami** (Red Mosque). There are also remnants of an ancient hamam, a ruined palace and a water reservoir. The southern side of the rock outcrop also holds huge cuneiform inscriptions as well as numerous *khachkars* (Armenian crosses) that can only be seen from Eski Van below. In the willow forest itself is **Sardur Burcu** (Sardur Tower; 840–830 BC). This large black stone rectangle sports cuneiform inscriptions in Assyrian praising the Urartian King Sardur I.

Van Museum MUSEUM
(Van Müzesi; Kale Yolu; ₺12.50; ☺8am-5pm) This gleaming glass structure at the foot of Van Castle, built after Van's original museum was damaged in the 2011 earthquakes, houses the world's pre-eminent collection of Urartian exhibits including exquisite gold jewellery and an array of bronze belts, helmets, horse armour and terracotta figures.

Van

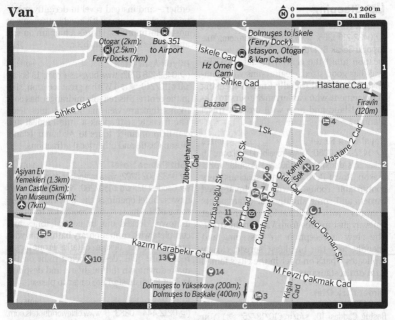

Van map legend:

Dolmuşes to İskele (Ferry Dock), İstasyon, Otogar & Van Castle

Otogar (2km); (2.5km) Ferry Docks (7km)

Bus 351 to Airport

İskele Cad

Hz Ömer Cami

Sıhke Cad

Hastane Cad

Bazaar

Firavîn (120m)

Sıhke Cad

Zübeydehanım Cad

30 Sk

1 Sk

Hastane 2 Cad

Aşiyan Ev Yemekleri (1.3km); Van Castle (5km); Van Museum (5km); (7km)

Yüzbaşıoğlu Sk

Kahvaltı Sok

Ordu Cad

Cumhuriyet Cad

PTT Cad

Hacı Osman Sk

Kazım Karabekir Cad

Dolmuşes to Yüksekova (200m); Dolmuşes to Başkale (400m)

M Fevzi Çakmak Cad

Kışla Cad

SOUTHEASTERN ANATOLIA VAN

Van

◎ Sights
1 Ulu Cami	D2

✪ Activities, Courses & Tours
2 Alkans Tours	A3

◻ Sleeping
3 Büyük Asur Oteli	C3
4 Dimet Park Otel	D2
5 Elite World Hotel	A3
6 Royal Berk Hotel	C2
7 Taht Palace Hotel	C2

8 Toprak Hotel	C1

✗ Eating
9 Kervansaray	C2
10 Kumru Ev Yemekleri	A3
11 Mevlana	C3
12 Sütçü Fevzi	D2
Sütçü Kenan	(see 12)

◆ Drinking & Nightlife
13 Lobby Terrace	B3
14 Niçe	C3

☞ Tours

Alkans Tours TOURS

(☏0530 349 2793, 0432-215 2092; www.eastern turkeytour.org; Uğur Plaza Fl 1/103, Abdurahman Gazi 1 Sokak; Hoşap, Çavuştepe and Akdamar Island day trip per person €30) This friendly local tour operator, run by the Alkan family, is a one-stop shop for any travel information you need in Van and the wider eastern Turkey region. It runs a range of group tours including a popular day trip taking in Hoşap Castle (p563), Çavuştepe (p563) and **Akdamar Island** (minimum four passengers) and regular multiday itineraries covering Turkey, Armenia and Georgia.

Multiday group trips include the 12-day 'Eastern Turkey' tour beginning in Trabzon and finishing in Gaziantep and the 11-day 'Between Ararat and the Caucasus' tour taking in eastern Turkey, Armenia and Georgia. Mt Ararat trekking tours (when the mountain is open for trekkers) can also be organised, as can both short and long custom-made itineraries for individuals and groups.

For any local transport information, Alkans should be your first port of call in Van.

To find its office, Uğur Plaza is in the modern office block on the corner of Kazım Karabekir Bulvarı and Abduraham Gazi 1 Sokak, directly opposite Elite World Hotel.

🛏 Sleeping

Toprak Hotel
HOTEL $

(☎0432-216 1365; www.toprakhotelvan.com; Yüzbaşıoğlu Sokak 8; s/d ₺90/150; 🛜) In a great location amid the central bazaar area, Toprak has good-sized, clean rooms with comfortable beds and friendly English-speaking management who can arrange tours to Akdamar Island and help with onward travel planning.

Royal Berk Hotel
HOTEL $

(☎0432-215 0050; www.royalberkhotel.com; 6 Sokak 5; s/d from ₺100/150; 🛜) Popular for a reason, Royal Berk combines spacious, very comfortable rooms – with swirl-patterned carpets and some slightly wacky art prints on walls – with a brilliant location in a quiet laneway just metres from Van's main street. The crew at reception are easygoing and friendly, and the breakfast spread closely replicates what's on offer in the city's famed *kahvaltı* restaurants.

Dimet Park Otel
HOTEL $

(☎0432-216 3637; www.dimetparkhotel.com; İrfan Baştuğ Caddesi 10; s/d/tr €10/18/25; 🛜) You get a lot of bang for your buck at the Dimet Park. Ignore the entirely weird staircase design feature – no, we don't understand why

BREAKFAST OF CHAMPIONS

Van is famed for its tasty *kahvaltı* (breakfast). Skip your hotel breakfast and head to Kahvaltı Sokak (Breakfast Street), a pedestrianised side street running parallel to Cumhuriyet Caddesi. Here you'll find the city's specialist breakfast cafes, including **Sütçü Kenan** (☎0432-216 8499; set menu ₺30; ⏱5am-2pm) and **Sütçü Fevzi** (☎0432-216 6618; set menu ₺30; ⏱5am-2pm).

On summer mornings the street literally heaves with punters digging into a breakfast spread of *otlu peynir* (cheese mixed with a tangy herb), *beyaz peynir* (a mild yellow cheese), honey from the highlands, olives, *kaymak* (clotted cream), local butter, tomatoes, cucumbers and *sucuklu yumurta* (omelette with sausage).

In June 2014, almost 52,000 hungry locals had breakfast at Van Castle, gaining the city the Guinness World Record for the planet's biggest breakfast.

either – and instead revel in decently maintained, clean rooms with good bathrooms at hostel-dorm prices. There's a hamam on-site and the restaurant sells beer.

Büyük Asur Oteli
HOTEL $$

(☎0432-216 8792; www.buyukasur.com; 13 Sokak; s/d ₺110/240; ❄🛜) With a great location, slap in the centre, this reliable midranger has cosy rooms that are well maintained and clean. The friendly staff speak a little English and can help organise tours to Akdamar Island, Hoşap Castle and other local attractions.

Taht Palace Hotel
HOTEL $$

(☎0432-502 8202; www.tahtpalace.com; Cumhuriyet Caddesi 92; s/d ₺150/260; 🛜) One of Van's newest hotel openings, the Taht Palace offers some of the most stylish rooms for this price in town, decked out in neutral tones and complete with contemporary bathrooms with pretty blue-tile design details. Front-facing rooms are quiet despite being right on the main downtown thoroughfare, and despite a lack of English, staff are eager to please.

Elite World Hotel
HOTEL $$$

(☎0212-444 0883; www.eliteworldhotels.com.tr; Kazım Karabekir Caddesi 54; s/d ₺300/400; ⊜❄@🛜🏊) Elite World overflows with business-traveller-friendly features including a bar, non-smoking rooms, and a spa, sauna and swimming pool. Combine this with its plush decor and you've got Van's most comfortable hotel.

🍴 Eating & Drinking

Kumru Ev Yemekleri
ANATOLIAN $

(☎0539 356 9524; Meçhul Asker Sokak, off Kazım Karabekir Caddesi; meals ₺16-23; ⏱8am-8pm Mon-Sat) Run by women, this little *lokanta* dishes up the best value home cooking in town. There are always *güveç* (meat and vegetable stew), *dolmas* (vegetables stuffed with rice or meat) and hearty chickpea dishes available and your choice of main comes with soup, rice and salad. If coming from Cumhuriyet Caddesi, turn left on the road just before Elite World Hotel to find it.

Firavîn
ANATOLIAN $

(Hastane Caddesi; portions ₺20-23; ⏱10am-6pm Mon-Sat) Translating to 'Lunch' in Kurdish, this *lokanta* offers an ever-changing daily menu of homestyle Kurdish cooking. It's very popular, so get there before 1pm for hearty local *güveç* options, *hakkari doğaba* (the region's 'wedding soup' made from buttermilk, yoghurt and rice) and *soğan dolması* (onions stuffed with meat).

WORTH A TRIP

DAY TRIPPING SOUTH OF VAN

A day excursion southeast of Van along the road to Başkale and Hakkari takes you to the Urartian site at Çavuştepe (25km from Van), and the spectacular Kurdish castle at Hoşap, 33km further along.

Hoşap Castle (Güzelsu) FREE perches atop a rocky outcrop alongside sleepy Güzelsu. Cross one of two bridges to the far side of the hill to reach the castle entrance, above which are superb lion reliefs. Looking east is a row of mud-brick defensive walls that once encircled the village. Built in 1643 by a local Kurdish chieftain, Mahmudi Süleyman, the castle has an impressive gateway in a round tower. There is no permanent guardian on-site so you need to phone for entry. Annoyingly, whoever is in charge of guardian duties changes regularly, though the phone number of the current guardian is often posted at the entrance.

The narrow hill on the left side of the highway at **Çavuştepe** (☉ sunrise-sunset) FREE was once crowned by the fortress-palace **Sarduri-Hinili**, home of the kings of Urartu and built between 764 and 735 BC by King Sardur II. These are the best-preserved foundations of any Urartian palace.

From the car park, the **yukarı kale** (upper fortress) is to the left, and the vast **aşağı kale** (lower fortress) to the right. Climb the rocky hill to the lower fortress temple ruins, marked by a gate of black basalt blocks polished to a gloss; a few blocks on the left-hand side are inscribed in cuneiform. Mehmet Kuşman, one of the only people who can understand Urartian, is often on hand to translate. Note other illustrations of Urartian engineering ingenuity, including the cisterns under the pathways, the storage vessels, the kitchen and palace. Down on the plains to the south are canals also created by the Urartians.

Public transport to Hoşap and Çavuştepe (₺10, 45 minutes) isn't straightforward. From Cumhuriyet Caddesi, it's possible to hop on a dolmuş to **Yüksekova** (at the dolmuş stand opposite Perihan AVM mall) or **Başkale** (at the dolmuş stand next to VAN AVM mall) and get out at Hoşap. Dolmuşes heading to Hakkari can also drop you off. After seeing the castle, flag down a dolmuş back to Çavuştepe, 500m off the highway, and then flag down a third dolmuş heading back to Van. This return section of the trip is highly problematic as dolmuşes are usually full and so won't pick you up. Because of this, and the Hoşap castle entry issue, it's easier to take a tour if you want to explore this area. Alkans Tours runs recommended day trips also including Akdamar Kilisesi.

Mevlana TURKISH **$**
(Maraş Caddesi; mains ₺14-32; ☉9am-midnight)
Always bustling with local families in the evening, Mevlana offers a menu of good-value kebaps and lamb chop plates.

★**Aşiyan Ev Yemekleri** ANATOLIAN **$$**
(☑0432-212 4190; Melen Bulvarı; set menu per person ₺40; ☉10am-10pm Mon-Sat) This is where you come to feast on a set menu that traverses the flavours of southeastern Turkey, including Van's own speciality dishes *perde pilavi* (a cake-shaped rice, chicken and currant pilaf encased in almond-encrusted dough) and *keledoş* (a porridge-like dish of mashed chickpeas and lentils, meat, white beet and drained yoghurt).

Kervansaray ANATOLIAN **$$**
(Cumhuriyet Caddesi; mains ₺22-40; ☉11am-11pm) Upstairs from the hustle and bustle of Cumhuriyet Caddesi, Kervansaray is Van's go-to spot for a more elegant and refined dining experience. Dive into a few shared plates of excellent meze as you peruse a menu containing a few local specialities. Fans of lamb should try the tender *kağıt kebap* (paper kebab), wrapped and cooked in paper.

Niçe BAR
(Maraş Caddesi; ☉noon-late) Get to know Van's student population over frosty glasses of Efes beer at this friendly bar. There's often live music on Friday nights after 9pm.

Lobby Terrace BAR
(Kazım Karabekir Caddesi; ☉noon-late) This multi-floored bar, cafe and restaurant is one of Van's most popular venues for a beer or two, with regular live music on weekend evenings. The restaurant does steak plates if you get peckish.

SERVICES FROM VAN OTOGAR

DESTINATION	FARE (₺)	DURATION (HR)	FREQUENCY
Doğubayazıt	30	2½	7am, 9am, noon & 4pm
Erciş	15	1¼	hourly
Erzurum	80-90	7	3 morning, 3 afternoon
Hakkari	40	4	hourly
Malatya	120	8½-9½	hourly
Şanlıurfa	120	10-11	3 morning, 2 afternoon, 2 evening
Tatvan	30	2	hourly

Getting There & Away

AIR

Van Ferit Melen Airport (Van Ferit Melen Havalimanı, VAN; İpek Yolu) is 8km to the southwest of the central city. A taxi to the airport costs about ₺40.

BOAT

A ferry crosses Lake Van between Tatvan and Van daily (₺11, four hours). From Van İskele (ferry dock) the boat leaves at 9am. Coming from Tatvan, it leaves at 4.30pm. 'İskele' dolmuşes ply the route from İskele Caddesi to the harbour (₺2.50).

BUS

Van Otogar (Özalp Yolu) is 3km northwest of the centre. The major bus companies have ticket offices on Cumhuriyet and Kazım Karabekir Caddesis. Many provide free *servises* to transfer passengers to and from the otogar. Frequent dolmuşes (minibuses with a prescribed route) zip between the otogar and the central city from their İskele Caddesi bus stop.

From the otogar you can also catch dolmuşes and buses to:

Gevaş – (₺7, about 45 minutes, 7am, 11am, 1pm, 3pm, 5.30pm and 7.30pm)

Tabriz (₺70, 6½ hours, 11am and noon) In Iran.

TRAIN

Van Train Station (Van Garı; http://tcdd.gov. tr; İstasyon Caddesi) is northwest of the centre near the otogar. Regular dolmuşes (marked 'İstasyon') run between İskele Caddesi in the central city and the train station.

There are two trains weekly to Tabriz (€14.30, 8½ hours) and Tehran (€24.90, 21½ hours) in Iran. The *Van-Tahran Treni* leaves on Monday at 9pm; the *Trans Asya Treni* on Thursday at 9.52pm.

Heading into Turkey from Iran, the *Van-Tahran Treni* leaves Tehran at 1pm on Sunday and Tabriz at 2am on Monday. The *Trans Asya Treni* departs from Tehran at 10pm on Wednesday and Tabriz at 11am on Thursday.

It's usually not possible to hop on the *Trans Asya Treni* at Van to head on to Ankara. It needs to be booked from Iran. Instead, head to Tatvan to catch the twice-weekly *Vangölü Ekspresi* to Ankara.

Getting Around

The dolmuş stand on İskele Caddesi has frequent services zipping to Van Castle, the otogar, the train station and the ferry dock.

Avis (☑ 0432-214 6375; www.avis.com.tr; Cumhuriyet Caddesi)

SULEYMAN CAKIR/SHUTTERSTOCK ©

Traditional İznik tiles (p588)

Understand Turkey

History

Fate has put Turkey at the junction of two continents. A land bridge, meeting point and battleground, it has seen many people – mystics, merchants, nomads and conquerors – moving between Europe and Asia since time immemorial. Many have left their mark, filling the physical landscape with Byzantine castles, Greek and Roman ruins, Seljuk caravanserais and Ottoman palaces, and the cultural landscape with remarkable and intriguing events, cultures and individuals.

Archaeologist Ian Hodder's *Çatalhöyük: The Leopard's Tale* is an account of the excavation of the site and vividly portrays life as it was during the city's heyday.

Early Cultures, Cities & Clashes

Archaeological finds indicate that Anatolia (the Turkish landmass in Asia) was inhabited by hunter-gatherers during the Palaeolithic era. Neolithic people carved the stone pillars at Göbek Tepe around 9500 BC. By the 7th millennium BC some folk formed settlements; Çatalhöyük arose around 6500 BC. Perhaps the first-ever city, it was a centre of innovation, with locals creating distinctive pottery. Relics can be seen at Ankara's Museum of Anatolian Civilisations.

During the Chalcolithic age, communities in southeast Anatolia absorbed Mesopotamian influences, including the use of metal tools. Across Anatolia more and larger communities sprung up and interacted. By 3000 BC advances in metallurgy led to the creation of various Anatolian kingdoms. One such was at Alacahöyük, in the heart of Anatolia, yet even this place showed Caucasian influence – evidence of trade beyond the Anatolian plateau.

Until the rediscovery of the ruins at Boğazkale in the 19th century, the Hittites were known only through several obscure references in the Old Testament.

Trade was increasing on the western coast too, where Troy was trading with the Aegean islands and mainland Greece. Around 2000 BC, the Hatti established a capital at Kanesh near Kayseri, ruling over a web of trading communities. Here for the first time Anatolian history materialises and becomes 'real', with clay tablets providing written records of dates, events and names.

No singular Anatolian civilisation had yet emerged, but the tone was set for millennia to come: cultural interaction, trade and war would be recurring themes in Anatolian history.

TIMELINE	c 9500 BC	c 6500 BC	c 4000–3000 BC
	Neolithic man creates the circular array of megaliths at Göbekli Tepe. Previously thought to be a medieval cemetery, the site is now considered the world's oldest place of pilgrimage yet discovered.	Founding of Çatalhöyük, one of the world's first cities. Over time 13 layers of houses are built, beehive style, interconnected and linked with ladders. At its peak the city houses around 8000.	Hattian culture develops at Alacahöyük during the early Bronze Age. The Hatti develop distinctive jewellery and metalwork.

Ages of Bronze: The Hittites

The Hatti soon declined and the Hittites swallowed their territory. From Alacahöyük, the Hittites shifted their capital to Hattuşa (near present-day Boğazkale) around 1800 BC. The Hittites' legacy consisted of their capital, as well as their state archives and distinctive artistic styles. By 1450 BC the kingdom, having endured internal ructions, re-emerged as an empire. In creating the first Anatolian empire, the Hittites were warlike but displayed other imperial trappings, ruling over vassal states while also displaying a sense of ethics and a penchant for diplomacy. This didn't prevent them overrunning Ramses II of Egypt in 1298 BC, but did allow them to patch things up by marrying the crestfallen Ramses to a Hittite princess.

The Hittite empire was harassed in later years by subject principalities, including Troy. The final straw was the invasion of the iron-smelting Greeks, generally known as the 'sea peoples'. The landlocked Hittites were disadvantaged during an era of burgeoning sea trade and lacked the latest technology: iron.

Meanwhile, a new dynasty at Troy became a regional power. The Trojans, in turn, were harried by the Greeks, which led to the Trojan War in 1250 BC. This allowed the Hittites breathing space but later arrivals hastened their demise. Some pockets of Hittite culture persisted. Later city-states created a neo-Hittite culture, which became the conduit for Mesopotamian religion and arts to reach Greece.

Homer, the Greek author of the *Iliad*, which told the story of the Trojan War, is believed to have been born in Smyrna (present-day İzmir) before 700 BC.

Classical Empires: Greece & Persia

Post-Hittite Anatolia was a patchwork of peoples, with both indigenous Anatolians and recent interlopers. In the east, the Urartians forged a kingdom near Lake Van. By the 8th century BC the Phrygians arrived in western Anatolia. Under King Gordius, of Gordian knot fame, the Phrygians created a capital at Gordion, their power peaking later under his son Midas. In 725 BC Gordion was put to the sword by horse-borne Cimmerians, a fate that even Midas' golden touch couldn't avert.

On the southwest coast, the Lycians established a confederation of city-states extending from modern-day Fethiye to Antalya. Inland, the Lydians dominated western Anatolia from their capital at Sardis and created the first-ever coinage.

Meanwhile, Greek colonies spread along the Mediterranean coast and Greek influence infiltrated Anatolia. Most of the Anatolian peoples were influenced by the Greeks: Phrygia's King Midas had a Greek wife, the Lycians borrowed the legend of the Chimera, and Lydian art was an amalgam of Greek and Persian art forms. The admiration was almost mutual: the Greeks were so impressed by the wealth of the Lydian King Croesus

Introducing the Ancient Greeks: From Bronze Age Seafarers to Navigators of the Western Mind by Edith Hall highlights how Greek communities scattered across Turkey and elsewhere carried the baton of human progress for many centuries.

c 2000 BC	c 1200 BC	547 BC	333 BC
The Hittites, an Indo-European people, arrive in Anatolia and conquer the Hatti, claiming their capital at Hattuşa. The Hittites go on to create a kingdom extending to Babylon and Egypt.	The destruction of Troy, in a conflict later immortalised in Homer's *Iliad*. For 10 years the Mycenaeans had besieged the city strategically placed above the Dardanelles and the key to Black Sea trade.	Cyrus of Persia overruns Anatolia, setting the scene for a long Greco-Persian rivalry. Later Darius I and Xerxes further Persian influence in Anatolia and forestall the expansion of Greek colonies.	Alexander the Great advances on the Persians and conquers most of Anatolia. Persian Emperor Darius abandons his wife, children and mother, who is so appalled she disowns him and 'adopts' Alexander.

Tradition states that St John retired to Ephesus to write the fourth gospel, bringing Mary with him. The indefatigable St Paul roamed across Anatolia spreading the word, capitalising on the Roman road system.

that they coined the expression 'as rich as Croesus', but the Lycians were the only Anatolian people they didn't deride as 'barbarians'.

Heightened Hellenic influence didn't go unnoticed. Cyrus, the Persian emperor, would not countenance this in his backyard. He invaded in 547 BC, initially defeating the Lydians, then extending control to the Aegean. Under emperors Darius I and Xerxes, the Persians checked the expansion of coastal Greek colonies. They also subdued the interior, ending the era of home-grown Anatolian kingdoms.

Ruling Anatolia through local proxies, the Persians didn't have it all their own way. There was periodic resistance from feisty Anatolians, such as the revolt of the Ionian city of Miletus in 494 BC. Allegedly fomented from Athens, the revolt was abruptly put down. The Persians used the connivance of Athens as a pretext to invade mainland Greece, but were routed at Marathon.

Alexander & After

Persian control continued until 334 BC, when Alexander and his adventurers crossed the Dardanelles, intent on relieving Anatolia of the Persian yoke. Sweeping down the coast, they defeated the Persians near Troy then pushed down to Sardis, which willingly surrendered. Having later besieged Halicarnassus (modern-day Bodrum), Alexander ricocheted ever-eastwards, disposing of another Persian force on the Cilician plain.

Julius Caesar made his famous 'Veni, vidi, vici' ('I came, I saw, I conquered') speech about a military victory at Zile, near Tokat, in 47 BC.

Alexander was more a conqueror than a nation-builder. When he died leaving no successor, his empire was divided in a flurry of civil wars. However, in his mission to remove Persian influence and bring Anatolia within the Hellenic sphere, Alexander was entirely successful. In his armies' wake, steady Hellenisation occurred, the culmination of a process begun centuries earlier. A formidable network of municipal trading communities spread across Anatolia, the most notable of which was Pergamum (now Bergama). The Pergamene kings were great warriors and patrons of the arts, and the most celebrated ruler was Eumenes II, who built much of what remains of Pergamum's acropolis. As notable as the

205 BC	133 BC	AD 45–60	330
The Lycian League is formed by a group of city-states along the Mediterranean coast, including Xanthos, Patara and Olympos. Later Phaselis joins, and the league persists after the imposition of Roman rule.	On his deathbed, Pergamene King Attalus III leaves his state to Rome. The Romans swiftly establish a capital at Ephesus, an already buzzing port, and capitalise on vigorous sea trade.	St Paul, originally from Antioch (modern Antakya), undertakes his long proselytising treks across Anatolia. St John and the Virgin Mary are thought to have ended up in Ephesus.	Constantine declares his 'New Rome', later called Constantinople, as the capital of the Eastern Roman Empire (Byzantium). A convert to Christianity, in 325 he hosted the First Council of Nicaea.

building of Hellenic temples and aqueducts in Anatolia was the gradual spread of the Greek language, which eventually extinguished native Anatolian languages.

The cauldron of Anatolian cultures continued to produce various kingdoms. In 279 BC the Celts romped in, establishing the kingdom of Galatia, centred on Ancyra (Ankara). To the northeast Mithridates carved out the kingdom of Pontus, centred on Amasya, and the Armenians (from the Lake Van region) reasserted themselves, having been granted autonomy under Alexander.

Meanwhile, the increasingly powerful Romans, based on the other side of the Aegean, eyed up Anatolia's rich trade networks.

Roman Rule

Roman legions defeated the Seleucid King Antiochus the Great at Magnesia (Manisa) in 190 BC. Later Pergamum, the greatest post-Alexandrian city, became the beachhead for the empire's embrace of Anatolia when King Attalus III died, bequeathing the city to Rome. By 129 BC, Ephesus was capital of the Roman province of Asia and within 60 years the Romans had extended their rule to the Persian border.

Over time, Roman might dissipated. In the late 3rd century AD Diocletian tried to steady the empire by splitting it into eastern and western administrative units, simultaneously attempting to wipe out Christianity. Both endeavours failed. The fledgling religion of Christianity spread, albeit clandestinely and subject to intermittent persecution.

Diocletian's reforms ultimately resulted in a civil war, which Constantine won. A convert to Christianity, Constantine was said to have been guided by angels to build a 'New Rome' on the ancient Greek town of Byzantium. The city came to be known as Constantinople (now İstanbul). By the end of the 4th century Christianity was the official religion of the empire.

Rome Falls, Byzantium Arises

Even with a new capital at Constantinople, the Roman Empire proved unwieldy. Once the steadying hand of Theodosius (379–95) was gone, the empire split. The western (Roman) half of the empire succumbed to decadence and 'barbarians'; the eastern half (Byzantium) prospered, adopting Christianity and the Greek language.

Under Justinian (527–65), Byzantium took the mantle of imperialism from Rome. The emperor built the Aya Sofya, codified Roman law, and extended his empire's boundaries to envelop southern Spain, North Africa and Italy. It was then that Byzantium became a distinct entity from Rome, although sentimental attachment to the idea of Rome remained: the Greek-speaking Byzantines still called themselves Romans, and later

> In 1054, the line along which the Roman Empire had split in 395 became the dividing line between Catholicism and Orthodox Christianity; a line that persists to this day.

> *Byzantium: The Surprising Life of a Medieval Empire* by Judith Herrin takes a thematic approach to life in the Byzantine realm and in doing so reveals the secrets of the little-understood empire.

395	412	527–65	654–76
Under Theodosius the Roman Empire becomes Christian, with paganism forbidden. Upon his death, the empire is split into east and west, along the line Diocletian had set a century earlier.	Theodosius II builds the land walls of Constantinople to protect the riches of his capital. They prove effective, withstanding multiple sieges.	During the reign of Justinian, Byzantium enjoys a golden age. His military conquests include much of North Africa and Spain. He also pursues reform within the empire and embarks on building programs.	Muslim Arab armies capture Ankara and besiege Constantinople. Arab incursions in the west are temporary but the eastern and southern fringes (Syria and Egypt) of the Byzantine domain are lost forever.

the Turks would refer to them as 'Rum'. Justinian's ambition eventually overstretched the empire, and plague and encroaching Slavic tribes curtailed further expansion.

Later, a drawn-out struggle with age-old rivals, the Persians, further weakened the Byzantines, leaving eastern Anatolia easy prey for the armies exploding out of Arabia. The Arabs took Ankara in 654 and by 669 had besieged Constantinople. Here was a new people, bringing a new language, civilisation and religion: Islam.

On the western front, Goths and Lombards advanced; by the 8th century Byzantium was pushed back into the Balkans and Anatolia. The empire hunkered down until Basil assumed the throne in 867 and boosted its fortunes, chalking up victories against Islamic Egypt, the Bulgars and Russia. Basil II (976–1025) earned the moniker the 'Bulgar Slayer' after allegedly putting out the eyes of 14,000 Bulgarian prisoners of war. When Basil died, the empire lacked anyone of his calibre – or ferocity, perhaps – and the era of Byzantine expansion comprehensively ended.

> Byzantium experienced centuries of jockeying for power through palace intrigues, shifting alliances and skulduggery. Its legacy lives on: in modern times describing something as 'Byzantine' means it is complex and fraught.

First Turkic Empire: The Seljuks

From about the 8th century, nomadic Turks had moved westward from Central Asia, encountering the Persians and converting to Islam. Vigorous and martial, the Turks swallowed up parts of the Abbasid empire, and built a kingdom of their own centred on Persia. Tuğrul, of the Turkish Seljuk clan, took the title of sultan in Baghdad, and from there the Seljuks began raiding Byzantine territory. In 1071 Tuğrul's son Alp Arslan faced down a Byzantine army at Manzikert. The nimble Turkish cavalry

867	976–1025	1071	1080
Basil I helps to restore Byzantium's fortunes, catalysing a resurgence in military power and a flourishing of the arts. He is known as the 'Macedonian' but is actually an Armenian from Thrace.	Under Basil II (the Bulgar Slayer), Byzantium reaches its high-tide mark. He overcomes internal crises, pushes the frontiers to Armenia in the east, retakes Italy and defeats the Bulgarians.	New arrivals the Seljuk Turks take on and defeat a large Byzantine force at Manzikert. The Seljuks don't immediately follow on their success but it is a body blow for the Byzantines.	The Armenians, fleeing the Seljuks in Anatolia, establish the Kingdom of Cilicia on the Mediterranean coast. The kingdom raises Armenian culture to new heights and lasts almost 300 years.

prevailed, laying Anatolia open to wandering Turkic bands and beginning the demise of the Byzantine Empire.

However, not everything went the Seljuks' way. The 12th and 13th centuries saw incursions by Crusaders, who established short-lived statelets at Antioch (modern-day Antakya) and Edessa (now Şanlıurfa). In a sideshow to the Seljuks, an unruly Crusader army sacked Constantinople, the capital of the Byzantines, ostensibly the Crusaders' allies. Meanwhile the Seljuks succumbed to power struggles and their empire fragmented.

The Seljuk legacy persisted in Anatolia in the Sultanate of Rum, centred on Konya. Celaleddin Rumi, the Sufi mystic who founded the Mevlevi, or whirling dervish, order, was an exemplar of the cultural and artistic heights reached in Konya. Although ethnically Turkish, the Seljuks were purveyors of Persian culture and art. They introduced woollen rugs to Anatolia, as well as remarkable architecture – still visible at Erzurum, Divriği, Amasya, Konya and Sivas. These buildings were the first truly Islamic art forms in Anatolia, and were to become the prototypes for Ottoman art.

In the meantime, the Mongol descendants of Genghis Khan rumbled through Anatolia, defeating a Seljuk army at Köse Dağ in 1243. Anatolia fractured into a mosaic of Turkish *beyliks* (principalities), but by 1300 a single Turkish *bey* (tribal leader), Osman, established a dynasty that would eventually end the Byzantine line.

Fledgling Ottoman State

Osman's bands flitted around the borderlands between Byzantine and Seljuk territory. In an era marked by destruction and dissolution, they provided an ideal that attracted legions of followers and quickly established an administrative and military model which allowed them to expand. From the outset they embraced all the cultures of Anatolia – as many Anatolian civilisations before them had done – and their traditions became an amalgam of Greek and Turkish, Islamic and Christian elements.

Seemingly invincible, the Ottomans forged westward, establishing a first capital at Bursa, then crossing into Europe and taking Adrianople (now Edirne) in 1362. By 1371 they had reached the Adriatic and in 1389 they met and vanquished the Serbs at Kosovo Polje, effectively taking control of the Balkans.

In the Balkans, the Ottomans encountered resolute Christian communities and absorbed them neatly into the state with the creation of the *millet* system, by which minority communities were officially recognised and allowed to govern their own affairs. However, neither Christian insolence nor military bravado were countenanced: Sultan Beyazıt trounced the armies of the last Crusade at Nicopolis in Bulgaria in 1396. Perhaps

Painting portraits of the great port cities of Smyrna (modern İzmir), Beirut and Alexandria, *Levant: Splendour and Catastrophe on the Mediterranean* by Philip Mansel tells of the rise and fall of these centres of Ottoman wealth and culture.

Subjects of the Sultan: Culture and Daily Life in the Ottoman Empire, by Suraiya Faroqhi, portrays what life was like for everyday Ottoman folk, looking at townships, ceremonies, festivals, food and drink, and storytelling in the empire.

1204	1207–70	1243	1300
The rabble of the Fourth Crusade sack Constantinople, an indication of the contempt with which the Western Christians regard the Eastern Orthodox Church.	The lifetime of Celaleddin Rumi, known as Mevlâna, founder of the Mevlevi Sufi order of whirling dervishes. A great mystic poet and philosopher, Rumi lives in Konya after fleeing the Mongols.	The Mongols rumble out of Central Asia, taking Erzurum and defeating the Seljuks at Köse Dağ. The Seljuk empire limps on and the Mongols depart, leaving only some minor states.	Near Eskişehir on the marches between the moribund Byzantines and the shell-shocked Seljuks, the leader of the Ottoman Turks, Osman I, comes to prominence.

taking his military victories for granted thereafter, Beyazıt unwisely taunted the Tatar warlord Tamerlane. The result was Beyazıt's capture and the defeat of his army, resulting in a serious setback to the burgeoning Ottoman Empire as Tamerlane lurched through Anatolia.

Ottomans Ascendant: Constantinople & Beyond

The dust settled slowly after Tamerlane dragged Beyazıt away. Beyazıt's sons wrestled for control until Mehmet I emerged victorious in 1413, and the Ottomans returned to the job at hand: expansion. With renewed momentum they scooped up the rest of Anatolia, rolled through Greece, made a first attempt at Constantinople and beat the Serbs a second time.

The Ottomans had regained their mojo by the time Mehmet II became sultan in 1451. Constantinople, the last redoubt of the Byzantines, was now encircled by Ottoman territory. Mehmet, as an untested sultan, had no choice but to claim it. He built a fortress on the Bosphorus, imposed a naval blockade and amassed his army, while the Byzantines appealed forlornly to Europe for help. After seven weeks of siege the city fell on 29 May 1453. Christendom shuddered at the seemingly unstoppable Ottomans and fawning diplomats declared Mehmet – now known as 'Fatih', or Conqueror – a worthy successor to earlier Roman and Byzantine emperors.

The Ottoman machine rolled on, alternating campaigns between eastern and western fronts. The janissary system, where Christian youths were converted and trained for the military, gave the Ottomans Europe's only standing army – an agile and highly organised force. Successive sultans expanded the realm, with Selim the Grim capturing the Hejaz in 1517, and with it Mecca and Medina, thus claiming for the Ottomans the status of guardians of Islam's holiest places. It wasn't all mindless militarism, however: Beyazıt II demonstrated the multicultural nature of the empire when he invited the Jews expelled by the Spanish Inquisition to İstanbul in 1492.

The Ottoman golden age came during Süleyman's 46-year reign (1520–66). A remarkable figure, Süleyman the Magnificent was lauded for codifying Ottoman law as well as military prowess. On the battlefield, the Ottomans enjoyed victories over the Hungarians and absorbed the Mediterranean coast of Algeria and Tunisia. Süleyman's legal code meanwhile was a visionary amalgam of secular and Islamic law, and his patronage saw the Ottomans reach their artistic zenith.

Süleyman was also notable as the first Ottoman sultan to marry. While previous sultans had enjoyed the comforts of concubines, Süleyman fell in love and married Roxelana, known as Hürrem Sultan. Sadly, monogamy did not make for domestic bliss. Palace intrigues brought about the

Defending Constantinople, Emperor Constantine XI placed a chain across the Golden Horn to prevent Ottoman ships entering. Mehmet II ordered his ships over land – rolled over oiled logs – to breach the blockade and demoralise the Byzantine defenders.

1324	1349	1396	1402
Osman dies while campaigning against the Byzantines at Bursa. The city becomes the first Ottoman capital, where Osman's son and successor, Orhan, rules over a rapidly expanding realm.	As allies of the Byzantines, the Ottomans, under Orhan, make their first military foray into Europe. Orhan has by now consolidated Islam as the religion of the Ottomans.	The Crusade of Nicopolis, a group of Eastern and Western European forces, aims to forestall the Turks marching into Europe with impunity. Ottoman forces abruptly defeat them; Europe is left unguarded.	Beyazıt, victor over the Crusade of Nicopolis, is besieging Constantinople, but diverts his armies to take on the Tatar warlord Tamerlane. His army is crushed and he is enslaved.

ARMENIANS OF ANATOLIA

The twilight of the Ottoman Empire saw human misery on an epic scale, but nothing has proved as enduringly melancholic and controversial as the fate of Anatolia's Armenians. The tale begins with eyewitness accounts, in April 1915, of Ottoman army units marching Armenian populations towards the Syrian desert. It ends with an Anatolian hinterland virtually devoid of Armenians. What happened in between remains a subject of huge controversy.

Armenians maintain that they were subjected to the 20th century's first orchestrated genocide; that 1.5 million Armenians were summarily executed or killed on death marches and that Ottoman authorities intended to remove the Armenian presence from Anatolia. To this day, Armenians demand a Turkish acknowledgment that the episode was a genocide. Turkey denies that the genocide occurred. It admits that thousands of Armenians died, but claims the order had been to relocate Armenians without intending to eradicate them. The deaths, according to Turkish officials, were due to disease and starvation, consequences of the chaos of war. Some also claim that Turks were subjected to genocide by Armenian militias.

A century on, the issue remains unresolved. The murder of outspoken Turkish-Armenian journalist Hrant Dink in 2007 by Turkish ultranationalists appeared to confirm that antagonism was insurmountable, but the event became an unlikely catalyst for the reconciliatory progress: thousands of Turks, bearing placards saying 'We are all Armenians', marched in solidarity with the slain journalist. And the anniversary of his assassination is commemorated by many Turks to this day.

There is also increasing contact between Turkish and Armenian artists, students, academics and civil-society groups. Political obstacles remain, however, with both sides finding it difficult to compromise, particularly as nationalistic voices tend to be loudest. The issue frequently reignites, causing diplomatic arguments and accusations, and as long as the question remains officially unresolved between Turkish and Armenian governments, it will continue to resurface. A brief diplomatic thaw, which included the signing of protocols aimed at normalising relations, ended in 2010. Since then, the list of UN countries to officially recognise the genocide has grown to 32. The most recent country to do so was the USA. In October 2019. President Erdoğan described the vote in the US House of Representatives as 'worthless' and said that Turkey would not recognise it.

The Turkish–Armenian border has been closed since 1993.

death of his first two sons, and the period after Roxelana's ascension became known as the 'Sultanate of Women'. A wearied Süleyman died campaigning on the Danube in 1566.

Sick Man of Europe

Determining exactly when or why the Ottoman decline set in is tricky, but some historians pinpoint the death of Süleyman. The sultans following Süleyman were not up to the task. His son by Roxelana, Selim, known disparagingly as 'the Sot', lasted only briefly as sultan, overseeing the

1453	1480–1	1512–17	1520–66
Mehmet II lays siege to Constantinople, coinciding with a lunar eclipse. The Byzantines interpret this as a fatal omen. Sure enough, the Turks are victorious after the city walls are breached.	Mehmet II endeavours to establish himself as a true heir to Roman glory by invading Italy. He succeeds in capturing Otranto in Puglia, but he dies before he can march on Rome.	Selim the Grim defeats the Persians at Çaldiran. He proceeds to take Syria and Egypt, assuming the mantle of Caliph, then captures the holy cities of Mecca and Medina.	The reign of Süleyman the Magnificent is the zenith of the Ottoman Empire. Süleyman leads his forces to take Budapest, Belgrade and Rhodes, doubling the empire's size.

naval catastrophe at Lepanto, which spelled the end of Ottoman naval supremacy. Süleyman was the last sultan to lead his army into the field. Those who came after him were sequestered in opulent palaces, having minimal experience of everyday life and little inclination to administer the empire. This, coupled with the inertia that was inevitable after 250 years of expansion, meant that Ottoman military might, once famously referred to by Martin Luther as irresistible, was declining.

Roxelana, the wife of Süleyman, has inspired many artistic works, including paintings, Joseph Haydn's *Symphony No 63* and novels in Ukrainian, English and French.

The siege of Vienna in 1683 was the Ottomans' last tilt at expansion. It failed. Thereafter it was a downward spiral. The empire remained vast and powerful, but was falling behind the West militarily and scientifically. Napoleon's 1799 Egypt campaign indicated that Europe was willing to take the battle to the Ottomans. Meanwhile, the Habsburgs in central Europe and the Russians were increasingly assertive. The Ottomans, for their part, remained inward-looking and unaware of the advances happening elsewhere.

It was nationalism, an idea imported from the West, that sped the Ottoman demise. For centuries manifold ethnic groups had coexisted relatively harmoniously in the empire, but the creation of nation-states in Europe sparked a desire among subject peoples to throw off the Ottoman 'yoke' and determine their own destinies. Soon, pieces of the Ottoman jigsaw came apart: Greece attained its freedom in 1830. In 1878 Romania, Montenegro, Serbia and Bosnia followed suit.

As the Ottoman Empire shrunk there were attempts at reform, but they were too little, too late. In 1876, Abdülhamid allowed the creation of an Ottoman constitution and the first-ever Ottoman parliament, but he used the events of 1878 as an excuse for overturning the constitution. His reign henceforth grew increasingly authoritarian.

It wasn't just subject peoples who were restless: educated Turks, too, looked for ways to improve their lot. In Macedonia the Committee for Union and Progress (CUP) was created. Reform-minded and influenced by the West, in 1908 the CUP, which came to be known as the 'Young Turks', forced Abdülhamid to abdicate and reinstate the constitution. However, any rejoicing by the Turks proved short-lived. The First Balkan War saw Bulgaria and Macedonia removed from the Ottoman map, with Bulgarian, Greek and Serbian troops advancing rapidly on İstanbul.

The Ottoman regime, once feared and respected, was now deemed the 'sick man of Europe'. European diplomats plotted how to cherry-pick the empire's choicest parts.

WWI & Its Aftermath

The military crisis saw three nationalistic CUP *paşas* (generals) take control of the ever-shrinking empire. They managed to push back the Balkan alliance and save İstanbul, before siding with the Central Powers in the looming world war. Consequently the Ottomans had to fend off the Western

1553	1571	1595–1603	1683
Mustafa, Süleyman's first-born, is strangled upon his father's orders. Allegedly, Süleyman's wife Roxelana conspired to have Mustafa killed so her own son could succeed to the throne.	The Ottoman navy is destroyed at Lepanto by resurgent European powers who are in control of Atlantic and Indian Ocean trade routes, and who are experiencing the advances of the Renaissance.	Stay-at-home sultan Mehmet III has 19 brothers strangled to protect his grasp on the throne. His successor Ahmet I institutes 'the Cage' to distract potential claimants with concubines and confections.	Sultan Mehmet IV besieges Vienna, ending in the rout of his army. By century's end, the Ottomans have sued for peace for the first time and have lost the Peloponnese, Hungary and Transylvania.

powers on multiple fronts: Greece in Thrace, Russia in northeast Anatolia, Britain in Arabia and a multinational force at Gallipoli on the Dardanelles. It was during this turmoil that the Armenian tragedy (p573) unfolded.

By the end of WWI the Turks were in disarray. The French, Italians, Greeks and Armenians, with Russian support, controlled parts of Anatolia. The Treaty of Sèvres in 1920 demanded the dismembering of the empire, with only a sliver of steppe left to the Turks. European triumphalism did not count on a Turkish backlash, but a Turkish nationalist movement developed, motivated by the humiliation of Sèvres. At the helm was Mustafa Kemal, the victorious commander at Gallipoli. He began organising resistance and established a national assembly in Ankara, far from opposing armies and meddling diplomats.

Meanwhile, a Greek force pushed out from İzmir. The Greeks saw an opportunity to realise their *megali idea* (great idea) of re-establishing the Byzantine Empire. They took Bursa and Edirne – just the provocation that Mustafa Kemal needed to galvanise Turkish support. After initial skirmishes, the Greeks pressed on for Ankara, but stubborn Turkish resistance stalled them at the Battle of Sakarya. The two armies faced off again at Dumlupınar. Here the Turks savaged the Greeks, sending them in retreat towards İzmir, where they were expelled from Anatolia amid pillage and looting.

Mustafa Kemal emerged as the hero of the Turkish people, realising the earlier dream of the 'Young Turks': to create a Turkish nation-state. The Treaty of Lausanne in 1923 undid the insult of Sèvres and saw foreign powers leave Turkey. The borders of the modern Turkish state were set.

Atatürk & the Republic

The Turks consolidated Ankara as their capital and abolished the sultanate. Mustafa Kemal assumed the newly created presidency of the secular republic, later taking the name Atatürk – literally, 'Father Turk'. Thereupon the Turks set to work. Mustafa Kemal's energy was apparently limitless; his vision was to see Turkey take its place among the modern, developed countries of Europe.

At the time, the country was devastated after years of war. The Atatürk era was one of enlightened despotism; he established the institutions of democracy while never allowing any opposition to impede him. His ultimate motivation was the betterment of his people, but one aspect of the Kemalist vision was to have enduring consequences: the insistence that the nation be solely Turkish. Encouraging national unity made sense, considering the nationalist separatist movements that had bedevilled the Ottoman Empire, but in doing so a cultural existence was denied the Kurds. Sure enough, within a few years a Kurdish revolt erupted, the first of several to recur throughout the 20th century.

In *Gallipoli*, historian Peter Hart takes a detailed look at the tragic WWI campaign, from its planning stages to the bloody disembarkations at Anzac Cove and the Allies' eventual retreat.

1760–90s	1826	1839	1876
Despite attempts to modernise and military training from France, the Ottomans lose ground to the Russians under Catherine the Great, who anoints herself protector of the Ottomans' Orthodox subjects.	Major attempts at reform under Mahmut II. He centralises the administration and modernises the army, resulting in the 'Auspicious Event' where the unruly Janissaries are put to the sword.	Reform continues with the Tanzimat, a charter of legal and political rights, the underlying principle of which is the equality of the empire's Muslim and non-Muslim subjects.	Abdülhamid II takes the throne. The National Assembly meets for the first time and a constitution is created, but Serbia and Montenegro, emboldened by the pan-Slavic movement, fight for independence.

FATHER OF THE MOTHERLAND

Many Western travellers remark on the Turks' devotion to Atatürk. In response, the Turks reply that the Turkish state is a result of his energy and vision: without him there would be no Turkey. From the era of Stalin, Hitler and Mussolini, Atatürk stands as a beacon of statesmanship and proves that radical reform, deftly handled, can be hugely successful.

The Turks' gratitude to Atatürk manifests itself throughout the land. He appears on stamps, banknotes and statues across the country. His name is affixed to innumerable bridges, airports and highways. And seemingly every house in which he spent a night, from the southern Aegean to the Black Sea, is now a museum; İzmir's is worth a visit.

Turkish schoolchildren learn by rote and can dutifully recite Atatürk's life story. But it may be that the history-book image of Atatürk is more simplistic than the reality. An avowed champion of Turkish culture, he preferred opera to Turkish music and was a Francophile. Though calling himself 'Father Turk', he had no offspring.

Years as a military man, reformer and public figure took their toll, and Atatürk died relatively young (aged 57) in 1938. His friend and successor as president, İsmet İnönü, ensured that Atatürk was lauded by his countrymen. The praise continues; any perceived insult to Atatürk is considered highly offensive and is illegal.

There are several outstanding Atatürk biographies: Patrick Kinross' *Ataturk: The Rebirth of a Nation* sticks closely to the official Turkish view; Andrew Mango's *Atatürk* is detached and detailed; while *Atatürk: An Intellectual Biography* by Şükrü Hanioğlu examines the intellectual currents that inspired him.

The desire to create homogenous nation-states on the Aegean also prompted population exchanges: Greek-speaking communities from Anatolia were shipped to Greece, while Muslim residents of Greece were transferred to Turkey. These exchanges brought great disruption and the creation of ghost villages, such as Kayaköy (Karmylassos) near Fethiye. The intention was to forestall ethnic violence, but it was a melancholy episode that hobbled the development of the new state. Turkey found itself without the majority of the educated elites of Ottoman society, many of whom had not been Turkish speakers.

Atatürk's vision gave the Turkish state a comprehensive makeover. Everything from headgear to language was scrutinised and where necessary reformed. Turkey adopted the Gregorian calendar, reformed its alphabet (replacing Arabic with Roman script), standardised the language, outlawed the fez, instituted universal suffrage and decreed that Turks should take surnames, something they had previously not had. By the time of his death in November 1938, Atatürk had, to a large degree, lived up to his name, spearheading the creation of the nation-state and dragging it into the modern era.

European observers referred to Anatolia as 'Turchia' as early as the 12th century. The Turks themselves didn't do this until the 1920s.

1908	1912–13	1915–18	1919–20
The Young Turks of the Committee for Union and Progress (CUP), based in Salonika, demand the reintroduction of the constitution. In the ensuing elections the CUP wins a convincing majority.	The First and Second Balkan Wars. An alliance of Serbian, Greek and Bulgarian forces take Salonika, previously the second city of the Ottoman Empire, and Edirne. The alliance later turns on itself.	Turks fight in WWI on the side of the Central Powers. Defending four fronts, they repel invaders only at Gallipoli; at war's end, a British fleet is positioned off the coast of İstanbul.	The Turkish War of Independence begins. The Treaty of Sèvres (1920) reduces Turkey to a strip of Anatolian territory, but the Turks, led by Mustafa Kemal (later Atatürk), rise to defend their homeland.

Working Towards Democracy

Though reform proceeded apace, Turkey remained economically and militarily weak, and Atatürk's successor, İsmet İnönü, avoided involvement in WWII. The war over, Turkey found itself allied with the USA. A bulwark against the Soviets, Turkey was of strategic importance and received significant US aid. The new friendship was cemented when Turkish troops fought in Korea, and Turkey became a member of NATO.

Meanwhile, democratic reform gained momentum. In 1950 the Democratic Party swept to power. Ruling for a decade, the Democrats failed to live up to their name and became increasingly autocratic; the army intervened in 1960 and removed them. Army rule lasted briefly, and resulted in the liberalisation of the constitution, but it set the tone for future decades. The military considered themselves the guardians of Atatürk's vision and stepped in on several occasions to ensure the republic stayed on what they felt was the right trajectory.

The 1960s and '70s saw the creation of political parties of all stripes, but profusion did not make for robust democracy. The late 1960s were characterised by left-wing activism and political violence, which prompted a move to the right by centrist parties. The army stepped in again in 1971, before handing power back in 1973.

Political chaos reigned through the '70s, and the military seized power again to re-establish order in 1980. They did this through the creation of the highly feared National Security Council, but they allowed elections in 1983. Here, for the first time in decades, was a happy result. Turgut Özal, leader of the Motherland Party (ANAP), won a majority and was able to set Turkey back on course. An astute economist and pro-Islamic, Özal made vital economic and legal reforms that brought Turkey in line with the international community and sowed the seeds of its future vitality.

Bruce Clark's *Twice a Stranger* is an investigation of the Greek–Turkish population exchanges of the 1920s. Analysing background events and interviewing those who were transported, Clark shines new light on the two countries' fraught relationship.

Turn of the Millennium

In 1991, Turkey supported the allied invasion of Iraq, with Özal allowing air strikes from bases in southern Anatolia. After decades in the wilderness, Turkey now affirmed its place in the international community and as an important US ally. At the end of the Gulf War millions of Iraqi Kurds fled into Anatolia. The exodus caught the attention of the international media, bringing the Kurdish issue into the spotlight, and resulting in the establishment of a Kurdish safe haven in northern Iraq. This, in turn, emboldened the Kurdistan Workers Party (PKK), which stepped up its violent campaign aimed at creating a Kurdish state. The Turkish military responded with an iron fist, such that the southeast effectively endured a civil war.

1922	1923	1938	1945–50
The Turks push back the Greek expeditionary force, which has advanced into Anatolia, and eject them from Smyrna (İzmir). Turkey reasserts independence and the European powers accede.	The Treaty of Lausanne, signed by general and statesman İsmet İnönü, undoes the wrongs of Sèvres. The Republic of Turkey is unanimously supported by the members of the National Assembly.	Atatürk dies, at the age of 57, in the Dolmabahçe Palace in İstanbul on 10 November. All the clocks in the palace are stopped at the time that he died: 9.05am.	After WWII, which the Turks avoided, the Truman Doctrine brings aid to Turkey on the condition of democratisation. Democratic elections are held (1950) and the Democratic Party emerges victorious.

PRESS FREEDOM (OR LACK THEREOF)

Turkey dropped to number 157 in a list of 180 countries in the 2019 World Press Freedom Index compiled by Reporters Without Borders (RSF), which was a source of serious concern to many in the Turkish and international communities. The RSF summarised the situation as a 'witch-hunt waged by President Recep Tayyip Erdoğan's government against its media critics', condemning the elimination of dozens of media outlets, the imprisonment of journalists and the acquisition of Turkey's biggest media group (the Doğan group) by a pro-government conglomerate in 2018. RSF also claimed that censorship of websites and online social media has reached unprecedented levels. Needless to say, the government emphatically denies that its actions are undemocratic or excessive, and alleges that the international media and RSF are biased against the government.

Meanwhile, Turgut Özal died suddenly in 1993, creating a power vacuum. Weak coalition governments followed throughout the 1990s, with a cast of figures flitting across the political stage. Tansu Çiller served for three years as Turkey's first female prime minister, but despite high expectations she did not solve the Kurdish issue or cure the ailing economy.

In December 1995 the religious Refah (Welfare) Party formed a government led by veteran politician Necmettin Erbakan. Heady with power, Refah politicians made Islamist statements that raised the ire of the military. In 1997 the military declared that Refah had flouted the constitutional ban on religion in politics. Faced with a so-called postmodern coup, the government resigned and Refah was disbanded.

The capture of PKK leader Abdullah Öcalan in early 1999 seemed like a good omen for the state after the torrid '90s, and many Turks believed that his capture would disillusion the PKK and cause its support base to wither. In August 1999, disastrous earthquakes struck İzmit, ending any premillennial optimism. The government's handling of the crisis was inadequate; however, the global outpouring of aid and sympathy did much to reassure Turks they were valued members of the world community.

An appetiser for those wanting to know more, Turkey: A Short History *by Norman Stone is a succinct and pacey wrap-up of the crucial events and personalities of Turkey's long history.*

Rise of the AKP

There was a spectacular collapse of the Turkish economy in 2001, leading to the government's electoral defeat in 2002. The victorious party was the moderate Adalet ve Kalkınma Partisi (Justice and Development Party; AKP), led by Recep Tayyip Erdoğan. Much of the support for the AKP had arisen in the burgeoning cities nicknamed the Anatolian Tigers, such as Konya and Kayseri. These cities of the interior were experiencing an economic boom, proof that the modernising and economic development projects begun earlier were finally bearing fruit.

1971	1980	1983	1985–99
Increasing political strife prompts the military to step in (again) to restore order. The military chief hands the prime minister a written ultimatum, thus this is known as a 'coup by memorandum'.	The third of Turkey's military coups, this time as the military moves to stop widespread street violence between left- and right-wing groups. The National Security Council is formed.	In elections after the 1980 coup, the Özal era begins. A pragmatic leader, Turgut Özal institutes economic reforms, encouraging foreign investment. Turkey opens to the West and tourism takes off.	Abdullah Öcalan establishes the Kurdistan Workers Party (PKK), an armed political group calling for a Kurdish state. There is a long, low-intensity war in southeast Anatolia until Öcalan's capture in 1999.

Elections in 2007 and 2011 had the same result, as did the municipal election in 2014. The result of the 2014 election was a disappointment to many secular and left-leaning Turks, as well as to former AKP supporters who had changed their political allegiance as a result of the government's handling of the 2013 Gezi Park protests in İstanbul. The protests, initially about a city development plan, became widespread expressions of dissatisfaction with the government, and were violently dispersed.

After Gezi, local authorities cracked down on any political demonstrations that were seen as anti-government. Turkish media outlets seen to be anti-government were also targeted, with some being forcibly closed or taken over by the government. Many writers, journalists and editors were charged with serious crimes, including membership of a terror organisation, espionage and revealing confidential documents. Charges under Article 301 of the Turkish penal code, which make it a punishable offence to insult Turkishness or various official Turkish institutions (including the president), were particularly prevalent.

A coup d'état staged by a small faction of the military in July 2016 was defeated when members of the public took to the streets to defend the democratically elected AKP government. The government and many Turks believed that the coup had been orchestrated by US-based Islamic cleric Fethullah Gülen, a former close ally of Erdoğan. Official reprisals

Turkey: What Everyone Needs to Know, by İstanbul-based journalist Andrew Finkel, explores the ins and outs of Turkish culture, society and politics.

THE KURDISH SITUATION

The results of the June 2015 national elections, when the pro-Kurdish HDP (Peoples' Democratic Party) led by Figen Yüksekdağ and Kurdish politician Selahattin Demirtaş won 13% of the vote, seemed indicative of a greater acceptance of Kurdish voices within Turkey as a whole but resulted in the AKP government turning its back on many of the political concessions it had previously offered to the Kurdish community, leading to a resurgence in Kurdish anti-government feeling and political activism. Selahattin Demirtaş and Figen Yüksekdağ have been in jail since late 2016, accused of terrorism and spreading anti-Turkish propaganda. The European Commission of Human Rights has questioned the validity of their detention.

In October 2019 Turkish armed forces launched an offensive into Northeastern Syria aimed at expelling members of the predominantly Kurdish Syrian Democratic Forces (SDF) from the border area. The Turkish government alleges that the SDF is associated with the Kurdistan Workers Party (PKK), which it considers to be a terrorist organisation, and that the SDF's presence on the border is a threat to Turkey's national security. Turkey's actions have been greeted with anger and concern by members of the Kurdish community both within Turkey and elsewhere, and is likely to worsen the already fraught relationship between Turkish Kurds and their national government.

1997	2002	2005	2007–11
The coalition government headed by Necmettin Erbakan's Islamically inspired Refah (Welfare) Party is disbanded, apparently under military pressure, in what has been called a 'postmodern coup'.	Recep Tayyip Erdoğan's new Justice and Development Party (AKP) wins a landslide election victory, a reflection of the Turkish public's disgruntlement with the established parties. The economy recovers.	EU-accession talks begin, and economic and legal reforms begin to be implemented. Resistance to Turkish membership by some EU states leads to a decrease in approval by some Turks.	Further resounding election victories for the AKP, which increases its share of the vote, as well as winning two referenda in favour of amending the constitution.

DIPLOMATIC RELATIONS

The European refugee crisis prompted a controversial deal in March 2016 for Turkey to take Syrian refugees back from the EU, adding to the two million already in camps on the Syrian border and elsewhere, and to close the people-smuggling routes from Turkey's Aegean coast to the Greek islands. In exchange, Turks were to be granted easier access to the EU, and Turkey would receive financial aid and the acceleration of its EU membership application. However, increasingly strained relations between the AKP and Europe (largely to do with human rights issues) has meant that the deal hasn't been fully implemented. The government's ever-increasing diplomatic, economic and military ties with Russia make any full rapprochement with the EU extremely unlikely, and its purchase of the Russian S-400 surface-to-air missile system has also seriously damaged Turkey's relations with the US and NATO.

against anyone suspected of being a Gülenist, coup perpetrator or coup supporter were draconian, with thousands arrested, media outlets closed down and universities and schools purged.

As the 21st century hits its stride, Turkey is in an economic decline after two decades of unprecedented growth and prosperity. This is having a major impact, with inflation spiralling, businesses failing and unemployment numbers rising. Most Turks blame the current dire state of the economy on the national government's poor economic management and on the major diminution of tourist arrivals that followed the terrorism attacks and failed military coup d'état of 2016. The inflation rate, which averaged 18.17% in 2019, was the tenth highest in the world and the highest in Europe at that time. Social tensions are high as a consequence, with resentment against the millions of Syrian refugees who are in the country growing and long-standing issues such as the Kurdish conflict festering.

This and the ongoing government assaults on civil rights in the country has led to many Turks revising their wholehearted support for the AKP and President Erdoğan. The AKP's dominance was considerably weakened in the 2019 Turkish local elections with the CHP, the main opposition party, taking power in five of Turkey's six largest cities.

Throughout 2020 and 2021, as the pandemic deepened Turkey's economic problems, criticism continued to grow. Both the government's COVID response (in particular the decision to exempt foreign tourists from restrictions during national lockdowns) and its reaction to the İzmir earthquake in October 2020 and the forest fires and Black Sea flash floods of July and August 2021, angered many Turks. Whether any of this signals a shift in Turkey's next national government parliamentary elections, remains to be seen.

2013	2015	2016	2021
Criticism of the AKP mounts during the Gezi Park protests, when demonstrations against an AKP-supported development project in İstanbul cause weeks of unrest, with at least four deaths.	The general election results in a hung parliament. In a snap election six months later, the AKP reasserts its dominance, but without the majority needed to call a referendum on rewriting the constitution.	As the Syrian war sends millions of refugees into Turkey, ISIS suicide bombers target İstanbul. In July, military factions launch a failed coup attempt. Government reprisals are swift, draconian and ongoing.	Turkey suffers its worst forest fires in the Republic's history, with 240 separate fires destroying 170,000 hectares of forest.

Architectural Wonders

Turkey's rich architectural heritage has been moulded by the rise and fall of countless civilisations who have settled here over millennia. From a Neolithic temple-complex through to the imperial monuments of both the Byzantine and Ottoman eras, the dizzying array of architectural styles on display reveals how diverse cultural influences have inspired and shaped the human-built history stamped across this land.

Ancient (9500BC–550BC)

The earliest Anatolian architectural remnants, the carved megaliths of Göbekli Tepe, date back to approximately 10,000 BC. The mud-brick constructions of Çatalhöyük (p440), which were accessed through their roofs, were first constructed around 7500 BC. Alacahöyük (p424), dating from 4000 BC, was characterised by more complex buildings. By the time Troy (p174) was established in 3000 BC, temple design began to advance while in the treeless southeast, a distinctive 'beehive' construction technique developed, which can still be seen at Harran.

Later, the remnants of hefty gates, walls and ramparts of Hattuşa (the Hittite capital from 1660 BC; p421) reveal an increasing sophistication in working with the landscape.

Ottoman architectural styles spread beyond the boundaries of modern Turkey. There are still Ottoman constructions – mosques, fortresses, mansions and bridges – throughout the Balkans.

Greek & Roman (550BC–AD330)

The architects of ancient Greece displayed a heightened sense of planning and sophistication in design and construction, incorporating vaults and arches into their buildings. Later the Romans built upon the developments of the Greeks. The Romans were also accomplished road builders, establishing a comprehensive network linking trading communities.

Fine examples of classical Greco-Roman architecture can be seen today at the theatre of Aspendos (p369), the nymphaeum at Sagalassos (p315), Bergama's Acropolis (p198) area, and Letoön's (p338) fine temples. Other superb sites include Afrodisias (p309), Termessos (p370), Patara (p340) and Hierapolis (p303).

CAPITAL OF ROMAN ASIA

Ephesus (Efes) (p227) is the pre-eminent example of Roman city construction in Turkey; its flagstoned streets, gymnasium, sewerage system, mosaics and theatre form a neat set-piece of Roman design and architecture.

A prosperous trading city, Ephesus was endowed with significant buildings. The Temple of Artemis, boasting a forest of mighty columns, was one of the Wonders of the Ancient World, but was later destroyed under orders of a Byzantine archbishop. The Great Theatre (p229), one of the biggest in the Roman world, is evidence of Roman expertise in theatre design and acoustics, while the Library of Celsus (p232) is ingeniously designed to appear larger than it actually is.

Byzantine (AD330–1071)

Ecclesiastical construction distinguishes Byzantine architecture from that of the pagan Greeks. The Byzantines developed church design while working in new media, such as brick and plaster, and displaying a genius for dome construction, as seen in the Aya Sofya (p64).

Mosaics were a principal Byzantine design feature; fine examples can be seen in the Hatay Archaeology Museum (p395) or in situ at the Chora Church (p104; now called the Kariye Mosque) in İstanbul, which features a sumptuous array of mosaics. An example of the burgeoning skill of Byzantine civil engineers is the Basilica Cistern (p83), also in İstanbul.

In the east, Armenian stonemasons developed their own distinctive architectural style. The 10th-century church at Akdamar is a stunning example, while the site of Ani (p524) includes fascinating ruins and remnants.

For a scholarly investigation of the challenges faced by Byzantine architects see *The Master Builders of Byzantium* by Robert Ousterhout.

Seljuk (1071–1300)

The architecture of the Seljuks reveals significant Persian influences in design and decorative flourishes, including Kufic lettering and intricate stonework. The Seljuks created cosmopolitan styles incorporating elements of nomadic Turkic design traditions with Persian know-how and the Mediterranean-influenced architecture of the Anatolian Greeks.

The Seljuks left a legacy of magnificent mosques and *medreses* (seminaries), distinguished by their elaborate entrances; you can see the best of them in Konya (p434), Sivas (p431) and Divriği (p434). As patrons of the Silk Road, the Seljuks also built a string of caravanserais through Anatolia; two of the best examples are Sultanhanı and Sultan Han. The Anatolian countryside is also dotted with the grand conical *türbe* (tombs) of the Seljuks, such as those at Konya, Battalgazi (p551) and on both shores of Lake Van.

In the southeast, competitors to the Seljuks, the Artuklu Turks created the cityscapes of Mardin (p552) and Hasankeyf (p555), featuring distinctive honey-toned stonework and brick tombs, while also embellishing and adding to the imposing black basalt walls of Diyarbakır.

Ottoman (1300–1750)

From the 14th century, as the Ottomans expanded across Anatolia, they became increasingly influenced by Byzantine styles, especially ecclesiastical architecture. Ottoman architects absorbed Byzantine influences, particularly the use of domes, and incorporated them into their exist-

IMPERIAL MOSQUES

The rippling domes and piercing minarets of mosques are the quintessential image of Turkey for many travellers. The most impressive mosques, in size and grandness, are the imperial mosques commissioned by members of the royal households.

Each imperial mosque had a *külliye*, or collection of charitable institutions, clustered around it. These might include a hospital, asylum, orphanage, *imaret* (soup kitchen), hospice for travellers, *medrese* (seminary), library, baths and a cemetery in which the mosque's imperial patron and other notables could be buried. Over time, many of these buildings were demolished or altered, but İstanbul's Süleymaniye Mosque (p96) complex still has much of its *külliye* intact.

The design, perfected by the revered Ottoman architect Mimar Sinan during the reign of Süleyman the Magnificent, proved so durable that it is still being used, with variations, for mosque construction all over Turkey.

Dolmabahçe Palace (p107), İstanbul

ing Persian architectural repertoire to develop a completely new style: the T-shape plan. The Üç Şerefeli Mosque (p151) in Edirne became the model for other mosques. One of the first forays into the T-plan, it was the first Ottoman mosque to have a wide dome and a forecourt with an ablutions fountain.

Aside from mosques, the Ottomans also developed a distinctive style of domestic architecture, consisting of multistorey houses with a stone ground floor topped by protruding upper floors balanced on carved brackets. These houses featured separate private and public areas (*haremlik* and *selamlık* respectively), and often included woodwork detailing on ceilings and joinery, ornate fireplaces and expansive rooms lined with *sedirs* (low benches) ideal for the communal interaction that was a feature of Ottoman life. Cities including Amasya (p426), Safranbolu (p415) and Muğla (p282) still feature houses of this design.

In later centuries in İstanbul, architects developed the *yalı* (grand seaside mansions constructed solely of wood) to which notable families would escape at the height of summer. Prime examples are still visible on the Bosphorus.

The visually stunning *Constantinople: İstanbul's Historical Heritage*, by Stéphane Yerasimos, provides history and context to many of the city's magnificent buildings.

Turkish Baroque & Neoclassical (1750–1920)

From the mid-18th century, rococo and baroque influences hit Turkey, resulting in a pastiche of curves, frills, scrolls and murals that's sometimes described as 'Turkish baroque'. The period's archetype is the extravagant Dolmabahçe Palace (p107). Although building mosques was considered passé, the later Ottomans still adored pavilions where they could enjoy the outdoors; the Küçüksu Kasrı (p113) in İstanbul is a good example.

In the 19th and early 20th centuries, foreign or foreign-trained architects began to concoct a neoclassical blend: European architecture mixed in with Turkish baroque and some concessions to classic Ottoman style. Vedat Tek, a Turkish architect educated in Paris, built the capital's central post office, a melange of Ottoman elements and European symmetry. His style is sometimes seen as part of the first nationalist architecture movement, part of the modernisation project of the early Turkish republic. This movement sought to create a 'national' style specific to Turkey by drawing on Ottoman design elements and melding them with modern European styles.

Turkey: Modern Architectures in History, by Sibel Bozdoğan and Esra Akcan, examines the philosophy and impact of architecture in the new Turkey.

Notable buildings in this style include the Ethnography Museum (p406) in Ankara and Bebek Mosque (p113) in İstanbul. Sirkeci Train Station, by the German architect Jachmund, is another example of this eclectic neoclassicism.

Modern (1920–present)

The rapid growth that Turkey has experienced since the 1940s has seen a profusion of bland, grey apartment blocks and office buildings pop up in Anatolian cities and towns. Yet even these, taken in context of the Turkish landscape, climate and bustle of convivial neighbourhood interaction, have a distinctive quality all their own.

During the 1940s and '50s a new nationalist architecture movement developed as Turkish-trained architects working on government buildings sought to create a homegrown style reflecting Turkish tradition and the aspirations of the new republic. This architecture tended to be sturdy and monumental; examples include the Anıt Kabir (p401) in Ankara and the Çanakkale Şehitleri Anıtı (Çanakkale Martyrs' Memorial; p163) at Gallipoli.

Since the 1990s there has been more private-sector investment in architecture, leading to a diversification of building styles. The Levent business district in İstanbul has seen the mushrooming of shimmering office towers, and other futuristic buildings have arisen, such as the Esenboğa Airport in Ankara.

The most interesting development in recent decades is that Turks have begun to take more notice of their history, particularly the Ottoman era. This has meant reclaiming their architectural heritage, especially those parts of it that can be turned into dollars via the tourism industry. These days many restoration projects – in Sultanahmet and other parts of İstanbul, but also in cities across the country such as Antakya, Antalya and Tokat – are focused on classic Ottoman style.

Arts & Culture

Turkey's rich and diverse artistic traditions display influences of the many cultures and civilisations that have waxed and waned in Anatolia over the centuries. Internationally, it may still be best known for its textile and ceramic artisan heritage but the country's contemporary artists, writers, and filmmakers are making a name for themselves by finding inspiration in Turkey's long history and commenting in their work on the country's role in the world today.

Carpets

The art form that travellers are most likely to associate with Turkey is the carpet – there are few visitors who do not end up in a carpet shop at some time.

The carpets that travellers know and love are the culmination of an ages-old textile-making tradition. Long ago Turkic nomads weaved tents and saddle bags and established carpet-making techniques on the Central Asian steppes.

As in many aspects of their culture, the Turks adopted and adapted from other traditions. Moving ever-westward, the Turks eventually brought hand-woven carpets, into which they incorporated Persian designs and Chinese cloud patterns, to Anatolia in the 12th century.

Within Anatolia, distinctive regional designs evolved. Uşak carpets, with star and medallion motifs, were the first to attract attention in Europe: Renaissance artist Holbein included copies of them in his paintings. Thereafter, carpet-making gradually shifted from cottage industry to big business. Village women still weave carpets but usually work to fixed contracts, using a pattern and being paid for their final effort rather than for each hour of work.

Fearing the loss of old carpet-making methods, the Ministry of Culture has sponsored projects to revive weaving and dyeing methods. One scheme is the Natural Dye Research and Development Project (Doğal Boya Arıştırma ve Geliştirme Projesi). Some shops keep stocks of these 'project carpets', which are usually high quality.

Literature

Only in the last century has Turkey developed a tradition of novel writing, but there is a wealth of writing by Turks and about Turkey that offers insight into the country and its people.

The Turkish literary canon is made up of warrior epics, mystical verses (including those of Rumi, founder of the Mevlevi order of whirling dervishes), and the elegies of wandering *aşık* (minstrels). Travellers may encounter tales of Nasreddin Hoca, a semi-legendary quasi-holy man noted for his quirky humour and left-of-centre 'wisdom'.

Yaşar Kemal was the first Turkish novelist to win international attention, writing gritty novels of rural life. His *Memed, My Hawk*, a tale of impoverished Anatolian villagers, won him nomination for the Nobel Prize in Literature.

Panoramic Photographs of Turkey, by noted film director Nuri Bilge Ceylan, is a limited-edition book of stunningly beautiful mages of Turkish landscapes and cityscapes.

One of Turkey's biggest cultural exports in recent years has been *Muhteşem Yüzyıl* (literally 'Magnificent Century'), a sumptuous TV series detailing the life and loves of sultan Süleyman the Magnificent, which has attracted an enormous audience in Turkey and elsewhere.

ORHAN PAMUK: NOBEL LAUREATE

The biggest name in Turkish literature is Orhan Pamuk. Long feted in Turkey, Pamuk has built a worldwide audience since first being translated in the 1990s. He is an inventive prose stylist, creating elaborate plots and finely sketched characters while dealing with the issues confronting contemporary Turkey.

His *Black Book* is an existential whodunit told through a series of newspaper columns, while *My Name is Red* is a 16th-century murder mystery that also philosophises on conceptions of art. In his nonfiction *İstanbul: Memories and the City,* Pamuk ruminates on his complex relationship with the beguiling city. *Cevdet Bey and His Sons,* one of his earliest works, was translated into English for the first time in 2014.

His 2008 novel, *The Museum of Innocence,* details an affair between wealthy Kemal and shop girl Füsun in İstanbul. In 2012 Pamuk opened a museum (p103) in İstanbul based on that in the novel and displaying the ephemera of everyday life in the mid-20th century. His 2015 novel *A Strangeness in My Mind* again returned to the city to track the life of an İstanbul seller of *boza* (drink made from water, sugar and fermented grain) over four decades and illustrates Pamuk's uncanny ability to evoke the ambience of modern Turkey.

Pamuk was awarded the Nobel Prize in Literature in 2006, becoming the first Turk to have won a Nobel Prize.

Irfan Orga's autobiographical *Portrait of a Turkish Family,* set during the late Ottoman/early Republican era, describes the collapse of his well-to-do İstanbullu family. In *The Caravan Moves On* Orga offers a glimpse of rural life in the 1950s as he travels with nomads in the Taurus Mountains.

Recently, the prolific Turkish-American writer and academic Elif Şafak has attracted an international following. Her controversial and acclaimed *The Bastard of Istanbul* centres on the Armenian tragedy while *The Forty Rules of Love* retells the story of Rumi and Shams of Tabriz. Both were bestsellers in Turkey. Most of her works, including her 2019 novel *10 Minutes 38 Seconds in this Strange World,* deal with issues confronting modern Turkey.

Ayşe Kulin has a huge following and her novels have been translated widely. *Last Train to İstanbul* is her novel of Turkish diplomats' attempts to save Jewish families from the Nazis, while *Farewell* is set during the era of Allied occupation after WWI.

Hakan Günday is one of the rising stars of Turkey's literary scene. His 2013 novel *More* is an unflinching look at the refugee crisis and human trafficking.

One of the giants of Turkish literature was Evliya Çelebi, who travelled the Ottoman realm for 40 years and produced a 10-volume travelogue from 1630. A recent edition, *An Ottoman Traveller,* presents a selection of his quirky observations.

Music

Even in the era of YouTube and pervasive Western cultural influences, Turkish musical traditions and styles have remained strong and homegrown stars continue to emerge.

Pop, Rock, Experimental

You'll hear Turkish pop everywhere: in taxis, bars and long-distance buses. With its skittish rhythms and strident vocals, it's undeniably energetic and distinctive.

Sezen Aksu is lauded as the queen of Turkish pop music, releasing a string of albums in diverse styles since the 1970s. However, it is Tarkan, the pretty-boy pop star, who has achieved most international recognition. His 1994 album, *A-acayıpsın,* sold mightily in Turkey and Europe, establishing him as Turkey's biggest-selling pop sensation. 'Şımarık', released in 1999, became his first European number one. He continues to release albums and his metrosexual hip-swivelling ensures he remains a household name in Turkey.

Burhan Öçal is one of the country's finest percussionists. His seminal *New Dream* is a funky take on classical Turkish music, and his Trakya All-Stars albums are investigations of the music of his native Thrace.

Mercan Dede has released a string of albums incorporating traditional instruments and electronic beats. In a similar vein, BaBa ZuLa create a fusion of dub, *saz* (Turkish lute) and pop – accompanied by live belly dancing.

Notable rock bands include Duman and Mor ve Ötesi. maNga play an intriguing mix of metal, rock and Anatolian folk. Their 2012 album *e-akustik* is worth seeking out.

Rap is becoming increasingly popular in the country, with artists often motivated by their unhappiness with the current political and social state of the country. A good example is 2019's 'Susamam (I Can't Stay Silent)', a 15-minute song collaboration by 19 Turkish rap artists including Şanışer, Fuat, Ados, Hayki, Server Uraz, Beta, Tahribad-ı İsyan, Sokrat St, Ozbi, Deniz Tekin, Sehabe, Yeis Sensura, Aspova, Defkhan, Aga B, Mirac, Mert Şenel and Kamufle. Released on YouTube, it received more than 25 million views and more than a million likes in the first week of its release.

Folk

Turkish folk music includes various subgenres that may be indistinguishable to unschooled ears. Ensembles consist of *saz* (a traditional stringed instrument, similar to a lute) accompanied by various drums and flutes. Arrangements include plaintive vocals and swelling choruses. Names to look out for include female Kurdish singers Aynur Doğan and the ululating Rojin, whose hit 'Hejaye' has an addictive, singalong chorus.

Fasıl is a lightweight version of Ottoman classical. This is the music you hear at *meyhanes* (taverns), usually played by gypsies. This skittish music is played with clarinet, *kanun* (zither), *darbuka* (a drum shaped like an hourglass), *ud* (Arabic lute) and violin.

Cinema

The Turkish film industry itself came of age in the 1960s and '70s, when films with a political edge were being made alongside innumerable lightweight Bollywood-style movies, labelled *Yeşilçam* movies. During the 1980s, the film industry went into decline as TV siphoned off audiences, but during the 1990s Turkish cinema re-emerged.

Yılmaz Güney was the first Turkish filmmaker to attract international attention. Joint winner of the best film award at Cannes in 1982, his film *Yol* explored the dilemmas of men on weekend-release from prison,

> The biggest cinema event in the Turkish calendar, the International Antalya Film Festival (www.antalyaff.com/en), also known as the Altın Portakal (Golden Orange) Film Festival, brings together film industry figures, glitterati and a range of Turkish and international films for one week towards the end of each year.

A CINEMA AUTEUR IN ANATOLIA

Internationally, Nuri Bilge Ceylan has become the most widely recognised Turkish director. Since emerging in 2002 with *Uzak* (Distant), a meditation on the lives of migrants in Turkey, he has been a consistent favourite at international film festivals. *Uzak* won the Grand Prix at Cannes in 2003; he also won Best Director at Cannes in 2008 for *Üç Maymun* (Three Monkeys).

His 2011 release, *Once Upon a Time in Anatolia*, with brooding landscape shots and quirky dialogue, is an intriguing all-night search for a corpse in the Turkish backwoods. In 2014 he won the Palme d'Or at the Cannes Film Festival with *Winter Sleep*. His most recent film is *The Wild Pear Tree* (2018), which follows a would-be writer as he returns to the rural village near Çanakkale where he grew up.

a tragic tale that Turks were forbidden to watch until 2000. Güney's uncompromising stance led to confrontations with authorities and several stints in prison. He died in exile in France in 1984.

Turkish directors have comedic flair, too. Yılmaz Erdoğan's *Vizontele* is a wry look at the arrival of the first TV in Hakkari, a remote town in the southeast. *Düğün Dernek* is similarly quirky and entertaining. Ferzan Özpetek received international acclaim for *Hamam* (Turkish Bath), which follows a Turk living in Italy who reluctantly travels to İstanbul after he inherits a hamam.

Fatih Akin captured the spotlight after winning the Golden Bear award at the 2004 Berlin Film Festival with *Duvara Karşı* (Head On), a gripping telling of Turkish immigrant life in Germany. He followed this with *Edge of Heaven,* again pondering the Turkish experience in Germany. In 2010 Semih Kaplanoğlu won the Golden Bear award with *Bal* (Honey), a coming-of-age tale in the Black Sea region; while Reha Erdem's *Jîn* is an intriguing allegory.

In 2015 Turkish-French director Deniz Gamze Ergüven caused quite a stir with her critically acclaimed and controversial debut film *Mustang,* which tells the story of five sisters rebelling against their family's conservatism. The film went on to be nominated for the Academy Award for Best Foreign Language Film.

Visual Arts

Turkey does not have a long tradition of painting or portraiture. Turks channelled their artistic talents into textile- and carpet-making, as well as *ebru* (paper marbling), calligraphy and ceramics. İznik became a centre for tile production from the 16th century. The exuberant tiles that adorn İstanbul's Blue Mosque and other Ottoman-era mosques hail from İznik. You'll find examples of *ebru*, calligraphy and ceramics in bazaars across Turkey.

İstanbul is the place to see what modern Turkish artists are up to: head to İstanbul Modern (p92), the Pera Museum (p103), ARTER (p92), and SALT Beyoğlu (p92) and the Akbank Art Centre (p120) to see well-curated exhibitions.

Ara Güler (1928–2018) was one of Turkey's most respected photographers. For almost 60 years he has documented Turkish life; his book *Ara Güler's İstanbul* is a poignant photographic record of the great city.

Dance

Turkey boasts a range of folk dances, ranging from the frenetic to the hypnotic, and Turks tend to be enthusiastic and unselfconscious dancers, swivelling hips and shaking shoulders in ways entirely different from Western dance styles.

Folk dance can be divided into several broad categories. Originally a dance of central Anatolia, the *halay* is led by a dancer waving a handkerchief, and can be seen especially at weddings and in *meyhanes* when everyone has downed plenty of rakı. The *horon,* from the Black Sea region, is most eye catching – it involves plenty of Cossack-style kicking.

The *sema* (dervish ceremony) of the whirling dervishes is not unique to Turkey, but it's here that you are most likely to see it performed.

The Peoples of Turkey

Turkey has a population of almost 84 million, the great majority of whom are Muslim and Turkish. Kurds form the largest minority, but there is an assortment of other groups – both Muslim and non-Muslim – leading some to say Turkey is comprised of 40 nations. Whether Muslim or Christian, Turkish, Kurdish or otherwise, the peoples of Turkey tend to be family-focused, easy going, hospitable, gregarious and welcoming.

Turks

The first mentions of the Turks were in medieval Chinese sources, which record them as the Tujue in 6th-century Mongolia. The modern Turks descended from Central Asian tribes that moved westward through Eurasia over 1000 years ago. As such the Turks retain cultural links with various peoples through southern Russia, Azerbaijan, Iran, the nations of Central Asia and western China.

As they moved westward Turkic groups encountered the Persians and converted to Islam. The Seljuks established the Middle East's first Turkic empire. The Seljuks' defeat of the Byzantines in 1071 opened up Anatolia to wandering Turkish groups, accelerating the westward drift of the Turks. Over succeeding centuries, Anatolia became the core of the Ottoman Empire and of the modern Turkish Republic. During the Ottoman centuries, Turkish rule extended into southeast Europe so today there are people of Turkish descent in Cyprus, Iraq, Macedonia, Greece, Bulgaria and Ukraine.

Linguistic connections with peoples in Central Asia and the Balkans means that Turks can merrily chat to locals all the way from Novi Pazar in Serbia to Kashgar in China. Turkish is one of the Turkic languages, a family of languages spoken by over 150 million people across Eurasia.

Various (not exactly academically rigorous) theories state that the Turks are descendants of Japheth, the grandson of Noah. The Ottomans themselves claimed that the founder of the Ottoman dynasty, Osman I, could trace his genealogy back through 52 generations to Noah.

Kurds

Kurds have lived for millennia in the mountains where the modern borders of Turkey, Iran, Iraq and Syria meet. Turkey's Kurdish minority is estimated at over 15 million people. Sparsely populated southeastern

IN THE FAMILY WAY

Turks retain a strong sense of family and community. One endearing habit is to use familial titles to embrace friends, acquaintances and even strangers. A teacher may address his student as çocuğum (my child); passers-by call elderly men in the street amca (uncle); and elderly women are comfortable being called teyze (auntie) by strangers.

Males and females of all ages address older men and women as abi (older brother) and abla (older sister), which is charming in its simplicity. It's also common for children to call elder male family friends dede (grandfather).

These terms are a sign of respect but also of inclusiveness. Perhaps this intimacy explains how the sense of community persists amid the tower blocks of sprawling cities, where most Turks now live.

Anatolia is home to perhaps eight million Kurds, while seven million more live elsewhere in the country, largely integrated into mainstream Turkish society. The majority of Turkish Kurds are Sunni Muslims.

Despite having lived side by side with Turks for centuries, the Kurds retain a distinct culture and folklore and speak a language related to Persian. Some Kurds claim descent from the Medes of ancient Persia. The Kurds have their own foundation myth which is associated with Nevruz, the Persian New Year (21 March).

The short documentary *Mountain of Servants* by Daniel Lombroso takes a look at how the Mardin region's dwindling community of Syriac Christians attempt to keep their heritage alive.

The struggle between Kurds and Turks has been very well documented. Kurds fought alongside the Turks during the battle for independence in the 1920s, but they were not guaranteed rights as a minority under the 1923 Treaty of Lausanne. The Turkish state was decreed to be homogeneous – inhabited solely by Turks – hence the Kurds were denied a cultural existence. After the fragmentation, along ethnic lines, of the Ottoman Empire, such an approach may have seemed prudent, but as the Kurds were so numerous problems swiftly arose.

Until the start of the 21st century, the Turkish government refused to recognise the existence of the Kurds, insisting they were 'Mountain Turks'. Even today the census form and identity cards do not allow anyone to identify as Kurdish. However, this lack of recognition has begun to be addressed in recent years and there are now Kurdish newspapers, books and media outlets, and the Kurdish language is taught in some schools.

SEPARATISM OR THE 'BROTHERHOOD' OF PEOPLES?

In 1978 Abdullah Öcalan formed the Kurdistan Workers Party (PKK), which became the most enduring – and violent – Kurdish organisation that Turkey had seen. The PKK remains outlawed. Many Kurds, while not necessarily supporting the demands of the PKK for a separate Kurdish state, wanted to be able to read newspapers in their own language, teach their children their language and watch Kurdish TV. The Turkish government reacted to the PKK's violent tactics and territorial demands by branding calls for Kurdish rights as 'separatism'. Strife escalated until much of southeastern Anatolia was in a permanent state of emergency. After 15 years of fighting and suffering and the deaths of over 30,000 people, Öcalan was captured in Kenya in 1999.

In the early 2000s, following Öcalan's arrest, an increasingly reasoned approach by both the military and government went some way towards making progress on the 'Kurdish question'. In 2002 the Turkish government approved broadcasts in Kurdish and gave the go-ahead for Kurdish to be taught in language schools, and emergency rule was lifted in the southeast. The government's 2009 'Kurdish opening' was an attempt to address the social and political roots of the issue.The creation of TRT6, a government-funded Kurdish-language TV channel, was hailed as a positive initiative. In early 2013 the government entered into negotiations with Öcalan, which resulted in both sides announcing an end to the armed struggle.

But the ceasefire wouldn't hold. By mid-2015, with the war in Syria spilling over Turkey's border, violence between government forces and the PKK erupted again. By the end of the year tit-for-tat skirmishes had descended into drawn-out urban clashes in several cities in eastern Turkey. More than 200,000 people have been displaced by the current fighting, irreparable damage has been caused to historic city centres such as Diyarbakır, and the conflict reverberated through the entirety of Turkey in 2016 with a series of deadly bomb attacks on Ankara, Bursa and İstanbul claimed by TAK (Kurdistan Freedom Falcons; a PKK splinter group). In the current climate – and especially with the continued detention of Öcalan and politicians Selahattin Demirtaş and Figen Yüksekdağ, former leaders of the Peoples' Democratic Party (HDP) – the hope of finally resolving and ending the 40-year conflict seems a long way off.

ISLAM IN TURKEY

For many travellers, Turkey is their first experience of Islam. While it may seem 'foreign', Islam actually shares much with Christianity and Judaism. Like Christians, Muslims believe that Allah (God) created the world, pretty much according to the biblical account. They also revere Adam, Noah, Abraham, Moses and Jesus as prophets, although they don't believe Jesus was divine. Muslims call Jews and Christians 'People of the Book', meaning those with a revealed religion (in the Torah and Bible) that preceded Islam.

Where Islam differs from Christianity and Judaism is in the belief that Islam is the 'perfection' of these earlier traditions. Although Moses and Jesus were prophets, Mohammed was the greatest and last, to whom Allah communicated his final revelation.

Islam has diversified into many versions over the centuries; however, the five 'pillars' of Islam – the profession of faith, daily prayers, alms giving, the fasting month of Ramazan, pilgrimage to Mecca – are shared by the entire Muslim community.

Islam is the most widely held belief in Turkey, however many Turks take a relaxed approach to religious duties and practices. Fasting during Ramazan is widespread and Islam's holy days and festivals are observed, but for many Turks Islamic holidays are the only times they'll visit a mosque. Turkish Muslims have also absorbed and adapted other traditions over the years, so it's not uncommon to see Muslims praying at Greek Orthodox shrines, while the Alevis, a heterodox Muslim minority, have developed a tradition combining elements of Anatolian folklore, Sufism and Shia Islam.

Muslim Minorities

Turkey is home to several other Muslim minorities, both indigenous and recent arrivals, most of whom are regarded as Turks, but who nonetheless retain aspects of their culture and native tongue.

Laz & Hemşin

The Black Sea region is home to the Laz and Hemşin peoples, two of the largest Muslim minorities after the Kurds.

The Laz mainly inhabit the valleys between Trabzon and Rize. East of Trabzon you can't miss the women in their maroon-striped shawls. Laz men were once among the most feared of Turkish warriors. Once Christian but now Muslim, the Laz are a Caucasian people speaking a language related to Georgian. They are renowned for their sense of humour and business acumen.

Like the Laz, the Hemşin were originally Christian. They mainly come from the far-eastern end of the Black Sea coast, although perhaps no more than 15,000 still live there; most have migrated to the cities where they earn a living as bread and pastry cooks. In and around Ayder, Hemşin women are easily identified by their leopard-print scarves coiled into elaborate headdresses.

Others

The last link to the wandering Turkic groups who arrived in Anatolia in the 11th century, the Yörük maintain a nomadic lifestyle around the Taurus Mountains. Named from the verb *yürümek* (to walk), the Yörük move herds of sheep between summer and winter pastures.

In Turkey's far southeast, along the Syrian border, there are communities of Arabic speakers. Throughout Turkey there are also various Muslim groups that arrived from the Caucasus and the Balkans during the later years of the Ottoman Empire. These include Circassians, Abkhazians, Crimean Tatars, Bosnians, and Uighurs from China.

The Turkic Speaking Peoples, edited by Ergün Çağatay and Doğan Kuban, is a monumental doorstop of a volume investigating, in full colour, the traditions and cultures of Turkic groups across Eurasia.

Turkey hosts the largest refugee population in the world with an estimated 4 million refugees living within its borders in 2019 according to the UNHCR. Most are from Syria but there are also substantial communities from Afghanistan and Iraq.

Non-Muslim Groups

The Ottoman Empire was notable for its large Christian and Jewish populations. These have diminished considerably in the last century.

There has been a Jewish presence in Anatolia for over 2000 years. A large influx of Jews arrived in the 16th century, fleeing the Spanish Inquisition. Today most of Turkey's Jews live in İstanbul and İzmir, and a few still speak Ladino, a Judaeo-Spanish language.

Armenians have lived in Anatolia for a very long time; a distinct Armenian people existed by the 4th century, when they became the first nation to collectively convert to Christianity. The Armenians created their own alphabet and established various kingdoms in the borderlands between the Byzantine, Persian and Ottoman empires. Until 1915 there were significant communities throughout Anatolia. The controversy (p573) surrounding the Armenians in the final years of the Ottoman Empire means that relations between Turks and Armenians remain predominantly sour. About 70,000 Armenians still live in Turkey, mainly in İstanbul and in pockets in Anatolia, particularly Diyarbakır.

Turkish-Armenian relations are tense, but there are occasionally signs of rapprochement. In recent times Armenian churches on Akdamar Island and in Diyarbakır have been refurbished. There have been services held in the refurbished churches (annually on Akdamar) attracting Armenian worshippers from across the border.

The Greeks are Turkey's other significant Christian minority. Greek populations once lived throughout the Ottoman realm, but after the population exchanges of the early Republican era and acrimonious events in the 1950s, the Greeks were reduced to a small community in İstanbul.

Rugged southeastern Anatolia is also home to ancient Christian communities. These include adherents of the Syriac Orthodox Church, who speak Aramaic and whose historical homeland is Tür Abdin, east of Mardin. There are also some Chaldean Catholics remaining in Diyarbakır.

Since the 1950s there has been a steady movement of people into urban areas, so today 92% of the population lives in cities. Cities such as İstanbul have turned into pervasive sprawls, their historic hearts encircled by rings of largely unplanned new neighbourhoods.

Landscapes & Wildlife

Turkey has one foot in Europe and another in Asia, its two parts separated by İstanbul's famous Bosphorus Strait, the Sea of Marmara and the Dardanelles. Given this position at the meeting of continents, Turkey boasts a rich environment with flora and fauna ranging from Kangal dogs to purple bougainvillea. Unfortunately, the country faces the unenviable challenge of balancing environmental management with rapid economic growth and urbanisation, and to date it's done a sloppy job.

The Land

Boasting 7200km of coastline, snow-capped mountains, rolling steppes, vast lakes and broad rivers, Turkey is stupendously diverse. Eastern Thrace (European Turkey) makes up a mere 3% of its 769,632 sq km land area; the remaining 97% is Anatolia (Asian Turkey).

The country's western edge is the Aegean coast, lined with coves and beaches and the Aegean islands, most belonging to Greece and within a few kilometres of mainland Turkey. Inland, western Anatolia has the vast Lake District and Uludağ (Great Mountain, 2543m), one of over 50 Turkish peaks above 2000m.

The Mediterranean coast is backed by the jagged Taurus Mountains. East of Antalya, it opens up into a fertile plain before the mountains close in again after Alanya.

Central Anatolia consists of a vast high plateau of rolling steppes, broken by mountain ranges and Cappadocia's fantastical valleys of fairy chimneys (rock formations). Like the Mediterranean, the Black Sea is often hemmed in by mountains, and the coastline is frequently rugged and vertiginous. At the eastern end, Mt Kaçkar (Kaçkar Dağı; 3937m) is the highest point in the Kaçkar range, where peaks and glaciers ring mountain lakes and *yaylalar* (mountain pastures).

Mountainous and somewhat forbidding, the rest of northeastern Anatolia is also wildly beautiful, from Yusufeli's valleys via the steppes around Kars to snow-capped Mt Ararat (Ağrı Dağı; 5137m), dominating the area bordering Iran, Armenia and Azerbaijan. Southeastern Anatolia offers windswept rolling steppe, jagged outcrops of rock, and the extraordinary alkaline, mountain-ringed Lake Van (Van Gölü).

Wildlife

Birds

Some 400 species of bird are found in Turkey, with about 250 of these passing through on migration from Africa to Europe. Spring and autumn are particularly good times to see the feathered commuters. Eager birdwatchers flock here to spot wallcreepers, masked shrike and Rüppell's warbler, and to tick the elusive Caspian snowcock off their list. There are several *kuş cennetleri* (bird sanctuaries) dotted about the country.

Endangered Species

Anatolia's lions, beavers and Caspian tigers are extinct, and its lynx, striped hyena and Anatolian leopard have all but disappeared.

Kangal dogs were originally bred to protect sheep from wolves and bears on mountain pastures. People wandering off the beaten track, especially in eastern Turkey, are sometimes startled by these huge, yellow-coated, black-headed animals, with optional spiked collar to protect against wolves. Their mongrel descendants live on Turkey's streets.

A leopard was shot in Diyarbakır province in 2013, following a dramatic clifftop battle with a shepherd; the only previous sightings were in Siirt province in 2010 and outside Beypazarı in 1974. The Caucasian (Persian) leopard that has traditionally been found here is also close to extinction. Another feline, the beautiful, pure-white Van cat, often with one blue and one amber eye, has come close to becoming endangered in its native Turkey. The Anatolian wild sheep, unique to the Konya region, has protected status.

In good news, a breeding program at Birecik's semi-wild colony of northern bald ibis has managed to raise population numbers of this critically endangered species and released 241 birds into the wild in 2018.

Rare loggerhead turtles nest on various Mediterranean beaches, including Anamur, Patara, İztuzu Beach at Dalyan, and the Göksu Delta. A few rare Mediterranean monk seals live around Foça, but you would be lucky to see them and the International Union for Conservation of Nature has listed the species as critically endangered. Greenpeace has criticised Turkey for not following international fishing quotas relating to Mediterranean bluefin tuna, which is facing extinction.

Turkey's 58 'nature monuments' are mostly protected trees, including 1500- to 2000-year-old cedars in Finike, southwest of Antalya; a 1000-year-old plane tree in İstanbul; and a 700-year-old juniper at 2100m near Gümüşhane, south of Trabzon.

Plants

Turkey is one of the world's most biodiverse temperate-zone countries. Not only does its fertile soil produce an incredible range of fruit and vegetables, it is blessed with an exceptionally rich flora: over 9000 species, over a third endemic and many found nowhere else on earth.

Common trees and plants are pine, cypress, myrtle, laurel, rosemary, lavender, thyme and, on the coast, purple bougainvillea, introduced from South America. Isparta is one of the world's leading producers of attar of roses, a valuable oil extracted from rose petals and used in perfumes and cosmetics.

National Parks & Reserves

In recent years, thanks to EU aspirations, Turkey has stepped up its environmental protection practices. It has 14 Ramsar sites (wetlands of international importance) and is a member of Cites, which covers international trade of endangered species. There are now almost 100 areas designated as *milli parkı* (national parks), nature reserves and nature parks, where the environment is supposedly protected, and hunting controlled. Sometimes the regulations are carefully enforced, but in other cases problems such as litter-dropping picnickers persist.

The action of wind and water on *tuff* (rock composed of compressed volcanic ash, thrown for miles around by prehistoric eruptions) created Cappadocia's fairy chimneys. As traditional agriculture declines, the pigeon houses dotting the rock formations, once used to harvest the birds' droppings for use as fertiliser, are increasingly disused.

Tourism is not well developed in the national parks, which are rarely well set up with facilities. It is not the norm for footpaths to be clearly marked, and camping spots are often unavailable. Most of the well-frequented national parks are as popular for their historic monuments as they are for the surrounding natural environment.

Environmental Issues

Lack of finances and poor education have placed the environment a long way down Turkey's list of priorities, and environmental laws are often inadequately enforced. But there are glimmers of improvement, largely due to the country endeavouring to comply with EU environmental legislation. Turkey also ratified the Kyoto protocol in 2009.

Nuclear Turkey

The government's construction of a nuclear power plant to be opened by 2023 is of concern to environmentalists, with the European Parliament calling on Turkey to halt construction due to its concerns that neighbours Greece and Cyprus were not consulted about the project and its environmental and safety impact. Despite local protests, the initial

EARTHQUAKE DANGER

Turkey lies on at least three active earthquake fault lines: the North Anatolian, the East Anatolian and the Aegean. Most of Turkey lies south of the North Anatolian fault line, which runs roughly parallel with the Black Sea coast. As the Arabian and African plates to the south push northward, the Anatolian plate is shoved into the Eurasian plate and squeezed west towards Greece.

More than 25 major earthquakes, measuring up to 7.8 on the Richter scale, have been recorded since 1939. A 7.6-magnitude quake in 1999 hit İzmit (Kocaeli) and Adapazarı (Sakarya) in northwestern Anatolia, killing more than 18,000. A 7.1-magnitude earthquake shook Van in 2011, killing more than 600, injuring over 4000 and damaging over 11,000 buildings, with thousands left homeless.

If a major quake struck İstanbul, much of the city would be devastated, due to unlicensed, jerry-built construction. When a 5.8-magnitude earthquake hit in 2019, no deaths or major damage were caused, but it highlighted how ill-prepared the city was, with many locals hitting the phone and social networking sites rather than evacuating their houses.

construction phase for the site of the Russian-built Akkuyu plant, which is on the eastern Mediterranean coast, has begun and the project has attracted media attention due to reports that its concrete foundations have been cracking and may therefore be unsafe. The country's seismic vulnerabilities increase the risk posed by nuclear reactors.

The government says the plants will aid economic growth and and reduce dependency on natural gas supplies from Russia and Iran.

The Bosphorus

One of the biggest environmental challenges facing Turkey is the threat from maritime traffic along the Bosphorus. The 1936 Montreux Convention decreed that, although Turkey has sovereignty over the strait, it must permit the free passage of shipping through it. At that time, perhaps a few thousand ships a year passed through, but this has risen to over 45,000 vessels annually; around 10% are tankers, which carry over 100 million tonnes of hazardous substances through the strait every year.'

There have already been serious accidents, including the 1979 *Independenta* collision with another vessel, which killed 43 people and spilt and burnt some 95,000 tonnes of oil (around 2½ times the amount spilt by the infamous *Exxon Valdez* in Alaska). In 2018 a historic *yalı* on the Asian shore was extensively damaged when an out-of-control Maltese-flagged tanker crashed into it. Fortunately, no-one was injured.

Following the Gulf of Mexico disaster in 2010, the Turkish government renewed its efforts to find alternative routes for oil transportation. Its ambitious plans include a US$12 billion canal to divert tankers, which would see the creation of two new cities by the Bosphorus. There is already an 1800km-long pipeline between Baku, Azerbaijan and the Turkish eastern Mediterranean port of Ceyhan, and construction of a new 1000km pipeline between Kirkuk in Iraq and Ceyhan to replace a former pipeline was announced in 2019.

Construction

Rampant development is taking a terrible toll on the environment. Mega-construction projects, including İstanbul's Yavuz Sultan Selim Bridge and the ongoing construction of the city's third airport, the first stage of which opened in 2019, are contributing to mass deforestation in the Bosphorus region. On the Aegean and Mediterranean coasts, spots such as Kuşadası and Marmaris (once pleasant fishing villages) have been overwhelmed by urban sprawl and are in danger of losing all appeal.

Despite its environmental shortcomings, Turkey is doing well at beach cleanliness, with 463 beaches and 22 marinas qualifying for Blue Flag status; see www.blueflag.org.

Dams

Short of water and electricity, Turkey is one of the world's major builders of dams. There are already more than 600 dams and many more on the way, with controversy surrounding new and proposed developments. The gigantic Southeastern Anatolia Project, known as GAP, is one of Turkey's major construction efforts. Harnessing the headwaters of the Tigris and Euphrates Rivers, it's creating a potential political time bomb, causing friction with the arid countries downstream that also depend on this water. Iraq, Syria and Georgia have all protested, and a UN report said the project is in danger of violating human rights.

Inside Turkey itself, one of the most controversial components of the GAP project is the İlisu Dam, which was scheduled to submerge the historic town of Hasankeyf in 2020. Due to the project plans, the town featured on the World Monuments Watch list of the planet's 100 most endangered sites in 2008 (not the first or last time Turkey has appeared on the list). Despite both local and international opposition, work towards the dam completion continues to steamroll ahead. Although the town's major monuments – relics of a time it was a Silk Road commercial centre on the border of Anatolia and Mesopotamia – are now hidden under a layer of scaffolding, readying to be moved to higher ground, it's estimated that 80% of the town's ruins will vanish under the dam water, along with their atmospheric setting on the Tigris river and dozens of other villages. Up to 80,000 people will be displaced, many of them Kurds and minority groups.

In northeast Anatolia a separate dam project harnessing the Çorah River has already changed the face of the region's valley landscapes and signalled the end of the river's white-water rafting activities. The opening of the project's Yusefeli Dam will see the current town of Yusefeli disappear beneath the water.

The ruins of the world's oldest-known spa settlement, Allianoi, disappeared beneath the waters of the Yortanlı Dam in 2011.

Other Issues

Turkey's environmental shortcomings are vast. Blue recycling bins are an increasingly common sight on the streets of İstanbul, but the government still has a long way to go in terms of educating its citizens and businesses.

The country's once-rich fishing waterways are in rapid decline due to commercial overfishing and water pollution. A recent seasonal fishing ban enforced during the summer months is seen by many as shutting the gate after the horse has bolted. Despite the potential for renewable energy in Turkey, multiple new coal-fired power plants are on the proposal table to keep up with the country's expanding development needs.

Issues for Turkey to address as part of its bid to join the EU include water treatment, waste-water disposal, food safety, soil erosion, deforestation, degradation of biodiversity, air quality, industrial pollution control and risk management, climate change and nature protection.

The documentary *Polluting Paradise* is a poignant comment on Turkey's environmental issues, telling the heartbreaking story of director Fatih Akın's father's village, which was wrecked by a waste landfill site.

Southwest Turkey, especially around Köyceğiz, is one of the last remaining sources of *Liquidambar orientalis* (frankincense trees). Their resin, once used by the Egyptians in embalming, is exported for use in perfume and incense. The world's last remaining populations of *Phoenix theophrastii* (Datça palm) grow in southwest Turkey and Crete.

İstanbul Airport (p610)

Survival Guide

Directory A–Z

Accessible Travel

Improvements are being made but Turkey is a challenging destination for disabled (*özürlü*) travellers. Although ramps have been installed in many public buildings (including at museums and other historic sites), wide doorways and properly equipped toilets remain rare, as are Braille and audio information at sights. Crossing most streets is particularly challenging as everyone does so at their peril.

Airlines and the top hotels and resorts have some provision for wheelchair (*tekerlekli sandalye*) access, and ramps are beginning to appear in some smaller hotels (though they're often ridiculously steep). Dropped kerb edges are being introduced to cities, especially in western Turkey – in places such as Edirne, Bursa and İzmir they seem to have been sensibly designed. Selçuk, Bodrum and Fethiye have been identified as relatively user-friendly towns for people with mobility issues because their pavements and roads are fairly level.

In İstanbul, the tram, metro, funicular railways and catamaran ferries are the most wheelchair-accessible forms of public transport. İstanbul Deniz Otobüsleri's (İDO) Sea Bus catamaran ferries, which cross the Sea of Marmara and head up the Bosphorus from İstanbul, are generally accessible. Ankara and İzmir's metros are also accessible.

The YHT (high-speed) trains between İstanbul, Eskişehir, Konya and Ankara are fully accessible with disabled-access lifts to platforms, access on to trains and on-board toilets. However, many of the older trains that service the rest of the country are still boarded by steps. Urban and intercity buses often accommodate wheelchairs, but fully accessible vehicles are uncommon.

Turkish Airlines offers a 20% discount on most domestic flights, and 25% on international fares, to travellers with minimum 40% disability, and in some cases to their companions. The bigger bus and ferry companies also often offer discounts.

Businesses and resources serving travellers with disabilities include the following:

Accessible Turkey (www.accessibleturkey.org) Wide range of package tours and day tours for wheelchair users plus hotel booking and transport services.

Hotel Rolli (www.hotel-rolli.de) Resort in Anamur, specifically designed for mobility-impaired people.

Mephisto Voyage (www.mephistovoyage.com) Offers hiking tours for wheelchair users in the Cappadocia and Taurus Mountain regions utilising the Joëlette wheelchair system.

Turkey Accessible Travel (www.turkeyaccessibletravel.com) Wheelchair-accessible airport transfers, tours and transport services in İstanbul and the İzmir (Selçuk, Kuşadası, Ephesus) area.

PRACTICALITIES

Newspapers *Hürriyet Daily News* (www.hurriyetdailynews.com) and *Daily Sabah* (www.sabahenglish.com) are English-language newspapers.

Magazines *Cornucopia* (www.cornucopia.net) is a glossy magazine in English about Turkey published twice yearly; Turkish Airlines' in-flight monthly, *Skylife* (www.skylife.com/en), is also worth a read.

Radio TRT broadcasts news daily, in languages including English, on radio and at www.trtworld.com.

TV Digiturk (www.digiturk.com.tr) offers numerous Turkish and international satellite TV channels.

Weights & Measures Turkey uses the metric system.

THE ART OF BARGAINING

Traditionally, when customers enter a Turkish shop to make a significant purchase, they're offered a comfortable seat and a drink (çay, coffee or a soft drink). There is some general chit-chat, then a discussion of the shop's goods, then of the customer's tastes, preferences and requirements. Finally, a number of items are displayed for the customer's inspection.

The customer asks the price; the shop owner gives it. The customer looks doubtful and makes a counter-offer 25% to 50% lower. This procedure goes back and forth several times before a price acceptable to both parties is arrived at. It's considered bad form to haggle over a price, come to an agreement and then change your mind.

If you can't agree on a price, it's perfectly acceptable to say goodbye and walk out of the shop. In fact, walking out is one of the best ways to test the authenticity of the last offer. If shopkeepers know you can find the item elsewhere for less, they'll probably call after you and drop their price. Even if they don't stop you, there's nothing to prevent you from returning later and buying the item for what they quoted.

To bargain effectively you must be prepared to take your time and you must know something about the items in question, including their market price. The best way to learn is to look at similar goods in several shops, asking prices but not making counter-offers. Always stay good-humoured and polite when you are bargaining – if you do this the shopkeeper will too. When bargaining, you can often get a discount by offering to buy several items at once, by paying in a strong major currency, or by paying in cash. Note that if you enter a shop with a tour guide you will always have to pay more for an item as the shopkeeper has to count the guide's commission fee into the price.

If you don't have sufficient time to shop around, follow the age-old rule: find something you like at a price you're willing to pay, buy it, enjoy it, and don't worry about whether or not you received the world's lowest price.

In general, you shouldn't bargain in food shops, restaurants or over public transport costs. Outside tourist areas, hotels may expect to 'negotiate' the room price with you. In tourist areas hotel owners are usually fairly clear about their prices, although if you're travelling in winter or staying a long time, it's worth asking about *indirim* (discounts).

Download Lonely Planet's free Accessible Travel guide from http://lptravel.to/AccessibleTravel.

Customs Regulations

Imports

Jewellery and items valued over US$15,000 should be declared, to ensure you can take them out when you leave. Goods including the following can be imported duty-free:

➡ 200 cigarettes

➡ 200g of tobacco

➡ 1kg each of coffee, instant coffee, chocolate and sugar products

➡ 500g of tea

➡ 1L of alcohol exceeding 22% volume, 2L of alcoholic beverages max 22% volume

➡ Five bottles of perfume (max 120ml each)

➡ Personal electronic devices, but only one of each type

➡ Unlimited currency

➡ Souvenirs/gifts worth up to €300 (€145 if aged under 15)

Exports

➡ Buying and exporting genuine antiquities is illegal.

➡ Carpet shops should be able to provide a form certifying that your purchase is not an antiquity.

➡ Ask for advice from vendors you buy from.

➡ Keep receipts and paperwork.

Discount Cards

The Ministry of Culture and Tourism offers various discount cards covering museums and sights. Visit https://muze.gov.tr/MuseumPass for more information.

Museum Pass: İstanbul (p140) The five-day card (₺220) offers a good saving on entry to the city's major sights including Topkapı Palace, and allows holders to skip admission queues.

Museum Pass: Cappadocia The three-day card (₺130) covers the region's major sights including Göreme Open-Air Museum.

Museum Pass: The Aegean The seven-day card (₺220) covers 60 museums and sights from İzmir to Fethiye, including Ephesus and Pergamum.

Museum Pass: The Mediterranean The seven-day card (₺220) covers 50 museums and sights east from Fethiye to Adana, including Xanthos, Patara and Aspendos.

Museum Pass: Turkey The 15-day card (₺375) covers some 300 museums and sights nationwide, from Topkapı Palace to Ani.

İstanbulkart (p143) The rechargeable travel card offers substantial savings on İstanbul's public transport.

The following offer discounts on accommodation, eating, entertainment, transport and tours. They are available in Turkey but easier to get in your home country.

International Student Identity Card (www.isic.org)

International Youth Travel Card (www.isic.org)

International Teacher Identity Card (www.isic.org)

Electricity

➡ Electrical current is 230V AC, 50Hz.

➡ You can buy plug adaptors at most electrical shops.

➡ A universal AC adaptor is also a good investment.

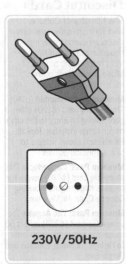

230V/50Hz

Embassies & Consulates

➡ Many embassies and consulates in Turkey only open for consular issues (visas, lost passports) for a set number of hours per day. Many also require you to have made an appointment beforehand.

➡ Embassies of some Muslim countries may open Sunday to Thursday.

➡ To ask the way to an embassy, say: '[Country] *büyükelçiliği nerede?*'.

➡ The embassies listed below are all in Ankara. There are consulates in other Turkish cities.

Australian Embassy (Avustralya Büyükelçiliği; ☑for initial appointment 0312-459 9500; www.turkey.embassy.gov.au; 7th fl, MNG Bldg, Uğur Mumcu Caddesi 88, Gaziosmanpaşa; ☺by appointment only 8.30am-4.45pm Mon-Fri)

Azerbaijani Embassy (Azerbaycan Büyükelçiliği; ☑0312-491 1681; http://ankara.mfa.gov.az; Diplomatik Site, Bakü Sokak 1, Oran; ☺9am-noon & 4-5pm Mon-Fri)

Bulgarian Embassy (Bulgaristan Büyükelçiliği; ☑0312-467

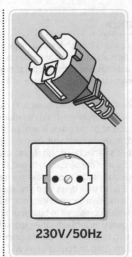

230V/50Hz

2071; www.mfa.bg/embassies/turkey; Atatürk Bulvarı 124, Kavaklıdere; ☺9am-noon Mon-Fri)

Canadian Embassy (Kanada Büyükelçiliği; ☑0312-409 2700; http://turkey.gc.ca; Cinnah Caddesi 58, Çankaya; ☺by appointment only 8.30-11.30am Mon-Fri)

Dutch Embassy (Hollanda Büyükelçiliği; ☑0312-409 1800; www.hollandavesen.nl; Hollanda Caddesi 5, off Turan Güneş Bulvarı; ☺by appointment only 8.30am-4pm Mon-Fri)

French Embassy (Fransa Büyükelçiliği; ☑9-11am only 0312-455 4545; www.ambafrance-tr.org; Paris Caddesi 70, Kavaklıdere; ☺9am-12.45pm Mon-Fri)

Georgian Embassy (Gürcistan Büyükelçiliği; ☑0312-491 8030; www.turkey.mfa.gov.ge; Diplomatik Site, Kılıç Ali Sokak 12, Oran; ☺9am-noon Mon-Fri)

German Embassy (Almanya Büyükelçiliği; ☑0312-455 5100; www.ankara.diplo.de; Atatürk Bulvarı 114, Kavaklıdere; ☺9am-4pm Mon-Thu, 9am-2pm Fri)

Greek Embassy (Yunanistan Büyükelçiliği; ☑0312-448 0647; www.mfa.gr/ankara; Zia Ür Rahman Caddesi 9-11, Gaziosmanpaşa; ☺9am-2pm Mon-Fri)

Iranian Embassy (İran İslam Cumhuriyeti Büyükelçiliği; ☑0312-468 2821; http://iranembassy-tr.ir; Tahran Caddesi 10, Kavaklıdere; ☺8.30am-noon Mon-Fri)

Iraqi Embassy (Irak Büyükelçiliği; ☑0312-468 7421; www.irakkonsoloslugu.net/ankara-buyukeliciligi; Turan Emeksiz Sokak 11, Gaziosmanpaşa; ☺9am-noon Mon-Fri)

Irish Embassy (İrlanda Büyükelçiliği; ☑for initial appointment 0312-459 1000; www.embassyofireland.org.tr; 1st fl, MNG Bldg, Uğur Mumcu Caddesi 88, Gaziosmanpaşa; ☺9am-1pm & 2-5pm Mon-Fri)

New Zealand Embassy (Yeni Zelanda Büyükelçiliği; ☑0312-446 3333; www.nzembassy.com/turkey; Kizkulesi Sokak

11, Gaziosmanpaşa; ⊙8.30am-5pm Mon-Fri)

Russian Embassy (Rusya Büyükçiliği; ☑0312-439 2183; www.turkey.mid.ru; Andrey Karlov Sokağı 5, Çankaya; ⊙by appointment only 9.30am-noon Mon, Wed & Fri)

UK Embassy (Birleşik Krallık Büyükçiliği; ☑0312-455 3344; www.gov.uk/world/ turkey; Şehit Ersan Caddesi 46a, Çankaya; ⊙consular section 9am-noon Mon-Fri)

US Embassy (ABD Büyükçiliği; ☑0312-455 5555; https:// tr.usembassy.gov; Atatürk Bulvarı 110, Kavaklıdere; ⊙by appointment only 9am-4pm Mon-Fri)

Insurance

➡ A travel insurance policy covering theft, loss and medical expenses is recommended.

➡ A huge variety of policies is available; check small print.

➡ Some policies exclude 'dangerous activities', which can include scuba diving, motorcycling and even trekking.

➡ Some policies may not cover you if you travel to regions of the country where your government warns against travel, such as areas near the Syrian border.

➡ If you cancel your trip on the advice of an official warning against travel, your insurer may not cover you.

➡ Look into whether your regular health insurance and motor insurance will cover you in Turkey.

Internet Access

➡ Throughout Turkey, the majority of accommodation options of all standards offer free wi-fi. Note that it can often be slow.

➡ Wi-fi networks are also found at locations from cafes and carpet shops to otogars (bus stations) and ferry terminals.

➡ Some major websites such as Wikipedia are currently banned. While in the country, you currently cannot book Turkish accommodation using www.booking.com due to a ban.

➡ Note that although virtual private networks (VPNs) are officially banned in Turkey, many internet users within the country use them regularly. Some popular VPN apps (many of the free-to-use ones) have been successfully blocked, but more powerful apps continue to work fine.

Internet Cafes

➡ Internet cafe numbers are declining with the proliferation of wi-fi and hand-held devices.

➡ They are typically open from 9am until midnight, and charge around ₺2 an hour (İstanbul ₺3). Many are used only by gamers.

➡ Connection speeds vary, but are generally fast.

➡ Viruses are rife.

➡ English keyboards are few and far between. Nearly all have Turkish keyboards, on which 'ı' occupies the position occupied by 'i' on English keyboards.

➡ On Turkish keyboards, create the @ symbol by holding down the 'q' and ALT keys at the same time.

Language Courses

İstanbul is the most popular place to learn Turkish, though there are also courses in Ankara, İzmir, Antalya and other places. Try to sit in on a class before you commit, as the quality of your experience definitely depends on the teacher and your classmates.

Private tuition is more expensive, but tutors advertise at http://istanbul.craigslist. org. Many books and online resources are available; the books and CDs by David and Asuman Pollard in the 'Teach

Yourself' series are recommended. Schools include the following:

Dilmer (www.dilmer.com) İstanbul.

International House (www. ilsizmir.com) İzmir.

Tömer (http://tomer.ankara. edu.tr) Alanya, Ankara, Antalya, Bursa, İstanbul and İzmir.

Turkish Language Center (www. turkishlanguagecenter.com) İzmir.

Legal Matters

Officially, you need to carry your passport (and, if applicable, a photocopy of your e-visa) with you at all times. Security stops (operated by both the police and military) are frequent throughout the country on the roads. It is also becoming common for foreigners to be targeted for a stop-and-search at otogars in the south of the country.

There are laws against lese-majesty (p604) and buying and smuggling antiquities (p604). Recreational drugs, including cannabis, are illegal. Being caught with cannabis can result in a jail sentence of up to two years (first-time offenders are often fined and given probation). Turkish jails are not places where you want to spend any time, particularly in their current horribly overcrowded state.

If you are arrested in Turkey you have the right to request an interpreter and to contact your country's embassy. The Turkish judicial system grants all defendants the right to legal representation, a trial and appeal.

LGBTIQ+ Travellers

Homosexuality is not a criminal offence in Turkey, and people have been legally permitted to change gender since 1988, but there are no laws protecting LGBTIQ+ people from discrimination, same-sex marriage is not recognised and prejudice remains strong, with sporadic reports of violence towards LGBTIQ+ people.

In recent years, there has been a surge in government authorities cracking down on LGBTIQ+ focused events. İstanbul's Pride Parade has been banned by the authorities since 2015 with marchers facing police action against them. Ankara banned all public LGBTIQ+ events in 2017 and 2018 (the ban was lifted in 2019 but a Pride event at Ankara's Middle East Technical University in May 2019 was stopped by police and 19 marchers were arrested) and in 2019 Pride events in various other Turkish cities were also banned. The LGBTIQ+ dating app Grindr has been banned in Turkey since 2013.

For LGBTIQ+ travellers, discretion is recommended. Same-gender couples will have no problem booking a double room together, though they should avoid the very cheap local hotel end of the market, particularly once away from the main tourist centres. Overt displays of affection in public should be avoided (though the same goes for opposite-gender couples). Despite a growing sense of conservatism that has seen some popular LGBTIQ+ bars close down, İstanbul still has a flourishing gay scene while Ankara and İzmir both have much smaller, but vibrant, scenes.

For more on the challenges facing LGBTIQ+ people in Turkey, visit www.outrightinternational.org/region/turkey.

İstanbul Pride Travel (www.everydayturkeytours.com/gay/) LGBTIQ+ owned İstanbul travel agent. As well as the usual caboodle of tour options, runs private evening tours of İstanbul's LGBTIQ+ nightlife scene.

Kaos GL (www.kaosgl.org) Based in Ankara, this LGBTIQ+ rights organisation publishes a gay-and-lesbian magazine and its website has news and information in English.

Lambdaistanbul (www.lambdaistanbul.org) The Turkish branch of the International Lesbian, Gay, Bisexual, Trans and Intersexual Association.

LGBTI News Turkey (www.lgbtinewsturkey.com) News and links.

Maps

Maps are widely available at tourist offices and bookshops, although quality maps are hard to find. In İstanbul, try the bookshops on İstiklal Caddesi or Yeniçarşı Caddesi in Beyoğlu.

Mep Medya's city and regional maps are recommended, as are its touring maps including the following:

➡ *Türkiye Karayolları Haritası* (1:1,200,000) A sheet map of the whole country

➡ *Adım Adım Türkiye Yol Atlası* (Step by Step Turkey Road Atlas; 1:400,000)

Money

Turkey's currency is the Türk Lirası (Turkish lira; ₺). The lira comes in notes of five, 10, 20, 50, 100 and 200, and coins of one, five, 10, 25 and 50 kuruş and one lira. Lack of small change is a problem; try to keep a supply of coins and small notes for minor payments.

ATMS

ATMs dispense Turkish lira, and occasionally euros and US dollars, to Visa, MasterCard, Cirrus and Maestro card holders. Look for these logos on machines, which are found in most towns. Machines generally offer instructions in foreign languages including English.

It's possible to get around Turkey using only ATMs if you draw out money in the towns to tide you through the villages that don't have them. Also keep some cash in reserve for the inevitable day when the machine throws a wobbly. If your card is swallowed by a stand-alone ATM booth, it may be tricky to get it back. The booths are often run by franchisees rather than by the banks themselves.

Credit Cards

Visa and MasterCard are widely accepted by hotels, shops and restaurants, although often not by pensions and local restaurants outside the main tourist areas. You can also get cash advances on these cards. Amex is less commonly accepted outside top-end establishments. Inform your credit-card provider of your travel plans; otherwise transactions may be stopped, as credit-card fraud does happen in Turkey.

Changing Money

The Turkish lira is weak against Western currencies, and you will probably get a better exchange rate in Turkey than elsewhere. The lira is virtually worthless outside Turkey, so make sure you spend it all before leaving.

US dollars and euros are the easiest currencies to change, although most exchange offices, all post offices (PTTs) and many banks will change other major currencies such as Australian dollars, UK pounds and Japanese yen.

You'll get better rates at exchange offices, which often don't charge commission, and at post offices than at banks. Exchange offices operate in tourist and market areas, with better rates often found in the latter. Plentiful shops and hotels in tourist areas will exchange money.

Banks are more likely to change minor currencies, although they tend to make heavy weather of it. Turkey has no black market.

Foreign Currencies

Euros and US dollars are the most readily accepted foreign currencies. Shops, hotels and restaurants in many tourist areas accept these and taxi drivers will take them for big journeys.

Opening Hours

The following are standard opening hours.

Tourist information 9am–12.30pm and 1.30pm–5pm Monday to Friday

Restaurants 11am–10pm

Bars 4pm–late

Nightclubs 11pm–late

Shops 9am–6pm Monday to Friday (longer in tourist areas and big cities – including weekend opening)

Government departments, offices and banks 8.30am–noon and 1.30pm–5pm Monday to Friday

Most museums close on Monday; from April to October, many have extended hours. Other businesses with seasonal variations include bars, which are likely to stay open later in summer than in winter, and tourist offices in popular locations, which open for longer hours and

sometimes at weekends during summer.

The working day shortens during the holy month of Ramazan. Devoutly religious cities such as Konya and Kayseri virtually shut down during noon prayers on Friday (the Muslim sabbath); apart from that, Friday is a normal working day.

Photography

People in Turkey are generally receptive to having their photo taken. The major exception is when they are praying or performing other religious activities. Photographing military sites and similar installations is banned. There is typically prominent 'no photography' signage in these areas.

Check out the best-selling *Lonely Planet's Guide to Travel Photography* for tips on taking great travel photos.

Post

Turkish *postanes* (post offices) are indicated by black-on-yellow 'PTT' signs. Most post offices open Monday to Friday from around 8.30am to noon and 1.30pm to 5pm, but a few offices in major cities have extended opening hours.

Letters take between one and four weeks to get to/from Turkey.

When posting letters, the *yurtdışı* slot is for mail to

foreign countries, *yurtiçi* for mail to other Turkish cities, and *şehiriçi* for local mail. Visit www.ptt.gov.tr for more information.

Parcels

If you are shipping something from Turkey, don't close your parcel before it has been inspected by a customs official. Take packing and wrapping materials with you to the post office.

Parcels take around one month to arrive.

International couriers including DHL also operate in Turkey.

Public Holidays

New Year's Day (Yılbaşı) 1 January

National Sovereignty & Children's Day (Ulusal Egemenlik ve Çocuk Günü) 23 April

Labor & Solidarity Day (May Day) 1 May

Şeker Bayramı (Sweets Holiday) See the table below.

Commemoration of Atatürk, Youth & Sports Day (Gençlik ve Spor Günü) 19 May

Democracy and National Solidarity Day 15 July

Kurban Bayramı (Festival of the Sacrifice) See the table on p603

Victory Day (Zafer Bayramı) 30 August

Republic Day (Cumhuriyet Bayramı) 29 October

MAJOR ISLAMIC HOLIDAYS

The rhythms of Islamic practice are tied to the lunar calendar, which is slightly shorter than its Gregorian equivalent, so the Muslim calendar begins around 11 days earlier each year. The following dates are approximate.

ISLAMIC YEAR	START OF RAMAZAN	ŞEKER BAYRAMI (AFTER RAMAZAN FINISHES)	KURBAN BAYRAMI	ISLAMIC NEW YEAR	PROPHET'S BIRTHDAY
2022	2 Apr	1-3 May	9-12 Jul	30-31 Jul (1442)	8-9 Oct
2023	22 Mar	20-22 Apr	29 Jun-1 Jul	19-20 Jul (1443)	27-28 Sep
2024	11 Mar	9-11 Apr	18-21 Jun	8-9 Jul (1444)	16 Sep

Safe Travel

Although Turkey's reputation as a safe travel destination was tarnished by both a spate of high-profile terrorist attacks between 2015 and 2017, and 2016's attempted coup, it is by no means a dangerous country to visit. Exercise common sense vigilance and do not travel within 10km of the border with Syria.

➡ The likelihood of being caught in a terrorist incident (p604) remains small.

➡ Be aware of the lese-majesty (p604) rule about not insulting the Turkish Republic.

➡ In conservative areas, women should be aware of cultural differences in the way men and women interact – if in doubt, follow the lead of local women.

Assaults

A small number of sexual assaults targeting tourists are reported each year. Most happen in tourist resort towns along the Mediterranean coast, though assaults against travellers have also occurred in hotels in central and eastern Anatolia. Check forums and do a little research in advance if you are travelling alone or heading off the beaten track.

Demonstrations

Marches and demonstrations are a regular sight in Turkish cities, especially İstanbul. These are best avoided as they can lead to clashes with the police.

Flies & Mosquitoes

In high summer (late June to August), mosquitoes are troublesome even in İstanbul; they can make a stay along the coast a nightmare. Some hotel rooms come equipped with nets and/or plug-in bug-busters, but it's a good idea to bring some insect repellent and mosquito coils.

Lese-Majesty

The laws against insulting, defaming or making light of the Turkish Republic, the Turkish flag, the Turkish government, the Turkish people and the Turkish president are taken very seriously. Making derogatory remarks, even in the heat of a quarrel, can be enough to get a foreigner carted off to jail.

Scams & Druggings

Various scams operate in İstanbul. In the most notorious, normally targeted at single men, a pleasant local guy befriends you in the street and takes you to a bar. After a few drinks, and possibly the attention of some ladies, to whom you offer drinks, the bill arrives. The prices are astronomical and the proprietors can produce a menu showing the same prices. If you don't have enough cash, you'll be frogmarched to the nearest ATM. If this happens to you, report it to the tourist police; some travellers have taken the police back to the bar and received a refund.

A less common variation on this trick involves the traveller having their drink spiked and waking up in an unexpected place with their belongings, right down to their shoes, missing.

Single men should not accept invitations from unknown folk in large cities without sizing the situation up carefully. You could invite your new-found friends to a bar of *your* choice; if they're not keen to go, chances are they are shady characters.

The spiking scam has also been reported on overnight trains, with passengers getting robbed. Turks are often genuinely sociable and generous travelling companions, but be cautious about accepting food and drinks from people you are not 100% sure about.

ANTIQUITIES

Do not buy coins or other artefacts offered to you by touts at ancient sites such as Ephesus and Perge. It is a serious crime here, punishable by long prison terms, and the touts are likely in cahoots with the local police.

SHOE CLEANERS

In Sultanahmet, İstanbul, if a shoe cleaner walking in front of you drops his brush, don't pick it up. He will insist on giving you a 'free' clean in return, before demanding an extortionate fee.

Traffic

As a pedestrian, note that some Turks are aggressive, dangerous drivers; 'right of way' doesn't compute with many motorists, despite the little green man on traffic lights. Give way to vehicles in all situations, even if you have to jump out of the way.

Terrorism

The terrorist attacks of 2015 to 2017 illustrated the heightened terrorism risk in Turkey. Most of the higher profile attacks – including the June 2016 Atatürk Airport attack and the January 2017 Reina nightclub attack, both in İstanbul – were carried out by militants linked to Islamic State (ISIS). The terrorist group, often referred to as Daesh in Turkey, stated that at least two of the attacks were aimed at harming Turkey's tourist industry, in retaliation for the country's active role in the US coalition against ISIS. Other major attacks in Ankara and İstanbul, as well as bombings in Adana and Bursa, were carried out by the TAK (Kurdistan Freedom Falcons), a splinter group from the PKK (Kurdistan Workers' Party).

In the same time frame, a ceasefire between the Turkish state and the PKK ended in July 2015. The PKK, considered a terrorist organisation by the USA and the EU, wants greater rights and autonomy for Turkey's Kurdish population. Since the end of the ceasefire, the PKK has carried out a spate of car

GOVERNMENT TRAVEL ADVICE
....

For the latest travel information log on to the following websites.

Australian Department of Foreign Affairs and Trade (www.smartraveller.gov.au)

Dutch Ministry of Foreign Affairs (www.minbuza.nl)

German Federal Foreign Office (www.auswaertiges-amt.de)

Global Affairs Canada (www.travel.gc.ca)

Japanese Ministry of Foreign Affairs (www.mofa.go.jp)

New Zealand Ministry of Foreign Affairs and Trade (www.safetravel.govt.nz)

UK Foreign & Commonwealth Office (www.fco.gov.uk/travel)

US Department of State's Bureau of Consular Affairs (https://travel.state.gov)

bombings and other attacks in the southeast region, most aimed at Turkish military and government targets. Keep up to date with the current situation if travelling in the southeast. Although much of the ongoing conflict happens far away from traveller routes in remote, mountainous areas, there has been fighting and attacks in urban centres such as Diyarbakır.

However, it is worth remembering that, as with the atrocities seen in Western cities, these attacks are random; the chance of being caught in an incident is statistically low, so keep things in perspective amid the media coverage.

BORDER AREAS

In October 2019 the Turkish government began a controversial cross-border military operation into northeastern Syria to dislodge Kurdish control over the Syrian border region. Due to both the chance of getting caught up in Turkish military operations and of being kidnapped by militants from Syria, all travel within 10km of the Syrian border should be avoided. At the time of writing, the UK Foreign & Commonwealth Office advised against all travel in this border region and that only essential travel should be undertaken to Şırnak and Hakkari provinces (along the Iraq border), Hatay province, Diyarbakır province

and Tunceli province (in the mountains of the southeast). Both the US Department of State's Bureau of Consular Affairs and the Australian Department of Foreign Affairs and Trade advise their citizens to not travel within 10km of the Syrian or Iraqi border, to reconsider all travel in the southeast and to exercise a high degree of caution throughout the country.

Safety Standards

Turkey is not a safety-conscious country: holes in pavements go unmended; precipitous drops go unguarded; seat belts are not always worn; lifeguards on beaches are rare; and dolmuş (minibus with a prescribed route) drivers negotiate bends while counting out change.

Street Crime

Incidents such as bag-snatching, bag-slashing, pickpocketing and mugging remain much rarer than in other destinations. Nevertheless they do occur, often perpetrated by young men or boys in busy areas such as bazaars and transport terminals. Practice common sense precautions such as wearing your bag with the strap across your body and carrying your phone or wallet in your front rather than your back pocket, particularly in big cities such as İstanbul, İzmir and Ankara.

Smoking

Turks love smoking and there's even a joke about the country's propensity for puffing: Who smokes more than a Turk? Two Turks.

➡ Smoking in enclosed public spaces is officially banned, and punishable by a fine.

➡ In İstanbul, along the Mediterranean coastline and in other tourism centres such as Cappadocia, the ban is, for the most part, strictly adhered to in hotels, restaurants and bars, although bars sometimes relax the rules as the evening wears on.

➡ Off the tourist trail, the smoking ban isn't so stridently enforced. Many hotel rooms have ashtrays, though the public areas are smoke-free, and some restaurants still allow smoking inside.

➡ Public transport is meant to be smoke-free, although plenty of bus drivers still smoke at the wheel. Don't take seats in the first two rows of intercity buses if you're affected by smoke.

Telephone

The country code is +90 and the international access code is +00. Within Turkey, numbers starting with 444 don't require area codes and, wherever you call from, are charged at the local rate.

Mobile Phones

If your cell phone is unlocked, you can purchase a prepaid SIM card (SIM *kart*) package with credit and data. There are three major networks: Turkcell (www.turkcell.com.tr), Vodafone (www.vodafone.com.tr) and Türk Telekom (www.turktelekom.com.tr). You'll need your passport when purchasing.

All three networks offer 30-day bundle deals of SIM, data and credit orientated towards tourists. Turkcell's Tourist Welcome Pack includes SIM, 20GB data, 1000 SMS messages and 200 minutes of calls for ₺149.

Non-tourist-orientated bundle deals offering between 6GB and 10GB of data usually cost between ₺90 and ₺120.

➡ All Turkish mobile numbers start with a four-digit number beginning with 05.

➡ Reception is generally excellent throughout Turkey but Turkcell's coverage is best, especially out east.

➡ Turkish SIM cards can be used in a foreign phone for 120 days. The network will automatically detect and bar your phone after this time period.

➡ SIM cards and *kontör* (credit) are widely available – at street-side kiosks and shops as well as mobile phone outlets. *Kontör* can also be purchased at cash registers of many supermarkets and shops.

➡ Be aware that buying a Turkish SIM package is always more expensive at the airport.

LONG STAYS

Anyone wanting to use a foreign mobile phone in Turkey for longer than 120 days needs to register their phone. The process is convoluted and expensive, costing ₺1500. For a run-down on the process, go to https://yellali.com/advice/question/235/ how-do-i-register-a-mobile-phone-in-turkey.

Time

➡ Eastern European Summer Time all year round (GMT/UTC plus three hours).

➡ Turkish bus timetables and so on use the 24-hour clock, but Turks rarely use it when speaking.

Toilets

➡ Most hotels, restaurants and tourist sites have sit-down toilets.

➡ Squat toilets – with a conventional flush, or a tap and jug – are common in public facilities such as bus stations and out-of-the-way tourist sites.

➡ Toilet paper is sometimes unavailable, so keep some with you.

➡ Many sink taps are unmarked and reversed (cold on the left, hot on the right).

➡ Public toilets can usually be found at major attractions and transport hubs; most require a payment of between ₺1 and ₺2.

➡ In an emergency it's worth remembering that mosques have basic toilets (for both men and women).

➡ You can flush paper down most toilets but in some places this may flood the premises. This is the case in much of İstanbul's old city. If you're not sure, play it safe and dispose of the paper in the bin provided. Signs often advise patrons to use the bin. This may seem slightly gross to the uninitiated, but many Turks (as well as people from other Middle Eastern and Asian countries) use a jet spray of water to clean themselves after defecating, applying paper to pat dry. The used paper is thus just damp, rather than soiled.

Tourist Information

GoTurkey (www.goturkey.com) Official Turkey travel website with plenty of flashy photography and content to inspire trip planning.

Ministry of Culture and Tourism (www.kultur.gov.tr) Official portal with information on Turkish culture and tourism activities.

Müze (www.muze.gov.tr/en) Information on every major museum and sight in the country.

Tourist Offices

Every Turkish town of any size has an official tourist office run by the Ministry of Culture and Tourism. Levels of helpfulness vary wildly – some staff may have sketchy knowledge of the area, and few speak fluent English. Tour operators, pension owners and so on are often better sources of information.

Visas

➡ Nationals of countries including Argentina, Austria, Belgium, Brazil, Denmark, Finland, France, Germany, Greece, Israel, Italy, Japan, Malaysia, the Netherlands, New Zealand, Poland, South Korea, Spain, Sweden, Switzerland and the UK don't need a visa to visit Turkey. A stamp upon entry grants multiple-entry for up to 90 days.

➡ Russians can enter without a visa for up to 60 days.

➡ Nationals of countries including Australia, Canada, China, India, Ireland, Mexico, Norway, South Africa, Taiwan and the USA need a visa, which should be purchased online at www.evisa.gov.tr before travelling.

➡ Depending on nationality, tourist visas are issued as either multiple-entry or single-stay and for periods of between 30 and 90 days.

➜ Visa fees are US$20 to US$60, depending on nationality.

➜ For most nationalities who receive a visa-free, multiple-entry, 90-day stay and those that receive a 90-day, multiple-entry visa, the visa is valid 180 days from the date of issue for a maximum stay of 90 days. This means you can spend three months in Turkey within one six-month period; when you leave, after having used up your 90 days, you can't re-enter for three months. Check the Ministry of Foreign Affairs (www.mfa.gov.tr, www.evisa.gov.tr) for more information.

Tourist Visa Process

➜ On the official Turkish government e-visa site (www.evisa.gov.tr), you must enter details of your passport and date of arrival in Turkey, click on the link in the verification email and pay with a Mastercard or Visa credit or debit card. No photos required.

➜ Having completed this process, the e-visa can be downloaded in Adobe PDF format; a link is also emailed so it can be printed out later. It is recommended that you print out the e-visa to show on arrival in Turkey; keep it while in the country.

➜ It's also recommended that applications are made at least 48 hours before departure.

➜ Although many Western nationals can also obtain a visa on arrival in Turkey, this is not recommended as travellers have reported extra charges and bad experiences with the customs officials. Cash cannot be used.

COVID Requirements for Foreign Visitors

➜ Entry and travel requirements in response to the COVID-19 pandemic continue to evolve. Currently all travellers must fill out the Turkey entrance form at https://register.health.gov.tr and provide proof of either/both (depending on country) vaccination or a negative PCR test to enter.

➜ The PDF generated after completing the Turkey entrance form will display your HES (Hayat Eve Sığar) code – a personal tracking code run through Turkey's Ministry of Health.

➜ Although it's technically not mandatory for foreign visitors to use a HES code, in reality you will need to show your HES code to gain access to shopping malls, some museums and to buy inter-city bus and train tickets.

➜ Some cities (and provinces) that run their city-bus, metro and tram network through a transport travelcard system have made it mandatory to register your HES code with their travelcard if you want to use their public transport system. See p618 for information on how to do this.

Residency Permits

➜ Turkey doesn't issue tourist visa extensions as 90-day tourist stays are granted as the norm for most nationalities.

➜ If you want to stay longer in the country, you need to apply for a residence permit *(ikamet tezkeresi)* for touristic purposes. This permit does not allow you to work in Turkey.

➜ Various other types of residence permits, such as work permits and spousal permits are available and are generally supported and applied for through your employer or spouse.

➜ Touristic residency permits are typically valid for one year; the price varies according to the applicant's nationality and office of application, with charges starting at around ₺400 including administrative charges.

APPLYING FOR TOURISTIC RESIDENCY

Applications for a touristic residency permit are submitted online (https://e-ikamet.goc.gov.tr) after which you'll receive an interview time at the residency office where you apply. Application rules change regularly and are not applied consistently. For a first-time application you need:

➜ A Turkish tax ID number.

➜ A bank statement to give evidence of enough money to support yourself. The amount required varies between regions of Turkey. It's usually between ₺15,000 and ₺20,000 to safely qualify for a full year's permit.

➜ Proof of accommodation such as a rental contract (usually needs to be notarised).

➜ Certificate of address registration from your local Population Registry Office (Nüfus Müdürlüğü).

➜ Passport photos.

➜ Health insurance: note that travel insurance and foreign health insurance are not accepted. The insurer must be a Turkish company. A year of insurance costs about ₺600. You'll need to enter your insurance policy details on the online application.

➜ Criminal background check.

➜ Health check-up at a Turkish state hospital (costs from ₺300).

➜ Photocopies of your passport information page and Turkish entry stamp page.

The process can be confusing and the staff unhelpful in locations such as İstanbul; those working behind the desks in cities such as İzmir and Nevşehir are reputedly more helpful. Due to the amount of applications in İstanbul, there can be a wait between your online application and interview time.

Little English is spoken, so take a Turkish-speaking friend with you if possible.

If your application is successful, your touristic residency card will be posted to you (it usually takes two weeks). Due to the cost and time involved in the process, it's generally not worth applying unless you're applying for a year.

More details are available at the websites YellAli (https://yellali.com/advice) and Yabangee (https://yabangee.com/get-your-residence-permit-guide).

Volunteering

Culture Routes in Turkey (http://cultureroutesinturkey.com) In April and May volunteers help waymark and repair Turkey's hiking trails such as the Lycian Way and St Paul Trail.

European Youth Portal (https://europa.eu/youth/volunteering/organisations_en) Database of European Union–accredited opportunities.

Gençtur (www.genctur.com.tr) Organises voluntourism including farmstays, with offices in İstanbul and Berlin.

Ta Tu Ta (www.tatuta.org) Turkey's branch of WWOOF (World Wide Opportunities on Organic Farms) organises work on dozens of organic farms around the country, where you receive accommodation and board in exchange for labour.

Women Travellers

Travelling in Turkey is straightforward for women, provided you follow some simple guidelines.

Accommodation

➡ Outside tourist areas, the very cheapest hotels, as well as often being fleapits, are generally not suitable for lone women. Stick with the upper end of the budget category or family-oriented midrange hotels.

➡ If conversation in the lobby grinds to a halt as you enter, the hotel is not likely to be a great place for a woman.

➡ If there is a knock on your hotel door late at night, don't open it; in the morning, complain to the manager.

➡ We recommend female travellers stick to official campsites and camp where there are plenty of people around – especially out east. If you do otherwise, you will be taking a risk.

Clothing

Tailor your behaviour and your clothing to your surrounds. Look at what local women are wearing. On the streets of Beyoğlu in İstanbul and in the resort towns of the Mediterranean coast you'll see skimpy tops, tight jeans, shorts and short skirts. In more rural areas of western Turkey and as you head east, clothing becomes more conservative.

There is absolutely no need to don a headscarf, but away from heavily touristed destinations, wearing long pants and a T-shirt with at least a cap-sleeve will garner less unwanted attention.

When entering mosques, you should wear long pants or a skirt, a long-sleeved top/shirt that doesn't show cleavage and don a headscarf. At many larger mosques, headscarves are available to borrow from a box at the entrance.

Holiday Romances

Holiday romances between foreign female travellers and Turkish men are so common – particularly in the coastal resort towns along the Mediterranean coast and in Cappadocia – they're somewhat a cliché. Use normal common sense judgement that you'd use back home when entering into a holiday relationship. There are occasional cases of men exploiting these relationships by inventing sob stories and asking for financial help, and

numerous cases of married men, posing as single, entering into short relationships with foreign females.

Regional Differences

Turkey is a large country with distinct differences in attitudes and levels of conservatism. While many cities and towns are vibrantly cosmopolitan in outlook, in rural areas, particularly in the east, life is much more traditional and a solo female traveller is something of a curiosity.

Having a banter with men in restaurants and shops in tourist-focused destinations can be fun, and many men won't necessarily think much of it. In less-visited towns and villages, it's worth being more cautious. Keenly observe your surroundings and make judgement calls based on the local atmosphere. In small towns where public life on the street seems very male-orientated, keep conversations with men on a slightly more formal level to avoid being misconstrued.

Transport

On long-distance buses and trains, lone female travellers are never assigned seats next to a male.

Although rare, there have been cases of male passengers or conductors on long-distance night buses harassing female travellers. If this happens to you complain loudly, making sure that others on the bus hear. Repeat your complaint on arrival at your destination; you have a right to be treated with respect.

On dolmuşes, both within cities and between local towns, you can usually sit anywhere, but on some routes in rural areas the passengers will rearrange themselves as people get on and off so that a solo female isn't sitting next to an unrelated male.

It's not usually normal for a female to sit beside the driver in a dolmuş. When using taxis, most lone Turkish women will sit in the back, not the front seat. Follow their lead, as getting into the seat beside the driver can be occasionally misinterpreted as a come-on.

Sanitary Products

Tampons are easy to find in the big cities of western Turkey and in tourist-orientated regions, but if you're heading east, or into a very rural area, stock up before you go. Even in the big eastern cities they can be difficult to find. Note that if you need to buy from an *eczane* (pharmacy), tampons are usually kept hidden so you need to ask for them.

Work

Outside professional fields such as academia and the corporate sector, bagging a job in Turkey is tough. Most people teach English or nanny.

Check whether potential employers will help you get a work permit. Many employers, notably language schools, are happy to employ foreigners on an informal basis, but unwilling to organise work permits due to the time and money involved in the bureaucratic process. This necessitates working illegally on a tourist visa/residence permit. The '90 days within 180 days' regulation stipulated by most tourist visas (for more on this, see www.mfa.gov.tr/visa-information-for-foreigners.en.mfa) rules out the option of cross-border 'visa runs' to pick up a new visa on re-entry to Turkey.

Locals also occasionally report illegal workers, and there have even been cases of English teachers being deported.

Job hunters may pick up leads on the following foreign resident and advertising websites:

➡ www.istanbul.angloinfo.com

➡ https://istanbul.craigslist.org

➡ www.sahibinden.com

➡ www.turkeycentral.com

➡ https://yabangee.com

Nannying

One of the most lucrative non-specialist jobs open to foreigners is nannying for the wealthy urban elite, or looking after their teenage children and helping them develop their language skills.

There are opportunities for English, French and German speakers, and openings for young men as well as women, all mostly in İstanbul.

You must be prepared for long hours, demanding employers and spoilt children.

Accommodation is normally included, and the digs will likely be luxurious. However, living with the family means you are always on call, and you may be based in the suburbs.

Teaching English

You can earn a decent living, mostly in İstanbul and the other major cities, as an English teacher at a university or a school. Good jobs require a university degree and TEFL (Teaching English as a Foreign Language) certificate or similar.

For job-hunting resources, log onto www.eslcafe.com, which has a Turkey forum, and www.tefl.com.

If you want to proactively contact potential employers, Wikipedia has lists of universities and private schools in Turkey.

DERSHANE

There are lots of jobs at *dershane* (private schools), which pay good wages and offer attractions such as accommodation (although it may be on or near the school campus in the suburbs) and work permits. Some even pay for your flight to Turkey and/or flights home.

Unless a teacher has dropped out before the end of their contract, these jobs are mostly advertised around May and June, when employers are recruiting in preparation for the beginning of the academic year in September. Teachers are contracted until the end of the academic year in June.

LANGUAGE SCHOOLS

Teaching at a language school is not recommended. Many have been found to be institutions untroubled by professional ethics.

Tourism

Travellers sometimes work illegally for room and board in pensions, bars and other businesses in tourist areas. These jobs are generally badly paid and only last a few weeks, but some visitors find they are a fun way to stay in a place and get to know the locals. Given that they will be in direct competition with unskilled locals for such employment, and working in the public eye, there is a danger of being reported to authorities and deported.

Working Visas

➡ All the legwork and paperwork involved with obtaining a work permit is usually carried out by your Turkish employer.

➡ The visa can be obtained in Turkey or from a Turkish embassy or consulate.

➡ The separate Turkish government 'turquoise card' program, which grants long-term residence with the right to work, is aimed only at top-tier science, technology, business, sports and arts professionals and those who make a large monetary investment in Turkey.

Transport

GETTING THERE & AWAY

Flights, cars and tours can be booked online at lonely planet.com/bookings.

Entering Turkey

Some nationalities don't need a tourist visa. Most that do can purchase a tourist e-visa online before travelling. See p606 for more on visas.

Passport

Make sure your passport will still have at least six months' validity after you enter Turkey.

Air

It's a good idea to book flights months in advance if you plan to arrive in Turkey any time from April until late August. If you plan to visit a resort, check with travel

agents for flight and accommodation deals. Sometimes you can find cheap flights with Turkish carriers and smaller airlines.

Airports

The main international airports are in western Turkey.

İstanbul Airport (☏444 1442, Whatsapp 0549 563 3434; www.istairport.com/en; Terminal Caddesi 1, Arnavutköy) The city's mammoth new airport opened in 2019. It's located in Arnavutköy, 42km northwest of Sultanahmet.

Sabiha Gökçen International Airport (SAW, Sabiha Gökçen Havalimanı; ☏0216-588 8888; www.sabihagokcen.aero/homepage; Pendik) This smaller airport on İstanbul's Asian side receives international flights and is popular with budget carriers.

Antalya International Airport (Antalya Havalimanı; ☏0242-444 7423; www.aytport.com; Serik Caddesi) Receives flights from across Turkey and Europe.

Adnan Menderes Airport (☏0232-455 0000; www.adnanmenderesairport.com; 🛈) There are many flights to İzmir's Adnan Menderes Airport from European destinations.

Milas-Bodrum Airport (BJV; ☏0252 523 0101) Receives flights from all over Europe, mostly with charters and budget airlines in summer, and from İstanbul and Ankara with the Turkish airlines.

Dalaman International Airport (☏0252-792 5555; www.yda.aero) Seasonal flights from many European cities, and year-round from İstanbul.

Ankara Esenboğa Airport (Ankara Esenboğa Havalimanı, ESB; ☏0312-590 4000; www.esenbogaairport.com; Özal Bulvarı, Balıkhisar) Numerous international and domestic connections from Ankara, although İstanbul's airports offer more choice.

Airlines

Turkish Airlines (☏1800-874 8875; www.turkishairlines.com), the national carrier, has

---

CLIMATE CHANGE & TRAVEL

Every form of transport that relies on carbon-based fuel generates CO_2, the main cause of human-induced climate change. Modern travel is dependent on aeroplanes, which might use less fuel per kilometre per person than most cars but travel much greater distances. The altitude at which aircraft emit gases (including CO_2) and particles also contributes to their climate change impact. Many websites offer 'carbon calculators' that allow people to estimate the carbon emissions generated by their journey and, for those who wish to do so, to offset the impact of the greenhouse gases emitted with contributions to portfolios of climate-friendly initiatives throughout the world. Lonely Planet offsets the carbon footprint of all staff and author travel.

extensive international and domestic networks, which include its budget subsidiaries **Sun Express** (☑444 0797; www.sunexpress.com) and **Anadolu Jet** (☑444 2538; www.anadolujet.com/tr). It is generally considered a safe airline, and its operational safety is certified by the International Air Transport Association (IATA).

AUSTRALIA & NEW ZEALAND
You can fly from the main cities in Australia and New Zealand to İstanbul, normally via Dubai, Qatar, Kuala Lumpur or Singapore.

Travellers wanting to head straight to the coast or start their Turkey trip further inland should note that you can now fly direct to Adana, Ankara and İzmir via Qatar on **Qatar Airways** (www.qatarairways.com).

You can often get affordable flights with European airlines, if you're prepared to change flights in Europe.

CONTINENTAL EUROPE
There's not much variation in fares from one European airport to another, with the exception of Germany, which has the biggest Turkish community outside Turkey, enabling some great deals.

Most European national carriers fly direct to İstanbul. Cheaper indirect flights can be found, for example changing in Frankfurt or Munich en route from Amsterdam to İstanbul.

Budget airlines such as Turkey's **Pegasus Airlines** (☑0888-228 1212; www.flypgs.com/en) fly between several European cities and the major Turkish airports. From Germany, Sun Express is often the cheapest option.

EASTERN EUROPE
Turkish Airlines and Pegasus Airlines both have regular flights to cities in Bulgaria, Russia and Ukraine.

MIDDLE EAST & ASIA
From Central Asia and the Middle East, there are good connections with Turkish Airlines or the Asian or Middle Eastern country's national carrier. Cheaper flights are often found with regional budget carriers such as Pegasus Airlines.

Affordable flights from further afield normally travel to İstanbul via Dubai or Qatar.

UK & IRELAND
The major carriers, Turkish Airlines, Pegasus Airlines and **British Airways** (www.britishairways.com) have plentiful direct flights. The cheapest flights are usually out of London airports.

Charter flights are a good option, particularly at the beginning and end of the peak summer holiday season.

USA & CANADA
Turkish Airlines has direct flights between Toronto and Montreal (Canada) and several USA cities. Most other flights connect with İstanbul-bound flights in the UK or continental Europe, so it's worth looking at European and British airlines in addition to North American airlines.

Another option is to cross the Atlantic to, say, London or Frankfurt, and continue on a separate ticket with a budget carrier.

Land
Turkey has land borders with Armenia, the Azerbaijani enclave of Nakhchivan, Bulgaria, Georgia, Greece, Iran, Iraq and Syria.

Turkey's relationships with most of its neighbours tend to be tense, which can affect when and where you can cross. Check for the most up-to-date information; sources of information include Lonely Planet's Thorn Tree forum (www.lonelyplanet.com/thorntree), your embassy in Turkey and the Turkish embassy in your country.

Border Crossings
If you're travelling by train or bus, expect to be held up at the border for two to three hours – or even longer if your fellow passengers don't have their paperwork in order. You'll usually have to disembark and endure paperwork and baggage checks on both sides of the border. Security at the crossings to/from countries to the east and southeast (Georgia, Azerbaijan/Nakhchivan, Iran and Iraq) is tightest. The process is prolonged by a trainload of passengers or the long lines of trucks and cars that build up at some crossings.

Crossing the border into Turkey with your own vehicle should be fairly straightforward, providing your paperwork is in order.

ARMENIA
At the time of writing, the Turkey–Armenia border was closed. The only way to go is via Georgia.

AZERBAIJAN
The Borualan–Sadarak crossing, east of Iğdır (Turkey), leads to the Azerbaijani enclave of Nakhchivan (Nahçıvan in Turkish; p527). Nakhchivan is separated from the rest of Azerbaijan by Armenia, which has no diplomatic relations with Azerbaijan. The only way to get from Nakhchivan to the rest of Azerbaijan is to fly.

Bus
Buses run from İstanbul and Trabzon to Baku via Georgia. Otherwise, head to Tbilisi (Georgia) and change there.

There are regular buses and dolmuşes (minibuses with a prescribed route) from Iğdır to Nakhchivan.

Alpar (☑0212-658 1851; www.alparturizm.com.tr) runs direct from İstanbul to Baku from Aksaray Emniyet Otogar (US$50, 3pm Monday to Saturday).

Metro Turizm (☑0850-222 3455; www.metroturizm.com.tr) runs the same route from Aksaray Emniyet Otogar (₺230, 2pm daily).

Train
Passenger services run on the Kars–Tbilisi–Baku route.

BULGARIA & EASTERN EUROPE
Bulgarian border guards only occasionally allow pedestrians to cross the frontier. There are three border crossings:

Kapitan Andreevo–Kapıkule This 24-hour post is the main crossing – and the world's second-busiest land border crossing. Located 18km northwest of Edirne (Turkey) on the E80 and 9km from Svilengrad (Bulgaria).

Lesovo–Hamzabeyli Some 25km northeast of Edirne, this is favoured by big trucks and should be avoided.

Malko Tărnovo–Aziziye Some 70km northeast of Edirne via Kırklareli and 92km south of Burgas (Bulgaria), this is only useful for those heading to Bulgaria's Black Sea resorts.

Bus
Approximately half a dozen companies have daily departures between İstanbul and eastern European destinations including Albania, Bulgaria, Hungary, Kosovo, North Macedonia, Slovakia and Romania.

Alpar buses depart 8.30pm daily to Plovdiv (₺100) and Sofia (₺130) and 5pm Monday to Saturday to Pristina in Kosovo (€40) from Esenler Otogar. From Bayrampaşa Otogar it runs daily services to Ohrid in North Macedonia (€40, 7pm).

Huntur (☑0554 342 0409; www.huntur.com.tr) has departures at 6pm and 10.30pm daily to Plovdiv (₺120) and

Sofia (₺150) from Esenler Otogar.

Metro Turizm offers two morning and three evening services to Plovdiv (₺115) and Sofia (₺150) from Bayrampaşa Otogar. One evening service goes via Edirne Otogar. Also direct buses to Albania, Hungary and Slovakia.

Train
The nightly *İstanbul–Sofya Ekspresi* to Sofia (Bulgaria) departs Halkalı station at 9.40pm (June to September) or 10.40pm (October to May); ticket prices start at €27.88. To get to Halkalı from central İstanbul, catch the Marmaray from Sirkeci Station (13 stops, 40 minutes). Ticket holders can also catch a free *servis* (shuttle bus) from Sirkeci Station to Halkalı, which leaves at 8pm (June to September) or 9.30pm (October to May).

The *Bosfor Ekspresi* to Bucharest (Romania) operates from June to September with carriages attached to the *İstanbul–Sofya Ekspresi* until the train routes split in Bulgaria. Tickets start at €31.40.

GEORGIA
Sarp The main 24-hour crossing, on the Black Sea coast between Hopa (Turkey) and Batumi (Georgia).

Türkgözü Near Posof (Turkey), north of Kars and southwest of Akhaltsikhe (Georgia). The border is open 6am to 6pm.

Aktaş South of Türkgözü, this crossing between Ardahan and Akhalkalaki (Georgia) reduces the driving time to Armenia. It's usually open 6am to 6pm.

Bus
Several bus companies depart from İstanbul, Ankara and other cities to Batumi, Kutaisi and Tbilisi.

Closer to Georgia, buses and dolmuşes run from Trabzon via Rize, Pazar and Hopa to the border at Sarp (and vice versa). Although many

of the buses advertise the route as ending in Batumi, the Sarp border is usually the final stop. This is because crossing the border by bus normally takes about an hour so it's quicker to walk through and pick up transportation on the far side.

There's one daily bus each way between Ardahan (Turkey) and Akhaltsikhe (Georgia) via Türkgözü. In theory it continues to/from Tbilisi, but it doesn't always do so.

Three daily dolmuşes connect Ardahan and Akhalkalaki (Georgia) via Aktaş, stopping at Çıldır between Ardahan and the border.

Golden Turizm (☑444 1153; www.goldenturizm.com.tr) has one daily bus at 6pm to Tbilisi (₺220) from İstanbul's Aksaray Emniyet Otogar. From Trabzon, one daily service at 12.30pm to Tbilisi (₺130).

Metro Turizm has daily services from İstanbul's Aksaray Emniyet Otogar to Tbilisi (₺200) at noon and 6pm.

Train
Passenger trains run between Kars and Tbilisi.

GREECE & WESTERN EUROPE
Greek and Turkish border guards allow you to cross the frontier on foot. The following are open 24 hours.

Kastanies–Pazarkule About 9km southwest of Edirne.

Kipi–İpsala Located 29km northeast of Alexandroupolis (Greece) and 35km west of Keşan (Turkey).

Bus
The most direct services to İstanbul are from Greece, though there are also a few direct buses from Germany and Austria. If you're travelling from other European countries, you'll likely have to catch a connecting bus.

Alpar has a service from İstanbul's Bayrampaşa Otogar to Thessaloniki (€35, daily at 9pm), as does while

Metro Turizm (₺230, 10am and 10pm).

Car & Motorcycle
The E80 highway makes its way through the Balkans to Edirne and İstanbul, then on to Ankara. Using the car ferries from Italy and Greece can shorten driving times from Western Europe, but at a price.

From Alexandroupolis, the main road leads to Kipi-İpsala, then to Keşan and east to İstanbul or south to Gallipoli, Çanakkale and the Aegean.

IRAN
Gürbulak–Bazargan This busy post, 35km southeast of Doğubayazıt (Turkey), is open 24 hours.

Esendere–Sero Southeast of Van, this border is usually open from 8am to midnight. Check locally, and with government travel advisories, before using due to the security situation in this area.

Bus
There are regular buses from İstanbul and Ankara. Metro Turizm has a daily service to Tabriz and Tehran (₺220, noon) from Ankara.

From Doğubayazıt Catch a dolmuş to Gürbulak, then walk or catch a shared taxi across the border. It's Iran's busiest border crossing, and Turkey's second busiest. The crossing might take up to an hour, although tourists are normally waved through without much fuss. Change any unused Turkish lira in Bazargan, as it's harder to do so in Tabriz and Tehran. There are onward buses from Bazargan.

From Van There are direct buses to Tabriz via Urmia.

An alternative route into Iran is to go via Iğdır then through the Azerbaijani enclave of Nakhchivan to the Iranian border at Jolfa (p527).

Train
In 2019, both trains between Van and Tehran and the weekly *Trans Asya Treni* (€40.90, 2.25pm Wednesday) between Ankara and Tehran (via Van) began operating again.

From Tehran, the Tehran–Tabriz–Van train service leaves Tehran at 1pm every Sunday and the *Trans Asya Treni* on Wednesday at 10pm.

IRAQ
Between Silopi (Turkey) and Zakho (Kurdish Iraq), there's no town or village at the Habur–Ibrahim al-Khalil crossing and you can't walk across it. Although the border crossing itself falls outside of the 10km zone along the Syrian border that most government travel advisories recommend avoiding, Silopi, and the road to the town, sits within this zone, so using this border is not recommended due to security reasons.

There are direct daily buses from Diyarbakır to Erbil (₺150, nine hours) via Dohuk in Kurdish Iraq, and from Cizre.

More hassle than the bus, a taxi from Silopi to Zakho costs between US$50 and US$70. Your driver will manoeuvre through a maze of checkpoints and handle the paperwork. On the return journey, watch out for taxi drivers slipping contraband into your bag.

SYRIA
Travel within the 10km zone north of the Syrian border is not recommended due to a volatile security situation and Turkish military offensives in northern Syria. Of the several border crossings into Syria, many are either closed or only have restricted access.

Sea
Departure times change between seasons, with fewer ferries running in the winter. The routes available also change from year to year. A good starting point for information is **Ferrylines** (www.ferrylines.com).

From the Aegean and Mediterranean coasts, day trips on ferries to Greece are popular. Remember to take your passport, and check you have a multiple-entry Turkish visa so you can get back into the country at the end of the day. (Most e-visas allow multiple entries, but visas differ depending on nationality.)

Routes
Ayvalık–Lesvos (Midilli), Greece (www.erturk.com.tr/en, www.turyolonline.com)

Bodrum–Kalymnos, Kos, Rhodes and Symi, Greece (www.bodrumexpresslines.com, www.bodrumferryboat.com, www.erturk.com.tr/en, www.rhodesferry.com)

Çeşme–Chios, Greece (www.erturk.com.tr/en, www.chiossunrisetours.com.tr)

Karasu (northeast from İstanbul)–Chornomorsk (Odessa), Ukraine (www.sealines.com.tr, www.ukrferry.com/eng)

Kaş–Meis (Kastellorizo), Greece (www.erturk.com.tr/en, www.meisexpress.com)

Kuşadası–Samos, Greece (www.bareltravel.com, www.meandertravel.com)

Marmaris–Rhodes (www.marmarisferry.com, www.rhodesferry.com)

Taşacu–Girne, Northern Cyprus (www.kibrisdenizcilik.com)

Turgutreis–Kalymnos and Kos (www.bodrumexpresslines.com, www.bodrumferryboat.com)

GETTING AROUND

Air
Turkey is well connected by air throughout the country, although many flights go via the hubs of İstanbul or Ankara. Competition between the domestic airlines keeps tickets affordable.

Airlines in Turkey

Anadolu Jet (☑444 2538; www.anadolujet.com/tr) The Turkish Airlines subsidiary serves a large network of some 40 airports across the country.

Pegasus Airlines (☑0888-228 1212; www.flypgs.com/en) Turkey's main budget carrier with a country-wide network of of some 30 airports, including far-flung eastern spots such as Erzurum and Kars.

Sun Express (☑444 0797; www.sunexpress.com) The Turkish Airlines subsidiary has a useful network of about 20 airports, with most flights from Antalya and İzmir.

Turkish Airlines (☑1800-874 8875; www.turkishairlines.com) State-owned Turkish Airlines provides the main domestic network, covering airports from Çanakkale to Erzurum.

Bicycle

Turkish cycling highlights include spectacular scenery, easy access to archaeological sites – which you may have all to yourself in some obscure corners – and the curiosity and hospitality of locals, especially out east.

Bicycles and parts Good-quality spare parts are generally only available in İstanbul and Ankara. Bisan (www.bisan.com.tr) is the main bike manufacturer in Turkey, but you can buy international brands in shops such as Delta Bisiklet (www.deltabisiklet.com), which has branches in İstanbul, Ankara, İzmir, Antalya, Konya and Kayseri. Delta services bicycles and can send parts throughout the country.

Hazards These include Turkey's notorious road-hog drivers, rotten road edges and, out east, stone-throwing children, wolves and ferocious Kangal dogs. Avoid main roads between cities; secondary roads are safer and more scenic.

Hire You can hire bikes for short periods in tourist towns along the coast, in Eğirdir and in Cappadocia.

Maps The best map for touring by bike is the *Köy Köy Türkiye Yol Atlası,* available in bookshops in İstanbul.

Transport You can sometimes transport your bike by bus or ferry free of charge, although some will charge for the space it takes up. Trains generally do not accept bikes.

Boat

İstanbul Deniz Otobüsleri (☑0850-222 4436; www.ido.com.tr) and **BUDO** (Bursa Deniz Otobüsleri, Bursa Sea Buses; https://budo.burulas.com.tr) operate passenger and car ferries across the Sea of Marmara, with routes to/from İstanbul including:

➜ Eminönü–Mudanya (for Bursa)

➜ Eminönü–Armutlu

➜ Kadıköy–Güzelyalı (for Bursa)

➜ Yenikapı–Bandırma, Güzelyalı (for Bursa), Princes' Islands, Yalova

Gestaş (www.gdu.com.tr) operates passenger and car ferries across the Dardanelles and to/from the Turkish Aegean islands of Bozcaada and Gökçeada.

Bus

Turkey's intercity bus system is as good as any you'll find, with modern, comfortable coaches crossing the country at all hours and for decent prices. On the journey, you'll be treated to hot and cold drinks and usually snacks, and some bus company conductors will attempt to douse you in liberal sprinklings of the Turks' beloved *kolonya* (lemon cologne).

Companies

These are some of the major companies, with extensive route networks:

İstanbul Seyahat (☑0850-222 5959; https://istanbulseyahat.com.tr) Serves Ankara, İstanbul and destinations throughout Thrace and Marmara.

Kamil Koç (☑0224-294 5562; www.kamilkoc.com.tr) Serves most major cities and towns throughout western and central Anatolia and along the Black Sea coast.

Metro Turizm (☑0850-222 3455; www.metroturizm.com.tr) Serves most cities and major towns throughout Turkey.

Pamukkale Turizm (☑0850-333 3535; www.pamukkale.com.tr) Extensive network on the Aegean coast.

Süha Turizm (☑0850-250 3838; www.suhaturizm.com.tr) Extensive network serving the Mediterranean coast, central Anatolia, the Black Sea and the southeast.

Cost

Bus fares are subject to fierce competition between companies and bargains such as student discounts may be offered. Prices reflect what the market will bear, so the fare from a big city to a village is likely to be different to the fare in the opposite direction.

To check which companies service a route and compare prices and times, see www.obilet.com and www.neredennereye.com. Neither offers a complete list of all bus services, but they give you a decent idea of what is available.

Tickets

Although you can usually walk into an otogar (bus station) and buy a ticket for the next bus, it's wise to plan ahead on public holidays, at weekends and during the school holidays from mid-June to mid-September. You can buy seats in advance at bus company offices and online with many of the companies. Note that some bus company online booking processes are convoluted and a few don't let you use foreign passport numbers as ID, so it's usually easier to book in person.

At the otogar When you enter bigger otogars prepare for a few touts offering buses to the destination of your choice. It's usually a good idea to stick to the reputable big-name companies. You may pay a bit more, but you can be more confident the bus is well maintained, will run on time and will have a relief driver on really long hauls. For shorter trips, some companies have big regional networks.

Men and women Unrelated men and women are not supposed to sit together, but the bus companies rarely enforce this in the case of foreigners. Couples may be asked if they are married without having to produce any proof of wedlock or both travellers may find their tickets marked with *bay* (man). Solo male and female travellers will only be assigned a seat next to a passenger of their own gender.

Refunds Getting a refund can be difficult; exchanging it for another ticket with the same company is easier.

Identification Take your passport/ID when booking tickets, as many bus companies now ask to see it. Also keep your passport with you on the journey for security checks.

All seats can be reserved, and your ticket will bear a specific seat number. The ticket agent will have a chart of the seats with those already sold crossed off. They will often assign you a seat, but if you ask to look at the chart and choose a place, you can avoid sitting in the following black spots:

At the front On night buses you may want to avoid the front row of seats behind the driver, which have little legroom, plus you may have to inhale the driver's

cigarette smoke and listen to them chatting to their conductor into the early hours.

Above the wheels Can get bumpy.

In front of the middle door Seats don't recline.

Behind the middle door Little legroom.

At the back Can get stuffy, and may have 'back of the cinema' connotations if you are a lone woman.

Otogars

Most Turkish cities and towns have a bus station, called the otogar, *garaj* or *terminal*, generally located on the outskirts. Besides intercity buses, otogars often handle dolmuşes (minibuses with a prescribed route) to outlying districts or villages. Most have an *emanetçi* (left luggage) room, which you can use for a nominal fee.

Don't believe taxi drivers at otogars who tell you there is no bus or dolmuş to your destination; they may be trying to trick you into taking their taxi. Check with the bus and dolmuş operators.

Cities where the otogar is out of the centre generally have one or more central terminals for dolmuş services to nearby towns – often called Eski Otogar (old bus station), because it used to be the main bus station.

SERVIS

Because most bus stations are some distance from the town or city centre, the bus companies sometimes provide free *servis* (shuttle buses). These take you to the bus company's office or another central location, possibly with stops en route to drop off other passengers. Ask *'Servis var mı?'* ('Is there a *servis*?').

Leaving town Ask about the *servis* when you buy your ticket at the bus company's central office; they will likely instruct you to arrive at the office an hour before the official departure time.

Drawbacks This service saves you a taxi or local public trans-

port fare to the otogar, but involves a lot of hanging around. If you only have limited time in a location, a taxi fare may be a good investment.

Scams Pension owners may try to convince you the private minibus to their pension is a *servis*. Taxi drivers may say the *servis* has left or isn't operating in the hope of convincing you that their cab is the only option. If you do miss a *servis*, inquire at the bus company office – they normally run regularly.

Car & Motorcycle

Driving around Turkey gives you unparalleled freedom to explore the marvellous countryside and coastline, and to follow back roads to hidden villages and obscure ruins.

Bear in mind that Turkey is a huge country and covering long distances by car will eat up your time and money. Consider planes, trains and buses for long journeys, and cars for localised travel.

Public transport is a much easier and less stressful way of getting around the traffic-clogged cities.

Automobile Associations

Turkey's main motoring organisation is the Türkiye Turing ve Otomobil Kurumu (Turkish Touring & Automobile Club; www.turing.org.tr).

Motorcyclist website Horizons Unlimited (www.horizonsunlimited.com/country/turkey) also has Turkey-related information and contacts.

Motorcyclists may want to check out One More Mile Riders Turkey (www.ommriders.com), a community resource for riding in Turkey.

Bring Your Own Vehicle

You can bring your vehicle into Turkey for six months without charge. Ensure you have your car's registration papers, tax number and insurance policy with you. The fact that you brought a vehicle to Turkey will be marked in your passport to ensure you take it back out again.

Checkpoints

Roadblocks are common in eastern Turkey, with police checking vehicles and paperwork are in order. In southeastern Anatolia you may encounter military roadblocks, and roads are sometimes closed completely if there is trouble ahead.

Driving Licences

Drivers must have a valid driving licence. Your own national licence should be sufficient, but an international driving permit (IDP) may be useful if your licence is from a country likely to seem obscure to a Turkish police officer.

Fines

You may be stopped by blue-uniformed *trafik polis*, who can fine you on the spot for speeding. If you know you have done nothing wrong and the police appear to be asking for money, play dumb. You'll probably have to pay up if they persist, but insisting on proof of payment may dissuade them from extracting a fine destined only for their pocket. If they don't ask for on-the-spot payment, contact your car-rental company (or mention the incident when you return the vehicle), as it can pay the fine and take the money from your card. Do the same in the case of fines for other offences, such as not paying a motorway toll.

Fuel & Spare Parts

Turkey has the world's second-highest petrol prices. Petrol/diesel cost about ₺6.50 per litre. Petrol stations are widespread across most of the country. Service staff (rather than drivers) pump the petrol. Many will also clean your windscreen (tip around ₺5). In remoter

parts of central and eastern Anatolia, it's a good idea to have a full tank when you start out in the morning.

Yedek parçaları (spare parts) are readily available in the major cities, especially for European models. Elsewhere, you may have to wait a day or two for parts to be ordered and delivered. Ingenious Turkish mechanics can contrive to keep some US models in service. The *sanayi bölgesi* (industrial zone) on the outskirts of every town generally has a repair shop; for tyre repairs find an *oto lastikçi* (tyre repairer).

Spare motorcycle parts may be hard to come by everywhere except major cities.

Hire

You need to be at least 21 years old, with a year's driving experience, to hire a car in Turkey. Most car-hire companies require a credit card. Most hire cars have standard (manual) transmission; you'll pay more for automatic. The majority of the big-name companies charge hefty one-way fees, starting at around ₺150 and climbing to hundreds of euros for longer distances.

The big international companies – including Avis, Budget, Europcar, Hertz, National and Sixt – operate in the main cities and towns, and most airports. Particularly in eastern Anatolia, stick to the major companies, as the local agencies often do not have insurance. Even some of the major operations are actually franchises in the east, so check the contract carefully, particularly the section relating to insurance. Ask for a copy in English.

If your car incurs any accident damage, or if you cause any, do not move the car before finding a police officer and obtaining a *kaza raporu* (accident report). Contact your car-rental company as soon as possible. In the case of an accident, your hire-car insurance may be void if it

can be shown you were operating under the influence of alcohol or drugs, were speeding, or if you did not submit the required accident report within 48 hours to the rental company.

Insurance

You must have international insurance, covering third-party damage, if you are bringing your own car into the country (further information is available at www.turing.org.tr/international -traffic-insurance-green card/). Buying it at the border is a straightforward process (one month car/motorcycle €59.06/47.25).

When hiring a car, 100%, no-excess insurance is increasingly the only option on offer. If this is not the only option, the basic, mandatory insurance package should cover damage to the vehicle and theft protection – with an excess, which you can reduce or waive for an extra payment.

As in other countries, insurance generally does not cover windows and tyres. You will likely be offered cover for an extra few euros a day.

Road Conditions

Road surfaces and signage are generally excellent – on the main roads, at least. There are good *otoyols* (motorways) connecting major cities across the country.

Elsewhere, roads are being steadily upgraded, although they still tend to be worst in the east, where severe winters play havoc with the surfaces. In northeastern Anatolia, road conditions change from year to year; seek local advice before setting off on secondary roads. There are frequent roadworks in the northeast; even on main roads traffic can crawl along at 30km/h. Dam building and associated road construction in the Artvin/Yusufeli area can cause waits of up to half an hour on some roads. Ask locally about the timing of your journey; on some roads, traffic flows according to a regular timetable, posted at the roadside.

In winter, from December 1 to April 1, winter (snow) tyres are officially obligatory on vehicles throughout the country though local authorities decide whether to enforce the law. During a bad winter, in every region outside of the Aegean and Mediterranean Coast winter tyres are very much a necessity. The police may stop you in more remote areas to check you're properly prepared for emergencies. In mountainous areas such as northeastern Anatolia, landslides and rockfalls are a danger, caused by wet weather and snow-melt in spring. Between İstanbul and Ankara, be aware of the fog belt around Bolu that can seriously reduce visibility, even in summer.

Road Rules

In theory, Turks drive on the right and yield to traffic approaching from the right. In practice, they often drive in the middle and yield to no one. Maximum speed limits, unless otherwise posted, are 50km/h in towns, 90km/h on highways and 120km/h on *otoyols* (motorways).

Safety

Turkey's roads are not particularly safe, and claim about 10,000 lives a year. Turkish drivers can be impatient and incautious, rarely use their indicators and pay little attention to anyone else's, drive too fast both on the open road and through towns, and have an irrepressible urge to overtake – including on blind corners.

To survive on Turkey's roads:

➡ Drive cautiously and defensively.

➡ Do not expect your fellow motorists to obey road signs or behave in a manner you would generally expect at home.

➡ Avoid driving at night, when you won't be able to see potholes, animals, or even vehicles driving without lights, with lights missing, or stopped in the middle of the road. Drivers sometimes flash their lights to announce their approach.

➡ Rather than trying to tackle secondary, gravel roads when visiting remote sights, hire a taxi for the day. It's an extra expense, but the driver should know the terrain and the peace of mind is invaluable.

Tolls

Turkey has a motorway toll system, known as HGS (Hızlı Geçiş Sistemi – 'fast transit system'). Paying tolls should be automatic if you hire a car in Turkey; the vehicle should be equipped with an electronic-chip sticker or a small plastic toll transponder. You simply pay the rental company a flat fee of about €10 for unlimited use of the *otoyols*. Confirm that the car is equipped with a device, which should be located in the top centre of the windscreen. If it is not, you will likely end up with a fine.

If you are driving your own car, you must register the vehicle and buy credit at the earliest opportunity in a branch of the PTT (post office).

Dolmuşes & Midibuses

As well as providing transport within cities and towns, dolmuşes (minibuses with a prescribed route) run between places; you'll usually use them to travel between small towns and villages. Ask, '[Your destination] *dolmuş var mı?*' (Is there a dolmuş to [your destination]?). Most dolmuşes have a set departure timetable; in some remote destinations they wait until every seat is taken before leaving. To let the driver know that you want to hop out, say '*inecek var*' (someone wants to get out).

Midibuses generally operate on routes that are too long for dolmuşes, but not popular enough for full-size buses. They often have narrow seats with rigid upright backs, which can be uncomfortable on long stretches.

Local Transport
City Buses

Most cities and larger towns have swapped to a local pre-paid transport card system for municipal public transport. In this case, it is sometimes impossible to buy single *bilets* (tickets). Instead you purchase a card and credit from either a kiosk (usually found at major bus terminals and transfer points and sometimes at shops near bus stops), or from automatic machines at bus stops. For towns where you can still purchase single tickets, they're usually purchased in advance from the same places. A single fare is normally between ₺1.75 and ₺2.50, except in İstanbul where it is ₺5.

Private buses sometimes operate on the same routes as municipal buses; they are usually older, and accept either cash or tickets.

Local Dolmuş

Dolmuşes are minibuses or, occasionally, *taksi dolmuşes* (shared taxis) that operate on set routes within a city. They're usually faster and only slightly more expensive than the bus. Unlike city buses, which are run by the municipality, dolmuşes are privately run so fares are paid to the driver either when you board or when you get off. In larger cities, dolmuş stops are marked by signs; look for a 'D' and text reading '*Dolmuş İndirme Bindirme Yeri*' (Dolmuş Boarding and Alighting Place). Stops are usually conveniently located near major squares, terminals and intersections.

Metro

Several cities have underground metros, including İstanbul, İzmir, Bursa and Ankara. These are usually quick and simple to use, although you may have to go through the ticket barriers to find a route map. To use most, you need to purchase the city's transport card and some credit. A couple also offer single-use tickets. Fares are usually between ₺2.50 and ₺5.

Taxi

Turkish taxis are fitted with digital meters. If your driver doesn't start theirs, mention it right away by saying 'saatiniz' (your meter). Check your driver is running the right rate, which varies from city to city. The gece (night) rate is 50% more than the gündüz (daytime) rate, but some places, including İstanbul, do not have a night rate.

Some taxi drivers – particularly in İstanbul – try to demand a flat payment from foreigners. In this situation, drivers sometimes offer a decent fare; for example to take you to an airport, where they can pick up a good fare on the return journey. It is more often the case that they demand an exorbitant amount, give you grief and refuse to run the meter. If this happens find another cab and, if convenient, complain to the police. Generally, only when you are using a taxi for a private tour involving waiting time (eg to an archaeological site) should you agree on a set fare, which should work out cheaper than using the meter. In tourist areas, taxi companies normally have set fees for longer journeys written in a ledger at the rank – they can be haggled down a little. Always confirm such fares in advance to avoid argument later.

Tram

Several cities including İstanbul, Antalya, Eskişehir, Kayseri and Konya have tramvays (trams), which are a quick and efficient way of getting around. Usually fares are paid by purchasing that city's transport card or with single tickets (both bought from kiosks or automatic machines). Single fares are usually between ₺2.50 and ₺3.50 except in İstanbul where fares are ₺5.

Transport Cards & HES Codes

Currently in many cities that use a transport card system for municipality-run transport (bus, tram, metro) it's mandatory for your HES code (p607) to be registered to your transport card. Without registration, you will not be able to use that city's public transport system.

Each city has created an individual online registration system. Some of them are:

Antalya https://hes.antalyakart.com.tr/

İstanbul https://kisisellestirme.istanbulkart.istanbul/

Muğla Province (covering Bodrum, Fethiye and Marmaris) https://hes.mugla.bel.tr/

Tours

Every year we receive complaints from travellers who feel they have been fleeced by local travel agents, especially some of those operating in Sultanahmet, İstanbul. However, there are plenty of good agents alongside the sharks. Figure out a ballpark figure for doing the same trip yourself, and shop around before committing.

Recommended operators include the following:

Alkans Tours (Map p561; ☑0530 349 2793, 0432-215 2092; www.easternturkeytour.org; Uğur Plaza Fl 1/103, Abdurahman Gazi 1 Sokak) Eastern Turkey Van-based specialist with recommended scheduled multiday group tours taking in central Anatolia, Cappadocia, the northeast, the southeast and the Black Sea as well as custom-made private itineraries. Also covers Georgia and Armenia.

Bougainville Travel (Map p348; ☑0242-836 3737; www.bougainville-turkey.com; İbrahim Serin Caddesi 10) Long-established English-Turkish tour operator based in Kaş, offering a range of Mediterranean activities and tours.

Crowded House Tours (☑0286-814 1565; www.crowdedhousegallipoli.com; Zubeyde Hanim Meydani 28) Tours of the Gallipoli Peninsula and other areas, including Cappadocia and Ephesus. Based in Eceabat.

Hassle Free Travel Agency (Map p170; ☑0286-213 5969; www.anzachouse.com; Cumhuriyet Meydanı 59) Tours of the Gallipoli Peninsula and other parts of western Turkey, plus gület (traditional wooden sailing boat) cruises. Based in Çanakkale and İstanbul.

Heritage Travel (Map p446; ☑0384-271 2687; www.turkishheritagetravel.com; Uzundere Caddesi; ◷9.30am-5.30pm) Cappadocia specialist with bundles of group day-tour and activity options in the region. Recommended for tailor-made private tours across Turkey.

İstanbul Walks (Map p88; ☑0212-516 6300, 0554 335 6622; www.istanbulwalks.com; 1st fl, Şifa Hamamı Sokak 1, Küçük Ayasofya) The folks behind İstanbul Walks also run short tours to popular sights such as Antalya, Ephesus and Pamukkale as well as day trips from İstanbul to Troy, Gallipoli and Bursa.

Kirkit Voyage (☑0384-511 3259; www.kirkit.com; Atatürk Caddesi 50; ◷9am-6pm) Cappadocia specialist offering customised tours around Turkey, including İstanbul and Ephesus. French spoken, too.

Middle Earth Travel (Map p446; ☑0384-271 2559; www.middleearthtravel.com; Adnan Menderes Caddesi) Nationwide outdoor specialist with scheduled group hiking tours along the Lycian Way, St Paul Trail, in the Kaçkar Mountains (Kaçkar Dağları) and Cappadocia as well as biking and mountaineering tours. Based in Göreme.

Train

Train travel through Turkey is becoming increasingly popular as improvements are made. A high-speed (YHT) network now links İstanbul, Ankara, Eskişehir and Konya with more lines under construction. Of all the long-distance regular trains, the *Doğu Ekspresi* between Ankara and Kars has become a tourism focal point and should be booked as far in advance as possible.

If you're on a budget, an overnight train journey is a great way to save accommodation costs. Many fans also appreciate no-rush travel experiences such as the stunning scenery rolling by and meeting fellow passengers. Occasional unannounced hold-ups and toilets gone feral by the end of the long journey are all part of the adventure.

The Turkish State Railways website is http://tcdd.gov.tr.

Classes

Turkey's high-speed trains (*Yüksek Hızlı Treni*, known as YHT) are ultra-modern, air-conditioned and as comfortable as they come. There are two Pullman seat classes: economy and business. For most people, economy is spacious enough so there's no need to upgrade. Snacks and drinks are available on a trolley service and there's a cafe-car as well.

On regular trains, depending on the route, classes are either Pullman seating in air-conditioned carriages with reclining seats, or a mix of Pullman seating cars and *küşet* (couchette) wagons, which have shared four-person compartments with seats that fold down into shelf-like beds. Some lines

also have *yataklı vagons* (sleeping car) one- and two-bed compartments, with a washbasin, bedding, fridge and even a shared shower. Many regular trains have restaurant cars.

Costs

Train tickets are usually about half the price of bus tickets, with the exception of high-speed services (which are around 5% to 10% cheaper). A return ticket is 20% cheaper than two singles. Students (though you may need a Turkish student card), ISIC cardholders and seniors (60 years plus) get a 20% discount. Children under eight travel free and under-12s are half-price. Teenagers also have a discounted *genç* (youth) fare.

InterRail Global and One Country passes and Balkan Flexipass cover the Turkish railway network, as do the Eurail Global and Select passes. Train Tour Cards, available at major stations, allow unlimited travel on Turkish intercity trains for a month. There are also Tour Cards covering just high-speed trains, intercity trains (apart from sleeping and couchette wagons) or couchettes and sleeping cars.

Long-Distance Trips

The following are useful routes for travellers:

HIGH-SPEED ROUTES

➡ İstanbul Söğütlüçeşme–Eskişehir–Ankara

➡ İstanbul Söğütlüçeşme–Eskişehir–Konya

➡ Ankara–Konya

REGULAR TRAIN ROUTES

➡ Ankara–Eskişehir–İzmir

➡ Ankara–Kayseri–Sivas–Erzurum–Kars

➡ Ankara–Kayseri–Sivas–Malatya–Tatvan

➡ Ankara–Kayseri–Sivas–Malatya–Diyarbakır

➡ Eskişehir–Denizli

➡ İzmir–Konya

➡ Kayseri–Adana

➡ Konya–Adana

➡ Malatya–Adana

Network

The Turkish State Railways network covers the country fairly well, with the notable exception of the coastlines. For the Aegean and Mediterranean coasts you can travel by train to İzmir and take the bus from there.

From İstanbul, you can access the rest of the Anatolian train network by taking a high-speed (YHT) train to Ankara, Eskişehir or Konya. There are four İstanbul train stations where you can board; İstanbul Söğütlüçeşme in Kadıköy is the most useful for travellers. Heading direct to/from Sabiha Gökçen International Airport, use İstanbul Pendik (25km southeast of the centre).

Reservations

It is wise to buy your seat at least a few days before travelling. For the *yataklı* (sleeping car) wagons, reserve as far in advance as possible, especially if a religious or public holiday is looming. Weekend trains tend to be busiest.

You can buy tickets at stations (only major stations for sleeping car tickets), through travel agencies and, with more difficulty, at http://tcdd.gov.tr. The website www.seat61.com/Turkey2 gives step-by-step instructions for navigating the transaction.

Timetables

You can double-check train departure times, which do change, at http://tcdd.gov.tr.

Timetables sometimes indicate stations rather than cities, eg Basmane rather than İzmir.

Health

BEFORE YOU GO

Health Insurance

Turkish doctors generally expect payment in cash. Find out in advance if your travel insurance will reimburse you for overseas health expenditures or, less likely, pay providers directly. If you are required to pay upfront, keep all documentation. Some policies ask you to call a centre in your home country (reverse charges) for an immediate assessment of your problem. It's also worth ensuring your insurance covers ambulances and transport. Not all policies cover emergency medical evacuation home or to a hospital in a major city, which may be necessary in a serious emergency.

Medical Checklist

Consider packing the following in your medical kit:

➡ acetaminophen/ paracetamol (Tylenol) or aspirin

➡ adhesive or paper tape

➡ antibacterial cream or ointment

➡ antibiotics (if travelling off the beaten track)

➡ antidiarrhoeal drugs (eg loperamide)

➡ antihistamines (for hay fever and allergic reactions)

➡ anti-inflammatory drugs (eg ibuprofen)

➡ bandages, gauze and gauze rolls

➡ DEET-based insect repellent for the skin

➡ insect spray for clothing, tents and bed nets

➡ water purification tablets

➡ oral rehydration salts (eg Dioralyte)

➡ pocket knife, scissors, safety pins and tweezers

➡ steroid cream or cortisone

➡ sunblock (it's expensive in Turkey)

➡ syringes and sterile needles (if travelling to remote areas)

➡ thermometer

RECOMMENDED VACCINATIONS

The following are recommended as routine for travellers, regardless of the region they are visiting:

➡ diphtheria-tetanus-polio

➡ influenza

➡ measles-mumps-rubella (MMR)

➡ varicella (chickenpox)

Hepatitis A and B shots are also recommended for travellers to Turkey

Rabies is endemic in Turkey, so if you will be travelling off the beaten track, consider an antirabies vaccination.

Malaria is still found from May to October in the provinces of Diyarbakır, Mardin and Şanlıurfa, however, the risk of travellers catching malaria is low.

Get vaccinations four to eight weeks before departure, and ask for an International Certificate of Vaccination or Prophylaxis (ICVP or 'yellow card'), listing all the vaccinations you've received.

Websites

Consult your government's travel health website before departure, if one is available. The Health section at www.lonelyplanet.com/turkey has further information.

IN TURKEY

Availability & Cost of Health Care

The best private hospitals in major centres offer world-class service but they are expensive. Smaller private hospitals don't always have high standards of care and their state-run equivalents even less so. The bigger private hospitals in cities often offer a translator service for foreign patients. Apart from that, English (and other foreign languages) is minimal.

Hospitals & clinics Medicine, and even sterile dressings or intravenous fluids, may need to be bought from a local pharmacy. Nursing care is frequently rudimentary, as family often look after Turkish patients.

Dentists Ask for local recommendations as standards vary. The best offer world-class service. There is a risk of hepatitis B and HIV transmission via poorly sterilised equipment, so watch the tools in use carefully.

Pharmacists For minor illnesses, pharmacists can often provide advice.

Infectious Diseases

Diphtheria

Spread through Close respiratory contact.

Symptoms & effects A high temperature and severe sore throat. Sometimes a membrane forms across the throat, requiring a tracheotomy to prevent suffocation.

Prevention The vaccine is given as an injection, normally with tetanus and in many countries as a routine childhood jab. Recommended for those likely to be in close contact with the local population in infected areas.

Hepatitis A

Spread through Contaminated food (particularly shellfish) and water.

> ### TAP WATER
>
> Turkish tap water is officially safe to drink. However, due to heavy chlorination use in the filtration process, which makes it taste less than delicious, and old plumbing infrastructure of metal rather than plastic pipes in many towns and cities (which can create health hazards due to pipe rust and calcification), many Turks refuse to drink it. Many of the mild stomach complaints travellers have in Turkey are blamed on the water. To avoid plastic bottle waste, consider bringing along a water bottle with an inbuilt filtration system.

Symptoms & effects Jaundice, dark urine, a yellow colour to the whites of the eyes, fever and abdominal pain. Although rarely fatal, it can cause prolonged lethargy and delayed recovery.

Prevention Vaccine given as an injection, with a booster extending the protection offered. Available in some countries as a combined single-dose vaccine with hepatitis B or typhoid.

Hepatitis B

Spread through Infected blood, contaminated needles and sexual intercourse.

Symptoms & effects Jaundice and liver problems (occasionally failure).

Prevention The vaccine is worth considering for Turkey, where the disease is endemic. Many countries give it as part of routine childhood vaccinations.

Leishmaniasis

Spread through The bite of an infected sandfly or dog. More prevalent in areas bordering Syria.

Symptoms & effects A slowly growing skin lump or ulcer. It may develop into a serious, life-threatening fever, usually accompanied by anaemia and weight loss.

Leptospirosis

Spread through The excreta of infected rodents, especially rats. It is unusual for travellers to be affected unless living in poor sanitary conditions.

Symptoms & effects Fever, jaundice, and hepatitis and renal failure that may be fatal.

Malaria

Spread through Mosquito bites. The risk is minimal to zero in all regions of Turkey except southeastern Turkey, where it's considered low risk.

Symptoms & effects Malaria almost always starts with marked shivering, fever and sweating. Muscle pain, headache and vomiting are common. Symptoms may occur anywhere from a few days to three weeks after a bite by an infected mosquito. The illness can start while you are taking preventative tablets, if they are not fully effective, or after you have finished taking your tablets. Malaria symptoms can be mistaken for flu by travellers who return home during winter.

Prevention Most travel health advisories for Turkey council awareness of risk and protection (covering up and using repellent) for travellers heading to the southeast region rather than antimalarial drugs due to the low risk. Check with your doctor before travelling.

Rabies

Spread through Bites or licks on broken skin from an infected animal.

Symptoms & effects Initially, pain or tingling at the site of the bite, with fever, loss of appetite and headache. With 'furious' rabies, there is a growing sense of anxiety, jumpiness, disorientation, neck stiffness, sometimes seizures or convulsions, and hydrophobia (fear of water). 'Dumb' rabies (less common) affects the spinal cord, causing muscle paralysis then heart and lung failure. If untreated, both forms are fatal.

Prevention People travelling to remote areas, where a reliable source of post-bite vaccine is not available within 24 hours, should be vaccinated. Any bite, scratch or lick from a warm-blooded, furry animal should immediately be thoroughly cleaned. If you have not been vaccinated and you get bitten, you will need a course of injections starting as soon as possible after the injury. Vaccination does not provide immunity, it merely buys you more time to seek medical help.

Tuberculosis

Spread through Close respiratory contact and, occasionally, infected milk or milk products.

Symptoms & effects Can be asymptomatic, although symptoms can include a cough, weight loss or fever months or even years after exposure. An X-ray is the best way to confirm if you have tuberculosis.

Prevention BCG vaccine is recommended for those likely to be mixing closely with the local population – visiting family, planning a long stay, or working as a teacher or healthcare worker. As it's a live vaccine, it should not be given to pregnant women or immunocompromised individuals.

Typhoid

Spread through Food or water contaminated by infected human faeces.

Symptoms & effects Initially, usually a fever or a pink rash on the abdomen. Septicaemia (blood poisoning) may also occur.

Prevention Vaccination given by injection. In some countries, an oral vaccine is available.

Environmental Hazards

Heat Illness

Causes Sweating heavily, fluid loss and inadequate replacement of fluids and salt. Particularly

common when you exercise outside in a hot climate.

Symptoms & effects Headache, dizziness and tiredness.

Prevention Drink sufficient water (you should produce pale, diluted urine). By the time you are thirsty, you are already dehydrated.

Treatment Replace fluids by drinking water, fruit juice or both, and cool down with cold water and fans. Treat salt loss by consuming salty fluids, such as soup or broth, and adding a little more table salt to foods.

Heatstroke

Causes Extreme heat; high humidity; dehydration; drug or alcohol use or physical exertion in the sun. Occurs when the body's heat-regulating mechanism breaks down.

Symptoms & effects An excessive rise in body temperature; sweating stops; irrational and hyperactive behaviour; and eventually loss of consciousness and death.

Treatment Rapidly cool down by spraying the body with water and using a fan. Emergency fluid intake and replacing electrolytes by intravenous drip are usually also required.

Insect Bites & Stings

Causes Mosquitoes, sandflies (located around the Mediterranean beaches), scorpions (found in arid or dry climates), bees and wasps (in the Aegean and Mediterranean coastal areas, particularly around Marmaris), and centipedes.

Symptoms & effects Even if mosquitoes do not carry malaria, they can cause irritation and infected bites. Sandflies have a nasty, itchy bite, and occasionally carry leishmaniasis or Pappataci fever. Turkey's small white scorpions can give a painful sting that will bother you for up to 24 hours.

Prevention DEET-based insect repellent. Citronella candles. Cover up with light-coloured clothing. Avoid riversides and marshy areas from late after-

noon onwards. Take a mosquito head net and bed net.

Treatment Antihistamine cream to sooth and reduce inflammation.

Snake Bites

Prevention Do not walk barefoot or stick your hands into holes or cracks when exploring nature or touring overgrown ruins and little-visited historic sites.

Treatment Do not panic: half of those bitten by venomous snakes are not actually injected with poison (envenomed). Immobilise the bitten limb with a splint (eg a stick) and bandage the site with firm pressure. Do not apply a tourniquet, or cut or suck the bite. Note the snake's appearance for identification purposes, and get medical help as soon as possible so that antivenene can be given.

Travellers' Diarrhoea

To prevent diarrhoea, avoid tap water unless it has been boiled, filtered or chemically disinfected (with iodine or purification tablets). Eat fresh fruit or vegetables only if they're cooked or you have peeled them yourself, and avoid dairy products that might contain unpasteurised milk. Buffet meals are risky since food may not be kept hot enough; meals freshly cooked in front of you in a busy restaurant are safer.

If you develop diarrhoea, drink plenty of fluids, and preferably an oral rehydration solution containing salt and sugar. A few loose stools don't require treatment, but if you start having more than four or five motions a day, you should take an antidiarrhoeal agent (such as loperamide) or, if that's unavailable, an antibiotic (usually a quinolone drug). If diarrhoea is bloody, persists for more than 72 hours or is accompanied by fever, shaking chills or severe abdominal pain, you should seek medical attention.

Language

Turkish belongs to the Ural-Altaic language family. It's the official language of Turkey and Northern Cyprus, and has approximately 70 million speakers worldwide.

Pronouncing Turkish is pretty simple for English speakers as most Turkish sounds are also found in English. If you read our coloured pronunciation guides as if they were English, you should be understood just fine. Note that the symbol ew represents the sound 'ee' pronounced with rounded lips (as in 'few'), and that the symbol uh is pronounced like the 'a' in 'ago'. The Turkish r is always rolled and v is pronounced a little softer than in English.

Word stress is quite light in Turkish – in our pronunciation guides the stressed syllables are in italics.

BASICS

Hello.
Merhaba.   mer·ha·ba

Goodbye.
Hoşçakal.   hosh·cha·kal
(said by person leaving)

Güle güle.   gew·le gew·le
(said by person staying)

Yes.
Evet.   e·vet

No.
Hayır.   ha·yuhr

WANT MORE?

For in-depth language information and handy phrases, check out Lonely Planet's *Turkish Phrasebook*. You'll find it at **shop.lonelyplanet.com**.

Excuse me.
Bakar mısınız.   ba·kar muh·suh·nuhz

Sorry.
Özür dilerim.   er·zewr dee·le·reem

Please.
Lütfen.   lewt·fen

Thank you.
Teşekkür ederim.   te·shek·kewr e·de·reem

You're welcome.
Birşey değil.   beer·shay de·eel

How are you?
Nasılsınız?   na·suhl·suh·nuhz

Fine, and you?
İyiyim, ya siz?   ee·yee·yeem ya seez

What's your name?
Adınız nedir?   a·duh·nuhz ne·deer

My name is ...
Benim adım ...   be·neem a·duhm ...

Do you speak English?
İngilizce   een·gee·leez·je
konuşuyor   ko·noo·shoo·yor
musunuz?   moo·soo·nooz

I understand.
Anlıyorum.   an·luh·yo·room

I don't understand.
Anlamıyorum.   an·la·muh·yo·room

ACCOMMODATION

Where can I find a ...?	Nerede ... bulabilirim?	ne·re·de ... boo·la·bee·lee·reem
campsite	kamp yeri	kamp ye·ree
guesthouse	misafirhane	mee·sa·feer·ha·ne
hotel	otel	o·tel
pension	pansiyon	pan·see·yon
youth hostel	gençlik hosteli	gench·leek hos·te·lee

How much is it per night/person?
Geceliği/Kişi · ge·je·lee·ee/kee·shee
başına ne kadar? · ba·shuh·na ne ka·dar

Is breakfast included?
Kahvaltı dahil mi? · kah·val·tuh da·heel mee

Do you have a ...?	... odanız var mı?	... o·da·nuz var muh
single room	Tek kişilik	tek kee·shee·leek
double room	İki kişilik	ee·kee kee·shee·leek

air conditioning	klima	klee·ma
bathroom	banyo	ban·yo
window	pencere	pen·je·re

DIRECTIONS

Where is ...?
... nerede? · ... ne·re·de

What's the address?
Adresi nedir? · ad·re·see ne·deer

Could you write it down, please?
Lütfen yazar · lewt·fen ya·zar
mısınız? · muh·suh·nuhz

Can you show me (on the map)?
Bana (haritada) · ba·na (ha·ree·ta·da)
gösterebilir · gers·te·re·bee·leer
misiniz? · mee·seen·neez

It's straight ahead.
Tam karşıda. · tam kar·shuh·da

at the traffic lights
trafik · tra·feek
ışıklarından · uh·shuhk·la·ruhn·dan

at the corner	köşeden	ker·she·den
behind	arkasında	ar·ka·suhn·da
far (from)	uzak	oo·zak
in front of	önünde	er·newn·de
near (to)	yakınında	ya·kuh·nuhn·da
opposite	karşısında	kar·shuh·suhn·da
Turn left.	Sola dön.	so·la dern
Turn right.	Sağa dön.	sa·a dern

EATING & DRINKING

What would you recommend?
Ne tavsiye · ne tav·see·ye
edersiniz? · e·der·see·neez

What's in that dish?
Bu yemekte neler var? · boo ye·mek·te ne·ler var

I don't eat ...
... yemiyorum. · ... ye·mee·yo·room

Cheers!
Şerefe! · she·re·fe

KEY PATTERNS

To get by in Turkish, mix and match these simple patterns with words of your choice:

When's (the next bus)?
(Sonraki otobüs) · (son·ra·kee o·to·bews)
ne zaman? · ne za·man

Where's (the market)?
(Pazar yeri) nerede? · (pa·zar ye·ree) ne·re·de

Where can I (buy a ticket)?
Nereden (bilet · ne·re·den (bee·let
alabilirim)? · a·la·bee·lee·reem)

I have (a reservation).
(Rezervasyonum) · (re·zer·vas·yo·noom)
var. · var

Do you have (a map)?
(Haritanız) · (ha·ree·ta·nuhz)
var mı? · var muh

Is there (a toilet)?
(Tuvalet) var mı? · (too·va·let) var muh

I'd like (the menu).
(Menüyü) · (me·new·yew)
istiyorum. · ees·tee·yo·room

I want to (make a call).
(Bir görüşme · (beer ger·rewsh·me
yapmak) · yap·mak)
istiyorum. · ees·tee·yo·room

Do I have to (declare this)?
(Bunu beyan · (boo·noo be·yan
etmem) gerekli mi? · et·mem) ge·rek·lee mee

I need (assistance).
(Yardıma) · (yar·duh·ma)
ihtiyacım var. · eeh·tee·ya·juhm var

That was delicious!
Nefisti! · ne·fees·tee

The bill/check, please.
Hesap lütfen. · he·sap lewt·fen

I'd like a table for ...	... bir masa ayırtmak istiyorum.	... beer ma·sa a·yuhrt·mak ees·tee·yo·room
(eight) o'clock	Saat (sekiz) için	sa·at (se·keez) ee·cheen
(two) people	(İki) kişilik	(ee·kee) kee·shee·leek

Key Words

appetisers	mezeler	me·ze·ler
bottle	şişe	shee·she
bowl	kase	ka·se
breakfast	kahvaltı	kah·val·tuh
(too) cold	(çok) soğuk	(chok) so·ook

cup	fincan	feen·jan
delicatessen	şarküteri	shar·kew·te·ree
dinner	akşam yemeği	ak·sham ye·me·ee
dish	yemek	ye·mek
food	yiyecek	yee·ye·jek
fork	çatal	cha·tal
glass	bardak	bar·dak
grocery	bakkal	bak·kal
halal	helal	he·lal
high chair	mama sandalyesi	ma·ma san·dal·ye·see
hot (warm)	sıcak	suh·jak
knife	bıçak	buh·chak
kosher	koşer	ko·sher
lunch	öğle yemeği	er·le ye·me·ee
main courses	ana yemekler	a·na ye·mek·ler
market	pazar	pa·zar
menu	yemek listesi	ye·mek lees·te·see
plate	tabak	ta·bak
restaurant	restoran	res·to·ran
spicy	acı	a·juh
spoon	kaşık	ka·shuhk
vegetarian	vejeteryan	ve·zhe·ter·yan

Meat & Fish

anchovy	hamsi	ham·see
beef	sığır eti	suh·uhr e·tee
calamari	kalamares	ka·la·ma·res
chicken	piliç/ tavuk	pee·leech/ ta·vook
fish	balık	ba·luhk
lamb	kuzu	koo·zoo
liver	ciğer	jee·er
mussels	midye	meed·ye
pork	domuz eti	do·mooz e·tee
veal	dana eti	da·na e·tee

Fruit & Vegetables

apple	elma	el·ma
apricot	kayısı	ka·yuh·suh
banana	muz	mooz
capsicum	biber	bee·ber
carrot	havuç	ha·vooch
cucumber	salatalık	sa·la·ta·luhk
fruit	meyve	may·ve
grape	üzüm	ew·zewm
melon	kavun	ka·voon

olive	zeytin	zay·teen
onion	soğan	so·an
orange	portakal	por·ta·kal
peach	şeftali	shef·ta·lee
potato	patates	pa·ta·tes
spinach	ıspanak	uhs·pa·nak
tomato	domates	do·ma·tes
watermelon	karpuz	kar·pooz

Other

bread	ekmek	ek·mek
cheese	peynir	pay·neer
egg	yumurta	yoo·moor·ta
honey	bal	bal
ice	buz	booz
pepper	kara biber	ka·ra bee·ber
rice	pirinç/ pilav	pee·reench/ pee·lav
salt	tuz	tooz
soup	çorba	chor·ba
sugar	şeker	she·ker
Turkish delight	lokum	lo·koom

Drinks

beer	bira	bee·ra
coffee	kahve	kah·ve
(orange) juice	(portakal) suyu	(por·ta·kal soo·yoo)
milk	süt	sewt
mineral water	maden suyu	ma·den soo·yoo
soft drink	alkolsüz içecek	al·kol·sewz ee·che·jek
tea	çay	chai
water	su	soo
wine	şarap	sha·rap
yoghurt	yoğurt	yo·oort

Signs	
Açık	Open
Bay	Male
Bayan	Female
Çıkışı	Exit
Giriş	Entrance
Kapalı	Closed
Sigara İçilmez	No Smoking
Tuvaletler	Toilets
Yasak	Prohibited

EMERGENCIES

Help!
İmdat! eem·dat

I'm lost.
Kayboldum. kai·bol·doom

Leave me alone!
Git başımdan! geet ba·shuhm·dan

There's been an accident.
Bir kaza oldu. beer ka·za ol·doo

Can I use your phone?
Telefonunuzu te·le·fo·noo·noo·zoo
kullanabilir miyim? kool·la·na·bee·leer mee·yeem

Call a doctor!
Doktor çağırın! dok·tor cha·uh·ruhn

Call the police!
Polis çağırın! po·lees cha·uh·ruhn

I'm ill.
Hastayım. has·ta·yuhm

It hurts here.
Burası ağrıyor. boo·ra·suh a·ruh·yor

I'm allergic to (nuts).
(Çerezlere) (che·rez·le·re)
alerjim var. a·ler·zheem var

SHOPPING & SERVICES

I'd like to buy ...
... almak istiyorum. ... al·mak ees·tee·yo·room

I'm just looking.
Sadece bakıyorum. sa·de·je ba·kuh·yo·room

May I look at it?
Bakabilir miyim? ba·ka·bee·leer mee·yeem

The quality isn't good.
Kalitesi iyi değil. ka·lee·te·see ee·yee de·eel

How much is it?
Ne kadar? ne ka·dar

It's too expensive.
Bu çok pahalı. boo chok pa·ha·luh

Do you have something cheaper?
Daha ucuz birşey da·ha oo·jooz beer·shay
var mı? var muh

There's a mistake in the bill.
Hesapta bir he·sap·ta beer
yanlışlık var. yan·luhsh·luhk var

Question Words		
How?	*Nasıl?*	na·seel
What?	*Ne?*	ne
When?	*Ne zaman?*	ne za·man
Where?	*Nerede?*	ne·re·de
Which?	*Hangi?*	han·gee
Who?	*Kim?*	keem
Why?	*Neden?*	ne·den

ATM	*bankamatik*	ban·ka·ma·teek
credit card	*kredi kartı*	kre·dee kar·tuh
post office	*postane*	pos·ta·ne
signature	*imza*	eem·za
tourist office	*turizm*	too·reezm
	bürosu	bew·ro·soo

TIME & DATES

What time is it?	*Saat kaç?*	sa·at kach
It's (10) o'clock.	*Saat (on).*	sa·at (on)
Half past (10).	*(On) buçuk.*	(on) boo·chook

in the morning	*öğleden evvel*	er·le·den ev·vel
in the afternoon	*öğleden sonra*	er·le·den son·ra
in the evening	*akşam*	ak·sham
yesterday	*dün*	dewn
today	*bugün*	boo·gewn
tomorrow	*yarın*	ya·ruhn

Monday	*Pazartesi*	pa·zar·te·see
Tuesday	*Salı*	sa·luh
Wednesday	*Çarşamba*	char·sham·ba
Thursday	*Perşembe*	per·shem·be
Friday	*Cuma*	joo·ma
Saturday	*Cumartesi*	joo·mar·te·see
Sunday	*Pazar*	pa·zar

January	*Ocak*	o·jak
February	*Şubat*	shoo·bat
March	*Mart*	mart
April	*Nisan*	nee·san
May	*Mayıs*	ma·yuhs
June	*Haziran*	ha·zee·ran
July	*Temmuz*	tem·mooz
August	*Ağustos*	a·oos·tos
September	*Eylül*	ay·lewl
October	*Ekim*	e·keem
November	*Kasım*	ka·suhm
December	*Aralık*	a·ra·luhk

TRANSPORT

Public Transport

At what time	*... ne zaman*	*... ne za·man*
does the ...	*kalkacak/*	kal·ka·jak/
leave/arrive?	*varır?*	va·ruhr
boat	*Vapur*	va·poor
bus	*Otobüs*	o·to·bews
plane	*Uçak*	oo·chak
train	*Tren*	tren

Numbers

1	*bir*	beer
2	*iki*	ee·kee
3	*üç*	ewch
4	*dört*	dert
5	*beş*	besh
6	*altı*	al·tuh
7	*yedi*	ye·dee
8	*sekiz*	se·keez
9	*dokuz*	do·kooz
10	*on*	on
20	*yirmi*	yeer·mee
30	*otuz*	o·tooz
40	*kırk*	kuhrk
50	*elli*	el·lee
60	*altmış*	alt·muhsh
70	*yetmiş*	et·meesh
80	*seksen*	sek·sen
90	*doksan*	dok·san
100	*yüz*	yewz
1000	*bin*	been

Does it stop at (Maltepe)?
(Maltepe'de) (mal·te·pe·de)
durur mu? doo·roor moo

What's the next stop?
Sonraki durak son·ra·kee doo·rak
hangisi? han·gee·see

Please tell me when we get to (Beşiktaş).
(Beşiktaş'a) (be·sheek·ta·sha)
vardığımızda var·duh·uh·muhz·da
lütfen bana lewt·fen ba·na
söyleyin. say·le·yeen

I'd like to get off at (Kadıköy).
(Kadıköy'de) inmek (ka·duh·kay·de) een·mek
istiyorum. ees·tee·yo·room

I'd like a ...	*(Bostancı'ya)*	(bos·tan·juh·ya)
ticket to	*... bir bilet*	... beer bee·let
(Bostancı).	*lütfen.*	lewt·fen
1st-class	*Birinci*	bee·reen·jee
	mevki	mev·kee
2nd-class	*İkinci*	ee·keen·jee
	mevki	mev·kee
one-way	*Gidiş*	gee·deesh
return	*Gidiş-*	gee·deesh·
	dönüş	der·newsh
first	*ilk*	eelk
last	*son*	son
next	*geleçek*	ge·le·jek

I'd like	*... bir yer*	... beer yer
a/an ... seat.	*istiyorum.*	ees·tee·yo·room
aisle	*Koridor*	ko·ree·dor
	tarafında	ta·ra·fuhn·da
window	*Cam kenarı*	jam ke·na·ruh
cancelled	*iptal*	eep·tal
	edildi	e·deel·dee
delayed	*ertelendi*	er·te·len·dee
platform	*peron*	pe·ron
ticket office	*bilet*	bee·let
	gişesi	gee·she·see
timetable	*tarife*	ta·ree·fe
train station	*istasyon*	ees·tas·yon

Driving & Cycling

I'd like to	*Bir ...*	beer ...
hire a ...	*kiralamak*	kee·ra·la·mak
	istiyorum.	ees·tee·yo·room
4WD	*dört çeker*	dert che·ker
bicycle	*bisiklet*	bee·seek·let
car	*araba*	a·ra·ba
motorcycle	*motosiklet*	mo·to·seek·let
bike shop	*bisikletçi*	bee·seek·let·chee
child seat	*çocuk*	cho·jook
	koltuğu	kol·too·oo
diesel	*dizel*	dee·zel
helmet	*kask*	kask
mechanic	*araba*	a·ra·ba
	tamircisi	ta·meer·jee·see
petrol/gas	*benzin*	ben·zeen
service	*benzin*	ben·zeen
station	*istasyonu*	ees·tas·yo·noo

Is this the road to (Taksim)?
(Taksim'e) giden (tak·see·me) gee·den
yol bu mu? yol boo moo

(How long) Can I park here?
Buraya (ne kadar boo·ra·ya (ne ka·dar
süre) park sew·re) park
edebilirim? e·de·bee·lee·reem

**The car/motorbike has broken down
(at Osmanbey).**
Arabam/ a·ra·bam/
Motosikletim mo·to·seek·le·teem
(Osmanbey'de) (os·man·bay·de)
bozuldu. bo·zool·doo

I have a flat tyre.
Lastiğim patladı. las·tee·eem pat·la·duh

I've run out of petrol.
Benzinim bitti. ben·zee·neem beet·tee

GLOSSARY

acropolis – hilltop citadel and temples of a classical Hellenic city

ada(sı) – island

agora – open space for commerce and politics in a Greco-Roman city

Anatolia – the Asian part of Turkey; also called *Asia Minor*

arasta – row of shops near a mosque, the rent from which supports the mosque

Asia Minor – see *Anatolia*

bahçe(si) – garden

bedesten – vaulted, fireproof market enclosure where valuable goods are kept

belediye (sarayı) – municipal council, town hall

bey – polite form of address for a man; follows the name

bilet – ticket

bulvar(ı) – boulevard or avenue; often abbreviated to 'bul'

cadde(si) – street; often abbreviated to 'cad'

cami(i) – mosque

caravanserai – large fortified way-station for (trade) caravans

çarşı(sı) – market, bazaar; sometimes town centre

çay bahçesi – tea garden

dağ(ı) – mountain

deniz – sea

dervish – member of Mevlevi Muslim brotherhood

dolmuş – shared taxi; can be a minibus or sedan

döviz (bürosu) – currency exchange (office)

emir – Turkish tribal chieftain

eski – old (thing, not person)

ev pansiyonu – pension in a private home

geçit, geçidi – (mountain) pass

gişe – ticket kiosk

göl(ü) – lake

gület – traditional Turkish wooden yacht

hamam(ı) – Turkish bathhouse

han(ı) – see *caravanserai*

hanım – polite form of address for a woman

haremlik – family/women's quarters of a residence; see also *selamlık*

hisar(ı) – fortress or citadel

imam – prayer leader, Muslim cleric

iskele(si) – jetty, quay

kale(si) – fortress, citadel

kapı(sı) – door, gate

kaplıca – thermal spring or baths

kaya – cave

KDV – katma değer vergisi, Turkey's value-added tax

kebapçı – place selling kebaps

kervansaray(ı) – Turkish for *caravanserai*

kilim – flat-weave rug

kilise(si) – church

köfte – meatballs

köfteci – *köfte* maker or seller

konak, konağı – mansion, government headquarters

köprü(sü) – bridge

köşk(ü) – pavilion, villa

köy(ü) – village

kule(si) – tower

külliye(si) – mosque complex including seminary, hospital and soup kitchen

kümbet – vault, cupola, dome; tomb topped by this

liman(ı) – harbour

lokanta – eatery serving ready-made food

mağara(sı) – cave

mahalle(si) – neighbourhood, district of a city

medrese(si) – Islamic theological seminary or school attached to a mosque

mescit, mescidi – prayer room, small mosque

meydan(ı) – public square, open place

meyhane – tavern, wine shop

mihrab – niche in a mosque indicating the direction of Mecca

milli parkı – national park

müze(si) – museum

nargile – traditional water pipe (for smoking); hookah

necropolis – city of the dead, cemetery

oda(sı) – room

otobüs – bus

otogar – bus station

Ottoman – of or pertaining to the Ottoman Empire, which lasted from the end of the 13th century to the end of WWI

pansiyon – pension, B&B, guesthouse

paşa – general, governor

pastane – pastry shop (patisserie); also *pastahane*

pazar(ı) – weekly market, bazaar

peribacalar – fairy chimneys (rock formation)

pideci – pide maker or seller

plaj – beach

Ramazan – Islamic holy month of fasting

saray(ı) – palace

sedir – bench seating that doubled as a bed in Ottoman houses

şehir – city; municipality

sema – *dervish* ceremony

semahane – hall where whirling *dervish* ceremonies are held

servis – shuttle minibus service to and from the *otogar*

sokak, sokağı – street or lane; often abbreviated to 'sk'

Sufi – Muslim mystic, member of a mystic (*dervish*) brotherhood

Thrace – the European part of Turkey

tramvay – tram

tuff, tufa – soft stone laid down as volcanic ash

türbe(si) – tomb, grave, mausoleum

yayla – highland pastures

yol(u) – road, way

Behind the Scenes

SEND US YOUR FEEDBACK

We love to hear from travellers – your comments keep us on our toes and help make our books better. Our well-travelled team reads every word on what you loved or loathed about this book. Although we cannot reply individually to your submissions, we always guarantee that your feedback goes straight to the appropriate authors, in time for the next edition. Each person who sends us information is thanked in the next edition – the most useful submissions are rewarded with a selection of digital PDF chapters.

Visit **lonelyplanet.com/contact** to submit your updates and suggestions or to ask for help. Our award-winning website also features inspirational travel stories, news and discussions.

Note: We may edit, reproduce and incorporate your comments in Lonely Planet products such as guidebooks, websites and digital products, so let us know if you don't want your comments reproduced or your name acknowledged. For a copy of our privacy policy visit lonelyplanet.com/privacy.

OUR READERS

Many thanks to the travellers who used the last edition and wrote to us with helpful hints, useful advice and interesting anecdotes:

Ali Ozguven, Anthony Sheppard, Babur Karaoglu, Emre Deliveli, Hilary Swift, Jacques Amateis, Jeff Randall, Jeremy Star, Jeremy Thomas, Julie Woods, Kenneth Padley, Luc Carnier, Malgorzata Sinica, Maria Casanovas, Marie-Eve Pages, Murathan Arslancan, Nathan Geffen, Ozge Kalaycioglu, Sain Alizada, Simon Lemon, Sylvia Bartels, Will Joneyau Chan, Yasar Ozkul

WRITER THANKS

Jessica Lee

A huge *çok teşekkürler* to Deniz Aşık and family, İbrahim Ağartan, and Sabahattin Alkan for advice and local knowledge. A big cheers to Kuki Taylor and Kristen Post for coming along for bits of the journey and Lauren Pucci for exceptional chauffeur services on those bits. Also thanks to Yvette Koç, who put up with my random Turkish grammar queries, Angela Şişman, Ruth Lockwood, Diane Nelson and fellow writers Brett Atkinson, Virginia Maxwell and Mark Elliott.

Brett Atkinson

Returning to explore one of my favourite countries is always a pleasure, and special thanks for this trip must go to Jennifer Hattam,

Selin Rozanes, Ceylan Zera and Sabahattin Alkan. Thanks also for the ongoing and unwavering hospitality I enjoyed along the way, and to the editorial and commissioning team at Lonely Planet. *Serefe!* (Cheers!) to my talented co-authors Virginia, Jess, Iain, Mark and Steve, and final love and thanks to Carol and my family back home in Yeni Zelanda.

Mark Elliott

In Turkey enormous thanks are due to dozens of people, notably Onur, Mehmet in Kars, Sali at Giresun, Nuri in Amasra, Murat and the mystery drivers in Doğubayazıt, Can in İnebolu, Serhad in Samsun, Serkan in Ünye, Jane in Ardahan, the Toprak crew at Sarıkamış, Murat and Beyza at Yason Kilesesi, Adele and Inis at Maçka, Aydın at Fatsa, Sven at Barhal, and Mohammad and Sammet in Trabzon. Love and infinite thanks, too, to my wonderful family and especially to the lovely Sally for joining me on the most special journey of all – life.

Steve Fallon

Çok teşekkürler to those who provided assistance, ideas and/or hospitality along the way in the eastern Mediterranean, including Mehmet Şirin in Kızkalesi, Hüseyin Algumuş and Hikmet Oğuzcan in Tarsus and Nilüfer Sucu in Arsuz. As always, I'd like to dedicate my share of this to now-husband Michael Rothschild, with love and gratitude and hopes for even better times in Kördere.

Virginia Maxwell

Many thanks to Pat Yale, Mehmet Umur, Emel Güntaş, Özlem Tuna, Atilla Tuna, Faruk Boyacı, Tahir Karabaş, Jen Hartin, Eveline Zoutendijk, Monica Fritz, Jennifer Gaudet, Ken Dakan, Max Handsaker and the many others who shared their knowledge and love of İstanbul with me. Thanks, too, to Peter Handsaker, who held the fort at home.

Iain Stewart

Thanks to the hospitable Turks along the Aegean and Mediterranean coasts for making this trip such a pleasure. In particular to Ercan and family in Selçuk, Mustafa Akkan in Kaş, the Çirali gang for the yoga, and all the Lonely Planet teams in Dublin, London and Melbourne.

ACKNOWLEDGEMENTS

Climate map data adapted from Peel MC, Finlayson BL & McMahon TA (2007) 'Updated World Map of the Köppen-Geiger Climate Classification', *Hydrology and Earth System Sciences*, 11, 1633–44.

Illustrations pp68-9, pp78-9 and pp230-1 by Javier Zarracina.

Cover photograph: Yeşil Cami, Bursa; Ivan Vdovin/AWL Images ©.

THIS BOOK

This 16th edition of Lonely Planet's *Turkey* guidebook was researched and written by Jessica Lee, Brett Atkinson, Mark Elliott, Steve Fallon, Virginia Maxwell and Iain Stewart. The previous edition was written by James Bainbridge, Brett, Steve, Jessica, Virginia, Hugh McNaughtan and John Noble. This guidebook was produced by the following:

Senior Product Editors Daniel Bolger, Kate Chapman, Jessica Ryan

Cartographers Alison Lyall, Anthony Phelan

Product Editors Carolyn Boicos, Lauren O'Connell

Book Designer Ania Bartoszek, Fergal Condon

Assisting Editors Michelle Bennett, Alex Conroy, Emma Gibbs, Carly Hall, Kate James, Rosie Nicholson, James Smart, Gabrielle Stefanos

Assisting Cartographers David Connolly, Hunor Csutoros, Rachel Imeson, James Leversha

Cover Researcher Brendan Dempsey-Spencer

Thanks to Fergal Condon, Gemma Graham, Paul Harding, Karen Henderson, Sandie Kestell, Darren O'Connell, Charlotte Orr, Genna Patterson, Ambika Shree, Angela Tinson

Index

Map Legend

Sights

- Beach
- Bird Sanctuary
- Buddhist
- Castle/Palace
- Christian
- Confucian
- Hindu
- Islamic
- Jain
- Jewish
- Monument
- Museum/Gallery/Historic Building
- Ruin
- Shinto
- Sikh
- Taoist
- Winery/Vineyard
- Zoo/Wildlife Sanctuary
- Other Sight

Activities, Courses & Tours

- Bodysurfing
- Diving
- Canoeing/Kayaking
- Course/Tour
- Sento Hot Baths/Onsen
- Skiing
- Snorkelling
- Surfing
- Swimming/Pool
- Walking
- Windsurfing
- Other Activity

Sleeping

- Sleeping
- Camping
- Hut/Shelter

Eating

- Eating

Drinking & Nightlife

- Drinking & Nightlife
- Cafe

Entertainment

- Entertainment

Shopping

- Shopping

Information

- Bank
- Embassy/Consulate
- Hospital/Medical
- Internet
- Police
- Post Office
- Telephone
- Toilet
- Tourist Information
- Other Information

Geographic

- Beach
- Gate
- Hut/Shelter
- Lighthouse
- Lookout
- Mountain/Volcano
- Oasis
- Park
- Pass
- Picnic Area
- Waterfall

Population

- Capital (National)
- Capital (State/Province)
- City/Large Town
- Town/Village

Transport

- Airport
- Border crossing
- Bus
- Cable car/Funicular
- Cycling
- Ferry
- Metro station
- Monorail
- Parking
- Petrol station
- Subway station
- Taxi
- Train station/Railway
- Tram
- Underground station
- Other Transport

Routes

- Tollway
- Freeway
- Primary
- Secondary
- Tertiary
- Lane
- Unsealed road
- Road under construction
- Plaza/Mall
- Steps
- Tunnel
- Pedestrian overpass
- Walking Tour
- Walking Tour detour
- Path/Walking Trail

Boundaries

- International
- State/Province
- Disputed
- Regional/Suburb
- Marine Park
- Cliff
- Wall

Hydrography

- River, Creek
- Intermittent River
- Canal
- Water
- Dry/Salt/Intermittent Lake
- Reef

Areas

- Airport/Runway
- Beach/Desert
- Cemetery (Christian)
- Cemetery (Other)
- Glacier
- Mudflat
- Park/Forest
- Sight (Building)
- Sportsground
- Swamp/Mangrove

Note: Not all symbols displayed above appear on the maps in this book

Virginia Maxwell

İstanbul Although based in Australia, Virginia spends at least half of her year updating Lonely Planet destination coverage across the globe. The Mediterranean is her major area of interest – she has covered Spain, Italy, Turkey, Syria, Lebanon, Israel, Egypt, Morocco and Tunisia for Lonely Planet – but she also covers Finland, Bali, Armenia, the Netherlands, the USA and Australia. Follow her @maxwellvirginia on Instagram and Twitter. Virginia also wrote the Understand Turkey chapters.

Iain Stewart

Ephesus, Bodrum & the South Aegean; Antalya & the Turquoise Coast Iain trained as journalist in the 1990s and then worked as a news reporter and a restaurant critic in London. He started writing travel guides in 1997 and has since penned more than 60 books for destinations as diverse as Ibiza and Cambodia. Iain's contributed to Lonely Planet titles including Mexico, Indonesia, Central America, Croatia, Vietnam, Bali & Lombok and Southeast Asia. He also writes regularly for the Independent, Observer and Daily Telegraph and tweets at @iaintravel. He'll consider working anywhere there's a palm tree or two and a beach of a generally sandy persuasion. Iain lives in Brighton (UK) within firing range of the city's wonderful south-facing horizon.

OUR STORY

A beat-up old car, a few dollars in the pocket and a sense of adventure. In 1972 that's all Tony and Maureen Wheeler needed for the trip of a lifetime – across Europe and Asia overland to Australia. It took several months, and at the end – broke but inspired – they sat at their kitchen table writing and stapling together their first travel guide, *Across Asia on the Cheap*. Within a week they'd sold 1500 copies. Lonely Planet was born.

Today, Lonely Planet has offices in the USA, Ireland and China, with a network of over 2000 contributors in every corner of the globe. We share Tony's belief that 'a great guidebook should do three things: inform, educate and amuse'.

OUR WRITERS

Jessica Lee

Western Anatolia, Central Anatolia, Cappadocia, Southeastern Anatolia In 2011 Jessica swapped a career as an adventure-tour leader for writing and since then her travels for Lonely Planet have taken her across Africa, the Middle East and Asia. She has lived in the Middle East since 2007 and tweets @jessofarabia. Jessica has contributed to Lonely Planet's *Egypt, Turkey, Cyprus, Morocco, Marrakesh, Middle East, Abu Dhabi, Europe, Africa, Cambodia* and *Vietnam* guidebooks and her writing has appeared in *Wanderlust* magazine, the *Daily Telegraph*, the *Independent*, *BBC Travel* and Lonelyplanet.com. Jessica also wrote the Plan and Survival Guide chapters.

Brett Atkinson

Thrace & Marmara, İzmir & the North Aegean Brett is based in Auckland, New Zealand, but is frequently on the road for Lonely Planet. He's a full-time travel and food writer specialising in adventure travel, unusual destinations and surprising angles on more well-known destinations. Craft beer and street food are Brett's favourite reasons to explore places, and he is featured regularly on the Lonely Planet website, and in newspapers, magazines and websites across New Zealand and Australia. Since becoming a Lonely Planet author in 2005, Brett has covered areas as diverse as Vietnam, Sri Lanka, the Czech Republic, New Zealand, Morocco and the South Pacific. Brett also wrote the Plan Your Trip chapters.

Mark Elliott

Black Sea Coast, Northeastern Anatolia Mark had already lived and worked on five continents when, in the pre-internet dark ages, he started writing travel guides. He has since authored (or co-authored) around 70 books, including dozens for Lonely Planet. He also acts as a travel consultant, occasional tour leader, video presenter, public speaker, art critic, wine taster, interviewer and blues harmonicist.

Steve Fallon

Eastern Mediterranean With a house in Kalkan on the Turquoise Coast of the Mediterranean, Steve considers Turkey to be a second home. This assignment took him to the other side of that coast, the Eastern Mediterranean, where he stepped back in time at Tarsus, marvelled at the collections in the new museums of Adana and Mersin, and rediscovered the beauty and tranquillity of Arsuz. OK, *Türkçe'yi hala mağara adamı gibi konuşuyor* (he still speaks Turkish like a caveman), but no Turk has called him Tarzan. At least not yet. Find Steve at www.steveslondon.com.

OVER PAGE MORE WRITERS

Published by Lonely Planet Global Limited
CRN 554153
16th edition – May 2022
ISBN 978 1 78657 800 6
© Lonely Planet 2022   Photographs © as indicated 2022
10 9 8 7 6 5 4 3 2 1
Printed in Singapore